Introduction

This edition of the New Testament
Study Bible, the beginning of a new generation of study Bibles. Its purpose is to help you discover ways to relate the Word of God to you and the world you live in. This Bible makes it easy to bring the Word into your own world by taking you right into the world of the Bible.

The Word In Life Study Bible helps you get a clear understanding of God's Word by focusing on the surroundings of the biblical narrative. Stimulating articles get you thinking about how to relate the teachings of God's Word to life. The articles raise questions about what it means to live for God in today's world—about what a believer's role in the world is—and about how the Word in one life can touch the lives of others.

Features about the people, places, and customs of Jesus' world make the teachings of the Bible more vivid. You'll find friends in the Word of God. You'll feel at home where they lived. You'll discover that people aren't much different now than they were two thousand years ago. And you'll see that God's Word is more useful than you ever realized.

Explore the following pages and take a closer look at *The Word In Life Study Bible*—what it's meant to do, what it looks like, and how it works. Remember that the Bible is the heart of this book, and the articles and features are "helps"—helps to assist *you* in *your* study. So raise *your* questions. Write questions and comments in the margins. Bring your heart, mind, and soul to this book.

CONTENTS

BOOK ABBREVIATIONS IN BIBLICAL ORDER

OLD TESTAMENT:

Genesis	Gen.
Exodus	Ex.
Leviticus	Lev.
Numbers	Num.
Deuteronomy	Deut.
Joshua	Josh.
Judges	Judg.
Ruth	Ruth
1 Samuel	1 Sam.
2 Samuel	2 Sam.
1 Kings	1 Kin.
2 Kings	2 Kin.
1 Chronicles	1 Chr.
2 Chronicles	2 Chr.
Ezra	Ezra
Nehemiah	Neh.
Esther	Esth.
Job	Job
Psalms	Ps.
Proverbs	Prov.
Ecclesiastes	Eccl.
Song of Solomon	Song
Isaiah	Is.
Jeremiah	Jer.
Lamentations	Lam.
Ezekiel	Ezek.
Daniel	Dan.
Hosea	Hos.
Joel	Joel
Amos	Amos
Obadiah	Obad.
Jonah	Jon.
Micah	Mic.
Nahum	Nah.
Habakkuk	Hab.
Zephaniah	Zeph.
Haggai	Hag.
Zechariah	Zech.
Malachi	Mal.

NEW TESTAMENT:

Matthew	Matt.
Mark	Mark
Luke	Luke
John	John
Acts	Acts
Romans	Rom.
1 Corinthians	1 Cor.
2 Corinthians	2 Cor.
Galatians	Gal.
Ephesians	Eph.
Philippians	Phil.
Colossians	Col.
1 Thessalonians	1 Thess.
2 Thessalonians	2 Thess.
1 Timothy	1 Tim.
2 Timothy	2 Tim.
Titus	Titus
Philemon	Philem.
Hebrews	Heb.
James	James
1 Peter	1 Pet.
2 Peter	2 Pet.
1 John	1 John
2 John	2 John
3 John	3 John
Jude	Jude
Revelation	Rev.

ALPHABETICAL KEY TO BOOK ABBREVIATIONS

Acts	Acts
Amos	Amos
1, 2 Chr.	1, 2 Chronicles
Col.	Colossians
1, 2 Cor.	1, 2 Corinthians
Dan.	Daniel
Deut.	Deuteronomy
Eccl.	Ecclesiastes
Eph.	Ephesians
Esth.	Esther
Ex.	Exodus
Ezek.	Ezekiel
Ezra	Ezra
Gal.	Galatians
Gen.	Genesis
Hab.	Habakkuk
Hag.	Haggai
Heb.	Hebrews
Hos.	Hosea
Is.	Isaiah
James	James
Jer.	Jeremiah
Job	Job
Joel	Joel
John	John
1, 2, 3 John	1, 2, 3 John
Jon.	Jonah
Josh.	Joshua
Jude	Jude
Judg.	Judges
1, 2 Kin.	1, 2 Kings
Lam.	Lamentations
Lev.	Leviticus
Luke	Luke
Mal.	Malachi
Mark	Mark
Matt.	Matthew
Mic.	Micah
Nah.	Nahum
Neh.	Nehemiah
Num.	Numbers
Obad.	Obadiah
1, 2 Pet.	1, 2 Peter
Phil.	Philippians
Philem.	Philemon
Prov.	Proverbs
Ps.	Psalms
Rev.	Revelation
Rom.	Romans
Ruth	Ruth
1, 2 Sam.	1, 2 Samuel
Song	Song of Solomon
1, 2 Thess.	1, 2 Thessalonians
1, 2 Tim.	1, 2 Timothy
Titus	Titus
Zech.	Zechariah
Zeph.	Zephaniah

Why This Kind of Publication?

Someone has well said that Scripture was not written merely to be studied, but to change our lives. Likewise, James exhorts us to be "doers of the word, and not merely hearers" (James 1:22). And Jesus said, "My Father is glorified by this, that you bear much fruit and become my disciples" (John 15:8). Clearly, the point of God's Word is not to make us "smarter sinners" but to help us become more like Jesus Christ by making the Word of God part of our lives.

However, applying biblical truth in this day and age is far from easy. In the first place, the fact that the Bible was written thousands of years ago in a different culture can sometimes make it difficult to understand. And even if we grasp what the writers were saying to their original readers, we still must make the connection to our own situation today. In the end, many people wonder: can Scripture really make any difference in our complex, modern world? Yes it can, and this publication helps to show the way. ◆

A "User-Friendly" Study Bible

The Word In Life Study Bible helps you understand the biblical text.

Before you can apply Scripture, you must understand what Scripture means. That's why The Word In Life Study Bible *provides the kind of information you'll need to make sense of what the biblical text is talking about. The articles and other information (see below) provide the "who, what, when, where, how, and why" behind scores of passages, in an interesting, easy-to-understand way. Not only do they offer insight into the text, they also help you to understand the context of those passages, so that you can connect the words and events of biblical times with today.*

The Word In Life Study Bible helps you apply Scripture to everyday life.

"Wow! This is the kind of Bible I need in my life," one reader said. "It just makes Scripture come alive. It's contemporary. It's relevant." As you read The Word In Life Study Bible, *you won't have to search and struggle for ways to apply God's Word; the articles suggest numerous possibilities for how Scripture makes a difference. That's especially helpful if you're one who is strapped for time or likes to quickly get to the point.*

The Word In Life Study Bible challenges you to develop your own thinking.

You won't find pat answers or a "packaged" theology in this study Bible. Instead, the articles are designed to provoke your thinking by relating the text of Scripture to the issues of today, providing information to guide your thinking. Sometimes the commentary will raise a question without answering it; sometimes it will suggest possible answers. Sometimes you may disagree with particular interpretations—that's okay. The articles don't pretend to address every issue raised by the biblical text or to solve every theological problem. But they're designed to make you think!

THE WORD IN LIFE STUDY BIBLE INTRODUCES YOU TO THE PEOPLE OF SCRIPTURE.

For too many readers, the Bible can seem dull and lifeless, a book that only scholars and mystics might find interesting. But Scripture comes alive once we discover the people in the text. The Word In Life Study Bible *is designed to help you do that, to "make friends" with some of the fascinating characters that God chose to include in His Word. Almost fifty of them receive special attention through "Personality Profiles" that summarize what we know of them (see below). Even though these people lived long ago, you'll find that you have far more in common with them than you have differences. They experienced many of the same things you do. By learning what God did in their lives, you'll gain insight into what God is doing in yours.*

THE WORD IN LIFE STUDY BIBLE MAKES THE BIBLE EASY TO READ.

"I know I should read the Bible more, but to be honest, I just don't have time!" Have you ever felt that way? If so, The Word In Life Study Bible *is for you. It was designed for busy people. In the first place, you'll enjoy how easy it is to read the New Revised Standard Version. A modern translation that seeks "to put the message of the Scriptures in simple, enduring words and expressions," the NRSV presents the eternal Word of God in everyday language that people can understand. You'll also find the material presented in bite-size units, with section headings to mark the text. The Scriptures are accompanied not by long, drawn-out treatises, but by straight-to-the-point articles and other information presented in simple, easily grasped terms.* ◆

◆ ◆

FEATURES TO LOOK FOR

INTRODUCTORY ARTICLES

At the beginning of a book of the Bible you'll find information that explains why the book is important and what to pay attention to as you read it. You'll learn something of the background behind the book, including who the author and original readers were. You'll also get an idea of the issues the book addresses through a table of contents that describes some of the articles you'll find alongside the text.

Consider This

(symbols enlarged)

As mentioned above, God intended His Word to change people's lives. That's why occasionally you'll find a symbol that refers you to a nearby article relating in some way to the text indicated. These articles help to explain the Scriptural passages and highlight the significance of biblical truths for modern readers. In articles with this symbol, ways are offered for you to **consider** *how the passage applies to your life and the world around you. You may arrive at understandings different from, or in addition to, those presented in the articles.*

For Your Info

This symbol indicates articles that primarily offer **information** *about the text or its cultural context. Knowing the background of a biblical passage will help you understand it more accurately and make it more useful to you.*

Personality Profiles

One of the goals that the editors of The Word In Life Study Bible *had in developing their material was to introduce readers to the* **people** *of the Scriptures, including those who lived and worked in public places. One of the important ways that this study Bible does that is through personality profiles that highlight various individuals. These are not biographies, but summaries of what the Bible tells us about the person, what can be reasonably inferred from the text, and what other sources report about his or her life and legacy.*

You Are There

One of the most important windows on understanding the text of Scripture is knowing the **places** *where the events occurred. Unfortunately, ancient localities are unknown to most modern readers. The cities of Acts, for example, are little more than dots on a map for most of us. Yet when we examine the geography of the New Testament, we discover that the first-century Roman world was quite a bit like our own. The articles indicated by the "you are there" symbol will take you to places that you may never have "visited" before. Sometimes there's also information about what life was like for the people who lived there.*

A Closer Look

Sometimes the best way to understand a text of Scripture is to **compare** *the text to a related passage and/or its connected article. That's why you'll find symbols that "advertise" companion passages and articles that provide insight into the passage indicated.*

Quote Unquote

Occasionally you might be interested in knowing what someone else besides the writers of Scripture had to say about an idea raised in the biblical text, or about the text itself. That's not to suggest that these **quotations** *from various authors are on a par with Scripture. But one way to gain perspective on the implications of a passage is to read what someone has written, and then use that to reflect on what God has said.*

Themes to Consider

In designing The Word In Life Study Bible, *the editors wanted to create a resource that would help people deal with the issues of today, not yesterday. To that end, they identified a number of themes to highlight. Articles and other information provide a starting point for thought, study, and discussion of the following important areas:*

Work

For most of us, work is the most dominating area of life. It determines where we'll live, what kind of lifestyle we'll have, even who our friends will be. Yet how many of us are aware of how much the Bible says about work and workplace issues?

Economics

Who can doubt the importance of economic issues in a world increasingly tied together in a giant global marketplace? Of course, Scripture wasn't written to be an economics textbook. Nevertheless, it gives us principles relating to wealth, money, value, service, the environment, and other topics affecting both public policy and personal financial decisions.

Ethics

This is the issue of right and wrong, of integrity and character. In a day when truth and values have become relative, we need to return to God's unchanging Word as our basic standard for ethical conduct and commitments.

Ethnicity

One has only to glance at a map of our modern world to recognize the impact of racial and ethnic differences. The landscape is strewn with wars, conflicts, and problems tied to long-standing ethnic tensions. How should Christians respond, especially living in an increasingly diverse society? As the early church discovered, the gospel has enormous implications for how we relate to others from different backgrounds.

The Church

Enormous opportunities and critical choices face the church today. A fresh look at the church's beginnings and its impact on the first-century world can offer valuable guidelines for the church's impact on the twenty-first-century world.

Laity

Elton Trueblood has pointed out that the first Reformation put the Word of God back into the hands of the people of God; now we face the prospect of a "second reformation" that can put the *work* of God back into the hands of the people of God. This means that "everyday" believers can participate in carrying out God's work and find meaning and value in their efforts.

The Family

Building marriages and families that honor God has perhaps never been harder than today. That's why *The Word In Life Study Bible* highlights passages, principles, and people that show us the fundamental truths—and the honest realities—of building healthy family relationships in a fallen world.

The City

Today for the first time in history, more people live in metropolitan than in rural areas. That has enormous implications for how Christians engage the world. Yet many believers have adopted a negative view of the city; some even see it as an evil. But when we read the Bible, we discover that the gospel "conquered" the Roman world by penetrating its major cities. The same thing can happen today.

Witness

One thing is certain about evangelism: both non-Christians and Christians feel uncomfortable with it. Yet Jesus has sent His followers into the world to communicate His message of salvation. Fortunately, the Bible gives us guidelines for carrying out the task in a way that is winsome, sensitive, and effective.

Women

One of the most significant developments in recent culture has been the growing awareness of and sensitivity to issues and concerns of women—their dignity, their needs, and their rights. *The Word In Life Study Bible* places a special emphasis on the many women of the Scriptures and their significant contribution to the ministry of Jesus and the growth of the church. It also highlights the condition of women in the ancient world and the biblical teaching that pertains to the lives of women both then and now.

The themes mentioned above are just some of the ones that are touched on. It wouldn't be possible to classify them all. But as you use The Word In Life Study Bible, *New Testament edition, it will stir up your thinking and show you other areas in which to apply God's Word to life.* ◆

How to Use the Symbol System

The section above concerning "Features to Look For" mentions four symbols that are used to designate various kinds of articles, tables, or related material in The Word In Life Study Bible.

From time to time as you read the biblical text, you will see one of those four symbols along the left side of the text, accompanied by a box containing information that will lead you to a feature that has to do with the biblical passage you are reading.

If the feature you are being sent to is on one of the two pages you are opened to (called a "spread"), then the box next to the symbol by the text will contain just chapter-and-verse information, designating one verse (for example, 1:10) or a range of verses (1:1–16). No page number is given. Just look on the spread you are opened to for a matching symbol accompanied by a box containing the name of the symbol (such as CONSIDER THIS) and matching chapter-and-verse information.

1:1–16 1 A
Je
the son of Abraham.
2 Abraham was the fa
of Jacob, and Jacob the

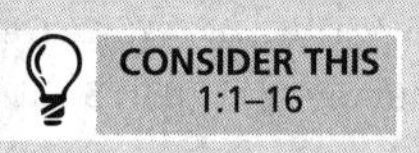

Don't skip this genealogy a
includes it for at least three

If the feature you are being sent to is someplace other than the spread you are opened to, then the box next to the symbol by the text will contain chapter-and-verse information and a page number. Just look on the designated page for a matching symbol accompanied by a box containing the name of the symbol and matching chapter-and-verse information.

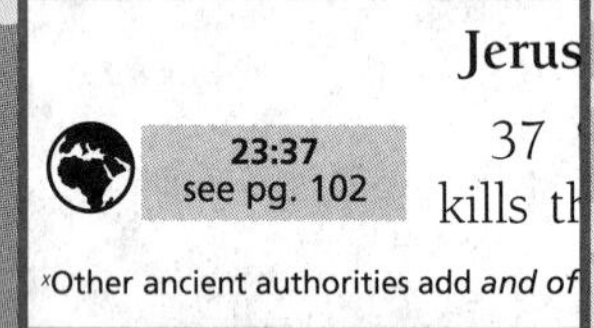

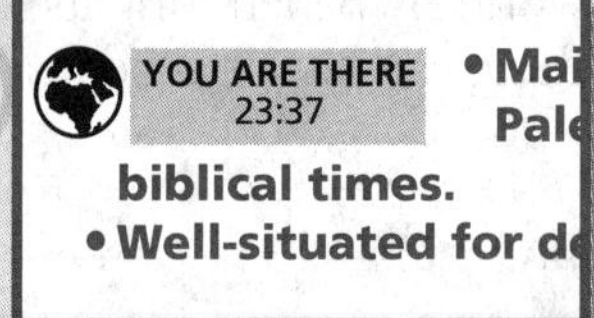

YOU ARE THERE
23:37
• Mai
Pale
biblical times.
• Well-situated for de

New Revised Standard Version Footnotes

> with a brother or sister,[a] you will be liable to ju
> if you insult[b] a brother or sister,[c] you will be

As you read, you will often see a raised letter in the biblical text. Each raised letter designates a New Revised Standard Version footnote, to be found at the foot of the column of text. (The footnotes are lettered from *a* to *z*, and then begin again with *a*.) Each footnote is also marked with the same raised letter, followed by the information in the footnote.

> the last penny.
>
> [a]Gk *a brother;* other ancient authorities add *without cause* [b]Gk *say Raca* t
> term of abuse) [c]Gk *a brother* [d]Gk *Gehenna* [e]Gk *your brother* [f]Gk lack

The footnotes of the New Revised Standard Version contain helpful information about significant textual variations and alternative translations, as well as words and phrases from Greek, the original language of the New Testament. Language notes are indicated by the abbreviation Gk ("Greek") and give the Greek word or phrase that underlies the English translation.

Occasionally, an article or feature in *The Word In Life Study Bible* will refer to a verse that is located not in the New Revised Standard Version text itself, but in a footnote. The box next to the symbol by the text will contain chapter-and-verse information and the raised letter of the footnote (such as "note *v*").

> **23:13, note *v*** 13 "But woe to you, scribes a
> isees, hypocrites! For you loc
> out of the kingdom of heaven. For you do not go

The feature you are being sent to will have a matching symbol accompanied by a box containing the name of the symbol along with matching chapter-and-verse and raised letter information.

> **CONSIDER THIS**
> 23:13, note *v*
> **Jesus chastised the Pharisees for growing fat at the expense of widows (v. 14). Unfortunately, not much has changed from that day to this. We**

To receive the most benefit from this feature, you should read the footnote as well (in this case, footnote *v*).

Other Features

Maps

Many maps appear throughout The Word In Life Study Bible. *They are designed to provide relevant geographical information in an accessible and easy-to-read format, on the same pages with the biblical text and related features.*

A number of locator maps *show you quickly where a certain place is with regard to its surrounding area.*

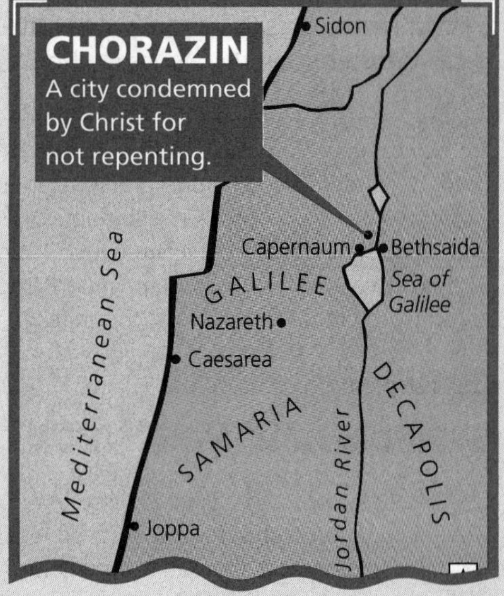

THE TWELVE

Apostle	Description
Simon (Peter) (Mark 1:16)	Fisherman from Galilee, Andrew's brother
Andrew (John 1:40)	Fisherman from Galilee, Peter's brother
James	Son of Zebedee, brother to John; from Capernaum
John (Introduction to John)	Son of Zebedee, brother to James; from Capernaum
Philip	From Bethsaida
Bartholomew	From [illegible] in [illegible]

Tables

Information is often presented in the form of tables or lists, showing at a glance how various facts and ideas relate to each other.

In the back of *The Word In Life Study Bible*, New Testament edition, are four handy reference features:

Themes to Study (p. 938)

A list of *themes to study* includes information about articles and their related texts, arranged by subject. Using this feature, you can read in connected fashion the material that relates to certain themes or issues.

Index to Key Passages (p. 957)

This index directs you to passages in the New Testament that pertain to a variety of practical and spiritual topics. Passages are listed alphabetically within each topic by brief content summaries.

The Four Gospels Side by Side (p. 964)

This table shows the parallel passages in the four Gospels. By referring to it, you can find out what all four Gospels say about an event in the life of Jesus.

Jobs and Occupations Index (p. 971)

People in the Bible had to work for a living too. This feature describes the occupations mentioned in the Bible and offers a revealing glimpse into the daily lives of men and women in biblical times. You'll see many resemblances to the work world of today.

Introduction to The New Revised Standard Version, New Testament

To The Reader

This preface is addressed to you by the Committee of translators, who wish to explain, as briefly as possible, the origin and character of our work. The publication of our revision is yet another step in the long, continual process of making the Bible available in the form of the English language that is most widely current in our day. To summarize in a single sentence: the New Revised Standard Version of the Bible is an authorized revision of the Revised Standard Version, published in 1952, which was a revision of the American Standard Version, published in 1901, which, in turn, embodied earlier revisions of the King James Version, published in 1611.

The need for issuing a revision of the Revised Standard Version of the Bible arises from three circumstances: (*a*) the acquisition of still older Biblical manuscripts, (*b*) further investigation of linguistic features of the text, and (*c*) changes in preferred English usage. Consequently, in 1974 the Policies Committee of the Revised Standard Version, which is a standing committee of the National Council of the Churches of Christ in the U.S.A., authorized the preparation of a revision of the entire RSV Bible.

For the New Testament the Committee has based its work on the most recent edition of the *Greek New Testament*, prepared by an interconfessional and international committee and published by the United Bible Societies (1966; 3rd ed. corrected, 1983; information concerning changes to be introduced into the critical apparatus of the forthcoming 4th edition was available to the Committee). As in that edition, double brackets are used to enclose a few passages that are generally regarded to be later additions to the text, but which we have retained because of their evident antiquity and their importance in the textual tradition. Only in very rare instances have we replaced the text or the punctuation of the Bible Societies' edition by an alternative that seemed to us to be superior. Here and there in the footnotes the phrase, "Other ancient authorities read," identifies alternative readings preserved by Greek manuscripts and early versions. Alternative renderings of the text are indicated by the word "Or."

As for the style of English adopted for the present revision, among the mandates given to the Committee in 1980 by the Division of Education and Ministry of the National Council of Churches of Christ (which now holds the copyright of the RSV Bible) was the directive to continue in the tradition of the King James Bible, but to introduce such changes as are warranted on the basis of accuracy, clarity, euphony, and current English usage. Within the constraints set by the original texts and by the mandates of the Division, the Committee has followed the maxim, "As literal as possible, as free as necessary." As a consequence, the New Revised Standard Version (NRSV) remains essentially a literal translation. Paraphrastic renderings have been adopted only sparingly, and then chiefly to compensate for a deficiency in the English language—the lack of a common gender third person singular pronoun.

During the almost half a century since the publication of the RSV, many in the churches have become sensitive to the danger of linguistic sexism arising from the inherent bias of the English language toward the masculine gender, a bias that in the case of the Bible has often restricted or obscured the meaning of the original text. The mandates from the Division specified that, in references to men and women, masculine-oriented language should be eliminated as far as this can be done without altering passages that reflect the historical situation of ancient patriarchal culture. As can be appreciated, more than once the Committee found that the several mandates stood in tension and even in conflict. The various concerns had to be balanced case by case in order to provide a faithful and acceptable rendering without using contrived English. In the vast majority of cases, however, inclusiveness has been attained by simple rephrasing or by introducing plural forms when this does not distort the meaning of the passage. Of course, in narrative and in parable no attempt was made to generalize the sex of individual persons.

It will be seen that in prayers addressed to God the archaic second person singular pronouns (*thee*, *thou*, *thine*) and verb forms (*art*, *hast*, *hadst*) are no longer used. Although some readers may regret this change, it should be pointed out that in the original languages neither the Old Testament nor the New makes any linguistic distinction between addressing a human being and addressing the Deity. Furthermore, in the tradition of the King James Version one will not expect to find the use of capital letters for pronouns that refer to the Deity—such capitalization is an unnecessary innovation that has only recently been introduced into a few English translations of the Bible. Finally, we have left to the discretion of the licensed publishers such matters as section headings, cross-references, and clues to the pronunciation of proper names.

This new version seeks to preserve all that is best in the English Bible as it has been known and used through the years. It is intended for use in public reading and congregational worship, as well as in private study, instruction, and meditation. We have resisted the temptation to introduce terms and phrases that merely reflect current moods, and have tried to put the message of the Scriptures in simple, enduring words and expressions that are worthy to stand in the great tradition of the King James Bible and its predecessors. It is the hope and prayer of the translators that this version of the Bible may continue to hold a large place in congregational life and to speak to all readers, young and old alike, helping them to understand and believe and respond to its message.

For the Committee,
Bruce M. Metzger

THE BOOKS OF THE NEW TESTAMENT

that your faith itself feels under siege, pay attention to 1 and 2 Peter! They were written for Christians in the crucible.

2 PETER—We Can Count on God 843

When we're being persecuted, sometimes it seems that just enduring it is all we can do. Coping may look like our only alternative to caving in. This letter offers great comfort to "coping Christians" by showing that we can rely on God, His Word, and the ultimate return of Jesus.

1 JOHN—Tough Love 849

John is often described as the "apostle of love" and 1, 2, and 3 John as the "love letters" of the New Testament. But these writings are not about sentimentalism. They're about "tough love," love that shoots straight, even if it hurts, because it cares for others and wishes them the best.

2 JOHN—The Test of Truth 863

Ideas and spiritual claims need to be given a simple but crucial litmus test: what do they say about Jesus? As believers today confront an onslaught of religious systems in a pluralistic society, this letter is particularly relevant.

3 JOHN—Imitate What Is Good 865

This letter confronts disloyalty in the church in a striking way. John sets descriptions of two leaders side by side and then encourages the reader to "imitate what is good." Apparently John felt confident that a sensible person would know which man was worthy of imitation.

JUDE—The New Testament's Exposé of False Teachers 867

Using graphic word pictures and recalling a rogue's gallery of deceivers from years gone by, Jude documents a history of subversive forces that threatened to destroy the early church. In reading this letter, we are reminded that Christianity is no game.

REVELATION—Christ, the Lord of History 873

How will history end? That's the theme of this last book in the New Testament, which pulls the curtain back to reveal God's ultimate plan for the world. What we find is a dramatic tale told in highly symbolic language. Nevertheless, its point is easily grasped: Christ will be revealed as the Lord of history.

. . . the Messiah, who is over all,
God blessed forever. Amen.
—*Romans 9:5*

FAITH IMPACTS THE WORLD

The workplace today includes many specific occupations, as it did in biblical times. See the Jobs and Occupations Index *on* page 971 *for a detailed look at what work was like for the people of the Bible. You might see some parallels to your own situation.*

Faith Impacts the World

Jesus not only affects one's private life, but one's public life as well. Christ's followers can recover that dimension of the gospel today. We can discover how to live out our faith in visible, public ways, as "God's own people" (1 Pet. 2:9–10), in order to powerfully impact our culture. But in doing so we need to consider: How does faith impact *the world?*

It helps to understand how our world operates. We can start by identifying three components of the "global village" in which we live and work:

(1) *The workplace*, made up of businesses, governments, and services.
(2) *Communities*, involving groupings of people such as cities, neighborhoods, and especially families.
(3) *Systems*, such as laws, traditions, and values, that support work and community life.

The world of (1) work and employment can be divided into three general sectors, as shown by the three towers in the accompanying diagram on page xx: business, government, and service. Each sector contains thousands of specific occupations and there is much overlap. Gatekeepers, power brokers, and other leaders exist for each sector.

The more general, and in many ways less formal, sectors of (2) community and family are represented by the larger horizontal disc that supports the workplace.

The undergirdings of society, (3) systems, are not as easily observed. They exist conceptually in our minds and hearts, quietly supporting and influencing the institutions, systems, and peoples of the world. Policies, traditions, values, laws, beliefs—like pilings sunk deep into the ground under tall buildings—are powerful supports that provide a foundation for society.

Some parts of the foundation are permanent in their value. But sometimes, as illustrated by the decaying columns, the nature of the foundation changes as unreliable supports crumble and the stronger foundations are relied upon even more and fortified if possible.

Behind it all is the sovereign God who sustains creation. Faith in Him enables truly meaningful social progress, as believers move back and forth between gathering for worship and scattering for engagement with the world.

How, Then, Does Christian Faith Impact the World?

Three ways that Christ's message impacts our world are:

(1) *Through followers of Christ.* These are individuals with an active faith who live out the gospel and proclaim it to the world through:

- sharing Christ by word and deed in their relationships and lifestyles;
- the proper handling of responsibilities and resources in their personal possession;

(continued)

(continued)

- informal networks of friendships, care groups, and guilds;
- active participation in the structures of society;
- recognized leaders who influence others in the society.

(2) *Through Christian institutions and structures.* In many cultures, believers have the privilege of owning or controlling organizations that present the gospel and its implications to the society. Some of these include:

- local churches, whose members and attenders can influence the larger community;
- service organizations that render human aid such as medical care, education, and help to the poor;
- media outlets, such as magazines, radio and television stations, and publishing houses.

(3) *Through lobbying and advocacy.* Here Christians attempt to influence the values of society and the people and institutions that determine them. This can mean either affirming support for beliefs with which Christians agree or restraining and resisting influences that seem opposed to Scripture. Christian advocacy might include:

- voting;
- running for office or supporting candidates and legislation;
- lobbying leaders and institutions to affect policies, procedures, and activities;
- pressing for business and community development that benefits people and their surroundings;
- demonstrating publicly for or against various activities;
- taking legal action.

We see that faith impacts more than just individuals. Jesus used images such as salt, light, leaven, and seeds to describe His kingdom's effect on the world. His gospel not only transforms persons but also institutions and the value structures that undergird society.

Evil and sin certainly pervade the world. In response, Jesus has sent us into the world to have influence for His sake (Mark 16:15). Through our work, our families, our prayers for the world and its leaders, our activity as good citizens, and our involvement in the structures of society, we can present Christ's message and have impact on a world that needs Him now more than ever. ◆

New Testament Panelists Speak Out on the Issues

Imagine that we could observe a panel discussion including the major writers of the New Testament. We might ask them to explain how the gospel affects the issues of our day.

Naturally, we can't listen to such a discussion in person, but we can observe the writers' statements in Scripture, and try to estimate how they would respond.

That's what the table below does. It offers some scriptural comments by six New Testament writers as they relate to eight topics treated in The Word In Life Study Bible. *It also refers you to various annotations in which the passages and others are discussed.*

Use this table as a starting point for your own study of the issues. Examine the authors' statements in context and see what else they and the other New Testament writers have to say about applying biblical truth to everyday life.

Matthew	
Race and Ethnicity	•Matthew opens with a family tree of Jesus' ancestors. See "Jesus' Roots," Matt. 1:1–16. •The writer shows Jesus breaking through a wall of hatred and separation between Jews and Gentiles. See "Jews, Gentiles, and Jesus," Matt. 15:24.
The Church	•Christ's kingdom advances as His people live the gospel throughout the world. See "The King Declares His Kingdom," Matt. 4:17.
Laity	•Christ doesn't look for perfect people, but rather faithful people who will experience His forgiveness and grow. See "Would You Choose These for Leaders?" Matt. 26:35–74.
Witness	•It's easy to say that Jesus cares for the whole world. But sometimes it's easier to follow a pattern of religion that fits comfortably into our own culture. See "To All the Nations," Matt. 28:19.
Gender	•In certain remarks of Jesus we see an understanding of women and childbearing that varies from what was offered by the culture of His day. See "A New Respect for Women," Matt. 5:32.
Public Systems	•Matthew records a number of statements by Jesus that sound extreme to our ears (5:22, 30, 37, 39–42). How can we make sense out of them? See "The Morality of Christ," Matt. 5:17–48. •Believers today need to discover how to live out faith in visible, public ways, in order to have an impact in the world. See "The Public Side of Our Faith," Matt. 14:13–14.

Continued

Continued

Matthew	
Work	•One story that Jesus told offers an important lesson about success. See "True Success Means Faithfulness," Matt. 25:14–30.
The City	•Matthew called Jerusalem "the holy city," but it was also noisy, dirty, and smelly, not unlike cities today. How could such a city be considered "holy"? See "Can a Noisy, Dirty, Smelly City Also Be Holy?" Matt. 4:5. •Jesus used two symbols—salt and light—to remind us that following Him involves a person's public life, particularly through work and participation in the community. See "Sulfa Drugs and Street Lights," Matt. 5:13–16.

Mark	
Race and Ethnicity	•Jesus' Galilean roots demonstrated that His gospel was not just for the elite, but for everyone. See "Jesus the Galilean," Mark 1:14. •Jesus' encounter with a distraught woman gave His disciples a powerful lesson about dealing with foreigners. See "Jesus and Ethnicity," Mark 7:24–30.
The Church	•Jesus calls people to Him who are insignificant according to traditional ideas of importance. See "Significance for Little People," Mark 2:3–17.
Laity	•Is your significance tied too closely to achievements? God calls us to a far more stable basis for significance. See "A Kingdom Perspective on Significance," Mark 13:33.
Witness	•Mark shows that we must avoid the trap of evaluating our faith by how others respond to our communication of it. See "Is Your Witness Falling on Deaf Ears?" Mark 4:3–20.
Gender	•A question about divorce reveals that Jewish women in the first century were far more restricted than men in their grounds for divorce. See "Divorce," Mark 10:2–12.
Public Systems	•At times people have used a statement by Jesus to avoid caring for the poor. But is that what Jesus had in mind? See "Always the Poor," Mark 14:7.
Work	•Like His earthly father before Him, Jesus worked to make a living. See "Jesus the Carpenter," Mark 6:3. •Jesus modeled a principle that many of us today could stand to practice more—the principle of rest. See "Why Not Rest a While?" Mark 6:31.
The City	•No individual Christian can meet all of the desperate needs in today's cities. But does God really ask us to? See "People Priorities in the City," Mark 5:21–43.

LUKE	
Race and Ethnicity	•Luke shows that the Lord's salvation is for "all peoples," both Jews and Gentiles. See "An International Savior," Luke 2:29–31.
The Church	•The original leaders of the church were not exactly prize recruits for a new spiritual movement. See "Can Laity Get the Job Done?" Luke 9:1–62. •In the book of Acts, Luke goes on to demonstrate that God uses empowered laypeople like the Twelve—and like us today—to do His work. See "The Extraordinary Acts of Ordinary People," Introduction to Acts.
Laity	•Powerful results come from experienced believers mentoring younger believers in the faith. See "Discipleship—Or Mentoring?" Acts 9:26–30. •Dozens of churches sprang up in the first century, thanks to the Holy Spirit's coordinated use of three tentmakers, a fiery evangelist, and countless unnamed laity. See "The Ephesus Approach," Acts 19:8–41.
Witness	•What is the gospel, and why was it significant for Jesus—and us—to proclaim it? See "What Is the Gospel?" Luke 7:22. •God may have placed you in a strategic position to bring the gospel to someone. See "Where Has God Placed You?" Acts 8:26–39.
Gender	•If you're a man, are you growing in your appreciation of women as God's creation? Do you esteem the women God brings your way? See "Those Women Again!" Luke 24:11.
Public Systems	•Jesus' first sermon before His hometown crowd moves us to ask: Whom are we reaching out to with the good news about Christ? What issues does Jesus' gospel address in our times? See "Jesus' First Sermon Included Surprises," Luke 4:16–27.
Work	•Jesus saw His followers in the grip of a common way of thinking—competing to prove their significance. See "Competition versus Compassion," Luke 9:46–48. •Luke provides three examples to show that Christlike values don't always produce financial gain in the marketplace. See "People, Property, and Profitability," Acts 16:19.
The City	•When some people came to ask Jesus whether He was the Messiah, they found Him ministering among people who were just getting by on the margins of society. See "The Underclass," Luke 7:20–23. •Luke's account in Acts demonstrates that one reason Christianity prevailed in the Roman world was that it planted churches in dozens of the empire's major cities. See "Churches—Keys to the Cities," Acts 11:22.

John

Race and Ethnicity	•Jesus refused to play ethnic games when there was a matter of eternal life and death at stake. See "Ethnic Games with Religious Roots," John 4:19–23.
The Church	•To be effective, believers must remain "on line" with Jesus, drawing from His resources and obeying His commands. See "The Network," John 15:1–10. •John records a prayer of Jesus that shows that engagement with the world, not isolation, is His desire for His church. See "Called into the World," John 17:18.
Laity	•Have you ever struggled with doubts or tough questions about Christ, the Christian faith, or the church? See "Skeptics Welcome," John 20:24–31.
Witness	•John presents back-to-back accounts that show two of the many different ways in which Jesus dealt with people. See "The Gospel in a Pluralistic Society," John 3:21. •One thing is certain about evangelism: both non-Christians and Christians feel uncomfortable with it. See "Whose Job Is Evangelism?" John 16:8.
Gender	•An attempt to humiliate a woman before Jesus results in His setting a new standard for judgment. See "A Double Standard?" John 8:2–3. •Will there ever be an end to discrimination, elitism, and injustice? Will people ever regard each other as equals? See "Finally, Full Equality," Rev. 5:9–10.
Public Systems	•John's Gospel presents another man named John whose behavior seems to repudiate the common measures of success in our society. See "Success," John 3:30.
Work	•A statement by Jesus shows that God is a worker who continues to maintain the creation and provide for His creatures. See "God—The Original Worker," John 5:17. •John envisions "a new heaven and a new earth" in which work will be free of the painful toil and drudgery that now characterizes it. See "Fresh Fruit Salad!" Rev. 22:2.
The City	•Jesus tapped into one of the most powerful concepts of the Old Testament—the idea that a specific place on earth is made special because of God's presence there. See "Sacred Space," John 1:51. •In the book of Revelation, John presents Babylon as more than a city, but as an entire world system in rebellion against God. See "A Symbol of Evil," Rev. 14:8.

PETER	
Race and Ethnicity	•An officer of Rome's occupation troops in Palestine came to faith, and Peter realized that God wants Gentiles in the church. See "Ethnic Walls Break Down," Acts 10:44–45. •Peter paints a family portrait of God's people. See "God's Family Album," 1 Pet. 2:9–10.
The Church	•Peter's memorable declaration led to an important statement about the foundation on which the church is built. See "'You Are the Messiah,'" Mark 8:27–33. •Peter urges clergy to maintain the utmost integrity when it comes to finances. See "Don't Fleece the Flock," 1 Pet. 5:2.
Laity	•Do you ever doubt God's willingness to forgive you over and over again? Peter might easily have felt that way. But Jesus reconnected with him and called him to genuine love and the continuation of His work. See "Forgiveness Abounds," John 21:15–23.
Witness	•At Pentecost, Peter proclaimed the message of Christ to a crowd of unbelievers in the best way he knew how, being faithful to the truth. The speech produced dramatic results. See "Carrots, Not Sticks," Acts 2:37–38.
Gender	•Peter recalls a heroine of the Old Testament as a model of good works and courageous faith. See "Sarah," 1 Pet. 3:6.
Public Systems	•Faced with a conflict between human authority and God's authority, Peter showed how believers can strike a balance between the two. See "'We Must Obey God Rather than Any Human Authority,'" Acts 5:22–32.
Work	•Peter reminds us that the church is not a business, and when it imports marketplace practices, it needs to carefully evaluate them by the Scriptures. See "The Business of the Church," 1 Pet. 5:2–4.
The City	•Peter witnessed the birth of an international, multilingual church when he preached the gospel at Pentecost. See "Pluralism at Pentecost," Acts 2:5.

PAUL	
Race and Ethnicity	•It took Paul years to reevaluate his cultural perspectives and bring them in line with the heart of God. See "From Persecutor to Apostle," Gal. 1:13–17. •Race is one of three major social distinctions that no longer matter in Christ. See "We Are Family!" Gal. 3:28.
The Church	•Suppose Paul were to visit your church—not the physical building, but the people. How would he evaluate your group? See "This Building Gets Landmark Status," Eph. 2:19–22.
Laity	•Paul didn't see himself as a super-saint. On the contrary, he grew in the faith with some difficulty. His view of himself changed over time. See "Hope for You: Watch Paul Grow!" Gal. 1:11–24. •The vast majority of a church's faithful worshipers probably are available for ministries outside the church, out in the world among unbelievers. See "Is Your Church Upside-down or Right Side Up?" 1 Thess. 2:13–14.
Witness	•Rome was the greatest superpower of its day. Perhaps that's why Paul described the gospel to the believers there in terms of power—God's power to save. It's a gospel powerful enough to handle the empire, big enough to address issues on a global scale. See "The Super-Powerful Gospel," Introduction to Romans.
Gender	•The gospel requires a different understanding of sex and marriage than the one held by the surrounding culture. See "A New View of Sexuality," 1 Cor. 7:3–6. •Gender is one of three major social distinctions that no longer matter in Christ. See "We Are Family!" Gal. 3:28.
Public Systems	•Paul used his Roman citizenship to protect his rights, showing that there's no need to allow discrimination to hinder one's practice of the faith. See "Faith and Rights," Acts 22:25–29. •Paul offers some helpful perspectives on how to respond to the systems in which we live. See "Governmental Authority," Rom. 13:2.
Work	•Paul's statement recalling the curse that God leveled on creation reminds us of the commonly held idea that God imposed work as a curse to punish Adam and Eve's sin. But is that completely correct? See "Is Work a Curse?" Rom. 8:20. •What determines the spiritual value of a job? How does God assign significance? See "Are Some Jobs More Important Than Others?" 1 Cor. 12:28–31.
The City	•Paul intentionally went to cities. We see that the gospel has implications for the urban setting. See "Paul's Urban Strategy," Acts 16:4. •While there is a place for human responsibility, Paul tells us that people—including authorities—are not the ultimate enemy. See "Who Is the Enemy?" Eph. 6:10–13.

25 IMPORTANT FIGURES IN THE NEW TESTAMENT

One key to understanding the New Testament is to observe the people in the text, especially the way they relate to God and His work in the world. Obviously they lived in a somewhat different culture two thousand years ago. Yet, are the issues they faced, the questions they asked, the personalities they displayed, and the triumphs and failures they experienced really much different from our own?

Below, you are invited to examine twenty-five of the important figures in the New Testament. Some are models to follow; make them your friends and mentors. Others illustrate pitfalls to avoid; learn from their mistakes! Either way, study the fears and foibles, great deeds and misdeeds of these twenty-five, and allow the Scriptures to come alive through the personalities that God included in His Word.

(Italic titles and references indicate Personality Profiles.)

25 IMPORTANT FIGURES IN THE NEW TESTAMENT	
JESUS **Son of God**	•See: Matt. 16:16; 26:62–66; John 8:58. •Read: Ten Myths series, Myth #1: "Jesus Christ Was Only a Great Moral Teacher," Matt. 13:34–35.
Savior	•See: Matthew; Mark; Luke (especially 4:18–19); John. •Read: "An International Savior," Luke 2:29–31.
Lord	•See: Phil. 2:9–11. •Read: "Is Jesus Really Lord of All?" Luke 6:1–5; "Christ, the Lord of the World," Col. 1:15–18.
Messiah	•See: Matt. 16:16. •Read: "You Are the Messiah," Mark 8:27–33.
Teacher of the Kingdom	•See: Matt. 5–7. •Read: "The King Declares His Kingdom," Matt. 4:17; "Work-World Stories Describe the Kingdom," Matt. 13:1.
Example for believers	•See: John 13:12–17; Phil. 2:5; 1 Pet. 2:21–23. •Read: "What It Means To Be Like Jesus," Matt. 10:25.
PAUL **A leader of the church**	•See: Acts 13–28. •Read: *"Saul," Acts 13:2–3; "Paul," Acts 13:2–3.* *Continued*

Continued

25 Important Figures in the New Testament	
Mentor of numerous believers	•See: 1 Cor. 4:16; 11:1; 2 Tim. 2:2. •Read: "Discipleship—Or Mentoring?" Acts 9:26–30.
Apostle to the Gentiles	•See: Acts 9:15; Gal. 1:16; 2:9. •Read: "Paul Turns to the Gentiles," Acts 13:44–48; "Paul the Jew—Teacher of the Gentiles," 2 Tim. 1:3.
Business partner in tentmaking	•See: Acts 18:1–3. •Read: "Paul's 'Real' Job," Acts 18:1–3.
Author of more than a dozen New Testament letters	•See: Romans through Philemon, and (traditionally) Hebrews.
PETER **Disciple of Jesus**	•See: Matt. 10:2; John 1:40–42; 21:15–19. •Read: "The Twelve," Matt. 10:2; *"Simon Peter," Mark 1:16.*
A leader of the church	•See: Acts 1–15.
Evangelist	•See: Acts 2:14–42. •Read: "Off to a Good Start," Acts 2:1; "Ethnic Walls Break Down," Acts 10:44–45.
Author of two New Testament letters	•See: 1 and 2 Peter.
MARY, Jesus' Mother **Mother of Jesus**	•See: Matt. 1:18—2:23; Luke 1:26–56; 2:1–52. •Read: *"Mary, the Mother of Jesus," Luke 1:26–56.*
International refugee	•See: Matt. 2:13–15, 19–23. •Read: "Asian-born Jesus Becomes a Refugee in Africa," Matt. 2:13–15.
PONTIUS PILATE **Roman procurator of Judea**	•See: John 18:28–40. •Read: "New Testament Political Rulers," Luke 3:1; "Roman Politics in the First Century A.D.," Luke 22:25.
Ruler who condemned Jesus to death	•See: John 19:1–16.
MARY of Magdala **Devoted follower of Jesus**	•See: Luke 8:1–3. •Read: *"Mary of Magdala," Luke 8:2.*
First person to see the resurrected Jesus	•See: Mark 16:9–10; John 20:14–18.

Continued

Continued

25 Important Figures in the New Testament

JAMES **Brother of Jesus**	•See: Matt. 13:55; Gal. 1:19. •Read: *"James," Introduction to James.*
A leader of the church	•See: Acts 15:13–21; 21:18; Gal. 2:9.
Author of a New Testament letter	•See: James.
ELIZABETH **Mother of John the Baptist**	•See: Luke 1:5–25, 39–45, 57–66. •Read: *"Elizabeth," Luke 1:24.*
HEROD THE GREAT **King of Judea for Rome**	•See: Matt. 2:1–12. •Read: "The Herods," Acts 12:1–2.
Ruler who ordered the slaughter of babies in and near Bethlehem	•See: Matt. 2:16–18. •Read: "City Kids Die over Adult Matters," Matt. 2:16–18.
HERODIAS **Wife of Herod Antipas**	•See: Matt. 14:3. •Read: "Hateful Herodias," Matt. 14:3; "The Herods," Acts 12:1–2.
Schemer behind the execution of John the Baptist	•See: Matt. 14:1–12; Mark 6:17–28.
BARNABAS **Landowner in the early church**	•See: Acts 4:36–37. •Read: *"Barnabas," Acts 4:36–37.*
Mentor to Paul	•See: Acts 9:27; 11:22, 30; 12:25. •Read: "Barnabas—A Model for Mentoring," Acts 9:27.
Leader in the early church	•See: Acts 14:12–18.
TIMOTHY **Associate of Paul**	•See: Acts 16:3–7; 1 Thess. 1:1; 3:6. •Read: *"Timothy," Introduction to 2 Timothy.*
Project leader at Ephesus	•See: 1 Tim. 1:3; 4:6–16. •Read: "Discipleship—Or Mentoring?" Acts 9:26–30; "The Ephesus Approach," Acts 19:8–41.
Cross-cultural worker	•See: Acts 16:1–3.

Continued

Continued

25 Important Figures in the New Testament	
PRISCILLA and AQUILA **Tent manufacturers**	•See: Acts 18:1–3. •Read: "Paul's 'Real' Job," Acts 18:1–3; *"Priscilla and Aquila," Rom. 16:3–5.*
Coworkers with Paul	•See: Acts 18:18–19; Rom. 16:3–5. •Read: "The Ephesus Approach," Acts 19:8–41.
Mentors to Apollos	•See: Acts 18:24–28. •Read: "Discipleship—Or Mentoring?" Acts 9:26–30; *"Apollos," Acts 18:24–28.*
LUKE **Gentile doctor**	•See: Col. 4:14. •Read: *"Luke," Introduction to Luke.*
Paul's associate	•See: Acts 16:10–17 ("we"); Philem. 24.
Author of Luke and Acts	•See: Luke 1:1–4; Acts 1:1. •Read: Introductions to Luke and Acts.
JUDAS ISCARIOT **Disciple of Jesus and treasurer of the Twelve**	•See: Matt. 10:4; John 12:6; 13:29. •Read: "The Twelve," Matt. 10:2; *"Judas Iscariot," Matt. 26:14.*
Betrayer of Jesus	•See: Luke 22:3–6, 47–53; John 13:21–30; 18:1–3. •Read: "Judas Iscariot, the Betrayer," Matt. 26:14–16.
ONESIMUS **Runaway slave of Philemon befriended by Paul and returned as a fellow believer**	•See: Philemon. •Read: Introduction to Philemon; *"Onesimus," "Philemon," both at Introduction to Philemon.*
LYDIA **Businesswoman of Philippi**	•See: Acts 16:14. •Read: *"Lydia," Acts 16:14–15.*
Host to the first church in Europe	•See: Acts 16:15, 40.
MATTHEW **Tax collector of Capernaum**	•See: Matt. 9:9. •Read: *"Matthew," Introduction to Matthew;* "Who Were Those Tax Collectors?" Matt. 9:10; "Taxes," Mark 12:14.
Disciple of Jesus	•See: Matt. 9:9–13; 10:3; Luke 5:27–32. •Read: "A Rich Man Enters the Kingdom," Matt. 9:9–13; "The Twelve," Matt. 10:2.
Author of Matthew	•Read: Introduction to Matthew.

Continued

25 Important Figures in the New Testament	
MARY of Bethany **Sister of Martha and Lazarus**	•See: Luke 10:38–42; John 11:1. •Read: *"Mary of Bethany," John 11:1–2.*
Devoted follower of Jesus	•See: Matt. 26:6–13; Mark 14:3–9; Luke 10:38–42; John 11:2; 12:1–8. •Read: "A Parting Gift," Mark 14:3–9.
MARTHA of Bethany **Sister of Mary and Lazarus**	•See: Luke 10:38–42; John 11:1. •Read: *"Martha of Bethany," Luke 10:38–42.*
A practical woman and follower of Jesus	•See: Luke 10:38–42; John 11:20–28.
ANANIAS and SAPPHIRA **Members of the early church who lied to the Holy Spirit**	•See: Acts 5:1–11. •Read: *"Ananias and Sapphira," Acts 5:1.*
PHILIP **Deacon (worker) in the early church**	•See: Acts 6:5. •Read: *"Philip the Evangelist," Acts 8:5–13.*
Communicator of the gospel	•See: Acts 8:4–13, 26–40. •Read: "The Conversion of Samaritans to the Gospel—and of Peter and John to Samaritans," Acts 8:4–25.
Father of daughters who prophesied	•See: Acts 21:8–9. •Read: "The Four Daughters of Philip," Acts 21:9.
APOLLOS **Eloquent speaker and itinerant lecturer**	•See: Acts 18:24—19:1. •Read: *"Apollos," Acts 18:24–28.*
Leader in the early church	•See: Acts 18:27–28; 1 Cor. 1:12; 4:1–6; 16:12. •Read: "Discipleship—Or Mentoring?" Acts 9:26–30; "The Ephesus Approach," Acts 19:8–41.

In addition to the ones mentioned above, the New Testament tells of numerous other prominent figures, including some from the Old Testament. See if you can identify the "biblical VIP'S" described in "Fathers and Prophets," Heb. 1:1, and "Who Are These People?" Heb. 11:2.

A Month-Long Journey with Jesus

Whatever else *The Word In Life Study Bible* accomplishes, the most important thing it could do for you is to help you know Jesus Christ. Nothing matters more than your relationship with Him. To help you get acquainted with Jesus, here are 31 readings (one for each day of the month) listed in the order of their appearance in the New Testament.

Day 1
Matt. 1:18—2:23
Jesus is born, then becomes a refugee as an evil king seeks to destroy Him. Finally His family returns home.

Day 2 **Matt. 4:1–11** Jesus confronts very real temptations.	*Day 3* **Matt. 13:54–58** Jesus faces rejection based on His family, their work, and the small size of His hometown.	*Day 4* **Matt. 23:1–39** Jesus speaks out against deceit, pride, and hypocrisy.	*Day 5* **Matt. 25:31–46** Jesus judges according to mercy and compassion rather than outward displays of spirituality.	*Day 6* **Mark 4:1–41** Jesus begins to explain the kingdom of God, using stories and images from the workplace.
Day 7 **Luke 2:1–52** Luke describes events connected with Jesus' birth—and tells of an incident during a boyhood trip to Jerusalem.	*Day 8* **Luke 4:14–37** Jesus goes public with His purpose, and immediately encounters opposition.	*Day 9* **Luke 6:17–49** Jesus teaches basic truths about attitudes, true charity, evaluating others, and making wise choices.	*Day 10* **Luke 9:18–36** Jesus talks with His followers about who He is.	*Day 11* **Luke 22:1—24:53** Jesus is betrayed, judged, executed, buried, resurrected, and reconnected with His followers.
Day 12 **John 1:1–18** John, one of Jesus' followers, describes how God became a man through Christ—full of grace and truth.	*Day 13* **John 5:19–47** Jesus explains His relationship with His Father and the implications for us.	*Day 14* **John 6:35–51** Jesus teaches that He is the bread of life, and tells how people can find Him.	*Day 15* **John 8:12–30** Jesus announces that He is the light of the world.	*Day 16* **John 10:1–18** Jesus says that He is the good shepherd who seeks His Father's lost sheep.
Day 17 **John 11:1—12:8** John describes Jesus' relationship with some of His friends, and their profound love and care for each other.	*Day 18* **John 14:1—15:8** Jesus explains that He is our source of spiritual life and productivity—the way to God.	*Day 19* **John 21:15–25** Jesus loved even the man who had denied Him and was jealous of another disciple.	*Day 20* **Acts 2:22–42** Peter explains Christ to a massive crowd in Jerusalem, and welcomes 3,000 people into the faith.	*Day 21* **Rom. 5:1–21** Paul explains how Christ sets people free from sin and makes them acceptable to God.
Day 22 **1 Cor. 15:1–28** Paul teaches about Christ's resurrection and the destruction of our enemy, death.	*Day 23* **Eph. 1:3–14** Paul describes Christ's work for us from three vantage points: before creation, in the present, and in eternity.	*Day 24* **Phil. 2:5–16** Paul explains the choices Christ made in order to become a man, as well as the choices we should make in following Him.	*Day 25* **Col. 1:15–22** Paul states that Christ is Lord of all—yesterday, today, and tomorrow.	*Day 26* **1 Thess. 4:13—5:11** Paul explains that Jesus will return and bring history to its culmination.
Day 27 **Heb. 1:1—2:18** The author of Hebrews describes Christ's complete and wonderful work on our behalf.	*Day 28* **Heb. 4:14—5:10** Christ has experienced every kind of test or trial we will ever face.	*Day 29* **Heb. 9:23—10:18** Jesus takes away sin, once and for all. Forgiveness is ours in Him.	*Day 30* **1 Pet. 1:1–12** Peter tells us that our salvation in Christ is a reality that even the angels and Old Testament prophets did not understand.	*Day 31* **Rev. 5:1–14; 22:1–21** Christ will rule heaven and earth and will welcome believers to an eternity with Him.

THE NEW COVENANT

commonly called

THE NEW TESTAMENT

of

OUR LORD AND SAVIOR

JESUS CHRIST

New Revised Standard Version

Marching Orders!

No other person has ever touched the world in quite the way Jesus did. And no other book of the New Testament records Jesus' teaching in quite the way Matthew does. Built around five major addresses that Jesus gave to His followers, Matthew records the essence of Christ's message, the core commands that He not only wanted His people to live by, but to spread to "all nations . . . teaching them to obey everything that I have commanded you" (Matt. 28:19–20).

Thus Matthew contains marching orders for Christ's followers today. He sends us into the world to have impact—not the impact of coercion or force, but the irresistible influence of lives that reflect His ways, His love, and His values.

How appropriate, then, that Matthew leads off the New Testament. All of the books that follow are God's Word, but Matthew sets the pace. It highlights the agenda of our Lord: "everything that I have commanded you."

The Gospel According to

Matthew

Christ sends us into the world to have impact.

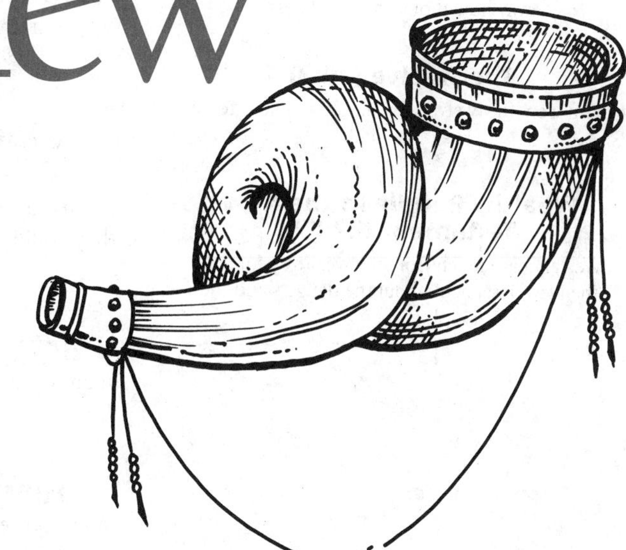

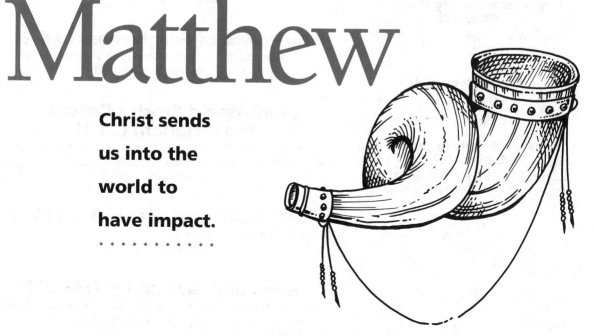

CONTENTS

People You'll Meet in Matthew

Articles

Servant-Leaders (20:25–28)

Jesus revealed a unique style of authority—that whoever wishes to be great should become a "slave."

Whitewashed Tombs (23:27–28)

Jesus used a grim, arresting image to denounce His self-righteous enemies.

◆ ◆

A Global Gospel with a Jewish Accent

For centuries, Jews had waited for a Messiah. They based their expectations on numerous Old Testament promises. For example, God told Abraham, the father of the nation, that through him "all the families of the earth [would] be blessed" (Gen. 12:3). To David, God's choice for Israel's king, God promised an enduring kingdom (2 Sam. 7:16). Through the prophets God renewed His pledge and provided details about the One who would fulfill it (Is. 7:14; 9:6–7; Dan. 2:44; 7:13–14).

Over the years, various figures came and went, some claiming to be the Messiah, others regarded by the people as likely candidates. But none proved convincing. None quite fulfilled the expectations of either the religious scholars who carefully studied the Scriptures, or the people who developed popular conceptions of what the Chosen One would accomplish.

What about the rabbi Jesus? He claimed to be God's Son. He performed extraordinary miracles that seemed to indicate divine power. He also taught with unprecedented authority and attracted a devoted band of followers. Yet hadn't He been rejected by the nation's leaders? Didn't He die a criminal's death? How, then, did He fulfill the promises of God? Was He really Israel's Messiah?

Matthew's Gospel answers with a resounding yes! He fills his account with Old Testament prophecies that point to Jesus as God's Chosen One (Matt. 1:23; 2:6, 15, 18, 23 to mention just a few). He wants his fellow Jews to study their Scriptures and find Jesus to be the Christ, the son of David, the son of Abraham, and the Son of God.

However, Matthew is not so much a Jewish Gospel as a global Gospel with a Jewish accent. In Jesus, all of us can find hope, no matter what our ethnic background. ◆

MATTHEW, THE SOCIAL OUTCAST

As a tax collector, Matthew was a member of a group that other Jews detested. Tax collectors were perceived not only as cheats, but mercenaries working for the Romans. Condemned by the religious leaders as unrighteous and ostracized by the general public as frauds and traitors, they found friends only among prostitutes, criminals, and other outcasts.

Yet Jesus selected Matthew to follow Him (Matt. 9:9). Scripture gives no indication why, but it does record the Lord's comment, "Go and learn what this means, 'I desire mercy, not sacrifice' [Hos. 6:6]. For I have come to call not the righteous but sinners" (v. 13). Apparently the call of Matthew was an act of pure mercy on the Lord's part—a choice that outraged self-satisfied religionists like the Pharisees.

They also criticized Jesus' willingness to attend a dinner that Matthew threw for Him (vv. 10–11). But Jesus knew whom He had come to help and where to find them. In Matthew, He had a direct entrée into the underworld of Jewish society, a class of people untouched by the religious legalists but deeply in need of a Savior. As the Great Physician (v. 12), Jesus was neither condoning nor glorifying lifestyles of sin, but merely reaching out to people who knew that they were sick and, as matters stood, completely lost. Matthew showed that Jesus can save anyone—that is, anyone who admits he needs saving. ◆

It's no wonder that Jews at the time of Jesus despised anyone associated with taxation: they were probably paying no less than 30 or 40 percent of their income on taxes and religious dues. *See "Taxes," Mark 12:14.*

Another tax collector who responded to Jesus was Zacchaeus of Jericho. *See Luke 19:1–10.*

PERSONALITY PROFILE: MATTHEW

Also known as: Levi. His given name, Matthew, meant "gift of Yahweh [the Hebrew term indicating God]."

Home: Capernaum (headquarters of Jesus' ministry); later Damascus, Syria.

Family: His father was Alphaeus.

Occupation: Tax collector; later an author, and pastor of a church in Damascus.

Special interests: Collecting Jesus' sermons and stories. He preserved them in a book that some call a new Torah because Jesus fulfilled so much Old Testament prophecy and restated much of the Mosaic Law.

Best known today as: The author of one of the Gospels, according to tradition.

HE SAW A MAN CALLED MATTHEW SITTING AT THE TAX BOOTH.
—Matthew 9:9

A Christian Torah

Tradition holds that after Jesus' departure, Matthew established a mostly Jewish church in or near Damascus of Syria and became its pastor. If so, his Gospel may have been a manual for Christian discipleship organized in a way that resembles the Pentateuch, the five books of Moses—Genesis, Exodus, Leviticus, Numbers, and Deuteronomy.

*In Jesus' day, the Pentateuch was known as the Torah, which means "instruction" or "law." Moses warned the people to carefully observe all the words of the Law, the commandments of God (Deut. 32:46). The English word "law" does not convey all that Moses intended. Both the hear*ing *and the doing of the Law made the Torah. It was a manner of life, a way to live based on the covenant that God made with His people.*

In the same way, Matthew balances the teaching of Christ with the application of that truth in day-to-day life. He builds his material around five major speeches that Jesus gave, producing a sort of five-volume "Christian Torah":

5:1—7:27	*The Sermon on the Mount, given to a large crowd*
9:35—10:42	*Instructions to the Twelve, chosen by Christ*
13:1–52	*Parables of the kingdom, given on a crowded beach*
18:1–35	*Instructions on community, given to the disciples*
24:1—25:46	*The Olivet Discourse, also given to the disciples*

Before and after each of these teaching sections are action sections in which Jesus and His followers carry out God's Word. The book climaxes with what has been called the Great Commission, where Jesus instructs the Eleven to go throughout the world and make disciples, "teaching them to observe *everything that I have* commanded *you" (28:16–20, emphasis added). Discipleship involves not only truth believed, but truth applied.*

It's interesting how Matthew ties Jesus' earthly life to the history of Israel. For example, Jesus fled to Egypt as an infant (Matt. 2:13–15) just as Israel dwelt in Egypt beginning with Joseph (Gen. 39:1). Jesus was tempted by the devil in a wilderness (Matt. 4:1–11) just as Israel was tested in the wilderness (Ex. 15:22—32:35). The point is that Jesus was not some detached, heaven-sent Savior untouched by the pain that Israel experienced. On the contrary, Jesus was a full-fledged Hebrew who fulfilled the name Immanuel, "God with us" (Matt. 1:23).

Yet Matthew also shows Jesus reaching out to non-Jews and other "undesirables." In fact, Jesus' own ancestry was laced with "sinners" and "foreigners" (see "The Women in Jesus' Genealogy," Matt. 1:3–6). As a former tax collector, Matthew knew better than most that Jesus came "to call not the righteous, but sinners" to repentance (9:13). The pastor/author wanted his congregation to understand that God's salvation is offered both to Jew and to Gentile. ◆

THE LAND OF THE GOSPELS

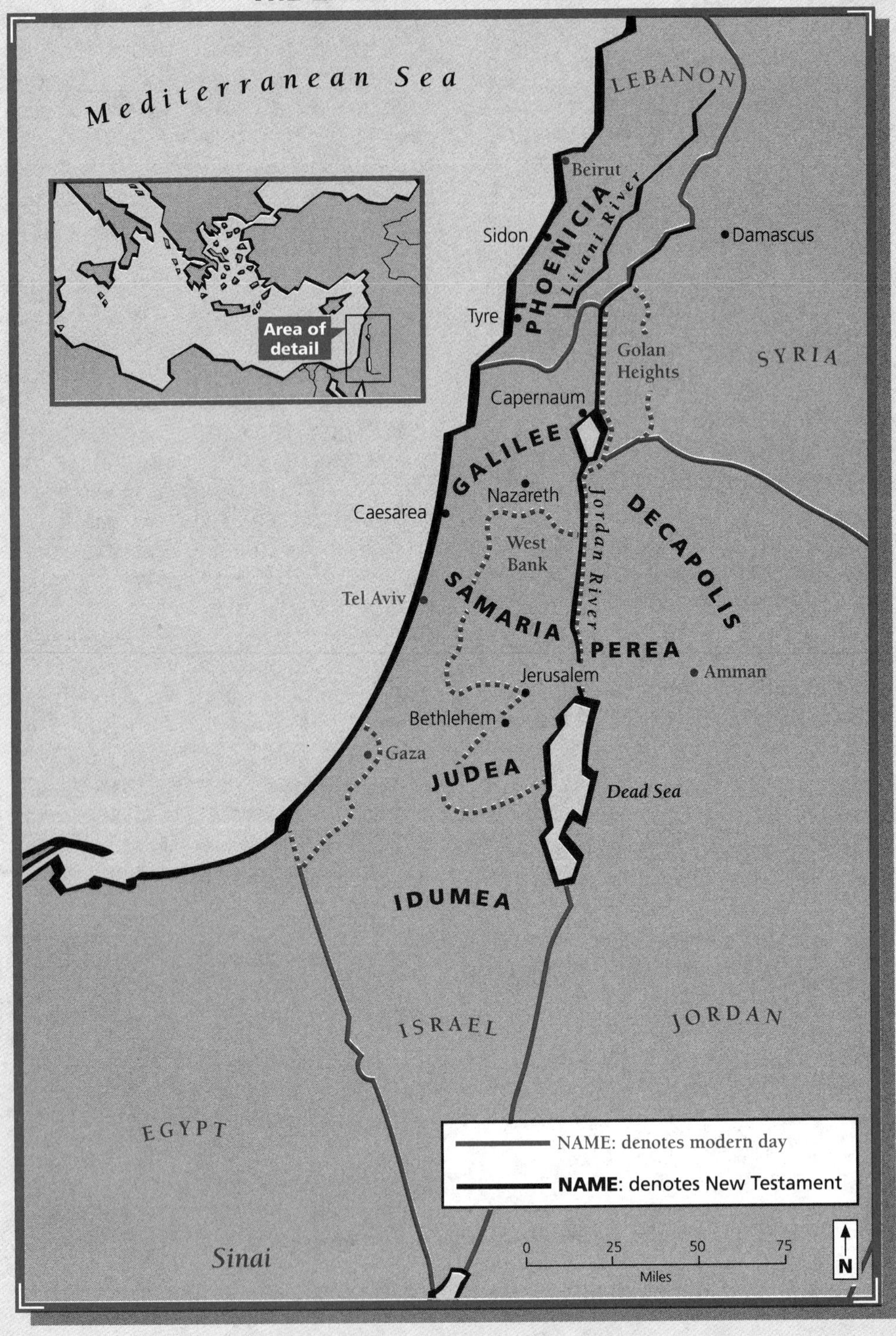
Mediterranean Sea
LEBANON
Beirut
PHOENICIA
Litani River
Sidon
Damascus
Tyre
Area of detail
Golan Heights
SYRIA
Capernaum
GALILEE
Nazareth
Caesarea
Jordan River
DECAPOLIS
West Bank
SAMARIA
Tel Aviv
PEREA
Jerusalem
Amman
Bethlehem
Gaza
JUDEA
Dead Sea
IDUMEA
ISRAEL
JORDAN
EGYPT
NAME: denotes modern day
NAME: denotes New Testament
Sinai
0
25
50
75
Miles
N

The Background of the Messiah

1:1–16 1 An account of the genealogy[a] of
Jesus the Messiah,[b] the son of David,
the son of Abraham.
2 Abraham was the father of Isaac, and Isaac the father
of Jacob, and Jacob the father of Judah and his brothers,
1:3–6 see pg. 8 3 and Judah the father of Perez and Zerah
by Tamar, and Perez the father of
Hezron, and Hezron the father of Aram, 4 and Aram the father of Aminadab, and Aminadab the father of Nahshon,
and Nahshon the father of Salmon, 5 and Salmon the father
of Boaz by Rahab, and Boaz the father of Obed by Ruth,
and Obed the father of Jesse, 6 and Jesse the father of King
David.
And David was the father of Solomon by the wife of
Uriah, 7 and Solomon the father of Rehoboam, and Rehoboam the father of Abijah, and Abijah the father of

(Bible text continued on page 9)

[a]Or *birth* [b]Or *Jesus Christ*

Jesus' Roots

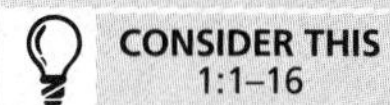

CONSIDER THIS 1:1–16 *Matthew opens with a family tree of Jesus' ancestors (vv. 1–16). Don't skip this genealogy and begin at v. 18! Matthew includes it for at least three important reasons:*

(1) To show that God's Son was also a real, flesh-and-blood human. This was a crucial concept for Matthew's first-century readers (see "Jesus, the Son of . . . ," Luke 3:23–38).

(2) To show that Jesus was the long-awaited Messiah of Israel. Notice the prominence of David and Abraham.

(3) To show that Jesus is also the international Christ, the Savior of the whole world. His genealogy reaches beyond Jews to include several ethnic groups that populated the Middle East during Israel's Old Testament history (see the accompanying article, "The Women In Jesus' Genealogy"). Jesus came to "make disciples of all nations" (Matt. 28:19).

What It Means To Be Like Jesus

CONSIDER THIS 1:1–17 *Jesus indicated that those who follow Him will become like Him (10:25). What does it mean to* **"be like Jesus"** *in today's complex world? Matthew paints eight portraits of what Christlikeness looks like, including:*

#1: To Be Like Jesus Means TO ACCEPT OUR ROOTS

Jesus' family tree hides nothing. His heritage was multiethnic and included several unattractive or embarrassing individuals. Indeed, the circumstances surrounding His own birth might have raised questions in the minds of some. But Jesus never denied His ancestry or allowed others to shame Him. If we want to be like Him, we need to understand and accept our roots in terms of culture, race, gender, and reputation. Moreover, like Jesus we want to avoid demeaning anyone else's heritage.

For a summary of all eight portraits of Christlikeness, see "What It Means to Be Like Jesus" at 10:25. The next item in the series can be found at 1:18—2:23.

CONSIDER THIS
1:3–6

THE WOMEN IN JESUS' GENEALOGY

Much has been made of the virgin Mary, but Matthew's genealogy (vv. 1–16) highlights four other women in Jesus' family. They were touched by scandal and remembered as "sinners" and "foreigners." Their inclusion can be an encouragement to us.

Tamar (v. 3; Gen. 38:1–30)

- Left a widow by Er, the firstborn son of Judah.
- Married Onan, Judah's second son, who refused to consummate the marriage and also died, leaving her childless—and therefore without means of support.
- Sent away to her home village by her father-in-law, Judah, who avoided responsibility to provide another husband.
- Eventually resorted to trickery, acting as a prostitute to cause Judah to father an heir and thereby provide economic security. The child also continued the line that eventually led to Jesus. Exposed as the father, irresponsible Judah acknowledged that Tamar was "more in the right than I" (Gen. 38:26).

Rahab (v. 5; Josh. 2:1–24; 6:22–25)

- A Canaanite harlot in Jericho.
- Protected two Hebrew spies in exchange for her own protection from the Israelites, who surrounded the city.
- Later married a Hebrew and gave birth to Boaz, David's great-grandfather.
- Praised in the New Testament as a person of faith (Heb. 11:31) and faithful action (James 2:25).

Ruth (v. 5; Ruth 1:1—4:22)

- A woman of Moab. Although Moab and Israel recognized kinship through Lot, the two nations remained enemies from the Exodus events when Moab resisted rather than assisted the Israelites (Ex. 23:3–5).
- Widowed when her Jewish husband died, and left without sons.
- Migrated to Israel with her mother-in-law, Naomi.
- Married Boaz (Rahab's son) and became the mother of Obed, making her David's great-grandmother. In effect, hostile Israel joined hated Moab to bring about God's will.

The Wife of Uriah (v. 6; 2 Sam. 11:1—12:25)

- Unnamed by Matthew, but known to be Bathsheba, wife of Uriah the Hittite.
- Attracted the eye of King David while bathing in ritual obedience on her roof, cleansing herself from her monthly flow.
- Summoned by the king, who committed adultery with her.
- Suffered the murder of her husband by David and the loss of the child that David had fathered.
- Married David, giving birth to a second child, Solomon, who became David's successor. (If Bathsheba was a Hittite like her first husband, then Solomon was half-Jew, half-Gentile. However, she was likely a Hebrew who married a Hittite sojourner.)

Jesus is the Messiah for women as well as men—even for women with (supposedly) checkered pasts and tainted bloodlines. He is the Messiah for all people, regardless of gender, race, or background. ◆

Matthew offers plenty of evidence to show Jesus' global connections. See Matt. 8:10.

Asaph,[c] 8and Asaph[c] the father of Jehoshaphat, and Jehoshaphat the father of Joram, and Joram the father of
Uzziah, 9and Uzziah the father of Jotham, and Jotham the
father of Ahaz, and Ahaz the father of Hezekiah, 10and
Hezekiah the father of Manasseh, and Manasseh the father
of Amos,[d] and Amos[d] the father of Josiah, 11and Josiah the
father of Jechoniah and his brothers, at the time of the deportation to Babylon.
12 And after the deportation to Babylon: Jechoniah was
the father of Salathiel, and Salathiel the father of Zerubbabel, 13and Zerubbabel the father of Abiud, and Abiud the
father of Eliakim, and Eliakim the father of Azor, 14and
Azor the father of Zadok, and Zadok the father of Achim,
and Achim the father of Eliud, 15and Eliud the father of
Eleazar, and Eleazar the father of Matthan, and Matthan the
father of Jacob, 16and Jacob the father of Joseph the husband of Mary, of whom Jesus was born, who is called the
Messiah.[e]

1:1–17 see pg. 7

17 So all the generations from Abraham to David are fourteen generations;
and from David to the deportation to Babylon, fourteen
generations; and from the deportation to Babylon to the
Messiah,[e] fourteen generations.

The Birth of the Messiah

1:18—2:23 see pg. 10

18 Now the birth of Jesus the Messiah[f] took place in this way. When his
mother Mary had been engaged to Joseph, but before they
lived together, she was found to be with child from the
Holy Spirit. 19Her husband Joseph, being a righteous man
and unwilling to expose her to public disgrace, planned to
dismiss her quietly. 20But just when he had resolved to do
this, an angel of the Lord appeared to him in a dream and
said, "Joseph, son of David, do not be afraid to take Mary as
your wife, for the child conceived in her is from the Holy
Spirit. 21She will bear a son, and you are to name him Jesus,
for he will save his people from their sins." 22All this took
place to fulfill what had been spoken by the Lord through
the prophet:

1:23

23 "Look, the virgin shall conceive and
bear a son,
and they shall name him Emmanuel,"
which means, "God is with us." 24When Joseph awoke from
sleep, he did as the angel of the Lord commanded him; he
took her as his wife, 25but had no marital relations with her
until she had borne a son;[g] and he named him Jesus.

[c]Other ancient authorities read *Asa* [d]Other ancient authorities read *Amon* [e]Or *the Christ* [f]Or *Jesus Christ* [g]Other ancient authorities read *her firstborn son*

What's in a Name?

CONSIDER THIS 1:23 **Jesus was and is Immanuel, "God with us" (v. 23). God comes to us as people and lives in our world, rather than having us try the impossible of going to Him. Jesus does not take us out of the turmoil and pain of daily life, but rather walks *with us* as we live life.**

It's a mistake to think of salvation as escape from the world instead of engagement with the world. God has a job for us to do right where we live and work. That's where Jesus is *with us;* that's where He gives us power (see Acts 1:8).

The name of Jesus played a powerful role in a five-act drama of which early Christians were a part. See "Jesus—The Name You Can Trust," Acts 3:1.

A Poor Family Comes into Wealth

CONSIDER THIS 2:11 **What happened to the gifts presented to Jesus by the wise men (v. 11)? Scripture doesn't say. Clearly they reflected the Magi's worship of Christ at His birth. Yet we can speculate that they may have provided the means for His family's flight to Egypt (vv. 13–15).**

The angel's warning and instructions to Joseph were sudden and unexpected. There was no time to save enough money for such a long journey—if saving was even an option. The family, after all, was poor (see "A Poor Family's Sacrifice," Luke 2:22–24). In fact, the costly gifts probably represented more wealth than either spouse had seen in a lifetime.

God promises to provide what is necessary for His children and to care for their needs (Matt. 6:19–34). In this instance, offerings of worship may have paid for a journey to Egypt and a new life in a strange land.

What It Means To Be Like Jesus

CONSIDER THIS 1:18—2:23 *Jesus indicated that those who follow Him will become like Him (10:25). What does it mean to* **"be like Jesus"** *in today's complex world? Matthew paints eight portraits of what Christlikeness looks like, including:*

#2: To Be Like Jesus Means TO ENGAGE THE WORLD'S PAIN

Jesus' entry into human life was fraught with awkward tensions and human dilemmas: a miraculous but nevertheless embarrassing conception, an earthly father who was considering a quiet divorce, an outraged king resorting to infanticide, an early childhood in a strange culture, and a return to a homeland that remained hostile and dangerous. We, too, are all born into some troubles and circumstances. If we want to be like Jesus, we need to face up to the world and remain very much in it, despite all its troubles.

For a summary of all eight portraits of Christlikeness, see "What It Means to Be Like Jesus" at 10:25. The next item in the series can be found at 3:1–17.

Wise Men Visit

2 In the time of King Herod, after Jesus was born in
Bethlehem of Judea, wise men[h] from the East came to
Jerusalem, 2asking, "Where is the child who has been born
king of the Jews? For we observed his star at its rising,[i]
2:3 and have come to pay him homage."
3When King Herod heard this, he was
frightened, and all Jerusalem with him; 4and calling together all the chief priests and scribes of the people, he inquired of them where the Messiah[j] was to be born. 5They
told him, "In Bethlehem of Judea; for so it has been written
by the prophet:
6 'And you, Bethlehem, in the land of Judah,
are by no means least among the rulers of Judah;
for from you shall come a ruler
who is to shepherd[k] my people Israel.' "
7 Then Herod secretly called for the wise men[h] and
learned from them the exact time when the star had appeared. 8Then he sent them to Bethlehem, saying, "Go and
search diligently for the child; and when you have found
him, bring me word so that I may also go and pay him
homage." 9When they had heard the king, they set out; and
there, ahead of them, went the star that they had seen at its
rising,[i] until it stopped over the place where the child was.
10When they saw that the star had stopped,[l] they were over-
2:11 see pg. 9 whelmed with joy. 11On entering the
house, they saw the child with Mary his
mother; and they knelt down and paid him homage. Then,
opening their treasure chests, they offered him gifts of gold,
frankincense, and myrrh. 12And having been warned in a
dream not to return to Herod, they left for their own country by another road.

The Family Flees to Egypt

2:13–15 13 Now after they had left, an angel of
the Lord appeared to Joseph in a dream

[h]Or astrologers; Gk magi [i]Or in the East [j]Or the Christ [k]Or rule [l]Gk saw the star

Herod the Great

A CLOSER LOOK 2:3 *Herod the Great (v. 3) was a highly ambitious leader who would stop at nothing to advance or protect his position. He routinely disposed of his enemies—even one of his wives and three of his sons. So it was no surprise that his immediate thought upon hearing the wise men's question—"Where is the child who has been born king of the Jews?" (v. 2)—was to plan the infant's extermination. Read more about this ruler's infamy and the bloody family he came from in "The Herods," Acts 12:1–2.*

and said, "Get up, take the child and his mother, and flee to
Egypt, and remain there until I tell you; for Herod is about
to search for the child, to destroy him." 14Then Joseph[m] got
up, took the child and his mother by night, and went to
Egypt, 15and remained there until the death of Herod. This
was to fulfill what had been spoken by the Lord through
the prophet, "Out of Egypt I have called my son."

Herod Slaughters Infants

2:16–18 see pg.12

16 When Herod saw that he had been
tricked by the wise men,[n] he was infuri-
ated, and he sent and killed all the children in and around
Bethlehem who were two years old or under, according to
the time that he had learned from the wise men.[n] 17Then
was fulfilled what had been spoken through the prophet
Jeremiah:

18 "A voice was heard in Ramah,
wailing and loud lamentation,
Rachel weeping for her children;
she refused to be consoled, because they are no more."

The Family Returns to Nazareth

19 When Herod died, an angel of the Lord suddenly appeared in a dream to Joseph in Egypt and said, 20"Get up,
take the child and his mother, and go to the land of Israel,

[m]Gk *he* [n]Or *astrologers;* Gk *magi*

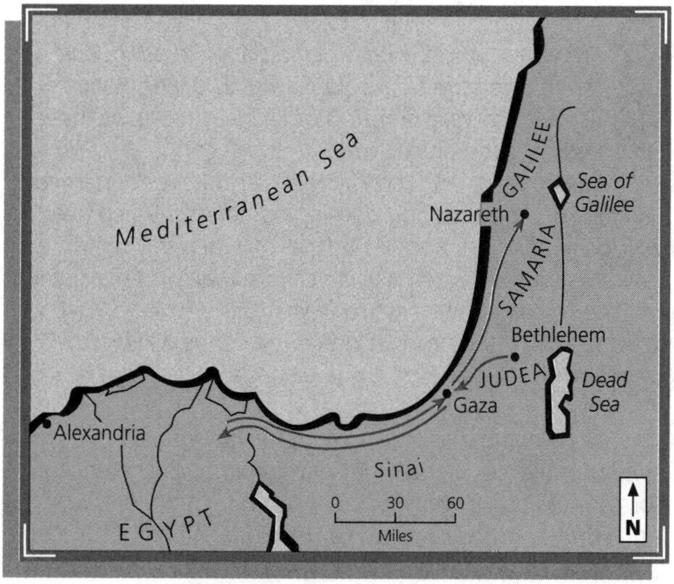

TO EGYPT AND BACK

"OUT OF EGYPT I HAVE CALLED MY SON." —Matthew 2:15

ASIAN-BORN JESUS BECOMES A REFUGEE IN AFRICA

YOU ARE THERE 2:13–15

Have you ever thought of Jesus as an intercontinental political refugee? He was, according to the Christmas story in vv. 13–15. Through His parents, the Asian-born Jesus sought political asylum in Africa, avoiding the infanticide ordered by King Herod, the ruthless ruler of Palestine.

The text doesn't say where the family stayed. Perhaps they were absorbed into the one million Jews estimated to have lived in Alexandria at that time. Wherever they ended up, we know that Jesus, perhaps close to two years old at the start of the journey (2:16), spent at least some of His formative years in Egypt, displaced from His homeland. And when the family migrated back to Palestine (2:22–23), they did not settle in a privileged neighborhood, but in Nazareth in rural Galilee.

Jesus can identify with the many migrating peoples of the world today. He is an international Savior who knows the pain of forced migration. That is indeed good news for those who have been displaced by natural disasters, famine, or political unrest.

Herod shared a reputation for villainy with others in his family. See "The Herods," Acts 12:1–2.

for those who were seeking the child's life are dead." 21Then
Joseph[o] got up, took the child and his mother, and went to
the land of Israel. 22But when he heard that Archelaus was
ruling over Judea in place of his father Herod, he was afraid
to go there. And after being warned in a dream, he went
away to the district of Galilee. 23There he made his home in
a town called Nazareth, so that what had been spoken
through the prophets might be fulfilled, "He will be called a
Nazorean."

The Ministry of John the Baptist

3:1–17

3 In those days John the Baptist appeared in the wilderness of Judea,
proclaiming, 2"Repent, for the kingdom of heaven has come
near."[p] 3This is the one of whom the prophet Isaiah spoke
when he said,

"The voice of one crying out in the wilderness:
'Prepare the way of the Lord,
make his paths straight.' "

3:4

4Now John wore clothing of camel's hair
with a leather belt around his waist, and
his food was locusts and wild honey. 5Then the people of
Jerusalem and all Judea were going out to him, and all the

[o]Gk *he* [p]Or *is at hand*

John the Street Preacher

CONSIDER THIS 3:4 **Would John the Baptist (v. 4) have been comfortable using today's media to proclaim his startling message? Probably not. Even for his own day he reflected none of the outward trappings of a successful ministry. He was not the head rabbi of a large city synagogue. He was not dressed in fine clothes. He did not sport a fine chariot. Nor did he enjoy sumptuous meals with leading citizens.**

Nevertheless, news about him spread far and wide, and people from throughout the region around Jerusalem and the Jordan came to hear him.

John illustrates the truth of Paul's words that "God chose what is weak in the world to shame the strong" (1 Cor. 1:27).

For the follower of Christ, how does success relate to wealth? See "Christians and Money," 1 Tim. 6:6–19.

CONSIDER THIS
2:16–18

City Kids Die over Adult Matters

In the tragic account in vv. 16–18, we read of an entire village of baby boys being slaughtered, due to the insane rage of a jealous king. The story reminds us that growing numbers of children today die needlessly for the sins of adults.

Like Rachel (v. 18), mothers all over the world, particularly in urban ghettos and developing nations, weep over their dead children. Rachel had lots of experience with tears. Her father tricked her fiancé into marrying her sister and she remained childless for years (Gen. 29:1—30:24). Later, Jeremiah the prophet described her as wailing over the exiled tribes (Jer. 31:15, the passage quoted by Matthew).

The weeping and wailing in Bethlehem must have gone on for days. It could not have been quickly silenced, nor could Rachel's wailing be comforted. The babies of Bethlehem and the people in exile had a common bond: in both cases, innocent people suffered as a result of the proud, ungodly acts of powerful leaders.

region along the Jordan, [6]and they were baptized by him in
the river Jordan, confessing their sins.
7 But when he saw many Pharisees and Sadducees coming for baptism, he said to them, "You brood of vipers!
Who warned you to flee from the wrath to come? [8]Bear
fruit worthy of repentance. [9]Do not presume to say to yourselves, 'We have Abraham as our ancestor'; for I tell you,
God is able from these stones to raise up children to Abraham. [10]Even now the ax is lying at the root of the trees;
every tree therefore that does not bear good fruit is cut
down and thrown into the fire.

3:11 see pg. 14

11 "I baptize you with[q] water for repentance, but one who is more powerful
than I is coming after me; I am not worthy to carry his sandals. He will baptize you with[q] the Holy Spirit and fire.
[12]His winnowing fork is in his hand, and he will clear his
threshing floor and will gather his wheat into the granary;
but the chaff he will burn with unquenchable fire."

John Baptizes Jesus

13 Then Jesus came from Galilee to John at the Jordan,
to be baptized by him. [14]John would have prevented him,
saying, "I need to be baptized by you, and do you come to

[q]Or *in*

Jesus can offer particular comfort to those who grieve the loss of a child. In effect, the babies of Bethlehem died for Him. He must have carried the pain of that throughout His life and onto the cross. It doubtless shaped His special concern for children (compare Matt. 18:6–7). And His concerned activity toward them beckons us to find ways to serve children today.

Matthew's retelling of this slaughter is a very significant part of the Christmas story. In a powerful way, it reminds city kids today that they need not die in vain: Jesus lived and died for them, too. ◆

What It Means To Be Like Jesus

CONSIDER THIS 3:1–17 *Jesus indicated that those who follow Him will become like Him (10:25). What does it mean to* **"be like Jesus"** *in today's complex world? Matthew paints eight portraits of what Christlikeness looks like, including:*

#3: To Be Like Jesus Means TO COMMIT OURSELVES TO OTHER BELIEVERS

John the Baptist was not your average individual. He was an unexpected child. He lived in the wilderness—the "other side of the tracks" for that day. He wore strange clothing and ate strange food. He was pugnacious, even offensive at times. Yet he helped launch Jesus' career. In return, Jesus had nothing but praise for him (11:7–15). If we want to be like Jesus, we must not pick and choose our brothers and sisters in God's family. We need to embrace other believers and demonstrate our unity in Christ, no matter how awkward or inconvenient.

For a summary of all eight portraits of Christlikeness, see "What It Means to Be Like Jesus" at 10:25. The next item in the series can be found at 4:1–11.

THE POWER OF HUMILITY

CONSIDER THIS 3:11 **How difficult is it for you to accept and admit that others are mightier than you? If you regard strength as the power to dominate, you'll always be intimidated by those who seem to have more than you—more expertise, more experience, more energy, more intelligence.**

John held a different understanding of strength (v. 11). He saw it as a gift from God to be used for divine purposes. That gave him tremendous power in his community (v. 5). His humility gave him the capacity to serve and to welcome others—in this case, Jesus—as valuable associates.

Like John, Paul challenged believers to cultivate humility. Not a groveling, abject demeanor, but rather an acknowledgment of what one is. See "Humility—The Scandalous Virtue," Phil. 2:3.

me?" 15But Jesus answered him, "Let it be so now; for it is
proper for us in this way to fulfill all righteousness." Then
he consented. 16And when Jesus had been baptized, just as
he came up from the water, suddenly the heavens were
opened to him and he saw the Spirit of God descending
like a dove and alighting on him. 17And a voice from
heaven said, "This is my Son, the Beloved,[r] with whom I
am well pleased."

The Temptation of Jesus

4:1–11 see pg. 16

4 Then Jesus was led up by the Spirit
into the wilderness to be tempted by
the devil. 2He fasted forty days and forty nights, and after-
4:3
wards he was famished. 3The tempter
came and said to him, "If you are the
Son of God, command these stones to become loaves of
bread." 4But he answered, "It is written,

'One does not live by bread alone,
but by every word that comes from the mouth of
God.' "

[r]Or *my beloved Son*

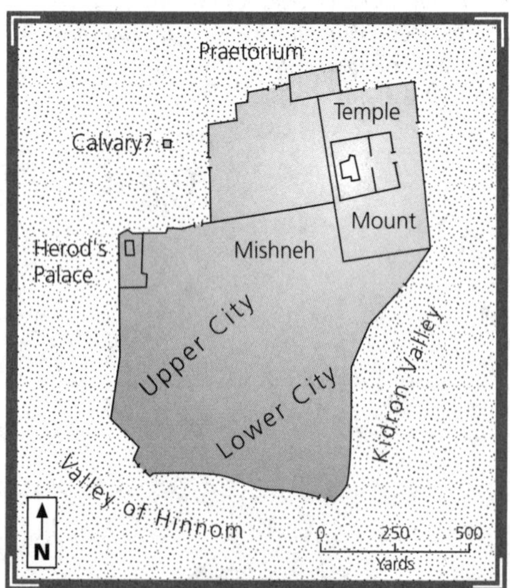

JERUSALEM

CAN A NOISY, DIRTY, SMELLY CITY ALSO BE HOLY?

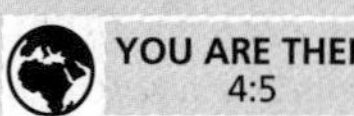

Matthew called Jerusalem "the holy city" (v. 5), but it was also noisy, dirty, and smelly. Gehenna, the town garbage dump and home to countless lepers, lay just outside the gates in a deep, narrow ravine, the Valley of Hinnom. Refuse, waste materials, and dead animals were burned there. Fires continually smouldered, and with the right wind, rank smells drifted north, blanketing the city and the temple mount with noxious odors.

How could such a city be considered "holy"? Because God's presence was there, in the temple. That made it "sacred space" to the Hebrews (see John 1:51).

4:5

5 Then the devil took him to the holy
city and placed him on the pinnacle of
the temple, 6saying to him, "If you are the Son of God,
throw yourself down; for it is written,

'He will command his angels concerning you,'
and 'On their hands they will bear you up,
so that you will not dash your foot against a stone.' "

7Jesus said to him, "Again it is written, 'Do not put the Lord
your God to the test.' "

4:8–10
see pg. 16

8 Again, the devil took him to a very
high mountain and showed him all the
kingdoms of the world and their splendor; 9and he said to
him, "All these I will give you, if you will fall down and
worship me." 10Jesus said to him, "Away with you, Satan!
for it is written,

'Worship the Lord your God,
and serve only him.' "

11Then the devil left him, and suddenly angels came and
waited on him.

Jesus Begins His Ministry

4:12–25
see pg. 17

12 Now when Jesus[s] heard that John
had been arrested, he withdrew to Gali-
lee. 13He left Nazareth and made his home in Capernaum
by the sea, in the territory of Zebulun and Naphtali, 14so
that what had been spoken through the prophet Isaiah
might be fulfilled:

15 "Land of Zebulun, land of Naphtali,
on the road by the sea, across the Jordan, Galilee of
the Gentiles—
16 the people who sat in darkness
have seen a great light,
and for those who sat in the region and shadow of death
light has dawned."

4:17
see pg. 18

17From that time Jesus began to proclaim, "Repent, for the kingdom of
heaven has come near."[t]

Jesus Calls Disciples

4:18–22
see pg. 17

18 As he walked by the Sea of Galilee, he saw two brothers, Simon, who
is called Peter, and Andrew his brother, casting a net into
the sea—for they were fishermen. 19And he said to them,

(Bible text continued on page 17)

[s]Gk *he* [t]Or *is at hand*

"You Don't Understand!"

CONSIDER THIS
4:3

How often we hear someone dismiss the implications of faith for day-to-day life with the retort, "You don't understand! I live in the real world, where things are tough. They play by a different set of rules there. Christianity is all well and good, but isn't it a bit simplistic when it comes to real life?"

The account of the temptation in vv. 1–11 offers a response to that sort of thinking. It shows that Jesus *does* understand real life. He faced real temptations—the same temptations that show up every day in the "real world."

Some people think that because He did not give in to what was offered, He must not have been "really" tempted; therefore, He can't "really" understand our situation. But that won't do. Scripture affirms that Satan's devices were real temptations that really tempted Him. And because He was able to resist them, He is able to help us do the same (Heb. 2:18). He completely understands our feelings—and how to do what is right in spite of them.

Temptation is not sin, but giving in is. See "Tired of Praying?" Luke 11:5–13.

Few teachings in Scripture have more practical, day-to-day implications than the truth that people are fallen, temptable, and subject to thinking and doing wrong. "Pay Attention to Temptation!" at 1 Cor. 10:12–13, explores the importance of that for Christians in today's workplace.

What It Means To Be Like Jesus

CONSIDER THIS 4:1–11 *Jesus indicated that those who follow Him will become like Him (10:25). What does it mean to* **"be like Jesus"** *in today's complex world? Matthew paints eight portraits of what Christlikeness looks like, including:*

#4: To Be Like Jesus Means TO ADMIT OUR VULNERABILITY TO TEMPTATION

Matthew's inclusion of the temptation is remarkable. It shows that the sinless Lord of the universe was tempted, just as we are (Heb. 4:15–16). If we want to be like Jesus, we must accept that temptation is real—as is the possibility of overcoming temptation. But we need to be open about our struggles. In doing so we honor God, recognize the power of sin, and encourage others to do likewise.

For a summary of all eight portraits of Christlikeness, see "What It Means to Be Like Jesus" at 10:25. The next item in the series can be found at 4:12–25.

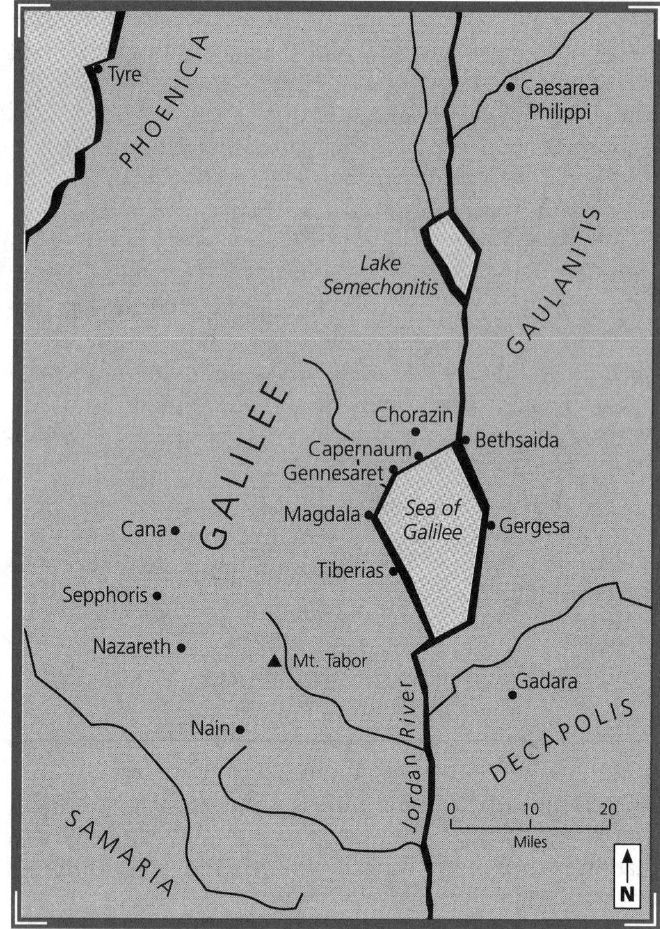

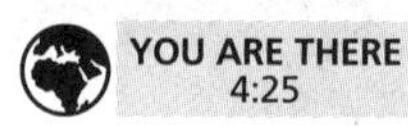

JESUS' GALILEAN MINISTRY

Wealth's Temptation

CONSIDER THIS 4:8–10 **For us who live in a materialistic culture, it's good to recognize that the desire for wealth and all that it symbolizes—prestige, power, luxury, authority—can be a powerful tool in Satan's hands. It was one of three strategies that the devil used to try to draw Christ away from His mission (vv. 8–10).**

Are you tempted by desires that are closely tied to wealth? If so, Christ's response in v. 10 challenges you to ask: Who or what are you going to worship and serve?

Opportunities for temptation sometimes seem endless. Yet Scripture offers several alternatives for dealing with temptation as we find it. See "Pay Attention to Temptation," 1 Cor. 10:12–13.

Most of Jesus' followers were not wealthy, but a few notable ones were. From them we can learn a great deal about the dangers and the disciplines of money. See the survey, "Wealthy People in the New Testament," Matt. 27:57.

"Follow me, and I will make you fish for people." 20Im-
mediately they left their nets and followed him. 21As he
went from there, he saw two other brothers, James son of
Zebedee and his brother John, in the boat with their father
Zebedee, mending their nets, and he called them. 22Imme-
diately they left the boat and their father, and followed him.

Galilean Ministry

4:23

23 Jesus[u] went throughout Galilee,
teaching in their synagogues and pro-
claiming the good news[v] of the kingdom and curing every
disease and every sickness among the people. 24So his fame
spread throughout all Syria, and they brought to him all the
sick, those who were afflicted with various diseases and
pains, demoniacs, epileptics, and paralytics, and he cured
them. 25And great crowds followed him
from Galilee, the Decapolis, Jerusalem,
Judea, and from beyond the Jordan.

4:25

The Sermon on the Mount

5:1—7:27 see pg. 20

5:2 see pg. 21

5 When Jesus[w] saw the crowds, he
went up the mountain; and after he
sat down, his disciples came to him.
2Then he began to speak, and taught
them, saying:

The Beatitudes

5:3 see pg. 22

3 "Blessed are the poor in spirit, for
theirs is the kingdom of heaven.
4 "Blessed are those who mourn, for they will be comforted.

(Bible text continued on page 20)

[u]Gk *He* [v]Gk *gospel* [w]Gk *he*

What It Means To Be Like Jesus

CONSIDER THIS 4:12–25 *Jesus indicated that those who follow Him will become like Him (10:25). What does it mean to* **"be like Jesus"** *in today's complex world? Matthew paints eight portraits of what Christlikeness looks like, including:*

#5: To Be Like Jesus Means TO PROCLAIM THE MESSAGE OF CHRIST

Jesus' life was *not* an open book, readable by all. To be sure, He lived a perfect, model life. But even that could not stand alone as an undeniable witness. His actions needed interpretation. So He supplemented His good *deeds* with good *news*. In the same way, we need to verbally declare our faith if we want to be like Christ. Certainly we need to back up our words with a Christlike lifestyle. But what we tell others gives meaning to our quiet walk and good deeds.

For a summary of all eight portraits of Christlikeness, see "What It Means to Be Like Jesus" at 10:25. The next item in the series can be found at 5:1—7:27.

"I WILL MAKE YOU FISH FOR PEOPLE."
—Matthew 4:19

The Fishermen

The fishermen Jesus called (vv. 18–22) eventually became members of an inner circle of Jesus' followers. See "The Twelve," Matt. 10:2.

Galilee

A CLOSER LOOK 4:23

Though Jesus launched His ministry in Galilee (v. 23) with great energy, there is little evidence that His message ever took firm root there after He left. See "Galilee," Mark 1:14.

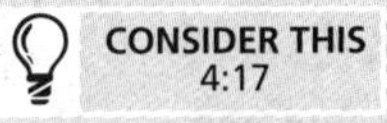

THE KING DECLARES HIS KINGDOM

Jesus initiated His public life with a simple but stiff challenge to repentance (v. 17). It was actually a familiar message—identical, in fact, to the message of John the Baptist, Jesus' forerunner (Matt. 3:2). Both urged their listeners to repent, to change their minds and hearts, not merely for the sake of change, but in light of what they called "the kingdom."

Jesus Is the King

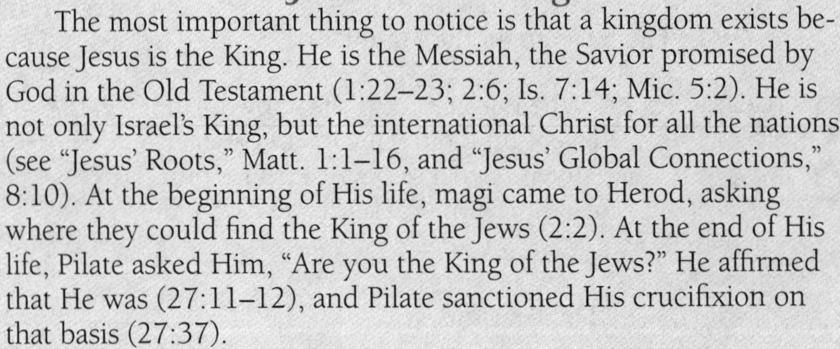

The most important thing to notice is that a kingdom exists because Jesus is the King. He is the Messiah, the Savior promised by God in the Old Testament (1:22–23; 2:6; Is. 7:14; Mic. 5:2). He is not only Israel's King, but the international Christ for all the nations (see "Jesus' Roots," Matt. 1:1–16, and "Jesus' Global Connections," 8:10). At the beginning of His life, magi came to Herod, asking where they could find the King of the Jews (2:2). At the end of His life, Pilate asked Him, "Are you the King of the Jews?" He affirmed that He was (27:11–12), and Pilate sanctioned His crucifixion on that basis (27:37).

So in 4:17–25, the King was declaring His kingdom. Foretold by Scripture and announced by John, Jesus had come to establish His rule. However, He disappointed the expectations of many people—both then and now.

Where Is the Kingdom?

For a few brief decades, Israel had enjoyed a relatively prosperous, peaceful monarchy under David and his son, Solomon. Some Old Testament passages prophesied that the Messiah would reestablish that sort of kingdom. Was now the time? Would Jesus overthrow the iron rule of the Romans and set up a political state? He did not. In fact, He told the Roman governor Pilate that His kingdom was not of this world, that He did not have an army fighting on His behalf (John 18:36). And He told the Pharisees that the kingdom was not something tangible and observable, but was within them (Luke 17:20).

Then is Christ's kingdom simply a spiritual concept, a powerful but abstract ideal? No, because He made a definite promise to His disciples that they would rule the tribes of Israel in His kingdom (Matt. 19:23, 28). They apparently took Him literally (Acts 1:6).

When Is the Kingdom?

No less puzzling is the question of when the kingdom has or will come. As they began their ministries, John the Baptist and Jesus declared that the kingdom "has come near." But a few years later, when Jesus' followers asked whether He was ready to restore Israel's kingdom, He put them off; that was something that only His Father could know, He told them (Acts 1:6–7). Sometimes the kingdom seemed to be a present reality (Matt. 12:28; 13:18–23; 21:43). At other times, it seemed to be a hope for the future (16:28; 20:20–23; 26:29).

Even today, theologians stridently debate over whether and in what form the kingdom has already been established, is currently in the process of being formed, is coming in the future, or is not coming at all. Like most questions that cannot be answered definitively to everyone's satisfaction, agreements are few and positions strongly defended.

What Is the Kingdom?

Is there any simple way to understand this puzzling doctrine of the kingdom? Probably not. Jesus' followers have not ceased to puzzle over His statements about it since the moment they were made. But most would generally agree that Christ's kingdom began in some way with His first coming. It continues to advance as His people live the gospel message throughout the world. However, it will not realize its ultimate completion until He returns.

What Difference Does It Make?

Whatever else we can say, the kingdom has to do with whatever Christ the King rules. That's why Jesus began His ministry with a call to repentance. Repentance means to change one's mind or purpose. In terms of the kingdom, it involves:

(1) A change in one's allegiance. If Christ is the King, He deserves our honor, loyalty, and obedience. We put ourselves under His authority and power. Whatever He says, we determine to do. That's the point of the oft-repeated lines in the Lord's Prayer, "Your kingdom come. Your will be done, on earth as it is in heaven" (Matt. 6:10). Kingdom people submit their own will to the will of the King.

(2) A change in one's expectations. One of the difficulties people have with the idea of a kingdom is that it doesn't appear to be in place yet. The world seems to grow farther away from God by the day. As a result, it's easy to live for the here and now, as if this present life is all that matters. But the hope of the kingdom is that there is far more to life than what we see right now. Jesus made extraordinary promises in regard to a future kingdom, not only for Israel, but for all who follow Him as King. The kingdom may not yet be fulfilled completely, but it has been established and will last forever (6:13, note *m*).

(3) A change in one's values. Our culture values achievement, success, independence, and image. Other cultures value other qualities. But the values of the kingdom reflect what matters to the King. Jesus described a number of His values in Matthew 5:3–10, a section of the Sermon on the Mount known as the Beatitudes (or, as some call them, the "beautiful attitudes"). Kingdom people adopt the King's values and make choices that reflect those values—in their jobs, families, and communities.

(4) A change in one's priorities. The real test of people's values is how they spend their time and money. Jesus spoke directly to that issue in terms of the kingdom (6:24–34). He did not demean the value of work or diminish the need for material goods. But He challenged His followers to bring kingdom values into their day-to-day lives. "Strive first for the kingdom" (6:33) puts a Christlike perspective on one's work and its outcomes.

(5) A change in one's lifelong mission. Some people are driven to accomplish great tasks with their lives. Others live aimlessly from day to day, lacking purpose or direction. Either way, Jesus affects the outlook of a person's life. He gives His followers purpose and a mission—to live as subjects of the kingdom and promote kingdom values in everyday life and work. Ultimately, He wants His followers to extend His message to the ends of the earth, so that all people have the opportunity to give their allegiance to Him as their Savior and King (28:18–20). ◆

What It Means To Be Like Jesus

CONSIDER THIS 5:1—7:27 *Jesus indicated that those who follow Him will become like Him (10:25). What does it mean to* **"be like Jesus"** *in today's complex world? Matthew paints eight portraits of what Christlikeness looks like, including:*

#6: To Be Like Jesus Means TO COMMIT TO CHANGED THINKING AND BEHAVIOR

In His Sermon on the Mount, Jesus explained the values of the kingdom. Money, prayer, relationships, possessions, information, and power were a few of the categories He redefined from God's perspective. He showed that following Him will involve radical change for most of us. It may mean undoing the way we've always done things and rethinking traditional sources of wisdom from our parents and culture. To become like Jesus involves a tough-minded review of our values and a thorough change in our behavior.

For a summary of all eight portraits of Christlikeness, see "What It Means to Be Like Jesus" at 10:25. The next item in the series can be found at 8:1—9:38.

 5:5

5 "Blessed are the meek, for they will
inherit the earth.
6 "Blessed are those who hunger and thirst for righteousness, for they will be filled.
7 "Blessed are the merciful, for they will receive mercy.
8 "Blessed are the pure in heart, for they will see God.
9 "Blessed are the peacemakers, for they will be called
children of God.
10 "Blessed are those who are persecuted for righteousness' sake, for theirs is the kingdom of heaven.
11 "Blessed are you when people revile you and persecute you and utter all kinds of evil against you falsely[x] on
my account. 12Rejoice and be glad, for your reward is great
in heaven, for in the same way they persecuted the
prophets who were before you.

"You Are Salt and Light"

5:13–16 see pg. 24

13 "You are the salt of the earth; but if
salt has lost its taste, how can its saltiness be restored? It is no longer good for anything, but is
thrown out and trampled under foot.
14 "You are the light of the world. A city built on a hill
cannot be hid. 15No one after lighting a lamp puts it under
the bushel basket, but on the lampstand, and it gives light
to all in the house. 16In the same way, let your light shine
before others, so that they may see your good works and
give glory to your Father in heaven.

The Morality of Christ

5:17–48 see pg. 24

17 "Do not think that I have come to
abolish the law or the prophets; I have
come not to abolish but to fulfill. 18For truly I tell you, until
heaven and earth pass away, not one letter,[y] not one stroke
of a letter, will pass from the law until all is accomplished.
19Therefore, whoever breaks[z] one of the

5:19 see pg. 23

least of these commandments, and
teaches others to do the same, will be called least in the

(Bible text continued on page 22)

[x]Other ancient authorities lack *falsely* [y]Gk *one iota* [z]Or *annuls*

The Meek

A CLOSER LOOK 5:5 *Nearly every society and every city in biblical times had a large* underclass, *people scraping by on the margins of society (v. 5). Jesus intentionally directed much of His life and ministry to that disadvantaged group. See Luke 7:22.*

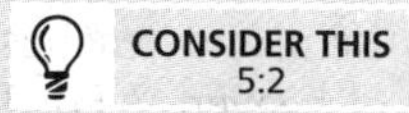

THE SERMON ON THE MOUNT

"Repent, for the kingdom of heaven has come near," Jesus warned as He began His public ministry in Galilee (Matt. 4:17). His message quickly spread and huge crowds came to hear Him from Galilee, from nearby Syria and the Decapolis, and from as far away as Jerusalem, Judea, and east of the Jordan River (vv. 24–25).

They came to hear about a kingdom. Instead, Jesus talked about a lifestyle—the lifestyle of those who intend to live in the kingdom. As perhaps thousands gathered on a hillside (or "mountain," 5:1; the exact location is unknown), Jesus began to fill out the implications of His appeal for repentance. It would mean far more than an outward show of piety. Indeed, Jesus urged His listeners to make such a complete change of heart and life that they would "be perfect, therefore, as your heavenly Father is perfect" (v. 48).

Jesus may have spoken the contents of Matthew 5–7, known as the Sermon on the Mount, on more than one occasion. It is possible that the address lasted for some time as He described the new lifestyle of the kingdom, holding it up like a jewel with many facets, to be examined from many different angles. On the other hand, bits and pieces of the sermon can be found throughout the Gospels. Like any good teacher, Jesus probably repeated much of His teaching at other times and places in order to drive home the message.

The Sermon on the Mount contains the core of Jesus' moral and ethical teaching:

The Beatitudes (5:3–12). True happiness comes from looking at life from God's perspective, which is often the reverse of the human point of view.

Salt and Light (5:13–16). Jesus wants His followers to influence the moral and spiritual climate of the world.

The Morality of the Kingdom (5:17–48). Jesus' listeners were familiar with the Old Testament Law and with the many traditions added by generations of legal scholars. But Jesus revealed a morality that went beyond the letter of the Law to its spirit.

Spiritual Disciplines (6:1–18). Practicing religion certainly involves behavior, but it goes beyond an outward show of spirituality to the hidden quality of one's character.

Treasures on Earth (6:19–34). Our relationship to money and material possessions reveals much about our relationship to God. Jesus does not denounce worldly goods, but He urges His listeners to place ultimate value on the treasures of heaven.

Judging Right and Wrong (7:1–6). Most of us are quick to point out the moral flaws of others. Jesus warns us to pay more attention to our own.

Asking and Receiving (7:7–12). When we approach God with a request, we can expect Him to deal with us as a loving father deals with his child. And just as God deals with us in love, He expects us to deal with others in love.

A Challenge to Obedience (7:13–29). Jesus wraps up His message with a challenge to change. The alternatives are clear: living a lifestyle that is worthy of the kingdom, resulting in life and joy; or ignoring the way of Christ, resulting in death and disaster.

In this manner, Jesus described the lifestyle of the kingdom. When He was finished, Matthew says that the people were "astounded" at His teaching (7:28; literally "overwhelmed" or "stunned"). They had come to hear a new teacher, but this one exceeded their expectations. His voice had an unusual but unmistakable ring of authority (v. 29). And no wonder: they were listening to the King Himself! ◆

kingdom of heaven; but whoever does them and teaches
them will be called great in the kingdom of heaven. 20 For I
tell you, unless your righteousness exceeds that of the
scribes and Pharisees, you will never enter the kingdom of
heaven.

21 "You have heard that it was said to those of ancient
times, 'You shall not murder'; and 'whoever murders shall
be liable to judgment.' 22 But I say to you that if you are angry with a brother or sister,[a] you will be liable to judgment;
and if you insult[b] a brother or sister,[c] you will be liable to
the council; and if you say, 'You fool,' you will be liable to
the hell[d] of fire. 23 So when you are offering your gift at the
altar, if you remember that your brother or sister[e] has something against you, 24 leave your gift there before the altar
and go; first be reconciled to your brother or sister,[e] and
then come and offer your gift. 25 Come to terms quickly
with your accuser while you are on the way to court[f] with
him, or your accuser may hand you over to the judge, and
the judge to the guard, and you will be thrown into prison.
26 Truly I tell you, you will never get out until you have paid
the last penny.

[a]Gk *a brother*; other ancient authorities add *without cause* [b]Gk *say Raca to* (an obscure term of abuse) [c]Gk *a brother* [d]Gk *Gehenna* [e]Gk *your brother* [f]Gk lacks *to court*

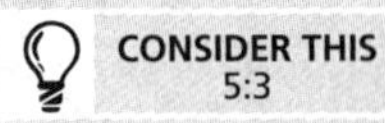

CONSIDER THIS
5:3

The Way Up Is Down

Of all the virtues Christ commended in the Beatitudes, it is significant that the first is humility, being "poor in spirit" (v. 3). That underlies all the others:

- *You cannot mourn (v. 4) without appreciating how insufficient you are to handle life in your own strength. That is humility.*
- *You cannot be meek (v. 5) unless you have needed gentleness yourself. Knowing that need is humility.*
- *You cannot hunger and thirst for righteousness (v. 6) if you proudly think of yourself as already righteous. Longing to fill that spiritual appetite demands humility. In a parable that Luke recorded, a humble tax collector prayed, "God, be merciful to me, a sinner!" He went away justified, unlike a proud Pharisee who boasted of his righteousness (Luke 18:13).*
- *You cannot be merciful (Matt. 5:7) without recognizing your own need for mercy. Jesus said that it's the person who is forgiven much that loves much (Luke 7:47). To*

27 "You have heard that it was said, 'You shall not commit adultery.' 28But I say to you that everyone who looks at
a woman with lust has already committed adultery with her
in his heart. 29If your right eye causes you to sin, tear it out
and throw it away; it is better for you to lose one of your
members than for your whole body to be thrown into hell.[g]
30And if your right hand causes you to sin, cut it off and
throw it away; it is better for you to lose one of your members than for your whole body to go into hell.[g]
31 "It was also said, 'Whoever divorces his wife, let him
give her a certificate of divorce.' 32But I
say to you that anyone who divorces his
wife, except on the ground of unchastity, causes her to
commit adultery; and whoever marries a divorced woman
commits adultery.
33 "Again, you have heard that it was said to those of ancient times, 'You shall not swear falsely, but carry out the
vows you have made to the Lord.' 34But I say to you, Do
not swear at all, either by heaven, for it is the throne of

5:32 see pg. 26

(Bible text continued on page 26)

[g]*Gk* *Gehenna*

confess your sin and ask God and others for forgiveness takes humility.

- *You cannot be pure in heart (Matt. 5:8) if your heart is filled with pride. God promises to exalt the humble, not the proud (James 4:10).*
- *You cannot be a peacemaker (Matt. 5:9) if you believe that you are always right. To admit your own fallibility takes humility. Peace results when both warring parties move toward each other.*
- *Finally, identifying with Christ no matter what the reaction of others (vv. 10–12) demands a certain death to yourself and a renunciation of your own rights. Standing up under persecution demands Christlike humility.* ◆

Humility is the scandalous virtue! See Phil. 2:3.

What About the Old Testament Law?

CONSIDER THIS 5:19

Jesus' critics claimed that His teaching encouraged people to violate the Mosaic Law, allowing them to get away with sin. Actually, He warned people to avoid the ways of religious hypocrites. While making an outward show of righteousness they took ethical shortcuts and carried out wicked schemes. In this portion of the the Sermon on the Mount (vv. 17–20), Jesus turned the tables on His opponents by appealing to the Law as the basis for His moral code—not the Law as they taught it, but as God intended it.

Jesus' words are crucial for Christians today. While God does not require us to live by the specific regulations of the Old Testament Law, He still expects us to honor Old Testament morality. What might that look like in today's ethically complicated marketplace? See "Ten Commandments for Practical Living," James 2:8–13.

The Old Testament Law was part of the covenant that set Israel apart as God's people. It governed their worship, their relationship to God, and their social relationships with one another. See "The Law," Rom. 2:12.

CONSIDER THIS
5:13–16

SULFA DRUGS AND STREET LIGHTS

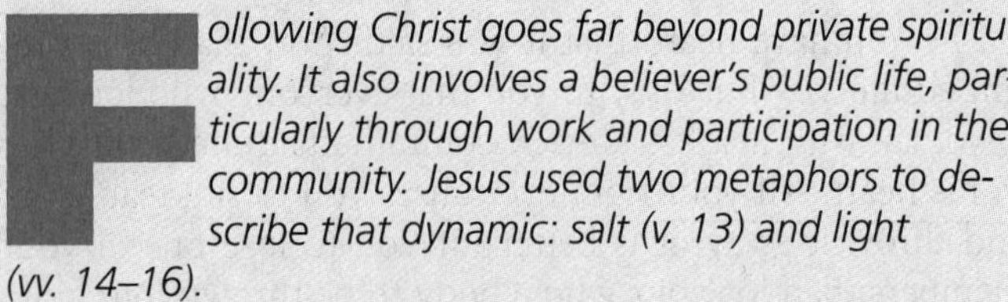
Following Christ goes far beyond private spirituality. It also involves a believer's public life, particularly through work and participation in the community. Jesus used two metaphors to describe that dynamic: salt (v. 13) and light (vv. 14–16).

In Jesus' day, salt was used to preserve foods like fish from decay. In the same way, believers can help to preserve society from moral and spiritual decay. Of course, in our culture, salt has given way to chemical preservatives (many of which have come under attack in recent years for their alleged role in causing cancer). So Jesus might use a different metaphor were He speaking today.

Perhaps He would talk in terms of an infection-fighting drug, such as an antibiotic like penicillin, or the sulfa drugs developed in the '40s that have proved so valuable in fighting meningitis and pneumonia. Christians can help to ward off spiritual infections and diseases in the larger society. One of the most powerful arenas for influence is the workplace, particularly jobs that affect values, laws, and public opinion. That's why believers need to pursue careers in education, government, and journalism, among many others. They may not be able to transform the entire society, but they can use whatever influence they have to promote Christlike values and hinder evil.

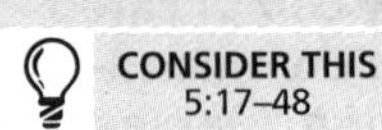
CONSIDER THIS
5:17–48

THE MORALITY OF CHRIST

"Jesus was a great moral teacher. Mainly He taught that people should love each other." Have you ever heard someone summarize Christ's life and ministry that way?

It is true that Jesus was a great moral teacher. But of course, He was much more—He was also the Son of God (see "Ten Myths of Christianity, Myth #1: Jesus Christ Was Only a Great Moral Teacher," Matt. 13:34–35). Likewise, He certainly taught that people should love each other. But He taught a great deal more. In this section of the Sermon on the Mount (5:17–48), we discover much about Jesus' concept of morality.

Unfortunately, numerous misunderstandings have come from this passage. Jesus makes a number of statements that sound extreme to our ears (vv. 22, 30, 37, 39–42). How can we make sense out of them?

First, it's important to know that when Jesus referred to "the Law" and "the Prophets" (v. 17), He was referring to the express moral teaching of the Old Testament. His listeners were Jews, so their moral conduct and character were governed by those Scriptures. At least, they were supposed to be.

Jesus also called His followers "the light of the world" (v. 14), an image that fits perfectly into modern society. The Lord's first-century listeners would be astonished at the availability and importance of light in our culture. We use it not only to illuminate but also to communicate. Thus, Jesus wants us as His followers to shine, to be visible and attractive, not to bring attention to ourselves, but to bring people to God (v. 16). Again, our vocations are one of the primary means we have to reflect Christ to others.

Jesus' teaching here challenges us as His followers to ask: How are we engaging our society? What spiritual infections are we fighting to overcome? What positive changes are we trying to promote? What impact for God are we having through our work? Have we lost our saltiness (v. 13)? Are we standing like burned-out street lights, ineffective and waiting to be removed? Or are we shining brilliantly with the love and truth of Christ? ◆

Spreading Christ's message involves far more than just broadcasting a statement or a set of facts. See "Faith Impacts the World," Mark 16:15–16.

In reality, the people were taught a heavily doctored version of Scripture by many of their leaders. Sometimes these teachers stressed the letter of the Law, rather than its spirit, and sometimes they favored their own traditions over the actual teaching of God (12:9–12; 15:1–9). And sometimes they actually perverted the Law to suit their own ends (19:3–8). No wonder Jesus labeled them hypocrites and warned people not to follow their example (23:1–36).

That helps to explain the formula that Jesus uses here: "You have heard that it was said . . . but I say to you" (vv. 21–22, 27–28, 33–34, 38–39, 43–44). The people had heard the Law and the Prophets, but not in their purity. By contrast, Jesus spoke with integrity and authority to five areas of morality: murder (vv. 21–26), adultery (vv. 27–32), vows and oaths (vv. 33–37), vengeance (vv. 38–42), and love and hate (vv. 43–47).

Framing these remarks is an introduction in which the Lord appealed to His listeners to fulfill the Law (vv. 17–20) and a conclusion in which He challenged them to act as the Father would act (v. 48). ◆

"YOU HAVE HEARD THAT IT WAS SAID. . . . BUT I SAY TO YOU. . . ."
—Matthew 5:21–22

God, 35or by the earth, for it is his footstool, or by
Jerusalem, for it is the city of the great King. 36And do not
swear by your head, for you cannot make one hair white or
black. 37Let your word be 'Yes, Yes' or 'No, No'; anything
more than this comes from the evil one.[h]

5:38–42 see pg. 28

38 "You have heard that it was said,
'An eye for an eye and a tooth for a
tooth.' 39But I say to you, Do not resist an evildoer. But if
anyone strikes you on the right cheek, turn the other also;
40and if anyone wants to sue you and take your coat, give
your cloak as well; 41and if anyone forces you to go one
mile, go also the second mile. 42Give to everyone who begs
from you, and do not refuse anyone who wants to borrow
from you.

5:43–48

43 "You have heard that it was said,
'You shall love your neighbor and hate
your enemy.' 44But I say to you, Love your enemies and
pray for those who persecute you, 45so that you may be
children of your Father in heaven; for he makes his sun rise
on the evil and on the good, and sends rain on the righteous and on the unrighteous. 46For if you love those who
love you, what reward do you have? Do not even the tax
collectors do the same? 47And if you greet only your brothers and sisters,[i] what more are you doing than others? Do
not even the Gentiles do the same? 48Be perfect, therefore,
as your heavenly Father is perfect.

Spiritual Disciplines

6:1–4 see pg. 29

6 "Beware of practicing your piety before others in order to be seen by

(Bible text continued on page 29)

[h]*Or evil* [i]*Gk your brothers*

A New Respect for Women

CONSIDER THIS 5:32 *Greek, Roman, and Jewish laws of Jesus' day afforded men many opportunities to divorce their wives. Perhaps the most painful for the women was infertility. But in vv. 31–32, Jesus insisted on a different understanding of women—and the relative importance of childbearing. Only the severing of the marriage bond through sexual immorality was to be grounds for divorce, not the lack of an heir.*

Living the Way God Wants Us To

A CLOSER LOOK 5:43–48 *Jesus' moral standard seems high. But it's not to be reached by just our own ability. When we are Christ's, we are made into new creatures. The Holy Spirit lives through us as we become more like Jesus. See "New Creatures with New Character," Gal. 5:22–23.*

There are two reasons not to feel frustrated by the expectations we see here: First, eternal life is not earned but is God's gift. Second, godly principles enable us to live stable, joyful lives. See "Rules That Lead to Joy," 1 John 2:3–6.

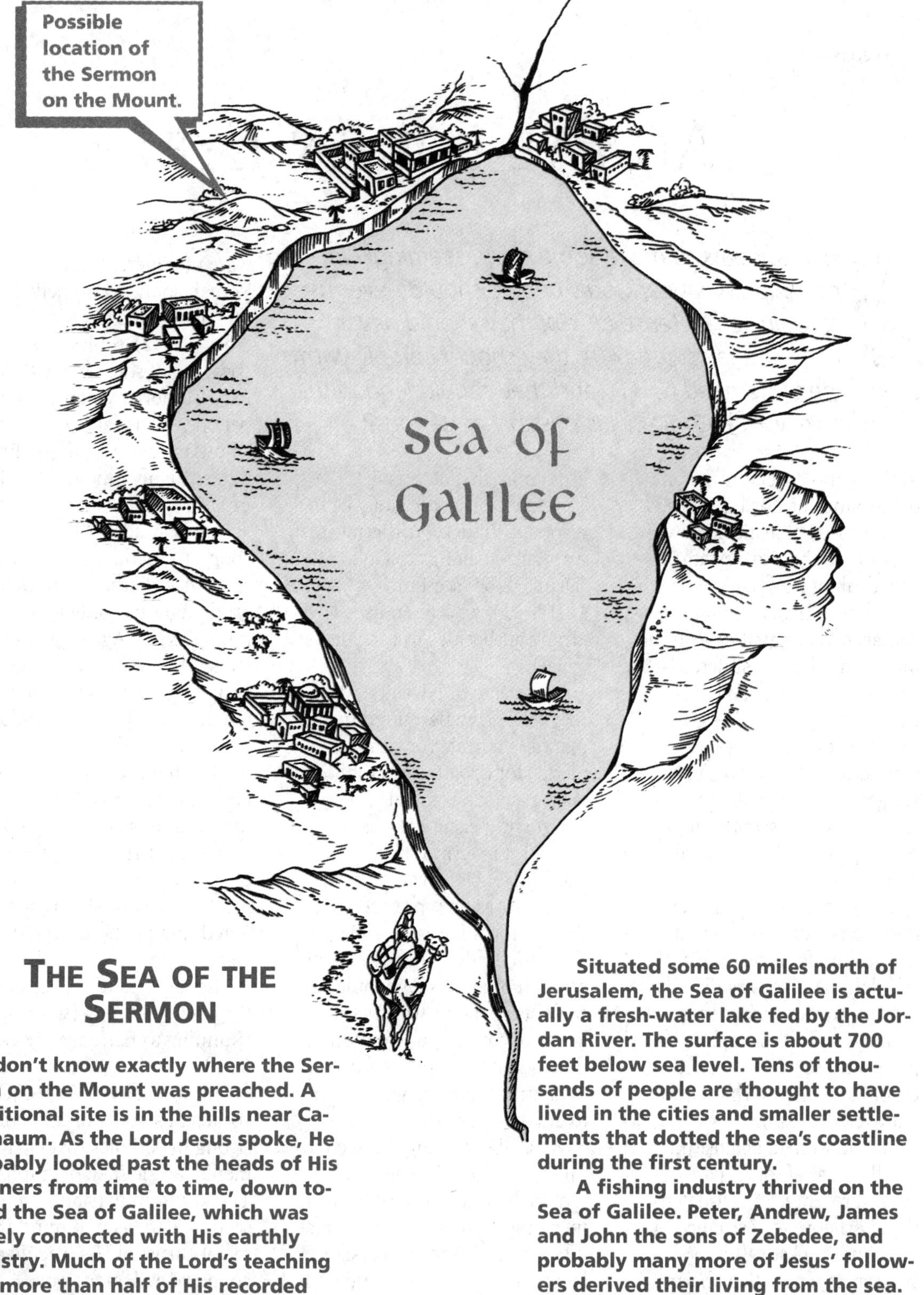

THE SEA OF THE SERMON

We don't know exactly where the Sermon on the Mount was preached. A traditional site is in the hills near Capernaum. As the Lord Jesus spoke, He probably looked past the heads of His listeners from time to time, down toward the Sea of Galilee, which was closely connected with His earthly ministry. Much of the Lord's teaching and more than half of His recorded miracles occurred on or around this body of water.

Situated some 60 miles north of Jerusalem, the Sea of Galilee is actually a fresh-water lake fed by the Jordan River. The surface is about 700 feet below sea level. Tens of thousands of people are thought to have lived in the cities and smaller settlements that dotted the sea's coastline during the first century.

A fishing industry thrived on the Sea of Galilee. Peter, Andrew, James and John the sons of Zebedee, and probably many more of Jesus' followers derived their living from the sea. For more information see "The World of the Fishermen," Luke 5:1–11.

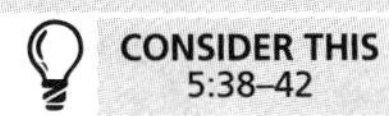

AN EYE FOR AN EYE

Jesus appears to make some stark, seemingly impossible demands: God's people should never use force in self-defense (v. 39); they should never contest a lawsuit (v. 40); they should comply with every type of demand (v. 41); and they should lend without reserve (v. 42). Could Jesus possibly be serious?

In this part of the Sermon on the Mount, the Lord is addressing the issue of justice. He was alluding to the Old Testament Law dealing with *public* vengeance. The Law limited damages in criminal cases to no more than the loss suffered—"an eye for an eye" (v. 38; Ex. 21:24–25). Nevertheless, as might be expected, people tended to justify *personal* vengeance by appealing to the same texts. We would call it "taking the law into your own hands."

But Jesus' morality challenged that. To be sure, some circumstances call for resistance and self-defense. The Law did allow for self-protection in certain situations; for instance, it did not punish those who defended themselves against thieves after dark (Ex. 22:2–3).

But He warned against the needless use of force, particularly in revenge. In self-defense, the alternative to resistance may be injury or death. But in vengeance, one inflicts harm even though immediate danger is past. A slap on the cheek is little more than an insult. There's no place for violence in response to that. Furthermore, vengeance belongs to God (Deut. 32:35; see Rom. 12:19–21), who often uses governing authorities to carry it out (13:4).

In the case of lawsuits (Matt. 5:40), the Law permitted demanding a tunic (or shirt) in pledge for a loan, but prohibited taking a cloak (or coat) overnight, because it was needed for warmth (Ex. 22:26–27). However, Jesus' listeners commonly pressed for the cloak—for ruinous damages—almost literally "suing the pants off each other," as we would say. But Christ's point was that if lawsuits have to go to extremes, they ought to be in the extreme of charity. (Paul argued similarly in 1 Cor. 6:1–8.)

What about going the second mile (Matt. 5:41)? The word "compels" is a technical term meaning "to requisition or press into service." Ancient Persian law permitted postal carriers to *compel* private citizens to help carry their loads. The Romans were no different; for example, Roman soldiers compelled Simon of Cyrene to carry Jesus' cross (27:32). So Jesus was speaking of someone with legitimate authority who might compel one of His followers to go a "thousand paces," or one Roman mile, roughly nine-tenths of an English mile.

How should a believer respond to such requests? With resistance? Perhaps complying grudgingly, but only to a minimum degree? Again, Jesus challenged His followers to grace and integrity. Imagine the reputation that Christians would have if we always did twice what the law required! What would tax auditors think if we not only followed the rules, but paid more than the law required of us? What would our employers think if we consistently rendered double the expected service?

The same pattern holds in the case of lending (v. 42; see "Running to Extremes," Luke 6:29).

Throughout vv. 17–48, Jesus speaks in stark contrasts and strong hyperboles (overstatements for the sake of emphasis). The key to understanding this section is to keep in mind the major thrust of His teaching: good not evil, grace not vengeance, love not hatred. That is the morality of Christ. ◆

them; for then you have no reward from your Father in
heaven.
2 "So whenever you give alms, do not sound a trumpet
before you, as the hypocrites do in the synagogues and in
the streets, so that they may be praised by others. Truly I
tell you, they have received their reward. 3But when you
give alms, do not let your left hand know what your right
hand is doing, 4so that your alms may be done in secret;
and your Father who sees in secret will reward you.[j]
5 "And whenever you pray, do not be like the hypocrites;
for they love to stand and pray in the synagogues and at the
street corners, so that they may be seen by others. Truly I
tell you, they have received their reward. 6But whenever
you pray, go into your room and shut the door and pray to
your Father who is in secret; and your Father who sees in
secret will reward you.[j]
7 "When you are praying, do not heap up empty phrases
as the Gentiles do; for they think that they will be heard because of their many words. 8Do not be like them, for your
Father knows what you need before you ask him.
9 "Pray then in this way:

Our Father in heaven,
hallowed be your name.
10 Your kingdom come.
Your will be done,
on earth as it is in heaven.

6:11

11 Give us this day our daily bread.[k]
12 And forgive us our debts,
as we also have forgiven our debtors.

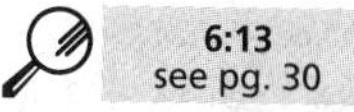
6:13
see pg. 30

13 And do not bring us to the time of
trial,[l]
but rescue us from the evil one.[m]

14For if you forgive others their trespasses, your heavenly
Father will also forgive you; 15but if you do not forgive others, neither will your Father forgive your trespasses.

[j]Other ancient authorities add *openly* [k]*Or our bread for tomorrow* [l]*Or us into temptation* [m]*Or from evil.* Other ancient authorities add, in some form, *For the kingdom and the power and the glory are yours forever. Amen.*

Our Daily Bread

A CLOSER LOOK
6:11

The request for daily bread (v. 11) acknowledges that God ultimately provides for our needs. He gives us skills and strength, jobs and income, and a world rich with resources to that end. For more on God's provision, see "God—The Original Worker," John 5:17.

ANONYMOUS DONORS

CONSIDER THIS 6:1–4

Jesus' words in vv. 1–4 challenge a lot of what goes on today in fund-raising and charitable causes. As any fund-raiser knows, one of the biggest motivations for people who give large gifts is the prestige that results.

Jesus questioned that spirit of giving, however. He detested people who made a great show of presenting their gifts in the temple and elsewhere (Mark 12:41–44) as if they were generous and upright, but behind the scenes practiced the worst sorts of greed and immorality (Matt. 23:23–24). He was not attacking giving but hypocrisy.

How can we be sure that we are giving with the right motives? One way is to give anonymously (6:3–4). That way, our gifts will affect no one's opinion of us one way or the other. The matter will stay between us and God—and He can evaluate our motives.

"DO NOT BE LIKE THE HYPOCRITES."
—Matthew 6:5

16 "And whenever you fast, do not look dismal, like the
hypocrites, for they disfigure their faces so as to show others that they are fasting. Truly I tell you, they have received
their reward. 17But when you fast, put oil on your head and
wash your face, 18so that your fasting may be seen not by
others but by your Father who is in secret; and your Father
who sees in secret will reward you.[n]

Treasures on Earth

6:19–34

19 "Do not store up for yourselves
treasures on earth, where moth and rust[o]
consume and where thieves break in and steal; 20but store
up for yourselves treasures in heaven, where neither moth
nor rust[o] consumes and where thieves do not break in and

[n]Other ancient authorities add *openly* [o]Gk *eating*

Do Not Lead Us into Temptation

A CLOSER LOOK 6:13

God has committed Himself to helping His children avoid, flee, confess, and resist temptation (v. 13). See "Pay Attention to Temptation!" at 1 Cor. 10:12–13.

CONSIDER THIS 6:19–34

Don't Worry!

Of the texts in Scripture that discuss money and work, vv. 19–34 are among the most frequently cited. Unfortunately, they are often used to imply that Jesus was against money and considered everyday work a distraction to things that "really" matter.

However, a careful reader will notice that Jesus condemned worry, not work (vv. 25, 27–28, 31, 34). He never told us to stop working. Rather, He called us to correctly focus our faith on God, the ultimate supplier of our needs (v. 32).

God provides for people in many ways. The most common is through everyday work. He expects us to work diligently with whatever resources He gives us (2 Thess. 3:6–12). Of course, sometimes that normal means of provision fails for a variety of reasons: ill health, divorce from or death of a provider, loss of a job, natural disaster, changing markets, and other circumstances beyond our control.

It is precisely the fear of those possibilities that tempts us to worry so much and forget about trusting God. Why rely on Him, we figure, if He can't keep us from troubles like that? Why not just rely on ourselves and trust to our

steal. 21For where your treasure is, there your heart will be
also.
22 "The eye is the lamp of the body. So, if your eye is
healthy, your whole body will be full of light; 23but if your
eye is unhealthy, your whole body will be full of darkness.
If then the light in you is darkness, how great is the darkness!
24 "No one can serve two masters; for a slave will either hate the one and love the other, or be devoted to the
one and despise the other. You cannot serve God and
wealth.[p]
25 "Therefore I tell you, do not worry about your life,
what you will eat or what you will drink,[q] or about your
body, what you will wear. Is not life more than food, and
the body more than clothing? 26Look at the birds of the air;
they neither sow nor reap nor gather into barns, and yet
your heavenly Father feeds them. Are you not of more
value than they? 27And can any of you by worrying add a
single hour to your span of life?[r] 28And why do you worry
about clothing? Consider the lilies of the field, how they

[p] Gk *mammon* [q] Other ancient authorities lack *or what you will drink* [r] Or *add one cubit to your height*

own devices? All the while we forget that God never promised that we wouldn't face hard times, and that He has many ways to help us through them when we do: family members, church communities, neighbors, charities, inheritances, even public agencies and non-profit groups.

Certainly we need to pay attention to our physical and material needs. But Jesus urged us to stop worrying about things so that they dominate our lives and values. We can't do that and serve God at the same time (v. 24). Instead, we need to redirect our focus onto God's kingdom and righteousness (v. 33). That means adopting the values of the King and bringing Him into our work and lives. Jesus said that's what "really" matters. ◆

God has given work as a gift to be used in service to others. See "People at Work," Heb. 2:7.

Contrary to what many people think, work is not a curse. See "Is Work a Curse?" Rom. 8:20–22.

Bringing Christ into our everyday work has a tangible effect on how we do our jobs. See "Your 'Workstyle,'" Titus 2:9–10.

"FOR WHERE YOUR TREASURE IS, THERE YOUR HEART WILL BE ALSO."
—Matthew 6:21

Judge Not!

CONSIDER THIS 7:1–5 **What was Jesus calling for when He ordered His followers to "not judge" (v. 1)? Did He want us to close our eyes to error and evil? Did He intend that managers forgo critical performance reviews of their employees? Or that news editors and art critics pull their punches? Or that juries refrain from judgment? Should we decline any assessment of others, since none of us is perfect?**

No, those would all be misapplications of Jesus' teaching. In the first place, He was not commanding blind acceptance, but grace toward others. Since all of us are sinners, we need to stop bothering with the failings of others and start attending to serious issues of our own (vv. 3–5). His words here extend His earlier exposé of hypocrisy (6:1–18). Don't blame or put down others while excusing or exalting yourself, Jesus was saying.

Is there room, then, to assess others, especially when we know we are not perfect? Yes, but only in Jesus' way: with empathy and fairness (7:12) and with a readiness to freely and fully forgive (Matt. 6:12, 14). When we are called upon to correct others, we should act like a good doctor whose purpose is to bring healing—not like an enemy who attacks.

Scripture gives clear guidelines to believers in cases where judgments need to be rendered. See Matt. 18:15–17; 1 Cor. 6:1–8; and Gal. 6:1–5.

grow; they neither toil nor spin, 29yet I tell you, even Solomon in all his glory was not clothed like one of these. 30But if God so clothes the grass of the field, which is alive today and tomorrow is thrown into the oven, will he not much more clothe you—you of little faith? 31Therefore do not worry, saying, 'What will we eat?' or 'What will we drink?' or 'What will we wear?' 32For it is the Gentiles who strive for all these things; and indeed your heavenly Father knows that you need all these things. 33But strive first for the kingdom of God[s] and his[t] righteousness, and all these things will be given to you as well.

34 "So do not worry about tomorrow, for tomorrow will bring worries of its own. Today's trouble is enough for today.

"Do Not Judge"

7:1–5

7 "Do not judge, so that you may not be judged. 2For with the judgment you make you will be judged, and the measure you give will be the measure you get. 3Why do you see the speck in your neighbor's[u] eye, but do not notice the log in your own eye? 4Or how can you say to your neighbor,[v] 'Let me take the speck out of your eye,' while the log is in your own eye? 5You hypocrite, first take the log out of your own eye, and then you will see clearly to take the speck out of your neighbor's[u] eye.

6 "Do not give what is holy to dogs; and do not throw your pearls before swine, or they will trample them under foot and turn and maul you.

Asking and Receiving

7 "Ask, and it will be given you; search, and you will find; knock, and the door will be opened for you. 8For everyone who asks receives, and everyone who searches finds, and for everyone who knocks, the door will be opened. 9Is there anyone among you who, if your child asks for bread, will give a stone? 10Or if the child asks for a fish, will give a snake? 11If you then, who are evil, know how to give good gifts to your children, how much more will your Father in heaven give good things to those who ask him!

7:12

12 "In everything do to others as you would have them do to you; for this is the law and the prophets.

[s]Other ancient authorities lack *of God* [t]Or *its* [u]Gk *brother's* [v]Gk *brother*

A Challenge to Obedience

13 "Enter through the narrow gate; for the gate is wide and the road is easy[w] that leads to destruction, and there are many who take it. 14For the gate is narrow and the road is hard that leads to life, and there are few who find it.

15 "Beware of false prophets, who come to you in sheep's clothing but inwardly are ravenous wolves. 16You will know them by their fruits. Are grapes gathered from thorns, or figs from thistles? 17In the same way, every good tree bears good fruit, but the bad tree bears bad fruit. 18A good tree cannot bear bad fruit, nor can a bad tree bear good fruit. 19Every tree that does not bear good fruit is cut down and thrown into the fire. 20Thus you will know them by their fruits.

21 "Not everyone who says to me, 'Lord, Lord,' will enter the kingdom of heaven, but only the one who does the will of my Father in heaven. 22On that day many will say to me, 'Lord, Lord, did we not prophesy in your name, and cast out demons in your name, and do many deeds of power in your name?' 23Then I will declare to them, 'I never knew you; go away from me, you evildoers.'

24 "Everyone then who hears these words of mine and acts on them will be like a wise man who built his house on rock. 25The rain fell, the floods came, and the winds blew and beat on that house, but it did not fall, because it had been founded on rock. 26And everyone who hears these words of mine and does not act on them will be like a foolish man who built his house on sand. 27The rain fell, and the floods came, and the winds blew and beat against that house, and it fell—and great was its fall!"

28 Now when Jesus had finished saying these things,

7:29 see pg. 34

the crowds were astounded at his teaching, 29for he taught them as one having authority, and not as their scribes.

Jesus Heals a Leper

8 When Jesus[x] had come down from the mountain, great crowds followed him; 2and there was a leper[y] who

8:2 see pg. 35

came to him and knelt before him, saying, "Lord, if you choose, you can make me clean." 3He stretched out his hand and touched him,

[w]Other ancient authorities read *for the road is wide and easy* [x]Gk *he* [y]The terms *leper* and *leprosy* can refer to several diseases

QUOTE UNQUOTE

CONSIDER THIS 7:12 *The "golden rule" (v. 12) is one of the best known teachings of Scripture. The great Reformer, Martin Luther, applied it specifically to the workplace:*

If you are a manual laborer, you find that the Bible has been put in your workshop, into your hand, into your heart. It teaches and preaches how you should treat your neighbor. Just look at your tools—at your needle or thimble, . . . your goods, your scales or yardstick or measure—and you will read this statement inscribed on them. Everywhere you look it stares at you. Nothing you handle every day is so tiny that it does not continually tell you this, if only you will listen. Indeed, there is no shortage of preaching. You have as many preachers as you have transactions, goods, tools, and other equipment in your house and home. All this is continually crying out to you: "Friend use me in your relations with your neighbor just as you would want your neighbor to use his property in his relations with you."

Martin Luther

Jesus had much more to say about the Law and the Prophets (v. 12). See "The Morality of Christ," Matt. 5:17–48.

JESUS' AUTHORITY

CONSIDER THIS 7:29

Scribes were members of a learned class in Israel who studied the Scriptures and tradition, and who served as copyists, editors, and teachers (see Luke 20:39). But while they held positions of authority, Jesus was a person of authority (v. 29). His authority was a function of who He was, not of what He had learned.

saying, "I do choose. Be made clean!" Immediately his leprosy[z] was cleansed. 4Then Jesus said to him, "See that you
say nothing to anyone; but go, show yourself to the priest,
and offer the gift that Moses commanded, as a testimony to
them."

Jesus Heals a Centurion's Servant

8:5–13

5 When he entered Capernaum, a
centurion came to him, appealing to him
6and saying, "Lord, my servant is lying at home paralyzed,
in terrible distress." 7And he said to him, "I will come and
cure him." 8The centurion answered, "Lord, I am not worthy to have you come under my roof; but only speak the

[z]The terms *leper* and *leprosy* can refer to several diseases

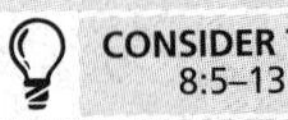

CONSIDER THIS 8:5–13

UNDER AUTHORITY

The centurion pointed out that, like Jesus, he was also "a man under authority" (v. 9). The encounter between the two suggests several lessons of authority and leadership:

(1) Effective leaders willingly admit when they need help (v. 5). The centurion faced a problem that went beyond his own considerable power. But he was willing to go outside his resources to enlist Jesus to deal with the situation.

(2) Effective leaders respond to matters of the heart and spirit (vv. 6, 8). The centurion was moved by compassion for his suffering servant, and perceived that Jesus had insight and power that went beyond a physician's skill.

(3) Effective leaders are able to approach others on their terms (vv. 5, 8). The centurion came in faith, pleading with Jesus to help his servant. As a Roman officer, he could have ordered Jesus, or offered Him money. But instead, he approached the Lord in a manner consistent with His nature.

(4) Effective leaders understand and accept the nature of authority (v. 9). The centurion understood what submission is all about. When he issued a command, his soldiers simply obeyed. He recognized that Jesus had the same authority over illness.

(5) Effective leaders invest trust in those under their authority (vv. 9–10). Great leaders display great faith in their people. The centurion trusted that Jesus could do what He said He would do.

word, and my servant will be healed. 9For I also am a man
under authority, with soldiers under me; and I say to one,
'Go,' and he goes, and to another, 'Come,' and he comes,
and to my slave, 'Do this,' and the slave
does it." 10When Jesus heard him, he
was amazed and said to those who followed him, "Truly I
tell you, in no one[a] in Israel have I found such faith. 11I tell
you, many will come from east and west and will eat with
Abraham and Isaac and Jacob in the kingdom of heaven,
12while the heirs of the kingdom will be thrown into the
outer darkness, where there will be weeping and gnashing
of teeth." 13And to the centurion Jesus said, "Go; let it be
done for you according to your faith." And the servant was
healed in that hour.

8:10 see pg. 36

(Bible text continued on page 37)

[a]Other ancient authorities read *Truly I tell you, not even*

(6) Effective leaders know who to trust (v. 10). Trust is only as useful as the trustworthiness of the one in whom it is placed. The centurion's faith was marvelous because it was invested in the right person—Jesus. Leadership based on blind faith, either in others or in a system, is foolhardy.

In light of these observations:

- *Do you rely too much on your own competence, or do you honestly assess both your strengths and your weaknesses?*
- *Do you respond to people only in terms of "the facts," or are you sensitive to the feelings and unexpressed needs of others (as well as your own)?*
- *Are you willing to meet and work with people on their terms, in their arena? Or must everyone come to you and play by your rules?*
- *Are you willing to be in charge, but unwilling to submit?*
- *In whom and in what do you place your faith?* ◆

Centurions played a powerful role in Rome's occupation of Palestine. See Mark 15:39.

In praising the centurion, Jesus tweaked the ethnic attitudes of the Jews. A Gentile with greater faith than any of them? Scandalous! See "A Soldier's Surprising Faith," Luke 7:1–10.

LEPROSY

FOR YOUR INFO 8:2

Lepers like the man mentioned in v. 2 were common in the ancient world. They suffered from a slowly progressing, ordinarily incurable skin disease that was believed to be highly contagious and therefore greatly feared. As a result, anyone who appeared to have leprosy, even if the symptoms were caused by some other condition, was banished from the community.

True leprosy is caused by a bacterium that spreads across the skin, creating sores, scabs, and white shining spots. The most serious problem, however, is a loss of sensation. Without the ability to feel, lepers injure their tissue, leading to further infection, deformity, muscle loss, and eventual paralysis. Fortunately, modern medicine has all but eliminated the disease.

Old Testament Law was quite detailed in its instructions regarding recognition and quarantine of leprous persons. Priests became the central figures for diagnosis, care of patients, and taking sanitary precautions to protect the rest of the community. The Law required that a leper be isolated from the rest of society (Lev. 13:45–46). Infected persons were required to wear mourning clothes, leave their hair in disorder, keep their beards covered, and cry "Unclean! Unclean!" so that others could avoid them. Any contact would defile the person who touched a leper.

Sometimes lepers were miraculously cured, as in the case of Moses (Ex. 4:7), Miriam, his sister (Num. 12:10), and Naaman (2 Kin. 5:1,10).

In the New Testament, Jesus intentionally healed lepers as a sign to vindicate His ministry. On one occasion He healed ten, but only one returned to thank Him (Luke 17:11–15).

CONSIDER THIS
8:10

JESUS' GLOBAL CONNECTIONS

While Matthew's Gospel portrays Jesus in terms of His Jewish roots, it also shows that Jesus is an international Savior, a Messiah for the whole world. Notice some of Jesus' global connections:

Jesus' Roots (Matt. 1:1–16)

Jesus' genealogy includes at least two, and possibly three, Gentiles:

- David's great-great-grandmother, Rahab, a Canaanite prostitute of Jericho (Matt. 1:5; Josh. 2:1–24; 6:22–25).
- David's great-grandmother Ruth, a Moabite (Matt. 1:5; Ruth 1:1—4:22).
- Perhaps David's lover, Bathsheba, wife of Uriah the Hittite whom David murdered (Matt. 1:6; 2 Sam. 11:1—12:25). It is possible that Bathsheba was also a Hittite, though more likely she was a Hebrew who married a Hittite sojourner.

Wise Men from the East (Matt. 2:1–12)

In Matthew, the first worshipers of the baby Jesus were not Jews but Gentiles from the East. These wise men (*magi*) may have been astrologers from Persia (modern-day Iran). They came looking for the King of the Jews—their Messiah!

The Flight to Egypt (Matt. 2:13–14)

Egypt, a Gentile nation, provided a refuge for the infant Messiah from an outraged Herod the Great. In the same way, centuries before, Egypt had saved Jacob's family from starvation and had become a home where the family grew into a nation (Gen. 41:46—46:7).

Jesus' Childhood in Galilee (Matt. 2:22–23)

Jesus grew up in Nazareth, a small town of Galilee in the northern part of Palestine. The region was called Galilee of the Gentiles because of its mixed population (Matt. 4:15). Jesus began His ministry there, and many of His early followers were Gentiles from Syria and the Decapolis, a Gentile region (4:23–25).

"Undesirables" in Matthew

Jesus broke with many discriminatory traditions of His culture, reaching out to Samaritans, Gentiles, and other undesirables, as the following table of passages from Matthew shows:

A VARIETY OF PEOPLE AND RESPONSES

Text	People Involved	Jesus' Response
8:2–4	A leper, physically diseased and religiously unclean	Touched him when others would not
8:5–10	A Roman centurion	Healed his servant; praised his great faith
8:28–34	Two demon-possessed men from a Gentile region	Delivered them when the town rejected them
9:9–13	Matthew, a tax collector, and his disreputable friends	Called Matthew; dined with his friends
9:20–22	A hemorrhaging woman	Healed her; praised her faith
11:20–24	Tyre, Sidon, and Sodom (Gentile cities)	Said that in the judgment they will fare better than unrepentant "religious" cities
12:39–42	Nineveh and the Queen of the South	Praised their repentance; said they would judge the generation of Jews that knew Jesus
14:34–36	People of Gennesaret, a Gentile region	Healed their sick
15:21–28	A Canaanite woman from the region of Tyre and Sidon	Healed her daughter; praised her great faith

◆

The roots of hostility between Jews and Gentiles stretched deep into Israel's history. See "Jews, Gentiles, and Jesus," Matt. 15:24.

Peter's Mother-in-Law Healed

8:14–15

14 When Jesus entered Peter's house,
he saw his mother-in-law lying in bed
with a fever; 15he touched her hand, and the fever left her,
and she got up and began to serve him. 16That evening they
brought to him many who were possessed with demons;
and he cast out the spirits with a word, and cured all who
were sick. 17This was to fulfill what had been spoken
through the prophet Isaiah, "He took our infirmities and
bore our diseases."

Following Jesus Has Its Costs

18 Now when Jesus saw great crowds around him, he
gave orders to go over to the other side. 19A scribe then approached and said, "Teacher, I will follow you wherever you

8:20 see pg. 38

go." 20And Jesus said to him, "Foxes
have holes, and birds of the air have
nests; but the Son of Man has nowhere to lay his head."
21Another of his disciples said to him, "Lord, first let me go
and bury my father." 22But Jesus said to him, "Follow me,
and let the dead bury their own dead."

Jesus Calms a Storm

8:23–27

23 And when he got into the boat, his
disciples followed him. 24A windstorm
arose on the sea, so great that the boat was being swamped
by the waves; but he was asleep. 25And they went and woke
him up, saying, "Lord, save us! We are perishing!" 26And
he said to them, "Why are you afraid, you of little faith?"
Then he got up and rebuked the winds and the sea; and
there was a dead calm. 27They were amazed, saying, "What
sort of man is this, that even the winds and the sea obey
him?"

Two Demoniacs Healed

28 When he came to the other side, to the country of the
Gadarenes,[b] two demoniacs coming out of the tombs met
him. They were so fierce that no one could pass that way.

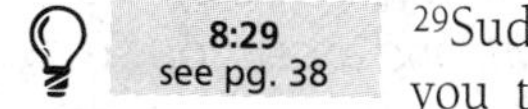

29Suddenly they shouted, "What have
you to do with us, Son of God? Have

[b]Other ancient authorities read *Gergesenes;* others, *Gerasenes*

A Surprise in Peter's Household

CONSIDER THIS 8:14–15

Households in Jesus' day tended to be much larger than those of today, with more children and more relatives from the extended family.

But Peter's home (v. 14) was somewhat unusual in that his mother-in-law lived with the family. Peter was not required by law or custom to provide her with a home. A widow usually moved back to her father's home, if he were still alive, or else joined a son's household.

It was fortunate for Peter's mother-in-law that Peter befriended Jesus. The Lord's compassion extended to widowed mothers-in-law even when He was a house guest! He healed her from her fever and she began to serve Him—a response that indicated a changed life and a deeply grateful attitude.

Does your faith cause you to respond to the needs of others like Jesus did?

The Storms of Galilee

A CLOSER LOOK 8:23–27

Galilee was and is the site of frequent violent storms such as the one described in vv. 23–27. For an explanation of this phenomenon, see the diagram, "What Kind of Storm Was This?" at Luke 8:22.

JESUS—A HOMELESS MAN?

CONSIDER THIS 8:20 **Jesus was born poor and lived poor. His comment in v. 20 even suggests that He was homeless. He never celebrated poverty, but He did ask His followers to forsake the common belief that real security comes from having wealth (Matt. 6:19–34).**

Does that seem too difficult for those of us living in a society that craves financial security and independence? If so, consider that Christ is not asking us to do anything that He did not do Himself. He wants us to learn to hold what we have very lightly.

you come here to torment us before the time?" 30 Now a
large herd of swine was feeding at some distance from
them. 31 The demons begged him, "If you cast us out, send
us into the herd of swine." 32 And he said to them, "Go!" So
they came out and entered the swine; and suddenly, the
whole herd rushed down the steep bank into the sea and
perished in the water. 33 The swineherds ran off, and on going into the town, they told the whole story about what had
happened to the demoniacs. 34 Then the whole town came
out to meet Jesus; and when they saw him, they begged him
9 to leave their neighborhood. 1 And after getting into a
boat he crossed the sea and came to his own town.

Jesus Heals a Paralytic

2 And just then some people were carrying a paralyzed
man lying on a bed. When Jesus saw their faith, he said to

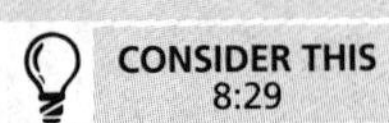

CONSIDER THIS 8:29

SPIRITUAL REALITIES BEYOND YOU

Jesus often encountered demons like those that possessed the men at Gadara (vv. 28–34). The mention of demons affirms the reality of powerful spiritual forces in the universe. Scripture has much to say about angels and demons.

Angels *are presented as members of an order of heavenly beings who are superior to humans in power and intelligence (Heb. 2:7; 2 Pet. 2:11). However, unlike God they are not all-powerful or all-knowing (Ps. 103:20; 2 Thess. 1:7). God often sends them to announce good news, such as the birth of Jesus (Luke 1:30–31), or to warn of coming dangers, such as the destruction of Sodom (Gen. 18:16—19:29).*

Angels played a particularly active role in the events surrounding Jesus' birth, resurrection, and ascension. They:

- *counseled Joseph to wed Mary (Matt. 1:20);*
- *warned Joseph to flee to Egypt with Mary and the Christ child (2:13);*
- *instructed Joseph to return the family to Palestine (2:19);*
- *foretold to Zechariah the birth of John the Baptist (Luke 1:11–38);*
- *announced to shepherds the birth of Christ (2:8–15);*
- *appeared to Jesus in the Garden of Gethsemane to strengthen Him (Luke 22:43);*

the paralytic, "Take heart, son; your sins are forgiven."
3Then some of the scribes said to themselves, "This man is
9:4–8 blaspheming." 4But Jesus, perceiving
their thoughts, said, "Why do you think
evil in your hearts? 5For which is easier, to say, 'Your sins
are forgiven,' or to say, 'Stand up and walk'? 6But so that
you may know that the Son of Man has authority on earth
to forgive sins"—he then said to the paralytic—"Stand up,
take your bed and go to your home." 7And he stood up and
went to his home. 8When the crowds saw it, they were
filled with awe, and they glorified God, who had given
such authority to human beings.

Matthew Follows Jesus

9 As Jesus was walking along, he saw a man called
Matthew sitting at the tax booth; and he said to him, "Follow me." And he got up and followed him.

(Bible text continued on page 41)

◆ ◆ ◆ ◆ ◆ ◆ ◆ ◆ ◆ ◆ ◆ ◆ ◆ ◆ ◆

- *rolled back the stone from Jesus' empty tomb (Matt. 28:2);*
- *appeared to women at the empty tomb to announce Jesus' resurrection (Luke 24:4–7, 23; John 20:12);*
- *promised Jesus' return after His ascension (Acts 1:9–11).*

Since Pentecost, the frequency of angelic activity in human affairs appears to have diminished, perhaps because of the larger role played by the Holy Spirit in the lives of believers.

***Demons** are presented as the personification of evil. Sometimes they are described as fallen angels that have been cast out of heaven. They seek to undermine the cause of righteousness in the world. Scripture describes them with various names: "unclean spirits" (Mark 6:7), "evil spirits" (Luke 7:21; Acts 19:12–13), "spirit of divination" (Acts 16:16), "deceitful spirits" (1 Tim. 4:1), and "spirit of error" (1 John 4:6).* ◆

Scripture presents demons not as mythological creatures, but as real beings involved in historical events. See "Demons," Luke 11:14.

The Power of Forgiveness

CONSIDER THIS 9:4–8 **The crowd that watched Jesus heal the paralytic responded enthusiastically to His dramatic display of power (v. 8). But they overlooked His more significant ability to forgive sins—a power that deeply troubled the scribes (vv. 2–3).**

The power of forgiveness is immeasurable. Jesus challenged us as His followers to forgive others who have wronged or hurt us (6:14–15; 18:21–35). That may seem like a simple act, but anyone who has struggled with pain and anger knows that it takes enormous power to authentically forgive—to lay aside one's hurt and reach out to an offender with the embrace of a pardon. On the other side, forgiveness can release the wrongdoer from paralyzing guilt and even turn around the course of that person's life (James 5:19–20).

Forgiveness is as powerful and liberating as the healing of a paralytic. And it's a power that Jesus has delegated to His followers (John 20:23).

We are called to forgive others as Christ has forgiven us. See Col. 3:13.

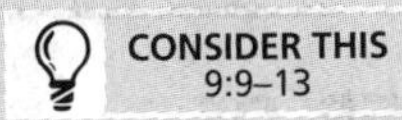
CONSIDER THIS
9:9–13

A Rich Man Enters the Kingdom

Jesus said it would be hard for the rich to enter the kingdom of heaven (Matt. 19:23). The remark has led some to believe that rich people can't enter the kingdom, and others to feel that Jesus was opposed to wealth and the wealthy. But Matthew's response to Jesus' call (9:9–13) contradicts both of those assumptions.

The incident recorded here contrasts sharply with Jesus' encounter with the rich young ruler (Matt. 19:16–30; Mark 10:17–31; Luke 18:18–30). In many ways, the ruler seemed to make a more likely prospect than Matthew for membership in Jesus' burgeoning movement. (See table below.)

Yet despite the young ruler's apparent edge, it was Matthew who ended up following Jesus. The other "went away grieving" (19:22). What accounts for the difference? For one thing, the wealthy young man clearly perceived himself as already righteous (19:17–20). He felt that he was able to meet God's requirements on his own merits (19:16). But no one had to convince Matthew that he needed the Great Physician (9:11–12). As a tax collector, he was among the most despised members of Jewish society.

Yet there was a more fundamental difference between these two men, a difference that depended on Jesus' attitude more than on theirs. His words to the Pharisees explained the matter clearly: " 'I desire mercy, not sacrifice.' For I have come to call not the righteous but sinners" (v. 13). In calling Matthew but turning away the rich young ruler, Jesus demonstrated in real-life parables precisely this point: that salvation depends on the mercy of God, not on the merits or sacrifice of people.

In the end, the crucial difference between the rich man who followed and the rich man who rejected was the merciful choice of God. Of course, none of us knows that choice beforehand. Therefore, we as believers need to be equally eager to present the gospel of Christ to everyone, rich or poor, wise or foolish, mighty or weak. ◆

Two Different Rich Men

Rich Young Ruler	Matthew
Probably enjoyed inherited wealth	Rich most likely because of his work as a tax collector
Had lived a good life	Like most tax collectors, was probably dishonest and ruthless
Came to Jesus	Sat at his tax table; Jesus approached him
Displayed interest in spiritual things	Was collecting money when Jesus found him
Indicated a willingness to make sacrifices to gain eternal life	Gave no such indication

Scripture has much to say to believers about their wealth. See "Christians and Money," 1 Tim. 6:6–19, and "Getting Yours," James 5:1–6.

9:10
10 And as he sat at dinner[c] in the
house, many tax collectors and sinners
came and were sitting[d] with him and his disciples. 11When
the Pharisees saw this, they said to his disciples, "Why does
9:9–13
your teacher eat with tax collectors and
sinners?" 12But when he heard this, he
said, "Those who are well have no need of a physician, but
those who are sick. 13Go and learn what this means, 'I desire mercy, not sacrifice.' For I have come to call not the
righteous but sinners."

The Old and the New

14 Then the disciples of John came to him, saying, "Why
do we and the Pharisees fast often,[e] but your disciples do
not fast?" 15And Jesus said to them, "The wedding guests
cannot mourn as long as the bridegroom is with them, can
they? The days will come when the bridegroom is taken
away from them, and then they will fast. 16No one sews a
piece of unshrunk cloth on an old cloak, for the patch pulls
away from the cloak, and a worse tear is made. 17Neither is
new wine put into old wineskins; otherwise, the skins
burst, and the wine is spilled, and the skins are destroyed;
but new wine is put into fresh wineskins, and so both are
preserved."

Four Dramatic Healings

18 While he was saying these things to them, suddenly a
leader of the synagogue[f] came in and knelt before him, saying, "My daughter has just died; but come and lay your
hand on her, and she will live." 19And Jesus got up and
9:20–22 see pg. 43
followed him, with his disciples. 20Then
suddenly a woman who had been suffer-
ing from hemorrhages for twelve years came up behind him
and touched the fringe of his cloak, 21for she said to herself,
"If I only touch his cloak, I will be made well." 22Jesus
turned, and seeing her he said, "Take heart, daughter; your
faith has made you well." And instantly the woman was
9:23 see pg. 43
made well. 23When Jesus came to the
leader's house and saw the flute players
and the crowd making a commotion, 24he said, "Go away;
for the girl is not dead but sleeping." And they laughed at
him. 25But when the crowd had been put outside, he went
in and took her by the hand, and the girl got up. 26And the
report of this spread throughout that district.

(Bible text continued on page 43)

[c]Gk *reclined* [d]Gk *were reclining* [e]Other ancient authorities lack *often* [f]Gk lacks *of the synagogue*

Who Were Those Tax Collectors?

CONSIDER THIS 9:10 **Tax collectors (v. 10) were agents or contract workers who collected taxes for the government during Bible times. Some translations incorrectly call them "publicans," but publicans were wealthy men, usually non-Jewish, who contracted with the Roman government to be responsible for the taxes of a particular district. They were often backed by military force. By contrast, tax collectors were employed by publicans to do the actual collecting of monies. They were Jews, usually not very wealthy.**

Tax collectors gathered several different types of taxes. Depending on the kind of rule in a given Jewish province, Rome levied a land tax, a poll tax, even a tax for the operation of the temple (Matt. 17:24–27). Some provinces, like Galilee, were not under an imperial governor, so their taxes remained in the province rather than going to the imperial treasury at Rome. Perhaps these inequities prompted the Pharisees in Judea (an imperial province) to ask Jesus, "Is it lawful to pay taxes to the emperor, or not?" (Matt. 22:17).

As a class, tax collectors were despised by their fellow Jews, and were generally associated with "sinners" (Matt. 9:10–11; Mark 2:15). They often gathered more than the government required and pocketed the excess amount—a practice that John the Baptist specifically preached against (Luke 3:12–13). But tax collectors were also hated because their fellow citizens viewed them as mercenaries working for the Roman oppressors.

In Jesus' day, Jews were probably paying no less than 30 or 40 percent of their income on taxes and religious dues. See "Taxes," Mark 12:14.

Zacchaeus was called the chief tax collector in Jericho, which may mean he was a publican. Nevertheless, he responded to Jesus' call. See Luke 19:1–10.

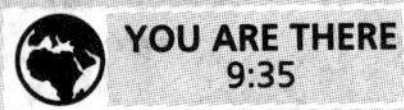

JESUS—A CITY PREACHER

Popular opinion frequently regards the Bible in general and the ministry of Jesus in particular in rural terms. Perhaps it's the Christmas story, with its quaint references to a donkey, a manger, and shepherds. Perhaps it's the memorable parables, such as the sower and the seed, the wheat and the weeds, and the prodigal son. Perhaps it's Jesus' origins in a small town. Whatever the cause, the popular image of Jesus and His world seems fixed on a rural environment. But that is somewhat misleading.

Palestine in Jesus' day was undergoing rapid urban development. Its population of around 2.5 to 3 million people lived in numerous preindustrial cities and towns that revolved around Jerusalem, the hub of the region. The Holy City had a population conservatively estimated by modern scholars at between 55,000 and 90,000. (Josephus, a first-century Jewish historian, placed the number at 3 million; the Talmud gives an incredible 12 million.)

So as Jesus carried out His ministry, He focused on the urban centers of Palestine (v. 35; 11:1; Luke 4:43; 13:22) and visited Jerusalem at least three times. This brought Him into contact with a greater number and wider variety of people than He would have encountered in a purely rural campaign—women, soldiers, religious leaders, the rich, merchants, tax collectors, Gentiles, prostitutes, beggars, and the poor. These He attracted in large crowds as He visited each city.

Jesus' urban strategy established a model for His disciples and the early church. When He sent the disciples on preaching tours, He directed them toward cities (Matt. 10:5, 11–14; Luke 10:1, 8–16). And later, the movement spread throughout the Roman empire by using an urban strategy that planted communities of believers in no less than 40 cities by the end of the first century (see "Churches—Keys to the Cities," Acts 11:22).

In light of the vital role that cities played in the ministry of Jesus, we who follow Him today need to ask: What are we doing to relate the message of Christ to our increasingly urban, multicultural, and pluralistic world? Our Lord's example in urban Palestine has much to teach us. ◆

Jerusalem dominated life in first-century Palestine. To find out why, see Matt. 23:37.

Don't miss the explosive start of the worldwide church! See "A Surprising First Fulfillment of Acts 1:8," Acts 2:8–11.

An urban strategy for ministry can be explosive—and unpredictable. See "The Ephesus Approach: How the Gospel Penetrates a City," Acts 19:8–41.

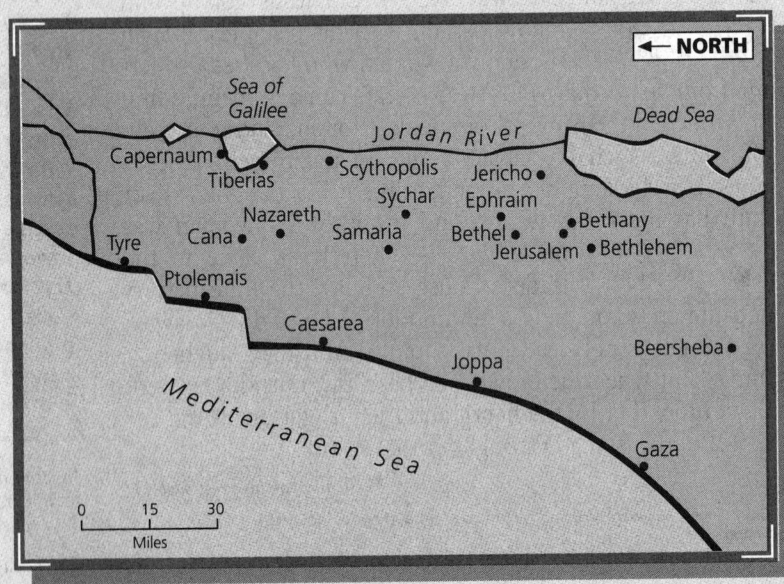

CITIES OF PALESTINE IN CHRIST'S TIME

27 As Jesus went on from there, two blind men followed
him, crying loudly, "Have mercy on us, Son of David!"
28When he entered the house, the blind men came to him;
and Jesus said to them, "Do you believe that I am able to do
this?" They said to him, "Yes, Lord." 29Then he touched
their eyes and said, "According to your faith let it be done
to you." 30And their eyes were opened. Then Jesus sternly
ordered them, "See that no one knows of this." 31But they
went away and spread the news about him throughout that
district.

32 After they had gone away, a demoniac who was mute
was brought to him. 33And when the demon had been cast
out, the one who had been mute spoke; and the crowds
were amazed and said, "Never has anything like this been
seen in Israel." 34But the Pharisees said, "By the ruler of the
demons he casts out the demons."[g]

[g]Other ancient authorities lack this verse

THE MOURNERS

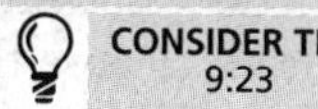

CONSIDER THIS 9:23 *In the ancient world, paid professional mourners (v. 23), most often women, aided families in their public expression of grief upon the death of a loved one. They composed poems or dirges praising the deceased, which they chanted to the accompaniment of a flute or other musical instrument in an attempt to stir the audience emotionally. They usually wore sackcloth and scattered dust in the air and on their heads. Weeping, wailing, and beating their breasts, they created an unmistakable tone of grief. There was no denial of death or distancing themselves from loss.*

THE HEMORRHAGING WOMAN

CONSIDER THIS 9:20–22 **For twelve years the woman in vv. 20–22 had sought a cure for her condition. Perhaps worse than the drain on her physical strength and finances was the stigma of uncleanness. Jews considered women ritually unclean during menstruation, and whoever touched a menstruating woman was made unclean until evening. If a woman experienced bleeding other than at her normal menses, she was considered unclean until the bleeding stopped (Lev. 15:19–27). That meant exclusion from participating in the life and worship of the community.**

Scripture is silent on the source of this woman's livelihood. Perhaps she lived off an inheritance, or perhaps she was divorced and her dowry had been returned to her. Whatever her means of support, it was gone. Jesus was her last hope.

So she approached Him, breaking a rule that made it an unclean person's responsibility to keep away from others. In desperation, she reached out and touched Jesus.

Perceiving that power had gone out from Him, Jesus sought her out. Perhaps as she explained her disease the crowd backed away, not wanting to contaminate themselves. But Jesus didn't withdraw. Rather He drew her to Him with the affectionate term "daughter" and sent her away in peace, healed at last.

Who are the "untouchables" in your world? Who is desperately trying to reach out for help? How can you respond to their needs with Christlikeness?

WHAT IT MEANS TO BE LIKE JESUS

CONSIDER THIS 8:1—9:38 *Jesus indicated that those who follow Him will become like Him (10:25). What does it mean to* **"be like Jesus"** *in today's complex world? Matthew paints eight portraits of what Christlikeness looks like, including:*

#7: To Be Like Jesus Means TO SERVE OTHERS

The Sermon on the Mount (Matt. 5–7) was immediately followed by "deeds in the valley" (Matt. 8–9). Christlike values lead to servant actions—and it was obedient action that Jesus cared about, not just sermonizing (7:21–29). Jesus modeled how to *do* the will of God by actively serving more than 25 different people (chs. 8–9). These included such undesirables as lepers, an officer of the Roman occupation troops, the sick, the demon-possessed, cave dwellers, tax collectors, and a diseased, outcast woman. If we want to be like Jesus, we need to befriend those who are weak, under oppression, or without Christ. Like Him, we need to become a friend of "sinners" (11:19). He offered much more than religious information—He served them.

For a summary of all eight portraits of Christlikeness, see "What It Means to Be Like Jesus" at 10:25. The next item in the series can be found at 10:1–42.

Jesus Feels Compassion for the Crowds

9:35 see pg. 42

35 Then Jesus went about all the cities
and villages, teaching in their syna-
gogues, and proclaiming the good news of the kingdom,
and curing every disease and every sickness. 36When he
saw the crowds, he had compassion for them, because they
were harassed and helpless, like sheep without a shepherd.
37Then he said to his disciples, "The harvest is plentiful,
but the laborers are few; 38therefore ask
the Lord of the harvest to send out laborers into his harvest."

8:1—9:38

The Twelve

10:1–42

10 Then Jesus[h] summoned his
twelve disciples and gave them
authority over unclean spirits, to cast them out, and to cure
every disease and every sickness. 2These
are the names of the twelve apostles:
first, Simon, also known as Peter, and his brother Andrew;
James son of Zebedee, and his brother John; 3Philip and
Bartholomew; Thomas and Matthew the tax collector;
James son of Alphaeus, and Thaddaeus;[i] 4Simon the
Cananaean, and Judas Iscariot, the one who betrayed
him.

10:2

Jesus Sends and Warns the Twelve

5 These twelve Jesus sent out with the following instructions: "Go nowhere among the Gentiles, and enter no town
of the Samaritans, 6but go rather to the lost sheep of the
house of Israel. 7As you go, proclaim the
good news, 'The kingdom of heaven has
come near.'[j] 8Cure the sick, raise the dead, cleanse the lepers,[k] cast out demons. You received without payment; give
without payment. 9Take no gold, or silver, or copper in
your belts, 10no bag for your journey, or two tunics, or sandals, or a staff; for laborers deserve their food. 11Whatever
town or village you enter, find out who in it is worthy, and
stay there until you leave. 12As you enter the house, greet
it. 13If the house is worthy, let your peace come upon it; but
if it is not worthy, let your peace return to you. 14If anyone
will not welcome you or listen to your words, shake off
the dust from your feet as you leave that house or town.
15Truly I tell you, it will be more tolerable for the land of
Sodom and Gomorrah on the day of judgment than for that
town.
16 "See, I am sending you out like sheep into the midst

10:7–10 see pg. 46

[h]Gk *he* [i]Other ancient authorities read *Lebbaeus,* or *Lebbaeus called Thaddaeus* [j]Or *is at hand* [k]The terms *leper* and *leprosy* can refer to several diseases

of wolves; so be wise as serpents and innocent as doves.
17Beware of them, for they will hand you over to councils
and flog you in their synagogues; 18and you will be dragged
before governors and kings because of me, as a testimony
to them and the Gentiles. 19When they hand you over, do
not worry about how you are to speak or what you are to
say; for what you are to say will be given to you at that
time; 20for it is not you who speak, but the Spirit of your
Father speaking through you. 21Brother will betray brother
to death, and a father his child, and children will rise
against parents and have them put to death; 22and you will
be hated by all because of my name. But the one who endures to the end will be saved. 23When they persecute you
in one town, flee to the next; for truly I tell you, you will
not have gone through all the towns of Israel before the Son
of Man comes.

(Bible text continued on page 47)

◆ ◆ ◆ ◆ ◆ ◆ ◆ ◆ ◆ ◆ ◆ ◆ ◆ ◆ ◆

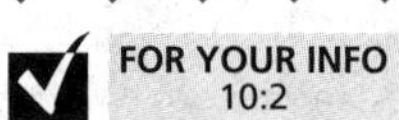

THE TWELVE

Apostle	Description
Simon (Peter) (Mark 1:16)	Fisherman from Galilee, Andrew's brother
Andrew (John 1:40)	Fisherman from Galilee, Peter's brother
James	Son of Zebedee, brother to John; from Capernaum
John (Introduction to John)	Son of Zebedee, brother to James; from Capernaum
Philip	From Bethsaida
Bartholomew (Nathanael)	From Cana in Galilee
Thomas (Didymus)	Possibly also a fisherman
Matthew (Levi) (Matt. 9:9)	Tax collector in Capernaum; son of Alphaeus, possibly James' brother
James	Son of Alphaeus, possibly Matthew's brother
Lebbaeus Thaddeus (Judas)	May have taken the name Thaddeus ("warm-hearted") because of the infamy that came to be attached to the name Judas
Simon (the Cananite)	From Cana; one of the Zealots, Jewish revolutionaries who opposed Rome
Judas Iscariot (Matt. 26:14)	From Kerioth, and possibly the only Judean among the Twelve

(Biblical references are to Personality Profiles.)

Matthew called these twelve "apostles." What did that term mean? See 2 Cor. 11:5.

WHAT IT MEANS TO BE LIKE JESUS

Jesus indicated that those who follow Him will become like Him (10:25). What does it mean to **"be like Jesus"** *in today's complex world? Matthew paints eight portraits of what Christlikeness looks like, including:*

#8: To Be Like Jesus Means TO AFFIRM OTHER LEADERS

Jesus invested Himself in the development of other people, particularly the Twelve. He gave them responsibility and authority, resisting the temptation to get the job done "right" by doing it Himself. In doing so, He accepted the risk that they might fail. Of course, He gave them adequate preparation before sending them out, and on their return He affirmed them on their successful completion of the mission. Jesus calls us to help others grow. If we want to be like Him, we will share the joys and risks of working together with our brothers and sisters.

For a summary of all eight portraits of Christlikeness, see "What It Means to Be Like Jesus" at 10:25. This is the last item in the series.

CONSIDER THIS
10:7–10

A PRAYER OF THE LAITY

He was born into a noble family in Assisi, Italy in 1182. Although christened Giovanni Bernadone, he went by the nickname Francis—a reminder that his merchant father had been away in France when he was born. The privileges of his childhood fostered a pursuit of wealth, education, and fun, and when he came of age he joined the army as the simplest avenue to achieving those goals.

But young Francis' life took a dramatic turn when serious illness interrupted his plans. While convalescing, he took a new and profound interest in religion. Once on his feet, he made a pilgrimage to Rome, a common discipline for the spiritually devoted.

But he was shocked at what he found there. Lepers and beggars languished in cathedrals fallen into disrepair. Moved to compassion and inspired by his newfound faith, he exercised one of the few options available to concerned laity at the time: he sold his horse and some of his father's cloth supplies and gave the money to a local priest, assuming that the cleric would restore the buildings. But to his surprise, the priest rejected the gift when he learned that it had come from the Bernadone family's commercial ventures. To make matters worse, Francis' father disowned him upon learning of his actions.

Penniless, he managed to find refuge with a bishop. But he continued his mission to the poor, begging enough money over a two-year span to repair four church buildings. It was during that period that he heard a sermon on Matthew 10:7–10. The text galvanized his thinking, and he made a decision to live the rest of his life as a beggar, serving the poor through preaching and healing.

His example motivated others to follow. A wealthy woman from Assisi began a sister movement, as well as one for married laity. Those who joined were reacting against widespread corruption in the church and a general confusion about the meaning and practice of spirituality for laypeople. Not all of the newcomers were sincere. Some tried to introduce changes away from a singleminded focus on the poor and unbelievers. And, as the movement became fashionable, Francis had to constantly resist the clergy's attempts to bring the work under their auspices and "upgrade" the status of the lay workers to agents of the church.

The spirit of Francis' vision was captured in a prayer that he penned, "Make me an instrument of Thy peace." Today, it has become quite well known. Perhaps its popularity springs from its simple yet eloquent statement of the aspirations of a very concerned and committed layperson who determined to make a difference for God in the world as he found it. ◆

The Prayer of St. Francis

Lord,
Make me an instrument of Thy peace;
Where there is hatred, let me sow love;
Where there is injury, pardon;
Where there is doubt, faith;
Where there is despair, hope;
Where there is darkness, light; and
Where there is sadness, joy.
Divine Master,
Grant that I may not so much
seek to be consoled as to console;
To be understood as to understand;
To be loved as to love;
For it is in giving that we receive;
It is in pardoning that we are pardoned;
And it is in dying
that we are born to eternal life.

24 "A disciple is not above the teacher, nor a slave
10:25 above the master; 25 it is enough for the
disciple to be like the teacher, and the
slave like the master. If they have called the master of
the house Beelzebul, how much more will they malign
those of his household!
26 "So have no fear of them; for nothing is covered up
that will not be uncovered, and nothing secret that will not
become known. 27 What I say to you in the dark, tell in the
light; and what you hear whispered, proclaim from the
housetops. 28 Do not fear those who kill the body but cannot kill the soul; rather fear him who can destroy both soul
and body in hell.[l] 29 Are not two sparrows sold for a penny?
Yet not one of them will fall to the ground apart from your
Father. 30 And even the hairs of your head are all counted.
31 So do not be afraid; you are of more value than many
sparrows.
32 "Everyone therefore who acknowledges me before
others, I also will acknowledge before my Father in heaven;
33 but whoever denies me before others, I also will deny before my Father in heaven.
34 "Do not think that I have come to bring peace to the
earth; I have not come to bring peace, but a sword.
35 For I have come to set a man against his father,
and a daughter against her mother,
and a daughter-in-law against her mother-in-law;
36 and one's foes will be members of one's own household.
37 Whoever loves father or mother more than me is not worthy of me; and whoever loves son or daughter more than
me is not worthy of me; 38 and whoever does not take up
the cross and follow me is not worthy of me. 39 Those who
find their life will lose it, and those who lose their life for
my sake will find it.
40 "Whoever welcomes you welcomes me, and whoever
welcomes me welcomes the one who sent me. 41 Whoever
welcomes a prophet in the name of a prophet will receive a
prophet's reward; and whoever welcomes a righteous person in the name of a righteous person will receive the reward of the righteous; 42 and whoever gives even a cup of
cold water to one of these little ones in the name of a disciple—truly I tell you, none of these will lose their reward."

Jesus Speaks about John the Baptist

11 Now when Jesus had finished instructing his twelve
disciples, he went on from there to teach and proclaim his message in their cities.

[l] Gk *Gehenna*

What It Means To Be Like Jesus

CONSIDER THIS 10:25 **Jesus' statement in v. 25 implies that His disciples will be like Him. To His first-century followers, that included the prospect of persecution and martyrdom. But what else does it mean to "be like Jesus," especially for Christians in today's marketplace? Eight portraits in Matthew's eye-witness account give us some clues:**

#1: To be like Jesus means to accept our roots (1:1–17).

#2: To be like Jesus means to engage the world's pain and struggle (1:18—2:23).

#3: To be like Jesus means to commit ourselves to other believers, no matter how "weird" they appear to be (3:1–17).

#4: To be like Jesus means to admit our vulnerability to temptation (4:1–11).

#5: To be like Jesus means to openly proclaim the message of Christ (4:12–25).

#6: To be like Jesus means to commit ourselves to changed thinking and behavior (5:1—7:27).

#7: To be like Jesus means to serve others, especially those who are oppressed or without Christ (8:1—9:38).

#8: To be like Jesus means to affirm others in leadership (10:1–42).

For more on each of these points, see the articles at the texts indicated.

Some Surprising Evidence

CONSIDER THIS 11:2–6 **John the Baptist wanted reassurance about who Jesus was and what He was doing (vv. 2–3). Jesus replied with a list of things He had done that revealed God's presence, power, and love (vv. 4–5). The most telling evidence was His work among the poor, the downtrodden, and the needy.**

Our culture today wants to know whether Christ is still alive among His people. Like John, observers are asking whether those of us who claim to be Christ's followers are truly of God, or whether they should look elsewhere. They especially pay attention to our posture toward the poor. So it's worth asking: Are we as involved and concerned with the material needs of our neighbors as we are with their spiritual needs? Do we respond to physical needs as intentionally as Christ did, even if we have only material help to offer rather than miracles of healing? Is there unmistakable evidence of Christ working within us?

Scripture has a great deal to say about Christians' responsibilities to the poor and needy. See "I Have Not Coveted," Acts 20:33–38; "Giving It All Away," 1 Cor. 13:3; "Christ Became Poor," 2 Cor. 8:9; and "Take a Cardiogram," 1 John 3:16–21.

11:2–6

2 When John heard in prison what
the Messiah[m] was doing, he sent word by
his[n] disciples 3and said to him, "Are you the one who is to
come, or are we to wait for another?" 4Jesus answered
them, "Go and tell John what you hear and see: 5the blind
receive their sight, the lame walk, the lepers[o] are cleansed,
the deaf hear, the dead are raised, and the poor have good
news brought to them. 6And blessed is anyone who takes
no offense at me."

7 As they went away, Jesus began to speak to the crowds
about John: "What did you go out into the wilderness to
look at? A reed shaken by the wind? 8What then did you go
out to see? Someone[p] dressed in soft robes? Look, those
who wear soft robes are in royal palaces. 9What then did
you go out to see? A prophet?[q] Yes, I tell you, and more
than a prophet. 10This is the one about whom it is written,

'See, I am sending my messenger ahead of you,
who will prepare your way before you.'

11Truly I tell you, among those born of women no one has
arisen greater than John the Baptist; yet the least in the
kingdom of heaven is greater than he. 12From the days of
John the Baptist until now the kingdom of heaven has suffered violence,[r] and the violent take it by force. 13For all the
prophets and the law prophesied until John came; 14and if
you are willing to accept it, he is Elijah who is to come.
15Let anyone with ears[s] listen!

16 "But to what will I compare this generation? It is like
children sitting in the marketplaces and calling to one another,

17 'We played the flute for you, and you did not dance;
we wailed, and you did not mourn.'

18For John came neither eating nor drinking, and they say,
'He has a demon'; 19the Son of Man came eating and drinking, and they say, 'Look, a glutton and a drunkard, a friend
of tax collectors and sinners!' Yet wisdom is vindicated by
her deeds."[t]

Unbelieving Cities Condemned

20 Then he began to reproach the cities in which most
of his deeds of power had been done, because they did
not repent. 21"Woe to you, Chorazin!
Woe to you, Bethsaida! For if the
deeds of power done in you had been done in Tyre and

11:21

[m]Or *the Christ* [n]Other ancient authorities read *two of his* [o]The terms *leper* and *leprosy* can refer to several diseases [p]Or *Why then did you go out? To see someone* [q]Other ancient authorities read *Why then did you go out? To see a prophet?* [r]Or *has been coming violently* [s]Other ancient authorities add *to hear* [t]Other ancient authorities read *children*

Sidon, they would have repented long ago in sackcloth
and ashes. 22But I tell you, on the day of judgment it
will be more tolerable for Tyre and Sidon than for you.
23And you, Capernaum,
will you be exalted to heaven?
No, you will be brought down to Hades.
For if the deeds of power done in you had been done in
Sodom, it would have remained until this day. 24But I tell
you that on the day of judgment it will be more tolerable
for the land of Sodom than for you."

An Invitation

25 At that time Jesus said, "I thank[u] you, Father, Lord of
heaven and earth, because you have hidden these things
from the wise and the intelligent and have revealed them to
infants; 26yes, Father, for such was your gracious will.[v] 27All
things have been handed over to me by my Father; and no
one knows the Son except the Father, and no one knows
the Father except the Son and anyone to whom the Son
chooses to reveal him.
28 "Come to me, all you that are weary and are carrying
heavy burdens, and I will give you rest. 29Take my yoke
upon you, and learn from me; for I am gentle and humble
in heart, and you will find rest for your souls. 30For my
yoke is easy, and my burden is light."

Sabbath Controversies

12:1–13

12 At that time Jesus went through
the grainfields on the sabbath;
his disciples were hungry, and they began to pluck heads of
grain and to eat. 2When the Pharisees saw it, they said to
him, "Look, your disciples are doing what is not lawful to
do on the sabbath." 3He said to them, "Have you not read
what David did when he and his companions were hungry?
4He entered the house of God and ate the bread of the Presence, which it was not lawful for him or his companions to
eat, but only for the priests. 5Or have you not read in the
law that on the sabbath the priests in the temple break the
sabbath and yet are guiltless? 6I tell you, something greater
than the temple is here. 7But if you had known what this

[u]Or *praise* [v]Or *for so it was well-pleasing in your sight*

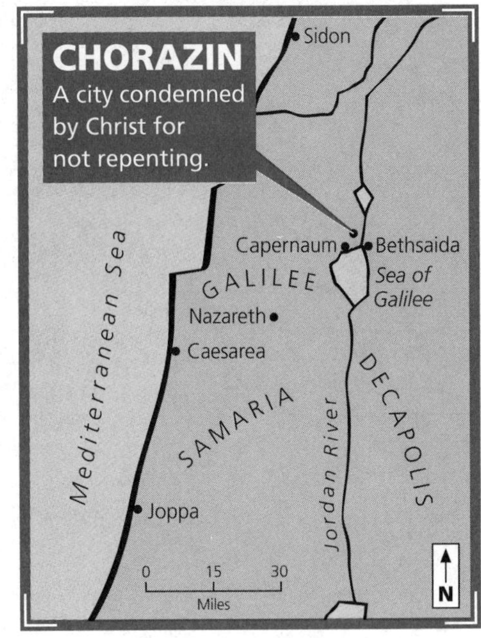

CHORAZIN

YOU ARE THERE 11:21

- **A town north of the Sea of Galilee, built on the basalt hills two and one-half miles north of Capernaum.**
- **Name means "secret."**
- **Mentioned in the Talmud as a distribution point for wheat.**
- **Known for the black, volcanic rock ruins of its synagogue. The famed *cathedra Mosis,* a carved judgment seat of Moses (compare Matt. 23:2), has been found there (in modern-day Khirbet Kerazeh).**

Why This Anger?

A CLOSER LOOK 12:1–13

What was it that so enraged the Pharisees when they saw the disciples picking grain and Jesus healing a man's withered hand? And why did Jesus refuse to allow their grumbling to go unchallenged? See "Jesus Confronts the Legalists," Luke 6:1–11.

means, 'I desire mercy and not sacrifice,' you would not
have condemned the guiltless. [8]For the Son of Man is lord
of the sabbath."
9 He left that place and entered their synagogue; [10]a man
was there with a withered hand, and they asked him, "Is it
lawful to cure on the sabbath?" so that they might accuse
him. [11]He said to them, "Suppose one of you has only one
sheep and it falls into a pit on the sabbath; will you not lay
hold of it and lift it out? [12]How much more valuable is a
human being than a sheep! So it is lawful to do good on the
sabbath." [13]Then he said to the man, "Stretch out your
hand." He stretched it out, and it was restored, as sound
as the other. [14]But the Pharisees went
out and conspired against him, how
to destroy him.

12:14

Jesus Seeks a Low Profile

15 When Jesus became aware of this, he departed. Many
crowds[w] followed him, and he cured all of them, [16]and he

[w]Other ancient authorities lack *crowds*

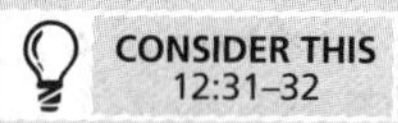

NO FORGIVENESS!

People speak of committing the "unpardonable sin," but in His severe comments to the Pharisees (vv. 31–32), Jesus indicated that it is more than just a figure of speech—it is a matter with eternal consequences!

Can people ever sin so badly that God cannot forgive them? The answer is yes and no. It's important to realize that the blood of Jesus Christ on the cross paid for all of the sin of the world (John 1:29; Rom. 5:12–21; 8:3). There is no sin that God has not overcome through Christ. That means that no one ever has to fear going beyond the scope of God's grace or power. Sometimes people despair because they have committed certain sins that to them seem unforgivable. But no matter what their failure has been, God can and will forgive their sin if they come to Him in repentance (Acts 2:38; 1 John 1:9).

At the same time, it is possible to willfully place oneself beyond the grace of God—to persist in rebellion and sin and resist His call to repentance. This, essentially, is what the Pharisees and other Jewish leaders did (compare Acts 7:51–52). Jesus had healed a demon-possessed man by the power of the Holy Spirit (v. 28). His enemies claimed that He cast them out by the power of Satan ("Beelze-

ordered them not to make him known. 17This was to fulfill
what had been spoken through the prophet Isaiah:

18 "Here is my servant, whom I have chosen,
my beloved, with whom my soul is well pleased.
I will put my Spirit upon him,
and he will proclaim justice to the Gentiles.
19 He will not wrangle or cry aloud,
nor will anyone hear his voice in the streets.
20 He will not break a bruised reed
or quench a smoldering wick
until he brings justice to victory.
21 And in his name the Gentiles will hope."

Political Intrigue

The Pharisees feared Jesus as much as they hated Him. They were concerned that His popularity might have political repercussions, drawing Roman troops to the area and causing the loss of what little independence the nation had. So they plotted to destroy Him. The mastermind behind their plans was Caiaphas the high priest, a Sadducee rather than a Pharisee, but equally opposed to Jesus. Find out more about this man at Matt. 26:3.

bul," v. 24). The accusation was evidence that they had rejected Him.

It also slandered the Holy Spirit, revealing their spiritual blindness, a warping and perversion of their moral nature that put them beyond hope of repentance and faith—and therefore beyond forgiveness.

Is there an "unpardonable sin?" Not for those who cry out like the tax collector in a parable of Jesus, "God, be merciful to me, a sinner!" (Luke 18:13). But those who, like the Pharisee in the same parable (as well the Pharisees in this incident), trust to their own self-righteousness, reject Christ, and slander His Holy Spirit—they reveal a spiritual cancer so advanced that they are beyond any hope of healing and forgiveness. ◆

Our culture tends to dismiss demon possession as a quaint, archaic way of trying to explain physical and psychological conditions. But the Bible presents demons and demon possession not as myth, but as reality. See "Demons," Luke 11:14.

"HOW MUCH MORE VALUABLE IS A HUMAN BEING THAN A SHEEP!"
—Matthew 12:12

Allegations of Satanism

22 Then they brought to him a demoniac who was blind
and mute; and he cured him, so that the one who had been
mute could speak and see. 23All the crowds were amazed
and said, "Can this be the Son of David?" 24But when the
Pharisees heard it, they said, "It is only by Beelzebul, the
ruler of the demons, that this fellow casts out the demons."
25He knew what they were thinking and said to them,
"Every kingdom divided against itself is laid waste, and no
city or house divided against itself will stand. 26If Satan
casts out Satan, he is divided against himself; how then will
his kingdom stand? 27If I cast out demons by Beelzebul, by
whom do your own exorcists[x] cast them out? Therefore
they will be your judges. 28But if it is by the Spirit of God

[x]Gk *sons*

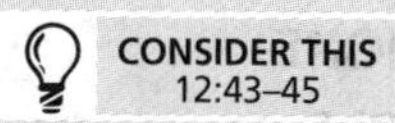

TURNING BACK IS AWFUL

Do you intend to overcome evil? If so, make sure to replace it with good or else, as Jesus warns, the evil may return with its friends, producing more evil than ever (vv. 43–45).

This teaching warns us to persevere in the journey of faith. That can be hard to do when everything in us wants to quit, the way an exhausted long-distance runner wants to drop out of a marathon. Besides (we reason), look how far we've already come!

Yes, but God's goal is not just to make us nicer people or better people, but to make us Christlike *people. That won't happen completely until we're with Him. For now, He wants us to keep growing in that direction. Stopping short can bring disaster. In a warning similar to Jesus' words here, the writer of Hebrews urges us to "go on toward perfection" and describes in sobering words the fate of those who "have fallen away" (Heb. 6:1–12).*

Fortunately, God lends us help to prevent us from falling back. As Hebrews also says, He disciplines us for our good. His stern efforts can feel harsh, but they are the loving protection of a caring Father (12:3–11). ◆

It is dangerous to compare ourselves with others when evaluating our worth. God has a better way of self-assessment. See "Do You Suffer from 'Comparisonitis'?" Rom. 12:3.

that I cast out demons, then the kingdom of God has come
to you. [29]Or how can one enter a strong man's house and
plunder his property, without first tying up the strong man?
Then indeed the house can be plundered. [30]Whoever is not
with me is against me, and whoever does not gather with
12:31–32 see pg. 50
me scatters. [31]Therefore I tell you, people will be forgiven for every sin and
blasphemy, but blasphemy against the Spirit will not be forgiven. [32]Whoever speaks a word against the Son of Man
will be forgiven, but whoever speaks against the Holy Spirit
will not be forgiven, either in this age or in the age to come.

33 "Either make the tree good, and its fruit good; or
make the tree bad, and its fruit bad; for the tree is known
by its fruit. [34]You brood of vipers! How can you speak good
things, when you are evil? For out of the abundance of the
heart the mouth speaks. [35]The good person brings good
things out of a good treasure, and the evil person brings
evil things out of an evil treasure. [36]I tell you, on the day of
judgment you will have to give an account for every careless word you utter; [37]for by your words you will be justified, and by your words you will be condemned."

38 Then some of the scribes and Pharisees said to him,
"Teacher, we wish to see a sign from you." [39]But he answered them, "An evil and adulterous generation asks for a
sign, but no sign will be given to it except the sign of the
prophet Jonah. [40]For just as Jonah was three days and three
nights in the belly of the sea monster, so for three days and
three nights the Son of Man will be in the heart of the
earth. [41]The people of Nineveh will rise up at the judgment
with this generation and condemn it, because they repented
at the proclamation of Jonah, and see, something greater
than Jonah is here! [42]The queen of the South will rise up at
the judgment with this generation and condemn it, because
she came from the ends of the earth to listen to the wisdom
of Solomon, and see, something greater than Solomon is
here!

12:43–45

43 "When the unclean spirit has gone
out of a person, it wanders through wa-
terless regions looking for a resting place, but it finds none.
[44]Then it says, 'I will return to my house from which I
came.' When it comes, it finds it empty, swept, and put in
order. [45]Then it goes and brings along seven other spirits
more evil than itself, and they enter and live there; and the
last state of that person is worse than the first. So will it be
also with this evil generation."

(Bible text continued on page 55)

Family Loyalty

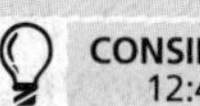

CONSIDER THIS 12:46–50 *Ancient society placed great emphasis on faithfulness to blood relatives. So Jesus' words in vv. 48–50 must have sounded quite foreign to the crowd. He seemed to be breaking with tradition and disowning His family. But notice: Jesus didn't deny that the woman and the men at the door were His family. He merely pushed beyond the normal understanding of family to a larger reality—the claims of spiritual kinship. This new "family" included anyone who does the will of the Father in heaven.*

In no way was Jesus denying the value or benefits of solid family relationships. See "The Family: A Call to Long-Term Work," Eph. 5:21.

CONSIDER THIS
13:1

Work-World Stories Describe the Kingdom

Jesus captivated His listeners by presenting truth in terms that they could understand. Here in chapter 13 we find no less than eight different images from the work world. Clearly, Jesus knew how to relate to the world in which everyday people lived and worked.

No wonder: Jesus probably spent most of His life working in His family's carpentry business. We know almost nothing of His youth from adolescence until He began His public ministry at about age 30. But we know that His father was a carpenter (Matt. 13:55) and that Jesus also practiced the trade (Mark 6:3). Carpenters worked with wood, metal, and stone to produce furniture and farm implements, and constructed houses and public buildings.

Jesus may have continued His occupation even after He began to teach and travel. Rabbis (or teachers) of the day commonly spent anywhere from one-third to one-half of their time working (most likely with their hands) to provide for themselves. And while Jesus' opponents, many of them rabbis, attacked Him on numerous grounds, they never accused Him of laziness or free-loading. Indeed, He was known to them as a carpenter.

That reputation passed on to the early church. One writer described Jesus as "working as a carpenter when among men, making ploughs and yokes, by which He taught the symbols of righteousness and an active life."

Little wonder, then, that Jesus' teaching was filled with work-place images and analogies such as those recorded here. Using parables—brief tales illustrating moral principles—He frequently spoke about the nature of His kingdom. Matthew 13 collects eight of these as listed below (with possible interpretations):

(1) *The parable of the soils (vv. 1–23)* addresses the receptivity of those who hear about the kingdom.

(2) *The parable of the wheat and the weeds (vv. 24–30)* warns that people who pretend to be part of the kingdom may be able to fool others, but they can't fool God.

(3) *The parable of the mustard seed (vv. 31–32)* is a promise that the kingdom would become a force to be reckoned with. Do not despise small beginnings!

(4) *The parable of the yeast (v. 33)* describes the influence of the kingdom: it quietly but effectively spreads among people and accomplishes significant results.

(5) *The parable of the hidden treasure (v. 44)* puts a value on the kingdom: it's the most important thing one can possess.

(6) *The parable of the pearl of great price (vv. 45–46)* also describes the kingdom's value: it's worth sacrificing everything in order to possess it.

(continued on next page)

Family Loyalty

12:46–50
see pg. 53

46 While he was still speaking to the crowds, his mother and his brothers were standing outside, wanting to speak to him. 47Someone told him, "Look, your mother and your brothers are standing outside, wanting to speak to you."[y] 48But to the one who had told him this, Jesus[z] replied, "Who is my mother, and who are my brothers?" 49And pointing to his disciples, he said, "Here are my mother and my brothers! 50For whoever does the will of my Father in heaven is my brother and sister and mother."

Parables by the Sea: Soils

13:1

13 That same day Jesus went out of the house and sat beside the sea. 2Such great crowds gathered around him that he got into a boat and sat there, while the whole crowd stood on the beach. 3And he told them many things in parables, saying: "Listen! A sower went out to sow. 4And as he sowed, some seeds fell on the path, and the birds came and ate them up. 5Other seeds fell on rocky ground, where they did not have much soil, and they sprang up quickly, since they had no depth of soil. 6But when the sun rose, they were scorched; and since they had no root, they withered away. 7Other seeds fell among thorns, and the thorns grew up and choked them. 8Other seeds fell on good soil and brought forth grain, some a hundredfold, some sixty, some thirty. 9Let anyone with ears[a] listen!"

The Purpose of Parables

10 Then the disciples came and asked him, "Why do you speak to them in parables?" 11He answered, "To you it has been given to know the secrets[b] of the kingdom of heaven, but to them it has not been given. 12For to those who have, more will be given, and they will have an abundance; but from those who have nothing, even what they have will be taken away. 13The reason I speak to them in parables is that 'seeing they do not perceive, and hearing they do not listen, nor do they understand.' 14With them indeed is fulfilled the prophecy of Isaiah that says:

[y]Other ancient authorities lack verse 47 [z]Gk *he* [a]Other ancient authorities add *to hear*
[b]Or *mysteries*

(continued from previous page)

(7) *The parable of the net* (vv. 47–50) warns that a day of reckoning is coming, when those who accept the kingdom will be separated from those who reject it.

(8) *The parable of the householder* (vv. 51–52) places a responsibility on those who understand about the kingdom to share their insight with others.

Jesus' stories connected with the real world of agriculture (sowing, harvesting, growing), the food industry (baking, fishing), real estate (land purchasing, home ownership), and retailing (the sale of pearls). His images and language helped bring His message alive to common people. It showed clearly that God takes an interest in the workplace, and desires people to serve Him in the "secular" arena.

Work is one of the most important means that believers today have to accomplish God's purposes. See "Faith Impacts the World," Mark 16:15–16.

Like Jesus, Paul was able to support himself through a "secular" occupation. See "Paul's 'Real' Job," Acts 18:1–3.

If Jesus might have supported Himself while carrying out His ministry, is there any reason why modern Christian leaders shouldn't at least consider that as an option today? See "Paying Vocational Christian Workers," 1 Cor. 9:1–23.

'You will indeed listen, but never understand,
and you will indeed look, but never perceive.
15 For this people's heart has grown dull,
and their ears are hard of hearing,
and they have shut their eyes;
so that they might not look with their eyes,
and listen with their ears,
and understand with their heart and turn—
and I would heal them.'
16But blessed are your eyes, for they see, and your
ears, for they hear. 17Truly I tell you, many
prophets and righteous people longed to see what
you see, but did not see it, and to hear what you
hear, but did not hear it.

Soils Explained

18 "Hear then the parable of the sower.
19When anyone hears the word of the kingdom
and does not understand it, the evil one comes and
snatches away what is sown in the heart; this is
what was sown on the path. 20As for what was
sown on rocky ground, this is the one who hears
the word and immediately receives it with joy;
21yet such a person has no root, but endures only
for a while, and when trouble or persecution arises
on account of the word, that person immediately falls away.[c] 22As for what was sown among
thorns, this is the one who hears the word, but
the cares of the world and the lure of wealth
choke the word, and it yields nothing. 23But as
for what was sown on good soil, this is the
one who hears the word and understands it,
who indeed bears fruit and yields, in one case
a hundredfold, in another sixty, and in another
thirty."

Wheat and Weeds

24 He put before them another parable: "The
kingdom of heaven may be compared to someone
who sowed good seed in his field; 25but while
everybody was asleep, an enemy came and sowed
weeds among the wheat, and then went away. 26So
when the plants came up and bore grain, then the
weeds appeared as well. 27And the slaves of the
householder came and said to him, 'Master, did
you not sow good seed in your field? Where, then,
did these weeds come from?' 28He answered, 'An
enemy has done this.' The slaves said to him, 'Then
do you want us to go and gather them?' 29But he
replied, 'No; for in gathering the weeds you would
uproot the wheat along with them. 30Let both of
them grow together until the harvest; and at harvest time I will tell the reapers, Collect the weeds
first and bind them in bundles to be burned, but
gather the wheat into my barn.' "

A Mustard Seed

31 He put before them another parable: "The
kingdom of heaven is like a mustard seed that
someone took and sowed in his field; 32it is the
smallest of all the seeds, but when it has grown it
is the greatest of shrubs and becomes a tree, so that
the birds of the air come and make nests in its
branches."

Yeast

13:33
see pg. 58

33 He told them another
parable: "The kingdom of
heaven is like yeast that a woman took and mixed
in with[d] three measures of flour until all of it was
leavened."

The Use of Parables

13:34–35

34 Jesus told the crowds all
these things in parables; without
a parable he told them nothing. 35This was to fulfill
what had been spoken through the prophet:[e]
"I will open my mouth to speak in parables;
I will proclaim what has been hidden from
the foundation of the world."[f]

Wheat and Weeds Explained

36 Then he left the crowds and went into the
house. And his disciples approached him, saying,
"Explain to us the parable of the weeds of the
field." 37He answered, "The one who sows the
good seed is the Son of Man; 38the field is
the world, and the good seed are the children of
the kingdom; the weeds are the children of the evil
one, 39and the enemy who sowed them is the devil;
the harvest is the end of the age, and the reapers
are angels. 40Just as the weeds are collected and
burned up with fire, so will it be at the end of the

(Bible text continued on page 58)

[c]Gk *stumbles* [d]Gk *hid in* [e]Other ancient authorities read *the prophet Isaiah* [f]Other ancient authorities lack *of the world*

MYTH #1

10 MYTHS ABOUT CHRISTIANITY

MYTH: JESUS CHRIST WAS ONLY A GREAT MORAL TEACHER

Many people today accept a number of myths about Christianity, with the result that they never respond to Jesus as He really is. This is one of ten articles that speak to some of those misconceptions. For a list of all ten, see 1 Tim. 1:3–4.

People marveled at the teaching of Jesus. Whether He spoke in interesting parables (v. 34) or gave more straightforward, extended discourses (for instance, Matt. 5–7), people followed Him everywhere, hanging on His every word (Matt. 7:28). "Never has anyone spoken like this!" His listeners remarked (John 7:46). And they were right. Jesus was a master teacher and communicator.

Moreover, beyond simply teaching the highest moral and spiritual principles ever known, Jesus actually *lived* them. He told people to love their enemies; He forgave those who crucified Him. He told people to lay down their lives for others; He laid down His own life for the world. He told people not to worry about material possessions; He owned no more than the clothes on His back. Jesus' example makes Him the most remarkable of all teachers.

And yet that legacy almost makes it too easy for people to dismiss Him, ignoring both His message and His person: "Jesus? Yes, He was a great moral teacher." What they really mean is that, for them, Jesus was *only* a teacher—a great teacher, perhaps the greatest the world has ever seen, but a teacher and nothing more.

Neither He nor His followers would allow for that. Jesus was either very much more than a great teacher or else very much less than one. For in addition to His great moral precepts, He made astonishing claims that no other sane person has ever made, and behaved in ways that no other decent human has. For instance:

- He claimed to forgive people's sins (Matt. 9:2; Luke 7:47–48).
- He accepted people's worship (Matt. 8:2–3; 9:18–19; 14:33).
- He said that He alone was the way to God, the truth of God, and the life of God (John 5:40; 6:44; 7:16–17; 14:6).
- He said that He had come to seek and to save the lost (Luke 19:10).
- He promised that He would rise from the dead (Matt. 20:19; 27:63).
- He claimed that humanity would ultimately be accountable to Him (Matt. 7:21–23; 25:31–46).
- He claimed to be God and allowed others to call Him God (Matt. 16:15–16; 26:63–64; John 8:58).

These are astonishing claims. Any teacher who would make them had better be telling the truth or else He would be the worst of all liars and neither great nor moral.

The evidence suggests that Jesus was telling the truth. For in addition to His explicit claims are the implicit claims of fulfilled Old Testament prophecies and the performance of supernatural miracles. And there is also the fact that countless others who have examined His words and actions have come away convinced that He was not merely a great moral teacher, but the very Son of God. Among them have been determined and supposedly unshakable skeptics like Thomas and adamant opponents like the brilliant Saul of Tarsus who ended up becoming His most ardent follower.

(continued on next page)

(continued from previous page)

To believe that Jesus was simply a great moral teacher is untenable. As C. S. Lewis put it,

A man who was merely a man and said the sort of things Jesus said would not be a great moral teacher. He would either be a lunatic—on a level with the man who says he is a poached egg—or else He would be the Devil of Hell. You must make your choice. Either this man was, and is, the Son of God: or else a madman or something worse. You can shut Him up for a fool, you can spit at Him and kill Him as a demon; or you can fall at His feet and call Him Lord and God. But let us not come with any patronizing nonsense about His being a great human teacher. He has not left that open to us. He did not intend to.

(C. S. Lewis, *Mere Christianity,* p. 56) ◆

age. 41The Son of Man will send his angels, and they will
collect out of his kingdom all causes of sin and all evildoers,
42and they will throw them into the furnace of fire,
where there will be weeping and gnashing of teeth. 43Then
the righteous will shine like the sun in the kingdom of their
Father. Let anyone with ears[g] listen!

Hidden Treasure

44 "The kingdom of heaven is like
treasure hidden in a field, which someone
found and hid; then in his joy he goes and sells all that
he has and buys that field.

[g]Other ancient authorities add *to hear*

◆ ◆ ◆ ◆ ◆ ◆ ◆ ◆ ◆ ◆ ◆ ◆ ◆ ◆ ◆

Fifty Pounds of Flour

CONSIDER THIS 13:33

Perhaps when Jesus told the parable of the yeast (v. 33), laughter rippled through the crowd from the women who were listening. "Doesn't He know anything about baking?" *they might have chuckled—or maybe Jesus was humoring them with an inside joke.*

Jewish women did not use fresh yeast each day to leaven their barley or wheat bread, but a small piece of fermented dough from the previous day's batch. However, three measures was an enormous amount of flour—close to fifty pounds! How could that much flour be leavened by the usual amount of previously leavened dough?

Jesus' parable—and its point—must have come to mind every day afterwards as the women kneaded their dough. Fifty pounds of flour leavened by such a small amount of dough . . . the kingdom of God brought about by way of such a small number of faithful people.

Two other images that Jesus used to describe the influence His followers can have on society were salt and light. See "Sulfa Drugs and Street Lights," Matt. 5:13–16.

On another occasion, Jesus talked about leaven in a much more negative connection. See "Danger Ahead," Mark 8:14–21.

A Pearl of Great Value

45 "Again, the kingdom of heaven is like a merchant in search of fine pearls; 46on finding one pearl of great value, he went and sold all that he had and bought it.

A Net

47 "Again, the kingdom of heaven is like a net that was thrown into the sea and caught fish of every kind; 48when it was full, they drew it ashore, sat down, and put the good into baskets but threw out the bad. 49So it will be at the end of the age. The angels will come out and separate the evil from the righteous 50and throw them into the furnace of fire, where there will be weeping and gnashing of teeth.

Master of a Household

51 "Have you understood all this?" They an-
13:52 see pg. 60
swered, "Yes." 52And he said to them, "Therefore every scribe who has been trained for the kingdom of heaven is like the master of a household who brings out of his treasure what is new and what is old." 53When Jesus had finished these parables, he left that place.

Jesus Dishonored in His Own Country

54 He came to his hometown and began to teach the people[h] in their synagogue, so that they were astounded and said, "Where did this man get this wisdom and these deeds of power? 55Is not this the carpenter's son? Is not his mother called Mary? And are not his brothers James and Joseph and Simon and Judas? 56And are not all his sisters with us? Where then did this man get all this?" 57And they took offense at him. But Jesus said to them, "Prophets are not without honor except in their own country and in their own house." 58And he did not do many deeds of power there, because of their unbelief.

Herod Executes John the Baptist

14:1 see pg. 61

14 At that time Herod the ruler[i] heard reports about Jesus; 2and he said to his servants, "This is John the Baptist; he has been raised from the dead, and for this reason these
14:3 see pg. 61
powers are at work in him." 3For Herod had arrested John, bound him, and put

(Bible text continued on page 61)

[h]Gk *them* [i]Gk *tetrarch*

The Incomparable Value of the Kingdom

CONSIDER THIS 13:44–46 **The two parables in vv. 44–46 describe the incomparable value of the kingdom. Nothing was worth more, Jesus told His followers. Nothing is too great to sacrifice for it—certainly not material wealth (Matt. 6:33; 19:16–30).**

In light of Jesus' words here, maybe it's worth pausing to reflect on your own life and choices. What has your commitment to Christ cost you? Or has it cost you anything? Has it made any difference in decisions about your career, lifestyle, investments, or purchases? What would you sell in order to gain the King and His kingdom (v. 46)?

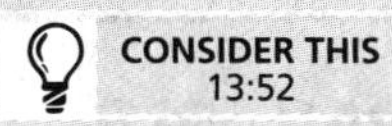

Treasures New and Old

One of the most exciting aspects of Christian truth is that it is inexhaustible. One can never come to the end of it. No matter how long we may have been in the faith, no matter how much theology we may master, we can never come to the end of what God has revealed in Christ and in the Bible. Jesus spoke to this fact in His parable of the householder (v. 52).

The key to understanding this parable is the question Jesus asked His followers: "Have you understood all this?" (v. 51). "These things" refers to the series of parables on the kingdom that He had just told (vv. 1–50). Amazingly, the disciples answered yes. Apparently they thought they had absorbed everything Jesus had to say.

But how could they? They could not possibly perceive the vast implications of these stories for day-to-day life, let alone the theological issues involved in a doctrine as complex as the kingdom. Theologians still debate these matters (see "The King Declares His Kingdom," Matt. 4:17).

Jesus recognized that the disciples were claiming more insight than they actually possessed. So He gave them the parable of the householder to characterize the situation.

Householders were what we would call heads of households, persons with authority over what went on in a given home.

If one were to visit the home, the master of the house might bring out some of the treasures of the home to delight and impress his guest. He might bring out something old—perhaps one of the family heirlooms—or something new—maybe a recent purchase.

Jesus likened His disciples to heads of the family in possession of His truth. Over the years they would tell people about the "old treasures"—the basics of the gospel—and about "new treasures"—the way in which His teaching applied to new situations.

In effect, they would be like scribes "trained for the kingdom of heaven" (v. 52). Scribes were a learned class of scholars who studied the Scriptures and served as copyists, editors, and teachers. They occupied a prestigious position, as only ordained teachers could transmit and create religious tradition. Just as the Jewish scribes studied the Law, recalling old truths recognized for centuries as well as "new" truths that applied Scripture to the demands of new situations, so the disciples were storing up Jesus' teaching and—someday—would repeat it to others, write it down, and teach from it, passing on "things new and old."

Today we possess the written record of these treasures. But like Jesus' first disciples, we can find both old and new. As we confront situations, we can look back to the "old" truths, the fundamental things that never change, and we can also discern how to apply biblical truth to new issues in ways that are fresh and alive. ◆

To become a scribe required constant study, often beginning at age 14 and continuing to the age of 40. Learn more about these elite scholars of Jewish society at Luke 20:39.

him in prison on account of Herodias, his brother Philip's
wife,[j] 4because John had been telling him, "It is not lawful
for you to have her." 5Though Herod[k] wanted to put him to
death, he feared the crowd, because they regarded him as a

14:6–10

prophet. 6But when Herod's birthday
came, the daughter of Herodias danced
before the company, and she pleased Herod 7so much that
he promised on oath to grant her whatever she might ask.
8Prompted by her mother, she said, "Give me the head of
John the Baptist here on a platter." 9The king was grieved,
yet out of regard for his oaths and for the guests, he commanded it to be given; 10he sent and had John beheaded in
the prison. 11The head was brought on a platter and given
to the girl, who brought it to her mother. 12His disciples
came and took the body and buried it; then they went and
told Jesus.

Jesus Feeds 5,000

14:13–14 see pg. 62

13 Now when Jesus heard this, he
withdrew from there in a boat to a de-
serted place by himself. But when the crowds heard it, they
followed him on foot from the towns. 14When he went
ashore, he saw a great crowd; and he had compassion for
them and cured their sick. 15When it was evening, the disciples came to him and said, "This is a deserted place, and
the hour is now late; send the crowds away so that they
may go into the villages and buy food for themselves." 16Je-
sus said to them, "They need not go away; you give them
something to eat." 17They replied, "We have nothing here
but five loaves and two fish." 18And he said, "Bring them
here to me." 19Then he ordered the crowds to sit down on
the grass. Taking the five loaves and the two fish, he looked
up to heaven, and blessed and broke the loaves, and gave

[j]Other ancient authorities read *his brother's wife* [k]Gk *he*

Herod the Tetrarch

A CLOSER LOOK 14:1

The son of King Herod, Herod Antipas inherited the title of "tetrarch" (ruler of a fourth part; see Luke 9:7). Read about his infamous family in "The Herods," Acts 12:1–2.

Herod's Rash Promise

A CLOSER LOOK 14:6–10

Charmed by his stepdaughter and no doubt intoxicated, Herod rashly made a promise that cost John the Baptist his life (vv. 6–10). "A Reckless Choice" at Mark 6:23, discusses how decisions with far-reaching consequences are often made in haste, in a flush of wild excitement.

HATEFUL HERODIAS

CONSIDER THIS 14:3

Herodias (v. 3) was a powerful woman. The wife of the Roman-appointed ruler of Galilee and Perea, she enjoyed privilege and position. But one thing she had no control over was the outspoken tongue of John the Baptist.

John had publicly condemned Herodias' marriage to Herod Antipas. A granddaughter of Herod the Great, Herodias had first married her father's brother, Herod Philip I. But she left Philip to marry his half-brother, Herod Antipas, who divorced his wife to marry Herodias.

John denounced their immorality, and Herodias was determined to silence the troublesome prophet. So she persuaded Herod to have John arrested and imprisoned. However, she could not convince her husband to execute the man.

Eventually, however, an opportunity presented itself when Herod's lust led him to foolishly promise Herodias' daughter Salome anything (v. 7). The extent of Herodias' evil and cunning is evident from her daughter's unusual request. Imagine the control she must have had over the girl's mind!

The Bible records terrible stories truthfully. This woman's choice, to use her daughter to work her vengeance on an innocent man, ranks among the worst.

them to the disciples, and the disciples gave them to the
crowds. 20And all ate and were filled; and they took up
what was left over of the broken pieces, twelve baskets full.
21And those who ate were about five thousand men, besides
women and children.

Jesus Walks on Water

22 Immediately he made the disciples get into the boat
and go on ahead to the other side, while he dismissed the
crowds. 23And after he had dismissed the crowds, he went
up the mountain by himself to pray. When evening came,

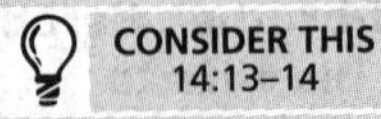
CONSIDER THIS
14:13–14

THE PUBLIC SIDE OF OUR FAITH

For many persons Christianity has developed into a private spirituality—prayers, private devotions and Bible reading, self-examination and confession, personal holiness, individual acts of charity, and so on. This is all to the good, inasmuch as Christ is a Person who seeks a relationship with individuals.

But what about the public side of our faith? For example:

- *How do we as believers live as Christians in the public arenas—work, community, relationships, civic responsibilities, and so on?*
- *What about our communities of faith, such as our churches? How vibrant and strategic is our collective witness as God's people to a watching world?*

he was there alone, 24but by this time the boat, battered by
the waves, was far from the land,[l] for the wind was against
14:25 see pg. 64 them. 25And early in the morning he
came walking toward them on the sea.
26But when the disciples saw him walking on the sea, they
were terrified, saying, "It is a ghost!" And they cried out in
fear. 27But immediately Jesus spoke to them and said, "Take
heart, it is I; do not be afraid."
28 Peter answered him, "Lord, if it is you, command me
to come to you on the water." 29He said, "Come." So Peter
got out of the boat, started walking on the water, and came

[l]Other ancient authorities read *was out on the sea*

- *In what ways do we as believers influence our society as a whole—its institutions, its needs, and its values?*

These are broad, complex questions that have no easy answers. But we cannot afford to ignore them—not when we consider the public side of Jesus' ministry. Unlike others of His day who withdrew from society to practice and perfect their own, private spirituality (such as the Essenes, Matt. 16:1), Jesus actively engaged His culture. He participated in its rituals. He focused His work on its cities (see "Jesus—A City Preacher," Matt. 9:35). He interacted with its leaders. He welcomed its crowds (as seen here in vv. 13–14). He particularly reached out to its poor—not only the financially poor but the "poor in spirit," those left behind, those left without hope.

In short, Jesus not only affects our private lives, but our public lives as well. We need to recover that dimension of the gospel today. As believers we are no longer simply individuals, but have been made part of a "royal priesthood" and a "holy nation." Out of those who were once "not a people," we are now "God's people" (1 Pet. 2:9–10). We need to discover how to live out our faith in visible, public ways, as the collective people of God, in order to powerfully impact our world. ◆

Jesus used two metaphors to describe a believer's public life, particularly work and participation in the community. See "Sulfa Drugs and Street Lights," Matt. 5:13–16.

HE SAW A GREAT CROWD; AND HE HAD COMPASSION FOR THEM. . .
—Matthew 14:14

toward Jesus. 30But when he noticed the strong wind,[m] he
became frightened, and beginning to sink, he cried out,
"Lord, save me!" 31Jesus immediately reached out his hand
and caught him, saying to him, "You of little faith, why did
you doubt?" 32When they got into the boat, the wind
ceased. 33And those in the boat worshiped him, saying,
"Truly you are the Son of God."

Many Healed in Gennesaret

34 When they had crossed over, they came to land at
Gennesaret. 35After the people of that place recognized him,
they sent word throughout the region and brought all who
were sick to him, 36and begged him that they might touch

[m]Other ancient authorities read *the wind*

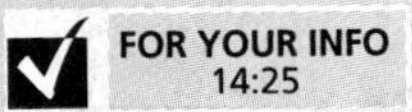

FOR YOUR INFO
14:25

Telling Time

Matthew records that Jesus came walking on the sea "early in the morning" (v. 25), indicating that the disciples had spent virtually the entire night struggling with the stormy conditions!

In those days, time was not reckoned as precisely as it is today. In cultures that lacked electricity and were far more agriculturally based than our own, time was an approximation. Thus when the men of Jabesh Gilead came to Saul for help, he promised them, "Tomorrow, by the time the sun is hot, you shall have deliverance" (1 Sam. 11:9), indicating that reinforcements would arrive sometime in mid-morning. Likewise, God is said to have walked in the garden of Eden "at the time of the evening breeze" (Gen. 3:8).

However, the Hebrews did divide the period of daylight (yom) *into 12 hours, as follows:*

Sunrise	*6:00 a.m.*
1st hour	*7:00 a.m.*
2nd hour	*8:00 a.m.*
3rd hour	*9:00 a.m.*
4th hour	*10:00 a.m.*
5th hour	*11:00 a.m.*
6th hour	*12:00 noon*
7th hour	*1:00 p.m.*
8th hour	*2:00 p.m.*

even the fringe of his cloak; and all who touched it were
healed.

Debates over Tradition

15:1–3

15 Then Pharisees and scribes came
to Jesus from Jerusalem and said,
2"Why do your disciples break the tradition of the elders?
For they do not wash their hands before they eat." 3He answered them, "And why do you break the commandment
of God for the sake of your tradition? 4For God said,[n]
'Honor your father and your mother,' and, 'Whoever speaks

[n]Other ancient authorities read *commanded, saying*

9th hour .... 3:00 p.m.
10th hour..................... 4:00 p.m.
11th hour..................... 5:00 p.m.
12th hour..................... 6:00 p.m.

Obviously these times could vary substantially, depending on the season. To complicate matters, the Romans reckoned the day (as we do) in two twelve-hour periods beginning at midnight and noon.

Nighttime was divided into "watches," so called because of the changing shifts of watchmen who stood guard on city walls and at the gates. In the New Testament, the influence of the Romans created four watches estimated as follows (again depending on the season):

Beginning around . . .
1st watch..................... 6:00 p.m.
2nd watch .... 9:00 p.m.
3rd watch..................... midnight
4th watch..................... 3:00 a.m. ◆

TRADITION

CONSIDER THIS 15:1–3 Tradition. Is it the bedrock of intelligent change or the stumbling block to any change? Should leaders embrace and personify traditional values, or should they be mavericks, breaking with tradition and striking out in new directions?

Jesus rebuked the scribes and Pharisees for allowing their rabbinic traditions to actually supersede the express commands of God (v. 3). The specific issue here was a tradition about ritual washings connected with the preparation and serving of food. Not only must one's hands be washed, but also the bowls, cups, pitchers, and other utensils.

In modern American culture we do not follow the rigid pronouncements of a priestly class. Yet there are numerous traditions and expectations—most of which are unspoken—that govern our behavior in powerful ways. This creates tension for believers in the workplace, particularly managers. They are called upon to be both sustainers and breakers of tradition. There are no simple formulas to help one decide how to respond to tradition, but it might help to reflect on questions such as:

- **What values and principles does the tradition seek to embody? How do those square with the values of Christ?**
- **Why does the tradition exist? Why is it maintained? Are there any major objections to it?**
- **In maintaining a tradition, who benefits and who suffers? If it changes, who might be helped or hurt? How would the organization be affected?**

Tradition is an important area in which faith impacts the world. See Mark 16:15–16.

evil of father or mother must surely die.' 5But you say that
whoever tells father or mother, 'Whatever support you
might have had from me is given to God,'[o] then that person
need not honor the father.[p] 6So, for the sake of your tradition, you make void the word[q] of God. 7You hypocrites! Isaiah prophesied rightly about you when he said:

8 'This people honors me with their lips,
but their hearts are far from me;
9 in vain do they worship me,
teaching human precepts as doctrines.' "

Jesus Denounces the Pharisees

10 Then he called the crowd to him and said to them,
"Listen and understand: 11it is not what goes into the
mouth that defiles a person, but it is what comes out of the
mouth that defiles." 12Then the disciples approached and
said to him, "Do you know that the Pharisees took offense
when they heard what you said?" 13He answered, "Every
plant that my heavenly Father has not planted will be uprooted. 14Let them alone; they are blind guides of the
blind.[r] And if one blind person guides another, both will
fall into a pit." 15But Peter said to him, "Explain this parable
to us." 16Then he said, "Are you also still without understanding? 17Do you not see that whatever goes into the
mouth enters the stomach, and goes out into the sewer?
18But what comes out of the mouth proceeds from the
heart, and this is what defiles. 19For out of the heart come
evil intentions, murder, adultery, fornication, theft, false
witness, slander. 20These are what defile a person, but to eat
with unwashed hands does not defile."

A Canaanite Woman's Plea

15:21-28

21 Jesus left that place and went
away to the district of Tyre and Sidon.
22Just then a Canaanite woman from that region came out
and started shouting, "Have mercy on me, Lord, Son of
David; my daughter is tormented by a demon." 23But he did
not answer her at all. And his disciples came and urged
him, saying, "Send her away, for she keeps shouting after

(Bible text continued on page 68)

[o]Or *is an offering* [p]Other ancient authorities add *or the mother* [q]Other ancient authorities read *law*; others, *commandment* [r]Other ancient authorities lack *of the blind*

Persistence Pays Off

CONSIDER THIS 15:21-28 **Jesus took His disciples to the seacoast towns of Tyre and Sidon (v. 21), probably to rest (Mark 7:24). As far as we can tell, He had no intention of preaching or healing in that area.**

But as so often happens when one has no intention of being available, someone interrupted His vacation. Today, phone calls prove to be the major source of interruptions. But in ancient times it was worse: interruptions arrived at one's doorstep and stayed until someone answered.

In this instance, a woman who supposedly had no claim on Jesus' attention begged Him to deliver her daughter from demons. She had probably already tried to heal the girl and failed. In ancient societies, women usually tended the sick and nursed the dying.

Jesus hardly encouraged this woman. As He pointed out, she had no ethnic or religious claim on Him. But somehow she recognized that He was capable of doing what she could not—heal her daughter. In the end, her courage, faith, and sheer persistence won out.

How persistent are you in crying out to God for people who matter a lot to you? Like the woman, will you keep coming back to God in faith?

Jesus' treatment of the woman seems a contradiction to His image. She came in utter sincerity and with great respect, yet He put her off with severe words. Why would He do that? See "Jesus and Ethnicity," Mark 7:24–30.

On another occasion, Jesus told His followers an interesting story about the need for persistence in prayer. See Luke 18:1–8.

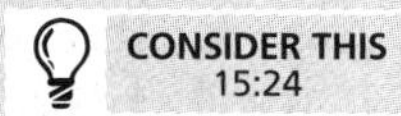
CONSIDER THIS
15:24

JEWS, GENTILES, AND JESUS

At the time Jesus was born, Hebrews saw the world divided into two types of people—Jews and everyone else. Jews regarded foreigners (known as Gentiles, or "nations") as morally unclean and spiritually lost. Jews were God's people; Gentiles were not. The attitude was well expressed by Peter upon meeting Cornelius, a Roman centurion: "You yourselves know that it is unlawful for a Jew to associate with or to visit a Gentile" (Acts 10:28).

The roots of this separation stretched deep into Israel's history. One important development occurred in about 450 B.C. when a remnant of Jews returned from captivity in Babylon to rebuild Jerusalem. Their leader, Ezra the priest, called for purification from all pagan influences, such as foreign-born wives (Ezra 10:2–4).

Later, after centuries of domination by the Greeks and Romans, Jews developed a hatred for all Gentiles and tried to avoid contact with foreigners. According to Tacitus, a Roman historian, "they regard the rest of mankind with all the hatred of enemies" (*Histories*, v. 5).

In Matthew's Gospel we see a recognition of the tension between the two groups. He presents Jesus as the long-awaited Christ of the Jews (Matt. 15:24). Jesus fulfilled numerous Old Testament messianic prophecies (for example, Matt. 1:23; 2:6, 14, 18, 23). But Matthew also shows Jesus breaking through the Jew/Gentile wall of hatred and separation. Jesus dealt with Jews and Gentiles alike, shattering the caste system of His day—and shocking His Jewish brothers.

What ethnic or racial walls would Jesus tear down in the modern era? Perhaps He would have joined black slaves in the United States and lived among them as an equal. Perhaps He would have violated the customs of segregation and eaten with blacks in white restaurants earlier in this century. Perhaps He would open His door to Haitians in Miami, Chinese in Vancouver, or Vietnamese in Houston. Perhaps He would make friends with Palestinians in Israel, or reach out to Moslems in Iraq and Iran. Perhaps He would heal both Roman Catholics and Protestants in Northern Ireland.

Racism and ethnic hatred have never been God's desire. They come from the sin of men and women. Jesus repudiated such sin wherever He found it. As Matthew shows, His heart is for all the nations. ◆

While Matthew's Gospel portrays Jesus in terms of His Jewish roots, it also shows that Jesus is an international Savior, a Messiah for the whole world. See "Jesus' Global Connections," Matt. 8:10.

Part-Jew, part-Gentile, Samaritans were treated with unusual scorn by their Hebrew cousins. See John 4:4.

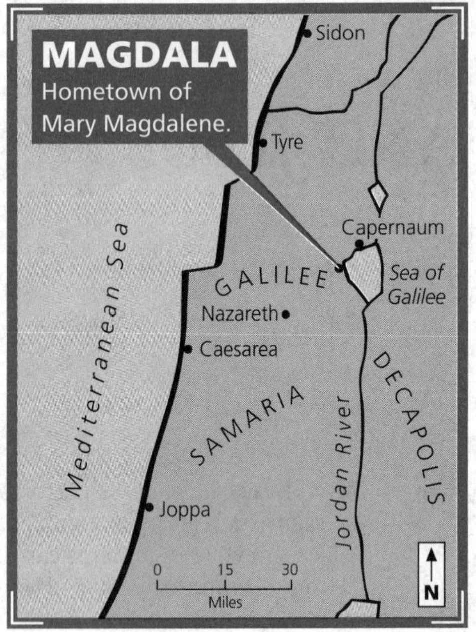

MAGDALA

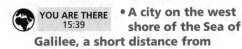

- A city on the west shore of the Sea of Galilee, a short distance from Tiberias.
- Also known as Taricheae and called *Migdal* ("tower"), suggesting its significance militarily.
- A flourishing center of the region's fishing industry, shipping salted and pickled fish to Jerusalem, Damascus, and even as far away as Spain.
- Also known for agriculture, shipbuilding, and trade.
- Mostly Gentile in population and very wealthy.
- Boasted a hippodrome (stadium for chariot racing).
- Modern-day Mejdel the likely site of the ancient city.

15:24 see pg. 67

us." [24]He answered, "I was sent only to
the lost sheep of the house of Israel."
[25]But she came and knelt before him, saying, "Lord, help
me." [26]He answered, "It is not fair to take the children's
food and throw it to the dogs." [27]She said, "Yes, Lord, yet
even the dogs eat the crumbs that fall from their masters'
table." [28]Then Jesus answered her, "Woman, great is your
faith! Let it be done for you as you wish." And her daughter
was healed instantly.

Jesus Heals on a Mountain

29 After Jesus had left that place, he passed along the
Sea of Galilee, and he went up the mountain, where he sat
down. [30]Great crowds came to him, bringing with them the
lame, the maimed, the blind, the mute, and many others.
They put them at his feet, and he cured them, [31]so that the
crowd was amazed when they saw the mute speaking, the
maimed whole, the lame walking, and the blind seeing.
And they praised the God of Israel.

Jesus Feeds 4,000

32 Then Jesus called his disciples to him and said, "I
have compassion for the crowd, because they have been
with me now for three days and have nothing to eat; and I
do not want to send them away hungry, for they might faint
on the way." [33]The disciples said to him, "Where are we to
get enough bread in the desert to feed so great a crowd?"
[34]Jesus asked them, "How many loaves have you?" They
said, "Seven, and a few small fish." [35]Then ordering the
crowd to sit down on the ground, [36]he took the seven
loaves and the fish; and after giving thanks he broke them
and gave them to the disciples, and the disciples gave them
to the crowds. [37]And all of them ate and were filled; and
they took up the broken pieces left over, seven baskets full.
[38]Those who had eaten were four thousand men, besides

15:39

women and children. [39]After sending
away the crowds, he got into the boat
and went to the region of Magadan.[s]

Leaders Ask for a Sign

16:1 see pg. 70

16 The Pharisees and Sadducees
came, and to test Jesus[t] they
asked him to show them a sign from heaven. [2]He answered

[s]Other ancient authorities read *Magdala* or *Magdalan* [t]Gk *him*

them, "When it is evening, you say, 'It will be fair weather,
for the sky is red.' [3]And in the morning, 'It will be stormy
today, for the sky is red and threatening.' You know how to
interpret the appearance of the sky, but you cannot interpret the signs of the times.[u] [4]An evil and adulterous generation asks for a sign, but no sign will be given to it except
the sign of Jonah." Then he left them and went away.

"Beware of the Yeast of the Pharisees"

5 When the disciples reached the other side, they had
forgotten to bring any bread. [6]Jesus said to them, "Watch
out, and beware of the yeast of the Pharisees and Sadducees." [7]They said to one another, "It is because we have
brought no bread." [8]And becoming aware of it, Jesus said,
"You of little faith, why are you talking about having no
bread? [9]Do you still not perceive? Do you not remember
the five loaves for the five thousand, and how many baskets
you gathered? [10]Or the seven loaves for the four thousand,
and how many baskets you gathered? [11]How could you fail
to perceive that I was not speaking about bread? Beware of
the yeast of the Pharisees and Sadducees!" [12]Then they understood that he had not told them to beware of the yeast
of bread, but of the teaching of the Pharisees and Sadducees.

"You Are the Messiah"

16:13–20

13 Now when Jesus came into the district of Caesarea Philippi, he asked his
disciples, "Who do people say that the Son of Man is?"
[14]And they said, "Some say John the Baptist, but others Elijah, and still others Jeremiah or one of the prophets." [15]He
said to them, "But who do you say that I am?" [16]Simon Peter answered, "You are the Messiah,[v] the Son of the living
God." [17]And Jesus answered him, "Blessed are you, Simon
son of Jonah! For flesh and blood has not revealed this to

(Bible text continued on page 72)

[u]Other ancient authorities lack [2]*When it is . . . of the times* [v]Or *the Christ*

"YOU CANNOT INTERPRET THE SIGNS OF THE TIMES." —Matthew 16:3

Standing at the Gates of Hell

A CLOSER LOOK 16:13–20 *When Jesus queried His disciples as to His identity (vv. 13, 15), they were standing in the shadow of a city named in honor of Rome's emperor. See "You Are the Messiah," Mark 8:27–33, and "Caesarea," Acts 10:24.*

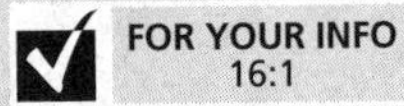

PARTY POLITICS OF JESUS' DAY

What were the politics of Jesus? We may speculate on what His preferences might be today. But what political ideals did He favor during His earthly life? What leaders did He endorse, if any? What causes did He support? For that matter, was political choice even an issue for Him? Did politics even matter?

In the end, it would be difficult if not impossible to determine any satisfactory answers. Jesus seemed acutely aware of the power brokers in His society. He also showed remarkable skill at political gamesmanship. But He never addressed or practiced politics in any formal sense. And He lived in a system completely different from our own.

However, even if we cannot know precisely what Jesus' affiliations were, we can at least understand some of the political dynamics at work in Palestine in the first half of the first century. For example, we know that there were at least five major political parties among the Hebrews of that day.

The Herodians—Loyal Defenders of the Status Quo

- Took their name from Herod the Great (37–4 B.C.) and his supporters. (See "The Herods," Acts 12:1–2.)
- Supported the adoption of Graeco-Roman culture and policies in Palestine.
- Like the Pharisees, favored local political autonomy. Fearing military intervention by Rome, they stridently resisted challengers to the status quo, such as the Zealots, John the Baptist, Jesus, and the apostles.
- Joined forces with other parties in the plot to eliminate Jesus (Matt. 22:16; Mark 3:6; 12:13).

The Pharisees—Religious Legalists

- Probably derived from a group of the faithful called the *Hasidim*.
- Name means "to separate."
- Shared similar views with the Essenes, but chose to stay within the

larger society. Nevertheless, many chose to study the Law on their own, having lost respect for the priesthood as a result of its corruption.

- Many served on the council (see Acts 6:12).
- Considered the doctors of the Law; scribes were considered laymen.
- Collected and preserved the Talmud and the Mishnah, voluminous products of oral tradition and Old Testament commentary.
- By reputation, legalistic and fanatically devoted to rabbinic tradition. Some even refused to eat with non-Pharisees for fear of being contaminated by food not rendered ritually clean.
- Like the Herodians, favored local political autonomy.
- Differed with the Sadducees over the doctrine of the resurrection.
- Understood the coming kingdom as a literal fulfillment of the promise to David for a King to reign over Israel forever.
- Maintained an elaborate theology of angels, believing them to intervene in human affairs.

The Sadducees—The Urban Elite

- May have derived from Zadok, high priest under King David.
- Tended to represent the aristocrats, priests, merchants, and urban elite in Jerusalem and other cities in Judea.
- Hostile to Jesus and His followers.
- Many served on the council. Most of the high priests in the days of Jesus and the apostles were Sadducees.
- Denied the resurrection or life after death, along with the doctrines of everlasting punishment and a literal kingdom.
- Denied that God controls history, insisting on free will and the responsibility of humans to make wise choices according to the Law.
- Held only to the Law of Moses (the first five books of the Old Testament) as supremely authoritative.
- Denied the existence of angels.

The Zealots—Firebrands of Revolution

- Ardent nationalists who awaited an opportunity to revolt against Rome.
- Resisted paying taxes to Rome or to the temple.
- One particular tax revolt against Rome, led by Judas the Galilean (6 B.C.), secured Galilee's reputation as a seedbed of revolutionaries.
- Blamed by some for the collapse of Judea to Rome in the war of A.D. 66–70. Josephus, a Jewish historian, claimed that they degenerated into mere assassins or *sicarii* ("dagger-men").
- Sided with the Pharisees in supporting Jewish Law.
- Opposed the Herodians and Sadducees, who tried to maintain the political status quo.
- Intolerant of the Essenes and later the Christians for their tendencies toward nonviolence.
- Two recruited by Jesus were Judas Iscariot and Simon the Cananite.

The Essenes—Detached Purists

- A sect of ascetics that thrived between the middle of the second century B.C. until the Jewish-Roman war in A.D. 66–70.
- Once members of the *Hasidim*, but unlike the Pharisees separated from society, withdrawing into monastic communities like Qumran where the Dead Sea scrolls were found.
- Known today mostly through secondary sources.
- Lived in societies that held property in common.
- Believed in the immortality of the soul, angels, and an elaborate scheme of end-times prophecies. Some were looking for as many as three different Messiahs.
- Known for celibacy, pacifism, opposition to slavery, caring for their own sick and elderly, trading only within their own sect, simplicity in meals and dress, and the rejection of all ostentatious display.
- Paid more attention to ceremonial purity than did even the Pharisees, and carefully guarded the Sabbath.
- Practiced ritual baptism and a communal dinner called the messianic banquet.
- May have influenced some early Christian practices and rituals. ◆

In addition to the regional and local politics of Palestine, Jesus and His followers lived under the enormous influence of Rome. See "Roman Politics in the First Century A.D.," Luke 22:25.

16:18

you, but my Father in heaven. 18And I
tell you, you are Peter,[w] and on this rock[x]
I will build my church, and the gates of Hades will not prevail against it. 19I will give you the keys of the kingdom of heaven, and whatever you bind on earth will be bound in heaven, and whatever you loose on earth will be loosed in
heaven." 20Then he sternly ordered the disciples not to tell anyone that he was[y] the Messiah.[z]

Following Jesus Means Sacrifice

21 From that time on, Jesus began to show his disciples that he must go to Jerusalem and undergo great suffering at the hands of the elders and chief priests and scribes, and be killed, and on the third day be raised.

16:22–23 see pg. 74

22And Peter took him aside and began to rebuke him, saying, "God forbid it, Lord! This must never happen to you."
23But he turned and said to Peter, "Get behind me, Satan! You are a stumbling block to me; for you are setting your mind not on divine things but on human things."

24 Then Jesus told his disciples, "If any want to become my followers, let them deny themselves and take up their cross and follow me.
25For those who want to save their life will lose it, and those who lose their life for my sake will
find it. 26For what will it profit them if they gain the whole world but forfeit their life? Or what will they give in return for their life?

27 "For the Son of Man is to come with his angels in the glory of his Father, and then he will repay everyone for
what has been done. 28Truly I tell you, there are some standing here who will not taste death before they see the Son of Man coming in his kingdom."

"FOR WHAT WILL IT PROFIT THEM IF THEY GAIN THE WHOLE WORLD BUT FORFEIT THEIR LIFE?" —Matthew 16:26

The Transfiguration

17 Six days later, Jesus took with him Peter and James and his brother John and led them up a high mountain, by themselves.
2And he was transfigured before them, and his face shone like the sun, and his clothes became dazzling white.
3Suddenly there appeared to them Moses and Elijah, talking with him.
4Then Peter said to

(Bible text continued on page 74)

[w]Gk *Petros* [x]Gk *petra* [y]Other ancient authorities add *Jesus* [z]Or *the Christ*

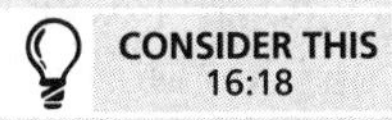

"THE GATES OF HELL"

Jesus referred to "the gates of Hades" (hell) in His bold statement to Peter (v. 18). For Matthew's original readers, the word "gates" held special significance.

Ancient cities erected walls to protect themselves from invaders. Here and there along the walls they inserted massive gates to allow traffic in and out. In times of trouble, they could close the gates against attacking armies or bandits.

City gates, then, tended to be thoroughfares through which communications and commerce passed with frequency. Not surprisingly, bazaars and forums tended to congregate around a city's gates, so that they became an important arena in a town's public life. Goods were traded there and decision-makers gathered to hear news and deliberate on events of the day. Such gates exist to this day in some cities of the world.

Given this phenomenon, "gates" became a metaphor signifying the economic and political life of a walled city. The influential and powerful did their business "in the gates." For example, the husband of the virtuous women of Proverbs 31 is "known in the city gates, taking his seat among the elders of the land" (Prov. 31:23). Boaz, the intended husband of Ruth, went to the gate to buy a marriage license (Ruth 4:1–12; also Deut. 25:7). War plans were devised and military treaties signed in the gates (Judg. 5:8, 11). Kings sat in the gates to address their people (2 Sam. 19:8). Even conspirators against kings hatched their plots and were exposed in the gates (Esth. 2:19–23).

So when Jesus spoke of the gates of Hades, He was drawing on a powerful image. Matthew's original readers would have seen it as a political metaphor, the way we use the terms *City Hall*, *the White House*, or *the Capitol* today. For them, the gates of Hades were not just a spiritual abstraction but actual forces of evil at work among human systems—the Roman government, for instance. While not evil in and of itself, first-century government was quickly becoming corrupted and also anti-Christian.

Jesus was alluding to a spiritual warfare of cosmic proportions. His followers are pitted against the powers of hell itself, which not only attack individual believers but seek to corrupt institutions, enlisting them in their campaign against Christ. Satan's guises can take many forms, as a look at any day's news will attest. (See "Spiritual Realities Beyond You," Matt. 8:29.)

Fortunately, Jesus also promised that in the end the gates of Hades would not succeed. That offers great hope to believers who live in difficult places and contend for good against powerful entities that, in ways known and unknown, are backed by spiritual forces of wickedness. In the midst of the fight Jesus has declared: "I will build my church!" ◆

Jesus, "Lord, it is good for us to be here; if you wish, I[a] will
make three dwellings[b] here, one for you, one for Moses,
and one for Elijah." 5 While he was still
speaking, suddenly a bright cloud over-

17:5 see pg. 76

shadowed them, and from the cloud a voice said, "This is
my Son, the Beloved;[c] with him I am well pleased; listen to
him!" 6 When the disciples heard this, they fell to the
ground and were overcome by fear. 7 But Jesus came and
touched them, saying, "Get up and do not be afraid." 8 And
when they looked up, they saw no one except Jesus himself
alone.

9 As they were coming down the mountain, Jesus ordered them, "Tell no one about the vision until after the
Son of Man has been raised from the dead." 10 And the disciples asked him, "Why, then, do the scribes say that Elijah
must come first?" 11 He replied, "Elijah is indeed coming
and will restore all things; 12 but I tell you that Elijah has already come, and they did not recognize him, but they did
to him whatever they pleased. So also the Son of Man is

[a]Other ancient authorities read *we* [b]Or *tents* [c]Or *my beloved Son*

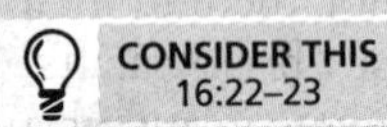

Living Within Your Limits

Are you impulsive? Are you quick to step forward with a plan of action? As the exchange between Peter and the Lord in vv. 22–23 shows there were times when Peter liked to take charge quickly and set the agenda for himself and others. But just as often he found himself in over his head:

- *When Jesus came walking on water to a storm-tossed boat that held His terrified disciples, Peter demanded that He show that it was He by bidding Peter also to walk on water. After a few steps, Peter noticed the wind and the waves and promptly sank, requiring Jesus to rescue him again (Matt. 14:22–32).*
- *He overstated his commitment to Christ, claiming that "even though I must die with you, I will not deny you" (26:35). Yet only a few hours later he denied having any association with the Lord (26:69–75).*
- *He took charge of defending Jesus against Roman soldiers when they came to arrest Him—even though he*

about to suffer at their hands." 13Then the disciples understood that he was speaking to them about John the Baptist.

Jesus Cures an Epileptic Boy

14 When they came to the crowd, a man came to him,
knelt before him, 15and said, "Lord, have mercy on my son,
for he is an epileptic and he suffers terribly; he often falls
into the fire and often into the water. 16And I brought him
to your disciples, but they could not cure him." 17Jesus answered, "You faithless and perverse generation, how much
longer must I be with you? How much longer must I put
up with you? Bring him here to me." 18And Jesus rebuked
the demon,[d] and it[e] came out of him, and the boy was
cured instantly. 19Then the disciples came to Jesus privately
and said, "Why could we not cast it out?" 20He said to
them, "Because of your little faith. For truly I tell you, if
you have faith the size of a[f] mustard seed, you will say to

(Bible text continued on page 77)

[d]Gk *it or him* [e]Gk *the demon* [f]Gk *faith as a grain of*

had failed to watch and pray with Christ as had been requested (26:36–46; John 18:1–11).

- *He refused to allow Jesus to wash his feet at the Last Supper, then called on Him to wash his hands and his head as well (John 13:5–11).*

Eventually Peter's leadership skills were captured in a more controlled spirit and he became a significant figure in the early church. Despite many false starts as a result of Peter's impetuous nature, Jesus enlisted this impulsive but loyal follower to "feed my sheep" (John 21:17).

Have your personality and skills become more mature and thoughtful? Or are you still in the raw stage, ready to jump at the first idea that occurs to you? ◆

Peter was not the only man who made an unlikely candidate for Jesus' "leadership training program." See "Would You Choose These for Leaders?" Matt. 26:35–74.

"YOU FAITHLESS AND PERVERSE GENERATION, HOW MUCH LONGER MUST I BE WITH YOU?" —Matthew 17:17

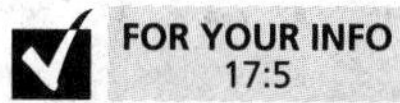
FOR YOUR INFO
17:5

THE NAMES OF JESUS

The voice that the disciples heard during the Transfiguration said that Jesus was "my Son, the Beloved" (v. 5). This term indicates a unique relationship that Jesus has with God the Father. Elsewhere Scripture calls Jesus by other names and titles to indicate other aspects of His nature, character, and roles:

Name or Title	Description
Adam (1 Cor. 15:45)	The first Adam brought death through sin; Jesus, "the last Adam," brought life through His righteousness.
The Alpha and the Omega (Rev. 21:6)	Jesus is eternal, "the beginning and the end." Alpha is the first letter in the Greek alphabet, omega is the last.
Apostle (Heb. 3:1)	"Messenger." Jesus came to bring the good news of salvation to humanity.
The bread of life (John 6:35, 48)	Jesus is the heavenly manna, the spiritual food, given by the Father to those who ask for it.
The cornerstone (Eph. 2:20)	Jesus is the foundation of the church.
The Chief Shepherd (1 Pet. 5:4)	The title that Peter called Jesus, indicating His oversight of His "flock," the church.
The Messiah (Matt. 1:1, 17; 16:16; Luke 2:11; John 1:40)	From the Greek word *Christos*, "Messiah" or "Anointed One." Jesus fulfills the Old Testament promise of a Messiah.
The consolation of Israel (Luke 2:25)	Jesus came to bring comfort to the nation (Is. 40:1–2).
The firstborn from the dead (Col. 1:18)	Jesus overcame death in order to give life to believers.
The firstborn of all creation (Col. 1:15)	As God's Son, Jesus rules over everything that exists.
The good shepherd (John 10:11, 14; compare Heb. 13:20)	An image that Jesus used to describe His relationship to His people.
The head of the body, the church (Eph. 1:22–23; 4:15–16; Col. 1:18)	Jesus is the leader of His people and the source of their life.
High Priest (Heb. 3:1)	Like the Old Testament high priest, Jesus stands between God and people to offer an acceptable sacrifice for sin.
The Holy One of God (Mark 1:24; John 6:69)	Jesus is the sinless Messiah promised by God.
I AM (John 8:58)	A name by which God made Himself known to Moses (Ex. 3:14), related to the verb "to be."
The image of the invisible God (Col. 1:15)	Jesus expresses God in bodily form.
Immanuel (Matt. 1:23)	"God is with us" (Is. 7:14).
Jesus (Matt. 1:21; Luke 1:30; Acts 9:5)	The name that God instructed Joseph and Mary to call their Son.
King of kings and Lord of lords (Rev. 19:16)	The formal title that Jesus has received, indicating His supremacy as the one to whom "every knee should bend" (Phil. 2:9–11).
King of the Jews (Matt. 2:2; 27:11–12; John 19:19)	As Messiah, Jesus is Israel's king, fulfilling God's promises to David (2 Sam. 7:12–16).
The Lamb of God (John 1:29, 35)	Jesus became the atoning sacrifice for sin.
The light of the world (John 9:5)	Jesus brings truth and hope to light in the midst of spiritual darkness.
Lord (Luke 2:11; 1 Cor. 2:8; Phil. 2:11)	A title indicating ultimate sovereignty.
Mediator between God and men (1 Tim. 2:5)	Jesus reestablishes the relationship between God and people.

Continued

this mountain, 'Move from here to there,' and it will move;
and nothing will be impossible for you."[g]

Jesus Predicts His Betrayal

22 As they were gathering[h] in Galilee, Jesus said to them,
"The Son of Man is going to be betrayed into human hands,
23and they will kill him, and on the third day he will be
raised." And they were greatly distressed.

Jesus and Taxation

17:24–27 see pg. 78

24 When they reached Capernaum,
the collectors of the temple tax[i] came to
Peter and said, "Does your teacher not pay the temple tax?"[i]
25He said, "Yes, he does." And when he came home, Jesus
spoke of it first, asking, "What do you think, Simon? From
whom do kings of the earth take toll or tribute? From their
children or from others?" 26When Peter[j] said, "From others," Jesus said to him, "Then the children are free. 27How-
ever, so that we do not give offense to them, go to the sea

[g]Other ancient authorities add verse 21, *But this kind does not come out except by prayer and fasting* [h]Other ancient authorities read *living* [i]Gk *didrachma* [j]Gk *he*

Continued

Name or Title	Description
The only Son of the Father (John 1:14)	Jesus is God's only-begotten and unique Son.
The Prophet (Mark 6:15; John 7:40; Acts 3:22)	Jesus is the leader that God promised to "raise up" like Moses (Deut. 18:15, 18–19).
Rabbi (John 1:38; 3:2)	Friends and enemies alike recognized Jesus as Teacher.
Savior (Luke 1:47; 2:11)	Jesus came to save people from their sins.
Seed (of Abraham; Gal. 3:16)	God made promises to Abraham and his "Seed," whom Paul identified as Christ (Gen. 13:15; 17:8).
The Son of Abraham (Matt. 1:1)	Jesus descended from Abraham and fulfills the promises of God to Abraham (Gen. 22:18).
The Son of David (Matt. 1:1)	Jesus descended from David and fulfills the promises of God to David (2 Sam. 7:12–16).
The Son of God (John 1:24; 9:35–37)	Jesus is one of three Persons of the Trinity (Father, Son, and Holy Spirit).
The Son of Man (Matt. 18:11; John 1:51)	Though fully God, Jesus took on a human body (compare Phil. 2:5–8).
The Word (John 1:1; Rev. 19:13)	Jesus is fully God and therefore is the full expression of God.

and cast a hook; take the first fish that comes up; and when
you open its mouth, you will find a coin;[k] take that and
give it to them for you and me."

"Who Is Greatest in the Kingdom?"

18 At that time the disciples came to Jesus and asked,
"Who is the greatest in the kingdom of heaven?"
2He called a child, whom he put among them, 3and said,
"Truly I tell you, unless you change and become like children, you will never enter the kingdom of heaven. 4Who-
ever becomes humble like this child is the greatest in the
kingdom of heaven. 5Whoever welcomes one such child in
my name welcomes me.
6 "If any of you put a stumbling block before one of

[k]Gk *stater;* the stater was worth two didrachmas

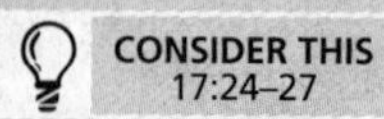

CONSIDER THIS 17:24–27

JESUS AND TAXATION

The odd episode in vv. 24–27 turns out to be a subtle and winsome reminder that Jesus claimed to be God. It's also a lesson in the proper exercise of moral liberty.

The temple tax of half a shekel was assessed annually on all Jews 20 years old and above. It paid for the support of the temple system (Ex. 30:13–15). Apparently Jesus and Peter had not yet paid their taxes, though Peter's response to the tax collectors indicated that they soon would (Matt. 17:24–25).

The irony, however, is that the temple tax collectors were demanding taxes from the Messiah Himself! How ludicrous—as Jesus pointed out in His question to Peter about who is taxed by a ruler (v. 25). As God's Son, Jesus was the Lord of the temple; technically, He was exempt from taxation.

God put His stamp of approval on Jesus' reasoning with the miracle of the coin (v. 27). Peter found "a coin"

these little ones who believe in me, it would be better for
you if a great millstone were fastened around your neck
and you were drowned in the depth of the sea. 7Woe to the
world because of stumbling blocks! Occasions for stumbling are bound to come, but woe to the one by whom the
stumbling block comes!

18:8–9

8 "If your hand or your foot causes
you to stumble, cut it off and throw it
away; it is better for you to enter life maimed or lame than
to have two hands or two feet and to be thrown into the
eternal fire. 9And if your eye causes you to stumble, tear it
out and throw it away; it is better for you to enter life with
one eye than to have two eyes and to be thrown into the
hell[l] of fire.

10 "Take care that you do not despise one of these little

[l]Gk *Gehenna*

◆ ◆ ◆ ◆ ◆ ◆ ◆ ◆ ◆ ◆ ◆ ◆ ◆ ◆ ◆ ◆

(a stater, a four-drachma coin) in the fish's mouth—the exact amount needed for the two of them. The collectors were satisfied, and the transaction cost Peter and Jesus nothing.

But consider: Jesus voluntarily paid the tax to avoid offending the religious leaders that the collectors represented (v. 27). In doing so, He demonstrated something about how His followers should live.

We as Christians are properly free in many areas because of our relationship with God. We are not bound by legalistic rules about eating, drinking, or special observances. Nonetheless, we must be careful not to use our liberty in a manner that offends other people. If the Son of God paid a voluntary tax in order to avoid offending those who did not understand who He was, how much more should we, as God's children, bend over backwards at times to avoid offending those who do not understand our liberty? ◆

Scripture offers help for believers in handling the "gray" areas of life in which God has prescribed no specific behavior. See "Matters of Conscience," Rom. 14:1–23; and "Gray Areas," 1 Cor. 8:1–13.

There were so many taxes during Jesus' time that the Jews were probably paying between 30 and 40 percent of their income on taxes and religious dues. See "Taxes," Mark 12:14.

Exaggerating to Make a Point

CONSIDER THIS 18:8–9

Was Jesus speaking literally when He told His followers to cut off their hand or foot if it caused them to sin (v. 8)? Did He intend for them actually to rip out their eye if it caused them to sin (v. 9)? No, Jesus was using a customary teaching method called *hyperbole*—exaggerating to make a point. He frequently spoke in that manner, perhaps to hold His listeners' attention, to touch their imagination, or to show a bit of humor.

After all, it's a bit silly to imagine what would happen if people actually followed these instructions literally. It's hard to sin without using a hand, a foot, or an eye, so it wouldn't be long before we all would be paralyzed and blind. Without our faculties, we simply couldn't function. And that's precisely Jesus' point. Sin makes it difficult if not impossible to function spiritually in the way God created us. Moreover, sin can do what no amputation can—keep us from God. That's why, to catch Jesus' serious point, it *would* be better to do without an arm or a leg than to live forever apart from God.

ones; for, I tell you, in heaven their angels continually see
the face of my Father in heaven.[m] 12What do you think? If a
shepherd has a hundred sheep, and one of them has gone
astray, does he not leave the ninety-nine on the mountains
and go in search of the one that went astray? 13And if he
finds it, truly I tell you, he rejoices over it more than over
the ninety-nine that never went astray. 14So it is not the will
of your[n] Father in heaven that one of these little ones
should be lost.

15 "If another member of the church[o] sins against you,[p]
go and point out the fault when the two of you are alone. If
the member listens to you, you have regained that one.[q]
16But if you are not listened to, take one or two others
along with you, so that every word may be confirmed by
the evidence of two or three witnesses. 17If the member refuses to listen to them, tell it to the church; and if the offender refuses to listen even to the church, let such a one be
to you as a Gentile and a tax collector. 18Truly I tell you,
whatever you bind on earth will be bound in heaven, and
whatever you loose on earth will be loosed in heaven.
19Again, truly I tell you, if two of you agree on earth about
anything you ask, it will be done for you by my Father in
heaven. 20For where two or three are gathered in my name,
I am there among them."

About Forgiveness

18:21–35

21 Then Peter came and said to him,
"Lord, if another member of the church[r]
sins against me, how often should I forgive? As many as
seven times?" 22Jesus said to him, "Not seven times, but, I
tell you, seventy-seven[s] times.

23 "For this reason the kingdom of heaven may be compared to a king who wished to settle accounts with his
slaves. 24When he began the reckoning, one who owed him
ten thousand talents[t] was brought to him; 25and, as he
could not pay, his lord ordered him to be sold, together
with his wife and children and all his possessions, and payment to be made. 26So the slave fell on his knees before
him, saying, 'Have patience with me, and I will pay you
everything.' 27And out of pity for him, the lord of that slave
released him and forgave him the debt. 28But that same
slave, as he went out, came upon one of his fellow slaves
who owed him a hundred denarii;[u] and seizing him by the
throat, he said, 'Pay what you owe.' 29Then his fellow slave
fell down and pleaded with him, 'Have patience with me,

[m]Other ancient authorities add verse 11, *For the Son of Man came to save the lost* [n]Other ancient authorities read *my* [o]Gk *If your brother* [p]Other ancient authorities lack *against you* [q]Gk *the brother* [r]Gk *if my brother* [s]Or *seventy times seven* [t]A talent was worth more than fifteen years' wages of a laborer [u]The denarius was the usual day's wage for a laborer

Seventy Times Seven—Still Not Enough!

CONSIDER THIS 18:21–35 **If Peter gasped when Jesus told him to forgive his brother up to seventy times seven times (v. 22), he must have gagged when he heard the parable that followed.**

The first servant owed 10,000 talents to the king (v. 24). The second servant owed 100 denarii to the first servant (v. 28). This was an extraordinary difference in indebtedness. A talent was a lot of money, perhaps $1,000 in today's currency. But in that culture, it probably represented far more. A talent equalled 6,000 denarii, and one denarius was what a common laborer could earn in one day, about 16¢ to 18¢.

So the first servant owed at least $10 million, but from the standpoint of common wages, *he would have had to work 60 million days to pay off his debt!* By contrast, the second servant owed $16 to $18, which he could earn in 100 days. In other words, the first servant owed the king more than the second servant owed the first servant by a ratio of at least 600,000-to-1!

Somehow, after Jesus finished that parable, seventy times seven probably didn't look so bad to Peter!

The power of forgiveness is immeasurable. It is a power that Jesus used often and even delegated to His followers. See "The Power of Forgiveness," Matt. 9:4–8.

The talent was one of several units of money in the ancient world. See the table, "Money in the New Testament," Rev. 16:21.

and I will pay you.' 30But he refused; then he went and
threw him into prison until he would pay the debt. 31When
his fellow slaves saw what had happened, they were greatly
distressed, and they went and reported to their lord all that
had taken place. 32Then his lord summoned him and said
to him, 'You wicked slave! I forgave you all that debt because you pleaded with me. 33Should you not have had
mercy on your fellow slave, as I had mercy on you?' 34And
in anger his lord handed him over to be tortured until he
would pay his entire debt. 35So my heavenly Father will
also do to every one of you, if you do not forgive your
brother or sister[v] from your heart."

Marriage and Divorce

19:1–15 see pg. 82

19 When Jesus had finished saying
these things, he left Galilee and
went to the region of Judea beyond the Jordan. 2Large
crowds followed him, and he cured them there.

3 Some Pharisees came to him, and to test him they
asked, "Is it lawful for a man to divorce his wife for any
cause?" 4He answered, "Have you not read that the one who
made them at the beginning 'made them male and female,'
5and said, 'For this reason a man shall leave his father and
mother and be joined to his wife, and the two shall become
one flesh'? 6So they are no longer two, but one flesh. Therefore what God has joined together, let no one separate."
7They said to him, "Why then did Moses command us to
give a certificate of dismissal and to divorce her?" 8He said
to them, "It was because you were so hard-hearted that
Moses allowed you to divorce your wives, but from the beginning it was not so. 9And I say to you, whoever divorces
his wife, except for unchastity, and marries another commits adultery."[w]

(Bible text continued on page 84)

[v]Gk *brother* [w]Other ancient authorities read *except on the ground of unchastity, causes her to commit adultery;* others add at the end of the verse *and he who marries a divorced woman commits adultery*

"WHAT GOD HAS JOINED TOGETHER, LET NO ONE SEPARATE."
—Matthew 19:6

Please Bless Our Children

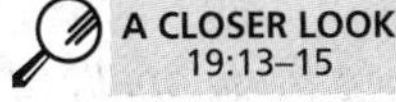

In Jesus' day it was customary to ask famous rabbis to bless one's children. See "The Friend of Children" at Mark 10:13–16.

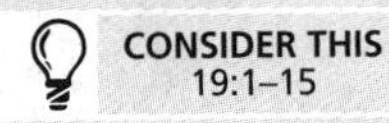

CONSIDER THIS
19:1–15

THE CHALLENGE OF COMMITMENT

Commitment is in jeopardy these days. Some even call it the "C" word, as if to shame it as something we won't even acknowledge. After all, the demands and costs are too great. Today, convenience usually wins out over the sacrifice involved in being committed to someone or something.

The situation was no less confused in Jesus' day. As He began to unveil a new way of life for His followers, critics appeared and challenged Him on the difficulties of keeping the marriage commitment (vv. 3, 7). Even His disciples quivered as they perceived the costs of maintaining one's marriage vows (v. 10). Later, they wanted to send away some bothersome children in order to deal with more "important" things (v. 13). It seems that Jesus was surrounded by men who were a little unsure about domestic matters.

The discussion of divorce followed appropriately on the heels of Jesus' remarks about the merits of boundless forgiveness (18:21–35). What better way to lead into the topic of commitment? Jesus didn't ignore the problems and failures of human relationships. Those very shortcomings are what make forgiveness—and commitment—crucial.

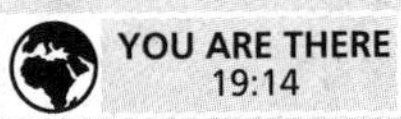

YOU ARE THERE
19:14

CHILDREN AND CHILDCARE

When Jesus welcomed the little children (v. 14), He was making a major statement to everyone standing by about the value and significance of children.

Perhaps the disciples, who rebuked the mothers who brought their babies to Jesus (v. 13), had adopted the prevailing Graeco-Roman view of childhood as an insignificant phase of life. To be sure, children were necessary for a family's survival, but they were not valued for their own sake.

Indeed, unwanted infants in pagan cultures were routinely abandoned on roadsides and at garbage dumps. Tragically, gender and economics often determined an infant's fate: more girls than boys were exposed since girls represented a future financial burden while boys could eventually contribute to the family's income.

Most exposed infants died but a few were rescued and raised to become slaves, gladiators, or prostitutes. Children were held in such low esteem in Jesus' time that some professional beggars collected exposed children, mutilated them, and then used their misery to gain sympathy and thus increase profits from their begging.

However, among the Jews children were traditionally

Those lessons were reinforced in Jesus' next encounter, with a rich man who wanted to ensure his possession of eternal life (19:16–30). The man proposed rule-keeping as the standard by which he should be judged, but Jesus countered with an appeal for service (v. 21). True wealth involved a higher commitment—serving the Lord and others rather than the idol of material gain (vv. 23, 29).

Followers of Christ need to be known for their commitment—to marriage, to family, to community, to work, above all to Christ. Such loyalty often means messy obedience, but it is the way of Christ. How desperately that is needed in a day when people make vows of convenience rather than commitment. ◆

Commitment makes all the difference when it comes to family relationships. See "The Family: A Call to Long-Term Work," Eph. 5:21—6:4.

Commitment is one of the hallmarks of a godly "workstyle." See Titus 2:9–10.

Peter echoed Jesus' words on marital faithfulness in his instructions to husbands, 1 Pet. 2:11–17.

considered a blessing from God, and childlessness a curse. In fact, children were so desired that barrenness was grounds for divorce.

Jewish fathers had ultimate authority over all aspects of their children's lives, but both fathers and mothers were instructed by the Law to nurture and care for their children. Fathers were particularly obligated to teach their children God's commands and to raise them as members of God's chosen people (Deut. 6:6–8). In return, children were obliged to honor both mother and father (5:16).

Mothers usually took care of infants who typically nursed until the age of two or three. In some wealthy Greek and Roman homes, women employed wet nurses and, as the children grew, slaves who were assigned to their total care. Poor women, however, worked while their babies hung from slings on their backs. But as soon as the children were old enough, they were taught to help.

First-century women did not have to confront the childcare dilemma faced by many today. Their work and their homes were tightly linked, so they did not have to surmount the challenges of specialization and separation. ◆

"LET THE LITTLE CHILDREN COME TO ME. . . ."
—Matthew 19:14

10 His disciples said to him, "If such is the case of a man
with his wife, it is better not to marry." 11But he said to
them, "Not everyone can accept this teaching, but only
those to whom it is given. 12For there are eunuchs who
have been so from birth, and there are eunuchs who have
been made eunuchs by others, and there are eunuchs who
have made themselves eunuchs for the sake of the kingdom
of heaven. Let anyone accept this who can."

Jesus Blesses Children

19:13–15 see pg. 81

13 Then little children were being
brought to him in order that he might
lay his hands on them and pray. The disciples spoke sternly

19:14 see pg. 82

to those who brought them; 14but Jesus
said, "Let the little children come to me,
and do not stop them; for it is to such as these that the
kingdom of heaven belongs." 15And he laid his hands on
them and went on his way.

"IT IS EASIER FOR A CAMEL TO GO THROUGH THE EYE OF A NEEDLE THAN FOR SOMEONE WHO IS RICH TO ENTER THE KINGDOM OF GOD." —Matthew 19:24

A Rich Young Man's Question

19:16–26

16 Then someone came to him and
said, "Teacher, what good deed must I
do to have eternal life?" 17And he said to him, "Why do you
ask me about what is good? There is only one who is good.
If you wish to enter into life, keep the commandments."
18He said to him, "Which ones?" And Jesus said, "You shall
not murder; You shall not commit adultery; You shall not
steal; You shall not bear false witness; 19Honor your father
and mother; also, You shall love your neighbor as yourself."
20The young man said to him, "I have kept all these;[x] what
do I still lack?" 21Jesus said to him, "If you wish to be perfect, go, sell your possessions, and give the money[y] to the
poor, and you will have treasure in heaven; then come, follow me." 22When the young man heard this word, he went
away grieving, for he had many possessions.

[x]Other ancient authorities add *from my youth* [y]Gk lacks *the money*

"What Do I Still Lack?"

The rich young ruler asked the classic question of many who appear to have it all: "What do I still lack?" (v. 20). "The Man Who Had It All—Almost" (Mark 10:17–27) discusses the Lord's mysterious response and challenging perspective on wealth. In a similar situation (Luke 10:25–37), Jesus urged people to put feet on their good intentions.

23 Then Jesus said to his disciples, "Truly I tell you, it
will be hard for a rich person to enter the kingdom of
heaven. 24Again I tell you, it is easier for a camel to go
through the eye of a needle than for someone who is rich to
enter the kingdom of God." 25When the disciples heard
this, they were greatly astounded and said, "Then who can
be saved?" 26But Jesus looked at them and said, "For mortals it is impossible, but for God all things are possible."

Rewards for the Twelve

27 Then Peter said in reply, "Look, we have left everything and followed you. What then will we have?" 28Jesus
said to them, "Truly I tell you, at the renewal of all things,
when the Son of Man is seated on the throne of his glory,
you who have followed me will also sit on twelve thrones,
19:29
judging the twelve tribes of Israel. 29And
everyone who has left houses or brothers
or sisters or father or mother or children or fields, for my
name's sake, will receive a hundredfold,[z] and will inherit
eternal life. 30But many who are first will be last, and the
last will be first.

A Parable about Wages

20:1–16 see pg. 86

20 "For the kingdom of heaven is
like a landowner who went out
early in the morning to hire laborers for his vineyard. 2After
agreeing with the laborers for the usual daily wage,[a] he sent
them into his vineyard. 3When he went out about nine
o'clock, he saw others standing idle in the marketplace;
4and he said to them, 'You also go into the vineyard, and I
will pay you whatever is right.' So they went. 5When he
went out again about noon and about three o'clock, he did
the same. 6And about five o'clock he went out and found
others standing around; and he said to them, 'Why are you
standing here idle all day?' 7They said to him, 'Because no
one has hired us.' He said to them, 'You also go into the
vineyard.' 8When evening came, the owner of the vineyard
said to his manager, 'Call the laborers and give them their
pay, beginning with the last and then going to the first.'
9When those hired about five o'clock came, each of them
received the usual daily wage.[a] 10Now when the first came,

[z]Other ancient authorities read *manifold* [a]Gk *a denarius*

A Pushy Mother

CONSIDER THIS 20:20–23 **Overzealous mothers are not exclusive to the twentieth century, as the incident in vv. 20–23 makes clear. The woman's name remains unknown; she is remembered only as the mother of Zebedee's sons (James and John). Perhaps she was so caught up in managing her sons' lives that she had no other life, and therefore required no other designation than "mother." Naturally, she would have claimed that she only wanted what was best for her sons.**

But when Jesus found out what she was seeking, He gave her and her sons a warning. He knew that suffering had to come before glory. Could James and John endure that suffering? The two men were quick to promise that they would. (Perhaps their mother prompted them to say so by giving them a stern look.) Jesus assured them that they would have the chance to back up their words.

Perhaps later James and John regretted making such bold promises. But how often are we like them—eager to promise whatever we have to in order to get what we want? Perhaps worse, how often do we push our children into things based on our own needs for pride and significance?

An Eternal Inheritance

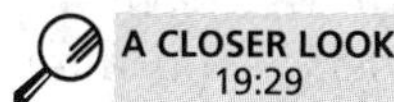
A CLOSER LOOK 19:29

To have Christ is to have everything *(v. 29). "What's in It for Me?" (Eph. 1:11) describes the inheritance we will enjoy as God's children.*

they thought they would receive more; but each of them
also received the usual daily wage.[b] 11And when they received it, they grumbled against the landowner, 12saying,
'These last worked only one hour, and you have made them
equal to us who have borne the burden of the day and the
scorching heat.' 13But he replied to one of them, 'Friend, I
am doing you no wrong; did you not agree with me for the
usual daily wage?[b] 14Take what belongs to you and go; I
choose to give to this last the same as I give to you. 15Am I
not allowed to do what I choose with what belongs to me?
Or are you envious because I am generous?'[c] 16So the last
will be first, and the first will be last."[d]

[b]Gk *a denarius* [c]Gk *is your eye evil because I am good?* [d]Other ancient authorities add *for many are called but few are chosen*

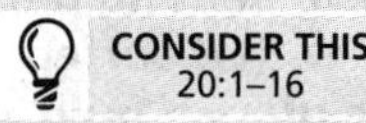

CONSIDER THIS
20:1–16

Jesus and Unjust Pay

Anyone who feels that they are not paid what they are worth can appreciate the reaction of the workers in the parable Jesus told (vv. 1–16). He spoke of an employer who hired workers for a full day, others for two-thirds of a day, others for half a day, and others for even less. Yet he paid them all the same (v. 9–11)! Naturally those who had worked longer demanded, "What's going on here?" (vv. 11–12). Good question!

The first thing to notice is that none of the workers was employed before the landowner hired them (vv. 3, 6, 7). The fact that they got a job was due to the employer's goodwill, not to anything they brought to the situation. Furthermore, the landowner promised the first group fair wages of a day's pay (a denarius, *v. 2; see "Money in the New Testament," Rev. 16:21) and the rest an undetermined amount ("whatever is right"). As it turned out, he paid everyone an entire day's wage.*

Jesus was trying to help His followers grasp something important about grace in the kingdom of God. They had been asking about the kingdom's makeup and benefits earlier (Matt. 19:16, 25, 27). Jesus was not encouraging unjust pay scales and discrimination. He was merely illustrating the nature of God's grace in terms that His followers could understand.

In the kingdom of God, grace is given because of the nature of the Giver, not the worthiness of the recipient. Receiving God's grace is a privilege for sinners—who, after all, really deserve nothing but condemnation. ◆

Jesus Predicts His Death

17 While Jesus was going up to Jerusalem, he took the
twelve disciples aside by themselves, and said to them on
the way, 18“See, we are going up to Jerusalem, and the Son
of Man will be handed over to the chief priests and scribes,
and they will condemn him to death; 19then they will hand
him over to the Gentiles to be mocked and flogged and
crucified; and on the third day he will be raised.”

A Mother’s Big Request

20:20–23 see pg. 85

20 Then the mother of the sons of
Zebedee came to him with her sons, and
kneeling before him, she asked a favor of him. 21And he
said to her, “What do you want?” She said to him, “Declare
that these two sons of mine will sit, one at your right hand
and one at your left, in your kingdom.” 22But Jesus answered, “You do not know what you are asking. Are you
able to drink the cup that I am about to drink?”[e] They said
to him, “We are able.” 23He said to them, “You will indeed
drink my cup, but to sit at my right hand and at my left,
this is not mine to grant, but it is for those for whom it has
been prepared by my Father.”
24 When the ten heard it, they were angry with the two
brothers. 25But Jesus called them to him
and said, “You know that the rulers of
the Gentiles lord it over them, and their great ones are
tyrants over them. 26It will not be so among you; but whoever wishes to be great among you must be your servant,
27and whoever wishes to be first among you must be your
slave; 28just as the Son of Man came not
to be served but to serve, and to give his
life a ransom for many.”

20:25–28

20:28 see pg. 88

[e]Other ancient authorities add *or to be baptized with the baptism that I am baptized with?*

The Dangerous Road to Jericho

A CLOSER LOOK 20:29 *Jericho was notorious for the beggars and thieves who camped nearby, plundering travelers along the narrow, winding mountain road up to Jerusalem. See Luke 10:30.*

SERVANT-LEADERS

CONSIDER THIS 20:25–28 **Responding to a controversy among the disciples (vv. 25–28), Jesus revealed a unique style of authority—servant leadership. What does it mean to be a “slave” in order to become great (v. 27)? What does it mean to define leadership in terms of servanthood? Jesus suggested that both involve seeking the highest good for others—good as evaluated from God’s perspective.**

In light of Jesus’ own example—particularly in giving up His own life as a “ransom for many” (v. 28)—we can observe that servant leadership means:

- **seeing ourselves as called by God to serve/lead others.**
- **knowing intimately the people we serve/lead.**
- **caring deeply about the people we serve/lead.**
- **being willing to sacrifice our own convenience to meet the needs of the people we serve/lead.**

QUOTE UNQUOTE

CONSIDER THIS 20:28 *Just as Jesus came to serve, He calls His followers to a life of service:*

That Christianity should be equated in the public mind, inside as well as outside the Church, with "organized religion" merely shows how far we have departed from the New Testament. For the last thing the Church exists to be is an organization for the religious. Its charter is to be the servant of the world.

John A.T. Robinson, *Honest To God*

Two Blind Men Healed at Jericho

20:29 see pg. 87

29 As they were leaving Jericho, a
large crowd followed him. 30There were
two blind men sitting by the roadside. When they heard
that Jesus was passing by, they shouted, "Lord,[f] have mercy
on us, Son of David!" 31The crowd sternly ordered them to
be quiet; but they shouted even more loudly, "Have mercy
on us, Lord, Son of David!" 32Jesus stood still and called
them, saying, "What do you want me to do for you?"
33They said to him, "Lord, let our eyes be opened." 34Moved
with compassion, Jesus touched their eyes. Immediately
they regained their sight and followed him.

Jesus Enters Jerusalem

21:1

21 When they had come near
Jerusalem and had reached Beth-
phage, at the Mount of Olives, Jesus sent two disciples,

[f]Other ancient authorities lack *Lord*

Sheep Gate
Possible route of Jesus' entry into temple area.
Temple Mount
Jerusalem
Kidron Valley
Mt. of Olives
Road from Bethphage
N
0 250 500
Yards

YOU ARE THERE 21:1 **JESUS' ENTRY**

Jesus used a powerful image when He compared true leadership to slavery. See "Slaves," Rom. 6:16.

[2]saying to them, "Go into the village ahead of you, and immediately you will find a donkey tied, and a colt with her;
untie them and bring them to me. [3]If anyone says anything
to you, just say this, 'The Lord needs them.' And he will
send them immediately.[g]" [4]This took place to fulfill what
had been spoken through the prophet, saying,

5 "Tell the daughter of Zion,
Look, your king is coming to you,
humble, and mounted on a donkey,
and on a colt, the foal of a donkey."

[6]The disciples went and did as Jesus had directed them;
[7]they brought the donkey and the colt, and put their cloaks
on them, and he sat on them. [8]A very
large crowd[h] spread their cloaks on the
road, and others cut branches from the trees and spread
them on the road. [9]The crowds that went ahead of him and
that followed were shouting,

21:8–11 see pg. 90

"Hosanna to the Son of David!
Blessed is the one who comes in the name of the Lord!
Hosanna in the highest heaven!"

[10]When he entered Jerusalem, the whole city was in turmoil, asking, "Who is this?" [11]The crowds were saying,
"This is the prophet Jesus from Nazareth in Galilee."

Jesus Cleanses the Temple

12 Then Jesus entered the temple[i] and drove out all who
were selling and buying in the temple, and he overturned
the tables of the money changers and the seats of those who
sold doves. [13]He said to them, "It is written,

'My house shall be called a house of prayer';
but you are making it a den of robbers."

14 The blind and the lame came to him in the temple,
and he cured them. [15]But when the chief priests and the
scribes saw the amazing things that he did, and heard[j] the
children crying out in the temple, "Hosanna to the Son of
David," they became angry [16]and said to him, "Do you hear

(Bible text continued on page 92)

[g]Or *'The Lord needs them and will send them back immediately.'* [h]Or *Most of the crowd*
[i]Other ancient authorities add *of God* [j]Gk lacks *heard*

"'MY HOUSE SHALL BE CALLED A HOUSE OF PRAYER'; BUT YOU ARE MAKING IT A DEN OF ROBBERS." —Matthew 21:13

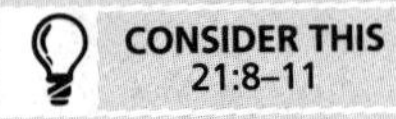

A New Style of Fame

If you've ever encountered a famous person, you may have felt somewhat intimidated, especially if that person seemed arrogant. People of status and image can easily make us feel inferior, as if we have nothing to offer by comparison. No wonder we long for the traits of compassion and humility in society's leaders.

Jesus became famous among His own people. But as He entered Jerusalem, the capital of Palestine, He modeled a new style for handling acclaim from the crowd. The city was wild with excitement during its peak season of tourists and celebration. What a moment for Jesus to bring His campaign to a climax! He even had the prophecies of Zechariah 9:9 and Isaiah 62:11 to bolster His confidence.

But instead of a parade of chariots and trumpets and a well-orchestrated ceremony, Jesus chose to ride into town on a donkey, a common beast of burden; no prancing warhorse for Him! And instead of walking arm-in-arm with powerful city officials and other celebrities, He was accompanied only by a small band of common fishermen, rural Galileans, and even a former tax collector. For once, the common folks had a parade (Matt. 21:8, 10).

Once arrived at the end of the parade route, Jesus did

A Challenge to Authority

Sooner or later, almost all leaders have their authority questioned. Sometimes they are challenged directly, but more often indirectly by rumor and innuendo.

Jesus faced a direct challenge to His authority from the chief priests and elders, the top leadership in Israel (vv. 23–27). In this instance He didn't argue with them, but simply tossed the ball back into their court. He showed that one very effective way of responding to threatening questions is to ask questions in return.

But observe two aspects of the interaction between Jesus and the Jewish leaders:

(1) The motives of the challengers. *The scribes and Pharisees had no interest in an honest understanding of the nature or source of Jesus' authority. They were only concerned with protecting their own interests and power. In light of their behavior, you might ask yourself whether you ever question or resist people in authority over you because you are afraid or jealous of them.*

not go to the halls of the powerful. Instead He marched into the place of worship, a national center for the Jews. There He overthrew the tables of unjust businesses that manipulated the poor and made the temple a place of moneymaking (vv. 12–13). He focused on the blind, the lame, and children (vv. 14–16). And when He completed the day's tasks, He spent the night not in the fashionable home of a city leader but in a humble house in a nearby suburb, Bethany (v. 17).

Jesus' final activities before His death focused on those most ready to hear of His love, forgiveness, and hope—the little people in (or even outside) the system of privilege and power (Luke 4:18).

Do you know people who need to be invited to join the humble King's procession? Are there coworkers, neighbors, or family members who need to receive good news through you? How are you dealing with the temptation to rub shoulders only with the powerful and elite? ◆

Jesus liked to surround Himself with relatively average people of little social standing or influence. See "The Little People at Jesus' Death," Matt. 27:32.

(2) The security of Jesus. *Jesus was neither upset nor caught off guard by His attackers. For one thing, He had endured their criticism before, and no doubt expected it to increase. But He also knew with absolute certainty about the very thing that His challengers were attacking: He knew who He was and whose authority He wielded (28:18). His response is a reminder that intimidation is something we allow to occur. People may threaten and confront us, but only we allow ourselves to feel fear. The real question is, are we certain who we are as followers of the King?* ◆

To understand more about Jesus' sense of identity, see "Being Like Jesus," Matt. 10:25.

" 'BLESSED IS THE ONE WHO COMES IN THE NAME OF THE LORD!' "
—Matthew 21:9

what these are saying?" Jesus said to them, "Yes; have you
never read,

'Out of the mouths of infants and nursing babies
you have prepared praise for yourself'?"

17He left them, went out of the city to Bethany, and spent
the night there.

Jesus Curses a Fig Tree

18 In the morning, when he returned to the city, he was
hungry. 19And seeing a fig tree by the side of the road, he
went to it and found nothing at all on it but leaves. Then he
said to it, "May no fruit ever come from you again!" And
the fig tree withered at once. 20When the disciples saw it,

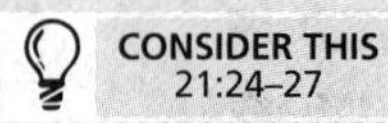
CONSIDER THIS
21:24–27

IS EVASION ETHICAL?

As you deal with people at work and in your family, you no doubt encounter situations where it might seem better not to reveal the whole truth. What should you do? Is anything less than the actual, complete truth ever ethical or biblical? Can believers practice cunning when Scripture calls us to be honest (for example, Eph. 4:15, 25, 29)?

Christ faced this dilemma when certain leaders challenged His authority (Matt. 21:23). He replied by asking them a question that was almost impossible for them to answer (vv. 24–27). Was He being fair?

Observe the context. Jesus' inquisitors were powerful religious leaders who felt threatened by His assault on their hypocrisies and His impact on the people. He had just challenged one of their sources of revenue by throwing the money changers out of the temple (vv. 12–17). Now they were launching a counterassault by challenging His authority.

Rather than being unethically evasive, Jesus was merely diverting an evil plot in a discrete manner by posing a difficult question. A simple yes or no answer would have played right into their hands. It probably would have touched off a confrontation prematurely. Jesus was more interested in accomplishing His long-range purposes than in exposing these hateful leaders on the spot.

Have you developed the ability to discern the gray areas of conflict and competition? Do you take a long-term view when you face confrontation? ◆

they were amazed, saying, "How did the fig tree wither at
once?" [21]Jesus answered them, "Truly I tell you, if you have
faith and do not doubt, not only will you do what has been
done to the fig tree, but even if you say to this mountain,
'Be lifted up and thrown into the sea,' it will be done.
[22]Whatever you ask for in prayer with faith, you will receive."

Priests and Elders Challenge Jesus' Authority

21:23–27 see pg. 90

23 When he entered the temple, the
chief priests and the elders of the people
came to him as he was teaching, and said, "By what authority are you doing these things, and who gave you this au-

21:24–27

thority?" [24]Jesus said to them, "I will also
ask you one question; if you tell me the
answer, then I will also tell you by what authority I do
these things. [25]Did the baptism of John come from heaven,
or was it of human origin?" And they argued with one another, "If we say, 'From heaven,' he will say to us, 'Why
then did you not believe him?' [26]But if we say, 'Of human
origin,' we are afraid of the crowd; for all regard John as a
prophet." [27]So they answered Jesus, "We do not know." And
he said to them, "Neither will I tell you by what authority I
am doing these things.

A Parable about Two Sons

28 "What do you think? A man had two sons; he went to
the first and said, 'Son, go and work in the vineyard today.'
[29]He answered, 'I will not'; but later he changed his mind
and went. [30]The father[k] went to the second and said the
same; and he answered, 'I go, sir'; but he did not go.

21:31–32 see pg. 94

[31]Which of the two did the will of his
father?" They said, "The first." Jesus said
to them, "Truly I tell you, the tax collectors and the prostitutes are going into the kingdom of God ahead of you.
[32]For John came to you in the way of righteousness and
you did not believe him, but the tax collectors and the
prostitutes believed him; and even after you saw it, you did
not change your minds and believe him.

A Parable about a Vineyard Owner

33 "Listen to another parable. There was a landowner
who planted a vineyard, put a fence around it, dug a wine
press in it, and built a watchtower. Then he leased it to tenants and went to another country. [34]When the harvest time
had come, he sent his slaves to the tenants to collect his
produce. [35]But the tenants seized his slaves and beat one,

[k]Gk *He*

" 'THE STONE THAT THE BUILDERS REJECTED HAS BECOME THE CORNERSTONE. . . .' "
—Matthew 21:42

killed another, and stoned another. 36Again he sent other
slaves, more than the first; and they treated them in the
same way. 37Finally he sent his son to them, saying, 'They
will respect my son.' 38But when the tenants saw the son,
they said to themselves, 'This is the heir; come, let us kill
him and get his inheritance.' 39So they seized him, threw
him out of the vineyard, and killed him. 40Now when the
owner of the vineyard comes, what will he do to those tenants?" 41They said to him, "He will put those wretches to a
miserable death, and lease the vineyard to other tenants
who will give him the produce at the harvest time."
42 Jesus said to them, "Have you never read in the scriptures:

'The stone that the builders rejected
has become the cornerstone;[l]
this was the Lord's doing,
and it is amazing in our eyes'?

43Therefore I tell you, the kingdom of God will be taken
away from you and given to a people that produces the
fruits of the kingdom.[m] 44The one who falls on this stone
will be broken to pieces; and it will crush anyone on whom
it falls."[n]

[l]Or *keystone* [m]Gk *the fruits of it* [n]Other ancient authorities lack verse 44

CONSIDER THIS
21:31–32

"Prostitutes Are Going into the Kingdom"

Jesus' startling statement about prostitutes (vv. 31–32) was not an endorsement of that lifestyle but a condemnation of the self-righteousness and especially the unbelief of Israel's religious leaders. Faith was the key to the kingdom; yet even prostitutes were showing more faith in Christ than those who were viewed as "righteous."

Prostitution has been a part of religious rites since at least 3,000 B.C. In Babylon, Syria, Canaan, Arabia, and Phoenicia intercourse with a temple prostitute was believed to induce fertility among humans, animals, and crops. The historian Herodotus tells of a Babylonian custom that required every woman to sit in the temple of the goddess Ishtar until chosen by a stranger for sexual relations. A desirous man would toss a coin in a woman's lap. If she accepted the coin and his sexual advances, she would have paid her obligation to the goddess and be free to return to her normal life.

In Israel, however, ritual prostitution was forbidden (Deut. 23:17). Laws existed to prevent priests from marrying prostitutes (Lev. 21:7), and income from prostitution could not be used to pay vows in the temple (Deut. 23:18).

45 When the chief priests and the Pharisees heard his parables, they realized that he was speaking about them. 46They wanted to arrest him, but they feared the crowds, because they regarded him as a prophet.

A Parable about a Rejected Invitation

22:2–14

22 Once more Jesus spoke to them
in parables, saying: 2"The king-
dom of heaven may be compared to a king who gave a
wedding banquet for his son. 3He sent his slaves to call
those who had been invited to the wedding banquet, but
they would not come. 4Again he sent other slaves, saying,
'Tell those who have been invited: Look, I have prepared
my dinner, my oxen and my fat calves have been slaughtered, and everything is ready; come to the wedding banquet.' 5But they made light of it and went away, one to his
farm, another to his business, 6while the rest seized his
slaves, mistreated them, and killed them. 7The king was enraged. He sent his troops, destroyed those murderers, and
burned their city. 8Then he said to his slaves, 'The wedding

Nevertheless, commercial prostitutes practiced their trade rather freely in Hebrew society. They were easily recognizable by their hairstyle, head ornaments, or perhaps a special mark on their foreheads. Their clothing and jewelry signaled their availability, and like streetwalkers everywhere, they frequented particular locales well known as meeting spots. Payments were accepted in money, grain, wine, or livestock. It was even common to accept a pledge until the payment could be fulfilled.

In Jesus' day, prostitutes endured the particular condemnation of the religious elite, especially the Pharisees, who avoided all outward contact with such people. By contrast, Jesus became known as a friend of sinners who welcomed those in need of forgiveness (Matt. 11:19; Luke 7:36–50). His words on this occasion showed that people don't have to become religiously "proper" before they can believe. God responds to faith no matter how troubled one's personal life may be. What an encouragement to start now to put trust in Jesus and be among the first in the kingdom! ◆

Worse than Rude

CONSIDER THIS 22:2–14

Jesus' parable of the king's wedding feast for his son (vv. 2–14) turns on an important detail of Jewish marriage custom. Wedding hosts sent out two invitations for a wedding. The first was sent far in advance to let people know that a wedding was being prepared and they were invited. This was necessary because weddings were major events that could last as long as a week. Furthermore, it took time for the replies to come back.

When all the preparations were complete, messengers were sent out with a second invitation telling the guests that the feast was ready and it was time for the celebration to begin. To turn down that second invitation—which was the one the guests in the parable refused (v. 3)—was not merely bad manners. It was considered a rejection of the host family's hospitality and a complete insult to their dignity.

God had sent Israel an early "invitation" to His Son's wedding through the Old Testament Law and prophets. Now that Jesus had arrived, proclaiming the second invitation, the nation was rejecting Him—a perilous choice.

Trick Questions Foiled

CONSIDER THIS 22:23–33 **Have you ever seen someone try to manipulate someone else by asking for one thing in order to get another? Perhaps you've tried to outwit or embarrass someone with a less-than-direct approach.**

The Sadducees did precisely that when they tried to trap Jesus in front of a crowd (vv. 23–33). Using the subject of serial marriage relationships, they attempted to paint Him into a corner on His teaching about the resurrection, a belief that they rejected (v. 23).

Jesus confronted them on their thinly veiled pretext and at the same time affirmed the resurrection. He even used the very Scriptures they loved to quote: v. 32 is from Exodus 3:6. Jesus refused to let them get away with using subtle inferences to twist things to their own advantage. He cut to the heart of the matter.

There's nothing wrong with being discreet, using inference, or stating things subtly and diplomatically. Some situations call for planting seed ideas in someone else's thinking, then allowing time for the idea to take shape. Here, however, Jesus was challenging selfish manipulation and trickery which had no benefit for others.

Are you known as a speaker of truth among your peers? Are there ways you could be more forthright and helpful in your communications?

Speaking truth in love is one of the main characteristics of Christlike character. See Eph. 4:15.

is ready, but those invited were not worthy. 9Go therefore
into the main streets, and invite everyone you find to the
wedding banquet.' 10Those slaves went out into the streets
and gathered all whom they found, both good and bad; so
the wedding hall was filled with guests.
11 "But when the king came in to see the guests, he noticed a man there who was not wearing a wedding robe,
12and he said to him, 'Friend, how did you get in here without a wedding robe?' And he was speechless. 13Then the
king said to the attendants, 'Bind him hand and foot, and
throw him into the outer darkness, where there will be
weeping and gnashing of teeth.' 14For many are called, but
few are chosen."

Jesus Confounds His Challengers

15 Then the Pharisees went and plotted to entrap him in
what he said. 16So they sent their disciples to him, along
with the Herodians, saying, "Teacher, we know that you are
sincere, and teach the way of God in accordance with truth,
and show deference to no one; for you do not regard people with partiality. 17Tell us, then, what you think. Is it lawful to pay taxes to the emperor, or not?" 18But Jesus, aware
of their malice, said, "Why are you putting me to the test,
you hypocrites? 19Show me the coin used for the tax." And
they brought him a denarius. 20Then he said to them,
"Whose head is this, and whose title?" 21They answered,
"The emperor's." Then he said to them, "Give therefore to
the emperor the things that are the emperor's, and to God
the things that are God's." 22When they heard this, they
were amazed; and they left him and went away.
22:23–33 23 The same day some Sadducees
came to him, saying there is no resurrec-
tion;[o] and they asked him a question, saying, 24"Teacher,
Moses said, 'If a man dies childless, his brother shall marry
the widow, and raise up children for his brother.' 25Now
there were seven brothers among us; the first married, and
died childless, leaving the widow to his brother. 26The second did the same, so also the third, down to the seventh.
27Last of all, the woman herself died. 28In the resurrection,
then, whose wife of the seven will she be? For all of them
had married her."
29 Jesus answered them, "You are wrong, because you
know neither the scriptures nor the power of God. 30For in
the resurrection they neither marry nor are given in marriage, but are like angels[p] in heaven. 31And as for the resurrection of the dead, have you not read what was said to you

[o]Other ancient authorities read *who say that there is no resurrection* [p]Other ancient authorities add *of God*

by God, 32'I am the God of Abraham, the God of Isaac, and
the God of Jacob'? He is God not of the dead, but of the living." 33And when the crowd heard it, they were astounded
at his teaching.

The Greatest of the Commandments

22:34–40
see pg. 98

34 When the Pharisees heard that he
had silenced the Sadducees, they gath-
ered together, 35and one of them, a lawyer, asked him a
question to test him. 36"Teacher, which commandment in
the law is the greatest?" 37He said to him, " 'You shall love
the Lord your God with all your heart, and with all your
soul, and with all your mind.' 38This is the greatest and first
commandment. 39And a second is like it: 'You shall love
your neighbor as yourself.' 40On these two commandments
hang all the law and the prophets."

Jesus Silences the Pharisees

41 Now while the Pharisees were gathered together, Jesus asked them this question: 42"What do you think of the
Messiah?[q] Whose son is he?" They said to him, "The son of
David." 43He said to them, "How is it then that David by
the Spirit[r] calls him Lord, saying,
44 'The Lord said to my Lord,
"Sit at my right hand,
until I put your enemies under your feet" '?
45If David thus calls him Lord, how can he be his son?"
46No one was able to give him an answer, nor from that day
did anyone dare to ask him any more questions.

Jesus Denounces the Scribes and Pharisees

23:1–30

23 Then Jesus said to the crowds
and to his disciples, 2"The scribes
and the Pharisees sit on Moses' seat; 3therefore, do whatever they teach you and follow it; but do not do as they do,
for they do not practice what they teach. 4They tie up heavy
burdens, hard to bear,[s] and lay them on the shoulders of
others; but they themselves are unwilling to lift a finger to
move them. 5They do all their deeds to be seen by others;
for they make their phylacteries broad and their fringes
long. 6They love to have the place of honor at banquets and
the best seats in the synagogues, 7and to be greeted with re-

[q]Or *Christ* [r]Gk *in spirit* [s]Other ancient authorities lack *hard to bear*

QUOTE UNQUOTE

CONSIDER THIS
23:1–30

Jesus denounced the Pharisees for their abuse of spiritual authority. Perhaps their daily contact with religion made them callous to it:

Someone has said, "None are so unholy as those whose hands are cauterized with holy things"; sacred things may become profane by becoming matters of the job.

C.S. Lewis, Letter to Sheldon Vanauken, Jan. 5, 1951

spect in the marketplaces, and to have people call them
rabbi. 8But you are not to be called rabbi, for you have one
teacher, and you are all students.[t] 9And call no one your father on earth, for you have one Father—the one in heaven.
10Nor are you to be called instructors, for you have one instructor, the Messiah.[u] 11The greatest among you will be
your servant. 12All who exalt themselves will be humbled,
and all who humble themselves will be exalted.

Woe to the Scribes and Pharisees

23:13, note v

13 “But woe to you, scribes and Pharisees, hypocrites! For you lock people
out of the kingdom of heaven. For you do not go in your-

[t]Gk *brothers* [u]Or *the Christ*

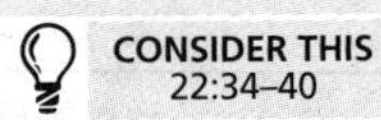

WHAT KIND OF LOVE IS THIS?

“Love” is a very confusing concept these days. People use the word “love” to describe very different relationships: people “love” their dog . . . a certain type of car . . . a brand of pizza . . . a sexually intimate partner . . . another person for whom they have deep feelings. What can “love” possibly mean if it applies equally well to dogs, machines, food, sex, or close companions?

The Bible is not confused or vague about the powerful concept it calls love. Greek, the international language of Jesus’ day and the language in which the New Testament was written, had four distinct words for love, each with its own shade of meaning:

(1) Erōs *denoted the relationship between male and female, including physical desire, craving, and longing. That word for love is not used in the New Testament.*

(2) Stergos *described affection and was applied especially to the mutual love between family members. It is not used in the New Testament either.*

(3) Philos *reflected the care and concern that friends have for each other, what we would call brotherly love. Peter spoke of this kind of love when he and Jesus discussed his future task of serving others (John 21:15–17).*

selves, and when others are going in, you stop them.[v]
15Woe to you, scribes and Pharisees, hypocrites! For you
cross sea and land to make a single convert, and you make
the new convert twice as much a child of hell[w] as yourselves.

16 "Woe to you, blind guides, who say, 'Whoever swears
by the sanctuary is bound by nothing, but whoever swears
by the gold of the sanctuary is bound by the oath.' 17You
blind fools! For which is greater, the gold or the sanctuary
that has made the gold sacred? 18And you say, 'Whoever
swears by the altar is bound by nothing, but whoever
swears by the gift that is on the altar is bound by the oath.'
19How blind you are! For which is greater, the gift or the altar that makes the gift sacred? 20So whoever swears by the
altar, swears by it and by everything on it; 21and whoever

(Bible text continued on page 101)

[v]Other authorities add here (or after verse 12) verse 14, *Woe to you, scribes and Pharisees, hypocrites! For you devour widows' houses and for the sake of appearance you make long prayers; therefore you will receive the greater condemnation* [w]Gk Gehenna

◆ ◆ ◆ ◆ ◆ ◆ ◆ ◆ ◆ ◆ ◆ ◆ ◆ ◆ ◆ ◆

(4) Agapē *described a unique type of supreme love involving a conscious and deliberate choice to do good for another, a commitment based on the willful choice of the lover, not the qualities of the person receiving the love.* Agapē *love is perhaps best seen in God's love for the world (John 3:16) and in the love that God calls believers to display (1 Cor. 13:1–13).*

When Jesus recalled the greatest of the commandments, both of which had to do with love (Matt. 22:34–40), He was calling for agapē *love, a sustained and conscious choice to graciously serve God, neighbor, and self, expecting nothing in return. Followers of Christ learn this kind of love as God loves them first. He then commands us to live in the same way toward others (1 John 3:11–24). God's love empowers us to love by choice rather than just emotion or senses, and to sustain our love even in the face of hostility or rejection.*

*God wants to deliver a new kind of love—*agapē *love—to families, workplaces, and communities through His people. Who around you needs that kind of intentional touch of compassion and grace?* ◆

Growing Fat at the Poor's Expense

CONSIDER THIS 23:13, note *v* **Jesus chastised the Pharisees for growing fat at the expense of widows (v. 14). Unfortunately, not much has changed from that day to this. We still see people with lots of power but few scruples grow rich by dislodging widows and other less powerful folks from what little they own.**

Sadly, there are loan sharks and other flimflam artists who con the poor. But there are also more respectable businesspeople whose activities can hurt the powerless. For example, occasionally some "urban renewal projects" have driven the poor from one slum to another in a frantic search for housing that costs more than before.

Then there are those who buy, sell, close down, and bankrupt companies with little regard for the impact on workers or communities, whose only motive appears to be personal financial gain.

Jesus never condemned business or investment. But His stiff rebuke of the Pharisees challenges any of us involved in finance and deal-making to carefully weigh the ethics of our choices. Woe to us if we devour the resources of the disadvantaged.

Scripture has much more to say about our use and abuse of wealth. See "Christians and Money," 1 Tim. 1:6–19; and "Getting Yours," James 5:1–6.

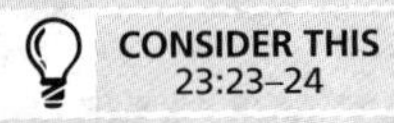

TITHING

Jesus' words to the Pharisees (v. 23) raise the issue of tithing. Should Christians today pay tithes? Or are we free from that practice?

For that matter, what is a *tithe*? The word means "a tenth part." In the Old Testament, God commanded the Israelites to give tithes—one-tenth of their produce or income—for one of three reasons:

(1) To support the Levites, who were responsible for the tabernacle and worship (Num. 18:20–24).

(2) To support various feasts and sacrifices (Deut. 14:22–27), some of which lasted more than one or two days and were times of joyous celebration and thanksgiving.

(3) To establish a pool of resources to help the poor, orphans and widows, and strangers in the land (Deut. 14:28–29).

In the New Testament, neither Christ nor the apostles gave any explicit instructions about tithing. However, Jesus clearly endorsed it, as He did all the Law (v. 23; Matt. 5:17–20). He denounced the hypocritical way that the Pharisees ignored the "weightier matters" of the Law—justice, mercy, and faith. But those "heavy duty" issues by no means negated such "lightweight matters" as tithing.

So what is the place of tithing for believers today? Several principles might be considered:

(1) As Christians, our allegiance is not to the Old Testament Law, which was primarily given to Israel, but to Christ.

(2) Our giving needs to spring from a love of Christ, not a slavish obedience to a percentage standard. When Abraham gave the first tithe recorded in the Bible (Gen. 14:17–20), he did it as an expression of gratitude for God's deliverance of him in battle. Throughout Scripture, loving God and worshiping Him are at the heart of tithing.

(3) All of what we have ultimately comes from and belongs to God—not just what we give away, but also what we keep. So He has total claim on 100 percent of our income, not just 10 percent.

(4) Ten percent makes a great starting point for giving. However, studies indicate that as a group, Christians in the United States give nowhere near that much of their income away—to ministries or charities of any kind. In fact, while per capita income has increased, church members have actually *decreased* their contributions to churches.

(5) The New Testament is clear that vocational Christian workers have a right to financial support from those to whom they minister (1 Cor. 9:13–14; Gal. 6:6). Likewise, many churches and other ministries assist the poor, orphans and widows, and strangers. So it seems legitimate to expect believers to donate money to those causes.

(6) No matter how much we give or to whom, Matt. 23:23 indicates that our first priority should be to ensure that justice is carried out around us, that we show mercy to our "neighbors," and that we practice our faith and not just talk about it. In the end, it is through our obedience that Jesus increases our faith. ◆

swears by the sanctuary, swears by it and by the one who
dwells in it; 22and whoever swears by heaven, swears by the
throne of God and by the one who is seated upon it.

23:23–24

23 "Woe to you, scribes and Pharisees,
hypocrites! For you tithe mint, dill, and
cummin, and have neglected the weightier matters of the
law: justice and mercy and faith. It is these you ought to
have practiced without neglecting the others. 24You blind
guides! You strain out a gnat but swallow a camel!

25 "Woe to you, scribes and Pharisees, hypocrites! For
you clean the outside of the cup and of the plate, but inside
they are full of greed and self-indulgence. 26You blind Pharisee! First clean the inside of the cup,[x] so that the outside
also may become clean.

23:27–28

27 "Woe to you, scribes and Pharisees,
hypocrites! For you are like white-
washed tombs, which on the outside look beautiful, but inside they are full of the bones of the dead and of all kinds
of filth. 28So you also on the outside look righteous to others, but inside you are full of hypocrisy and lawlessness.

29 "Woe to you, scribes and Pharisees, hypocrites! For
you build the tombs of the prophets and decorate the
graves of the righteous, 30and you say, 'If we had lived in
the days of our ancestors, we would not have taken part
with them in shedding the blood of the prophets.' 31Thus
you testify against yourselves that you are descendants of
those who murdered the prophets. 32Fill up, then, the measure of your ancestors. 33You snakes, you brood of vipers!
How can you escape being sentenced to hell?[y] 34Therefore I
send you prophets, sages, and scribes, some of whom you
will kill and crucify, and some you will flog in your synagogues and pursue from town to town, 35so that upon you
may come all the righteous blood shed on earth, from the
blood of righteous Abel to the blood of Zechariah son of
Barachiah, whom you murdered between the sanctuary and
the altar. 36Truly I tell you, all this will come upon this generation.

Jerusalem's Refusal

23:37
see pg. 102

37 "Jerusalem, Jerusalem, the city that
kills the prophets and stones those who

[x]Other ancient authorities add *and of the plate* [y]Gk *Gehenna*

Whitewashed Tombs

CONSIDER THIS 23:27–28 *Jesus drew upon a grim, arresting image in His denunciation of the self-righteous Pharisees (vv. 27–28). At the end of a Jewish funeral procession, which everyone was obliged to join, the body was placed on a rock shelf in a tomb. Once the flesh had decomposed, the bones would be collected and removed, allowing the shelf to be reused. Since Jews were made ritually unclean by touching graves (Num. 19:16), rocks used to seal tombs were whitewashed as a warning to stay away. The glaze gave the tombs a clean image on the outside—even though there were decomposing corpses on the inside.*

Jesus Weeps for the Children

A CLOSER LOOK 23:37–39 *Jesus wanted to gather together the lost children of Jerusalem (v. 37). Was He speaking only in spiritual terms? See "Good Men Care," Luke 13:34.*

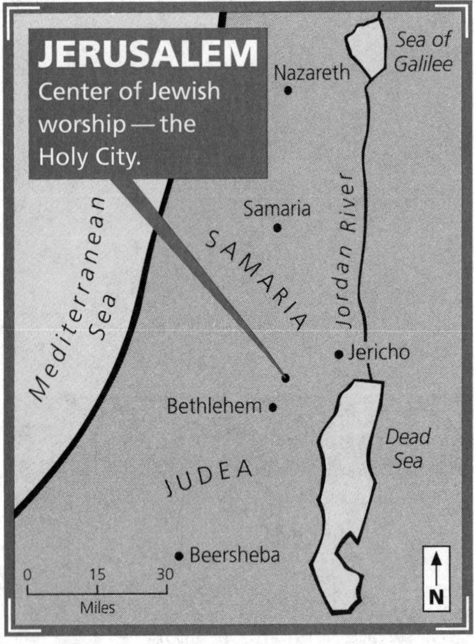

JERUSALEM

YOU ARE THERE 23:37

- Main city of Palestine in biblical times.
- Well-situated for defense on two triangular ridges that converged to the south, bordered by the Kidron Valley on the east and the Valley of Hinnom on the west.
- Appears in the Bible as early as Abraham (Gen. 14:18), though the site had probably been inhabited for centuries before.
- Captured by David and made the capital of Israel.
- Site of Solomon's temple and, in the first century, Herod's temple.
- Estimated population in Jesus' day probably 60,000 to 70,000, though estimates range from 40,000 to 12 million.
- Besieged and destroyed by Rome in A.D. 70.
- Relatively small geographically, but a sizable metropolitan area with numerous suburban towns.

(continued on next page)

are sent to it! How often have I desired to gather your children together as a hen gathers her brood under her wings,
and you were not willing! 38See, your house is left to you,
desolate.[z] 39For I tell you, you will not
see me again until you say, 'Blessed is the
one who comes in the name of the Lord.' "

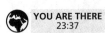

23:37–39 see pg. 101

Jesus Predicts the Temple's Destruction

24 As Jesus came out of the temple and was going
away, his disciples came to point out to him the
buildings of the temple. 2Then he asked them, "You see all
these, do you not? Truly I tell you, not one stone will be left
here upon another; all will be thrown down."

3 When he was sitting on the Mount of Olives, the disciples came to him privately, saying, "Tell us, when will this
be, and what will be the sign of your coming and of the end
of the age?" 4Jesus answered them, "Beware that no one
leads you astray. 5For many will come in my name, saying,
'I am the Messiah!'[a] and they will lead many astray. 6And
you will hear of wars and rumors of wars; see that you are
not alarmed; for this must take place, but the end is not
yet. 7For nation will rise against nation, and kingdom
against kingdom, and there will be famines[b] and earthquakes in various places: 8all this is but the beginning of
the birth pangs.

Terrible Times to Come

9 "Then they will hand you over to be tortured and will
put you to death, and you will be hated by all nations because of my name. 10Then many will fall away,[c] and they
will betray one another and hate one another. 11And many
false prophets will arise and lead many astray. 12And because of the increase of lawlessness, the love of many will
grow cold. 13But the one who endures to the end will be
saved. 14And this good news[d] of the kingdom will be proclaimed throughout the world, as a testimony to all the nations; and then the end will come.

15 "So when you see the desolating sacrilege standing in
the holy place, as was spoken of by the prophet Daniel (let
the reader understand), 16then those in Judea must flee to
the mountains; 17the one on the housetop must not go
down to take what is in the house; 18the one in the field
must not turn back to get a coat. 19Woe to those who are
pregnant and to those who are nursing infants in those
days! 20Pray that your flight may not be in winter or on a
sabbath. 21For at that time there will be great suffering,
such as has not been from the beginning of the world until

[z] Other ancient authorities lack *desolate* [a] Or *the Christ* [b] Other ancient authorities add *and pestilences* [c] Or *stumble* [d] Or *gospel*

now, no, and never will be. 22And if those days had not
been cut short, no one would be saved; but for the sake of
the elect those days will be cut short. 23Then if anyone says
to you, 'Look! Here is the Messiah!'[e] or 'There he is!'—do
not believe it. 24For false messiahs[f] and false prophets will
appear and produce great signs and omens, to lead astray, if
possible, even the elect. 25Take note, I have told you beforehand. 26So, if they say to you, 'Look! He is in the wilderness,' do not go out. If they say, 'Look! He is in the inner
rooms,' do not believe it. 27For as the lightning comes from
the east and flashes as far as the west, so will be the coming
of the Son of Man. 28Wherever the corpse is, there the vultures will gather.

29 "Immediately after the suffering of those days
the sun will be darkened,
and the moon will not give its light;
the stars will fall from heaven,
and the powers of heaven will be shaken.

30Then the sign of the Son of Man will appear in heaven,
and then all the tribes of the earth will mourn, and they
will see 'the Son of Man coming on the clouds of heaven'
with power and great glory. 31And he will send out his angels with a loud trumpet call, and they will gather his elect
from the four winds, from one end of heaven to the other.

32 "From the fig tree learn its lesson: as soon as its
branch becomes tender and puts forth its leaves, you know
that summer is near. 33So also, when you see all these
things, you know that he[g] is near, at the very gates. 34Truly I
tell you, this generation will not pass away until all these
things have taken place. 35Heaven and earth will pass away,
but my words will not pass away.

Faithful and Foolish Living

36 "But about that day and hour no one knows, neither
the angels of heaven, nor the Son,[h] but only the Father.
37For as the days of Noah were, so will be the coming of the
Son of Man. 38For as in those days before the flood they
were eating and drinking, marrying and giving in marriage,

[e]Or *the Christ* [f]Or *christs* [g]Or *it* [h]Other ancient authorities lack *nor the Son*

(continued from previous page)

THE HOLY CITY

For centuries before and after Christ, Jerusalem has been viewed as more than just a city. It stands as a great symbol of the Bible and the Near East. As the center of Judaism and Hebrew culture, it bore the brunt of Jesus' dramatic cry of anguish over its rejection of Him (Matt. 23:37–38). In fact, in only a few years, Jerusalem would be completely destroyed by the Romans.

Jesus visited Jerusalem several times. Yet its population as a whole never did respond to the Son of God. Nor did it accept Christ's followers later when they tried to penetrate it with His message. Known as the Holy City (Matt. 4:5), Jerusalem nevertheless rejected the Holy One of Israel, the Messiah.

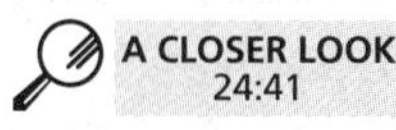

A CLOSER LOOK 24:41

An Everyday Task

Jesus promised that His return would burst into common, everyday life, as pictured in two women grinding grain (v. 41). See Luke 17:35.

The first headquarters of the early church was at Jerusalem, but the city's supremacy was short-lived. See "Jerusalem—Merely the Beginning," Acts 1:12–26.

until the day Noah entered the ark, 39and they knew nothing until the flood came and swept them all away, so too
will be the coming of the Son of Man. 40Then two will be in

24:41
see pg. 103

the field; one will be taken and one will
be left. 41Two women will be grinding
meal together; one will be taken and one will be left. 42Keep
awake therefore, for you do not know on what day[i] your
Lord is coming. 43But understand this: if the owner of the
house had known in what part of the night the thief was
coming, he would have stayed awake and would not have
let his house be broken into. 44Therefore you also must be
ready, for the Son of Man is coming at an unexpected hour.
45 "Who then is the faithful and wise slave, whom his
master has put in charge of his household, to give the other
slaves[j] their allowance of food at the proper time? 46Blessed
is that slave whom his master will find at work when he arrives. 47Truly I tell you, he will put that one in charge of all
his possessions. 48But if that wicked slave says to himself,
'My master is delayed,' 49and he begins to beat his fellow
slaves, and eats and drinks with drunkards, 50the master of
that slave will come on a day when he does not expect him
and at an hour that he does not know. 51He will cut him in
pieces[k] and put him with the hypocrites, where there will
be weeping and gnashing of teeth.

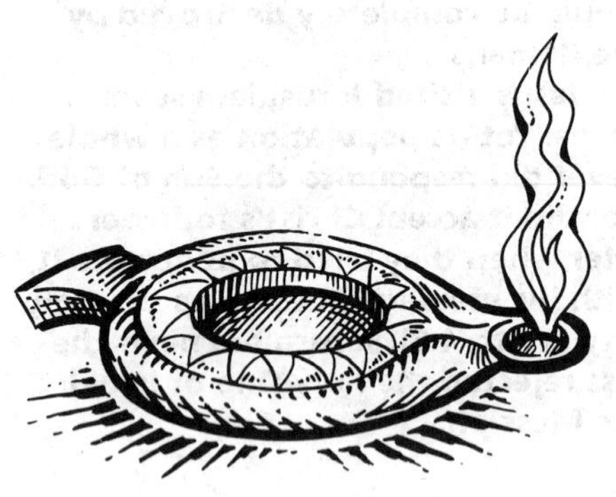

A Parable about Ten Bridesmaids

25 "Then the kingdom of heaven will be like this. Ten
bridesmaids[l] took their lamps and went to meet the
bridegroom.[m] 2Five of them were foolish, and five were
wise. 3When the foolish took their lamps, they took no oil
with them; 4but the wise took flasks of oil with their lamps.
5As the bridegroom was delayed, all of them became
drowsy and slept. 6But at midnight there was a shout,
'Look! Here is the bridegroom! Come out to meet him.'
7Then all those bridesmaids[l] got up and trimmed their
lamps. 8The foolish said to the wise, 'Give us some of your
oil, for our lamps are going out.' 9But the wise replied, 'No!
there will not be enough for you and for us; you had better
go to the dealers and buy some for yourselves.' 10And while
they went to buy it, the bridegroom came, and those who
were ready went with him into the wedding banquet; and
the door was shut. 11Later the other bridesmaids[l] came also,
saying, 'Lord, lord, open to us.' 12But he replied, 'Truly I tell
you, I do not know you.' 13Keep awake therefore, for you
know neither the day nor the hour.[n]

[i]Other ancient authorities read *at what hour* [j]Gk *to give them* [k]Or *cut him off* [l]Gk *virgins* [m]Other ancient authorities add *and the bride* [n]Other ancient authorities add *in which the Son of Man is coming*

A Parable about Investment

14 "For it is as if a man, going on a journey, summoned
his slaves and entrusted his property to them; 15to one he
gave five talents,[o] to another two, to another one, to each
according to his ability. Then he went away. 16The one who
had received the five talents went off at once and traded
with them, and made five more talents. 17In the same way,
the one who had the two talents made two more talents.
18But the one who had received the one talent went off and
dug a hole in the ground and hid his master's money. 19Af-
ter a long time the master of those slaves came and settled
accounts with them. 20Then the one who had received the
five talents came forward, bringing five more talents, saying, 'Master, you handed over to me five talents; see, I have
made five more talents.' 21His master said to him, 'Well
done, good and trustworthy slave; you have been trustworthy in a few things, I will put you in charge of many things;
enter into the joy of your master.' 22And the one with the
two talents also came forward, saying, 'Master, you handed
over to me two talents; see, I have made two more talents.'
23His master said to him, 'Well done, good and trustworthy
slave; you have been trustworthy in a few things, I will put
you in charge of many things; enter into the joy of your
25:14–30 master.' 24Then the one who had received the one talent also came forward,
saying, 'Master, I knew that you were a harsh man, reaping
where you did not sow, and gathering where you did not
scatter seed; 25so I was afraid, and I went and hid your talent in the ground. Here you have what is yours.' 26But his
master replied, 'You wicked and lazy slave! You knew, did
you, that I reap where I did not sow, and gather where I did
not scatter? 27Then you ought to have invested my money
with the bankers, and on my return I would have received
what was my own with interest. 28So take the talent from
him, and give it to the one with the ten talents. 29For to all
those who have, more will be given, and they will have an
abundance; but from those who have nothing, even what
they have will be taken away. 30As for this worthless slave,

[o]A talent was worth more than fifteen years' wages of a laborer

TRUE SUCCESS MEANS FAITHFULNESS

CONSIDER THIS 25:14–30 **The story of the talents (vv. 14–30) is about the kingdom of heaven (v. 14), but it offers an important lesson about success. God measures our success not by what we have, but by what we do with what we have—for all that we have is a gift from Him. We are really only managers to whom He has entrusted resources and responsibilities.**

The key thing He looks for is *faithfulness* (vv. 21, 23), doing what we can to obey and honor Him with whatever He has given us. We may or may not be "successful" as our culture measures success, in terms of wealth, prestige, power, or fame. In the long run that hardly matters. What counts is whether we have faithfully served God with what He has entrusted to us. By all means we must avoid wasting our lives, the way the third servant wasted his talents, by failing to carry out our Master's business.

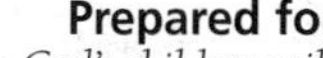

A CLOSER LOOK 25:34

Prepared for You

God's children will enjoy an inheritance that is beyond comprehension. See "What's In It for Me?" at Eph. 1:11.

A talent was worth a lot of money. See "Seventy Times Seven—Still Not Enough," Matt. 18:21–35.

Jesus told a different version of this parable in Luke 19:15–27.

The Final Exam

CONSIDER THIS 25:31–46 Have you ever wondered whether God is going to give you a "final exam" when you stand before Him? If you pass you go to heaven, but if you fail . . . ? Fortunately, Jesus has already taken that exam for us—and passed (Eph. 2:4–10). Nevertheless, Matt. 25:31–46 reveals a final exam for the nations at Christ's return with one six-part question:

Exam for the Nations		
Were you a friend of Jesus when He was *hungry*?	yes	no
Were you a friend of Jesus when He was *thirsty*?	yes	no
Were you a friend of Jesus when He was *a stranger*?	yes	no
Were you a friend of Jesus when He was *naked*?	yes	no
Were you a friend of Jesus when He was *sick*?	yes	no
Were you a friend of Jesus when He was *in prison*?	yes	no

The point is that those being examined at that time will have made certain choices: whether or not to feed the hungry, to give drink to the thirsty, to befriend the strangers, to clothe the naked, to heal the sick, to befriend the prisoners. Who ever said that life was a series of meaningless choices? And who can say that the evidence Christ will look for at His return is not the same evidence He wants to see in believers today? To love Jesus is to love all who need our care.

Who are those in need nearest you? See "Who Was the Neighbor?" Luke 10:37.

throw him into the outer darkness, where there will be weeping and gnashing of teeth.'

Judgment of the Nations

25:31–46

31 "When the Son of Man comes in his glory, and all the angels with him,
then he will sit on the throne of his glory. 32All the nations
will be gathered before him, and he will separate people
one from another as a shepherd separates the sheep from
the goats, 33and he will put the sheep at his right hand and
the goats at the left. 34Then the king will
say to those at his right hand, 'Come,
you that are blessed by my Father, inherit the kingdom prepared for you from the foundation of the world; 35for I was
hungry and you gave me food, I was thirsty and you gave
me something to drink, I was a stranger and you welcomed
me, 36I was naked and you gave me clothing, I was sick and
you took care of me, I was in prison and you visited me.'
37Then the righteous will answer him, 'Lord, when was it
that we saw you hungry and gave you food, or thirsty and
gave you something to drink? 38And when was it that we
saw you a stranger and welcomed you, or naked and gave
you clothing? 39And when was it that we saw you sick or in

25:34 see pg. 105

Personality Profile: Caiaphas

FOR YOUR INFO 26:3 **Also known as:** Joseph. His given name, Caiaphas, meant "a searcher."

Home: Jerusalem.

Occupation: High priest of Israel from A.D. 18 to 36.

Family: His father-in-law was Annas, also a high priest. Both father and son were Sadducees (see "Party Politics of Jesus' Day," Matt. 16:1) from aristocratic families in Israel.

Special interests: Maintaining the political and religious status quo.

Best known today as: The judge at the trial leading to Jesus' crucifixion.

prison and visited you?' 40And the king will answer them,
'Truly I tell you, just as you did it to one of the least of
these who are members of my family,[p] you did it to me.'
41Then he will say to those at his left hand, 'You that are accursed, depart from me into the eternal fire prepared for
the devil and his angels; 42for I was hungry and you gave
me no food, I was thirsty and you gave me nothing to
drink, 43I was a stranger and you did not welcome me,
naked and you did not give me clothing, sick and in prison
and you did not visit me.' 44Then they also will answer,
'Lord, when was it that we saw you hungry or thirsty or a
stranger or naked or sick or in prison, and did not take care
of you?' 45Then he will answer them, 'Truly I tell you, just

[p] Gk *these my brothers*

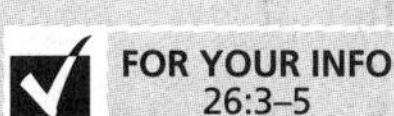

FOR YOUR INFO
26:3–5

CAIAPHAS, THE RELIGIOUS POWER BROKER

As the high priest, Caiaphas was the most influential member of the Sanhedrin, or council, the highest ruling body and supreme court of the Jews (see "Stephen's Trial and Murder," Acts 6:12). However, while the position afforded him vast authority, it provided little job security. High priests served at the whim of Rome, and between 37 B.C. and A.D. 67, the empire appointed no fewer than 28 men to the position. The fact that Caiaphas held onto the job for 18 years is a tribute to his political savvy and, some felt, was evidence that he was in league with Rome.

There may be some truth to that, but if so, his concern was not to protect Rome's interests as much as Israel's. He feared lest the slightest civil disorder would mobilize Roman troops and lead to the nation's downfall. So when Jesus came, drawing the attention of vast numbers of the people and performing astounding miracles, especially the raising of Lazarus, Caiaphas determined that He would have to be destroyed (John 11:45–50).

This led to a well conceived plot in which Jesus was arrested, an illegal trial was held, and false evidence was brought against Him (Matt. 26:3–4, 57–68). By playing Pilate the Roman governor and Herod the Jewish king against each other, and by whipping up the people into a mob (Luke 22:66—23:25), Caiaphas triumphantly orchestrated Jesus' conviction leading to execution.

To Caiaphas' amazement, however, the sparks that he thought he had doused flamed up again with renewed power. The apostles began preaching the gospel in Jerusalem (and beyond) with great effect. And, like Jesus, they began performing miracles that not only drew the people's attention, but their response to the message about Christ (Acts 3:1—4:13). ◆

as you did not do it to one of the least of these, you did not
do it to me.' 46And these will go away into eternal punishment, but the righteous into eternal life."

Leaders Plot to Kill Jesus

26 When Jesus had finished saying all these things, he
said to his disciples, 2"You know that after two days
the Passover is coming, and the Son of Man will be handed
over to be crucified."

26:3 see pg. 106

3 Then the chief priests and the elders
of the people gathered in the palace of
the high priest, who was called Caiaphas, 4and they con-

26:3–5 see pg. 107

spired to arrest Jesus by stealth and kill
him. 5But they said, "Not during the festival, or there may be a riot among the people."

A Woman Anoints Jesus for Burial

26:6–13

6 Now while Jesus was at Bethany in
the house of Simon the leper,[q] 7a woman
came to him with an alabaster jar of very costly ointment,

26:8–9

and she poured it on his head as he sat
at the table. 8But when the disciples saw
it, they were angry and said, "Why this waste? 9For this
ointment could have been sold for a large sum, and the
money given to the poor." 10But Jesus, aware of this, said to
them, "Why do you trouble the woman? She has performed
a good service for me. 11For you always have the poor with
you, but you will not always have me. 12By pouring this
ointment on my body she has prepared me for burial.
13Truly I tell you, wherever this good news[r] is proclaimed in
the whole world, what she has done will be told in remembrance of her."

(Bible text continued on page 110)

[q]The terms *leper* and *leprosy* can refer to several diseases [r]Or *gospel*

Preparing Jesus for His Death

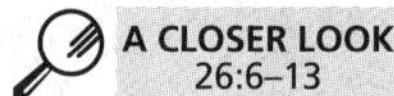

A CLOSER LOOK 26:6–13

The woman who anointed Jesus turns out to have been Mary, Lazarus' sister. See "Funeral Preparations," John 12:1–8.

Squandering Wealth on Worship

A CLOSER LOOK 26:8–9

What the disciples saw as waste (vv. 8–9) the Lord saw as worship. The tension still exists. Is it right for a community of believers to spend millions on new church facilities when there are so many poor and homeless on the streets? Moreover, don't they, too, deserve the benefits of art and beauty? "A Parting Gift" (Mark 14:3–9) says more about this incident at Simon's home.

Personality Profile: Judas Iscariot

FOR YOUR INFO 26:14

Name meant: "Praise of the Lord."

Home: Probably Kerioth in southern Judah.

Family: His father was Simon Iscariot.

Occupation: Unknown, although he may have had some background in finance or accounting; he kept track of the money box for Jesus and the other disciples; John calls him a thief (John 12:6).

Best known then and now as: The disciple who betrayed Jesus to His enemies.

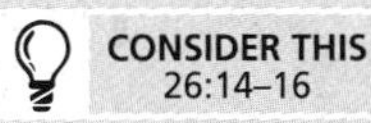

CONSIDER THIS 26:14–16

Judas Iscariot, the Betrayer

The New Testament never mentions Judas Iscariot without reminding the reader that he was the man who betrayed Jesus (for example, Matt. 10:4; Mark 3:19; John 12:4). Consequently, to this day the name Judas is a symbol of betrayal.

Why did he do it? His portrayal in the Gospels suggests that he had a keen interest in money. But the amount that the priests paid him—30 pieces of silver—was relatively small. Besides, he had access to the disciples' money box and apparently was known for helping himself to its contents (John 12:6).

Some have suggested that Judas thought that his betrayal would force Jesus into asserting His true power and overthrowing the Romans. Others have suggested that Judas became convinced that Jesus was a false Messiah and that the true Messiah was yet to come. Or perhaps he was upset over Jesus' seemingly casual attitude toward the Law in regard to associating with sinners and violating the Sabbath.

In the end, no one knows what Judas' exact motives were for turning against Jesus. He remains a shadowy figure in the Gospel accounts, unknown by his companions, unfaithful to his Lord, and unmourned in his death. ◆

Judas took his own life. Ironically, his death was memorialized in the purchase of a plot of ground for a cemetery. See "Field of Blood," Acts 1:19.

The New Testament mentions several other Judases. One was a brother of Jesus and probably the author of the book of Jude (Matt. 13:55). See the introduction to Jude.

Judas Sells Out

26:14
see pg. 109

26:14–16
see pg. 109

14 Then one of the twelve, who was
called Judas Iscariot, went to the chief
priests [15]and said, "What will you give
me if I betray him to you?" They paid
him thirty pieces of silver. [16]And from that moment he began to look for an opportunity to betray him.

A Final Passover Meal

17 On the first day of Unleavened Bread the disciples
came to Jesus, saying, "Where do you want us to make the
preparations for you to eat the Passover?" [18]He said, "Go
into the city to a certain man, and say to him, 'The Teacher
says, My time is near; I will keep the Passover at your
house with my disciples.' " [19]So the disciples did as Jesus
had directed them, and they prepared the Passover meal.
20 When it was evening, he took his place with the
twelve;[s] [21]and while they were eating, he said, "Truly I tell
you, one of you will betray me." [22]And they became greatly

[s]Other ancient authorities add *disciples*

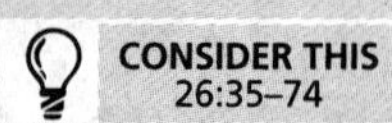
CONSIDER THIS
26:35–74

WOULD YOU CHOOSE THESE FOR LEADERS?

Jesus was close to the end of His earthly ministry. His life was about to come to an agonizing end at the hands of bitter opponents. Shortly thereafter, those He had trained would be assuming the reins of His new movement.

That transition period would prove to be rather awkward. It didn't help that it was forced on the group by hostile outsiders. But the most troubling aspect was what happened to Jesus' associates, the ones who would have to carry His banner into the future. During those final days and hours, they began to fall apart:

- *Bravado caused them to overstate their commitment (v. 35). When the moment of truth came, they deserted the Lord (v. 56).*
- *Even though the Lord asked them to keep watch with Him during His final hours of freedom, they fell asleep twice (vv. 40, 43).*
- *At the very moment when Jesus was standing trial and enduring mockery and beatings, Peter, who had led the others in declaring their loyalty (v. 35), denied any association with Him (vv. 69–75).*

In short, the disciples hardly seem to have had the "right stuff" for continuing the important work that Jesus

distressed and began to say to him one after another,
"Surely not I, Lord?" 23 He answered, "The one who has
dipped his hand into the bowl with me will betray me.
24 The Son of Man goes as it is written of him, but woe to
that one by whom the Son of Man is betrayed! It would
have been better for that one not to have been born." 25 Judas, who betrayed him, said, "Surely not I, Rabbi?" He
replied, "You have said so."

26 While they were eating, Jesus took a loaf of bread,
and after blessing it he broke it, gave it to the disciples, and
said, "Take, eat; this is my body." 27 Then he took a cup, and
after giving thanks he gave it to them, saying, "Drink from
it, all of you; 28 for this is my blood of the[t] covenant, which
is poured out for many for the forgiveness of sins. 29 I tell
you, I will never again drink of this fruit of the vine until
that day when I drink it new with you in my Father's kingdom."

30 When they had sung the hymn, they went out to the
Mount of Olives.

31 Then Jesus said to them, "You will all become deserters because of me this night; for it is written,

[t]Other ancient authorities add *new*

began. Yet, even after all that He went through, Jesus returned to that very group of followers after His resurrection and declared that they were still His chosen representatives, the ones appointed to continue His work. He even affirmed His commitment to stick with them to the end (28:19–20).

Jesus' treatment of the disciples shows that failure is not the unforgivable act. In fact, it seems to be the crucible out of which character is formed. It is certainly not a sifting-out process to eliminate weak or useless people. Christ does not look for perfect people, but rather faithful *people who can experience His forgiveness and grow.*

Do you stick with people even though they stumble? Do you allow the shortcomings of your spouse, children, boss, coworkers, and neighbors to open up bright futures? Do you give yourself *freedom to fail?* ◆

The Twelve were all men. But women also played an important role in Jesus' life and ministry. See "The Women Who Followed Jesus," Luke 8:1–3.

God has always valued faithfulness over perfection when it comes to handing out acclaim. See "The Hall of Faithfulness," Heb. 11:1–40.

Praying in a Workplace

CONSIDER THIS 26:36 *Jesus chose a familiar place of work in which to pray one of His final prayers (v. 36). The area around Jerusalem was rich with olive groves, and many people were employed at the commercial oil presses, or gethsemanes, to produce the city's only export product.*

The particular garden mentioned here was a place to which Jesus often went alone or with His disciples for prayer or relaxation. As a result, Judas had no trouble finding Him when he led the party to arrest Him (John 18:1–2). The exact site of the garden is unknown, but it may have been located on the Mount of Olives, just east of Jerusalem across the Kidron Valley, opposite the temple (Mark 13:3; John 18:1).

'I will strike the shepherd,
and the sheep of the flock will be scattered.'
32But after I am raised up, I will go ahead of you to Galilee." 33Peter said to him, "Though all become deserters
because of you, I will never desert you." 34Jesus said
to him, "Truly I tell you, this very night, before the cock
26:35–74 see pg. 110
crows, you will deny me three times."
35Peter said to him, "Even though I must
die with you, I will not deny you." And so said all the disciples.

Jesus Prays in the Garden of Gethsemane

26:36 see pg. 111
36 Then Jesus went with them to a
place called Gethsemane; and he said to
his disciples, "Sit here while I go over there and pray." 37He
took with him Peter and the two sons of Zebedee, and began to be grieved and agitated. 38Then he said to them, "I
am deeply grieved, even to death; remain here, and stay
awake with me." 39And going a little farther, he threw himself on the ground and prayed, "My Father, if it is possible,
let this cup pass from me; yet not what I want but what you
want." 40Then he came to the disciples and found them
sleeping; and he said to Peter, "So, could you not stay
26:41
awake with me one hour? 41Stay awake
and pray that you may not come into the
time of trial;[u] the spirit indeed is willing, but the flesh is
weak." 42Again he went away for the second time and
prayed, "My Father, if this cannot pass unless I drink it,
your will be done." 43Again he came and found them sleeping, for their eyes were heavy. 44So leaving them again, he
went away and prayed for the third time, saying the same
words. 45Then he came to the disciples and said to them,
"Are you still sleeping and taking your rest? See, the hour is
at hand, and the Son of Man is betrayed into the hands of
sinners. 46Get up, let us be going. See, my betrayer is at
hand."

Jesus Betrayed

47 While he was still speaking, Judas, one of the twelve,

[u]Or *into temptation*

"PUT YOUR SWORD BACK INTO ITS PLACE; FOR ALL WHO TAKE THE SWORD WILL PERISH BY THE SWORD."
—Matthew 26:52

Lest You Enter into Temptation

A CLOSER LOOK 26:41

Prayer is one of the most important strategies believers can use to avoid temptation (v. 41). Only by God's help can we resist. See "Pay Attention to Temptation!" at 1 Cor. 10:12–13.

arrived; with him was a large crowd with swords and clubs,
from the chief priests and the elders of the people. 48Now
the betrayer had given them a sign, saying, "The one I will
kiss is the man; arrest him." 49At once he came up to Jesus
and said, "Greetings, Rabbi!" and kissed him. 50Jesus said to
him, "Friend, do what you are here to do." Then they came
and laid hands on Jesus and arrested him. 51Suddenly, one
of those with Jesus put his hand on his sword, drew it, and
struck the slave of the high priest, cutting off his ear.
52Then Jesus said to him, "Put your sword back into its
place; for all who take the sword will perish by the sword.
53Do you think that I cannot appeal to my Father, and he
will at once send me more than twelve legions of angels?
54But how then would the scriptures be fulfilled, which say
it must happen in this way?" 55At that hour Jesus said to the
crowds, "Have you come out with swords and clubs to arrest me as though I were a bandit? Day after day I sat in the
temple teaching, and you did not arrest me. 56But all this
has taken place, so that the scriptures of the prophets may
be fulfilled." Then all the disciples deserted him and fled.

Jesus Is Brought Before the High Priest

57 Those who had arrested Jesus took him to Caiaphas
the high priest, in whose house the scribes and the elders
had gathered. 58But Peter was following him at a distance,
as far as the courtyard of the high priest; and going inside,
he sat with the guards in order to see how this would end.
26:59–68 59Now the chief priests and the whole
council were looking for false testimony
against Jesus so that they might put him to death, 60but
they found none, though many false witnesses came forward. At last two came forward 61and said, "This fellow
said, 'I am able to destroy the temple of God and to build it
in three days.' " 62The high priest stood up and said, "Have
you no answer? What is it that they testify against you?"
63But Jesus was silent. Then the high priest said to him, "I
put you under oath before the living God, tell us if you are
the Messiah,[v] the Son of God." 64Jesus said to him, "You
have said so. But I tell you,

From now on you will see the Son of Man
seated at the right hand of Power
and coming on the clouds of heaven."

65Then the high priest tore his clothes and said, "He has
blasphemed! Why do we still need witnesses? You have
now heard his blasphemy. 66What is your verdict?" They
answered, "He deserves death." 67Then they spat in his face

[v]Or *Christ*

No Right Answers

CONSIDER THIS 26:59–68 **Have you ever been trapped in a situation where there is no good alternative? Jesus faced that as He stood trial before Caiaphas and the Jewish elders (v. 59). They were determined to do away with Him by any means, even resorting to false witnesses (vv. 59–62). The situation was so distorted and malicious that there was no good response. So Jesus remained silent (v. 63).**

As their anger intensified, the high priest placed Jesus "under oath before the living God" (v. 63). This meant that Jesus was bound by Law to answer and answer truthfully. In effect, Caiaphas was coercing a response. Jesus rewarded him by giving the very response he expected and wanted—a claim to be "the Messiah, the Son of God." This sent His accusers into a frenzy as it allowed them to impose their prearranged verdict (vv. 65–68).

Some situations cannot be salvaged. There is no way out and the worst happens. Like Jesus, however, believers can take hope that even in those moments, God remains in control. Ultimately, He will see that justice is done (Rom. 12:19).

TAINTED MONEY

CONSIDER THIS 27:3–10 **The chief priests knew that the coins tossed back at them by Judas were unacceptable to God (v. 6). It was blood money, money they had paid to apprehend their enemy, Jesus (26:14–16). Yet they turned around and used it to buy a cemetery for the poor—a good deed, yet hypocritical all the same.**

Do you ever present "tainted" money to the Lord—money not necessarily obtained through outright crime, but perhaps through deception, shady deal-making, or dirty politics? When we donate money to churches, missions, schools, ministries to the poor, and the like, we hide nothing from God. He knows all of our motives. He knows whether our gifts are from the first and best of what we've accumulated, or whether we're giving "leftovers." He knows whether our gifts cost us little or nothing (2 Sam. 24:21–24). And He certainly knows—and hates—whatever we have come by unjustly (Mal. 1:6–14). We deceive no one but ourselves if we pretend to honor God while giving Him the fruit of unrighteousness.

The early church found out just how much God disapproves of tainted money. See "Real Estate Deal Deadly," Acts 5:2–10.

and struck him; and some slapped him, 68 saying, "Prophesy
to us, you Messiah![w] Who is it that struck you?"

Peter Denies Knowing Jesus

69 Now Peter was sitting outside in the courtyard. A
servant-girl came to him and said, "You also were with
Jesus the Galilean." 70 But he denied it before all of them,
saying, "I do not know what you are talking about."
71 When he went out to the porch, another servant-girl saw
him, and she said to the bystanders, "This man was with
Jesus of Nazareth."[x] 72 Again he denied it with an oath, "I do
not know the man." 73 After a little while the bystanders
came up and said to Peter, "Certainly you are also one of
them, for your accent betrays you." 74 Then he began to
curse, and he swore an oath, "I do not know the man!" At
that moment the cock crowed. 75 Then Peter remembered
what Jesus had said: "Before the cock crows, you will deny
me three times." And he went out and wept bitterly.

Jesus Is Taken to Pilate

27 When morning came, all the chief priests and the
elders of the people conferred together against Jesus in order to bring about his death. 2 They bound him, led
him away, and handed him over to Pilate the governor.

Judas Hangs Himself

27:3–10

3 When Judas, his betrayer, saw that
Jesus[y] was condemned, he repented and
brought back the thirty pieces of silver to the chief priests
and the elders. 4 He said, "I have sinned by betraying innocent[z] blood." But they said, "What is that to us? See to it
yourself." 5 Throwing down the pieces of silver in the temple, he departed; and he went and hanged himself. 6 But the
chief priests, taking the pieces of silver, said, "It is not lawful to put them into the treasury, since they are blood
money." 7 After conferring together, they used them to buy
the potter's field as a place to bury foreigners. 8 For this reason that field has been called the Field of Blood to this day.
9 Then was fulfilled what had been spoken through the
prophet Jeremiah,[a] "And they took[b] the thirty pieces of silver, the price of the one on whom a price had been set,[c] on
whom some of the people of Israel had set a price, 10 and
they gave[d] them for the potter's field, as the Lord commanded me."

[w] Or *Christ* [x] Gk *the Nazorean* [y] Gk *he* [z] Other ancient authorities read *righteous* [a] Other ancient authorities read *Zechariah* or *Isaiah* [b] Or *I took* [c] Or *the price of the precious One* [d] Other ancient authorities read *I gave*

Jesus Before Pilate

11 Now Jesus stood before the governor; and the governor asked him, "Are you the King of the Jews?" Jesus said,
"You say so." 12But when he was accused by the chief
priests and elders, he did not answer. 13Then Pilate said to
him, "Do you not hear how many accusations they make
against you?" 14But he gave him no answer, not even to a
single charge, so that the governor was greatly amazed.
15 Now at the festival the governor was accustomed
to release a prisoner for the crowd, anyone whom they
27:16 wanted. 16At that time they had a notorious prisoner, called Jesus[e] Barabbas. 17So
after they had gathered, Pilate said to them, "Whom do you
want me to release for you, Jesus[e] Barabbas or Jesus who is
called the Messiah?"[f] 18For he realized that it was out of
jealousy that they had handed him over. 19While he was sitting on the judgment seat, his wife sent word to him, "Have
nothing to do with that innocent man, for today I have suffered a great deal because of a dream about him." 20Now
the chief priests and the elders persuaded the crowds to ask
for Barabbas and to have Jesus killed. 21The governor again
said to them, "Which of the two do you want me to release
for you?" And they said, "Barabbas." 22Pilate said to them,
"Then what should I do with Jesus who is called the Messiah?"[f] All of them said, "Let him be crucified!" 23Then he
asked, "Why, what evil has he done?" But they shouted all
the more, "Let him be crucified!"
24 So when Pilate saw that he could do nothing, but
rather that a riot was beginning, he took some water and
washed his hands before the crowd, saying, "I am innocent
of this man's blood;[g] see to it yourselves." 25Then the people
as a whole answered, "His blood be on us and on our children!" 26So he released Barabbas for them; and after flogging Jesus, he handed him over to be crucified.

Soldiers Mock Jesus

27 Then the soldiers of the governor took Jesus into the
governor's headquarters,[h] and they gathered the whole cohort around him. 28They stripped him and put a scarlet
robe on him, 29and after twisting some thorns into a crown,

(Bible text continued on page 117)

[e]Other ancient authorities lack *Jesus* [f]Or *the Christ* [g]Other ancient authorities read *this righteous blood*, or *this righteous man's blood* [h]Gk *the praetorium*

**BUT HE GAVE HIM NO ANSWER, NOT EVEN TO A SINGLE CHARGE, SO THAT THE GOVERNOR WAS GREATLY AMAZED.
—Matthew 27:14**

The Prisoner Barabbas

A CLOSER LOOK 27:16

But for a remarkable set of circumstances, the "notorious prisoner, called Jesus Barabbas" (v. 16) probably would have remained unknown to history. See "'Not This Man but Barabbas!'" Mark 15:7.

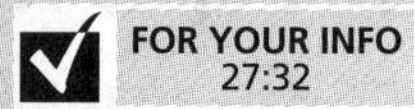
FOR YOUR INFO
27:32

THE LITTLE PEOPLE AT JESUS' DEATH

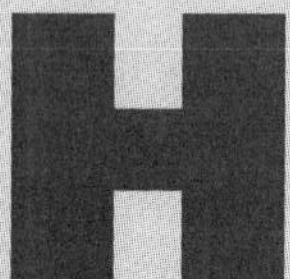

Have you ever noticed that Jesus tended to surround Himself with or be surrounded by relatively average people of little social standing or influence?

At Jesus' birth, various kinds of "little people" were involved: a minor priest and his barren wife, a small town girl and a poor carpenter, shepherds, an elderly woman, and others. A similar cast appeared during Jesus' final days and hours, including Simon, who was compelled to carry His cross (v. 32). Many of these people showed curiosity about Christ, demonstrated understanding and loyalty, or provided needed services and acts of compassion. (See table below.)

Unlike many who rise to positions of prominence and leadership, Jesus never lost touch with the little people of society. He did not insulate Himself from difficulties by surrounding Himself with the powerful, the wealthy, and the privileged. His birth, life, and death involved countless ordinary folks who could perceive His message about true values and needs.

Are you in touch with the unnamed and unnoticed? How can you serve them? What can you learn from them? ◆

ORDINARY PEOPLE WHO SAW JESUS TO THE CROSS	
Simon the leper, who had been an untouchable outcast	Hosts Jesus as his house guest (Matt. 26:6)
An unnamed woman (probably Mary of Bethany; see John 11:2; compare 12:1–8)	Uses expensive ointment to anoint Jesus' head (26:7)
An unnamed homeowner in Jerusalem	Opens his home to Jesus and the Twelve for their last meal together (26:18)
The disciples, Jesus' chosen successors from rural Galilee	Overstate their faith (26:35); join Jesus in a garden during the final hours before His arrest (26:40, 43, 56)
An unnamed servant girl	Asks Peter about his association with Jesus (26:69)
Another girl in the crowd	Also asks Peter about his association with Jesus (26:71)
Unnamed crowd members	Also enquire about Peter's association with Jesus (26:71)
Judas	Betrays Christ; later breaks down with guilt and commits suicide (27:3–5)
Barabbas, a convicted criminal	Is freed instead of Jesus due to a mob's demands (27:16, 26)
Simon of Cyrene, a man in the watching crowd	Is conscripted to carry Jesus' cross (27:32)
Two dying robbers	Are executed with Jesus (27:38, 44)
An unnamed crowd member	Offers Jesus a drink as He is in His death throes (27:48)
An unnamed Roman centurion	Observes that Jesus must be the Son of God (27:54)
Some loyal women from Galilee	Look on from afar (27:55–56)

they put it on his head. They put a reed in his right hand
and knelt before him and mocked him, saying, "Hail, King
of the Jews!" 30They spat on him, and took the reed and
struck him on the head. 31After mocking him, they stripped
him of the robe and put his own clothes on him. Then they
led him away to crucify him.

The Crucifixion

27:32 32 As they went out, they came upon
a man from Cyrene named Simon; they
compelled this man to carry his cross. 33And when they
came to a place called Golgotha (which means Place of a
Skull), 34they offered him wine to drink, mixed with gall;
but when he tasted it, he would not drink it. 35And when
they had crucified him, they divided his clothes among
themselves by casting lots;[i] 36then they sat down there and
kept watch over him. 37Over his head they put the charge
against him, which read, "This is Jesus, the King of the
Jews."

38 Then two bandits were crucified with him, one on his
right and one on his left. 39Those who passed by derided[j]
him, shaking their heads 40and saying, "You who would destroy the temple and build it in three days, save yourself! If
you are the Son of God, come down from the cross." 41In
the same way the chief priests also, along with the scribes
and elders, were mocking him, saying, 42"He saved others;
he cannot save himself.[k] He is the King of Israel; let him
come down from the cross now, and we will believe in him.
43He trusts in God; let God deliver him now, if he wants to;
for he said, 'I am God's Son.' " 44The bandits who were crucified with him also taunted him in the same way.

45 From noon on, darkness came over the whole land[l]
until three in the afternoon. 46And about three o'clock Jesus
cried with a loud voice, "Eli, Eli, lema sabachthani?" that is,
"My God, my God, why have you forsaken me?" 47When
some of the bystanders heard it, they said, "This man is
calling for Elijah." 48At once one of them ran and got a
sponge, filled it with sour wine, put it on a stick, and gave
it to him to drink. 49But the others said, "Wait, let us see
whether Elijah will come to save him."[m] 50Then Jesus cried
again with a loud voice and breathed his last.[n] 51At that moment the curtain of the temple was torn in two, from top to
bottom. The earth shook, and the rocks were split. 52The
tombs also were opened, and many bodies of the saints

(Bible text continued on page 119)

[i]Other ancient authorities add *in order that what had been spoken through the prophet might be fulfilled, "They divided my clothes among themselves, and for my clothing they cast lots."* [j]Or *blasphemed* [k]Or *is he unable to save himself?* [l]Or *earth* [m]Other ancient authorities add *And another took a spear and pierced his side, and out came water and blood* [n]Or *gave up his spirit*

THEY PUT A REED IN HIS RIGHT HAND AND KNELT BEFORE HIM AND MOCKED HIM.
—Matthew 27:29

WEALTHY PEOPLE IN THE NEW TESTAMENT

Most of Jesus' followers were not wealthy, but a few notable ones, like Joseph of Arimathea (v. 57), were. We can learn a great deal from the wealthy people recorded in the New Testament, about the dangers and the disciplines of money.

Persons	What They Did With Their Wealth	Lessons To Be Learned
Zacchaeus the tax collector (Luke 19:1–10)	• Before faith, cheated citizens and abused the poor. • After faith, repented and made restitution.	(1) Ill-gotten gain must be repaid. (2) God saves and changes us—all the way down to our pocketbooks.
Joseph of Arimathea (Matt. 27:57–61; Mark 15:42–46; Luke 23:50–53)	• Pre-paid his own funeral. • Donated his tomb for the burial of Jesus.	(3) Forsaking treasures on earth for the kingdom will be rewarded.
Women supporters of Christ (Luke 8:1–3*; 23:55—24:10; Mark 15:40; 16:1)	• Supported Jesus' work. • Assisted in His burial (probably donated expensive perfume).	(4) Generosity characterizes those who follow Jesus.
Roman centurion who believed (Matt. 8:5–13; Luke 7:5)	• Showed kindness toward the Jews. • Paid for the building of a synagogue. • Showed compassion for his ill servant.	(5) When we love people it shows in the things we do and the projects we support.
Rich young ruler (Matt. 19:16–30; Mark 10:17–31; Luke 18:18–30)	• Unwilling to part with his wealth when tested by Jesus.	(6) Those who cling to wealth have difficulty getting into the kingdom. (7) Righteousness cannot be earned, but must be received as a gift. (8) "Many who are first will be last, and the last will be first."
Philemon (Philem. 1*)	• Owned slaves and other property. • Forgave a runaway slave, both morally and financially.	(9) People are more valuable than property.
Joseph, called Barnabas (Acts 4:36–37*)	• Sold land and gave the proceeds to believers.	(10) Partnership in the gospel may mean putting your money where believers hurt.
Ananias and Sapphira (Acts 5:1–11*)	• Sold land and tried to deceive the church about the proceeds to gain a reputation.	(11) God is not fooled by gracious appearances but sees the heart and acts accordingly.
Rich Christians written about by James (James 2:1–7)	• Exploited the tendency of some to cater to them because of their wealth. • Dragged other believers into court and slandered Jesus' name.	(12) God favors those who are rich in faith; they will inherit the kingdom.
Lydia (Acts 16:13–15*, 40)	• Hosted the first church in Europe in her home.	(13) We should use our resources and homes to accomplish God's purposes.
Cornelius the centurion (Acts 10:1–48*)	• Generous to the poor. • Sought out Peter concerning the faith.	(14) Fear of God should prompt us to admit our own need for a Savior.
The Ethiopian treasurer (Acts 8:26–40)	• Nurtured his belief in God by traveling to Jerusalem. • Invited Philip to explain more about the faith.	(15) Stewardship of money and study of Scripture go hand in hand—as do business trips and worship services.
Simon the Sorcerer (Acts 8:9–25)	• Longed for spiritual power and thought it could be bottled and sold.	(16) The gifts of God cannot be bought.

Your checkbook is a diary of your values. God calls believers to be compassionate, merciful, and just to all. Does your checkbook reflect such values? Does it show a pattern of godly concern for people?

Wealth is a major topic in the New Testament. Jesus often warned about its dangers. See Matt. 6:24; Mark 10:17–31; and Luke 12:13–21. Likewise, Paul challenged believers to use their resources in a Christlike way. See "Christians and Money," 1 Tim. 6:6–19.

***See profiles of these people at the texts indicated.**

who had fallen asleep were raised. 53 After his resurrection they came out of the tombs and entered the holy city and appeared to many. 54 Now when the centurion and those with him, who were keeping watch over Jesus, saw the earthquake and what took place, they were terrified and said, "Truly this man was God's Son!"[o]

55 Many women were also there, looking on from a distance; they had followed Jesus from

27:56

Galilee and had provided for him. 56 Among them were Mary Magdalene, and Mary the mother of James and Joseph, and the mother of the sons of Zebedee.

Jesus Is Buried in a Borrowed Tomb

27:57

57 When it was evening, there came a rich man from Arimathea, named Joseph, who was also a disciple of

27:58–61

27:59–60

Jesus. 58 He went to Pilate and asked for the body of Jesus; then Pilate ordered it to be given to him. 59 So Joseph took the body and wrapped it in a clean linen cloth 60 and laid it in his own new tomb, which he had hewn in the rock. He then rolled a great stone to the door of the tomb and went away. 61 Mary Magdalene and the other Mary were there, sitting opposite the tomb.

62 The next day, that is, after the day of Preparation, the chief priests and the Pharisees gathered before Pilate 63 and said, "Sir, we remember what that impostor said while he was still alive, 'After three days I will rise again.' 64 Therefore command the tomb to be made secure until the third day; otherwise his disciples may go and steal him away, and tell the people, 'He has been raised from the dead,' and the last deception would be worse than the first." 65 Pilate said to them, "You have a guard[p] of soldiers; go, make it as secure as you can."[q] 66 So they went with the guard and made the tomb secure by sealing the stone.

The Resurrection

28:1–10
see pg. 120

28 After the sabbath, as the first day of the week was dawning, Mary Magdalene and the other Mary went to see the tomb. 2 And suddenly there was a great earthquake; for an angel of the Lord, descending from heaven, came and rolled back the stone and sat on it. 3 His appearance was like lightning, and his clothing white as snow. 4 For fear of him the guards shook and became like dead men. 5 But the angel said to the women, "Do not be afraid; I know that you are looking for Jesus who

28:6
see pg. 121

was crucified. 6 He is not here; for he has been raised, as he said. Come, see the place where he[r] lay. 7 Then go quickly and tell his disciples, 'He has been raised from the dead,[s] and indeed he is going ahead of you to Galilee; there you will see him.' This is my message for you." 8 So they left the tomb quickly with fear and great joy, and ran to tell his disciples. 9 Suddenly Jesus met them and said, "Greetings!" And they came to him, took hold of his feet, and worshiped him. 10 Then Jesus said to them, "Do not be afraid; go and tell my brothers to go to Galilee; there they will see me."

(Bible text continued on page 121)

[o] Or *a son of God* [p] Or *Take a guard* [q] Gk *you know how* [r] Other ancient authorities read *the Lord* [s] Other ancient authorities lack *from the dead*

Mary—A Common Name for Some Uncommon Women

A CLOSER LOOK 27:56

At least six Marys are mentioned in the New Testament. Why was the name so common? See "Why So Many Marys?" Mark 15:40.

For a listing of other women who followed Jesus, see Luke 8:1.

A Borrowed Tomb

A CLOSER LOOK 27:58–61

Just as God provided for Jesus' needs at His birth (see "A Poor Family Comes into Wealth," Matt. 2:11), He provided for His needs in death (27:57–61). "A Burial Fit for a King" at Mark 15:42—16:1 talks about the gift of a borrowed tomb.

Expensive Funerals

A CLOSER LOOK 27:59–60

It is common for people to spend a great deal on funerals, sometimes more than they should. See "A Burial Fit for a King," Mark 15:42—16:1, for more on honoring the dead without breaking the bank.

CONSIDER THIS
28:1–10

MYTH #2

10 MYTHS ABOUT CHRISTIANITY

MYTH: THERE IS NO EVIDENCE THAT JESUS ROSE FROM THE DEAD

Many people today accept a number of myths about Christianity, with the result that they never respond to Jesus as He really is. This is one of ten articles that speak to some of those misconceptions. For a list of all ten, see 1 Tim. 1:3–4.

All four Gospels give an account of Jesus' resurrection (vv. 1–10; Mark 16:1–18; Luke 24:1–12; John 20:1–29). Moreover, the rest of the New Testament speaks with a tremendous sense of confidence about an empty tomb and the triumph of Christ over death.

And no wonder. If true, the resurrection is the most amazing news the world has ever heard. It means there is a God after all. It means that Jesus really is God's Son. It means that Christ is alive—today—and we can know Him and be touched by His life and power. It means that we need not fear death the way we once did; we are not destined to oblivion but to spend eternity with God. It also means that knowing God is of the utmost importance right now, while we can.

These are important implications, so the question of whether Jesus actually rose from the dead is crucial. At least four lines of evidence indicate that He did:

(1) *Jesus really was dead.* Every source we have indicates that Jesus was publicly executed before large crowds. He was certified as dead by both a centurion in charge of the execution—a professional whose job it was to determine that death had taken place—and by the regional governor, Pilate, who sent to have the matter checked. This is an important point because some skeptics claim that Jesus was not really dead, that He was only near death but revived in the cool of the tomb.

(2) *The tomb was found empty.* Jesus was buried in a new tomb, one that had never before been used (John 19:41). That means it was in perfect condition and would have been easy to locate. But when Jesus' friends arrived on the second morning after His death, His body was gone. All the accounts agree on this.

The empty tomb was no less astonishing to Jesus' enemies than it was to His friends. His enemies had been working for years to see Him dead and buried. Having accomplished their goal, they took pains to post a guard and seal the tomb with an enormous boulder. Nevertheless, on Easter morning the tomb was found empty.

Who emptied it? Either men or God. If men, which ones? Jesus' enemies would have been the least likely to have stolen the body. Even if they had, they would certainly have produced it later to refute the claims of the disciples that Jesus was alive. What about Jesus' friends? Unlikely, since the accounts show them to have been very demoralized after the crucifixion. Nor would they have willingly suffered persecution and death for what they knew to be a lie.

(3) *Jesus appeared after His death to many witnesses.* In a garden, on a road, in an upstairs room, by a lake—each of the Gospels recounts Jesus' post-resurrection appearances to His fearful, doubting followers over a period of forty days. Were these hallucinations? That seems implausible, since they happened to too many people, among them hardheaded fishermen, steadfast women, civil servants, and the ultimate skeptic, Thomas.

(4) *Countless people have encountered the living Jesus and been changed by Him.* The resurrection is not simply a matter of intellectual curiosity or theological argument, but of personal experience. From the first century to today there have been innumer-

(continued on next page)

The Guards Are Bribed

11 While they were going, some of the guard went into
the city and told the chief priests everything that had happened. 12After the priests[t] had assembled with the elders,
they devised a plan to give a large sum of money to the soldiers, 13telling them, "You must say, 'His disciples came by
night and stole him away while we were asleep.' 14If this
comes to the governor's ears, we will satisfy him and keep
you out of trouble." 15So they took the money and did as
they were directed. And this story is still told among the
Jews to this day.

(Bible text continued on page 123)

[t]Gk *they*

(continued from previous page)

able people who have turned from being totally opposed or indifferent to Christianity to being utterly convinced that it is true. What changed them? They met the living Jesus. He has invited them to respond to Him in faith and challenged them to live according to His way. Jesus is as alive now as He was that first Easter morning. He still invites people to know Him today. ◆

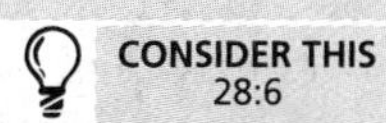

Don't Miss God's Help

Do you feel uneasy when it comes to religion and spirituality? Do issues of faith and morality create fear? The women who went to the tomb on the first Easter Sunday were terribly frightened by what they found—or rather, by what they didn't *find, for the tomb was empty (v. 6)!*

Fortunately, God understands when spiritual matters invade the safety of our world. He offers help to overcome our fears and deal with whatever has come our way. For Mary and Mary Magdalene, He sent an angel to comfort and enlighten them about the reality of Christ's resurrection. He also sent an angel to Joseph, the earthly father of Jesus, when he was troubled by his fiancée's miraculous pregnancy (1:18–25).

So it was for many others in Scripture, who were no less troubled by spiritual events and truths than many of us are today. In addition to angels, God's help has included other people, dramatic and even miraculous demonstrations of His power, direct promises, and the enormous comfort of His Word. These helps show that God appreciates the impact of spiritual light suddenly shining in a dark world. He helps us overcome the shock not only of what *He has spoken, but* that *He has spoken.*

The question remains, will we respond to His message? No matter how awkward we may feel about matters of faith, we dare not avoid them. God opens up these scary places in our lives only because He wants to restore us to Himself. ◆

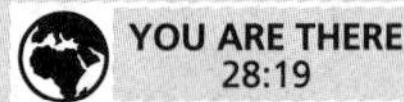

To All the Nations

Jesus sent His followers to make disciples of all the nations (ethnē, *"peoples"; v. 19). That mandate may seem obvious to us today. After all, we live at the end of 2,000 years of Christian outreach based on this and similar passages. Christianity now is an overwhelmingly Gentile religion subscribed to by roughly one-third of the world's population. And with modern technology, it appears to be a relatively simple task to expand that outreach even further.*

Yet in many ways we are just like Jesus' original disciples. They wanted a local hero, a Messiah just for Israel, one who would follow their customs and confirm their prejudices. So they were no doubt stunned by the scope and far-reaching implications of the global, cross-cultural vision that Jesus now presented. He was turning out to be more than the King of the Jews; He was the international Christ, the Savior of the entire world.

Actually, Jesus had been showing them this since the beginning of His ministry. Matthew recorded again and again His work among the Gentiles (Matt. 8:10; 15:24). The writer even cited Isaiah 42:1–4, that Jesus would "proclaim justice to the Gentiles [nations] . . . and in his name the Gentiles will hope" (12:14–21). Yet the disciples had a hard time believing it. Could their Lord really be interested in "all nations"? They certainly weren't.

(continued on next page)

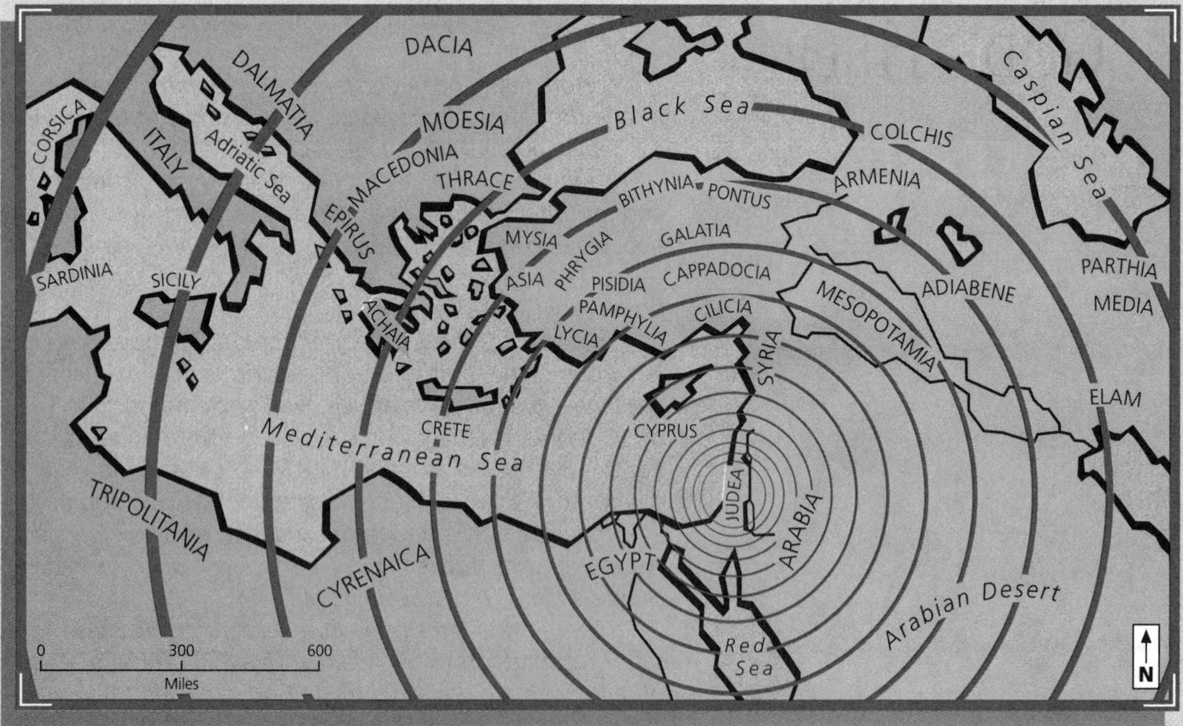

"To All the Nations"

Jesus Sends His Followers into the World

16 Now the eleven disciples went to Galilee, to the
mountain to which Jesus had directed them. 17When they
28:18 saw him, they worshiped him; but some
doubted. 18And Jesus came and said to
them, "All authority in heaven and on earth has been given
28:19 to me. 19Go therefore and make disciples
of all nations, baptizing them in the
name of the Father and of the Son and of the Holy Spirit,
20and teaching them to obey everything that I have commanded you. And remember, I am with you always, to the
end of the age."[u]

[u]Other ancient authorities add *Amen*

Jesus' Power

A CLOSER LOOK 28:18 *The power that gave Jesus authority and that He promised to His followers (vv. 18–19) was not the power of force or political authority. It was an ability to accomplish a very specific task. See "Power," Acts 1:8.*

(continued from previous page)

Are we? It's easy to pay lip service to the idea that Jesus cares for the whole world. But isn't it easier to follow a Christ that fits comfortably into our own culture?

Culture, after all, is the key. Jesus told His Galilean followers to "make disciples," and they did—*Jewish* disciples. But they experienced profound culture shock when the Holy Spirit brought new groups into the fellowship, including Hellenist disciples (Acts 6:1–7), Samaritan disciples (8:4–25), and eventually even Gentile disciples of all kinds (10:1—11:18; 15:1–21).

Today the bulk of new disciples are non-white and non-Western. Not surprisingly, they bring very different cultural perspectives into the church. So one of the greatest challenges believers will face in the coming years is the same one that the original disciples faced at the inauguration of the movement: to not only believe but to *accept* that Jesus really is for all the nations. ◆

One of the key people responsible for helping communicate the message about Christ throughout the Roman world was "Luke, the Gentile Author." Find out more about him at the introduction to Luke.

The spread of the gospel to "all nations" began in an explosive way just a few days after Jesus' words in Matthew 28. See "A Surprising First Fulfillment of Acts 1:8," Acts 2:8–11.

As the gospel spread to people of different cultures, there was always the danger of believers going their separate ways. That's why Paul challenged Christians to pursue unity in the body of Christ and charity among the peoples of the world. See "Are We One People?" Rom. 11:13–24.

The Action-oriented Christ

There are four Gospels. Which one should you read first? Probably the Gospel of Mark. Even though it is placed second among the four, it's an ideal book for "entry-level" readers. Like a television drama, Mark's Gospel portrays the life of Jesus in simple, straightforward, action-packed vignettes. In fact, *action* is the hallmark of the book: Jesus reveals Himself here more by what He does than by what He says.

If you like stories, you'll love reading Mark. The author opens with a view of crowds streaming into the wilderness to be baptized by John the Baptist (1:4–5). A close-up shows John predicting the coming of the Messiah (1:6–8). Then Jesus appears, and John baptizes Him (1:9–11). Dissolve to another wilderness setting, where Jesus endures a lonely vigil as Satan tests Him, wild beasts haunt Him, and angels attend Him (1:12–13). Time passes, and arid wilderness gives way to seaside Galilee, where Jesus launches His ministry with an appeal for repentance (1:14–15).

And so it goes, as Mark heaps up scenes of an action-oriented Christ, going places and doing things. The overall message is that Jesus is the Son of God (1:1, 11; 9:7; 14:61–62; 15:39) who came "not to be served but to serve, and to give his life a ransom for many" (10:45).

The Gospel According to Mark

Jesus is the Son of God who came to serve.

C O N T E N T S

Mark's Vivid Portrayal of People

A R T I C L E S

Life—The Big Picture (12:28–34)

Unfortunately, many Christians have developed some dangerous attitudes that push God to the fringes of their lives. Some popular myths need to be explored—and exploded.

A Parting Gift (14:3–9)

Sensing that her days with Jesus were drawing to a close, a woman poured out a costly gift of oil worth about a year's wages.

Why So Many Marys? (15:40)

Mary was a popular name in first-century Palestine. It honored one of Israel's most famous women.

Faith Impacts the World (16:15–16)

Jesus had global impact in mind for His followers. But spreading Christ's message and having an impact requires that we understand how our world operates.

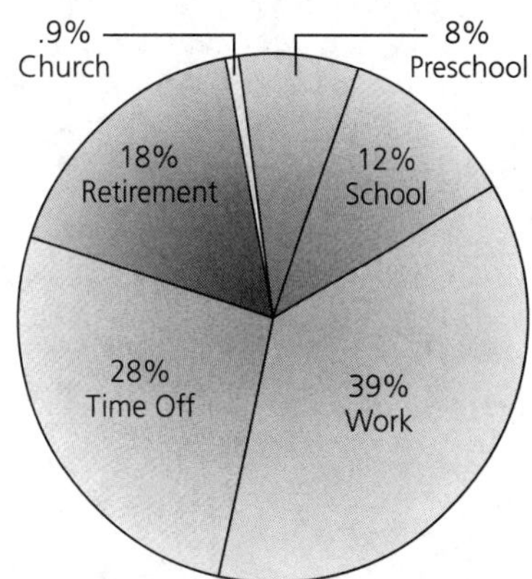

HOW THE TYPICAL 75-YEAR-OLD AMERICAN WILL HAVE SPENT LIFE

TALES OF THE FISHERMAN

The vivid, direct style of Mark's Gospel and its attention to detail provide a sense of authenticity and immediacy that could come only from an eyewitness to the events recorded. But was Mark himself a participant in the story? Probably not.

The book never mentions the name of its author. However, in about A.D. 125, Papias, bishop of Hierapolis in Asia Minor, claimed that Mark created this Gospel by writing down Peter's recollections of Jesus' life. Subsequent tradition agrees with Papias in ascribing the book to Mark.

So possibly what we have here are the memoirs of Peter. Ministering to Christians in Rome, he may have recalled his memories of Jesus in order to create a Gospel for Christians under persecution by Nero. If so, it's no wonder that the narrative reads so easily: as a fisherman, Peter was probably quite skilled in holding an audience with a good story.

Fortunately, Mark wrote it all down. Mark had not followed Jesus during His lifetime—though he may have been present at the arrest of Jesus, leaving an "anonymous signature" in the story of a young man who fled naked (Mark 14:51–52). Mark was a native of Jerusalem, and the church often met for prayer at his mother's house (Acts 12:12). Thanks to his cousin Barnabas (Col. 4:10), he was mentored in the faith (Acts 15:37–39) and became a valued associate of Paul (2 Tim. 4:11) and Peter (1 Pet. 5:13). Mark probably traveled with Peter to Rome, where tradition holds that he composed his Gospel in the early 60s. ◆

John Mark

Church tradition holds that John Mark was known to have stumpy fingers. Evidently that did not impede him from writing the first Gospel. Turn to Acts 15:37 to learn more about the man Peter described as "my son" (1 Pet. 5:13).

John the Baptist Prepares the Way

1 The beginning of the good news[a] of Jesus Christ, the
Son of God.[b]
2 As it is written in the prophet Isaiah,[c]
"See, I am sending my messenger ahead of you,[d]
who will prepare your way;
3 the voice of one crying out in the wilderness:
'Prepare the way of the Lord,
make his paths straight,' "
4John the baptizer appeared[e] in the wilderness, proclaiming
a baptism of repentance for the forgive-
ness of sins. 5And people from the whole
Judean countryside and all the people of Jerusalem were
going out to him, and were baptized by him in the river
Jordan, confessing their sins. 6Now John
was clothed with camel's hair, with a
leather belt around his waist, and he ate locusts and wild
honey. 7He proclaimed, "The one who is more powerful
than I is coming after me; I am not worthy to stoop down

1:5

1:6

(Bible text continued on page 130)

[a]Or *gospel* [b]Other ancient authorities lack *the Son of God* [c]Other ancient authorities read *in the prophets* [d]Gk *before your face* [e]Other ancient authorities read *John was baptizing*

John, a Voice Crying in the Wilderness

All four Gospels present John as a preacher in the wilderness (Matt. 3:1; Mark 1:4; Luke 3:2; John 1:23). Even in his own day he must have seemed odd. He lived in the wild. He ate locusts and honey. He seemed given to extremes of humility—for example, declaring that "[Jesus] must increase, but I must decrease" (John 3:30), and that he was not worthy even to loose Jesus' sandal strap (1:27).

But the main thing that impressed people about John was that he fearlessly preached a message of repentance to any who would listen—and many did. Crowds flocked to hear him from throughout Judea, including the main city of Jerusalem. In addition to everyday folk, he attracted great sinners like the tax gatherers, respectable socialites like the religious leaders, and even Gentiles like the Roman soldiers. What was his winsome message? "Brood of vipers! Who warned you to flee from the wrath to come?" (Luke 3:7).

As one might have expected, he eventually offended the wrong person—Herodias, wife of the King Herod (see "Hateful Herodias," Matt. 14:3). John condemned the

Personality Profile: John the Baptist

FOR YOUR INFO 1:6 **In his day, often confused with:** The Old Testament prophet, Elijah; one of the other prophets; the Messiah.

Home: Born and raised in a town of Judah, but lived most of his adult life in the Judean wilderness, near the Jordan River.

Family: Son of Zechariah and Elizabeth.

Occupation: Preacher and prophet.

Best known today for: Preparing the way for Jesus the Messiah.

royal couple for their illicit marriage. Outraged, Herodias had her husband arrest the prophet and badgered him to execute him. But the king refused, fearing to kill a man he knew to be holy and just. However, Herodias knew ways to accomplish her evil ends, and eventually had her way (Mark 6:14–29).

John's influence continued to live on after his death. Several of his disciples became followers of Jesus (for example, Andrew, John 1:35–40). And nearly 30 years later, when Paul arrived at Ephesus to preach the gospel, he encountered a group of John's disciples (Acts 19:1–7).

The last of the Old Testament prophets, John was declared by Jesus to be the greatest of men (Matt. 11:11–14). He fulfilled the purpose for which he was sent—to pave the way for Jesus. ◆

Even evaluated by the standards of his own day, John the Baptist reflected none of the outward trappings of a successful ministry. See "John the Street Preacher," Matt. 3:4, to learn about the "wealth" of John.

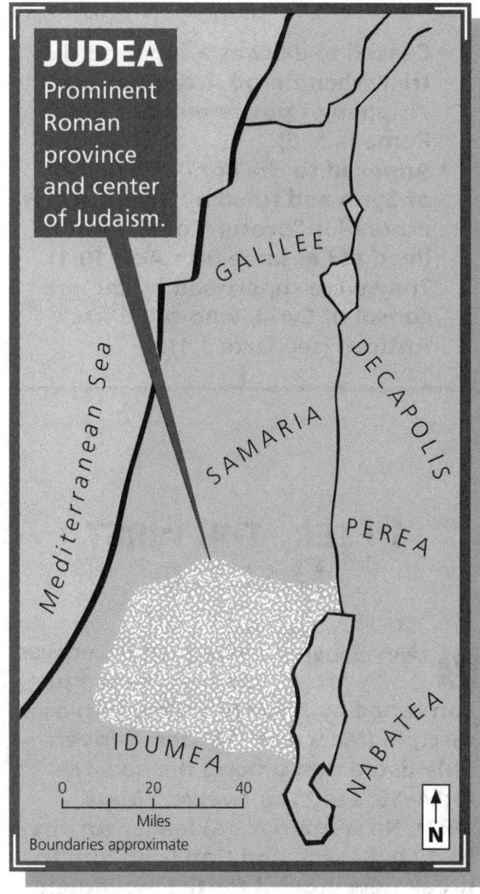

Judea

YOU ARE THERE 1:5

- **The most prominent Roman province of Palestine in the first century.**
- **Contained four distinctive types of land: coastal plains near the Mediterranean Sea, lowlands in the south, hill country, and desert.**
- **Named by the Greeks and Romans from a term used of the Hebrew captives who had returned to the promised land after the Babylonian exile, most of whom were of the tribe of Judah.**
- **Under the Persians, a district administered by a governor, usually a Jew (Ezra 5:8; Hag. 1:14; 2:2).**

(continued on next page)

(continued from previous page)

- **Ceased to exist as a separate district when Herod Archelaus was stripped of power and banished to Rome (A.D. 6).**
- **Annexed to the Roman province of Syria and ruled by imperial governors (or "procurators") who lived at Caesarea (see Acts 10:1). They were supervised by the proconsul of Syria, who ruled from Antioch (see Luke 3:1).**

PETER, THE FIRST DISCIPLE

FOR YOUR INFO 1:16

Fisherman Peter was the first known person called by Jesus to follow Him as a disciple (Mark 1:16–18) and is invariably listed first among the apostles (3:14–16; see "The Twelve," Matt. 10:2). He was a natural leader for the early believers, and God used him to break new ground for the movement that Jesus initiated. Among Peter's "firsts":

- **First apostle to recognize Jesus as the Christ (Matt. 16:13–17).**
- **First ordinary person to walk on water (Matt. 14:28–30).**
- **First apostle to see the risen Lord (Luke 24:34; 1 Cor. 15:5).**
- **Preached the first sermon after the coming of the Holy Spirit (Acts 2:14–40).**
- **First apostle to break the barrier between Jews and Gentiles (Acts 10:1—11:18).**
- **First apostle to be associated with the writing of a Gospel. Early church tradition says that Peter died in Rome. Papias (A.D. 125) claimed that Peter's preaching led his interpreter, Mark, to write the first Gospel.**

and untie the thong of his sandals. 8I have baptized you
with[f] water; but he will baptize you with[f] the Holy Spirit."

John Baptizes Jesus

9 In those days Jesus came from Nazareth of Galilee and
was baptized by John in the Jordan. 10And just as he was
coming up out of the water, he saw the heavens torn apart
and the Spirit descending like a dove on him. 11And a voice
came from heaven, "You are my Son, the Beloved;[g] with you
I am well pleased."

Jesus Faces Temptation in the Wilderness

1:12–13

12 And the Spirit immediately drove
him out into the wilderness. 13He was in

(Bible text continued on page 132)

[f]Or *in* [g]Or *my beloved Son*

The "Real" World

A CLOSER LOOK 1:12–13

Jesus understands real life. He faced real temptations—the same temptations that show up every day in the "real" world. See "You Don't Understand!" at Matt. 4:3.

PERSONALITY PROFILE: SIMON PETER

Also known as: Simon (his given name); renamed Cephas (Aramaic), or Peter (Greek), or "The Rock" or "Rocky" (English) by Christ.

Home: Bethsaida and Capernaum on the north shore of the Sea of Galilee.

Family: His father's name was Jonah; his younger brother was Andrew; he was married and his wife traveled with him as he spread the message about Jesus.

Occupation: Commercial fisherman; later one of Jesus' first representatives.

Best known today for: His declaration that Jesus was the Christ, and his denial of Christ.

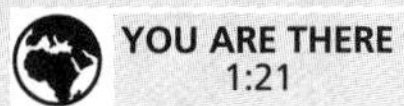

The Synagogue

In Jesus' day, synagogues (v. 21) were common throughout Palestine. Synagogues (from the Greek sunagōgē, *meaning "a leading or bringing together") were local congregations of Jews that met for the reading and explanation of Scripture and for prayer. The original emphasis was not on preaching but instruction in the law of Moses.*

Synagogues began during the Babylonian captivity experience. Lacking a temple but longing for communion with God, Jewish captives in Babylon met in local groups for worship and Torah reading. Some of the captives eventually returned to their land, where Zerubbabel rebuilt the temple and Ezra the scribe promoted the reading of the Law and prayer (Neh. 8). But many Jews remained in Persia and spread elsewhere, notably to Alexandria, Egypt. Both in and outside of Palestine, Jews continued to meet in synagogues, which became centers of community life.

Some synagogues functioned as local courts of justice which could sentence offenders as well as inflict the punishment of scourging (Matt. 10:17; 23:34). They also became grammar schools teaching children to read. And much of Jewish social life revolved around synagogue activities.

By Jesus' time, synagogues were well-established and had customary officials, including:

Elders, a board made up of devout and respected men who regulated the policies of the synagogue. Custom seated the elders in the chief seats at the front of the synagogue (see Matt. 23:6).

A ruler of the synagogue, appointed by the elders, whose duty was to attend to matters concerning the building and the planning of the services. There could be more than one ruler. On one occasion, a ruler named Jairus approached Jesus about healing his daughter (Mark 5:21–43).

The minister (chazzan), who had charge of the sacred scrolls kept in the ark, attended to the lamps, and kept the building clean. If an offender was found guilty by the council of elders, this official was the one who administered the number of lashes prescribed for the scourging.

During the week he taught children how to read.

The delegate of the congregation. This was not a permanent office. Before each service the ruler chose a capable person to read the Scripture lesson, lead in prayer, and preach or comment on the Scripture. Jesus was selected for this office in the synagogue in Nazareth (Luke 4:16–20).

The interpreter. The Scriptures were written in Hebrew, but by Jesus' day most Jews in Palestine spoke Aramaic, a language related to Hebrew but different enough to call for an interpreter.

Almoners, two or three persons who received money or other necessities for the poor.

A synagogue could not be formed unless there were at least ten Jewish men in the community—apparently a condition met in a great many towns throughout the Roman world, as Paul found synagogues at Damascus (Acts 9:2), Salamis (13:5), Antioch in Pisidia (13:14), Iconium (14:1), Thessalonica (17:1), Berea (17:10), Athens (17:16–17), and Ephesus (19:1, 8). Indeed, whenever Paul entered a city to preach the gospel, he invariably spoke first in the synagogue before reaching out to the larger community.

Not surprisingly, synagogue worship had a profound influence on Christian worship. The Jewish service began with a recitation of the *shema* by the

(continued on next page)

(continued from previous page)

people. *Shema* ("Hear") is the first Hebrew word in the passage, "Hear, O Israel: The Lord our God, the Lord is one!" (Deut. 6:4–9). The speaker for the day then led the congregation in prayer as they stood facing Jerusalem with hands extended. At the close of the prayer the people said "Amen."

The chosen speaker stood and read the Law while the interpreter translated it into Aramaic. Then a passage from the Prophets was read and translated. For the commentary or sermon, the speaker usually sat down. After the sermon, a priest, if one was present, pronounced a benediction and the people said "Amen." Since the earliest Christians were Jews, they tended to follow this synagogue pattern in their own assemblies. ◆

the wilderness forty days, tempted by Satan; and he was
with the wild beasts; and the angels waited on him.

Jesus Launches His Ministry

1:14

14 Now after John was arrested, Jesus
came to Galilee, proclaiming the good
news[h] of God,[i] 15and saying, "The time is fulfilled, and the
kingdom of God has come near;[j] repent, and believe in the
good news."[h]

Jesus Calls Fishermen to Follow Him

1:16 see pg. 130

16 As Jesus passed along the Sea of
Galilee, he saw Simon and his brother
Andrew casting a net into the sea—for they were fishermen. 17And Jesus said to them, "Follow me and I will make
you fish for people." 18And immediately they left their nets
and followed him. 19As he went a little farther, he saw
James son of Zebedee and his brother John, who were in
their boat mending the nets. 20Immediately he called them;
and they left their father Zebedee in the boat with the hired
men, and followed him.

[h]Or *gospel* [i]Other ancient authorities read *of the kingdom* [j]Or *is at hand*

JESUS THE GALILEAN

In New Testament times there were two Galilees, upper and lower. Jesus of Nazareth grew up in densely populated lower Galilee. Among its urban centers He carried out most of His ministry (Mark 1:14). In fact, as many as eleven of His twelve disciples may have come from that region, the exception being Judas Iscariot (see "The Twelve," Matt. 10:2).

Galilee represented the periphery of traditional Jewish life, a cultural frontier between the Hebraic and Graeco-Roman worlds. As a result, Galileans were scorned by their neighbors in Judea. Judeans used the term "Galilean" as a synonym for fool, heathen, sinner, or worse. Most significantly for Jesus, they were certain that no prophet could come from Galilee (John 7:52).

Yet, a prophet did come from Galilee. It was there that Jesus announced the character of His message (Luke 4:14–19) and demonstrated its power. He performed at least 33 known miracles there, and of 32 recorded parables, 19 were spoken in Galilee.

Demons Are Cast Out at Capernaum

1:21 see pg. 131

21 They went to Capernaum; and
when the sabbath came, he entered the
synagogue and taught. 22They were astounded at his teaching, for he taught them as one having authority, and not as
the scribes. 23Just then there was in their synagogue a man
with an unclean spirit, 24and he cried out, "What have you
to do with us, Jesus of Nazareth? Have you come to destroy
us? I know who you are, the Holy One of God." 25But Jesus
rebuked him, saying, "Be silent, and come out of him!"
26And the unclean spirit, convulsing him and crying with a
loud voice, came out of him. 27They were all amazed, and
they kept on asking one another, "What is this? A new
teaching—with authority! He[k] commands even the unclean
spirits, and they obey him." 28At once his fame began to
spread throughout the surrounding region of Galilee.

Jesus Heals Simon's Mother-in-Law

1:29–31 see pg. 134

29 As soon as they[l] left the synagogue,
they entered the house of Simon and An-
drew, with James and John. 30Now Simon's mother-in-law
was in bed with a fever, and they told him about her at

[k]Or *A new teaching! With authority he* [l]Other ancient authorities read *he*

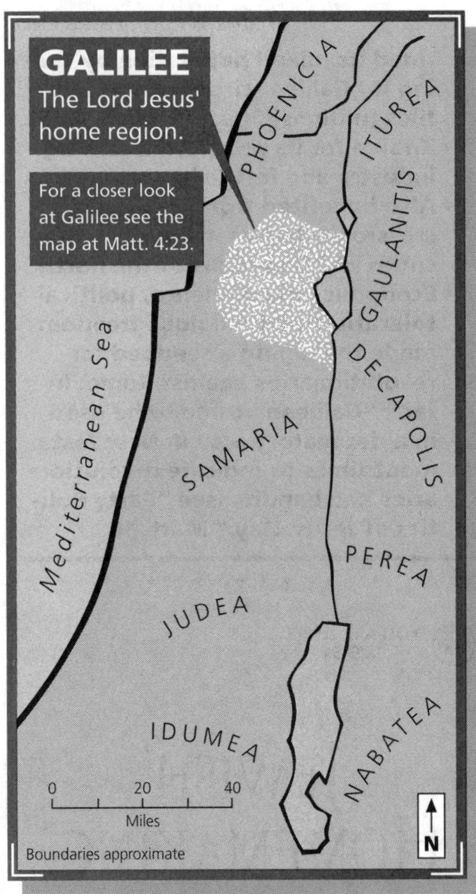

In short, the Galilee district was also the arena for Jesus' public ministry. He demonstrated that His gospel was not just for the elite, but for all. It was for those living at the margins of traditional, acceptable society. It did not start at the top and move down, but at the bottom and moved up, from the periphery to the center.

And yet, there is little evidence that His message ever took firm root in Galilee after He left. His predictions about Capernaum, Chorazin, and other Galilean cities came true (Matt. 11:20–24). In their unbelief they rejected Him—their one and only Prophet and King. ◆

"Can any good thing come out of Galilee?" Jesus' enemies cried. To find out, see John 7:52.

The Sea of Galilee was no place to be caught in a storm. Sudden outbursts of violent weather occur there to this day. See "What Kind of Storm Was This?" Luke 8:22–25.

GALILEE

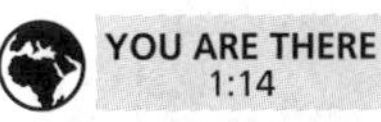

- **The Roman province of northern Palestine extending from Mount Hermon in the north to Mount Carmel in the south, between the Mediterranean Sea and the Jordan River.**
- **Unlike Judea, remained under the rule of the Herods (see Acts 12:1–2) during the first half of the first century.**
- **Herod the Great depopulated Judea by resettling Jews in new or rebuilt cities in Samaria and Galilee.**
- **Galilee, meaning "circuit," "district," or "cylinder," was surrounded and heavily influenced by Gentiles. Jews to the south de-**

(continued on next page)

(continued from previous page)

rided its mixed population by calling it "Galilee [circle] of the Gentiles [nations]" (Is. 9:1; Matt. 4:15).
- **Known for its prosperous fishing industry and fertile lands.**
- **Also benefited from trade as a crossroads between Egypt to the south and Damascus to the north.**
- **Economic independence, political toleration, and religious freedom made the region a seedbed for revolutionaries against Rome. In fact, "Galilean" came to be used in a derogatory way in New Testament times to indicate revolutionaries and bandits (see "Party Politics of Jesus' Day," Matt. 16:1).**

once. 31He came and took her by the hand and lifted her
up. Then the fever left her, and she began to serve them.

Many Healed in Galilee

32 That evening, at sundown, they
brought to him all who were sick or possessed with demons. 33And the whole city was gathered
around the door. 34And he cured many who were sick with

The Great Physician

A CLOSER LOOK 1:32–34

Throughout His ministry, Jesus healed many people whose diseases made them outcasts of society. On the other hand, He also healed several well-connected folks whose maladies were of prime concern to their families, friends, and employers. See " 'Who Sinned?': Health and Disease in the Bible," John 9:2–3.

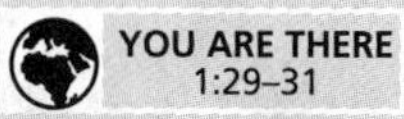

Jewish Homemaking

Mark recounts Jesus' visit to the home of two of His new followers, Simon and Andrew. There He healed Simon's mother-in-law, after which, the text says, "she began to serve them." Her service likely involved far more than cooking a meal.

In Jewish homes of the day, work began at sunrise. After a simple breakfast of curds and bread, the women went to the nearest well or stream to fill their jars with fresh water for the day's needs.

Some of the water was used to make the daily bread. The women ground kernels of wheat or barley by hand on the family millstone (see "Grinding the Grain," Luke 17:35), then added water and some of the previous day's dough that had yeast in it. Kneaded and left to rise, the dough was shaped into several large, flat disks and baked in the household oven. The oven was fueled by grasses and brush gathered by the women and their children.

Other chores included spinning wool, weaving, making clothes and linens, mending, washing, producing pottery and other utensils for cooking, and preparing food. Far more than hobbies, these tasks were absolutely necessary to the family's survival. In that pre-industrial society, each household had to rely on its own labor and skills. Women acquired these from their mothers and in turn passed them on to their children.

Perhaps for that reason, first-century Jewish women enjoyed a "seamlessness" in their lives between work and home: the two were not separate categories of life, but

various diseases, and cast out many demons; and he would
not permit the demons to speak, because they knew him.
35 In the morning, while it was still very dark, he got up
and went out to a deserted place, and there he prayed.
36And Simon and his companions hunted for him. 37When
they found him, they said to him, "Everyone is searching
for you." 38He answered, "Let us go on to the neighboring
towns, so that I may proclaim the message there also; for
that is what I came out to do." 39And he went throughout
Galilee, proclaiming the message in their synagogues and
casting out demons.
40 A leper[m] came to him begging him, and kneeling[n] he
said to him, "If you choose, you can make me clean."
41Moved with pity,[o] Jesus[p] stretched out his hand and

[m]The terms *leper* and *leprosy* can refer to several diseases [n]Other ancient authorities lack *kneeling* [o]Other ancient authorities read *anger* [p]Gk *he*

parts of an integrated whole. Caring for children and providing for essentials such as food and clothing were highly valued in Hebrew culture.

Nor was a woman's work confined to material needs. The wife provided essential leadership in the home, shaping the cultural and religious values of her children. Formal schooling was rare, so she tutored them in craft skills and literacy. She was also expected to help them follow the customs and faith of Israel. It was through her that her children's Jewish heritage was determined.

The woman was responsible for preparing the home for the Sabbath. She filled the lamps with olive oil, prepared Sabbath food and special treats, and collected an extra day's water. No wonder that on each Sabbath, as part of the evening ceremony, her husband would recite to her Proverbs 31:10–31, an acknowledgement of her vital and varied work. ◆

Women were the primary caregivers to infants and children. See "Children and Childcare," Matt. 19:14.

Not all first-century women centered their lives around domestic responsibilities totally. Lydia was a successful businesswoman in the purple trade (see profile at Acts 16:14) and Priscilla manufactured tents with her husband (see profile at Rom. 16:3–5).

Evidence from the first century reveals that women worked as wool workers, midwives, hairdressers, nurses, vendors, entertainers, political leaders, and even construction workers. See "Women and Work in the Ancient World," 1 Cor. 7:32–35.

"LET US GO ON TO THE NEIGHBORING TOWNS. . . ." —Mark 1:38

touched him, and said to him, "I do choose. Be made
clean!" [42]Immediately the leprosy[q] left him, and he was
made clean. [43]After sternly warning him he sent him away
at once, [44]saying to him, "See that you say nothing to anyone; but go, show yourself to the priest, and offer for your
cleansing what Moses commanded, as a testimony to
them." [45]But he went out and began to proclaim it freely,
and to spread the word, so that Jesus[r] could no longer go
into a town openly, but stayed out in the country; and people came to him from every quarter.

Persistence Brings Healing and Forgiveness

2 When he returned to Capernaum after some days,
it was reported that he was at home. [2]So many gathered
around that there was no longer room for them, not even in
front of the door; and he was speaking the word to them.
2:3–17 [3]Then some people[s] came, bringing to
him a paralyzed man, carried by four of
them. [4]And when they could not bring him to Jesus
because of the crowd, they removed the roof above him;
and after having dug through it, they let down the mat on
which the paralytic lay. [5]When Jesus saw their faith, he said
to the paralytic, "Son, your sins are forgiven." [6]Now some
of the scribes were sitting there, questioning in their hearts,
[7]"Why does this fellow speak in this way? It is blasphemy!
Who can forgive sins but God alone?" [8]At once Jesus
perceived in his spirit that they were discussing these
questions among themselves; and he said to them, "Why do
you raise such questions in your hearts? [9]Which is easier, to
say to the paralytic, 'Your sins are forgiven,' or to say, 'Stand
up and take your mat and walk'? [10]But so that you may
know that the Son of Man has authority on earth to forgive
sins"—he said to the paralytic— [11]"I say to you, stand up,
take your mat and go to your home." [12]And he stood up,
and immediately took the mat and went out before all of
them; so that they were all amazed and glorified God,
saying, "We have never seen anything like this!"

THE WHOLE CROWD GATHERED AROUND HIM, AND HE TAUGHT THEM.
—Mark 2:13

Levi (Matthew) Called

13 Jesus[t] went out again beside the sea; the whole crowd
gathered around him, and he taught them. [14]As he was
walking along, he saw Levi son of Alphaeus sitting at the

(Bible text continued on page 138)

[q]The terms *leper* and *leprosy* can refer to several diseases [r]Gk *he* [s]Gk *they* [t]Gk *He*

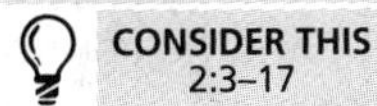

SIGNIFICANCE FOR LITTLE PEOPLE

Who really counts in life? Do those without position, power, health, or wealth really matter? Or is their only hope in somehow climbing to the top of the heap?

Each of the four Gospel writers helps the reader meet the significant people in Jesus' life. Most were distinctly insignificant when evaluated by the traditional criteria for importance. The paralytic let down from the roof (v. 3), for example, blended into the background until touched by Jesus. Likewise, the rest were generally not wealthy or famous, nor were they social, business, or government leaders. They were little people of the world with problems and needs similar to ours.

Note the cluster of people in each of the writers' first few chapters:

Matthew

- Four women touched by scandal (1:3, 5–6)
- A young couple dealing with a complicated engagement (1:18–21)
- Three advisors from a foreign government (2:1–12)
- Countless baby boys who are slaughtered (2:16–18)
- A wilderness man who becomes Jesus' forerunner (3:1–17)

Mark

- Four fishermen (1:16–20)
- A man oppressed by a demon (1:23–27)
- A feverish mother-in-law (1:29–31)
- Many sick and oppressed (1:32–34)
- An outcast leper (1:40–42)
- A paralytic (2:1–12)
- A despised tax-collector (2:13–17)

Luke

- A barren elderly couple (1:5–25)
- An expectant couple (1:26–38)
- A baby born amid confusion (1:57–80)
- Startled shepherds (2:8–20)
- An aged, saintly man (2:25–35)
- An elderly widow with a gift of prophecy (2:36–38)

John

- A puzzling religious pioneer (1:19–35)
- Two fishermen (1:35–42)
- The fishermen's friend (1:43–44)
- A skeptical critic (1:45–51)
- An enquirer who prefers a low profile (3:1–21)
- A minority woman touched by scandal (4:1–42)
- A nobleman's ill son (4:46–54)

As Scripture introduces the Savior, it shows us lots of little people, and for good reason: the people ready for God's help are not the ones insulated from trouble by possessions, health, or status, but those who know their needs. Brokenness makes one ready to turn to God for help. In Him is the forgiveness and hope that can overcome human limitation.

Are you trapped in the world's system of climbing over others to gain significance? Or have you allowed God to help you break that bondage? If so, are you following Jesus among the "little people," wherever they are struggling and groping for help? ◆

QUOTE UNQUOTE

CONSIDER THIS 2:17 *One modern-day writer intentionally seeks to broaden her appeal, in the spirit of Jesus' words about who it was He came to help:*

I do not write my books for either Christians or women. If I understand the Gospel, it tells us that we are to spread the Good News to all four corners of the world, not limiting the giving of light to people who already have seen the light. If my stories are incomprehensible to Jews or Muslims or Taoists, then I have failed as a Christian writer. We do not draw people to Christ by loudly discrediting what they believe, by telling them how wrong they are and how right we are, but by showing them a light that is so lovely that they want with all their hearts to know the source of it.

Madeleine L'Engle, *Walking On Water,* p. 122

tax booth, and he said to him, "Follow me." And he got up
and followed him.

Jesus Dines with Levi and His Friends

15 And as he sat at dinner[u] in Levi's[v] house, many tax
collectors and sinners were also sitting[w] with Jesus and his
disciples—for there were many who followed him. 16When
the scribes of[x] the Pharisees saw that he was eating with
sinners and tax collectors, they said to his disciples, "Why
2:17 does he eat[y] with tax collectors and sinners?" 17When Jesus heard this, he said
to them, "Those who are well have no need of a physician,
but those who are sick; I have come to call not the righteous but sinners."

Cloth and Wineskins

18 Now John's disciples and the Pharisees were fasting;
and people[z] came and said to him, "Why do John's disciples
and the disciples of the Pharisees fast, but your disciples do
not fast?" 19Jesus said to them, "The wedding guests cannot
fast while the bridegroom is with them, can they? As long
as they have the bridegroom with them, they cannot fast.
20The days will come when the bridegroom is taken away
from them, and then they will fast on that day.
21 "No one sews a piece of unshrunk cloth on an old
cloak; otherwise, the patch pulls away from it, the new
from the old, and a worse tear is made. 22And no one puts
new wine into old wineskins; otherwise, the wine will burst
the skins, and the wine is lost, and so are the skins; but one
puts new wine into fresh wineskins."[a]

Sabbath Controversies

2:23—3:6 23 One sabbath he was going through
the grainfields; and as they made their
way his disciples began to pluck heads of grain. 24The Pharisees said to him, "Look, why are they doing what is not
lawful on the sabbath?" 25And he said to them, "Have you
never read what David did when he and his companions

[u]Gk *reclined* [v]Gk *his* [w]Gk *reclining* [x]Other ancient authorities read *and* [y]Other ancient authorities add *and drink* [z]Gk *they* [a]Other ancient authorities lack *but one puts new wine into fresh wineskins*

No Tolerance for Intolerance

A CLOSER LOOK 2:23—3:6 *Some Pharisees were like some intolerant religionists of our own day, and Jesus refused to put up with them. See "Jesus Confronts the Legalists," Luke 6:1–11, for a discussion of the Sabbath controversies.*

were hungry and in need of food? 26He entered the house
of God, when Abiathar was high priest, and ate the bread of
the Presence, which it is not lawful for any but the priests
to eat, and he gave some to his companions." 27Then he
said to them, "The sabbath was made for humankind, and
not humankind for the sabbath; 28so the Son of Man is lord
even of the sabbath."

3 Again he entered the synagogue, and a man was there
who had a withered hand. 2They watched him to see
whether he would cure him on the sabbath, so that they
might accuse him. 3And he said to the man who had the
withered hand, "Come forward." 4Then he said to them, "Is
it lawful to do good or to do harm on the sabbath, to save
life or to kill?" But they were silent. 5He looked around at
them with anger; he was grieved at their hardness of heart
and said to the man, "Stretch out your hand." He stretched
it out, and his hand was restored. 6The Pharisees went out
and immediately conspired with the Herodians against him,
how to destroy him.

"THE SABBATH WAS MADE FOR HUMANKIND, AND NOT HUMANKIND FOR THE SABBATH."
—Mark 2:27

Massive Crowds Follow Jesus

7 Jesus departed with his disciples to the sea, and a great
multitude from Galilee followed him; 8hearing all that he
was doing, they came to him in great numbers from Judea,
Jerusalem, Idumea, beyond the Jordan, and the region
around Tyre and Sidon. 9He told his disciples to have a boat
ready for him because of the crowd, so that they would not
crush him; 10for he had cured many, so that all who had
diseases pressed upon him to touch him. 11Whenever the
unclean spirits saw him, they fell down before him and
shouted, "You are the Son of God!" 12But he sternly ordered
them not to make him known.

Jesus Calls the Twelve

3:13–19

13 He went up the mountain and
called to him those whom he wanted,
and they came to him. 14And he appointed twelve, whom
he also named apostles,[b] to be with him, and to be sent out
to proclaim the message, 15and to have authority to cast out

[b]Other ancient authorities lack *whom he also named apostles*

A Diverse Group

A CLOSER LOOK 3:13–19

The twelve that Jesus appointed to be His followers came from an interesting variety of backgrounds. See Matt. 10:2.

demons. 16So he appointed the twelve:[c] Simon (to whom he
gave the name Peter); 17James son of Zebedee and John the
brother of James (to whom he gave the name Boanerges,
that is, Sons of Thunder); 18and Andrew, and Philip, and
Bartholomew, and Matthew, and Thomas, and James son of
Alphaeus, and Thaddaeus, and Simon the Cananaean,
19and Judas Iscariot, who betrayed him.

"WHO ARE MY MOTHER AND MY BROTHERS?" —Mark 3:33

Scribes Call Jesus Satanic

Then he went home; 20and the crowd came together
again, so that they could not even eat. 21When his family
heard it, they went out to restrain him, for people were
3:22 saying, "He has gone out of his mind."
22And the scribes who came down from
Jerusalem said, "He has Beelzebul, and by the ruler of the
demons he casts out demons." 23And he called them to
him, and spoke to them in parables, "How can Satan cast
out Satan? 24If a kingdom is divided against itself, that kingdom cannot stand. 25And if a house is divided against itself,
that house will not be able to stand. 26And if Satan has risen
up against himself and is divided, he cannot stand, but his
end has come. 27But no one can enter a strong man's house
and plunder his property without first tying up the strong
man; then indeed the house can be plundered.
28 "Truly I tell you, people will be forgiven for their sins
and whatever blasphemies they utter; 29but whoever blasphemes against the Holy Spirit can never have forgiveness,
but is guilty of an eternal sin"— 30for they had said, "He
has an unclean spirit."

[c]Other ancient authorities lack *So he appointed the twelve*

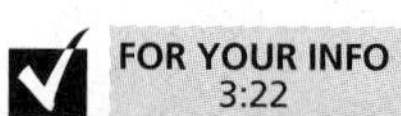

PAGAN GODS IN THE NEW TESTAMENT

Name	Description	Reference
BEELZEBUL	A heathen god considered by the Jews to be the supreme evil spirit	Mark 3:22
DIANA	In Roman mythology, the goddess of the moon, hunting, wild animals, and virginity	Acts 19:24, 27–28
HERMES	The Greek god of commerce, science, invention, cunning, eloquence, and theft	Acts 14:12
MAMMON	The Aramaic word for *riches*, personified by Jesus as a false god	Luke 16:9, 11
MOLOCH	National god of the Ammonites whose worship involved child sacrifice	Acts 7:43
REMPHAN	An idol worshiped by Israel in the wilderness	Acts 7:43
TWIN BROTHERS	In Greek mythology, the twin sons of Zeus	Acts 28:11
ZEUS	The supreme god of the ancient Greeks	Acts 14:12–13

"Who Are My Mother and Brothers?"

3:31–35

31 Then his mother and his brothers
came; and standing outside, they sent to
him and called him. 32A crowd was sitting around him; and
they said to him, "Your mother and your brothers and sisters[d] are outside, asking for you." 33And he replied, "Who
are my mother and my brothers?" 34And looking at those
who sat around him, he said, "Here are my mother and my
brothers! 35Whoever does the will of God is my brother and
sister and mother."

Parables by the Sea: Soils

4 Again he began to teach beside the sea. Such a very
large crowd gathered around him that he got into a
boat on the sea and sat there, while the whole crowd was
beside the sea on the land. 2He began to
teach them many things in parables, and
in his teaching he said to them: 3"Listen!
A sower went out to sow. 4And as he
sowed, some seed fell on the path, and the birds came and
ate it up. 5Other seed fell on rocky ground, where it did not
have much soil, and it sprang up quickly, since it had no
depth of soil. 6And when the sun rose, it was scorched; and
since it had no root, it withered away. 7Other seed fell
among thorns, and the thorns grew up and choked it, and
it yielded no grain. 8Other seed fell into good soil and
brought forth grain, growing up and increasing and yielding thirty and sixty and a hundredfold." 9And he said, "Let
anyone with ears to hear listen!"

4:2 see pg. 144

4:3–20 see pg. 142

The Purpose of Parables

10 When he was alone, those who were around him
along with the twelve asked him about the parables. 11And
he said to them, "To you has been given the secret[e] of the
kingdom of God, but for those outside, everything comes
in parables; 12in order that

'they may indeed look, but not perceive,
and may indeed listen, but not understand;
so that they may not turn again and be forgiven.' "

13 And he said to them, "Do you not understand this
parable? Then how will you understand all the parables?
14The sower sows the word. 15These are the ones on the
path where the word is sown: when they hear, Satan imme-

[d]Other ancient authorities lack *and sisters* [e]Or *mystery*

For or Against Family?

CONSIDER THIS 3:31–35 **Conflict seems inevitable within families. Family members can always find something to disagree about—personal values, current events, politics, possessions, sex, money, feelings. Why do some of the most bitter fights occur between people who married for love? How can people who are so familiar with each other sometimes find themselves so far apart?**

One reason is that families are unions of sinners, and sinners will be themselves no matter how intense their love and commitment for each other (1 John 1:8, 10). This has been so from the beginning: the first eight families in Scripture displayed many kinds of dysfunction, revealing their condition as sinful human beings. Perhaps God recorded their stories to let us know that even though He instituted the family unit, families are made up of sinners who will inevitably hurt each other.

Was Jesus "too good" to associate with His family of origin? His words in Mark 3:33–35 might seem to imply that. But He was merely distinguishing between human expectations about how families should relate and what the values of the kingdom had to say about family relations. He was not against His own parents and siblings; He just wanted to stress obedience to God.

"His own people" had already shown that they understood very little about Jesus or the values of His kingdom (vv. 20–21). They were limited by their own sinfulness, and needed God's help like everyone else.

Scripture has much to say about healthy ways families can interrelate. See "The Family: A Call to Long-term Work," Eph. 5:21.

diately comes and takes away the word that is sown in
them. [16]And these are the ones sown on rocky ground:
when they hear the word, they immediately receive it with
joy. [17]But they have no root, and endure only for a while;
then, when trouble or persecution arises on account of the
word, immediately they fall away.[f] [18]And others are those
sown among the thorns: these are the ones who hear the
word, [19]but the cares of the world, and the lure of wealth,
and the desire for other things come in and choke the
word, and it yields nothing. [20]And these are the ones sown
on the good soil: they hear the word and accept it and bear
fruit, thirty and sixty and a hundredfold."

Warnings

21 He said to them, "Is a lamp brought in to be put under the bushel basket, or under the bed, and not on the
lampstand? [22]For there is nothing hidden, except to be disclosed; nor is anything secret, except to come to light. [23]Let
anyone with ears to hear listen!" [24]And he said to them,
"Pay attention to what you hear; the measure you give will

[f]Or *stumble*

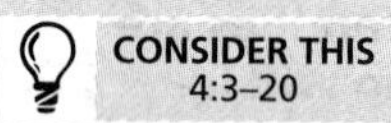

CONSIDER THIS
4:3–20

Is Your Witness Falling on Deaf Ears?

Do you find some of your coworkers or neighbors totally uninterested in the Christian faith? Are some even openly hostile? Have you become a target for their venom?

Jesus called us to be His witnesses (Acts 1:6–8), but that is not a call to convert others. Conversion is the responsibility of the Holy Spirit (John 16:8–11). That means that we need not measure our success in witnessing by the number who respond. If that were the case, Jesus would have often been considered a failure: many who heard Him—and even some who followed Him—turned out to be uninterested (John 6:60–66).

The fact is that people are in various conditions when it comes to spiritual matters, as Jesus' story of the four kinds of soils illustrates (Mark 4:3–20). One thing we as "farmers" can't do is change the soil. But we can offer good seed and do the best we can to nurture whatever faith sprouts up (1 Cor. 3:7–9). One way to do that is by continually working out our faith in day-to-day life (Phil. 2:12–13; James 2:14–26), making it available for others to consider rather than hiding it (Mark 4:21–23). How others react is between them and God.

be the measure you get, and still more will be given you.
25For to those who have, more will be given; and from
those who have nothing, even what they have will be taken
away."

A Growing Seed

26 He also said, "The kingdom of God is as if someone
would scatter seed on the ground, 27and would sleep and
rise night and day, and the seed would sprout and grow, he
does not know how. 28The earth produces of itself, first the
stalk, then the head, then the full grain in the head. 29But
when the grain is ripe, at once he goes in with his sickle,
because the harvest has come."

A Mustard Seed

30 He also said, "With what can we compare the kingdom of God, or what parable will we use for it? 31It is like a
mustard seed, which, when sown upon the ground, is the

(Bible text continued on page 145)

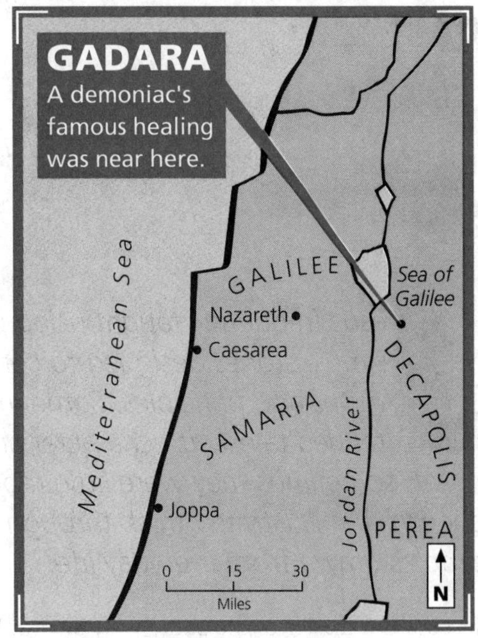

GADARA

YOU ARE THERE 5:1

- **A town located six miles southeast of the Sea of Galilee, east of the Jordan on the edge of the Arabian desert.**
- **Surrounding region known as the country of the Gadarenes (Mark 5:1; Luke 8:26) or Gergesenes (Matt. 8:28), but see the textual footnotes for variants.**

That's not to suggest that we should be detached or uncaring about others and their responses. Scripture challenges us to love others as we have been loved. One way is to make available to them our experience of faith—and make ourselves available to God to be used with anybody, anywhere, anytime.

We ought to avoid the trap of evaluating our faith by how others respond to us. The Spirit of God converts people—we don't. If we do, our converts are on shaky ground. The story is told of an evangelist traveling on an airplane who sat across the aisle from a noisy drunk. After watching the fellow carry on for a while, the minister's seatmate turned and sarcastically remarked, "I understand he's one of your converts!"

The evangelist replied, "Must be. If he were God's, he wouldn't act that way." ◆

The Holy Spirit is the great evangelist, but Scripture also urges us to work with the Spirit in influencing others with the gospel. To understand our role in this joint venture, see "Whose Job Is Evangelism?" John 16:8.

One of the most important ways that we can give evidence of our faith in Christ is through the way we do our work. See "Your 'Workstyle,'" Titus 2:9–10.

FOR YOUR INFO
4:2

PARABLES

Jesus frequently taught using parables (v. 2), short, simple stories designed to communicate spiritual truths and principles. Sometimes these were extended tales with character and plot development; sometimes they were little more than figures of speech that illustrated truth through comparisons or examples drawn from everyday life.

Jesus was a master of the parabolic form, but He was not the first to use parables. Several appear in the Old Testament. For example: Nathan's parable of a rich man who took a small ewe lamb belonging to a poor man (2 Sam. 12:1–4); the wise woman of Tekoa's parable of a widow whose two sons fought until one was killed (2 Sam. 14:5–7); and Solomon's parable of the sluggard (Prov. 24:30–34).

The advantage of stories like these is that they impress the listener with a vivid, imaginative picture of the truth. That doesn't mean, however, that they are always easy to understand. Even Jesus' disciples were sometimes confused as to the meaning of His parables (Matt. 13:24–30, 36–43). Furthermore, Jesus sometimes spoke in parables to reveal truth to His followers but to conceal it from those who had rejected Him (Matt. 13:10–17; Mark 4:10–12; Luke 8:9–10). Like a double-edged sword, His words cut two ways—enlightening those who sought the truth but blinding the disobedient.

Interpreting Parables

Most of Jesus' parables have one central point, and there is no need for fanciful, speculative interpretation. To find that central meaning, it helps if we as modern-day readers can understand what the parable meant in the time of Jesus and relate the story to His proclamation of the kingdom and to His miracles. After all, the parables were more than simple folk stories; they were expressions of Christ's view of God, humanity, salvation, and the new epoch which began with His ministry.

A good example of this approach are the parables dealing with the four "lost" things in Luke 15:3–32: the lost sheep, the lost coin, and the two lost sons. The context shows that Jesus told these stories while eating with tax collectors and sinners (vv. 1–2). The Pharisees and scribes, the religious elite of the day, were criticizing Him because, in their view, He was transgressing the Law.

In response, Jesus told the three parables. God rejoices more, He said, over the repentance of one sinner (such as those sitting with Him at the table) than over "ninety-nine just persons who need no repentance" (v. 7; such as the religious professionals who congratulated themselves on their own self-achieved "goodness"). Likewise, the prodigal son (vv. 11–24) illustrated the tax collectors and sinners, while the older son (vv. 25–32) illustrated the scribes and Pharisees.

Parables are one of the most engaging forms of teaching in Scripture. If you or someone you know has struggled with understanding and applying God's truth, you might consider reading the parables. In a powerful way, they stimulate the imagination and bring eternal truth to everyday life. ◆

Jesus probably spent most of His life working in His family's carpentry business. No wonder He knew how to present truth in terms that normal people could understand. *See "Work-World Stories Describe the Kingdom," Matt. 13:1.*

smallest of all the seeds on earth; 32yet when it is sown it grows up and becomes the greatest of all shrubs, and puts forth large branches, so that the birds of the air can make nests in its shade."

The Use of Parables

4:33–34

33 With many such parables he spoke the word to them, as they were able to hear it; 34he did not speak to them except in parables, but he explained everything in private to his disciples.

Jesus Stills a Great Storm

35 On that day, when evening had come, he said to them, "Let us go across to the other side." 36And leaving the crowd behind, they took him with them in the boat, just as he was. Other boats were with him. 37A great windstorm arose, and the waves beat into the boat, so that the boat was already being swamped. 38But he was in the stern, asleep on the cushion; and they woke him up and said to him, "Teacher, do you not care that we are perishing?" 39He woke up and rebuked the wind, and said to the sea, "Peace! Be still!" Then the wind ceased, and there was a dead calm. 40He said to them, "Why are you afraid? Have you still no faith?" 41And they were filled with great awe and said to one another, "Who then is this, that even the wind and the sea obey him?"

A Demoniac Finds Help

5:1
see pg. 143

5 They came to the other side of the sea, to the country of the Gerasenes.[g] 2And when he had stepped out of the boat, immediately a man out of the tombs with an unclean spirit met him. 3He lived among the tombs; and no one could restrain him any more, even with a chain; 4for he had often been restrained with shackles and chains, but the chains he wrenched apart, and the shackles he broke in pieces; and no one had the strength to subdue him. 5Night and day among the tombs and on the mountains he was always howling and bruising himself with stones. 6When he saw Jesus from a distance, he ran and bowed down before him; 7and he shouted at the top of his voice, "What have you to do with me, Jesus, Son of the Most High God? I adjure you by God,

[g]Other ancient authorities read *Gergesenes*; others, *Gadarenes*

Faith Unfolds Slowly

CONSIDER THIS 4:33–34 **How much do you understand about the faith? Do you wish you knew more? Perhaps others intimidate you with their knowledge and familiarity with Scripture.**

If so, Jesus' work with His disciples (vv. 33–34) can lend some helpful perspective. Just as our biological lives unfold slowly, so do our spiritual lives. God offers us what we can understand as soon as we can handle it, but not before. Most parents would consider explicit lessons on sexuality to be premature for preschoolers. Likewise, driving lessons for first graders would be inappropriate. And some athletic activities can cause great damage if children engage in them too early in their development. In the same way, God holds back certain lessons until we're mature enough to handle them.

Jesus called the disciples to follow Him one day at a time (Luke 9:23). But He also promised them that the Spirit would come later and lead them into truths that they could not handle then (John 16:12–16). Like those first disciples, we as Jesus' modern-day followers are not to know the end from the beginning, but to learn something from Him every day, applying it to our lives. Faith is not a badge to be worn or knowledge to be flaunted, but a little seed to be nurtured (vv. 26–32).

Jesus told a parable to illustrate the way in which His followers would slowly understand spiritual truth. See "Treasures New and Old," Matt. 13:52.

do not torment me." 8For he had said to him, "Come out of
the man, you unclean spirit!" 9Then Jesus[h] asked him,
"What is your name?" He replied, "My name is Legion; for
we are many." 10He begged him earnestly not to send them
out of the country. 11Now there on the hillside a great herd
of swine was feeding; 12and the unclean spirits[i] begged him,
"Send us into the swine; let us enter them." 13So he gave
them permission. And the unclean spirits came out and entered the swine; and the herd, numbering about two thousand, rushed down the steep bank into the sea, and were
drowned in the sea.

14 The swineherds ran off and told it in the city and in
the country. Then people came to see what it was that had
happened. 15They came to Jesus and saw the demoniac sitting there, clothed and in his right mind, the very man who
had had the legion; and they were afraid. 16Those who had
seen what had happened to the demoniac and to the swine
reported it. 17Then they began to beg Jesus[j] to leave their
neighborhood. 18As he was getting into the boat, the man
who had been possessed by demons begged him that he
might be with him. 19But Jesus[h] refused, and said to him,
"Go home to your friends, and tell them how much the
Lord has done for you, and what mercy he has shown you."

(Bible text continued on page 148)

[h]*Gk he* [i]*Gk they* [j]*Gk him*

The City of the Dead

Gadara was either the site of or near the site of Jesus' dramatic healing of a man possessed by demons calling themselves Legion (Mark 5:1–20; Matt. 8:28–34; Luke 8:26–39). Matthew records that Jesus healed two demon-possessed men; Mark and Luke refer to only one.

At any rate, the incident took place at a "necropolis," or city of the dead (Mark 5:2–3, 5). Then as now, certain people lived among the dead. The Gospels say that the demon-possessed man had been driven away from normal society. In modern Cairo, nearly one million people live in cemeteries, with houses literally built on tombs. The arrangement continues a long-standing practice in the Middle East.

But not only does this dramatic story take place at a necropolis, it follows an equally riveting incident—the stilling of the storm (4:35–41). Mark shows that Jesus was the master of both the storm at sea and the storm inside the head of the poor cemetery dweller.

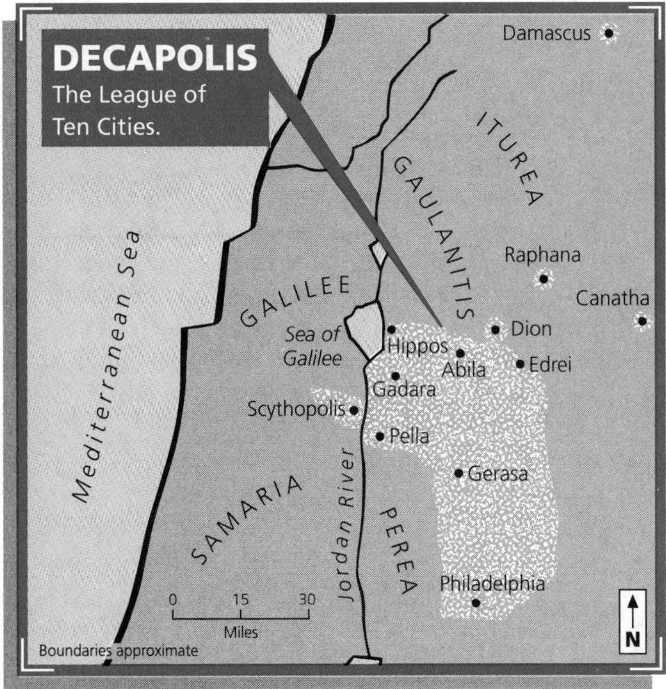

The man, or rather the demons, identified themselves as Legion (5:9). Roman legions of between 5,000 and 6,000 soldiers marched along the King's Highway that ran from the Gulf of Aqaba north to Syria, through the Decapolis—right beside the lakeside cemetery where the man lived. In a similar way, thousands of demonic spirits marched through the man's body, tormenting him day and night.

Jesus cast them out, and they entered a herd of pigs which they drowned in the lake (vv. 11–13). Some have used this incident to accuse Jesus of being both environmentally and economically insensitive. But to Jesus, one demented person was worth more than a herd of pigs or the economic impact of losing them. He didn't cause their loss—the demons did—or approve of it, but He permitted it in order to save the man. Here as elsewhere, He showed that people matter more than products or profits. ◆

Decapolis

YOU ARE THERE 5:20

- **The region also known as the Transjordan east of Galilee and Samaria.**
- **Name means "League of Ten Cities." Alphabetically, these included:**
  - **Canatha**
  - **Damascus, the chief city (see Acts 9:2)**
  - **Dion**
  - **Gadara**
  - **Gerasa (modern Jerash, Jordan)**
  - **Hippos**
  - **Pella, an ancient settlement not mentioned in the Bible, but a sanctuary for Christians during the Jewish-Roman War of A.D. 67–70**
  - **Philadelphia (Old Testament Rabbah or Rabbath Ammon, chief city of the Ammonites, perpetual enemies of the Israelites since at least the thirteenth century B.C.; present-day Amman)**
  - **Raphana**
  - **Scythopolis**
  - **and later, Abila and Edrei.**
- **Accessed in Roman times by the King's Highway and three other major roads, making it a major trade route in the empire.**
- **Region tended to favor Greek culture more than Hebrew.**
- **Visited by Jesus, who drew large crowds mostly of Gentiles (Matt. 4:25; Mark 5:20; 7:31). Word no doubt spread quickly through the transportation links afforded by the league.**

5:20 see pg. 147

20And he went away and began to proclaim in the Decapolis how much Jesus
had done for him; and everyone was amazed.

Jairus Pleads for His Daughter

5:21–43

5:22–23

21 When Jesus had crossed again in
the boat[k] to the other side, a great crowd
gathered around him; and he was by the
sea. 22Then one of the leaders of the synagogue named Jairus came and, when he saw him, fell at
his feet 23and begged him repeatedly, "My little daughter is
at the point of death. Come and lay your hands on her, so

[k]Other ancient authorities lack *in the boat*

A CLOSER LOOK 5:26

A Desperate Woman

Whether the woman with the hemorrhage lived off an inheritance or perhaps was divorced and supported herself from the dowry that would have been returned to her, her livelihood was exhausted. Jesus was her last hope. Fortunately, He did not disappoint her. See "The Hemorrhaging Woman," Matt. 9:20–22.

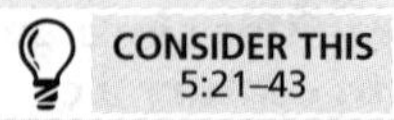

CONSIDER THIS 5:21–43

People Priorities in the City

Believers today can feel overwhelmed as they look at the many needs in the world around them. Where should they start? How can they make any difference? Who needs help the most?

Jesus modeled several lessons in dealing with the needs of people when He disembarked from His sail across the Sea of Galilee (v. 21). He found Himself confronted by two individuals with critical needs: a well-off, well-connected, and well-respected synagogue ruler whose twelve-year-old daughter was terminally ill (vv. 22–24); and an obscure elderly woman who had spent her livelihood on an ineffectual medical system, yet still suffered from chronic bleeding (vv. 25–28).

The man, with all his connections, got to Jesus first. But as Jesus was on His way across town, the woman—unnamed, unannounced, and, from the crowd's point of view, unwanted—grabbed Him. It was the desperate act of someone who knew she was going to die unless a miracle of some sort took place.

A little girl who had been living for twelve years (v. 42) and an old lady who had been dying for twelve years (v. 25). What would Jesus do?

To complicate matters, the woman's touch rendered

that she may be made well, and live." 24So he went with
him.

A Desperate Woman Reaches Out to Jesus

And a large crowd followed him and pressed in on him.
25Now there was a woman who had been suffering from
hemorrhages for twelve years. 26She had
endured much under many physicians,
and had spent all that she had; and she was no better, but
rather grew worse. 27She had heard about Jesus, and came
up behind him in the crowd and touched his cloak, 28for
she said, "If I but touch his clothes, I will be made well."
29Immediately her hemorrhage stopped; and she felt in her
body that she was healed of her disease. 30Immediately
aware that power had gone forth from him, Jesus turned
about in the crowd and said, "Who touched my clothes?"
31And his disciples said to him, "You see the crowd pressing
in on you; how can you say, 'Who touched me?' " 32He

5:26

Jesus ritually unclean (Lev. 15:25–27). Technically, He was now prohibited from helping the little girl until the next day. But neither the woman nor Jesus cared about that in the least: she was more amazed at her immediate healing, and Jesus was aware that His power had been activated (vv. 29–30). He was able to distinguish the incidental touch of the crowd from the person who reached out in faith.

Jesus called her "daughter" (v. 34). Perhaps He was referring to her Jewish ancestry. He called a woman in a similar situation a daughter of Abraham (Luke 13:16). But the term also put her on an equal footing with the daughter of the ruler—and put Jesus in sympathy with Jairus as a parent in pain. Perhaps that's why Jairus continued to trust Jesus even as his crisis worsened (vv. 35–36).

No individual Christian can meet all the desperate needs in today's urban arena. But does God really ask us to? If Jesus' example in Mark 5 is any indication, we need to do what we can to respond to the individuals He sends our way. We also need to remember that chronically ill old ladies mean just as much to God as bright, privileged schoolgirls. ◆

A Respected Leader Takes a Risk

CONSIDER THIS 5:22–23

Personal crises can cause us to break with our peers and cultural traditions in order to seek help. Jairus (v. 22) risked his job as the ruler of the synagogue by turning to Jesus. This leader was well-known in his town, and his actions were carefully watched by people. But he was desperate to save his daughter's life, so he went to Jesus as a last resort.

Jesus was a controversial rabbi. Some Jews followed Him, but many others took great offense at His teaching (3:6). So when Jairus fell at Jesus' feet, he must have known that some in his synagogue would sharply criticize him.

When Jesus arrived at Jairus' home, He took the daughter by the hand. In doing so, He risked a violation of Jewish custom. By touching her dead body, Jesus was making Himself ritually unclean. Moreover, by touching a woman, He was doing something that Jewish men, and particularly rabbis, were told not to do.

Jairus risked his secure, prestigious job because he loved his daughter more than his career. Jesus risked His reputation as a teacher in order to bring the daughter back to life.

Whom do you love enough to risk your career for?

Jesus the Carpenter

CONSIDER THIS 6:3 **Like His earthly father before Him, Jesus worked as a carpenter (v. 3). Possibly He continued to practice His trade while traveling about to teach and heal.**

He certainly derived no income from His ministry. Only officials of the temple and religious courts drew salaries. The rest of the religious teachers and leaders were either independently wealthy or supported themselves through a trade or profession.

Jesus did receive support from several wealthy women (see "The Women Who Followed Jesus," Luke 8:1–3). And He was welcomed as a guest into many homes. But of all the complaints that His enemies lodged against Him—that He failed to keep the Sabbath, that He ate and drank with sinners, that He made Himself out to be God—they never accused Him of being lazy. Indeed, Jesus' own townsfolk were amazed at His teaching because He was "just a carpenter."

One Pharisee who joined the Christian movement supported himself by manufacturing tents. See "Paul's 'Real' Job," Acts 18:1–3.

If Jesus may have supported Himself through "secular" employment while carrying out His ministry, is there any reason why modern Christian leaders shouldn't at least consider that as an option today? See "Paying Vocational Christian Workers," 1 Cor. 9:1–23.

looked all around to see who had done it. 33But the woman,
knowing what had happened to her, came in fear and trembling, fell down before him, and told him the whole truth.
34He said to her, "Daughter, your faith has made you well;
go in peace, and be healed of your disease."

Jesus Heals Jairus' Daughter

35 While he was still speaking, some people came from
the leader's house to say, "Your daughter is dead. Why trouble the teacher any further?" 36But overhearing[l] what they
said, Jesus said to the leader of the synagogue, "Do not fear,
only believe." 37He allowed no one to follow him except Peter, James, and John, the brother of James. 38When they
came to the house of the leader of the synagogue, he saw a
commotion, people weeping and wailing loudly. 39When he
had entered, he said to them, "Why do you make a commotion and weep? The child is not dead but sleeping."
40And they laughed at him. Then he put them all outside,
and took the child's father and mother and those who were
with him, and went in where the child was. 41He took her
by the hand and said to her, "Talitha cum," which means,
"Little girl, get up!" 42And immediately the girl got up and
began to walk about (she was twelve years of age). At this
they were overcome with amazement. 43He strictly ordered
them that no one should know this, and told them to give
her something to eat.

Unbelief in Jesus' Own Country

6 He left that place and came to his hometown, and his
disciples followed him. 2On the sabbath he began to
teach in the synagogue, and many who heard him were
astounded. They said, "Where did this man get all this?
What is this wisdom that has been given to him? What
6:3 deeds of power are being done by his
hands! 3Is not this the carpenter, the son
of Mary[m] and brother of James and Joses and Judas and
Simon, and are not his sisters here with us?" And they took
offense[n] at him. 4Then Jesus said to them, "Prophets are not
without honor, except in their hometown, and among their
own kin, and in their own house." 5And he could do no
deed of power there, except that he laid his hands on a few
sick people and cured them. 6And he was amazed at their
unbelief.

[l]Or *ignoring;* other ancient authorities read *hearing* [m]Other ancient authorities read *son of the carpenter and of Mary* [n]Or *stumbled*

The Twelve Are Sent Out

Then he went about among the villages teaching. 7He
called the twelve and began to send them out two by two,
and gave them authority over the unclean spirits. 8He ordered them to take nothing for their journey except a staff;
no bread, no bag, no money in their belts; 9but to wear sandals and not to put on two tunics. 10He said to them,
"Wherever you enter a house, stay there until you leave the
place. 11If any place will not welcome you and they refuse
to hear you, as you leave, shake off the dust that is on your
feet as a testimony against them." 12So they went out and
proclaimed that all should repent. 13They cast out many
demons, and anointed with oil many who were sick and
cured them.

Herod Hears and Fears

6:14
6:14–16

14 King Herod heard of it, for Jesus'[o]
name had become known. Some were[p]
saying, "John the baptizer has been raised from the dead;
and for this reason these powers are at
work in him." 15But others said, "It is Elijah." And others said, "It is a prophet, like one of the
prophets of old." 16But when Herod heard of it, he said,
"John, whom I beheaded, has been raised."

The Murder of John the Baptist

17 For Herod himself had sent men who arrested John,
bound him, and put him in prison on account of Herodias,
his brother Philip's wife, because Herod[q] had married her.
18For John had been telling Herod, "It is not lawful for you
to have your brother's wife." 19And Herodias had a grudge
against him, and wanted to kill him. But she could not,
20for Herod feared John, knowing that he was a righteous
and holy man, and he protected him. When he heard him,
he was greatly perplexed;[r] and yet he liked to listen to him.
21But an opportunity came when Herod on his birthday

[o]Gk *his* [p]Other ancient authorities read *He was* [q]Gk *he* [r]Other ancient authorities read *he did many things*

* * *

Herod the Tetrarch

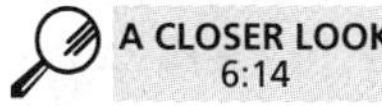

A CLOSER LOOK 6:14

Called King Herod in v. 14, this man was also known as Herod Antipas or, with his formal title, Herod the tetrarch (ruler of a fourth part; *see Luke 9:7). The son of Herod the Great, he came from a line of brilliant but immoral rulers. Don't miss "The Herods," Acts 12:1–2.*

"YOU REMIND ME OF . . ."

CONSIDER THIS 6:14–16 **Jesus' reputation traveled far and wide, even to the king (v. 14). But who was this Man with such extraordinary power and authority? Herod and his counselors compared Jesus to some very special people—John the Baptist, Elijah, the Old Testament prophets.**

Their exercise in trying to identify Jesus raises an interesting question: When others observe you and the way you use power and authority, to whom do they compare you? How might someone complete the sentence, "When I think of [*YOUR NAME*], I'm most reminded of . . . " whom?

A RECKLESS CHOICE

CONSIDER THIS 6:23 **Someone has well said that there are good decisions and there are quick decisions, but there are few good quick decisions. Herod made a very bad decision on the spur of the moment when he rewarded his stepdaughter with a blank check (v. 23).**

It's easy to condemn Herod for his foolishness. Yet how often we act in a similar manner, making decisions that have the most far-reaching consequences in haste, in a flush of wild excitement. Carried away by our passions, we choose impulsively, to our misfortune.

Herod's mistake is easily understood. He was drunk, he was distracted, he was impulsive by nature. Believers ought never to make their decisions in such a manner. As Paul challenges us, we need to live as wise people, not as fools (Eph. 5:14–17).

Why Not Rest a While?

CONSIDER THIS 6:31 **When the Twelve returned from their preaching tour (vv. 7, 12, 30), Jesus took them aside for a bit of rest and relaxation (v. 31). In doing so, He modeled a principle that many of us today could stand to practice more—the principle of rest.**

Rest may seem to be the last thing we need, given industry's obsession with productivity and our culture's reputation as a "leisure society." But God wants us to adopt His values, not the values of our culture. One thing He values is leisure. He values work as well (see "God—The Original Worker," John 5:17 and "People at Work," Heb. 2:7). But rest is something God Himself does (Gen. 2:2), which means that rest is good in and of itself. In fact, God actually commanded His people Israel to rest (Ex. 20:8–11).

Have you determined how much time you actually need to spend at work? Have you carefully considered how to balance your time and energy between workplace commitments and your family? Are you perhaps working too much, not because the job demands it, but because you won't trust God to supply your needs through a reasonable amount of work? Perhaps you need to take Jesus' advice: "Come aside . . . and rest a while."

gave a banquet for his courtiers and officers and for the
leaders of Galilee. 22When his daughter Herodias[s] came in
and danced, she pleased Herod and his guests; and the king
said to the girl, "Ask me for whatever you wish, and I will
6:23 see pg. 151
give it." 23And he solemnly swore to her,
"Whatever you ask me, I will give you,
even half of my kingdom." 24She went out and said to her
mother, "What should I ask for?" She replied, "The head of
John the baptizer." 25Immediately she rushed back to the
king and requested, "I want you to give me at once the
head of John the Baptist on a platter." 26The king was
deeply grieved; yet out of regard for his oaths and for the
guests, he did not want to refuse her. 27Immediately the
king sent a soldier of the guard with orders to bring John's[t]
head. He went and beheaded him in the prison, 28brought
his head on a platter, and gave it to the girl. Then the girl
gave it to her mother. 29When his disciples heard about it,
they came and took his body, and laid it in a tomb.

Jesus Feeds 5,000

30 The apostles gathered around Jesus, and told him all
6:31
that they had done and taught. 31He said
to them, "Come away to a deserted place
all by yourselves and rest a while." For many were coming
and going, and they had no leisure even to eat. 32And they
went away in the boat to a deserted place by themselves.
33Now many saw them going and recognized them, and
they hurried there on foot from all the towns and arrived
ahead of them. 34As he went ashore, he saw a great crowd;
and he had compassion for them, because they were like
sheep without a shepherd; and he began to teach them
many things. 35When it grew late, his disciples came to him
and said, "This is a deserted place, and the hour is now
very late; 36send them away so that they may go into the
surrounding country and villages and buy something for
themselves to eat." 37But he answered them, "You give them
something to eat." They said to him, "Are we to go and buy
two hundred denarii[u] worth of bread, and give it to them to
eat?" 38And he said to them, "How many loaves have you?
Go and see." When they had found out, they said, "Five,
and two fish." 39Then he ordered them to get all the people
to sit down in groups on the green grass. 40So they sat
down in groups of hundreds and of fifties. 41Taking the five
loaves and the two fish, he looked up to heaven, and
blessed and broke the loaves, and gave them to his disciples

[s]Other ancient authorities read *the daughter of Herodias herself* [t]Gk *his* [u]The denarius was the usual day's wage for a laborer

to set before the people; and he divided the two fish among
them all. 42And all ate and were filled; 43and they took up
twelve baskets full of broken pieces and of the fish. 44Those
who had eaten the loaves numbered five thousand men.

Jesus Walks on Water

6:45

45 Immediately he made his disciples
get into the boat and go on ahead to the
other side, to Bethsaida, while he dismissed the crowd.
46After saying farewell to them, he went up on the mountain to pray.
47 When evening came, the boat was out on the sea,
and he was alone on the land. 48When he saw that they
were straining at the oars against an adverse wind, he came
towards them early in the morning, walking on the sea. He
intended to pass them by. 49But when they saw him walking on the sea, they thought it was a ghost and cried out;
50for they all saw him and were terrified. But immediately
he spoke to them and said, "Take heart, it is I; do not be
afraid." 51Then he got into the boat with them and the wind
ceased. And they were utterly astounded, 52for they did not
understand about the loaves, but their hearts were hardened.

Many Healed in Gennesaret

6:53
see pg. 154

53 When they had crossed over, they
came to land at Gennesaret and moored
the boat. 54When they got out of the boat, people at once
recognized him, 55and rushed about that whole region and
began to bring the sick on mats to wherever they heard he
was. 56And wherever he went, into villages or cities or
farms, they laid the sick in the marketplaces, and begged
him that they might touch even the fringe of his cloak; and
all who touched it were healed.

Jesus Answers the Pharisees

7 Now when the Pharisees and some of the scribes who
had come from Jerusalem gathered around him, 2they
noticed that some of his disciples were eating with defiled
hands, that is, without washing them. 3(For the Pharisees,
and all the Jews, do not eat unless they thoroughly wash
their hands,[v] thus observing the tradition of the elders; 4and
they do not eat anything from the market unless they wash

[v]Meaning of Gk uncertain

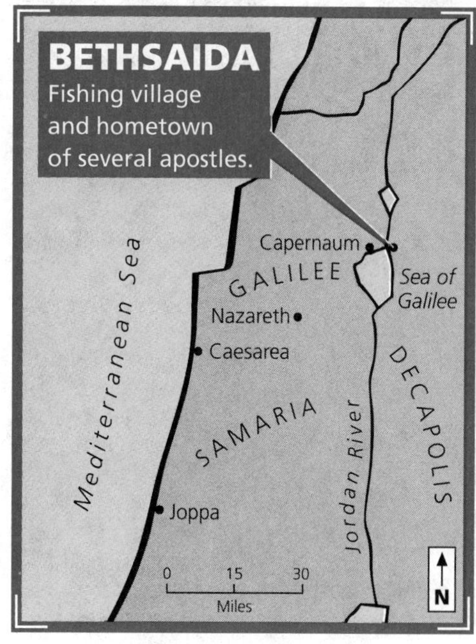

BETHSAIDA

YOU ARE THERE 6:45

- **A town (or possibly two) located on the north shore of the Sea of Galilee (modern-day Golan Heights).**
- **Name in Aramaic meant "fish town" (not the same as *Bethesda,* having to do with wells and healing).**
- **Located near the Decapolis (Mark 5:20), total population for the surrounding seaside area was greater in the first century than today.**
- **In New Testament times, the entire city was employed in the fishing industry.**
- **Situated near the heavily used King's Highway running alongside the Sea of Galilee.**
- **Home town to several of the apostles: brothers James and John, Simon and Andrew, and Philip.**
- **Inhabitants denounced by Jesus for their lack of faith (Matt. 11:21; Luke 10:13).**
- **Possible home of the early Christian sign of the fish.**

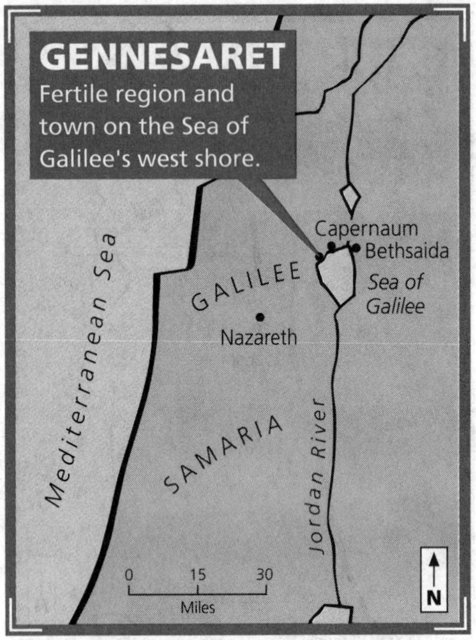

GENNESARET

YOU ARE THERE 6:53

- A plain extending a mile from the Sea of Galilee along a five-mile section of the north shore.
- Name means "garden of riches"; the district's rich, loamy soil caused figs, olives, palms, and other trees to grow well there.
- Also the name of a town on the west shore, the fortified city of Naphtali (Josh. 19:35), often called by its Hebrew name, *Chinnereth.*

it;[w] and there are also many other traditions that they
observe, the washing of cups, pots, and bronze kettles.[x])
5So the Pharisees and the scribes asked him, "Why do your
disciples not live[y] according to the tradition of the elders,
but eat with defiled hands?" 6He said to them, "Isaiah
prophesied rightly about you hypocrites, as it is written,

'This people honors me with their lips,
but their hearts are far from me;
7 in vain do they worship me,
teaching human precepts as doctrines.'

8You abandon the commandment of God and hold to human tradition."

7:9–13

9 Then he said to them, "You have a
fine way of rejecting the commandment
of God in order to keep your tradition! 10For Moses said,
'Honor your father and your mother'; and, 'Whoever speaks
evil of father or mother must surely die.' 11But you say that
if anyone tells father or mother, 'Whatever support you
might have had from me is Corban' (that is, an offering to
God[z])— 12then you no longer permit doing anything for a
father or mother, 13thus making void the word of God
through your tradition that you have handed on. And you
do many things like this."

14 Then he called the crowd again and said to them,
"Listen to me, all of you, and understand: 15there is nothing
outside a person that by going in can defile, but the things
that come out are what defile."[a]

17 When he had left the crowd and entered the house,
his disciples asked him about the parable. 18He said to
them, "Then do you also fail to understand? Do you not see
that whatever goes into a person from outside cannot defile,
19since it enters, not the heart but the stomach, and
goes out into the sewer?" (Thus he declared all foods
clean.) 20And he said, "It is what comes out of a person that
defiles. 21For it is from within, from the human heart, that
evil intentions come: fornication, theft, murder, 22adultery,
avarice, wickedness, deceit, licentiousness, envy, slander,
pride, folly. 23All these evil things come from within, and
they defile a person."

Jesus Heals a Gentile Woman's Daughter

7:24

24 From there he set out and went
away to the region of Tyre.[b] He entered a
house and did not want anyone to know he was there. Yet

[w]Other ancient authorities read *and when they come from the marketplace, they do not eat unless they purify themselves* [x]Other ancient authorities add *and beds* [y]Gk *walk* [z]Gk lacks *to God* [a]Other ancient authorities add verse 16, *"Let anyone with ears to hear listen"* [b]Other ancient authorities add *and Sidon*

he could not escape notice, 25but a woman whose little
daughter had an unclean spirit immediately heard about
him, and she came and bowed down at his feet. 26Now the
woman was a Gentile, of Syrophoenician origin. She
begged him to cast the demon out of her
daughter. 27He said to her, "Let the chil-
dren be fed first, for it is not fair to take the children's food
and throw it to the dogs." 28But she answered him, "Sir,[c]
even the dogs under the table eat the children's crumbs."
29Then he said to her, "For saying that, you may go—the
demon has left your daughter." 30So she went home, found
the child lying on the bed, and the demon gone.

7:24–30 see pg. 156

A Deaf and Mute Man Healed

31 Then he returned from the region of Tyre, and went
by way of Sidon towards the Sea of Galilee, in the region of
the Decapolis. 32They brought to him a deaf man who had
an impediment in his speech; and they begged him to lay
his hand on him. 33He took him aside in private, away from
the crowd, and put his fingers into his ears, and he spat
and touched his tongue. 34Then looking up to heaven, he
sighed and said to him, "Ephphatha," that is, "Be opened."
35And immediately his ears were opened, his tongue was
released, and he spoke plainly. 36Then Jesus[d] ordered them
to tell no one; but the more he ordered them, the more
zealously they proclaimed it. 37They were astounded beyond measure, saying, "He has done everything well; he
even makes the deaf to hear and the mute to speak."

Jesus Feeds 4,000

8 In those days when there was again a great crowd
without anything to eat, he called his disciples and said
to them, 2"I have compassion for the crowd, because they
have been with me now for three days and have nothing to
eat. 3If I send them away hungry to their homes, they will
faint on the way—and some of them have come from a
great distance." 4His disciples replied, "How can one feed
these people with bread here in the desert?" 5He asked

(Bible text continued on page 157)

[c]Or *Lord*; other ancient authorities prefix *Yes* [d]Gk *he*

Honor Your Parents

CONSIDER THIS 7:9–13 *Giving equal honor to both father and mother (v. 10) was a requirement of the Law (Ex. 20:12). Indeed, the Law decreed stiff punishment for those who cursed their parents (Lev. 20:9). According to Jewish wisdom literature, only a fool would disobey his mother or mock his father (Prov. 30:17).*

Nevertheless, the scribes and the Pharisees of Jesus' day had found a way around these commands, at least in part (Mark 7:11–12). Their man-made tradition was more important than keeping the Law. No wonder Jesus called them hypocrites (v. 6).

A Beautiful Vacation Spot

A CLOSER LOOK 7:24 *Apparently Jesus' trip to Tyre and Sidon was meant to be a pleasant rest at the seashore (v. 24). He picked a beautiful spot for a spiritual retreat. See "Tyre and Sidon" at Luke 6:17.*

CONSIDER THIS
7:24–30

JESUS AND ETHNICITY

Jesus' encounter with the Syrophoenician woman (vv. 24–30; Matt. 15:21–28) could raise some troubling questions about racial and ethnic attitudes. His treatment of the woman seems to be a contradiction of His image as the international Christ, the Savior of the whole world. Notice:

THE CONVERSATION OF JESUS AND THE SYROPHOENICIAN WOMAN	
The Gentile Woman...	**But Jesus...**
•Sought Jesus out (v. 25).	•Tried to hide from her (v. 24).
•Begged mercy for her demon-possessed daughter (vv. 25–26; Matt. 15:22).	•Ignored her cries (Matt. 15:23). •Seemed to agree with His disciples that she should be sent away (Matt. 15:23–24).
•Called Him "Lord" (v. 28; Matt. 15:25) and "Son of David" (Matt. 15:22). •Worshiped Him (v. 25; Matt. 15:25).	•Said He only came for the Jews (Matt. 15:24).
•Did not object to being called a dog (v. 28; Matt. 15:27).	•Implied that she was a dog (Jews frequently referred to Gentiles as "dogs"; v. 27; Matt. 15:26). •Implied that because she was not a Jew, she was not a child of God and could not be helped (Matt. 15:24, 26).
•Asked only for the "crumbs" left over from Jesus' work with the Jews (v. 28; Matt. 15:27).	

Finally, because of the woman's persistent faith, Jesus praised her and healed her daughter (v. 29; Matt. 15:28).

But what are we to make of His treatment of her? The woman came in utter sincerity and with great respect, yet Jesus rebuffed her with hard words. Why would He do that? Does God want us to relate to people from other races and ethnic groups like that?

Perhaps the key is to consider that Jesus' words were intended less for the woman's ears than for His disciples'. Maybe it was to them, not the woman, that He said, "I was sent only to the lost sheep of the house of Israel" (Matt. 15:24). They wanted Him to heal her daughter and send her away, but He refused—by appealing to their own national pride and exclusivism.

In other words, Jesus may have turned this incident into a living parable to show His disciples how hardened they were in their attitudes against Gentiles. Tyre, the setting for this story, was only 50 miles from the Galilee region where most of the Twelve had grown up. But it was an entirely different culture, dominated by Greek influences and populated almost exclusively by Gentiles. Many of them had already come south to learn more about Jesus (Mark 3:8). Now Jesus was taking His followers north on a crash course in cross-cultural awareness.

So upon encountering the woman, it could be that Jesus treated her the way His disciples would have treated her. Perhaps He wanted to illustrate in a way they would never forget that despite rejection, Gentiles like the woman deeply hungered for God's grace and power. In the end, Jesus' high praise for the woman's faith and the healing of her daughter repudiated the notion that God was concerned only with Israel.

How would Jesus have to treat someone today to illustrate prejudice among His followers? ◆

Racism and ethnic hatred have never been God's desire, and Jesus repudiated such sin wherever He found it. *See "Jews, Gentiles, and Jesus," Matt. 15:24.*

them, "How many loaves do you have?" They said, "Seven."
6Then he ordered the crowd to sit down on the ground;
and he took the seven loaves, and after giving thanks he
broke them and gave them to his disciples to distribute;
and they distributed them to the crowd. 7They had also a
few small fish; and after blessing them, he ordered that
these too should be distributed. 8They ate and were filled;
and they took up the broken pieces left over, seven baskets
full. 9Now there were about four thousand people. And he
sent them away. 10And immediately he got into the boat
with his disciples and went to the district of Dalmanutha.[e]

The Pharisees Demand a Sign

8:11–12 see pg. 158

11 The Pharisees came and began to
argue with him, asking him for a sign
from heaven, to test him. 12And he sighed deeply in his
spirit and said, "Why does this generation ask for a sign?
Truly I tell you, no sign will be given to this generation."
13And he left them, and getting into the boat again, he went
across to the other side.

Jesus Warns His Disciples

8:14–21 see pg. 160

14 Now the disciples[f] had forgotten to
bring any bread; and they had only one
loaf with them in the boat. 15And he cautioned them, saying, "Watch out—beware of the yeast of the Pharisees and
the yeast of Herod."[g] 16They said to one another, "It is because we have no bread." 17And becoming aware of it, Jesus
said to them, "Why are you talking about having no bread?
Do you still not perceive or understand? Are your hearts
hardened? 18Do you have eyes, and fail to see? Do you have
ears, and fail to hear? And do you not remember? 19When I
broke the five loaves for the five thousand, how many baskets full of broken pieces did you collect?" They said to
him, "Twelve." 20"And the seven for the four thousand, how
many baskets full of broken pieces did you collect?" And
they said to him, "Seven." 21Then he said to them, "Do you
not yet understand?"

A Blind Man Healed at Bethsaida

22 They came to Bethsaida. Some people[h] brought a
blind man to him and begged him to touch him. 23He took
the blind man by the hand and led him out of the village;

(Bible text continued on page 159)

[e]Other ancient authorities read *Mageda* or *Magdala* [f]Gk *they* [g]Other ancient authorities read *the Herodians* [h]Gk *They*

"How many loaves do you have?"
—Mark 8:5

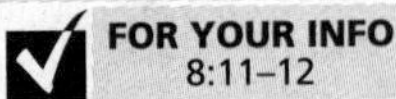

THE MIRACLES OF JESUS

"No sign [miracle] will be given to this generation," Jesus declared to the Pharisees (v. 12). Jesus wanted to avoid giving in to his opponents' demand for a miracle, but He had performed plenty of miracles already and would perform many more, as the following table shows:

Miracle	Matthew	Mark	Luke	John
Healed a leper	8:2–4	1:40–45	5:12–16	
Healed a centurion's servant	8:5–13		7:1–10	
Healed Peter's mother-in-law	8:14–15	1:29–31	4:38–39	
Healed the sick in the evening	8:16–17	1:32–34	4:40–41	
Stilled the storm	8:23–27	4:35–41	8:22–25	
Cast out demons and sent them into swine	8:28–34	5:1–20	8:26–39	
Healed a paralytic	9:1–8	2:1–12	5:18–26	
Raised Jairus' daughter	9:18–19, 23–26	5:22–24, 35–43	8:40–42, 49–56	
Healed a woman with a hemorrhaging	9:20–22	5:25–34	8:43–48	
Healed two blind men	9:27–31			
Healed a demon-possessed, mute man	9:32–33			
Healed a man with a withered hand	12:9–14	3:1–6	6:6–11	
Healed a demon-possessed, blind, and mute man	12:22		11:14	
Fed more than 5,000 people	14:13–21	6:30–44	9:10–17	6:1–14
Walked on the Sea of Galilee	14:22–27	6:45–52		6:16–21
Enabled Peter to walk on the Sea of Galilee	14:28–33			
Healed the Syro-Phoenician woman's daughter	15:21–28	7:24–30		
Fed more than 4,000 people	15:32–39	8:1–10		
Healed an epileptic boy	17:14–18	9:17	9:38–42	
Sent Peter to find a coin in a fish's mouth	17:24–27			
Healed two blind men near Jericho	20:29–34			
Caused a fig tree to wither	21:18–19	11:12–14, 20–21		
Returned from the dead	28:1–10	16:1–14	24:1–43	20:1–29
Cast out an unclean spirit		1:23–28	4:33–37	
Healed a deaf mute		7:31–37		
Healed the blind man at Bethsaida		8:22–26		
Healed blind Bartimaeus		10:46–52	18:35–43	
Escaped from a hostile crowd			4:28–30	
Caused a great catch of fish			5:1–11	
Raised a widow's son at Nain			7:11–17	
Healed an infirm, bent woman			13:11–13	

Continued

and when he had put saliva on his eyes and laid his hands
on him, he asked him, "Can you see anything?"
24And the
man[i] looked up and said, "I can see people, but they look
like trees, walking."
25Then Jesus[i] laid his hands on his eyes
again; and he looked intently and his sight was restored,
and he saw everything clearly.
26Then he sent him away to
his home, saying, "Do not even go into the village."[j]

Peter Calls Jesus "the Messiah"

8:27 see pg. 161

27 Jesus went on with his disciples to
the villages of Caesarea Philippi; and on
the way he asked his disciples, "Who do people say that I
am?"
28And they answered him, "John the Baptist; and

8:27–33 see pg. 162

others, Elijah; and still others, one of the
prophets."
29He asked them, "But who
do you say that I am?" Peter answered him, "You are the

[i]Gk *he* [j]Other ancient authorities add *or tell anyone in the village*

"Do you not yet understand?" —Mark 8:21

Continued

Miracle	Matthew	Mark	Luke	John
Healed a man with dropsy			14:1–4	
Healed ten lepers			17:11–19	
Healed Malchus' ear			22:47–51	18:10
Turned water into wine				2:1–11
Healed a nobleman's son				4:46–54
Healed an infirm man at Bethsaida				5:1–15
Healed a man born blind				9:1–41
Raised Lazarus				11:1–44
Caused a second great catch of fish				21:1–14

Even though Jesus performed astonishing miracles, most of His Jewish brothers and sisters rejected Him as their Messiah. Today many people reject Christianity on similar grounds, claiming that Christianity and science conflict. See "Ten Myths about Christianity, Myth #3: Science Is in Conflict with Christian Faith," John 4:48.

Messiah."[k] 30And he sternly ordered them not to tell anyone
about him.

Jesus Rebukes Peter

31 Then he began to teach them that the Son of Man
must undergo great suffering, and be rejected by the elders,
the chief priests, and the scribes, and be killed, and after
three days rise again. 32He said all this quite openly. And
Peter took him aside and began to rebuke him. 33But turning and looking at his disciples, he rebuked Peter and said,
"Get behind me, Satan! For you are setting your mind not
on divine things but on human things."

Discipleship Is Costly

34 He called the crowd with his disciples, and said to
them, "If any want to become my followers, let them deny

[k]Or *the Christ*

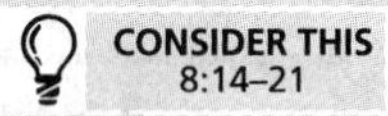

DANGER AHEAD

Yeast, or leaven, is a powerful fungus that can cause a lump of dough to rise into bread, ferment liquids into alcohol, or cause painful infections. When Jesus spoke of yeast in His comments about the Pharisees and Herod (v. 15), His disciples were quite confused. What could He mean? What was the leaven of the Pharisees and Herod?

Jesus reminded His followers of His miracles of feeding the five thousand and the four thousand (vv. 19–21; 6:35–44; 8:1–9). What was the response of the Pharisees? They disputed with Him and tried to test Him by appealing for a miracle (v. 11). In short, they refused to believe—despite the miraculous provision of meals for more than nine thousand people! Furthermore, they were already in league with Herod and his supporters to destroy Jesus (3:6; 12:13), just as Herod had done away with John the Baptist (6:14–29).

Clearly, Jesus was warning His followers against the insidious infection of unbelief. Like yeast in dough, a lack of faith can permeate one's life until it breaks out in open rebellion against God. No wonder the Lord was so dis-

themselves and take up their cross and follow me. 35For
those who want to save their life will lose it, and those who
lose their life for my sake, and for the sake of the gospel,[l]
will save it. 36For what will it profit them to gain the whole
world and forfeit their life? 37Indeed, what can they give in
return for their life? 38Those who are ashamed of me and of
my words[m] in this adulterous and sinful generation, of
them the Son of Man will also be ashamed when he comes
9:1–13 see pg. 162
9 in the glory of his Father with the
holy angels." 1And he said to them,
"Truly I tell you, there are some standing here who will not
taste death until they see that the kingdom of God has
come with[n] power."

Jesus Is Transfigured

2 Six days later, Jesus took with him Peter and James
and John, and led them up a high mountain apart, by

[l]Other ancient authorities read *lose their life for the sake of the gospel* [m]Other ancient authorities read *and of mine* [n]Or *in*

pleased with the disciples' lack of perception (8:17–18). Perhaps the yeast of unbelief was already at work among them. After all, they had apparently failed to understand the significance of a feeding miracle the first time around (6:52); now they were missing it a second time!

Jesus had grave concern about the condition of His followers' faith. He knew that there was danger ahead. Powerful enemies would lay hold of Him, and the disciples would be sorely tested. No wonder He took measures to keep a low profile (vv. 26, 30). He wanted to avoid exposing these men to the full force of His opponents before their faith was ready to handle such a trial.

None of us knows what dangers lie ahead for our faith. We may be headed for trials and challenges that we never imagined. Is our faith ready to meet whatever challenges come our way? Or have we let the yeast of unbelief gain a foothold, breaking down our trust in God and spreading resistance to Him throughout our life? ◆

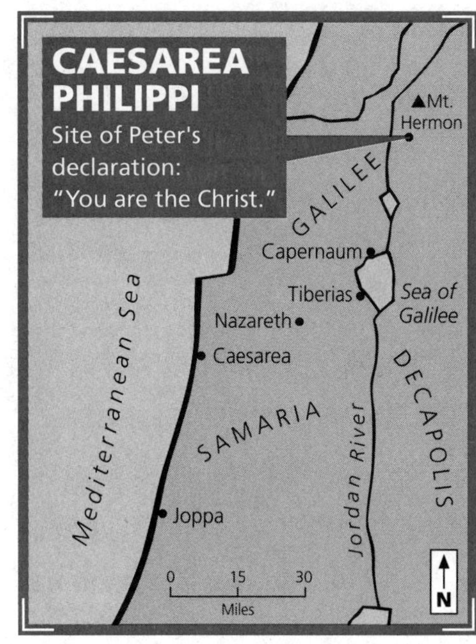

Caesarea Philippi

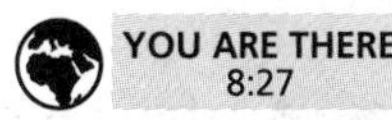

- **City on the southwestern slope of Mount Hebron in northern Palestine.**
- **Known as Paneas (or Panias) in New Testament times, but renamed by Philip the tetrarch in honor of Caesar Augustus.**
- **Not to be confused with Caesarea, Herod's seaport jewel on the Mediterranean (see Acts 8:40; 10:1).**
- **Perhaps the northernmost extent of Jesus' ministry.**
- **High cliffs nearby housed a cave dedicated to the Greek god Pan. Other rock cuts held statues dedicated to the mythical nymphs.**

themselves. And he was transfigured before them, 3and his
clothes became dazzling white, such as no one[o] on earth
could bleach them. 4And there appeared to them Elijah
with Moses, who were talking with Jesus. 5Then Peter said
to Jesus, "Rabbi, it is good for us to be here; let us make
three dwellings,[p] one for you, one for Moses, and one for
Elijah." 6He did not know what to say, for they were terrified. 7Then a cloud overshadowed them, and from the
cloud there came a voice, "This is my Son, the Beloved;[q] listen to him!" 8Suddenly when they looked around, they saw
no one with them any more, but only Jesus.
9 As they were coming down the mountain, he ordered
them to tell no one about what they had seen, until after

[o]Gk *no fuller* [p]Or *tents* [q]Or *my beloved Son*

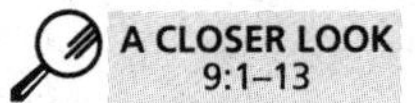

The "A" Team?

The actions of Peter, James, and John during the Transfiguration (vv. 1–13) raise questions as to their fitness for leadership. But Jesus not only kept them and the rest of the Twelve on His team, He kept all of them as His first team! He showed that undeveloped rookies can be developed into servant-leaders—over time. *See "Can Laity Get the Job Done?" Luke 9:1–62.*

"You Are the Messiah"

Peter's memorable declaration, "You are the Messiah" (v. 29) was made near Caesarea Philippi (v. 27), a town named in honor of Caesar Augustus.

In Old Testament times, the city was a center of the Canaanites' Baal worship. Later the Greeks substituted their god Pan for Baal, and later the Romans used it to develop worship of their emperors.

Significantly, Jesus took His followers outside of Palestine to a center of pagan, Gentile deities, where He asked them two vital questions:

- *"Who do people say that I am?" (v. 27).*
- *"Who do you say that I am?" (v. 29).*

The answer to the first question was easy enough. People believed that He was more or less a powerful religious leader such as John the Baptist, Elijah, or one of the Old Testament prophets. Even King Herod's counselors saw Him that way (6:14–16).

But Peter had finally settled in His own mind who Jesus was, so he immediately stepped forward to answer the

the Son of Man had risen from the dead. [10]So they kept the
matter to themselves, questioning what this rising from
the dead could mean. [11]Then they asked him, "Why do the
scribes say that Elijah must come first?" [12]He said to them,
"Elijah is indeed coming first to restore all things. How then
is it written about the Son of Man, that he is to go through
many sufferings and be treated with contempt? [13]But I tell
you that Elijah has come, and they did to him whatever
they pleased, as it is written about him."

A Young Boy with a Spirit Healed

14 When they came to the disciples, they saw a great
crowd around them, and some scribes arguing with them.
[15]When the whole crowd saw him, they were immediately
overcome with awe, and they ran forward to greet him.
[16]He asked them, "What are you arguing about with them?"
[17]Someone from the crowd answered him, "Teacher, I
brought you my son; he has a spirit that makes him unable
to speak; [18]and whenever it seizes him, it dashes him down;

second question: "You are the Messiah, the Son of the living God" (8:29; Matt. 16:16).

It may be that Jesus looked at the great rock cliffs standing nearby as He replied, "Blessed are you, Simon, son of Jonah! . . . And I tell you, you are Peter ['Rock'], and on this rock I will build my church" (Matt. 16:17–18).

Some have understood "rock" to mean the bedrock of faith, like the faith Peter was demonstrating here. Others believe that Peter himself (and for some, the other disciples as well) was the rock, the key figure on whom the church was to stand, and that his successors have continued that foundational role. Another view, based on the language Jesus used, is that Jesus made a word play on Peter's name to indicate Himself as the Rock on which His church is built.

The key point of the incident, however, is that Jesus is the Christ. Standing in the shadow of a city named in honor of Rome's emperor, Jesus was declared to be the the very Son of God. He was more than just the Messiah of the Jews; He was the Savior of the whole world. ◆

"THIS IS MY SON, THE BELOVED; LISTEN TO HIM!"
—Mark 9:7

Are You Confused about Greatness, Too?

CONSIDER THIS 9:33–37 **Significance is a tricky achievement. Too often it is built upon fame, money, marketing, power, position, or possessions.**

The disciples were caught up in a value system based on these things, which caused them to compete with each other (v. 34). In fact, the dispute over greatness resurfaced later (10:35–45). The quest for significance through power was an insidious problem.

Jesus noticed His followers' thinking and challenged it (9:35). He pointed out that true greatness is in serving others rather than outdoing them. Later He suggested the same thing to a rich ruler (10:21).

To drive His point home, Jesus gathered a child in His arms and said that to welcome a child is to welcome both Christ and His Father (vv. 36–37). No wonder the apostle Paul, in writing to believers in Galatia, identified many childlike characteristics as highly valued works of the Spirit (Gal. 5:22–25). He contrasted those traits with some ugly ones that often accompany competition (Gal. 5:16–21).

Do you need to rework your value system? Are you addicted to fame and fortune? A good test is to ask yourself, *Where do children and the poor stand among my priorities?*

One of the most debilitating diseases of the modern world is "comparisonitis"—the tendency to measure one's worth by comparing oneself to other people. Do you suffer from it? Find out at Rom. 12:3.

and he foams and grinds his teeth and becomes rigid; and I
asked your disciples to cast it out, but they could not do
so." 19He answered them, "You faithless generation, how
much longer must I be among you? How much longer
must I put up with you? Bring him to me." 20And they
brought the boy[r] to him. When the spirit saw him, immediately it convulsed the boy,[r] and he fell on the ground and
rolled about, foaming at the mouth. 21Jesus[s] asked the father, "How long has this been happening to him?" And he
said, "From childhood. 22It has often cast him into the fire
and into the water, to destroy him; but if you are able to do
anything, have pity on us and help us." 23Jesus said to him,
"If you are able!—All things can be done for the one who
believes." 24Immediately the father of the child cried out,[t] "I
believe; help my unbelief!" 25When Jesus saw that a crowd
came running together, he rebuked the unclean spirit, saying to it, "You spirit that keeps this boy from speaking and
hearing, I command you, come out of him, and never enter
him again!" 26After crying out and convulsing him terribly,
it came out, and the boy was like a corpse, so that most of
them said, "He is dead." 27But Jesus took him by the hand
and lifted him up, and he was able to stand. 28When he had
entered the house, his disciples asked him privately, "Why
could we not cast it out?" 29He said to them, "This kind can
come out only through prayer."[u]

Jesus Predicts His Death

30 They went on from there and passed through Galilee.
He did not want anyone to know it; 31for he was teaching
his disciples, saying to them, "The Son of Man is to be betrayed into human hands, and they will kill him, and three
days after being killed, he will rise again." 32But they did
not understand what he was saying and were afraid to ask
him.

A Discussion about Rank

9:33–37

33 Then they came to Capernaum;
and when he was in the house he asked
them, "What were you arguing about on the way?" 34But
they were silent, for on the way they had argued with one
another who was the greatest. 35He sat down, called the
twelve, and said to them, "Whoever wants to be first must
be last of all and servant of all." 36Then he took a little child
and put it among them; and taking it in his arms, he said to

[r]Gk *him* [s]Gk *He* [t]Other ancient authorities add *with tears* [u]Other ancient authorities add *and fasting*

them, 37“Whoever welcomes one such child in my name
welcomes me, and whoever welcomes me welcomes not me
but the one who sent me.”

Taking Sides

38 John said to him, “Teacher, we saw someone[v] casting
out demons in your name, and we tried to stop him, because he was not following us.” 39But Jesus said, “Do not
stop him; for no one who does a deed of power in my
name will be able soon afterward to speak evil of me.
40Whoever is not against us is for us. 41For truly I tell you,
whoever gives you a cup of water to drink because you bear
the name of Christ will by no means lose the reward.
42 “If any of you put a stumbling block before one of
these little ones who believe in me,[w] it would be better for
you if a great millstone were hung around your neck and
you were thrown into the sea. 43If your hand causes you to
stumble, cut it off; it is better for you to enter life maimed
than to have two hands and to go to hell,[x] to the unquenchable fire.[y] 45And if your foot causes you to stumble, cut it
off; it is better for you to enter life lame than to have two
feet and to be thrown into hell.[x, y] 47And if your eye causes
you to stumble, tear it out; it is better for you to enter the
kingdom of God with one eye than to have two eyes and to
be thrown into hell,[x] 48where their worm never dies, and
the fire is never quenched.
49 “For everyone will be salted with fire.[z] 50Salt is good;
but if salt has lost its saltiness, how can you season it?[a]
Have salt in yourselves, and be at peace with one another.”

“WHOEVER WANTS TO BE FIRST MUST BE LAST OF ALL. . . .”
—Mark 9:35

Jesus Teaches about Divorce

10 He left that place and went to the region of Judea
and[b] beyond the Jordan. And crowds again gathered
around him; and, as was his custom, he again taught them.

10:2–12
see pg. 166

2 Some Pharisees came, and to test him
they asked, “Is it lawful for a man to divorce his wife?” 3He answered them, “What did Moses
command you?” 4They said, “Moses allowed a man to write
a certificate of dismissal and to divorce her.” 5But Jesus said

[v]Other ancient authorities add *who does not follow us* [w]Other ancient authorities lack *in me* [x]Gk *Gehenna* [y]Verses 44 and 46 (which are identical with verse 48) are lacking in the best ancient authorities [z]Other ancient authorities either add or substitute *and every sacrifice will be salted with salt* [a]Or *how can you restore its saltiness?* [b]Other ancient authorities lack *and*

to them, "Because of your hardness of heart he wrote this
commandment for you. 6But from the beginning of creation, 'God made them male and female.' 7'For this reason a
man shall leave his father and mother and be joined to his
wife,[c] 8and the two shall become one flesh.' So they are no
longer two, but one flesh. 9Therefore what God has joined
together, let no one separate."

10 Then in the house the disciples asked him again
about this matter. 11He said to them, "Whoever divorces his
wife and marries another commits adultery against her;
12and if she divorces her husband and marries another, she
commits adultery."

DIVORCE

CONSIDER THIS 10:2–12 *In the first century, Jewish men were allowed to divorce their wives for many different reasons (v. 2). Depending on which interpretation of the Torah one followed, a man could even send his wife away if she burned a meal.*

By contrast, women were far more restricted in their grounds for divorce. One of the few had to do with her husband's occupation. If he were a copper smelter, tanner, or dung collector, she could get a divorce, even if she knew before she married what his trade was, on the grounds that she couldn't have known how awful the smell would be.

Jesus Lets Children Come to Him

10:13–16

13 People were bringing little children
to him in order that he might touch
them; and the disciples spoke sternly to them. 14But when
Jesus saw this, he was indignant and said to them, "Let the
little children come to me; do not stop them; for it is to
such as these that the kingdom of God belongs. 15Truly I
tell you, whoever does not receive the kingdom of God as a
little child will never enter it." 16And he took them up in
his arms, laid his hands on them, and blessed them.

A Rich Man Asks about Eternal Life

10:17–27 see pg. 168

17 As he was setting out on a journey,
a man ran up and knelt before him, and
asked him, "Good Teacher, what must I do to inherit eternal life?" 18Jesus said to him, "Why do you call me good?
No one is good but God alone. 19You know the commandments: 'You shall not murder; You shall not commit adultery; You shall not steal; You shall not bear false witness;
You shall not defraud; Honor your father and mother.' "
20He said to him, "Teacher, I have kept all these since my
youth." 21Jesus, looking at him, loved him and said, "You
lack one thing; go, sell what you own, and give the money[d]
to the poor, and you will have treasure in heaven; then
come, follow me." 22When he heard this, he was shocked
and went away grieving, for he had many possessions.

Jesus Speaks about Riches

23 Then Jesus looked around and said to his disciples,
"How hard it will be for those who have wealth to enter the

[c]Other ancient authorities lack *and be joined to his wife* [d]Gk lacks *the money*

kingdom of God!" 24And the disciples were perplexed at
these words. But Jesus said to them again, "Children, how
hard it is[e] to enter the kingdom of God! 25It is easier for a
camel to go through the eye of a needle than for someone
who is rich to enter the kingdom of God." 26They were
greatly astounded and said to one another,[f] "Then who can
be saved?" 27Jesus looked at them and said, "For mortals it
is impossible, but not for God; for God all things are possible."

Rewards for the Twelve

28 Peter began to say to him, "Look, we have left everything and followed you." 29Jesus said, "Truly I tell you,
there is no one who has left house or brothers or sisters or
mother or father or children or fields, for my sake and for
the sake of the good news,[g] 30who will not receive a hundredfold now in this age—houses, brothers and sisters,
mothers and children, and fields with persecutions—and in
the age to come eternal life. 31But many who are first will
be last, and the last will be first."

Jesus Again Predicts His Death

10:32–37 see pg. 169

32 They were on the road, going up to
Jerusalem, and Jesus was walking ahead
of them; they were amazed, and those who followed were
afraid. He took the twelve aside again and began to tell
them what was to happen to him, 33saying, "See, we are going up to Jerusalem, and the Son of Man will be handed
over to the chief priests and the scribes, and they will condemn him to death; then they will hand him over to the
Gentiles; 34they will mock him, and spit upon him, and flog
him, and kill him; and after three days he will rise again."

James and John's Request

35 James and John, the sons of Zebedee, came forward
to him and said to him, "Teacher, we want you to do for us
whatever we ask of you." 36And he said to them, "What is it
you want me to do for you?" 37And they said to him, "Grant
us to sit, one at your right hand and one at your left, in
your glory." 38But Jesus said to them, "You do not know
what you are asking. Are you able to drink the cup that I
drink, or be baptized with the baptism that I am baptized

[e]Other ancient authorities add *for those who trust in riches* [f]Other ancient authorities read *to him* [g]Or *gospel*

The Friend of Children

CONSIDER THIS 10:13–16 *In Jesus' day it was common for mothers to ask famous rabbis to bless their children. This blessing involved the rabbi touching the child, particularly on the head or the shoulder.*

Mark did not explain why the disciples tried to keep the children away. Perhaps they viewed the little ones as ritually unclean, or, like most of society, unworthy of an important man's attention.

But Jesus rebuked the disciples and invited the children into His arms (v. 16). The way that He spoke to them and embraced them must have shocked those who stood by. Such tenderness and respect were rarely given children in that society.

Perhaps the disciples had adopted the prevailing Graeco-Roman view of childhood as an insignificant phase of life. Children were not valued for their own sake. See "Children and Childcare," Matt. 19:14.

with?" 39They replied, "We are able." Then Jesus said to
them, "The cup that I drink you will drink; and with the
baptism with which I am baptized, you will be baptized;
40but to sit at my right hand or at my left is not mine to
grant, but it is for those for whom it has been prepared."
41 When the ten heard this, they began to be angry with
James and John. 42So Jesus called them and said to them,
"You know that among the Gentiles those whom they recognize as their rulers lord it over them, and their great ones
are tyrants over them. 43But it is not so among you; but
whoever wishes to become great among you must be your
servant, 44and whoever wishes to be first among you must
be slave of all. 45For the Son of Man came not to be served
but to serve, and to give his life a ransom for many."

Blind Bartimaeus Sees

10:46

46 They came to Jericho. As he and
his disciples and a large crowd were leav-
ing Jericho, Bartimaeus son of Timaeus, a blind beggar, was

CONSIDER THIS
10:17–27

THE MAN WHO HAD IT ALL—ALMOST

He was young, well-mannered, well-educated, and well-off. He was sincere, honest, and above reproach. Maybe he also had an engaging personality and a winsome smile. Certainly Jesus found him likable; He even tried to recruit him (v. 21). He was the man who had everything—except eternal life. And he could have had that, too. All he had to do was get rid of his money and follow Jesus.

But it wasn't to be. Elsewhere Jesus had said that no one can serve both God and money (Matt. 6:24). Here was living proof of that principle. In coming to Jesus, the rich young ruler came to a fork in the road. He had to choose which one he would serve—money or Jesus. Apparently he chose money.

Jesus never condemned people for being rich. Nor does Scripture condemn the possession or the accumulation of money. But Jesus warned people about what He called "the lure of wealth" (Mark 4:19). He understood the powerful but ultimately fatal attraction of money as a substitute for God.

Jesus perceived that tendency in the rich young ruler.

sitting by the roadside. 47When he heard that it was Jesus of
Nazareth, he began to shout out and say, "Jesus, Son of
David, have mercy on me!" 48Many sternly ordered him to
be quiet, but he cried out even more loudly, "Son of David,
have mercy on me!" 49Jesus stood still and said, "Call him
here." And they called the blind man, saying to him, "Take
heart; get up, he is calling you." 50So throwing off his cloak,
he sprang up and came to Jesus. 51Then Jesus said to him,
"What do you want me to do for you?" The blind man said
to him, "My teacher,[h] let me see again." 52Jesus said to him,
"Go; your faith has made you well." Immediately he regained his sight and followed him on the way.

The Triumphal Entry into Jerusalem

11:1
see pg. 170

11 When they were approaching
Jerusalem, at Bethphage and

[h]Aramaic *Rabbouni*

Jericho

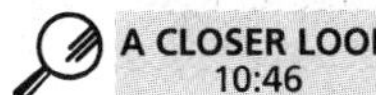

Blind Bartimaeus (v. 46) was but one of countless beggars who lined the road to Jericho in Jesus' day. See "Jericho" at Luke 10:30.

The man was placing far too much value on his wealth. So Jesus told him to give it away, to free himself from its entanglements. It's worth noting that Jesus did not give that same advice to every other rich person He encountered. But it was a requirement for this young ruler.

There are many rich young rulers today, people who have or are well on their way to having relatively sizable assets. Some are Christians and some are not. But sooner or later they all must answer the question that this man asked Jesus: "What must I do to inherit eternal life?" (10:17).

Jesus' response is still the same: there's nothing you can do, only God can give eternal life (v. 27). But He gives it freely and graciously to those who follow Him (vv. 29–30). However, that's especially hard for the rich (v. 23). They have a competing offer, and it's very attractive. ◆

Scripture offers an alternative to greed. See "Christians and Money," 1 Tim. 6:6–19.

No Better than Gentiles

CONSIDER THIS
10:32–37

On the final trip to Jerusalem, something of a power struggle began to emerge among Jesus' disciples. James and John were the first to try to obtain positions of power in the coming kingdom (vv. 35–37).

Jesus rebuked them in an interesting way. He compared them to the leaders of the Gentiles that they so despised (v. 42)—people like Pilate and Augustus and all their governors, tax collectors, soldiers, and centurions. The disciples detested those people as living only for themselves. Yet Jesus implied that this was the way His disciples were acting when they jockeyed for positions of power. The comparison must have challenged them to the core. Jesus was telling them, "You are no different than Gentiles!"

BETHPHAGE
"Place of young figs," suburb of Jerusalem.

Jordan River
Jericho
Bethabara
Jerusalem
Bethany
Qumran
Bethlehem
0 15 Miles
Dead Sea
N

BETHPHAGE

YOU ARE THERE 11:1

- **A village near Bethany, along the road from Jerusalem to Jericho (possibly modern Moslem town of Abu Dis); or perhaps somewhere between Bethany and the Mount of Olives.**
- **A "suburb" of Jerusalem.**
- **Name in Aramaic meant "place of young figs," a species that never appeared ripe, even when edible—perhaps giving rise to Jesus' parable of the unripe figs (Mark 11:12–14, 20–26; see "Bethany," John 11:1).**
- **First stop in Jesus' triumphal entry into Jerusalem (Mark 11:1; Matt. 21:1; Luke 19:29).**
- **Modern-day Bethphage hosts a Franciscan monastery (see "A Prayer of the Laity," Matt. 10:7–10).**

Bethany, near the Mount of Olives, he sent two of his disciples [2]and said to them, "Go into the village ahead of you,
and immediately as you enter it, you will find tied there a
colt that has never been ridden; untie it and bring it. [3]If
anyone says to you, 'Why are you doing this?' just say this,
'The Lord needs it and will send it back here immediately.' "
[4]They went away and found a colt tied near a door, outside
in the street. As they were untying it, [5]some of the bystanders said to them, "What are you doing, untying the
colt?" [6]They told them what Jesus had said; and they allowed them to take it. [7]Then they brought the colt to Jesus

11:1–11

and threw their cloaks on it; and he sat
on it. [8]Many people spread their cloaks
on the road, and others spread leafy branches that they had
cut in the fields. [9]Then those who went ahead and those
who followed were shouting,

"Hosanna!
Blessed is the one who comes in the name of the Lord!
10 Blessed is the coming kingdom of our ancestor David!
Hosanna in the highest heaven!"

11 Then he entered Jerusalem and went into the temple;
and when he had looked around at everything, as it was already late, he went out to Bethany with the twelve.

Jesus Curses a Fig Tree

11:12–25

12 On the following day, when they
came from Bethany, he was hungry.
[13]Seeing in the distance a fig tree in leaf, he went to see
whether perhaps he would find anything on it. When he
came to it, he found nothing but leaves, for it was not the
season for figs. [14]He said to it, "May no one ever eat fruit
from you again." And his disciples heard it.

Jesus Drives Merchants from the Temple

15 Then they came to Jerusalem. And he entered the
temple and began to drive out those who were selling and
those who were buying in the temple, and he overturned
the tables of the money changers and the seats of those who
sold doves; [16]and he would not allow anyone to carry any-

A Parade for the Common People

A CLOSER LOOK 11:1–11

For once, the common folks in Jerusalem had a parade (vv. 8–9). But the Man they celebrated traveled into town in a manner unlike any other celebrity they had seen. See "A New Style of Fame," Matt. 21:8–11.

thing through the temple. [17]He was teaching and saying, "Is
it not written,

'My house shall be called a house of prayer for all the
nations'?

But you have made it a den of robbers."

[18]And when the chief priests and the scribes heard it, they
kept looking for a way to kill him; for they were afraid of
him, because the whole crowd was spellbound by his
teaching. [19]And when evening came, Jesus and his disciples[i]
went out of the city.

Lessons from the Cursed Fig Tree

20 In the morning as they passed by, they saw the fig
tree withered away to its roots. [21]Then Peter remembered
and said to him, "Rabbi, look! The fig tree that you cursed
has withered." [22]Jesus answered them, "Have[j] faith in God.
[23]Truly I tell you, if you say to this mountain, 'Be taken up
and thrown into the sea,' and if you do not doubt in your
heart, but believe that what you say will come to pass, it
will be done for you. [24]So I tell you, whatever you ask for
in prayer, believe that you have received[k] it, and it will be
yours.

25 "Whenever you stand praying, forgive, if you have
anything against anyone; so that your Father in heaven may
also forgive you your trespasses."[l]

Leaders Question Jesus' Authority

27 Again they came to Jerusalem. As he was walking in
the temple, the chief priests, the scribes, and the elders
came to him [28]and said, "By what authority are you doing
these things? Who gave you this authority to do them?"
[29]Jesus said to them, "I will ask you one question; answer
me, and I will tell you by what authority I do these things.
[30]Did the baptism of John come from heaven, or was it of
human origin? Answer me." [31]They argued with one another, "If we say, 'From heaven,' he will say, 'Why then did
you not believe him?' [32]But shall we say, 'Of human origin'?"—they were afraid of the crowd, for all regarded John
as truly a prophet [3]So they answered Jesus, "We do not
know." And Jesus said to them, "Neither will I tell you by
what authority I am doing these things."

[i] Gk *they*: other ancient authorities read *he* [j] Other ancient authorities read *"If you have* [k] Other ancient authorities read *are receiving* [l] Other ancient authorities add verse 26, *"But if you do not forgive, neither will your Father in heaven forgive your trespasses."*

JESUS AND THE FIG TREE

CONSIDER THIS 11:12–25 **Why did Jesus destroy an innocent fig tree and then promise mountain-moving powers (vv. 12–14, 20–24)? The context of these events and statements is important. Jesus and His disciples were entering Jerusalem, where He was about to be killed (Mark 15). When He came upon the fig tree, He used it as an illustration and a warning of what ultimately awaits those who oppose the kingdom of God—like the Jewish leaders of that day. Rather than bearing useful fruit, the nation was misusing its privileges as God's people (11:12–18).**

Cursing the fig tree was not a wanton act of environmental destruction but a teaching method for Jesus' disciples. They would soon be very confused and frightened by events. Perhaps the memory of that graphic illustration would help.

As for moving mountains into the sea by prayer, Jesus was talking about the power of forgiveness (v. 25). He was not holding out false hopes of the free use of power to one's personal advantage. Instead, He was showing the significance of moving heaven and earth with another power—forgiving one's enemies.

Jesus frequently used contrasts to highlight spiritual truths. In Matt. 6:5–15, for example, He spoke of attention-getting prayers on the one hand (v. 5) and unseen prayers of forgiveness on the other (vv. 6, 14–15).

The power of forgiveness is immeasurable. It's a power that Jesus has delegated to us as His followers. See "The Power of Forgiveness," Matt. 9:4–8.

A Parable about a Vineyard Owner

12:1–12

12 Then he began to speak to them
in parables. “A man planted a
vineyard, put a fence around it, dug a pit for the wine
press, and built a watchtower; then he leased it to tenants
and went to another country. 2When the season came, he
sent a slave to the tenants to collect from them his share of
the produce of the vineyard. 3But they seized him, and beat
him, and sent him away empty-handed. 4And again he sent
another slave to them; this one they beat over the head and
insulted. 5Then he sent another, and that one they killed.
And so it was with many others; some they beat, and others
they killed. 6He had still one other, a beloved son. Finally
he sent him to them, saying, ‘They will respect my son.’
7But those tenants said to one another, ‘This is the heir;
come, let us kill him, and the inheritance will be ours.’ 8So
they seized him, killed him, and threw him out of the vineyard. 9What then will the owner of the vineyard do? He will
come and destroy the tenants and give the vineyard to others. 10Have you not read this scripture:
‘The stone that the builders rejected
has become the cornerstone;[m]
11 this was the Lord’s doing,
and it is amazing in our eyes’?”
12 When they realized that he had told this parable
against them, they wanted to arrest him, but they feared the
crowd. So they left him and went away.

“SO THEY SEIZED HIM, KILLED HIM, AND THREW HIM OUT OF THE VINEYARD.” —Mark 12:8

A Test Regarding Taxes

13 Then they sent to him some Pharisees and some
Herodians to trap him in what he said.
12:14
14And they came and said to him,
“Teacher, we know that you are sincere, and show deference to no one; for you do not regard people with partiality,
but teach the way of God in accordance with truth. Is it

(Bible text continued on page 174)

[m]Or *keystone*

Who Owns What?

A CLOSER LOOK 12:1–12 *The parable of the vineyard owner (vv. 1–12) challenges the idea that our significance is determined by how much we own and how much what we own is worth. See “Owners or Tenants?” Luke 20:9–19.*

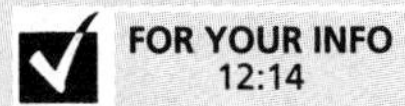

TAXES

When the Pharisees and Herodians tested Jesus with a question about taxes (v. 14), they were raising a highly explosive issue. Feelings of resentment over taxes ran extremely deep among the Jews, who were heavily taxed.

Taxes may have originated with the custom of giving presents for protection from harm (Gen. 32:13–21; 33:10; 43:11).

In Egypt, Joseph warned of seven years of famine after seven years of abundance. Pharaoh then put him in charge of raising revenues. He collected a 20 percent tax to store up food and buy land for Pharaoh—during the famine as well as the time of plenty (Gen. 47:20–26).

During the Exodus, Moses asked for voluntary contributions to construct the tabernacle (Ex. 25:2; 35:5, 21). The Law prescribed that every male over the age of 20 was to give half a shekel for the service of the tabernacle (Ex. 30:11–16).

When Israel asked Samuel for a king, he warned the people that heavy taxes would result—10 percent of nearly everything the people produced, as well as confiscation of land and servants. "In that day you will cry out because of your king, whom you have chosen for yourselves," he predicted (1 Sam. 8:14–18). His words came true almost right away.

Under David and Solomon, several taxes were established: a 10 percent tax on the produce of land and livestock (1 Sam. 8:15, 17); compulsory military service for one month each year (1 Chr. 27:1); import duties (1 Kin. 10:15); and tribute paid by subject peoples (2 Sam. 8:6; 2 Kin. 3:4). The taxes became so oppressive under Solomon that they contributed to the split in the kingdom after his death (1 Kin. 12:4).

When the Persians came, they set up a new system. Instead of paying tribute, each province in the Persian Empire was required to collect its own taxes. Persian rulers called *satraps* collected taxes for their own provinces, from which they paid a fixed amount into the royal treasury. Revenues were derived from tribute, custom, and toll (Ezra 4:13). Priests and religious servants were exempt (Ezra 7:24). A tax was also collected for maintenance of the governor's household. Again, the taxes were crushing. Many people were forced to mortgage their fields and vineyards, and some even sold their own children into slavery (Neh. 5:1–5).

During the period between the Old and the New Testament, the Jews were first under the Egyptian Ptolemaic rule (301–198 B.C.) and later under the Syrian Seleucid rule (198–63 B.C.). Under the Ptolemies, taxing privileges were farmed out to the highest bidders. People came to Alexandria from the various provinces to bid for the privilege of collecting taxes from their own people. Contractors would tax their people up to double the amount required by law in order to make a handsome profit. These tax collectors were even given military assistance to enforce their demands.

The same type of system probably continued under the Syrians. A poll tax, a salt tax, and a crown tax were enforced during this time. The Syrians taxed as much as one-third of the grain, one-half of the fruit, and a portion of the tithes which the Jews paid to support the temple.

When the Romans captured Jerusalem in 63 B.C., a tax of 10,000 talents was temporarily imposed on the Jews. Julius

(continued on next page)

lawful to pay taxes to the emperor, or not? 15Should we pay
them, or should we not?" But knowing their hypocrisy, he
said to them, "Why are you putting me to the test? Bring
me a denarius and let me see it." 16And they brought one.
Then he said to them, "Whose head is this, and whose title?" They answered, "The emperor's." 17Jesus said to them,
"Give to the emperor the things that are the emperor's, and
to God the things that are God's." And they were utterly
amazed at him.

Jesus Confounds the Sadducees

12:18–27

18 Some Sadducees, who say there is
no resurrection, came to him and asked
him a question, saying, 19"Teacher, Moses wrote for us that
if a man's brother dies, leaving a wife but no child, the
man[n] shall marry the widow and raise up children for his
brother. 20There were seven brothers; the first married and,
when he died, left no children; 21and the second married
her and died, leaving no children; and the third likewise;
22none of the seven left children. Last of all the woman herself died. 23In the resurrection[o] whose wife will she be? For
the seven had married her."

24 Jesus said to them, "Is not this the reason you are
wrong, that you know neither the scriptures nor the power
of God? 25For when they rise from the dead, they neither
marry nor are given in marriage, but are like angels in
heaven. 26And as for the dead being raised, have you not
read in the book of Moses, in the story about the bush, how
God said to him, 'I am the God of Abraham, the God of
Isaac, and the God of Jacob'? 27He is God not of the dead,
but of the living; you are quite wrong."

The Greatest of the Commandments

12:28–34

28 One of the scribes came near and
heard them disputing with one another,

(Bible text continued on page 176)

[n]Gk *his brother* [o]Other ancient authorities add *when they rise*

(continued from previous page)

Caesar later reformed the system by reducing taxes and levying no tax during the sabbatic years. But soon the Herods came to power.

The Herods instituted a poll tax and a tax on fishing rights. Customs were collected on trade routes by men like Levi in Capernaum (Matt. 9:9; Mark 2:14; Luke 5:27). The city may have also been a place for port duties and fishing tolls. Some items sold for 1,000 per cent above their original prices because of all the taxes. There may have been a sales tax on slaves, oil, clothes, hides, and furs.

Over and above these taxes were religious dues, generally between 10 and 20 percent of a person's income before government tax. As a result, during Jesus' time, the Jews were probably paying between 30 and 40 percent of their income on taxes and religious dues.

No wonder the Pharisees asked, "Is it lawful to pay taxes to the emperor, or not?" ◆

Jesus' example in paying taxes proves instructive. See "Jesus and Taxation," Matt. 17:24–27.

How Would You Respond?

A CLOSER LOOK 12:18–27

As the Sadducees saw Jesus gaining popularity and influence, they schemed to undo Him with trick questions (vv. 18–27). If you had been in His shoes, would you have known how to respond to their trickery? See "Retaliation Foiled," Luke 20:20–26.

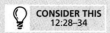

CONSIDER THIS
12:28–34

LIFE—THE BIG PICTURE

When Jesus recited the greatest of the commandments (vv. 29–30), He repeated the word "all" four times. What aspects of life was He including? Later, Paul emphasized that "all things were created" through and for Christ (Col. 1:15–18, emphasis added). How much of "all" is all?

Here's how a typical American who lives to be 75 years old will have spent life:

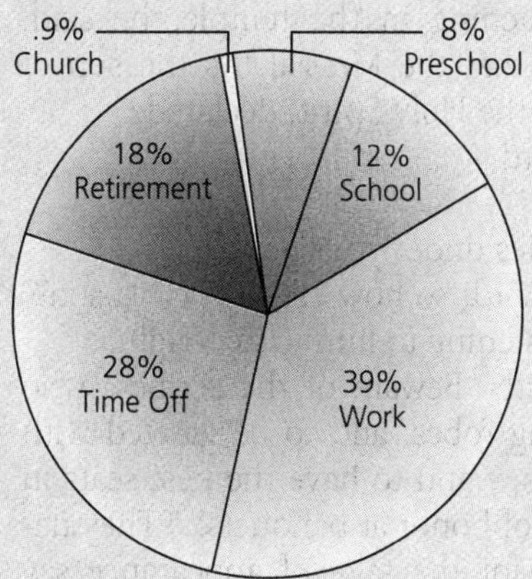

In light of this use of time, when does a person "love the Lord God" as Jesus commanded? Is that limited to what one does for an hour or so on Sunday morning? If so, then worship takes up a mere 3,900 hours, or 0.9 percent, of one's waking life—assuming that one goes to church *every* Sunday for 75 years!

Is that what Jesus or Paul had in mind? No, Christ is Lord of *all* of life—not just Sunday mornings, but weekdays, too, including time at work. Furthermore, He is Lord not only of our time, but of our money and possessions as well. Unfortunately, many Christians in the West have developed some dangerous attitudes in these areas that push God to the fringes of life. For example:

Myth: One-seventh of our time belongs to God. Some Christians speak of Sunday as "the Lord's day," a day for religion. And so it might be if Christians worshiped from sunup to sundown. But for most people Sunday worship means an hour-long service before an afternoon of televised sporting events. Thus the "day of worship" is effectively reduced to less than one-twentieth of the week.

That was never what God intended. Originally, the seventh day or Sabbath rest was viewed as the completion of the week, not a break or separation from the work week. It was a time for review, celebration, and restoration.

Yet already by Jesus' day there were major distortions regarding the Sabbath. It had become a day of legalistic ritual. Jesus sought to restore it as a day of compassion and worship (Luke 6:1–11; John 5:1–18).

Dedicating *all* of our time to God does not mean apportioning so much to family, so much to a job, so much for ourselves, and a little left over for God. No, all 168 hours of the week, all 52 weeks of the year, and all of the years of a lifetime belong to God and are on loan to us to manage for Him.

Myth: Ten percent of our money belongs to God. Some Christians believe that God expects them to give a flat 10 percent of their income to church and other ministries. The reality is that on the average, American believers give only 2.3 percent of their income to religious or charitable causes of any kind.

The underlying principle that needs to be considered is that God has given us the ability to earn money, so actually all 100 percent of our earnings belong to Him. We are called to manage our money—not just what we give away, but what we keep, too—according to His values. Tithing was intended as a discipline to remind God's people that all of what they have or earn belongs to Him. Originally a voluntary activity (Gen. 14:13–24; 28:20–22), it was intended for the care of others and as a representation of the worship of God (Deut. 26:1–19).

(continued on next page)

(continued from previous page)

Tithing was never intended to replace obedience to *all* of God's commands (Matt. 23:23–24).

Myth: Only some real estate belongs to God. Too many Christians have fallen into a dangerous pattern of identifying a few buildings as the Lord's property—religious institutions like churches, schools, and church-owned hospitals. By implication, other real estate is ours to do with as we please.

However, Scripture opposes that view. Paul says that "all things have been created through him and for him" (Col. 1:16). Even our bodies are "temples of God" (1 Cor. 6:19). God calls us to serve Him in *all* that we do (Col. 3:17). Therein lies the path to true blessing, peace, and truth. Christ has come to break our bondage to anything less. Equipped by His Spirit within us and instructed by His written Word, we can live *wholly* for the kingdom. ◆

and seeing that he answered them well, he asked him, "Which commandment is the first of all?" [29]Jesus answered, "The first is, 'Hear, O Israel: the Lord our God, the Lord is one; [30]you shall love the Lord your God with all your heart, and with all your soul, and with all your mind, and with all your strength.' [31]The second is this, 'You shall love your neighbor as yourself.' There is no other commandment greater than these." [32]Then the scribe said to him, "You are right, Teacher; you have truly said that 'he is one, and besides him there is no other'; [33]and 'to love him with all the heart, and with all the understanding, and with all the strength,' and 'to love one's neighbor as oneself,'—this is much more important than all whole burnt offerings and sacrifices." [34]When Jesus saw that he answered wisely, he said to him, "You are not far from the kingdom of God." After that no one dared to ask him any question.

Jesus Turns the Tables on the Pharisees

35 While Jesus was teaching in the temple, he said, "How can the scribes say that the Messiah[p] is the son of David? [36]David himself, by the Holy Spirit, declared,

'The Lord said to my Lord,
"Sit at my right hand,
until I put your enemies under your feet." '

[37]David himself calls him Lord; so how can he be his son?" And the large crowd was listening to him with delight.

38 As he taught, he said, "Beware of the scribes, who like to walk around in long robes, and to be greeted with respect in the marketplaces, [39]and to have the best seats in the synagogues and places of honor at banquets! [40]They devour widows' houses and for the sake of appearance say long prayers. They will receive the greater condemnation."

A Poor Widow's Contribution

12:41–44

41 He sat down opposite the treasury, and watched the crowd putting money into the treasury. Many rich people put in large sums. [42]A poor widow came and put in two small copper coins, which are worth a penny. [43]Then he called his disciples and said to them, "Truly I tell you, this poor widow has put in more than all those who are contributing to the treasury. [44]For all of them have contributed out of their abundance; but she out of her

12:43–44

[p]Or the Christ

poverty has put in everything she had, all she had to live
on."

Jesus Predicts the Temple's Destruction

13:1–37
see pg. 178

13 As he came out of the temple,
one of his disciples said to him,
"Look, Teacher, what large stones and what large buildings!" 2Then Jesus asked him, "Do you see these great
buildings? Not one stone will be left here upon another; all
will be thrown down."

Signs of the End

3 When he was sitting on the Mount of Olives opposite
the temple, Peter, James, John, and Andrew asked him privately, 4"Tell us, when will this be, and what will be the sign
that all these things are about to be accomplished?" 5Then
Jesus began to say to them, "Beware that no one leads you
astray. 6Many will come in my name and say, 'I am he!'[q] and
they will lead many astray. 7When you hear of wars and rumors of wars, do not be alarmed; this must take place, but
the end is still to come. 8For nation will rise against nation,
and kingdom against kingdom; there will be earthquakes in
various places; there will be famines. This is but the beginning of the birth pangs.
9 "As for yourselves, beware; for they will hand you over
to councils; and you will be beaten in synagogues; and you
will stand before governors and kings because of me, as a
testimony to them. 10And the good news[r] must first be proclaimed to all nations. 11When they bring you to trial and
hand you over, do not worry beforehand about what you
are to say; but say whatever is given you at that time, for it
is not you who speak, but the Holy Spirit. 12Brother will betray brother to death, and a father his child, and children
will rise against parents and have them put to death; 13and
you will be hated by all because of my name. But the one
who endures to the end will be saved.
14 "But when you see the desolating sacrilege set up
where it ought not to be (let the reader understand), then

[q]Gk *I am* [r]Gk *gospel*

Down to Her Last Penny

A CLOSER LOOK 12:41–44 *The poor widow in v. 42 was so destitute that she was literally in danger of death. For more on this incident, see "How Poor Was the Widow?" Luke 21:1–4.*

It's All Relative

CONSIDER THIS 12:43–44 **What did Jesus mean when He said that the widow had put more money into the treasury than anyone else (v. 43)? Clearly, He was indicating that economic value is relative. The widow's contribution would have been nothing but spare change to the rich who preceded her. But to her, two mites represented enormous value. It was "*everything* she had, *all* she had to live on" (v. 44, italics added). Replacing it would be difficult, if not impossible; as a poor widow, she was probably unemployable. Giving it to God meant that she could not use it to buy her next crust of bread.**

But Jesus indicated that God placed moral rather than economic value on her tiny offering. Her gift showed that she was giving herself entirely to God and trusting in Him to meet her needs. Her use of money disclosed the moral and spiritual condition of her heart.

those in Judea must flee to the mountains; 15the one on the
housetop must not go down or enter the house to take anything away; 16the one in the field must not turn back to get
a coat. 17Woe to those who are pregnant and to those who
are nursing infants in those days! 18Pray that it may not be
in winter. 19For in those days there will be suffering, such
as has not been from the beginning of the creation that God
created until now, no, and never will be. 20And if the Lord
had not cut short those days, no one would be saved; but
for the sake of the elect, whom he chose, he has cut short
those days. 21And if anyone says to you at that time, 'Look!
Here is the Messiah!'[s] or 'Look! There he is!'—do not believe it. 22False messiahs[t] and false prophets will appear and
produce signs and omens, to lead astray, if possible, the
elect. 23But be alert; I have already told you everything.

24 "But in those days, after that suffering,
the sun will be darkened,
and the moon will not give its light,
25 and the stars will be falling from heaven,
and the powers in the heavens will be shaken.

[s]Or *the Christ* [t]Or *christs*

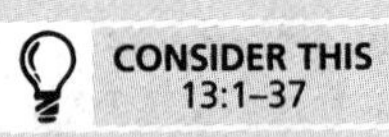

CONSIDER THIS
13:1–37

ISSUES FOR DOOMSDAY

As you look at events in the world today, you may feel anxious about how history is going to turn out. Perhaps you're confused and troubled about end times. The buildup of weapons, the warnings of religious prophets of doom, shaky economies, and the turmoil of nations may feel very unsettling.

Jesus' words in Mark 13 (and Matt. 24:1–51 and Luke 21:5–36) speak to these issues. They left an indelible impression on His followers. What touched off the discussion was the disciples' comments on the solidity and significance of a downtown building (Mark 13:1). Jesus replied by noting how temporary such structures actually are (v. 2). Later, in a quiet setting (v. 3), He went into far more detail about the end of history as we know it and the stresses believers would undergo (vv. 4–37). Rather than avoid the topic, He spoke of:

- *deception, wars, earthquakes, and famines as the beginning of sorrows (vv. 5–8).*
- *how His followers would experience testing as His witnesses before councils, governors, and kings (vv. 9–11).*
- *how family members would turn against each other (vv. 12–13).*

26Then they will see 'the Son of Man coming in clouds' with
great power and glory. 27Then he will send out the angels,
and gather his elect from the four winds, from the ends of
the earth to the ends of heaven.

28 "From the fig tree learn its lesson: as soon as its
branch becomes tender and puts forth its leaves, you know
that summer is near. 29So also, when you see these things
taking place, you know that he[u] is near, at the very gates.
30Truly I tell you, this generation will not pass away until all
these things have taken place. 31Heaven and earth will pass
away, but my words will not pass away.

32 "But about that day or hour no one knows, neither
the angels in heaven, nor the Son, but
only the Father. 33Beware, keep alert;[v] for
you do not know when the time will come. 34It is like a
man going on a journey, when he leaves home and puts his
slaves in charge, each with his work, and commands the
doorkeeper to be on the watch. 35Therefore, keep awake—
for you do not know when the master of the house will

13:33 see pg. 180

(Bible text continued on page 181)

[u]Or *it* [v]Other ancient authorities add *and pray*

"FOR IN THOSE DAYS THERE WILL BE SUFFERING. . . ."
—Mark 13:19

- *how distress and deception would eventually reign, but such times would be limited by God (vv. 14–25).*
- *His eventual return for His own (vv. 15–31).*
- *the fact that no one knows precisely when He will return—and thus the need for His followers to be watchful and dutiful in serving God (vv. 32–37).*

Jesus contrasted the strength and beauty of a downtown building with the faithful loyalty and service of His followers (vv. 2, 9, 13, 33–37). Human structures will inevitably crumble and fall, but the righteous works of God will last forever. Therefore, believers ought to stand firm, serving God faithfully—not just building monuments to their own accomplishments, and certainly not falling prey to the seductive dangers of the times. ◆

Paul emphasized exactly the same things as Jesus when he wrote his second letter to the Thessalonians and addressed the issue of troubled times (2 Thess. 2:1–17).

CONSIDER THIS
13:33

A Kingdom Perspective on Significance

Jesus wants His followers to evaluate turbulent times of change (v. 33) not just from the perspective of history but even more from the perspective of His kingdom. As believers, we are citizens of eternity. Therefore, our confidence needs to be rooted in something far more important than our positions and achievements here and now. It's not that the here and now has no importance. But as we live our lives, God wants us to be loyal workers for His kingdom, serving the people He sends our way.

Is your significance tied too closely to achievements—building buildings, reaching business goals, acquiring material possessions, climbing career ladders? There's nothing inherently wrong with these. But if you lost them, would your confidence completely crumble? If your sense of worth depends on them, what happens when you reach the top of the ladder, only to discover that the ladder is leaning against the wrong wall?

The problem is that our world has a system of values that is upside down from the way God determines value. It lacks any sense of what Scripture describes as "calling," or what Christians later termed "vocation"—a perspective that God has called and equipped people to serve Him through their work in the world. Instead, our culture encourages us to climb a work/identity ladder that is ultimately self-serving, and often self-destructive.

Climbing that ladder can be very misleading. The higher one goes, the more one's identity, value, and security tend to depend on the nature of one's work. But what happens if we lose our position, titles, or high-level compensation? Perhaps this explains why severe emotional problems—drug and alcohol abuse, abuse of spouse and children, divorce, even suicide—often accompany job loss. If our significance relies on our job, then it dies with our job.

God calls us to a far more stable basis for significance. He wants us to establish our identity in the fact that we are His children, created by Him to carry out good works as responsible people in His kingdom (Eph. 2:10). This is our calling or vocation from God. According to Scripture, our calling:

- is irrevocable (Rom. 11:29).
- is from God; He wants to let us share in Christ's glory (2 Thess. 2:14).
- is a function of how God has designed us (Eph. 2:10).
- is an assurance that God will give us everything we need to serve Him, including the strength to remain faithful to Him (1 Cor. 1:7–9).
- is what we should be proclaiming as our true identity (1 Pet. 2:5, 9).
- carries us through suffering (1 Pet. 2:19–21).
- is rooted in peace, no matter what the circumstances in which we find ourselves (1 Cor. 7:15–24).
- is focused on eternal achievements, not merely temporal ones (Phil. 3:13—4:1).

Above all else, believers are called to character development, service to others, and loyalty to God. These can be accomplished wherever we live or work, whatever our occupational status or position in society. If we pursue these, we can enjoy great satisfaction and significance. No matter what happens on the job, we can join Paul in saying, "We know that all things work together for good for those who love God, who are called according to his purpose" (Rom. 8:28). ◆

come, in the evening, or at midnight, or at cockcrow, or at
dawn, [36]or else he may find you asleep when he comes suddenly. [37]And what I say to you I say to all: Keep awake."

Leaders Plot to Do Away with Jesus

14 It was two days before the Passover and the festival
of Unleavened Bread. The chief priests and the
scribes were looking for a way to arrest Jesus[w] by stealth
and kill him; [2]for they said, "Not during the festival, or
there may be a riot among the people."

A Woman Anoints Jesus with Costly Oil

14:3–9

3 While he was at Bethany in the
house of Simon the leper,[x] as he sat at
the table, a woman came with an alabaster jar of very costly
ointment of nard, and she broke open the jar and poured
the ointment on his head. [4]But some were there who said to
one another in anger, "Why was the ointment wasted in
this way? [5]For this ointment could have been sold for more
than three hundred denarii,[y] and the money given to the
poor." And they scolded her. [6]But Jesus said, "Let her alone;
why do you trouble her? She has performed a good service

14:7 see pg. 182

for me. [7]For you always have the poor
with you, and you can show kindness to
them whenever you wish; but you will not always have me.

14:3–9

[8]She has done what she could; she has
anointed my body beforehand for its
burial. [9]Truly I tell you, wherever the good news[z] is proclaimed in the whole world, what she has done will be told
in remembrance of her."

Judas Betrays Jesus

10 Then Judas Iscariot, who was one of the twelve, went
to the chief priests in order to betray him to them. [11]When

[w]Gk *him* [x]The terms *leper* and *leprosy* can refer to several diseases [y]The denarius was the usual day's wage for a laborer [z]Or *gospel*

A Parting Gift

CONSIDER THIS 14:3–9 **What the disciples saw as waste (vv. 4–9) the Lord saw as worship. The woman's gift of costly oil was worth about one year's average wages, yet she poured it out, apparently sensing that her days with Jesus were drawing to a close.**

This incident raises the issue of how one's material wealth enters into worship. While Jesus was still physically present and available to her, the woman did "what she could" (v. 8). She took one of her most valuable possessions and gave it to Jesus in an unusual act of devotion. A waste? Not to the One she honored by it.

Today Jesus is not physically among us. Yet while we are alive, we control a certain measure of the world's resources. So we might ask: What act of worship might we give while we have opportunity? How might we honor the Lord materially?

There are no easy answers. But did Jesus give us a clue when He told His disciples that just as the woman had done Him "a good service," so they could do good to the poor at any time (v. 6)?

The woman's act was the first step in preparing Jesus' body for the grave. See "A Burial Fit for a King," Mark 15:42—16:1.

Important Preparations

A CLOSER LOOK 14:3–9 *It's difficult for us today to appreciate the significance that burial rituals had for ancient peoples (v. 8). Nearly every ancient religion gave explicit and sometimes elaborate instructions for preparing and burying the dead. See "Funeral Preparations," John 12:1–8.*

they heard it, they were greatly pleased, and promised to give him money. So he began to look for an opportunity to betray him.

The Upper Room

12 On the first day of Unleavened Bread, when the Passover lamb is sacrificed, his disciples said to him, "Where do you want us to go and make the preparations for you to eat the Passover?" [13]So he sent two of his disciples, saying to them, "Go into the city, and a man carrying a jar of water will meet you; follow him, [14]and wherever he enters, say to the owner of the house, 'The Teacher asks, Where is my guest room where I may eat the Passover with my disciples?' [15]He will show you a large room upstairs, furnished and ready. Make preparations for us there." [16]So the disciples set out and went to the city, and found everything as he had told them; and they prepared the Passover meal.

17 When it was evening, he came with the twelve. [18]And when they had taken their places and were eating, Jesus said, "Truly I tell you, one of you will betray me, one who is eating with me." [19]They began to be distressed and to say to him one after another, "Surely, not I?" [20]He said to them, "It is one of the twelve, one who is dipping bread[a] into the bowl[b] with me. [21]For the Son of Man goes as it is written of him, but woe to that one by whom the Son of Man is betrayed! It would have been better for that one not to have been born."

22 While they were eating, he took a loaf of bread, and after blessing it he broke it, gave it to them, and said, "Take; this is my body." [23]Then he took a cup, and after giving thanks he gave it to them, and all of them drank from it. [24]He said to them, "This is my blood of the[c] covenant, which is poured out for many. [25]Truly I tell you, I will never again drink of the fruit of the vine until that day when I drink it new in the kingdom of God."

26 When they had sung the hymn, they went out to the Mount of Olives. [27]And Jesus said to them, "You will all become deserters; for it is written,

'I will strike the shepherd,
and the sheep will be scattered.'

[28]But after I am raised up, I will go before you to Galilee." [29]Peter said to him, "Even though all become deserters, I will not." [30]Jesus said to him, "Truly I tell you, this day, this very night, before the cock crows twice, you will deny me

ALWAYS THE POOR

CONSIDER THIS 14:7 *Unfortunately, some people use Jesus' statement in v. 7 as an escape hatch to avoid caring for the poor. "Jesus Himself said there will always be poor people," the logic goes, "so what good does it do to offer aid? The problem won't go away." But Jesus had nothing of the sort in mind. On the contrary, He was mandating that we should always care for those who have need.*

[a]Gk lacks *bread* [b]Other ancient authorities read *same bowl* [c]Other ancient authorities add *new*

three times." 31But he said vehemently, "Even though I must
die with you, I will not deny you." And all of them said the
same.

Jesus Prays in the Garden of Gethsemane

14:32 32 They went to a place called Gethsemane; and he said to his disciples, "Sit
here while I pray." 33He took with him Peter and James and
John, and began to be distressed and agitated. 34And he
said to them, "I am deeply grieved, even to death; remain
here, and keep awake." 35And going a little farther, he
threw himself on the ground and prayed that, if it were
possible, the hour might pass from him. 36He said, "Abba,[d]
Father, for you all things are possible; remove this cup from
me; yet, not what I want, but what you want." 37He came
and found them sleeping; and he said to Peter, "Simon, are
14:38 you asleep? Could you not keep awake
one hour? 38Keep awake and pray that
you may not come into the time of trial;[e] the spirit indeed is
willing, but the flesh is weak." 39And again he went away
and prayed, saying the same words. 40And once more he
came and found them sleeping, for their eyes were very
heavy; and they did not know what to say to him. 41He
came a third time and said to them, "Are you still sleeping
and taking your rest? Enough! The hour has come; the Son
of Man is betrayed into the hands of sinners. 42Get up, let
us be going. See, my betrayer is at hand."

"THE SPIRIT INDEED IS WILLING, BUT THE FLESH IS WEAK." —Mark 14:38

Judas Brings About Jesus' Arrest

43 Immediately, while he was still speaking, Judas, one
of the twelve, arrived; and with him there was a crowd with
swords and clubs, from the chief priests, the scribes, and
the elders. 44Now the betrayer had given them a sign, say-

[d]Aramaic for *Father* [e]Or *into temptation*

Gethsemane

A CLOSER LOOK 14:32 *Jesus chose a familiar place of work in which to pray (v. 32). See, "Praying in a Workplace," Matt. 26:36.*

Watch and Pray!

A CLOSER LOOK 14:38 *Jesus told His disciples to pray to avoid succumbing to temptation (v. 38). He knew that only God could help them avoid, flee, confess, and resist it. See "Pay Attention to Temptation!" at 1 Cor. 10:12–13.*

ing, "The one I will kiss is the man; arrest him and lead him
away under guard." 45So when he came, he went up to him
at once and said, "Rabbi!" and kissed him. 46Then they laid
hands on him and arrested him. 47But one of those who
stood near drew his sword and struck the slave of the high
priest, cutting off his ear. 48Then Jesus said to them, "Have
you come out with swords and clubs to arrest me as though
I were a bandit? 49Day after day I was with you in the temple teaching, and you did not arrest me. But let the scriptures be fulfilled." 50All of them deserted him and fled.
51 A certain young man was following him, wearing
nothing but a linen cloth. They caught hold of him, 52but
he left the linen cloth and ran off naked.

Jesus Taken to the High Priest

14:53–64
53 They took Jesus to the high priest;
and all the chief priests, the elders, and
the scribes were assembled. 54Peter had followed him at a
distance, right into the courtyard of the high priest; and he

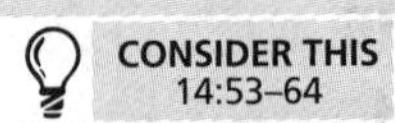

Is There Enough Evidence to Convict You?

Are you a "closet" Christian, an undercover follower of Christ, keeping your faith a secret? Would your friends or coworkers describe you as a loyal believer? Is there any evidence that could be used to convict you of practicing the faith?

The religious and political leaders of Israel wanted to rid themselves of Jesus. They tried every means possible to convict Him of a crime. They paid an informant from among Jesus' own followers—but he returned their money and declared the Lord to be innocent (vv. 43–46; Matt. 27:3–5). They orchestrated an armed mob to intimidate Him—but He kept His cool and restrained His followers (Matt. 26:51–54). The leaders even presented witnesses to testify against Him in court—but the witnesses either perjured themselves or contradicted each other (Mark 14:55–56).

People tried to convict Jesus of a crime—something bad—for which they lacked even a shred of evidence. Suppose you were on trial instead of Jesus. What would be some of the best evidence against you, that you were "guilty" of following Christ—something good, and something for which there should be evidence? Would

was sitting with the guards, warming himself at the fire.
55Now the chief priests and the whole council were looking
for testimony against Jesus to put him to death; but they
found none. 56For many gave false testimony against him,
and their testimony did not agree. 57Some stood up and
gave false testimony against him, saying, 58"We heard him
say, 'I will destroy this temple that is made with hands, and
in three days I will build another, not made with hands.' "
59But even on this point their testimony did not agree.
60Then the high priest stood up before them and asked Jesus, "Have you no answer? What is it that they testify
against you?" 61But he was silent and did not answer. Again
the high priest asked him, "Are you the Messiah,[f] the Son of
the Blessed One?" 62Jesus said, "I am; and

'you will see the Son of Man
seated at the right hand of the Power,'
and 'coming with the clouds of heaven.' "

63Then the high priest tore his clothes and said, "Why do
we still need witnesses? 64You have heard his blasphemy!

[f]*Or the Christ*

ALL OF THEM DESERTED HIM AND FLED.
—Mark 14:50

there be anything conclusive? Here is a checklist to consider:

EVIDENCE OF FOLLOWING JESUS

- ____ Displays the "beautiful attitudes" described by Jesus in His Sermon on the Mount (Matt. 5:3–16).
- ____ Thinks with a transformed mind, expresses a spirit of genuine love, and shows respect for authority (Rom. 12:1–2; 13:1–7).
- ____ Reflects the "lifestyle of love" (1 Cor. 13).
- ____ Displays the fruits of the Spirit described by Paul (Gal. 5:22–26).
- ____ Looks out for the interests of others in the humility of Christ (Phil. 2:1–4).
- ____ Rejoices always, prays without ceasing, and in everything gives thanks (1 Thess. 5:16–18).
- ____ Carries out works of faith and compassion (James 2:14–17), controls the tongue (3:1–11), and is known for wisdom (3:13).
- ____ Holds to the truth about Jesus (2 John 4, 3 John 3–4) and defends it (Jude 3).

Is there enough evidence to convict you of faith in Christ? ◆

What is your decision?" All of them condemned him as deserving death. 65Some began to spit on him, to blindfold
him, and to strike him, saying to him, "Prophesy!" The
guards also took him over and beat him.

Peter Denies His Lord

66 While Peter was below in the courtyard, one of the
servant-girls of the high priest came by. 67When she saw Peter warming himself, she stared at him and said, "You also
were with Jesus, the man from Nazareth." 68But he denied
it, saying, "I do not know or understand what you are talking about." And he went out into the forecourt.[g] Then the
cock crowed.[h] 69And the servant-girl, on seeing him, began
again to say to the bystanders, "This man is one of them."
70But again he denied it. Then after a little while the bystanders again said to Peter, "Certainly you are one of them;
for you are a Galilean." 71But he began to curse, and he
swore an oath, "I do not know this man you are talking
about." 72At that moment the cock crowed for the second
time. Then Peter remembered that Jesus had said to him,
"Before the cock crows twice, you will deny me three
times." And he broke down and wept.

[g]Or *gateway* [h]Other ancient authorities lack *Then the cock crowed*

ALL OF THEM CONDEMNED HIM AS DESERVING DEATH. —Mark 14:64

PERSONALITY PROFILE: BARABBAS

FOR YOUR INFO 15:7

Name meant: "Son of Abbas."

Home: Unknown, but because he was a revolutionary, he might have been from Galilee, known as a seedbed for resistors against Rome (see "Galilee," Mark 1:14).

Occupation: Unknown, but he may have worked as a member of the Zealots, ardent nationalists who wanted to throw off Roman occupation of Palestine.

Best known today for: Being released instead of Jesus by Pilate (v. 15).

Jesus Brought Before Pilate

15 As soon as it was morning, the chief priests held a consultation with the elders and scribes and the whole council. They bound Jesus, led him away, and handed him over to Pilate. 2Pilate asked him, "Are you the King of the Jews?" He answered him, "You say so." 3Then the chief priests accused him of many things. 4Pilate asked him again, "Have you no answer? See how many charges they bring against you." 5But Jesus made no further reply, so that Pilate was amazed.

"NOT THIS MAN BUT BARABBAS!"

But for a remarkable set of circumstances, Barabbas probably would have remained unknown to history. He was just another one of the sicarii ("dagger-men") who assassinated Roman officials in the vain hope of driving them out of Palestine. Occasionally, when political conditions were right, such men managed to gain a small following and create serious trouble. For example, in 6 B.C. Judas the Galilean led a tax revolt. But the Romans quickly executed him and scattered his followers.

In a similar way, the authorities had arrested Barabbas and others on charges of insurrection and murder (Mark 15:7; Luke 23:19). The prisoners knew well what fate awaited them—crucifixion, a grisly form of execution that the Romans reserved for political criminals. The public spectacle of nailing rebels to an upraised cross was a potent deterrent to political opposition.

But Barabbas was not to die in that manner. The arrest of Jesus, the political maneuverings of Caiaphas the high priest (see "Caiaphas, the Religious Power Broker," Matt. 26:3) and of Herod and Pilate (23:6–12), and the custom of releasing a prisoner during the feast of the Passover (Mark 15:6) combined to open a way for Barabbas to go free.

What finally secured his liberty were the cries of the mob to have him released (John 18:40). Pilate found it hard to believe that they actually preferred Barabbas, and when they kept demanding that Jesus be crucified, Pilate asked, "Shall I crucify your King?" (19:15). At that point the chief priests claimed, "We have no king but the emperor," and the governor released Barabbas. What a peculiar irony that a revolutionary against Rome should be released by the cry, "We have no king but the emperor." ◆

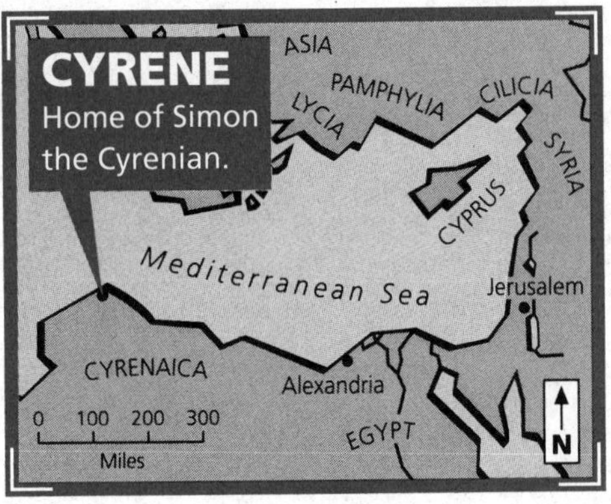

CYRENE

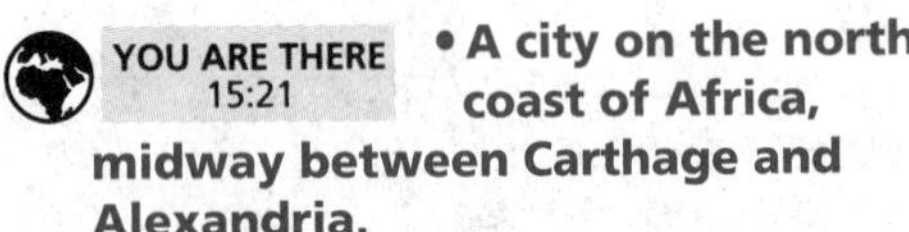

YOU ARE THERE 15:21

- A city on the north coast of Africa, midway between Carthage and Alexandria.
- Under the Romans, capital of the province of Cyrenaica (ancient and modern Libya).
- Built on beautiful tableland 2,000 feet above sea level but only 16 miles from the sea.
- A major crossroads for trade, commerce, and tourism.
- Renowned as an intellectual center.
- In New Testament times, home to a large Jewish population.
- Site of a Jewish revolt in A.D. 115–116 in which 200,000 people were killed.
- Stricken by a disastrous earthquake in A.D. 365.
- Invaded by the Arabs in A.D. 642.
- Uninhabited today.

6 Now at the festival he used to release a prisoner for
15:7 see pg. 186
them, anyone for whom they asked.
7Now a man called Barabbas was in
prison with the rebels who had committed murder during
the insurrection. 8So the crowd came and began to ask Pilate to do for them according to his custom. 9Then he answered them, "Do you want me to release for you the King
of the Jews?" 10For he realized that it was out of jealousy
that the chief priests had handed him over. 11But the chief
priests stirred up the crowd to have him release Barabbas
for them instead. 12Pilate spoke to them again, "Then what
do you wish me to do[i] with the man you call[j] the King of
the Jews?" 13They shouted back, "Crucify him!" 14Pilate
asked them, "Why, what evil has he done?" But they
shouted all the more, "Crucify him!" 15So Pilate, wishing to
satisfy the crowd, released Barabbas for them; and after
flogging Jesus, he handed him over to be crucified.

Soldiers Mock Jesus

16 Then the soldiers led him into the courtyard of the
palace (that is, the governor's headquarters[k]); and they
15:17–20
called together the whole cohort. 17And
they clothed him in a purple cloak; and
after twisting some thorns into a crown, they put it on him.
18And they began saluting him, "Hail, King of the Jews!"
19They struck his head with a reed, spat upon him, and
knelt down in homage to him. 20After mocking him, they
stripped him of the purple cloak and put his own clothes
on him. Then they led him out to crucify him.

The Crucifixion

15:21
21 They compelled a passer-by, who
was coming in from the country, to carry
his cross; it was Simon of Cyrene, the father of Alexander
and Rufus. 22Then they brought Jesus[l] to the place called
Golgotha (which means the place of a skull). 23And they of-

[i]Other ancient authorities read *what should I do* [j]Other ancient authorities lack *the man you call* [k]Gk *the praetorium* [l]Gk *him*

A CLOSER LOOK 15:17–20

Mocked by Wealth

The outrageous incident in vv. 17–20 is a reminder that the symbols of wealth can be used to send many kinds of messages—including mockery and disrespect, as happened here. See "Discrimination on the Basis of Wealth," John 19:1–6.

fered him wine mixed with myrrh; but he did not take it.
15:24
24 And they crucified him, and divided
his clothes among them, casting lots to
decide what each should take.
25 It was nine o'clock in the morning when they crucified him. 26 The inscription of the charge against him read,
"The King of the Jews." 27 And with him they crucified two
bandits, one on his right and one on his left.[m] 29 Those who
passed by derided[n] him, shaking their heads and saying,
"Aha! You who would destroy the temple and build it in
three days, 30 save yourself, and come down from the cross!"
31 In the same way the chief priests, along with the scribes,
were also mocking him among themselves and saying, "He
saved others; he cannot save himself. 32 Let the Messiah,[o] the
King of Israel, come down from the cross now, so that we
may see and believe." Those who were crucified with him
also taunted him.
33 When it was noon, darkness came over the whole
land[p] until three in the afternoon. 34 At three o'clock Jesus
cried out with a loud voice, "Eloi, Eloi, lema sabachthani?"
which means, "My God, my God, why have you forsaken
me?"[q] 35 When some of the bystanders heard it, they said,
"Listen, he is calling for Elijah." 36 And someone ran, filled a
sponge with sour wine, put it on a stick, and gave it to him
to drink, saying, "Wait, let us see whether Elijah will come
to take him down." 37 Then Jesus gave a loud cry and
breathed his last. 38 And the curtain of the temple was torn
15:39 see pg. 190
in two, from top to bottom. 39 Now when
the centurion, who stood facing him,
saw that in this way he[r] breathed his last, he said, "Truly
this man was God's Son!"[s]
15:40 see pg. 192
40 There were also women looking on
from a distance; among them were Mary
Magdalene, and Mary the mother of James the younger and
of Joses, and Salome. 41 These used to follow him and provided for him when he was in Galilee; and there were many
other women who had come up with him to Jerusalem.

[m]Other ancient authorities add verse 28, *And the scripture was fulfilled that says, "And he was counted among the lawless."* [n]Or *blasphemed* [o]Or *the Christ* [p]Or *earth* [q]Other ancient authorities read *made me a reproach* [r]Other ancient authorities add *cried out and* [s]Or *a son of God*

Jesus Died Poor

A CLOSER LOOK 15:24

Jesus not only was born poor and lived poor, He died poor. The soldiers tore the clothes off his back and divided them among themselves (v. 24), leaving Him with not a single material possession to pass on to His family or friends. "Jesus—A Homeless Man?" (Matt. 8:20) addresses His lack of earthly wealth and what that means for us today.

SIMON OF CYRENE

As Jesus staggered under the weight of His cross, Roman soldiers pressed into service a man known as Simon the Cyrenean to help Him (Mark 15:21). Little is known of this man who came to the Lord's aid, but he had probably made the pilgrimage from his home in Africa to Jerusalem for the Passover. Perhaps after the dramatic events in which he played a small part he stayed, like many Hellenistic Jews, until Pentecost. We know that men from Cyrene were among the crowd that witnessed the birth of the church (Acts 2:10).

We suspect that Simon became a believer, because Mark recorded his sons' names, Alexander and Rufus. (Alexander was probably a popular name among the Cyreneans; Alexander the Great had captured the city in 331 B.C.) Paul mentioned Rufus, along with his mother, in his greetings to the Romans (Rom. 16:13). Thus the family was well known to the early church.

Jesus Is Buried

15:42—16:1

42 When evening had come, and since
it was the day of Preparation, that is, the
day before the sabbath, 43Joseph of Arimathea, a respected
member of the council, who was also himself waiting expectantly for the kingdom of God, went boldly to Pilate and
asked for the body of Jesus. 44Then Pilate wondered if he
were already dead; and summoning the centurion, he asked
him whether he had been dead for some time. 45When he
learned from the centurion that he was dead, he granted
the body to Joseph. 46Then Joseph[t] bought a linen cloth,
and taking down the body,[u] wrapped it in the linen cloth,
and laid it in a tomb that had been hewn out of the rock.
He then rolled a stone against the door of the tomb. 47Mary
Magdalene and Mary the mother of Joses saw where the
body[u] was laid.

[t]Gk *he* [u]Gk *it*

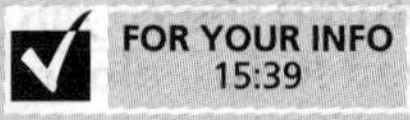

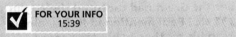

FOR YOUR INFO
15:39

CENTURIONS

Roman centurions (v. 39) were non-commissioned officers who commanded battle groups called "centuries," each comprising at least 100 men. Akin to sergeants in a modern army, centurions often led Rome's local police forces in occupied territories.

Centurions were responsible for keeping track of individuals who posed a threat to Rome's security. Because Jesus drew thousands of people to hear Him, He was perhaps kept under surveillance. That may account for the accurate knowledge that one officer seemed to have of Him (Luke 7:1–10).

The Roman Army

1 Contubernum	=	*8 soldiers*		
1 Century	=	*10 Contubernums*	=	*80 to 100 men*
1 Cohort	=	*6 Centuries*	=	*500 to 600 men*
1 Legion	=	*10 Cohorts*	=	*6,000 men*

At the time of Jesus, Rome had an estimated 500,000 troops in its army.

Legions were placed in two major Roman cities of Palestine, Sebaste in Samaria and Caesarea on the Mediterranean. A military force was also kept in Jerusalem at the Antonia fortress, guarding Herod's temple palace.

An Angel Announces the Resurrection

16:1–8 see pg. 194

16 When the sabbath was over,
Mary Magdalene, and Mary the
mother of James, and Salome bought spices, so that they
might go and anoint him. 2And very early on the first day
of the week, when the sun had risen, they went to the
tomb. 3They had been saying to one another, "Who will roll
away the stone for us from the entrance to the tomb?"
4When they looked up, they saw that the stone, which was
very large, had already been rolled back. 5As they entered
the tomb, they saw a young man, dressed in a white robe,
sitting on the right side; and they were alarmed. 6But he
said to them, "Do not be alarmed; you are looking for Jesus
of Nazareth, who was crucified. He has been raised; he is
not here. Look, there is the place they laid him. 7But go, tell
his disciples and Peter that he is going ahead of you to
Galilee; there you will see him, just as he told you." 8So

◆ ◆ ◆ ◆ ◆ ◆ ◆ ◆ ◆ ◆ ◆ ◆ ◆ ◆ ◆ ◆

During Jewish feasts, Rome moved additional troops into the city to ensure order.

It was to a Gentile Roman centurion and his troops that fell the gruesome task of crucifying Jesus and the two men with Him. The officer had likely observed Jesus' trial, final march to the execution, crucifixion, and response to the crowd that mocked Him. He had seen the sky turn black at midday, felt the earth quake, and heard Jesus' last, exhausted death cry. A Gentile who probably had little regard for Hebrew religion, he was left with no doubt that the man he had seen die was not only "innocent" (Luke 23:47), but was in fact the very Son of God (Mark 15:39; Matt. 27:54). ◆

Another centurion who responded to the message about Christ was Cornelius. Read about him at Acts 10:1.

A Burial Fit for a King

CONSIDER THIS 15:42—16:1 **How much should you spend on a funeral? A fortune, or only enough to pay for the barest essentials?**

The four Gospel writers recorded that Jesus' body was treated as a rich man's corpse might be—which is not surprising since rich people buried Him:

- ***Joseph of Arimathea* bought fine linen to wrap the body in before laying it in his own very expensive tomb (v. 43–46; Matt. 27:60).**
- ***Nicodemus* helped with the arrangements and brought 100 pounds of myrrh and aloes, costly substances used to perfume and wrap the body (John 19:39).**
- ***Women who had supported Jesus* in His ministry, including Mary Magdalene, Mary the mother of James, and Salome, prepared spices and fragrant oils to place on the body as soon as the Sabbath was over (Mark 16:1; Luke 23:56).**

Those who took charge of Jesus' burial did so out of love, not guilt. And under the circumstances, they obviously were not trying to make a prideful show of their wealth. Rather they honestly expressed their grief, devotion, respect, adoration, and desire to protect the Lord's body from His enemies. They did what they could according to their desires and financial resources, and in keeping with the laws, customs, and traditions of their day.

The first step in preparing Jesus' body for the grave was actually a woman's curious act of devotion. See "A Parting Gift," Mark 14:3–9.

It is difficult for us today to appreciate the significance that burial rituals had for ancient peoples. See "Funeral Preparations," John 12:1–8.

QUOTE UNQUOTE

CONSIDER THIS
16:15

Some Christians today feel that the church is not fulfilling the bold mandate prescribed by Christ in v. 15:

The modern religious crisis . . . is its fearful retreat into the comfortable womb of community, where there is no outward mission, and where the retreating community inevitably begins to die—as if a fetus from within chooses its own abortion.

National Catholic Reporter, October 27, 1989, p. 1

they went out and fled from the tomb, for terror and amazement had seized them; and they said nothing to anyone, for they were afraid.[v]

THE SHORTER ENDING OF MARK

⟦And all that had been commanded them they told briefly to those around Peter. And afterward Jesus himself sent out through them, from east to west, the sacred and imperishable proclamation of eternal salvation.[w]⟧

THE LONGER ENDING OF MARK

Jesus Appears to Many Witnesses

9 ⟦Now after he rose early on the first day of the week,
he appeared first to Mary Magdalene, from whom he had cast
out seven demons. 10She went out and told those who had

[v]Some of the most ancient authorities bring the book to a close at the end of verse 8. One authority concludes the book with the shorter ending; others include the shorter ending and then continue with verses 9-20. In most authorities verses 9-20 follow immediately after verse 8, though in some of these authorities the passage is marked as being doubtful. [w]Other ancient authorities add *Amen*

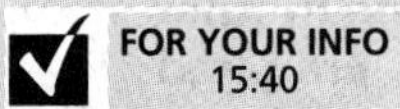

FOR YOUR INFO
15:40

WHY SO MANY MARYS?

In reading the New Testament, one discovers that Mary was a popular name in first-century Palestine. For example, we find:

- *Mary of Nazareth, the mother of Jesus (Luke 1:26—2:52).*
- *Mary of Bethany, the sister of Martha and Lazarus (Luke 10:38–42; John 11). She anointed Jesus with perfume before His death (John 12:3).*
- *Mary of Magdala, a financial supporter of Jesus (Luke 8:2–3). The Lord had cast seven demons out of her. She watched Jesus' crucifixion and was the first witness of His resurrection (Mark 15:40; 16:9).*
- *Mary the mother of James and Joses. She was present at Jesus' crucifixion and was probably the same woman described as the "other" Mary (Matt. 27:61; 28:1) and Mary the wife of Clopas (John 19:25).*
- *Mary the mother of Mark, making her a relative of Barnabas (Acts 12:12; Col. 4:10).*
- *Mary of Rome, known simply as a woman who worked hard for Paul and his companions (Rom. 16:6).*

Why were so many Jewish women named Mary? The name is the Greek form of the Hebrew Miriam, *which was the name of one of Israel's most famous women:*

been with him, while they were mourning and weeping.
11But when they heard that he was alive and had been seen
by her, they would not believe it.
12 After this he appeared in another form to two of
them, as they were walking into the country. 13And they
went back and told the rest, but they did not believe them.

Final Instructions

14 Later he appeared to the eleven themselves as they
were sitting at the table; and he upbraided them for their
lack of faith and stubbornness, because they had not believed those who saw him after he had
16:15
risen.[x] 15And he said to them, "Go into
all the world and proclaim the good news[y] to the whole

(Bible text continued on page 195)

[x]Other ancient authorities add, in whole or in part, *And they excused themselves, saying, "This age of lawlessness and unbelief is under Satan, who does not allow the truth and power of God to prevail over the unclean things of the spirits. Therefore reveal your righteousness now"—thus they spoke to Christ. And Christ replied to them, "The term of years of Satan's power has been fulfilled, but other terrible things draw near. And for those who have sinned I was handed over to death, that they may return to the truth and sin no more, that they may inherit the spiritual and imperishable glory of righteousness that is in heaven."* [y]Or *gospel*

- *Miriam was the sister of Moses (Num. 26:59) and one of the nation's first prophets (Ex. 15:20).*
- *She, her brother, and Aaron were the leadership team that God appointed to lead Israel out of Egypt and through the wilderness toward the Promised Land (Mic. 6:4).*
- *Miriam displayed courage early in life when she saved her baby brother from death (Ex. 2:4–7).*
- *Later, after Israel escaped across the Red Sea from the Egyptian army, she helped lead the people in songs of celebration and praise (Ex. 15:20–21).*
- *However, on one occasion she spoke against Moses. As a consequence she experienced God's judgment by contracting leprosy. For seven days she was shut out of the camp, the time required before a person healed of leprosy could rejoin the community (Num. 12:1–15).*
- *While she was on "forced sick leave," the people remained in one place until she returned to her work of leading the people (Num. 12:15).* ◆

Faith Impacts the World

CONSIDER THIS 16:15–16 **Jesus sent His followers into "all the world" (v. 15). Clearly He had global impact in mind. But spreading Christ's message involves more than just broadcasting a statement or set of facts. How does faith *impact* the world?**

One way is through followers of Christ who live out the gospel and proclaim it to the world. That's why the lifestyles and relationships of believers are so important. People are watching to see how we as Christians handle our responsibilities and resources. Is there any evidence that Christ really makes a difference in our lives?

Another way is through Christian institutions, such as local churches, parachurch organizations, and the Christian media. If you work or volunteer for one of these kinds of organizations, you have an important opportunity to touch the needs of the world with Christ's love and power.

A third sphere of influence is through lobbying and advocacy. Here Christians attempt to influence the institutions and people that control society. This might mean something as simple as voting, or something as complex as running for office or working to enact a particular piece of legislation. In our culture, Christians have the right to participate actively in public policy decisions, and we should use that right in ways that we believe honor the Lord.

As we attempt to take Christ's message to "all the world," it helps to understand how our world operates. See the diagram located at pages xx–xxii, "Faith Impacts the World," to find out more about how we can be salt and light in a world that needs Jesus.

EVIDENCE FOR THE RESURRECTION—JESUS' APPEARANCES

Dead people don't ordinarily rise again. History stands on the fact that death is inevitable, and no human can avoid it. But Jesus broke that cycle. He conquered death by rising from the grave (vv. 1–8), and verified His resurrection by appearing to many of His followers:

RESURRECTION APPEARANCES			
Who Sees Him	**Where**	**When**	**Reference**
Mary Magdalene, Mary the mother of James, and **Salome**	At the tomb	Early Sunday morning	Matt. 28:1–10; Mark 16:1–8; Luke 24:1–12; John 20:1–9
Mary Magdalene	At the tomb	Early Sunday morning	Mark 16:9–11; John 20:11–18
Peter	Jerusalem	Sunday	Luke 24:34; 1 Cor. 15:5
Two travelers	Road to Emmaus	Midday Sunday	Luke 24:13–32
Ten disciples	Upper room	Sunday evening	Mark 16:14; Luke 24:36–43; John 20:19–25
Eleven disciples	Upper room	One week later	John 20:26–29; 1 Cor. 15:5
Seven disciples	Fishing in Galilee	Dawn	John 21:1–23
Eleven disciples	Galilee	Much later	Matt. 28:16–20; Mark 16:15–18
500 followers	Probably Galilee	Later	1 Cor. 15:6
James the apostle	Unknown	Later	1 Cor. 15:7
Disciples, leading women, Jesus' brothers, and others	Mount of Olives	40 days after the resurrection	Luke 24:46–53; Acts 1:3–14
Saul of Tarsus	Road to Damascus	Midday, years later	Acts 9:1–9; 1 Cor. 15:8

As Christians we can have hope in life after death because Jesus broke the bondage of death (1 Cor. 15:12–24, 35–58). ◆

The resurrection is the most amazing news the world has ever heard. For more on this most incredible event of history, see "Ten Myths About Christianity, Myth #2: There Is No Evidence that Jesus Rose from the Dead," Matt. 28:1–10.

16:15–16
see pg. 193

creation. 16The one who believes and is
baptized will be saved; but the one who
does not believe will be condemned. 17And these signs will
accompany those who believe: by using my name they will
cast out demons; they will speak in new tongues; 18they
will pick up snakes in their hands,[z] and if they drink any
deadly thing, it will not hurt them; they will lay their hands
on the sick, and they will recover."

The Ascension and Its Effect

19 So then the Lord Jesus, after he had spoken to them,
was taken up into heaven and sat down at the right hand of
God. 20And they went out and proclaimed the good news
everywhere, while the Lord worked with them and confirmed the message by the signs that accompanied it.[a]]

[z]Other ancient authorities lack *in their hands* [a]Other ancient authorities add *Amen*

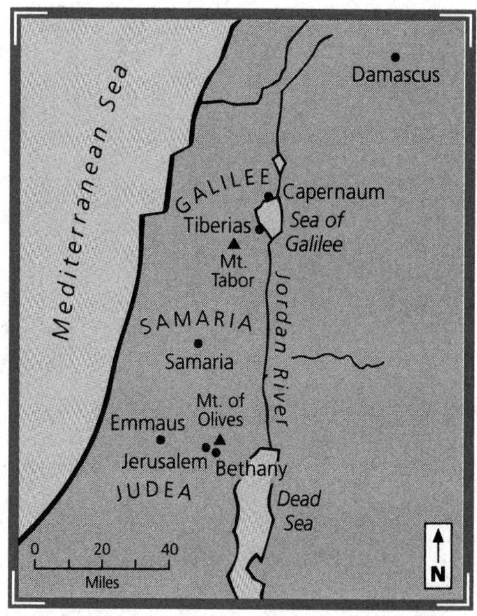

RESURRECTION APPEARANCES

The Global Gospel

Who was Jesus of Nazareth and what difference does it make? That's the question Luke answers in this carefully researched account that reads like a newspaper serial of the life of Christ.

Luke tells a story that has universal appeal. The Jesus that he portrays reaches out to people of every class and background—Jews, Samaritans, Gentiles, Roman soldiers, the poor, women, children, the powerful, the powerless, the sick, the fearful, the devout, the irreligious. He has something to offer everyone. Perhaps that's why some of today's most popular selections of Scripture come from this book—the Christmas story, the Good Samaritan, the Prodigal Son.

Jesus of Nazareth was a carpenter from an obscure town in an insignificant Roman province. Nevertheless, Luke will help you discover Him to be the international Christ whose words and works have global implications.

The Gospel According to

Luke

The Jesus that he portrays reaches out to people of every class and background.

C O N T E N T S

Whom Did Jesus Touch?

A R T I C L E S

Who Was the Neighbor? (10:37)

One of Jesus' most popular parables reduces an abstract theological question to a simple, practical challenge: "Go and do likewise!"

Watch Out for Greed! (12:15)

Jesus warned us to guard against *covetousness*—longing for what we don't have. He was not telling us to watch for it in others, but in ourselves.

Set for Life—But What about Eternity? (16:19–31)

It can be a dangerous thing to have it made in this life. With wealth, status, and power, who needs God?

◆ ◆

Luke, the Gentile Author

To the best of our knowledge, the entire Bible, Old Testament and New, was composed by Hebrew writers, with the exception of one man—the "beloved physician," Luke. A Greek from Antioch of Syria (according to one tradition), he was well educated and thoroughly acquainted with the Roman world. His writings, the Gospel of Luke and Acts, show a far more cultured form of Greek than the rest of the New Testament.

How did Luke come to write nearly one-fourth of the New Testament? He probably began by traveling with Paul on parts of his second, third, and final journeys. At three places in Acts, the narrative changes to the first person ("we," Acts 16:10–17; 20:5—21:18; 27:1—28:16). That probably indicates that Luke was personally present during those episodes.

While Paul was imprisoned at Caesarea for two years (Acts 24:24–27), Luke may have used the time to visit Galilee and Judea, gathering firsthand accounts of Jesus' life. He may have interviewed Mary, Jesus' mother, as his account describes details of her pregnancy and motherhood that the other three Gospel writers leave out: for example, her song of praise (Luke 1:46–55) and her habit of reflection on the events of which she was a part (2:19, 51). Who better to pay attention to the virgin birth from Mary's point of view than a physician?

Luke 1:1 implies that the doctor may also have visited Matthew, Mark, or John, the other Gospel writers, or perhaps others from the Twelve who remained in Palestine. Whoever his sources were, Luke's detailed descriptions indicate that they were actual participants. There was no need to resort to legends and hearsay. Instead, writing as a disciplined, careful historian and inspired by the Holy Spirit, Luke compiled the material into a skillfully crafted document, "an orderly account of the events that have been fulfilled . . ." (1:1).

If, as is probable, Luke was a Gentile, then it's no surprise that his Gospel seems to highlight Gentiles and their response to Jesus. For example, Matthew traces Jesus' genealogy back to Abraham, the father of the Jews (Matt. 1:2), but Luke traces it back to Adam, the father of the human race (Luke 3:38). Furthermore, Luke's narrative continues into Acts, where He shows the gospel moving beyond its Jewish origins to include peoples of every race.

One early source states that Luke had no wife or children, which would have made it easy for him to travel with Paul. Elsewhere Paul refers to him affectionately as a "fellow worker" (Philem. 24), a term of high esteem. ◆

The Gospel of Luke is only volume one of a two-volume set. Volume two begins at Acts 1:1.

The First of Two Volumes

By the time Nero ascended to the title of Caesar over an increasingly troubled realm, the Christian movement had spread to most of the Roman empire's major cities. Yet the authorities did not at first view the new religion as a significant threat. Indeed, they still regarded it as a minor sect of Judaism. Nevertheless, the Christians' insistence on the divinity of Christ and their refusal to pay homage to the emperors eventually brought state-supported persecution.

Against this backdrop Luke wrote his Gospel and the book of Acts. The two-part narrative could have been intended as a legal document for the apostle Paul, who awaited trial at Rome (Acts 22:11; 25:11; 28:30–31). In his Gospel, Luke presents "all that Jesus did and taught" (Acts 1:1). In Acts, he goes on to describe how Jesus' followers continued their Lord's work.

The key link between these two accounts is the Holy Spirit. While John's Gospel has much to say about the person of the Spirit, Luke-Acts emphasizes the activity of the Spirit in the ministry of Jesus and the early church. In the Gospel, John the Baptist and his parents are filled with the Spirit (Luke 1:15, 41, 67), as is Simeon (2:25–35). Jesus begins His ministry in "the power of the Spirit" (4:14; also 4:1, 18; 10:21), and He promises the Spirit to His disciples in their hour of need (12:12). Jesus is not alone; the Spirit is always with Him, within Him, empowering Him to accomplish God's purpose. ◆

Personality Profile: Luke

Also known as: The "beloved physician" (Col. 4:14).

Home: Antioch of Syria; later Philippi and other cities where Christian communities were started.

Background: Born into a cultured, educated Gentile family.

Profession: Primarily a physician, though he became a historian and author, and even did some evangelism.

Best known today for: Writing about one-fourth of the New Testament (Luke and Acts). His works emphasize the impact of the gospel on people considered "second-class" in Jewish culture at the time—Gentiles, women, the poor—as well as the topics of prayer and the work of the Holy Spirit.

LUKE, THE BELOVED PHYSICIAN. . . .
—Colossians 4:14

Luke's Preface

1:1–4

1 Since many have undertaken to
set down an orderly account of the
events that have been fulfilled among us, 2just as they were
handed on to us by those who from the beginning were
eyewitnesses and servants of the word, 3I too decided, after
investigating everything carefully from the very first,[a] to
write an orderly account for you, most excellent
Theophilus, 4so that you may know the truth concerning
the things about which you have been instructed.

An Angel Promises Zechariah a Son

1:5

5 In the days of King Herod of Judea,
there was a priest named Zechariah, who
belonged to the priestly order of Abijah. His wife was a descendant of Aaron, and her name was Elizabeth. 6Both of
them were righteous before God, living blamelessly according to all the commandments and regulations of the Lord.
7But they had no children, because Elizabeth was barren,
and both were getting on in years.
8 Once when he was serving as priest before God and
his section was on duty, 9he was chosen by lot, according to
the custom of the priesthood, to enter the sanctuary of the
Lord and offer incense. 10Now at the time of the incense offering, the whole assembly of the people was praying outside. 11Then there appeared to him an angel of the Lord,
standing at the right side of the altar of incense. 12When
Zechariah saw him, he was terrified; and fear overwhelmed

1:5–25 see pg. 202

him. 13But the angel said to him, "Do not
be afraid, Zechariah, for your prayer has
been heard. Your wife Elizabeth will bear you a son, and
you will name him John. 14You will have joy and gladness,
and many will rejoice at his birth, 15for he will be great in
the sight of the Lord. He must never drink wine or strong
drink; even before his birth he will be filled with the Holy
Spirit. 16He will turn many of the people of Israel to the
Lord their God. 17With the spirit and power of Elijah he
will go before him, to turn the hearts of parents to their

(Bible text continued on page 203)

[a]Or *for a long time*

King Herod

King Herod, also known as Herod the Great, was highly intelligent, charming, and a brilliant politician. Yet his memory lives in infamy for the violence, incest, and intrigue that marked his family. Read about it in "The Herods," Acts 12:1–2.

Jesus Is for Gentiles, Too

CONSIDER THIS 1:1–4 **Luke's Gospel (as well as Acts) is addressed to someone named Theophilus. Little is known about this person, though speculation abounds. Was this an individual or a group of believers? Was Theophilus, which means "lover of God," his given name or a name taken after conversion (a common practice)? The title "most excellent" (Luke 1:3) indicates prominence and a high rank in Roman society. However, the title is dropped in Acts 1:1. Did Theophilus lose his position in the intervening years?**

One thing seems apparent: Luke was writing to and for a Gentile reader. In fact, a major emphasis of the account is that the gospel is not just for a select nation. Jesus offers forgiveness and salvation freely to all humanity, regardless of race, gender, or social merit. Luke shows that the good news is for:

- **Samaritans (Luke 9:52–56; 10:30–37; 17:11–19)**
- **Gentiles (2:32; 4:25–27; 7:1–9; 10:1; 24:47)**
- **Jews (1:32–33, 54)**
- **Women (1:26–56; 7:36–50; 8:1–3; 10:38–42)**
- **Outcasts such as tax collectors, widows, lepers, and the disabled (3:12; 4:27; 5:27–32; 7:11–15, 22–23, 37–50; 14:1–6; 15:1; 17:12; 19:2–10)**
- **The poor (1:53; 2:7; 6:20; 7:22)**
- **The rich (19:2; 23:50–51)**

Personality Profile: Zechariah

FOR YOUR INFO 1:5–25

Often confused with: Zechariah, the name of dozens of other men in the Bible, as well as the priest who was murdered in the temple, also called Zacharias (Matt. 23:35; Luke 11:51).

Home: The Judean hill country.

Family: Descended from Abijah, who was a priest in David's day and a descendent of Aaron. His wife was Elizabeth, also from a family of priestly descent. John the Baptist was their son.

Occupation: Priest and therefore a local leader in his town's religious community.

Best known today for: Faltering in his faith when God was answering his prayer.

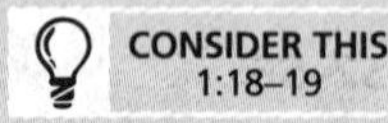

Can You Be Trusted?

Told by the angel Gabriel that he and his wife would have a son, Zechariah expressed doubt (v. 18) based on their advanced age. But implicit in his comments was a lack of trust in Gabriel himself. The angel responded with the simple statement, "I am Gabriel, I stand in the presence of God." No appeal to evidence; no attempt at persuasion. Just a simple declaration of his position before God. That alone was enough to ensure that the messenger was absolutely trustworthy.

Were Gabriel a liar, God would have banished him long before. But his continued presence before God indicated that he must have been truthful, as none but the truthful can stand in God's presence.

Consider the implications of that for the character of believers today. If we know God, we are to be like Him (2 Pet. 1:3–4; 1 John 3:2). As He is faithful and true (Rev. 3:14; 19:11; 22:6), we must be faithful and true. Wouldn't it be something if the claim "I am a Christian" were enough to establish one's integrity!

Yet that is far from the case today. For example, how

children, and the disobedient to the wisdom of the righteous, to make ready a people prepared for the Lord."

1:18–19

18Zechariah said to the angel, "How will I
know that this is so? For I am an old
man, and my wife is getting on in years." 19The angel
replied, "I am Gabriel. I stand in the presence of God, and I
have been sent to speak to you and to bring you this good
news. 20But now, because you did not believe my words,
which will be fulfilled in their time, you will become mute,
unable to speak, until the day these things occur."
21 Meanwhile the people were waiting for Zechariah,

Personality Profile: Elizabeth

FOR YOUR INFO 1:24

Home: Hill country of Judea.

Family: Descended from a priestly family; wife of Zechariah, a priest; mother of John the Baptist; a relative of Mary of Nazareth.

Occupation: Homemaker.

Best known today as: The mother of John the Baptist.

many "Christian businesspeople" bring disrepute to the name of Christ by failing to pay their bills, abusing contracts, performing sloppy work, or making excuses rather than fulfilling commitments? Even some churches and Christian ministries cheat vendors, short-change visiting speakers and musicians, misrepresent their finances, or pay employees far below a fair wage for their work.

What a tragedy! If Gabriel's confident statement is any indication of the integrity that should mark God's workers, then it ought to be that one need only be identified as a Christian to erase all doubt. Of all people, Christ's followers should pursue an unimpeachable reputation for integrity. ◆

"I won't hire Christians!" says one business owner, himself a believer. See 1 Tim. 6:1–2.

How you do your job can make the gospel attractive to coworkers and customers. What impression are you making? See "Your 'Workstyle,'" Titus 2:9–10.

". . . To make ready a people prepared for the Lord."
—Luke 1:17

and wondered at his delay in the sanctuary. [22]When he did
come out, he could not speak to them, and they realized
that he had seen a vision in the sanctuary. He kept motioning to them and remained unable to speak. [23]When his
time of service was ended, he went to his home.

1:24 see pg. 203

24 After those days his wife Elizabeth
conceived, and for five months she re-
mained in seclusion. She said, [25]"This is what the Lord has
done for me when he looked favorably on me and took
away the disgrace I have endured among my people."

Mary Learns that She Will Bear the Messiah

26 In the sixth month the angel Gabriel was sent by God

1:27

to a town in Galilee called Nazareth, [27]to
a virgin engaged to a man whose name
was Joseph, of the house of David. The virgin's name was

The Maidservant of the Lord

When Gabriel appeared to Mary of Nazareth (Luke 1:26–38), she was perhaps no more than 15 years old. His startling announcement—that she would soon bear the very Son of the Highest—meant the end of a normal life. Mary's name would forever be on the lips of gossips and rumormongers. Joseph, her husband-to-be, could decide to end their betrothal through a public, humiliating divorce. Even if he "dismiss her quietly" (Matt. 1:19), she would still have to return in shame to her father's home or else survive on her own by whatever means she could.

Faced with these ruinous prospects that she had neither caused nor sought, Mary would have had plenty of reason to balk at Gabriel's message. Instead she accepted her assignment: "Let it be with me according to your word" (Luke 1:38). Her response was submissive obedience to the clearly revealed will of God. It was her duty as one of God's people.

Preparations and Follow Through

After Gabriel's departure, Mary took practical action by visiting her relative, Elizabeth, during the third trimester before John's birth (Luke 1:39–56). She might well have helped Elizabeth prepare items for the coming baby, even as she herself produced or acquired what she would need in her new home with Joseph. We can imagine that Mary

1:26–56
see pg. 206

Mary. 28And he came to her and said,
"Greetings, favored one! The Lord is with
you."[b] 29But she was much perplexed by his words and
pondered what sort of greeting this might be. 30The angel
said to her, "Do not be afraid, Mary, for you have found favor with God. 31And now, you will conceive in your womb
and bear a son, and you will name him Jesus. 32He will be
great, and will be called the Son of the Most High, and the
Lord God will give to him the throne of his ancestor David.
33He will reign over the house of Jacob forever, and of his
kingdom there will be no end." 34Mary said to the angel,
"How can this be, since I am a virgin?"[c] 35The angel said to
her, "The Holy Spirit will come upon you, and the power of
the Most High will overshadow you; therefore the child to
be born[d] will be holy; he will be called Son of God. 36And
now, your relative Elizabeth in her old age has also conceived a son; and this is the sixth month for her who was
said to be barren. 37For nothing will be impossible with

[b]Other ancient authorities add *Blessed are you among women* [c]Gk *I do not know a man*
[d]Other ancient authorities add *of you*

learned much from this older, righteous woman as she listened to her and observed her marriage to Zechariah.

Once Jesus was born and the family set up housekeeping in Nazareth (2:39–40), Mary apparently settled into a fairly routine life as a homemaker. (The tasks involved are described in "Jewish Homemaking," Mark 1:29–31.) As she carried out responsibilities such as drawing water, baking bread, and spinning wool, she would have tied her Baby on her back or carried Him in a sling over her shoulder.

Luke was careful to record the family's obedience to Jewish law in having Jesus circumcised (2:21), in regard to Mary's purification (2:22), and in the presentation of Jesus and a sacrifice at the temple (2:22–24). Assuming that such observance carried over into the home, Mary probably provided Jesus' earliest instruction in the ways and values of the Hebrews.

Empty Nest

The New Testament mentions little of Mary's life after Jesus' birth. She is not listed among the earliest followers; indeed, Jesus seemed to treat her with some remoteness (8:19–21; 11:27–28). Nevertheless, she stood at the cross (John 19:25–27) and was among the first believers in Acts who awaited the Holy Spirit (Acts 1:14). ◆

BETROTHAL

FOR YOUR INFO 1:27

Engagement or betrothal (v. 27) was a mutual agreement for a future marriage (Deut. 20:7; Jer. 2:2). Not to be entirely equated with the *modern* concept of engagement, betrothal followed the selection of the bride by the prospective husband. The contract was negotiated by a friend or agent representing the bridegroom and by the parents representing the bride. It was confirmed by oaths and was accompanied with presents to the bride and often to the bride's parents.

Betrothal was celebrated by a feast. In some instances, it was customary for the bridegroom to place a ring on the bride's finger as a token of love and fidelity. In Hebrew custom, betrothal was actually part of the marriage process. A change of intention by one of the partners after he or she was betrothed was a serious matter, subject in some instances to a fine.

Betrothal was much more closely linked with marriage than our modern engagement. But the actual marriage took place only when the bridegroom took the bride to his home and the marriage was consummated in the sexual union.

What Kind of "Hill Country" Was This?

YOU ARE THERE 1:39 **Mary's journey into the Judean hill country was no leisurely stroll along a country road. Given the difficulties and dangers that the landscape posed, her support network—Elizabeth and family—must have been especially valuable to her.**

The mountainous terrain that she traversed did have a certain rugged beauty: desert yellows, a glimpse of the Dead Sea, violet-red mountains, and perhaps a few groves of fruit trees grown on terraced slopes. One main north-south road linked the region's principal cities—Jerusalem to the north, Bethlehem, Beth-zur, and Hebron to the south.

Beyond that, the hill country was rather bleak. The eastern slopes were mostly impassable desert, stretching 10 to 15 miles from their highest point, 3000 feet near Hebron, down to the Dead Sea, the lowest point on earth at 1,300 feet below sea level. The vast wasteland was broken only by imposing cliffs and canyons and a few forts and oases, such as En Gedi. It was an area fit for fugitives, rebels, and hermits—but certainly not for a pregnant woman.

1:38 see pg. 204
God." 38 Then Mary said, "Here am I, the
servant of the Lord; let it be with me according to your word." Then the angel departed from her.

Elizabeth and Mary Praise God

1:39
39 In those days Mary set out and
went with haste to a Judean town in the
hill country, 40 where she entered the house of Zechariah
and greeted Elizabeth. 41 When Elizabeth heard Mary's
greeting, the child leaped in her womb. And Elizabeth was
filled with the Holy Spirit 42 and exclaimed with a loud cry,
"Blessed are you among women, and blessed is the fruit of
your womb. 43 And why has this happened to me, that the
mother of my Lord comes to me? 44 For as soon as I heard
the sound of your greeting, the child in my womb leaped
for joy. 45 And blessed is she who believed that there would
be[e] a fulfillment of what was spoken to her by the Lord."

1:46–55
46 And Mary[f] said,
"My soul magnifies the Lord,
47 and my spirit rejoices in God my Savior,
48 for he has looked with favor on the lowliness of his
servant.

[e] Or *believed, for there will be* [f] Other ancient authorities read *Elizabeth*

Personality Profile: Mary, the Mother of Jesus

FOR YOUR INFO 1:26–56 **Also known as:** Miryam (of Nazareth); the Virgin.

Sometimes confused with: Mary of Bethany, the sister of Martha and Lazarus (John 11:1; 12:1–8); Mary, the mother of James and Joses (Matt. 27:55–61); and Mary, the mother of John Mark (Acts 12:12).

Home: Nazareth.

Family: Married to Joseph; they had four other sons—James, Joses, Judas, and Simon—as well as daughters; she was a relative of Elizabeth, John the Baptist's mother.

Occupation: Homemaker.

Best known today as: The mother of Jesus.

Surely, from now on all generations will call me
blessed;
49 for the Mighty One has done great things for me,
and holy is his name.
50 His mercy is for those who fear him
from generation to generation.
51 He has shown strength with his arm;
he has scattered the proud in the thoughts of their
hearts.
52 He has brought down the powerful from their thrones,
and lifted up the lowly;
53 he has filled the hungry with good things,
and sent the rich away empty.
54 He has helped his servant Israel,
in remembrance of his mercy,
55 according to the promise he made to our ancestors,
to Abraham and to his descendants forever."
56 And Mary remained with her about three months and
then returned to her home.

John the Baptist Is Born

57 Now the time came for Elizabeth to give birth, and
she bore a son. 58Her neighbors and relatives heard that the
Lord had shown his great mercy to her, and they rejoiced
with her.
59 On the eighth day they came to circumcise the child,
and they were going to name him Zechariah after his father.
60But his mother said, "No; he is to be called John." 61They
said to her, "None of your relatives has this name." 62Then
they began motioning to his father to find out what name
he wanted to give him. 63He asked for a writing tablet and
wrote, "His name is John." And all of them were amazed.
64Immediately his mouth was opened and his tongue freed,
and he began to speak, praising God. 65Fear came over all
their neighbors, and all these things were talked about
throughout the entire hill country of Judea. 66All who heard
them pondered them and said, "What then will this child
become?" For, indeed, the hand of the Lord was with him.
67 Then his father Zechariah was filled with the Holy
Spirit and spoke this prophecy:
68 "Blessed be the Lord God of Israel,
for he has looked favorably on his people and
redeemed them.
69 He has raised up a mighty savior[g] for us
in the house of his servant David,
70 as he spoke through the mouth of his holy prophets
from of old,

[g]*Gk a horn of salvation*

A Public Statement

CONSIDER THIS
1:46–55

Mary's song (vv. 46–55) crackles with implications for society. Known as the Magnificat (from magnificare, *the first word in the Latin version), it praises the Lord for the great things He has done (v. 49). But notice who it is He helps: the lowly, including Mary (vv. 48–49, 52); those who fear Him (v. 50); the hungry (v. 53); and Israel (v. 54). By contrast, He scatters the proud (v. 51); puts down the mighty (v. 52); and sends away the rich empty (v. 53).*

Jesus' birth is good news for the poor. In fact, He Himself was born into poverty (see 2:24). So here, as elsewhere in Luke's account, the poor are valued. They can identify with Jesus, right from His birth. They identify with the hope that "His mercy is for those who fear him from generation to generation" (v. 50).

What does it mean to "fear" the Lord? See Luke 12:4–7.

For more on the poverty of Jesus and his family, see "A Poor Family Comes into Wealth," Matt. 2:11, and "Jesus—A Homeless Man?" Matt. 8:20.

Wealth was an important topic for Jesus. See "Don't Worry!" Matt. 6:19–34. Later, James warned those who live lavish lifestyles while ignoring their hurting neighbors that they are storing up judgment for themselves. See "Getting Yours," James 5:1–6.

THE CENSUS

FOR YOUR INFO 2:1–3 **Just as the United States numbers its population every ten years, so governments in biblical times kept track of their citizens. Four censuses or registrations are mentioned in Scripture: under Moses (Num. 1:1–3), under David (1 Chr. 21:1–2), upon the Hebrews' return from captivity under Ezra and Nehemiah (Ezra 2:1–67; Neh. 7:4–72), and the one mentioned here in vv. 1–3, when Quirinius was imperial legate in the Roman province of Syria.**

Censuses were important for taxation, administration, military planning and conscription, recruitment of (sometimes forced) labor for public works projects, and for tithes and offerings to maintain religious institutions. Caesar Augustus used censuses to inventory the resources and needs of his empire, to raise money, and to determine where to allocate his troops. The Romans are believed to have held an empire-wide census every 14 years, and Luke could have been referring to one of those.

In biblical times, as today, censuses had major political implications. They certainly aided the strategic delivery of services. But registration was experienced by many as a tool of exploitation and oppression, especially where government was maintained without the choice of the governed and with little concern for their welfare. Such was the case in Israel under the Romans.

Nevertheless, God used a census to bring Joseph and Mary to Bethlehem, where Jesus was born, in fulfillment of His plan.

71 that we would be saved from our enemies and from
the hand of all who hate us.
72 Thus he has shown the mercy promised to our
ancestors,
and has remembered his holy covenant,
73 the oath that he swore to our ancestor Abraham,
to grant us 74that we, being rescued from the hands of
our enemies,
might serve him without fear, 75in holiness and
righteousness
before him all our days.
76 And you, child, will be called the prophet of the Most
High;
for you will go before the Lord to prepare his ways,
77 to give knowledge of salvation to his people
by the forgiveness of their sins.
78 By the tender mercy of our God,
the dawn from on high will break upon[h] us,
79 to give light to those who sit in darkness and in the
shadow of death,
to guide our feet into the way of peace."
80 The child grew and became strong in spirit, and he
was in the wilderness until the day he appeared publicly to
Israel.

The Birth of Jesus

2:1

2 In those days a decree went out
from Emperor Augustus that all the
world should be registered. 2This was the first registration

2:1–3

and was taken while Quirinius was governor of Syria. 3All went to their own
towns to be registered. 4Joseph also went from the town of
Nazareth in Galilee to Judea, to the city of David called
Bethlehem, because he was descended from the house and
family of David. 5He went to be registered with Mary, to
whom he was engaged and who was expecting a child.
6While they were there, the time came for her to deliver her
child. 7And she gave birth to her firstborn son and wrapped
him in bands of cloth, and laid him in a manger, because
there was no place for them in the inn.
8 In that region there were shepherds living in the fields,
keeping watch over their flock by night. 9Then an angel of
the Lord stood before them, and the glory of the Lord
shone around them, and they were terrified. 10But the angel
said to them, "Do not be afraid; for see—I am bringing you

[h]Other ancient authorities read *has broken upon*

2:11 good news of great joy for all the people:
[11]to you is born this day in the city of
David a Savior, who is the Messiah,[i] the Lord. [12]This will be
a sign for you: you will find a child wrapped in bands of
cloth and lying in a manger." [13]And suddenly there was
with the angel a multitude of the heavenly host,[j] praising
God and saying,
[14] "Glory to God in the highest heaven,
and on earth peace among those whom he favors!"[k]

[i]Or *the Christ* [j]Gk *army* [k]Other ancient authorities read *peace, goodwill among people*

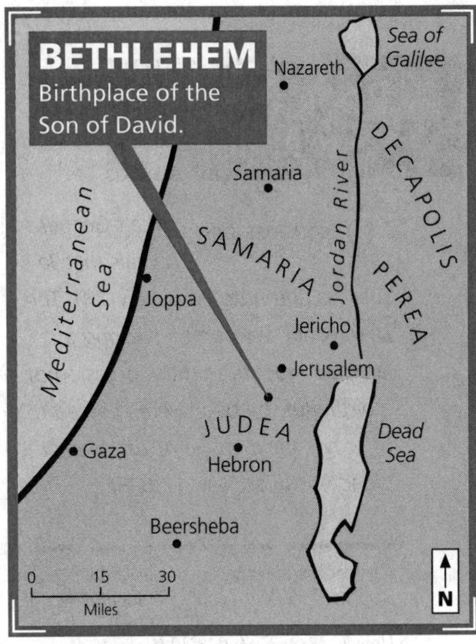

Personality Profile: Augustus

FOR YOUR INFO 2:1 **Also known as:** Gaius Octavius, his given name (born 63 B.C.); renamed Octavian; given the title Augustus in 27 B.C when he became emperor of Rome.

Home: A small town in Italy, but eventually Rome as the seat of power.

Family: Julius Caesar was his great-uncle by marriage. When Caesar was murdered in 44 B.C., Octavius was named his adopted son and heir, and even called the "son of a god." His first wife was Scribonia, whom he married for political reasons and hated. His second wife, Livia Drusilla, he loved although he cheated on her. His daughter Julia he exiled for moral offenses. His adopted son, Tiberius, was his aide and eventual heir.

Profession: Emperor of Rome and leader of its many institutions.

Best known today for: Bringing decades of civil war to an end and establishing Rome as a unified world power. Patient, shrewd, and a master of propaganda, he was a genius in administration and overhauled every aspect of Roman life—even the roads. During his 44-year reign, he established the *Pax Romana* ("Peace of Rome"), a state of control in which Roman culture flourished worldwide.

Bethlehem

YOU ARE THERE 2:11

- **The name of two towns mentioned in Scripture, the most famous of which was the birthplace of Jesus, five miles south of Jerusalem.**
- **Name means "House of Bread." The district was known for its agriculture.**
- **Called the City of David because of its association with Israel's second king (1 Sam. 17:12). The prophet Samuel anointed David king there, and David never lost his affection for the city.**
- **Predicted to be the birthplace of the Messiah (Mic. 5:2).**
- **The site of Jesus' birth was likely a cave near the town (sometimes stables were built into caves). Helena, mother of Constantine, erected the Church of the Nativity at the reputed birthplace in A.D. 330. Today a successor church, built by Emperor Justinian (A.D. 527–565), still stands.**

A Poor Family's Sacrifice

CONSIDER THIS 2:22–24 *Luke's Gospel reveals that Jesus was born into poverty (v. 24). The Law required a woman to bring a lamb as a sacrifice on the occasion of a birth. But the poor were allowed to offer two inexpensive turtledoves or pigeons instead (Lev. 12:6–8).*

For more on the poverty of Jesus and his family, see "A Poor Family Comes into Wealth," Matt. 2:11, and "Jesus—A Homeless Man?" Matt. 8:20.

15 When the angels had left them and gone into heaven,
the shepherds said to one another, "Let us go now to Bethlehem and see this thing that has taken place, which the
Lord has made known to us." 16So they went with haste
and found Mary and Joseph, and the child lying in the
manger. 17When they saw this, they made known what had
been told them about this child; 18and all who heard it were
amazed at what the shepherds told them. 19But Mary treasured all these words and pondered them in her heart.
20The shepherds returned, glorifying and praising God for
all they had heard and seen, as it had been told them.

Jesus Is Presented in the Temple

21 After eight days had passed, it was time to circumcise
the child; and he was called Jesus, the name given by the
angel before he was conceived in the womb.

 **2:22–24**

22 When the time came for their purification according to the law of Moses,
they brought him up to Jerusalem to present him to the
Lord 23(as it is written in the law of the Lord, "Every firstborn male shall be designated as holy to the Lord"), 24and
they offered a sacrifice according to what is stated in the
law of the Lord, "a pair of turtledoves or two young pigeons."

2:25–35

25 Now there was a man in Jerusalem
whose name was Simeon;[l] this man was
righteous and devout, looking forward to the consolation of
Israel, and the Holy Spirit rested on him. 26It had been revealed to him by the Holy Spirit that he would not see
death before he had seen the Lord's Messiah.[m] 27Guided by
the Spirit, Simeon[n] came into the temple; and when the
parents brought in the child Jesus, to do for him what was
customary under the law, 28Simeon[o] took him in his arms
and praised God, saying,

 **2:29–31**

29 "Master, now you are dismissing
your servant[p] in peace,
according to your word;
30 for my eyes have seen your salvation,
31 which you have prepared in the presence of all
peoples,
32 a light for revelation to the Gentiles
and for glory to your people Israel."

33 And the child's father and mother were amazed at
what was being said about him. 34Then Simeon[l] blessed
them and said to his mother Mary, "This child is destined
for the falling and the rising of many in Israel, and to be a
sign that will be opposed 35so that the inner thoughts of

[l] *Gk Symeon* [m] *Or the Lord's Christ* [n] *Gk In the Spirit, he* [o] *Gk he* [p] *Gk slave*

An International Savior

CONSIDER THIS 2:29–31 *Simeon declared the international significance of the baby Jesus. The Lord's salvation is for "all peoples," both Jews and Gentiles. The old man's blessing was not his own invention, but came from the Holy Spirit (mentioned three times in vv. 25–27).*

many will be revealed—and a sword will pierce your own
soul too."

2:36–38 see pg. 213

36 There was also a prophet, Anna[q]
the daughter of Phanuel, of the tribe of
Asher. She was of a great age, having lived with her husband seven years after her marriage, 37then as a widow to
the age of eighty-four. She never left the temple but worshiped there with fasting and prayer night and day. 38At
that moment she came, and began to praise God and to
speak about the child[r] to all who were looking for the redemption of Jerusalem.

Young Jesus Visits the Teachers

39 When they had finished everything required by the
law of the Lord, they returned to Galilee, to their own town
of Nazareth. 40The child grew and became strong, filled
with wisdom; and the favor of God was upon him.
41 Now every year his parents went to Jerusalem for the

2:42 see pg. 213

festival of the Passover. 42And when he
was twelve years old, they went up as
usual for the festival. 43When the festival was ended and
they started to return, the boy Jesus stayed behind in
Jerusalem, but his parents did not know it. 44Assuming that
he was in the group of travelers, they went a day's journey.
Then they started to look for him among their relatives and
friends. 45When they did not find him, they returned to

2:46–47 see pg. 212

Jerusalem to search for him. 46After three
days they found him in the temple, sit-
ting among the teachers, listening to them and asking them
questions. 47And all who heard him were amazed at his understanding and his answers. 48When his parents[s] saw him
they were astonished; and his mother said to him, "Child,
why have you treated us like this? Look, your father and I
have been searching for you in great anxiety." 49He said to
them, "Why were you searching for me? Did you not know
that I must be in my Father's house?"[t] 50But they did not
understand what he said to them. 51Then he went down
with them and came to Nazareth, and was obedient to
them. His mother treasured all these things in her heart.
52 And Jesus increased in wisdom and in years,[u] and in
divine and human favor.

John the Baptist Begins His Ministry

3:1 see pg. 214

3 In the fifteenth year of the reign of
Emperor Tiberius, when Pontius Pi-
late was governor of Judea, and Herod was ruler[v] of Galilee,

[q] Gk *Hanna* [r] Gk *him* [s] Gk *they* [t] *Or be about my Father's interests?* [u] Or *in stature*
[v] Gk *tetrarch*

SIMEON

CONSIDER THIS 2:25–35 **There was nothing special about Simeon that qualified him to take up the Christ child in his arms and bless Him (v. 28). To our knowledge he was not an ordained religious leader, he had no credentials or special authority. He was simply a "just and devout" man who had a close walk with the Holy Spirit (vv. 25–27).**

Thus, Simeon, whose name means "God hears," is an example of how God honors those who engage in lifetimes of quiet prayer and constant watchfulness. Simeon was a man of patient faith, yet his wait for the Messiah must have seemed interminable. He likely had many opportunities for doubt, as numerous would-be Messiahs sounded false alarms in the land.

Yet somehow he knew that the Redeemer would first come not as a great, heavenly champion wrapped in banners of nationalism, nor with a political agenda of violence, but as a Baby carried in the arms of His parents. His kingdom would prove to be a stumbling block to some and the Rock of salvation to others, both Jew and Gentile. Simeon also knew that the young couple standing before him would be hurt by the controversy that would eventually surround their Son (vv. 34–35).

and his brother Philip ruler[w] of the region of Ituraea and
Trachonitis, and Lysanias ruler[w] of Abilene, 2during the
high priesthood of Annas and Caiaphas, the word of God
came to John son of Zechariah in the wilderness. 3He went

[w]Gk *tetrarch*

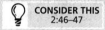

CONSIDER THIS
2:46–47

JESUS THE STUDENT

What kind of student was Jesus? Did He come into the world already knowing everything He needed to know? Was He able to acquire knowledge without even studying? The snapshot of Jesus in the temple (vv. 46–47) suggests otherwise. Though He apparently held His seniors spellbound with questions and responses, He nevertheless went through a lifelong process of education, learning and growing through "on-the-job training" from expert teachers.

Luke paints a picture of Jesus as a model Jewish student. The rabbis He encountered at Jerusalem were the preeminent experts in Judaism who researched, developed, and applied the body of Hebrew and rabbinical tradition to issues of the day. Some were members of the council, the governing tribunal of Judea. These teachers were fond of waxing eloquent on religious and legal questions in the temple courtyard for the benefit of any who would listen (Matt. 6:5; 7:28–29; 23:1–7).

Nevertheless, Jesus made strategic use of these authorities during His visit to the big city for Passover. Now age 12, He was considered a man. So He went to the temple to learn all He could about the Law of God. He proved to be an avid student, listening carefully and asking questions about His Father's business (Luke 2:49). Rather than embarrass His parents and offend His teachers by spouting off what He knew, He humbly subjected Himself to the discipline of education (v. 51). His turn to teach would come later. For now, He accepted the role of a learner.

It's a good example for all of us who must go through school and learn on the job. Like Jesus, we need to learn all we can from the best teachers we can find, showing ourselves to be teachable, with an attitude of humility. ◆

Jesus' teachers were probably among an elite class of scholars called scribes, who spent their entire lives studying the Law and tradition. See Luke 20:39.

The council, which included many of the temple rabbis, was the highest ruling body and supreme court of the Jews. See Acts 6:12.

into all the region around the Jordan, proclaiming a baptism of repentance for the forgiveness of sins, 4as it is written in the book of the words of the prophet Isaiah,
"The voice of one crying out in the wilderness:
'Prepare the way of the Lord,
make his paths straight.
5 Every valley shall be filled,
and every mountain and hill shall be made low,
and the crooked shall be made straight,
and the rough ways made smooth;
6 and all flesh shall see the salvation of God.' "
7 John said to the crowds that came out to be baptized
by him, "You brood of vipers! Who warned you to flee from
the wrath to come? 8Bear fruits worthy of repentance. Do
not begin to say to yourselves, 'We have Abraham as our
ancestor'; for I tell you, God is able from these stones to
raise up children to Abraham. 9Even now the ax is lying at
the root of the trees; every tree therefore that does not bear
good fruit is cut down and thrown into the fire."
10 And the crowds asked him, "What then should we
do?" 11In reply he said to them, "Whoever has two coats
must share with anyone who has none; and whoever has

(Bible text continued on page 215)

ANNA

FOR YOUR INFO 2:36–38

Prophets such as Anna (vv. 36–38) were known for their spiritual wisdom and the proclamation of God's word to the people. Anna spent her time in the temple, serving God through fasting and prayers. When Joseph and Mary brought Jesus to the temple for presentation, Anna recognized Him as the One who would bring redemption to Israel.

No doubt many of Anna's prayers over the years had expressed a longing for God's Anointed. Her many years in the temple had probably given her a keen knowledge of the Scriptures, which were read there regularly.

Along with Simeon, Anna helped to testify to Jesus as God's Redeemer. Her testimony as a woman would have counted for little in Jewish courts of the day. But Luke includes her in his Gospel, perhaps to highlight one of the changes that Jesus the

(continued on page 215)

FOR YOUR INFO 2:42

JEWISH FESTIVALS

Festival of	Month on Jewish Calendar	Day	Corresponding Month	References
Passover	Nisan	14	Mar.–Apr.	Ex. 12:1–14; Matt. 26:17–20
*Unleavened Bread	Nisan	15–21	Mar.–Apr.	Ex. 12:15–20
Firstfruits	Nisan or Sivan	16 6	Mar.–Apr. May–June	Lev. 23:9–14; Num. 28:26
*Pentecost (Harvest or Weeks)	Sivan	6 (50 days after barley harvest)	May–June	Deut. 16:9–12; Acts 2:1
Trumpets, *Rosh Hashanah*	Tishri	1, 2	Sept.–Oct.	Num. 29:1–6
Day of Atonement, *Yom Kippur*	Tishri	10	Sept.–Oct.	Lev. 23:26–32; Heb. 9:7
*Tabernacles (Booths or Ingathering)	Tishri	15–22	Sept.–Oct.	Neh. 8:13–18; John 7:2
Dedication (Lights), *Hanukkah*	Chislev	25 (8 days)	Nov.–Dec.	John 10:22
Purim (Lots)	Adar	14, 15	Feb.–Mar.	Esth. 9:18–32

*The three major festivals for which all males of Israel were required to travel to the temple in Jerusalem (Ex. 23:14–19)

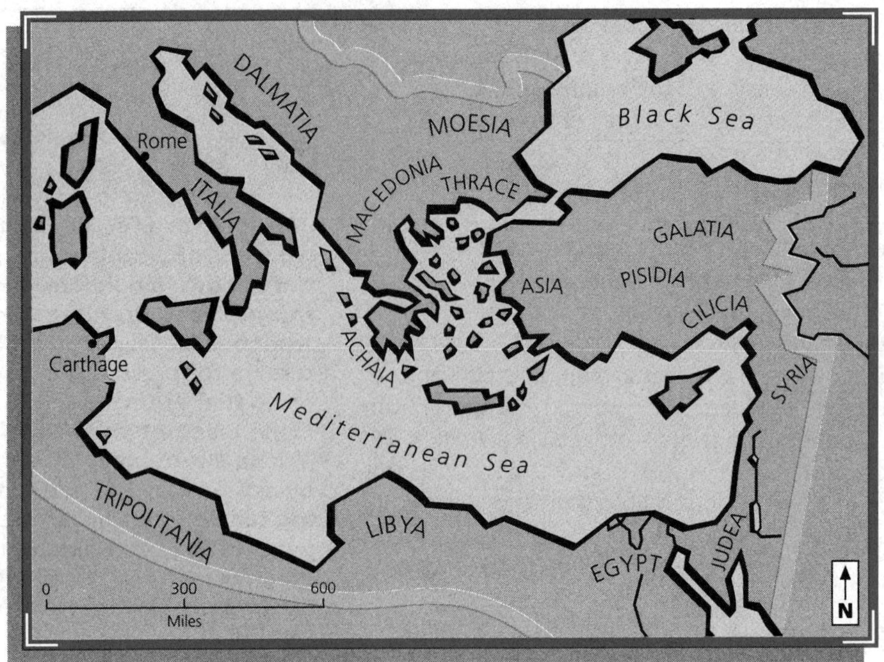

ROMAN POWER IN BIBLE LANDS

NEW TESTAMENT POLITICAL RULERS

We can almost name the day on which Jesus began His public ministry, thanks to Luke's list of Roman officials (v. 1). The accompanying table shows some of the other major political leaders of the Roman Empire and Palestine in the first century.

The Roman empire was far less centralized than most. For all its size and age, its bureaucracy and army were relatively small. For nearly a thousand years the system worked. But much depended on the good will of client kingdoms. Those that complied with Rome's wishes were treated leniently. By granting them a degree of autonomy, Rome could concentrate its limited armed forces on trouble spots. Rebellions were brutally crushed, creating a strong deterrent to revolt and an incentive to remain loyal to the emperor and his empire. ◆

What powers did Rome's government hold over Jesus and His fellow citizens in Judea? See "Roman Politics in the First Century A.D.," Luke 22:25.

food must do likewise." 12Even tax collectors came to be
baptized, and they asked him, "Teacher, what should we
do?" 13He said to them, "Collect no more than the amount
3:14 see pg. 216
prescribed for you." 14Soldiers also asked
him, "And we, what should we do?" He
said to them, "Do not extort money from anyone by threats
or false accusation, and be satisfied with your wages."

(continued from page 213)

Redeemer wanted to bring about among His followers. No longer should they regard women as untrustworthy witnesses, but as full members of a new community of faith in Christ.

Another woman became an important witness after Jesus' resurrection. See "Mary the Reliable Witness," Luke 8:2.

NEW TESTAMENT POLITICAL RULERS

Roman Emperor	Rulers of Palestine		
	Herod the Great (37–4 B.C.)		
	Judea	Galilee and Perea	Other Provinces
Augustus Caesar (31 B.C.–A.D. 14)	Archelaus (4 B.C.–A.D. 6)	Herod Antipas (4 B.C.–A.D. 39)	Herod Philip II (4 B.C.–A.D. 34) (Iturea and Trachonitis)
	Coponius (A.D. 6–8)		Lysanias (Dates uncertain) (Abilene)
	Ambivius (A.D. 9–12)		
	Annius Rufus (A.D. 12–15)		
Tiberius Caesar (A.D. 14–37)	Valerius Gratus (A.D. 15–26)		
	Pontius Pilate (A.D. 26–36)		
Caligula (A.D. 37–41)	Marcellus (A.D. 37)		
	Herod Agrippa I (A.D. 37–44)		
Claudius (A.D. 41–54)	Cuspius Fadus (A.D. 44–46)		
	Tiberius Alexander (A.D. 46–48)	Herod Agrippa II (Began to rule in A.D. 34 in other provinces and in A.D. 39 in Galilee and Perea.)	
	Ventidius Cumanus (A.D. 48–52)		
	M. Antonius Felix (A.D. 52–60)		
Nero (A.D. 54–68)	Porcius Festus (A.D. 60–62)		
	Clodius Albinus (A.D. 62–64)		
	Gessius Florus (A.D. 64–66)		
Galba, Otho, Vitellius (A.D. 68–69)	Jewish Revolt (A.D. 66–70)		
Vespasian (A.D. 69–79)			
Titus (A.D. 79–81)			
Domitian (A.D. 81–96)			

15 As the people were filled with expectation, and all
were questioning in their hearts concerning John, whether
he might be the Messiah,[x] 16John answered all of them by
saying, "I baptize you with water; but one who is more
powerful than I is coming; I am not worthy to untie the
thong of his sandals. He will baptize you with[y] the Holy
Spirit and fire. 17His winnowing fork is in his hand, to clear
his threshing floor and to gather the wheat into his granary;
but the chaff he will burn with unquenchable fire."

18 So, with many other exhortations, he proclaimed the
good news to the people. 19But Herod the ruler,[z] who had
been rebuked by him because of Herodias, his brother's
wife, and because of all the evil things that Herod had
done, 20added to them all by shutting up John in prison.

Jesus Is Baptized

21 Now when all the people were baptized, and when
Jesus also had been baptized and was praying, the heaven
was opened, 22and the Holy Spirit descended upon him in
bodily form like a dove. And a voice came from heaven,
"You are my Son, the Beloved;[a] with you I am well
pleased."[b]

The Genealogy of Jesus

3:23–38

23 Jesus was about thirty years old
when he began his work. He was the son
(as was thought) of Joseph son of Heli, 24son of Matthat,
son of Levi, son of Melchi, son of Jannai, son of Joseph,
25son of Mattathias, son of Amos, son of Nahum, son of
Esli, son of Naggai, 26son of Maath, son of Mattathias, son
of Semein, son of Josech, son of Joda, 27son of Joanan, son
of Rhesa, son of Zerubbabel, son of Shealtiel,[c] son of Neri,
28son of Melchi, son of Addi, son of Cosam, son of El-
madam, son of Er, 29son of Joshua, son of Eliezer, son of
Jorim, son of Matthat, son of Levi, 30son of Simeon, son of
Judah, son of Joseph, son of Jonam, son of Eliakim, 31son of
Melea, son of Menna, son of Mattatha, son of Nathan, son

[x] *Or the Christ* [y] *Or in* [z] *Gk tetrarch* [a] *Or my beloved Son* [b] Other ancient authorities read *You are my Son, today I have begotten you* [c] *Gk Salathiel*

THREE DANGERS OF POWER

CONSIDER THIS 3:14 **Like fire, power can be used to accomplish good. But always lurking in its shadow is the temptation of abuse—to use power for self-centered gains that harm others, and to avoid accountability for that harm. Responding to the Roman soldiers who policed Jerusalem (v. 14), John raised three issues in regard to the abuse of power:**

(1) Intimidation. **We can use our power to push others around, especially those who are too weak or afraid to push back. Using power in that way is ungodly and harmful. Ultimately such power users destroy themselves, for their subordinates serve them without loyalty and with increasing resentment.**

(2) False accusations. **We can use our power to make snap decisions and judgments. But power used in that way keeps us in the dark, since others will be too afraid to tell us when we're wrong. When things go awry, it's all too easy to start blaming people under us and around us.**

(3) Discontent. **If we use our power in self-centered, hurtful ways, we'll tend to increase our appetite for power and seek more, perhaps by pressuring superiors or by cheating and stealing.**

The power of the gospel is a complete contrast to the power of intimidation, blame, and discontent. See "Power," Acts 1:8.

of David, [32]son of Jesse, son of Obed, son of Boaz, son of
Sala,[d] son of Nahshon, [33]son of Amminadab, son of Admin,
son of Arni,[e] son of Hezron, son of Perez, son of Judah,
[34]son of Jacob, son of Isaac, son of Abraham, son of Terah,
son of Nahor, [35]son of Serug, son of Reu, son of Peleg, son

3:36–38 see pg. 219

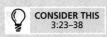

of Eber, son of Shelah, [36]son of Cainan,
son of Arphaxad, son of Shem, son of
Noah, son of Lamech, [37]son of Methuselah, son of Enoch,
son of Jared, son of Mahalaleel, son of Cainan, [38]son of
Enos, son of Seth, son of Adam, son of God.

[d]Other ancient authorities read *Salmon* [e]Other ancient authorities read *Amminadab, son of Aram*; others vary widely

◆ ◆

CONSIDER THIS
3:23–38

JESUS, THE SON OF . . .

Have you ever been tempted to skip over vv. 23–38 as just another boring genealogy? Why, you may ask, did God fill up pages of Scripture with passages like this one, or its counterpart in Matt. 1:1–16? Why not just get right to the story?

One answer is that these verses were a major piece of the story. For one thing, they demonstrated Jesus' descent from King David, establishing His credentials as Messiah. Also, they showed that Jesus was fully human. Nowadays skeptics question the divinity of Christ. By contrast, some in the first century doubted whether Jesus was really human. Perhaps He was just an immaterial Spirit being, they said, a "heavenly Jesus" who only appeared to be human.

To answer that challenge, Luke and other church leaders stressed Christ's biological and personal roots. The first few chapters of Luke and Matthew, for example, describe Jesus' infancy to show that He was born just like any other flesh-and-blood human being (even though His conception was miraculous). Luke especially highlights Jesus' mother, Mary, and His earthly father, Joseph. He also grounds the story in a precise moment of Roman and Jewish history (Luke 3:1–2).

Today, many of us are eager to trace our genealogy and discover our roots, the stock of people from which we've come. Luke does us a favor by cataloging Jesus' roots. He shows us that not only was Jesus the Son of God, He was also the Son of Man. He is one of us! ◆

Be sure to compare Luke's list of Jesus' forebears with "Jesus' Roots," Matt. 1:1–16.

Jesus Faces 40 Days of Temptation

4:1–13

4:1–13

4 Jesus, full of the Holy Spirit,
returned from the Jordan and was
led by the Spirit in the wilderness,
2where for forty days he was tempted by
the devil. He ate nothing at all during those days, and when
they were over, he was famished. 3The devil said to him, "If
you are the Son of God, command this stone to become a
loaf of bread." 4Jesus answered him, "It is written, 'One
does not live by bread alone.' "

4:5–8 see pg. 220

5 Then the devil[f] led him up and
showed him in an instant all the king-
doms of the world. 6And the devil[f] said to him, "To you I
will give their glory and all this authority; for it has been
given over to me, and I give it to anyone I please. 7If you,
then, will worship me, it will all be yours." 8Jesus answered
him, "It is written,

[f]Gk *he*

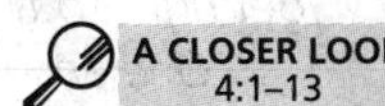

A CLOSER LOOK 4:1–13

Real Temptation?

Was Jesus really tempted, the same way that people are tempted today in the "real" world? To find out, see "You Don't Understand!" Matt. 4:3.

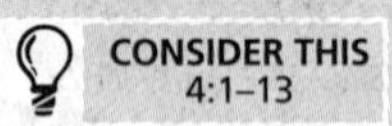

CONSIDER THIS 4:1–13

Under the Circumstances

In addition to the substance of what was happening when Satan tempted Jesus, we see an environmental aspect in this passage as well. Jesus was tempted in three very different settings:

(1) In a barren desert (vv. 1–4). *In the ancient world, deserts were believed to be inhabited by spirits that engaged in never-ending warfare. In fact, some of the early church fathers went into desert caves as a way to engage in spiritual warfare and develop spiritual disciplines. Unfortunately, they sometimes lost contact with the everyday world in which life has to be lived.*

Centuries earlier, Israel had run into major problems in the desert, rebelling against God and wandering for forty years before entering the promised land (Num. 14:29–35).

(2) On a mountain (vv. 5–8). *A mountain setting may seem an unlikely environment for temptation. But in the ancient world, many religious shrines were carved or carried into mountains, where they became sources of idolatry and superstition. Today, mountain retreats, even those*

'Worship the Lord your God,
and serve only him.' "
9 Then the devil[g] took him to Jerusalem, and placed him
on the pinnacle of the temple, saying to him, "If you are the
Son of God, throw yourself down from here, 10for it is written,
'He will command his angels concerning you,
to protect you,'
11and
'On their hands they will bear you up,
so that you will not dash your foot against a stone.' "
12Jesus answered him, "It is said, 'Do not put the Lord your
God to the test.' " 13When the devil had finished every test,
he departed from him until an opportune time.

Jesus Starts His Work and Meets Rejection

14 Then Jesus, filled with the power of the Spirit, returned to Galilee, and a report about him spread through
all the surrounding country. 15He began to teach in their
synagogues and was praised by everyone.

[g]Gk *he*

owned and operated by religious organizations, can become like shrines that tempt people to run away from problems. It's easy to prefer an exciting, memorable "mountain-top experience" to the grinding reality of day-to-day life in the "valley." Retreats and vacations can be valuable, but they can also become a vain religion if they are used to avoid reality.

(3) In Jerusalem, a city (vv. 9–13). *Like us, Jesus was tempted to take command of a city. Any city—especially "the holy city"—can sorely tempt a person with power. Power itself is morally neutral, but like fire it has grave potential to destroy people when mishandled. One has only to review the political history of cities like New York, Chicago, Hong Kong, or Beirut to appreciate that grim reality.*

Jesus' temptation touched the environment in three different ways. What environments pose temptations—and opportunities—for you? ◆

Jesus' Family Experienced Pain, Too

CONSIDER THIS 3:36–38 **Luke's review of Jesus' forebears shows His direct association with broken people—a fact that offers hope to anyone struggling with inherited pain. Very early in the record we find family members with deep problems:**

- ***Adam* (v. 38) was cast out of an ideal situation because he disobeyed in the garden of Eden (Gen. 3:23, 24).**
- ***Seth* (v. 38) was a baby conceived out of the grief caused by one brother's murder and another's alienation. Seth was named as a substitute child by his grieving mother (Gen. 4:25).**
- ***Noah* (v. 36) brings us to the Bible's first case of alcohol abuse. He caused embarrassment to his sons during a drunken stupor in which he lay naked (Gen. 9:20–23).**

The people listed in Luke's genealogy are more than just names on a list. Each was a person who needed God's rescue from sin and unhealth.

Like Luke, Matthew begins his account of Jesus' life with a family tree marked by human frailty. See "Jesus' Roots," Matt. 1:1–16, and "The Women in Jesus' Genealogy," Matt. 1:3–6.

"It Will All Be Yours"

CONSIDER THIS 4:5–8 **Satan promised to give Jesus authority over all the kingdoms of the world. "The father of lies" spoke the truth when he boldly declared, "It has been given over to me, and I give it to anyone I please" (v. 6). He neglected, of course, to mention *who* had delivered the world powers to him—God the Son Himself, who possessed authority over the entire created universe (Col. 1:15–17)!**

No wonder Jesus turned him down, one might say. But notice: Jesus did not respond by laying claim to His rightful authority. No, rather than focusing on the substance of the offer, He responded to its cost. To accept it would have required idolatry—a violation of His Father's unique position as the Lord God who *alone* deserves worship.

Jesus' response compels us to ask: When we receive an enticing offer that, in effect, promises "it will all be yours" (v. 7), what do we focus on—the benefits or the costs? The benefits may be extremely attractive. But what are the costs? Does it involve "selling out" our Lord by compromising His commands, His values, or His honor? If so, then the cost is simply too high, and we need to respond as Jesus did.

Matthew and Mark also record Jesus' temptation (Matt. 4:1–11; Mark 1:12–13). It was a major event in His life and preparation for ministry. Moses, too, confronted the "passing pleasures of sin," but like Jesus he resisted (Heb. 11:24–26).

4:16–27

16 When he came to Nazareth, where
he had been brought up, he went to the
synagogue on the sabbath day, as was his custom. He stood

4:17 see pg. 222

up to read, 17and the scroll of the
prophet Isaiah was given to him. He

4:17–21 see pg. 222

unrolled the scroll and found the place
where it was written:

4:18 see pg. 223

18 "The Spirit of the Lord is upon me,
because he has anointed me
to bring good news to the poor.
He has sent me to proclaim release to the captives
and recovery of sight to the blind,
to let the oppressed go free,
19 to proclaim the year of the Lord's favor."
20And he rolled up the scroll, gave it back to the attendant,
and sat down. The eyes of all in the synagogue were fixed
on him. 21Then he began to say to them, "Today this scripture has been fulfilled in your hearing." 22All spoke well of
him and were amazed at the gracious words that came from
his mouth. They said, "Is not this Joseph's son?" 23He said
to them, "Doubtless you will quote to me this proverb,
'Doctor, cure yourself!' And you will say, 'Do here also in
your hometown the things that we have heard you did at
Capernaum.' " 24And he said, "Truly I tell you, no prophet
is accepted in the prophet's hometown. 25But the truth is,
there were many widows in Israel in the time of Elijah,
when the heaven was shut up three years and six months,
and there was a severe famine over all the land; 26yet Elijah
was sent to none of them except to a widow at Zarephath in
Sidon. 27There were also many lepers[h] in Israel in the time
of the prophet Elisha, and none of them was cleansed except Naaman the Syrian." 28When they heard this, all in the
synagogue were filled with rage. 29They got up, drove him
out of the town, and led him to the brow of the hill on
which their town was built, so that they might hurl him off
the cliff. 30But he passed through the midst of them and
went on his way.

A Demon Is Cast Out at Capernaum

4:31 see pg. 225

31 He went down to Capernaum, a
city in Galilee, and was teaching them on
the sabbath. 32They were astounded at his teaching, because he spoke with authority. 33In the synagogue there was
a man who had the spirit of an unclean demon, and he

(Bible text continued on page 222)

[h]The terms *leper* and *leprosy* can refer to several diseases

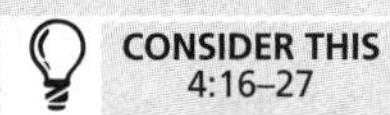
CONSIDER THIS
4:16–27

JESUS' FIRST SERMON INCLUDED SURPRISES

Jesus launched His public ministry with a dramatic first sermon in the synagogue at Nazareth. Using Isaiah 61:1–2 as His text, He announced that He *was the One anointed by the Spirit to preach the gospel (v. 18), the good news.*

Jesus also said that the "year of the Lord's favor" had come (v. 19), a reference to the Old Testament concept of the Jubilee Year (Lev. 25:8–19). Every fifty years, the Israelites were to set their slaves free, cancel each other's debts, and restore lands to their original owners. Apparently Jesus intended to make a dramatic difference in the lives of people, not only spiritually, but sociologically and economically as well.

Jesus' claims startled the hometown crowd for at least two reasons. First, He reminded His listeners of whom the good news was for: the poor, the brokenhearted, the captives (or prisoners), the blind, and the oppressed. At first, the people welcomed these words (v. 22). Perhaps they understood Jesus figuratively to mean them.

But soon they began to question His right to make such claims. "We know this fellow, don't we?" they asked in effect (v. 22). "Isn't He Joseph's boy? Isn't He one of us? Can He really be the One to fulfill Isaiah's prophecy?" They doubted His credentials.

Jesus rose to the occasion by throwing them another curve ball: "I'm especially impressed with the poor widow of Sidon," one might paraphrase His words (vv. 25–26). "She reminds Me that God often works outside of Israel; He even works in the lives of women. I'm also impressed with Naaman [v. 27]. He reminds me that God works in the lives of Syrian generals. Both cases indicate that prophets like Elijah and Elisha frequently had to go to the nations outside Israel to find people who would respond to God."

Such a radical message disturbed that small-town community. They loved the way that young Jesus read the Bible. But they were likely also concerned with preserving religious orthodoxy and reversing the region's reputation as a seedbed of radicals and "sinners" who were ignorant and/or disrespectful of the Law. Jesus' words might well have represented a threat to the image they wanted to project to the watching world. Once Jesus' neighbors realized what He was really saying—that His heroes and models were not always the usual Jewish models—they determined to reject Him. In fact, in their rage they almost killed Him (vv. 28–29).

The reaction of Jesus' hometown crowd moves us to ask: Whom are we reaching out to with the good news about Christ? What issues does Jesus' gospel address in our times? Are we like the Nazareth listeners, so committed to preserving the status quo that God has to go around us to accomplish His work? Nothing could be more tragic than that Jesus would pass through our midst and go on His way (v. 30). ◆

Jesus had a great deal to say about how we as His people should respond to those in need around us. See "Some Surprising Evidence," Matt. 11:2–6.

"Here Am I; Send Me!"

FOR YOUR INFO 4:17–21

It was a time of greatness for Judah. King Uzziah had ruled for 52 years—longer than any previous king of Judah or Israel. Wise, pious, and powerful, the ruler had extended the nation's territory and brought about great prosperity. Most importantly, he had sought the Lord, influenced by a prophet named Zechariah who encouraged him to honor and obey God (2 Chr. 26:5).

Yet upon Uzziah's death, the Lord appeared to Isaiah in a vision and warned that the nation was about to undergo His judgment. "Whom shall I send [to give this message to the people]?" He asked. "Who will go for us?" Isaiah replied, "Here am I; send me!" (Is. 6:8).

So God sent Isaiah to Judah, knowing that most of the people would reject his message (v. 10). Jesus found in the record of Isaiah's call a prediction of His own rejection by the people of His day (Matt. 13:14–15). Yet at the same time, no other Old Testament prophet made as many references to the coming Messiah as did Isaiah.

According to a popular Jewish tradition, Isaiah met his death by being sawed in half during the reign of the evil king Manasseh of Judah. The writer to the Hebrews may have had that in mind as he listed some of the heroes of the faith (Heb. 11:37–38).

One of Isaiah's major emphases was the Messiah as a suffering servant, a role that Jesus fulfilled. See Luke 24:27.

cried out with a loud voice, 34"Let us alone! What have you
to do with us, Jesus of Nazareth? Have you come to destroy
us? I know who you are, the Holy One of God." 35But Jesus
rebuked him, saying, "Be silent, and come out of him!"
When the demon had thrown him down before them, he
came out of him without having done him any harm.
36They were all amazed and kept saying to one another,
"What kind of utterance is this? For with authority and
power he commands the unclean spirits, and out they
come!" 37And a report about him began to reach every
place in the region.

Jesus Heals Simon's Mother-in-Law

38 After leaving the synagogue he entered Simon's
house. Now Simon's mother-in-law was suffering from a
high fever, and they asked him about her. 39Then he stood
over her and rebuked the fever, and it left her. Immediately
she got up and began to serve them.

Jesus Travels and Heals

4:40 see pg. 224

40 As the sun was setting, all those
who had any who were sick with various
kinds of diseases brought them to him; and he laid his
hands on each of them and cured them. 41Demons also

Personality Profile: Isaiah

FOR YOUR INFO 4:17

Name means: "Salvation of the LORD"

Home: Probably Jerusalem.

Family: May have been related to the royal house of Judah; married to a woman he called "the prophetess" (Is. 8:3); two sons, Shear-jashub ("A Remnant Shall Return") and Maher-shalal-hash-baz ("Speed the Spoil, Hasten the Booty").

Occupation: Early years spent as an official of King Uzziah of Judah; later called to be a prophet.

Best known today as: The Old Testament prophet who so vividly predicted the coming of the Messiah.

came out of many, shouting, "You are the Son of God!" But
he rebuked them and would not allow them to speak, because they knew that he was the Messiah.[i]
42 At daybreak he departed and went into a deserted
place. And the crowds were looking for him; and when
they reached him, they wanted to prevent him from leaving
them. 43But he said to them, "I must proclaim the good
news of the kingdom of God to the other cities also; for I
was sent for this purpose." 44So he continued proclaiming
the message in the synagogues of Judea.[j]

Fish Caught and Fishermen Called

5:1–11 see pg. 228

5 Once while Jesus[k] was standing
beside the lake of Gennesaret, and
the crowd was pressing in on him to hear the word of God,
2he saw two boats there at the shore of the lake; the fishermen had gone out of them and were washing their nets.
3He got into one of the boats, the one belonging to Simon,
and asked him to put out a little way from the shore. Then
he sat down and taught the crowds from the boat. 4When
he had finished speaking, he said to Simon, "Put out into
the deep water and let down your nets for a catch." 5Simon
answered, "Master, we have worked all night long but have
caught nothing. Yet if you say so, I will let down the nets."
6When they had done this, they caught so many fish that
their nets were beginning to break. 7So they signaled their
partners in the other boat to come and help them. And they
came and filled both boats, so that they began to sink. 8But
when Simon Peter saw it, he fell down at Jesus' knees, saying, "Go away from me, Lord, for I am a sinful man!" 9For
he and all who were with him were amazed at the catch of
fish that they had taken; 10and so also were James and
John, sons of Zebedee, who were partners with Simon.
Then Jesus said to Simon, "Do not be afraid; from now on
you will be catching people." 11When they had brought
their boats to shore, they left everything and followed him.

Jesus Heals a Leper

5:12–15 see pg. 229

12 Once, when he was in one of the
cities, there was a man covered with lep-
rosy.[l] When he saw Jesus, he bowed with his face to the
ground and begged him, "Lord, if you choose, you can

[i] Or *the Christ* [j] Other ancient authorities read *Galilee* [k] Gk *he* [l] The terms *leper* and *leprosy* can refer to several diseases

THE SPIRIT OF THE LORD IS UPON . . . YOU!

CONSIDER THIS 4:18 **If you've ever assumed that God's work in the world is accomplished primarily by ordained clergy, then you need to look carefully at Jesus' words to the hometown crowd of Nazareth. "The Spirit of the Lord is upon me," He declared, applying an Old Testament prophecy to Himself (vv. 18–19; Is. 61:1–2). "Today this scripture has been fulfilled in your hearing" (v. 21).**

The promise fulfilled was that the Messiah had come and would do all of the things foretold in the ancient text. But the text went on to make more promises about what would happen *after* the Messiah's initial work: "You shall be called priests of the LORD, you shall be named ministers of our God" (Is. 61:6).

This would be a profound change. The tasks of "ministry" would no longer be done just by priests, rabbis, or clergy, but by all of God's people. Just as the Spirit of the Lord had come upon Christ, enabling Him to accomplish God's work, so the Spirit would enable Christ's followers to accomplish God's work, too.

If you are a believer in Christ, God has empowered you with His Spirit. Are you carrying out His assignments for you?

Paul affirmed the idea of everyday believers carrying out the work of God in Eph. 4:12–13. Likewise, Peter calls us "a holy priesthood" in 1 Pet. 2:9–10.

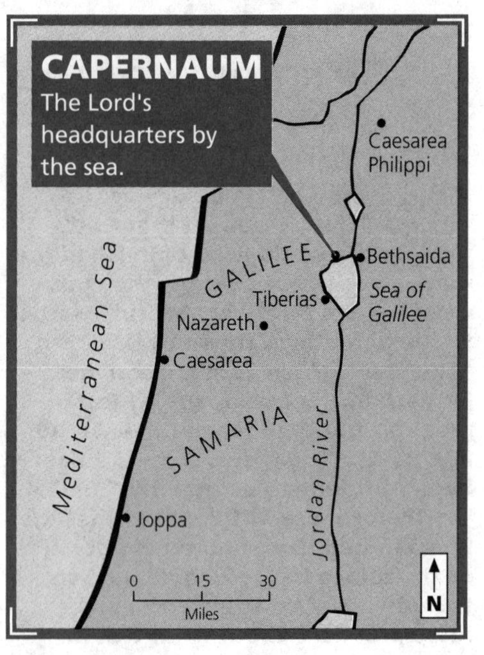

make me clean." 13Then Jesus[m] stretched out his hand,
touched him, and said, "I do choose. Be made clean." Immediately the leprosy[n] left him. 14And he ordered him to
tell no one. "Go," he said, "and show yourself to the priest,
and, as Moses commanded, make an offering for your
cleansing, for a testimony to them." 15But now more than
ever the word about Jesus[o] spread abroad; many crowds
would gather to hear him and to be cured of their diseases.
16But he would withdraw to deserted places and pray.

A Paralyzed Man Brought to Jesus

5:17–26 see pg. 227

17 One day, while he was teaching,
Pharisees and teachers of the law were
sitting near by (they had come from every village of Galilee
and Judea and from Jerusalem); and the power of the Lord

[m]Gk *he* [n]The terms *leper* and *leprosy* can refer to several diseases [o]Gk *him*

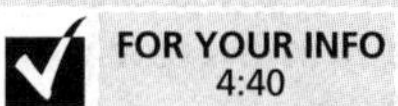

FOR YOUR INFO 4:40

He Healed Them All

Jesus backed up His claim of being the Messiah by healing the sick (v. 40). Later, His followers used similar miracles to verify their message. Not only did healing demonstrate Christ's divine power over disease and infirmity, it revealed God's heart of compassion. The Great Physician and the apostles treated people with:

Disabilities or Conditions from Birth

- *paralyzed (Matt. 9:1–8; Acts 9:32–35)*
- *blind (Matt. 9:27–31; Mark 8:22–25; 10:46–52; Luke 7:21; 18:35–43; John 9:1–12)*
- *unable to speak (Matt. 9:32–34)*
- *epileptic (Matt. 17:14–21)*
- *deaf and unable to speak (Mark 7:31–37)*
- *lame (John 5:1–15; Acts 3:1–11; 14:8–10)*
- *a deformed hand (Matt. 12:9–13)*

Diseases of a Permanent or Semi-permanent Nature

- *a woman with a flow of blood (Matt. 9:20–22)*
- *a leper (Matt. 8:1–4; Luke 5:12–14; 17:11–17)*
- *a woman bent over with an 18-year infirmity (Luke 13:11–16)*
- *a man with dropsy, or swelling (Luke 14:1–6)*

was with him to heal.[p] 18Just then some men came, carrying
a paralyzed man on a bed. They were trying to bring him in
and lay him before Jesus;[q] 19but finding no way to bring
him in because of the crowd, they went up on the roof and
let him down with his bed through the tiles into the middle
of the crowd[r] in front of Jesus. 20When he saw their faith,
he said, "Friend,[s] your sins are forgiven you." 21Then the
scribes and the Pharisees began to question, "Who is this
who is speaking blasphemies? Who can forgive sins but
God alone?" 22When Jesus perceived their questionings, he
answered them, "Why do you raise such questions in your
hearts? 23Which is easier, to say, 'Your sins are forgiven you,'
or to say, 'Stand up and walk'? 24But so that you may know
that the Son of Man has authority on earth to forgive
sins"—he said to the one who was paralyzed—"I say to
you, stand up and take your bed and go to your home."

[p]Other ancient authorities read *was present to heal them* [q]Gk *him* [r]Gk *into the midst* [s]Gk *Man*

◆ ◆ ◆ ◆ ◆ ◆ ◆ ◆ ◆ ◆ ◆ ◆ ◆ ◆ ◆

Spiritual and Psychological Conditions

- *demon-possessed (Matt. 8:28–34; Mark 5:1–20; 9:14–29; Luke 4:33–37; 7:21; Acts 5:12–16; 16:16–18; 19:11–12)*
- *demon-possessed, blind, and unable to speak (Matt. 12:22)*

Sickness

- *those with unspecified sickness (Matt. 14:34–36; Mark 1:32–34; Luke 4:40; 7:21; Acts 5:12–16; 19:11–12)*
- *people afflicted with a fever (Mark 1:29–31; John 4:46–54)*
- *a man suffering from dysentery (Acts 28:7–8)*

Death

- *Jairus' daughter (Mark 5:22–24, 35–43)*
- *the widow of Nain's son (Luke 7:11–17)*
- *Lazarus (John 11:38–44)*
- *Tabitha of Joppa (Acts 9:36–43)*
- *Eutychus (Acts 20:9–12)* ◆

The Bible mentions more than 40 specific diseases or disabilities and alludes frequently to sickness and health issues generally. It seems to accept that concerns over physical health are universal, inescapable, and problematic. See " 'Who Sinned?' Health and Disease in the Bible," John 9:2–3.

CAPERNAUM

YOU ARE THERE 4:31

- **The most important, prosperous city on the northwestern shore of the Sea of Galilee.**
- **Name means "village of Nahum" (not the Old Testament prophet).**
- **Economic and political hub of the Galilee region in the first century A.D. Situated on a road from Jerusalem to Damascus, it was a crossroads of international trade and commerce and was near the border between the tetrarchies of Philip and Herod Antipas.**
- **Blessed with fertile land and a mild climate. The area grew date palms, walnut trees, olives, figs, wheat, and wildflowers, and today even grows bananas.**
- **Offered many options for employment: agriculture, trade, fishing, even tax collection, a lucrative but not well-respected enterprise (Matt. 9:9–17).**
- **Center of Jesus' Galilean ministry, and called by Matthew Jesus' "own town" (Matt. 9:1–2). Two of Jesus' disciples are known to have had a home there, Simon Peter and Andrew (Mark 1:29–31; Luke 4:38).**
- **Archaeological excavations have uncovered ruins of a synagogue built on the site of the city's synagogue of Jesus' time. One block away is the foundation of an early church that excavators are convinced was built on the site of Peter's house (Mark 1:9; 8:14; Luke 4:38), the place where Jesus often stayed while in Capernaum.**

The densely populated Galilee region figured prominently in Jesus' life. He carried out most of His ministry there, and as many as eleven of His twelve disciples may have come from the region. See "Galilee," Mark 1:14.

25Immediately he stood up before them, took what he had
been lying on, and went to his home, glorifying God.
26Amazement seized all of them, and they glorified God and
were filled with awe, saying, "We have seen strange things
today."

Levi Follows Jesus and Hosts a Dinner

27 After this he went out and saw a tax collector named
Levi, sitting at the tax booth; and he said to him, "Follow
me." 28And he got up, left everything,
and followed him.

5:28–29 see pg. 230

29 Then Levi gave a great banquet for him in his house;
and there was a large crowd of tax collectors and others sitting at the table[t] with them. 30The Pharisees and their
scribes were complaining to his disciples, saying, "Why do
you eat and drink with tax collectors and sinners?" 31Jesus
answered, "Those who are well have no need of a physician, but those who are sick; 32I have come to call not the
righteous but sinners to repentance."

"New wine must be put into fresh wineskins. . . ." —Luke 5:38

New Wine and Old Wineskins

33 Then they said to him, "John's disciples, like the disciples of the Pharisees, frequently fast and pray, but your
disciples eat and drink. 34Jesus said to them, "You cannot
make wedding guests fast while the bridegroom is with
them, can you? 35The days will come when the bridegroom
will be taken away from them, and then they will fast in
those days." 36He also told them a para-
ble: "No one tears a piece from a new
garment and sews it on an old garment; otherwise the new
will be torn, and the piece from the new will not match the
old. 37And no one puts new wine into old wineskins; otherwise the new wine will burst the skins and will be spilled,
and the skins will be destroyed. 38But new wine must be
put into fresh wineskins. 39And no one after drinking old
wine desires new wine, but says, 'The old is good.' "[u]

5:36–39 see pg. 231

Plucking Grain on the Sabbath

6:1–11 see pg. 230

6 One sabbath[v] while Jesus[w] was
going through the grainfields, his
disciples plucked some heads of grain, rubbed them in

[t]Gk *reclining* [u]Other ancient authorities read *better;* others lack verse 39 [v]Other ancient authorities read *On the second first sabbath* [w]Gk *he*

their hands, and ate them. 2But some of the Pharisees said,
"Why are you doing what is not lawful[x] on the sabbath?"
3Jesus answered, "Have you not read what David did when
he and his companions were hungry? 4He entered the
house of God and took and ate the bread of the Presence,
which it is not lawful for any but the priests to eat, and
gave some to his companions?" 5Then he
said to them, "The Son of Man is lord of
the sabbath."

6:1–5 see pg. 232

Doing Good on the Sabbath

6 On another sabbath he entered the synagogue and
taught, and there was a man there whose right hand was
withered. 7The scribes and the Pharisees watched him to
see whether he would cure on the sabbath, so that they
might find an accusation against him. 8Even though he
knew what they were thinking, he said to the man who had
the withered hand, "Come and stand here." He got up and
stood there. 9Then Jesus said to them, "I ask you, is it lawful to do good or to do harm on the sabbath, to save life or
to destroy it?" 10After looking around at all of them, he said
to him, "Stretch out your hand." He did so, and his hand
was restored. 11But they were filled with fury and discussed
with one another what they might do to Jesus.

Twelve Named as Apostles

6:12–16

12 Now during those days he went out
to the mountain to pray; and he spent
the night in prayer to God. 13And when day came, he called
his disciples and chose twelve of them, whom he also
named apostles: 14Simon, whom he named Peter, and his
brother Andrew, and James, and John, and Philip, and
Bartholomew, 15and Matthew, and Thomas, and James son
of Alphaeus, and Simon, who was called the Zealot, 16and
Judas son of James, and Judas Iscariot, who became a trai-
tor.

[x]Other ancient authorities add *to do*

The Twelve: Similar or Diverse?

A CLOSER LOOK 6:12–16

On the one hand, the twelve disciples were a rather similar group: all men, all Jews, and all but one (Judas Iscariot) apparently from Galilee. On closer inspection, however, they turn out to be fairly different in their backgrounds and outlook. See "The Twelve" at Matt. 10:2 to find out more about Jesus' diverse followers.

Are You a Friend of Someone in Need?

CONSIDER THIS 5:17–26

The news was out: help was available for the sick! But a certain paralyzed man had no way to get to it. Physically disabled people like him were not only immobile, but usually poor. Useless to society and lacking help from the government, they invariably lived as social outcasts.

But some men knew of this man's dilemma and came to his need. They helped him get to a house where Jesus was teaching. Yet enormous crowds made access impossible. Fortunately, the men were determined and resourceful: they literally tore the roof off in order to connect their friend with the Helper (v. 19).

Jesus noticed "*their* faith" (v. 20, italics added) and healed the paralyzed man.

Is there someone near you who is cut off from needed services—health care, transportation, access to community resources, financial assistance, or advocacy in the workplace? Can you band together with others to provide what is needed in the tradition of the unnamed but faithful helpers described in Luke 5?

Crowds Come from Near and Far

6:17
see pg. 233

17 He came down with them and
stood on a level place, with a great crowd
of his disciples and a great multitude of people from all
Judea, Jerusalem, and the coast of Tyre and Sidon. 18They
had come to hear him and to be healed of their diseases;
and those who were troubled with unclean spirits were
cured. 19And all in the crowd were trying to touch him, for
power came out from him and healed all of them.

(Bible text continued on page 230)

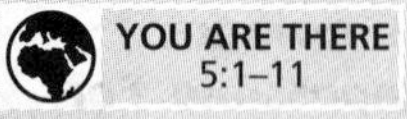

THE WORLD OF THE FISHERMEN

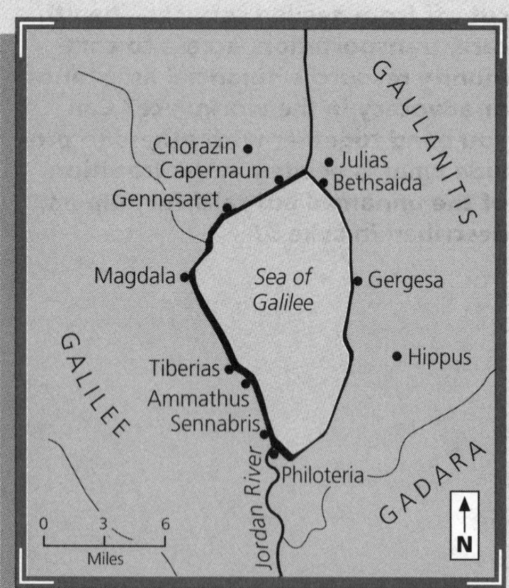

THE SEA OF GALILEE

Even though several of Jesus' disciples came from "Fish Town," He denounced it for its lack of faith. See "Bethsaida," Mark 6:45.

Fishing on the Sea of Galilee was big business. This now-famous body of water, 8 miles wide and 13 miles long, lay beside a fertile plain renowned for its agriculture. In Jesus' day, nine cities crowded its shorelines, each with no less than 15,000 citizens, possibly making the region's total population greater than Jerusalem's.

The names of the Galilean towns reflect the importance of fishing to the life and economy of the area. For example, at Tarichaea, "the place of salt fish," workers packed fish for shipment to Jerusalem and export to Rome. Bethsaida—from which at least four fishermen left their nets to follow Jesus (Matt. 4:18–22; John 1:44)—means "fish town"; most of the town was employed in the fishing industry.

Shoals just offshore were a fisherman's paradise. In Jesus' day, hundreds of fishing boats trawled the lake. Galileans ate little meat besides fish. It came highly salted, as there was no other way of preserving the "catch of the day."

Two kinds of nets were used—the sagēnē *and the* amphiblēstron. *The* sagēnē *(Matt. 13:47) was larger. Fitted with both weighted and buoyant material, it was used for trawling. In water, it stood almost upright and bagged fish as it was dragged behind a boat. The smaller* amphiblēstron *was shaped like an umbrella and was used for casting off the side of a boat (see Mark 1:16).*

The fisherman's day did not end with a return to shore. Mending and washing nets, preserving fish, maintaining boats and supplies, training and supervising crews, and negotiating with merchants and others in the shipping industry made for long, tiring hours. ◆

What Does Leprosy Have to Do with AIDS?

In Jesus' day, leprosy was a slowly progressing, chronic, highly infectious, incurable skin disease with large social implications. Today, leprosy is rare thanks to sulfone drugs and better hygiene. Now known as Hansen's Disease, the once-dreaded malady has been virtually eliminated. Much of that medical work has been done by Christians who followed Jesus' example in reaching out to a class of people that society had rejected (vv. 12–15; compare 17:11–15).

Now the world struggles with acquired immune deficiency syndrome (AIDS), a scourge that bears some remarkable similarities to leprosy. Biologically the diseases are quite different. But like the lepers of the ancient world, many AIDS sufferers are socially ostracized out of fear that they will contaminate others.

The situation is complicated by the fact that many AIDS cases have resulted from sex outside of monogamous, heterosexual marriage or from intravenous drug abuse—behaviors that oppose biblical precepts and principles. That introduces a moral dimension to the problem. But if there are moral issues involved in the spread of AIDS, there is also a moral issue involved in determining a Christlike response to AIDS.

In biblical times, leprosy was thought to be very contagious and hereditary. It was also believed to be a divine punishment for sin, even though the actual instances of that, such as Miriam (Num. 12:9–10) and Uzziah (2 Chr. 26:16–23), were exceptional. The Law was very specific about the diagnosis and treatment of leprosy (see Lev. 13). If a priest detected suspicious symptoms—pimples, scabs, sores, nodules, or white spots on the skin "like snow"—he ordered a quarantine of the infected person for seven days to protect the rest of the society. If the symptoms did not fade away within a week, another week of quarantine was prescribed.

Weeks could drag into months and months into years. Quarantined persons became social outcasts, living outside the Israelite camp. They fended for themselves as best they could. Some perhaps received occasional supplies from relatives, but most were reduced to begging.

Those who actually had the dreaded disease slowly wasted away. As the disease took away sensation, they easily injured themselves without feeling pain, leading to deformity and "half-eaten flesh" (Num. 12:12) and, eventually, death.

Quarantines never cured a leper. Only divine intervention could. God healed Moses (Ex. 4:6–7), Miriam (Num. 12:11–15), and Naaman (2 Kin. 5:1–15) in order to reveal His power and call people to follow Him. So when Jesus healed lepers, it demonstrated His divine nature and caused people to turn to Him.

What would Jesus do today? Surely His compassionate treatment of lepers is instructive for those of us living in a day of AIDS. We may debate the extent to which AIDS is a consequence of sinful choices and acts. But we can and should continue to seek for a cure, just as leprosy was eventually cured through modern medicine. In the meantime, believers need to consider what a Christlike response would be to those with AIDS. Jesus reached out to lepers with love and healing. What compassionate, redemptive responses can we show toward our own, modern-day "lepers"? ◆

Levi's Feast—A Career Transition Party

CONSIDER THIS
5:28–29

As Levi was about to leave his professional life to follow the Lord, he came up with an interesting idea: a feast where some of the power brokers of the society—who happened to be his friends—could meet his new friend, Jesus. Maybe it could be compared to an office good-bye party—but with a surprise guest! Can your coworkers detect any of your loyalty to Christ?

Jesus Pronounces Blessings

6:20–26

20 Then he looked up at his disciples and said:

"Blessed are you who are poor,
for yours is the kingdom of God.
21 "Blessed are you who are hungry now,
for you will be filled.
"Blessed are you who weep now,
for you will laugh.

22 "Blessed are you when people hate you, and when
they exclude you, revile you, and defame you[y] on account
of the Son of Man. 23Rejoice in that day and leap for joy, for
surely your reward is great in heaven; for that is what their
ancestors did to the prophets.

[y]Gk *cast out your name as evil*

The Blessing—and Woes—of Wealth

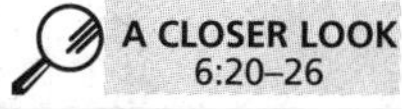

The blessings of vv. 20–23, contrasted with the woes of vv. 24–26, should warn us to reflect carefully on God's perspective on wealth and poverty. *See "Don't Worry!" at Matt. 6:19–34 for more on this issue.*

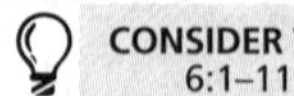

Jesus Confronts the Legalists

A pleasant day's hike through the grainfields turned sour when Jesus and His disciples ran into some Pharisees (vv. 1–2). Ever on the lookout for infractions of their traditions especially by Jesus and His followers, these legalists objected to the disciples "harvesting" grain in violation of the Sabbath. Never mind the group's hunger. For that matter, never mind that they were obviously snacking: after all, how could a handful of tiny heads of wheat or barley make a satisfying meal?

But the Pharisees would take Scripture out of context or add to it in order to condemn people for normal, God-given behavior. They ignored God's love and the freeness of His grace.

The Pharisees had lost sight of the intent of the Law and had taken upon themselves the impossible task of earning God's favor through moral perfectionism. The more they labored to "keep the Law," the more they wrapped themselves in an ever-expanding cloak of man-made rules and regulations. Worse, they judged everyone around them by their impossible standards.

Jesus Pronounces Woes

24 "But woe to you who are rich,
for you have received your consolation.
25 "Woe to you who are full now,
for you will be hungry.
"Woe to you who are laughing now,
for you will mourn and weep.

26 "Woe to you when all speak well of you, for that is what their ancestors did to the false prophets.

"Love Your Enemies"

6:27–31 see pg. 234

27 "But I say to you that listen, Love
your enemies, do good to those who hate
you, [28]bless those who curse you, pray for those who abuse

6:29 see pg. 234

you. [29]If anyone strikes you on the
cheek, offer the other also; and from
anyone who takes away your coat do not withhold even
your shirt. [30]Give to everyone who begs from you; and if
anyone takes away your goods, do not ask for them again.
[31]Do to others as you would have them do to you.

Jesus challenged them by using the very Scriptures they claimed to honor (vv. 3–4). Furthermore, according to Matthew's account of this incident, Jesus questioned their basic attitudes, which seemed to have more to do with ritual than with the mercy that God values (Matt. 12:7).

Yet the critics only seemed to harden in their legalism, continuing to dog Jesus' steps on another Sabbath, when He visited one of their synagogues (vv. 6–7).

Now as then, legalists may be the hardest people to reach with the message of God's love. Jesus never won the Pharisees over as a group. But neither did He allow their abuse of Scripture or people to go unchallenged. ◆

The Sabbath controversies raise legitimate questions: How should Christians observe a day of rest? Is it okay to work on Sundays? See "Are Sundays Special?" Rom. 14:5–13, and "The Sabbath," Heb. 4:1–13.

Does Change Threaten You?

CONSIDER THIS 5:36–39

A stubborn allegiance to old habits and traditions can sometimes seriously hinder maturing faith. Every believer should pay attention to that, because new life in Christ inevitably leads to innovation and timely change. Fear of change is understandable, but too much fear may be a sign of sinful resistance or of clinging to the past only because it feels safe and familiar.

Jesus understood our human tendency toward predictability and the natural resistance to new things. He also knew that not all changes are good, and He never advocated change for the sake of change. But He warned against making tradition, particularly religious tradition, the standard by which all things should be tested (vv. 36–39). His parable of the wineskins pleads for at least the openness to consider something new. It affirms timely change in matters of growth and new life.

Are you resistant to the dynamics of change in your life, work, family, or church? If so, could you be resisting the very work of God or the ongoing dynamic of life itself? Pay attention to Jesus' image of the wineskins!

Is Jesus Really Lord of All?

CONSIDER THIS 6:1–5 Is Jesus Lord of only the things we dedicate to Him, or is He Lord of everything and everyone? Are some things more "sacred" than others?

To the Pharisees, the Sabbath day was so sacred that they could not accept Jesus and His friends gathering a handful of grain and eating it on that day (v. 1). Jesus was violating their extreme view of the separation between rest and work. He added to their consternation by reminding them of King David who entered the temple and ate the ceremonial showbread (vv. 3–4; 1 Sam. 21:1–6).

Jesus was not only challenging the Pharisees' view of holiness, He was establishing Himself as the Lord of the Sabbath, and in fact of all creation (v. 5; Col. 1:15–18). As Lord, He was free to determine what was permissible on the Sabbath day of rest. More importantly, as Lord He will not be boxed in by people's categories of "sacred" and "secular." He is Lord of *all.*

In what areas of life do we try to keep Jesus from being Lord? How do we try to limit His authority in order to preserve our own views and further our own interests?

When we say that Jesus is Lord of all, how much of "all" is all? See "Life—The Big Picture," Mark 12:28–34.

32 "If you love those who love you, what credit is that to
you? For even sinners love those who love them. 33If you
do good to those who do good to you, what credit is that to
you? For even sinners do the same. 34If you lend to those
from whom you hope to receive, what credit is that to you?
Even sinners lend to sinners, to receive as much again.
35But love your enemies, do good, and lend, expecting
nothing in return.[z] Your reward will be great, and you will
be children of the Most High; for he is kind to the ungrateful and the wicked. 36Be merciful, just as your Father is
merciful.

"Do Not Judge"

37 "Do not judge, and you will not be judged; do not
condemn, and you will not be condemned. Forgive, and
you will be forgiven; 38give, and it will be given to you. A
good measure, pressed down, shaken together, running
over, will be put into your lap; for the measure you give
will be the measure you get back."
39 He also told them a parable: "Can a blind person
guide a blind person? Will not both fall into a pit? 40A disciple is not above the teacher, but everyone who is fully qualified will be like the teacher. 41Why do you see the speck in
your neighbor's[a] eye, but do not notice the log in your own
eye? 42Or how can you say to your neighbor,[b] 'Friend,[b] let
me take out the speck in your eye,' when you yourself do
not see the log in your own eye? You hypocrite, first take
the log out of your own eye, and then you will see clearly
to take the speck out of your neighbor's[a] eye.

A Tree Is Known by Its Fruit

43 "No good tree bears bad fruit, nor again does a bad
tree bear good fruit; 44for each tree is known by its own
fruit. Figs are not gathered from thorns, nor are grapes
picked from a bramble bush. 45The good person out of the
good treasure of the heart produces good, and the evil person out of evil treasure produces evil; for it is out of the
abundance of the heart that the mouth speaks.

The Foundation of a House

46 "Why do you call me 'Lord, Lord,' and do not do
what I tell you? 47I will show you what someone is like who
comes to me, hears my words, and acts on them. 48That

[z]Other ancient authorities read *despairing of no one* [a]Gk *brother's* [b]Gk *brother*

one is like a man building a house, who dug deeply and
laid the foundation on rock; when a flood arose, the river
burst against that house but could not shake it, because it
had been well built.[c] 49But the one who hears and does not
act is like a man who built a house on the ground without a
foundation. When the river burst against it, immediately it
fell, and great was the ruin of that house."

A Centurion's Great Faith

7 After Jesus[d] had finished all his sayings in the
hearing of the people, he entered Capernaum. 2A centurion there had a slave whom he valued highly, and who
was ill and close to death. 3When he heard about Jesus, he
sent some Jewish elders to him, asking him to come and
heal his slave. 4When they came to Jesus, they appealed to
him earnestly, saying, "He is worthy of having you do this
for him, 5for he loves our people, and it is he who built our
synagogue for us." 6And Jesus went with them, but when
he was not far from the house, the centurion sent friends to
say to him, "Lord, do not trouble yourself, for I am not
worthy to have you come under my roof; 7therefore I did
not presume to come to you. But only speak the word, and
let my servant be healed. 8For I also am a man set under
authority, with soldiers under me; and I say to one, 'Go,'
and he goes, and to another, 'Come,' and he comes, and to

7:1–10 see pg. 235

my slave, 'Do this,' and the slave does
it." 9When Jesus heard this he was
amazed at him, and turning to the crowd that followed
him, he said, "I tell you, not even in Israel have I found
such faith." 10When those who had been sent returned to
the house, they found the slave in good health.

A Dead Man Raised at Nain

7:11 see pg. 237

11 Soon afterwards[e] he went to a town
called Nain, and his disciples and a large
crowd went with him. 12As he approached the gate of the
town, a man who had died was being carried out. He was
his mother's only son, and she was a widow; and with her
was a large crowd from the town. 13When the Lord saw her,
he had compassion for her and said to her, "Do not weep."
14Then he came forward and touched the bier, and the
bearers stood still. And he said, "Young man, I say to you,

(Bible text continued on page 236)

[c]Other ancient authorities read *founded upon the rock* [d]Gk *he* [e]Other ancient authorities read *Next day*

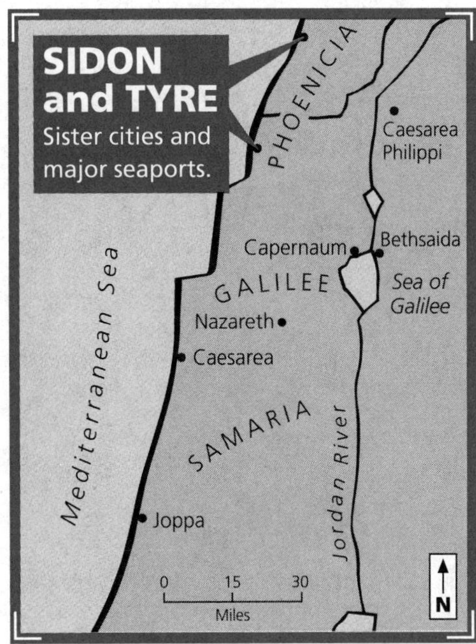

Tyre and Sidon

YOU ARE THERE 6:17

- **Sister cities and major seaports about 20 miles apart on the Mediterranean coast, in Phoenicia (modern Lebanon) north of Galilee.**
- **Tyre (*rock*) was a rocky, coastal city on the mainland and a small island city just offshore; Sidon (*fishery*), built on a hill, stretched across several small islands connected by bridges.**
- **Introduced pagan practices to Israel and resisted conquest.**
- **Frequently denounced by Hebrew prophets.**
- **Renowned for shipping and shipbuilding, fishing, purple (an expensive dye; see "Lydia," Acts 16:14), masonry, carpentry, pottery, and glassware.**
- **Used by Jesus to warn His Hebrew listeners: had Tyre and Sidon received the attention that cities like Chorazin and Capernaum did, their pagan citizens would have been converted (Luke 10:13–16).**

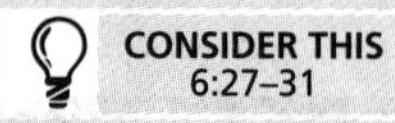
CONSIDER THIS
6:27–31

Love My *Enemies?*

The Law commanded Hebrews to love their neighbors (Lev. 19:18), but Jesus challenged His followers to love even their enemies (v. 27). Later He would be asked, "Who is my neighbor?" (Luke 10:29). Here we might ask, "Who are our enemies?"

Many believers today might think of our enemies as those we find unpleasant, people we just don't like. But that's not strong enough. By "enemies" Jesus meant those we actually hate, *and those who* hate us, *for whatever reason.*

Jesus' listeners didn't need to look far to understand who it was He was talking about. Verse 17 notes that a huge crowd had gathered around Him, including Gentiles from the seacoast cities of Tyre and Sidon. These centers of Baal worship had troubled the Hebrews for generations by introducing pagan ideas and practices. Elsewhere, Roman occupation troops held sway over the region, exploiting the Jews through oppressive taxation and political manipulation.

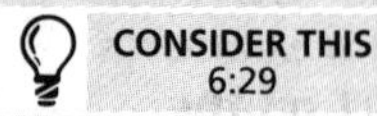
CONSIDER THIS
6:29

Running to Extremes

Did Christ intend for us to take what He said in vv. 27–36 literally? *It sounds noble to love our enemies, bless those who curse us, and pray for those who spite us. But what about physical abuse, robbery, or endless appeals for help (vv. 29–30)? Surely He didn't mean those words the way they sound. Or does Christianity encourage people to run to dangerous extremes?*

It's legitimate to notice that Jesus often used hyperbole and stark contrasts in His comments here (see "The Sermon on the Mount," Matt. 5:2). So when we read Jesus' words today, it's easy to set up all kinds of exceptions and qualifications to soften them. But in the process, do we miss His point? Do we distort His message?

Jesus was not calling here for unhealthy responses, nor setting forth a political or social agenda, nor offering a statement of public policy, nor constructing a model for business and finance. Instead, He posed a tough challenge to His followers—to those who listen (v. 27): What difference does our faith make in the way we respond to people in need? That's the key—our response to human need. That shows the true condition of our hearts. Do we respond to people as God Himself does, with mercy (v. 36)?

The test comes when we are faced with extremes. As

So it was immediately clear to the crowd who their enemies were—who was likely to curse and shame them (v. 28), who was likely to strike and rob them (v. 29), and who was likely to exploit them (v. 30). "Love your enemies," Jesus told them. Love those you hate, and who hate you.

Those of us who follow Jesus in today's world also have "enemies." Basically we are no different from those first believers. If we look carefully, we will recognize people we hate, *and who* hate *us. The bitterness may spring from racial, ethnic, political, economic, moral, gender, religious, or ideological conflicts. But they go beyond mere likes and dislikes. So Jesus' challenge to us is the same: "Love your enemies. Love those you hate, and who hate you."* ◆

On another occasion Jesus came back to the issue of loving one's neighbor. See Luke 10:27.

◆ ◆ ◆ ◆ ◆ ◆ ◆ ◆ ◆ ◆ ◆ ◆ ◆ ◆ ◆ ◆

Jesus pointed out, it's easy to love those who love us (v. 32). It's easy to give when we know we'll get back (v. 34). But God loves people who do not love Him, and gives to those who will never even thank Him, let alone give back to Him (v. 35).

Even God's enemies have needs that only He can meet. In His mercy, He meets those needs. Do we? When faced with people in genuine need, do we look only at their character, and base our response on that alone? Or do we look at their needs and do what we can to meet them?

We may question how far Jesus wants us to go in the various situations described in vv. 29–30. But we need never question how far God is willing to go to show mercy. That's what we need to take literally and imitate practically. ◆

Many misunderstandings have arisen from Jesus' statements in vv. 27–36. His words sound extreme to our ears. How can we make sense of them? See "The Morality of Christ," Matt. 5:17–48.

A Soldier's Surprising Faith

CONSIDER THIS
7:1–10

Jesus stepped on the toes of His Jewish listeners by praising a Roman centurion's faith (v. 9). He was impressed that the centurion—a soldier who knew all about power and authority—recognized Jesus' power and authority over disease. He marveled at the officer's faith. It was a faith that had such trust in Jesus that only His command was needed.

But with all the mention of authority, the centurion expressed humility: "I am not worthy to have you come under my roof" (v. 6). What can we learn from the centurion's humility, faith, and recognition of Jesus' authority?

rise!" 15The dead man sat up and began to speak, and Jesus[f]
gave him to his mother. 16Fear seized all of them; and they
glorified God, saying, "A great prophet has risen among
us!" and "God has looked favorably on his people!" 17This
word about him spread throughout Judea and all the surrounding country.

"The Least in the Kingdom"

18 The disciples of John reported all these things to him.
So John summoned two of his disciples 19and sent them to
the Lord to ask, "Are you the one who is to come, or are we
7:20–23
to wait for another?" 20When the men
had come to him, they said, "John the
Baptist has sent us to you to ask, 'Are you the one who is to
come, or are we to wait for another?' " 21Jesus[f] had just then
cured many people of diseases, plagues, and evil spirits,
7:22 see pg. 238
and had given sight to many who were
blind. 22And he answered them, "Go and
tell John what you have seen and heard: the blind receive
their sight, the lame walk, the lepers[g] are cleansed, the deaf
hear, the dead are raised, the poor have good news brought
to them. 23And blessed is anyone who takes no offense at
me."

[f]Gk *he* [g]The terms *leper* and *leprosy* can refer to several diseases

The Underclass

Nearly every society and every city in biblical times had a large underclass*—people scraping by on the margins of society. Tending to congregate in the cities, the underclass included those who were poor, sick, disabled, blind, mentally ill, demon-possessed, widowed, and orphaned. It included runaways, castaways, lepers, and refugees. Lacking resources to provide for even their basic needs, many turned to begging, stealing, menial labor, slavery, and prostitution. Few cultures made provision for these desperate, destitute wanderers, and so they remained largely powerless to change their condition.*

Yet it was to the underclass that Jesus intentionally directed much of His life and ministry. They were among the "blessed" in His opening remarks in the Sermon on the Mount (Matt. 5:3–10). And He declared that He had come to bring them good news in his inaugural sermon at Nazareth (Luke 4:17–18). So it was no surprise that when John's questioning disciples came to ask whether He was

24 When John's messengers had gone, Jesus[h] began to
speak to the crowds about John:[i] "What did you go out
into the wilderness to look at? A reed shaken by the wind?
7:25 25What then did you go out to see?
Someone[j] dressed in soft robes? Look,
those who put on fine clothing and live in luxury are in
royal palaces. 26What then did you go out to see? A
prophet? Yes, I tell you, and more than a prophet. 27This is
the one about whom it is written,

'See, I am sending my messenger ahead of you,
who will prepare your way before you.'

28I tell you, among those born of women no one is greater
than John; yet the least in the kingdom of God is greater
than he." 29(And all the people who heard this, including
the tax collectors, acknowledged the justice of God,[k] because they had been baptized with John's baptism. 30But by
refusing to be baptized by him, the Pharisees and the
lawyers rejected God's purpose for themselves.)
31 "To what then will I compare the people of this

(Bible text continued on page 240)

[h]Gk he [i]Gk him [j]Or Why then did you go out? To see someone [k]Or praised God

John Who?

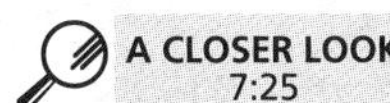

Even for his own day, John's ministry had none of the outward trappings of success. See "John the Street Preacher," Matt. 3:4.

indeed the Messiah, they found Him ministering among the underclass (7:20–21).

Nor was it any surprise that the early church continued this outreach. They used their resources to meet material needs among their own members (Acts 2:44–45; 4:32, 34–35). They attracted the sick and afflicted (5:12–16). They appointed leaders to manage social programs for widows (6:1–6). They sent famine relief (11:27–30). They urged new leaders to remember the poor (Gal. 2:10). They even evaluated their success in part by how much they collected in charitable contributions (Rom. 15:26–27).

To what extent will Christians today follow in the footsteps of Jesus and the first believers? Our cities, like theirs, are filling up with an underclass. How can we offer "good news" to them? Can we touch their bodies as well as their souls? Do we take them as seriously as our Savior did? ◆

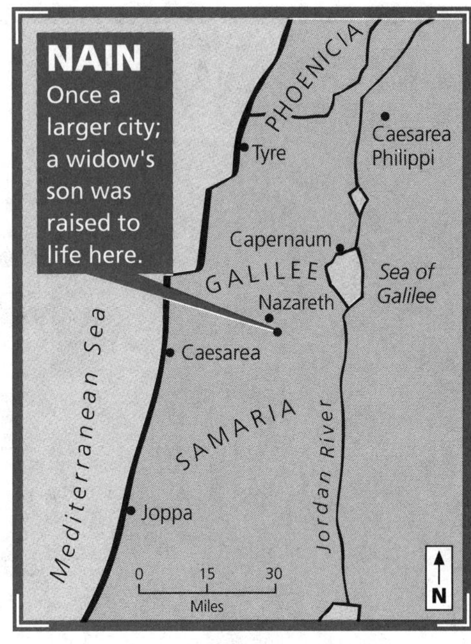

NAIN

YOU ARE THERE 7:11

- **Town in southwest Galilee, overlooking the Plain of Esdraelon.**
- **Name means *pleasant* or *delightful.* The view was certainly pleasant, and a spring contributed to groves of olives and figs.**
- **A small village now, though probably larger at the time of Jesus' visit (7:11).**
- **Located near numerous caves and tombs.**

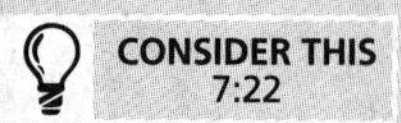

What Is the Gospel?

Fewer and fewer people today understand the meaning and significance of the term "gospel." To many it is little more than a category of the music industry or a vague religious term. Yet you are reading The Gospel *According to Luke. And Jesus told John's followers that one way they could tell He was the Messiah was that because of His coming, "the poor have* good news (the gospel) *brought to them" (v. 22, emphasis added).*

What is the gospel, and why was it significant for Jesus to preach it? The Greek word *euangelion* can be translated *gospel* or *good news* or *the good news proclaimed*. From the standpoint of the New Testament, the ultimate good news is that Jesus Christ has come as the Messiah, the Savior of the world. He has come to save people from sin and restore them to God.

The Good News

That is indeed good news because it speaks to the very bad news that apart from God's intervention, all the world would be lost and without hope. As Paul declared in Romans, his monumental work explaining the gospel, "All have sinned and fall short of the glory of God" (Rom. 3:23). The good news is that "while we still were sinners Christ died for us" (5:8). Indeed, Christ's death, which dealt with sin, and His resurrection from the dead form the core of the gospel message and ground that message in historical events (1 Cor. 15:1–4).

Obviously, though, Jesus had not yet gone to the cross at the time John's followers came, asking whether He was the Christ. Nevertheless, His message of the kingdom was good news because it revealed that God was finally bringing about the salvation promised in the Old Testament. Jesus' coming was like a fireman arriving on the scene of a fire or an emergency medical team arriving at an accident. The situation was not yet remedied, but the remedy was at hand. That was good news!

The Gospel for the Poor

But Jesus said it was especially good news for the poor (Luke 7:22). He had told the hometown crowd at Nazareth the same thing, that He had come "to bring good news to the poor" (4:18). Likewise, in the Sermon on the Mount He taught, "Blessed are you who are poor, for yours is the kingdom of God" (Luke 6:20). In what sense was Jesus' message of the kingdom particularly for the poor?

You might say Jesus was announcing an "upside-down kingdom." Whereas the kingdoms of the world are set up by and for the powerful and the advantaged, His kingdom was offered to the destitute, the wretched, the broken, and the hopeless, to those stripped of their dignity and self-respect. The poor in spirit were not merely the humble, but the humiliated, those who have had their spirits crushed and are knocked down by circumstances.

The poor were easy to spot in Jesus' day. They included widows and orphans, slaves and prisoners, the sick and demon-possessed, the homeless and the hungry. In our own day we could add people grieving the loss of a loved one or the end of a marriage, those who have lost jobs, or those who have been victimized by crime or injustice.

To these Jesus preached good news. He invited them to become part of a new family, a new community, the church. The rich are invited as well, but as in the parable of the slighted invitation, most reject the offer, feeling sufficient in themselves to take care of their needs (see "Worse than Rude," Matt. 22:2–14).

But those who accept Jesus' invitation do so by believing in His work on the cross on their behalf. That involves more than mere intellectual agreement to a theoretical truth. It means admitting their sinful condition and placing trust in Jesus to deal with their sin. It means entering into a vital relationship with the living Christ Himself.

The Purpose of the Gospel

When people believe, Christ begins to fashion them into a community of faith, the body of Christ (Eph. 2:1—3:11; 1 Pet. 2:9–10). His ultimate purpose in the gospel is to create a new people who live out the message, relationships, and values of His kingdom, a kingdom in which justice replaces injustice, community replaces rugged individualism, and compassion reigns over competition and neglect of others.

Thus the gospel is not merely a private relationship with God, but a public expression of godliness as well. The good news about Jesus certainly affects one's personal life, transforming individual attitudes and habits. But it challenges us to look beyond our own self-interests to the interests of others, both those in our network of relationships and in the world in general (Rom. 12:3–8; Eph. 4:1–16; Phil. 2:1–11). To embrace the gospel is to live no longer for oneself, but to live for Christ.

Spreading the Gospel

Moreover, Christ has commissioned His followers to spread the good news about Him throughout the world. This involves both the verbal proclamation of gospel truth and the demonstration of gospel reality in the lives of believers. Both can happen in a variety of ways: through preaching and teaching, through Christian worship and daily disciplines of spiritual life, through works of mercy and programs of compassion that meet basic human needs, or through believers taking moral stands (see "Faith Impacts the World," Mark 16:15).

The Four Gospels

During the second century, the term "gospel" came to mean the authoritative message about Jesus that the apostles had left and especially the four written accounts of His life and teaching, Matthew, Mark, Luke, and John. Mark was probably the first to be written, but all were created to be more than mere biographies about an historical figure. Each portrays the Lord in a particular way to show His saving significance for all people and to call them to respond in faith to His good news. ◆

THE GOOD NEWS
WHILE WE WERE STILL SINNERS CHRIST DIED FOR US....

Simon's Spoiled Party

CONSIDER THIS 7:36–50 *The incident in vv. 36–50 contrasts a respectable Pharisee, Simon, against a disreputable, unnamed woman. Luke describes her as a "sinner" (v. 37), a general term describing both those who failed to keep the ritual laws as well as those who flaunted the moral laws. How she gained entrance to Simon's feast is unclear.*

The religious leader was probably restricted from even talking to the woman. Extensive Jewish religious laws had developed in the first century to ensure moral purity. Many men suspected women of being sexually aggressive and eager to trap unsuspecting men. So Jewish men in general and teachers of the Law in particular—such as Simon and Jesus—were to have as little to do with women as possible.

Jesus knew what kind of life the woman lived, possibly by her hairstyle and the clothes she wore. Yet He accepted her anyway, violating taboos against speaking with her or allowing her to touch Him. In return, she gave to Jesus what Simon, the host, should have given—a kiss of welcome, a washing of the feet, and oil for the skin. These comforts were not merely symbolic but practical expressions of hospitality.

generation, and what are they like? 32They are like children
sitting in the marketplace and calling to one another,

'We played the flute for you, and you did not dance;
we wailed, and you did not weep.'

33For John the Baptist has come eating no bread and drinking no wine, and you say, 'He has a demon'; 34the Son of
Man has come eating and drinking, and you say, 'Look, a
glutton and a drunkard, a friend of tax collectors and sinners!' 35Nevertheless, wisdom is vindicated by all her children."

A Sinner at Simon's Dinner

7:36–50

36 One of the Pharisees asked Jesus[l]
to eat with him, and he went into the
Pharisee's house and took his place at the table. 37And a
woman in the city, who was a sinner, having learned that he
was eating in the Pharisee's house, brought an alabaster jar
of ointment. 38She stood behind him at his feet, weeping,
and began to bathe his feet with her tears and to dry them
with her hair. Then she continued kissing his feet and
anointing them with the ointment. 39Now when the Pharisee who had invited him saw it, he said to himself, "If this
man were a prophet, he would have known who and what
kind of woman this is who is touching him—that she is a
sinner." 40Jesus spoke up and said to him, "Simon, I have
something to say to you." "Teacher," he replied, "Speak."
41"A certain creditor had two debtors; one owed five hundred denarii,[m] and the other fifty. 42When they could not
pay, he canceled the debts for both of them. Now which of
them will love him more?" 43Simon answered, "I suppose
the one for whom he canceled the greater debt." And Jesus[n]
said to him, "You have judged rightly." 44Then turning toward the woman, he said to Simon, "Do you see this
woman? I entered your house; you gave me no water for
my feet, but she has bathed my feet with her tears and
dried them with her hair. 45You gave me no kiss, but from
the time I came in she has not stopped kissing my feet.
46You did not anoint my head with oil, but she has
anointed my feet with ointment. 47Therefore, I tell you, her
sins, which were many, have been forgiven; hence she has
shown great love. But the one to whom little is forgiven,

[l] Gk *him* [m] The denarius was the usual day's wage for a laborer [n] Gk *he*

loves little." 48Then he said to her, "Your sins are forgiven."
49But those who were at the table with him began to say
among themselves, "Who is this who even forgives sins?"
50And he said to the woman, "Your faith has saved you; go
in peace."

Many Women Provide for Jesus

8:1–3 see pg. 242

8 Soon afterwards he went on through
cities and villages, proclaiming and
bringing the good news of the kingdom of God. The twelve

8:2 see pg. 243

were with him, 2as well as some women
who had been cured of evil spirits and
infirmities: Mary, called Magdalene, from whom seven
demons had gone out, 3and Joanna, the wife of Herod's
steward Chuza, and Susanna, and many others, who provided for them[o] out of their resources.

A Parable about a Sower

8:4 see pg. 244

4 When a great crowd gathered and
people from town after town came to
him, he said in a parable: 5"A sower went out to sow his
seed; and as he sowed, some fell on the path and was trampled on, and the birds of the air ate it up. 6Some fell on the
rock; and as it grew up, it withered for lack of moisture.
7Some fell among thorns, and the thorns grew with it and
choked it. 8Some fell into good soil, and when it grew, it
produced a hundredfold." As he said this, he called out,
"Let anyone with ears to hear listen!"

The Purpose of Parables

9 Then his disciples asked him what this parable meant.
10He said, "To you it has been given to know the secrets[p] of
the kingdom of God; but to others I speak[q] in parables, so
that

'looking they may not perceive,
and listening they may not understand.'

The Parable of the Sower Explained

11 "Now the parable is this: The seed is the word of
God. 12The ones on the path are those who have heard;
then the devil comes and takes away the word from their

(Bible text continued on page 243)

[o]Other ancient authorities read *him* [p]Or *mysteries* [q]Gk lacks *I speak*

"YOUR FAITH HAS SAVED YOU; GO IN PEACE."
—Luke 7:50

The Women Who Followed Jesus

FOR YOUR INFO 8:1–3 **The Gospel writers show us that many women, frequently overlooked, were among the followers of Jesus. Several appear by name:**

Mary, called Magdalene (Matt. 27:56; Mark 15:40; Luke 8:2; 24:10). Invariably mentioned first, perhaps because of her dramatic healing or because she was the most prominent.

Joanna, the wife of Chuza (Luke 8:3; 24:10). Chuza managed the king's household, so Joanna had access to Herod's court — infamous for its extravagant parties and sexual immorality (see "The Herods," Acts 12:1-2).

Susanna (Luke 8:3).

Mary, the mother of James and Joses (Matt. 27:56; Mark 15:40; Luke 24:10).

Salome (Mark 15:40).

The mother of the sons of Zebedee (James and John; Matt. 27:56). Remembered for her request that Christ allow her sons to sit in favored positions in His kingdom (Matt 20:20-24).

In addition to the above, the writers state clearly that "many" other women followed Jesus (for example, see Matt. 27:55; Mark 15:41; Luke 8:3; 24:1). Luke indicates that women provided materially for Jesus and the disciples—a curious statement in that Jewish women of the time generally did not have much control over their families' resources. Nor did women commonly travel with a rabbi (see "Jesus—A Rabbi for Women, Too," 23:49). Indeed, strict codes tended to distance Jewish leaders from women, so much so that by Jesus' time a rabbi was not even to speak to his wife in public.

But Jesus apparently thought little of such taboos. There is no indication that He discouraged women from being His followers. They listened to His teaching, accompanied Him in His travels, stood by Him at His crucifixion, gave witness to His resurrection, and eventually helped spread His message throughout the Roman world. ◆

Just as women assisted Jesus in His life and ministry, so they played a major role in the early church. See "Women and the Growth of Christianity," Phil. 4:3.

hearts, so that they may not believe and be saved. [13]The
ones on the rock are those who, when they hear the word,
receive it with joy. But these have no root; they believe only
for a while and in a time of testing fall away. [14]As for what
fell among the thorns, these are the ones who hear; but as
they go on their way, they are choked by the cares and
riches and pleasures of life, and their fruit does not mature.
[15]But as for that in the good soil, these are the ones who,
when they hear the word, hold it fast in an honest and
good heart, and bear fruit with patient endurance.

A Lamp on a Lampstand

16 "No one after lighting a lamp hides it under a jar, or
puts it under a bed, but puts it on a lampstand, so that
those who enter may see the light. [17]For nothing is hidden
that will not be disclosed, nor is anything secret that will
not become known and come to light. [18]Then pay attention
to how you listen; for to those who have, more will be
given; and from those who do not have, even what they
seem to have will be taken away."

Jesus' Mother and Brothers Come to Him

 8:19–21

19 Then his mother and his brothers
came to him, but they could not reach

Who Is My Family?

Was Jesus disowning his family (v. 21)? Was He ashamed of His disbelieving relatives? See "Family Loyalty" at Matt. 12:46–50.

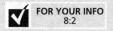

Personality Profile: Mary of Magdala

 FOR YOUR INFO 8:2

Also known as: Mary Magdalene.

Home: Raised in Magdala, a large town on the Sea of Galilee.

Best known today for: Being freed from seven demons by Jesus and becoming one of His most devoted followers.

Mary the Reliable Witness

The Gospels mention Mary of Magdala by name more than any other female disciple. One reason may be the dramatic turnaround in her life that the Lord brought about by casting out seven demons. She responded by supporting His ministry and joining with several other women who traveled with Him (Luke 8:1–3).

Mary's loyalty proved unwavering right to the end. While the Twelve fled after Jesus' arrest, Mary stood by at His crucifixion (Matt. 27:56; Mark 15:40; John 19:25). She also helped prepare His body for burial (Matt. 27:61; Mark 15:47; Luke 23:55). Perhaps it was to reward her undying devotion that the Lord allowed her to be the first person to meet Him after His resurrection (Mark 16:9–10; John 20:14–18).

Curiously, however, the disciples refused to believe Mary's report of the risen Lord. In fact, they dismissed it as an "idle tale" (Mark 16:11; Luke 24:11). Perhaps their skepticism betrayed long-held doubts about Mary's credibility: after all, hadn't she been possessed by seven demons? Moreover, Jewish culture raised its men to consider the testimony of women as inferior.

Nevertheless, Jesus chose Mary to report the good news of His resurrection to His other followers. Later, He rebuked them for their unwillingness to believe her (Mark 16:14). Thanks to Him, she was a changed person. Moreover, she was a reliable witness, having proven her trustworthiness through her perseverance and steadfastness in the face of danger and doubt.

him because of the crowd. 20And he was told, "Your mother
and your brothers are standing outside, wanting to see
you." 21But he said to them, "My mother and my brothers
are those who hear the word of God and do it."

". . . HEAR THE WORD OF GOD AND DO IT."
—Luke 8:21

A Great Storm Obeys Jesus

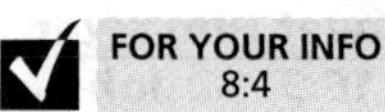
8:22–25 see pg. 246

22 One day he got into a boat with his
disciples, and he said to them, "Let us go
across to the other side of the lake." So they put out, 23and
while they were sailing he fell asleep. A windstorm swept
down on the lake, and the boat was filling with water, and
they were in danger. 24They went to him and woke him up,
shouting, "Master, Master, we are perishing!" And he woke
up and rebuked the wind and the raging waves; they
ceased, and there was a calm. 25He said to them, "Where is
your faith?" They were afraid and amazed, and said to one

FOR YOUR INFO 8:4

THE PARABLES OF JESUS CHRIST	Matthew	Mark	Luke
Lamp Under a Basket	5:14–16	4:21, 22	8:16, 17 11:33–36
A Wise Man Builds on Rock and a Foolish Man Builds on Sand	7:24–27		6:47–49
Unshrunk (New) Cloth on an Old Garment	9:16	2:21	5:36
New Wine in Old Wineskins	9:17	2:22	5:37, 38
The Sower	13:3–23	4:2–20	8:4–15
The Tares (Weeds)	13:24–30		
The Mustard Seed	13:31, 32	4:30–32	13:18, 19
The Yeast	13:33		13:20, 21
The Hidden Treasure	13:44		
The Pearl of Great Price	13:45, 46		
The Dragnet	13:47–50		
The Lost Sheep	18:12–14		15:3–7
The Unforgiving Servant	18:23–35		
The Laborers in the Vineyard	20:1–16		
The Two Sons	21:28–32		
The Wicked Vinedressers	21:33–45	12:1–12	20:9–19
The Wedding Feast	22:2–14		
The Fig Tree	24:32–44	13:28–32	21:29–33
The Wise and Foolish Bridesmaids	25:1–13		

another, "Who then is this, that he commands even the
winds and the water, and they obey him?"

A Demoniac Healed

26 Then they arrived at the country of the Gerasenes,[r]
which is opposite Galilee. 27As he stepped out on land, a
man of the city who had demons met him. For a long time
he had worn[s] no clothes, and he did not live in a house but
in the tombs. 28When he saw Jesus, he fell down before
him and shouted at the top of his voice, "What have you to
do with me, Jesus, Son of the Most High God? I beg you,
do not torment me"— 29for Jesus[t] had commanded the unclean spirit to come out of the man. (For many times it had
seized him; he was kept under guard and bound with
chains and shackles, but he would break the bonds and be
driven by the demon into the wilds.) 30Jesus then asked
him, "What is your name?" He said, "Legion"; for many

[r]Other ancient authorities read *Gadarenes;* others, *Gergesenes* [s]Other ancient authorities read *a man of the city who had had demons for a long time met him. He wore* [t]Gk *he*

THE PARABLES OF JESUS CHRIST (cont.)	Matthew	Mark	Luke
The Talents	25:14–30		
The Growing Seed		4:26–29	
The Absent Householder		13:33–37	
The Creditor and Two Debtors			7:41–43
The Good Samaritan			10:30–37
A Friend in Need			11:5–13
The Rich Fool			12:16–21
The Watchful Slaves			12:35–40
The Faithful Slave and the Unfaithful Slave			12:42–48
The Barren Fig Tree			13:6–9
The Great Dinner			14:16–24
Building a Tower and a King Making War			14:25–35
The Lost Coin			15:8–10
The Lost Son			15:11–32
The Dishonest Manager			16:1–13
The Rich Man and Lazarus			16:19–31
Unprofitable Slaves			17:7–10
The Persistent Widow			18:1–8
The Pharisee and the Tax Collector			18:9–14
The Ten Pounds			19:11–27

demons had entered him. 31They begged him not to order
them to go back into the abyss.
32 Now there on the hillside a large herd of swine was
feeding; and the demons[u] begged Jesus[v] to let them enter
these. So he gave them permission. 33Then the demons
came out of the man and entered the swine, and the herd
rushed down the steep bank into the lake and was
drowned.
34 When the swineherds saw what had happened, they
ran off and told it in the city and in the country. 35Then
people came out to see what had happened, and when they
came to Jesus, they found the man from whom the demons
had gone sitting at the feet of Jesus, clothed and in his right
mind. And they were afraid. 36Those who had seen it told
them how the one who had been possessed by demons had
been healed. 37Then all the people of the surrounding
country of the Gerasenes[w] asked Jesus[v] to leave them; for
they were seized with great fear. So he got into the boat and

[u]Gk *they* [v]Gk *him* [w]Other ancient authorities read *Gadarenes;* others, *Gergesenes*

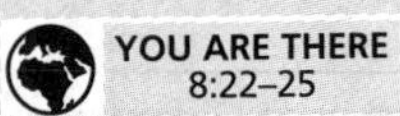

WHAT KIND OF STORM WAS THIS?

The Sea of Galilee was no place to be caught in a storm. The kind of weather that caught Jesus and His disciples occurs there to this day. As one traveler described it:

> The sun had scarcely set when the wind began to rush down towards the lake, and it continued all night long, with increasing violence, so that when we reached the shore the next morning the face of the lake was like a huge, boiling caldron . . . .
>
> We had to double-pin all the tent-ropes, and frequently were obliged to hang on with our whole weight upon them to keep the quivering tabernacle from being carried up bodily into the air.

The reason for such gale-force winds is the surrounding landscape. The lake is 700 feet below sea level, and is fed by rivers that have cut deep ravines surrounded by flat plains that are in turn hedged in by mountains. The ravines act like wind siphons or tunnels, gathering cooler air from the mountains as it crosses the plains. When the air mass runs into the hot lake shore, violent storms are whipped up with no warning.

Several of the disciples were experienced fishermen, well acquainted with such storms. However, they had never seen winds like those that attacked their boat (v. 23), for they turned to the Lord in utter terror, certain that all

returned. 38The man from whom the demons had gone
begged that he might be with him; but Jesus[x] sent him
8:38–39 away, saying, 39"Return to your home,
and declare how much God has done for
you." So he went away, proclaiming throughout the city
how much Jesus had done for him.

A Girl Restored to Life and a Woman Healed

40 Now when Jesus returned, the crowd welcomed him,
for they were all waiting for him. 41Just then there came a

[x]Gk *he*

The First Gentile Evangelist?

A CLOSER LOOK 8:38–39 *The restored man was most likely a Gentile from the city of Gadara (vv. 38–39). Jesus sent him back home to tell his family and friends of God's power and grace—possibly making him the first known Gentile evangelist. See "Gadara," Mark 5:1.*

"DECLARE HOW MUCH GOD HAS DONE FOR YOU." —Luke 8:39

was lost. Yet their fear of the wind and the waves gave way to wonder and awe when Jesus turned and calmed the sea. ◆

Jesus drew most of His followers from the Galilee region, and carried out most of His ministry there. See "Galilee," Mark 1:14.

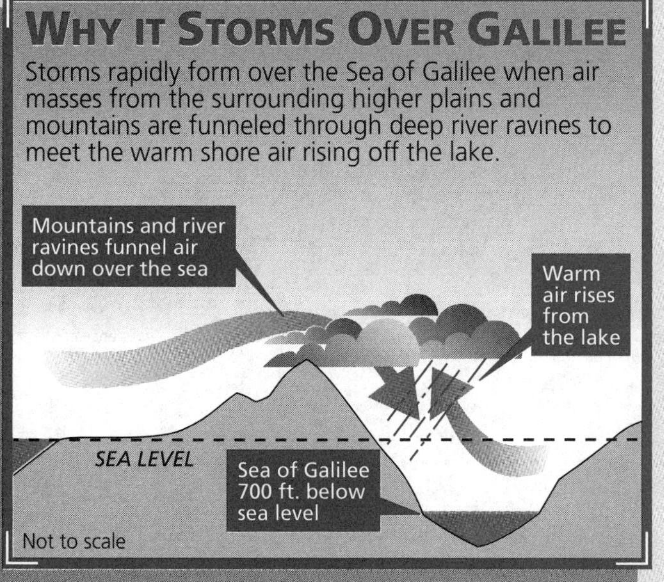
WHY IT STORMS OVER GALILEE
Storms rapidly form over the Sea of Galilee when air masses from the surrounding higher plains and mountains are funneled through deep river ravines to meet the warm shore air rising off the lake.
Mountains and river ravines funnel air down over the sea
Warm air rises from the lake
SEA LEVEL
Sea of Galilee 700 ft. below sea level
Not to scale

man named Jairus, a leader of the synagogue. He fell at
Jesus' feet and begged him to come to his house, 42for he
had an only daughter, about twelve years old, who was dying.

8:43–44 As he went, the crowds pressed in on
him. 43Now there was a woman who had
been suffering from hemorrhages for twelve years; and
though she had spent all she had on physicians,[y] no one
could cure her. 44She came up behind him and touched the
fringe of his clothes, and immediately her hemorrhage
stopped. 45Then Jesus asked, "Who touched me?" When all
denied it, Peter[z] said, "Master, the crowds surround you
and press in on you." 46But Jesus said, "Someone touched
me; for I noticed that power had gone out from me."
47When the woman saw that she could not remain hidden,
she came trembling; and falling down before him, she declared in the presence of all the people why she had
touched him, and how she had been immediately healed.
48He said to her, "Daughter, your faith has made you well;
go in peace."

49 While he was still speaking, someone came from the
leader's house to say, "Your daughter is dead; do not trouble
the teacher any longer." 50When Jesus heard this, he
replied, "Do not fear. Only believe, and she will be saved."
51When he came to the house, he did not allow anyone to
enter with him, except Peter, John, and James, and the
child's father and mother. 52They were all weeping and
wailing for her; but he said, "Do not weep; for she is not
dead but sleeping." 53And they laughed at him, knowing
that she was dead. 54But he took her by the hand and called
out, "Child, get up!" 55Her spirit returned, and she got up
at once. Then he directed them to give her something to
eat. 56Her parents were astounded; but he ordered them to
tell no one what had happened.

"YOUR FAITH HAS MADE YOU WELL; GO IN PEACE." —Luke 8:48

Jesus Sends Out the Twelve

9:1–62 9 Then Jesus[a] called the twelve
together and gave them power and

(Bible text continued on page 250)

[y]Other ancient authorities lack *and had spent all she had on physicians* [z]Other ancient authorities add *and those who were with him* [a]Gk *he*

A Desperate Grasp for Help

A CLOSER LOOK 8:43–44 *For more on this woman's attempt to find relief, see "A Desperate Woman," Mark 5:26.*

CONSIDER THIS
9:1–62

CAN LAITY GET THE JOB DONE?

Are you surprised by Jesus' choice of His leadership team? A close reading of Luke 9 suggests that the Twelve were not exactly prize recruits for a new spiritual movement. They showed some frightening patterns and embarrassing traits that might cause a manager to wonder, "Who hired these people? How in the world can they possibly get the job done?"

Jesus recruited them, and He delegated real power and authority to them to get the job done (v. 1), not just token responsibilities, as often happens when leaders "delegate" tasks to subordinates (vv. 2–6). When they reported back from their first assignment (v. 10), He took them aside for a "performance review" at a private place near Bethsaida, a small fishing village on the north of Galilee and hometown to several team members. From that point, the Twelve made eight identifiable mistakes that we might assume would disqualify them from leadership:

(1) *They acted from a short-sighted vision.* When their retreat was interrupted by a crowd eager to meet Jesus, all they could see was their limited resources in a desert place (vv. 12–13).

(2) *Some of them fell asleep at a moment of great opportunity.* When Jesus met with Moses and Elijah, two of the greatest leaders in Israel's history, Peter, James, and John were caught napping (vv. 28–32).

(3) *They tried to preserve the status quo.* Peter wanted to hang on to a good experience and build monuments to it (vv. 33–36).

(4) *They gave way to fear of the unknown.* Jesus healed an epileptic boy, but fear caused the Twelve not to ask questions when they were confused (vv. 43–45).

(5) *They competed to see who would be top dog.* The disciples argued over greatness and privilege rather than concern themselves with serving others. Contrast that with Jesus' treatment of seekers, especially "children" and "the least" (vv. 46–48).

(6) *They dallied in partisan politics.* Encountering a rival teacher, the disciples tried to claim exclusive rights to God's activity. By contrast, Jesus included any and all who were sincerely interested in serving God in His name (vv. 49–50).

(7) *They plotted a dirty tricks campaign.* When their ethnic enemies proved inhospitable, the Twelve turned vicious. Jesus replied by issuing one of His strongest rebukes (vv. 51–56).

(8) *They bit off more than they could chew.* As they traveled along, Jesus' followers overstated their commitment; in the end they failed to deliver what they promised (vv. 57–62).

Despite these shortcomings, Jesus not only kept the Twelve on His team, He kept them as His first team! He showed that undeveloped rookies can be developed into servant-leaders—over time. Even though they were weak, competitive, self-centered, unrealistic about themselves, and insensitive to others, He kept working with them. The Lord's hopes were rewarded, but only after His death and resurrection. Luke 9 is merely the beginning of the story. The outcome can be found in Acts, where Luke goes on to show that God uses empowered laypeople like the Twelve—and like us today—to do His work.

Can we as laity do the work of God? Absolutely! But as we do, we need to take a serious look at ourselves and ask God to help us purge out those mistaken attitudes that we share with Jesus' early leaders. ◆

Who were the twelve men that Jesus chose to spread His message in Luke 9? See "The Twelve," Matt. 10:2.

authority over all demons and to cure diseases, [2]and he sent
them out to proclaim the kingdom of God and to heal. [3]He
said to them, "Take nothing for your journey, no staff, nor
bag, nor bread, nor money—not even an extra tunic.
[4]Whatever house you enter, stay there, and leave from
there. [5]Wherever they do not welcome you, as you are leaving that town shake the dust off your feet as a testimony
against them." [6]They departed and went through the villages, bringing the good news and curing diseases everywhere.

Herod Seeks to See Jesus

9:7

7 Now Herod the ruler[b] heard about
all that had taken place, and he was perplexed, because it was said by some that John had been
raised from the dead, [8]by some that Elijah had appeared,
and by others that one of the ancient prophets had arisen.
[9]Herod said, "John I beheaded; but who is this about whom
I hear such things?" And he tried to see him.

Jesus Feeds 5,000

10 On their return the apostles told Jesus[c] all they had
done. He took them with him and withdrew privately to a
city called Bethsaida. [11]When the crowds found out about
it, they followed him; and he welcomed them, and spoke to
them about the kingdom of God, and healed those who
needed to be cured.
12 The day was drawing to a close, and the twelve came
to him and said, "Send the crowd away, so that they may go
into the surrounding villages and countryside, to lodge and
get provisions; for we are here in a deserted place." [13]But he
said to them, "You give them something to eat." They said,
"We have no more than five loaves and two fish—unless we
are to go and buy food for all these people." [14]For there
were about five thousand men. And he said to his disciples,
"Make them sit down in groups of about fifty each." [15]They
did so and made them all sit down. [16]And taking the five
loaves and the two fish, he looked up to heaven, and
blessed and broke them, and gave them to the disciples to
set before the crowd. [17]And all ate and were filled. What
was left over was gathered up, twelve baskets of broken
pieces.

[b]Gk *tetrarch* [c]Gk *him*

Herod's Curiosity

CONSIDER THIS 9:7 **Herod's interest in Jesus (vv. 7–9) is a reminder that pragmatic politicians often seem at a loss when it comes to the subtle doctrines of religion. Just as his father Herod the Great was "frightened" at the birth of the Christ child (Matt. 2:3), so Herod Antipas was "perplexed" by Jesus.**

The ruler wanted to find out exactly who it was he was dealing with. No sooner had he done away with John the Baptist than this new figure, Jesus, had appeared. The speculations of his advisors must have exasperated him, for while they put a religious "spin" on events, they explained nothing.

The tragedy is that even when Herod eventually got his wish and met Jesus face to face, Jesus remained an enigma to him (Luke 23:7–9). No doubt the Lord recognized that Herod's curiosity was not born of faith. Politicians, whose job it is to wield power, have often perceived the extraordinary power in religion, and many have sought to either eliminate it or make it their ally. Such was likely the case with Herod. His interest in Jesus surely had more to do with political expediency than any religious sincerity.

So it was with most of the other authorities that encountered Jesus, His followers, and the gospel. None of them recognized who it was they were dealing with; if they had, Paul later wrote, "they would not have crucified the Lord of glory" (1 Cor. 2:8).

Herod Antipas was given Galilee and Perea to rule, inheriting the title of "tetrarch" (ruler of a fourth part). *Rome liked to divide conquered territories into four parts under separate rulers. For more on the infamous family of Herod, see the article at Acts 12:1–2.*

Peter Recognizes Jesus as the Messiah

18 Once when Jesus[d] was praying alone, with only the
disciples near him, he asked them, "Who do the crowds say
that I am?" 19They answered, "John the Baptist; but others,
Elijah; and still others, that one of the ancient prophets has
arisen." 20He said to them, "But who do you say that I am?"
Peter answered, "The Messiah[e] of God."

Jesus Predicts His Death

21 He sternly ordered and commanded them not to tell
anyone, 22saying, "The Son of Man must undergo great suffering, and be rejected by the elders, chief priests, and
scribes, and be killed, and on the third day be raised."
23 Then he said to them all, "If any want to become my
followers, let them deny themselves and take up their cross
daily and follow me. 24For those who want to save their life
will lose it, and those who lose their life for my sake will
9:25 save it. 25What does it profit them if they
gain the whole world, but lose or forfeit
themselves? 26Those who are ashamed of me and of my
words, of them the Son of Man will be ashamed when he
comes in his glory and the glory of the Father and of the
holy angels. 27But truly I tell you, there are some standing
here who will not taste death before they see the kingdom
of God."

The Transfiguration

28 Now about eight days after these sayings Jesus[d] took
with him Peter and John and James, and went up on the
mountain to pray. 29And while he was praying, the appearance of his face changed, and his clothes became dazzling
white. 30Suddenly they saw two men, Moses and Elijah,
talking to him. 31They appeared in glory and were speaking
of his departure, which he was about to accomplish at
Jerusalem. 32Now Peter and his companions were weighed
down with sleep; but since they had stayed awake,[f] they
saw his glory and the two men who stood with him. 33Just
as they were leaving him, Peter said to Jesus, "Master, it is
good for us to be here; let us make three dwellings,[g] one for
you, one for Moses, and one for Elijah"—not knowing what
he said. 34While he was saying this, a cloud came and overshadowed them; and they were terrified as they entered the
cloud. 35Then from the cloud came a voice that said, "This

[d]*Gk he* [e]*Or The Christ* [f]*Or but when they were fully awake* [g]*Or tents*

THE REAL BOTTOM LINE

CONSIDER THIS 9:25 **Businesspeople commonly talk about the "bottom line," usually meaning the *financial* bottom line. In v. 25 Christ challenges us to look at another bottom line—the final accounting each of us will give to God for how we have spent our lives.**

Clearly one can be very successful from a human point of view and yet be finally lost. Moreover, a careless Christian's works will be judged adversely. That can happen both actively and passively. Actively, we can sell out to the world's values by lying to a customer, cheating on a deal, or running over others to advance our position. Passively, we can drift away from God by leaving Him out of our work and lives, or perhaps by sacrificing our families in order to pursue wealth and status. Either way, the "bottom line" is clear: we will bring ourselves to ultimate loss.

Jesus had more to say about what really matters to God in the story of the talents. See "True Success Means Faithfulness," Matt. 25:14–30.

is my Son, my Chosen;[h] listen to him!" 36 When the voice
had spoken, Jesus was found alone. And they kept silent
and in those days told no one any of the things they had
seen.

Jesus Heals a Boy with a Demon

37 On the next day, when they had come down from the
mountain, a great crowd met him. 38 Just
9:38–42
then a man from the crowd shouted,
"Teacher, I beg you to look at my son; he is my only child.
39 Suddenly a spirit seizes him, and all at once he[i] shrieks. It
convulses him until he foams at the mouth; it mauls him
and will scarcely leave him. 40 I begged your disciples to cast
it out, but they could not." 41 Jesus answered, "You faithless
and perverse generation, how much longer must I be with
you and bear with you? Bring your son here." 42 While he
was coming, the demon dashed him to the ground in con-

[h]Other ancient authorities read *my Beloved* [i]Or *it*

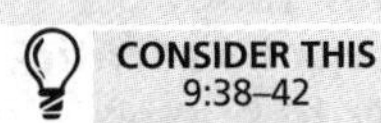

CONSIDER THIS
9:38–42

WHATEVER BECAME OF "DEMON POSSESSION"?

For all the good they've contributed to the healing professions and pastoral care, some theories of psychology have done a great disservice by dismissing the reality of evil and the devil. That presents a problem for those who read the Bible's accounts of demon possession (for example, vv. 38–42) and believe that demonic powers can play a hand in physical illnesses.

Some schools of psychology reduce religious experience to nothing but unconscious drives projected onto the external world. Satan, they say, is no more than a personification of one's deepest, darkest emotions. Likewise, God is reduced to the embodiment of a fully authenticated self, parental ideals, social mores, or universal symbols of goodness.

Without question, a genuine encounter with God or with Satan may involve intense emotional and psychological experiences. But that does not make either one any less real. The existence of Satan and demons is assumed in scores of scriptural texts. (A demon was thought to be a fallen angel or spirit that joined with Satan in his futile rebellion against God.) At war with Jesus and His followers, it was belived these evil powers played a major role in such events as the fall, the flood, and Jesus' crucifixion, and would figure in the tribulations that will someday wrack the earth and in the final judgment.

The Gospels record several dozen encounters between

vulsions. But Jesus rebuked the unclean spirit, healed the boy, and gave him back to his father. [43]And all were astounded at the greatness of God.

Jesus Again Predicts His Death

While everyone was amazed at all that he was doing, he said to his disciples, [44]"Let these words sink into your ears: The Son of Man is going to be betrayed into human hands."
[45]But they did not understand this saying; its meaning was concealed from them, so that they could not perceive it. And they were afraid to ask him about this saying.

Teaching about Rank

9:46–48

46 An argument arose among them as to which one of them was the greatest.
[47]But Jesus, aware of their inner thoughts, took a little child and put it by his side, [48]and said to them, "Whoever wel-

Jesus and the powers of evil. In many of those instances, demon possession had produced any number of physical maladies and manifestations:

- *deafness (Mark 9:25)*
- *muteness (Matt. 12:22; Mark 9:17–25)*
- *bodily deformity (Luke 13:10–17)*
- *blindness (Matt. 12:22)*
- *convulsions (Luke 9:39)*

Ailments like these did not automatically imply demon possession. In fact, distinctions were made between possession and physical illness unrelated to evil spirits (Matt. 4:24; 10:8; Mark 1:32; Luke 6:17–18).

By casting out demons and restoring people both physically and spiritually, Jesus showed that the kingdom of God was as real as, and more powerful than, the forces of Satan (Matt. 10:7–8; 12:28). Today, that same work has been delegated to the church (Luke 10:17; Acts 16:18). Psychology is often helpful in the task, but it is no match for the kingdom of darkness. Only the "whole armor of God" can help believers prevail (Eph. 6:10–18). ◆

One of Jesus' primary purposes was to overcome the power of Satan, which is why He regularly challenged the demonic realm. *See "Demons," Luke 11:14.*

COMPETITION VERSUS COMPASSION

CONSIDER THIS 9:46–48

Do you compete to prove your significance? Do you crave greatness? Do you measure your self-worth not only by whether you win, but by how much?

Jesus saw that His followers were in the grip of this common way of thinking (v. 46). So He placed a child in front of them and affirmed that childlikeness is more desirable to God than competition. He went so far as to state that welcoming the child in His name would be like welcoming Him. While the disciples aspired to positions of power and prestige, their Lord exalted the humble act of serving a child as more important.

Jesus calls us to follow a very different value system than our world's. Position, success, and beating the competition fade in comparison to caring for those around us who are weak and forgotten. He beckons us as His followers to replace competition with compassion.

Who near you needs affirmation and help?

comes this child in my name welcomes me, and whoever
welcomes me welcomes the one who sent me; for the least
among all of you is the greatest."
49 John answered, "Master, we saw someone casting out
demons in your name, and we tried to stop him, because
he does not follow with us." 50But Jesus said to him, "Do
not stop him; for whoever is not against you is for you."

Samaritans Reject Jesus

9:51–56

51 When the days drew near for him
to be taken up, he set his face to go to
Jerusalem. 52And he sent messengers ahead of him. On
their way they entered a village of the Samaritans to make
ready for him; 53but they did not receive him, because his
face was set toward Jerusalem. 54When his disciples James

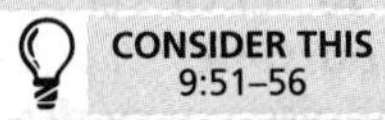

CONSIDER THIS
9:51–56

CONDEMNATION OR COMPASSION?

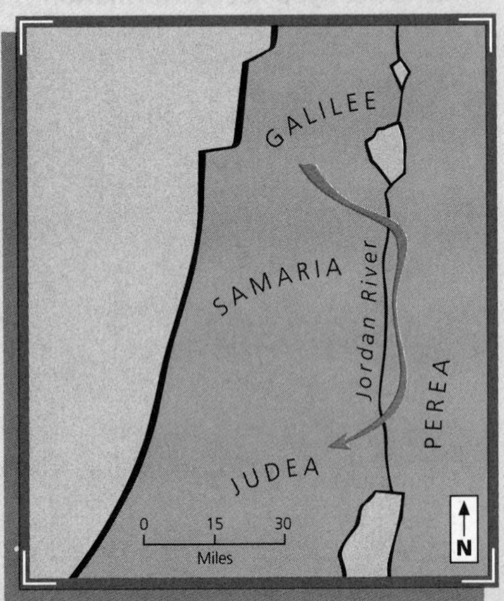

BYPASSING SAMARIA

Heading south from Galilee to Jerusalem (v. 51), Jesus traveled with His disciples through Samaria (v. 52). Prejudiced against the Samaritans (John 4:9), Jews commonly bypassed this region by journeying down the east bank of the Jordan River. But Jesus deliberately chose the more direct route, as if to seek out conflict rather than avoid it.

Confrontation erupted at the first village. The Samaritans did not want Jesus or His followers there, nor did the disciples want to be there. Neither group could see past the other's ethnic identity. But the disciples turned exceptionally ugly. Insulted by the villagers' rejection of their Lord, they were itching to call down fire from heaven—with the justification (according to most manuscripts), "as Elijah did."

Their response shows how terribly destructive centuries of hatred and bitterness can be. No wonder Jesus utterly rebuked this response. He realized that His followers were blinded by their presumption of religious and ethnic superiority. In rebuke, He reminded them of His mission: to save lives—even Samaritan lives—not to destroy them.

We as Jesus' followers today need to consider this incident carefully. Who do we regard with condemnation rather than compassion? Is it someone of another race or a different ideology? Our differences may arise from legitimate concerns. But if we would just as soon see someone

and John saw it, they said, "Lord, do you want us to command fire to come down from heaven and consume them?"[j]
55But he turned and rebuked them. 56Then[k] they went on to
another village.

The Costs of Discipleship

57 As they were going along the road, someone said to him, "I will follow you wherever you go." 58And Jesus said to him, "Foxes

9:58

[j]Other ancient authorities add *as Elijah did* [k]Other ancient authorities read *rebuked them, and said, "You do not know what spirit you are of, 56for the Son of Man has not come to destroy the lives of human beings but to save them." Then*

Nowhere to Lay His Head

A CLOSER LOOK 9:58

Like John the Baptist before Him, Jesus lived without a home (v. 58). He was born into relative poverty and never left it (2:24). For more on Jesus' lifestyle, see "A Poor Family Comes into Wealth," Matt. 2:11, and "Jesus—A Homeless Man?" Matt. 8:20.

eliminated in order to reinforce our feelings of ethnic, racial, moral, theological, or spiritual superiority, then we need the rebuke of Jesus' words: "You do not know what spirit you are of" (v. 56, note).

As we read in John 3:17, "God did not send the Son into the world to condemn the world, but in order that the world might be saved through him." ◆

This incident was only one in a series of courses that Jesus taught on relating to Samaritans. His next lesson proved to be one of the most memorable. See "Who Was the Neighbor?" Luke 10:37.

The disciples had grown up in a culture deeply divided along ethnic lines. To find out more about the Samaritan minority, see "'Jews Have No Dealings with Samaritans,'" John 4:9.

"THE SON OF MAN HAS NOWHERE TO LAY HIS HEAD." —Luke 9:58

have holes, and birds of the air have nests; but the Son of
Man has nowhere to lay his head." 59To another he said,
"Follow me." But he said, "Lord, first let me go and bury
my father." 60But Jesus[l] said to him, "Let the dead bury their
own dead; but as for you, go and proclaim the kingdom of
God." 61Another said, "I will follow you, Lord; but let me
first say farewell to those at my home." 62Jesus said to him,
"No one who puts a hand to the plow and looks back is fit
for the kingdom of God."

Jesus Sends Out Seventy Workers

10:1 **10** After this the Lord appointed
seventy[m] others and sent them
on ahead of him in pairs to every town and place where he

[l]Gk *he* [m]Other ancient authorities read *seventy-two*

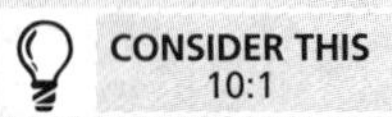

CONSIDER THIS
10:1

DELEGATION AND AFFIRMATION

Is delegation hard for you? When faced with a choice between letting others do a task or doing it yourself, do you tend to sigh, "It's easier to do it myself"? Do you give others, such as coworkers, relatives, or friends, not only the responsibility but the needed authority to get the job done—even if it means seeing it done their way instead of yours?

Certainly Jesus had more reason than any of us to avoid delegating His work to others. When it came to proclaiming His kingdom, He had every right to lack confidence in His band of followers. He had experienced their failings firsthand (Luke 9:10–50). Yet He sent out seventy workers with full appointment to preach and heal on His behalf (10:1, 16).

In doing so, Jesus affirmed the often heard but less often practiced concept of people and their development as the most important task of a manager. Certainly He gave the seventy workers detailed instructions before sending them off (vv. 2–12). But a study of His discipleship methods shows that He was just as concerned with their growth as He was that the task be accomplished or done in a certain way.

Jesus accomplished the work He came to do. He hardly needed seventy neophytes to help Him! But He was clear that people matter, and that His disciples would grow only if they held real responsibility and authority. No wonder the seventy returned "with joy," excited by their experiences (v. 17). They would never be the same again.

Whom do you need to give more responsibility to and affirm with greater encouragement? ◆

himself intended to go. 2 He said to them, "The harvest is
plentiful, but the laborers are few; therefore ask the Lord of
the harvest to send out laborers into his harvest. 3 Go on
your way. See, I am sending you out like lambs into the
midst of wolves. 4 Carry no purse, no bag, no sandals; and
greet no one on the road. 5 Whatever house you enter, first
say, 'Peace to this house!' 6 And if anyone is there who
shares in peace, your peace will rest on that person; but if
not, it will return to you. 7 Remain in the same house, eating
and drinking whatever they provide, for the laborer deserves to be paid. Do not move about from house to house.
8 Whenever you enter a town and its people welcome you,
eat what is set before you; 9 cure the sick who are there, and
say to them, 'The kingdom of God has come near to you.'[n]
10 But whenever you enter a town and they do not welcome
you, go out into its streets and say, 11 'Even the dust of your
town that clings to our feet, we wipe off in protest against
you. Yet know this: the kingdom of God has come near.'[o]
12 I tell you, on that day it will be more tolerable for Sodom
than for that town.

13 "Woe to you, Chorazin! Woe to you, Bethsaida! For if
the deeds of power done in you had been done in Tyre and
Sidon, they would have repented long ago, sitting in sackcloth and ashes. 14 But at the judgment it will be more
10:15 tolerable for Tyre and Sidon than for you.
15 And you, Capernaum,

will you be exalted to heaven?
No, you will be brought down to Hades.

16 "Whoever listens to you listens to me, and whoever
rejects you rejects me, and whoever rejects me rejects the
one who sent me."

The Joy of Jesus

17 The seventy[p] returned with joy, saying, "Lord, in your
name even the demons submit to us!" 18 He said to them, "I
watched Satan fall from heaven like a flash of lightning.
19 See, I have given you authority to tread on snakes and
scorpions, and over all the power of the enemy; and nothing will hurt you. 20 Nevertheless, do not rejoice at this, that
the spirits submit to you, but rejoice that your names are
written in heaven."

21 At that same hour Jesus[q] rejoiced in the Holy Spirit[r]
and said, "I thank[s] you, Father, Lord of heaven and earth,
because you have hidden these things from the wise and
the intelligent and have revealed them to infants; yes, Father, for such was your gracious will.[t] 22 All things have

[n] Or *is at hand for you* [o] Or *is at hand* [p] Other ancient authorities read *seventy-two* [q] Gk *he* [r] Other authorities read *in the spirit* [s] Or *praise* [t] Or *for so it was well-pleasing in your sight*

Capernaum, City of Unfulfilled Potential

YOU ARE THERE 10:15 **Jesus visited Capernaum after performing His first miracle at nearby Cana (John 2:1–12). His ministry in Capernaum was a fulfillment of Old Testament prophecy concerning the Messiah (Is. 9:1; Matt. 4:13–15). Jesus wanted the people of Capernaum to embrace His message with wholehearted faith. In addition to their bondage to the Romans, to their economic systems, to their petty political factions and kingdoms, and to their religious traditions, they were also in bondage to sin. He wanted them to turn to Him for salvation and deliverance and to reflect His light to the surrounding peoples, strategically located as they were.**

But the majority of Galileans were not responsive to His warnings to repent (Matt. 4:17), despite the many miracles He performed there. In the end, Jesus denounced Capernaum, along with her neighbors, Chorazin and Bethsaida (Matt. 11:23–24), prophesying that they would all come to ruin (Luke 10:13–15). His words were fulfilled when the prosperous city was destroyed during the Jewish-Roman war of A.D. 66–70. Rebuilt later as a center of Judaism, Capernaum was destroyed for good by the Arabs in the seventh century.

been handed over to me by my Father; and no one knows
who the Son is except the Father, or who the Father is except the Son and anyone to whom the Son chooses to reveal him."
23 Then turning to the disciples, Jesus[u] said to them privately, "Blessed are the eyes that see what you see! 24For I
tell you that many prophets and kings desired to see what
you see, but did not see it, and to hear what you hear, but
did not hear it."

A Parable about a Good Samaritan

25 Just then a lawyer stood up to test Jesus.[v] "Teacher,"
he said, "what must I do to inherit eternal life?" 26He said to
him, "What is written in the law? What do you read there?"
10:27–28
27He answered, "You shall love the Lord
your God with all your heart, and with
all your soul, and with all your strength, and with all your
mind; and your neighbor as yourself." 28And he said to
him, "You have given the right answer; do this, and you
will live."
29 But wanting to justify himself, he asked Jesus, "And
10:30
who is my neighbor?" 30Jesus replied, "A
man was going down from Jerusalem to
Jericho, and fell into the hands of robbers, who stripped
him, beat him, and went away, leaving him half dead.
10:30–37
31Now by chance a priest was going
down that road; and when he saw him,
he passed by on the other side. 32So likewise a Levite, when
he came to the place and saw him, passed by on the other
side. 33But a Samaritan while traveling came near him; and
when he saw him, he was moved with pity. 34He went to
him and bandaged his wounds, having poured oil and wine
on them. Then he put him on his own animal, brought him
10:35
to an inn, and took care of him. 35The
next day he took out two denarii,[w] gave
them to the innkeeper, and said, 'Take care of him; and
when I come back, I will repay you whatever more you
spend.' 36Which of these three, do you think, was a neigh-

[u]Gk *he* [v]Gk *him* [w]The denarius was the usual day's wage for a laborer

Love Your Neighbor

CONSIDER THIS 10:27–28 **How easy it is to excuse ourselves when we see someone in need by thinking, "There's no reason why I should get involved. Those people are strangers, and I have no obligation to them."**

But Scripture doesn't let us off that easily. Obviously we can't help every needy person we come across. Or can we? We can at least pray! At any rate, the lawyer's restatement of Leviticus 19:18 (v. 27) and Christ's response (v. 28) show that in fact we do have an obligation to strangers—even though we've made no commitments to them.

As Jesus goes on to show in the parable of the good Samaritan (vv. 29–37), we who intend to follow Him have a responsibility to everyone in the human race, because everyone is our neighbor. We are to demonstrate "mercy" to all (v. 37). Or, as Paul later wrote, "work for the good of all" (Gal. 6:10).

It is not enough to love just one's neighbor, however. Jesus challenges His followers to love even their enemies, Luke 6:27–31.

Heartstrings and Purse Strings

A CLOSER LOOK 10:35 *Heartstrings and purse strings are often tied together. The Samaritan was praised for mercy, but one way he showed it was through generosity (v. 35). For more on the ties between the heart and wealth, see "Don't Worry!" Matt. 6:19–34; "Christians and Money," 1 Tim. 6:6–19; and "Getting Yours," James 5:1–6.*

bor to the man who fell into the hands of the robbers?"
10:37 see pg. 261 [37]He said, "The one who showed him
mercy." Jesus said to him, "Go and do
likewise."

Jesus at Martha and Mary's House

10:38 38 Now as they went on their way, he
entered a certain village, where a woman
named Martha welcomed him into her home. [39]She had a
sister named Mary, who sat at the Lord's feet and listened to
what he was saying. [40]But Martha was distracted by her
many tasks; so she came to him and asked, "Lord, do you
not care that my sister has left me to do all the work by my-

The Village of Bethany

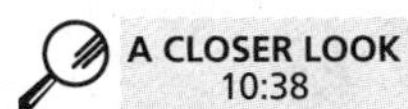
A CLOSER LOOK 10:38

The "certain village" that Jesus visited (v. 38) was Bethany, a suburb of Jerusalem and a favorite stopover for Jesus on His trips to and from the city. Find out more about Bethany at John 11:18.

The Good Neighbor

CONSIDER THIS 10:30–37

The parable in vv. 30–37 is set along the road from Jerusalem to Jericho. Descending through rugged, mountainous terrain, the route was ideal for ambush. There were many hiding places for bandits and little likelihood of help for the unfortunate victim.

But even though the story takes place in a rural setting, it speaks to a number of important urban issues: racial and ethnic divisions, violent crime, even the struggle of small businesses to collect on their debts.

The parable is Jesus' answer to the lawyer's question, "And who is my neighbor?" The neighbor was the one who "showed mercy." That neighbor was the Samaritan—the ethnic outsider.

His example challenges us as modern Christians, especially those of us living in cities among countless victims like the hapless man in the parable, to consider how we can be neighbors. How can we "go and do likewise"?

Jericho

YOU ARE THERE 10:30

- **Ancient city located northeast of Jerusalem on the west bank of the Jordan River.**
- **Name means "city of palms" (Deut. 34:3).**
- **Made famous by the Old Testament report of its dramatic defeat by Joshua and the Israelites (Josh. 6:1–21).**
- **Site of Herod the Great's winter palace.**
- **Notorious for the beggars and thieves who camped nearby, plundering travelers along the narrow, winding mountain road up to Jerusalem.**

Herod was fond of building projects, but is remembered more for political corruption. See "The Herods," Acts 12:1–2.

self? Tell her then to help me." [41]But the Lord answered her,
"Martha, Martha, you are worried and distracted by many
10:38–42 things; [42]there is need of only one thing.[x]
Mary has chosen the better part, which
will not be taken away from her."

[x]Other ancient authorities read *few things are necessary, or only one*

"YOUR KINGDOM COME."
—Luke 11:2

PERSONALITY PROFILE: MARTHA OF BETHANY

CONSIDER THIS 10:38–42

Home: Bethany, near Jerusalem.

Family: Sister of Mary and Lazarus (John 11:1).

Occupation: Homemaker.

Known today for: Being "distracted" in her preparations when Jesus and His disciples came to visit.

MARTHA, THE "PRACTICAL" ONE

Jesus' visit to Martha's home (Luke 10:38–42) has given rise to a caricature of Martha as obsessively "practical," as opposed to Mary, her "spiritual" sister. In fact, some would use this incident to reinforce a hierarchy of "spiritual" concerns over "secular" ones: it is more important to "sit at Jesus' feet"—that is, to engage in religious pursuits such as prayer or attending church—than to be "distracted" with everyday tasks such as work or household chores.

But it would be unfair to read Jesus' words to Martha as a rebuke for her preparations. After all, He had come as a guest to her home with His disciples. Someone was obligated to prepare a meal—a large meal. Assuming Jesus and the twelve, plus Mary, Martha, and Lazarus, there were at least 17 hungry people. No wonder Martha was "distracted [literally, drawn away*] by her many tasks" (v. 40). She could not sit and chat with her guests if she was to prepare the food.*

So what was Jesus getting at in vv. 41–42? Only this: that in addition to her marvelous preparations, Martha needed to add spiritual sensitivity. He was in no way set-

Instructions on Prayer

11 He was praying in a certain place, and after he had
finished, one of his disciples said to him, "Lord,
teach us to pray, as John taught his disciples." 2He said to
them, "When you pray, say:

Father,[y] hallowed be your name.
Your kingdom come.[z]
3 Give us each day our daily bread.[a]
4 And forgive us our sins,
for we ourselves forgive everyone indebted to us.
And do not bring us to the time of trial."[b]

11:5–13 see pg. 264

5 And he said to them, "Suppose one
of you has a friend, and you go to him at
midnight and say to him, 'Friend, lend me three loaves of
bread; 6for a friend of mine has arrived, and I have nothing
to set before him.' 7And he answers from within, 'Do not
bother me; the door has already been locked, and my children are with me in bed; I cannot get up and give you anything.' 8I tell you, even though he will not get up and give
him anything because he is his friend, at least because of his
persistence he will get up and give him whatever he needs.

(Bible text continued on page 263)

[y]Other ancient authorities read *Our Father in heaven* [z]A few ancient authorities read *Your Holy Spirit come upon us and cleanse us.* Other ancient authorities add *Your will be done, on earth as in heaven* [a]Or *our bread for tomorrow* [b]Or *us into temptation.* Other ancient authorities add *but rescue us from the evil one* (or *from evil*)

ting up a dichotomy between the sacred and the secular, but merely emphasizing that in the midst of her busyness, Martha should not lose sight of who He was and why He had come. Without question, Mary had that insight, and Jesus was keen to preserve it.

Apparently Martha profited from Jesus' exhortation, for when her brother Lazarus died, she recognized His ability as the Christ to raise him from the dead (John 11:27).

Like Martha, we today are called on to strike a balance between faithful, diligent service in our day-to-day responsibilities and a constant attitude of dependence on the Lord. ◆

What was involved in Martha's preparations for her guests? See "Jewish Homemaking," Mark 1:29–31.

Are you quiet, withdrawn, or shy? If so, Martha's sister, Mary, may be a model for you. She demonstrates that preaching sermons or leading movements are not the only ways to follow Jesus. See John 11:1.

Who Was the Neighbor?

CONSIDER THIS 10:37 **The parable of the good Samaritan (vv. 30–37) is one of Jesus' most popular. It reduces an abstract theological question, "What shall I do to inherit eternal life" (v. 25), to a simpler, more practical challenge: "Go and do likewise [i.e., show mercy]" (v. 37).**

The story begins with the lawyer's self-justifying question, "Who is my neighbor?" But Jesus turned the question around: "Which of these three do you think was neighbor to him who fell among the thieves?" What matters, Jesus implied, is not identifying needs, but meeting them. The question is not *Who is my neighbor?*, but rather *Am I a neighbor to others?*

What makes the story so poignant, however, is the contrast between the Jewish priest and Levite who avoid the half-dead victim, and the Samaritan who shows him compassion. Jesus was playing on the deep-seated animosity that existed between the two groups (see "Samaria," John 4:4). He knew His listeners would find it hard enough to show mercy, but unthinkable that a Samaritan would illustrate how. Prejudiced people find it almost impossible to think that their ethnic enemies might be compassionate human beings.

Jesus' challenge to "go and do likewise" is a test for us as we consider the many racial and ethnic divisions in the world today. God is interested in mercy, not maintaining prejudice.

Jesus' own disciples were blinded by ethnic pride. They thought Samaritans ought to be destroyed. See "Condemnation or Compassion?" Luke 9:51–56.

On another occasion, a Samaritan set an example in faith. See "Where Are the Others?" Luke 17:11–19.

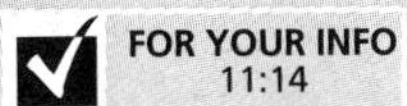

DEMONS

Popular culture tends to dismiss demons as nothing but an imaginative fantasy. But Scripture presents demons not as mythological creatures, but as the reality of evil in historical events. That reality of evil could not—and cannot—be ignored. Jesus, for example, frequently encountered demons during His ministry, as in the case of the demon-possessed mute (v. 14).

DEMONS in the NEW TESTAMENT

- unclean spirits (Matt. 10:1; Mark 6:7)
- Legion, probably a collective name for a group of demons rather than the name of a single demon (Mark 5:9; Luke 8:30)
- wicked or evil spirits (Luke 7:21; Acts 19:12–13)
- a spirit of divination (Acts 16:16)
- deceiving spirits (1 Tim. 4:1)
- the spirit of error (1 John 4:6)
- spirits of demons (Rev. 16:14)

The Bible often views demons as fallen angels who joined with Satan in rebellion against God. The Bible does not explicitly discuss their origin, but the New Testament does speak of the fall and later imprisonment of a group of angels (2 Pet. 2:4; Jude 6). Their rebellion apparently occurred before God's creation of the world. Afterward, Satan and his followers roamed the new creation, eventually contaminating the human race with wickedness (Gen. 3; Matt. 25:41; Rev. 12:9). To this day they continue to oppose God's purposes and undermine the cause of righteousness.

Demon Possession

One of Jesus' primary purposes was to overcome the power of Satan, which is why He regularly challenged the demonic realm (Matt. 12:25–29; Luke 11:17–22; John 12:31; 1 John 3:8). One of His most compassionate activities was to release persons possessed by demons.

Again, our culture tends to dismiss demon possession as a quaint, archaic way of trying to explain physical and psychological conditions. But the Bible never suggests that all ailments are the result of demonic activity, only that demons can afflict people with physical symptoms such as muteness (Matt. 12:22; Mark 9:17, 25), deafness (Mark 9:25), blindness (Matt. 12:22), and bodily deformity (Luke 13:10–17). The Gospels actually distinguish between sickness and demon possession (Matt. 4:24; Mark 1:32; Luke 6:17–18).

Demons can also cause mental and emotional problems (Matt. 8:28; Acts 19:13–16). The demon-possessed might rant and rave (Mark 1:23–24; John 10:20), have uncontrolled fits (Luke 9:37–42; Mark 1:26), and behave in an antisocial manner (Luke 8:27, 35).

In casting out demons, Jesus and His disciples used methods that differed radically from the mystical rites so often employed in that time. Through His simple command Jesus expelled them (Mark 1:25; 5:8; 9:25). His disciples did the same, adding only the authority of Jesus' name to their command (Luke 10:17; Acts 16:18). Even some who were not His followers invoked the Lord's power (Luke 9:49; Acts 19:13).

Despite these straightforward

(continued on next page)

9 "So I say to you, Ask, and it will be given you; search, and you will find; knock, and the door will be opened for you. 10For everyone who asks receives, and everyone who searches finds, and for everyone who knocks, the door will be opened. 11Is there anyone among you who, if your child asks for[c] a fish, will give a snake instead of a fish? 12Or if the child asks for an egg, will give a scorpion? 13If you then, who are evil, know how to give good gifts to your children, how much more will the heavenly Father give the Holy Spirit[d] to those who ask him!"

Jesus' Power Called Satanic

11:14

14 Now he was casting out a demon that was mute; when the demon had gone out, the one who had been mute spoke, and the crowds were amazed. 15But some of them said, "He casts out demons by Beelzebul, the ruler of the demons." 16Others, to test him, kept demanding from him a sign from heaven. 17But he knew what they were thinking and said to them, "Every kingdom divided against itself becomes a desert, and house falls on house. 18If Satan also is divided against himself, how will his kingdom stand? —for you say that I cast out the demons by Beelzebul. 19Now if I cast out the demons by Beelzebul, by whom do your exorcists[e] cast them out? Therefore they will be your judges. 20But if it is by the finger of God that I cast out the demons, then the kingdom of God has come to you. 21When a strong man, fully armed, guards his castle, his property is safe. 22But when one stronger than he attacks him and overpowers him, he takes away his armor in which he trusted and divides his plunder. 23Whoever is not with me is against me, and whoever does not gather with me scatters.

24 "When the unclean spirit has gone out of a person, it wanders through waterless regions looking for a resting place, but not finding any, it says, 'I will return to my house from which I came.' 25When it comes, it finds it swept and put in order. 26Then it goes and brings seven other spirits more evil than itself, and they enter and live there; and the last state of that person is worse than the first."

Obedience More Important than Family Ties

11:27–28
see pg. 265

27 While he was saying this, a woman in the crowd raised her voice and said to him, "Blessed is the womb that bore you and the breasts that nursed you!" 28But he said, "Blessed rather are those who hear the word of God and obey it!"

[c]Other ancient authorities add *bread, will give a stone; or if your child asks for* [d]Other ancient authorities read *the Father give the Holy Spirit from heaven* [e]Gk *sons*

(continued from previous page)

means, Jesus' enemies accused Him of being in alliance with Satan's kingdom (Mark 3:22; Luke 11:15; John 8:48). The same accusation was made against Jesus' forerunner, John the Baptist (Matt. 11:18; Luke 7:33). But Jesus' works of goodness and righteousness showed that these claims could not be true (Matt. 12:25–29; Luke 11:17–22).

The Final Victory

Following the resurrection of Jesus and His return to heaven, demons have continued their warfare against Him and His followers (Rom. 8:38–39; Eph. 6:12). Yet Satan and his allies will ultimately be overthrown by God. After Christ returns, the devil and his angels will be defeated and thrown into the lake of fire and brimstone (Matt. 25:41; Rev. 20:10)—a doom with which the demons are quite familiar (Matt. 8:29). God will achieve the final victory in a conflict that has been going on since the beginning of time. ◆

Some theories of psychology have tried to cast doubt on the reality of evil and the devil. That presents a problem for some who read the Bible's accounts of demon possession. See "Whatever Became of 'Demon Possession'?" Luke 9:38–42.

Tired of Praying?

CONSIDER THIS 11:5–13 **Do you ever feel impatient with God? Does He seem late in answering your requests or meeting your needs?**

Jesus spoke to the issues of how to pray, how long to pray, and how long God might take to respond. One day His disciples asked Him to teach them to pray (v. 1). He told a story about someone with a need who was

(continued on next page)

Jesus Warns the Crowds

29 When the crowds were increasing, he began to say,
"This generation is an evil generation; it asks for a sign, but
no sign will be given to it except the sign of Jonah. 30For
just as Jonah became a sign to the people of Nineveh, so
the Son of Man will be to this generation. **11:31**
31The queen of the South will rise at the
judgment with the people of this generation and condemn
them, because she came from the ends of the earth to listen
to the wisdom of Solomon, and see, something greater than
Solomon is here! 32The people of Nineveh will rise up at
the judgment with this generation and condemn it, because

FOR YOUR INFO 11:31

Who Was the Queen of Sheba?

The Queen of Sheba, known in the New Testament as the Queen of the South (v. 31), visited Solomon to examine his wisdom (1 Kin. 10:1–13). She ruled a country that was most likely in southwest Arabia, a mighty commercial power specializing in the trade of perfume and incense. During her visit, she probably negotiated a trade agreement as well as provisions for safe passage of her merchants' caravans through Israel's territory.

Having heard astonishing reports of Solomon's wisdom and splendor, she found him exceeding his reputation. In response, she worshiped the God of Israel (1 Kin. 10:9) and presented Solomon with an abundance of gold, jewels, and more spices than the kingdom had ever received before. In exchange, Solomon was equally generous, giving her "every desire that she expressed, as well as what he gave her out of Solomon's royal bounty" (1 Kin. 10:13).

Commenting on her story, Jesus warned His listeners that this queen would rise up in judgment on their generation. When she came to Solomon and saw his greatness, her response was not jealousy or denial, but awe and thanksgiving. She acknowledged Solomon's greatness and honored his God. By contrast, Jesus' generation had met one greater than Solomon—the Messiah Himself—and its response had been unbelief (v. 29; compare Matt. 12:38). So He predicted that a woman who ruled a powerful country would someday put them to shame because she, like Solomon, was wise. ◆

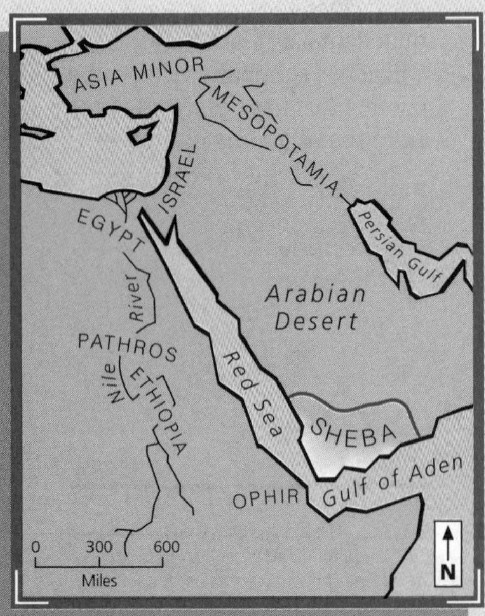

SHEBA

Women played a major role in Jesus' life and work. See "The Women around Jesus," John 19:25.

they repented at the proclamation of Jonah, and see, something greater than Jonah is here!
33 "No one after lighting a lamp puts it in a cellar,[f] but
on the lampstand so that those who enter may see the light.
34Your eye is the lamp of your body. If your eye is healthy,
your whole body is full of light; but if it is not healthy, your
body is full of darkness. 35Therefore consider whether the
light in you is not darkness. 36If then your whole body is
full of light, with no part of it in darkness, it will be as full
of light as when a lamp gives you light with its rays."

Pharisees and Lawyers Rebuked

37 While he was speaking, a Pharisee invited him to
dine with him; so he went in and took his place at the
table. 38The Pharisee was amazed to see that he did not first
wash before dinner. 39Then the Lord said to him, "Now you
Pharisees clean the outside of the cup and of the dish, but
inside you are full of greed and wickedness. 40You fools!
Did not the one who made the outside make the inside
also? 41So give for alms those things that are within; and
see, everything will be clean for you.

11:42

42 "But woe to you Pharisees! For you
tithe mint and rue and herbs of all kinds,
and neglect justice and the love of God; it is these you
ought to have practiced, without neglecting the others.
43Woe to you Pharisees! For you love to have the seat of
honor in the synagogues and to be greeted with respect in
the marketplaces. 44Woe to you! For you are like unmarked
graves, and people walk over them without realizing it."
45 One of the lawyers answered him, "Teacher, when
you say these things, you insult us too." 46And he said,
"Woe also to you lawyers! For you load people with burdens hard to bear, and you yourselves do not lift a finger to
ease them. 47Woe to you! For you build the tombs of the
prophets whom your ancestors killed. 48So you are witnesses and approve of the deeds of your ancestors; for they
killed them, and you build their tombs. 49Therefore also the
Wisdom of God said, 'I will send them prophets and apostles, some of whom they will kill and persecute,' 50so that
this generation may be charged with the blood of all the
prophets shed since the foundation of the world, 51from the
blood of Abel to the blood of Zechariah, who perished between the altar and the sanctuary. Yes, I tell you, it will be

[f]Other ancient authorities add *or under the bushel basket*

The Tithe

A CLOSER LOOK 11:42 *"Tithing" (Matt. 23:23–24) explains the tithe that Jesus was talking about in v. 42.*

(continued from previous page)

very persistent in asking a neighbor for help (vv. 5–8).

The story makes it clear that our ability to ask does not equal God's response or its timing. God is not a celestial bellhop waiting at our beck and call. Neither does He rely on us to define our needs, outline solutions, or say when or how He should act. No, God does those for us—which is just as well since He is all-wise.

God delights in His children developing the habit and freedom of asking Him for help (vv. 9–10). But He won't leave us trapped in our limited perception of the situation (vv. 11–13). Sooner or later He will answer our prayers, but in His own time. He asks us to trust Him to know what is needed and when.

Our calling, then, is to ask—even persistently—and to grow in the process. One of the surprising benefits of praying is how much *we* change. Sometimes, that in itself is the answer to our prayers.

Who Is Blessed?

CONSIDER THIS 11:27–28 *Notice how Jesus responded to the praise of His mother (vv. 27–28). He didn't deny that she was blessed, but focused attention on the real source of blessing—hearing and doing the Word of God. Mary was an outstanding model of that at the time of His conception, since she both heard and responded to God's words to her (see "The Maidservant of the Lord," Luke 1:26–56).*

The Right Kind of Fear

CONSIDER THIS 12:4–7 **Every culture seems to be afraid of someone. The Hebrews feared and hated the Romans because of the ruthless might of their occupation troops. Eventually those fears were realized as Rome viciously destroyed Jerusalem in A.D. 70 (see "Jerusalem Surrounded," Luke 21:20). In recent years, the West feared destruction from Soviet nuclear missiles. Today there is growing alarm and outrage over drug- and gang-related violence in cities.**

But in Luke 12:4–7 we see that Jesus redefines fear by rearranging our view so we look at things from God's perspective. He draws upon the Old Testament concept of the "fear of the Lord" (Prov. 1:7). This is not a fawning, cringing dread that keeps us wallowing in anxiety, but a respect for who God is—the One who holds ultimate power. When we have a balanced view of God, it puts our thinking in a proper framework. We view everybody and everything in relation to God's holiness, righteousness, and love. We can't ignore physical threats and violence, but we dare not ignore the One who holds sway over our eternal destiny.

Will You Get What's Coming to You?

CONSIDER THIS 12:13–15 **The man we read of in v. 13 appealed to Jesus for justice. He wanted to make sure that he was going to get his inheritance. But Jesus turned the issue**

(continued on next page)

charged against this generation. [52]Woe to you lawyers! For
you have taken away the key of knowledge; you did not enter yourselves, and you hindered those who were entering."
53 When he went outside, the scribes and the Pharisees
began to be very hostile toward him and to cross-examine
him about many things, [54]lying in wait for him, to catch
him in something he might say.

Hypocritical Leaders Warned Against

12 Meanwhile, when the crowd gathered by the
thousands, so that they trampled on one another,
he began to speak first to his disciples, "Beware of the yeast
of the Pharisees, that is, their hypocrisy. [2]Nothing is covered up that will not be uncovered, and nothing secret that
will not become known. [3]Therefore whatever you have said
in the dark will be heard in the light, and what you have
whispered behind closed doors will be proclaimed from the
housetops.

12:4–7
4 "I tell you, my friends, do not fear
those who kill the body, and after that
can do nothing more. [5]But I will warn you whom to fear:
fear him who, after he has killed, has authority[g] to cast into
12:6–7 see pg. 268
hell.[h] Yes, I tell you, fear him! [6]Are not
five sparrows sold for two pennies? Yet
not one of them is forgotten in God's sight. [7]But even the
hairs of your head are all counted. Do not be afraid; you are
of more value than many sparrows.
8 "And I tell you, everyone who acknowledges me before others, the Son of Man also will acknowledge before
the angels of God; [9]but whoever denies me before others
will be denied before the angels of God. [10]And everyone
who speaks a word against the Son of Man will be forgiven;
but whoever blasphemes against the Holy Spirit will not be
forgiven. [11]When they bring you before the synagogues, the
rulers, and the authorities, do not worry about how[i] you
are to defend yourselves or what you are to say; [12]for the
Holy Spirit will teach you at that very hour what you ought
to say."

A Parable about a Rich Fool

12:13–15
13 Someone in the crowd said to him,
"Teacher, tell my brother to divide the
family inheritance with me." [14]But he said to him, "Friend,

[g]Or *power* [h]Gk *Gehenna* [i]Other ancient authorities add *or what*

12:15
see pg. 269

who set me to be a judge or arbitrator
over you?" 15And he said to them, "Take
care! Be on your guard against all kinds of greed; for one's
life does not consist in the abundance of possessions."
16Then he told them a parable: "The land of a rich man produced abundantly. 17And he thought to himself, 'What
should I do, for I have no place to store my crops?' 18Then
he said, 'I will do this: I will pull down my barns and build
larger ones, and there I will store all my grain and my
goods. 19And I will say to my soul, 'Soul, you have ample
goods laid up for many years; relax, eat, drink, be merry.'
20But God said to him, 'You fool! This very night your life is
being demanded of you. And the things you have prepared,
whose will they be?' 21So it is with those who store up treasures for themselves but are not rich toward God."

Priorities and Comforts of the Kingdom

12:22–34

22 He said to his disciples, "Therefore
I tell you, do not worry about your life,
what you will eat, or about your body, what you will wear.
23For life is more than food, and the body more than clothing. 24Consider the ravens: they neither sow nor reap, they
have neither storehouse nor barn, and yet God feeds them.
Of how much more value are you than the birds! 25And can
any of you by worrying add a single hour to your span of
life?[j] 26If then you are not able to do so small a thing as
that, why do you worry about the rest? 27Consider the
lilies, how they grow: they neither toil nor spin;[k] yet I tell
you, even Solomon in all his glory was not clothed like one
of these. 28But if God so clothes the grass of the field, which
is alive today and tomorrow is thrown into the oven, how
much more will he clothe you—you of little faith! 29And do
not keep striving for what you are to eat and what you are
to drink, and do not keep worrying. 30For it is the nations
of the world that strive after all these things, and your Father knows that you need them. 31Instead, strive for his[l]
kingdom, and these things will be given to you as well.
32 "Do not be afraid, little flock, for it is your Father's

[j]Or *add a cubit to your stature* [k]Other ancient authorities read *Consider the lilies; they neither spin nor weave* [l]Other ancient authorities read *God's*

Don't Worry!

A CLOSER LOOK 12:22–34

This passage raises important questions about the impact of wealth on our lives. See "Don't Worry!" Matt. 6:19–34.

(continued from previous page)

from the material to the spiritual. He was far more concerned about the man's covetous spirit than his family's estate.

The Old Testament, which governed Hebrew life, had a great deal to say about family estates and the succession of land and property. Sometimes Christians have understood such teaching as merely foreshadowing the spiritual inheritance of New Testament believers. But our earthly, material estates are not to be treated as insignificant. An inheritance is a responsibility that God wants both parents and children to view and manage properly.

Here, Jesus showed grave concern that the man did not view his physical inheritance properly, but rather with a greedy attitude—a major problem because it threatened his spiritual inheritance, his eternal destiny.

The Lord's response and the parable following it (vv. 16–21) challenge us to ask: What is our perspective on the inheritance coming to us in this world? Will it be a blessing and a resource to be managed responsibly before God? Or, like this man and the man in the parable, are we trying to fashion a life out of the abundance of our possessions? If so, we need to pay attention to vv. 20–21.

There are three kinds of inheritance in Scripture: the earthly inheritance, such as the kind mentioned in this passage; the believer's inheritance "in Christ" (see "What's In It for Me?" Eph. 1:11); and Christ's inheritance of the redeemed children of God (see Eph. 1:18).

Jesus told another story about an inheritance: A son squandered his portion of the estate—but it turned out to be the best thing that could happen. See Luke 15:11–32.

Jesus frequently changed the subject from material concerns to spiritual ones. See, for example, Luke 4:5–8; 8:19–21; 10:38–42; 11:27–28.

good pleasure to give you the kingdom. 33Sell your possessions, and give alms. Make purses for yourselves that do
not wear out, an unfailing treasure in heaven, where no
thief comes near and no moth destroys. 34For where your
treasure is, there your heart will be also.

12:35–48
see pg. 270

35 "Be dressed for action and have
your lamps lit; 36be like those who are
waiting for their master to return from the wedding banquet, so that they may open the door for him as soon as he
comes and knocks. 37Blessed are those slaves whom the
master finds alert when he comes; truly I tell you, he will
fasten his belt and have them sit down to eat, and he will
come and serve them. 38If he comes during the middle of
the night, or near dawn, and finds them so, blessed are
those slaves.

39 "But know this: if the owner of the house had known
at what hour the thief was coming, he[m] would not have let
his house be broken into. 40You also must be ready, for the
Son of Man is coming at an unexpected hour."

A Parable about a Faithful Manager

41 Peter said, "Lord, are you telling this parable for us or
for everyone?" 42And the Lord said, "Who then is the faith-

[m]Other ancient authorities add *would have watched and*

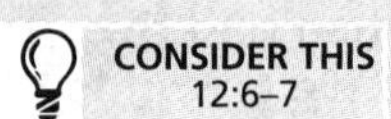
CONSIDER THIS
12:6–7

GOD AND THE ENVIRONMENT

In the middle of warning people against hypocrisy, Jesus made an interesting comparison. He said that God values people more than He values sparrows (vv. 6–7). The point is that people matter to God. But so do the rest of God's creatures. Indeed, "not one of them is forgotten."

Scripture clearly shows God's intense concern for every aspect of the creation, particularly its conservation. For example:

- *In the beginning, God commanded Adam and Eve to cultivate and keep the garden. That kind of stewardship ruled out wanton destruction (Gen. 2:15).*
- *Later, God was sorry that He had created humanity because of their total wickedness (Gen. 6:5–6). So He determined to destroy everyone through a flood. However, He saved not only Noah and his family, but the other creatures as well (Gen. 6:13–14, 19–22).*
- *After the flood, God made a covenant with both people and animals that "never again shall all flesh be cut off by the waters of a flood" (Gen. 9:8–11).*

ful and prudent manager whom his master will put in
charge of his slaves, to give them their allowance of food at
the proper time? [43]Blessed is that slave whom his master
will find at work when he arrives. [44]Truly I tell you, he will
put that one in charge of all his possessions. [45]But if that
slave says to himself, 'My master is delayed in coming,' and
if he begins to beat the other slaves, men and women, and
to eat and drink and get drunk, [46]the master of that slave
will come on a day when he does not expect him and at an
hour that he does not know, and will cut him in pieces,[n]
and put him with the unfaithful. [47]That slave who knew
what his master wanted, but did not prepare himself or do
what was wanted, will receive a severe beating. [48]But the
one who did not know and did what deserved a beating
will receive a light beating. From everyone to whom much
has been given, much will be required; and from the one to
whom much has been entrusted, even more will be demanded.

49 "I came to bring fire to the earth, and how I wish it
were already kindled! [50]I have a baptism with which to be
baptized, and what stress I am under until it is completed!
[51]Do you think that I have come to bring peace to the
earth? No, I tell you, but rather division! [52]From now on

[n]Or *cut him off*

- *Later, God instructed the Hebrews to allow their cropland to be rested (left fallow) every seventh year in order to rejuvenate it and preserve it (Ex. 23:10–11; Lev. 25:2–7; 26:34–35).*
- *The Law also forbade the unnecessary destruction of fruit and nut trees and the killing of mother birds, even for food (Deut. 20:19–20; 22:6–7).*

Without question, God cares about what He has created. And He has charged us to wisely manage those resources (Gen. 1:26), for our good and for His glory. As we face increasingly complex environmental issues, we need to view the earth as a sacred trust from God's hands, for which He will hold us accountable. If He cares about every single bird on the planet, shouldn't we? ◆

WATCH OUT FOR GREED!

CONSIDER THIS 12:15 **Jesus gave a direct, unequivocal command to guard against *covetousness* (v. 15)—longing for something we don't have, especially for what belongs to someone else. He was not telling us to watch for it in others, but in ourselves.**

According to this verse and the following parable, covetousness, or greed, is based on the foolish belief that what matters in life is how much one has. It may be money (as is the case here), or status, power, intelligence, beauty, even spiritual blessings; it is possible to covet anything that can be acquired. The idea is that having that thing will make us content. But biblically, only God can—and will—satisfy our real needs, as Jesus goes on to show (12:22–31).

To covet is to be discontented with what God brings our way. Yet our consumer-oriented culture excels at stoking the fires of discontent. In subtle yet powerful ways, we come to believe that whatever we have, it's not enough. We need more, we need bigger, we need better.

So more than ever, we need to pay attention to Jesus' warning: *Watch out for greed!*

Sometimes people attempt to enlist God in their selfish pursuit of material things. See "The Dangers of Prosperity Theology," 1 Tim. 6:3–6.

If we're supposed to avoid covetousness, what does a lifestyle of contentment look like? See Phil. 4:10–13.

What's wrong with wanting more? Paul warns us to watch out—we could be worshipping idols! See "Do-It-Yourself Idolatry," Col. 3:5.

AUTHORITY AND RESPONSIBILITY

CONSIDER THIS 12:35–48 All of us must deal with authority and responsibility. The parables Jesus told (vv. 35–48) talk about the believer's faithfulness to God. But they also remind us of faithful conduct on the job.

To be sure, our work relationships are more complicated—and civilized—than those between slaves and masters. But in light of the principles raised in this passage, we might ask: Are we as productive when our supervisors are gone as when they are looking over us? Do we try to anticipate their needs and desires, or do we wait until told what to do? Do we pray for our bosses and the work we do under them?

Jesus has a high regard for faithfulness. In this passage He challenges us to carry out our spiritual responsibilities in a faithful, diligent way. But clearly we need to fulfill our everyday work responsibilities with the same reliable, faithful spirit.

Paul explicitly challenges workers to diligence, whether or not the boss is around (Eph. 6:5–8). Moreover, faithfulness is a mark of a Christlike "workstyle." See Titus 2:9–10.

five in one household will be divided, three against two and
two against three; 53they will be divided:

father against son
and son against father,
mother against daughter
and daughter against mother,
mother-in-law against her daughter-in-law
and daughter-in-law against mother-in-law."

The Signs of the Times

12:54–56

54 He also said to the crowds, "When
you see a cloud rising in the west, you
immediately say, 'It is going to rain'; and so it happens.
55And when you see the south wind blowing, you say,
'There will be scorching heat'; and it happens. 56You hypocrites! You know how to interpret the appearance of earth
and sky, but why do you not know how to interpret the
present time?
57 "And why do you not judge for yourselves what is
right? 58Thus, when you go with your accuser before a
magistrate, on the way make an effort to settle the case,[o] or
you may be dragged before the judge, and the judge hand
you over to the officer, and the officer throw you in prison.
59I tell you, you will never get out until you have paid the
very last penny."

The Need for Repentance

13 At that very time there were some present who told
him about the Galileans whose blood Pilate had
mingled with their sacrifices. 2He asked them, "Do you
think that because these Galileans suffered in this way they
were worse sinners than all other Galileans? 3No, I tell you;
but unless you repent, you will all perish as they did. 4Or
those eighteen who were killed when the tower of Siloam
fell on them—do you think that they were worse offenders
than all the others living in Jerusalem? 5No, I tell you; but
unless you repent, you will all perish just as they did."
6 Then he told this parable: "A man had a fig tree
planted in his vineyard; and he came looking for fruit on it
and found none. 7So he said to the gardener, 'See here! For
three years I have come looking for fruit on this fig tree,
and still I find none. Cut it down! Why should it be wasting the soil?' 8He replied, 'Sir, let it alone for one more year,

[o]Gk *settle with him*

until I dig around it and put manure on it. 9If it bears fruit
next year, well and good; but if not, you can cut it down.' "

A Crippled Woman Finds Help

10 Now he was teaching in one of the synagogues on the
13:10–17 see pg. 272
sabbath. 11And just then there appeared
a woman with a spirit that had crippled
her for eighteen years. She was bent over and was quite unable to stand up straight. 12When Jesus saw her, he called
her over and said, "Woman, you are set free from your ail-
ment." 13When he laid his hands on her, immediately she
stood up straight and began praising God. 14But the leader
of the synagogue, indignant because Jesus had cured on the
sabbath, kept saying to the crowd, "There are six days on
which work ought to be done; come on those days and be
cured, and not on the sabbath day." 15But the Lord answered him and said, "You hypocrites! Does not each of
you on the sabbath untie his ox or his donkey from the
manger, and lead it away to give it water? 16And ought not
this woman, a daughter of Abraham whom Satan bound for
eighteen long years, be set free from this bondage on the
sabbath day?" 17When he said this, all his opponents were
put to shame; and the entire crowd was rejoicing at all the
wonderful things that he was doing.

A Parable about a Mustard Seed

13:18–21 see pg. 272
18 He said therefore, "What is the
kingdom of God like? And to what
should I compare it? 19It is like a mustard seed that someone took and sowed in the garden; it grew and became a
tree, and the birds of the air made nests in its branches."

A Parable about Hidden Yeast

20 And again he said, "To what should I compare the
kingdom of God? 21It is like yeast that a woman took and
mixed in with[p] three measures of flour until all of it was
leavened."

The Exclusivity of the Kingdom

13:22–23 see pg. 273
22 Jesus[q] went through one town and
village after another, teaching as he made
his way to Jerusalem. 23Someone asked him, "Lord, will

[p]Gk *hid in* [q]Gk *He*

Current Affairs

CONSIDER THIS 12:54–56 **In vv. 54–56, Jesus rebuked the people of Israel for their failure to recognize the real issues and forces at work among them. Many were farmers and fishermen who were quite skilled at discerning when the weather was about to change. But they failed to detect the momentous message and change that Christ was now bringing to the earth.**

What about you? Are you up on current affairs, yet unaware of God's global work and purposes? Are you quick to read the winds of change at your job, in the economy, in politics, and in public opinion, while you fail to observe God's Word regarding your work, your relationships, and your family? Are you up on all the latest gossip about celebrities, yet ignorant of what the Lord of the universe is up to?

only a few be saved?" He said to them, 24"Strive to enter
through the narrow door; for many, I tell you, will try to
enter and will not be able. 25When once the owner of the
house has got up and shut the door, and you begin to stand
outside and to knock at the door, saying, 'Lord, open to us,'
then in reply he will say to you, 'I do not know where you
come from.' 26Then you will begin to say, 'We ate and drank
with you, and you taught in our streets.' 27But he will say, 'I
do not know where you come from; go away from me, all
you evildoers!' 28There will be weeping and gnashing of
teeth when you see Abraham and Isaac and Jacob and all
the prophets in the kingdom of God, and you yourselves
thrown out. 29Then people will come from east and west,
from north and south, and will eat in the kingdom of God.
30Indeed, some are last who will be first, and some are first
who will be last."

Jesus Mourns over Jerusalem

31 At that very hour some Pharisees came and said to
him, "Get away from here, for Herod wants to kill you."

The Value of a Disabled Woman

CONSIDER THIS 13:10–17 **The incident in vv. 10–17 put the ruler of the synagogue and his fellow rabbis to shame. Jesus rebuked them for showing more concern for their animals than for a disabled woman. They grumbled about profaning the Sabbath, but Jesus pointed out that *any* time is appropriate to meet a genuine need; *any* day—even the Sabbath—is a proper day for acts of mercy.**

Actually, of all the days on which the woman could have been given rest from her affliction, the Sabbath—a day of rest—was perhaps the most appropriate.

(continued on next page)

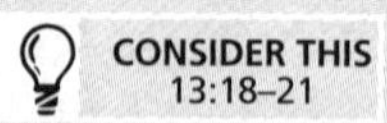

Little Things Mean a Lot

Do you tend to be impressed by bigness? Do you measure something's significance by whether it's bigger than anything else? Have you noticed the impact of little things, like the usefulness of a pinhead or the danger of a little bit of electricity in the wrong place?

Jesus described the kingdom and faith as starting out small, but ultimately having a big effect (vv. 18–21; 17:6; Matt. 13:31; 17:20; Mark 4:31). He likened the kingdom to a small seed that grows into a tree-like plant, just as today we speak of the acorn becoming an oak tree. He also borrowed an image from the baking industry, likening the kingdom to yeast or to leaven, a piece of fermented dough that was added to a new batch, causing it to rise.

In our own culture, where people tend to equate significance with magnitude, these parables remind us of the power of small but potent faith and of simple but solid kingdom values. Paul listed these lasting things: love, joy, peace, patience, kindness, goodness, faithfulness, gentleness, and self-control (Gal. 5:22–23).

God's challenge to us as His people is not to be impressed by power, success, or super-achievement, but to give ourselves to the so-called little things, the things of His kingdom. Therein lies ultimate significance. ◆

32He said to them, "Go and tell that fox for me,[r] 'Listen, I
am casting out demons and performing cures today and tomorrow, and on the third day I finish my work. 33Yet today,
tomorrow, and the next day I must be on my way, because
it is impossible for a prophet to be killed outside of
Jerusalem.' 34Jerusalem, Jerusalem, the
city that kills the prophets and stones
those who are sent to it! How often have I desired to gather
your children together as a hen gathers her brood under
her wings, and you were not willing! 35See, your house is
left to you. And I tell you, you will not see me until the
time comes when[s] you say, 'Blessed is the one who comes in
the name of the Lord.' "

13:34

Jesus Heals on the Sabbath

14 On one occasion when Jesus[t] was going to the
house of a leader of the Pharisees to eat a meal on
the sabbath, they were watching him closely. 2Just then, in
front of him, there was a man who had
dropsy. 3And Jesus asked the lawyers and
Pharisees, "Is it lawful to cure people on the sabbath, or
not?" 4But they were silent. So Jesus[t] took him and healed
him, and sent him away. 5Then he said to them, "If one of

14:1–6 see pg. 274

[r]Gk lacks *for me* [s]Other ancient authorities lack *the time comes when* [t]Gk *he*

Good Men Care

CONSIDER THIS 13:34

Jesus cried out as He came upon Jerusalem, mourning the lost children of Israel (v. 34). Clearly He was speaking of "children" in spiritual terms. But spiritual desolation is often reflected in outward ways. The fastest growing category of street people today are the children of the homeless in our cities. What would be Jesus' cry upon seeing them? What is our own response?

This was not the last time that Jesus would mourn over Jerusalem. See Luke 19:41.

(continued from previous page)

Jesus put a name on the legalists' attitude and behavior: hypocrisy. He wanted everyone to see that the outward appearance of righteousness often masks inner unrighteousness.

Jesus faced a similar situation somewhat earlier. He was no less direct in His condemnation of legalism. See "Jesus Confronts the Legalists," Luke 6:1–11.

Sorting Out Membership

CONSIDER THIS 13:22–23

Do you try to sort out who is saved and who is not? Do you find yourself making judgments about people's faith and its quality?

One of Jesus' followers asked Him how many others were being saved (v. 23). The Lord's response turned the questioner's attention away from others and toward his own quality of faith and the implications of that (vv. 24–30). Jesus even said that outward association with Him is not enough to ensure salvation (vv. 26–27). And He warned that those who seem to be the least likely candidates for the kingdom will enter ahead of others (v. 30).

Are you spending more energy trying to nail down who is and isn't going to heaven than on developing a walk with Christ that encourages others to pursue Him as Savior?

you has a child[u] or an ox that has fallen into a well, will you
14:1–6 not immediately pull it out on a sabbath
day?" 6And they could not reply to this.

A Parable about Seating at a Dinner

7 When he noticed how the guests chose the places of
honor, he told them a parable. 8"When you are invited by
someone to a wedding banquet, do not sit down at the
place of honor, in case someone more distinguished than
you has been invited by your host; 9and the host who invited both of you may come and say to you, 'Give this person your place,' and then in disgrace you would start to
take the lowest place. 10But when you are invited, go and
sit down at the lowest place, so that when your host comes,
he may say to you, 'Friend, move up higher'; then you will
be honored in the presence of all who sit at the table with
you. 11For all who exalt themselves will be humbled, and
those who humble themselves will be exalted."
14:12–14 12 He said also to the one who had
invited him, "When you give a luncheon
or a dinner, do not invite your friends or your brothers or
your relatives or rich neighbors, in case they may invite you
in return, and you would be repaid. 13But when you give a
banquet, invite the poor, the crippled, the lame, and the
blind. 14And you will be blessed, because they cannot repay
you, for you will be repaid at the resurrection of the righteous."

A Parable about a Slighted Invitation

15 One of the dinner guests, on hearing this, said to
him, "Blessed is anyone who will eat bread in the kingdom

[u]Other ancient authorities read *a donkey*

THE LETTER AND THE SPIRIT

CONSIDER THIS 14:1–6 **The Sabbath-day controversy (vv. 1–6) shows a tension between the letter of the Law and its spirit. The Old Testament was clear about keeping the Sabbath holy by resting from work (Ex. 20:8–11). But Jesus was known for doing the "work" of healing on the Sabbath (Luke 13:10–17). Was He breaking the Law or not? The lawyers and Pharisees couldn't say (v. 6).**

Jesus let them stew over the issue, but clearly He was convinced that He was acting well within the Law. If He appeared to break it, it was only because His enemies paid more attention to superficial, external ways of "keeping" the Law than to its underlying moral spirit. Furthermore, over the centuries their predecessors had heaped up countless traditions on top of the Law, creating a mammoth set of expectations that no one could fulfill.

In our own day, even believers sometimes try to live by a rigid set of dos and don'ts that go beyond the clear teaching of Scripture. Like the Pharisees, we are tempted to be more concerned about the externals of the faith than the larger principles of "justice and the love of God" (Luke 11:42). Given His treatment of the self-righteous Pharisees, what would Jesus say to us?

What does it mean to keep the Sabbath holy? See "Are Sundays Special?" Rom. 14:5–13, and "The Sabbath," Heb. 4:1–13.

"Do You Mind If I Heal?"

A CLOSER LOOK 14:1–6 *Jesus sparked plenty of controversy by healing on the Sabbath. His question in v. 3 appears ironic, as if asking "permission" to perform a miracle of mercy. Maybe His recent encounter with a synagogue ruler was still fresh in His mind (13:10–17).*

Jesus never won many legalists to His cause. But neither did He allow their abuse of Scripture or people to go unchallenged. See "Jesus Confronts the Legalists," Luke 6:1–11.

Care for the Poor

A CLOSER LOOK 14:12–14 *"Some Surprising Evidence" at Matt. 11:2–6 explores our responsibility toward the poor.*

14:16–24

of God!" 16Then Jesus[v] said to him,
"Someone gave a great dinner and in-
vited many. 17At the time for the dinner he sent his slave to
say to those who had been invited, 'Come; for everything is
ready now.' 18But they all alike began to make excuses. The
first said to him, 'I have bought a piece of land, and I must
go out and see it; please accept my regrets.' 19Another said,
'I have bought five yoke of oxen, and I am going to try
them out; please accept my regrets.' 20Another said, 'I have
just been married, and therefore I cannot come.' 21So the
slave returned and reported this to his master. Then the
owner of the house became angry and said to his slave, 'Go
out at once into the streets and lanes of the town and bring
in the poor, the crippled, the blind, and the lame.' 22And
the slave said, 'Sir, what you ordered has been done, and
there is still room.' 23Then the master said to the slave, 'Go
out into the roads and lanes, and compel people to come
in, so that my house may be filled. 24For I tell you,[w] none of
those who were invited will taste my dinner.' "

More about the Costs of Discipleship

14:25–32

25 Now large crowds were traveling
with him; and he turned and said to
them, 26"Whoever comes to me and does not hate father
and mother, wife and children, brothers and sisters, yes,
and even life itself, cannot be my disciple. 27Whoever does
not carry the cross and follow me cannot be my disciple.
28For which of you, intending to build a tower, does not
first sit down and estimate the cost, to see whether he has
enough to complete it? 29Otherwise, when he has laid a
foundation and is not able to finish, all who see it will begin to ridicule him, 30saying, 'This fellow began to build
and was not able to finish.' 31Or what king, going out to
wage war against another king, will not sit down first and
consider whether he is able with ten thousand to oppose
the one who comes against him with twenty thousand? 32If
he cannot, then, while the other is still far away, he sends a
delegation and asks for the terms of peace. 33So therefore,

[v]Gk *he* [w]The Greek word for *you* here is plural

The Cost of Following Jesus

CONSIDER THIS 14:25–32 **Following Jesus has its privileges—but also its costs, as vv. 25–32 reveal:**

- **The cost of *service* (v. 26). Jesus' followers must serve Him before all others.**
- **The cost of *sacrifice* (v. 27). Jesus' followers must subordinate their own interests to the interests of Christ.**
- **The cost of *self-assessment* (vv. 28–30). Jesus' followers must be fully in touch with who they are and how Christ has equipped and empowered them to do what He asks.**
- **The cost of *strategy* (vv. 31–33). Jesus' followers must think through the issues and have the courage to act in the face of uncertainty.**

Excuse Me!

The guests in Jesus' parable asked to be excused from the feast (v. 18). Jesus' listeners undoubtedly recognized that this was a gross impropriety. See *"Worse than Rude," Matt. 22:2–14.*

none of you can become my disciple if you do not give up all your possessions.

34 "Salt is good; but if salt has lost its taste, how can its saltiness be restored?[x] 35It is fit neither for the soil nor for the manure pile; they throw it away. Let anyone with ears to hear listen!"

A Parable about a Lost Sheep

15:1–31

15 Now all the tax collectors and sinners were coming near to listen to him. 2And the Pharisees and the scribes were grumbling and saying, "This fellow welcomes sinners and eats with them."

3 So he told them this parable: 4"Which one of you, having a hundred sheep and losing one of them, does not leave the ninety-nine in the wilderness and go after the one that is lost until he finds it? 5When he has found it, he lays it on his shoulders and rejoices. 6And when he comes home, he calls together his friends and neighbors, saying to them, 'Rejoice with me, for I have found my sheep that was lost.' 7Just so, I tell you, there will be more joy in heaven over one sinner who repents than over ninety-nine righteous persons who need no repentance.

A Parable about a Lost Coin

15:8–10

8 "Or what woman having ten silver coins,[y] if she loses one of them, does not light a lamp, sweep the house, and search carefully until she finds it? 9When she has found it, she calls together her friends and neighbors, saying, 'Rejoice with me, for I have found the coin that I had lost.' 10Just so, I tell you, there is joy in the presence of the angels of God over one sinner who repents."

A Parable about a Lost Son

11 Then Jesus[z] said, "There was a man who had two sons. 12The younger of them said to his father, 'Father, give me the share of the property that will belong to me.' So he divided his property between them. 13A few days later the younger son gathered all he had and traveled to a distant country, and there he squandered his property in dissolute living. 14When he had spent everything, a severe famine

[x]Or *how can it be used for seasoning?* [y]Gk *drachmas*, each worth about a day's wage for a laborer [z]Gk *he*

Confused Value?

CONSIDER THIS 15:1–31 *In Luke 15, Jesus tells three parables about a lost sheep (vv. 4–7), a lost coin (vv. 8–10), and a lost son (vv. 11–32). Each story reflects God's concern for lost people, the tremendous value He places on every individual, and the great joy He feels "over one sinner who repents" (v. 10).*

In the first two stories, Jesus points out the natural value that humans place on their possessions. A shepherd loses one sheep out of a hundred (only 1 percent of his flock), yet he goes out and scours the countryside until he finds it and returns it to the fold. Likewise, a woman loses one coin out of ten (only 10 percent of her collection), yet she searches high and low until she finds it.

But in the third story, the loss is a worthless son—not unlike the tax collectors and sinners listening to Jesus (v. 1). We can imagine that Jesus' critics, the Pharisees, found it easy to write off such unrighteous people. Surely they were hopelessly lost in sin and shame.

But Jesus' parable shows that God views every sinner with compassion, not as merely a possession, but as a person—indeed, as a lost but loved son. He longs for each one to return to Him.

took place throughout that country, and he began to be in
need. 15So he went and hired himself out to one of the citizens of that country, who sent him to his fields to feed the
pigs. 16He would gladly have filled himself with[a] the pods
that the pigs were eating; and no one gave him anything.
17But when he came to himself he said, 'How many of my
father's hired hands have bread enough and to spare, but
here I am dying of hunger! 18I will get up and go to my father, and I will say to him, "Father, I have sinned against
heaven and before you; 19I am no longer worthy to be
called your son; treat me like one of your hired hands." '
20So he set off and went to his father. But while he was still
far off, his father saw him and was filled with compassion;
he ran and put his arms around him and kissed him.
21Then the son said to him, 'Father, I have sinned against
heaven and before you; I am no longer worthy to be called
your son.'[b] 22But the father said to his slaves, 'Quickly, bring
out a robe—the best one—and put it on him; put a ring on
his finger and sandals on his feet. 23And get the fatted calf
and kill it, and let us eat and celebrate; 24for this son of
mine was dead and is alive again; he was lost and is found!'
And they began to celebrate.

15:25–30 see pg. 278

25 "Now his elder son was in the
field; and when he came and ap-
proached the house, he heard music and dancing. 26He
called one of the slaves and asked what was going on. 27He
replied, 'Your brother has come, and your father has killed
the fatted calf, because he has got him back safe and
sound.' 28Then he became angry and refused to go in. His
father came out and began to plead with him. 29But he answered his father, 'Listen! For all these years I have been
working like a slave for you, and I have never disobeyed
your command; yet you have never given me even a young
goat so that I might celebrate with my friends. 30But when
this son of yours came back, who has devoured your property with prostitutes, you killed the fatted calf for him!'
31Then the father[c] said to him, 'Son, you are always with
me, and all that is mine is yours. 32But we had to celebrate
and rejoice, because this brother of yours was dead and has
come to life; he was lost and has been found.' "

A Parable about a Dishonest Manager

16:1–13 see pg. 278

16 Then Jesus[c] said to the disciples,
"There was a rich man who had
a manager, and charges were brought to him that this man
was squandering his property. 2So he summoned him and

[a]Other ancient authorities read *filled his stomach with* [b]Other ancient authorities add *treat me as one of your hired servants* [c]Gk *he*

The Woman Who Searched as God Searches

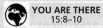

YOU ARE THERE 15:8–10

The impact of the parable in vv. 8–10 is easily lost on us as modern readers, who think nothing of tossing a penny in a fountain or losing a quarter in a pay phone. We need to understand that the lost coin was probably a drachma, *a Greek coin worth a day's wage. How many of us would not search high and low to find a missing paycheck? That's what the woman in the parable was doing.*

Actually, her coin was probably part of a set of ten silver coins. The women of Jesus' day commonly wore such collections as jewelry. So not only had she lost a valuable coin, she had a flawed piece of jewelry. What bride today does not get down on her hands and knees to search the carpet or the yard to find her missing diamond? That's what this woman was doing.

Jesus likens her search for the precious coin to God's search for each one of us.

A Shrewd Manager

CONSIDER THIS 16:1–13 **What is the point of the parable in vv. 1–13? Was Christ commending the manager (or steward) for cheating his boss (v. 8)? No, He was merely observing that people go to great lengths to secure favorable treatment when they are in legal or financial trouble. They may cheat others or pervert the law to do it, but in a way their conduct reveals a certain wisdom, a prudent concern for oneself. If only they took similar pains with their eternal destiny (vv. 9–12)!**

Verse 9 speaks of "dishonest wealth." Jesus was not implying that money (mammon) is inherently evil, only that material wealth is temporal in nature and will not go with us into eternal life. It will be "gone." Therefore, we should use our wealth wisely in this life. In fact, we should "make friends" with it—that is, use it in a

(continued on next page)

said to him, 'What is this that I hear about you? Give me an
accounting of your management, because you cannot be
my manager any longer.' 3Then the manager said to himself, 'What will I do, now that my master is taking the position away from me? I am not strong enough to dig, and I
am ashamed to beg. 4I have decided what to do so that,
when I am dismissed as manager, people may welcome me
into their homes.' 5So, summoning his master's debtors one
by one, he asked the first, 'How much do you owe my master?' 6He answered, 'A hundred jugs of olive oil.' He said to
him, 'Take your bill, sit down quickly, and make it fifty.'
7Then he asked another, 'And how much do you owe?' He
replied, 'A hundred containers of wheat.' He said to him,
'Take your bill and make it eighty.' 8And his master commended the dishonest manager because he had acted
shrewdly; for the children of this age are more shrewd in
dealing with their own generation than are the children of
light. 9And I tell you, make friends for yourselves by means
of dishonest wealth[d] so that when it is gone, they may welcome you into the eternal homes.[e]
10 "Whoever is faithful in a very little is faithful also in
much; and whoever is dishonest in a very little is dishonest
also in much. 11If then you have not been faithful with the
dishonest wealth,[d] who will entrust to you the true riches?

[d]Gk *mammon* [e]Gk *tents*

Are You the Elder Brother?

If you grew up in the church or have been a believer for many years, it's worth looking carefully at the prodigal son's elder brother (v. 25). He's one of the most intriguing characters in all of Jesus' parables—a case study in what can happen to people who have been around religion for a long time.

In contrast to the father, who shows nothing but mercy to his long lost son who has finally come home, the elder brother sneers at the joy and celebration heaped on his brother. He is not merely jealous, but outraged at what he perceives as injustice. How could the father kill the fatted calf just because his wayward, ne'er-do-well son had come back, while seeming to neglect the faithful, diligent loyalty of his other son (vv. 29–30)?

That was the attitude of the Pharisees who were among those listening to this story (vv. 2–3). And in a larger sense, it would become the attitude of many Jews as the gospel spread to the Gentiles (for example, Acts 11:1–3). How could Jesus be so friendly toward known

12And if you have not been faithful with what belongs to
another, who will give you what is your own? 13No slave
can serve two masters; for a slave will either hate the one
and love the other, or be devoted to the one and despise the
other. You cannot serve God and wealth."[f]

Jesus Denounces the Pharisees

14 The Pharisees, who were lovers of money, heard all
this, and they ridiculed him. 15So he said to them, "You are
those who justify yourselves in the sight of others; but God
knows your hearts; for what is prized by human beings is
an abomination in the sight of God.
16 "The law and the prophets were in effect until John
came; since then the good news of the kingdom of God is
proclaimed, and everyone tries to enter it by force.[g] 17But it
is easier for heaven and earth to pass away, than for one
stroke of a letter in the law to be dropped.
18 "Anyone who divorces his wife and marries another
commits adultery, and whoever marries a woman divorced
from her husband commits adultery.

The Rich Man and Lazarus

16:19–31 see pg. 280

19 "There was a rich man who was
dressed in purple and fine linen and who

(Bible text continued on page 281)

[f]Gk *mammon* [g]Or *everyone is strongly urged to enter it*

(continued from previous page)

way that brings others into the kingdom of Christ (vv. 8–9).

Jesus' words in vv. 10–11 make it plain that He is not denouncing money. On the contrary, our level of responsibility in His kingdom will depend on how we manage the resources that God gives us in this life. In fact, we might ask: What condition are our finances in? Are we overseeing our material resources prudently and faithfully?

The "bottom line" of this passage is found in vv. 12–13. All our earthly goods ultimately come from God and belong to Him. They are not really ours; we only manage them on His behalf. Any other outlook leads to a divided mind. We can't serve God if we're convinced that our money and property belong to us. We'll inevitably end up serving them.

sinners, such as the tax gatherers, and so distant from people like the Pharisees who carefully practiced the finer points of the Law? How could God be compassionate toward Gentiles, while the Jews, who had been His people for generations, were passed by?

Have you ever felt that more concern is shown for "lost" than for "faithful" persons? Have you ever felt that more attention is paid to new converts than to those who have followed biblical teaching all their lives? If so, Jesus' parable contains a comfort and a challenge. The comfort is that God never forgets who His children are and has great treasures stored up for them (v. 31). The challenge is to maintain a proper perspective—the perspective of compassion and mercy that is at the heart of the Father (v. 32). ◆

We can't serve God and wealth. See "Don't Worry!" Matt. 6:19–34.

Jesus encountered a man who had a "divided mind" about money—and it cost the fellow everything. See "The Man Who Had It All—Almost," Mark 10:17–27.

CONSIDER THIS
16:19–31

Set for Life—But What about Eternity?

The parable in vv. 19–31 draws a stark contrast between the rich man and the poor beggar Lazarus. The key to understanding it is to notice who Jesus told it to—the Pharisees, whom Luke describes as "lovers of money" (v. 14). Like the rich man, they were set for life—but not for eternity. They displayed an image of righteousness but were actually hypocrites (v. 15). Careful to preserve the letter of a greatly expanded Mosaic tradition, they violated the spirit of the Mosaic Law. They rejected God's love and compassion embodied in Jesus Christ (v. 31).

So Jesus told the parable to rebuke them. He was not saying that all the poor will go to heaven and all the rich will go to hell. He was warning those who live as though this life were all that matters: they are playing with fire!

Clearly, it is a dangerous thing to have it made in this life. The insensitive rich man received his "good things" during his lifetime (v. 25). He was like the men described in Psalm 17:14 "whose portion in life is in this world," but have no portion in the life to come. Likewise, Psalm 73 talks about the wicked who appear to have it all: They live above the everyday problems that everyone else faces. They wear their pride like jewelry. They have more wealth than they can possibly use. Yet they belittle those who live hand-to-mouth. With all of their status and power they strut through life, giving not a care for God. Who needs Him?

But in eternity, the tables turn, as the rich man discovers to his horror (v. 23). The parable concludes on an ominous note. Jesus describes the hardness of people who are determined to reject God. Despite plenty of evidence to warn them that they are headed for ruin, they persist in their ways—just as the Pharisees did.

This grim parable moves one to ask: "What portion do I value most in life? Which am I more interested in—being set for life or set for eternity?" The writer of Psalm 73 made his commitment clear (vv. 25–26):

> Whom have I in heaven but you?
> And there is nothing on earth
> that I desire other than
> you.
> My flesh and my heart may fail,
> but God is the strength of
> my heart and my portion
> forever. ◆

Modern believers do well to carefully study what Paul wrote about money, given the emphasis on material things in our culture. See "Christians and Money," 1 Tim. 6:6–19.

feasted sumptuously every day. 20And at his gate lay a poor man named Lazarus, covered with sores, 21who longed to satisfy his hunger with what fell from the rich man's table; even the dogs would come and lick his sores. 22The poor man died and was carried away by the angels to be with Abraham.[h] The rich man also died and was buried. 23In Hades, where he was being tormented, he looked up and saw Abraham far away with Lazarus by his side.[i] 24He called out, 'Father Abraham, have mercy on me, and send Lazarus to dip the tip of his finger in water and cool my tongue; for I am in agony in these flames.' 25But Abraham said, 'Child, remember that during your lifetime you received your good things, and Lazarus in like manner evil things; but now he is comforted here, and you are in agony. 26Besides all this, between you and us a great chasm has been fixed, so that those who might want to pass from here to you cannot do so, and no one can cross from there to us.' 27He said, 'Then, father, I beg you to send him to my father's house— 28for I have five brothers—that he may warn them, so that they will not also come into this place of torment.' 29Abraham replied, 'They have Moses and the prophets; they should listen to them.' 30He said, 'No, father Abraham; but if someone goes to them from the dead, they will repent.' 31He said to him, 'If they do not listen to Moses and the prophets, neither will they be convinced even if someone rises from the dead.' "

Forgiveness

17 Jesus[j] said to his disciples, "Occasions for stumbling are bound to come, but woe to anyone by whom they come! 2It would be better for you if a millstone were hung around your neck and you were thrown into the sea than for you to cause one of these little ones to stumble. 3Be on your guard! If another disciple[k] sins, you must rebuke the offender, and if there is repentance, you must forgive. 4And if the same person sins against you seven times a day, and turns back to you seven times and says, 'I repent,' you must forgive."

About Faith and Faithfulness

17:5–10

5 The apostles said to the Lord, "Increase our faith!" 6The Lord replied, "If you had faith the size of a[l] mustard seed, you could say to this mulberry tree, 'Be uprooted and planted in the sea,' and it would obey you.

[h]Gk *to Abraham's bosom* [i]Gk *in his bosom* [j]Gk *He* [k]Gk *your brother* [l]Gk *faith as a grain of*

DOING YOUR DUTY

CONSIDER THIS 17:5–10 **Jesus' words in vv. 6–10 raise many puzzling questions. Did He intend that we should never thank people for doing what is expected of them? Should workers never expect praise for doing their jobs? Why are the workers "worthless" if in fact they did what was their duty? Should we always do more than expected? Was this a sermon on initiative and creativity? Who was Jesus addressing, bosses or employees?**

Actually, He was responding to the disciples' request for more faith (v. 5). That's a key to understanding this passage. Jesus had just challenged His followers to forgive others freely and repeatedly (17:1–4). But they replied, "Increase our faith," as if it took great faith to forgive.

But it does not. Forgiveness is not some supernatural ability that only God can give. It is not the product of great faith, but rather of simple obedience. That's what the servant in the parable must do—obey his master. It doesn't take great trust on the part of the servant to get a meal prepared; it just takes doing it. In the same way, forgiveness is *expected* of us as Christ's followers, since Christ has forgiven us. We are *obligated* to forgive others, so there's no reward attached to it.

The disciples expected a payoff for following Jesus (9:46–48; Matt. 20:20–28). But Jesus wanted them to see that following Him *was* a reward in itself!

WHERE ARE THE OTHERS?

CONSIDER THIS 17:11–19 **Once again Jesus chose a route that made it likely that He would encounter Samaritans (v. 11; see map at Luke 9:51–56). And once again Luke's account has to do with the tension between Jews and Samaritans.**

It's easy to see why Jesus would ask, "But the other nine, where are they?" (v. 17). He was amazed at their lack of gratitude. But why did He call the one man who did return a "foreigner"? Luke singles out the fact that he was a Samaritan. That meant that he and Jesus were divided by a cultural wall that was virtually impenetrable. In fact, it was said to be unlawful for a Jew even to associate with a "foreigner" (compare Acts 10:28). Yet Jesus openly violated that taboo as He marveled at the Samaritan's thankful heart.

What of the other nine? Were they not Samaritans as well? Possibly, since this incident was taking place in or near Samaria. But is it not equally possible, given Luke's comment and Jesus' remark, that the other nine were not Samaritans, but Jews who had been driven away from the Jewish community to the Samaritans because of their leprous condition?

If so, their ingratitude was inexcusable. There was no racial wall separating them from Jesus. The only barrier had been their leprosy—and Jesus had removed that. They had every reason to turn in faith toward the Lord; but instead they turned away.

By contrast, a man who had every reason to stay away from Jesus returned and gave glory to God. As a

(continued on next page)

7 "Who among you would say to your slave who has just come in from plowing or tending sheep in the field, 'Come here at once and take your place at the table'? [8]Would you not rather say to him, 'Prepare supper for me, put on your apron and serve me while I eat and drink; later you may eat and drink'? [9]Do you thank the slave for doing what was commanded? [10]So you also, when you have done all that you were ordered to do, say, 'We are worthless slaves; we have done only what we ought to have done!' "

Ten Lepers Healed in Samaria

17:11–19

11 On the way to Jerusalem Jesus[m] was going through the region between Samaria and Galilee. [12]As he entered a village, ten lepers[n] approached him. Keeping their distance, [13]they called out, saying, "Jesus, Master, have mercy on us!" [14]When he saw them, he said to them, "Go and show yourselves to the priests." And as they went, they were made clean. [15]Then one of them, when he saw that he was healed, turned back, praising God with a loud voice. [16]He prostrated himself at Jesus'[o] feet and thanked him. And he was a Samaritan. [17]Then Jesus asked, "Were not ten made clean? But the other nine, where are they? [18]Was none of them found to return and give praise to God except this foreigner?" [19]Then he said to him, "Get up and go on your way; your faith has made you well."

The Kingdom of God and the Day of the Lord

20 Once Jesus[m] was asked by the Pharisees when the kingdom of God was coming, and he answered, "The kingdom of God is not coming with things that can be observed; [21]nor will they say, 'Look, here it is!' or 'There it is!' For, in fact, the kingdom of God is among[p] you."

22 Then he said to the disciples, "The days are coming when you will long to see one of the days of the Son of Man, and you will not see it. [23]They will say to you, 'Look there!' or 'Look here!' Do not go, do not set off in pursuit. [24]For as the lightning flashes and lights up the sky from one side to the other, so will the Son of Man be in his day.[q] [25]But first he must endure much suffering and be rejected by this generation. [26]Just as it was in the days of Noah, so too it will be in the days of the Son of Man. [27]They were eating and drinking, and marrying and being given in marriage,

[m]Gk *he* [n]The terms *leper* and *leprosy* can refer to several diseases [o]Gk *his* [p]Or *within* [q]Other ancient authorities lack *in his day*

until the day Noah entered the ark, and the flood came and
destroyed all of them. 28Likewise, just as it was in the days
of Lot: they were eating and drinking, buying and selling,
planting and building, 29but on the day that Lot left Sodom,
it rained fire and sulfur from heaven and destroyed all of
them 30—it will be like that on the day that the Son of Man
is revealed. 31On that day, anyone on the housetop who has
belongings in the house must not come down to take them
away; and likewise anyone in the field must not turn back.
17:32 32Remember Lot's wife. 33Those who try
to make their life secure will lose it, but
those who lose their life will keep it. 34I tell you, on that
night there will be two in one bed; one will be taken and
17:35 see pg. 284 the other left. 35There will be two women
grinding meal together; one will be taken
and the other left."[r] 37Then they asked him, "Where, Lord?"
He said to them, "Where the corpse is, there the vultures
will gather."

A Parable about an Unjust Judge

18 Then Jesus[s] told them a parable about their need to
pray always and not to lose heart. 2He said, "In a
certain city there was a judge who neither feared God nor
had respect for people. 3In that city there was a widow who
kept coming to him and saying, 'Grant me justice against
my opponent.' 4For a while he refused; but later he said to
himself, 'Though I have no fear of God and no respect for
anyone, 5yet because this widow keeps bothering me, I will
grant her justice, so that she may not wear me out by continually coming.' "[t] 6And the Lord said, "Listen to what the
unjust judge says. 7And will not God grant justice to his
chosen ones who cry to him day and night? Will he delay
long in helping them? 8I tell you, he will quickly grant justice to them. And yet, when the Son of Man comes, will he
find faith on earth?"

A Pharisee and a Tax Collector

18:9–14 see pg. 285 9 He also told this parable to some
who trusted in themselves that they were
righteous and regarded others with contempt: 10"Two men
went up to the temple to pray, one a Pharisee and the other
a tax collector. 11The Pharisee, standing by himself, was
praying thus, 'God, I thank you that I am not like other

[r]Other ancient authorities add verse 36, *"Two will be in the field; one will be taken and the other left."* [s]Gk *he* [t]*Or so that she may not finally come and slap me in the face*

(continued from previous page)

result, he received what the other nine did not: spiritual healing, and not just physical. How open are you to that healing?

At times Jesus chose to take His disciples through Samaria and challenged their prejudices—sometimes with explosive results. See "Condemnation or Compassion?" Luke 9:51–56.

Lepers were common in the ancient world. They suffered from a slowly progressing, ordinarily incurable skin disease that was believed to be highly contagious and therefore greatly feared. Anyone who appeared to have leprosy, even if the symptoms were caused by some other condition, was banished from the community. See Matt. 8:2.

The Infamous Mrs. Lot

CONSIDER THIS 17:32 *Jesus warned His followers to remember Lot's wife (v. 32). By including this instruction in his Gospel, Luke made sure we would do that!*

Mrs. Lot was forced to leave her prosperous home in Sodom, taking only what she could carry. Angels had come to warn her and her husband of God's impending judgment on the city. They told her not to look back—not to linger, not to long for her old way of life. But she did and as a result, judgment fell on her as well: she was turned into a pillar of salt (Gen. 19:15–26).

The example of Lot's wife reminds us that the return of Christ will be just as sudden as the judgment on Sodom—and the consequences of longing for an old way of life just as severe.

people: thieves, rogues, adulterers, or even like this tax collector. 12I fast twice a week; I give a tenth of all my income.'
13But the tax collector, standing far off, would not even
look up to heaven, but was beating his breast and saying,
'God, be merciful to me, a sinner!' 14I tell you, this man
went down to his home justified rather than the other; for
all who exalt themselves will be humbled, but all who
humble themselves will be exalted."

"All who humble themselves will be exalted." —Luke 18:14

"Let the Little Children Come to Me"

18:15–17

15 People were bringing even infants
to him that he might touch them; and
when the disciples saw it, they sternly ordered them not to
do it. 16But Jesus called for them and said, "Let the little
children come to me, and do not stop them; for it is to such
as these that the kingdom of God belongs. 17Truly I tell
you, whoever does not receive the kingdom of God as a little child will never enter it."

Jesus Encounters a Rich Ruler

18:18–30
see pg. 286

18 A certain ruler asked him, "Good
Teacher, what must I do to inherit eter-

Please Bless Our Children

A CLOSER LOOK 18:15–17

In Jesus' day it was customary to ask famous rabbis to bless one's children. See "The Friend of Children" at Mark 10:13–16.

Grinding the Grain

YOU ARE THERE 17:35

Jesus' allusion to two women grinding grain (v. 35) speaks to the suddenness of His return in the middle of ordinary, everyday life. Grinding grain was a daily task, as meal was not stored in large quantities. It was a job reserved for women in Jewish culture. Most households owned their own hand-mill, a round, medium-sized stone that rotated around a wooden post inserted through a hole in the center. It could be worked by one woman but was easiest with two (v. 35). One woman fed in the grain while the other worked the stone to crush the hulls. The task required little mental effort but a lot of muscle.

nal life?" 19Jesus said to him, "Why do you call me good?
No one is good but God alone. 20You know the commandments: 'You shall not commit adultery; You shall not murder; You shall not steal; You shall not bear false witness;
Honor your father and mother.' " 21He replied, "I have kept
all these since my youth." 22When Jesus heard this, he said
to him, "There is still one thing lacking. Sell all that you
own and distribute the money[u] to the poor, and you will
have treasure in heaven; then come, follow me." 23But when
he heard this, he became sad; for he was very rich. 24Jesus
looked at him and said, "How hard it is for those who have
wealth to enter the kingdom of God! 25Indeed, it is easier
for a camel to go through the eye of a needle than for someone who is rich to enter the kingdom of God."

26 Those who heard it said, "Then who can be saved?"
27He replied, "What is impossible for mortals is possible for
God."

Rewards for Self-Sacrifice

28 Then Peter said, "Look, we have left our homes and
followed you." 29And he said to them, "Truly I tell you,
there is no one who has left house or wife or brothers or
parents or children, for the sake of the kingdom of God,
30who will not get back very much more in this age, and in
the age to come eternal life."

Jesus Predicts His Death

31 Then he took the twelve aside and said to them, "See,
we are going up to Jerusalem, and everything that is written
about the Son of Man by the prophets will be accomplished. 32For he will be handed over to the Gentiles; and
he will be mocked and insulted and spat upon. 33After they
have flogged him, they will kill him, and on the third day
he will rise again." 34But they understood nothing about all
these things; in fact, what he said was hidden from them,
and they did not grasp what was said.

A Blind Man Healed Near Jericho

18:35–43
see pg. 287

35 As he approached Jericho, a blind
man was sitting by the roadside begging.

[u]Gk lacks *the money*

Comparisonitis Will Kill You

CONSIDER THIS 18:9–14

How do you establish your identity? Are you always comparing yourself to others? If so, you suffer from "comparisonitis," a malady that can kill you! Consider the Pharisee in Jesus' parable (vv. 9–14). He was so proud of himself that he started off his prayer with a comparison: "God, I thank you that I am not like other people."

Do you do that? Do you try to build up your self-esteem by looking down on others less fortunate or gifted than you? If so, you are standing on shaky ground because your identity becomes uncertain. You can never be sure about yourself on those terms. Sooner or later, someone is bound to come along who is better than you in some way. You also risk loneliness, because no one cultivates friends by always finding fault with others in order to feel better about oneself.

In contrast to the Pharisee, the second man in Jesus' parable looked to God in order to see himself properly. Doing so exposed his sin but it also brought about God's forgiveness and restoration. This man shows us the path to true identity. It is based on honesty about ourselves and becoming like Christ.

Paul was aware of how deadly "comparisonitis" can be. That's why he offers an antidote for it. See "Do You Suffer from 'Comparisonitis'?" Rom. 12:3.

Holding Wealth or Serving Others?

CONSIDER THIS 18:18–30 **Do you feel that your life would be better if only you were wealthy? Would your friends describe you as generous? These two issues were at stake in the encounter between Jesus and the rich young ruler (vv. 18–30). The young man was wealthy enough for this life, but he wanted to know about eternal life. He was confident that he was living a clean life, but he was fearful of his destiny and came seeking security for his future.**

Jesus did not challenge the young ruler's claims about his life, but rather focused on what was most important to him—his wealth. *Was it available for others?* was the probing question. Jesus made service to others the indication of fitness for eternal life. Real wealth involves following Jesus, living not to be served but to serve others and to gives one's life for others (Matt. 20:28).

This episode poses a challenge: Where is your attention focused, on accumulation or servanthood?

Jesus perceived that the rich young ruler placed far too much value on his wealth and told him to give it away. Jesus did not give that same advice to every other rich person He encountered. But it was a requirement for this young man. See "The Man Who Had It All—Almost," Mark 10:17–27.

36When he heard a crowd going by, he asked what was happening. 37They told him, "Jesus of Nazareth[v] is passing by." 38Then he shouted, "Jesus, Son of David, have mercy on me!" 39Those who were in front sternly ordered him to be quiet; but he shouted even more loudly, "Son of David, have mercy on me!" 40Jesus stood still and ordered the man to be brought to him; and when he came near, he asked him, 41"What do you want me to do for you?" He said, "Lord, let me see again." 42Jesus said to him, "Receive your sight; your faith has saved you." 43Immediately he regained his sight and followed him, glorifying God; and all the people, when they saw it, praised God.

Zacchaeus Believes

19:1–10 see pg. 288

19 He entered Jericho and was passing through it. 2A man was there named Zacchaeus; he was a chief tax collector and was rich. 3He was trying to see who Jesus was, but on account of the crowd he could not, because he was short in stature. 4So he ran ahead and climbed a sycamore tree to see him, because he was going to pass that way. 5When Jesus came to the place, he looked up and said to him, "Zacchaeus, hurry and come down; for I must stay at your house today." 6So he hurried down and was happy to welcome him. 7All who saw it began to grumble and said, "He has gone to be the guest of one who is a sinner." 8Zacchaeus stood there and said to the Lord, "Look, half of my possessions, Lord, I will give to the poor; and if I have defrauded anyone of anything, I will pay back four times as much." 9Then Jesus said to him, "Today salvation has come to this house, because he too is a son of Abraham. 10For the Son of Man came to seek out and to save the lost."

A Parable about a Wicked Slave

19:11–27 see pg. 289

11 As they were listening to this, he went on to tell a parable, because he was near Jerusalem, and because they supposed that the kingdom of God was to appear immediately. 12So he said, "A nobleman went to a distant country to get royal power for himself and then return. 13He summoned ten of his slaves, and gave them ten pounds,[w] and said to them, 'Do business with these until I come back.' 14But the citizens of his country hated him and sent a delegation after him, saying, 'We do not want this man to rule over us.' 15When he returned,

[v]Gk *the Nazorean* [w]The mina, rendered here by *pound,* was about three months' wages for a laborer

having received royal power, he ordered these slaves, to whom he had given the money, to be summoned so that he might find out what they had gained by trading. 16The first came forward and said, 'Lord, your pound has made ten more pounds.' 17He said to him, 'Well done, good slave! Because you have been trustworthy in a very small thing, take charge of ten cities.' 18Then the second came, saying, 'Lord, your pound has made five pounds.' 19He said to him, 'And you, rule over five cities.' 20Then the other came, saying, 'Lord, here is your pound. I wrapped it up in a piece of cloth, 21for I was afraid of you, because you are a harsh man; you take what you did not deposit, and reap what you did not sow.' 22He said to him, 'I will judge you by your own words, you wicked slave! You knew, did you, that I was a harsh man, taking what I did not deposit and

19:23

reaping what I did not sow? 23Why then did you not put my money into the

Banking

FOR YOUR INFO 19:23

When Jesus incorporated a bank into his parable of the talents (v. 23), He was referring to a relatively recent development in Jewish society. Institutional banking was not known in ancient Israel until the time of the Babylonian captivity (586 B.C.) because money as such did not exist at that time. Lending money at interest (a traditional function of banks) was forbidden in the Law (Ex. 22:25; Deut. 23:19–20). People protected their valuables by burying them or depositing them in temples or palaces.

During the captivity the Israelites became familiar with Babylonian banking practices. Some Jews joined the industry and became prominent bank officers. By New Testament times banking had become an established institution.

Although Jesus' parable shows that bankers received money for safekeeping and also paid interest, the most common New Testament reference to banking is to moneychanging (Matt. 21:12).

Holy Interruptions

CONSIDER THIS 18:35–43

How full is your schedule? Is it booked so tightly that only an act of God seems able to force an adjustment?

Jesus certainly had a demanding task with lots of responsibility. God sent Him to earth to gain salvation for all and to launch the church—and gave Him little more than three years to do it! Yet somehow Jesus' value system allowed for what we would call interruptions. People barged into His presence, even when His associates tried to prevent them.

Such was the case for a blind beggar by a roadside near Jericho (vv. 35–38). The man called out to Jesus as He and his leadership team were on their way to major events in Jerusalem. Then as now, well-traveled roads were cluttered with such inconveniences. Some tried to ignore the beggar, or at least keep him away. But amazingly, Jesus stopped and met the man's needs.

It's interesting that Jesus' very next encounter, with a known government crook, was also an interruption (Luke 19:1–10). Yet again, Jesus set aside His travel plans and turned aside to Zacchaeus' home to talk with him and meet his family and friends.

Do you have room for others in your life, especially the "little people" such as your children, an entry-level employee, a visitor to your church, or someone poor? When Jesus took time to serve a forgotten castaway, it caused everyone nearby to give praise to God (v. 43). Watch out for God's holy interruptions!

A Remedy for Tax Fraud

CONSIDER THIS 19:1–10 Luke describes Zacchaeus as a tax collector (v. 2). His first-century readers would have understood that to mean that Zacchaeus was a cheating, corrupt lackey of the Roman government. In fact, he was a *chief* tax collector, which probably meant that he was "public enemy number one" to the Jews in Jericho, even worse than the notorious bandits on the city's main highway.

But Jesus reached out to the curious Zacchaeus, prompting him to change his ways. In fact, Zacchaeus came up with his own formula for making restitution on the tax fraud he had practiced: a 400 percent rebate to those he had knowingly cheated, plus half of his net worth to go to the poor (v. 8). By paying restitution, he showed a new respect for the Old Testament Law (Ex. 22:1). Giving away his possessions was not a requirement of the Law, but it revealed his change of heart.

Imagine a corrupt public official or shady corporate financier today following that formula. Imagine a pastor challenging a businessperson in his congregation to repay four times what was made on a crooked deal. It sounds simplistic. But Zacchaeus was truly repentant. He was like the tax collector Jesus had recently mentioned in a parable who cried out, "God, be merciful to me, a sinner!" (18:13).

Zacchaeus may have been a higher-ranking "publican" rather than an ordinary tax collector. Either way, he would have been despised by the citizens of Jericho. See "Who Were Those Tax Collectors," Matt. 9:10, and "Taxes," Mark 12:14.

bank? Then when I returned, I could have collected it with
interest.' 24He said to the bystanders, 'Take the pound from
him and give it to the one who has ten pounds.' 25(And
they said to him, 'Lord, he has ten pounds!') 26'I tell you, to
all those who have, more will be given; but from those who
have nothing, even what they have will be taken away.
27But as for these enemies of mine who did not want me to
be king over them—bring them here and slaughter them in
my presence.' "

Jesus' Triumphal Entry into Jerusalem

28 After he had said this, he went on ahead, going up to
Jerusalem.
29 When he had come near Bethphage and Bethany, at
the place called the Mount of Olives, he sent two of the disciples, 30saying, "Go into the village ahead of you, and as
you enter it you will find tied there a colt that has never
been ridden. Untie it and bring it here. 31If anyone asks
you, 'Why are you untying it?' just say this, 'The Lord needs
it.' " 32So those who were sent departed and found it as he
had told them. 33As they were untying the colt, its owners
asked them, "Why are you untying the colt?" 34They said,
"The Lord needs it." 35Then they brought it to Jesus; and after throwing their cloaks on the colt, they set Jesus on it.
36As he rode along, people kept spreading their cloaks on
the road. 37As he was now approaching the path down from
the Mount of Olives, the whole multitude of the disciples
began to praise God joyfully with a loud voice for all the
deeds of power that they had seen, 38saying,

"Blessed is the king
  who comes in the name of the Lord!
Peace in heaven,
  and glory in the highest heaven!"

39Some of the Pharisees in the crowd said to him, "Teacher,
order your disciples to stop." 40He answered, "I tell you, if
these were silent, the stones would shout out."

Jesus Weeps over Jerusalem

19:41–46 see pg. 290

41 As he came near and saw the city,
he wept over it, 42saying, "If you, even
you, had only recognized on this day the things that make
for peace! But now they are hidden from your eyes. 43In-
deed, the days will come upon you, when your enemies
will set up ramparts around you and surround you, and
hem you in on every side. 44They will crush you to the
ground, you and your children within you, and they will

not leave within you one stone upon another; because you
did not recognize the time of your visitation from God."[x]

Jesus Purges the Temple

45 Then he entered the temple and began to drive out
those who were selling things there; 46and he said, "It is
written,

'My house shall be a house of prayer';
but you have made it a den of robbers."

47 Every day he was teaching in the temple. The chief
priests, the scribes, and the leaders of the people kept looking for a way to kill him; 48but they did not find anything
they could do, for all the people were spellbound by what
they heard.

Jesus' Authority Questioned

20 One day, as he was teaching the people in the
temple and telling the good news, the chief priests
and the scribes came with the elders 2and said to him, "Tell
us, by what authority are you doing these things? Who is it
who gave you this authority?" 3He answered them, "I will
also ask you a question, and you tell me: 4Did the baptism
of John come from heaven, or was it of human origin?"
5They discussed it with one another, saying, "If we say,
'From heaven,' he will say, 'Why did you not believe him?'
6But if we say, 'Of human origin,' all the people will stone
us; for they are convinced that John was a prophet." 7So
they answered that they did not know where it came from.
8Then Jesus said to them, "Neither will I tell you by what
authority I am doing these things."

A Parable about Wicked Tenants

20:9–19
see pg. 290

9 He began to tell the people this
parable: "A man planted a vineyard, and
leased it to tenants, and went to another country for a long
time. 10When the season came, he sent a slave to the tenants in order that they might give him his share of the produce of the vineyard; but the tenants beat him and sent him
away empty-handed. 11Next he sent another slave; that one
also they beat and insulted and sent away empty-handed.
12And he sent still a third; this one also they wounded and

[x]Gk lacks *from God*

A Job to Do

CONSIDER THIS 19:11–27 **The parable recorded in vv. 12–27 describes a case of absentee ownership and on-site management. Actually, it reflected the government in Palestine, in which Rome "owned" the region but left it in the hands of local governors, such as the infamous Herods (see Acts 12:1–2).**

The reason that Jesus told this story is given in v. 11: the kingdom of God would be delayed, and He wanted His followers to know some of the implications of that delay. Chief among them is that we as believers have a job to do. We've been given resources to manage until the Lord returns (v. 13). These include our skills, jobs, time, wealth, mental capacities, physical bodies, and so on. Eventually we will give a full accounting for how we have used these (v. 15).

Jesus delivered this lesson in the form of a parable and was obviously talking about more than the management of money. Yet it's clear that He expects His followers to live out their everyday, temporal lives with an eye toward His return. He will ask us what we have done with our lives, and reward us accordingly.

This story is very similar to the parable of the talents, Matt. 25:14–30, probably a story that Jesus told frequently.

Rom. 14:12 and 1 Pet. 4:5 also speak of the accounting believers will make to God for what He has entrusted to us.

threw out. [13]Then the owner of the vineyard said, 'What
shall I do? I will send my beloved son; perhaps they will respect him.' [14]But when the tenants saw him, they discussed
it among themselves and said, 'This is the heir; let us kill
him so that the inheritance may be ours.' [15]So they threw
him out of the vineyard and killed him. What then will the
owner of the vineyard do to them? [16]He will come and destroy those tenants and give the vineyard to others." When
they heard this, they said, "Heaven forbid!" [17]But he looked
at them and said, "What then does this text mean:

'The stone that the builders rejected
has become the cornerstone'?[y]

[18]Everyone who falls on that stone will be broken to pieces;
and it will crush anyone on whom it falls." [19]When the
scribes and chief priests realized that he had told this parable against them, they wanted to lay hands on him at that
very hour, but they feared the people.

[y]Or *keystone*

Compassion and Anger in One Person?

CONSIDER THIS 19:41–46

It isn't easy to show both compassion and anger in appropriate ways. With most people it seems like it's one or the other, often in extremes—sugar-coated sentimentality or vicious, destructive rage, neither of which helps anyone.

In vv. 41–46, we see that Jesus acted out of both compassion and anger. As He drew near Jerusalem and saw the plight of its people, He was moved to grief, and His eyes filled with tears (v. 41). But before long He saw one source of the city's problem—the unjust moneychangers in

(continued on next page)

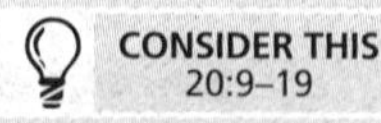

CONSIDER THIS 20:9–19

Owners or Tenants?

Are we the owners of possessions like money, houses, land, cars, clothing, TV sets, and so forth? Our culture tells us that we are. In fact, many messages tell us that significance is determined by how much we own and how much what we own is worth.

But the parable of the vineyard owner (vv. 9–19) challenges that way of looking at things. Jesus tells of tenants or workers who scheme to steal a vineyard from its owner rather than return its produce to him. They value the land, the trees, and the fruit more than people—they beat the owner's representatives (vv. 10–12)—and even more than life itself—they kill the owner's own son (vv. 14–15).

In the same way, the community leaders among Jesus' listeners harbored the same desire to kill Him (v. 19). At that point, however, they were prevented from acting by the rest of the people. But eventually they would have their way. Just as their forebears had rejected the prophets that God had sent, so they would now reject God's own Son in a futile effort to keep the nation under their control. But they would only succeed in bringing down God's judgment.

Jesus Tested about Tax Payment

20:20–26

20 So they watched him and sent
spies who pretended to be honest, in or-
der to trap him by what he said, so as to hand him over to
the jurisdiction and authority of the governor. [21]So they
asked him, "Teacher, we know that you are right in what
you say and teach, and you show deference to no one, but
teach the way of God in accordance with truth. [22]Is it lawful for us to pay taxes to the emperor, or not?" [23]But he perceived their craftiness and said to them, [24]"Show me a
denarius. Whose head and whose title does it bear?" They
said, "The emperor's." [25]He said to them, "Then give to the
emperor the things that are the emperor's, and to God the
things that are God's." [26]And they were not able in the presence of the people to trap him by what he said; and being
amazed by his answer, they became silent.

Jesus Tested about Resurrection

27 Some Sadducees, those who say there is no resurrection, came to him [28]and asked him a question, "Teacher,

◆ ◆ ◆ ◆ ◆ ◆ ◆ ◆ ◆ ◆ ◆ ◆ ◆ ◆ ◆ ◆

This parable challenges us to consider what God has entrusted to our care, and what He expects from us. No matter what He has given us, we are like tenants; the true Owner of all things is the Creator God. He has loaned us our lives, our families, our skills, and all our resources. He calls us to manage those gifts in a way that honors Him.

That means that we must resist getting so tied to our possessions and the accumulation of more possessions that we are tempted to resort to evil or even violence to keep them. We must hold things with the attitude of tenants, keeping in mind who really owns them—God who loaned them to us for His glory and the service of others. ◆

One of the most important resources that God has entrusted to us is our work. Whatever we do for a living, God wants us to do it as though we were working for Him. See "Who's the Boss?" Col. 3:22–24, and "People at Work," Heb. 2:7.

The Bible has much to offer believers today about how they handle their wealth. See "Christians and Money," 1 Tim. 6:6–19.

(continued from previous page)

the temple. With stern but controlled anger, He drove them out, taking care to put a name on their offense: "robbery" (vv. 45–46).

As you consider Jesus' responses in these two situations, it's worth asking: What moves you to tears? What injustices make you indignant? What productive or corrective action do you take in light of how you feel? Do you even allow yourself to react emotionally to the pain around you, or do you choose detached, dispassionate analysis or just plain apathy?

RETALIATION FOILED

CONSIDER THIS 20:20–26

When highly competitive people are overshadowed or intimidated they often resort to ugly tactics to try to regain their superiority. An unhealthy need for importance, success, and power can bring out the worst in anyone. Have you noticed this pattern among coworkers, family members, or yourself?

As community leaders saw Jesus once again gaining popularity and influence, they schemed to ensnare Him (vv. 9–19). They even enlisted agents for their plot (v. 20). Unfortunately, there always seems to be a ready supply of help for evil designs.

But Jesus refused to stoop to their methods (vv. 23–25). As they tried to undo Him, He foiled their plans with grace and truth.

Do you know how to respond to trickery or evil when it is intended for you?

Scripture challenges us that rather than being overcome by evil, we should overcome evil with good. See "Do Not Avenge Yourself," Rom. 12:19–21.

Moses wrote for us that if a man's brother dies, leaving a
wife but no children, the man[z] shall marry the widow and
raise up children for his brother. [29]Now there were seven
brothers; the first married, and died childless; [30]then the
second [31]and the third married her, and so in the same way
all seven died childless. [32]Finally the woman also died. [33]In
the resurrection, therefore, whose wife will the woman be?
For the seven had married her."

20:34

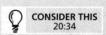

34 Jesus said to them, "Those who belong to this age marry and are given in
marriage; [35]but those who are considered worthy of a place
in that age and in the resurrection from the dead neither
marry nor are given in marriage. [36]Indeed they cannot die
anymore, because they are like angels and are children of
God, being children of the resurrection. [37]And the fact that

(Bible text continued on page 294)

[z]Gk *his brother*

"THOSE WHO BELONG TO THIS AGE MARRY AND ARE GIVEN IN MARRIAGE."
—Luke 20:34

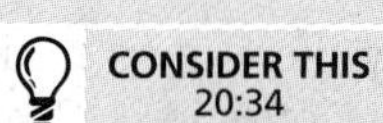

FAMILIES OF THE GOSPELS

As Jesus affirmed in His reply to the scheming Sadducees, marriages and families are fundamental institutions of life (v. 34). The Gospels support that view by portraying many different kinds of families, some large, some quite small. As the accompanying chart shows, some faced severe difficulties and "dysfunctions" not unlike those that families face today. The New Testament openly addresses these conditions and offers honest hope.

Judging by Acts and the New Testament letters, acceptance of the faith seemed often to be a decision of an entire family or clan during the early days of the church. See "Families of the Early Church," Acts 16:31–34.

FAMILIES OF THE GOSPELS

Gospel Appearances: Matthew Mark Luke John

Family Name	Description
•Zechariah •His wife Elizabeth •Son John the Baptist	The father is a temple priest on a rotating basis. He and his wife face a surprise pregnancy late in life that poses unique problems, especially for him. Later, their son John announces the arrival of the long-awaited Messiah.
•Joseph •His wife Mary •Jesus •Other sons and daughters	The father is a carpenter in the Galilean village of Nazareth. He and his fiancée face the delicate challenge of a supernatural pregnancy during their engagement. Their Child is delivered in a common stable and they become political refugees because of the new Baby. They struggle to understand their growing Son.
•Peter •His brother Andrew •Peter's mother-in-law	The family runs a fishing business on Lake Galilee. The two sons leave the business to follow Jesus. Later Peter's mother-in-law becomes sick as Jesus visits Peter's home.
•Zebedee •His wife, the mother of James and John •James •John	The family has a fishing business along with Peter's family on Lake Galilee. The mother approaches Jesus about positions of power for her sons in His kingdom. Both sons eventually hold significant leadership positions in the growing movement.
•The Herods	Powerful provincial rulers of Roman Palestine; the family name is remembered for violence, incest, and political intrigue. Herod the Great responds viciously to rumors of a new king born in the realm. Herod Antipas becomes a lover of his niece Herodias, who had been married to his brother Philip before leaving him for Antipas. The couple murders John the Baptist for criticizing their relationship.
•A Canaanite woman •Her demonized daughter	A despised minority woman displays relentless faith, winning Christ's approval and help for her daughter.
•A man •His epileptic son	Jesus heals the afflicted boy after His disciples could not.
•Jairus •His wife •His 12-year-old daughter	The father is a synagogue ruler who turns to Jesus when his daughter is on the verge of dying. When Jesus arrives the child is dead, but Jesus restores her to life.
•Anna	An 84-year-old widow and prophetess who serves in the temple rejoices to see the Christ child.
•A Roman centurion of Capernaum	Jesus heals his highly valued servant.
•A widow of Nain •Her only son	Jesus shows compassion on the woman by restoring her dead son to life.
•Joanna •Chuza, her husband	The wife of Herod's steward provides money for Jesus and joins several other women as His followers.
•Mary •Her sister Martha •Their brother Lazarus	Mary treats Jesus as a valued spiritual director. Sister Martha serves Him as a diligent worker. Brother Lazarus becomes a close friend. When he dies, Jesus restores him to life.
•A woman of Samaria •Her five previous husbands •Her lover	She meets Jesus at a well in Samaria and discovers Him to be the Living Water.
•A royal official of Cana •His son	After Jesus restores the boy to health, the entire household believes in Him.
•A woman caught in adultery	Jesus protects her from vindictive religious leaders.
•A man born blind •His parents	After Jesus restores his sight, the man is ostracized by the religious leaders for remaining loyal to Jesus.

◆

the dead are raised Moses himself showed, in the story
about the bush, where he speaks of the Lord as the God of
Abraham, the God of Isaac, and the God of Jacob. 38 Now
he is God not of the dead, but of the living; for to him all of
20:39 them are alive." 39 Then some of the
scribes answered, "Teacher, you have
spoken well." 40 For they no longer dared to ask him another question.

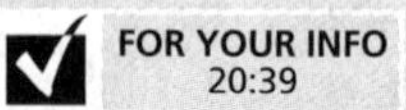

FOR YOUR INFO 20:39

SCRIBES

The scribes who challenged Jesus (v. 39) were members of a learned class in Israel who studied the Scriptures and served as copyists, editors, and teachers.

The era of the scribes began after the Jews returned from captivity in Babylon. Ezra the scribe directed that the Law be read before the entire nation (Neh. 8—10), signaling a return to exact observance of all the laws and rites that had been given. At first the priests were responsible for the scientific study and professional communication of this legal code. But that job eventually passed to the scribes. Unfortunately, their official interpretation of the meaning of the Law soon became more important than the Law itself.

From their position of strength, scribes began to enforce their rules and practices with binding authority. By the time of Jesus, they had become a new upper class. Large numbers of priests in Jerusalem joined the profession, including the Jewish historian, Josephus. Others came from the ordinary classes, including merchants, carpenters, tent makers, and even day laborers, like Hillel, who became a famous Jewish teacher. Most probably kept their former occupations, since scribes were not paid for their services and had to earn a living in other ways.

Prospective scribes went through a set course of study for several years, centered at Jerusalem. Students were in continual contact with the teacher, listening to his instruction. The disciple-scribe first had to master all the traditional material and a unique method of interpretation. The aim was to give the apprentice competence in making decisions on questions of religious legislation and justice.

The Question about David's Son

41 Then he said to them, "How can they say that the
Messiah[a] is David's son? 42For David himself says in the
book of Psalms,

'The Lord said to my Lord,
"Sit at my right hand,
43 until I make your enemies your footstool." '

44David thus calls him Lord; so how can he be his son?"
45 In the hearing of all the people he said to the[b] disciples, 46"Beware of the scribes, who like to walk around in
long robes, and love to be greeted with respect in the

[a]Or *the Christ* [b]Other ancient authorities read *his*

Within this course of study, according to tradition, there were "secrets" of interpretation to be learned, forbidden degrees of knowledge, which were not to be expounded before three or more persons. Some chapters in the Bible were to be explained only to sages, and certain teaching was hidden from the masses because they could not be trusted to understand and apply the Law.

Ordination required constant study, often beginning at age 14 and continuing to the age of 40. Once qualified, scribes could act as judges, be called rabbis, and occupy positions in law, government, and education. They joined the chief priests and aristocratic families who made up the Jewish council. They were held in great esteem by the people, as only ordained teachers could transmit and create the tradition.

Sometimes the Gospels refer to scribes as lawyers, a title identifying them as experts in the Mosaic Law (Matt. 22:35; Luke 7:30). In Jesus' day, they were usually associated with the Pharisees (Matt. 12:38; Mark 7:5; Luke 6:7). The two groups developed attitudes of pride based on their professional privileges. Jesus strongly warned against that posture and boldly attacked the religious hypocrisy of these religious leaders (Matt. 23). ◆

Luke records that the legal masters at Jerusalem were astonished at one boy's grasp of their material. *See "Jesus the Student," Luke 2:46–47.*

Jesus drew upon the image of a scribe in a parable He taught to show that we can never come to the end of what God has revealed. *See "Treasures New and Old," Matt. 13:52.*

**"NOW HE IS GOD NOT OF THE DEAD, BUT OF THE LIVING."
—Luke 20:38**

marketplaces, and to have the best seats in the synagogues
and places of honor at banquets. 47They devour widows'
houses and for the sake of appearance say long prayers.
They will receive the greater condemnation."

A Poor Widow's Contribution

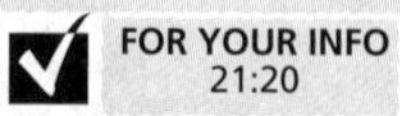

21 He looked up and saw rich
people putting their gifts into the
treasury; 2he also saw a poor widow put in two small cop-

FOR YOUR INFO 21:20

Jerusalem Surrounded

Those living in Jerusalem at the time of Christ had reason to believe His prediction that the city would eventually fall to an invading army (v. 20; see also 19:41–44). Political tensions were at a breaking point.

The Jews bitterly resented Rome's occupation of their homeland, which brought the corrupting influence of Greek culture, crushing taxes, and cruel government. Some, like the Zealots, fanned the flames of revolution by leading tax revolts and launching terrorist strikes against Roman troops and officials (see "Party Politics of Jesus' Day," Matt. 16:1).

The final chapter in the drama began in A.D. 66 when a skirmish broke out between Jews and Gentiles over the desecration of the synagogue at Caesarea. Unable to prevail politically, the Jews retaliated religiously by banning all sacrifices on behalf of foreigners, even for the emperor himself. Furthermore, access to the temple grounds at Jerusalem would be strictly limited to Jewish countrymen.

Meanwhile, the Roman procurator ordered an enormous payment from the temple treasury. The Jews balked and assumed that the ruler would back down. Instead, he unleashed troops on the city who raped and pillaged at will, even resorting to flogging and crucifixion. The slaughter claimed about 3,600 Jewish lives, including children.

The city went into riot. Arsonists torched official buildings along with the home of the high priest, long suspected of collusion with the empire. Elsewhere, Jews overran Roman fortresses and ambushed a legion of reinforcements, capturing arms for the revolt at Jerusalem. In the end, the Romans retreated, temporarily leaving the Holy City in the hands of the rebels.

per coins. [3]He said, "Truly I tell you, this poor widow has
put in more than all of them; [4]for all of them have contributed out of their abundance, but she out of her poverty
has put in all she had to live on."

Jesus Teaches about the End Times

5 When some were speaking about the temple, how it
was adorned with beautiful stones and gifts dedicated to
God, he said, [6]"As for these things that you see, the days

Yet no matter how brave or committed the Jewish revolutionaries may have been, they were no match for the professional armies of Rome. Emperor Nero dispatched Vespasian, his top general, to the region. Beginning in Galilee and working his way south, he systematically cut off Jerusalem's lines of supply—and escape—from Babylonia, the Mediterranean, and Egypt. By A.D. 70, he was poised to launch the final assault on Jerusalem.

However, Vespasian returned to Rome to succeed Nero as emperor, leaving his son Titus to complete the campaign. Advancing on the city from the north, the east, and the west, his legions erected siege walls and finally took the city, fulfilling Jesus' prophecy. Herod's temple was destroyed only three years after its completion (compare Luke 21:5–6), the priesthood and the council were abolished, and all Jews were expelled from the remains of the city.

Jesus wept to think of such carnage (Matt. 23:37–39). Today, as we read about Jesus' grim prediction and its tragic fulfillment in A.D. 70, we are challenged to ask a sobering question: If the destruction of Jerusalem came about just as Jesus said, what other prophecies did He make that might have to do with us, that we ought to take seriously? ◆

Jerusalem fell despite the fact that it was walled and well-situated for defense on two triangular ridges. See Matt. 23:37.

How Poor Was the Widow?

FOR YOUR INFO 21:1–4

Jesus called the widow in vv. 1–4 "poor." The word He used referred to a person so destitute that she was literally in danger of death.

It is hard to reckon what the two coins that she threw into the treasury would be worth in today's currency. But even in her day they were not much. Each copper coin was worth about one-thirty-second of a denarius, the daily wage of a soldier, which would be less than fifty cents today.

The important thing to note is that the two coins were "all she had to live on" (v. 4). She was truly destitute—the sort of widow who would later be eligible for support from the church (1 Tim. 5:5). Nevertheless, she gave generously to the temple. Jesus praised her for her faithfulness, even though it meant sacrifice.

In doing so, the Lord showed that God's accounting differs from ours. He pays attention to our attitudes in giving more than the absolute dollar amount of our gifts.

Widows were common in the ancient world, and usually poor, as their gender was a disadvantage in the ancient economies. However, Luke tells about one instance when the church stepped in to help struggling widows. See "A Growing Movement Confronts Ethnic Prejudice," Acts 6:2–6. See also "Widows," 1 Tim. 5:3.

will come when not one stone will be left upon another; all
will be thrown down."
7 They asked him, "Teacher, when will this be, and what
will be the sign that this is about to take place?" 8And he
said, "Beware that you are not led astray; for many will
come in my name and say, 'I am he!'[c] and, 'The time is
near!'[d] Do not go after them.
9 "When you hear of wars and insurrections, do not be
terrified; for these things must take place first, but the end
will not follow immediately." 10Then he said to them, "Nation will rise against nation, and kingdom against kingdom;
11there will be great earthquakes, and in various places
famines and plagues; and there will be dreadful portents
and great signs from heaven.
12 "But before all this occurs, they will arrest you and
persecute you; they will hand you over to synagogues and
prisons, and you will be brought before kings and governors because of my name. 13This will give you an opportunity to testify. 14So make up your minds not to prepare your
defense in advance; 15for I will give you words[e] and a wisdom that none of your opponents will be able to withstand
or contradict. 16You will be betrayed even by parents and
brothers, by relatives and friends; and they will put some of
you to death. 17You will be hated by all because of my
name. 18But not a hair of your head will perish. 19By your
endurance you will gain your souls.

"I WILL GIVE YOU WORDS AND A WISDOM. . . ." —Luke 21:15

21:20 see pg. 296

20 "When you see Jerusalem surrounded by armies, then know that its
desolation has come near.[f] 21Then those in Judea must flee
to the mountains, and those inside the city must leave it,
and those out in the country must not enter it; 22for these
are days of vengeance, as a fulfillment of all that is written.
23Woe to those who are pregnant and to those who are
nursing infants in those days! For there will be great distress on the earth and wrath against this people; 24they will
fall by the edge of the sword and be taken away as captives
among all nations; and Jerusalem will be trampled on by
the Gentiles, until the times of the Gentiles are fulfilled.
25 "There will be signs in the sun, the moon, and the
stars, and on the earth distress among nations confused by
the roaring of the sea and the waves. 26People will faint
from fear and foreboding of what is coming upon the
world, for the powers of the heavens will be shaken. 27Then
they will see 'the Son of Man coming in a cloud' with
power and great glory. 28Now when these things begin to
take place, stand up and raise your heads, because your redemption is drawing near."

[c]Gk *I am* [d]Or *at hand* [e]Gk *a mouth* [f]Or *is at hand*

29 Then he told them a parable: "Look at the fig tree and
all the trees; 30as soon as they sprout leaves you can see for
yourselves and know that summer is already near. 31So also,
when you see these things taking place, you know that the
kingdom of God is near. 32Truly I tell you, this generation
will not pass away until all things have taken place.
33Heaven and earth will pass away, but my words will not
pass away.

21:34–36

34 "Be on guard so that your hearts
are not weighed down with dissipation
and drunkenness and the worries of this life, and that day
catch you unexpectedly, 35like a trap. For it will come upon
all who live on the face of the whole earth. 36Be alert at all
times, praying that you may have the strength to escape all
these things that will take place, and to stand before the
Son of Man."

37 Every day he was teaching in the temple, and at night
he would go out and spend the night on the Mount of
Olives, as it was called. 38And all the people would get up
early in the morning to listen to him in the temple.

Judas Conspires to Betray Jesus

22 Now the festival of Unleavened Bread, which is
called the Passover, was near. 2The chief priests and
the scribes were looking for a way to put Jesus[g] to death,
for they were afraid of the people.

3 Then Satan entered into Judas called Iscariot, who was
one of the twelve; 4he went away and conferred with the
chief priests and officers of the temple police about how he
might betray him to them. 5They were greatly pleased and
agreed to give him money. 6So he consented and began to
look for an opportunity to betray him to them when no
crowd was present.

Jesus and the Twelve Eat the Passover

22:7

7 Then came the day of Unleavened
Bread, on which the Passover lamb had

[g]Gk *him*

PASSOVER

FOR YOUR INFO 22:7 **The Passover and Festival of Unleavened Bread (v. 7) was the first of three great festivals of the Hebrews.**

The name Passover recalls the deliverance of Israel from slavery in Egypt (Ex. 12:1—13:16). God sent His angel to kill all the firstborn sons of the Egyptians in order to persuade Pharaoh to let His people go. Hebrew families were instructed to sacrifice a lamb and smear its blood on the doorpost of their house as a signal to God that His angel should "pass over" them during the judgment.

Passover was observed on the fourteenth day of the first month, Abib (March-April), with the service beginning in the evening (Lev. 23:6). It was on the evening of this day that Israel left Egypt in haste. Unleavened bread was used in the celebration as a reminder that the people had no time to leaven their bread before they ate their final meal as slaves in Egypt.

In New Testament times, Passover became a pilgrim festival. Large numbers gathered in Jerusalem to observe the annual celebration. Thus an unusually large crowd was on hand to take part in the events surrounding Jesus' entry into the city (Luke 19:37–39) and His arrest, trial, and crucifixion (23:18, 27, 35, 48). Apparently many stayed on until the Festival of Pentecost, when they heard Peter's persuasive sermon (Acts 2:1–41).

Like the blood of the lambs which saved the Hebrews from destruction in Egypt, the blood of Jesus, the ultimate Passover Lamb, saves us from the power of sin and death.

The Cares of This Life

A CLOSER LOOK 21:34–36

Jesus warned us about becoming weighed down with the "cares of this life" (v. 34). He was not suggesting that everyday affairs are unimportant. But isn't it all too easy to get so wrapped up in the pressures and pace of life that we ignore our Lord? For more on this critical issue, see "Don't Worry!" Matt. 6:19–34.

In celebrating His final Passover meal, Jesus ate food that was highly symbolic. See Matt. 26:19.

Passover was one of three major festivals celebrated by the Jews. To find out about the others, see the table, "Jewish Festivals," Luke 2:42.

LEADERSHIP EQUALS HUMILITY?

CONSIDER THIS 22:24–27 **Are you in a position of leadership in your job, in government, in your family, or in your church? In vv. 24–27, Jesus shows that biblical leadership starts with humility, by *serving* others.**

The autocratic, authoritarian leadership style has fallen out of favor among many today. Yet a subtle, far more powerful approach has appeared, characterized by manipulation and selfish ambition. Masking their true intentions, many new-style "leaders" pretend to offer a "win-win" arrangement; but they have no real concern for others, except insofar as others can help them achieve their objectives.

Both styles are out of the question if we want to lead with Christ-likeness. He asks us to take the posture of a *servant*—to genuinely concern ourselves with the rights, the needs, and the welfare of those we lead. Christ Himself has provided the example of true servant-leadership: not to be served, but to serve and to give (Matt. 20:28).

Paul encouraged believers to develop the same attitude that Christ had. See "Humility—The Scandalous Virtue," Phil. 2:3.

to be sacrificed. 8So Jesus[h] sent Peter and John, saying, "Go
and prepare the Passover meal for us that we may eat it."
9They asked him, "Where do you want us to make preparations for it?" 10"Listen," he said to them, "when you have
entered the city, a man carrying a jar of water will meet
you; follow him into the house he enters 11and say to the
owner of the house, 'The teacher asks you, "Where is the
guest room, where I may eat the Passover with my disciples?"' 12He will show you a large room upstairs, already
furnished. Make preparations for us there." 13So they went
and found everything as he had told them; and they prepared the Passover meal.

14 When the hour came, he took his place at the table,
and the apostles with him. 15He said to them, "I have eagerly desired to eat this Passover with you before I suffer;
16for I tell you, I will not eat it[i] until it is fulfilled in the
kingdom of God." 17Then he took a cup, and after giving
thanks he said, "Take this and divide it among yourselves;
18for I tell you that from now on I will not drink of the fruit
of the vine until the kingdom of God comes." 19Then he
took a loaf of bread, and when he had given thanks, he
broke it and gave it to them, saying, "This is my body,
which is given for you. Do this in remembrance of me."
20And he did the same with the cup after supper, saying,
"This cup that is poured out for you is the new covenant in
my blood.[j] 21But see, the one who betrays me is with me,
and his hand is on the table. 22For the Son of Man is going
as it has been determined, but woe to that one by whom he
is betrayed!" 23Then they began to ask one another, which
one of them it could be who would do this.

22:24–27

22:25 see pg. 302

22:24–30

24 A dispute also arose among them
as to which one of them was to be
regarded as the greatest. 25But he said to
them, "The kings of the Gentiles lord it
over them; and those in authority over them are called
benefactors. 26But not so with you;
rather the greatest among you must be-
come like the youngest, and the leader like one who serves.
27For who is greater, the one who is at the table or the one
who serves? Is it not the one at the table? But I am among
you as one who serves.

28 "You are those who have stood by me in my trials;
29and I confer on you, just as my Father has conferred on
me, a kingdom, 30so that you may eat and drink at my table
in my kingdom, and you will sit on thrones judging the
twelve tribes of Israel.

[h]Gk *he* [i]Other ancient authorities read *never eat it again* [j]Other ancient authorities lack, in whole or in part, verses 19b-20 (*which is given . . . in my blood*)

31 "Simon, Simon, listen! Satan has demanded[k] to sift all
of you like wheat, 32but I have prayed for you that your
own faith may not fail; and you, when once you have
turned back, strengthen your brothers." 33And he said to
him, "Lord, I am ready to go with you to prison and to
death!" 34Jesus[l] said, "I tell you, Peter, the cock will not
crow this day, until you have denied three times that you
know me."

35 He said to them, "When I sent you out without a
purse, bag, or sandals, did you lack anything?" They said,
"No, not a thing." 36He said to them, "But now, the one who
has a purse must take it, and likewise a bag. And the one
who has no sword must sell his cloak and buy one. 37For I
tell you, this scripture must be fulfilled in me, 'And he was
counted among the lawless'; and indeed what is written
about me is being fulfilled." 38They said, "Lord, look, here
are two swords." He replied, "It is enough."

Jesus Prays on the Mount of Olives

22:39–46
see pg. 305

39 He came out and went, as was his
custom, to the Mount of Olives; and the
disciples followed him. 40When he reached the place, he
said to them, "Pray that you may not come into the time of
trial."[m] 41Then he withdrew from them about a stone's
throw, knelt down, and prayed, 42"Father, if you are willing,
remove this cup from me; yet, not my will but yours be
done." ⟦43Then an angel from heaven appeared to him and
gave him strength. 44In his anguish he prayed more
earnestly, and his sweat became like great drops of blood
falling down on the ground.⟧[n] 45When he got up from
prayer, he came to the disciples and found them sleeping
because of grief, 46and he said to them, "Why are you sleeping? Get up and pray that you may not come into the time
of trial."[m]

The Arrest of Jesus

47 While he was still speaking, suddenly a crowd came,
and the one called Judas, one of the twelve, was leading
them. He approached Jesus to kiss him; 48but Jesus said to
him, "Judas, is it with a kiss that you are betraying the Son
of Man?" 49When those who were around him saw what
was coming, they asked, "Lord, should we strike with the

(Bible text continued on page 306)

[k]*Or has obtained permission* [l]Gk *He* [m]*Or into temptation* [n]Other ancient authorities lack verses 43 and 44

The Quest for Greatness

CONSIDER THIS 22:24–30 **Is it wrong to desire greatness—to be a great salesperson, a great athlete, a great scholar, or a great performer? Shouldn't we all seek excellence in what we do? Does God not want us to experience great achievements?**

Jesus' words to the disciples in vv. 24–30 touch on this complex issue. As He did so often, the Lord challenged the motives of His followers rather than their desires. He realized that they wanted greatness for its own sake, in order to lord it over others. They sought position and power as means to personal gain, not service to others.

Jesus defined leadership for His disciples in a unique way. See "Servant-Leaders," Matt. 20:25–28.

FOR YOUR INFO 22:25

Roman Politics in the First Century A.D.

Jesus and His followers were well acquainted with the "kings of the Gentiles" and their authority (v. 25). Rome exercised a small but effective government over Judea and the other territories in its empire. The hierarchy of officials included:

Roman Leadership Positions

Position or title	Name and/or New Testament example	Description of position	Historical significance
Emperor or Caesar	Augustus Caesar, 31 B.C.–A.D. 14 (Luke 2:1); Tiberius, A.D. 14–37 (Luke 3:1); Gaius Caligula, A.D. 37–41; Claudius, A.D. 41–54 (Acts 18:2); Nero, A.D. 54–68; Galba, A.D. 68–69; Otho, A.D. 69; Vitellius, A.D. 69; Vespasian, A.D. 69–79; Titus, A.D. 79–81; Domitian, A.D. 81–96; Nerva, A.D. 96–98; Trajan, A.D. 98–117	•Sovereign ruler of the Roman Empire. •Augustus (Octavian) ruled with as much practicality and goodwill as possible. •A standing army was needed to preserve law and order only in those outlying provinces still struggling with conflict. Wherever possible, provincial rule was delegated to local authorities or to Roman senators, called proconsuls.	•The title *Caesar* was taken from the family name of Julius Caesar, father of the Roman Empire.
Proconsul or Senator	Junius Gallio in Achaia (Acts 18:12); Sergius Paulus in Cyprus (Acts 13:7–12)	•Rulers of the *senatorial* provinces. •The Senate met twice each month for legislative, administrative, and judicial purposes. •Senators were chosen by lot to rule in the provinces. •In the time of Augustus, the Senate comprised 600 members of the Roman aristocracy. •Proconsuls were appointed for one-year terms and tended to act expediently, enriching themselves before returning to Rome, where they remained politically active.	•Senatorial provinces were usually older, more stable, and nearer to Rome. Those named in the New Testament include Achaea, Asia, Bithynia, Crete, Cyrene, Cyprus, Macedonia, and Pontus. •Roman Law was approved by the Senate and implemented locally by procurators, proconsuls, and, when necessary, the Roman army. •When the silversmiths of Ephesus complained against Paul (Acts 19:38), proconsuls were mentioned as the appropriate officials to settle the dispute.
Procurator	Pilate (Luke 3:1); Felix (Acts 23:24); Festus (Acts 24:27)	•Relatively low-ranking rulers of the *imperial* provinces. •A procurator could gain political freedoms for the region he governed by demonstrating the area's loyalty to Rome and reverence for the emperor.	•Imperial provinces, such as Judea, tended to lie on the frontiers of the empire, in areas of conflict. •They required large standing armies to maintain order under the command of appointed governors.

(continued)

Procurator *(continued)*		•Privileges might include self–government, freedom from taxation, and freedom of religion. •The procurator had to maintain law and order in his jurisdiction, putting down any threat to the social order, and, if necessary, calling in the Roman army.	•Provinces mentioned in the New Testament include Judea, Syria, Galatia, Cappadocia and Egypt.
Legate (also called governor)	Quirinius, in Syria (Luke 2:2)	•A subordinate ruler under a proconsul who commanded troops, handled administrative tasks and, in the larger provinces, collected revenue.	•At the time of Augustus, there were 11 senatorial provinces (under senatorial supervision) and 21 imperial provinces (directly under the emperor or his agents).
Prefect (also called governor)		•Commanded non–Roman auxiliary troops and governed the smaller provinces, mostly as chief financial officers.	•Senators, procurators, legates, and prefects all preferred that local leaders handle most legal problems; theirs was the court of last resort.
King	Herod the Great (Matt. 2:1); Herod Agrippa (Acts 25:24)	•Under Rome, little more than puppet governors appointed by the emperor.	•Even Egypt was ruled by a viceroy representing Rome as a successor to the Pharaohs and the Ptolemaic dynasty (323–30 B.C.). They ruled in the wake of Alexander the Great.
Tetrarch	Herod Antipas (Matt. 14:1; Acts 13:1); Lysanias; Herod Philip (Luke 3:1)	•Literally "ruler of a fourth part." •The sons of Herod the Great disputed their father's will in 4 B.C. Archelaus received half of his father's territory, making him an ethnarch; Antipas and Philip both received one–fourth and became tetrarchs.	•*Tetrarch* came to designate any petty prince or local magistrate in the Middle East.
Praetorian Guard	Paul was "kept in Herod's Praetorium" (Acts 23:35)	•Official guard of the Roman emperor and the elite corps of the empire. •Their salaries and privileges exceeded those of other Roman soldiers.	•Originally stationed in Rome, the Praetorian Guard was later dispersed throughout the provinces. •The Guard was disbanded in the third century A.D., due to their threat to the emperor himself.
Centurion	The man who showed greater faith than any in Israel (Luke 7:2–10); the man who believed Jesus to be the Son of God after His death on the cross (Matt. 27:54; Mark 15:39; Luke 23:47)	•A non–commissioned officer commanding at least 100 soldiers. •Most served for life, much longer than the required 20 years. •Sixty centuries made up a *legion,* a force of 6,000 troops.	
Sergeant		•A local law enforcement officer.	

In addition to the kinds of officials listed, local leadership for each region might include priests, landlords, and merchant guilds. In Judea, rival factions attempted to gain influence with Rome, creating a dangerous instability. The conflicts came to a head after Jesus' departure, and Rome finally sent troops that laid siege to Jerusalem and destroyed it in A.D. 70. ◆

Luke mentions by name some of the Roman officials of the empire and Palestine in the first century. See "New Testament Political Rulers," Luke 3:1.

In addition to the Roman authorities listed here, there were at least five major political parties among the Jews in the first century A.D. See "Party Politics of Jesus' Day," Matt. 16:1.

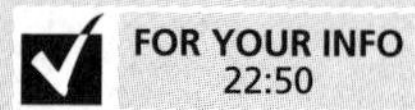

FOR YOUR INFO
22:50

Peter's Poor Aim

Total confusion reigned in the Garden of Gethsemane as Judas led a band to arrest Jesus. The chaos boiled over when Peter drew a sword and swept the air with a stroke that lopped off the ear of Malchus, one of the arresting party (v. 50; John 18:10).

Peter's impulsive act could have spelled disaster. Jesus and the Twelve were completely outnumbered and ill equipped to defend themselves against a mob that included soldiers from the Roman cohort. The arresting party might even have been looking for a pretext to use violence against this supposedly dangerous rabbi. Fortunately, Jesus acted swiftly to regain control of the situation by healing Malchus' ear and addressing the crowd (vv. 51–53).

Another stroke of fortune was probably Peter's bad aim. It's interesting that the account details an injury to Malchus' right ear. Modern readers might assume that Pe-

CONSIDER THIS
22:56–57

The Servant Girl

Fear of the truth and its consequences can lead even the strongest among us to hide behind lies and half-truths. So it was for Peter, the stouthearted fisherman and leader among the apostles. No doubt fearing for his life as he sat in the courtyard of the high priest's house, Peter denied to a servant girl that he had any connection with Jesus (vv. 56–57).

Normally Peter would have paid little attention to the young woman, who was merely a doorkeeper in Caiaphas' household (John 18:15–17; see "Caiaphas," Matt. 26:3). But having watched his Master's arrest and perhaps having learned from John, who gained him access to the courtyard, about the events taking place inside, Peter told an outright lie. Apparently he feared what the girl might say or do if he admitted to being one of Jesus' followers.

It's interesting to contrast this situation with Peter's later encounter with another doorkeeper, the servant girl Rhoda (Acts 12:1–17). On that occasion, it was not Peter who was afraid of the servant girl, but the servant girl who was astonished and overjoyed at seeing Peter, who had been miraculously delivered from jail. By that point, of

ter would have swung his sword laterally, with the blade parallel to the ground. But a first-century swordsman was more likely to sweep out his sword and come down on the head of an opponent with a vertical, chopping stroke. In battle, the idea was to place a well-aimed blow on the seam of an enemy's helmet, splitting it open and wounding the head.

Perhaps this was Peter's intention, but he aimed wide to the left. Perhaps, too, Malchus saw the blow coming and ducked to his left, exposing his right ear.

In any event, Peter caused no mortal injury. But he certainly drew attention to himself. Malchus happened to be a servant of Caiaphas, the high priest (see Matt. 26:3). Later, one of Malchus' relatives recognized Peter warming himself by a fire outside Pilate's court. "Did I not see you in the garden?" he asked suspiciously, a claim that Peter denied (John 18:26). ◆

◆ ◆ ◆ ◆ ◆ ◆ ◆ ◆ ◆ ◆ ◆ ◆ ◆ ◆ ◆ ◆

course, Peter had repented of denying Jesus and had received the Holy Spirit, who filled him with power and boldness to stand before not only the high priest (4:5–6, 18–21), but King Herod as well.

What place in your life is so vulnerable that you would tell an outright lie—even to someone that you would normally regard as inconsequential—rather than reveal the truth? Like Peter, are you afraid of the consequences of being identified with Jesus? If so, you need a dose of the Spirit's power to give you the courage to be honest (see Acts 1:8). ◆

The servant girl was among the many domestics of the ancient world who helped women attend to the chores of their households and provided care for children. Find out more about this large class of servants in "Slaves," Rom. 6:16.

Runaway slaves faced severe punishment, even death, if caught and returned to their masters. However, the gospel produced a different outcome for one slave and his owner. See the introduction to Philemon.

Prayerlessness Comes Before a Fall

CONSIDER THIS 22:39–46 **Temptation is tough. It's a test. It's an enticement to do wrong. It may involve great pleasure, a chance to escape risk, or illegitimate gain. Whatever the offering, it's usually attractive.**

But Scripture calls giving in to tempting opportunities sin. It even warns us that repeatedly giving way to temptation can result in falling away permanently with a total loss of interest in returning to God (Heb. 6:6–8, according to one interpretation). Clearly we need God's strength, and wisdom to flee (1 Cor. 6:18; 1 Tim. 6:11).

As Jesus and His closest companions faced great danger, they were afraid and tired (vv. 42–45). Jesus knew how vulnerable and confused that condition can make a person. He urged His followers to join Him in prayer so that they would not fall into temptation (v. 40). They could not face the trials to come without new strength from God.

Earlier Jesus had taught His followers to ask the Father not to lead them into temptation (Matt. 6:13). There is no sin in being tempted. In fact, temptation is a sign that our spiritual lives are strong enough to recognize values that conflict with godliness. But giving in is sin. That's why it's crucial to take time to declare to God our weakness, weariness, and need for help in the midst of testing.

It may also help to have others pray with us, just as Jesus did in His hour of need. Do you have others you can turn to for prayer in times of difficulty? Are you available when others have that need?

One of the best ways that we as believers can support each other is to be available for encouraging prayer. See "Are You a Friend of Someone in Need?" Luke 5:17–26.

22:50
see pg. 304

sword?" 50Then one of them struck the slave of the high priest and cut off his right ear. 51But Jesus said, "No more of this!" And he touched his ear and healed him. 52Then Jesus said to the chief priests, the officers of the temple police, and the elders who had come for him, "Have you come out with swords and clubs as if I were a bandit? 53When I was with you day after day in the temple, you did not lay hands on me. But this is your hour, and the power of darkness!"

"This is your hour, and the power of darkness!" —Luke 22:53

Peter Denies Knowing the Lord

54 Then they seized him and led him away, bringing him into the high priest's house. But Peter was following at a distance. 55When they had kindled a fire in the middle of the courtyard and sat down together, Peter sat among them.

22:56–57
see pg. 304

56Then a servant-girl, seeing him in the firelight, stared at him and said, "This man also was with him." 57But he denied it, saying, "Woman, I do not know him." 58A little later someone else, on seeing him, said, "You also are one of them." But Peter said, "Man, I am not!" 59Then about an hour later still another kept insisting, "Surely this man also was with him; for he is a Galilean." 60But Peter said, "Man, I do not know what you are talking about!" At that moment, while he was still speaking, the cock crowed. 61The Lord turned and looked at Peter. Then Peter remembered the word of the Lord, how he had said to him, "Before the cock crows today, you will deny me three times." 62And he went out and wept bitterly.

Jesus Is Beaten

63 Now the men who were holding Jesus began to mock him and beat him; 64they also blindfolded him and kept asking him, "Prophesy! Who is it that struck you?" 65They kept heaping many other insults on him.

Jesus Is Condemned by the Council

66 When day came, the assembly of the elders of the people, both chief priests and scribes, gathered together, and they brought him to their council. 67They said, "If you are the Messiah,[o] tell us." He replied, "If I tell you, you will

[o]Or *the Christ*

not believe; 68 and if I question you, you will not answer.
69 But from now on the Son of Man will be seated at the
right hand of the power of God." 70 All of them asked, "Are
you, then, the Son of God?" He said to them, "You say that
I am." 71 Then they said, "What further testimony do we
need? We have heard it ourselves from his own lips!"

Jesus Is Brought to Pilate and Herod

23:1–25

23 Then the assembly rose as a
body and brought Jesus[p] before
Pilate. 2 They began to accuse him, saying, "We found this
man perverting our nation, forbidding us to pay taxes to
the emperor, and saying that he himself is the Messiah, a
king."[q] 3 Then Pilate asked him, "Are you the king of the
Jews?" He answered, "You say so." 4 Then Pilate said to the
chief priests and the crowds, "I find no basis for an accusation against this man." 5 But they were insistent and said,
"He stirs up the people by teaching throughout all Judea,
from Galilee where he began even to this place."

6 When Pilate heard this, he asked whether the man was
a Galilean. 7 And when he learned that he was under
Herod's jurisdiction, he sent him off to Herod, who was

23:8

himself in Jerusalem at that time. 8 When
Herod saw Jesus, he was very glad, for
he had been wanting to see him for a long time, because he
had heard about him and was hoping to see him perform
some sign. 9 He questioned him at some length, but Jesus[r]
gave him no answer. 10 The chief priests and the scribes
stood by, vehemently accusing him. 11 Even Herod with his
soldiers treated him with contempt and mocked him; then
he put an elegant robe on him, and sent him back to Pilate.

(Bible text continued on page 309)

[p]Gk *him* [q]Or *is an anointed king* [r]Gk *he*

Herod Finally Meets Jesus

A CLOSER LOOK 23:8 *In v. 8, Herod Antipas finally meets an old nemesis. Having allowed himself to be manipulated into executing John the Baptist (Matt. 14:1–12; Mark 6:17–28), he was frightened by the coming of Jesus, wondering whether John had come back to life (Luke 9:7–9). Jesus' enemies tried to make use of that fear, but to no avail (13:31–33). For more on Herod and his infamous family, see "The Herods," Acts 12:1–2.*

Convenience Makes for Odd Choices

CONSIDER THIS 23:1–25 **Faced with difficulty, most of us tend to choose convenience and expediency over sacrifice and integrity, particularly when the personal costs are likely to be high. Our desire to avoid negative outcomes can stir up odd reactions in us.**

Jesus triggered some odd choices of convenience and expediency in the political system of Jerusalem. For example:

- **Two leaders who had been longtime enemies suddenly became allies and friends (v. 12).**
- **Pilate chose to free Barabbas, an insurrectionist and murderer (v. 19), and allow the execution of Jesus, the innocent man (v. 22), in order to maintain order and appease an angry mob (vv. 23–25).**
- **The rulers chose popularity with the people, and the people chose fawning subservience to the rulers, over justice for the accused (vv. 23–24; Matt. 27:20, 25; John 19:15).**

These kinds of sinful tendencies are part of the reason Christ came to die. He wants to save us from opportunistic, self-serving ways of life, because ultimately they lead to death. Evil alliances, political manipulation, rigged votes, and injustice are a stench in the nostrils of God (Is. 2:5—3:26).

As believers, we may have to make odd choices, too. But ours should be rooted in Christlike values of love, truth, and humility, rather than expedience, popularity, and selfishness.

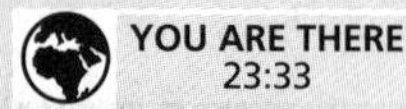

CRUCIFIXION

The Romans used one of the most painful methods of torture ever devised to put Jesus to death (v. 33). Crucifixion was used by many nations of the ancient world, including Assyria, Media, and Persia. The idea may have originated from the practice of hanging up the bodies of executed persons on stakes for public display. This discouraged civil disobedience and mocked defeated military foes (Gen. 40:19; 1 Sam. 31:8–13).

Ancient writers do not tell us much about when or how execution on a stake or cross came about, or how it was carried out. But we know that the Assyrians executed captured enemies by forcing their living bodies down onto pointed stakes. This barbaric cruelty was not actually crucifixion but impalement.

No one knows when the crossbeam was added. But Ezra 6:11 provides clear evidence that the Persians continued to use impalement as a method of execution. Likewise, the references to "hanging" in Esther 2:23 and 5:14 probably refer to either impalement or crucifixion. Rope hangings were not used in Persia during the biblical period. The word translated "gallows" refers not to a scaffold but to a pole or stake.

Crucifixion on a stake or cross was practiced by the Greeks, notably Alexander the Great, who hung 2,000 people on crosses when the city of Tyre was destroyed. During the period between Greek and Roman control of Palestine, the Jewish ruler Alexander Jannaeus crucified 800 Pharisees who opposed him. But such executions were condemned as detestable and abnormal even in that day as well as by the later Jewish historian, Josephus.

From the early days of the Roman Republic, death on the cross was used for rebellious slaves and bandits, although Roman citizens were rarely subjected to it. The practice continued well beyond the New Testament period as one of the supreme punishments for military and political crimes such as desertion, spying, revealing secrets, rebellion, and sedition. However, following the conversion of Constantine, the cross became a sacred symbol and its use as a means of execution was abolished.

Crucifixion involved attaching the victim with nails through the wrists or with leather thongs to a crossbeam attached to a vertical stake. Sometimes blocks or pins were put on the stake to give the victim support as he hung suspended from the crossbeam. At times the feet were also nailed to the vertical stake. As the victim hung dangling by the arms, blood could no longer circulate to his vital organs. Only by supporting himself on the seat or pin could he gain some relief.

But gradually exhaustion set in, and death followed, although usually not for several days. If the victim had been severely beaten, he would not live that long. To hasten death, the executioners sometimes broke the victim's legs with a club. Then he could no longer support his body to keep blood circulating, and death by suffocation quickly followed. Usually bodies were left to rot or to be eaten by scavengers.

To the Jewish people, crucifixion represented the most disgusting form of death: "anyone hung on a tree is under God's curse" (Deut. 21:23). Yet the Jewish council sought and obtained Roman authorization to have Jesus crucified (Mark 15:13–15).

The apostle Paul summed up the crucial importance of His manner of death when he wrote, "We proclaim Christ crucified, a stumbling block to Jews and foolishness to Gentiles, but to those who are called, both Jews and Greeks, Christ the power of God and the wisdom of God" (1 Cor. 1:23–24). Out of the ugliness and agony of crucifixion, God accomplished the greatest good of all—the redemption of sinners. ◆

12That same day Herod and Pilate became friends with each
other; before this they had been enemies.

Pilate Sentences Jesus to Death

13 Pilate then called together the chief priests, the leaders, and the people, 14and said to them, "You brought me
this man as one who was perverting the people; and here I
have examined him in your presence and have not found
this man guilty of any of your charges against him. 15Nei-
ther has Herod, for he sent him back to us. Indeed, he has
done nothing to deserve death. 16I will therefore have him
flogged and release him."[s]

18 Then they all shouted out together, "Away with this
fellow! Release Barabbas for us!" 19(This was a man who
had been put in prison for an insurrection that had taken
place in the city, and for murder.) 20Pilate, wanting to release Jesus, addressed them again; 21but they kept shouting,
"Crucify, crucify him!" 22A third time he said to them,
"Why, what evil has he done? I have found in him no
ground for the sentence of death; I will therefore have him
flogged and then release him." 23But they kept urgently demanding with loud shouts that he should be crucified; and
their voices prevailed. 24So Pilate gave his verdict that their
demand should be granted. 25He released the man they
asked for, the one who had been put in prison for insurrection and murder, and he handed Jesus over as they wished.

"HE HAS DONE NOTHING TO DESERVE DEATH."
—Luke 23:15

The Crucifixion

26 As they led him away, they seized a man, Simon of
Cyrene, who was coming from the country, and they laid
the cross on him, and made him carry it behind Jesus. 27A
great number of the people followed him, and among them
were women who were beating their breasts and wailing for
him. 28But Jesus turned to them and said, "Daughters of
Jerusalem, do not weep for me, but weep for yourselves
and for your children. 29For the days are surely coming
when they will say, 'Blessed are the barren, and the wombs
that never bore, and the breasts that never nursed.' 30Then
they will begin to say to the mountains, 'Fall on us'; and to

[s]Here, or after verse 19, other ancient authorities add verse 17, *Now he was obliged to release someone for them at the festival*

the hills, 'Cover us.' 31For if they do this when the wood is
green, what will happen when it is dry?"
32 Two others also, who were criminals, were led away
23:33 see pg. 308
to be put to death with him. 33When
they came to the place that is called The
Skull, they crucified Jesus[t] there with the criminals, one on
his right and one on his left. ⟦34Then Jesus said, "Father,
forgive them; for they do not know what they are doing."⟧[u]
And they cast lots to divide his clothing. 35And the people
stood by, watching; but the leaders scoffed at him, saying,
"He saved others; let him save himself if he is the Messiah[v]
of God, his chosen one!" 36The soldiers also mocked him,
coming up and offering him sour wine, 37and saying, "If
you are the King of the Jews, save yourself!" 38There was
also an inscription over him,[w] "This is the King of the
Jews."
39 One of the criminals who were hanged there kept de-

[t]Gk *him* [u]Other ancient authorities lack the sentence *Then Jesus . . . what they are doing* [v]Or *the Christ* [w]Other ancient authorities add *written in Greek and Latin and Hebrew* (that is, *Aramaic*)

CONSIDER THIS
23:49

Jesus—A Rabbi for Women, Too

Luke mentions that Jesus had a following among the women of His day (v. 49; see "The Women Who Followed Jesus," 8:1–3). From what we know about Jewish culture in the first century, their presence and loyalty probably offended many members of the community.

Jewish tradition frowned upon women studying with rabbis. Some rabbis actually considered it sinful to teach women the Law. Women were permitted in the synagogues, but custom required them to sit apart from the men. Menstruation made them unclean each month according to the Law (Lev. 15:19). Women were often viewed as the cause of men's sexual sins. To prevent any temptation, Jewish men were instructed not to speak to a woman in public—even to one's wife. And they were never to touch a woman in public.

But not only did Jesus speak to women in public (John 4:27), he dared to take them by the hand (Mark 5:41). He encouraged a woman who desired to follow Him, even when it conflicted with her household duties (Luke 10:42). And as He tried to help people understand the kingdom of

riding[x] him and saying, "Are you not the Messiah?[y] Save
yourself and us!" 40But the other rebuked him, saying, "Do
you not fear God, since you are under the same sentence of
condemnation? 41And we indeed have been condemned
justly, for we are getting what we deserve for our deeds, but
this man has done nothing wrong." 42Then he said, "Jesus,
remember me when you come into[z] your kingdom." 43He
replied, "Truly I tell you, today you will be with me in Paradise."

44 It was now about noon, and darkness came over the
whole land[a] until three in the afternoon, 45while the sun's
light failed;[b] and the curtain of the temple was torn in two.
46Then Jesus, crying with a loud voice, said, "Father, into
your hands I commend my spirit." Having said this, he
breathed his last. 47When the centurion saw what had
taken place, he praised God and said, "Certainly this man
was innocent."[c] 48And when all the crowds who had gathered there for this spectacle saw what had taken place, they

[x]Or *blaspheming* [y]Or *the Christ* [z]Other ancient authorities read *in* [a]Or *earth* [b]Or *the sun was eclipsed.* Other ancient authorities read *the sun was darkened* [c]Or *righteous*

"FATHER, INTO YOUR HANDS I COMMEND MY SPIRIT."
—Luke 23:46

God, He used illustrations that women as well as men could relate to.

Though excluded from the inner courts of the temple, Jewish women were welcome among Jesus' followers. He showed that rules of "clean" and "unclean" no longer determined who could approach God. He had come to open a new way, and everyone was welcome to participate. In doing so, He turned the world upside down.

What about your world? Do you see people—whether women or men—the way Jesus does? What one change would you need to make to treat someone more like the Savior did? ◆

Find out more about the significant part women played in Jesus' life and work in "The Women around Jesus," John 19:25. Women helped communicate the gospel throughout the Roman world. See "Women and the Growth of Christianity," Phil. 4:3, and "Paul's Female Coworkers," Rom. 16:12.

23:49
see pg. 310

returned home, beating their breasts.
[49]But all his acquaintances, including the
women who had followed him from Galilee, stood at a distance, watching these things.

Friends Bury Jesus in a Borrowed Tomb

23:50–56

50 Now there was a good and righteous man named Joseph, who, though a
member of the council, [51]had not agreed to their plan and
action. He came from the Jewish town of Arimathea, and he
was waiting expectantly for the kingdom of God. [52]This
man went to Pilate and asked for the body of Jesus. [53]Then
he took it down, wrapped it in a linen cloth, and laid it in a

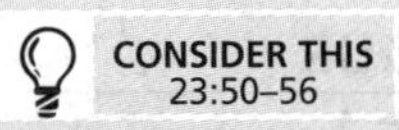

CONSIDER THIS
23:50–56

A Remarkable Coalition

We live in a world where groups of people tend to exclude others rather than include them. Seldom do people from vastly different backgrounds band together, unless it's to fight a common enemy. Distinctions such as race, money, position, language, and gender often keep people from cooperating with each other.

But for those who followed Jesus, divisive walls began to break down. As a result of His influence, people who were far apart socially began to come together for the benefit of others.

Such was the case at Jesus' burial. His death brought about a surprising coalition of persons from the Jewish community: two men who were prominent religious leaders, and two women who were from the common people (vv. 50–56). Who were these four persons?

> Joseph of Arimathea *was a wealthy community leader and a member of the Jewish council. He had access to Pilate and gained permission to take away Jesus' body. He helped prepare the body for burial and deliver it to his own tomb (vv. 50–53; Matt. 27:57–60; Mark 15:42–46).*

> Nicodemus *was also a member of the council (John 3:1–2). He challenged some of the accusations against*

rock-hewn tomb where no one had ever been laid. 54It was
the day of Preparation, and the sabbath was beginning.[d]
55The women who had come with him from Galilee followed, and they saw the tomb and how his body was laid.
56Then they returned, and prepared spices and ointments.
On the sabbath they rested according to the commandment.

The Resurrection

24 But on the first day of the week, at early dawn,
they came to the tomb, taking the spices that they
had prepared. 2They found the stone rolled away from the
tomb, 3but when they went in, they did not find the body.[e]

[d]Gk *was dawning* [e]Other ancient authorities add *of the Lord Jesus*

Jesus (John 7:50–51). After the Lord's death, he brought nearly 100 pounds of embalming supplies (John 19:39–42).

Mary Magdalene *came from Galilee. She had been healed of evil spirits by Jesus (Luke 8:2). Along with other women she observed the tragic ordeal of the crucifixion (23:49). After Joseph retrieved the body, she helped with the embalming (v. 56). Later, after Jesus' resurrection, she helped spread the amazing news that He was alive (24:10).*

Mary of Galilee *was the mother of James and Joses (Mark 15:40). Little else is known about her, but she played enough of a part in the burial coalition to have her participation recorded in Scripture.*

Does your faith connect you with people different from yourself? Believers often have more in common with other believers than they do with family, friends, or coworkers. That fact can sometimes be just the bit of evidence needed to make the faith attractive to its worst critics. ◆

Mary Magdalene and Mary of Galilee were only two of a number of Jesus' female followers. *See "The Women Who Followed Jesus," Luke 8:1–3.*

THEN THEY REMEMBERED HIS WORDS, AND. . .THEY TOLD ALL THIS. . . .
—Luke 24:8–9

Those Women Again!

CONSIDER THIS 24:11 **The discounting of women by men is a pattern that has persisted throughout history. Jesus' male disciples found it easy to dismiss Mary Magdalene, Joanna, Mary, and the other women when they reported the empty tomb and a conversation with the risen Lord (v. 11).**

The news should have been encouraging, given the confusion that dominated the group after their Master's cruel death. But the men rejected the words of these women. It didn't seem to matter that the women had followed Jesus just as closely and in fact had stood by Him through His ordeal rather than betray Him (as Judas had), or deny Him (as Peter had), or run away in fear (as all the men had).

Male skepticism of women's testimony raises questions about the masculine mind. Why are some men so insecure that they must exalt themselves over the other sex to feel significant? Can true companionship survive that kind of distrust? Sooner or later, men can expect to pay for that kind of abuse, especially since both male and female are created in God's image and vested with authority and responsibility together (Gen. 1:26–31; 2:18–25).

If you're a man, are you growing in your appreciation of woman as God's creation? Do you esteem the women God brings your way? Are you learning to listen to them, partner with them, and even follow their lead toward godliness?

4While they were perplexed about this, suddenly two men
in dazzling clothes stood beside them. 5The women[f] were
terrified and bowed their faces to the ground, but the men[g]
said to them, "Why do you look for the living among the
dead? He is not here, but has risen.[h] 6Remember how he
told you, while he was still in Galilee, 7that the Son of Man
must be handed over to sinners, and be crucified, and on
the third day rise again." 8Then they remembered his
words, 9and returning from the tomb, they told all this to
24:10 the eleven and to all the rest. 10Now it
was Mary Magdalene, Joanna, Mary the
mother of James, and the other women with them who told
24:11 this to the apostles. 11But these words
seemed to them an idle tale, and they did
not believe them. 12But Peter got up and ran to the tomb;
stooping and looking in, he saw the linen cloths by themselves; then he went home, amazed at what had happened.[i]

Jesus Appears on the Road to Emmaus

13 Now on that same day two of them were going to a
village called Emmaus, about seven miles[j] from Jerusalem,
14and talking with each other about all these things that
had happened. 15While they were talking and discussing,
Jesus himself came near and went with them, 16but their
eyes were kept from recognizing him. 17And he said to
them, "What are you discussing with each other while you
walk along?" They stood still, looking sad.[k] 18Then one of
them, whose name was Cleopas, answered him, "Are you
the only stranger in Jerusalem who does not know the
things that have taken place there in these days?" 19He
asked them, "What things?" They replied, "The things
about Jesus of Nazareth,[l] who was a prophet mighty in
deed and word before God and all the people, 20and how
our chief priests and leaders handed him over to be condemned to death and crucified him. 21But we had hoped
that he was the one to redeem Israel.[m] Yes, and besides all
this, it is now the third day since these things took place.
22Moreover, some women of our group astounded us. They
were at the tomb early this morning, 23and when they did
not find his body there, they came back and told us that

[f]Gk *They* [g]Gk *but they* [h]Other ancient authorities lack *He is not here, but has risen* [i]Other ancient authorities lack verse 12 [j]Gk *sixty stadia;* other ancient authorities read *a hundred sixty stadia* [k]Other ancient authorities read *walk along, looking sad?"* [l]Other ancient authorities read *Jesus the Nazorean* [m]Or *to set Israel free*

Mary—An Important Name

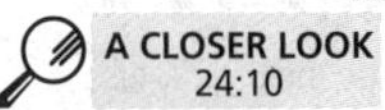

A CLOSER LOOK 24:10 *In naming their daughters Mary, Hebrew parents honored one of Israel's most famous women. See "Why So Many Marys?" Mark 15:40.*

they had indeed seen a vision of angels who said that he
was alive. [24]Some of those who were with us went to the
tomb and found it just as the women had said; but they did
not see him." [25]Then he said to them, "Oh, how foolish you
are, and how slow of heart to believe all that the prophets
have declared! [26]Was it not necessary that the Messiah[n]
should suffer these things and then enter into his glory?"
24:27 see pg. 316
[27]Then beginning with Moses and all the
prophets, he interpreted to them the
things about himself in all the scriptures.
28 As they came near the village to which they were going, he walked ahead as if he were going on. [29]But they
urged him strongly, saying, "Stay with us, because it is almost evening and the day is now nearly over." So he went
in to stay with them. [30]When he was at the table with them,
he took bread, blessed and broke it, and gave it to them.
[31]Then their eyes were opened, and they recognized him;
and he vanished from their sight. [32]They said to each other,
"Were not our hearts burning within us[o] while he was talking to us on the road, while he was opening the scriptures
to us?" [33]That same hour they got up and returned to
Jerusalem; and they found the eleven and their companions
gathered together. [34]They were saying, "The Lord has risen
indeed, and he has appeared to Simon!" [35]Then they told
what had happened on the road, and how he had been
made known to them in the breaking of the bread.

Jesus Appears to His Apostles

36 While they were talking about this, Jesus himself
stood among them and said to them, "Peace be with you."[p]
[37]They were startled and terrified, and thought that they
were seeing a ghost. [38]He said to them, "Why are you
frightened, and why do doubts arise in your hearts? [39]Look
at my hands and my feet; see that it is I myself. Touch me
and see; for a ghost does not have flesh and bones as you
see that I have." [40]And when he had said this, he showed
them his hands and his feet.[q] [41]While in their joy they were
disbelieving and still wondering, he said to them, "Have
you anything here to eat?" [42]They gave him a piece of
broiled fish, [43]and he took it and ate in their presence.

Final Instructions

44 Then he said to them, "These are my words that I
spoke to you while I was still with you—that everything
written about me in the law of Moses, the prophets, and the
24:45–49
psalms must be fulfilled." [45]Then he
opened their minds to understand the

[n]Or *the Christ* [o]Other ancient authorities lack *within us* [p]Other ancient authorities lack *and said to them, "Peace be with you."* [q]Other ancient authorities lack verse 40

His Last Words

CONSIDER THIS 24:45–49 **What would you like to be your last words to your closest family and friends? Whatever they might be, imagine the impact if you returned from the grave to speak them!**

Jesus did. He came back from the dead to give His followers a final word. As a result, His instructions carry unusual weight and have come to be known as the "Great Commission," because Jesus charged His followers with a mighty task. All four writers of His life provide a version of this mandate (vv. 45–49; Matt. 28:18–20; Mark 16:15–16; John 20:21–23; Acts 1:6–8). Jesus gives us the privilege and responsibility of telling the good news about His provision of forgiveness and eternal life to all who will listen.

Do your friends know what Christ has done for them? Do they know what He has done and is doing in your life? Can you afford to deprive them of having that good news so they can consider it for themselves?

scriptures, 46and he said to them, "Thus it is written, that
the Messiah[r] is to suffer and to rise from the dead on the
third day, 47and that repentance and forgiveness of sins is to
be proclaimed in his name to all nations,[s] beginning from
Jerusalem. 48You are witnesses of these
things. 49And see, I am sending upon
you what my Father promised; so stay
here in the city until you have been
clothed with power from on high."

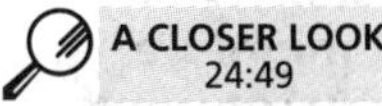
24:48 see pg. 318

24:49

[r]Or the Christ [s]Or nations. Beginning from Jerusalem you are witnesses

Wait for the Power!

A CLOSER LOOK 24:49 *Jesus told His followers to wait in Jerusalem for power (v. 49). He had a job for them to do, but they were not to attempt it through their own ability, but to wait for empowerment from God. See Acts 1:8 for a description of the power that Jesus promised.*

FOR YOUR INFO 24:27

THE SUFFERING CHRIST

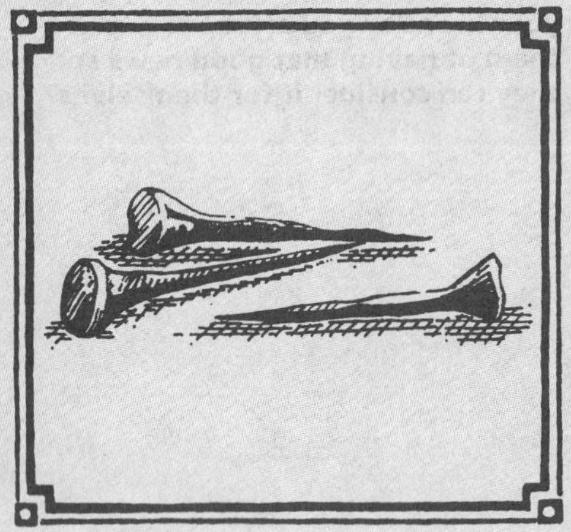

Would you be able to explain to someone where the Scriptures speak about Jesus, "beginning with Moses and all the prophets" (v. 27)? That's what the Lord did with two of His disciples on the road to Emmaus. He explained how the Old Testament—the only inspired Scriptures in existence at that time—foretold His coming as the Messiah.

An entire list of the Old Testament texts to which Jesus probably referred would be too lengthy to publish here. But one book that He undoubtedly spent a lot of time on was Isaiah. No other Old Testament prophet made as many references to the coming Messiah as did Isaiah. Notice his emphasis on the Messiah as a suffering servant, a role that Jesus fulfilled:

ISAIAH'S PROPHECY FULFILLED IN CHRIST

The Suffering Servant	Jesus
Would be widely rejected (53:1, 3)	Jesus came to His own people, but they did not accept Him (John 1:11; compare 12:37–38).
Would be disfigured by suffering (52:14; 53:2)	Pilate had Jesus scourged (beaten); Roman soldiers placed a crown of thorns on His head, struck Him on the head with a stick, and spat on Him (Mark 15:15, 17, 19).
Would voluntarily accept the pain, suffering, and death that sinners deserve (53:7–8)	As the Good Shepherd, Jesus laid down His life for His "sheep" (John 10:11; compare 19:30).
Would make atonement for sin through His blood (52:15)	Believers are redeemed and saved through the blood of Christ (1 Pet. 1:18–19).
	Continued

The Ascension

50 Then he led them out as far as Bethany, and, lifting
up his hands, he blessed them. 51While he was blessing
them, he withdrew from them and was carried up into
heaven.[t] 52And they worshiped him, and[u] returned to
Jerusalem with great joy; 53and they were continually in the
temple blessing God.[v]

[t]Other ancient authorities lack *and was carried up into heaven* [u]Other ancient authorities lack *worshiped him, and* [v]Other ancient authorities add *Amen*

Continued	
Would take upon Himself the grief of human sin and sorrow (53:4–5)	Jesus was delivered to death for our offenses (Rom. 4:25); He "bore our sins in his body on the cross" and by His wounds we were healed (1 Pet. 2:24–25).
Would die on behalf of "the iniquity [sin] of us all" (53:6, 8)	God made Jesus "who knew no sin" to be sin for us (2 Cor. 5:21).
Would die in order to make "intercession for the transgressors" (53:12)	Jesus was crucified between two robbers, one on His right and the other on His left (Mark 15:27–28; compare Luke 22:37). More generally, He is the one "Mediator between God and humankind" (1 Tim. 2:5).
Would be buried in a rich man's tomb (53:9)	Joseph of Arimathea placed the body of Jesus in his own new tomb (John 19:38–42).
Would bring salvation to those who believed in Him (53:10–11)	Jesus promised that whoever believes in Him would not perish but have everlasting life (John 3:16). The early church proclaimed that same message (Acts 16:31).
Would be exalted and extolled and be very high (52:13)	God has "highly exalted [Jesus] and given Him the name" of Lord, to whom "every knee should bend" (Phil. 2:9–11).

According to Jewish tradition, Isaiah underwent suffering of his own: he met his death by being sawed in half during the reign of the evil king Manasseh of Judah. Find out more about this major Old Testament prophet at Luke 4:17.

"I AM SENDING UPON YOU WHAT MY FATHER PROMISED."
—Luke 24:49

CONSIDER THIS
24:48

WITNESSING—JESUS' STYLE

Does evangelism make you nervous? If so, it will help to study carefully how Jesus interacted with people. Whom did He meet? How did He connect with them? Where did the encounters take place? Who initiated contact? What happened in the conversation?

Like Jesus' original followers, believers today are sent into the world to be His witnesses (v. 48; compare Matt. 28:18–20; Acts 1:8). We can learn much about how to handle that assignment by asking questions of the four narratives of Jesus' life—Matthew, Mark, Luke, and John. They include more than 40 meetings between Jesus and various individuals.

Who started the conversation?

In nine cases, Jesus initiated the conversations.

Examples:

- a Samaritan woman (John 4:7–42)
- a crippled beggar (John 5:1–15)

In 25 instances, it was the other party who started the discussion. Jesus responded to other people's inquiries.

Examples:

- a rich young ruler (Matt. 19:16–30)
- a demoniac (Mark 5:1–20)
- Jairus, a synagogue ruler (Mark 5:21–43)
- a hemorrhaging woman (Mark 5:24–34)

Other conversations were triggered by third parties.

Examples:

- tax collectors and other "sinners," invited to a party by Matthew (Matt. 9:9–13)
- Herod, introduced by Pilate (Luke 23:6–16)
- Nathaniel, invited by Philip (John 1:45–51)
- an adulterous woman brought by the scribes (John 8:1–11)

Where did the conversation take place?

The majority of Jesus' interactions occurred in the workplace.

Examples:

- with James and John (Matt. 4:21–22)
- with a Samaritan woman (John 4:7–42)
- with a lame man (John 5:1–15)

Many took place in homes.

Examples:

- at Peter's house with his mother-in-law (Mark 1:29–31)
- with a Syro-Phoenician woman (Mark 7:24–30)
- at Zacchaeus' house (Luke 19:1–10)

Few were in religious settings. Instead, Jesus talked with people about spiritual issues where they were most familiar. He did not need a special environment or control over the circumstances to discuss things of eternal significance.

What was discussed?

Jesus asked questions in more than half of the conversations He had. This is similar to God's first response to the first sinners in history, when He asked four questions of Adam and Eve (Gen. 3:9, 11, 13).

Examples:

- an adulterous woman (John 8:1–11)
- the scribes (Luke 5:17–26)
- His mother and brothers (Matt. 12:46–50)
- the Pharisees (Luke 6:6–11)

He connected with people's thoughts and feelings. He understood that new ideas need to be connected with existing frames of reference if they are to last. He seldom pressed for "closure" or a decision. Instead, He understood that time is required for ideas to simmer and for people to own them before they act on them.

What can we learn from Jesus' example?

- Jesus knew how to take initiative.
- Jesus responded to the initiatives of others.
- Jesus left room in his schedule for interruptions by friends and others enlisting his help.
- Jesus usually met people on their own turf.
- Jesus was interested in establishing common ground with others.

Witnessing is a science, an art, and a mystery. It involves connecting your faith with people's experience in a way that they can understand it, in their own time and manner. It means cooperating with whatever God's Spirit may be doing with them and leaving the results to Him. ◆

Both non-Christians and Christians seem to feel uncomfortable with evangelism. That's one reason why many believers remain silent when it comes to spiritual matters. *See "Whose Job Is Evangelism?" John 16:8.*

A Gospel for the Thinking Person

The first-century world was a swirl of ideas, values, and symbols, not unlike our own. John's is a Gospel that is especially good for the thinking person. Unlike Matthew, Mark, and Luke, which present comprehensive and similar ("synoptic") overviews of the Lord's life, John is a highly stylized arrangement of carefully selected events and words, all directed toward one major purpose: that readers might find life by believing in Jesus as the Christ. John's goal is not belief for its own sake, but belief in order to have *life* (John 20:30–31).

For that reason, this book is vitally important for modern-day Christians. We tend to apply our faith only to certain private and "religious" settings, but leave it behind when we go into the public arena. The message of John cuts through that way of thinking and living. Jesus is our bridge between that which is eternal, spiritual, and supernatural, and the everyday, human, natural world. He is the divine Word of God, yet He became human and lived our experience (1:1, 14).

How can our faith become relevant to the day-to-day circumstances we face? In the Gospel of John, Jesus shows us. He lived the message that He preached. And as we come to know Him and follow Him, we can experience the *life* that He gives.

The Gospel According to

John

Christ is the divine Word of God, yet He became human.

C O N T E N T S

Individuals Encounter Christ

A R T I C L E S

Under Authority (12:49)

Jesus modeled for us two principles of leading and following.

The Cost of Following Jesus (15:18–25)

Sooner or later, following Christ has a cost, and those who think they can get by without paying it are misguided. In fact, if there's no cost, is there really any genuine commitment?

Whose Job Is Evangelism? (16:8)

John shows that bringing people to faith is a cooperative effort between Christians and the Holy Spirit.

The Women around Jesus (19:25)

Women played a major part in Jesus' life and work. This listing summarizes their participation.

The Seven Signs of John's Gospel

A famous author once said that the key to good writing is not in knowing what to put into a story, but what to leave out. Imagine, then, the problem of writing down the story of Jesus, especially if you had been an eyewitness and even a participant in the events. Of all that Jesus said and did, what would you include? What would you leave out?

John solved the problem by determining what he wanted his Gospel to accomplish: he wanted his readers to know that "Jesus is the Messiah, the Son of God, and that through believing you may have life in his name" (John 20:31). To that end, he organized his account around seven miracles that Jesus performed, seven "signs" pointing to His divine nature:

The Signs and Their Meanings	
Turns water into wine (2:1–12)	Jesus is the source of life.
Heals a nobleman's son (4:46–54)	Jesus is master over distance.
Heals a lame man at the pool of Bethesda (5:1–17)	Jesus is master over time.
Feeds 5,000 (6:1–14)	Jesus is the bread of life.
Walks on water, stills a storm (6:15–21)	Jesus is master over nature.
Heals a man blind from birth (9:1–41)	Jesus is the light of the world.
Raises Lazarus from the dead (11:17–45)	Jesus has power over death.

The fact that there are seven sign miracles is significant. In the Jewish view of life, the number seven signified perfection or completion. John's Gospel presents the seven miracles like a diamond refracting seven bands of color. Upon closer inspection, each one turns out to be rooted in Old Testament understanding of the Messiah. John's point is that Jesus is perfect and complete. His miracles show His true colors—that He is the Messiah that Israel has been looking for, and that He alone offers eternal life.

This way of presenting things may seem strange to some modern readers. But the Gospel of John, though probably the last Gospel to be written, was Christianity's first statement of the message of Jesus in a way that would relate to the thought-forms of its day. It is more meticulously and artistically composed than any prize-winning narrative or award-winning film. ◆

JOHN—THE APOSTLE OF LOVE

John and his brother James came from the prosperous family of Zebedee, a successful fisherman who owned his own boat and had hired servants (Mark 1:19–20). Together with Simon and Andrew, with whom they were in partnership (Luke 5:10), the brothers became loyal followers of Jesus. Their mother Salome also joined the fellowship and supported Jesus' ministry (Mark 15:4–41; Luke 8:3).

Modern Christians regard John as the "apostle of love" because of the frequent appearance of that theme in his writings and because the Gospel of John refers to him as the disciple whom Jesus loved (John 13:23). But he certainly didn't start out as a model of charity.

Apparently headstrong and opinionated, Jesus dubbed John and his brother the Sons of Thunder (Mark 3:17). On one occasion they created a storm of protest and indignation from the other disciples by asking if they could sit on Jesus' right and left hands in glory (Mark 10:35–45). On another occasion they suggested calling down fire from heaven on an unreceptive Samaritan village; Jesus rebuked them (Luke 9:51–56).

Somehow John's exposure to Jesus worked an amazing change in his life. After the Lord's departure, he became a leader of the Christian movement, as might be expected. But now his perspective was different. When word came that the gospel had spread to the Samaritans, John was sent with Peter to investigate. Whereas before he had wanted to destroy Samaritans, now he helped bring them the Holy Spirit (Acts 8:14–25). The son of thunder had become a son of love!

Church tradition holds that after the execution of his brother James, John eventually migrated to Ephesus, from which he wrote or oversaw the writing of five New Testament documents. From there he was banished to the island of Patmos, but later returned to Ephesus where he died sometime after A.D. 98. ◆

PERSONALITY PROFILE: JOHN

Name means: "Yahweh is gracious."

Home: Probably raised in Capernaum on the north shore of the Sea of Galilee; later lived at Ephesus; banished to the island of Patmos in old age.

Family: Father was Zebedee; mother was probably Salome; younger brother of James. Salome and Mary may have been sisters (Matt. 27:56; John 19:25); if so, James and John would have been cousins to Jesus.

Occupation: Commercial fisherman; later, one of Jesus' disciples and a member of His inner circle; also an author of a Gospel, three New Testament letters, and Revelation.

Best known today for: His close relationship to Jesus, and his New Testament writings.

The Word

1 In the beginning was the Word, and the Word was with
God, and the Word was God. 2He was in the beginning
1:3 with God. 3All things came into being
through him, and without him not one
thing came into being. What has come into being 4in him
was life,[a] and the life was the light of all people. 5The light
shines in the darkness, and the darkness did not overcome
it.
6 There was a man sent from God, whose name was
John. 7He came as a witness to testify to the light, so that all
might believe through him. 8He himself was not the light,
but he came to testify to the light. 9The true light, which
enlightens everyone, was coming into the world.[b]
10 He was in the world, and the world came into being
through him; yet the world did not know him. 11He came
to what was his own,[c] and his own people did not accept
him. 12But to all who received him, who believed in his
name, he gave power to become children of God, 13who
were born, not of blood or of the will of the flesh or of the
will of man, but of God.
1:14 see pg. 326 14 And the Word became flesh and
lived among us, and we have seen his
glory, the glory as of a father's only son,[d] full of grace and
truth. 15(John testified to him and cried out, "This was he of
whom I said, 'He who comes after me ranks ahead of me
because he was before me.' ") 16From his fullness we have
all received, grace upon grace. 17The law indeed was given
through Moses; grace and truth came through Jesus Christ.
18No one has ever seen God. It is God the only Son,[e] who is
close to the Father's heart,[f] who has made him known.

The Testimony of John the Baptist

19 This is the testimony given by John when the Jews
sent priests and Levites from Jerusalem to ask him, "Who
are you?" 20He confessed and did not deny it, but confessed, "I am not the Messiah."[g] 21And they asked him,
"What then? Are you Elijah?" He said, "I am not." "Are you
the prophet?" He answered, "No." 22Then they said to him,
"Who are you? Let us have an answer for those who sent
us. What do you say about yourself?" 23He said,

[a]Or [3]*through him. And without him not one thing came into being that has come into being.* [4]*In him was life* [b]Or *He was the true light that enlightens everyone coming into the world* [c]Or *to his own home* [d]Or *the Father's only Son* [e]Other ancient authorities read *It is an only Son, God,* or *It is the only Son* [f]Gk *bosom* [g]Or *the Christ*

The Divine Partnership

CONSIDER THIS 1:3 **Christ was fully involved in the work of creation (v. 3). In fact, the totality of the Godhead worked together to bring the world into existence.**

Many people tend to think of God's divine partnership only in terms of the work of salvation. But the three members of the Godhead are just as involved in the ongoing work of providing and caring for all creatures and maintaining the created order. In fact, their creative work continues even now in the heavens, as God prepares eternal dwelling places for believers (John 14:2–3; Rev. 21:1–2, 5).

Remarkably, this working, Triune God invites people to work with Him as junior members in the partnership, to accomplish His work in the world. In our day-to-day jobs, God asks us to do only what He has been doing from the beginning.

Perhaps you've never thought of God as a worker, but that's how He first appears in Scripture. See "God—The Original Worker," John 5:17.

Your own work is an extension of God's work in the world. See "People at Work," Heb. 2:7.

"I am the voice of one crying out in the wilderness,
'Make straight the way of the Lord,' "
as the prophet Isaiah said.
24 Now they had been sent from the Pharisees. 25They
asked him, "Why then are you baptizing if you are neither
the Messiah,[h] nor Elijah, nor the prophet?" 26John answered

[h]*Or the Christ*

GOD AMONG US

CONSIDER THIS 1:14 *The first fourteen verses of John 1 were probably a hymn for the early church. They remind us that Jesus is God's* Word *(v. 1), "word" being a Greek term that means a* thought *expressed. Jesus is the human expression of God. He is light and flesh, to use John's metaphors (vv. 4–5, 14). To see Jesus is to see God, and to know Jesus is to experience God's grace and truth.*

It is no accident, then, that believers are called to practice community and witness publicly. The gospel is both what we say and how we live. Just as Christ became flesh and "lived among us," so we are to "flesh out" the good news about Christ in our everyday world.

PERSONALITY PROFILE: ANDREW

FOR YOUR INFO 1:40

Name means: "Manly."

Home: Bethsaida and Capernaum, on the northwest coast of the Sea of Galilee.

Family: Father's name was Jonah; brother was Simon Peter (see Mark 1:16).

Occupation: Fisherman; later one of Jesus' followers and, according to tradition, an apostle to Scythia (now Russia).

Known today as: The person who introduced Simon to the Lord.

ANDREW THE NETWORKER

In addition to working in his family's commercial fishing enterprise, Andrew followed the teaching of John the Baptist and was considered one of his disciples (John 1:35–40). Thus he heard John declare that Jesus was the Lamb of God—a clear reference to Him as the Messiah. Eager to know more about this new Teacher, Andrew pursued Jesus, prompting an invitation to spend an evening with Him. The meeting convinced Andrew that he had indeed met the long-awaited Christ.

The text is quite clear that the first thing Andrew did after coming to this conclusion was to find his brother, Simon, and tell him the extraordinary news: "We have found the Messiah!" He then brought his brother to meet Jesus (vv. 41–42).

Later, after Jesus called both of the brothers to follow Him as His disciples, Andrew and the others found themselves on one occasion confronted by thousands of people. Jesus asked His disciples where they could buy food for the crowd to eat, a proposition that staggered them.

them, "I baptize with water. Among you stands one whom
you do not know, 27the one who is coming after me; I am
1:28 not worthy to untie the thong of his sandal." 28This took place in Bethany across
the Jordan where John was baptizing.
29 The next day he saw Jesus coming toward him and
declared, "Here is the Lamb of God who takes away the sin
of the world! 30This is he of whom I said, 'After me comes a
man who ranks ahead of me because he was before me.' 31I
myself did not know him; but I came baptizing with water
for this reason, that he might be revealed to Israel." 32And
John testified, "I saw the Spirit descending from heaven like
a dove, and it remained on him. 33I myself did not know
him, but the one who sent me to baptize with water said to
me, 'He on whom you see the Spirit descend and remain is
the one who baptizes with the Holy Spirit.' 34And I myself
have seen and have testified that this is the Son of God."[i]

Jesus Recruits His First Followers

35 The next day John again was standing with two of his
disciples, 36and as he watched Jesus walk by, he exclaimed,

[i]Other ancient authorities read *is God's chosen one*

But Andrew had made the acquaintance of a boy with a handful of barley loaves and a couple of fish. He brought this meager supply to the attention of the Lord, who then multiplied it to feed the entire crowd of about 5,000 (6:4–14).

Shortly before Jesus' arrest, certain Greeks desired to meet Him. Once again, Andrew acted as a go-between, carrying their request to his Teacher (12:20–22). All of these incidents suggest that Andrew was a networker, a man who liked to put people together—and especially to put them together with Jesus. He serves as a model for believers today in bringing others to Christ.

Tradition holds that Andrew devoted the later years of his life to spreading the news about Jesus to Scythia, the region north of the Black Sea. Some say that he was martyred at Patrae in Achaia by crucifixion on an X-shaped cross. ◆

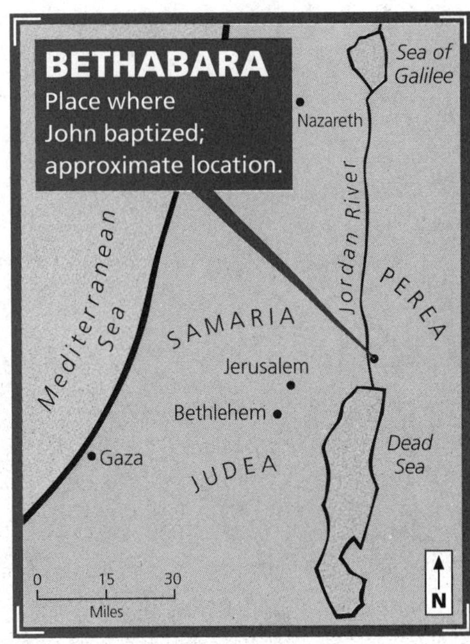

BETHABARA

YOU ARE THERE 1:28

- **A ford or crossing on the Jordan River at which John the Baptist carried out his work. The exact location is unknown.**
- **Name means "house of the ford," though it may also be another name for Bethany.**

"Look, here is the Lamb of God!" 37The two disciples heard
him say this, and they followed Jesus. 38When Jesus turned
and saw them following, he said to them, "What are you
looking for?" They said to him, "Rabbi" (which translated
means Teacher), "where are you staying?" 39He said to
them, "Come and see." They came and saw where he was
staying, and they remained with him that day. It was about
1:40 see pg. 326
four o'clock in the afternoon. 40One of
the two who heard John speak and fol-
lowed him was Andrew, Simon Peter's brother. 41He first
found his brother Simon and said to him, "We have found
the Messiah" (which is translated Anointed[j]). 42He brought
Simon[k] to Jesus, who looked at him and said, "You are Simon son of John. You are to be called Cephas" (which is
translated Peter[l]).

43 The next day Jesus decided to go to Galilee. He
found Philip and said to him, "Follow me." 44Now Philip
1:45
was from Bethsaida, the city of Andrew
and Peter. 45Philip found Nathanael and
said to him, "We have found him about whom Moses in the
law and also the prophets wrote, Jesus son of Joseph from
1:46
Nazareth." 46Nathanael said to him, "Can
anything good come out of Nazareth?"

[j]Or *Christ* [k]Gk *him* [l]From the word for *rock* in Aramaic (*kepha*) and Greek (*petra*), respectively

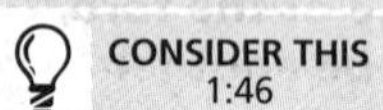

NAZARETH—THE OTHER SIDE OF THE TRACKS

Nazareth was a community on "the other side of the tracks." Located less than five miles from Sepphoris, the splendid capital city of Galilee, it knew quite well the impact on Palestine of Greek culture and Roman wealth and power. Yet Nazareth shared in none of those benefits. Its situation on a steep promontory ensured that its citizens would remain outsiders in the city below.

Someone has said that "God made the garden, evil men made the city, but the devil made the small town." Little towns can be vicious with rumors, gossip, and memories that refuse to die. They can also prove remarkably resistant to change. Nazareth in Jesus' day was possibly that kind of town.

Nevertheless, God chose Nazareth as the place where Jesus would grow up and invest most of His life. That fact demonstrates that while God cares deeply about cities, He also invests in small communities and various kinds of neighborhoods. Nazareth is a gift to anyone who comes from an unfashionable place, such as a dying inner city or

Philip said to him, "Come and see." 47When Jesus saw
Nathanael coming toward him, he said of him, "Here is
truly an Israelite in whom there is no deceit!" 48Nathanael
asked him, "Where did you get to know me?" Jesus answered, "I saw you under the fig tree before Philip called
you." 49Nathanael replied, "Rabbi, you are the Son of God!
You are the King of Israel!" 50Jesus answered, "Do you believe because I told you that I saw you under the fig tree?
You will see greater things than these."
51And he said to him, "Very truly, I tell
you,[m] you will see heaven opened and the angels of God ascending and descending upon the Son of Man."

1:51 see pg. 330

A Marriage Feast at Cana

2 On the third day there was a wedding in Cana of Galilee, and the
mother of Jesus was there. 2Jesus and his disciples had also
been invited to the wedding. 3When the
wine gave out, the mother of Jesus said
to him, "They have no wine." 4And Jesus said to her,
"Woman, what concern is that to you and to me? My hour

2:1 see pg. 331

2:3 see pg. 332

(Bible text continued on page 331)

[m]Both instances of the Greek word for *you* in this verse are plural

a declining rural town. Nazareth says that such a person, too, can receive God's love and serve the world.

If they want to, that is. Nazareth chose to reject its home-grown leader in dramatic fashion (Luke 4:16–30). Jesus left and as far as we know, never went back. However, His mother and brothers remained. They had to endure the scorn of their neighbors, who may have circulated rumors about Jesus' birth and His mental condition. The family might have suspected that Jesus' career would end in a martyr's death. For a while, even His brothers doubted His claims (John 7:5).

Can anything good come out of a Nazareth? Or out of a seedy neighborhood? Or out of an abandoned, forgotten piece of real estate? In Jesus, we see the answer is yes! ◆

Galilee, the province in which Nazareth was located, was a seedbed for revolutionaries against Rome. See "Galilee," Mark 1:14.

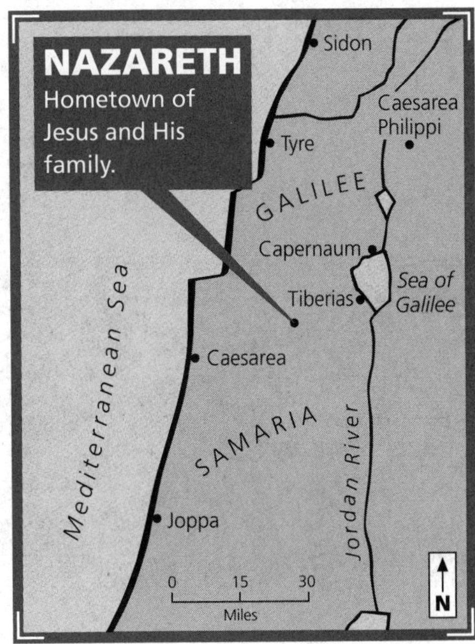

NAZARETH

YOU ARE THERE 1:45

- **Name meant "watchtower"; also "shoot" or "sprout."**
- **Close enough to the main trade routes to maintain contact with the outside world, but its remote location contributed to a certain aloofness and independence. Its people, for example, spoke a crude dialect of Aramaic.**
- **Not highly regarded, as reflected in Nathanael's remark, "Can anything good come out of Nazareth?" (John 1:46).**
- **Hometown of Joseph and Mary and boyhood home of Jesus.**
- **Today, Nazareth is a mostly Arab village of about 65,000 to 70,000 residents. Tours frequent the Church of the Carpenter and a house in which Jesus allegedly grew up.**
- **Recent archaeological digs have uncovered sites for numerous Roman garrisons and cities within five miles of Nazareth.**

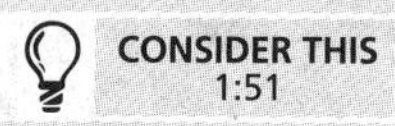
CONSIDER THIS
1:51

SACRED SPACE

In His conversation with Nathanael, Jesus alluded to the Old Testament incident we call Jacob's ladder (v. 51; Gen. 28:12). Jacob had a dream in which angels passed to and from heaven, where God stood and repeated promises He had made to Jacob's father and grandfather. Waking up, Jacob exclaimed, "Surely, the Lord is in this place."

By reminding Nathanael of that story, Jesus tapped into one of the most powerful concepts of Old Testament theology—the idea that a specific place on earth is made special because of God's presence there. To the Hebrews, wherever God or His representatives touched the ground, that spot became "Bethel," or sacred space (literally, "House of God"). They built altars in those places to commemorate God's visitation.

Jesus told Nathanael that someday angels would ascend and descend upon *Him*. That put a radically new twist on things: now there was not only sacred space, but a sacred *Person*. Eventually, that truth came to have enormous implications, such as:

(1) *Those who have Christ become temples of God.* We as believers become sacred space, or better yet, sacred people because of God's presence within us. Paul described us as "temple[s] of the Holy Spirit" (1 Cor. 6:19).

(2) *Every place that we take Jesus becomes a special place.* God is in Christ and Christ is in us, so wherever we are—in the city, in the marketplace, at home—that place becomes sacred space because Christ is there, *in us*. As a result . . .

(3) *We can view our workplaces, neighborhoods, and communities from a new perspective.* We don't have to write them off as "secular" territory. And no longer are cathedrals and churches the only hallowed buildings in town. An office with Christians in it who expect God to work there becomes as special a place as any religious shrine. Even a fig tree can become the place where God carries out His purposes, as Nathanael discovered (John 1:50). Furthermore . . .

(4) *We need no longer view the inner city as throw-away real estate or a God-forsaken ghetto.* Any neighborhood, no matter how scarred and broken, can become a Bethel. If Christ's people are there, Christ is there. That sort of vision can transform a community and lend its

(continued on next page)

has not yet come." 5His mother said to the servants, "Do
whatever he tells you." 6Now standing there were six stone
water jars for the Jewish rites of purification, each holding
twenty or thirty gallons. 7Jesus said to them, "Fill the jars
with water." And they filled them up to the brim. 8He said
to them, "Now draw some out, and take it to the chief
steward." So they took it. 9When the steward tasted the water that had become wine, and did not know where it came
from (though the servants who had drawn the water knew),
the steward called the bridegroom 10and said to him,
"Everyone serves the good wine first, and then the inferior
wine after the guests have become drunk. But you have
kept the good wine until now." 11Jesus
did this, the first of his signs, in Cana of

2:1–12

The Seven Signs of John's Gospel

WATER INTO WINE

CONSIDER THIS 2:1–12 *Jesus' miracle of turning water into wine (vv. 1–12) was loaded with symbolism. Its placement at the beginning of John's Gospel is significant.*

For Jews, wine represented life and abundance. No proper wedding would be without it. Wine symbolized the life of the party and the expectation of a good life to come for the newlyweds. But at Cana, just as the young couple prepared to launch a new life, the unthinkable happened—they ran out of wine. That may have been a common problem in that day, given that wedding festivities often lasted as long as a week. Nevertheless, it was discouraging and probably quite an embarrassment to the host. The party immediately began to wind down.

But Jesus seized the moment to reveal to His followers something of who He was. He produced wine from water. This was the first of His "signs," and explained the purpose of all seven: (1) to reveal His glory, and (2) to bring His disciples to faith in Him (v. 11).

(continued from previous page)

people significance and hope.

Jesus demonstrated the power of that new vision by going to the most sacred spot in Israel, the temple, and restoring it to its purpose of worship (2:13–22). Later He went to Samaria, to Mount Gerazim, the sacred place of the Samaritans (4:19–24), where He defined true worship. Then He went to a sacred pool in Jerusalem, Bethesda, where He healed a lame man (5:1–4). And so it goes throughout John's Gospel.

Sacred space is a vital concept for us who need a God as big as the city and as powerful as today's workplace. We carry with us the very Lord of the universe. He can make every place that we enter a place of grace and truth for us and for others. ◆

CANA

YOU ARE THERE 2:1

- **A town near Nazareth, exact location unknown, though possibly at modern Kirf Kenna, four miles north of Nazareth, or perhaps the ruined city of Khirbet Kana, nine miles north of Nazareth.**
- **Name meant "place of reeds"; at Kirf Kenna, water springs and shady fig trees are still found.**
- **Mentioned in Scripture only by John, as the site of Jesus' first recorded miracle (John 2:1–11; 4:46) and the home of Nathanael (21:2).**

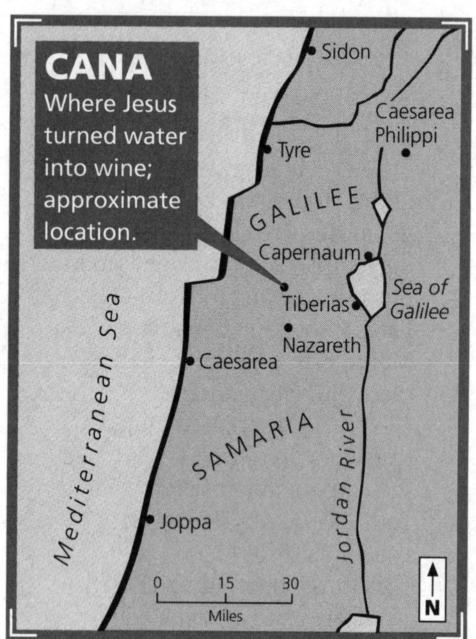

Galilee, and revealed his glory; and his disciples believed in
him.

2:12

12 After this he went down to Capernaum with his mother, his brothers, and
his disciples; and they remained there a few days.

Merchants Evicted from the Temple

13 The Passover of the Jews was near, and Jesus went up
to Jerusalem. [14]In the temple he found people selling cattle,
sheep, and doves, and the money changers seated at their

2:13–25

tables. [15]Making a whip of cords, he
drove all of them out of the temple, both
the sheep and the cattle. He also poured out the coins of
the money changers and overturned their tables. [16]He told
those who were selling the doves, "Take these things out of
here! Stop making my Father's house a marketplace!" [17]His
disciples remembered that it was written, "Zeal for your
house will consume me." [18]The Jews then said to him,

Good and Angry

A CLOSER LOOK 2:13–25

What injustices cause your blood to boil? Jesus showed how to be both compassionate and angry in appropriate ways (vv. 13–25). See "Compassion and Anger in One Person?" Luke 19:41–46.

WINEMAKING

YOU ARE THERE 2:3

Wine was a common beverage throughout biblical times. Galilee in particular was known for its cultivation of grapes and knowledge of the winemaking process.

Galilean women and children pressed grapes in a winepress dug out of limestone. Often an artificial cave constructed near the work area served as a wine cellar.

2:19–20 "What sign can you show us for doing
this?" 19Jesus answered them, "Destroy
this temple, and in three days I will raise it up." 20The Jews
then said, "This temple has been under construction for
forty-six years, and will you raise it up in three days?" 21But
he was speaking of the temple of his body. 22After he was
raised from the dead, his disciples remembered that he had
said this; and they believed the scripture and the word that
Jesus had spoken.
23 When he was in Jerusalem during the Passover festival, many believed in his name because they saw the signs
that he was doing. 24But Jesus on his part would not entrust
himself to them, because he knew all people 25and needed
no one to testify about anyone; for he himself knew what
was in everyone.

Nicodemus Visits Jesus by Night

3 Now there was a Pharisee named Nicodemus, a leader
of the Jews. 2He came to Jesus[n] by night and said to
him, "Rabbi, we know that you are a teacher who has come
from God; for no one can do these signs that you do apart
from the presence of God." 3Jesus answered him, "Very
truly, I tell you, no one can see the kingdom of God without being born from above."[o] 4Nicodemus said to him,
"How can anyone be born after having grown old? Can one
enter a second time into the mother's womb and be born?"
5Jesus answered, "Very truly, I tell you, no one can enter the
kingdom of God without being born of water and Spirit.
6What is born of the flesh is flesh, and what is born of the
Spirit is spirit.[p] 7Do not be astonished that I said to you,
'You[q] must be born from above.'[r] 8The wind[p] blows where it
chooses, and you hear the sound of it, but you do not
know where it comes from or where it goes. So it is with
everyone who is born of the Spirit." 9Nicodemus said to
him, "How can these things be?" 10Jesus answered him,
"Are you a teacher of Israel, and yet you do not understand
these things?
11 "Very truly, I tell you, we speak of what we know and
testify to what we have seen; yet you[s] do not receive our
testimony. 12If I have told you about earthly things and you
do not believe, how can you believe if I tell you about heavenly things? 13No one has ascended into heaven except the

(Bible text continued on page 335)

[n]Gk *him* [o]Or *born anew* [p]The same Greek word means both *wind* and *spirit* [q]The Greek word for *you* here is plural [r]Or *anew* [s]The Greek word for *you* here and in verse 12 is plural

What Happened to Mary?

CONSIDER THIS 2:12 **Jesus' mother, brothers, and disciples accompanied Him during His early travels to Capernaum (v. 12). But after this scene, Jesus' mother disappears from John's account until Jesus' crucifixion (19:25–27). Was Mary a follower of her Son? Perhaps not in the sense of one who traveled with Him. It could be that over time she came to understand better her Son's divine nature and call. After His departure, she was found among those in the upper room who prayed and waited for the promise of the Holy Spirit (Acts 1:14).**

Building the Temple

YOU ARE THERE 2:19–20 **During Jesus' time, the temple at Jerusalem was undergoing extensive reconstruction and renovation. Desiring favor among the Jews, King Herod pledged to build a magnificent temple that would perhaps recall some of the glory of Solomon's temple (1 Kin. 6:1). Work began in 19 B.C. and was carried on until A.D. 64.**

At first the priests opposed Herod, suspicious that his real intent was to either do away with the temple altogether or erect something profane in its place. But Herod proved he was serious, hiring 10,000 laborers and ordering 1,000 wagons for hauling cream-colored stone. When finished, the structure shone so brightly in the Mediterranean sun that it was difficult to look at directly.

Still the priests feared that this most sacred place would be profaned.

(continued on next page)

(continued from previous page)

So Herod had 1,000 of them trained as carpenters and masons so that only priestly hands would construct the Most Holy Place. Unfortunately, the priests themselves turned out to be their own worst enemies: poor craftsmen, they did work that sometimes collapsed and had to be replaced.

But it was an exercise in futility. In A.D. 70, Roman armies surrounded Jerusalem, captured it, and completely destroyed Herod's temple (see "Jerusalem Surrounded," Luke 21:20).

The temple was but one of many splendid edifices that the family of the Herods built while they governed Palestine. Unfortunately, they are remembered more for their infamous family history than their brilliant architectural achievements. See "The Herods," Acts 12:1–2.

CONSIDER THIS
3:21

THE GOSPEL IN A PLURALISTIC SOCIETY

Jesus' nighttime meeting with Nicodemus (vv. 1–21) and His midday encounter with the Samaritan woman (4:5–42) show two of the many different ways in which He dealt with people. Whether it had to do with a respected urban leader like Nicodemus or a hardened, street-wise loner like the woman of Samaria, Jesus approached people on their own terms, as individuals with unique concerns. He modeled for us what it means to live, work, and communicate the gospel message in a pluralistic society.

Nicodemus was an upper-class Jew, a Pharisee from one of the prominent families of Jerusalem. He approached Jesus, alone, at night. The Lord confronted him with his need to be "born again," then let him go away to think things over. The next time we see him, he is defending Jesus on a procedural matter (7:45–52). But Nicodemus apparently didn't openly identify with Jesus until after the crucifixion, when he helped prepare His body for burial (19:39).

The Samaritan woman, on the other hand, had lived a scandalous lifestyle with a succession of husbands and then with a live-in companion. As a result, her community despised her. She also probably came from mixed ancestry,

one who descended from heaven, the Son of Man.[t] 14And
just as Moses lifted up the serpent in the wilderness, so
must the Son of Man be lifted up, 15that whoever believes
in him may have eternal life.[u]
16 "For God so loved the world that he gave his only
Son, so that everyone who believes in him may not perish
but may have eternal life.
17 "Indeed, God did not send the Son into the world to
condemn the world, but in order that the world might be
saved through him. 18Those who believe in him are not
condemned; but those who do not believe are condemned
already, because they have not believed in the name of the
only Son of God. 19And this is the judgment, that the light
has come into the world, and people loved darkness rather
than light because their deeds were evil. 20For all who do
evil hate the light and do not come to the light, so that their
deeds may not be exposed. 21But those
who do what is true come to the light, so
that it may be clearly seen that their deeds have been done
in God."[u]

3:21

[t]Other ancient authorities add *who is in heaven* [u]Some interpreters hold that the quotation concludes with verse 15

for which the Jews despised her. She was spoken to by Jesus in broad daylight, in public, first by herself but later in the company of others. He told her of "living water" and the need to worship in spirit and truth. She responded much more quickly than Nicodemus. Furthermore, hers may have been not so much an individual choice as a clan decision (4:39–41).

John went on to record many other ways Jesus dealt with people, and many ways they responded to Him. Some became believers after they were fed (6:4–14), others after they were healed (9:1–38), and others after they had seen the resurrected Christ (20:24–29). Some responded to the Lord's miracles, others to His teaching. There was no one kind of response to Jesus.

We as believers today must present the gospel in an increasingly pluralistic world. Like Jesus, we need to use many different approaches. What are some of the creative means you can use to influence friends and coworkers for Christ? ◆

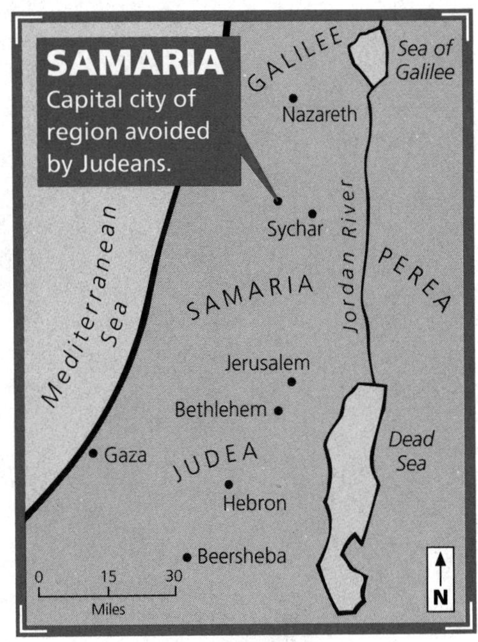

SAMARIA

YOU ARE THERE 4:4

- **The central province of Palestine under the Romans. Its key city, also called Samaria, had been the capital of the northern kingdom of Israel before its fall to Assyria (722 B.C.).**
- **Noted for rich, fertile farmlands that produced valuable grain crops, olives, and grapes.**
- **Served by five major roads, which encouraged trade with Phoenicia, Syria, and Egypt.**
- **Historically, a prime target of invaders due to its reputation for prosperity.**

Jesus taught His followers a series of courses on relating to Samaritans. For two of the more memorable, see "Condemnation or Compassion?" Luke 9:51–56, and "Who Was the Neighbor?" Luke 10:37.

In going from Jerusalem to the end of the earth, the gospel had to go through Samaria. See "Opportunities Look Like Barriers," Acts 1:4.

John the Baptist Teaches about Jesus

22 After this Jesus and his disciples went into the Judean countryside, and he spent some time there with them and baptized. 23John also was baptizing at Aenon near Salim because water was abundant there; and people kept coming and were being baptized 24—John, of course, had not yet been thrown into prison.

25 Now a discussion about purification arose between John's disciples and a Jew.[v] 26They came to John and said to him, "Rabbi, the one who was with you across the Jordan, to whom you testified, here he is baptizing, and all are going to him." 27John answered, "No one can receive anything except what has been given from heaven. 28You yourselves are my witnesses that I said, 'I am not the Messiah,[w] but I have been sent ahead of him.' 29He who has the bride is the bridegroom. The friend of the bridegroom, who stands and hears him, rejoices greatly at the bridegroom's voice. For

3:30

this reason my joy has been fulfilled. 30He must increase, but I must decrease."[x]

31 The one who comes from above is above all; the one who is of the earth belongs to the earth and speaks about earthly things. The one who comes from heaven is above all. 32He testifies to what he has seen and heard, yet no one accepts his testimony. 33Whoever has accepted his testimony has certified[y] this, that God is true. 34He whom God has sent speaks the words of God, for he gives the Spirit without measure. 35The Father loves the Son and has placed all things in his hands. 36Whoever believes in the Son has eternal life; whoever disobeys the Son will not see life, but must endure God's wrath.

"NO ONE CAN RECEIVE ANYTHING EXCEPT WHAT HAS BEEN GIVEN FROM HEAVEN."
—John 3:27

Jesus Encounters a Samaritan Woman

4 Now when Jesus[z] learned that the Pharisees had heard, "Jesus is making and baptizing more disciples than John" 2—although it was not Jesus himself but his disciples who baptized— 3he left Judea and started back to Galilee.

4:4 see pg. 335

4:5 see pg. 339

4But he had to go through Samaria. 5So he came to a Samaritan city called Sychar, near the plot of ground that Jacob had given to his son Joseph. 6Jacob's well was there, and Jesus, tired out by his journey, was sitting by the well. It was about noon.

(Bible text continued on page 338)

[v]Other ancient authorities read *the Jews* [w]Or *the Christ* [x]Some interpreters hold that the quotation continues through verse 36 [y]Gk *set a seal to* [z]Other ancient authorities read *the Lord*

CONSIDER THIS
3:30

SUCCESS

To what extent should Christ's followers today pursue success? John's declaration that "He must increase, but I must decrease" (v. 30) seems to repudiate the idea of personal achievement, recognition, or material gain—common measures of success in our society. Indeed, John himself showed none of the outward trappings of a successful ministry (see "John the Street Preacher," Matt. 3:4).

So should believers avoid success as the world defines it? Can people be successful in their careers as well as in their spiritual lives, or are the two mutually exclusive? Some Christians say that success on the job creates credibility for them to talk about Christ with coworkers. Others, however, claim that they have no interest in being successful. But is that a genuine conviction, or are they merely avoiding the rough-and-tumble of a competitive marketplace? Would God prefer that His people be *failures* on the job, in society, or in life?

Questions like these barely scratch the surface of the complex, emotional issue of success. The people of Jesus' day were no less interested in prospering than we are, even if they defined success in slightly different terms. So it's not surprising that Scripture speaks to human ambition and achievement. It seems to affirm at least three important principles, as illustrated by John the Baptist:

(1) *Success is always measured by a set of standards established by some person or group.* Many people of John's day felt that they were assured of the blessing of God simply because they were descendants of Abraham. Their religious leaders aggressively promoted and reinforced that idea (Matt. 3:7–9; Luke 3:8; John 8:39). John challenged them to reconsider that way of thinking. What mattered, he said, was faith in Jesus. That was the ultimate criterion by which God would measure people's lives. Thus, unbelief would result in the ultimate failure—eternal death (3:36).

(2) *Why and how we pursue success is just as important as whether or not we achieve it.* John's listeners were ordinary people caught up in the everyday scramble to get ahead. But in their pursuit of gain they tended to ignore the needs of others and to take ethical shortcuts. John challenged them to make internal changes (that is, to repent) and to demonstrate those changes in their day-to-day responsibilities through charity, honesty, and justice (Luke 3:8, 10–14).

John himself was able to carry out his ministry because he had the right perspective on the assignment that God had given him. He recognized that he was merely a forerunner to the Christ, not the Christ Himself (John 3:28–29). He knew that Jesus' ministry was going to grow and expand, slowly eliminating the need for John—hence his statement that "He must increase, but I must decrease."

(3) *Obtaining success always carries a cost.* John warned the people of God's judgment using a simple, well-known image: "Even now the ax is lying at the root of the trees; every tree therefore that does not bear good fruit is cut down and thrown into the fire" (Luke 3:9). Just as a lumberjack would lay his ax at the foot of a tree while he decided which trees in a forest to cut, so God had sent John and Jesus as His final messengers before letting His judgment fall.

The people could choose what they wanted to do—whether to continue in their self-satisfied ways of unbelief, or whether to turn toward God in repentance and obedience. Either way, there would be a cost involved. Unfortunately, most of them chose to reject John's message and later Jesus' message, with tragic results (see "Jerusalem Surrounded," Luke 21:20).

For John, the cost of faithfully proclaiming his message was imprisonment and, eventu-

(continued on next page)

7 A Samaritan woman came to draw water, and Jesus
said to her, “Give me a drink.” 8(His disciples had gone to

4:9 see pg. 340

the city to buy food.) 9The Samaritan
woman said to him, “How is it that you,
a Jew, ask a drink of me, a woman of Samaria?” (Jews do
not share things in common with Samaritans.)[a] 10Jesus answered her, “If you knew the gift of God, and who it is that
is saying to you, ‘Give me a drink,’ you would have asked
him, and he would have given you living water.” 11The
woman said to him, “Sir, you have no bucket, and the well
is deep. Where do you get that living water? 12Are you
greater than our ancestor Jacob, who gave us the well, and
with his sons and his flocks drank from it?” 13Jesus said to
her, “Everyone who drinks of this water will be thirsty
again, 14but those who drink of the water that I will give
them will never be thirsty. The water that I will give will become in them a spring of water gushing up to eternal life.”
15The woman said to him, “Sir, give me this water, so that I
may never be thirsty or have to keep coming here to draw
water.”

16 Jesus said to her, “Go, call your husband, and come
back.” 17The woman answered him, “I have no husband.”
Jesus said to her, “You are right in saying, ‘I have no husband’; 18for you have had five husbands, and the one you
have now is not your husband. What you have said is true!”

4:19–23 see pg. 341

19The woman said to him, “Sir, I see that
you are a prophet. 20Our ancestors wor-
shiped on this mountain, but you[b] say that the place where
people must worship is in Jerusalem.” 21Jesus said to her,
“Woman, believe me, the hour is coming when you will
worship the Father neither on this mountain nor in
Jerusalem. 22You worship what you do not know; we worship what we know, for salvation is from the Jews. 23But the
hour is coming, and is now here, when the true worshipers
will worship the Father in spirit and truth, for the Father
seeks such as these to worship him. 24God is spirit, and
those who worship him must worship in spirit and truth.”
25The woman said to him, “I know that Messiah is coming”
(who is called Christ). “When he comes, he will proclaim
all things to us.” 26Jesus said to her, “I am he,[c] the one who
is speaking to you.”

4:27 see pg. 342

27 Just then his disciples came. They
were astonished that he was speaking
with a woman, but no one said, “What do you want?” or,

4:4–42 see pg. 342

“Why are you speaking with her?”
28Then the woman left her water jar and

[a]Other ancient authorities lack this sentence [b]The Greek word for *you* here and in verses 21 and 22 is plural [c]Gk *I am*

(continued from previous page)

ally, execution (Matt. 14:1–12). Yet he gained a treasure all out of proportion to the price of martyrdom—-the praise of Christ (11:7–11).

So should believers pursue success? Judging from the experience of John the Baptist and the people who followed him, the issue seems to be not so much *whether* we should pursue it, but *how.* In light of John's message, it's worth considering three crucial questions:

- Who sets the standards by which I measure success?
- What are my motives and behavior in pursuing success?
- What price am I willing to pay to achieve success? ◆

Jesus told a parable in which He showed that “True Success Means Faithfulness.” See Matt. 25:14–30.

Like John, Paul challenged the idea of people looking out chiefly for Number One. See “Humility—The Scandalous Virtue,” Phil. 2:3.

went back to the city. She said to the people, 29"Come and
see a man who told me everything I have ever done! He
cannot be the Messiah,[d] can he?" 30They left the city and
were on their way to him.
31 Meanwhile the disciples were urging him, "Rabbi, eat
something." 32But he said to them, "I have food to eat that
you do not know about." 33So the disciples said to one another, "Surely no one has brought him something to eat?"
34Jesus said to them, "My food is to do the will of him who
sent me and to complete his work. 35Do you not say, 'Four
months more, then comes the harvest'? But I tell you, look
around you, and see how the fields are ripe for harvesting.
36The reaper is already receiving[e] wages and is gathering
fruit for eternal life, so that sower and reaper may rejoice
together. 37For here the saying holds true, 'One sows and
another reaps.' 38I sent you to reap that for which you did
not labor. Others have labored, and you have entered into
their labor."
39 Many Samaritans from that city believed in him because of the woman's testimony, "He told me everything I
have ever done." 40So when the Samaritans came to him,
they asked him to stay with them; and he stayed there two
days. 41And many more believed because of his word.
42They said to the woman, "It is no longer because of what
you said that we believe, for we have heard for ourselves,
and we know that this is truly the Savior of the world."

Jesus Heals an Official's Son

43 When the two days were over, he went from that
place to Galilee 44(for Jesus himself had testified that a
prophet has no honor in the prophet's own country).
45When he came to Galilee, the Galileans welcomed him,
since they had seen all that he had done in Jerusalem at the
festival; for they too had gone to the festival.
4:46–54 see pg. 343
46 Then he came again to Cana in
Galilee where he had changed the water
into wine. Now there was a royal official whose son lay ill
in Capernaum. 47When he heard that Jesus had come from
Judea to Galilee, he went and begged him to come down
4:48 see pg. 344
and heal his son, for he was at the point
of death. 48Then Jesus said to him, "Un-
less you[f] see signs and wonders you will not believe." 49The
official said to him, "Sir, come down before my little boy

[d]Or *the Christ* [e]Or [35]. . . *the fields are already ripe for harvesting.* [36]*The reaper is receiving* [f]Both instances of the Greek word for *you* in this verse are plural

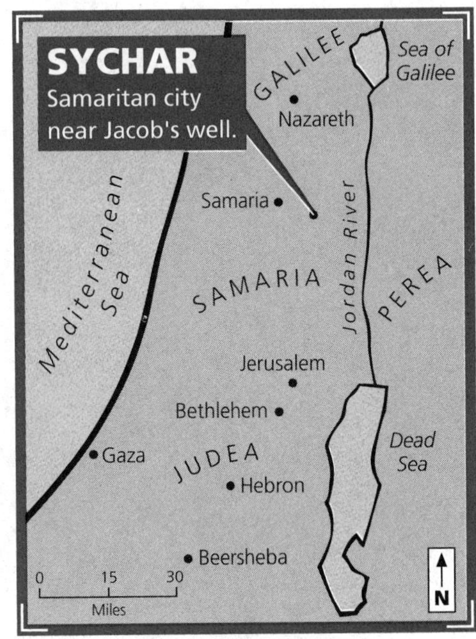

SYCHAR

YOU ARE THERE 4:5

- **A Samaritan city mentioned only once in the Bible (John 4:5).**
- **Exact location unknown, though it could be the same as ancient Askar, one mile north of Jacob's well, or possibly Shechem, a city of great historical significance (Gen. 33:18).**
- **Today some 300 Samaritan descendants live in Nablus, site of ancient Shechem.**

4:50

dies." 50Jesus said to him, "Go; your son
will live." The man believed the word
that Jesus spoke to him and started on his way. 51As he was
going down, his slaves met him and told him that his child
was alive. 52So he asked them the hour when he began to
recover, and they said to him, "Yesterday at one in the after-

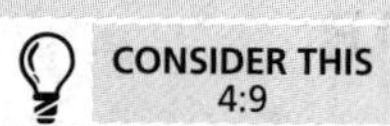

A CLOSER LOOK 4:50

A Wealthy Man Believes

The nobleman who sought Jesus' help (v. 46) became a true child of God because he believed the words of Christ (v. 50). His status with God was based on his faith, not his wealth. Anyone whose greatest aspiration is status and wealth, rather than faith, has embarked on a course that can only end in eternal poverty. See "Christians and Money," 1 Tim. 6:7–19, and "Getting Yours," James 5:1–6. To find out about some of the other wealthy people in the New Testament, see Matt. 27:57.

CONSIDER THIS 4:9

"Jews Have No Dealings with Samaritans"

Hatred between Jews and Samaritans was fierce and long-standing. In some ways, it dated all the way back to the days of the patriarchs. Jacob (or Israel) had twelve sons, whose descendants became twelve tribes. Joseph, his favorite, was despised by the other brothers (Gen. 37:3–4), and they attempted to do away with him.

But God intervened and not only preserved Joseph's life, but used him to preserve the lives of the entire clan. Before his death, Jacob gave Joseph a blessing in which he called him a "fruitful bough by a spring" (Gen. 49:22). The blessing was fulfilled, as the territory allotted to the tribes of Joseph's two sons, Ephraim ("doubly fruitful") and Manasseh, was the fertile land that eventually became Samaria.

Later, Israel divided into two kingdoms. The northern kingdom, called Israel, established its capital first at Shechem, a revered site in Jewish history, and later at the hilltop city of Samaria.

In 722 B.C. Assyria conquered Israel and took most of its people into captivity. The invaders then brought in Gentile colonists "from Babylon, Cuthah, Avva, Hamath, and from Sepharvaim" (2 Kin. 17:24) to resettle the land. The foreigners brought with them their pagan idols, which the remaining Jews began to worship alongside the God of Israel (2 Kin. 17:29–41). Intermarriages also took place (Ezra 9:1—10:44; Neh. 13:23–28).

noon the fever left him." 53The father realized that this was
the hour when Jesus had said to him, "Your son will live."
So he himself believed, along with his whole household.
54Now this was the second sign that Jesus did after coming
from Judea to Galilee.

Jesus Heals a Paralyzed Man

5:1–17 see pg. 343

5 After this there was a festival of the
Jews, and Jesus went up to Jerusalem.
2 Now in Jerusalem by the Sheep Gate there is a pool,
called in Hebrew[g] Beth-zatha,[h] which has five porticoes. 3In
these lay many invalids—blind, lame, and paralyzed.[i] 5One

(Bible text continued on page 345)

[g]That is, *Aramaic* [h]Other ancient authorities read *Bethesda*, others *Bethsaida* [i]Other ancient authorities add, wholly or in part, *waiting for the stirring of the water;* [4]*for an angel of the Lord went down at certain seasons into the pool, and stirred up the water; whoever stepped in first after the stirring of the water was made well from whatever disease that person had.*

Meanwhile, the southern kingdom of Judah fell to Babylon in 600 B.C. Its people, too, were carried off into captivity. But 70 years later, a remnant of 43,000 was permitted to return and rebuild Jerusalem. The people who now inhabited the former northern kingdom—the Samaritans—vigorously opposed the repatriation and tried to undermine the attempt to reestablish the nation. For their part, the full-blooded, monotheistic Jews detested the mixed marriages and worship of their northern cousins. So walls of bitterness were erected on both sides and did nothing but harden for the next 550 years.

There are countless modern parallels to the Jewish-Samaritan enmity—indeed, wherever peoples are divided by racial and ethnic barriers. Perhaps that's why the Gospels and Acts provide so many instances of Samaritans coming into contact with the message of Jesus. It is not the person from the radically different culture on the other side of the world that is hardest to love, but the nearby neighbor whose skin color, language, rituals, values, ancestry, history, and customs are different from one's own.

Jews had no dealings with the Samaritans. With whom do you have no dealings? ◆

Ethnic Games with Religious Roots

CONSIDER THIS 4:19–23 **Jesus must have made the woman at the well very uncomfortable when He spoke with such detailed, personal knowledge of her past (v. 17). Perhaps that's why she began to play ethnic games with Him, falling back on her religious roots (vv. 19–20).**

Nearby was Mount Ebal, where Joshua had renewed Israel's covenant with God (Josh. 8:30–35). According to the Jewish Torah (Deut. 27:4–6), Mount Ebal was also where Moses built an altar to celebrate the Israelites entering the Promised Land. But the Samaritans held that Mount Gerizim, also nearby, was the only true place of worship. The Samaritans built an altar there in 400 B.C., but the Jews destroyed it in 128 B.C. That only added to the historic enmity between the two groups—and provided ammunition for the woman to challenge Jesus.

Jesus understood this woman's need for ethnic identity and security. But He challenged her and her neighbors with a deeper issue—their need to turn to God and become true worshipers of Him. He refused to play ethnic games when there was a matter of eternal life and death at stake.

Jesus Speaks to a Woman

CONSIDER THIS
4:27

The disciples marveled that their rabbi was speaking to a woman (v. 27). In their day it was considered disreputable and beneath his dignity for a rabbi to speak to a woman in public. But Jesus chose a more inclusive posture than His religious peers.

Women were not the only group that Jesus reached out to in contrast to other rabbis. See "Please Bless Our Children," Matt. 19:13–15.

CONSIDER THIS
4:4–42

The Road Less Traveled

For Jews in Jesus' day, the main road to Jerusalem went around *Samaria. But He intentionally went* through *Samaria (v. 4), where He taught His disciples a lesson in cross-cultural communication.*

Finding a woman at Jacob's well in Sychar (vv. 5–7), Jesus struck up a conversation which quickly turned personal. Before long, the woman was on the verge of conversion. But Jesus understood that in her culture women lacked authority to make substantive decisions on their own. Those were made by men, often tribally, within clans. In fact, it was unusual for a man, particularly a rabbi, to hold serious conversation with a woman in public, as Jesus was doing. Perhaps that's one reason why the woman left as soon as the disciples showed up (vv. 27–28).

However, another reason was so that she could go and tell her "significant others," her network of family and friends, about Jesus (vv. 28–30). The woman left her waterpot at the well, maybe because she was in a hurry, though she may have left it there to avoid having to carry it around; after all, she clearly intended to return. At any rate, v. 28 specifically points out that she approached "the men" in the community first—perhaps a clue that they were indeed the decision makers.

The Seven Signs of John's Gospel

THE NOBLEMAN'S SON

CONSIDER THIS 4:46–54

The key to understanding the significance of Jesus' second sign miracle (vv. 46–54) is geography. The nobleman and his dying son lived in Capernaum, the main city of the Galilee region (see Luke 4:31). But Jesus was 20 miles away at Cana (where, significantly, His first sign miracle had taken place, John 2:1–12). That means that the nobleman walked a 40-mile round trip—a two-day trek by foot—to implore Jesus to heal his son. But Jesus merely spoke a word (v. 50), producing results 20 miles away, in a world that knew nothing of phones, faxes, or modems. No wonder the incident produced faith (v. 53). Jesus was the master of distance.

But it was also true that she had been married to or had lived with or been intimate with a number of the men in that clan (vv. 17–18). In that respect, she was like many persons today living in common-law marriages. Those connections might have made her a unique "gatekeeper" or social organizer in the community. She could unlock the village for Jesus. Once she did, He stayed there for two days (v. 43).

What does Jesus' example say about communicating the gospel message today? Northern European and American cultures tend to value individual choice. But elsewhere, many cultures are more clannish. Inter- and intra-family relationships have a powerful bearing on how the message will be received. Western believers need to respect that and use it to advantage as they cross over into cultures different from their own.

Jesus followed the less-traveled road directly into Samaria to bring not just an individual woman, but an entire community to faith. Have you chosen the road less traveled to walk with Jesus into cultures different than your own? ◆

The Seven Signs of John's Gospel

THE MAN AT BETHESDA

CONSIDER THIS 5:1–17

Jesus' third sign miracle revolves around the issue of time. The man at the pool of Bethesda had lain there for 38 years—an entire lifetime as a helpless cripple. Indeed, he had probably started lying there before Jesus was even born. Imagine the disappointment he must have experienced time after time when the angel stirred up the pool, but always he had arrived too late to experience healing. Yet Jesus healed him and immediately he was able to walk. Jesus showed Himself to be the master of time. However, was Israel ready for Him (v. 16)?

CONSIDER THIS
4:48

MYTH #3

10 MYTHS ABOUT CHRISTIANITY

MYTH: SCIENCE IS IN CONFLICT WITH CHRISTIAN FAITH

Many people today accept a number of myths about Christianity, with the result that they never respond to Jesus as He really is. This is one of ten articles that speak to some of those misconceptions. For a list of all ten, see 1 Tim. 1:3–4.

The people of Jesus' day demanded miraculous signs as a condition for belief (v. 48). Yet even though Jesus performed astonishing miracles, His Jewish brothers and sisters by and large rejected Him as their Messiah (1:11). Today many people reject Christianity on similar grounds. We live in a natural world, they say, a world that can be explained by science. Since Christianity relies on faith, it no longer applies in our modern, scientific world. In fact, Christianity and science conflict.

The interesting thing is that while many top scientists do not make this claim, many untrained people do. They have bought into a number of myths, including:

Science can be proved; Christianity cannot. The truth is that both science and Christianity deal with *evidence.* Science examines evidence about our world from things that we can see, touch, measure, and calculate. Christianity is based on evidence about our world from the life, teaching, death, and resurrection of Jesus. Both deal with matters that are very much open to examination.

Of course, it is a misconception that science can be "proved." The heart of the scientific method is to allow the evidence to lead one where it will. But in that case, one cannot "prove" a scientific hypothesis, but only support it with evidence. In fact, one of the fundamental tenets of science is that it takes only one contrary instance to bring down an entire hypothesis. For centuries Newton's theories of gravity seemed irrefutably "proven." Then along came Einstein. Today his thinking is giving way to new discoveries.

Science is progressive; Christianity resists progress. There is some truth to this—but only some. At certain times in history, Christianity has opposed ideas that seemed to challenge its worldview. Yet at other times Christianity—that is to say, Christians—have been (and still are) on the vanguard of scientific progress. Indeed, modern science is largely the product of inquiring believers.

Science is logical; Christianity involves a leap of faith. Without question there is a logic and an order in scientific inquiry. But the same is true for the philosophical, historical, ethical, and theological disciplines of Christianity. Our faith is not opposed to reason. At points it may go beyond reason. But it is a reasonable faith. It hangs together logically.

At the same time, science demands an element of faith. Faith is not, as one schoolboy defined it, believing what you know is not true; faith involves self-commitment on the basis of evidence. In science, one must commit oneself to the belief that the world we see and touch is real, that nature is uniform, and that it operates according to the principle of cause-and-effect. Without these prior "leaps of faith," reasonable though they are, one cannot undertake science.

Science deals with the laws of nature; Christianity thrives on miracles. If science involves a closed, physical universe with fixed, unalterable laws, then the concept of miracles, which in-

(continued on next page)

man was there who had been ill for thirty-eight years.
6When Jesus saw him lying there and knew that he had
been there a long time, he said to him, "Do you want to be
made well?" 7The sick man answered him, "Sir, I have no
one to put me into the pool when the water is stirred up;
and while I am making my way, someone else steps down
5:8–18
ahead of me." 8Jesus said to him, "Stand
up, take your mat and walk." 9At once
the man was made well, and he took up his mat and began
to walk.

Now that day was a sabbath. 10So the Jews said to the
man who had been cured, "It is the sabbath; it is not lawful
for you to carry your mat." 11But he answered them, "The
man who made me well said to me, 'Take up your mat and
walk.' " 12They asked him, "Who is the man who said to
you, 'Take it up and walk'?" 13Now the man who had been
healed did not know who it was, for Jesus had disappeared
in[j] the crowd that was there. 14Later Jesus found him in the
temple and said to him, "See, you have been made well! Do
not sin any more, so that nothing worse happens to you."
15The man went away and told the Jews that it was Jesus
5:16–17 see pg. 346
who had made him well. 16Therefore the
Jews started persecuting Jesus, because
5:17 see pg. 347
he was doing such things on the sabbath. 17But Jesus answered them, "My
Father is still working, and I also am working." 18For this
reason the Jews were seeking all the more to kill him, because he was not only breaking the sabbath, but was also
calling God his own Father, thereby making himself equal
to God.

Jesus Responds to His Critics

19 Jesus said to them, "Very truly, I tell you, the Son can
do nothing on his own, but only what he sees the Father
doing; for whatever the Father[k] does, the Son does likewise.
20The Father loves the Son and shows him all that he him-

[j]Or *had left because of* [k]Gk *that one*

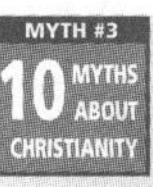

(continued from previous page)

volve the local, temporary suspension of natural laws, will prove intolerable. But that is a nineteenth-century view of science. Few scientists of stature today support such a view.

Moreover, the so-called "laws of nature" are not prescriptive but *descriptive.* They do not determine what may happen; they describe what normally does happen. Therefore, science can legitimately say that miracles do not usually occur in nature. But it would be illegitimate to claim that miracles are impossible. Such a claim speaks outside the limits of science. If God has really come into this world in Christ, is it so surprising that He would perform miracles, as the Gospels report?

Science is not in conflict with Christianity. To be sure, some scientists are. But other scientists are passionately committed Christians, just like people in other walks of life. There are reasons why people choose for or against Christ, but those reasons are found elsewhere than in science. ◆

"You Can't Get Healed on the Sabbath!"

A CLOSER LOOK 5:8–18 *Ever on the lookout for infractions of their traditions and especially eager to catch Jesus and His followers in sin, the Pharisees quibbled over a formerly lame man carrying his bed on the Sabbath (v. 10). Jesus' Sabbath-day miracles sparked no end of controversy with these legalists. But He refused to let their objections go unchallenged. See "Jesus Confronts the Legalists," Luke 6:1–11.*

Does God Work on Sundays?

CONSIDER THIS 5:16–17 **Jesus offered an odd retort to His critics in the controversy over observance of the Sabbath (vv. 16–17). Genesis 2:2–3 said that God "rested" from His work on the seventh day of creation and "hallowed" it, or set it apart as something special. Later, the third of the Ten Commandments made the seventh day a holy day, a Sabbath or day of rest in Israel (Ex. 20:8–11). Many Christians continue this practice today (on Sundays).**

According to rabbinical legal tradition, the healed man was violating the Sabbath rest by carrying his bed (v. 10), as was Jesus by healing him on that day (v. 16). But Jesus said that even God "breaks" His own Sabbath by continuing to work (v. 17). Even though He has completed the Creation, He continues to maintain it and provide for His creatures—even on Sundays.

The point was that it's never the wrong day to do good.

self is doing; and he will show him greater works than
these, so that you will be astonished. 21Indeed, just as the
Father raises the dead and gives them life, so also the Son
gives life to whomever he wishes. 22The Father judges no
one but has given all judgment to the Son, 23so that all may
honor the Son just as they honor the Father. Anyone who
does not honor the Son does not honor the Father who
sent him. 24Very truly, I tell you, anyone who hears my
word and believes him who sent me has eternal life, and
does not come under judgment, but has passed from death
to life.

25 "Very truly, I tell you, the hour is coming, and is now
here, when the dead will hear the voice of the Son of God,
and those who hear will live. 26For just as the Father has
life in himself, so he has granted the Son also to have life in
himself; 27and he has given him authority to execute judgment, because he is the Son of Man. 28Do not be astonished
at this; for the hour is coming when all who are in their
graves will hear his voice 29and will come out—those who
have done good, to the resurrection of life, and those who
have done evil, to the resurrection of condemnation.

30 "I can do nothing on my own. As I hear, I judge; and
my judgment is just, because I seek to do not my own will
but the will of him who sent me.

31 "If I testify about myself, my testimony is not true.
32There is another who testifies on my behalf, and I know
that his testimony to me is true. 33You sent messengers to
John, and he testified to the truth. 34Not that I accept such
human testimony, but I say these things so that you may be
saved. 35He was a burning and shining lamp, and you were
willing to rejoice for a while in his light. 36But I have a testimony greater than John's. The works that the Father has
given me to complete, the very works that I am doing, testify on my behalf that the Father has sent me. 37And the Father who sent me has himself testified on my behalf. You
have never heard his voice or seen his form, 38and you do
not have his word abiding in you, because you do not believe him whom he has sent.

39 "You search the scriptures because you think that in
them you have eternal life; and it is they that testify on my
behalf. 40Yet you refuse to come to me to have life. 41I do
not accept glory from human beings. 42But I know that you
do not have the love of God in[l] you. 43I have come in my
Father's name, and you do not accept me; if another comes
in his own name, you will accept him. 44How can you be-

(Bible text continued on page 348)

[l]Or *among*

CONSIDER THIS
5:17

God—The Original Worker

God is a worker! Perhaps you've never thought of Him that way. But that's how He first appears in Scripture. In the creation account (Gen. 1–2) He wears no end of occupational hats: strategic planner, designer, civil engineer, real estate developer, project manager, artist, and many more. Using these skills, He created something that was "very good" (1:31). How good? As good as God! No wonder the creation is said to "glorify," or praise God. His work is worth honoring, and it honors Him. (See Is. 43:7; 60:21.)

Furthermore, God continues to work (John 5:17), maintaining the creation and providing for His creatures. He also carries out the work of salvation. And He uses people to help Him accomplish these tasks. Think what that means:

(1) *Work itself is inherently good.* God didn't mind "getting His hands dirty," so to speak, in creating the universe. Genesis says He "worked" to bring it into existence (2:2). But that means work must be good in and of itself, since by definition, God can only do what is good. It also means work reflects the activity of God. The engineer who designs a bridge, the zoologist who studies animals, and the farmer who raises crops all carry out jobs that God did at the beginning of the world.

(2) *Your work is important; it matters.* The work that God gives you has dignity to it. In fact, God created you "in his image" (Gen. 1:26–27). Just as He works, so He has created you to work. Genesis even says that God has placed human beings in authority over the creation as His managers. As you use the abilities He's given you, you can be a partner, a coworker with Him to carry out His work.

For example, God can use: the nurse to meet the health needs of patients; the grocer to distribute food to customers; the researcher to provide accurate information; the lawyer to promote justice for clients; the career homemaker to nurture growing children. God values these kinds of jobs because they help to carry out His purposes in the world. These things matter to Him.

(3) *There's no such thing as "secular" or "sacred" work.* God certainly uses ministers and missionaries to meet spiritual and personal needs around the world. But they are not the only people doing "God's work." God is just as interested in the physical, emotional, intellectual, and other needs that people have. He also cares about the management of the earth itself. It takes all kinds of skills, and all kinds of people, to do what God wants done in the world.

(4) *You should do your work in a way that honors God.* Your work has dignity; you're created in God's image as a worker; you're a coworker with God; you have God-given abilities to carry out important tasks that He wants done. All of this says that what you do for work and how you do it should bring glory to God. He should be pleased with it—and with you as you do it. ◆

Our work isn't exactly the same as God's work, is it? See "Creation: 'Very Good,' But Not Sacred!" Heb. 11:3.

Doesn't Genesis say that God "rested" from His work? See "Does God Work on Sundays?" John 5:16–17.

Many people assume that work is a part of the curse. Is it? See Rom. 8:20–22.

lieve when you accept glory from one another and do not seek the glory that comes from the one who alone is God? 45Do not think that I will accuse you before the Father; your accuser is Moses, on whom you have set your hope. 46If you believed Moses, you would believe me, for he wrote about me. 47But if you do not believe what he wrote, how will you believe what I say?"

Jesus Feeds 5,000

6:1–14

6 After this Jesus went to the other side of the Sea of Galilee, also called the Sea of Tiberias.[m] 2A large crowd kept following him, because they saw the signs that he was doing for the sick. 3Jesus went up the mountain and sat down there with his disciples. 4Now the Passover, the festival of the Jews, was near. 5When he looked up and saw a large crowd coming toward him, Jesus said to Philip, "Where are we to buy bread for these people to eat?" 6He said this to test him, for he himself knew what he was going to do. 7Philip answered him, "Six months' wages[n] would not buy enough bread for each of them to get a little." 8One of his disciples, Andrew, Simon Peter's brother, said to him, 9"There is a boy here who has five barley loaves and two fish. But what are they among so many people?" 10Jesus said, "Make the people sit down." Now there was a great deal of grass in the place; so they[o] sat down, about five thousand in all. 11Then Jesus took the loaves, and when he had given thanks, he distributed them to those who were seated; so also the fish, as much as they wanted. 12When they were satisfied, he told his disciples, "Gather up the fragments left over, so that nothing may be lost." 13So they gathered them up, and from the fragments of the five barley loaves, left by those who had eaten, they filled twelve baskets. 14When the people saw the sign that he had done, they began to say, "This is indeed the prophet who is to come into the world."

6:14–15

Jesus Walks on Water

6:15–21

15 When Jesus realized that they were about to come and take him by force to make him king, he withdrew again to the mountain by himself.

16 When evening came, his disciples went down to the

[m]Gk *of Galilee of Tiberias* [n]Gk *Two hundred denarii*; the denarius was the usual day's wage for a laborer [o]Gk *the men*

The Seven Signs of John's Gospel

Feeding the 5,000

CONSIDER THIS 6:1–14

John writes that the crowd that followed Jesus did so in response to His miracles (v. 2), a link to the healing of the lame man in John 5:1–17. This leads to a fourth sign miracle, the feeding of the 5,000.

What Jesus did was remarkable in every way. Consider, for example, that even today very few facilities in the United States can accommodate 5,000 people for a sit-down meal. Yet Jesus miraculously provided for at least that many—with leftovers! John mentions that they filled twelve baskets—perhaps one for each disciple, or perhaps one for each of the twelve tribes of Israel. The overall result was faith: Jesus must be the Messiah, the crowd concluded (v. 14).

Yet doubt and rejection were soon to follow. Detractors pointed out that Jesus' lunch may have been impressive, but it was only one meal. By contrast, Moses had fed Israel in the wilderness for 40 years (vv. 30–31). Incredibly, they had missed the point of the sign: Jesus was not merely a deliveryman, He was the bread of life itself (vv. 32–58).

sea, 17got into a boat, and started across the sea to Capernaum. It was now dark, and Jesus had not yet come to
them. 18The sea became rough because a strong wind was
blowing. 19When they had rowed about three or four
miles,[p] they saw Jesus walking on the sea and coming near
the boat, and they were terrified. 20But he said to them, "It
is I;[q] do not be afraid." 21Then they wanted to take him into
the boat, and immediately the boat reached the land toward
which they were going.

"I Am the Bread of Life"

22 The next day the crowd that had stayed on the other
side of the sea saw that there had been only one boat there.
They also saw that Jesus had not got into the boat with his
disciples, but that his disciples had gone away alone.
23Then some boats from Tiberias came near the place where
they had eaten the bread after the Lord had given thanks.[r]
24So when the crowd saw that neither Jesus nor his disciples were there, they themselves got into the boats and
went to Capernaum looking for Jesus.
25 When they found him on the other side of the sea,
they said to him, "Rabbi, when did you come here?" 26Jesus
answered them, "Very truly, I tell you, you are looking for
me, not because you saw signs, but because you ate your
fill of the loaves. 27Do not work for the food that perishes,
but for the food that endures for eternal life, which the Son
of Man will give you. For it is on him that God the Father
has set his seal." 28Then they said to him, "What must we
do to perform the works of God?" 29Jesus answered them,
"This is the work of God, that you believe in him whom he
has sent." 30So they said to him, "What sign are you going
to give us then, so that we may see it and believe you?
What work are you performing? 31Our ancestors ate the
manna in the wilderness; as it is written, 'He gave them
bread from heaven to eat.' " 32Then Jesus said to them,
"Very truly, I tell you, it was not Moses who gave you the
bread from heaven, but it is my Father who gives you the
true bread from heaven. 33For the bread of God is that
which[s] comes down from heaven and gives life to the
world." 34They said to him, "Sir, give us this bread always."

6:35
see pg. 350

35 Jesus said to them, "I am the bread
of life. Whoever comes to me will never
be hungry, and whoever believes in me will never be thirsty.
36But I said to you that you have seen me and yet do not

[p]Gk *about twenty-five or thirty stadia* [q]Gk *I am* [r]Other ancient authorities lack *after the Lord had given thanks* [s]Or *he who*

Preventing Kingdom Confusion

CONSIDER THIS 6:14–15 **Throughout history people have longed for leaders to whom they can attach themselves. They often tie their own aspirations to the charisma and vision of a famous person, using that person to achieve their own ends, which are sometimes quite incompatible.**

Jesus knew the pattern well. He came to accomplish the work that His Father had given Him. But others quickly attached their own agendas and values to His plans (v. 15). Jesus resisted the mixed intentions of some of His followers and admirers because His kingdom differed fundamentally from their expectations.

What exactly was Jesus' concept of the kingdom, and what difference does it make for people today? See "The King Declares His Kingdom," Matt. 4:17.

The Seven Signs of John's Gospel

Miracles at Sea

CONSIDER THIS 6:15–21 *The fifth sign miracle that John included in his Gospel was a private affair for the disciples alone (vv. 15–21). What happened on the troubled Sea of Galilee revealed Jesus as master of the elements. John makes no explanatory comment on this incident, but its impact on the disciples is evident in Peter's words: "We have come to* believe and know *that you are the Holy One of God" (v. 69, emphasis added).*

believe. [37]Everything that the Father gives me will come to
me, and anyone who comes to me I will never drive away;
[38]for I have come down from heaven, not to do my own
will, but the will of him who sent me. [39]And this is the will
of him who sent me, that I should lose nothing of all that
he has given me, but raise it up on the last day. [40]This is indeed the will of my Father, that all who see the Son and believe in him may have eternal life; and I will raise them up
on the last day."

Jesus' Listeners Are Confounded

41 Then the Jews began to complain about him because
he said, "I am the bread that came down from heaven."
[42]They were saying, "Is not this Jesus, the son of Joseph,
whose father and mother we know? How can he now say, 'I
have come down from heaven'?" [43]Jesus answered them,

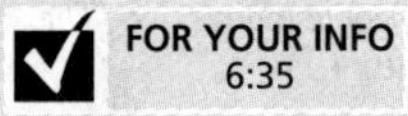

FOR YOUR INFO
6:35

The Bread of Life

When Jesus called Himself the "bread of life" (v. 35; also vv. 32–33, 41, 48), He was using as an image more than a staple of the diet, He was drawing on a rich symbol of Jewish life.

Bread played an important role in Israel's worship. During the celebration of Pentecost, two loaves of leavened bread were offered as sacrifices (Lev. 23:17). In the tabernacle, and later in the temple, the Levites placed twelve loaves of unleavened bread, or bread without yeast, before the Lord each week to symbolize God's presence with the twelve tribes (Ex. 25:30).

Throughout the Exodus, God miraculously sustained His people by sending manna from heaven each morning (Ex. 16). The bread-like manna was "a fine flaky substance, as fine as frost" (v. 14). It looked "like coriander seed, white" and tasted like "wafers made with honey" (v. 31) or "pastry prepared with oil" (Num. 11:8).

It was this manna that Jesus was recalling when He called Himself "the true bread from heaven" (John 6:32), "the bread that came down from heaven" (6:41), and the "bread of life" (vv. 48–51, 58). Symbolically, Jesus is the heavenly manna, the spiritual or supernatural food given by the Father to those who ask, seek, and knock (v. 45; Matt. 7:7–8).

6:44 "Do not complain among yourselves.
44No one can come to me unless drawn
by the Father who sent me; and I will raise that person up
on the last day. 45It is written in the prophets, 'And they
shall all be taught by God.' Everyone who has heard and
learned from the Father comes to me. 46Not that anyone
has seen the Father except the one who is from God; he has
seen the Father. 47Very truly, I tell you, whoever believes
has eternal life. 48I am the bread of life. 49Your ancestors ate
the manna in the wilderness, and they died. 50This is the
bread that comes down from heaven, so that one may eat of
it and not die. 51I am the living bread that came down from
heaven. Whoever eats of this bread will live forever; and
the bread that I will give for the life of the world is my
flesh."

52 The Jews then disputed among themselves, saying,
"How can this man give us his flesh to eat?" 53So Jesus said

◆ ◆ ◆ ◆ ◆ ◆ ◆ ◆ ◆ ◆ ◆ ◆ ◆ ◆ ◆ ◆

However, it's also interesting that Jesus' "bread of life discourse" (as John 6:26–58 is called) was given during Passover, also known as the Festival of Unleavened Bread (vv. 4, 22; see "Passover," Luke 22:7). Passover celebrated the deliverance of Israel from slavery in Egypt. On the night before leaving Egypt, the Israelites made unleavened bread, as they had no time to let their bread rise before taking flight (Ex. 12:8; 13:6–7).

In this context, Jesus had just fed at least 5,000 people (John 6:1–14), an event that led directly to the bread of life discourse (vv. 22–27). Clearly, He was indicating that He was God's provision for the people's deepest spiritual needs. Just as God had provided for His people as they came out of Egypt, so Jesus had provided physical food for the 5,000 and was ready to provide spiritual nourishment and life to all of them as well.

Tragically, the people balked at His teaching (vv. 30–31, 41–42, 52, 60). Their hearts were hardened in unbelief. Soon, many began to turn away (v. 66). But to those who believed, like Peter who declared, "You are the Holy One of God" (v. 69), Jesus gave abundant and eternal life. ◆

You Alone Can't Bring Them to Jesus

CONSIDER THIS 6:44 **Do you stagger under a heavy load of expectation that you alone (or that you primarily) are responsible for bringing your friends and coworkers to faith? Do you feel guilty because you can't get them converted? If so, you may be surprised to discover that not even Jesus felt that kind of load for the lost!**

While explaining how people enter the kingdom, Jesus clearly declared that it is God the Father who draws them (v. 44). That means that people's response to the gospel does not depend primarily on you or on Jesus. Elsewhere, Jesus taught that:

- **"Everything that the Father gives me will come to me" (v. 37).**
- **"No one can come to me unless it is granted by the Father" (v. 65).**

Clearly, the responsibility for conversion ultimately belongs to the Father. Then is there anything we can do as Christ's followers to motivate others toward the Savior? Yes, we can give evidence of how God works in our lives as we grow. We can offer clear, truthful information about the gospel as we have opportunity. And we can invite and even urge others to believe.

But the ultimate responsibility for salvation is God's, not ours. So relax! Live the faith, talk about it, and offer it to others. But let the dynamic of conversion be from God alone.

Unfortunately, some believers run to the other extreme: they fold their hands and shut their mouths when it comes to evangelism. After all, it's up to God to bring people to faith. Is that what Jesus intended? See "Whose Job Is Evangelism?" John 16:8.

to them, "Very truly, I tell you, unless you eat the flesh of the Son of Man and drink his blood, you have no life in you. [54]Those who eat my flesh and drink my blood have eternal life, and I will raise them up on the last day; [55]for my flesh is true food and my blood is true drink. [56]Those who eat my flesh and drink my blood abide in me, and I in them. [57]Just as the living Father sent me, and I live because of the Father, so whoever eats me will live because of me. [58]This is the bread that came down from heaven, not like that which your ancestors ate, and they died. But the one who eats this bread will live forever." [59]He said these things while he was teaching in the synagogue at Capernaum.

Many Followers Abandon Jesus

6:60–67

60 When many of his disciples heard it, they said, "This teaching is difficult; who can accept it?" [61]But Jesus, being aware that his disciples were complaining about it, said to them, "Does this offend you? [62]Then what if you were to see the Son of Man ascending to where he was before? [63]It is the spirit that gives life; the flesh is useless. The words that I have spoken to you are spirit and life. [64]But among you there are some who do not believe." For Jesus knew from the first who were the ones that did not believe, and who was the one that would betray him. [65]And he said, "For this reason I have told you that no one can come to me unless it is granted by the Father."

"WHOEVER EATS ME WILL LIVE BECAUSE OF ME." —John 6:57

Peter Declares that Jesus Is the Messiah

66 Because of this many of his disciples turned back and no longer went about with him. [67]So Jesus asked the twelve, "Do you also wish to go away?" [68]Simon Peter answered him, "Lord, to whom can we go? You have the words of eternal life. [69]We have come to believe and know that you are the Holy One of God."[t] [70]Jesus answered them,

[t]Other ancient authorities read *the Christ, the Son of the living God*

The Desertion of the Disciples

A CLOSER LOOK 6:60–67

Jesus attracted large crowds, and from them quite a number of disciples *or "learners." However, when His teaching became costly and hard to accept (v. 60), many deserted Him—but not all. To find out more about these dedicated followers, see "The Twelve," Matt. 10:2, and "The Women Who Followed Jesus," Luke 8:1–3.*

"Did I not choose you, the twelve? Yet one of you is a
devil." 71He was speaking of Judas son of Simon Iscariot,[u]
for he, though one of the twelve, was going to betray him.

Jesus' Brothers Doubt Him

7 After this Jesus went about in Galilee. He did not wish[v]
to go about in Judea because the Jews were looking for
7:2 an opportunity to kill him. 2Now the
Jewish festival of Booths[w] was near. 3So
his brothers said to him, "Leave here and go to Judea so
that your disciples also may see the works you are doing;
4for no one who wants[x] to be widely known acts in secret.
7:5 If you do these things, show yourself to
the world." 5(For not even his brothers
believed in him.) 6Jesus said to them, "My time has not yet
come, but your time is always here. 7The world cannot hate
you, but it hates me because I testify against it that its
works are evil. 8Go to the festival yourselves. I am not[y] going to this festival, for my time has not yet fully come." 9Af-
ter saying this, he remained in Galilee.

Jesus Attends the Festival of Booths

10 But after his brothers had gone to the festival, then he
also went, not publicly but as it were[z] in secret. 11The Jews
were looking for him at the festival and saying, "Where is
he?" 12And there was considerable complaining about him
among the crowds. While some were saying, "He is a good
man," others were saying, "No, he is deceiving the crowd."
13Yet no one would speak openly about him for fear of the
Jews.
14 About the middle of the festival Jesus went up into
the temple and began to teach. 15The Jews were astonished
at it, saying, "How does this man have such learning,[a] when
he has never been taught?" 16Then Jesus answered them,
"My teaching is not mine but his who sent me. 17Anyone
who resolves to do the will of God will know whether the

[u]Other ancient authorities read *Judas Iscariot son of Simon;* others, *Judas son of Simon from Karyot* (Kerioth) [v]Other ancient authorities read *was not at liberty* [w]Or *Tabernacles* [x]Other ancient authorities read *wants it* [y]Other ancient authorities add *yet* [z]Other ancient authorities lack *as it were* [a]Or *this man know his letters*

The Festival of Booths

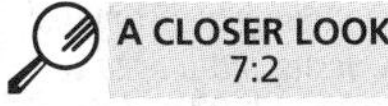

A CLOSER LOOK 7:2

The Festival of Booths (v. 2) was one of three great feast days in the life of the Hebrews. It offered Jesus an ideal moment of opportunity in which to declare Himself publicly. See "Jewish Festivals," Luke 2:42, and " 'We Interrupt This Program . . . ,' " John 7:37.

Does Anyone Believe You?

CONSIDER THIS 7:5

If you ever feel discouraged because family, friends, or coworkers refuse to accept the gospel, you may take some comfort from the fact that even Jesus' own brothers did not believe that He was the Christ (v. 5). Even though they had seen His miracles and listened to His teaching, they still balked at the idea of placing faith in Jesus as the Son of God.

This is important to notice, because it shows that the person who hears the gospel bears responsibility for responding in faith, while the person who shares the gospel bears responsibility for communicating with faithfulness. If we as believers ever start holding ourselves responsible for whether unbelievers accept or reject the message of Christ, we are headed for trouble!

That's not to suggest that we can be careless in our witness or ignore our credibility. Notice that Jesus' brothers rejected Him *in spite of* His works and words. Is that true of us? Or do people dismiss our faith because our lives show little evidence that what we say we believe is true or that it makes any difference to us?

Eventually, at least some of Jesus' brothers did believe in Him. James, probably the oldest, became a leader in the church (Acts 15:13–21) and wrote the New Testament letter that bears his name. Likewise, the author of Jude may have been the brother of Jesus. Ultimately, both urged Christians to practice and defend their *faith* (James 2:2–26; Jude 3).

Maybe you have decided that since it's up to God to bring people to faith, you can relax and keep quiet about the gospel. Is that a realistic attitude? See "Whose Job Is Evangelism?" John 16:8.

teaching is from God or whether I am speaking on my own.
[18]Those who speak on their own seek their own glory; but
the one who seeks the glory of him who sent him is true,
and there is nothing false in him.
19 "Did not Moses give you the law? Yet none of you
keeps the law. Why are you looking for an opportunity to
kill me?" [20]The crowd answered, "You have a demon! Who
is trying to kill you?" [21]Jesus answered
them, "I performed one work, and all of
you are astonished. [22]Moses gave you circumcision (it is, of
course, not from Moses, but from the patriarchs), and you
circumcise a man on the sabbath. [23]If a man receives circumcision on the sabbath in order that the law of Moses
may not be broken, are you angry with me because I healed
a man's whole body on the sabbath? [24]Do not judge by appearances, but judge with right judgment."
25 Now some of the people of Jerusalem were saying, "Is
not this the man whom they are trying to kill? [26]And here
he is, speaking openly, but they say nothing to him! Can it
be that the authorities really know that this is the Messiah?[b]
[27]Yet we know where this man is from; but when the Messiah[b] comes, no one will know where he is from." [28]Then
Jesus cried out as he was teaching in the temple, "You know
me, and you know where I am from. I have not come on
my own. But the one who sent me is true, and you do not
know him. [29]I know him, because I am from him, and he
sent me." [30]Then they tried to arrest him, but no one laid
hands on him, because his hour had not yet come. [31]Yet
many in the crowd believed in him and were saying,
"When the Messiah[b] comes, will he do more signs than this
man has done?"[c]
32 The Pharisees heard the crowd muttering such things
about him, and the chief priests and Pharisees sent temple
police to arrest him. [33]Jesus then said, "I will be with you a
little while longer, and then I am going to him who sent
me. [34]You will search for me, but you will not find me; and
where I am, you cannot come." [35]The Jews said to one another, "Where does this man intend to go that we will not

7:21–24

"DO NOT JUDGE BY APPEARANCES, BUT JUDGE WITH RIGHT JUDGMENT." —John 7:24

[b]Or *the Christ* [c]Other ancient authorities read *is doing*

Blind Guides

A CLOSER LOOK 7:21–24

Some Pharisees had grown so out of touch with the intent of the Law that they could no longer distinguish between appearance and reality. Jesus challenged them by appealing to the very Scriptures they held so dear (vv. 22–23). Here as elsewhere, He refused to let them abuse Him or others with their hypocrisy. See "Jesus Confronts the Legalists," Luke 6:1–11.

find him? Does he intend to go to the Dispersion among
the Greeks and teach the Greeks? 36What does he mean by
saying, 'You will search for me and you will not find me'
and 'Where I am, you cannot come'?"

Jesus Provides Living Water

7:37 see pg. 356

37 On the last day of the festival, the
great day, while Jesus was standing there,
he cried out, "Let anyone who is thirsty come to me, 38and
let the one who believes in me drink. As[d] the scripture has
said, 'Out of the believer's heart[e] shall flow rivers of living
water.' " 39Now he said this about the Spirit, which believers in him were to receive; for as yet there was no Spirit,[f]
because Jesus was not yet glorified.
40 When they heard these words, some in the crowd
said, "This is really the prophet." 41Others said, "This is the
Messiah."[g] But some asked, "Surely the Messiah[g] does not
come from Galilee, does he? 42Has not the scripture said
that the Messiah[g] is descended from David and comes from
Bethlehem, the village where David lived?" 43So there was a
division in the crowd because of him. 44Some of them
wanted to arrest him, but no one laid hands on him.
45 Then the temple police went back to the chief priests
and Pharisees, who asked them, "Why did you not arrest
him?" 46The police answered, "Never has anyone spoken
like this!" 47Then the Pharisees replied, "Surely you have
not been deceived too, have you? 48Has any one of the authorities or of the Pharisees believed in him? 49But this
crowd, which does not know the law—they are accursed."
50Nicodemus, who had gone to Jesus[h] before, and who was
one of them, asked, 51"Our law does not judge people without first giving them a hearing to find out what they are
doing, does it?" 52They replied, "Surely
you are not also from Galilee, are you?
Search and you will see that no prophet is to arise from
Galilee."

7:52

[d]*Or come to me and drink.* [38]*The one who believes in me, as* [e]Gk *out of his belly*
[f]Other ancient authorities read *for as yet the Spirit* (others, *Holy Spirit*) *had not been given* [g]*Or the Christ* [h]Gk *him*

No Prophet from Galilee

A CLOSER LOOK 7:52 *Pharisees and other citizens of Judea looked upon their brothers from Galilee with scorn. To them, a "Galilean" was a fool, heathen, sinner, or worse. See "Jesus the Galilean," Mark 1:14.*

A Double Standard?

CONSIDER THIS 8:2–3 **The woman presented to Jesus (v. 3) must have been utterly humiliated at being dragged into the temple by self-righteous men who were only using her to try to trick the Teacher they hated. According to the Law, adultery required capital punishment of *both* parties (Lev. 20:10). Did the accusers forget to bring the man? Or had they allowed a double standard to creep in?**

If so, Jesus refrained from challenging their hypocrisy, but He did set a new standard for judgment: Let someone perfect decide the case (v. 7; compare Matt. 5:48). Ironically, He was the only one who fit that qualification, and He did decide the case—declining to condemn the woman, but admonishing her to "go and sin no more."

Are there double standards in your moral judgments? Are you eager to point out the speck in someone else's eye, while ignoring the plank in your own (Matt. 7:4–5)? Or, perhaps, like the woman, you've experienced the forgiveness of God for grave offenses against His holiness. If so, live in His grace—and sin no more.

A Woman Caught in Adultery

8:2–3
see pg. 355

8 ⟦53Then each of them went
home, 1while Jesus went to the
Mount of Olives. 2Early in the morning he came again to
the temple. All the people came to him and he sat down
and began to teach them. 3The scribes and the Pharisees
brought a woman who had been caught in adultery; and
making her stand before all of them, 4they said to him,
"Teacher, this woman was caught in the very act of committing adultery. 5Now in the law Moses commanded us to
stone such women. Now what do you say?" 6They said this
to test him, so that they might have some charge to bring
against him. Jesus bent down and wrote with his finger on

CONSIDER THIS
7:37

"We Interrupt This Program . . ."

Jesus' cry in v. 37 was far more dramatic than most modern readers realize. He chose a time when Jerusalem was packed with holiday visitors and a crucial moment in the festivities when He could attract the most attention. It would be as if someone broke into the broadcast of a presidential state-of-the-union address or the kickoff of a Super Bowl to announce, "We interrupt this program to bring you a special report."

The annual Festival of Booths (or Tabernacles, or Tents, 7:2) swelled Jerusalem with an overflow of festive crowds. Every Jewish family within 20 miles of the city was required to move out of its home and live in a booth or tent in remembrance of Israel's wanderings in the wilderness. Many chose to move into the city for the week. Reunions and parties alternated with solemn processions from the temple down to the Pool of Siloam, a reservoir (9:7). Pushing its way through the crowded streets, the throng sang Psalms 113 to 118 in anticipation of God's righteous reign over Jerusalem.

Jesus chose to keep a low profile at this year's festival (7:2–10). He taught in the temple (v. 14), but waited for the right moment to declare Himself publicly. It came on the last day of the feast (v. 37), probably at the climax of the daily processional.

As on the previous six days, the high priest filled a goblet of water from Siloam and carried it back to the

the ground. 7When they kept on questioning him, he
straightened up and said to them, "Let anyone among you
who is without sin be the first to throw a stone at her."
8And once again he bent down and wrote on the ground.[i]
9When they heard it, they went away, one by one, beginning with the elders; and Jesus was left alone with the
woman standing before him. 10Jesus straightened up and
said to her, "Woman, where are they? Has no one condemned you?" 11She said, "No one, sir."[j] And Jesus said,
"Neither do I condemn you. Go your way, and from now
on do not sin again."]][k]

[i]Other ancient authorities add *the sins of each of them* [j]Or *Lord* [k]The most ancient authorities lack 7.53—8.11; other authorities add the passage here or after 7.36 or after 21.25 or after Luke 21.38, with variations of text; some mark the passage as doubtful.

temple, where he poured it out for all the people to see. Each day at that point the crowds chanted, "Oh, give thanks to the Lord*" (Ps. 118:1), and "Save us, we beseech you, O* Lord*! O* Lord*, we beseech you, give us sucess!" (118:25), and again, "Oh, give thanks to the* Lord*." Then they shook myrtle, willow, and palm branches toward the altar, as if to remind God of His promises. Then, after a pause, sacrifices were offered.*

On the last day, however, just after the crowds had not only waved their branches but, as was the custom, literally shook them to pieces in a frenzy of enthusiasm, a voice suddenly cried out: "Let anyone who is thirsty come to me, and let the one who believes in me drink" (John 7:37, emphasis added). Jesus' timing couldn't have been more perfect or His claim more explicit: He was declaring Himself to be none other than the long-awaited Christ who would pour out the Holy Spirit, as many in the crowd immediately recognized (vv. 39–43).

In many ways v. 37 acts as the pivot for John's account. From that point on, the hostility of Jesus' enemies mounted until they finally arrested Him (18:12) in vain hopes of shutting off the "living water." ◆

The festival of Tabernacles was one of three major festivals for the Hebrews of Jesus' day. *See "Jewish Festivals," Luke 2:42.*

"WHOEVER FOLLOWS ME WILL NEVER WALK IN DARKNESS BUT WILL HAVE THE LIGHT OF LIFE." —John 8:12

"I Am the Light of the World"

12 Again Jesus spoke to them, saying, "I am the light of
the world. Whoever follows me will never walk in darkness
but will have the light of life." 13Then the Pharisees said to
him, "You are testifying on your own behalf; your testimony
is not valid." 14Jesus answered, "Even if I testify on my own
behalf, my testimony is valid because I know where I have
come from and where I am going, but you do not know
where I come from or where I am going. 15You judge by human standards;[l] I judge no one. 16Yet even if I do judge, my
judgment is valid; for it is not I alone who judge, but I and
the Father[m] who sent me. 17In your law it is written that the
testimony of two witnesses is valid. 18I testify on my own
behalf, and the Father who sent me testifies on my behalf."
19Then they said to him, "Where is your Father?" Jesus an-

[l]Gk *according to the flesh* [m]Other ancient authorities read *he*

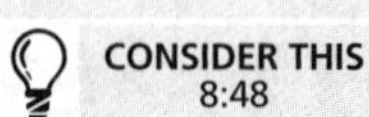

CONSIDER THIS
8:48

Jesus Is Called a Samaritan Demoniac

John 8 records a heated, even bitter, confrontation between Jesus and the Jews, led by the Pharisees. The Lord became particularly blunt with the religious leaders because they refused to accept His claims, imperiling not only their own spiritual standing but that of Israel.

Exchange between Jesus and the Pharisees

Jesus told the Pharisees...	The Pharisees responded...
I know where I came from and where I'm going (8:14–18).	You were born illegitimately (8:19).
You do not know God (8:19).	No response.
You will die in your sin (8:21, 24).	Who are You? (8:25).
[My] truth will make you free (8:31–32).	We've never needed freedom (8:33).
You are the slaves of sin (8:34–38).	We are children of Abraham (8:39).
You are murderers and liars, doing the deeds of your father (8:39–41).	We are not illegitimate [like You]; besides, God is our Father (8:41).
Your father is the devil, a murderer and liar (8:42–47).	You're nothing but a Samaritan and have a demon! (8:48).
I have power even over death (8:49–51).	Who do You think You are? (8:52–54).
My Father honors Me [as His Son]; but you are liars (8:54–56).	You're just a young upstart, yet You claim to have seen Abraham! (8:57).
I AM (8:58; compare Gen. 17:1; Ex. 3:14).	They picked up stones to throw at Him (8:59).

swered, "You know neither me nor my Father. If you knew me, you would know my Father also." [20]He spoke these words while he was teaching in the treasury of the temple, but no one arrested him, because his hour had not yet come.

21 Again he said to them, "I am going away, and you will search for me, but you will die in your sin. Where I am going, you cannot come." [22]Then the Jews said, "Is he going to kill himself? Is that what he means by saying, 'Where I am going, you cannot come'?" [23]He said to them, "You are from below, I am from above; you are of this world, I am not of this world. [24]I told you that you would die in your sins, for you will die in your sins unless you believe that I am he."[n] [25]They said to him, "Who are you?" Jesus said to them, "Why do I speak to you at all?[o] [26]I have much to say

(Bible text continued on page 361)

[n]Gk *I am* [o]Or *What I have told you from the beginning*

Calling Jesus a demon-crazed Samaritan was about the most insulting thing His opponents could think to say. "Samaritan" and "demoniac" were virtual synonyms in their minds. The names expressed all of the bitterness, rage, and contempt they felt toward Jesus.

By the way, what names would people call you as you stand for God's truth at your job or in your community? What hate words would you cringe to hear? ◆

Jews and Samaritans were deeply divided by ethnic barriers. In fact, they had almost no dealings with each other—not unlike many societies today. See John 4:4.

"YOU WILL DIE IN YOUR SINS UNLESS YOU BELIEVE THAT I AM HE."
—John 8:24

CONSIDER THIS
8:52–59

Many Men Would Be Gods, But Only One God Would Be Man

History is crowded with men who claimed to be gods. Christianity is unique in that it reveals that the one God became man, in the person of Jesus Christ. That is the dramatic import of Jesus' words, "Before Abraham was, I AM" (v. 58). I AM was an expression by which God was known to the Hebrews (Ex. 3:14). In using such words, Jesus was declaring that God Himself was standing before the crowd.

By contrast, consider others in history who wanted their followers to regard them as gods, or who were given such adulation after they died:

King Tutankhamen

The boy king of Egypt, who reigned during the fourteenth century B.C., was regarded as a god. We know a lot about him since the discovery in 1922 of his tomb of gold. He died at 18.

Alexander the Great

When the great military general of Macedonia overthrew the Persian Empire (c. 334–323 B.C.), he became a legend bigger than life. He attempted to fuse the Macedonians and the Persians into one master race of which he would be the supreme being. He demanded the same divine recognition from his subject people that they gave to the Greek gods, Heracles and Dionysus. Nevertheless, an illness claimed his life at age 33.

Julius Caesar

A Roman general and statesman, Caesar changed the course of the Graeco-Roman world by conquering Gaul (58–50 B.C.) and winning the Roman Civil War (49–45 B.C.). Crowned emperor, he had military and literary genius that was matched only by his carnal appetite. After his murder in 44 B.C. he was granted status as a god.

King Herod Agrippa I

The grandson of Herod the Great (see "The Herods," Acts 12:1–2) executed James the apostle and tried to do the same with Peter. Later, Agrippa's subjects in Tyre and Sidon, weary of his anger, attempted to make peace with him. Listening to one of his orations, they humored him by shouting, "The voice of a god and not of a man!" Apparently pleased with this sudden elevation in his status, he failed to correct their theology. God struck him for his arrogance so that he was eaten by worms and died (12:20–23).

Napoleon Bonaparte

The renowned French general and emperor made numerous reforms in government, education, and the military. The Napoleonic Code became a basis for civil law throughout the West. A military genius, he waged war and consolidated power throughout Europe (1800–1810). But he died in exile at age 51.

Vladimir Lenin

A militant Marxist, Lenin led the Bolshevik Revolution (1917) and became the first head of the former Soviet Union. His writings vastly expanded and promoted the Communist worldview, and he hoped they would stimulate other proletarian revolutions. He died at the age of 54 after a long, paralyzing illness. He was the closest thing to a "god" that the Soviets would allow. His body was put on view in Moscow.

(continued on next page)

about you and much to condemn; but the one who sent me
is true, and I declare to the world what I have heard from
him." 27They did not understand that he was speaking to
them about the Father. 28So Jesus said, "When you have
lifted up the Son of Man, then you will realize that I am
he,[p] and that I do nothing on my own, but I speak these
things as the Father instructed me. 29And the one who sent
me is with me; he has not left me alone, for I always do
what is pleasing to him." 30As he was saying these things,
many believed in him.

31 Then Jesus said to the Jews who had believed in him,
"If you continue in my word, you are truly my disciples;
32and you will know the truth, and the truth will make you
free." 33They answered him, "We are descendants of Abraham and have never been slaves to anyone. What do you
mean by saying, 'You will be made free'?"

34 Jesus answered them, "Very truly, I tell you, everyone
who commits sin is a slave to sin. 35The slave does not have
a permanent place in the household; the son has a place
there forever. 36So if the Son makes you free, you will be
free indeed. 37I know that you are descendants of Abraham;
yet you look for an opportunity to kill me, because there is
no place in you for my word. 38I declare what I have seen
in the Father's presence; as for you, you should do what
you have heard from the Father."[q]

39 They answered him, "Abraham is our father." Jesus
said to them, "If you were Abraham's children, you would
be doing[r] what Abraham did, 40but now you are trying to
kill me, a man who has told you the truth that I heard from
God. This is not what Abraham did. 41You are indeed doing
what your father does." They said to him, "We are not illegitimate children; we have one father, God himself." 42Jesus
said to them, "If God were your Father, you would love me,
for I came from God and now I am here. I did not come on
my own, but he sent me. 43Why do you not understand
what I say? It is because you cannot accept my word. 44You
are from your father the devil, and you choose to do your
father's desires. He was a murderer from the beginning and
does not stand in the truth, because there is no truth in
him. When he lies, he speaks according to his own nature,
for he is a liar and the father of lies. 45But because I tell the
truth, you do not believe me. 46Which of you convicts me
of sin? If I tell the truth, why do you not believe me?
47Whoever is from God hears the words of God. The reason
you do not hear them is that you are not from God."

[p]Gk *I am* [q]Other ancient authorities read *you do what you have heard from your father*
[r]Other ancient authorities read *If you are Abraham's children, then do*

(continued from previous page)

Adolf Hitler

The mad dictator of Nazi Germany (1932–45) was unequaled in his ability to wield hypnotic power over masses of people. He knew how to manipulate events and people to his own ends, but his attempts to build a master race resulted only in a holocaust of evil. He died by his own hand in 1945.

Only Jesus Backed Up His Claim

Many more pretenders could be listed. But only Jesus demonstrated that He was God by His words and actions. He healed the sick, raised the dead, forgave sins, and lived by the moral precepts that He taught. In fact, He fulfilled every code of righteousness without ever sinning. Most importantly, He backed up His claim of being God by conquering death. No one else in history has ever done that. Others have been regarded as divine, but all have fallen short of God's glory—except Jesus. ◆

8:48 see pg. 358
48 The Jews answered him, "Are we
not right in saying that you are a Samari-
tan and have a demon?" 49Jesus answered, "I do not have a
demon; but I honor my Father, and you dishonor me. 50Yet
I do not seek my own glory; there is one who seeks it and
he is the judge. 51Very truly, I tell you, whoever keeps my
8:52–59 see pg. 360
word will never see death." 52The Jews
said to him, "Now we know that you
have a demon. Abraham died, and so did the prophets; yet
you say, 'Whoever keeps my word will never taste death.'
53Are you greater than our father Abraham, who died? The
prophets also died. Who do you claim to be?" 54Jesus answered, "If I glorify myself, my glory is nothing. It is my Father who glorifies me, he of whom you say, 'He is our God,'
55though you do not know him. But I know him; if I would
say that I do not know him, I would be a liar like you. But I
do know him and I keep his word. 56Your ancestor Abraham rejoiced that he would see my day; he saw it and was
glad." 57Then the Jews said to him, "You are not yet fifty
years old, and have you seen Abraham?"[s] 58Jesus said to
them, "Very truly, I tell you, before Abraham was, I am."
59So they picked up stones to throw at him, but Jesus hid
himself and went out of the temple.

Jesus Heals a Man Born Blind

9:1–41

9:2–3

9 As he walked along, he saw a man
blind from birth. 2His disciples
asked him, "Rabbi, who sinned, this man
or his parents, that he was born blind?"
3Jesus answered, "Neither this man nor his parents sinned;
he was born blind so that God's works might be revealed in
him. 4We[t] must work the works of him who sent me[u] while
it is day; night is coming when no one can work. 5As long
as I am in the world, I am the light of the world." 6When he
had said this, he spat on the ground and made mud with
the saliva and spread the mud on the man's eyes, 7saying to
him, "Go, wash in the pool of Siloam" (which means Sent).
Then he went and washed and came back able to see. 8The
neighbors and those who had seen him before as a beggar
began to ask, "Is this not the man who used to sit and beg?"
9Some were saying, "It is he." Others were saying, "No, but
it is someone like him." He kept saying, "I am the man."
10But they kept asking him, "Then how were your eyes
opened?" 11He answered, "The man called Jesus made mud,

(Bible text continued on page 364)

The Seven Signs of John's Gospel

Jesus Heals the Blind Man

CONSIDER THIS
9:1–41

The sixth sign miracle featured in John's Gospel reveals Jesus as the light of the world (v. 5). He was also unique among the prophets in that none of them had cured blindness (vv. 30–33).

The healing of the blind man speaks to the problem of human suffering. Then as now, sickness was often assumed to be divine punishment for someone's sin. Like Job's counselors (Job 4:7–9; 8:2–8; 11:4–20), Jesus' disciples asked, "Whose sin caused this man's blindness?" (v. 2). But Jesus replied with a radically new truth: God can use human suffering to reveal His glory (v. 3). Jesus immediately showed what He was talking about by healing the man's blindness, thereby revealing Himself to be the Son of God.

[s]Other ancient authorities read *has Abraham seen you?* [t]Other ancient authorities read *I*
[u]Other ancient authorities read *us*

CONSIDER THIS
9:2–3

"WHO SINNED?" HEALTH AND DISEASE IN THE BIBLE

When Jesus' disciples asked Him whose sin had caused a man's blindness (v. 2), they were reflecting a common perception about health and disease in the ancient world. In their minds, physical maladies and suffering were the result of sin and/or God's judgment.

Viewed from our perspective 2,000 years later, their question seems quaint and simplistic. Yet was it really? Even with all of our culture's medical technology, we still wrestle the same issue: what is the ultimate cause of sickness and death? We may understand the scientific explanations and even know how to prevent or cure countless ills. But we still look for a larger meaning behind physical health and disease.

The Bible mentions more than 40 specific diseases or disabilities and alludes frequently to sickness and health issues generally. It seems to accept that concerns about physical health are universal, inescapable, and problematic.

The Great Physician

Jesus devoted considerable time and teaching to health issues, provoking many questions in the process. The most challenging aspect of His work was the miracles of physical healing that He performed. They confounded those who saw them first-hand no less than they trouble us today.

The Gospel writers make it clear that Jesus' first-century witnesses had no problem believing that He actually healed the sick and even raised the dead. They never accused Him of charlatanism. Apparently they accepted the miracles as miracles. But what they struggled with profoundly was the source of His power to perform them and the resulting implications. The curious wondered whether He might not be the Messiah (John 7:31); His enemies accused Him of being in league with the devil (8:48; 10:19–21; Matt. 9:34).

What most troubled people was that the miracles signaled the arrival of the kingdom of God. It was not the healings themselves that they anguished over, but what they were going to do with the One who claimed to be the Christ on the basis of those healings. Was He or wasn't He? And were they ready to receive Him or not?

Modern Skepticism

Today our culture challenges the credibility of the miraculous itself. Capable of accomplishing many physical feats once thought to be "impossible" (flying, curing leprosy, seeing inside the body noninvasively), and lacking many (some would say any) current examples of miracles, skeptics look for some "rational" explanation. "Perhaps Jesus knew more about the body than the average first-century Jew and cleverly manipulated physical forces in a way that people assumed the miraculous," some say. "Perhaps He only appeared to heal, duping the simple like so many modern-day pretenders. Perhaps the miracles never really occurred; they were simply imagined by later believers eager to embellish the myth of a God-man."

Other explanations have been put forth in the last two centuries. They all reflect the skepticism of our age. Yet in the end, one comes out at the same place as those who originally challenged the authority of the miracles: "If it is by the Spirit of God

(continued on next page)

spread it on my eyes, and said to me, 'Go to Siloam and
wash.' Then I went and washed and received my sight."
12They said to him, "Where is he?" He said, "I do not
know."
13 They brought to the Pharisees the man who had formerly been blind. 14Now it was a sabbath day when Jesus
made the mud and opened his eyes. 15Then the Pharisees
also began to ask him how he had received his sight. He
said to them, "He put mud on my eyes. Then I washed, and
now I see." 16Some of the Pharisees said, "This man is not
from God, for he does not observe the sabbath." But others
said, "How can a man who is a sinner perform such signs?"
And they were divided. 17So they said again to the blind
man, "What do you say about him? It was your eyes he
opened." He said, "He is a prophet."
18 The Jews did not believe that he had been blind and
had received his sight until they called the parents of the
man who had received his sight 19and asked them, "Is this
your son, who you say was born blind? How then does he
now see?" 20His parents answered, "We know that this is
our son, and that he was born blind; 21but we do not know
how it is that now he sees, nor do we know who opened
his eyes. Ask him; he is of age. He will speak for himself."
22His parents said this because they were afraid of the Jews;
for the Jews had already agreed that anyone who confessed
Jesus[v] to be the Messiah[w] would be put out of the synagogue. 23Therefore his parents said, "He is of age; ask him."
24 So for the second time they called the man who had
been blind, and they said to him, "Give glory to God! We
know that this man is a sinner." 25He answered, "I do not
know whether he is a sinner. One thing I do know, that
though I was blind, now I see." 26They said to him, "What
did he do to you? How did he open your eyes?" 27He answered them, "I have told you already, and you would not
listen. Why do you want to hear it again? Do you also want
to become his disciples?" 28Then they reviled him, saying,
"You are his disciple, but we are disciples of Moses. 29We
know that God has spoken to Moses, but as for this man,
we do not know where he comes from." 30The man answered, "Here is an astonishing thing! You do not know
where he comes from, and yet he opened my eyes. 31We
know that God does not listen to sinners, but he does listen
to one who worships him and obeys his will. 32Never since
the world began has it been heard that anyone opened the

[v]Gk *him* [w]Or *the Christ*

(continued from previous page)

that I cast out demons, then the kingdom of God has come to you" (Matt. 12:28). In other words, is it really the possibility of miracles that troubles moderns? Or is it the staggering probability that the One who performed them is in fact God Himself? ◆

Jesus and the Physical

- **Most of the healings that Jesus performed were intended to reveal His divine power and authority (John 9:2–3).**
- **He healed people from all walks of life, both the untouchables and the well-off and well-connected.**
- **He did not heal everyone (Matt. 13:58).**
- **He recognized and dealt with the emotional side of illness—feelings of sadness, anger, disorientation, anxiety, conflict, fear, and aggression.**
- **He exhibited patience, compassion, and courage when confronting the sick.**
- **He never used spells, charms, incantations, drugs, incense, or herbs to ward off evil spirits or to heal people of their diseases. His power came directly from His person.**
- **He drew a parallel between physical sickness and spiritual need (Mark 2:15–17).**
- **He often linked the healing of disease with faith and the forgiveness of sins.**
- **He refused to see all sickness as a sign of God's judgment.**
- **He refused to allow religious traditions and taboos to prevent Him from relieving pain and suffering.**

(continued on next page)

eyes of a person born blind. 33If this man were not from
God, he could do nothing." 34They answered him, "You
were born entirely in sins, and are you trying to teach us?"
And they drove him out.
35 Jesus heard that they had driven him out, and when
he found him, he said, "Do you believe in the Son of
Man?"[x] 36He answered, "And who is he, sir?[y] Tell me, so
that I may believe in him." 37Jesus said to him, "You have
seen him, and the one speaking with you is he." 38He said,
"Lord,[y] I believe." And he worshiped him. 39Jesus said, "I
came into this world for judgment so that those who do not
see may see, and those who do see may become blind."
40Some of the Pharisees near him heard this and said to
him, "Surely we are not blind, are we?" 41Jesus said to
them, "If you were blind, you would not have sin. But now
that you say, 'We see,' your sin remains.

"I Am the Good Shepherd"

10 "Very truly, I tell you, anyone who does not enter
the sheepfold by the gate but climbs in by another
way is a thief and a bandit. 2The one who enters by the gate
is the shepherd of the sheep. 3The gatekeeper opens the
gate for him, and the sheep hear his voice. He calls his own
sheep by name and leads them out. 4When he has brought
out all his own, he goes ahead of them, and the sheep follow him because they know his voice. 5They will not follow
a stranger, but they will run from him because they do not
know the voice of strangers." 6Jesus used this figure of
speech with them, but they did not understand what he
was saying to them.
7 So again Jesus said to them, "Very truly, I tell you, I am
the gate for the sheep. 8All who came before me are thieves
and bandits; but the sheep did not listen to them. 9I am the
gate. Whoever enters by me will be saved, and will come in
and go out and find pasture. 10The thief comes only to steal
and kill and destroy. I came that they may have life, and
have it abundantly.
11 "I am the good shepherd. The good shepherd lays
down his life for the sheep. 12The hired hand, who is not
the shepherd and does not own the sheep, sees the wolf
coming and leaves the sheep and runs away—and the wolf

[x]Other ancient authorities read *the Son of God* [y]*Sir* and *Lord* translate the same Greek word

(continued from previous page)

- **His power to heal threatened the established authorities.**
- **His immediate followers experienced the same power over physical maladies, a sign that their message was from God.**
- **Sometimes illness and death showed God's judgment (Acts 5:1–11; 12:19–23).**
- **His followers were not spared from physical afflictions. God used their sufferings to form character.**
- **We can look forward to a time when suffering, sorrow, pain, and disease will come to an end (Rom. 8:18; Rev. 21:4).**

Not only did healing demonstrate Christ's divine power over disease and infirmity, it revealed God's heart of compassion. "He Healed Them All" (Luke 4:40) lists some of the diseases and disabilities that Jesus and His followers treated.

THE POWER OF SELF-SACRIFICE

CONSIDER THIS 10:17–18 **What does power look like in the lives of people you know? Does it mean aggressively making things happen? Does it mean political or financial muscle? Jesus described His power as the right and ability to lay down His life for others (vv. 17–18).**

For whom or what would you lay down your life? Is there a cause so noble or people so dear that you would willingly let go of life itself? The world may not view that kind of self-sacrifice as power. But we who follow Christ can know the profound power of love—looking out not only for our own interests, but also for the interests of others (Phil. 2:4).

Jesus' first followers experienced a dynamic power that changed the world. See "Power," Acts 1:8.

THE FESTIVAL OF THE DEDICATION

FOR YOUR INFO 10:22 **The festival of the Dedication (v. 22) was a minor feast held in the Jewish month of Chislev (November-December). We know it today as Hanukkah, or the festival of Lights. It was not a feast prescribed by Old Testament Law. Rather it originated as a celebration of the cleansing of the temple after its desecration by Antiochus Epiphanes, one of the cruelest rulers of all time.**

A member of the Seleucid dynasty of Syria, Antiochus IV (175–164 B.C.) was surnamed Epiphanes, meaning "God manifest." His enemies, however, called him Epimanes, or "madman." Enterprising and ambitious, he desired to unify his empire by spreading Greek civilization and culture. This brought him into direct conflict with the Jews.

In a show of utter contempt for their religion, Antiochus erected an altar to the Greek god Zeus over the altar in the temple at Jerusalem. He also forced Jews to participate in heathen festivities and ordered them put to death if caught with the Law in their possession.

In 165 B.C., a man named Judas Maccabeus led a successful revolt that overthrew Seleucid domination of Palestine. The temple was cleansed on the 25th of Chislev, around December 25th by our calendar. Antiochus retreated to Persia, where, true to his nickname, he died a madman.

snatches them and scatters them. [13]The hired hand runs
away because a hired hand does not care for the sheep. [14]I
am the good shepherd. I know my own and my own know
me, [15]just as the Father knows me and I know the Father.
And I lay down my life for the sheep. [16]I have other sheep
that do not belong to this fold. I must bring them also, and
they will listen to my voice. So there will be one flock, one

10:17–18 see pg. 365

shepherd. [17]For this reason the Father
loves me, because I lay down my life in
order to take it up again. [18]No one takes[z] it from me, but I
lay it down of my own accord. I have power to lay it down,
and I have power to take it up again. I have received this
command from my Father."

19 Again the Jews were divided because of these words.
[20]Many of them were saying, "He has a demon and is out of
his mind. Why listen to him?" [21]Others were saying, "These
are not the words of one who has a demon. Can a demon
open the eyes of the blind?"

Jesus Attends the Festival of the Dedication

10:22

22 At that time the festival of the Dedication took place in Jerusalem. It was
winter, [23]and Jesus was walking in the temple, in the portico of Solomon. [24]So the Jews gathered around him and
said to him, "How long will you keep us in suspense? If
you are the Messiah,[a] tell us plainly." [25]Jesus answered, "I
have told you, and you do not believe. The works that I do
in my Father's name testify to me; [26]but you do not believe,
because you do not belong to my sheep. [27]My sheep hear
my voice. I know them, and they follow me. [28]I give them
eternal life, and they will never perish. No one will snatch
them out of my hand. [29]What my Father has given me is
greater than all else, and no one can snatch it out of the Father's hand.[b] [30]The Father and I are one."

10:31

31 The Jews took up stones again to
stone him. [32]Jesus replied, "I have shown
you many good works from the Father. For which of these
are you going to stone me?" [33]The Jews answered, "It is not
for a good work that we are going to stone you, but for
blasphemy, because you, though only a human being, are
making yourself God." [34]Jesus answered, "Is it not written
in your law,[c] 'I said, you are gods'? [35]If those to whom the
word of God came were called 'gods'—and the scripture

[z]Other ancient authorities read *has taken* [a]Or *the Christ* [b]Other ancient authorities read *My Father who has given them to me is greater than all, and no one can snatch them out of the Father's hand* [c]Other ancient authorities read *in the law*

cannot be annulled— 36can you say that the one whom the
Father has sanctified and sent into the world is blaspheming because I said, 'I am God's Son'? 37If I am not doing the
works of my Father, then do not believe me. 38But if I do
them, even though you do not believe me, believe the
works, so that you may know and understand[d] that the Father is in me and I am in the Father." 39Then they tried to
arrest him again, but he escaped from their hands.

Jesus Returns to the River Jordan

10:40–42 see pg. 369

40 He went away again across the Jordan to the place where John had been
baptizing earlier, and he remained there. 41Many came to
him, and they were saying, "John performed no sign, but
everything that John said about this man was true." 42And
many believed in him there.

Lazarus Raised from the Dead

11:1–2 see pg. 369

11:2 see pg. 370

11 Now a certain man was ill,
Lazarus of Bethany, the village of
Mary and her sister Martha. 2Mary was
the one who anointed the Lord with per-
fume and wiped his feet with her hair; her brother Lazarus
was ill. 3So the sisters sent a message to Jesus,[e] "Lord, he
whom you love is ill." 4But when Jesus heard it, he said,
"This illness does not lead to death; rather it is for God's
glory, so that the Son of God may be glorified through it."
5Accordingly, though Jesus loved Martha and her sister and
Lazarus, 6after having heard that Lazarus[f] was ill, he stayed
two days longer in the place where he was.
7 Then after this he said to the disciples, "Let us go to
Judea again." 8The disciples said to him, "Rabbi, the Jews
were just now trying to stone you, and are you going there
again?" 9Jesus answered, "Are there not twelve hours of
daylight? Those who walk during the day do not stumble,
because they see the light of this world. 10But those who
walk at night stumble, because the light is not in them."
11After saying this, he told them, "Our friend Lazarus has
fallen asleep, but I am going there to awaken him." 12The
disciples said to him, "Lord, if he has fallen asleep, he will
be all right." 13Jesus, however, had been speaking about his
death, but they thought that he was referring merely to

[d]Other ancient authorities lack *and understand*; others read *and believe* [e]Gk *him* [f]Gk *he*

Stoning

FOR YOUR INFO 10:31 *The intensity of the Jews' hostility against Jesus can be seen in their readiness to stone Him (v. 31; 8:59). Stoning was an ancient method of capital punishment reserved for the most serious crimes against the Mosaic Law, including:*

- *child sacrifice (Lev. 20:2).*
- *consultation with mediums and occultists (Lev. 20:27).*
- *blasphemy (Lev. 24:16).*
- *Sabbath-breaking (Num. 15:32–36).*
- *the worship of false gods (Deut. 13:10).*
- *rebellion against parents (Deut. 21:21).*
- *adultery (Ezek. 16:40).*
- *certain cases of direct disobedience against God's express command (Josh. 7:25).*

Stoning was usually carried out by the men of the community (Deut. 21:21) upon the testimony of at least two witnesses, who were to cast the first stones (17:5–7). The execution usually took place outside the camp or city (Lev. 24:14, 23; 1 Kin. 21:10, 13).

Jesus must have known He was headed for trouble when His enemies "gathered around" Him (literally, "closed in on Him,") as He walked in Solomon's porch (vv. 23–24). In the same way, a victim of stoning would be surrounded as the executioners cut all means of escape from their fury.

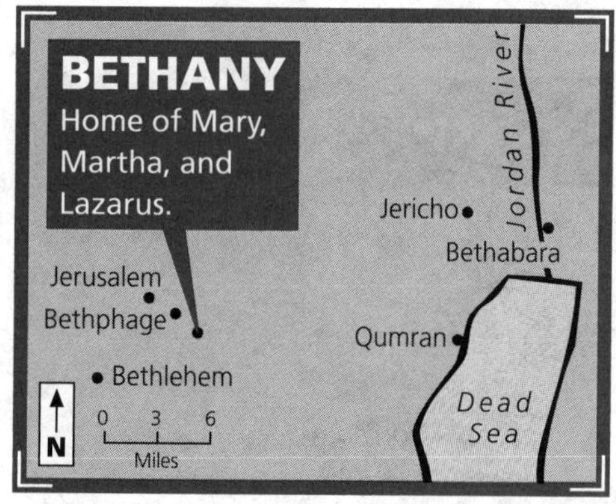

Bethany

YOU ARE THERE 11:18

- A village about two miles east of Jerusalem on the southeast slope of the Mount of Olives, on the road to Jericho.
- Name meant "house of an unripe fig," though its modern Arab

(continued on next page)

sleep. 14Then Jesus told them plainly, "Lazarus is dead.
15For your sake I am glad I was not there, so that you may
believe. But let us go to him." 16Thomas, who was called
the Twin,[g] said to his fellow disciples, "Let us also go, that
we may die with him."

(Bible text continued on page 370)

[g]Gk *Didymus*

Personality Profile: Lazarus

FOR YOUR INFO 11:1–45 **Not to be confused with:** The man named Lazarus in one of Jesus' parables (Luke 16:19–31).

Home: Bethany, near Jerusalem.

Family: Brother of Mary and Martha.

Occupation: Unknown.

Known today as: A man whom Jesus raised from the dead.

CONSIDER THIS 11:25

"I Am the Resurrection and the Life"

It was after the raising of Lazarus from the dead that the chief priests, Pharisees, and other religious leaders finally determined to put Jesus to death (John 11:53). Until now, the conflict between them and the upstart rabbi had been little more than a war of words. But the raising of Lazarus was an incredible miracle, witnessed by many. Jesus had raised at least two others, but those events had taken place in faraway Galilee (Mark 5:22–24, 35–43; Luke 7:11–17). By contrast, Lazarus' resurrection occurred in Bethany, a suburb of Jerusalem (John 11:18).

Not surprisingly, the miracle caused many to believe in Jesus (v. 45). It provided undeniable proof that Jesus' bold claim must be true: "I am the resurrection and the life . . . everyone who lives and believes in me will never die" (v. 25). Indeed, Lazarus became something of a curiosity, drawing numerous onlookers who wanted to see for themselves the man whom Jesus had brought back to life (12:9).

It was this kind of publicity that the leaders especially feared. Disputes over religious matters were one thing; a rapidly growing movement led by a popular Messiah-

Personality Profile: Mary of Bethany

FOR YOUR INFO 11:1–2 **Not to be confused with:** Mary, the mother of Jesus (Luke 1:26–56); Mary of Magdala (8:2); Mary, the mother of James and Joses (Matt. 27:55–61); Mary, the mother of John Mark (Acts 12:12).

Home: Bethany, a suburb of Jerusalem on the road to Jericho.

Family: Sister of Martha and Lazarus.

Best known today for: Sitting at Jesus' feet to worship and learn while her sister, Martha, served Him and His hungry disciples (Luke 10:38–42).

figure was something else. It was bound to have political repercussions, as the Romans were ever on the lookout for signs of rebellion (see "Jerusalem Surrounded," Luke 21:20).

It was Caiaphas the high priest (see Matt. 26:3) who saw the usefulness of that fact. Why sacrifice the entire nation for the sake of Jesus, when Jesus could be sacrificed for the sake of the nation (John 11:49–52)? Thus the religious leaders began to scheme how they might bring Jesus before the Romans and, hopefully, have Him put away on a charge of rebellion. And even though Lazarus had just been brought back from the dead, they plotted to do away with him as well, as he was living evidence of Jesus' power (12:10–11).

The plan succeeded brilliantly except for one detail that Caiaphas and his fellow leaders either overlooked or refused to believe: in arranging His death, they handed Him an opportunity to prove once and for all that He had spoken the truth when He said, "I am the resurrection and the life." ◆

(continued from previous page)

name is el-'Azariyeh, "home of Lazarus."

- **A favorite stopover for Jesus on His trips to and from Jerusalem. He stayed with His close friends Mary, Martha, and Lazarus.**
- **Modern Bethany offers a tomb site that some claim to be the authentic tomb of Lazarus, whom Jesus raised from the dead (John 11:1–44).**

A nearby village, Bethphage ("place of young figs") along with Bethany may have given rise to Jesus' parable of the unripe figs (Luke 13:6–9). See "Bethphage," Mark 11:1.

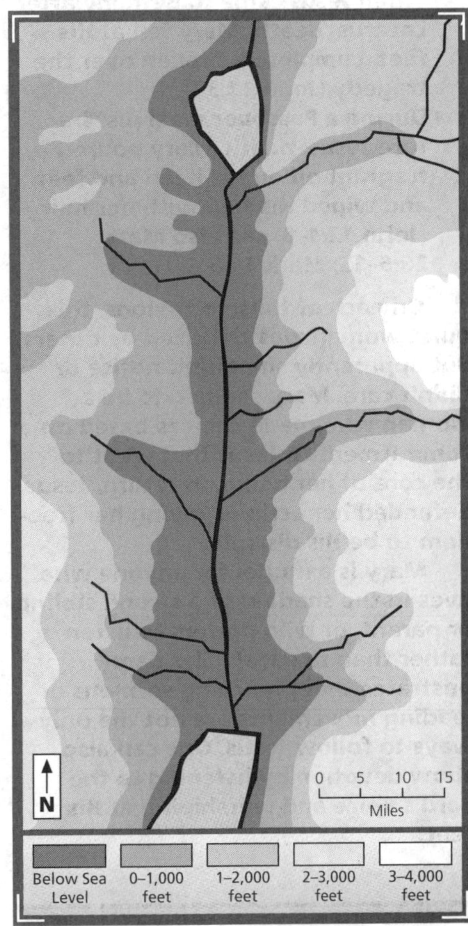

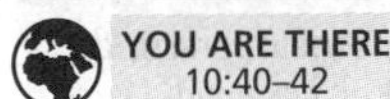
YOU ARE THERE 10:40–42

The Jordan River Valley

The Devoted Mary

CONSIDER THIS 11:2 **Scripture records only one sentence spoken by Mary of Bethany (John 11:32), and even that wasn't original: her sister Martha had already said the same thing (v. 21)! But what Mary may have lacked in outspokenness, she more than made up for in devotion to Jesus. All three portraits of her in the Gospels show her at the Lord's feet:**

- **During one of Jesus' visits to her home, Mary sat at His feet, listening (Luke 10:38–42).**
- **When Jesus came to Bethany after Lazarus' death, Mary fell at His feet, completely broken over the tragedy (John 11:32).**
- **During a Passover meal just before Jesus' death, Mary poured fragrant oil on His head and feet, and wiped His feet with her hair (John 12:1–8; see also Matt. 26:6–13; Mark 14:3–9).**

On each of these occasions, this quiet woman was criticized by others. But apparently she didn't notice or didn't care. Mary seemed to be a woman who made choices based on a commitment to Jesus that went to the core of her being. In return, Jesus defended her actions, giving her freedom to be His disciple.

Mary is a model for anyone who lives in the shadow of a strong sibling or parent, or who prefers to listen rather than to speak. She demonstrates that preaching sermons or leading movements are not the only ways to follow Jesus. One can also show devotion by listening to the Lord's voice and worshiping at His feet.

Mary's sister, Martha, was an industrious, practical woman who never hesitated to speak her mind. Learn more about her at Luke 10:38–42.

17 When Jesus arrived, he found that Lazarus[h] had
11:18 see pg. 368
already been in the tomb four days.
18Now Bethany was near Jerusalem,
some two miles[i] away, 19and many of the Jews had come to
Martha and Mary to console them about their brother.
20When Martha heard that Jesus was coming, she went and
met him, while Mary stayed at home. 21Martha said to Jesus, "Lord, if you had been here, my brother would not
have died. 22But even now I know that God will give you
whatever you ask of him." 23Jesus said to her, "Your brother
will rise again." 24Martha said to him, "I know that he will
11:25 see pg. 368
rise again in the resurrection on the last
day." 25Jesus said to her, "I am the resurrection and the life.[j] Those who believe in me, even though
they die, will live, 26and everyone who lives and believes in
me will never die. Do you believe this?" 27She said to him,
"Yes, Lord, I believe that you are the Messiah,[k] the Son of
God, the one coming into the world."
28 When she had said this, she went back and called her
sister Mary, and told her privately, "The Teacher is here and
is calling for you." 29And when she heard it, she got up
quickly and went to him. 30Now Jesus had not yet come to
the village, but was still at the place where Martha had met
him. 31The Jews who were with her in the house, consoling
her, saw Mary get up quickly and go out. They followed her
because they thought that she was going to the tomb to
weep there. 32When Mary came where Jesus was and saw
him, she knelt at his feet and said to him, "Lord, if you had
been here, my brother would not have died." 33When Jesus
saw her weeping, and the Jews who came with her also
weeping, he was greatly disturbed in spirit and deeply
moved. 34He said, "Where have you laid him?" They said to
him, "Lord, come and see." 35Jesus began to weep. 36So the
Jews said, "See how he loved him!" 37But some of them
said, "Could not he who opened the eyes of the blind man
have kept this man from dying?"
38 Then Jesus, again greatly disturbed, came to the
tomb. It was a cave, and a stone was lying against it. 39Jesus
said, "Take away the stone." Martha, the sister of the dead
man, said to him, "Lord, already there is a stench because
he has been dead four days." 40Jesus said to her, "Did I not
tell you that if you believed, you would see the glory of
11:17–45 see pg. 372
God?" 41So they took away the stone.
And Jesus looked upward and said, "Fa-

[h]Gk *he* [i]Gk *fifteen stadia* [j]Other ancient authorities lack *and the life* [k]Or *the Christ*

ther, I thank you for having heard me. [42]I knew that you always hear me, but I have said this for the sake of the crowd
standing here, so that they may believe that you sent me."
11:1–45 see pg. 368
[43]When he had said this, he cried with a
loud voice, "Lazarus, come out!" [44]The
dead man came out, his hands and feet bound with strips
of cloth, and his face wrapped in a cloth. Jesus said to
them, "Unbind him, and let him go."

Leaders Plot to Destroy Jesus

45 Many of the Jews therefore, who had come with Mary
and had seen what Jesus did, believed in him. [46]But some
of them went to the Pharisees and told them what he had
done. [47]So the chief priests and the Pharisees called a meeting of the council, and said, "What are we to do? This man
is performing many signs. [48]If we let him go on like this,
everyone will believe in him, and the Romans will come
11:49
and destroy both our holy place[l] and our
nation." [49]But one of them, Caiaphas,
who was high priest that year, said to them, "You know
nothing at all! [50]You do not understand that it is better for
you to have one man die for the people than to have the
whole nation destroyed." [51]He did not say this on his own,
but being high priest that year he prophesied that Jesus was
about to die for the nation, [52]and not for the nation only,
but to gather into one the dispersed children of God. [53]So
from that day on they planned to put him to death.
11:54
54 Jesus therefore no longer walked
about openly among the Jews, but went
from there to a town called Ephraim in the region near the
wilderness; and he remained there with the disciples.
55 Now the Passover of the Jews was near, and many
went up from the country to Jerusalem before the Passover
to purify themselves. [56]They were looking for Jesus and
were asking one another as they stood in the temple, "What
do you think? Surely he will not come to the festival, will

[l]Or *our temple*; Greek *our place*

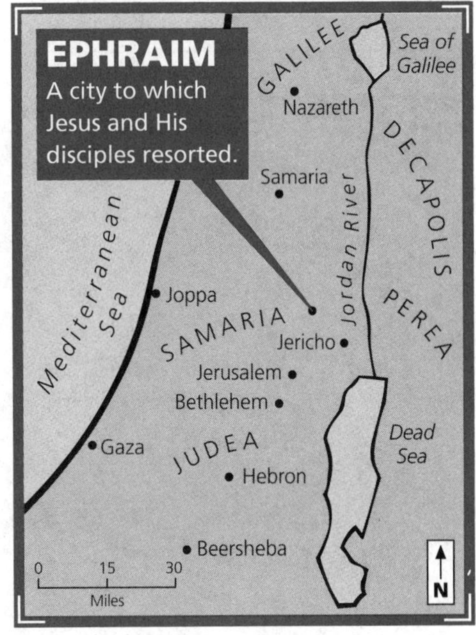

EPHRAIM

YOU ARE THERE 11:54

- **A city surrounded by mountains, four miles east of Bethel and fourteen miles northeast of Jerusalem.**
- **Also known as Ephron and Ephrain. Ephraim was of one of the twelve tribes of Israel.**
- **Name meant "doubly fruitful" or "double grain land."**
- **Identified with the Old Testament city of Ophrah (Josh. 18:23; 1 Sam. 13:17), at site of modern et-Taiyibeh.**

Caiaphas

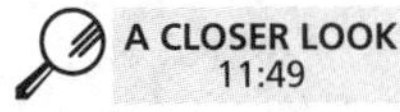

A CLOSER LOOK 11:49

Troubled by the confusion created by the raising of Lazarus, Caiaphas, the high priest, scorned his fellow leaders as know-nothings (v. 49). But what do we know about the man Caiaphas? See Matt. 26:3.

he?" 57Now the chief priests and the Pharisees had given orders that anyone who knew where Jesus[m] was should let
them know, so that they might arrest him.

Mary Anoints Jesus with Costly Oil

 12:1–8

12 Six days before the Passover
Jesus came to Bethany, the home
of Lazarus, whom he had raised from the dead. 2There they
gave a dinner for him. Martha served, and Lazarus was one
of those at the table with him. 3Mary took a pound of costly
perfume made of pure nard, anointed Jesus' feet, and wiped
them[n] with her hair. The house was filled with the fragrance
of the perfume. 4But Judas Iscariot, one
of his disciples (the one who was about
to betray him), said, 5"Why was this perfume not sold for
three hundred denarii[o] and the money given to the poor?"

[m]Gk *he* [n]Gk *his feet* [o]Three hundred denarii would be nearly a year's wages for a laborer

The Seven Signs of John's Gospel

Jesus Raises Lazarus

 **CONSIDER THIS** 11:17–45

The final sign miracle in John's Gospel is the climax of Jesus' signs: He raised Lazarus from the dead (vv. 41–44), proving to all that He was master even over death. The amazing thing was that this miracle led directly to the plot to arrest Him and put Him to death (vv. 46–53), along with Lazarus (12:10–11)!

YOU ARE THERE 12:1–8

Funeral Preparations

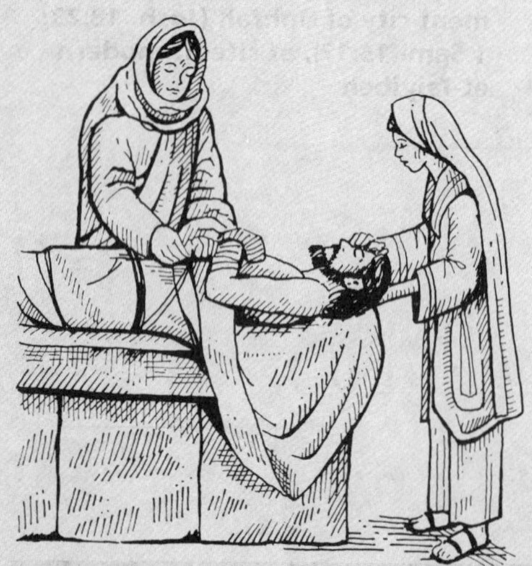

Jesus told the dinner crowd that Mary was preparing Him for His burial (v. 7). It's difficult for us today to appreciate the significance that burial rituals had for ancient peoples. Nearly every ancient religion gave explicit and sometimes elaborate instructions for preparing and burying the dead.

For Hebrews at the time of Christ, women and men participated in the mourning ritual, but women likely prepared the corpse for interment. First they washed the body, then scented it with fragrant oil, an act of devotion that might be repeated at the tomb.

The oil that Mary used on Jesus (v. 3) was probably nard, a perfume used by women. Imported from India, it was extremely costly and was known for its strong fragrance. It was the same perfume used by the woman that Solomon praised in his Song of Solomon (1:12; 4:13).

Washed and scented, the body was dressed in the person's own clothes or else wrapped in specially prepared sheets. Then, as soon as possible, it was carried upon a bier to the tomb. Relatives, friends, and professional mourners (see Matt. 9:23) formed a procession, and anyone meeting it was obliged to show honor to the

[6](He said this not because he cared about the poor, but because he was a thief; he kept the common purse and used
to steal what was put into it.) [7]Jesus said, "Leave her alone.
She bought it[p] so that she might keep it for the day of my
burial. [8]You always have the poor with you, but you do not
always have me."

The Curious Gather

9 When the great crowd of the Jews learned that he was
there, they came not only because of Jesus but also to see
Lazarus, whom he had raised from the dead. [10]So the chief
priests planned to put Lazarus to death as well, [11]since it
was on account of him that many of the Jews were deserting and were believing in Jesus.

[p]Gk lacks *She bought it*

Why Not Give to the Poor?

A CLOSER LOOK 12:4–7 *Judas Iscariot's greedy heart was clearly revealed in this incident (vv. 4–6). But Jesus responded with a puzzling statement (vv. 7–8). For an explanation, see "A Parting Gift," Mark 14:3–9.*

deceased and the relatives by joining. A eulogy was often delivered at the grave site.

The body was placed on a shelf in the tomb, which was then sealed by a heavy, tight-fitting slab. Jews were expected to visit the tomb often, partly as a precaution against burying someone who only seemed dead. ◆

For further details see "Burial" at 1 Cor. 15:42.

"YOU ALWAYS HAVE THE POOR WITH YOU, BUT YOU DO NOT ALWAYS HAVE ME." —John 12:8

A Parade Welcomes Jesus to Jerusalem

12 The next day the great crowd that had come to the
festival heard that Jesus was coming to Jerusalem. 13So they
took branches of palm trees and went out to meet him,
shouting,

"Hosanna!
Blessed is the one who comes in the name of the Lord—
the King of Israel!"

14Jesus found a young donkey and sat on it; as it is written:
15 "Do not be afraid, daughter of Zion.
Look, your king is coming,
sitting on a donkey's colt!"

16His disciples did not understand these things at first; but
when Jesus was glorified, then they remembered that these
things had been written of him and had been done to him.
17So the crowd that had been with him when he called
Lazarus out of the tomb and raised him from the dead continued to testify.[q] 18It was also because they heard that he
had performed this sign that the crowd went to meet him.
19The Pharisees then said to one another, "You see, you can
do nothing. Look, the world has gone after him!"

Jesus Sums Up His Teaching

12:20–36 20 Now among those who went up to
worship at the festival were some
Greeks. 21They came to Philip, who was from Bethsaida in
Galilee, and said to him, "Sir, we wish to see Jesus." 22Philip
went and told Andrew; then Andrew and Philip went and
told Jesus. 23Jesus answered them, "The hour has come for
the Son of Man to be glorified. 24Very truly, I tell you, unless a grain of wheat falls into the earth and dies, it remains
just a single grain; but if it dies, it bears much fruit. 25Those
who love their life lose it, and those who hate their life in
this world will keep it for eternal life. 26Whoever serves me
must follow me, and where I am, there will my servant be
also. Whoever serves me, the Father will honor.

27 "Now my soul is troubled. And what should I say—
'Father, save me from this hour'? No, it is for this reason
that I have come to this hour. 28Father, glorify your name."
Then a voice came from heaven, "I have glorified it, and I
will glorify it again." 29The crowd standing there heard it
and said that it was thunder. Others said, "An angel has

[q]Other ancient authorities read *with him began to testify that he had called. . .from the dead*

Jesus Excludes Only the Faithless

CONSIDER THIS 12:20–36 *Jesus was at an annual Jewish festival called Passover (12:1). It was a major feast, lasting several days and attended by people from all over the Roman Empire (see Luke 22:7).*

When Gentiles at the Passover requested a meeting with Jesus, He responded by telling His Jewish followers that He was going to draw all peoples to Himself (v. 32). Later He affirmed that nothing can save someone from judgment but faith in Him and His saving work on the cross (vv. 46, 48). Nothing else helps, nor does the lack of any other qualification prohibit anyone from coming to Jesus for salvation.

spoken to him." 30Jesus answered, "This voice has come for
your sake, not for mine. 31Now is the judgment of this
world; now the ruler of this world will be driven out. 32And
I, when I am lifted up from the earth, will draw all people[r]
to myself." 33He said this to indicate the kind of death he
was to die. 34The crowd answered him, "We have heard
from the law that the Messiah[s] remains forever. How can
you say that the Son of Man must be lifted up? Who is this
Son of Man?" 35Jesus said to them, "The light is with you
for a little longer. Walk while you have the light, so that the
darkness may not overtake you. If you walk in the darkness, you do not know where you are going. 36While you
have the light, believe in the light, so that you may become
children of light."

Unbelief Persists

After Jesus had said this, he departed and hid from them.
37Although he had performed so many signs in their presence, they did not believe in him. 38This was to fulfill the
word spoken by the prophet Isaiah:

"Lord, who has believed our message,
and to whom has the arm of the Lord been revealed?"

39And so they could not believe, because Isaiah also said,

40 "He has blinded their eyes
and hardened their heart,
so that they might not look with their eyes,
and understand with their heart and turn—
and I would heal them."

41Isaiah said this because[t] he saw his glory and spoke about
12:42–43
him. 42Nevertheless many, even of the
authorities, believed in him. But because
of the Pharisees they did not confess it, for fear that they
would be put out of the synagogue; 43for they loved human
glory more than the glory that comes from God.

Jesus Makes His Final Claims

44 Then Jesus cried aloud: "Whoever believes in me believes not in me but in him who sent me. 45And whoever
sees me sees him who sent me. 46I have come as light into
the world, so that everyone who believes in me should not
remain in the darkness. 47I do not judge anyone who hears

[r]Other ancient authorities read *all things* [s]Or *the Christ* [t]Other ancient witnesses read *when*

The Fear of Rejection

CONSIDER THIS 12:42–43 **As John points out in vv. 42–43, the Pharisees held a powerful grip on Jewish society in Jesus' day, stifling dissent through fear. Apparently Jesus had some support even at the highest levels of society. But it did Him no good, as fear of rejection overcame the impulse for justice and truth.**

Have you ever been embarrassed or afraid to identify publicly with Christ because of possible rejection by others, especially superiors? Scripture is clear that one price of authentic discipleship will almost certainly be some rejection and persecution (15:18–25; 2 Tim. 3:12). To believe that you can avoid any tough choices between acceptance by the world and loyalty to God is both naive and dangerous. If God does not hold your highest allegiance, how real can He be to you in any meaningful way?

The Pharisees were one of a number of major political parties among the Hebrews in the first century. See "Party Politics of Jesus' Day," Matt. 16:1.

The Order of the Towel

CONSIDER THIS 13:1–20

Leadership is a fascinating topic. Business books offer models of leadership as diverse as Attila the Hun, Oriental warlords, and Abraham Lincoln. But Jesus painted a different picture of leadership.

As He wrapped up His work, Jesus held a dinner for His closest associates. Instead of delivering a state-of-the-union address or naming a successor, He chose to leave His seat at the head of the table and pick up some household servant's equipment—a basin of water and a towel. He then washed the feet of every person at the table—even Judas, His betrayer (vv. 1–20). Foot-washing was usually performed by household servants as an act of hospitality to weary, dusty guests (compare Luke 7:44). Leaders and hosts did not stoop to such a menial task. But Jesus did.

(continued on next page)

my words and does not keep them, for I came not to judge
the world, but to save the world. 48The one who rejects me
and does not receive my word has a judge; on the last day
12:49 the word that I have spoken will serve as
judge, 49for I have not spoken on my
own, but the Father who sent me has himself given me a
commandment about what to say and what to speak. 50And
I know that his commandment is eternal life. What I speak,
therefore, I speak just as the Father has told me."

Jesus Washes the Disciples' Feet

13:1–20 13 Now before the festival of the
Passover, Jesus knew that his
hour had come to depart from this world and go to the Father. Having loved his own who were in the world, he
13:2–17 loved them to the end. 2The devil had already put it into the heart of Judas son of
Simon Iscariot to betray him. And during supper 3Jesus,
knowing that the Father had given all things into his hands,
and that he had come from God and was going to God, 4got
up from the table,[u] took off his outer robe, and tied a towel
around himself. 5Then he poured water into a basin and be-

[u]Gk *from supper*

CONSIDER THIS 12:49

Under Authority

Jesus faithfully represented His Father to the world (v. 49). Consider two implications of that for Christians today:

(1) As believers, we are to live under Christ's authority, and therefore we are responsible for faithfully representing Christ in our places of work. To do so we must be intimately familiar with Jesus—what He said, what His commands are, and what His purposes are. That means serious and continuous exploration of the Scriptures.

(2) As employees under human authorities, we are responsible for faithfully representing our organizations in general and our superiors in particular to other people. To do so we must be intimately familiar with the values, goals, policies, and procedures of our employers.

Neither of these is an easy assignment. It's all too common to misrepresent the statements of the Lord or our superiors to suit our own purposes. It's also easy to hear from them only what we want to hear.

gan to wash the disciples' feet and to wipe them with the
towel that was tied around him. 6He came to Simon Peter,
who said to him, "Lord, are you going to wash my feet?"
7Jesus answered, "You do not know now what I am doing,
but later you will understand." 8Peter said to him, "You will
never wash my feet." Jesus answered, "Unless I wash you,
you have no share with me." 9Simon Peter said to him,
"Lord, not my feet only but also my hands and my head!"
10Jesus said to him, "One who has bathed does not need to
wash, except for the feet,[v] but is entirely clean. And you[w]
are clean, though not all of you." 11For he knew who was to
betray him; for this reason he said, "Not all of you are
clean."
12 After he had washed their feet, had put on his robe,
and had returned to the table, he said to them, "Do you
know what I have done to you? 13You call me Teacher and
Lord—and you are right, for that is what I am. 14So if I,
your Lord and Teacher, have washed your feet, you also
ought to wash one another's feet. 15For I have set you an example, that you also should do as I have done to you.
16Very truly, I tell you, servants[x] are not greater than their
master, nor are messengers greater than the one who sent
them. 17If you know these things, you are blessed if you do

[v]Other ancient authorities lack *except for the feet* [w]The Greek word for *you* here is plural [x]Gk *slaves*

◆ ◆ ◆ ◆ ◆ ◆ ◆ ◆ ◆ ◆ ◆ ◆ ◆ ◆ ◆

Are there any checks and balances to guard against those temptations? Jesus modeled two principles for us. First, He asked questions and listened to answers: for example, with Nicodemus (3:1–21) and with the woman at the well (4:1–26). Furthermore, He was clear about His mission and secure in His position. As a result, He never felt compelled to prove or promote Himself. In this He differed from many of the leaders of His day, who "loved human glory more than the glory that comes from God" (12:43). ◆

Scripture has much more to say about our relationship to our employers. See "Who's the Boss?" Col. 3:22–24.

(continued from previous page)

Seated once again at the table, the Lord asked whether His followers understood what He had done (John 13:12). He then exhorted them to adopt the same posture of serving others, thereby following His example. He assured them that they would be blessed if they did (vv. 15–17).

Jesus still calls believers today to become members of the "Order of the Towel." As Christ's followers, we need to lead others by serving them.

In a related incident, Jesus spelled out what servant-leadership means. See "Servant-Leaders," Matt. 20:25–28.

A Model of Servant-Leadership

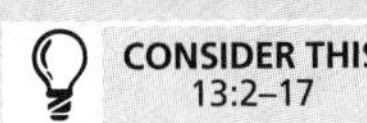

When Jesus washed His disciples' feet (vv. 3–5), He demonstrated a fundamental principle that He regularly stressed to His followers: To lead others, one must serve others. This is as true in public life and the business world as it is in the church. No number of corporate memos or rah-rah speeches exhorting workers to commit themselves to an organization or its clients will have as powerful an impact as a person of authority modeling consistently and clearly the attitude of a servant: placing others' needs before one's own, committing oneself to doing concrete things to meet those needs, and looking for neither favors nor reciprocity from the people one serves.

The Hallmark of Love

CONSIDER THIS 13:31–35 **A key test of our commitment to Christ is our love for other believers (vv. 31–35). It is not just our words that express our love, but our attitudes and actions as well. Jesus did not say that others would know we are His disciples by what we say, or how we dress, or what we know, or the label of our denomination. He said, "as I have loved you" (v. 34). Shortly afterward, He laid down His life for those first believers.**

". . . Have love for one another." —John 13:35

them. 18I am not speaking of all of you; I know whom I
have chosen. But it is to fulfill the scripture, 'The one who
ate my bread[y] has lifted his heel against me.' 19I tell you this
now, before it occurs, so that when it does occur, you may
believe that I am he.[z] 20Very truly, I tell you, whoever receives one whom I send receives me; and whoever receives
me receives him who sent me."

Judas Leaves to Betray Jesus

21 After saying this Jesus was troubled in spirit, and declared, "Very truly, I tell you, one of you will betray me."
22The disciples looked at one another, uncertain of whom
he was speaking. 23One of his disciples—the one whom Jesus loved—was reclining next to him; 24Simon Peter therefore motioned to him to ask Jesus of whom he was speaking. 25So while reclining next to Jesus, he asked him, "Lord,
who is it?" 26Jesus answered, "It is the one to whom I give
this piece of bread when I have dipped it in the dish."[a] So
when he had dipped the piece of bread, he gave it to Judas
son of Simon Iscariot.[b] 27After he received the piece of
bread,[c] Satan entered into him. Jesus said to him, "Do
quickly what you are going to do." 28Now no one at the
table knew why he said this to him. 29Some thought that,
because Judas had the common purse, Jesus was telling
him, "Buy what we need for the festival"; or, that he should
give something to the poor. 30So, after receiving the piece of
bread, he immediately went out. And it was night.

A New Commandment

13:31–35

31 When he had gone out, Jesus said,
"Now the Son of Man has been glorified,
and God has been glorified in him. 32If God has been glorified in him,[d] God will also glorify him in himself and will
glorify him at once. 33Little children, I am with you only a
little longer. You will look for me; and as I said to the Jews
so now I say to you, 'Where I am going, you cannot come.'
34I give you a new commandment, that you love one another. Just as I have loved you, you also should love one
another. 35By this everyone will know that you are my disciples, if you have love for one another."

[y]Other ancient authorities read *ate bread with me* [z]Gk *I am* [a]Gk *dipped it* [b]Other ancient authorities read *Judas Iscariot son of Simon*; others, *Judas son of Simon from Karyot* (Kerioth) [c]Gk *After the piece of bread* [d]Other ancient authorities lack *If God has been glorified in him*

Jesus Predicts Peter's Denial

36 Simon Peter said to him, "Lord, where are you going?" Jesus answered, "Where I am going, you cannot follow me now; but you will follow afterward." 37Peter said to
him, "Lord, why can I not follow you now? I will lay down
my life for you." 38Jesus answered, "Will you lay down your
life for me? Very truly, I tell you, before the cock crows, you
will have denied me three times.

"I Am the Way, and the Truth, and the Life"

14 "Do not let your hearts be troubled. Believe[e] in God,
believe also in me. 2In my Father's house there are
many dwelling places. If it were not so, would I have told
you that I go to prepare a place for you?[f] 3And if I go and
prepare a place for you, I will come again and will take you
to myself, so that where I am, there you may be also. 4And
you know the way to the place where I am going."[g]
5Thomas said to him, "Lord, we do not know where you are
going. How can we know the way?" 6Jesus said to him, "I
am the way, and the truth, and the life. No one comes to
the Father except through me. 7If you know me, you will
know[h] my Father also. From now on you do know him and
have seen him."

8 Philip said to him, "Lord, show us the Father, and we
will be satisfied." 9Jesus said to him, "Have I been with you
all this time, Philip, and you still do not know me? Whoever has seen me has seen the Father. How can you say,
'Show us the Father'? 10Do you not believe that I am in the
Father and the Father is in me? The words that I say to you
I do not speak on my own; but the Father who dwells in
me does his works. 11Believe me that I am in the Father and
the Father is in me; but if you do not, then believe me
14:12–13 because of the works themselves. 12Very
truly, I tell you, the one who believes in
me will also do the works that I do and, in fact, will do
greater works than these, because I am going to the Father.
13I will do whatever you ask in my name, so that the Father
may be glorified in the Son. 14If in my name you ask me[i] for
anything, I will do it.

[e]Or *You believe* [f]Or *If it were not so, I would have told you; for I go to prepare a place for you* [g]Other ancient authorities read *Where I am going you know, and the way you know* [h]Other ancient authorities read *If you had known me, you would have known* [i]Other ancient authorities lack *me*

Empowering Leadership

CONSIDER THIS 14:12–13 *Jesus' promise in vv. 12–13 shows that noble leadership seeks to empower others to achieve results even greater than the leader has achieved. The true leader seeks to achieve great goals more than great personal gain. Rather than being intimidated by his followers' potential, he rejoices in their growth, development, and achievements.*

Jesus used a unique style of authority to lead His disciples. To find out more about it, see "Servant-Leaders," Matt. 20:25–28.

With Us

CONSIDER THIS 14:16–18 *Jesus calls the Holy Spirit the Helper (vv. 16–17). The Greek word,* paraclete, *means "one called alongside to help." In giving us the Holy Spirit, Jesus shows that leadership is not so much the ability to walk ahead of someone as the willingness to walk* beside *someone. Followers need support as well as direction, a hand that helps as well as a finger that points.*

Peace in the Chaos

CONSIDER THIS 14:25–28 **We live in a turbulent world. Change is rapid and frequently dramatic. Jesus said that He alone can provide the help and peace we need to live and work with integrity and wholeness (vv. 25–28). Certainly our work cannot be depended on for that. No job is engaging enough, no position powerful enough, and no material rewards substantial enough to give us the kind of inner peace and confidence we long for. Only Christ will never leave us nor forsake us.**

The Holy Spirit Is Promised

15 "If you love me, you will keep[j] my commandments.
16 And I will ask the Father, and he will
give you another Advocate,[k] to be with
you forever. 17 This is the Spirit of truth, whom the world
cannot receive, because it neither sees him nor knows him.
You know him, because he abides with you, and he will be
in[l] you.

14:16–18 see pg. 379

18 "I will not leave you orphaned; I am coming to you.
19 In a little while the world will no longer see me, but you
will see me; because I live, you also will live. 20 On that day
you will know that I am in my Father, and you in me, and I
in you. 21 They who have my commandments and keep
them are those who love me; and those who love me will
be loved by my Father, and I will love them and reveal myself to them." 22 Judas (not Iscariot) said to him, "Lord, how
is it that you will reveal yourself to us, and not to the
world?" 23 Jesus answered him, "Those who love me will
keep my word, and my Father will love them, and we will
come to them and make our home with them. 24 Whoever

[j]Other ancient authorities read *me, keep* [k]Or *Helper* [l]Or *among*

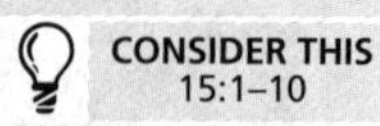
CONSIDER THIS 15:1–10

The Network

Computer networks have become important systems in today's competitive marketplace. They enable teams of workers in different offices, at regional sites, and even from around the world to join together on tasks that would otherwise be difficult if not impossible.

One way of setting up a network is to use a central computer to handle the main programming, storage, and communication functions, with remote workstations for individual input and retrieval. This is similar to the situation that Jesus described in His image of the vine and the branches (vv. 1–10):

(1) Jesus is the key (v. 1). *Like the central processing unit of a computer system, Jesus provides the life, the direction, and the commands for His followers, those of us "on-line."*

(2) To be effective, believers must maintain their relationship with Jesus (v. 4). *In order to use the features of a network, a user must remain attached to the network. If one "signs off," there is no more access to the central computer or to others in the network. Likewise, if we allow sin to disrupt our walk with Christ, we lose fellowship with Him and with other believers (1 John 1:6–7).*

does not love me does not keep my words; and the word that you hear is not mine, but is from the Father who sent me.

14:25–28

25 "I have said these things to you while I am still with you. [26]But the Advocate,[m] the Holy Spirit, whom the Father will send in my name, will teach you everything, and remind you of all that I have said to you. [27]Peace I leave with you; my peace I give to you. I do not give to you as the world gives. Do not let your hearts be troubled, and do not let them be afraid. [28]You heard me say to you, 'I am going away, and I am coming to you.' If you loved me, you would rejoice that I am going to the Father, because the Father is greater than I. [29]And now I have told you this before it occurs, so that when it does occur, you may believe. [30]I will no longer talk much with you, for the ruler of this world is coming. He has no power over me; [31]but I do as the Father has commanded me, so that the world may know that I love the Father. Rise, let us be on our way.

[m]Or *Helper*

(3) Jesus wants His followers to be productive (vv. 5–8). *Companies install computer networks so that their employees can get their work done. The systems cost too much to be treated as toys or to be underutilized. Correspondingly, the relationship that believers have with God was purchased through Christ's blood, so we need to take it seriously. Christ wants us to enjoy walking with Him, but He also wants us to accomplish His purposes.*

(4) To love Jesus is to follow His commands (vv. 9–10). *Occasionally network users receive an "error message" indicating that they have not followed the instructions of the program correctly. By the same token, Jesus has given us commands to follow, and the only way to experience His life and power is to obey those commands. To do so is not only practical, but an expression of our love for the Lord.*

Are you "on-line" with Jesus, drawing on His resources and obeying His commands? Is your life productive, accomplishing the tasks and responsibilities that He has assigned to you? ◆

"EVERY BRANCH THAT BEARS FRUIT HE PRUNES TO MAKE IT BEAR MORE FRUIT."
—John 15:2

QUOTE UNQUOTE

CONSIDER THIS 15:18–20 *Just as the world rejected Jesus, it will reject His followers (vv. 18–20). One writer offers a few reasons why:*

A real Christian is an odd number anyway. He feels supreme love for One whom he has never seen; talks familiarly every day to Someone he cannot see; expects to go to heaven on the virtue of Another; empties himself in order to be full; admits he is wrong so he can be declared right; goes down in order to get up; is strongest when he is weakest; richest when he is poorest; and happiest when he feels the worst. He dies so he can live; forsakes in order to have; gives away so he can keep; sees the invisible; hears the inaudible; and knows that which passeth knowledge.

A. W. Tozer

"I Am the True Vine"

15:1–10 see pg. 380

15 "I am the true vine, and my
Father is the vinegrower. 2He re-
moves every branch in me that bears no fruit. Every branch
that bears fruit he prunes[n] to make it bear more fruit. 3You
have already been cleansed[n] by the word that I have spoken
to you. 4Abide in me as I abide in you. Just as the branch
cannot bear fruit by itself unless it abides in the vine, neither can you unless you abide in me. 5I am the vine, you
are the branches. Those who abide in me and I in them
bear much fruit, because apart from me you can do nothing. 6Whoever does not abide in me is thrown away like a
branch and withers; such branches are gathered, thrown
into the fire, and burned. 7If you abide in me, and my
words abide in you, ask for whatever you wish, and it will
be done for you. 8My Father is glorified by this, that you
bear much fruit and become[o] my disciples. 9As the Father
has loved me, so I have loved you; abide in my love. 10If
you keep my commandments, you will abide in my love,
just as I have kept my Father's commandments and abide in
his love. 11I have said these things to you so that my joy
may be in you, and that your joy may be complete.

"Love One Another"

12 "This is my commandment, that you love one another as I have loved you. 13No one has greater love than
this, to lay down one's life for one's friends. 14You are my
friends if you do what I command you. 15I do not call you
servants[p] any longer, because the servant[q] does not know
what the master is doing; but I have called you friends, because I have made known to you everything that I have
heard from my Father. 16You did not choose me but I chose
you. And I appointed you to go and bear fruit, fruit that
will last, so that the Father will give you whatever you ask
him in my name. 17I am giving you these commands so that
you may love one another.

15:18–20

15:18–25

18 "If the world hates you, be aware
that it hated me before it hated you. 19If
you belonged to the world,[r] the world
would love you as its own. Because you
do not belong to the world, but I have chosen you out of
the world—therefore the world hates you. 20Remember the
word that I said to you, 'Servants[s] are not greater than their
master.' If they persecuted me, they will persecute you; if
they kept my word, they will keep yours also. 21But they

[n]The same Greek root refers to pruning and cleansing [o]Or *be* [p]Gk *slaves* [q]Gk *slave*
[r]Gk *were of the world* [s]Gk *Slaves*

will do all these things to you on account of my name, because they do not know him who sent me. 22If I had not
come and spoken to them, they would not have sin; but
now they have no excuse for their sin. 23Whoever hates me
hates my Father also. 24If I had not done among them the
works that no one else did, they would not have sin. But
now they have seen and hated both me and my Father. 25It
was to fulfill the word that is written in their law, 'They
hated me without a cause.'

26 "When the Advocate[t] comes, whom I will send to
you from the Father, the Spirit of truth who comes from the
Father, he will testify on my behalf. 27You also are to testify
because you have been with me from the beginning.

The Work of the Spirit

16 "I have said these things to you to keep you from
stumbling. 2They will put you out of the synagogues. Indeed, an hour is coming when those who kill you
will think that by doing so they are offering worship to
God. 3And they will do this because they have not known
the Father or me. 4But I have said these things to you so
that when their hour comes you may remember that I told
you about them.

"I did not say these things to you from the beginning, because I was with you. 5But now I am going to him who sent
me; yet none of you asks me, 'Where are you going?' 6But
because I have said these things to you, sorrow has filled
your hearts. 7Nevertheless I tell you the truth: it is to your
advantage that I go away, for if I do not go away, the Advocate[t] will not come to you; but if I go, I will send him to
16:8 see pg. 384
you. 8And when he comes, he will prove
the world wrong about[u] sin and righteousness and judgment: 9about sin, because they do not
believe in me; 10about righteousness, because I am going to
the Father and you will see me no longer; 11about judgment, because the ruler of this world has been condemned.

12 "I still have many things to say to you, but you cannot bear them now. 13When the Spirit of truth comes, he
will guide you into all the truth; for he will not speak on
his own, but will speak whatever he hears, and he will declare to you the things that are to come. 14He will glorify
me, because he will take what is mine and declare it to you.
15All that the Father has is mine. For this reason I said that
he will take what is mine and declare it to you.

(Bible text continued on page 386)

[t]Or *Helper* [u]Or *convict the world of*

The Cost of Following Jesus

CONSIDER THIS 15:18–25

Are you prepared to be *hated* because of your commitment to Jesus Christ? Perhaps you expect to be misunderstood occasionally or even chided by associates for "going overboard" on religion. But Jesus used strong words in vv. 18–25: "hate" and "persecute." He indicated that our true commitments will be made clear when they start to cost us something.

What has your faith cost you? A promotion or some other career opportunity? Criticism or even ostracism by coworkers or family? Legal action? Or nothing at all? Sooner or later, following Christ has a cost, and those who think they can get by without paying it are misguided. In fact, if there's no cost, is there really any genuine commitment? Jesus' words suggest not.

However, it's also possible for our actions or words to cause offense because they are inappropriate. In that case, the hostility we may receive is not persecution. Like Jesus (1:14), we are called to be people of grace and truth, not obnoxious and rude. True persecution involves unmerited hostility for doing good works in the pattern of Christ (1 Pet. 2:12–21).

Fear of rejection is one of the main reasons believers hesitate to declare their true colors. See John 12:42–43.

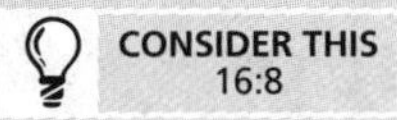
CONSIDER THIS
16:8

Whose Job Is Evangelism?

One thing is certain about evangelism: both non-Christians and Christians feel uncomfortable with it. Bring up the topic of religion (let alone the gospel) with your unbelieving workmates, and the atmosphere suddenly tenses up. It's as if spiritual matters are out of place in a professional setting.

Consequently, many Christians fold their hands and shut their mouths when it comes to evangelism. They've decided it's up to God to bring people to faith. But they're not going to participate in the process.

Of course, in a way it is up to God to bring about salvation, as v. 8 shows. The Holy Spirit is *the* great evangelist. Yet other passages urge us as believers to work *with* the Spirit in influencing others with the gospel. To understand our role in this joint venture, we need to rediscover the evangelistic work of the Spirit. This involves:

Common grace. No matter how bad things get in the world—plagued as it is with war, poverty, famine, disease, crime, family chaos, and so on—things would be far worse if it weren't for God's Spirit. The Spirit moves throughout the world, restraining the full onslaught of evil and promoting whatever is good. The Spirit does this for believers and unbelievers alike; hence the name, "common grace."

Because of this gracious work, the unbeliever is in a position to accept God's offer of salvation, and therefore benefits from divine grace whether salvation occurs or not (Ps. 104:24–30).

Spiritual awakening. Unaware that God restrains evil and promotes good, an unbeliever can be glib about life and unapproachable concerning spiritual issues. So the Spirit's job is to awaken the unbeliever to his or her true spiritual condition. The Spirit may use a disturbing conscience, a declining hope, or a gripping fear. Other instruments include the law, government, and human kindness (Is. 57:20–21; Joel 2:28–32; Rom. 2:1–6, 15–16).

Conviction of sin. When the Spirit pricks an unbeliever's conscience, there may be feelings of acute guilt and fear of God's judgment (John 16:8; Acts 5:1–11). Such a person can become quite hostile, and even attack nearby believers. This is important to know; rejection of the gospel does not necessarily reflect failure on our part as Christ's representatives (though anger is justifiable if we're insensitive in our approach).

Regeneration. This part of evangelism is one that Christians too often take credit for, even though it is the work of the Spirit. Regeneration involves the giving of new life to a lost sinner (John 3:5–8). Only the Spirit can do that. As believers, we can do nothing but help this birthing process along.

Sealing and equipping. Finally, the Spirit "seals" the new believer in Christ; that is, the Spirit confirms and guarantees the believer's place in God's family and provides assurance of salvation (2 Cor. 5:5; Eph. 1:13). Moreover, the Spirit equips the new Christian to live and act as Christ's follower by providing spiritual power and gifts, and bonding believers together. New appetites develop—a love for Scripture, a hatred of evil, and a desire to share the faith.

In light of these evangelistic efforts of God's Spirit, how can believers cooperate with God in evangelism? Here are four ways:

Identify with Christ. We can start by publicly (yet sensitively) acknowledging our life in Christ, declaring our spiritual commitments and convictions. We can also act with Christlike love toward others and demonstrate integrity in our work and lifestyle. And we can identify with the people of God. That doesn't mean we have to endorse everything that other Christians do. But we accept and affirm that we are part of God's family (John 13:14–15; 17:14–19; Phil. 3:17).

Proclaim the gospel. Jesus preached repentance and the forgiveness of sins. Similarly, He asks us to verbally communicate the gospel message to our relatives, friends, and coworkers. Naturally, we must avoid preaching more than we practice. However, evangelism demands more than a "silent witness." As important as it is, our lives alone are not enough to guide people toward Christ's work for them. We must also provide information that presents Christ's message clearly and persuasively (Matt. 4:17; Col. 1:26–29).

Appeal for a decision. God gives people a choice to accept or reject His salvation offer. Therefore, as the Spirit gives us opportunity, we should present the gospel and then ask the person to decide what to do with Jesus (2 Cor. 5:18–20). For instance: "Is there any reason why you can't give yourself to Jesus Christ and accept the work that He has done for you?" We can act as Christ's ambassadors, appealing to others to accept His gift of new life.

In a way we're like midwives, carefully assisting in a new birth. Obviously, timing is crucial. To try to force premature delivery by high-pressure tactics and insistence on a decision only produces hostility, sometimes even rejection. It can create lasting wounds that close people's minds to the gospel.

Nurture and train new believers. We can continue to work with the Spirit to help new Christians get established in their faith. As a mother nurtures her newborn child, so we can nurture a baby believer (1 Thess. 2:7–8; 2 Tim. 2:2). We can assist the person in resisting temptation, developing new values, building relationships with other Christians, and gaining insight into the Bible. We can invite the "newborn" to pray with us, discuss God's Word, and worship the Lord.

Evangelism, then, is a cooperative effort between the Holy Spirit and those of us who follow Christ. As we interact with our associates, we should consider: How is the Spirit working in this person, and how can I contribute to the process? We can act like farmers, sometimes sowing new seeds, other times watering what someone else has planted. Occasionally we must root out an offensive weed left by someone else. But always our objective should be to reap a harvest to the glory of God (see John 4:34–38; 1 Cor. 3:5–7). ◆

What is the gospel we are called to proclaim? See Luke 7:22.

How you do your job affects your coworkers' attitude toward your witness. See "Your 'Workstyle,'" Titus 2:9–10.

A Woman in Labor

CONSIDER THIS 16:21–22 **An alternative translation to *sorrow* (v. 21) is "pain." There were few options available to first-century women for pain relief during labor. Since births took place at home, all of the disciples had probably heard a woman scream out in pain while giving birth.**

As in most undeveloped countries today, childbearing in biblical times was often fatal for the child, the mother, or both. Many pagan women sought help from their gods, along with special charms, to protect them during pregnancy and delivery.

So Jesus was using a graphic metaphor by comparing the coming "pain" of His followers with that of a woman in labor. He was indicating that their pain could not be avoided. But He did give them a hope: He promised that they would see Him again, and when they did their joy would be as great as a woman whose baby has finally been delivered safely.

Do you live with the hope of seeing Jesus, even as you confront the pain of this world?

Temporary Sorrow, Then Permanent Joy

16 "A little while, and you will no longer see me, and
again a little while, and you will see me." [17]Then some of
his disciples said to one another, "What does he mean by
saying to us, 'A little while, and you will no longer see me,
and again a little while, and you will see me'; and 'Because I
am going to the Father'?" [18]They said, "What does he mean
by this 'a little while'? We do not know what he is talking
about." [19]Jesus knew that they wanted to ask him, so he
said to them, "Are you discussing among yourselves what I
meant when I said, 'A little while, and you will no longer
see me, and again a little while, and you will see me'?
[20]Very truly, I tell you, you will weep and mourn, but the
world will rejoice; you will have pain, but your pain will
16:21–22
turn into joy. [21]When a woman is in labor, she has pain, because her hour has
come. But when her child is born, she no longer remembers the anguish because of the joy of having brought a human being into the world. [22]So you have pain now; but I
will see you again, and your hearts will rejoice, and no one
will take your joy from you. [23]On that day you will ask
nothing of me.[v] Very truly, I tell you, if you ask anything of
the Father in my name, he will give it to you.[w] [24]Until now
you have not asked for anything in my name. Ask and you
will receive, so that your joy may be complete.

25 "I have said these things to you in figures of speech.
The hour is coming when I will no longer speak to you in
figures, but will tell you plainly of the Father. [26]On that day
you will ask in my name. I do not say to you that I will ask
the Father on your behalf; [27]for the Father himself loves
you, because you have loved me and have believed that I
came from God.[x] [28]I came from the Father and have come
into the world; again, I am leaving the world and am going
to the Father."

29 His disciples said, "Yes, now you are speaking plainly,
not in any figure of speech! [30]Now we know that you know
all things, and do not need to have anyone question you;
by this we believe that you came from God." [31]Jesus answered them, "Do you now believe? [32]The hour is coming,
indeed it has come, when you will be scattered, each one to
his home, and you will leave me alone. Yet I am not alone
because the Father is with me. [33]I have said this to you, so
that in me you may have peace. In the world you face persecution. But take courage; I have conquered the world!"

[v]Or *will ask me no question* [w]Other ancient authorities read *Father, he will give it to you in my name* [x]Other ancient authorities read *the Father*

Jesus Prays for His Followers Then

17:1

17 After Jesus had spoken these
words, he looked up to heaven
and said, "Father, the hour has come; glorify your Son so
that the Son may glorify you, 2since you have given him authority over all people,[y] to give eternal life to all whom you
have given him. 3And this is eternal life, that they may
know you, the only true God, and Jesus Christ whom you
have sent. 4I glorified you on earth by finishing the work
that you gave me to do. 5So now, Father, glorify me in your
own presence with the glory that I had in your presence before the world existed.
6 "I have made your name known to those whom you
gave me from the world. They were yours, and you gave
them to me, and they have kept your word. 7Now they
know that everything you have given me is from you; 8for
the words that you gave to me I have given to them, and
they have received them and know in truth that I came
from you; and they have believed that you sent me. 9I am
asking on their behalf; I am not asking on behalf of the
world, but on behalf of those whom you gave me, because
they are yours. 10All mine are yours, and yours are mine;
and I have been glorified in them. 11And now I am no
longer in the world, but they are in the world, and I am
coming to you. Holy Father, protect them in your name
that[z] you have given me, so that they may be one, as we are
one. 12While I was with them, I protected them in your
name that[z] you have given me. I guarded them, and not
one of them was lost except the one destined to be lost,[a] so
that the scripture might be fulfilled. 13But now I am coming
to you, and I speak these things in the world so that they
may have my joy made complete in themselves.[b] 14I have
given them your word, and the world has hated them because they do not belong to the world, just as I do not belong to the world. 15I am not asking you to take them out
of the world, but I ask you to protect them from the evil one.[c]
16They do not belong to the world, just as I do not belong
to the world. 17Sanctify them in the truth; your word is

(Bible text continued on page 389)

[y]Gk *flesh* [z]Other ancient authorities read *protected in your name those whom* [a]Gk *except the son of destruction* [b]Or *among themselves* [c]Or *from evil*

"I AM NOT ASKING YOU TO TAKE THEM OUT OF THE WORLD. . . ."
—John 17:15

Gethsemane

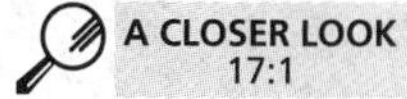

A CLOSER LOOK 17:1

Jesus' high priestly prayer recorded in this chapter was probably said in a familiar place of work. See "Praying in a Workplace," Matt. 26:36.

CONSIDER THIS
17:18

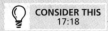

CALLED INTO THE WORLD

Should followers of Christ withdraw from the world to set up their own exclusive communities or retreat from society into "Christian ghettos"? Not if they are to fulfill Christ's prayer in v. 18. Engagement, not isolation, is His desire.

Some early Christians sought refuge in the catacombs of Rome. But that practice was only temporary, and they were forced there only by the most extreme persecutions. Normally, they could be found actively participating in the society.

Actually, Scripture recognizes a tension between separation and involvement. Passages like Romans 12:2 and 1 Peter 1:14–16 urge us to pursue a distinctive, holy lifestyle. Our commitments, character, and conduct should contrast vividly with those of people who do not know or follow God. On the other hand, Jesus calls us to live and work side by side with those very same people. He sends us *into the world* to make an impact (see Matt. 5:13–16, and "Faith Impacts the World," Mark 16:15).

Naturally, that can lead to conflict. If our loyalty is given to Christ, we can expect tension with others who follow a different course. Whether we undergo mild teasing and insults or open hostility and even violence, "normal" Christianity involves conflict with the world to which we are called (see 2 Tim. 3:12; 1 Pet. 4:12–14). Fortunately, the New Testament gives us plenty of examples to follow:

Jesus. The Lord Himself came into the world to offer a new relationship with God. He didn't have to. He could have remained in His heavenly position. Yet He voluntarily left it all to die for us, and to deliver to a rebellious humanity God's offer of forgiveness, love, and acceptance (Phil. 2:5–8).

When Christ came into the world, His listeners showed initial interest. Yet gradually most of them turned against Him. Knowing full well the fate that awaited Him, He entered Jerusalem, ready to face persecution, arrest, and even death. His followers tried to divert Him (Mark 8:31–33), but He was determined to follow God's call into the world. Isolation and safety were not options.

Paul. The church's greatest messenger started out hating anyone who followed Jesus. Yet Christ Himself stopped him in his vengeful tracks and redirected his life to become a globe-trotting messenger of faith and forgiveness.

However, Paul's first days as a Christian were spent in an isolated "retreat" in Arabia. But this withdrawal lasted only for a time, and only so that Saul could emerge as Paul, *the apostle.* He crisscrossed the empire, bringing the gospel to dozens of cities and towns. These encounters led to numerous misunderstandings, deportations, arrests, physical abuse, and attempts on his life. Probably Paul sometimes longed for the safer, quieter days of his Arabian retreat. But once he responded to God's call to engage the world, there was no turning back. He also challenged others to live, work, and witness among the lost (1 Cor. 4:16–20).

Peter. Peter struggled throughout his life to break out of the separatist mentality he had grown up with. He didn't like the prospect of suffering and rejection, and at times took steps to forestall it (see Mark 8:31–38; Luke 22:54–62; John 18:10–11). He liked even less the idea of sharing God's good news of salvation with Samaritans and Gentiles.

But Christ kept calling Peter back to re-engage the world (for example, see Acts 10). In the end, he learned the necessity and the value of suffering (1 Pet. 4:1–2) and called others to do likewise (2:11–12).

Barnabas. A respected landowner, Barnabas enjoyed a relatively "safe" calling as a

(continued on next page)

17:18 truth. [18]As you have sent me into the
world, so I have sent them into the
world. [19]And for their sakes I sanctify myself, so that they
also may be sanctified in truth.

Jesus Prays for His Followers Now

20 "I ask not only on behalf of these, but also on behalf
of those who will believe in me through their word, [21]that
they may all be one. As you, Father, are in me and I am in
you, may they also be in us,[d] so that the world may believe
that you have sent me. [22]The glory that you have given me I
have given them, so that they may be one, as we are one,
[23]I in them and you in me, that they may become completely one, so that the world may know that you have sent
me and have loved them even as you have loved me. [24]Fa-
ther, I desire that those also, whom you have given me,
may be with me where I am, to see my glory, which you
have given me because you loved me before the foundation
of the world.
25 "Righteous Father, the world does not know you, but
I know you; and these know that you have sent me. [26]I
made your name known to them, and I will make it
known, so that the love with which you have loved me may
be in them, and I in them."

Jesus Is Arrested

18:1–11 18 After Jesus had spoken these
words, he went out with his dis-
ciples across the Kidron valley to a place where there was a
garden, which he and his disciples entered. [2]Now Judas,
who betrayed him, also knew the place, because Jesus often
met there with his disciples. [3]So Judas brought a detachment of soldiers together with police from the chief priests
and the Pharisees, and they came there with lanterns and
torches and weapons. [4]Then Jesus, knowing all that was to
happen to him, came forward and asked them, "Whom are
you looking for?" [5]They answered, "Jesus of Nazareth."[e] Jesus replied, "I am he."[f] Judas, who betrayed him, was standing with them. [6]When Jesus[g] said to them, "I am he,"[f] they
stepped back and fell to the ground. [7]Again he asked them,
"Whom are you looking for?" And they said, "Jesus of
Nazareth."[e] [8]Jesus answered, "I told you that I am he.[f] So if
you are looking for me, let these men go." [9]This was to fulfill the word that he had spoken, "I did not lose a single one

[d]Other ancient authorities read *be one in us* [e]Gk *the Nazorean* [f]Gk *I am* [g]Gk *he*

(continued from previous page)

leader of the infant church in Jerusalem. But he accepted an assignment to visit Antioch and investigate rumors of Gentile converts to the predominantly Jewish movement. Sure enough, he found that God was bringing all nations into the fellowship. So he sought out Paul, an unknown, to help him establish the new converts in the faith (Acts 11:19–26). Later, they traveled to Jerusalem to defend and extend this new "worldly" thrust in the growing work of God (Acts 15). ◆

The Blessing of a Clean Conscience

CONSIDER THIS 18:1–11 **Would you feel free to welcome others to attempt to assassinate your character? Would you even help them? Jesus did. He had such a clean conscience and a secure trust in God that justice would ultimately prevail, and that His enemies could do no lasting harm, that He actually aided His accusers. He welcomed them (v. 4), identified Himself for them (vv. 5, 8), and even protected them from retaliation by His own loyalists (v. 11). Jesus demonstrated grace in the face of hostility.**

Jesus' innocence did not protect Him from suffering, pain, or death. But it gave Him a confidence rooted in a larger reality than life on earth. Because He answered to God's judgment (John 12:23–33; 14:1–4), He was free to suffer, even unjustly. He left justice up to God and did not resort to retaliation.

of those whom you gave me." [10]Then Simon Peter, who had a sword, drew it, struck the high priest's slave, and cut off his right ear. The slave's name was Malchus. [11]Jesus said to Peter, "Put your sword back into its sheath. Am I not to drink the cup that the Father has given me?"

12 So the soldiers, their officer, and the Jewish police arrested Jesus and bound him. [13]First they took him to Annas, who was the father-in-law of Caiaphas, the high priest that year. [14]Caiaphas was the one who had advised the Jews that it was better to have one person die for the people.

Peter Denies Knowing Jesus

15 Simon Peter and another disciple followed Jesus. Since that disciple was known to the high priest, he went with Jesus into the courtyard of the high priest, [16]but Peter was standing outside at the gate. So the other disciple, who was known to the high priest, went out, spoke to the woman who guarded the gate, and brought Peter in. [17]The woman said to Peter, "You are not also one of this man's disciples, are you?" He said, "I am not." [18]Now the slaves and the police had made a charcoal fire because it was cold, and they were standing around it and warming themselves. Peter also was standing with them and warming himself.

19 Then the high priest questioned Jesus about his disciples and about his teaching. [20]Jesus answered, "I have spoken openly to the world; I have always taught in synagogues and in the temple, where all the Jews come together. I have said nothing in secret. [21]Why do you ask me? Ask those who heard what I said to them; they know what I said." [22]When he had said this, one of the police standing nearby struck Jesus on the face, saying, "Is that how you answer the high priest?" [23]Jesus answered, "If I have spoken wrongly, testify to the wrong. But if I have spoken rightly, why do you strike me?" [24]Then Annas sent him bound to Caiaphas the high priest.

25 Now Simon Peter was standing and warming himself. They asked him, "You are not also one of his disciples, are you?" He denied it and said, "I am not." [26]One of the slaves of the high priest, a relative of the man whose ear Peter had cut off, asked, "Did I not see you in the garden with him?" [27]Again Peter denied it, and at that moment the cock crowed.

"I HAVE SPOKEN OPENLY TO THE WORLD; . . . I HAVE SAID NOTHING IN SECRET." —John 18:20

Jesus Is Taken to Pilate

28 Then they took Jesus from Caiaphas to Pilate's headquarters.[h] It was early in the morning. They themselves did
not enter the headquarters,[h] so as to avoid ritual defilement
and to be able to eat the Passover. 29So Pilate went out to
them and said, "What accusation do you bring against this
man?" 30They answered, "If this man were not a criminal,
we would not have handed him over to you." 31Pilate said
to them, "Take him yourselves and judge him according to
your law." The Jews replied, "We are not permitted to put
anyone to death." 32(This was to fulfill what Jesus had said
when he indicated the kind of death he was to die.)
33 Then Pilate entered the headquarters[h] again, summoned Jesus, and asked him, "Are you the King of the
Jews?" 34Jesus answered, "Do you ask this on your own, or
did others tell you about me?" 35Pilate replied, "I am not a
Jew, am I? Your own nation and the chief priests have
handed you over to me. What have you done?" 36Jesus answered, "My kingdom is not from this world. If my kingdom were from this world, my followers would be fighting
to keep me from being handed over to the Jews. But as it is,
18:37–38 my kingdom is not from here." 37Pilate
asked him, "So you are a king?" Jesus an-
swered, "You say that I am a king. For this I was born, and
for this I came into the world, to testify to the truth. Everyone who belongs to the truth listens to my voice." 38Pilate
asked him, "What is truth?"

After he had said this, he went out to the Jews again and
told them, "I find no case against him. 39But you have a
custom that I release someone for you at the Passover. Do
you want me to release for you the King of the Jews?"
18:40 40They shouted in reply, "Not this man,
but Barabbas!" Now Barabbas was a bandit.

[h]Gk *the praetorium*

QUOTE UNQUOTE

CONSIDER THIS 18:37–38 *Pilate tossed the question to Jesus, "What is truth?" (v. 38). As an unbeliever, Pilate had no basis for measuring ultimate truth.*

To the non-believer, the person who sees no cosmos in chaos, we are all the victims of the darkness which surrounds our choices; we have lost our way; we do not know what is right and what is wrong; we cannot tell our left hand from our right. There is no meaning.

Madeleine L'Engle, *Walking On Water,* p. 27

A Political Terrorist Goes Free

A CLOSER LOOK 18:40 *Barabbas was not only a robber (v. 40), he was a political terrorist, one of the sicarii ("dagger-men") who assassinated Roman officials in the vain hope of driving them out of Palestine. Find out more at Mark 15:7 about how this revolutionary escaped the usual punishment of crucifixion.*

Pilate Sends Jesus to Be Crucified

19:1–6

19 Then Pilate took Jesus and had him flogged. [2]And the soldiers wove a crown of thorns and put it on his head, and they dressed him in a purple robe. [3]They kept coming up to him, saying, "Hail, King of the Jews!" and striking him on the face. [4]Pilate went out again and said to them, "Look, I am bringing him out to you to let you know that I find no case against him." [5]So Jesus came out, wearing the crown of thorns and the purple robe. Pilate said to them, "Here is the man!" [6]When the chief priests and the police saw him, they shouted, "Crucify him! Crucify him!" Pilate said to them, "Take him yourselves and crucify him; I find no case against him." [7]The Jews answered him, "We have a law, and according to that law he ought to die because he has claimed to be the Son of God."

8 Now when Pilate heard this, he was more afraid than ever. [9]He entered his headquarters[i] again and asked Jesus,

19:10–11

"Where are you from?" But Jesus gave him no answer. [10]Pilate therefore said to him, "Do you refuse to speak to me? Do you not know that I have power to release you, and power to crucify you?" [11]Jesus answered him, "You would have no power over me unless it had been given you from above; therefore the one who handed me over to you is guilty of a greater sin." [12]From then on Pilate tried to release him, but the Jews cried out, "If you release this man, you are no friend of the emperor. Everyone who claims to be a king sets himself against the emperor."

13 When Pilate heard these words, he brought Jesus outside and sat[j] on the judge's bench at a place called The Stone Pavement, or in Hebrew[k] Gabbatha. [14]Now it was the day of Preparation for the Passover; and it was about noon. He said to the Jews, "Here is your King!" [15]They cried out, "Away with him! Away with him! Crucify him!" Pilate asked them, "Shall I crucify your King?" The chief priests answered, "We have no king but the emperor." [16]Then he handed him over to them to be crucified.

The Crucifixion

So they took Jesus; [17]and carrying the cross by himself, he went out to what is called The Place of the Skull, which in Hebrew[k] is called Golgotha. [18]There they crucified him,

[i]Gk *the praetorium* [j]Or *seated him* [k]That is, *Aramaic*

Discrimination on the Basis of Wealth

CONSIDER THIS 19:1–6 **The soldiers seemed to enjoy mocking Christ (vv. 2–3). But they were also mocking wealth and authority, perhaps having lived and worked too long under Rome's iron fist. The crown of thorns was a grisly caricature of the ultimate symbol of royalty. But the purple robe was the genuine item: the purple dye used to make it was very costly and only the very rich could afford it.**

This incident reminds us that wealth and its symbols can be used to send many kinds of messages. Frequently wealth is the starting point for deciding who should be respected, accepted, included, and honored, and who should not. Scripture explicitly states that sin lies at the root of such judgments (James 2:1–9).

Do you judge people, in your heart of hearts, by their possessions and financial achievements? Do you work hard at getting close to people of position and wealth? Do your friends come from many different levels on the social and economic ladder?

In Jesus' day, purple cloth was ranked in value with gold and was important not only for adorning emperors and temples but for tribute and international trade. See "The Trade in Purple," Acts 16:14.

There is a marked contrast between how our culture measures success and how God evaluates true success and wealth. See "Success," John 3:30, and "Christians and Money," 1 Tim. 6:7–19.

and with him two others, one on either side, with Jesus between them. 19Pilate also had an inscription written and put
on the cross. It read, "Jesus of Nazareth,[l] the King of the
Jews." 20Many of the Jews read this inscription, because the
place where Jesus was crucified was near the city; and it
was written in Hebrew,[m] in Latin, and in Greek. 21Then the
chief priests of the Jews said to Pilate, "Do not write, 'The
King of the Jews,' but, 'This man said, I am King of the
Jews.'" 22Pilate answered, "What I have written I have

19:23–24

written." 23When the soldiers had crucified Jesus, they took his clothes and di-
vided them into four parts, one for each soldier. They also
took his tunic; now the tunic was seamless, woven in one
piece from the top. 24So they said to one another, "Let us
not tear it, but cast lots for it to see who will get it." This
was to fulfill what the scripture says,

"They divided my clothes among themselves,
and for my clothing they cast lots."

19:25 see pg. 394

25And that is what the soldiers did.
Meanwhile, standing near the cross of
Jesus were his mother, and his mother's sister, Mary the
wife of Clopas, and Mary Magdalene. 26When Jesus saw his
mother and the disciple whom he loved standing beside
her, he said to his mother, "Woman, here is your son."
27Then he said to the disciple, "Here is your mother." And
from that hour the disciple took her into his own home.

28 After this, when Jesus knew that all was now finished, he said (in order to fulfill the scripture), "I am
thirsty." 29A jar full of sour wine was standing there. So they
put a sponge full of the wine on a branch of hyssop and
held it to his mouth. 30When Jesus had received the wine,
he said, "It is finished." Then he bowed his head and gave
up his spirit.

[l] Gk *the Nazorean* [m] That is, *Aramaic*

Seeing Behind Power

CONSIDER THIS 19:10–11 **Pilate assumed that he had more power than Jesus because he had authority to condemn Him to death (v. 10). But Jesus knew that all power ultimately comes from God, even the power of the state (v. 11; Rom. 13:1). Indeed, one of the reasons Jesus could submit to the injustices of His trial was that He was submitting to God's will (18:11). Pilate and those under him were merely exercising limited authority. Meanwhile, God's purposes were being fulfilled.**

What sort of power do you have—in your work, at home, in your community? Do you recognize that your authority ultimately comes from God, and that you are ultimately accountable to Him for the use of that power?

Submission to authority is never easy. Yet Scripture challenges believers to subject themselves to whatever governments they live under. See "Governmental Authority," Rom. 13:2.

Success or Failure?

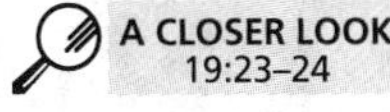

Would you consider your life a success if, at its conclusion, you had only the clothes on your back? That was the sum total of Jesus' wealth—and the soldiers took those away, leaving Him nothing (v. 24). For many of us, that kind of poverty would mark us as failures. "Jesus—A Homeless Man?" (Matt. 8:20) addresses the Lord's lack of earthly possessions and what that means for us today. As for the question What is success? *see "Christians and Money," 1 Tim. 6:7–19.*

31 Since it was the day of Preparation, the Jews did not
want the bodies left on the cross during the sabbath, especially because that sabbath was a day of great solemnity. So
they asked Pilate to have the legs of the crucified men broken and the bodies removed. 32Then the soldiers came and
broke the legs of the first and of the other who had been
crucified with him. 33But when they came to Jesus and saw
that he was already dead, they did not break his legs. 34In-
stead, one of the soldiers pierced his side with a spear, and
at once blood and water came out. 35(He who saw this has
testified so that you also may believe. His testimony is true,
and he knows[n] that he tells the truth.) 36These things occurred so that the scripture might be fulfilled, "None of his
bones shall be broken." 37And again another passage of
scripture says, "They will look on the one whom they have
pierced."

Jesus' Body Laid in Joseph's Tomb

38 After these things, Joseph of Arimathea, who was a disciple of Jesus,

[n]Or there is one who knows

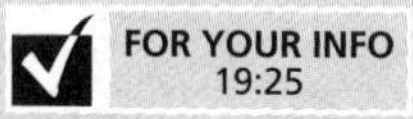

The Women Around Jesus

Jesus went to His death attended by a loyal following of women who had stood by Him throughout His ministry (v. 25). Women played a major part in Jesus' life and work. It was a woman or women who . . .

- *Nurtured Him as He grew up (Luke 2:51)*
- *Traveled with Him and helped finance His ministry (Luke 8:1–3)*
- *Listened to Him teach (Luke 10:39)*
- *Were featured in His parables (Matt. 13:33; 24:41)*
- *Shared the good news that He was the Messiah (John 4:28–30)*
- *Offered hospitality to Him and His companions (Mark 1:29–31)*
- *Were treated by Him with respect and compassion (John 4:5–27; 11:32–33)*
- *Were healed by Him (Matt. 9:20–22; Luke 13:10–17)*

though a secret one because of his fear of the Jews, asked
Pilate to let him take away the body of Jesus. Pilate gave
him permission; so he came and removed his body.
39Nicodemus, who had at first come to Jesus by night, also
came, bringing a mixture of myrrh and aloes, weighing
about a hundred pounds. 40They took the body of Jesus
and wrapped it with the spices in linen cloths, according to
the burial custom of the Jews. 41Now there was a garden in
the place where he was crucified, and in the garden there
was a new tomb in which no one had ever been laid. 42And
so, because it was the Jewish day of Preparation, and the
tomb was nearby, they laid Jesus there.

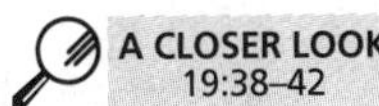

Jesus' Funeral

Jesus' body was treated as a rich man's corpse might be—which could be due to the fact that rich people buried Him. See "A Burial Fit for a King," Mark 15:42—16:1.

- *Were praised by Him for their faith (Mark 7:24–30)*
- *Were commended by Him for their generosity (Mark 12:41–44)*
- *Worshiped Him and prepared His body for burial before His crucifixion (Matt. 26:6–13)*
- *Stood by Him at the cross (Matt. 27:55; John 19:25)*
- *Assisted in His burial (Mark 16:1; Luke 23:55—24:1)*
- *First saw Him resurrected (John 20:16)*
- *Went to tell the rest of His followers that He was risen from the dead (John 20:18)* ◆

Meet some of the individual women who followed Jesus at Luke 8:1–3.

How were first-century women involved in the spread of the gospel? See "Women and the Growth of Christianity," Phil. 4:3.

HE WHO SAW THIS HAS TESTIFIED SO THAT YOU ALSO MAY BELIEVE. . . . HE KNOWS THAT HE TELLS THE TRUTH.
—John 19:35

Skeptics Welcome

CONSIDER THIS 20:24–31 **Have you ever struggled with doubts or troubling questions about Christ, the Christian faith, or the church? Do you sometimes feel that tough questions are not welcome or acceptable among believers?**

Thomas (v. 24) was a classic skeptic. Even though he had traveled with Jesus and learned from His teaching for at least three years, he needed time, evidence, and personal convincing before he would accept the resurrection (vv. 25–26). But Jesus responded to his doubt by inviting him to check it all out. He presented Himself for Thomas' inspection (vv. 26–27) and did not chide him for wanting to be certain.

Jesus seeks to honor the mind and heart of every seeker or doubter. He knows that easily developed loyalties often lack staying power. By contrast, many tenacious people who probe the corners of their doubts and fears finally reach the truth—and faith in the *truth* is what Christ desires. He even promised that the Spirit would aid those who seek it (16:12–16).

The encounter with Thomas welcomes every skeptic to bring his or her doubts to God. He delights in hearing our arguments and questions.

If you're a skeptic when it comes to issues of faith and God, you may find some friends in the Old Testament books of Habakkuk, Job, and Psalms.

The Resurrection

20:1–31

20 Early on the first day of the
week, while it was still dark,
Mary Magdalene came to the tomb and saw that the stone
had been removed from the tomb. 2So she ran and went to
Simon Peter and the other disciple, the one whom Jesus
loved, and said to them, "They have taken the Lord out of
the tomb, and we do not know where they have laid him."
3Then Peter and the other disciple set out and went toward
the tomb. 4The two were running together, but the other
disciple outran Peter and reached the tomb first. 5He bent
down to look in and saw the linen wrappings lying there,
but he did not go in. 6Then Simon Peter came, following
him, and went into the tomb. He saw the linen wrappings
lying there, 7and the cloth that had been on Jesus' head, not
lying with the linen wrappings but rolled up in a place by
itself. 8Then the other disciple, who reached the tomb first,
also went in, and he saw and believed; 9for as yet they did
not understand the scripture, that he must rise from the
dead. 10Then the disciples returned to their homes.

Jesus Appears to Mary and the Disciples

11 But Mary stood weeping outside the tomb. As she
wept, she bent over to look[o] into the tomb; 12and she saw
two angels in white, sitting where the body of Jesus had
been lying, one at the head and the other at the feet. 13They
said to her, "Woman, why are you weeping?" She said to
them, "They have taken away my Lord, and I do not know
where they have laid him." 14When she had said this, she
turned around and saw Jesus standing there, but she did
not know that it was Jesus. 15Jesus said to her, "Woman,
why are you weeping? Whom are you looking for?" Supposing him to be the gardener, she said to him, "Sir, if you
have carried him away, tell me where you have laid him,
and I will take him away." 16Jesus said to her, "Mary!" She
turned and said to him in Hebrew,[p] "Rabbouni!" (which

[o]Gk lacks *to look* [p]That is, *Aramaic*

The First Easter

A CLOSER LOOK 20:1–31 *John's account of that first Easter Sunday (vv. 1–31) is part of an important body of evidence pointing to the resurrection as a historical fact. See "Evidence for the Resurrection—Jesus' Appearances," Mark 16:1–8.*

means Teacher). 17 Jesus said to her, “Do not hold on to me,
because I have not yet ascended to the Father. But go to my
brothers and say to them, ‘I am ascending to my Father and
your Father, to my God and your God.’ ” 18 Mary Magdalene
went and announced to the disciples, “I have seen the
Lord”; and she told them that he had said these things to
her.

19 When it was evening on that day, the first day of the
week, and the doors of the house where the disciples had
met were locked for fear of the Jews, Jesus came and stood
among them and said, “Peace be with you.” 20 After he said
this, he showed them his hands and his side. Then the disciples rejoiced when they saw the Lord. 21 Jesus said to them
again, “Peace be with you. As the Father has sent me, so I
send you.” 22 When he had said this, he breathed on them
and said to them, “Receive the Holy Spirit. 23 If you forgive
the sins of any, they are forgiven them; if you retain the sins
of any, they are retained.”

20:24–31

24 But Thomas (who was called the
Twin[q]), one of the twelve, was not with
them when Jesus came. 25 So the other disciples told him,
“We have seen the Lord.” But he said to them, “Unless I see
the mark of the nails in his hands, and put my finger in the
mark of the nails and my hand in his side, I will not believe.”

26 A week later his disciples were again in the house,
and Thomas was with them. Although the doors were shut,
Jesus came and stood among them and said, “Peace be with
you.” 27 Then he said to Thomas, “Put your finger here and
see my hands. Reach out your hand and put it in my side.
Do not doubt but believe.” 28 Thomas answered him, “My
Lord and my God!” 29 Jesus said to him, “Have you believed
because you have seen me? Blessed are those who have not
seen and yet have come to believe.”

The Purpose of John's Gospel

20:30–31

30 Now Jesus did many other signs in
the presence of his disciples, which are
not written in this book. 31 But these are written so that you
may come to believe[r] that Jesus is the Messiah,[s] the Son of
God, and that through believing you may have life in his
name.

[q]Gk *Didymus* [r]Other ancient authorities read *may continue to believe* [s]Or *the Christ*

The Purpose of John's Gospel

A CLOSER LOOK 20:30–31

Whereas Luke tells his reader in the opening verses of Luke (1:1–4) and Acts (1:1–3) what those books are about and why he wrote them, John hangs the key to his Gospel at the back door of his narrative (John 20:30–31). That was a common practice in ancient writings. What we would call a preface was often placed at the end of a book, where it summarized the writer's purpose.

John's "preface" tells us that he wanted his readers to find faith and life from his narrative. That's why he included seven sign miracles that show Jesus as the authentic, life-giving Son of God. See "The Seven Signs of John's Gospel" in the introduction to the book.

Forgiveness Abounds

CONSIDER THIS 21:15–23 **Do you ever feel hopeless regarding your faith? Do you doubt God's willingness to forgive you over and over again?**

Peter (v. 15) might easily have felt that way. He had risen to a position of leadership among Jesus' followers. He had even been given the "keys of the kingdom" (Matt. 16:19). And he had positioned himself as the defender of Christ when Roman soldiers came to arrest Him (John 18:10). But when he felt the heat of a national trial, conviction, and death, Peter denied three times that he even knew Christ (18:15–18, 25–27) and afterward disappeared. What Jesus had predicted about him came true (John 13:31–38).

So when Jesus engaged Peter in a conversation on the shore (21:15–23), Peter might easily have felt that he was already disqualified from further service for the Lord. After all, as we would say, three strikes and you're out. But Jesus reconnected with Peter and called him to genuine love and the continuation of His work.

Second and third chances are not often available in families, communities, or workplaces. All you have to do is fail once too often, and you're gone. But Christ offers tangible love and boundless forgiveness—to those who own up to their failures and repent (Luke 7:47). Can we offer anything less to our coworkers, families, and friends?

Abundant forgiveness is something that Scripture stresses over and over for followers of Christ. See Matt. 18:21–22; Luke 17:3; Gal. 6:1.

A Great Catch of Fish

21 After these things Jesus showed himself again to the
disciples by the Sea of Tiberias; and he showed
himself in this way. [2]Gathered there together were Simon
Peter, Thomas called the Twin,[t] Nathanael of Cana in
Galilee, the sons of Zebedee, and two others of his disciples. [3]Simon Peter said to them, "I am going fishing." They
said to him, "We will go with you." They went out and got
into the boat, but that night they caught nothing.
4 Just after daybreak, Jesus stood on the beach; but the
disciples did not know that it was Jesus. [5]Jesus said to
them, "Children, you have no fish, have you?" They answered him, "No." [6]He said to them, "Cast the net to the
right side of the boat, and you will find some." So they cast
it, and now they were not able to haul it in because there
were so many fish. [7]That disciple whom Jesus loved said to
Peter, "It is the Lord!" When Simon Peter heard that it was
the Lord, he put on some clothes, for he was naked, and
jumped into the sea. [8]But the other disciples came in the
boat, dragging the net full of fish, for they were not far from
the land, only about a hundred yards[u] off.
9 When they had gone ashore, they saw a charcoal fire
there, with fish on it, and bread. [10]Jesus said to them,
"Bring some of the fish that you have just caught." [11]So Simon Peter went aboard and hauled the net ashore, full of
large fish, a hundred fifty-three of them; and though there
were so many, the net was not torn. [12]Jesus said to them,
"Come and have breakfast." Now none of the disciples
dared to ask him, "Who are you?" because they knew it was
the Lord. [13]Jesus came and took the bread and gave it to
them, and did the same with the fish. [14]This was now the
third time that Jesus appeared to the disciples after he was
raised from the dead.

Jesus Commissions Peter

21:15–23 15 When they had finished breakfast,
Jesus said to Simon Peter, "Simon son of
John, do you love me more than these?" He said to him,
"Yes, Lord; you know that I love you." Jesus said to him,
"Feed my lambs." [16]A second time he said to him, "Simon
son of John, do you love me?" He said to him, "Yes, Lord;
you know that I love you." Jesus said to him, "Tend my

[t]Gk *Didymus* [u]Gk *two hundred cubits*

21:15–17 sheep." 17 He said to him the third time, "Simon son of John, do you love me?" Peter felt hurt because he said to him the third time, "Do you love me?" And he said to him, "Lord, you know everything; you know that I love you." Jesus said to him, "Feed my sheep. 18 Very truly, I tell you, when you were younger, you used to fasten your own belt and to go wherever you wished. But when you grow old, you will stretch out your hands, and someone else will fasten a belt around you and take you where you do not wish to go." 19 (He said this to indicate the kind of death by which he would glorify God.) After this he said to him, "Follow me."

20 Peter turned and saw the disciple whom Jesus loved following them; he was the one who had reclined next to Jesus at the supper and had said, "Lord, who is it that is going to betray you?" 21 When Peter saw him, he said to Jesus, "Lord, what about him?" 22 Jesus said to him, "If it is my will that he remain until I come, what is that to you? Follow me!" 23 So the rumor spread in the community[v] that this disciple would not die. Yet Jesus did not say to him that he would not die, but, "If it is my will that he remain until I come, what is that to you?"[w]

24 This is the disciple who is testifying to these things and has written them, and we know that his testimony is true. 25 But there are also many other things that Jesus did; if every one of them were written down, I suppose that the world itself could not contain the books that would be written.

[v] Gk *among the brothers* [w] Other ancient authorities lack *what is that to you*

"DO YOU LOVE ME? . . . FEED MY SHEEP."
—John 21:17

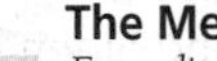

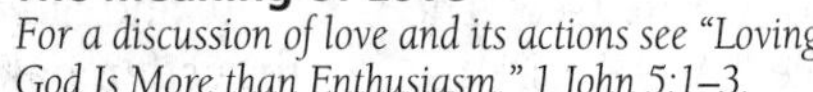

The Meaning of Love

A CLOSER LOOK 21:15–17

For a discussion of love and its actions see "Loving God Is More than Enthusiasm," 1 John 5:1–3.

TRADE IN ANCIENT ISRAEL

While the strip of land that Israel inhabited had little in the way of proven natural resources, its location geographically made it a strategic corridor through which much of the military and economic traffic between Europe, Asia, and Africa had to pass. As a result, Israel became a major factor in international trade and commerce and a much-prized possession of ancient empires.

The major route through Palestine was the "**way of the sea**" (Is. 9:1), an ancient and important highway that ran along the coast to Joppa before turning inland in the north (see "Travel," Acts 13:4). Despite their proximity to the Mediterranean, the Hebrews never liked the sea and never had a navy. Solomon built a **merchant fleet** to sail from Ezion Geber, a port and refinery on the Red Sea, but many of the crews were Phoenician (1 Kin. 9:27), and the ships often sailed with King Hiram's Phoenician fleet (1 Kin. 10:22).

What the Israelites gave up on the water, however, they more than made up for on the land. **Grain**, especially **wheat and barley**, grew abundantly in the shallow valleys along the foothills of Judea and Samaria and became major export crops. **Figs, grapes, and olives** were plentiful in the hill country of Judea.

Hebron produced magnificent **grapes** which it turned into large quantities of **raisins and wine** for domestic consumption and export. **Olives** were used as food or crushed for **cooking oil**. **Olive oil** was also used in lamps or as a body rub, making it a major product of the region.

Palestine also boasted large herds of **sheep and goats** from which **wool and cloth** were produced. **Fish** were taken along the Mediterranean coast and especially at the Sea of Galilee. Along the northern section of the Mediterranean coast could be found the **murex shell**, used to make a very valuable dye called **purple** (see "The Trade in Purple," Acts 16:14). Extensive **textile industries**, using both wool and the **linen** made from **flax** grown on the coastal plain, produced the distinctive Tyrian **purple cloth** that was in great demand throughout the Mediterranean world.

The southern end of the Jordan Valley was the source of a large and profitable **salt-mining industry**. **Asphalt or bitumen** was easily obtained from the **tar pits** in the Dead Sea area. This substance was used as **caulk** in boats and rafts, as **mortar** in building, and for making **monuments and jewelry**. Israel exported few metals except during the reign of Solomon when **copper mines** in Sinai and the **iron mines** in Syria were worked commercially. However, **timber** from the Lebanon mountains was a major trade item.

Little **pottery** was exported, except for simple containers for wine and oil. This may have been because Israelite pottery was more practical and less artistic than Philistine and Greek pottery. However, a major industry was the manufacture of **millstones** from the high-quality **basalt stone** found in the volcanic hills of northern Gilead. These were shipped as far away as Spain, Italy, and North Africa.

Ezekiel 27:1–24 lists numerous products that were traded through the city of Tyre (see "Tyre and Sidon," Luke 6:17): **fir, cedar, oak, ivory, ebony, fine embroidered linen, blue and purple cloth and clothes, white wool, finished garments and multicolored apparel, saddlecloths for riding, caulk, silver, gold, iron, tin, lead, vessels of bronze, emeralds, corals, rubies, precious stones, wheat, millet, honey, the herb cassia, spices, cane, oil, balm, horses, mules, lambs, rams, goats, wine, luxury goods, and slaves.** ◆

The Extraordinary Acts of Ordinary People

Tradition has assigned this book the title, "The Acts of the Apostles," as if Peter, Paul, and a handful of other spiritual giants alone carried out the significant work of the early church. But actually the account shows that the Holy Spirit *and a whole lot of ordinary people* took the message of Christ "to the ends of the earth."

This is one of the most timely books, because it illustrates what happens when everyday people, filled with God's power, apply their faith to everyday life and society.

The Acts of the Apostles

Everyday people, filled with God's power, apply their faith.

C O N T E N T S

People Just Like You

A R T I C L E S

Christ Collides with Culture

Acts shows the gospel's impact on a variety of cultures and societies as it builds into a movement. It internationalizes across gender, ethnic, lingual, geographic, occupational, and economic boundaries in places as diverse as . . .

***Jerusalem (1:12–26; 7:1–53; 8:1).* The Holy City witnesses the dramatic birth of the church but then gets left behind as the gospel spreads out across the Roman Empire.**

***Samaria (8:5).* Samaritans experience ethnic separation until a minority preacher invites them to join the community of faith.**

***Damascus (9:2).* A "political football" in the ancient world becomes an amplifier for the Christian message.**

***Tarsus (11:25).* The empire's second most important center of learning and the headquarters of the tent manufacturing industry produces one of Christianity's most influential messengers.**

***Antioch (13:1).* A multiethnic church in the third-largest city of the Roman Empire becomes headquarters for New Testament Christianity.**

***Cyprus (13:4).* This Mediterranean island was a frequent port of call for early Christian travelers.**

***Philippi (16:12).* A retirement community becomes the gateway to Christianity's march to the West.**

***Athens (17:15).* Curious philosophers lend an ear to the new message about Christ—but prefer debate to commitment.**

***Alexandria (18:24).* This center of education and scholarship is the source of the world's first popular translation of the Bible.**

***Ephesus (19:10).* A shrine of first-century paganism goes haywire when the gospel upsets its economy. ◆**

The Second of Two Volumes

Acts is the second volume of a two-part account. Luke's Gospel narrates "all that Jesus did and taught" (Acts 1:1). In Acts, Luke continues the account of what happened after Christ returned to heaven and His followers spread out across the Roman Empire.

However, the book ends abruptly, leading some scholars to suggest that Luke was working on or at least had planned a third installment. The message of Acts could have served two important purposes. First, it would have shown believers that rebellion and retaliation against Rome were not the way of Jesus. Instead, faithfulness to the message and lifestyle of the gospel was called for.

In addition, Luke may have written Acts (along with the Gospel of Luke) as a legal document for use in Paul's trial in Rome (see 22:11; 25:11; 28:30–31). His presentation of the Christian movement would have been evidence to show that believers posed no threat to the government. ◆

THE WORLD OF THE EARLY CHURCH

The Second of Two Volumes

1 In the first book, Theophilus, I wrote about all that
Jesus did and taught from the beginning 2until the day
when he was taken up to heaven, after giving instructions
through the Holy Spirit to the apostles whom he had
chosen. 3After his suffering he presented himself alive to
them by many convincing proofs, appearing to them
during forty days and speaking about the kingdom of God.
1:4 see pg. 406
4While staying[a] with them, he ordered
them not to leave Jerusalem, but to wait
there for the promise of the Father. "This," he said, "is what
you have heard from me; 5for John baptized with water, but
you will be baptized with[b] the Holy Spirit not many days
from now."

Jesus Ascends to Heaven

6 So when they had come together, they asked him,
"Lord, is this the time when you will restore the kingdom
to Israel?" 7He replied, "It is not for you to know the times
1:8
or periods that the Father has set by his
own authority. 8But you will receive
power when the Holy Spirit has come upon you; and you
will be my witnesses in Jerusalem, in all Judea and Samaria,
and to the ends of the earth." 9When he had said this, as
they were watching, he was lifted up, and a cloud took him
out of their sight. 10While he was going and they were gazing up toward heaven, suddenly two men in white robes
stood by them. 11They said, "Men of Galilee, why do you
stand looking up toward heaven? This Jesus, who has been
taken up from you into heaven, will come in the same way
as you saw him go into heaven."

Waiting—and Choosing a New Apostle

1:12–26 see pg. 408
12 Then they returned to Jerusalem
from the mount called Olivet, which is
1:13
near Jerusalem, a sabbath day's journey
away. 13When they had entered the city,
they went to the room upstairs where they were staying,
Peter, and John, and James, and Andrew, Philip and
Thomas, Bartholomew and Matthew, James son of

(Bible text continued on page 407)

[a]*Or eating* [b]*Or by*

POWER

CONSIDER THIS 1:8 **At the beginning of Acts, Jesus' followers appear confused and fearful. But by the end of the book they are well on their way to transforming the Roman world with the gospel. What accounts for this dramatic change? Verse 8 provides the answer: "You will receive *power.*" But notice:**

(1) The power promised was not force or political authority. **Israel had enjoyed superiority under David and Solomon, but those days were a distant memory. Jesus was not indicating a revival of political dominance. Instead, the word "power" means *ability* or *capacity.* Jesus promised that once the Holy Spirit came upon them, His followers would have a new ability.**

(2) The ability had more to do with being than doing. **The believers would "be witnesses," not just "do witnessing." Evangelism is a process, not just an event. It involves a total lifestyle, not just occasional efforts.**

(3) The power came from without, not from within. **The believers were not to manufacture their own ways of proclaiming the gospel, but to look for supernatural ability from the Spirit to make them effective in gospel presentation. The power came when the Holy Spirit arrived, not before.**

(4) The believers were to be witnesses to Christ, not to themselves. **They were to make disciples not to themselves but to the risen Lord (Matt. 28:18–20).**

The Apostles

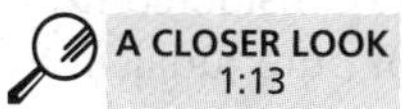

Who were these men who met with others in the upper room, waiting for the promise of the Spirit? See "The Twelve," Matt. 10:2.

CONSIDER THIS
1:4

Opportunities Look Like Barriers

A Grand Strategy

Speaking on the Mount of Olives at Bethany (vv. 4, 12), Jesus outlined a vision that would affect the whole world (v. 8). He began by pointing to the starting point of gospel penetration—Jerusalem, two miles to the west. From there the message would spread to the surrounding region, Judea, and its estranged cousin to the north, Samaria. Eventually it would reach the entire world (though the crowd in Acts 1 probably understood "the ends of the earth" as meaning the extent of the Roman Empire).

While Jesus' mandate sounds admirable today, it probably met with less than enthusiasm then. All of the places mentioned represented trouble and danger, both real and imagined. Jews—which almost all of Jesus' listeners were—were a small minority in the Roman Empire.

In fact, most of the apostles came from the Galilee region, north of Samaria. Galileans endured the scorn of their Jewish brothers from Judea, especially those from Jerusalem, who considered themselves more pure and orthodox, less contaminated by foreign influences. The lake region was derided as "Galilee of the Gentiles." Even the Galilean accent was chided.

Jerusalem

Jerusalem was not the apostles' home, but it was Judea's key city, center of its religious, political, economic, and cultural life. Jesus' crucifixion had recently taken place there. Leaders still plotted to stamp out what was left of His movement.

Yet Christ told His followers to start their witness there, in the place of greatest hostility and intimidation. They must have wondered: Could He protect them from the inevitable opposition they would encounter? Would they suffer the same terrible end that He had?

The Spread of the Gospel

Judea and Samaria

The relationship of Jerusalem to Judea was that of urban center to province, or of city to state. By penetrating the city, the gospel would also permeate the city's surroundings.

However, Jesus was careful to link Judea to Samaria, its cousin to the north. The two regions endured a bitter rivalry dating to the seventh century B.C., when the Assyrians colonized Samaria with non-Jews who intermarried with Israelites and thereby "corrupted" the race. Judea, which means "Jewish," considered itself the home of pure Judaism

(continued on next page)

Alphaeus, and Simon the Zealot, and Judas son of[c] James.
1:14 [14]All these were constantly devoting
themselves to prayer, together with cer-
tain women, including Mary the mother of Jesus, as well as
his brothers.
15 In those days Peter stood up among the believers[d]
(together the crowd numbered about one hundred twenty
persons) and said, [16]"Friends,[e] the scripture had to be fulfilled, which the Holy Spirit through David foretold concerning Judas, who became a guide for those who arrested
Jesus— [17]for he was numbered among us and was allotted
his share in this ministry." [18](Now this man acquired a field
with the reward of his wickedness; and falling headlong,[f] he
burst open in the middle and all his bowels gushed out.
1:19 see pg. 409 [19]This became known to all the residents
of Jerusalem, so that the field was called
in their language Hakeldama, that is, Field of Blood.) [20]"For
it is written in the book of Psalms,

'Let his homestead become desolate,
and let there be no one to live in it';

and

'Let another take his position of overseer.'

[21]So one of the men who have accompanied us during all
the time that the Lord Jesus went in and out among us,
[22]beginning from the baptism of John until the day when
he was taken up from us—one of these must become a witness with us to his resurrection." [23]So they proposed two,

[c]Or *the brother of* [d]Gk *brothers* [e]Gk *Men, brothers* [f]Or *swelling up*

◆ ◆ ◆ ◆ ◆ ◆ ◆ ◆ ◆ ◆ ◆ ◆ ◆ ◆ ◆

An Inclusive Prayer Meeting

CONSIDER THIS 1:14 *The first prayer meeting of the new movement was notable for its inclusiveness, particularly of women (v. 14). Jewish religious gatherings separated men and women and assigned them different roles. By contrast, the apostles were joined by women who had followed Christ, including His mother. Together they formed a unified group of dedicated followers. God intended all of them to be His witnesses.*

(continued from previous page)

and viewed Samaria with contempt. As John points out in his account of the woman at the well at Sychar, "Jews do not share things in common with Samaritans" (John 4:9).

In reaching Judea with the gospel, the Galilean apostles would have to surmount barriers of regional pride and cultural arrogance. But in moving into Samaria, they would have to overcome long-held ethnic prejudices.

The End of the Earth

Talk of the gospel spreading to "the ends of the earth" signaled the eventual inclusion of Gentiles—the ultimate shock to the apostles. In their mind, the world was divided into Jews and non-Jews (Gentiles or "foreigners"). Extremely orthodox Jews would have nothing to do with Gentiles. Even Jews like the apostles, who had grown up alongside of Gentiles, avoided contact as much as possible.

For the gospel to spread to the Gentiles, then, Jesus' followers would have to overcome centuries of racial, religious, and cultural prejudice and break down well-established walls of separation. Eventually they did—but not without great conflict and tension (see "Ethnic Walls Break Down," Acts 10:44–45; and "'Sure You're Saved . . . Sort Of,'" Acts 15:1–21). ◆

How strong was the antagonism between Jews and Samaritans? See " 'Jews Have No Dealings with Samaritans,' " John 4:9.

Joseph called Barsabbas, who was also known as Justus,
and Matthias. 24 Then they prayed and said, “Lord, you
know everyone's heart. Show us which one of these two
you have chosen 25 to take the place[g] in this ministry and
apostleship from which Judas turned aside to go to his own
place.” 26 And they cast lots for them, and the lot fell on
Matthias; and he was added to the eleven apostles.

The Day of Pentecost

2:1 see pg. 410

2 When the day of Pentecost had
come, they were all together in one
place. 2 And suddenly from heaven there came a sound like
the rush of a violent wind, and it filled the entire house
where they were sitting. 3 Divided tongues, as of fire, appeared among them, and a tongue rested on each of them.
4 All of them were filled with the Holy Spirit and began to
speak in other languages, as the Spirit gave them ability.

2:5 see pg. 410

5 Now there were devout Jews from
every nation under heaven living in

[g] Other ancient authorities read *the share*

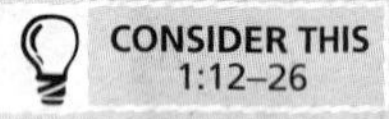

CONSIDER THIS 1:12–26

Jerusalem—Merely the Beginning

The first headquarters of the church was Jerusalem, but the city's supremacy was short-lived. By the time Paul returned there on his way to Rome (Acts 21:15—23:31), only a shadow remained of the Pentecostal euphoria that characterized the first believers. Three factors could account for this:

1. Jerusalem was not the leaders' home. *Home for most of Jesus' followers was the Galilee region to the north (see "Opportunities Look Like Barriers," 1:4; and "The Twelve," Matt. 10:2). While they set up headquarters in Jerusalem, they probably never viewed it with the same loyalty as their hometowns of Cana, Bethsaida, or Capernaum. In fact, the city and its leaders never ceased to oppose their efforts, beginning with the arrest of Peter and John (Acts 4:1–3) and climaxing with the arrest of Paul (21:30).*

2. Christianity in Jerusalem excluded rather than included. *Following Pentecost, the new believers enjoyed an unusual sense of community, sharing, and fellowship. But as Samaritans and Gentiles responded to the gospel, the Jewish believers struggled to accept them (10:1–48; 15:1–31).*

Jerusalem remained the center of a Judaistic Christianity that assumed Gentiles had to become like Jews to be

Jerusalem. 6And at this sound the crowd gathered and was
bewildered, because each one heard them speaking in the
native language of each. 7Amazed and astonished, they
2:8–11 see pg. 412
asked, "Are not all these who are speaking Galileans? 8And how is it that we
hear, each of us, in our own native language? 9Parthians,
Medes, Elamites, and residents of Mesopotamia, Judea and
Cappadocia, Pontus and Asia, 10Phrygia and Pamphylia,
Egypt and the parts of Libya belonging to Cyrene, and visitors from Rome, both Jews and proselytes, 11Cretans and
Arabs—in our own languages we hear them speaking about
God's deeds of power." 12All were amazed and perplexed,
saying to one another, "What does this mean?" 13But others
sneered and said, "They are filled with new wine."

Peter Speaks and Many Respond

14 But Peter, standing with the eleven, raised his voice
and addressed them, "Men of Judea and all who live in
Jerusalem, let this be known to you, and listen to what I

completely acceptable to God. As a result, the influence of the Jerusalem church waned as more and more Gentiles came to faith. Eventually Antioch eclipsed Jerusalem as the capital of New Testament Christianity (see "Antioch," 13:1).

3. The gospel was meant to be spread. *As Jesus' words predicted (1:8), the gospel would reach the ends of the earth. The spark that ignited in Galilee (Luke 4:14–22) would eventually explode in Jerusalem, home of Israel's religion and politics. Jerusalem would act as a springboard to launch the good news throughout the Mediterranean and eventually to Rome and beyond. Then the church would survive long after Jerusalem's destruction by the Romans in A.D. 70 (see "Jerusalem Surrounded," Luke 21:20).* ◆

For an introduction to the Holy City, see "Jerusalem," Matt. 23:37. Even though it waned as a center of Christian activity, Jerusalem figured prominently in the events of Acts. See "Stephen's New View of History," Acts 7:1–53, and "Rome or Bust," Acts 19:21.

Field of Blood

FOR YOUR INFO 1:19

The tragic end of Judas Iscariot, who betrayed Jesus (see Matt. 26:14), was memorialized in the purchase of a plot of ground for a cemetery, appropriately named the Field of Blood (Acts 1:19).

Matthew informs us that the field was purchased by the chief priests with the 30 pieces of silver which they had paid Judas for betraying Jesus. Remorseful at having betrayed innocent blood, Judas flung the money onto the floor of the temple and went out and hanged himself. The priests would not put the coins in the temple treasury because they were tainted with "blood money." So they used them instead to buy the potter's field in which to bury foreigners and strangers (Matt. 27:3–10).

As Luke words it in Acts 1:18, Judas "acquired a field with the reward of his wickedness." Matthew's account shows that Judas did not personally buy the field; he "bought" it only in the sense that his own money was used by the chief priests to purchase the land.

Tradition holds that this plot of ground is on the Hill of Evil Counsel, a level spot overlooking the Valley of Hinnom south of Jerusalem.

Off to a Good Start

FOR YOUR INFO 2:1 **The Spirit's timing for the launch of the church could not have been better. The drama that unfolds in Acts 2–3 coincides perfectly with the meaning and significance of the festival of Weeks (or Pentecost) then underway in Jerusalem. The diverse crowds that packed the city to celebrate the festival became a ready audience for the events that took place.**

There were three great annual festivals in Jewish life (see "Jewish Festivals," Luke 2:42): the festival of Unleavened Bread (or Passover), the festival of Weeks (or Harvest, or Pentecost), and the festival of Tabernacles (or Booths; see "'We Interrupt This Program . . . ,'" John 7:37). On all three occasions, thousands of Jews made pilgrimages to the temple at Jerusalem.

The festival of Weeks, or Pentecost, took its name from the fact that it occurred seven weeks, or fifty days, after Passover. Each family offered thanks to God for the just-completed grain harvest by giving the firstfruits of its produce to the temple priests. Pentecost was a day of celebration; no work was carried out. Everyone was expected to participate—husbands and wives, parents and children, servants, priests, widows, orphans, even visitors and foreigners. The days of slavery in Egypt were recalled, and the people were reminded to observe God's Law.

On this day, then, God's Spirit chose to descend on the 120 believers gathered in the upper room. The event followed by fifty days the death of Jesus on the cross and turned into a spiritual harvest: 3,000 people responded to Peter's proclamation of the gospel (Acts 2:41), becoming the firstfruits of the church.

say. [15]Indeed, these are not drunk, as you suppose, for it is
only nine o'clock in the morning. [16]No, this is what was
spoken through the prophet Joel:

17 'In the last days it will be, God declares,
that I will pour out my Spirit upon all flesh,
and your sons and your daughters shall prophesy,
and your young men shall see visions,
and your old men shall dream dreams.
18 Even upon my slaves, both men and women,
in those days I will pour out my Spirit;
and they shall prophesy.
19 And I will show portents in the heaven above
and signs on the earth below,
blood, and fire, and smoky mist.
20 The sun shall be turned to darkness
and the moon to blood,
before the coming of the Lord's great and glorious day.
21 Then everyone who calls on the name of the Lord shall be saved.'

22 "You that are Israelites,[h] listen to what I have to say:
Jesus of Nazareth,[i] a man attested to you by God with
deeds of power, wonders, and signs that God did through

[h]Gk *Men, Israelites* [i]Gk *the Nazorean*

Pluralism at Pentecost

CONSIDER THIS 2:5 *What happened at Pentecost began to reverse what happened at ancient Babel (Gen. 11:1–9). At Babel God confused the languages of the peoples and dispersed the nations abroad in order to stop their evil from multiplying. At Pentecost He brought Jews from many nations together in Jerusalem. Once again there was confusion (v. 6), but this time it came from the fact that everyone heard ordinary men and women, filled with the Holy Spirit, speaking in the various languages of the ancient world. Then an international, multilingual church was born when the onlookers heard the gospel preached and believed it.*

him among you, as you yourselves know— 23this man,
handed over to you according to the definite plan and fore-
knowledge of God, you crucified and killed by the hands of
those outside the law. 24But God raised him up, having
freed him from death,[j] because it was impossible for him to
be held in its power. 25For David says concerning him,
'I saw the Lord always before me,
for he is at my right hand so that I will not be shaken;
26 therefore my heart was glad, and my tongue rejoiced;
moreover my flesh will live in hope.
27 For you will not abandon my soul to Hades,
or let your Holy One experience corruption.
28 You have made known to me the ways of life;
you will make me full of gladness with your presence.'
29 "Fellow Israelites,[k] I may say to you confidently of
our ancestor David that he both died and was buried, and
his tomb is with us to this day. 30Since he was a prophet, he
knew that God had sworn with an oath to him that he
would put one of his descendants on his throne. 31Forésee-
ing this, David[l] spoke of the resurrection of the Messiah,[m]
saying,
'He was not abandoned to Hades,
nor did his flesh experience corruption.'
32This Jesus God raised up, and of that all of us are witnesses. 33Being therefore exalted at[n] the right hand of God,
and having received from the Father the promise of the
Holy Spirit, he has poured out this that you both see and
hear. 34For David did not ascend into the heavens, but he
himself says,
'The Lord said to my Lord,
"Sit at my right hand,
35 until I make your enemies your footstool." '
36Therefore let the entire house of Israel know with certainty that God has made him both Lord and Messiah,[o] this
Jesus whom you crucified."

Early Organization

2:37–38

37 Now when they heard this, they
were cut to the heart and said to Peter
and to the other apostles, "Brothers,[k] what should we do?"
38Peter said to them, "Repent, and be baptized every one of
you in the name of Jesus Christ so that your sins may be
forgiven; and you will receive the gift of the Holy Spirit.
39For the promise is for you, for your children, and for all

(Bible text continued on page 413)

[j]*Gk the pains of death* [k]*Gk Men, brothers* [l]*Gk he* [m]*Or the Christ* [n]*Or by* [o]*Or Christ*

Carrots, Not Sticks

CONSIDER THIS 2:37–38 **As believers, we are called to proclaim the message of Christ to unbelievers in the best way we know how, being faithful to the truth. That's really all that Peter did at Pentecost (vv. 14–36), but his speech produced dramatic results: the small band of Christ's followers added 3,000 believers that day (v. 41).**

In the same way, each of us needs to speak up as best we can when the opportunity presents itself. What we say will reflect our understanding of the faith at the time. We may not sound as impressive as Peter or a minister or some other believer. But at least our message will be authentic.

Notice that Peter did not call for an immediate response. Only after God's Spirit had "cut to the heart" those in the audience and they asked for help (v. 37) did he explain what they ought to do (v. 38).

In the same way we need to offer the "carrot" of truth to others—the facts of the gospel and our experience of it—and let the Holy Spirit wield the "stick" of conviction. We should strive for impact and understanding before pressing for a decision. That might take weeks or years, or just moments. But we need the sensitive timing of a midwife as we assist in the spiritual birthing process.

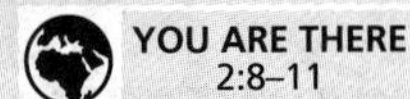

A Surprising First Fulfillment of Acts 1:8

The harvest festival of Pentecost brought together thousands of Jews (including converts to Judaism) from all over the Roman Empire. This made it possible to bring about at least a partial fulfillment of the promise of Acts 1:8—that the gospel would spread "to the ends of the earth"—much sooner than the apostles expected.

Nations of Pentecost

The 3,000 who converted following Peter's Pentecost speech (2:14–41) stayed for a while in Jerusalem but eventually returned to their homelands, taking their newfound faith with them.

Parthia: Included parts of modern-day Iran, Iraq, and Turkey. Part of the Persian Empire conquered by the Greeks in 330 B.C., it broke away in 250 B.C. and built an empire of its own. Even the Romans could not conquer it, and it became the other first-century superpower.

Media: A mountainous region southwest of Parthia. It aligned either with Assyria or Babylon to suit its interests. Like the Parthians, Medes were Indo-European peoples whose religion was the dualistic Zoroastrianism.

Elam: Home to an ancient people who struggled with the Babylonians, Assyrians, and Persians for control of Mesopotamia. After defeating the Northern Kingdom of Israel in 722 B.C., the Assyrians deported some Elamites to Samaria, and some Samaritan Jews to Elam.

Mesopotamia: The land between the Tigris and Euphrates Rivers in modern-day Iraq, homeland of the Jewish patriarch Abram (Abraham) and later of the feared Babylonians.

Judea: The Graeco-Roman name for the homeland of the Jews.

Cappadocia: A large Roman province in eastern Asia Minor, now Turkey.

Pontus: A Roman province in northern Asia Minor on the Black Sea coast. A mountainous region, it produced olives, grain, and timber.

Asia: A strategic Roman province that included the cities of Ephesus, Smyrna, and Pergamos, which vied for domination of the region. Its wealth and culture were legendary, and positions in its government were among the most prized in all the Roman Empire.

(continued on next page)

who are far away, everyone whom the Lord our God calls to him." [40]And he testified with many other arguments and exhorted them, saying, "Save yourselves from this corrupt generation." [41]So those who welcomed his message were baptized, and that day about three thousand persons were added. [42]They devoted themselves to the apostles' teaching and fellowship, to the breaking of bread and the prayers.

2:42–47 see pg. 415

43 Awe came upon everyone, because many wonders and signs were being done by the apostles. [44]All who believed were together and had all things in common; [45]they would sell their possessions and goods and distribute the proceeds[p] to all, as any had need. [46]Day by day, as they spent much time together in the temple, they broke bread at home[q] and ate their food with glad and generous[r] hearts, [47]praising God and having the goodwill of all the people. And day by day the Lord added to their number those who were being saved.

2:46–47 see pg. 414

Peter Heals a Lame Man

3:1 see pg. 416

3 One day Peter and John were going up to the temple at the hour of prayer, at three o'clock in the afternoon. [2]And a man lame from birth was being carried in. People would lay him daily at the gate of the temple called the Beautiful Gate so that he could ask for alms from those entering the temple. [3]When he saw Peter and John about to go into the temple, he asked them for alms. [4]Peter looked intently at him, as did John, and said, "Look at us." [5]And he fixed his attention on them, expecting to receive something from them. [6]But Peter said, "I have no silver or gold, but what I have I give you; in the name of Jesus Christ of Nazareth,[s] stand up and walk." [7]And he took him by the right hand and raised him up; and immediately his feet and ankles were made strong. [8]Jumping up, he stood and began to walk, and he entered the temple with them, walking and leaping and praising God. [9]All the people saw him walking and praising God, [10]and they recognized him as the one who used to sit and ask for alms at the Beautiful Gate of the temple; and they were filled with wonder and amazement at what had happened to him.

Peter Speaks Again

11 While he clung to Peter and John, all the people ran together to them in the portico called Solomon's Portico,

[p]Gk *them* [q]Or *from house to house* [r]Or *sincere* [s]Gk *the Nazorean*

(continued from previous page)

Phrygia: A large, mountainous, inland region divided by the Romans between Galatia in the east and Asia in the west.

Pamphylia: The southern coast of Asia Minor. Its name means "a region of every tribe."

Egypt: Homeland of the ancient north African empire. By the time of Christ an estimated one million Jews lived in Alexandria (Hebrews dispersed from Palestine after the fall of Israel to the Assyrians in 722 B.C. and of Judah to the Babylonians in 597–581 B.C.).

Libya and Cyrene: The same region as modern-day Libya on the northern coast of Africa. Founded by the Greeks, Cyrene was established by the Romans as the provincial capital of Libya. In New Testament times it was an intellectual center with a large Jewish population.

Rome: Capital of the empire, and therefore the symbolic center of Luke's world. ◆

3:12
see pg. 417
utterly astonished. 12When Peter saw it,
he addressed the people, "You Israelites,[t]
why do you wonder at this, or why do you stare at us, as
though by our own power or piety we had made him walk?
13The God of Abraham, the God of Isaac, and the God of
Jacob, the God of our ancestors has glorified his servant[u] Jesus, whom you handed over and rejected in the presence of
Pilate, though he had decided to release him. 14But you rejected the Holy and Righteous One and asked to have a

[t]Gk *Men, Israelites* [u]Or *child*

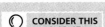

Reconnecting Sunday and Monday

*Does the faith you celebrate on Sunday sometimes feel disconnected from the "real world" you face on Monday? The newly formed group of believers (vv. 46–47) closed that gap by practicing a rhythm of two kinds of experiences—*gathering *for growth and worship balanced by* scattering *into the world for work and to communicate the gospel to non-Christian friends and coworkers.*

Notice this rhythm of gathering for refinement and scattering for engagement as we see it progressing in Acts 4—9:

Believers Gathered for Refinement	Believers Scattered for Engagement
Donate money from asset sales to care for their poor (4:36–37).	
Discipline those who practice deceit in giving to the poor (5:1–11).	
	Meet in public to care for the sick; many are converted (5:12–21).
	Are arrested and tried on charges of civil disobedience (5:22–42).
	Go to the Samaritans with the gospel; challenge Simon, a leading sorcerer (8:3–13).
Meet to discuss and confirm Samaritan work (8:14–17).	
Discipline a new believer for misuse of Holy Spirit (8:18–24).	
	Take the gospel to an Ethiopian government official on a highway (8:26–40).
Confirm and nurture the new faith of Saul (9:10–22).	
Accept Saul into the fellowship, even though he had persecuted them (9:26–28).	

murderer given to you, [15]and you killed the Author of life,
whom God raised from the dead. To this we are witnesses.
[16]And by faith in his name, his name itself has made this
man strong, whom you see and know; and the faith that is
through Jesus[v] has given him this perfect health in the presence of all of you.

17 "And now, friends,[w] I know that you acted in ignorance, as did also your rulers. [18]In this way God fulfilled
what he had foretold through all the prophets, that his

[v]Gk *him* [w]Gk *brothers*

This pattern continues throughout Acts as the narrative moves back and forth between internal meetings of the church and external encounters with the surrounding culture. The account includes more than twenty refinement narratives and more than fifty engagement narratives. We clearly see a connection between the development of faith and its delivery.

Believers today could help to reconnect Sundays and Mondays by moving through this same cycle. The gathering process might include worship services, praise gatherings, prayer meetings, fellowship over meals, and teaching for growth. Such encounters prepare us for Monday's world of work and responsibility, filled as it often is with pressures, conflicts, and opportunities to engage unbelievers as they inspect or perhaps even oppose our faith.

Rather than being disconnected, these two worlds need to be vitally connected. The refinement of our faith as we gather for growth supplies much-needed strength as we engage the world Monday through Saturday. On the other hand, the realities of life outside the fellowship can alert us to areas where we need to grow in faith.

Are you reconnecting Sunday and Monday by practicing this rhythm? Is there a link between the resources of your faith community and the demands of your world? Are there ways to improve the connections? ◆

New Life Means New Lifestyles

CONSIDER THIS 2:42–47

The converts from Peter's sermon remained in Jerusalem for a while, perhaps as guests of the handful of local believers. They celebrated their new life in Christ in five important ways (vv. 42–47):

(1) they listened to the apostles' teaching;
(2) they practiced community by sharing meals;
(3) they worshiped God with praise;
(4) they demonstrated lifestyle changes by sharing their possessions with each other; and
(5) they cared for each others' needs.

These essential behaviors of the first believers form a challenging summary of behaviors that should characterize believers today.

Messiah[x] would suffer. 19Repent therefore, and turn to God
so that your sins may be wiped out, 20so that times of refreshing may come from the presence of the Lord, and that
he may send the Messiah[y] appointed for you, that is, Jesus,
21who must remain in heaven until the time of universal
restoration that God announced long ago through his holy
prophets. 22Moses said, 'The Lord your God will raise up
for you from your own people[z] a prophet like me. You must
listen to whatever he tells you. 23And it will be that everyone who does not listen to that prophet will be utterly
rooted out of the people.' 24And all the prophets, as many

[x]Or *his Christ* [y]Or *the Christ* [z]Gk *brothers*

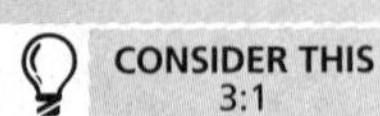
CONSIDER THIS
3:1

JESUS—THE NAME YOU CAN TRUST

Using none of the sophisticated marketing strategies of today's corporate giants, a small-town carpenter's name managed to become a byword in the first-century world. Why? Because there was power *in His name.*

Jesus *means "The Lord is salvation" or "The Lord delivers." Early Christians discovered just how true to His name Jesus was. In Acts 3—4, Luke records a sequence of events resembling a five-act drama, in which the name of Jesus features prominently.*

THE FIVE-ACT DRAMA OF ACTS 3—4

Act One, 3:1–10	The lame man healed at the gate.	He was healed in the name of Jesus (3:6).
Act Two, 3:11–26	Peter's sermon identifies Jesus with the "I Am" of Israel's history. Jesus is Lord!	Faith in the name of Jesus brings salvation (3:16, 26).
Act Three, 4:1–12	Peter and John imprisoned and tried.	No other name but Jesus can be called on to bring salvation to all the earth (4:12).
Act Four, 4:13–22	Peter and John warned and released.	Though opposed, the name of Jesus rings true—"God delivers" (4:18, 21).
Act Five, 4:23–37	The church responds by worshiping Jesus, caring for each other, and witnessing about Christ.	Signs and wonders continue to be done through the name of Jesus (4:30).

How is the name "Jesus" used in today's workplace? Probably not in the same way as recorded here! Why might that be? Is it possible that Christians today have lost confidence in the power behind Jesus' name? ◆

A related name, "Christian," was used to malign early believers. See "A New Reality Gets a New Name," Acts 11:26.

as have spoken, from Samuel and those after him, also predicted these days. 25You are the descendants of the
prophets and of the covenant that God gave to your ancestors, saying to Abraham, 'And in your descendants all the
families of the earth shall be blessed.' 26When God raised
up his servant,[a] he sent him first to you, to bless you by
turning each of you from your wicked ways."

Peter and John Arrested; More Respond

4 While Peter and John[b] were speaking to the people, the
priests, the captain of the temple, and the Sadducees
came to them, 2much annoyed because they were teaching
the people and proclaiming that in Jesus there is the
resurrection of the dead. 3So they arrested them and put
them in custody until the next day, for it was already
evening. 4But many of those who heard the word believed;
and they numbered about five thousand.

Peter and John Face the Council

4:5

5 The next day their rulers, elders,
and scribes assembled in Jerusalem,
6with Annas the high priest, Caiaphas, John,[c] and Alexander, and all who were of the high-priestly family. 7When
they had made the prisoners[d] stand in their midst, they inquired, "By what power or by what name did you do this?"
8Then Peter, filled with the Holy Spirit, said to them,
"Rulers of the people and elders, 9if we are questioned today because of a good deed done to someone who was sick
and are asked how this man has been healed, 10let it be
known to all of you, and to all the people of Israel, that this
man is standing before you in good health by the name of
Jesus Christ of Nazareth,[e] whom you crucified, whom God
raised from the dead. 11This Jesus[f] is

'the stone that was rejected by you, the builders;
it has become the cornerstone.'[g]

4:12 see pg. 418

12There is salvation in no one else, for
there is no other name under heaven
given among mortals by which we must be saved."

(Bible text continued on page 419)

[a]Or *child* [b]Gk *While they* [c]Other ancient authorities read *Jonathan* [d]Gk *them* [e]Gk *the Nazorean* [f]Gk *This* [g]Or *keystone*

Caiaphas

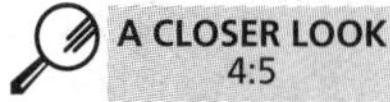

A CLOSER LOOK 4:5

This same Caiaphas had once himself been the high priest of Israel, making him the most influential member of the Jewish council. He figured prominently in the trial of Jesus. See Matt. 26:3.

SEIZING THE OPPORTUNITY

CONSIDER THIS 3:12

When God is at work, people will marvel. The people in Jerusalem marveled at the healing of a lame man (v. 11). People today may be just as surprised by social or personal changes that God brings about. Often that makes them ready and even eager to hear believers as we explain the message of Christ. Curiosity opens an opportunity for us to speak up. We can help "open the eyes" of others to see God's hand behind what they have observed, the way Peter did (3:12–26).

Of course, like Peter and John we may also trigger a hostile reaction from some (4:1–4). Our explanation might confront the anger or confusion that often accompanies conviction—the realization that one has offended God. But belonging to God means that we speak the truth anyway, no matter what the outcome.

CONSIDER THIS
4:12

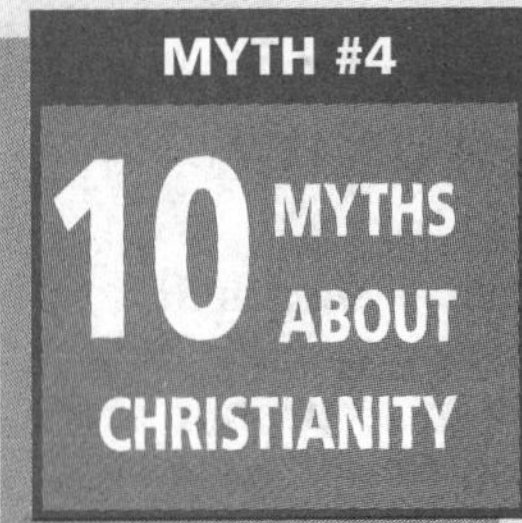

MYTH: IT DOESN'T MATTER WHAT YOU BELIEVE, ALL RELIGIONS ARE BASICALLY THE SAME

Many people today accept a number of myths about Christianity, with the result that they never respond to Jesus as He really is. This is one of ten articles that speak to some of those misconceptions. For a list of all ten, see 1 Tim. 1:3–4.

Peter describes the exclusiveness of Christianity by claiming that "there is no other name" that can save (v. 12). That doesn't play well in our pluralistic society where tolerance is a chief virtue. Indeed, many people feel that an exclusive commitment to any one religious system is pointless, since they assume that all religions are basically the same.

Most of us would never apply such reasoning to any other realm of life. Imagine a student saying, "It doesn't matter what answer I give in algebra, Latin, history, or geography. They all come to the same thing in the end."

So why do so many people apply the same shaky reasoning to religion? Perhaps one motivation is the strong desire to see everyone getting along in our global village. Christianity, Islam, Hinduism, Buddhism—all kinds of faiths drive the peoples of the world. If one system claims exclusivity, it's bound to create hostility among the others. But the fact is, religion is already one of the greatest sources there is of national and international conflicts—which seems incredibly odd if "all religions are basically the same." Obviously they are not.

Another reason why people accept this myth is because they think that faith itself is what really matters. One can believe in anything, they reason, as long as one believes in something. But they misunderstand faith. Faith is only as good as the object in which it is placed. Like a rope, it matters enormously what one attaches it to. One can believe in anything—but not just anything will reward one's commitment. Only what is true.

A third reason why people adopt the all-religions-are-the-same line of thinking is that it helps them avoid a decision. If all religions are the same, they don't have to choose any one. In other words, they can avoid religion altogether. How convenient!

But they are committing themselves to a deception. The assumption that we are all looking for God and will find Him in the end is false both to the nature of people and to the nature of God. In the first place, we are not all looking for God. Many people today have absolutely no interest in God or religion. They are not atheists, just committed secularists. Moreover, there are far more motives behind the practice of religion than a search or desire for God. Political power, tradition, standing in the community, a desire for increased fertility or wealth, even sexual gratification are among the forces driving countless people back to their centers of worship. Looking for God? Hardly.

Nor is there any guarantee that people will find Him in the end. If there is a God at all, He obviously lives in realms beyond us. Otherwise all of us would already know Him from birth. But the religions of the world, including today's New Age systems, recognize that people do not naturally and instinctively know God, which is why they promise their followers access to Him. The problem is, they offer competing and often conflicting versions of who God is and how we can know Him.

Christianity is unique in that it claims that instead of people gaining access to God, God has made Himself known to people. His ultimate self-disclosure was in Jesus Christ. No longer is He the unknown God. Although

(continued on next page)

4:13 13 Now when they saw the boldness
of Peter and John and realized that they
were uneducated and ordinary men, they were amazed and
recognized them as companions of Jesus. 14When they saw
the man who had been cured standing beside them, they
had nothing to say in opposition. 15So
4:15 they ordered them to leave the council
while they discussed the matter with one another. 16They
said, "What will we do with them? For it is obvious to all
who live in Jerusalem that a notable sign has been done
through them; we cannot deny it. 17But to keep it from
spreading further among the people, let us warn them to
speak no more to anyone in this name." 18So they called
them and ordered them not to speak or teach at all in the
name of Jesus. 19But Peter and John answered them,
"Whether it is right in God's sight to listen to you rather
than to God, you must judge; 20for we cannot keep from
speaking about what we have seen and heard." 21After
threatening them again, they let them go, finding no way to
punish them because of the people, for all of them praised
God for what had happened. 22For the man on whom this
sign of healing had been performed was more than forty
years old.

Peter and John Released

23 After they were released, they went to their friends[h]
and reported what the chief priests and the elders had said
to them. 24When they heard it, they raised their voices together to God and said, "Sovereign Lord, who made the
heaven and the earth, the sea, and everything in them, 25it
is you who said by the Holy Spirit through our ancestor
David, your servant:[i]

'Why did the Gentiles rage,
  and the peoples imagine vain things?
26 The kings of the earth took their stand,
  and the rulers have gathered together
    against the Lord and against his Messiah.'[j]

27For in this city, in fact, both Herod and Pontius Pilate,
with the Gentiles and the peoples of Israel, gathered together against your holy servant[i] Jesus, whom you
anointed, 28to do whatever your hand and your plan had

[h]Gk *their own* [i]Or *child* [j]Or *his Christ*

The Council

A CLOSER LOOK 4:15

In arguing their case before the council (v. 15), Peter and John were standing before the supreme court of the Jews. See "Stephen's Trial and Murder," Acts 6:12.

(continued from previous page)

"no one has ever seen God," Jesus "made him known" (John 1:18).

So does Christianity claim that all other religions are totally wrong? Of course not. Most have some measure of truth in them. Islam and Judaism in particular have a great deal of truth in them. They are like candles that bring a bit of light into a very dark world. Nevertheless, all religions pale into insignificance at the dawn that has come with Christ. He fulfills the hopes, the aspirations, the virtues, and the insights of whatever is true and good in all faiths. ◆

QUOTE UNQUOTE

CONSIDER THIS 4:13 *The council marveled that untrained "laymen" like Peter and John could speak with such boldness and authority (v. 13). Yet the same thing happens today:*

Most words of a clergyman are minimized [by non-clergy] simply because he is supposed to say them . . . . The contrast in effect is often enormous when a layman's remarks are taken seriously, even though he says practically the same words. His words are given full weight, not because he is a more able exponent, but because he is wholly free from any stigma of professionalism.

Elton Trueblood, *Your Other Vocation,* pp. 40–41

Being Renewed and Renewed

CONSIDER THIS 4:31 **A person of faith among non-believing coworkers can face misunderstanding, challenges to his or her values, or outright opposition. One's lifestyles, convictions, and even "workstyle" can trigger such responses. It can be very draining, like swimming against the tide.**

The new believers in Acts felt stress, too. They encountered the arrest of their leaders (4:1–3), rage and plots against them (4:25), and threats (4:21, 29). In response, they prayed together and were filled with the Holy Spirit yet again (v. 31). The previous filling (2:4) needed to be renewed.

As modern-day believers we, too, face the drain of unfriendly encounters in our lives and work. Like the Christians in Acts, we need to gather regularly for spiritual refueling. Worship services and small groups can provide that essential element, supplying the power we need to follow Christ in this world.

Do you have such a place? If not, consider gathering a small group of believers at your job or in your neighborhood to pray together and talk about life in Christ.

One church has a long history of linking prayer for its people with the work they carry out. See "Coventry," Heb. 10:19–25.

What is your "workstyle"? See Titus 2:9–10.

Sharing Things in Common

CONSIDER THIS 4:32–35 **The first Christians were extraordinarily generous. In fact, "everything they owned was held in common" (vv.**

(continued on next page)

predestined to take place. 29And now, Lord, look at their
threats, and grant to your servants[k] to speak your word
with all boldness, 30while you stretch out your hand to
heal, and signs and wonders are performed through the
4:31 name of your holy servant[l] Jesus."
31When they had prayed, the place in
which they were gathered together was shaken; and they
were all filled with the Holy Spirit and spoke the word of
God with boldness.

More Organizational Development

4:32–35 32 Now the whole group of those
who believed were of one heart and soul,
and no one claimed private ownership of any possessions,
but everything they owned was held in common. 33With
great power the apostles gave their testimony to the resurrection of the Lord Jesus, and great grace was upon them
all. 34There was not a needy person among them, for as
many as owned lands or houses sold them and brought the
proceeds of what was sold. 35They laid it at the apostles'
4:36–37 see pg. 422 feet, and it was distributed to each as any
had need. 36There was a Levite, a native
4:36–37 see pg. 422 of Cyprus, Joseph, to whom the apostles
gave the name Barnabas (which means
4:37—5:11 see pg. 422 "son of encouragement"). 37He sold a
field that belonged to him, then brought
the money, and laid it at the apostles' feet.
5:1 see pg. 423 5 But a man named Ananias, with the
consent of his wife Sapphira, sold a
5:2–10 piece of property; 2with his wife's knowledge, he kept back some of the proceeds,
and brought only a part and laid it at the apostles' feet.
3"Ananias," Peter asked, "why has Satan filled your heart to
lie to the Holy Spirit and to keep back part of the proceeds
of the land? 4While it remained unsold, did it not remain
your own? And after it was sold, were not the proceeds at
your disposal? How is it that you have contrived this deed
in your heart? You did not lie to us[m] but to God!" 5Now
when Ananias heard these words, he fell down and died.
And great fear seized all who heard of it. 6The young men
came and wrapped up his body,[n] then carried him out and
buried him.

7 After an interval of about three hours his wife came in,
not knowing what had happened. 8Peter said to her, "Tell
me whether you and your husband sold the land for such

[k] Gk *slaves* [l] Or *child* [m] Gk *to men* [n] Meaning of Gk uncertain

and such a price." And she said, "Yes, that was the price."
9Then Peter said to her, "How is it that you have agreed together to put the Spirit of the Lord to the test? Look, the
feet of those who have buried your husband are at the door,
and they will carry you out." 10Immediately she fell down at
his feet and died. When the young men came in they found
her dead, so they carried her out and buried her beside her
husband. 11And great fear seized the
whole church and all who heard of these
things.

5:1–11
see pg. 423

Growing Respect among the People

5:12–16
see pg. 424

12 Now many signs and wonders were
done among the people through the
apostles. And they were all together in Solomon's Portico.
13None of the rest dared to join them, but the people held
them in high esteem. 14Yet more than ever believers were
added to the Lord, great numbers of both men and women,
15so that they even carried out the sick into the streets, and
laid them on cots and mats, in order that Peter's shadow
might fall on some of them as he came by. 16A great number
of people would also gather from the towns around
Jerusalem, bringing the sick and those tormented by unclean spirits, and they were all cured.

REAL ESTATE DEAL DEADLY

CONSIDER THIS
5:2–10

If Sapphira's consent was required to sell the property (vv. 2, 9), it would have been unusual since first-century women's legal powers were limited compared to those of modern women. In any case, she knew about the sale and, unfortunately, the deceit. She chose to participate in it rather than oppose her husband and hold to the truth.

As a spouse, do you choose to "keep the peace" even when you know you are denying what is right?

(continued from previous page)

32–35), an ideal that pure communism advocated but never achieved. So were these first believers in some sense communists?

No. In the first place, they were not setting up an economic system here, but simply responding to each other with gracious, Christlike compassion. Such behavior was one powerful result of the outpouring of the Spirit (Acts 2:1–4). Unfortunately, not all New Testament believers demonstrated that kind of concern (5:1–11; 1 Cor. 6:8; James 4:1–2).

Furthermore, Scripture never mandates an equal distribution of goods, nor does it call for the elimination of property or ownership. This passage (along with 2:44–45) is a historical account, not a doctrinal treatise. It documents the work of God in building the early church.

In that day, as in ours, there were both rich and poor Christians (2 Cor. 8:2; 1 Tim. 6:17–19). And when the New Testament does address issues such as wealth, care for the poor, work, equality, widows, slaves, and public justice, it inevitably calls believers to compassion and generosity; but not to asceticism, the idea that one can become more godly through self-denial and renouncing worldly wealth. In fact, Paul warns against that (Col. 2:18–23). The Bible condemns the love of wealth, not its possession, as a root of all kinds of evil (1 Tim. 6:9–10).

Reading about these early Christians, modern believers are challenged to consider: Do we, with our much higher standard of living, show the same commitment to generosity as these believers? If we, too, are filled with the Spirit of Christ, then we ought to respond to the needs of people with the love of Christ.

Religious Leaders Try to Stop the Apostles

17 Then the high priest took action; he and all who were
with him (that is, the sect of the Sadducees), being filled
with jealousy, 18arrested the apostles and put them in the
public prison. 19But during the night an angel of the Lord
opened the prison doors, brought them out, and said,
20"Go, stand in the temple and tell the people the whole
message about this life." 21When they heard this, they entered the temple at daybreak and went on with their teaching.
When the high priest and those with him arrived, they
called together the council and the whole body of the elders of Israel, and sent to the prison to have them brought.
5:22–32 see pg. 425 22But when the temple police went there,
they did not find them in the prison; so
they returned and reported, 23"We found the prison securely locked and the guards standing at the doors, but
when we opened them, we found no one inside." 24Now
when the captain of the temple and the chief priests heard
these words, they were perplexed about them, wondering
what might be going on. 25Then someone arrived and announced, "Look, the men whom you put in prison are
standing in the temple and teaching the people!" 26Then the
captain went with the temple police and brought them, but

Wealth—Hold It Lightly

CONSIDER THIS 4:37—5:11 **Whether we own land, buildings, things, or cash, wealth is tricky to handle. How we hold these assets speaks volumes about our values. If we hold them too tightly, the results will likely be possessiveness, stinginess, manipulation, and elitism.**

Barnabas converted some land that he owned into a cash gift for needy believers (4:36–37). Notice how he *let go* of the money, laying it at the apostles' feet to be administered by them. By contrast, Ananias and Sapphira practiced a similar transaction for the same need, but lied about it (5:1–2). Apparently they wanted to look good among the believers, but they also wanted to secretly hold onto some of their money from the sale.

God calls us as believers to hold our resources lightly. After all, everything that we have comes from Him. He gives it to us as a trust to be managed—not a treasure to be hoarded.

Perhaps it was to avoid situations like the one mentioned in this passage that Jesus warned His followers that when doing a charitable deed, "Do not let your left hand know what your right hand is doing." See "Anonymous Donors," Matt. 6:1–4.

Barnabas—"Joe Encouragement"

CONSIDER THIS 4:36–37 **The apostles chose the perfect Christian name for Joses of Cyprus when they called him Barnabas—Son of Encouragement. Every appearance of Barnabas in Scripture finds him encouraging others in the faith. In fact, he serves as the supreme model for how**

(continued on next page)

Personality Profile: Barnabas

FOR YOUR INFO 4:36–37

Given name: Joses (Joseph).

Renamed (by the apostles): Barnabas, which means "Son of Encouragement."

Home: Cyprus.

Family: A Levite by background.

A primary responsibility: Landowner.

Best known today for: Recruiting and mentoring promising young leaders such as Saul and John Mark.

without violence, for they were afraid of being stoned by
the people.
27 When they had brought them, they had them stand
before the council. The high priest questioned them, 28say-
ing, "We gave you strict orders not to teach in this name,[o]
yet here you have filled Jerusalem with your teaching and
you are determined to bring this man's blood on us." 29But
Peter and the apostles answered, "We must obey God rather
than any human authority.[p] 30The God of our ancestors
raised up Jesus, whom you had killed by hanging him on a
tree. 31God exalted him at his right hand as Leader and Savior that he might give repentance to Israel and forgiveness
of sins. 32And we are witnesses to these things, and so is the
Holy Spirit whom God has given to those who obey him."
33 When they heard this, they were enraged and wanted
to kill them. 34But a Pharisee in the council named
Gamaliel, a teacher of the law, respected by all the people,
stood up and ordered the men to be put outside for a short
time. 35Then he said to them, "Fellow Israelites,[q] consider
carefully what you propose to do to these men. 36For some
time ago Theudas rose up, claiming to be somebody, and a
number of men, about four hundred, joined him; but he
was killed, and all who followed him were dispersed and
disappeared. 37After him Judas the Galilean rose up at the
time of the census and got people to follow him; he also
perished, and all who followed him were scattered. 38So in
the present case, I tell you, keep away from these men and

[o]Other ancient authorities read *Did we not give you strict orders not to teach in this name?* [p]Gk *than men* [q]Gk *Men, Israelites*

Personality Profile: Ananias and Sapphira

FOR YOUR INFO 5:1 **Names mean:** "God is gracious" (Ananias) and "beautiful" (Sapphira).

Not to be confused with: Ananias, the disciple in Damascus, who was the first believer to visit Saul after his dramatic conversion (Acts 9:10); Ananias the high priest (23:2).

Remembered today for: Lying to Peter about donating money to the church and being struck dead by the Holy Spirit for their deception.

(continued from previous page)

to mentor young believers. Numerous churches can trace their beginnings back to the efforts of "Joe Encouragement" (see "Discipleship—Or Mentoring?" and "Kingdom-Style Mentoring," Acts 9:26–30).

An interesting sidelight: Though Levites traditionally lived off the temple system, Barnabas had real estate. But on coming into the faith he sold it and donated the proceeds for the care of the poor (4:36–37). Later, he joined with Paul in refusing to make a living from the gospel (1 Cor. 9:6).

Ananias and Sapphira—Playing Games with God

CONSIDER THIS 5:1–11 **The dramatic account of Ananias and Sapphira (Acts 5:1–11) immediately after the mention of Barnabas (4:36–37) draws a stark contrast between two kinds of people. On the one hand, Barnabas serves as a positive model of sincere faith, as evidenced by his open-handed generosity. On the other hand, Ananias and Sapphira serve as negative models.**

Externally, they appeared the same. Like Barnabas, they sold land and brought money to the church, where they "laid it at the apostles' feet" (4:37; 5:2). But internally, they had a radically different commitment.

The sins that Peter named—lying to the Holy Spirit (v. 3) and testing the Spirit (v. 9)—indicate that they were playing games with God. Peter noted that the source of their deception was Satan. As the ultimate liar (John 8:44), Satan had filled their hearts with lies, in contrast to the Holy Spirit, who fills the heart with truth (14:16–17; Eph. 5:6–21). And like Israel, they were testing the Spirit (1 Cor. 10:1–13), testing the limits of

(continued on next page)

(continued from previous page)

what He would permit, trying to see how much they could get away with.

God dealt severely with this couple by making an example of them. As a result, fear came upon the church (Acts 5:5, 11)—not a cringing fear of dread, but a heightened respect for God's holiness, His moral purity. The incident still stands as a bold warning to believers today about relating to God. No one is perfect, and God forgives. But when given a chance to confess the truth, it's important to confess the truth, not lie as they did.

A Confusing Reputation

CONSIDER THIS 5:12–16 **Seeing loyalty to God's kingdom often triggers peculiar responses from unbelievers. Many will keep a safe distance, as happened to the early church (v. 13), while others enthusiastically join up (v. 14).**

What will bring the hesitant watchers across the line? Time, reasonable evidence, and the work of the Holy Spirit will. That's why we as believers need to give others space to sort things out. Many times quick transitions don't have lasting power.

We must not measure our evangelistic effectiveness by responses, but by whether we have been faithful in our witness. The commands of God must be our yardstick—not the reactions of others.

Believers are called to present the message of Christ in the best way they know how when the opportunity presents itself. See "Carrots, Not Sticks," Acts 2:37–38.

let them alone; because if this plan or this undertaking is of
human origin, it will fail; 39but if it is of God, you will not
be able to overthrow them—in that case you may even be
found fighting against God!"
They were convinced by him, 40and when they had called
in the apostles, they had them flogged. Then they ordered
them not to speak in the name of Jesus, and let them go.
41As they left the council, they rejoiced that they were considered worthy to suffer dishonor for the sake of the name.
42And every day in the temple and at home[r] they did not
cease to teach and proclaim Jesus as the Messiah.[s]

Ethnic Tensions

6:1 see pg. 426

6 Now during those days, when the
disciples were increasing in number,

[r]*Or from house to house* [s]*Or the Christ*

Leaders Start as Servants

CONSIDER THIS 6:5–6 *Two factors probably led to the neglect of the Hellenist (Greek-speaking) widows (v. 1): dramatic numerical growth and cultural prejudice by native-born Jews against their foreign-born brothers and sisters. Something had to be done, because first-century widows had almost no means of support. Sometimes a widow was left with no options but begging or prostitution to survive. Those in the church relied on the daily distribution of food.*

Church leaders appointed seven men, probably from among the Hellenists, to manage the program (vv. 5–6). Note that their first assignment in ministry involved what we might call "social work." In fact, it involved a task that their culture defined as women's or slaves' work—serving meals. We don't know what struggles that must have created, but perhaps the requirements of good character and being full of the Spirit and wisdom had something to do with what these men would need to break out of traditional cultural ways.

Having served well, at least some of these workers extended their service into cross-cultural evangelism (v. 8; 8:5–40).

from heaven flashed around him. 4He fell to the ground
and heard a voice saying to him, "Saul, Saul, why do you
persecute me?" 5He asked, "Who are you, Lord?" The reply
came, "I am Jesus, whom you are persecuting. 6But get up
and enter the city, and you will be told what you are to do."
7The men who were traveling with him stood speechless
because they heard the voice but saw no one. 8Saul got up
from the ground, and though his eyes were open, he could
see nothing; so they led him by the hand and brought him
into Damascus. 9For three days he was without sight, and
neither ate nor drank.

Ananias Reaches Out Cautiously

9:10 see pg. 440

10 Now there was a disciple in Damascus named Ananias. The Lord said to
him in a vision, "Ananias." He answered, "Here I am, Lord."
11The Lord said to him, "Get up and go to the street called
Straight, and at the house of Judas look for a man of Tarsus
named Saul. At this moment he is praying, 12and he has
seen in a vision[r] a man named Ananias come in and lay his
hands on him so that he might regain his sight." 13But Ananias answered, "Lord, I have heard from many about this
man, how much evil he has done to your saints in
Jerusalem; 14and here he has authority from the chief
priests to bind all who invoke your
name." 15But the Lord said to him, "Go,
for he is an instrument whom I have chosen to bring my
name before Gentiles and kings and before the people of Israel; 16I myself will show him how much he must suffer for
the sake of my name." 17So Ananias went
and entered the house. He laid his hands
on Saul[s] and said, "Brother Saul, the Lord Jesus, who appeared to you on your way here, has sent me so that you
may regain your sight and be filled with the Holy Spirit."
18And immediately something like scales fell from his eyes,
and his sight was restored. Then he got up and was baptized, 19and after taking some food, he regained his
strength.

9:15 see pg. 438

9:10–18 see pg. 438

Believers Doubt Saul's Conversion

For several days he was with the disciples in Damascus,
20and immediately he began to proclaim Jesus in the synagogues, saying, "He is the Son of God." 21All who heard

(Bible text continued on page 440)

[r]Other ancient authorities lack *in a vision* [s]Gk *him*

(continued from previous page)

vants at least thirty days by chariot. How long would he have stayed? A month? Then he faced a return trip. So he spent at least a quarter of a year to travel to Jerusalem to worship God.

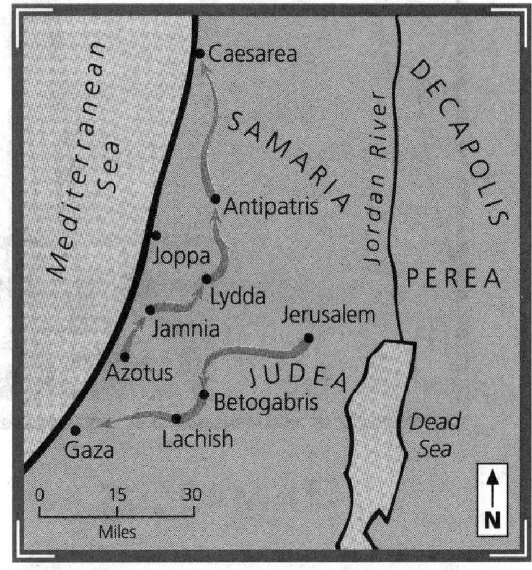

PHILIP AND THE ETHIOPIAN TREASURER

What he heard in the city about the followers of Jesus and their persecution is not recorded. But he responded warmly to Philip and the message about Christ, and became the first known witness—black or white—to Africa. For the second time in Acts 8, the gospel moved outside of the narrow confines of Jerusalem and Judea.

Once again God used Philip, the Greek-speaking Hellenist table-server, to accomplish the task rather than Peter, John, or the other apostles, who were just beginning to realize that the gospel reaches out to all peoples—Hellenists, Samaritans, even Gentiles of all colors and races.

Who was the curious man that the treasurer met on the road to Gaza? See "Philip the Evangelist," Acts 8:5–13.

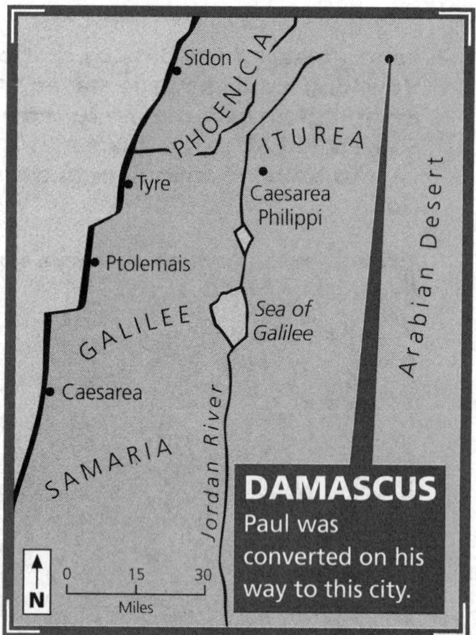

DAMASCUS

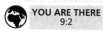

 YOU ARE THERE 9:2

- Major city of the "Decapolis," ten cities located east of the Jordan River.
- A transportation and commercial hub for Palestine and Egypt to the south, the Tigris and Euphrates River valleys to the east, and Antioch and Asia Minor to the north. It sat at the intersection of the two main international highways of the ancient Near East, the Way of the Sea and the King's Highway (see "Travel in the Ancient World," Acts 13:3–4).
- Flat, surrounded by hills, it was never easy to defend.
- Heavily populated by Jews, later by Christians.
- Under Rome, governed itself as a free city, minting its own coinage, which added to its commercial prospects.
- Walled and laid out in a rectangle, with two parallel streets running its length. One was (and is) "the street called Straight."

ANANIAS—SCARED BUT OBEDIENT

CONSIDER THIS 9:10–18 **Saul's reputation as a ruthless persecutor of Christians preceded him to Damascus (Acts 9:1, 10). Perhaps hearing that Saul was headed that way, Ananias mentally prepared himself to be hunted down, arrested, imprisoned, and ultimately martyred for following the new movement called the Way. In any case, he was no doubt stunned by the Lord's command to go and meet this dangerous enemy face-to-face! His words of protest indicate great fear.**

But twice God commanded, "Go" (vv. 11, 15), and to his credit, Ananias—scared as he may have been—went obediently to lay hands on Saul that he might receive the Holy Spirit, and to baptize him. As a result, he witnessed the spiritual birth of early Christianity's greatest spokesperson. He also saw a dramatic demonstration of the truth that God's grace can overcome anyone's background.

Ananias' story challenges believers today to consider: Who might God want us to approach with the message of His grace? Who that we know is the least likely to respond to Christ—yet just might if only someone would reach out in faith and obedience?

The man whom Ananias went to visit had been raised in a way that made him the perfect choice to lead the opposition against the growing Christian movement—but later to lead the movement itself. See "Saul" and "Paul," Acts 13:2–3.

A RADICALLY CHANGED PERCEPTION

CONSIDER THIS 9:15 **Have you ever avoided someone who seems dangerous? Ananias felt that way about Saul. He knew very well that Saul was a determined persecutor of believers, a government hit man assigned to purge the land of Christ's**

followers (9:1–2, 13–14). Saul terrified Ananias, and the frightened believer told God so.

But God assured him that the "impossible" can happen (v. 15). An enemy can become a partner. In fact, this particular enemy had changed and needed Ananias' help (vv. 17–18).

Do you harbor deep doubts about certain people, convinced that they will never change, never enter the faith? In light of Ananias' experience, perhaps it's time to review your perspective.

Another case in which an early believer needed to radically change his perception was Philemon, the owner of a runaway slave named Onesimus. See the Introduction to Philemon.

Barnabas—A Model for Mentoring

CONSIDER THIS 9:27

Barnabas' example serves as a textbook case in kingdom-style mentoring. This model mentor . . .

- **Befriended Saul (Paul) as a new believer (9:26–27).**
- **Recruited a forgotten Saul from his home in Tarsus to help him stabilize a new group of multiethnic believers at Antioch, a year-long project (11:25–26).**
- **Helped organize an international team of leaders in prayer, fasting, and decision-making. Result: he launched out with Paul to bring the gospel to peoples in the western empire (13:1–3).**
- **Moved Paul to the forefront of leadership. "Barnabas and Saul" (13:7) became "Paul and his companions" (13:13).**
- **Contended with ethnic hostility, personal attacks, and idol worship (13:46—14:20).**
- **Resisted well-meaning but misguided attempts at Lystra to make him and Paul into gods of Greek culture (14:8–18).**
- **Took the lead with Paul in defending Gentile believers before the Jerusalem church council (15:1–4, 12).**
- **Stood up to Paul over a negative assessment of young John Mark (15:36–38). Notice: Encouragers like Barnabas need not avoid conflict.**
- **Gave John Mark a second chance, taking him with him to Cyprus (15:39). He was vindicated several years later when Paul described John Mark as "useful in my ministry" (2 Tim. 4:11).**

The apostles chose the perfect Christian name for Joses of Cyprus when they called him Barnabas. Find out more about "Joe Encouragement" at Acts 4:36–37.

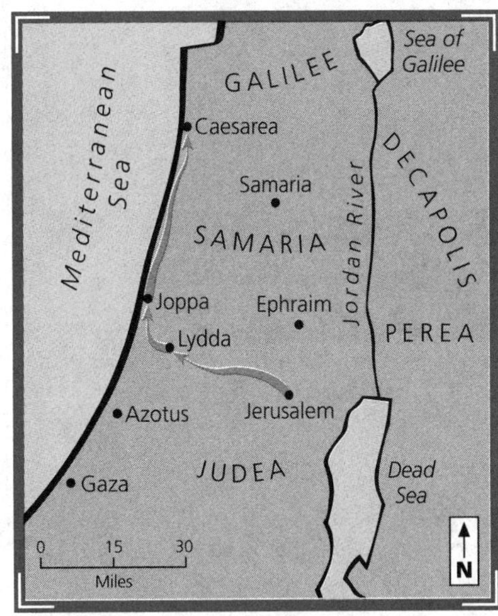

PETER'S JOURNEY TO THE SEA

Lydda

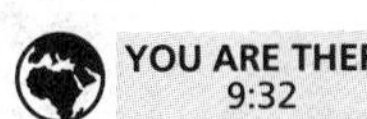

YOU ARE THERE 9:32

- **Known as Lod in Old Testament times (1 Chr. 8:12) and today.**
- **Variously occupied by Jews, Greeks, Romans, Arabs, and Crusaders.**
- **In Peter's day, renowned for its legacy of Jewish scholarship and commerce.**
- **Burned in A.D. 70 by the Romans.**
- **Became a center of Christianity in the fourth century.**
- **Captured from the Arabs by Israel in 1948 and settled by Jewish immigrants.**
- **Famous today for its defense industry, paper products, food preserves, and electrical appliances.**

him were amazed and said, "Is not this the man who made
havoc in Jerusalem among those who invoked this name?
And has he not come here for the purpose of bringing them

9:2–25
see pg. 442

bound before the chief priests?" 22 Saul
became increasingly more powerful and
confounded the Jews who lived in Damascus by proving
that Jesus[t] was the Messiah.[u]
23 After some time had passed, the Jews plotted to kill
him, 24 but their plot became known to Saul. They were
watching the gates day and night so that they might kill
him; 25 but his disciples took him by night and let him
down through an opening in the wall,[v] lowering him in a
basket.

9:26–30
see pg. 444

26 When he had come to Jerusalem,
he attempted to join the disciples; and
they were all afraid of him, for they did not believe that he

9:27
see pg. 439

was a disciple. 27 But Barnabas took him,
brought him to the apostles, and de-
scribed for them how on the road he had seen the Lord,
who had spoken to him, and how in Damascus he had spoken boldly in the name of Jesus. 28 So he went in and out
among them in Jerusalem, speaking boldly in the name of
the Lord. 29 He spoke and argued with the Hellenists; but
they were attempting to kill him. 30 When the believers[w]
learned of it, they brought him down to Caesarea and sent
him off to Tarsus.

[t]Gk *that this* [u]Or *the Christ* [v]Gk *through the wall* [w]Gk *brothers*

Where Has God Placed You?

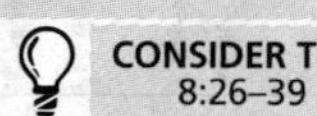

CONSIDER THIS 8:26–39 *The Ethiopian treasurer (v. 27) was strategically placed to bring the gospel to his people and their leaders. In the same way, God may have placed you in a strategic position to bring the gospel to someone.*

Are you taking advantage of that opportunity?

Personality Profile: Ananias the Disciple

FOR YOUR INFO 9:10 **Not to be confused with:** Ananias, the deceptive property owner (Acts 5:1); Ananias, the notorious high priest (23:2).

Home: Damascus in Syria.

Best known today as: The believer sent by God to bring into the faith Saul of Tarsus, the zealous government agent who persecuted Christians.

31 Meanwhile the church throughout Judea, Galilee, and
Samaria had peace and was built up. Living in the fear of
the Lord and in the comfort of the Holy Spirit, it increased
in numbers.

Peter Heals Aeneas and Raises Tabitha

9:32 see pg. 439

32 Now as Peter went here and there
among all the believers,[x] he came down
also to the saints living in Lydda. 33 There he found a man
named Aeneas, who had been bedridden for eight years, for
he was paralyzed. 34 Peter said to him, "Aeneas, Jesus Christ
heals you; get up and make your bed!" And immediately he
got up. 35 And all the residents of Lydda and Sharon saw
him and turned to the Lord.

9:36

36 Now in Joppa there was a disciple
whose name was Tabitha, which in
Greek is Dorcas.[y] She was devoted to good works and acts
of charity. 37 At that time she became ill and died. When
they had washed her, they laid her in a room upstairs.
38 Since Lydda was near Joppa, the disciples, who heard that
Peter was there, sent two men to him with the request,
"Please come to us without delay." 39 So Peter got up and
went with them; and when he arrived, they took him to the
room upstairs. All the widows stood beside him, weeping
and showing tunics and other clothing that Dorcas had
made while she was with them. 40 Peter put all of them

[x] Gk *all of them* [y] The name Tabitha in Aramaic and the name Dorcas in Greek mean *a gazelle*

"JESUS CHRIST HEALS YOU; GET UP AND MAKE YOUR BED!"
—Acts 9:34

PERSONALITY PROFILE: TABITHA

FOR YOUR INFO 9:36

Also known as: Dorcas, which means "gazelle."

Home: Joppa, the Mediterranean seaport (see accompanying map).

Special skills: Deft at sewing; she made clothing for destitute widows (Acts 9:36, 39).

Best known today for: Being raised from the dead by Peter, a miracle that demonstrated the gospel's truth and power (compare Mark 16:15–18; John 14:12–14).

outside, and then he knelt down and prayed. He turned to
the body and said, "Tabitha, get up." Then she opened her
eyes, and seeing Peter, she sat up. 41He gave her his hand
and helped her up. Then calling the saints and widows, he
showed her to be alive. 42This became
9:42
known throughout Joppa, and many be-
lieved in the Lord. 43Meanwhile he stayed in Joppa for
some time with a certain Simon, a tanner.

An Amplifier for the Gospel

Damascus was a political football in the ancient world, not unlike places today that are torn by rival claims of ownership.

Damascus turned out to be an important city in the life of the church. Christians fled there from the persecution that followed Stephen's death (Acts 8:1, 4). Their faith attracted the attention of the council in Jerusalem, and Saul, the zealous Pharisee in charge of the anti-Christian campaign, was dispatched to investigate and make arrests (9:1–2).

Saul's (that is, Paul's) dramatic conversion on the Damascus road has been celebrated throughout Christian history. Less well known is that Damascus became a strategic center for Paul and the gospel. Certainly the church there must have been powerfully encouraged by the incredible turn of events that Paul's conversion entailed. During his lengthy stay (three years, according to Gal. 1:17–18), he became a champion of the gospel and probably helped win many Damascenes to the faith—so much so that he was forced to flee the city, just as earlier he had forced others to run (9:23–25).

Nevertheless, Damascus continued to be an amplifier for the gospel, as travelers through the Decapolis heard the good news there and spread it throughout the ancient world. Tradition holds that the apostle Matthew became a Syrian pastor and established a church in or near the city. The gospel that he wrote reflects his concern for Syrian believers (see the Introduction to Matthew).

A Christian church can still be found in Damascus—on a street called Straight. The Antiochian Orthodox Church and the Syrian Orthodox Church are both headquartered there. ◆

Cities in general can be enormously strategic in amplifying the message of Christ. See "Boom Box," Acts 19:10.

An Ethnic Wall Comes Down

10:1

10 In Caesarea there was a man
named Cornelius, a centurion of
the Italian Cohort, as it was called. 2He was a devout man
who feared God with all his household; he gave alms generously to the people and prayed constantly to God. 3One afternoon at about three o'clock he had a vision in which he
clearly saw an angel of God coming in and saying to him,
"Cornelius." 4He stared at him in terror and said, "What is
it, Lord?" He answered, "Your prayers and your alms have
ascended as a memorial before God. 5Now send men to
Joppa for a certain Simon who is called Peter; 6he is lodging
with Simon, a tanner, whose house is by the seaside."
7When the angel who spoke to him had left, he called two
of his slaves and a devout soldier from the ranks of those
who served him, 8and after telling them everything, he sent
them to Joppa.

(Bible text continued on page 445)

Joppa

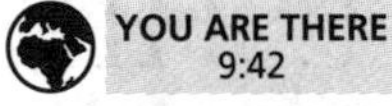

- **A Mediterranean seaport, the only natural harbor between Egypt and the Bay of Acco (Haifa).**
- **Named Joppa, or "beautiful," because of the way sunlight reflected off its buildings and city walls.**
- **Known today as Jaffa or Yafo, a southern suburb of Tel Aviv.**
- **Although ideally situated for Israel's maritime use, Joppa was rarely under Israel's control. As a result, the nation never developed much of a navy during Old Testament times, which prevented it from dominating the Mediterranean.**

Personality Profile: Cornelius

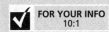

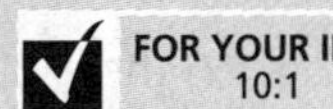

Home: Stationed in Caesarea, Rome's administrative center in Palestine.

Occupation: Centurion. A Roman officer was designated a centurion if he oversaw at least 100 soldiers. As head of the Italian Cohort, he probably had about 600 men under his command.

Known to be: God-fearing, prayerful, and generous. He was drawn to Jewish monotheism as opposed to the pagan idolatry and immorality common among Romans of that day.

Best known today as: The second recorded Gentile convert to Christianity (an Ethiopian treasurer was first, Acts 8:26–40). He sent men to fetch Simon Peter, 36 miles away, in response to a vision from God.

CONSIDER THIS
9:26–30

DISCIPLESHIP—OR MENTORING?

In the Great Commission (as it is frequently labeled; Matt. 28:19), Jesus commanded His disciples to "Go . . . and make disciples." The objective was not that they attract their own disciples, but that they win new followers of Jesus. Acts tells the story of how the Spirit-filled apostles obeyed that command.

But closely related to the making of disciples is the *mentoring* of leaders. Here in Acts 9 Saul's conversion starts one dynamic chain of mentoring that extends through the rest of the New Testament (see the accompanying diagram, "Kingdom-Style Mentoring").

"Mentoring" has become a buzzword among Western business and professional people. But the concept is as old as Homer's *Odyssey* (c. 900–810 B.C.), in which Odysseus entrusts to his friend, Mentor, the education of Telemachus, his son. A mentor, then, is a trusted counselor or guide—typically an older, more experienced person who imparts valuable wisdom to someone younger. Countless figures throughout history have recalled the powerful influence of mentors on their development.

The Old Testament is filled with mentoring relationships: Jethro, a wealthy livestock owner, helped his overworked son-in-law, Moses, learn to delegate authority (Ex. 18:1–27); Deborah, judge over Israel, summoned Barak to military leadership and helped him triumph over Jabin, a Canaanite king, bringing forty years of peace to the land (Judg. 4:4–24); Eli, a priest of the Lord (but a failure as a father) raised young Samuel to succeed him (1 Sam. 1:1—3:21); the prophet Elijah, who oversaw the evil end of Ahab and Jezebel, passed his office on to young Elisha, who received a double portion of his spirit (2 Kin. 2:1–15).

Barnabas, a wealthy landowner in the early church, became an advocate and guide for Saul, the former enemy and persecutor of the movement (Acts 9:26–30). Over time, with Barnabas' coaching and encouragement, Saul (later called Paul) became the central figure in the early spread of the gospel.

Close observation reveals four key functions of a kingdom-style mentor:

(1) Mentors *care* about those who follow them. Their primary interest is not what they can gain from the relationship, but with what they can give to it. They also realize how much they have to learn from their protégés. Ultimately, they fulfill Paul's admonition to look out not only for their own interests, but also for the interests of others (Phil. 2:4).

(2) Mentors *convey* wisdom and skill. Through modeling and coaching, and eventually by turning over responsibility to their followers, kingdom-style mentors seek to make their disciples more capable than the mentors have been (Matt. 10:25).

(3) Mentors *correct* their followers when they are wrong. An excellent example is Barnabas' challenge to Paul over taking John Mark along on the second missionary journey (Acts 15:36–39). Later Paul changed his perspective, and asked Timothy to bring John Mark to him (2 Tim. 4:11). Kingdom-style mentors do not avoid confrontation.

(4) Mentors *connect* their followers to significant others. As Acts 9 shows, Saul's entrée into the early church was Barnabas. Kingdom-style mentors introduce their protégés to relationships and resources that will further their development and increase their opportunities. ◆

Barnabas was so well regarded in the early church for his encouragement of others that his name was changed from Joses to Barnabas, which means "Son of Encouragement." Learn more about this model of kingdom-style mentoring at Acts 4:36–37.

9 About noon the next day, as they were on their journey and approaching the city, Peter went up on the roof to
pray. [10]He became hungry and wanted something to eat;
and while it was being prepared, he fell into a trance. [11]He
saw the heaven opened and something like a large sheet
coming down, being lowered to the ground by its four corners. [12]In it were all kinds of four-footed creatures and reptiles and birds of the air. [13]Then he heard a voice saying,
"Get up, Peter; kill and eat." [14]But Peter said, "By no means,
Lord; for I have never eaten anything that is profane or unclean." [15]The voice said to him again, a second time, "What
God has made clean, you must not call profane." [16]This
happened three times, and the thing was suddenly taken
up to heaven.

17 Now while Peter was greatly puzzled about what to
make of the vision that he had seen, suddenly the men sent
by Cornelius appeared. They were asking for Simon's house
and were standing by the gate. [18]They called out to ask

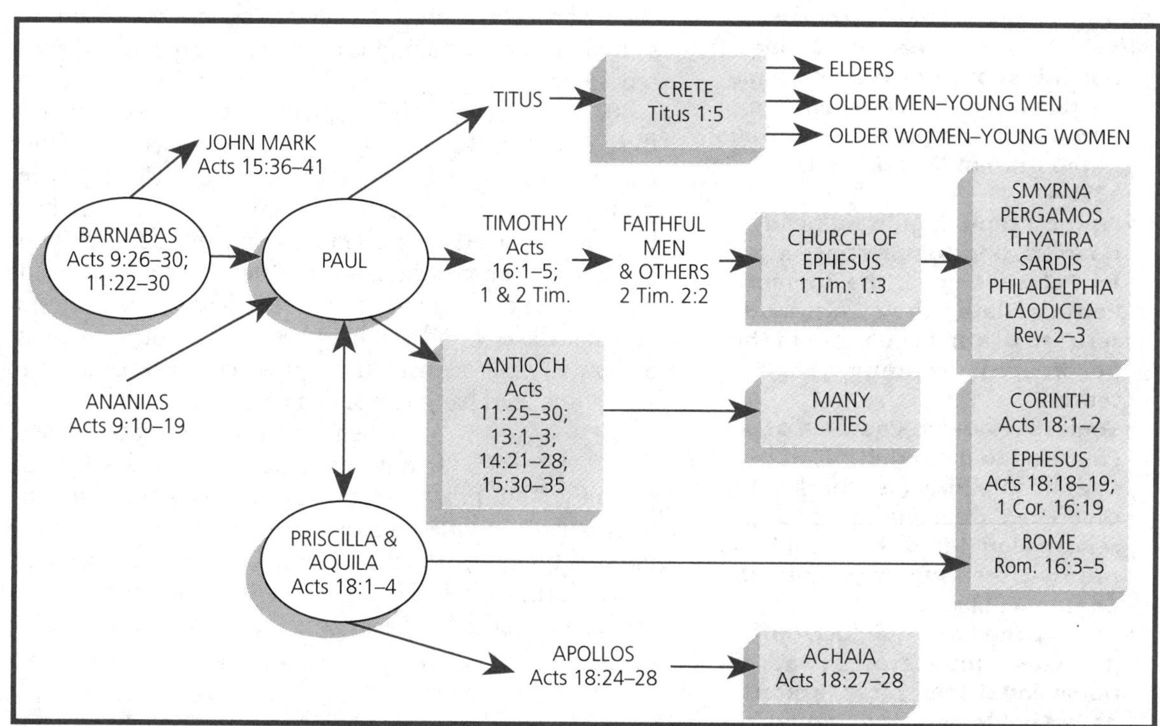

KINGDOM-STYLE MENTORING

Powerful results stem from experienced believers mentoring younger believers in the faith. Not only individuals, but entire communities benefit as the gospel transforms lives.

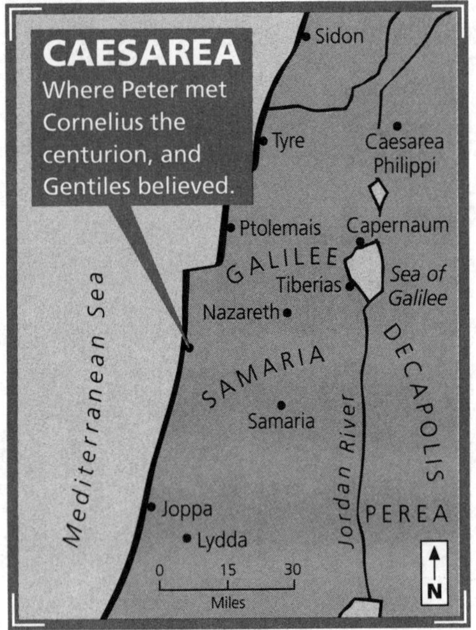

CAESAREA

YOU ARE THERE 10:24

- **Mediterranean seaport 60 miles northwest of Jerusalem, on a major caravan route between Tyre and Alexandria (Egypt; see "Travel in the Ancient World," Acts 13:3–4).**
- **Political capital, military headquarters, and commercial center for Palestine under the Romans. Pontius Pilate, who condemned Jesus to death, lived there in the governor's palace during his tenure.**
- **Sometimes called Caesarea of Palestine to distinguish it from Caesarea Philippi (see Mark 8:27).**
- **Given by Caesar Augustus to the Jewish king Herod the Great, who returned the favor by naming it Caesarea (22 B.C.).**
- **Herod added an aqueduct, amphitheater, hippodrome (track for horse and chariot races), colonnaded boulevard, and harbor (the city had no natural harbor).**
- **Herod also built a Roman temple**

(continued on next page)

whether Simon, who was called Peter, was staying there.
19While Peter was still thinking about the vision, the Spirit
said to him, "Look, three[z] men are searching for you. 20Now
get up, go down, and go with them without hesitation; for I
have sent them." 21So Peter went down to the men and
said, "I am the one you are looking for; what is the reason
for your coming?" 22They answered, "Cornelius, a centurion, an upright and God-fearing man, who is well spoken
of by the whole Jewish nation, was directed by a holy angel
to send for you to come to his house and to hear what you
have to say." 23So Peter[a] invited them in and gave them
lodging.

The next day he got up and went with them, and some of
the believers[b] from Joppa accompanied
him. 24The following day they came to
Caesarea. Cornelius was expecting them and had called together his relatives and close friends. 25On Peter's arrival
Cornelius met him, and falling at his feet, worshiped him.
26But Peter made him get up, saying, "Stand up; I am only a
mortal." 27And as he talked with him, he went in and found
that many had assembled; 28and he said to them, "You
yourselves know that it is unlawful for a Jew to associate
with or to visit a Gentile; but God has shown me that I
should not call anyone profane or unclean. 29So when I was
sent for, I came without objection. Now may I ask why you
sent for me?"

10:24

30 Cornelius replied, "Four days ago at this very hour, at
three o'clock, I was praying in my house when suddenly a
man in dazzling clothes stood before me. 31He said, 'Cornelius, your prayer has been heard and your alms have
been remembered before God. 32Send therefore to Joppa
and ask for Simon, who is called Peter; he is staying in the
home of Simon, a tanner, by the sea.' 33Therefore I sent for
you immediately, and you have been kind enough to come.
So now all of us are here in the presence of God to listen to
all that the Lord has commanded you to say."

10:34 see pg. 450

34 Then Peter began to speak to them:
"I truly understand that God shows no
partiality, 35but in every nation anyone who fears him and
does what is right is acceptable to him. 36You know the
message he sent to the people of Israel, preaching peace by
Jesus Christ—he is Lord of all. 37That message spread
throughout Judea, beginning in Galilee after the baptism

[z]One ancient authority reads *two*; others lack the word [a]Gk *he* [b]Gk *brothers*

that John announced: [38]how God anointed Jesus of
Nazareth with the Holy Spirit and with power; how he
went about doing good and healing all who were oppressed
by the devil, for God was with him. [39]We are witnesses to
all that he did both in Judea and in Jerusalem. They put
him to death by hanging him on a tree; [40]but God raised
him on the third day and allowed him to appear, [41]not to
all the people but to us who were chosen by God as witnesses, and who ate and drank with him after he rose from
the dead. [42]He commanded us to preach to the people and
to testify that he is the one ordained by God as judge of the
living and the dead. [43]All the prophets testify about him
that everyone who believes in him receives forgiveness of
sins through his name."

10:44–45 see pg. 448

44 While Peter was still speaking, the
Holy Spirit fell upon all who heard the
word. [45]The circumcised believers who had come with Peter were astounded that the gift of the Holy Spirit had been
poured out even on the Gentiles, [46]for they heard them
speaking in tongues and extolling God. Then Peter said,
[47]"Can anyone withhold the water for baptizing these people who have received the Holy Spirit just as we have?" [48]So
he ordered them to be baptized in the name of Jesus Christ.
Then they invited him to stay for several days.

Peter Defends His Visit to the Gentiles

11 Now the apostles and the believers[c] who were in
Judea heard that the Gentiles had also accepted the
word of God. [2]So when Peter went up to
Jerusalem, the circumcised believers[d]
criticized him, [3]saying, "Why did you go to uncircumcised
men and eat with them?" [4]Then Peter began to explain it to
them, step by step, saying, [5]"I was in the city of Joppa praying, and in a trance I saw a vision. There was something
like a large sheet coming down from heaven, being lowered
by its four corners; and it came close to me. [6]As I looked at
it closely I saw four-footed animals, beasts of prey, reptiles,
and birds of the air. [7]I also heard a voice saying to me, 'Get
up, Peter; kill and eat.' [8]But I replied, 'By no means, Lord;
for nothing profane or unclean has ever entered my mouth.'
[9]But a second time the voice answered from heaven, 'What
God has made clean, you must not call profane.' [10]This
happened three times; then everything was pulled up again

11:2–18 see pg. 451

(Bible text continued on page 450)

[c]Gk *brothers* [d]Gk lacks *believers*

(continued from previous page)

honoring Augustus. Filled with statues of the emperor, it offended the Jewish population, one of the prominent minority groups in the city.

- **Home to Philip the evangelist (see Acts 8:5).**
- **Paul kept there for two years in Herod's Praetorium, which housed an elite corps of Roman soldiers (23:23–35; 24:27), perhaps including Cornelius the centurion (see related article at 10:44–45).**
- **In the later Roman Empire, a major headquarters for the church and a center of learning.**

Herod the Great was politically astute but ruthless. He routinely exterminated his enemies, including one of his wives and three of his sons. See "The Herods," Acts 12:1–2.

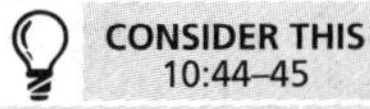

ETHNIC WALLS BREAK DOWN

A major breakthrough in race relations is described in Acts 10. For years a virtual wall between Jews and Gentiles had hampered the apostles in sharing Jesus with the Gentile world. But when Peter met Cornelius—an officer of Rome's occupation troops in Palestine—two conversions took place: Cornelius, his family, and his friends came to faith; and Peter came to realize that God wants Gentiles in the church.

God easily could have used Philip the evangelist (see 8:5) to bring the gospel to Cornelius. After all, he lived in Caesarea and had already shown his willingness to share the gospel across ethnic lines. But no, God called Peter to bring His message to the Roman centurion. Apparently He wanted to break down barriers against Gentiles in Peter's heart.

How Peter Saw Cornelius

- *Living in Caesarea,* Roman military capital of Palestine (10:1).
- *A centurion,* commander of 100 occupying Roman troops (10:1).
- *Of the Italian Cohort,* all men from Italy (10:1).
- *Gentile* (10:1).
- *Unclean,* like the unclean animals of the Old Testament dietary laws (10:11–16).
- *Unlawful for a Jew to visit,* as he was from another nation (10:28).
- *Uncircumcised,* therefore not right to eat with (11:3).

In Peter's mind, these factors disqualified Cornelius from serving him dinner, let alone coming to faith. But Peter was following a "narrow gospel."

God's intention had been that Hebrews would treat their Gentile neighbors cordially (Num. 35:15; Deut. 10:19; Ezek. 47:2). Of course, He also charged His people to exclude heathen practices, particularly idolatry (Lev. 18:24—19:4; Deut. 12:29–31). Intermarriage was condemned, though sometimes allowed (compare Ex. 34:16; Deut. 7:3; Ezra 9:12; 10:2–44; Neh. 10:30). But the main concern was moral purity.

Through rabbinic tradition strict separation became the rule. By Peter's day, four hundred years of Greek and Roman oppression had only hardened Jewish resolve to avoid as much contact as possible with foreigners.

Peter and the other Jewish believers brought these attitudes with them into the church, which made it almost impossible for them to reach out to Gentiles.

How God Saw Cornelius

- *Devout* (10:2).
- *A God-fearer,* along with his household (10:2).
- *Generous to the poor* (10:2).
- *A man of prayer* whose prayers and alms were received by God (10:2, 4).
- *Obedient to God's angel* (10:7–8).
- *Cleansed by God,* so not unclean (10:15).
- *Crucial for Peter to visit* (10:5, 19–20).

God's view of Cornelius was a contrast to Peter's. Because of Christ, God was ready to throw the doors of faith wide open to Gentiles: "What God has made clean, you must not call profane," He sternly declared to Peter (vv. 9–16). Because of Christ, the centurion could be "cleansed" from sin and be acceptable to God.

But Peter was confused. Should he break with his culture and visit this Gentile, violating traditional codes handed down as if carrying the force of God's law? He had at least two days to sort out his thoughts as he walked to Caesarea to meet Cornelius. His emotional struggle can be seen in his first words to the assembled group: "You yourselves know that it is unlawful for a Jew to associate with or to visit a Gentile" (v. 28).

But God broke down the wall in Peter's heart by pouring out the Holy Spirit on these Gentile believers (vv. 44–45).

Peter's New Perspective

- "I truly understand that *God shows no partiality*" (10:34, italics added).
- "But *in every nation* anyone who fears him . . . is acceptable to him" (10:35, italics added).
- "Jesus Christ . . . is Lord of *all*" (10:36, italics added).
- "*Everyone who believes* in him receives forgiveness of sins" (10:43, italics added).
- "Can *anyone* withhold the water for baptizing these people who have received the Holy Spirit *just as we have?*" (10:47, italics added).
- "God gave *them* the *same gift* that he gave us when we believed" (11:17, italics added).
- "*Who was I* that I could hinder God?" (11:17, italics added).

Breaking Down Barriers Today

Attitudes of prejudice and legalism trouble the church today just as they did the early church. Believers sometimes mingle cultural biases with biblical mandates, creating wrenching controversies over numerous sensitive issues. Certainly issues need to be addressed, particularly when essentials of the faith are at stake. But one of those biblical essentials is that believers eagerly seek out *all* people, look at them from God's perspective, love them for the gospel's sake, and rejoice over those that respond in faith. Can the church ever afford to wall itself off through fear or prejudice? Doing so would be to turn away from God's compassionate heart. ◆

The incident at Caesarea was not the first time that the early church had to deal with ethnic issues. See "A Growing Movement Confronts Ethnic Prejudice," Acts 6:2–6, and "Society's Divisions Affect Believers," Acts 6:1.

Peter's visit with Cornelius recalls an earlier meeting he had with Samaritans. See "The Conversion of Samaritans to the Gospel—and of Peter and John to Samaritans," Acts 8:4–25.

CONSIDER THIS
10:34

COME ONE, COME ALL!

God never shows partiality (v. 34), but people often do. Luke peppers his Acts account with incidents of ethnic tension and prejudice, and also their resolution in Christ. He shows that the door of faith is open to the whole world, Jews and Gentiles alike.

1:8 / Jesus sends His followers out "**to the ends of the earth.**"

2:5–12, 37–41 / 3,000 **Hellenist Jews** from throughout the Roman world come to faith at Pentecost.

6:1–7 / Reconciliation occurs between **Hellenist and native-born Jews.** Stephen, Philip, and other Hellenist leadership emerge.

8:1, 4 / Persecuted believers scatter from Jerusalem throughout **Samaria**, telling their story.

8:5–8 / Philip preaches the gospel to the **Samaritans**, who respond in multitudes.

8:14–17, 25 / Peter and John visit the new **Samaritan believers**, pray that they would receive the Spirit, and begin preaching in **Samaritan cities.**

8:26–40 / Philip meets a black official from **Ethiopia** and leads him to faith.

10:1–48 / Peter baptizes Cornelius, a **Roman centurion of Caesarea**, and his relatives and close friends after seeing the Spirit come upon them.

11:19–26 / The gospel spreads to **Antioch** and a multiethnic church is born.

13:1—14:26 / Barnabas and Saul (Paul) take the gospel to **Asia Minor**, preaching first in synagogues but then turning to the Gentiles.

15:1–33 / A meeting is held at Jerusalem to resolve controversy over the inclusion of **Gentiles** in the church.

16:1–4 / Paul recruits **Timothy**, a young believer from a mixed background.

17:16–34 / Paul preaches to the **intellectuals in Athens**, and some respond in faith.

18:5–11 / Paul turns to the **Gentiles in Corinth**, establishing a multiethnic church.

21:17–36 / Paul explains his **Gentile ministry** to the believers in Jerusalem, and takes Greeks into the temple, creating a riot.

to heaven. 11At that very moment three men, sent to me
from Caesarea, arrived at the house where we were. 12The
Spirit told me to go with them and not to make a distinction between them and us.[e] These six brothers also accompanied me, and we entered the man's house. 13He told us
how he had seen the angel standing in his house and saying, 'Send to Joppa and bring Simon, who is called Peter;
14he will give you a message by which you and your entire
household will be saved.' 15And as I began to speak, the
Holy Spirit fell upon them just as it had upon us at the beginning. 16And I remembered the word of the Lord, how he
had said, 'John baptized with water, but you will be baptized with the Holy Spirit.' 17If then God gave them the
same gift that he gave us when we believed in the Lord Jesus Christ, who was I that I could hinder God?" 18When
they heard this, they were silenced. And they praised God,
saying, "Then God has given even to the Gentiles the repentance that leads to life."

The Message Spreads to Antioch

11:19–26
see pg. 453

19 Now those who were scattered because of the persecution that took place
over Stephen traveled as far as Phoenicia, Cyprus, and Antioch, and they spoke the word to no one except Jews. 20But
among them were some men of Cyprus and Cyrene who,
on coming to Antioch, spoke to the Hellenists[f] also, proclaiming the Lord Jesus. 21The hand of the Lord was with
them, and a great number became believers and turned to

11:22
see pg. 452

the Lord. 22News of this came to the ears
of the church in Jerusalem, and they sent
Barnabas to Antioch. 23When he came and saw the grace of
God, he rejoiced, and he exhorted them all to remain faithful to the Lord with steadfast devotion; 24for he was a good
man, full of the Holy Spirit and of faith. And a great many

11:25
see pg. 454

people were brought to the Lord. 25Then
Barnabas went to Tarsus to look for Saul,

11:26
see pg. 455

26and when he had found him, he
brought him to Antioch. So it was that
for an entire year they met with[g] the church and taught a
great many people, and it was in Antioch that the disciples
were first called "Christians."

[e]Or *not to hesitate* [f]Other ancient authorities read *Greeks* [g]Or *were guests of*

Famine Relief for Judea

27 At that time prophets came down from Jerusalem to
11:28 Antioch. 28One of them named Agabus
stood up and predicted by the Spirit that

Personality Profile: Claudius

FOR YOUR INFO 11:28 **Also known as:** Tiberius Claudius Nero Germanicus (his full given name).

Home: Rome.

Family: Married and divorced three wives in succession, by whom he had five children. His fourth wife, Agrippina, fed him poison after forcing him to adopt her son, Nero, and proclaim him heir.

Profession: Fourth emperor of Rome (A.D. 41–54), crowned after the Praetorian Guard found him trembling in a corner following the murder of his predecessor, Caligula. Having been a sickly child and rather ugly and ill-mannered, he was considered unfit for public life.

Accomplishments: Planted Roman colonies throughout the empire; wrote some 30 books having to do with Roman history.

Regarded as: A fool. Seneca even wrote a satire entitled, *The Pumpkinification of the Divine Claudius.*

Best known today for: Putting down a riot "instigated by one Chrestus," which led to the expulsion of Jews and some Christians from Rome, including Aquila and Priscilla (Acts 18:1–2; see Rom. 16:3–5). A worldwide famine is also reported to have occurred during his reign (Acts 11:28).

For more on the powerful emperors and others who ruled the Roman Empire and Palestine in the first century, see "New Testament Political Rulers," Luke 3:1.

Conflict Resolution

CONSIDER THIS 11:2–18 **It seems that no matter what one does, conflicts are bound to happen. Peter's report of his visit to Cornelius aroused hostility and opposition among some of the believers at Jerusalem (vv. 2–3). His behavior in Joppa, socializing with the hated and feared Gentiles, was unacceptable—even scandalous.**

But Peter responded with a clear, honest description of what happened (vv. 4–17). He filled in the gaps in their understanding and gently interpreted his activities. As a result, he not only achieved understanding, but created acceptance and approval for the new converts (v. 18).

Is there a need for advocacy, interpretation, or gentle persuasion in your world? Can you be a source of grace and truth between adversaries?

Peter's encounter with the believers at Jerusalem was not the end of the controversy over Gentiles in the church. See "Sure You're Saved . . . Sort Of," Acts 15:1–21.

there would be a severe famine over all the world; and this
took place during the reign of Claudius. 29The disciples determined that according to their ability, each would send relief to the believers[h] living in Judea; 30this they did, sending
it to the elders by Barnabas and Saul.

Herod Executes James and Has Peter Arrested

12:1–2 see pg. 458

12 About that time King Herod laid
violent hands upon some who
belonged to the church. 2He had James, the brother of
John, killed with the sword. 3After he saw that it pleased
the Jews, he proceeded to arrest Peter also. (This was during the festival of Unleavened Bread.) 4When he had seized
him, he put him in prison and handed him over to four
squads of soldiers to guard him, intending to bring him out

[h]Gk *brothers*

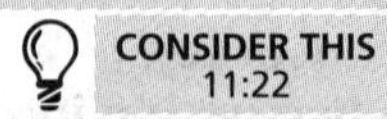

CHURCHES—KEYS TO THE CITIES

Christianity eventually prevailed as the dominant worldview and social force in the Roman world. One reason: it planted churches in dozens of the empire's major cities by the end of the first century. Christians spread the gospel "to the ends of the earth" (Acts 1:8) by establishing strategic, visible communities in urban areas such as Antioch (11:22, 26; see 13:1). These groups of believers stood apart from the culture in their beliefs and values, yet engaged the culture in their daily lives and work.

The New Testament word for "church," ekklēsia, *means assembly or congregation. In the Greek world, the* ekklēsia *was a public assembly called together by a herald to discuss legal issues and make community decisions. For example, Paul faced such a gathering at Ephesus, a town meeting that turned into a riot (19:32–41). But* ekklēsia *always referred to people—originally to the citizens of a city, and later to a gathering of believers. There is no evidence that it meant a church building until the fourth century* A.D.

Interestingly, eight times out of ten the New Testament uses the word ekklēsia *to refer to all of the believers in a specific city, such as "the church at Antioch" (13:1) or "the church of God that is in Corinth" (1 Cor. 1:2). Elsewhere it implies all Christian believers, regardless of geographic location or time in history—what is often called the universal (or catholic) church (Eph. 1:22; 3:10, 21; 5:23–32).*

to the people after the Passover. 5While Peter was kept in
prison, the church prayed fervently to God for him.

Peter Is Miraculously Released

6 The very night before Herod was going to bring him
out, Peter, bound with two chains, was sleeping between
two soldiers, while guards in front of the door were keeping
watch over the prison. 7Suddenly an angel of the Lord appeared and a light shone in the cell. He tapped Peter on the
side and woke him, saying, "Get up quickly." And the
chains fell off his wrists. 8The angel said to him, "Fasten
your belt and put on your sandals." He did so. Then he said
to him, "Wrap your cloak around you and follow me." 9Pe-
ter[i] went out and followed him; he did not realize that what
was happening with the angel's help was real; he thought

[i]Gk *He*

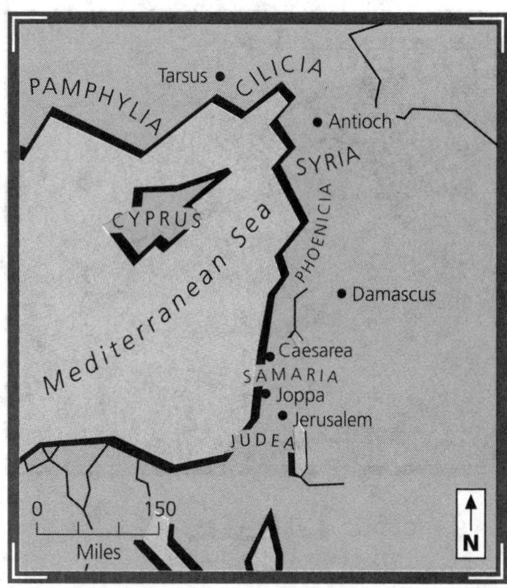

EARLY CHURCH EXPANSION

In forming churches, the early Christians did not drop out of society, nor did they form congregations that competed with each other for members (though sometimes members competed with each other, 1 Cor. 1:10–12). Instead, they lived and worked as members of the larger community. Meanwhile, they related to the other believers in their cities as members of a common family in Christ. This proved to be a radical concept—so powerful, in fact, that by the end of the second century, one author was able to write:

> *Christians are not distinguished from the rest of mankind by either country, speech, customs; the fact is, they nowhere settle in cities of their own; they use no peculiar language; they cultivate no eccentric mode of life . . . .*
>
> *Yet while they dwell in both Greek and non-Greek cities, as each one's lot was cast, and conform to the customs of the country in dress, food, and mode of life in general, the whole tenor of their way of living stamps it as worthy of admiration and admittedly extraordinary.*

This remarkable reputation of the early Christians compels modern believers to ask: What will the church today be remembered for? ◆

THE MOVEMENT EXPANDS BEYOND PALESTINE

YOU ARE THERE 11:19–26 **Though the apostles remained in Jerusalem, the majority of believers there scattered (v. 19) in the face of deadly attacks by Saul and others following Stephen's death (Acts 8:1–3; 9:1; 22:4–5; 26:10–11). As the Christians searched for places to rebuild their lives, some related the gospel to Jews only. But others who spoke Greek (like those from Cyprus and Cyrene, modern-day Libya) crossed ethnic barriers, particularly at Antioch.**

Jerusalem was never intended to be the headquarters of Christianity. *See "Jerusalem—Merely the Beginning," Acts 1:12–26, and "The Message Leaves Jerusalem," Acts 8:1.*

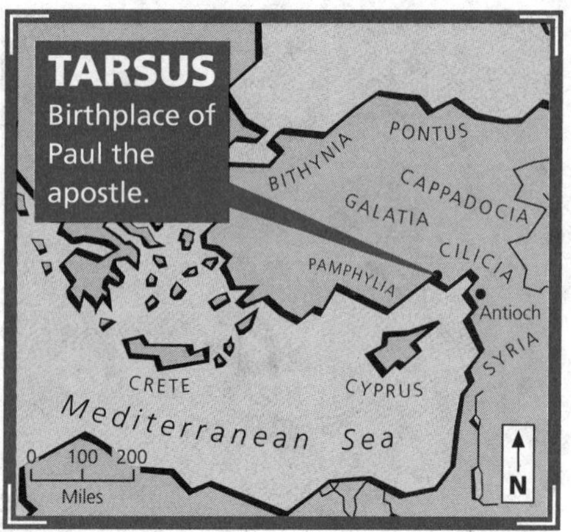

TARSUS

YOU ARE THERE 11:25

- **One of the world's oldest cities, with a continuous history dating back several thousand years.**
- **Capital of the province of Cilicia under the Romans, on the southeast coast of Asia Minor, with a culture heavily influenced by the Greeks.**
- **City where Cleopatra first met Mark Antony.**
- **A free city under Caesar Augustus, meaning it enjoyed self-government and tax-exempt status.**
- **Noted as a center of learning, with schools rivaling those of Alexandria.**
- **Center for the garment and tent-making industries. A goat hair fabric called cilicium was used to make tents. Paul may have picked up this trade as a boy.**
- **Population in Roman times may have been 500,000.**
- **A sizable Jewish population and synagogue by the first century.**

Tarsus' greatest claim to fame proved to be the apostle Paul. To learn more about this dynamic leader, see the profile at Acts 13:2–3.

he was seeing a vision. 10After they had passed the first and
the second guard, they came before the iron gate leading
into the city. It opened for them of its own accord, and they
went outside and walked along a lane, when suddenly the
angel left him. 11Then Peter came to himself and said, "Now
I am sure that the Lord has sent his angel and rescued me
from the hands of Herod and from all that the Jewish people were expecting."

12:12–17

12 As soon as he realized this, he went
to the house of Mary, the mother of John
whose other name was Mark, where many had gathered
and were praying. 13When he knocked at the outer gate, a
maid named Rhoda came to answer. 14On recognizing Peter's voice, she was so overjoyed that, instead of opening
the gate, she ran in and announced that Peter was standing
at the gate. 15They said to her, "You are out of your mind!"
But she insisted that it was so. They said, "It is his angel."
16Meanwhile Peter continued knocking; and when they
opened the gate, they saw him and were amazed. 17He motioned to them with his hand to be silent, and described for
them how the Lord had brought him out of the prison. And
he added, "Tell this to James and to the believers."[j] Then he
left and went to another place.
18 When morning came, there was no small commotion
among the soldiers over what had become of Peter. 19When

[j] *Gk brothers*

MARY'S HOUSE

CONSIDER THIS 12:12–17

Mary, John Mark's mother (v. 12), contributed immeasurably to the growth of the early church by opening her home as a meeting place for believers at Jerusalem. As homeowner and host she probably had a prominent role in the gatherings.

Like her nephew, Barnabas (see 4:36–37; Col. 4:10), Mary apparently enjoyed some wealth, as demonstrated by her employment of the maid Rhoda. Released from prison, Peter went immediately to this center of Christian activity.

Herod had searched for him and could not find him, he examined the guards and ordered them to be put to death.
Then he went down from Judea to Caesarea and stayed
there.

An Angel of the Lord Strikes Down Herod

20 Now Herod[k] was angry with the people of Tyre and
Sidon. So they came to him in a body; and after winning
over Blastus, the king's chamberlain, they asked for a reconciliation, because their country depended on the king's
country for food. 21On an appointed day Herod put on his
royal robes, took his seat on the platform, and delivered a
public address to them. 22The people kept shouting, "The
voice of a god, and not of a mortal!" 23And immediately, because he had not given the glory to God, an angel of the
Lord struck him down, and he was eaten by worms and
died.

Barnabas and Saul Are Sent Out

24 But the word of God continued to advance and gain
adherents. 25Then after completing their mission Barnabas
and Saul returned to[l] Jerusalem and brought with them
John, whose other name was Mark.

13:1 see pg. 461

13:1–3 see pg. 460

13:2–3 see pg. 456

13 Now in the church at Antioch
there were prophets and teachers: Barnabas, Simeon who was called
Niger, Lucius of Cyrene, Manaen a member of the court of Herod the ruler,[m] and
Saul. 2While they were worshiping the
Lord and fasting, the Holy Spirit said, "Set apart for me
Barnabas and Saul for the work to which I have called
them." 3Then after fasting and praying they laid their hands
on them and sent them off.

A Proconsul Believes

13:3–4 see pg. 462

13:5 see pg. 466

13:6 see pg. 466

4 So, being sent out by the Holy
Spirit, they went down to Seleucia; and
from there they sailed to Cyprus. 5When
they arrived at Salamis, they proclaimed
the word of God in the synagogues of the Jews. And they
had John also to assist them. 6When they
had gone through the whole island as far
as Paphos, they met a certain magician, a Jewish false
prophet, named Bar-Jesus. 7He was with the proconsul,
Sergius Paulus, an intelligent man, who summoned Barnabas and Saul and wanted to hear the word of God. 8But

(Bible text continued on page 458)

[k]Gk *he* [l]Other ancient authorities read *from* [m]Gk *tetrarch*

A New Reality Gets a New Name

CONSIDER THIS 11:26 **As Jesus' band of followers grew into a movement, they were called the Way (Acts 9:2), probably a reference to Christ's statement, "I am the way" (John 14:6). For the most part, members of the Way had been Jewish believers.**

But in Antioch there was an infusion of other ethnic groups, and observers were perplexed as to what to call the multicultural body. The new reality required a new name. Standard ethnic designations—Jews, Greeks, Romans, Gentiles—no longer fit. So the Antiochians seized on the one factor that united the diverse community—Christ. Actually, the term "Christians," or Christ-followers, was a sarcastic put-down (Acts 11:26). But the term stuck and even became a name of honor.

Are there perceptions of the faith where you live and work that are inadequate? Can you change some of those with a display of what following Christ actually involves? Are there ways in which coworkers, friends, or relatives can be touched by the faith, ways that will cause a breakthrough in understanding?

The name of Jesus held extraordinary power for the first believers. See "Jesus—The Name You Can Trust," Acts 3:1.

SAUL OF TARSUS

FOR YOUR INFO 13:2–3 **Few backgrounds could have better prepared Saul to be the chief persecutor of the early church. He was born at Tarsus—"an important city," as he liked to describe it (21:39)—a major Roman city on the coast of southeast Asia Minor. Tarsus was a center for the tentmaking industry, and perhaps that influenced Saul to choose that craft as an occupation. Teachers of the Law, which Saul eventually became, were not paid for their services and had to earn a living in other ways (see "Scribes," Luke 20:39).**

However, Saul said that he was "brought up" in Jerusalem "at the feet of Gamaliel," the most illustrious rabbi of the day (Acts 22:3) and a highly respected member of the Jewish council (5:34; see "The Council," Acts 6:12). In making that statement, Saul was describing a process of technical training in the Law that prepared him to become one of the Pharisees, the religious elite of Judaism. For many Jewish youth, the rigorous course of study began at age 14 and continued to the age of 40.

Apparently Saul was an apt pupil. He claimed to have outstripped his peers in enthusiasm for ancestral traditions and in his zeal for the Law (Phil. 3:4–6). Probably through Gamaliel, he had opportunity to observe the council and come to know many of its principals and some of its inner workings.

So it was that he chanced to be present when the conflict between the council and the early church came to a head in the stoning of Stephen (7:57—8:1). He had likely watched earlier encounters between the council and members of the Way, such as those with Peter and John (4:5–18; 5:17–40). But apparently the incident with Stephen galvanized his commitment to traditional Judaism and set him off on a mission to seek out and destroy as many believers as he could (8:1–3).

PERSONALITY PROFILE: SAUL

Also known as: Paul, perhaps his Roman name; but as far as we know, he was always called Saul prior to his conversion (see the accompanying profile on post-conversion Paul).

Home: Born at Tarsus (see Acts 11:25); brought up in Jerusalem (see Matt. 23:37).

Family: Saul was a Jew but was born a Roman citizen (Acts 22:28), which means his father, who was a Pharisee (23:6), must have been a Roman citizen before him.

Profession: Tentmaker by trade (see 18:1–3); trained as a Pharisee under Rabbi Gamaliel, he became the Jewish council's chief agent of anti-Christian activity.

Life-changing experience: Before his conversion—probably witnessing Stephen's defense before the council and subsequent execution by stoning (7:1—8:1).

Best known today for: His ardent persecution of Christians.

SAUL WAS RAVAGING THE CHURCH.
—Acts 8:3

Paul, the Apostle to the Gentiles

Ironically, Paul's background not only prepared him to be the early church's chief opponent, but also to become its leading spokesperson. Devout, energetic, outspoken, stubborn, and exacting, Paul became far more troublesome to the Jews than he had ever been to the Christians, not in terms of violence, but ideology. Indeed, he lived with a price on his head as his former colleagues among the Jews sought to destroy him (Acts 9:23–25, 29; 23:12–15; 2 Cor. 11:26, 32–33).

Perhaps the chief irony of Paul's life was his calling to be the "apostle to the Gentiles" (Acts 9:15; Gal. 1:16; 2:7–9). Paul had been a Pharisee, the very title meaning "to separate." Some Pharisees even refused to eat with non-Pharisees for fear of being contaminated by food not rendered ritually clean. They also separated from women, from lepers, from Samaritans, and especially from Gentiles (or "foreigners").

So for Paul to take the gospel to the Gentiles was a reversal of his life and a thorough repudiation of his background as a Pharisee. Perhaps three people proved invaluable in helping him make this dramatic change: Barnabas, who like Paul was a Hellenistic Jew and came from a Levite background—he embraced Paul and mentored him in the faith when no one else would come near him (see Acts 4:36–37); and Priscilla and Aquila, fellow tentmakers—they joined Paul in business in Corinth and probably discussed the faith and its implications with Paul much as they did with Apollos (18:1–3, 24–28; see Rom. 16:3–5).

Paul eventually became Christianity's leading evangelist and theologian. But even as his status in the church rose, his perspective on himself changed. At first he saw himself as an important Christian leader, but then as "the least of the apostles" (1 Cor. 15:9). Later he realized that he was capable of "nothing good" (Rom. 7:18) and was "the very least of all the saints" (Eph. 3:8). Finally he described himself as the "foremost" of sinners (1 Tim. 1:15)—and threw himself on God's mercy and grace.

The fearsome Pharisee of Pharisees became the fearless apostle to the Gentiles whose credo was, "Living is Christ and dying is gain" (Phil. 1:21).

Paul's transformation into the "apostle to the Gentiles" did not take place overnight. It took him at least ten years to reevaluate his cultural perspectives and bring them in line with the heart of God for the world. See "From Persecutor to Apostle," Gal. 1:13–17.

Personality Profile: Paul

Also known as: Saul, his Jewish name, perhaps given in memory of Israel's first king, a member of the tribe of Benjamin, to which Paul's family belonged; but following his conversion he was known as Paul.

Home: Settled in Antioch of Syria (see Acts 13:1), but traveled throughout the Roman empire, with extended stays in Corinth (see Introduction to 2 Corinthians) and Ephesus (see Introduction to Ephesians).

Family: Luke mentions a sister and her son (Acts 23:16).

Profession: Tentmaker by trade (see 18:1–3); he became not only a leader in the church, but its most well-known and widely traveled spokesperson, and a major New Testament writer.

Life-changing experience: A vision of Christ on the Damascus road, which led to his conversion and call as an apostle (9:1–31; Gal. 1:1–24).

Best known today as: The apostle to the Gentiles.

the magician Elymas (for that is the translation of his name)
opposed them and tried to turn the proconsul away from
the faith. 9But Saul, also known as Paul, filled with the Holy
Spirit, looked intently at him 10and said, "You son of the
devil, you enemy of all righteousness, full of all deceit and
villainy, will you not stop making crooked the straight

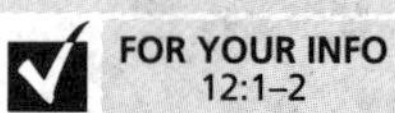
FOR YOUR INFO
12:1–2

THE HERODS

Backed by Roman authority, the family of the Herods exerted ruthless control over Palestine during the time of Christ and the founding of the church. Although they built many splendid edifices and strengthened Judea militarily, they are remembered infamously for a family history full of violence, incest, and political intrigue.

Antipater

- *Cunning, wealthy, ambitious.*
- *Leveraged Jewish civil unrest with Roman muscle to take control (47 B.C.).*
- *Installed his son Herod ("the Great") as governor of Judea.*
- *Died of poisoning.*

Herod the Great

- *Intelligent, charming in manners, a master of statecraft, and like his father, highly ambitious.*
- *Survived Jewish challenges to his rule through skillful politicking with Roman authorities, hard fighting, and extermination of his enemies, including one of his wives and three of his sons.*
- *Proclaimed king of the Jews by the Romans, a position he held at the birth of Christ (Matt. 2:1).*
- *Married a total of ten women who bore him at least 15 children.*
- *Rebuilt the temple to regain the Jews' favor. But he also built temples to pagan gods.*
- *Deteriorated mentally and physically in later years, but before dying divided his kingdom among three sons.*

Herod Archelaus

- *Oldest of Herod's sons, with the worst reputation.*
- *Given Judea by his father (Matt. 2:22).*
- *Angered the Jews by marrying his half-brother's widow.*
- *Deposed and banished in A.D. 6, leaving Judea a Roman province.*

paths of the Lord? 11And now listen—the hand of the Lord is against you, and you will be blind for a while, unable to see the sun." Immediately mist and darkness came over him, and he went about groping for someone to lead him by the hand. 12When the proconsul saw what had happened, he believed, for he

13:4–12 see pg. 464

Herod Antipas

- *Depicted in Scripture as wholly immoral.*
- *Given Galilee and Perea by his father, Herod the Great, inheriting the title of tetrarch (ruler of a fourth part).*
- *Childhood companion of Manaen, who was a leader in the church at Antioch (Acts 13:1).*
- *Divorced his first wife to marry Herodias, wife of his half-brother and also his niece.*
- *Maneuvered by Herodias into executing John the Baptist (Matt. 14:1–12; Mark 6:17–28).*
- *Exiled by Caligula after Herodias' brother Agrippa accused him of plotting against Rome.*

Herod Philip II

- *The one bright spot in the family—dignified, modest, and just.*
- *Given the northeastern territories of Iturea and the region of Trachonitis by his father Herod the Great (Luke 3:1).*

Herod Agrippa I

- *Grandson of Herod the Great.*
- *Installed by Caligula, he eventually ruled all of Jewish Palestine.*
- *Executed the apostle James and persecuted the early church (Acts 12:1–2).*
- *Struck down by God for his arrogance (12:21–23).*

Herod Agrippa II

- *Son of Agrippa I.*
- *Had an incestuous relationship with his sister, Bernice.*
- *Heard Paul's defense of his ministry (Acts 25:13—26:32).*
- *Fled Palestine for Rome during the Jewish revolts, where he died in A.D. 100.* ◆

Find out about the other major political leaders of the Roman Empire and Palestine in the first century in the table, "New Testament Political Rulers," Luke 3:1.

"WILL YOU NOT STOP MAKING CROOKED THE STRAIGHT PATHS OF THE LORD?"
—Acts 13:10

13:4–12 see pg. 465

was astonished at the teaching about the
Lord.

Barnabas and Paul Turn to the Gentiles

13:13 see pg. 468

13 Then Paul and his companions set
sail from Paphos and came to Perga in
Pamphylia. John, however, left them and returned to

13:13–14 see pg. 466

Jerusalem; 14but they went on from Perga
and came to Antioch in Pisidia. And on
the sabbath day they went into the synagogue and sat
down. 15After the reading of the law and
the prophets, the officials of the syna-

13:14–52 see pg. 466

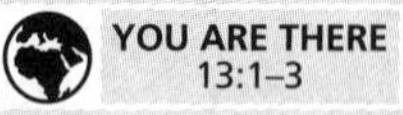

YOU ARE THERE 13:1–3

ANTIOCH: A MODEL FOR THE MODERN CHURCH?

Even though first-century Christians made regular pilgrimages to Jerusalem and met annually in the upper room, the city of Antioch—not Jerusalem—was the center of early Christianity. In fact, modern churches might consider Antioch as a model for what God's people ought to be and do.

Like most cities today, Antioch was racially diverse and culturally pluralistic. As a result, when the scattered believers arrived there (Acts 11:19–20), they had to wrestle with how to make the gospel meaningful for a diversity of groups. Four factors help to account for their success.

(1) They saw ethnic division as a barrier to overcome rather than a status quo to be maintained. *Antioch walled off the four dominant ethnic groups of its population, Greek, Syrian, African, and Jewish. But the gospel breaks down walls of separation and hostility (Eph. 2:14–22) and brings diverse peoples together in Christ. We know that the Antioch believers broke through the ethnic barriers because . . .*

(2) They soon had multiethnic leadership. *The church employed and deployed pastors, teachers, and evangelists who reflected the composition of the community. Notice the cross-section of the city represented by the leadership team in Acts 13:1:*

- *Barnabas, a Hellenist from Cyprus raised in a priestly family. Appropriately, he was the first major leader of the new group (see 4:36; 11:22–23).*
- *Simeon (Niger), an African.*
- *Lucius of Cyrene, also of African descent.*
- *Manaen, a childhood companion of Herod Antipas (the ruler who killed John the Baptist, Mark 6:17–28), per-*

gogue sent them a message, saying, "Brothers, if you have
any word of exhortation for the people, give it." 16So Paul
stood up and with a gesture began to speak:
"You Israelites,[n] and others who fear God, listen. 17The
God of this people Israel chose our ancestors and made the
people great during their stay in the land of Egypt, and
with uplifted arm he led them out of it. 18For about forty
years he put up with[o] them in the wilderness. 19After he
had destroyed seven nations in the land of Canaan, he gave
them their land as an inheritance 20for about four hundred

(Bible text continued on page 464)

[n]Gk *Men, Israelites* [o]Other ancient authorities read *cared for*

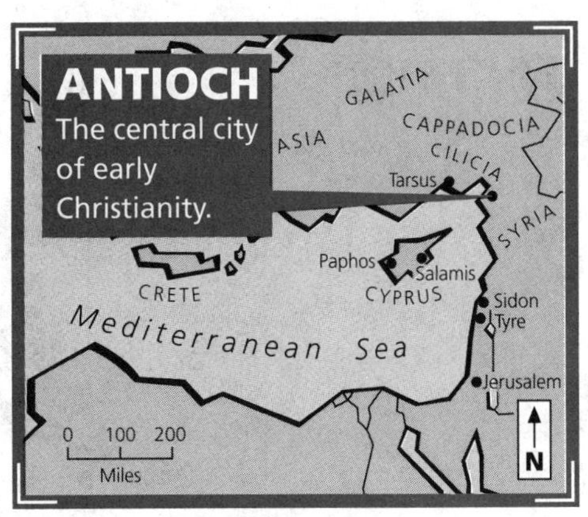

haps even a relative, and surely a privileged member of society.

- *Saul, a Hellenistic Jew from Tarsus with rabbinical training who had Roman citizenship. Note how Barnabas intentionally recruited this young, untried leader for the work (Acts 11:25–26).*

(3) They sent out ministry teams. *Just as the church at Antioch had been established by believers fleeing from Jerusalem, it, too, sent out ministry teams to tell the story of Jesus. Paul used Antioch as his base of operation for three successive tours (13:1–3; 15:36–41; and 18:22–23). Moreover, Antioch served as a crossroads for travelers from the Tigris and Euphrates River valleys to the east, Asia Minor to the north, and Egypt to the south. So the church was able to maintain an international outreach in its own hometown.*

(4) They joined together to accomplish projects of compassion. *A famine in Judea became an opportunity for the multiethnic Christians at Antioch to serve their predominantly Jewish brothers in Judea (11:27–30). Paul recognized how powerful the "politics of compassion" could be at uniting otherwise disconnected churches. "Remember the poor" became his rallying cry to bring together believers in Ephesus, Corinth, Thessalonica, Galatia, and Rome with those at Jerusalem (for example, 20:17–18, 35; 2 Cor. 8:1—9:15; Gal. 2:10).*

Overall, Antioch became the model for how the church ought to function when surrounded by diversity and cultural pluralism. ◆

ANTIOCH

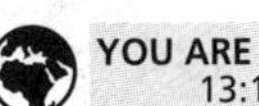
YOU ARE THERE 13:1

- **One of 16 cities named Antioch, sometimes called "Antioch of Syria" to distinguish it.**
- **Third largest city of the Roman empire, with 500,000 to 800,000 residents.**
- **Noted for its political power, bustling trade and commerce, a vibrant intellectual life, and religious tolerance.**
- **Divided by walls into four quadrants—Greek, Syrian, African, and Jewish.**
- **City where followers of the Way were first called "Christians" (Acts 11:26) and main headquarters of the early church.**
- **Known today as Antakiya in Turkey, a town of 35,000.**

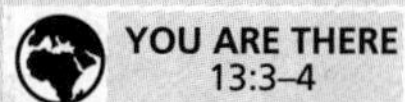

Travel in the Ancient World

As they set off on their travels for "the work" to which God had called them, Barnabas and Saul traveled through Seleucia (vv. 3–4), the seaport for Antioch. The city was important to the Romans because it provided access to one of the major east-west land trade routes of the Mediterranean region, the Way of the Sea.

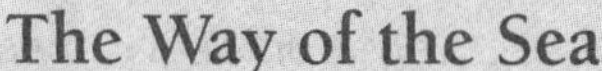

The Way of the Sea

The Way of the Sea (Is. 9:1), also called the "way of the land of the Philistines" (Ex. 13:17) and, later, the Via Maris, was the most important international highway throughout the biblical period. Originating in Egypt, it ran north along the coast to a pass over the Carmel ridge, through the Valley of Jezreel to Hazor, and eventually to Damascus. From there one could either head north through Syria toward Asia Minor, or east toward Mesopotamia, eventually linking up with the Euphrates River, which the highway followed to the Persian Gulf.

Many of the most important political and commercial centers of the ancient world were located along this road and its branches. Citizens thrived on supplying the needs and security of the many caravans traveling east and west.

However, it was the strategic military value of this roadway that ancient empires prized the most. By controlling a key city like Damascus or the passes at Megiddo and Hazor, an army could effectively shut down the way of the sea—or keep it open for its own troops or merchants. As a result, Palestine became a major factor in international politics and trade.

The King's Highway

A second major highway in the region was the King's Highway (Num. 20:17; 21:22). The northern portion was also called "the road to Bashan" (Num. 21:33; Deut. 3:1). The King's Highway ran north and south along the length of the Transjordanian Highlands, near the desert to the east of the Sea of Galilee, Jordan River, and the Dead Sea, and linked Damascus (and the Way of the Sea) with Elath on the Gulf of Aqaba.

This route provided a secondary road to Egypt and access to the spice routes of Arabia. It was often controlled by semi-nomadic people who prevented the founding of settlements along its length. In certain periods, however, the route was guarded by a network of fortresses.

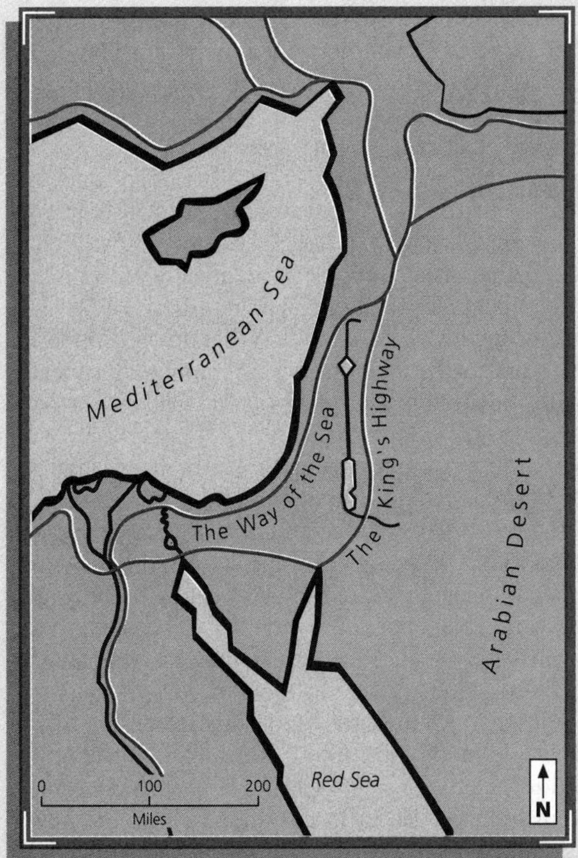

MAJOR LAND ROUTES

Secondary Road Systems

Within the region of Palestine, an internal system of roads provided communication between the many regions of the country. One north-south route, called the Way of the Wilderness of Edom and the Way of the Wilderness of Moab was located to the east of the King's Highway, along the fringe of the desert. It avoided the dry streambeds whose deep canyons divided the Transjordanian Highlands into its main geographical regions.

Other regional roads mentioned in the Bible include: "the way to the hill country of the Amorites" in the south (Deut. 1:19); "the way to Beth-shemesh" linking that city with Jerusalem (1 Sam. 6:9); "the route to Beth-horon," north of and parallel to the route to Beth-shemesh (1 Sam. 13:18).

For people of means or position, such as the Ethiopian treasurer (Acts 8:26–28), travel along these roads might be by chariot or by portable chairs (Song 3:6–10). Horses were used mostly for military purposes (Acts 23:23–24).

For most people, however, the only way to get about was on foot or donkeyback. Foot travelers could average about 16 miles a day. Thus under normal circumstances, the trip that Joseph and Mary took from Nazareth to Bethlehem (Luke 2:1–7) probably took at least five days.

Sea Journeys

For long distances, ship travel was common (Jon. 1; Acts 13:4; 27:1–44). In addition to Seleucia, some other major ports were beautiful Cyrene in northern Africa (see Mark 15:21); Caesarea of Palestine (see Acts 10:1); Tarsus, the hometown of Saul (see Acts 11:25); Corinth, perhaps the most celebrated city of the Roman Empire (see Introduction to 2 Corinthians); Syracuse, once home port of the world's best navy (see Acts 28:12); and Puteoli, gateway to Rome (see 28:13).

The islands of Crete (see Introduction to Titus) and especially Cyprus (see Acts 13:4) also served as major crossroads for shipping across the Mediterranean.

None of these locations, however, could top Alexandria for its reputation as a center of shipbuilding (see 18:24). Cargo ships usually had little room for passengers, though occasionally they carried voyagers on the open deck or in the hold with the cargo (Jon. 1:5). Paul sailed on such a vessel on the last leg of his trip to Rome (Acts 28:11).

Despite his earlier shipwreck (27:13–44) and his allusion to the various perils of travel (2 Cor. 11:26), travel in Paul's day was relatively simple and considerably safer than in the earlier times. The establishment of Roman control over the Mediterranean put an effective end to piracy and highway robbery in the region. Furthermore, the well-maintained Roman road system linked every corner of the empire and made travel much easier. ◆

Thanks to Israel's location on the Way of the Sea, it became a major exporter of agricultural goods. See "Trade in Ancient Israel" at the conclusion of John.

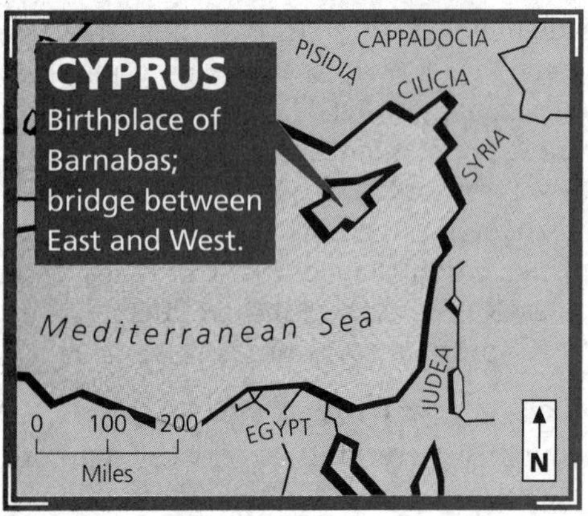

CYPRUS

YOU ARE THERE 13:4–12

- **First called Cyprus by the Greek poet, Homer; also known as "Copper Country."**
- **Its mostly Greek population was seldom independent of a stronger nation; accountable to Rome at the time of Christianity's rise.**
- **Dramatically variable climate—from warm water at sea level to snow in the mountains.**
- **Home to Barnabas (see Acts 4:36) and Mnason (21:16); a frequent port of call for early Christian travelers (11:19–20; 13:4–12). It was also where Barnabas took John Mark after separating from Paul (15:36–39).**
- **The modern Greek Orthodox Church honors Barnabas there as the patron saint of the Cyprus church.**

fifty years. After that he gave them judges until the time of
the prophet Samuel. 21Then they asked for a king; and God
gave them Saul son of Kish, a man of the tribe of Benjamin,
who reigned for forty years. 22When he had removed him,
he made David their king. In his testimony about him he
said, 'I have found David, son of Jesse, to be a man after my
heart, who will carry out all my wishes.' 23Of this man's
posterity God has brought to Israel a Savior, Jesus, as he
promised; 24before his coming John had already proclaimed
a baptism of repentance to all the people of Israel. 25And as
John was finishing his work, he said, 'What do you suppose
that I am? I am not he. No, but one is coming after me; I
am not worthy to untie the thong of the sandals[p] on his
feet.'

26 "My brothers, you descendants of Abraham's family,
and others who fear God, to us[q] the message of this salvation has been sent. 27Because the residents of Jerusalem and
their leaders did not recognize him or understand the
words of the prophets that are read every sabbath, they fulfilled those words by condemning him. 28Even though they
found no cause for a sentence of death, they asked Pilate to
have him killed. 29When they had carried out everything
that was written about him, they took him down from the
tree and laid him in a tomb. 30But God raised him from the
dead; 31and for many days he appeared to those who came
up with him from Galilee to Jerusalem, and they are now
his witnesses to the people. 32And we bring you the good
news that what God promised to our ancestors 33he has fulfilled for us, their children, by raising Jesus; as also it is
written in the second psalm,

'You are my Son;
today I have begotten you.'

34As to his raising him from the dead, no more to return to
corruption, he has spoken in this way,

'I will give you the holy promises made to David.'

35Therefore he has also said in another psalm,

'You will not let your Holy One experience corruption.'

36For David, after he had served the purpose of God in his
own generation, died,[r] was laid beside his ancestors, and
experienced corruption; 37but he whom God raised up experienced no corruption. 38Let it be known to you therefore, my brothers, that through this man forgiveness of sins
is proclaimed to you; 39by this Jesus[s] everyone who believes
is set free from all those sins[t] from which you could not be
freed by the law of Moses. 40Beware, therefore, that what
the prophets said does not happen to you:

[p]Gk *untie the sandals* [q]Other ancient authorities read *you* [r]Gk *fell asleep* [s]Gk *this* [t]Gk *all*

41 'Look, you scoffers!
Be amazed and perish,
for in your days I am doing a work,
a work that you will never believe, even if someone
tells you.' "
42 As Paul and Barnabas[u] were going out, the people
urged them to speak about these things again the next sabbath. 43When the meeting of the synagogue broke up,
many Jews and devout converts to Judaism followed Paul
and Barnabas, who spoke to them and urged them to continue in the grace of God.
13:44–48 44 The next sabbath almost the whole
city gathered to hear the word of the
Lord.[v] 45But when the Jews saw the crowds, they were filled

(Bible text continued on page 468)

[u]Gk *they* [v]Other ancient authorities read *God*

Some Prominent Women Oppose the Gospel

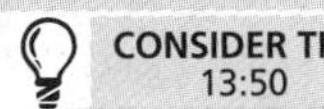

CONSIDER THIS 13:50 *The devout and prominent women who opposed Paul (v. 50) may have been Jews, but more likely they were Roman citizens.*

The first century saw tremendous changes in women's roles. Though Roman law technically kept a woman under a guardian, in practice it was easy for her to do as she pleased. In Asia Minor, women ran businesses, held municipal offices, and participated in public life. Women were gaining increasing wealth and, with it, influence. Those who had civic and social ambitions were heavily pressured to donate money for building projects, athletic contests, and religious cults.

The tragedy of the women of Pisidian Antioch was that once they gained access to the political and social power structures of their community, they used them to reject the gospel and protect their own interests.

Cyprus, a Geographic Hyphen

CONSIDER THIS 13:4–12 **In the first century—as well as today—Cyprus functioned much like a Heathrow, the international airport in England, hosting travelers who crisscrossed the ancient Mediterranean. These included Christians like Paul and Barnabas who sailed to Asia Minor, Greece, and Italy with the message of Christ.**

Cyprus was thus a "hyphen," a bridge between East and West. As such, its coastal cities were frequently exposed to new ideas and influences, which they tended to adopt, much like coastal cities today.

Modern Cyprus has become the offshore headquarters for many corporations, governmental agencies, nonprofit organizations, and ministries that used to be located in Beirut. In this way it still acts as a hyphen, contributing strategically to the flow of ideas and people between East and West.

Paul Turns to the Gentiles

CONSIDER THIS 13:44–48 *Paul's decision to turn to the Gentiles (v. 46) was a crossroads in the Christian movement. From then on, Paul extended the gospel as freely to Gentiles as to Jews.*

Salamis

YOU ARE THERE 13:5

- Principal city of ancient Cyprus, not to be confused with the town and island of Salamis off the coast of Greece.
- Boasted a deep water harbor which made the town a commercial success; now silted over.
- Traded in copper, flax, wine, fruit, and honey.
- Included an influential Jewish colony when Paul and Barnabas arrived on the first leg of their first journey.
- Traditional site of Barnabas' martyrdom at the hands of a Jewish mob.

Paphos

YOU ARE THERE 13:6

- Roman capital of Cyprus.
- Less significant than neighboring Salamis which had a better harbor.
- Site of a famous temple to the goddess Astarte (Greek Aphrodite, the goddess of beauty, love, and fertility).

Perga

YOU ARE THERE 13:13–14

- Capital city of Pamphylia, a Roman province on the southwest coast of Asia Minor.
- Situated inland to defend against pirates who roamed the coast.
- Boasted many structures typical of Graeco-Roman cities, including an acropolis, a walled lower city, colonnaded streets, an *agora,* or marketplace, public baths, a stadium seating 12,000, a theater, and a temple to the goddess Artemis (Roman Diana).
- The nearby port city of Attalia, founded by Rome in the second century B.C., eventually overshadowed Perga's waterway and prosperity. Perga fell into decay—its ruins are still visible—while Attalia (modern Adalia) remains to this day.
- Visited twice by Paul (Acts 13:13–14; 14:25). This was the first instance of Paul preaching in a predominantly pagan environment. There is no evidence that he had much success.

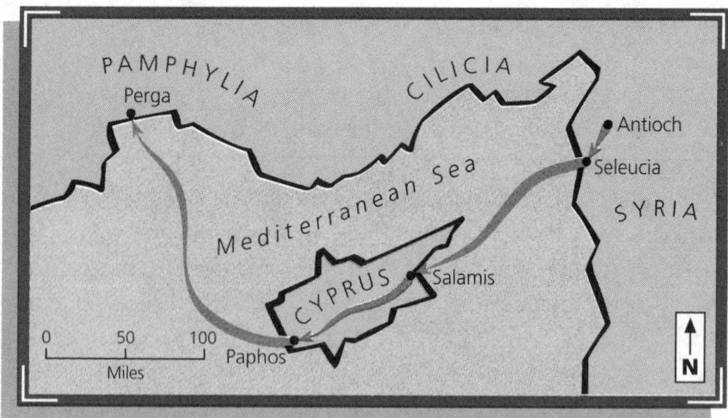

Paul's First Journey, Part One

Antioch in Pisidia

YOU ARE THERE 13:14–52

- One of 16 Antiochs in the ancient world.
- A commercial and administrative center on the east-west highway from Ephesus to Syria.
- Noted for its worship of pagan deities and a temple to Caesar Augustus.
- The city had a rare mix of native Phrygians, Greeks, Jews, and Roman colonists, making it one of the most ethnically diverse cities in the empire.
- Antioch's relative openness to the gospel, in contrast to the indifference of Perga, motivated Paul to begin a strategy that he frequently used elsewhere: speaking first to leading Jews and Gentile God-fearers at the synagogue, then mixing with the pagan Greeks and Roman colonists.

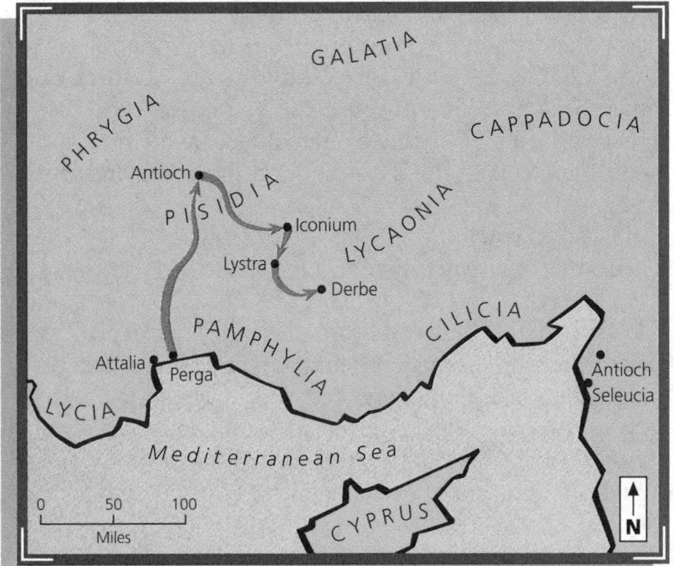

PAUL'S FIRST JOURNEY, PART TWO

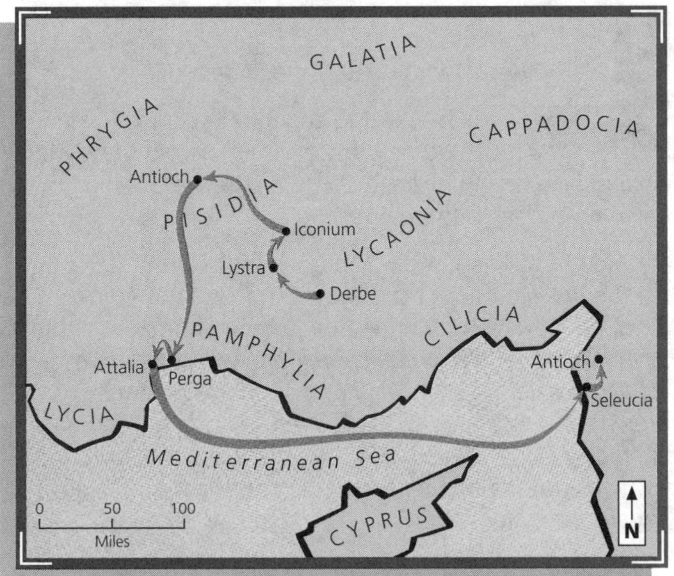

PAUL'S FIRST JOURNEY, PART THREE

ICONIUM

YOU ARE THERE 14:1

- Capital of the Roman province of Lycaonia in central Asia Minor.
- Largely Greek, the city was at one time named Claudiconium, reflecting privileges conferred by the Roman emperor Claudius.
- Several major routes—west to Antioch and Ephesus, south to Lystra and Derbe—led to and from this important crossroads.
- Bordering a huge plateau, Iconium was well watered and fertile, prospering from wheat fields and apricot and plum orchards.
- The Iconium church may have been the first to read Paul's letter to the Galatians, as well as the first letter of Peter.
- Known today as Konya, in Turkey.

LYSTRA

YOU ARE THERE 14:8

- An obscure town on the plains of Lycaonia in central Asia Minor, about 45 miles from the Mediterranean.
- Only 25 miles from Iconium but closer to Derbe in its politics and Roman culture.
- A Roman road system, the Via Sebaste, connected Lystra, Iconium, Derbe, and the other cities in the region.

DERBE

YOU ARE THERE 14:20

- A city in the southeastern part of the Roman province of Lycaonia.
- Now believed to be the unexcavated site of Kerti Huyuk in south central Asia Minor.
- Politically and culturally aligned with Lystra in the Roman province of Galatia.
- Home to Gaius, a traveling companion of Paul (Acts 20:4).
- Surviving inscriptions suggest a succession of bishops in Derbe. One of them, Daphnus, was present at the Council of Constantinople in A.D. 381. So apparently Paul's efforts in this little town were not in vain.

with jealousy; and blaspheming, they contradicted what
was spoken by Paul. [46]Then both Paul and Barnabas spoke
out boldly, saying, “It was necessary that the word of God
should be spoken first to you. Since you reject it and judge
yourselves to be unworthy of eternal life, we are now turning to the Gentiles. [47]For so the Lord has commanded us,
saying,

> ‘I have set you to be a light for the Gentiles,
> so that you may bring salvation to the ends of the
> earth.’ ”

48 When the Gentiles heard this, they were glad and
praised the word of the Lord; and as many as had been destined for eternal life became believers. [49]Thus the word of
the Lord spread throughout the region.
[50]But the Jews incited the devout women
of high standing and the leading men of the city, and stirred

13:50 see pg. 465

CONSIDER THIS
13:13

Why Did John Mark Go Home?

Luke does not tell us why John Mark returned to Jerusalem (v. 13), giving rise to all kinds of speculation. A few possibilities:

He was young and felt homesick. *Possibly, but we don’t know exactly how old Mark was. He had been to Antioch (12:25), but otherwise might never have been outside Palestine.*

He reacted negatively to the interaction with Gentiles. *On the first leg of the trip (Cyprus), cultural and ethnic overload may have set in. We know how controversial the inclusion of Gentiles in the church proved to be for believers at Jerusalem (15:1–29). If Mark departed because of prejudice, it might explain Paul’s refusal to take him on a later journey (15:37–38). On the other hand, he had worked with the multiethnic church at Antioch with no apparent problems (12:25).*

He didn’t want to work with Paul. *We know that Paul was a hard charger and that his standards were quite high. Perhaps Mark didn’t measure up, or perhaps the relational chemistry didn’t work, and so Mark decided to go home rather than endure a lengthy trip with a demanding person. But later Paul was eager to have him on board (2 Tim. 4:11) and included him among his fellow laborers (Philem. 24).*

He got seasick. *No evidence for that except that Mark left as soon as the party hit the mainland at Perga in Pamphylia. But why return home over seasickness?*

up persecution against Paul and Barnabas, and drove them
out of their region. 51So they shook the dust off their feet in
protest against them, and went to Iconium. 52And the disciples were filled with joy and with the Holy Spirit.

Conflict at Iconium

14:1 see pg. 467

14 The same thing occurred in Iconium, where Paul and Barnabas[w]
went into the Jewish synagogue and spoke in such a way
that a great number of both Jews and Greeks became believers. 2But the unbelieving Jews stirred up the Gentiles
and poisoned their minds against the brothers. 3So they remained for a long time, speaking boldly for the Lord, who
testified to the word of his grace by granting signs and
wonders to be done through them. 4But the residents of the
city were divided; some sided with the Jews, and some with

[w]Gk *they*

He was afraid. *In Antioch, Mark met a diverse community of believers who showed extraordinary concern and compassion for each other (see "Antioch: A Model for the Modern Church?" Acts 13:1–3). But on Cyprus he encountered characters like Elymas the sorcerer (13:6–12) and discovered that in gospel outreach, opponents use live ammunition. So he might have left out of fear.*

The pace was too hard. *Luke calls Mark an assistant (13:5), which probably involved making arrangements for travel, food, and lodging, and possibly some teaching. Again, Paul's pace may have outstripped the young man's capacities, and once they arrived at Perga he decided to throw in the towel. But this is pure speculation.*

Scripture doesn't tell us why John Mark made the decision to go home. But the encouraging thing is that his return didn't disqualify him from the faith or diminish his spirituality, no matter how strongly Paul felt about it later (15:38–39). With time and the encouragement of Barnabas, Mark developed into one of the key leaders of the early church who had a lasting impact on the faith. ◆

The man who "deserted" Paul and Barnabas turned out to be a key figure in the Christian movement—thanks to Barnabas. See "John Mark," Acts 15:37.

Confusing Responses

CONSIDER THIS 14:11–19

The gospel can trigger intense responses, both positive and negative. At Lystra, Barnabas and Paul were initially hailed as Greek gods after healing a crippled man (vv. 11–12). But at Iconium, their message offended some Jews (14:1–2), who viewed the apostles not as gods, but devils.

The good news can either raise a person's hopes or strike fear at levels that are hard to perceive. That's why believers today need to be ready for extreme reactions when they present the gospel.

Attalia

YOU ARE THERE 14:25

- **Key seaport on the coast of Pamphylia in south central Asia Minor, serving Perga, the regional capital, eight miles inland.**
- **Archaeologists have found evidence of a double wall, an ancient aqueduct, and a triple gateway constructed under the reign of Hadrian, who visited in A.D. 130.**
- **Alternately conquered by Turks and Europeans during the Crusades.**
- **Known today as Adalia (Antalya), this major seaport on Turkey's Gulf of Adalia is the "Turkish Riviera," with tourism the major industry.**

the apostles. 5And when an attempt was made by both
Gentiles and Jews, with their rulers, to mistreat them and to
stone them, 6the apostles[x] learned of it and fled to Lystra
and Derbe, cities of Lycaonia, and to the surrounding country; 7and there they continued proclaiming the good news.

Enthusiasm Turns to Violence

14:8
see pg. 467

8 In Lystra there was a man sitting
who could not use his feet and had never
walked, for he had been crippled from birth. 9He listened
to Paul as he was speaking. And Paul, looking at him intently and seeing that he had faith to be healed, 10said in a
loud voice, "Stand upright on your feet." And the man[y]

14:11–19
see pg. 469

sprang up and began to walk. 11When
the crowds saw what Paul had done,
they shouted in the Lycaonian language, "The gods have
come down to us in human form!" 12Barnabas they called
Zeus, and Paul they called Hermes, because he was the
chief speaker. 13The priest of Zeus, whose temple was just
outside the city,[z] brought oxen and garlands to the gates; he
and the crowds wanted to offer sacrifice. 14When the apostles Barnabas and Paul heard of it, they tore their clothes
and rushed out into the crowd, shouting, 15"Friends,[a] why
are you doing this? We are mortals just like you, and we
bring you good news, that you should turn from these
worthless things to the living God, who made the heaven
and the earth and the sea and all that is in them. 16In past
generations he allowed all the nations to follow their own
ways; 17yet he has not left himself without a witness in doing good—giving you rains from heaven and fruitful seasons, and filling you with food and your hearts with joy."
18Even with these words, they scarcely restrained the
crowds from offering sacrifice to them.

19 But Jews came there from Antioch and Iconium and
won over the crowds. Then they stoned Paul and dragged

14:20
see pg. 467

him out of the city, supposing that he
was dead. 20But when the disciples surrounded him, he got up and went into the city. The next
day he went on with Barnabas to Derbe.

> **"IT IS THROUGH MANY PERSECUTIONS THAT WE MUST ENTER THE KINGDOM OF GOD."**
> **—Acts 14:22**

Paul and Barnabas Retrace Their Steps

21 After they had proclaimed the good news to that city
and had made many disciples, they returned to Lystra, then
on to Iconium and Antioch. 22There they strengthened the
souls of the disciples and encouraged them to continue in
the faith, saying, "It is through many persecutions that we
must enter the kingdom of God." 23And after they had ap-

[x]Gk *they* [y]Gk *he* [z]Or *The priest of Zeus-Outside-the-City* [a]Gk *Men*

pointed elders for them in each church, with prayer and
fasting they entrusted them to the Lord in whom they had
come to believe.
24 Then they passed through Pisidia and came to Pam-
14:25 see pg. 469
phylia. 25When they had spoken the
word in Perga, they went down to At-
talia. 26From there they sailed back to Antioch, where they
had been commended to the grace of God for the work[b]
that they had completed. 27When they arrived, they called
the church together and related all that God had done with
them, and how he had opened a door of faith for the Gentiles. 28And they stayed there with the disciples for some
time.

A Controversy over Doctrine Boils Over

15:1–21 see pg. 472
15 Then certain individuals came
down from Judea and were
teaching the brothers, "Unless you are circumcised accord-
15:2
ing to the custom of Moses, you cannot
be saved." 2And after Paul and Barnabas
had no small dissension and debate with them, Paul and
Barnabas and some of the others were appointed to go up
to Jerusalem to discuss this question with the apostles and
the elders. 3So they were sent on their way by the church,
and as they passed through both Phoenicia and Samaria,
they reported the conversion of the Gentiles, and brought
great joy to all the believers.[c] 4When they came to
Jerusalem, they were welcomed by the church and the
apostles and the elders, and they reported all that God had
done with them. 5But some believers who belonged to the
sect of the Pharisees stood up and said, "It is necessary for
them to be circumcised and ordered to keep the law of
Moses."
15:6 see pg. 473
6 The apostles and the elders met together to consider this matter. 7After
there had been much debate, Peter stood up and said to
them, "My brothers,[d] you know that in the early days God
made a choice among you, that I should be the one through
whom the Gentiles would hear the message of the good
news and become believers. 8And God, who knows the human heart, testified to them by giving them the Holy Spirit,
just as he did to us; 9and in cleansing their hearts by faith
he has made no distinction between them and us. 10Now
therefore why are you putting God to the test by placing on
the neck of the disciples a yoke that neither our ancestors
nor we have been able to bear? 11On the contrary, we

[b]*Or committed in the grace of God to the work* [c]*Gk brothers* [d]*Gk Men, brothers*

Growth Leads to New Understanding

CONSIDER THIS 15:2 *An encounter with a different culture can sometimes force believers to evaluate what they believe and why. In Antioch the church ran into a pluralistic society made up of several different groups, prompting the question, "What about circumcision and the Law?" The council at Jerusalem came together to address that issue and formulate a biblical response (vv. 2, 6). In this sense Antioch could be called the mother not only of Christian missions and church government, but of biblical theology as well.*

"Antioch: A Model for the Modern Church?" tells this story in more detail, Acts 13:1–3.

Who Was the Leader?

CONSIDER THIS 15:12 *Note the order in which Luke mentions the two leaders in v. 12—Barnabas before Paul. Perhaps Barnabas took the lead before the council, rather than Paul, as compared to other settings (for instance, 13:13, 43, 46, 50; 15:2, 35).*

believe that we will be saved through the grace of the Lord
Jesus, just as they will."

15:12
see pg. 471

12 The whole assembly kept silence,
and listened to Barnabas and Paul as they
told of all the signs and wonders that God had done through
them among the Gentiles. 13After they finished speaking,
James replied, "My brothers,[e] listen to me. 14Simeon has related how God first looked favorably on the Gentiles, to
take from among them a people for his name. 15This agrees
with the words of the prophets, as it is written,

16 'After this I will return,
and I will rebuild the dwelling of David, which has
fallen;
from its ruins I will rebuild it,
and I will set it up,
17 so that all other peoples may seek the Lord—
even all the Gentiles over whom my name has been
called.
Thus says the Lord, who has been making these
things 18known from long ago.'[f]

[e]Gk *Men, brothers* [f]Other ancient authorities read *things. 18Known to God from of old are all his works.'*

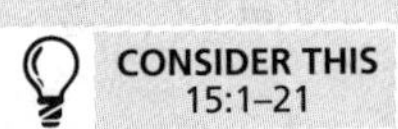

CONSIDER THIS
15:1–21

"Sure You're Saved . . . Sort Of"

In Acts 15 we see a simmering controversy that finally boiled over. The year was about A.D. 48. Paul and Barnabas had just returned to Antioch from their first preaching tour and reported the exciting news that God had opened the door of faith to the Gentiles (14:26–27). Now men who claimed to speak for the church in Judea came with a disturbing message: to be saved, Gentiles must become Jews. They must reject their ethnic backgrounds and instead accept the tenets of Hebrew religion and culture.

If true, that would mean that perhaps half the church at Antioch was not saved, along with the majority of new believers in the new churches established by Paul and Barnabas in Pisidia and Galatia. No wonder the debate that ensued created great tension and bitterness (15:2, 6–7, 24)!

Nor was it easily resolved. Paul reported that Peter went along with the error when the false teachers arrived. Even Barnabas was swayed (Gal. 2:11–16). The crisis was so great that Paul, Barnabas, and others journeyed to Jerusalem for a full-scale debate with the apostles and elders there.

The discussion turned on three important presentations:

19 Therefore I have reached the decision that we should not
trouble those Gentiles who are turning to God, 20 but we
should write to them to abstain only from things polluted
by idols and from fornication and from whatever has been
strangled[g] and from blood. 21 For in every city, for generations past, Moses has had those who proclaim him, for he
has been read aloud every sabbath in the synagogues."

A Letter of Reconciliation Is Sent

15:22–35
see pg. 474

22 Then the apostles and the elders,
with the consent of the whole church,
decided to choose men from among their members[h] and to
send them to Antioch with Paul and Barnabas. They sent
Judas called Barsabbas, and Silas, leaders among the
brothers, 23 with the following letter: "The brothers, both the
apostles and the elders, to the believers[i] of Gentile origin in
Antioch and Syria and Cilicia, greetings. 24 Since we have
heard that certain persons who have gone out from us,

(Bible text continued on page 475)

[g]Other ancient authorities lack *and from whatever has been strangled* [h]Gk *from among them* [i]Gk *brothers*

◆ ◆ ◆ ◆ ◆ ◆ ◆ ◆ ◆ ◆ ◆ ◆ ◆ ◆ ◆ ◆

(1) Peter's reminder of his meeting with Cornelius (Acts 10:1–48), in which God gave the Holy Spirit to Gentiles.

(2) Barnabas and Paul's account of their recent travels through Asia Minor, in which God worked miraculously among the Gentiles.

(3) James' conclusion that these events correlated with the prophetic words of Amos 9:11–12.

The conclusion, as described in the letter to the Galatians, was, "There is no longer Jew or Greek . . . slave or free . . . male and female; for all of you are one in Christ Jesus" (Gal. 3:28).

However, the issues of Acts 15 have continued to trouble the church in one form or another to this day. It is difficult to separate one's culture and worldview from one's understanding the gospel. Even in the church we often find our security in sameness and sometimes exclude those who differ. Diversity feels uncomfortable. But in light of Acts 15, we might consider what it would take to address our concerns honestly and biblically. ◆

Issues of Faith and Culture

CONSIDER THIS 15:6 **As the gospel expanded "to the ends of the earth" (Acts 1:8), the first Christians encountered new cultures that challenged accepted beliefs and practices. Then as now, the frontiers of mission required the church to meet as an international body to sort out issues of faith and culture (15:6).**

Some controversies involve "truth issues," others "love issues," and others both truth and love issues. Truth issues call for clarity of doctrine and understanding of Scripture. Love issues call for open-mindedness and toleration. The situation in Acts 15 required the early church to deal with both.

What issues in today's church are truth-related? What issues are love issues demanding tolerance for legitimate differences of opinion and practice? What issues demand the perspective of both truth and love?

CONSIDER THIS
15:22–35

A Church That Defies Market Research

As the twentieth century closes and the twenty-first century begins, the population of the United States is becoming increasingly diverse. Can the church prosper in a pluralistic society? Yes, judging by Acts. In fact, the response of the council at Jerusalem to an influx of Gentile believers (vv. 22–35) suggests that Christians must allow for cultural differences if they want their churches to thrive.

The collections of people who responded to the gospel and banded together in the first century defy much of modern market research and ideas about church growth. Modern thinking holds that groups of people with similar sociological backgrounds ("homogeneous" groups) grow more quickly than ones with different backgrounds ("heterogeneous") because like attracts like. Therefore, churches should target people of the same race, demographic profile, socioeconomic status, and so forth.

But the untidy collection of Acts believers seems to contradict that model. Churches sprouted up spontaneously in response to God's grace more than through social marketing.

Heterogeneous Backgrounds

- They came from *all classes* of society, from the wealthy and privileged to destitute beggars, slaves, and even criminals.
- They represented the *many cultures* of that day—Roman, Greek, Hebrew, African, Arab.
- They varied widely in their *political allegiances and power,* from government, military, and civic leaders to reactionaries, revolutionaries, and displaced refugees.
- Their *leadership* was male and female, old and young.
- They came from all manner of *religious traditions*—pagan sorcery and mystery cults, Greek and Roman mythology, idol worship, and Judaism.

A Diversity of Abilities and Callings

- *Landholders* such as Barnabas (4:34–37), Ananias and Sapphira (5:1–11), Mnason (21:16) and Publius (28:7–10).
- *Health care workers and therapists* including Dr. Luke (Acts 1:1; see also Col. 4:14; 2 Tim. 4:11).
- *Lecturers and teachers* such as Stephen (6:8–10), Philip (8:4–5), Priscilla and Aquila (18:26), Apollos (18:24–28), and of course Peter, Paul, and the other apostles.
- *Government officials and civic leaders,* including the Ethiopian treasurer (8:26–40), Saul before his conversion (8:3; 9:1–2; 26:9–11), the proconsul Sergius Paulus (13:6–12), a Philippian jailer (16:22–34), Dionysius (17:34), and Crispus (18:8).

Individual converts came from many other, equally diverse industries:

- Dorcas, who possibly worked in the *tailoring and garment industry* (9:36–42).
- Simon, employed in *leather tanning* (9:43).
- Cornelius, a centurion from the Italian Cohort of the *Roman military* (10:1–48).
- Rhoda, a *domestic* (12:12–17).
- Lydia, who *manufactured, imported, and exported clothing* for the rich (16:13–15, 40).
- *Tentmakers* Priscilla and Aquila (18:1–3).

Innovative Programs

- Advocacy by Barnabas on behalf of Saul (9:26–27); by Paul and Barnabas on behalf of a slave girl, freeing her from oppressive masters (16:16–21); and by Ephesian believers on behalf of Apollos (18:27–28).

(continued on next page)

though with no instructions from us, have said things to
disturb you and have unsettled your minds,[j] 25we have decided unanimously to choose representatives[k] and send
them to you, along with our beloved Barnabas and Paul,
26who have risked their lives for the sake of our Lord Jesus
Christ. 27We have therefore sent Judas and Silas, who themselves will tell you the same things by word of mouth. 28For
it has seemed good to the Holy Spirit and to us to impose
on you no further burden than these essentials: 29that you
abstain from what has been sacrificed to idols and from
blood and from what is strangled[l] and from fornication. If
you keep yourselves from these, you will do well.
Farewell."

30 So they were sent off and went down to Antioch.
When they gathered the congregation together, they delivered the letter. 31When its members[m] read it, they rejoiced at
the exhortation. 32Judas and Silas, who
were themselves prophets, said much to
encourage and strengthen the believers.[n] 33After they had
been there for some time, they were sent off in peace by the
believers[n] to those who had sent them.[o] 35But Paul and

15:32

[j]Other ancient authorities add *saying, 'You must be circumcised and keep the law,'* [k]Gk *men* [l]Other ancient authorities lack *and from what is strangled* [m]Gk *When they* [n]Gk *brothers* [o]Other ancient authorities add verse 34, *But it seemed good to Silas to remain there*

◆ ◆ ◆ ◆ ◆ ◆ ◆ ◆ ◆ ◆ ◆ ◆ ◆ ◆ ◆

PERSONALITY PROFILE: SILAS

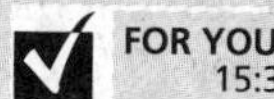

FOR YOUR INFO 15:32

Also known as: Silvanus, meaning "person of the woods."

First gained notice as: One of four church leaders from Jerusalem named to write and deliver to Antioch a pivotal decision on the status of Gentile converts (Acts 15:22).

Best known today as: Paul's traveling companion on his second journey after the apostle had rejected John Mark (15:36–41). Silas' Roman citizenship and ties to the Jerusalem church proved useful to their work as messengers of Christ. He also became Paul's literary assistant.

(continued from previous page)

- *Charity and hospitality,* often anonymously and on a large scale, to meet both social and spiritual needs (2:45; 4:32; 11:29–30; 28:13–15).
- *Ethnic reconciliation* as deacons acted on behalf of neglected widows (6:1–6); as Philip carried the gospel across ethnic barriers (8:4–17, 26–40); as Peter met with the Gentile, Cornelius, and defended his actions to the Jewish leaders at Jerusalem (10:1—11:30); as Paul and Barnabas brought together Gentiles and Jews at Antioch in Pisidia (13:46–52); as the council at Jerusalem accepted Gentiles into the faith, sending Judas and Silas as emissaries to welcome them (15:1–35); as Paul recruited Timothy into gospel work (16:1–5).

The early church was a diverse, grass-roots, from-the-ground-up movement that drew people together in surprising ways. It turned them inside out, toward one another in service and love. Its example challenges believers today to ask: How are we allowing for cultural differences in our pluralistic society? ◆

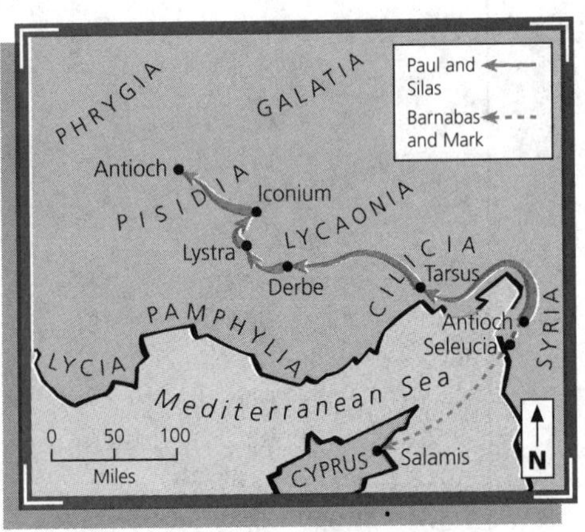

PAUL'S SECOND JOURNEY, PART ONE

Barnabas remained in Antioch, and there, with many others, they taught and proclaimed the word of the Lord.

Paul and Barnabas Part

36 After some days Paul said to Barnabas, "Come, let us
return and visit the believers[p] in every city where we proclaimed the word of the Lord and see
how they are doing." 37Barnabas wanted
to take with them John called Mark.
38But Paul decided not to take with them
one who had deserted them in Pamphylia and had not ac-

15:37 see pg. 478

15:37–39

[p]Gk *brothers*

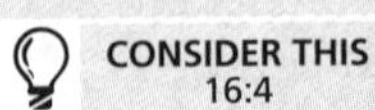

PAUL'S URBAN STRATEGY

Iconium. Lystra. Derbe. Philippi. Ephesus. Corinth. Antioch. Athens. For most people today, names like these indicate merely dots on a map. But they were major cities in the Roman world, centers of influence that attracted Christian messengers such as Paul (v. 4). The message of Christ was a message for the city—for its marketplace, arts, academies, councils, courts, prisons, temples, and synagogues.

Paul was from the beautiful coastal seaport of Tarsus, "an important city" as he described it (Acts 21:39; see 11:25), with an estimated half-million residents. He was brought up in Jerusalem, one of the largest cities in the empire. Thus he was no stranger to city life. In fact, as a spokesperson for the Christian movement, he preferred working in urban centers. This strategy offered several advantages:

(1) He could use a common language, Greek. *Older ethnic languages prevailed among rural peoples, but multicultural city dwellers spoke to each other in* koinē *("common") Greek.*

(2) He could anticipate greater receptivity. *Urban peoples were perhaps more likely to entertain new ideas and consider change.*

(3) He could influence networks. *As crossroads of communication and commerce, cities tended to amplify the Christian message to their surrounding areas (see "Boom Box," 19:10).*

(4) He could affect multiple ethnic groups. *The gospel is inclusive and multiethnic, uniting people of every background. Cities brought into close proximity Jews and Gentiles, men and women, rich and poor. The message of Christ brought them together.*

15:39 see pg. 478
companied them in the work. 39The disagreement became so sharp that they
parted company; Barnabas took Mark with him and sailed
away to Cyprus. 40But Paul chose Silas and set out, the believers[q] commending him to the grace of the Lord. 41He
went through Syria and Cilicia, strengthening the churches.

Timothy Is Recruited for the Work

16:1–3 see pg. 478
16 Paul[r] went on also to Derbe and
to Lystra, where there was a dis-
ciple named Timothy, the son of a Jewish woman who was

[q]Gk *brothers* [r]Gk *He*

(5) He could reach the workplace. *As a tentmaker, Paul identified with the great numbers of artisans who populated Roman cities. In fact, urban areas were often divided into districts according to crafts, and workers formed guilds to enhance their trades. Paul used these coalitions to advantage in spreading the message.*

(6) He could make use of the Roman legal system. *Paul believed that his message had relevance for the political, economic, and religious institutions of his day. As a Roman citizen, he expected—and even demanded—justice. He also used the courts to attract a larger audience for the gospel.*

Paul intentionally went to the cities. The gospel he proclaimed had implications for an urban setting. To him, the message of Christ spoke not only to the private individual, but to public society as well. Given the increasingly urban nature of the modern world, he would likely urge Christians today to pay attention to cities. Those who want to have influence will benefit from a careful study of Paul's urban strategy. ◆

From the very beginning, the church was known for its inclusiveness (see Acts 1:13). One of the best models could be found at Antioch (see Acts 13:1).

Christianity conquered Rome by invading its cities. It penetrated the cities by establishing dozens of urban churches by the end of the first century. See "Churches—Keys to the Cities," Acts 11:22.

To see how explosive—and unpredictable—Paul's urban strategy could be, read "The Ephesus Approach: How the Gospel Penetrated a City," Acts 19:8–41.

JOHN MARK—"USEFUL FOR MINISTRY"

CONSIDER THIS 15:37–39

John Mark is a case study in second chances. Spurned by Paul because he had gone home to Jerusalem instead of continuing on a journey to Asia Minor (Acts 13:13; 15:38), John Mark was fortunate in that his cousin was the mentoring model, Barnabas (see 4:36–37). Just as he had done with Paul when no one else would come near him, Barnabas took John Mark home with him to Cyprus where he nurtured him personally and spiritually.

Thanks to Barnabas, John Mark turned out to be a special gift to the early church. He became a valued associate of Peter and probably traveled with him to Rome, where tradition holds that he composed his Gospel by writing down Peter's memories of Jesus' life and teaching (see "Tales of the Fisherman," Introduction to Mark).

Paul also finally recognized the value of John Mark. Late in life, he wrote to Timothy, urging him to "get Mark and bring him with you, for he is useful in my ministry" (2 Tim. 4:11). Indeed he was. Early church tradition says that he was the first evangelist to Alexandria, Egypt, and the first bishop of that city. He won a great number of sincerely committed converts there.

Luke does not tell us why John Mark returned to Jerusalem, giving rise to all kinds of speculation. See "Why Did John Mark Go Home?" Acts 13:13.

a believer; but his father was a Greek. [2]He was well spoken
of by the believers[s] in Lystra and Iconium. [3]Paul wanted
Timothy to accompany him; and he took him and had him
circumcised because of the Jews who were in those places,
for they all knew that his father was a
Greek. [4]As they went from town to town,
they delivered to them for observance the decisions that
had been reached by the apostles and elders who were in
Jerusalem. [5]So the churches were strengthened in the faith
and increased in numbers daily.

16:4 see pg. 476

The Spirit Directs the Team Westward

6 They went through the region of Phrygia and Galatia,
having been forbidden by the Holy Spirit to speak the word

[s]Gk *brothers*

The Tension between Truth and Love

CONSIDER THIS 15:39

The account states that the split between Paul and Barnabas was contentious (v. 39), and the outcome was ugly. Paul was known to emphasize issues of truth, arguing for high doctrinal standards (see "Issues of Faith and Culture," Acts 15:6). Barnabas felt the same commitment to doctrinal purity, but when it came to people, it seems that the "Son of Encouragement" tended to emphasize issues of love. He was a risk-taker who held onto those who fell through the cracks. So it's not surprising that he embraced John Mark (15:39), just as he had embraced Paul when none of the other believers would touch him because of his past (11:25).

To Paul's credit, he later reconciled with John Mark and Barnabas (Col. 4:10–11; 2 Tim. 4:11).

Where do you tend to place your emphasis in the tension between truth and love? Are there times when your commitment to doctrinal truth causes you to forget that no matter how right or wrong others may be, they are people who need to be loved?

Timothy

A CLOSER LOOK 16:1–3

It's interesting that Paul recruited Timothy (vv. 1–3) for the same trip from which he had just rejected John Mark (15:37–41). What did he see in the young man from Lystra? See the profile at the Introduction to 2 Timothy. Eventually Timothy took on a major assignment—a multiethnic church at Ephesus. See "Discipleship—Or Mentoring?" Acts 9:26–30.

Personality Profile: John Mark

FOR YOUR INFO 15:37

Not to be confused with: John, one of the Twelve and a close friend of Jesus.

Family: Son of Mary, who owned a house in Jerusalem where the church often prayed (Acts 12:12–17); cousin to Barnabas (see 4:36–37; Col. 4:10). Peter referred to Mark as his "son" (1 Pet. 5:13).

Background: His family was wealthy enough to own a large home with at least one servant. It frequently hosted gatherings of believers.

Best known today for: Leaving Paul and Barnabas on their first gospel tour after visiting Cyprus (Acts 13:13); later writing the Gospel that bears his name, Mark.

16:7
see pg. 480

16:8
see pg. 480

in Asia. 7 When they had come opposite
Mysia, they attempted to go into Bithynia, but the Spirit of Jesus did not allow them; 8 so, passing by Mysia, they
went down to Troas. 9 During the night Paul had a vision:
there stood a man of Macedonia pleading with him and
saying, "Come over to Macedonia and help us." 10 When he
had seen the vision, we immediately tried to cross over to
Macedonia, being convinced that God had called us to proclaim the good news to them.

A Clothier Turns to Christ

16:12
see pg. 481
16:13
see pg. 480

11 We set sail from Troas and took a straight course to
Samothrace, the following day to Neapo-
lis, 12 and from there to Philippi, which is
a leading city of the district[t] of Macedonia and a Roman
colony. We remained in this city for
some days. 13 On the sabbath day we
went outside the gate by the river, where we supposed
there was a place of prayer; and we sat down and spoke to

[t]Other authorities read *a city of the first district*

Personality Profile: Lydia

FOR YOUR INFO
16:14–15

Home: Originally Thyatira (see Rev. 2:18), a large industrial city and leading exporter of purple dye; relocated to Philippi (see accompanying article), a Roman colony on a busy trade route.

Family: Unknown, though the text mentions her "household" (Acts 16:15).

Occupation: Owner of a business that traded in an exotic dye known as purple, along with cloth dyed in it.

Best known today for: Becoming the first known convert to Christianity in the West and hosting the first church in Europe in her home.

The Trade in Purple

FOR YOUR INFO
16:14

Lydia's hometown, Thyatira, was a thriving manufacturing and commercial center. Its trade in purple was renowned in the Roman world. The most expensive of dyes and a mark of wealth or royalty, purple came from the murex, a shellfish found only along the northeastern section of the Mediterranean coast. Purple cloth was ranked in value with gold and was important not only for adorning emperors and temples but for tribute and international trade.

We don't know when or why Lydia relocated to Philippi, but it was a smart business move. A Latin inscription found there mentions the dying trade and its economic importance to the city. Philippi was the leading Roman colony of the region, located on the major east-west highway connecting Europe to the Middle East. Its people were known for trying to outdo Rome in dress and manners.

Lydia probably belonged to a local dyer's guild, a professional association. Guilds sometimes involved such pagan customs and practices as worship of the trade's patron god, feasts using food sacrificed to idols, and loose sexual morality.

Lydia's conversion didn't change her occupation, but it dramatically changed her loyalty. Her business contacts likely introduced Paul to the "movers and shakers" of the Macedonian area.

To get better acquainted with Lydia and the church that met in her house, read Paul's letter to the Philippians.

Mysia

YOU ARE THERE 16:7

- A Roman province, the westernmost portion of Asia Minor (present-day Turkey).
- Never granted independent status, so its precise boundaries are unknown.
- Passively allied with the Trojans during the legendary Trojan War.
- Apparently of little interest to Paul, who hastily passed by Mysia on his way to Troas (Acts 16:8). No evidence of other Christian outreach here.

Troas

YOU ARE THERE 16:8

- A major city on the coast of Mysia in northwest Asia Minor (modern Turkey).
- Name means "the region around Troy"; the city was located on the rugged Troad Plain 10 miles south of legendary Troy.
- In Paul's day, called Alexandria Troas in honor of Alexander the Great.
- A key Roman seaport, offering the shortest route from Asia to Greece.
- Visited by Paul at least three times: en route to Macedonia (Acts 16:11); after his journey in Ephesus (20:6; 2 Cor. 2:12); and once when he left his cloak and books at the house of Carpus (2 Tim. 4:13).

A Turning Point in Western Civilization

Paul's vision and subsequent trip from Troas to Neapolis (Acts 16:9–11) proved to be a major fork in the road for Western civilization. One small step for Paul became one giant leap

(continued on next page)

16:14 see pg. 479

the women who had gathered there. 14A
certain woman named Lydia, a worshiper
of God, was listening to us; she was from the city of Thyatira and a dealer in purple cloth. The Lord opened her
16:14–15 see pg. 479
heart to listen eagerly to what was said
by Paul. 15When she and her household
were baptized, she urged us, saying, "If you have judged me to be faithful to the Lord, come and stay at my home." And she prevailed upon us.

A Different Approach

CONSIDER THIS 16:13

Paul began his ministry in Philippi among women he met by the river (v. 13). His normal approach was through the synagogues. But apparently Philippi lacked even ten male Jews, which was the required number to form a synagogue. Yet there were spiritually hungry women meeting for prayer. Perhaps they met outside the city because their monotheism was considered strange by the dominant pagan culture. At any rate, God answered their prayers by bringing the gospel to their community.

PAUL'S SECOND JOURNEY, PART TWO

A Slave-girl Finds Faith and Freedom

16:16–24
see pg. 482

16 One day, as we were going to the
place of prayer, we met a slave-girl who
had a spirit of divination and brought her owners a great
deal of money by fortune-telling. 17While she followed Paul
and us, she would cry out, "These men are slaves of the
Most High God, who proclaim to you[u] a way of salvation."
18She kept doing this for many days. But Paul, very much
annoyed, turned and said to the spirit, "I order you in the
name of Jesus Christ to come out of her." And it came out
that very hour.

16:19
see pg. 482

19 But when her owners saw that their
hope of making money was gone, they
seized Paul and Silas and dragged them into the marketplace before the authorities. 20When they had brought them
before the magistrates, they said, "These men are disturbing
our city; they are Jews 21and are advocating customs that
are not lawful for us as Romans to adopt or observe." 22The
crowd joined in attacking them, and the magistrates had
them stripped of their clothing and ordered them to be
beaten with rods. 23After they had given them a severe flogging, they threw them into prison and ordered the jailer to
keep them securely. 24Following these instructions, he put
them in the innermost cell and fastened their feet in the
stocks.

A Jailer and His Family Believe

25 About midnight Paul and Silas were praying and
singing hymns to God, and the prisoners were listening to
them. 26Suddenly there was an earthquake, so violent that
the foundations of the prison were shaken; and immediately all the doors were opened and everyone's chains were
unfastened. 27When the jailer woke up and saw the prison
doors wide open, he drew his sword and was about to kill
himself, since he supposed that the prisoners had escaped.
28But Paul shouted in a loud voice, "Do not harm yourself,
for we are all here." 29The jailer[v] called for lights, and rushing in, he fell down trembling before Paul and Silas. 30Then
he brought them outside and said, "Sirs, what must I do to

16:31–34
see pg. 484

be saved?" 31They answered, "Believe on
the Lord Jesus, and you will be saved,
you and your household." 32They spoke the word of the
Lord[w] to him and to all who were in his house. 33At the
same hour of the night he took them and washed their
wounds; then he and his entire family were baptized without delay. 34He brought them up into the house and set

[u]Other ancient authorities read *to us* [v]Gk *He* [w]Other ancient authorities read *word of God*

(continued from previous page)

for Christianity as it spread west, gaining a foothold at Philippi in Macedonia, moving on into Europe, and eventually pervading the entire western hemisphere.

PHILIPPI

YOU ARE THERE
16:12

- **A city in eastern Macedonia (modern Greece) 10 miles inland from the Aegean Sea.**
- **Name means "city of Philip."**
- **Founded in 356 B.C. by the great Macedonian king, Philip, father of Alexander the Great.**
- **Honored by Caesar Augustus with the placement of a Roman military colony with the pretentious name *Colonia Augusta Julia Philippensis.* Parcels of land were used to reward retired soldiers.**
- **A "gateway city" on the Egnatian Way, the highway connecting the Empire from east to west.**
- **At one time boasted vast gold and silver mines.**

PHILIPPI—GATEWAY FOR THE GOSPEL

Just as all roads led to Rome, so much of the traffic to Rome from the east funneled through Philippi, which served as a gateway to Greece and Italy. Thus the city served as a gateway for the gospel once a church was established there. However, Paul had not planned to visit Philippi until a timely vision persuaded him to change direction (Acts 16:9–10).

Pride, self-importance, and affluence marked the people he found there, as they basked in the city's rich political and military history.

To find out more about the church that Paul founded in Philippi, see his letter to the Philippians.

Be Willing to Pay the Price

CONSIDER THIS 16:16–24 **The gospel frequently challenges systems of privilege, oppression, and injustice. Such was the case in Paul's encounter with the slave girl at Philippi (vv. 16–24). She was imprisoned in a pathetic situation that afforded her no options. But when Paul**

(continued on next page)

food before them; and he and his entire household rejoiced that he had become a believer in God.

Paul and Silas Are Released

35 When morning came, the magistrates sent the police,
saying, "Let those men go." 36And the jailer reported the
message to Paul, saying, "The magistrates sent word to let
you go; therefore come out now and go in peace." 37But
Paul replied, "They have beaten us in public, uncondemned, men who are Roman citizens, and have thrown us
into prison; and now are they going to discharge us in secret? Certainly not! Let them come and take us out them-

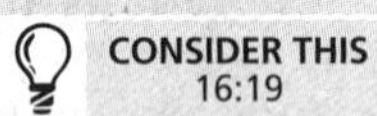

People, Property, and Profitability

The gospel can produce radical changes as it affects people, property, and profitability. Consider three instructive examples from Acts:

Simon "the Great" (Acts 8:9–13, 18–24)

- *A sorcerer with a large following.*
- *The gospel threatened his profitable business by demonstrating a greater power.*
- *Hoping to expand his repertoire, he offered to buy the apostles' power.*
- *Rebuked by the apostles, who called him to true repentance.*

The Slave Girl at Philippi (Acts 16:16–40)

- *Paul's gospel freed a fortune-teller from her occult bondage.*
- *Owned by a syndicate of investors, she had powers that earned them good money.*
- *Realizing their loss, they seized Paul and Silas and hauled them before the authorities.*
- *Punishment: beatings and jail.*
- *But lockup only led to further conversions.*
- *Morning brought embarrassment to the city as officials learned of the travelers' Roman citizenship.*

The Silversmiths at Ephesus (Acts 19:1–41)

- *Paul lectured daily in the hall of Tyrannus, resulting in many conversions.*
- *Sales of silver statues of Artemis (the Greek goddess of fertility) fell off, triggering an emergency "Chamber of Commerce" meeting.*
- *Artisans complained that Paul's gospel had reduced*

selves." 38The police reported these words to the magistrates, and they were afraid when they heard that they were
Roman citizens; 39so they came and apologized to them.
And they took them out and asked them to leave the city.
40After leaving the prison they went to Lydia's home; and
when they had seen and encouraged the brothers and sisters[x] there, they departed.

Converts and Conflict in Thessalonica

17:1

17 After Paul and Silas[y] had passed
through Amphipolis and Apollo-

(Bible text continued on page 486)

[x]Gk *brothers* [y]Gk *they*

(continued from previous page)

delivered her from demonic oppression, it broke not only the spiritual powers that dominated her, but the economic power of the syndicate that owned her.

Not surprisingly, the girl's bosses reacted to their loss and Paul paid for her liberation by going to jail. But despite the injustice, he and his team rejoiced with singing (v. 25) and were eventually vindicated (vv. 38–39).

Is there some whistle-blowing needed where you work or live? Are you willing to pay the price to bring equity or justice to others who are suffering?

trade, ruined their reputations, and impugned their goddess.

- *A riot was incited and Paul's associates were dragged before a lynch mob.*
- *The city clerk eventually restored peace and Paul quietly went on his way.*

Good Ethics—Not Always Good Business

Christlike values do not necessarily produce financial gain in the marketplace. Sometimes they produce just the opposite. Scripture has no argument with making a profit except when it compromises people or the truth. At that point the gospel raises questions that any responsible believer must face. For example, a contract goes unsigned because a Christian refuses to offer money under the table. A sale is lost because a Christian refuses to lie to a customer. A promotion slips by because a Christian sets limits on the intrusion of work into his or her family and personal life.

Make no mistake, many people are receptive toward Christian principles at home and church, and even on the job—as long as such principles cost nothing. But the test of Christian commitment often lies in what one is willing to sacrifice.

What have your Christian convictions cost you? If nothing, are you making tradeoffs that you can't afford to make? Do you sometimes value possessions or power more than people? ◆

How you apply your faith to your work is one of the most important ways you have of communicating Christ to others. See "Your 'Workstyle,'" Titus 2:9–10.

THESSALONICA

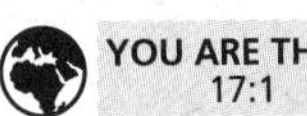

YOU ARE THERE 17:1

- **Chief city of Macedonia and capital city of its district, second only to Corinth as the commercial center of Greece.**
- **Located on the Thermaic Gulf and the main seaport for the region.**
- **Founded by Cassander, king of Macedonia, in 316 B.C. to resettle war refugees from 26 towns that he had destroyed.**
- **Granted free-city status by Rome, allowing it to levy its own taxes, mint its own coins, and appoint local magistrates, known as politarchs. (Jason and other believers were dragged before these officials, Acts 17:5–9.)**
- **Located on the Egnatian Way, a Roman road extending across Macedonia from the Adriatic Sea to the Aegean Sea. The highway, along with a well-situated harbor, brought much commercial and military traffic through the city.**

FOR YOUR INFO
16:31–34

Families of the Early Church

Among the first people to join the Christian movement in the West were the Philippian jailer and his entire family (vv. 31–34). Families played an interesting role in the spread of the gospel during the early days of the church. Judging by Acts and the New Testament letters, acceptance of the faith seemed often to be a decision of an entire family or clan.

Consider the impact of family life, for better or worse, on the faith and commitment of several families and singles recorded in Acts and the New Testament letters.

Families of the Early Church

Family Name	Description
•Ananias •His wife Sapphira	These landowners in the early church observe the praise heaped on Barnabas for selling property and donating the proceeds to the movement. In like manner, they sell property and represent to Peter that they, too, are donating the funds. However, their collusion to keep back part of the money is uncovered and the Holy Spirit strikes them dead.
•Philip •His four daughters	This man is one of seven selected to manage distribution of food to widows. An evangelist, he crosses ethnic barriers by taking the gospel to Samaria. Later, he hosts Paul and his fellow travelers at his home in Caesarea, where his four daughters prophesy.
•Simon	Little is known about this tanner of Joppa except that he hosts Peter in his home during the apostle's momentous trip to Caesarea to take the gospel to Cornelius, a Gentile centurion.
•Mary •John Mark, her son •Rhoda, their maid	A woman of some means makes her home in Jerusalem available as a center of Christian activity. When Peter is released from prison, he goes to her house, where believers are in prayer. John Mark travels with cousin Barnabas, Mary's nephew, and later writes the first surviving narrative of Jesus' life and teachings.
•Barnabas	This landowner, donor, and leader in the early church helps bring Saul into the fellowship of believers, mentors him in the faith, and later works with him in the spread of the movement. He also mentors and defends cousin John Mark. At Antioch, he helps stabilize a new church that crosses many ethnic barriers.

Continued

FAMILIES OF THE EARLY CHURCH

Family Name	Description
Continued	
•Eunice •Her mother Lois •Eunice's son Timothy •His unnamed father, a Gentile	A Jewish mother and grandmother instill faith in Timothy, the product of a mixed marriage. Chosen and mentored by Paul, he becomes a pastor and fellow worker in the spread of Christianity.
•Lydia •Her household	This upscale garment dealer of Philippi and her family become the first believers in Europe. Probably a Gentile, she hosts Paul and his fellow travelers in her home, risking social and economic rejection but helping to found a church.
•A jailer of Philippi •His household	Shaken by an earthquake and the apparent escape of his prisoners, this man, probably a retired Roman soldier, is about to take his own life when Paul and Silas offer him the gospel. His entire family believes and he welcomes the apostles into his home.
•Priscilla •Aquila, her husband	This couple, possibly a mixed marriage between a Roman woman and a Jewish man, become partners in the tent manufacturing business with Paul. Together they mentor a teacher named Apollos. They also help to lead congregations in Corinth, Rome, and Ephesus, at least some of which are in their home.
•Saul, later called Paul •His sister •Her son	A young Jewish man with Roman citizenship starts out as a well-trained Pharisee determined to stamp out the Christian movement. But a dramatic encounter with the risen Christ causes him to make a complete turnabout, and he ends up as the faith's most ardent and widely traveled spokesperson. Apparently his nephew and perhaps his sister join him in the faith.
•Felix •Drusilla, his third wife	This Roman procurator, or governor, of Judea marries the Jewish Drusilla, youngest daughter of Herod Agrippa I, linking him to the notorious Herod family (Acts 12:1–2). Like the Herods, he considers himself above the law because of his influence with the courts. When Paul is brought before him, he hopes to collect a bribe. Later, their son, Agrippa, dies at the eruption of Mount Vesuvius in A.D. 79.
•Herod Agrippa II •Bernice, his sister and lover	The son of Herod Agrippa I becomes Roman governor over part of Palestine. His sister Bernice first marries a man named Marcus, then her uncle Herod, king of Chalcis. After his death she marries Polemo, king of Cilicia, but deserts him shortly after the wedding. Making her way to Jerusalem, she becomes the lover of her brother, by whom she has two sons. During this time Paul is brought before the couple to make a defense. Later, during the Jewish revolt, Agrippa flees Palestine for Rome, where he rules in absentia. Meanwhile, Bernice becomes mistress of the victorious Roman general and emperor, Vespasian, then of his son Titus.
•Publius •His father	The leading citizen of Malta welcomes shipwrecked Paul and his fellow travelers to his estate, hosting the group for three days. Paul heals his father of feverish dysentery, thereby attracting many others with illnesses.
•Philemon •Apphia, possibly his wife •Onesimus, their runaway slave	Probably a businessman of Colosse, this man's family hosts church in their home. When Paul sends back his runaway slave, Onesimus, he is challenged to break with the normal discipline and regard him as a brother in the faith rather than a rebellious slave. According to tradition, Onesimus becomes the first bishop of Ephesus.
•Onesiphorus •His household	A relative unknown of Scripture, this man receives high praise from Paul for his diligence in seeking out the imprisoned apostle in Rome and bringing him refreshment and help there and in Ephesus.

◆

The Gospels also portray many different families. They faced issues not unlike the ones families face today. *See "Families of the Gospels," Luke 20:34.*

nia, they came to Thessalonica, where there was a synagogue of the Jews. 2And Paul went in, as was his custom,
and on three sabbath days argued with them from the
scriptures, 3explaining and proving that it was necessary for
the Messiah[z] to suffer and to rise from the dead, and saying,
"This is the Messiah,[z] Jesus whom I am proclaiming to
17:4
you." 4Some of them were persuaded
and joined Paul and Silas, as did a great
many of the devout Greeks and not a few of the leading
women. 5But the Jews became jealous, and with the help of
some ruffians in the marketplaces they formed a mob and
set the city in an uproar. While they were searching for Paul
and Silas to bring them out to the assembly, they attacked
Jason's house. 6When they could not find them, they
dragged Jason and some believers[a] before the city authorities,[b] shouting, "These people who have been turning the
world upside down have come here also, 7and Jason has
entertained them as guests. They are all acting contrary to
the decrees of the emperor, saying that there is another king
named Jesus." 8The people and the city officials were disturbed when they heard this, 9and after they had taken bail
from Jason and the others, they let them go.

More Conflict in Beroea

17:10 see pg. 488
10 That very night the believers[a] sent
Paul and Silas off to Beroea; and when
they arrived, they went to the Jewish synagogue. 11These
Jews were more receptive than those in Thessalonica, for
they welcomed the message very eagerly and examined the
scriptures every day to see whether these things were so.
12Many of them therefore believed, including not a few
Greek women and men of high standing. 13But when the
Jews of Thessalonica learned that the word of God had
been proclaimed by Paul in Beroea as well, they came there
too, to stir up and incite the crowds. 14Then the believers[a]
immediately sent Paul away to the coast, but Silas and Tim-
17:15 see pg. 489
othy remained behind. 15Those who conducted Paul brought him as far as
Athens; and after receiving instructions to have Silas and
Timothy join him as soon as possible, they left him.

Distress and Debate at Athens

17:15–34 see pg. 488
16 While Paul was waiting for them in
Athens, he was deeply distressed to see
17:17
that the city was full of idols. 17So he argued in the synagogue with the Jews and
the devout persons, and also in the marketplace[c] every day

[z]Or *the Christ* [a]Gk *brothers* [b]Gk *politarchs* [c]Or *civic center;* Gk *agora*

The Leading Women

CONSIDER THIS 17:4 *Thessalonica gave women more opportunities than most cities of the first-century world. Women there were known for their business contributions, their support of public projects, and their leadership in city government. When the gospel arrived, many of the "leading women" responded (v. 4), unlike their counterparts in Antioch of Pisidia (13:50). The difference is hard to explain, but it shows that success doesn't necessarily keep people from responding to the message of Christ.*

Thessalonica was named in honor of a woman, the wife of Cassander, sister of Alexander the Great, and daughter of Philip II of Macedonia.

with those who happened to be there. 18Also some Epicurean and Stoic philosophers debated with him. Some
said, "What does this babbler want to say?" Others said,
"He seems to be a proclaimer of foreign divinities." (This
was because he was telling the good news about Jesus and
the resurrection.) 19So they took him and brought him to
the Areopagus and asked him, "May we know what this
new teaching is that you are presenting? 20It sounds rather
strange to us, so we would like to know what it means."
21Now all the Athenians and the foreigners living there
would spend their time in nothing but telling or hearing
something new.

22 Then Paul stood in front of the Areopagus and said,
"Athenians, I see how extremely religious you are in every
way. 23For as I went through the city and looked carefully at
the objects of your worship, I found among them an altar
with the inscription, 'To an unknown god.' What therefore
you worship as unknown, this I proclaim to you. 24The
God who made the world and everything in it, he who is
Lord of heaven and earth, does not live in shrines made by
human hands, 25nor is he served by human hands, as
though he needed anything, since he himself gives to all
mortals life and breath and all things. 26From one ancestor[d]
he made all nations to inhabit the whole earth, and he allotted the times of their existence and the boundaries of the
places where they would live, 27so that they would search
for God[e] and perhaps grope for him and find him—though
indeed he is not far from each one of us. 28For 'In him we
live and move and have our being'; as even some of your
own poets have said,

'For we too are his offspring.'

29Since we are God's offspring, we ought not to think that
the deity is like gold, or silver, or stone, an image formed
by the art and imagination of mortals. 30While God has
overlooked the times of human ignorance, now he commands all people everywhere to repent, 31because he has
fixed a day on which he will have the world judged in
righteousness by a man whom he has appointed, and of
this he has given assurance to all by raising him from the
dead."

32 When they heard of the resurrection of the dead,
some scoffed; but others said, "We will hear you again
about this." 33At that point Paul left
them. 34But some of them joined him
and became believers, including Dionysius the Areopagite
and a woman named Damaris, and others with them.

17:34 see pg. 490

(Bible text continued on page 490)

[d]Gk *From one*; other ancient authorities read *From one blood* [e]Other ancient authorities read *the Lord*

ADAPT YOUR WITNESS!

CONSIDER THIS 17:17 *At Athens Paul addressed the Greeks in three very different settings—the synagogue, the Areopagus (the supreme tribunal), and the agora, or marketplace. This required three different approaches and points to Paul's great ability in the rhetorical arts.*

It's particularly interesting that Paul spoke out in the marketplace. As there apparently were few if any believers in Athens, he had to work "from the outside in" to present the gospel to Athenian workers. By contrast, believers today work in all levels of industry and commerce.

Paul's example raises a challenging question: Are you willing—and prepared—to represent Christ and His message and values where you work? Your faith cannot be a purely personal affair. God has appointed you to your workplace to carry the message of Christ to your coworkers and customers, just as he appointed Paul to go to the agora of Athens.

BEROEA

YOU ARE THERE
17:10

- A city in southwest Macedonia located along the major east-west trade route, 45 miles west of Thessalonica.
- Capital city of the Macedonian region.
- Large and prosperous at the time of Paul, it prospered even more later under Byzantine rule; by the time of the Ottoman Turks (sixteenth century A.D.) it had become Europe's chief trade center for the Middle East.
- Sopater, Paul's companion from Beroea (Acts 20:4), may have been converted when the fair-minded Beroeans searched the Scriptures daily (17:11).

PAUL'S SECOND JOURNEY, PART THREE

CONSIDER THIS
17:15–34

PAUL, APOSTLE TO THE INTELLECTUALS

At Athens the gospel collided with a centuries-old culture rooted in intellectualism and discourse. Certainly Paul had encountered Greek philosophy elsewhere; indeed, he had grown up with it in Tarsus. But his visit to Athens brought him into direct contact with the inheritors of the city's celebrated intellectual tradition (Acts 17:18).

Was Paul intimidated by the arrogance and cynicism of the leisurely Epicureans and Stoics (vv. 18–21)? Some believe that he was (based on passages like 1 Cor. 2:1–5). Yet even though he might have felt more apprehension addressing them than any other audience, Acts gives no hint that he felt inferior. On the contrary, he addressed them at their own forum, the Areopagus, building on common ground by discussing their altar "to an unknown god" and citing one of their poets (Acts 17:28).

Was Paul's strategy effective? If judged by the number of converts, no. Only a handful believed. The rest dismissed him immediately or else postponed judgment pending later discussion—which apparently never came, as Paul departed.

On that basis, some believe that the apostle was wrong for ever going to Athens. In fact, some contend that Paul was so disillusioned by the experience that for a

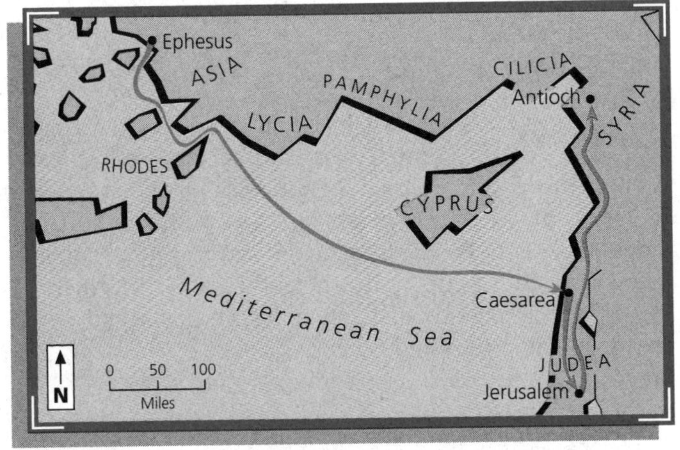

PAUL'S SECOND JOURNEY, PART FOUR

ATHENS
Cultural center of the Roman world.

time he left the ministry to make tents at Corinth (18:1–3). Supposedly, his words in 1 Cor. 1:18—2:5 denouncing philosophy as so much "foolosophy" reflect that view. As a result, some conclude that it is a waste of time to offer the gospel to intellectuals.

Luke doesn't tell us exactly why Paul left Athens, but nothing suggests disillusionment. He never "left" the ministry, just as he had never abandoned his trade, tentmaking (see "Paul's 'Real' Job," Acts 18:1–3). While working with Aquila and Priscilla at Corinth, Paul continued to preach in the synagogue and in the house of Justus (18:4, 7), a ministry that lasted more than 18 months (18:11). Later in Ephesus he followed the same pattern for two years (19:8–10).

Paul's approach to the Athenian intellectuals should encourage believers today to actively participate in universities and other centers of learning. Those that God calls to work within the academic disciplines have an outstanding model to follow—Paul, God's apostle to the intellectuals. ◆

Moses is another example that demonstrates "The Value of Learning," Acts 7:22.

ATHENS

YOU ARE THERE 17:15

- **Principal city of ancient Greece and capital of the district of Attica.**
- **Name derived from the Greek goddess Athena.**
- **Renowned in the ancient world for its philosophers, schools, and academies.**
- **As a free city, governed itself independently and paid no taxes to Rome.**
- **Though Paul won several converts to the gospel there, it may have been years later before a church began.**

Dionysius and Damaris

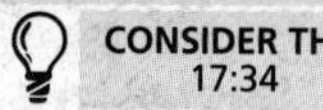

CONSIDER THIS 17:34 *Apparently none of the Epicurean or Stoic philosophers of Athens responded to Paul's message about Christ, but Luke does name a council member and a woman as the nucleus of a group that believed (v. 34).*

Dionysius was a member of the court and likely a person of some standing. Later writers name him as the first bishop of the church in Athens.

As for Damaris, it is remarkable that a woman should be among the first believers. Greek women of the day rarely took part in philosophical discourses. They generally stayed at home in seclusion while their husbands, freed by slaves from the menial tasks of life, pursued leisurely activities such as gymnastics, politics, and philosophy.

There are several possibilities to explain how Damaris managed to hear Paul and decide to follow Christ. One is that she was among a class of women known as hetairai, *specially trained companions to wealthy men who were educated in subjects usually reserved for men, such as rhetoric and philosophy. Their purpose was to entertain their partners. The role of* hetairai *was not as respected as that of wives, but they en-*

(continued on next page)

Partnership with Priscilla and Aquila

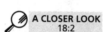

18:1–3 18:2

18 After this Paul[f] left Athens and
went to Corinth. 2There he
found a Jew named Aquila, a native of
Pontus, who had recently come from
Italy with his wife Priscilla, because Claudius had ordered
all Jews to leave Rome. Paul[g] went to see them, 3and, because he was of the same trade, he stayed with them, and
they worked together—by trade they were tentmakers.
4Every sabbath he would argue in the synagogue and would
try to convince Jews and Greeks.

[f]Gk *he* [g]Gk *He*

A Strategic Partnership

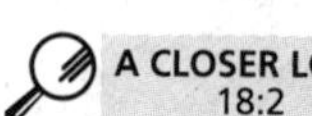

A CLOSER LOOK 18:2 *In teaming up with Priscilla and Aquila, Paul not only made a smart business move, he also cultivated lifelong friends. Find out more about this outstanding first-century couple by reading "Priscilla and Aquila," Rom. 16:3–5.*

Paul's "Real" Job

CONSIDER THIS 18:1–3 *Though the ministry today is viewed as a full-time profession, some of the first gospel workers earned all or part of their living through other occupations. Paul was a tentmaker (v. 3), a trade he may have learned as a boy in Tarsus (see 11:25 and "Saul," 13:1).*

That kind of "bivocationalism" is worth considering in today's world. Many minority pastors in urban settings work at second and third jobs, since their churches cannot support them financially. And in developing countries, "secular" skills are desperately needed in supplying food, shelter, and economic development.

Jesus also could have made His living through a "secular" job, as did most rabbis of His day. See "Jesus the Carpenter," Mark 6:3, and "Scribes," Luke 20:39.

If Paul supported himself through an occupation other than his ministry, shouldn't Christian workers today at least consider that as an option? See "Paying Vocational Christian Workers," 1 Cor. 9:1–23.

A Synagogue Official Believes

5 When Silas and Timothy arrived from Macedonia, Paul
was occupied with proclaiming the word,[h] testifying to the
Jews that the Messiah[i] was Jesus. 6When they opposed and
reviled him, in protest he shook the dust from his clothes[j]
and said to them, "Your blood be on your own heads! I am
innocent. From now on I will go to the
Gentiles." 7Then he left the synagogue[k]
and went to the house of a man named Titius[l] Justus, a
worshiper of God; his house was next door to the synagogue. 8Crispus, the official of the synagogue, became a believer in the Lord, together with all his household; and
many of the Corinthians who heard Paul became believers
and were baptized. 9One night the Lord
said to Paul in a vision, "Do not be
afraid, but speak and do not be silent; 10for I am with you,
and no one will lay a hand on you to harm you, for there
are many in this city who are my people." 11He stayed there a
year and six months, teaching the word of God among them.

18:7–8

18:9–10 see pg. 492

Jewish Leaders Oppose the Gospel

12 But when Gallio was proconsul of Achaia, the Jews
made a united attack on Paul and brought him before the

[h] Gk *with the word* [i] Or *the Christ* [j] Gk *reviled him, he shook out his clothes* [k] Gk *left there* [l] Other ancient authorities read *Titus*

(continued from previous page)

joyed far more freedom and opportunity—including the opportunity to attend the philosophical discussions held daily in the marketplace and the Areopagus (vv. 17, 19).

Of course, there is no way to know for certain whether Damaris was a hetaira. *But no matter what her role in the society was, she courageously went against the prevailing culture by siding with Paul, Dionysius, and the message about the resurrected Jesus.*

"Not Many Mighty" . . . But a Few

CONSIDER THIS
18:7–8

A majority of converts to early Christianity, at least those in Corinth, were from the lower classes; "not many were powerful," as Paul put it (1 Cor. 1:26–28).

But even if there were not many mighty, at least there were some. Several prominent citizens were attracted to the new religion, including Justus who lived next door to the synagogue (probably in a house of some size), Crispus, the ruler of the synagogue (Acts 18:7–8), and Erastus, the city treasurer (Rom. 16:23). Once again the gospel showed its incredible power to break down social barriers, creating a new people of God.

tribunal. 13They said, "This man is persuading people to
worship God in ways that are contrary to the law." 14Just as
Paul was about to speak, Gallio said to the Jews, "If it were
a matter of crime or serious villainy, I would be justified in
accepting the complaint of you Jews; 15but since it is a matter of questions about words and names and your own law,
see to it yourselves; I do not wish to be a judge of these
matters." 16And he dismissed them from the tribunal.

18:17

17Then all of them[m] seized Sosthenes, the
official of the synagogue, and beat him in
front of the tribunal. But Gallio paid no attention to any of
these things.

Paul Returns to Antioch

18:18

18 After staying there for a considerable time, Paul said farewell to the be-
lievers[n] and sailed for Syria, accompanied by Priscilla and
Aquila. At Cenchreae he had his hair cut, for he was under

[m]Other ancient authorities read *all the Greeks* [n]Gk *brothers*

Afraid in the City?

CONSIDER THIS 18:9–10 *The Lord's words to Paul (vv. 9–10) offer hope for believers who live and work in cities. While there are many evils in the city—as well as in the country—the city itself is not an evil. Nor does evil prefer urban over rural settings. In his nighttime vision, Paul derived comfort from the affirmation that God was at work in the city. It was not a strange place for him, nor a place of alienation and fear. He felt at home there.*

Today, cities continue to be strategic for the work of the church in an increasingly urbanized world. Believers might as well get used to living and working in them as God's people. After all, they will spend eternity in a heavenly city (Rev. 21:1–27)!

Paul intentionally went to the cities. The gospel he proclaimed had implications for an urban setting. See "Paul's Urban Strategy," Acts 16:4.

Sosthenes the Attorney

CONSIDER THIS 18:17 *Sosthenes (v. 17) could have been the prosecuting lawyer who brought the case against Paul—and lost. The unfortunate synagogue ruler was beaten in a moment of mob psychology.*

There is perhaps a happy ending to the story, however. A man named Sosthenes was with Paul a few years later in Ephesus, as the apostle was writing to the Corinthians. In his letter, Paul brings greetings from "our brother Sosthenes" (1 Cor. 1:1).

We cannot know whether they were one and the same Sosthenes, but the possibility that we are witnessing Paul's treatment of a former enemy brings us to ask: What is the role of the church today with regard to the oppressed and victimized? How does it handle targets of persecution—people who have been "beaten up" by the unfair and capricious systems of the world?

a vow. 19When they reached Ephesus, he left them there,
but first he himself went into the synagogue and had a discussion with the Jews. 20When they asked him to stay
longer, he declined; 21but on taking leave of them, he said,
"I[o] will return to you, if God wills." Then he set sail from
Ephesus.
22 When he had landed at Caesarea, he went up to
Jerusalem[p] and greeted the church, and then went down to
Antioch. 23After spending some time there he departed and
went from place to place through the region of Galatia[q] and
Phrygia, strengthening all the disciples.

Apollos Is Mentored in the Faith

18:24 see pg. 494
24 Now there came to Ephesus a Jew
named Apollos, a native of Alexandria.
He was an eloquent man, well-versed in the scriptures.

18:24–26 see pg. 494
25He had been instructed in the Way of
the Lord; and he spoke with burning

[o]Other ancient authorities read *I must at all costs keep the approaching festival in Jerusalem, but I* [p]Gk *went up* [q]Gk *the Galatian region*

Personality Profile: Apollos

FOR YOUR INFO 18:24–28

Name means: "Destroyer."

Home: Alexandria, Egypt.

Occupation: Itinerant teacher in the things of the Lord (though his doctrinal knowledge only went as far as John the Baptist); later became an evangelist at Corinth.

Known to be: Eloquent and extremely popular. The Corinthians set up a faction around him, and perhaps to avoid causing any further controversy or fuel any party spirit, he did not return to Corinth, despite Paul's request (1 Cor. 16:12).

Best known today for: Being taught "the Way of God . . . more accurately" by Priscilla and Aquila (Acts 18:26; see Rom. 16:3–5), after which he became even more "mighty in the Scriptures."

Cenchreae

YOU ARE THERE 18:18

- **Corinth's eastern seaport on the Saronic Gulf, used as a jumping-off point for trade with Asia. Sailors hauled small ships and their cargo across the Isthmus of Corinth on a man-made "ship road" rather than sailing 200 miles around the dangerous peninsula.**
- **Several temples to a variety of pagan deities have been excavated in the Cenchrean harbor.**
- **Shared Corinth's ethnic diversity, free-thinking spirit, and money-making entrepreneurship; also the site of the biennial Isthmian games, on which there was heavy betting.**
- **Home of Phoebe, who distinguished herself as courier of Paul's letter to Rome (Rom. 16:1–2).**
- **Site of modern Kichries, Greece.**

enthusiasm and taught accurately the things concerning
Jesus, though he knew only the baptism of John. 26He began to speak boldly in the synagogue; but when Priscilla
and Aquila heard him, they took him aside and explained
the Way of God to him more accurately. 27And when he
wished to cross over to Achaia, the believers[r] encouraged
him and wrote to the disciples to welcome him. On his arrival he greatly helped those who through grace had become believers, 28for he powerfully re-
futed the Jews in public, showing by the
scriptures that the Messiah[s] is Jesus.

18:24–28
see pg. 493

[r]Gk *brothers* [s]Or *the Christ*

Marketplace Mentors: Priscilla and Aquila

A CLOSER LOOK 18:24–26

Priscilla and Aquila served as spiritual mentors to Apollos (vv. 24–28), updating his theology and increasing his effectiveness in the spread of the gospel. For more on the importance of the mentoring process, see "Discipleship—Or Mentoring?" Acts 9:26–30. To learn about the couple with whom Paul partnered in business, see "Priscilla and Aquila," Rom. 16:3–5.

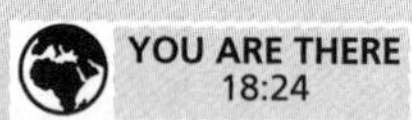

The Septuagint: Alexandria's Gift to Christianity

Scripture mentions Alexandria only four times (all in Acts: 6:9; 18:24; 27:6; 28:11). However, the city's influence on the New Testament and the church was far greater than these few references might lead one to believe, for Alexandria was the birthplace of the Greek Old Testament translation known as the Septuagint.

Scattered among the cities of the Alexandrian, Greek, and Roman Empires were millions of Hebrews. By the first century, more than one million lived in Egypt. In Alexandria they had separate districts from their Gentile neighbors, but nevertheless isolation from Jerusalem took its toll. Each successive generation moved further away from Judaism, adopting the Hellenistic ways of Alexandrian society.

The Septuagint was a response to this cultural assimilation. Tradition holds that Jewish leaders in Alexandria invited some 70 Greek-speaking elders from Israel to translate the Hebrew Scriptures into koinē*, the Greek commonly spoken as a trade language throughout the ancient world.*

Several legends attach the miraculous to their work, completed in the second century B.C. *One holds that the*

Paul Arrives at Ephesus

19 While Apollos was in Corinth, Paul passed through
the interior regions and came to Ephesus, where he
found some disciples. 2He said to them, "Did you receive
the Holy Spirit when you became believers?" They replied,
"No, we have not even heard that there is a Holy Spirit."
3Then he said, "Into what then were you baptized?" They
answered, "Into John's baptism." 4Paul said, "John baptized
with the baptism of repentance, telling the people to believe in the one who was to come after him, that is, in Jesus." 5On hearing this, they were baptized in the name of
the Lord Jesus. 6When Paul had laid his hands on them, the
Holy Spirit came upon them, and they spoke in tongues
and prophesied— 7altogether there were about twelve of
them.

Lectures in the Synagogue and the Hall of Tyrannus

19:8–41 see pg. 496

8 He entered the synagogue and for
three months spoke out boldly, and

(Bible text continued on page 498)

translators were inspired by the Holy Spirit. Another claims that the 70 worked independently, but when finished their versions matched in every detail. At any rate, the translation, known as the Septuagint (Latin, septuaginta, *or* LXX *for 70), was a scholarly feat of astounding importance.*

This "Alexandrian Greek Urban Bible" became the Bible of the early church. It was the Bible Peter quoted at Pentecost, and the Bible that Apollos had grown up with. Conceived in a world-class, pluralistic city, it was the first Bible translated into the language of the people, and encouraged the use of koinē *for the New Testament. Even today the Septuagint is the authorized Bible of the Greek Orthodox Church.*

In short, the Alexandrian translation made Scripture intelligible and readable to common people, both Jew and Gentile. As a result, it became an indispensable tool in the spread of the gospel throughout the Roman world. ◆

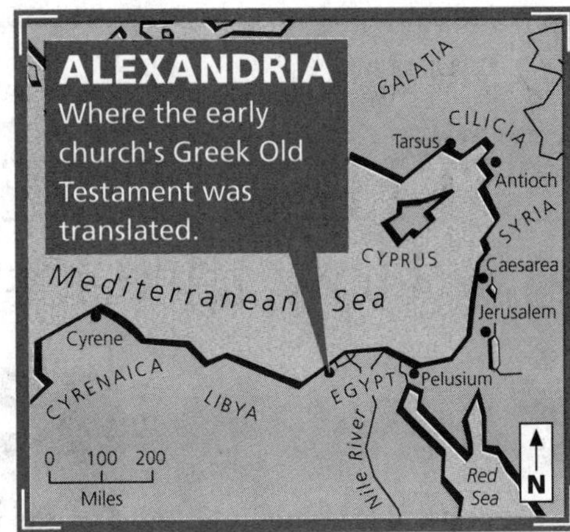

ALEXANDRIA

- **One of 21 cities founded by Alexander the Great named Alexandria or Alexander.**
- **Major port on the Nile delta, with a canal accessing the Mediterranean Sea.**
- **Perhaps the second-largest city of the Roman Empire, with a population of well over 300,000, over 500,000 counting slaves; Jews migrated there in large numbers.**
- **Renowned for shipbuilding (Acts 27:6; 28:11).**
- **Boasted the greatest "emporium," or trade center, of the ancient world. Exported papyrus, books, ivory, wood, glasswork, precious metals, bronze, perfumes, cosmetics, and domestic animals. Imported horses, wine and olive oil from Greece, timber from Cyprus, silk from Africa and the East, and precious stones.**
- **Site of a library housing 700,000 volumes, one of the "Seven Wonders of the Ancient World," making it the intellectual center of the Roman Empire.**
- **Birthplace of Apollos (18:24).**
- **John Mark, author of the second Gospel, may have founded a church there in A.D. 67. Later it became a major center of Christian philosophers and theologians.**

CONSIDER THIS
19:8–41

The Ephesus Approach: How the Gospel Penetrated a City

Evangelism in Ephesus was explosive and unpredictable. People from vastly different backgrounds formed a diverse coalition of believers who had a far-reaching impact on the city's culture and economy (v. 10).

Laypeople Laid a Foundation

Start-up began with **Priscilla and Aquila**, the entrepreneurial couple that Paul met in Corinth (Acts 18:1–3). Joining Paul's team, they sailed with him to Ephesus, a major city of 350,000. While he traveled to Palestine and Galatia, they remained and set up key contacts, working in the **tent manufacturing industry** (18:18–23).

One beneficiary of their efforts was **Apollos**, a powerful orator from Alexandria who stirred things up in Paul's absence. Eloquent in delivery but incomplete in his theology, he learned from them about Jesus. After mentoring him in the faith, they sent him to Greece where he strengthened the believers, including their old friends at Corinth (18:24–28; 1 Cor. 3:6).

The Message Took Hold

Returning to Ephesus, Paul encountered a new breed of **religious followers**. Like Apollos, they were unaware of Jesus, knowing

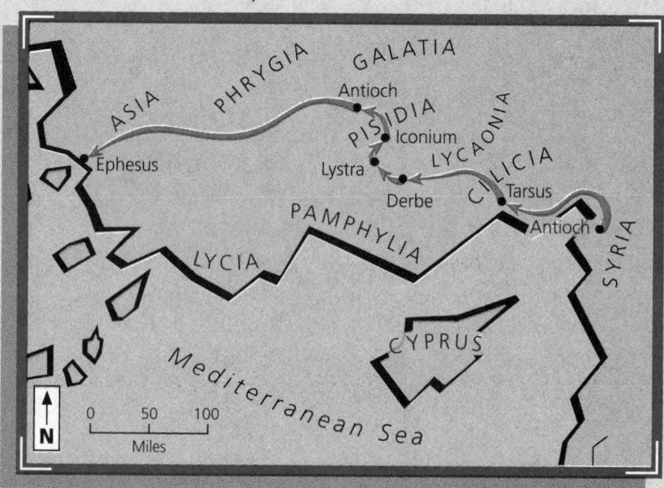

PAUL'S THIRD JOURNEY, PART ONE

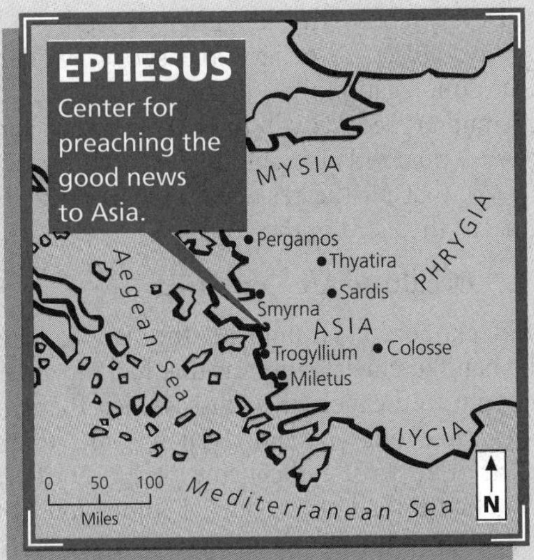

only of John the Baptist. But they became ecstatic as Paul related the fulfillment of John's ministry in Christ. Twelve of their number received the Holy Spirit, arousing the **religious establishment** (Acts 19:1–7).

Paul exploited the interest by initiating a three-month campaign in the local synagogue. However, his arguments met with opposition from some **synagogue members** who maligned the movement publicly. In response, Paul relocated to the **hall of Tyrannus** where for two years he engaged the Ephesians in a dialogue on Christianity during their midday, off-work hours (19:8–10).

Rapid Growth

Concentrated focus brought extraordinary results. The Christian message proved contagious among both **open-minded Jews and intellectually curious Gentiles**, impacting the city's **educational system**. **Residents and merchants** of Ephesus and from throughout Asia Minor were exposed. As word spread among **workers in regional commerce, the arts, and the transportation system**, "all . . . of Asia heard the word of the Lord" (19:10). Philemon's house church in Laodicea and probably other Asian churches were started by those attending Paul's "university lectureship."

Meanwhile, God validated Paul's message with dramatic miracles among the **sick and diseased**. This drew the notice of **health professionals**, including esoteric healing artists who become jealous. One group, the seven sons of Sceva, attempted to imitate the apostle through an occult ritual but were routed by the very powers over which they claimed to have mastery. The incident produced even more converts to Christianity, driving **occult practitioners and publishers** out of business (though not all; see 2 Tim. 3:8). The growing community of believers lit a bonfire that consumed magic books valued at no less than 400,000 hours of wages (Acts 19:11–20).

Economic Impact

At this point the civic leaders started receiving complaints from **artisans and craftsmen**, particularly **metalworkers**, about the economic impact of the message. Paul's meddlesome habit of attacking idolatry threatened the city's thriving **tourist trade**, centered around the internationally acclaimed temple to Artemis, one of the "Seven Wonders of the Ancient World." The metalworkers, led by Demetrius, mobilized the entire city to save a key industry. Recruiting their associates in **other trade guilds**, they fomented a riot and rushed to the amphitheater.

THE THEATER AT EPHESUS

This brought **City Hall** into the act. At great

(continued on next page)

(continued from previous page)

pains to keep law and order—as well as his job—a Rome-appointed civil servant finally silenced the crowd and urged them to use the **court system** for redress of their grievances. His tactic forestalled violence, bought time, and saved the economy. It also spared Paul and his companions (19:23–41).

An Established Community

The riot brought Paul's lecture series to an end, but not the impact of the gospel. Departing the city, he left behind a growing, dynamic church, pastored by his young protégé, **Timothy** (16:1–3; 1 Tim. 1:3). Not only did these believers continue to penetrate their own community with the message of Christ, they also reached out to the many **travelers** to and from their strategically placed import-export city—**tourists and religious pilgrims, shipping merchants, sailors and other transportation workers, military personnel, political refugees**. Dozens of churches sprang up throughout Asia Minor, thanks to the Holy Spirit's coordinated use of three tentmakers (Priscilla, Aquila, and Paul), a fiery evangelist (Apollos), and countless unnamed laity. ◆

With its magnificent temple to Artemis, Ephesus was a popular tourist spot in the ancient world. For more on Ephesus, see the Introduction to Ephesians.

The Ephesian outreach spawned numerous churches in Asia Minor. See "The Church at the End of the First Century A.D.," Rev. 1:20.

argued persuasively about the kingdom of God. 9When
some stubbornly refused to believe and spoke evil of the
Way before the congregation, he left them, taking the disciples with him, and argued daily in the lecture hall of Tyran-
19:10 nus.[t] 10This continued for two years, so
that all the residents of Asia, both Jews
and Greeks, heard the word of the Lord.

Occultists Are Converted

11 God did extraordinary miracles through Paul, 12so
that when the handkerchiefs or aprons that had touched his
skin were brought to the sick, their diseases left them, and
the evil spirits came out of them. 13Then some itinerant
Jewish exorcists tried to use the name of the Lord Jesus
over those who had evil spirits, saying, "I adjure you by the
Jesus whom Paul proclaims." 14Seven sons of a Jewish high
priest named Sceva were doing this. 15But the evil spirit
said to them in reply, "Jesus I know, and Paul I know; but
who are you?" 16Then the man with the evil spirit leaped on
them, mastered them all, and so overpowered them that
they fled out of the house naked and wounded. 17When
this became known to all residents of Ephesus, both Jews
and Greeks, everyone was awestruck; and the name of the
Lord Jesus was praised. 18Also many of those who became
believers confessed and disclosed their practices. 19A number of those who practiced magic collected their books and
burned them publicly; when the value of these books[u] was
calculated, it was found to come to fifty thousand silver
coins. 20So the word of the Lord grew mightily and prevailed.

The Gospel Challenges the Economy

19:21 see pg. 500

21 Now after these things had been
accomplished, Paul resolved in the Spirit
to go through Macedonia and Achaia, and then to go on to
Jerusalem. He said, "After I have gone there, I must also see
Rome." 22So he sent two of his helpers, Timothy and Erastus, to Macedonia, while he himself stayed for some time
longer in Asia.

19:23–27 19:24

23 About that time no little disturbance broke out concerning the Way. 24A
man named Demetrius, a silversmith
who made silver shrines of Artemis,
brought no little business to the artisans. 25These he gathered together, with the workers of the same trade, and said,

[t]Other ancient authorities read *of a certain Tyrannus, from eleven o'clock in the morning to four in the afternoon* [u]Gk *them*

"Men, you know that we get our wealth from this business.
26You also see and hear that not only in Ephesus but in almost the whole of Asia this Paul has persuaded and drawn
away a considerable number of people by saying that gods
made with hands are not gods. 27And there is danger not
only that this trade of ours may come into disrepute but
also that the temple of the great goddess Artemis will be
scorned, and she will be deprived of her majesty that
brought all Asia and the world to worship her."
28 When they heard this, they were enraged and
shouted, "Great is Artemis of the Ephesians!" 29The city was
filled with the confusion; and people[v] rushed together to
the theater, dragging with them Gaius and Aristarchus,
Macedonians who were Paul's travel companions. 30Paul
wished to go into the crowd, but the disciples would not let
him; 31even some officials of the province of Asia,[w] who
were friendly to him, sent him a message urging him not to
venture into the theater. 32Meanwhile, some were shouting
one thing, some another; for the assembly was in confusion, and most of them did not know why they had come

[v]Gk *they* [w]Gk *some of the Asiarchs*

Gospel and Property Conflicts

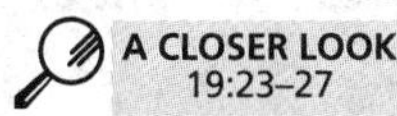

A CLOSER LOOK 19:23–27 *Scripture has no argument with making a profit except when it compromises people or the truth. See "People, Property, and Profitability," Acts 16:19.*

Personality Profile: Demetrius the Silversmith

FOR YOUR INFO 19:24 **Home:** Ephesus, a major tourist center renowned for its temple to Artemis, one of the "Seven Wonders of the Ancient World" (see Introduction to Ephesians).

Profession: Silversmith and union leader of the local craft guild, specializing in silver statues of the goddess Artemis.

Best known today for: Instigating a riot in Ephesus to get rid of Paul.

Boom Box

CONSIDER THIS 19:10 **Anyone who lives or works in a large urban center today is no doubt familiar with the boom box, an oversized stereo box popular among urban youth for the same reason that many adults find it obnoxious—it shatters all peace and quiet with rap and rhythm.**

When it comes to the gospel, a city itself can act like a boom box, amplifying the message to a level that cannot be ignored. As it reproduces the gospel's distinctive "sounds," city life exposes more and more people to the Good News.

That's what happened in Ephesus. The message reverberated out from that city such that "all the residents of Asia . . . heard the word of the Lord" (v. 10). This is not to say that *every Asian* heard the gospel, but that the gospel was heard *all over Asia.* By penetrating the city, the gospel penetrated the region.

19:33

together. 33Some of the crowd gave instructions to Alexander, whom the Jews
had pushed forward. And Alexander motioned for silence
and tried to make a defense before the people. 34But when
they recognized that he was a Jew, for about two hours all
of them shouted in unison, "Great is Artemis of the
Ephesians!" 35But when the town clerk had quieted the

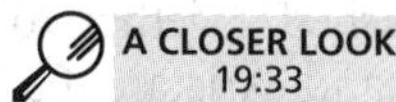

A CLOSER LOOK 19:33

Alexander

Paul later charged "Alexander the coppersmith," possibly this man, with doing him great harm. See "Alexander—A Confirmed Enemy," 2 Tim. 4:14–15.

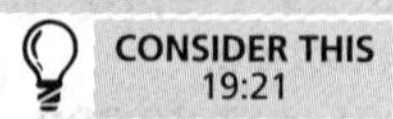

CONSIDER THIS 19:21

Rome or Bust

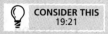

When Paul declared, "I must also see Rome" (v. 21), he wasn't talking about a tourist excursion; he was stating his bold intention to penetrate the capital of his world with the gospel. To him, Rome was a symbol of the center of power, the system that was driving the world. Jerusalem may have been important as a starting point, but the goal was Rome.

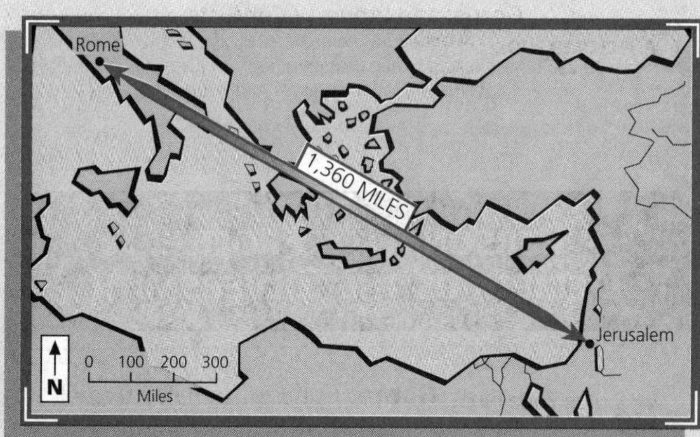

Jerusalem to Rome

In the center of Rome was a tall, marble obelisk indicating the distance from that point to every town in the empire—a graphic reminder of just how important Rome viewed itself. But Paul seemed to have a reverse model of that. Wherever he was, an internal marker seemed to remind him how far he was from Rome and how intent he

crowd, he said, "Citizens of Ephesus, who is there that does
not know that the city of the Ephesians is the temple
keeper of the great Artemis and of the statue that fell from
heaven?[x] 36Since these things cannot be denied, you ought to
be quiet and do nothing rash. 37You have brought these men
here who are neither temple robbers nor blasphemers of
our[y] goddess. 38If therefore Demetrius and the artisans with
him have a complaint against anyone, the courts are open,
and there are proconsuls; let them bring charges there
against one another. 39If there is anything further[z] you want
to know, it must be settled in the regular assembly. 40For we

[x]Meaning of Gk uncertain [y]Other ancient authorities read *your* [z]Other ancient authorities read *about other matters*

◆ ◆ ◆ ◆ ◆ ◆ ◆ ◆ ◆ ◆ ◆ ◆ ◆ ◆ ◆ ◆

was on getting there. The cities that he visited—including Jerusalem—became mileposts on his way to Rome.

The audacity of his plan is rather shocking: A tiny group living on the periphery of the Roman Empire aimed to conquer the cities and even the capital of the mightiest empire in world history with its new and strange beliefs. Incredibly, the movement prevailed!

That stunning achievement compels believers today to ask: What is our Rome? What are the forces shaping our world today? What is our strategy for gospel penetration? If Paul were alive today, where would he be headed as the strategic center of influence? Perhaps to the megacities of our world, like Mexico City with its 24 million people, half under the age of 15. Perhaps to Tokyo, the second largest city in the world and a major influence on the world's economy.

The point is that modern Christians walk in a tradition of people who declared, "We must get to Rome!" In the same way, we must not stay in our Jerusalems, our homes, our cultures. We are here for influence. We are here to spread the gospel. ◆

Paul's global vision came from Jesus, who sent His followers into "all the world." But spreading Christ's message involves more than just broadcasting a statement or set of facts. How does faith impact the world? *See Mark 16:15.*

Learn more about the imperial city at Acts 28:16.

An International Work Group

CONSIDER THIS 20:4 **The rapidly growing Christian movement recruited members from a wide variety of places. That created significant cultural diversity, as the traveling team mentioned in v. 4 shows. Note the rich differences of background:**

Macedonians

- **Sopater of Beroea (perhaps the same as Sosipater in Rom. 16:21)**
- **Aristarchus (Acts 27:2) and Secundus of Thessalonica**

Galatians

- **Gaius of Derbe**
- **Timothy of Lystra, the product of a mixed marriage (Acts 16:1; see Introduction to 2 Timothy)**

Asians

- **Tychicus, possibly from Ephesus (Eph. 6:21–22; Col. 4:7–8)**
- **Trophimus of Ephesus (Acts 21:29)**

Others

- **Luke the physician from Antioch in Syria, who possibly was writing the Acts account while on the trip (see Introduction to Luke)**
- **Paul of Tarsus, Jerusalem, and Antioch in Syria (see Acts 13:1)**

This varied coalition shows how the people of God have a foundation for unity beyond all other causes. The common faith can bridge differences that even circumstances like a depression, war, or natural disaster cannot. It fulfills Jesus' prayer for His followers that they would demonstrate a oneness that demands the world's attention (John 17:20–23).

are in danger of being charged with rioting today, since
there is no cause that we can give to justify this commotion." 41When he had said this, he dismissed the assembly.

Macedonian Believers Are Revisited

20 After the uproar had ceased, Paul sent for the disciples; and after encouraging them and saying
farewell, he left for Macedonia. 2When he had gone
through those regions and had given the believers[a] much
encouragement, he came to Greece, 3where he stayed for
three months. He was about to set sail for Syria when a plot
was made against him by the Jews, and so he decided to re-

20:4 see pg. 501

turn through Macedonia. 4He was accompanied by Sopater son of Pyrrhus
from Beroea, by Aristarchus and Secundus from Thessalonica, by Gaius from Derbe, and by Timothy, as well as by
Tychicus and Trophimus from Asia. 5They went ahead and
were waiting for us in Troas; 6but we sailed from Philippi
after the days of Unleavened Bread, and in five days we
joined them in Troas, where we stayed for seven days.

Eutychus Falls to His Death and Is Raised

20:7–12

7 On the first day of the week, when
we met to break bread, Paul was holding
a discussion with them; since he intended to leave the next
day, he continued speaking until midnight. 8There were
many lamps in the room upstairs where we were meeting.
9A young man named Eutychus, who was sitting in the
window, began to sink off into a deep sleep while Paul
talked still longer. Overcome by sleep, he fell to the ground
three floors below and was picked up dead. 10But Paul went
down, and bending over him took him in his arms, and
said, "Do not be alarmed, for his life is in him." 11Then Paul
went upstairs, and after he had broken bread and eaten, he
continued to converse with them until dawn; then he left.
12Meanwhile they had taken the boy away alive and were
not a little comforted.

Farewell to the Ephesian Elders

20:13

13 We went ahead to the ship and set
sail for Assos, intending to take Paul on
board there; for he had made this arrangement, intending

20:14

to go by land himself. 14When he met us
in Assos, we took him on board and

20:15

went to Mitylene. 15We sailed from there,
and on the following day we arrived op-

[a]Gk *given them*

Develop Faith Whenever You Can

CONSIDER THIS 20:7–12 The incidents at Troas (vv. 7–12) reflect a habit that believers do well to cultivate—gathering frequently in informal, small clusters to reflect on Scripture, pray, and support one another.

The working people of that key Roman seaport gathered around the visitors to spend an evening together and learn more about the faith. They were following a pattern established at the beginning of the movement, of coming together around the apostles' teaching, fellowship, the breaking of bread, and prayer (2:42). In fact, their appetite for the experience was insatiable: even the shock of Eutychus' fall could not deter them (vv. 9–11)!

Home- or work-based groups of believers have frequently been the foundation of significant Christian movements throughout history. It's worth asking: Do you meet regularly with peers at work, home, or church to sort out your faith and its application to your world?

Troas was the site of a pivotal decision in Christianity. See "A Turning Point in Western Civilization," Acts 16:8.

posite Chios. The next day we touched at Samos, and[b] the
20:15–16 see pg. 505
day after that we came to Miletus. 16For
Paul had decided to sail past Ephesus, so
that he might not have to spend time in Asia; he was eager
to be in Jerusalem, if possible, on the day of Pentecost.

17 From Miletus he sent a message to Ephesus, asking
the elders of the church to meet him. 18When they came to
him, he said to them:

"You yourselves know how I lived among you the entire
time from the first day that I set foot in Asia, 19serving the
Lord with all humility and with tears, enduring the trials
that came to me through the plots of the Jews. 20I did not
shrink from doing anything helpful, proclaiming the message to you and teaching you publicly and from house to
house, 21as I testified to both Jews and Greeks about repentance toward God and faith toward our Lord Jesus. 22And
now, as a captive to the Spirit,[c] I am on my way to
Jerusalem, not knowing what will happen to me there,
23except that the Holy Spirit testifies to me in every city that
imprisonment and persecutions are waiting for me. 24But I
do not count my life of any value to myself, if only I may
finish my course and the ministry that I received from the
Lord Jesus, to testify to the good news of God's grace.

25 "And now I know that none of you, among whom I
have gone about proclaiming the kingdom, will ever see my
face again. 26Therefore I declare to you this day that I am
not responsible for the blood of any of you, 27for I did not
shrink from declaring to you the whole purpose of God.
28Keep watch over yourselves and over all the flock, of
which the Holy Spirit has made you overseers, to shepherd
the church of God[d] that he obtained with the blood of his
own Son.[e] 29I know that after I have gone, savage wolves
will come in among you, not sparing the flock. 30Some even
from your own group will come distorting the truth in order to entice the disciples to follow them. 31Therefore be
alert, remembering that for three years I did not cease night
or day to warn everyone with tears. 32And now I commend
you to God and to the message of his grace, a message that
is able to build you up and to give you the inheritance
among all who are sanctified. 33I coveted no one's silver or
gold or clothing. 34You know for yourselves that I worked
with my own hands to support myself and my companions.
20:33–38 see pg. 506
35In all this I have given you an example
that by such work we must support the
weak, remembering the words of the Lord Jesus, for he
himself said, 'It is more blessed to give than to receive.' "

[b]Other ancient authorities add *after remaining at Trogyllium* [c]Or *And now, bound in the spirit* [d]Other ancient authorities read *of the Lord* [e]Or *with his own blood*; Gk *with the blood of his Own*

ASSOS

YOU ARE THERE 20:13

- **Seaport located on a volcanic hill, 700 feet in altitude, overlooking the Gulf of Adramyttium on the Aegean Sea.**
- **Also known as Assus.**
- **Site of modern Behram Köi in Turkey.**
- **Impressively fortified with a thick wall two miles long and 65 feet high; also boasted a theater, public baths, and a rectangular *agora*, or marketplace.**
- **Competed with other Greek cities for the largest shrine by building a Doric temple to Athena. Emperor worship was also prevalent; like most Greek cities, Assos wanted Caesar to look upon it favorably.**
- **Home to the philosopher Aristotle for three years (348–345 B.C.).**

MITYLENE

YOU ARE THERE 20:14

- **Chief city of the island of Lesbos off the coast of Asia Minor in the Aegean Sea.**
- **Name means "purity."**
- **Its sheltered, deep-water harbor faced the mainland, making it a logical overnight stay for anyone traveling along the coast.**
- **A favorite holiday resort for Roman soldiers.**

CHIOS

YOU ARE THERE 20:15

- **Small, mountainous island between Lesbos and Samos, just five miles off the coast of modern-day Turkey in the Aegean Sea.**
- **Modern Khios, meaning "open."**
- **Historically a "political football,"**

(continued on next page)

(continued from previous page)

wavering between conquest by empires, treaty alliances, and revolt for independence.

- **Renowned for its wine, wheat, citrus fruits, figs, and (today) the substance used in chewing gum.**
- **Claims to be the birthplace of Homer, the Greek poet to whom is ascribed *The Iliad* and *The Odyssey.* Tradition holds that he collected students at the foot of Chios' Mount Epos.**

SAMOS

- **Small, mountainous island in the Aegean Sea, separated from Asia Minor by the narrow Samos Strait.**
- **Important maritime island for Greece, later declared a free state by Rome.**
- **Known for producing fine wine, fruit, olives, and cotton.**

TROGYLLIUM

- **City 20 miles south of Ephesus, located on land that protrudes into the Aegean Sea within a mile of the island of Samos.**
- **Influenced by its neighbors to the north, the Lydians, who were the first to set up permanent retail shops and mint gold and silver coins to enhance economic activity.**
- **Some New Testament texts mention Trogyllium in Acts 20:15 (see 20:15, note p).**
- **A modern harbor in this region on the western tip of Trogyllium is designated St. Paul's Harbor.**

36 When he had finished speaking, he knelt down with
them all and prayed. 37There was much weeping among
them all; they embraced Paul and kissed him, 38grieving especially because of what he had said, that they would not
see him again. Then they brought him to the ship.

Paul Is Warned to Avoid Jerusalem

21:1 see pg. 508

21 When we had parted from them
and set sail, we came by a
straight course to Cos, and the next day to Rhodes, and
from there to Patara.[f] 2When we found a ship bound for
Phoenicia, we went on board and set sail. 3We came in
sight of Cyprus; and leaving it on our left, we sailed to Syria
and landed at Tyre, because the ship was to unload its cargo
there. 4We looked up the disciples and stayed there for
seven days. Through the Spirit they told Paul not to go on
to Jerusalem. 5When our days there were ended, we left
and proceeded on our journey; and all of them, with wives
and children, escorted us outside the city. There we knelt
down on the beach and prayed 6and said farewell to one
another. Then we went on board the ship, and they returned home.

21:7 see pg. 509

7 When we had finished[g] the voyage
from Tyre, we arrived at Ptolemais; and
we greeted the believers[h] and stayed with them for one day.

[f]Other ancient authorities add *and Myra* [g]Or *continued* [h]Gk *brothers*

PAUL'S THIRD JOURNEY, PART TWO

8The next day we left and came to Caesarea; and we went
into the house of Philip the evangelist, one of the seven,
21:9 see pg. 506
and stayed with him. 9He had four unmarried daughters[i] who had the gift of
prophecy. 10While we were staying there for several days, a
prophet named Agabus came down from Judea. 11He came
to us and took Paul's belt, bound his own feet and hands
with it, and said, "Thus says the Holy Spirit, 'This is the
way the Jews in Jerusalem will bind the man who owns this
belt and will hand him over to the Gentiles.' " 12When we
heard this, we and the people there urged him not to go up
to Jerusalem. 13Then Paul answered, "What are you doing,
weeping and breaking my heart? For I am ready not only to
be bound but even to die in Jerusalem for the name of the
Lord Jesus." 14Since he would not be persuaded, we remained silent except to say, "The Lord's will be done."
15 After these days we got ready and started to go up to
Jerusalem. 16Some of the disciples from Caesarea also came
along and brought us to the house of Mnason of Cyprus, an
early disciple, with whom we were to stay.

Paul Arrives in Jerusalem

17 When we arrived in Jerusalem, the brothers welcomed us warmly. 18The next day Paul went with us to visit
James; and all the elders were present. 19After greeting

[i] Gk *four daughters, virgins,*

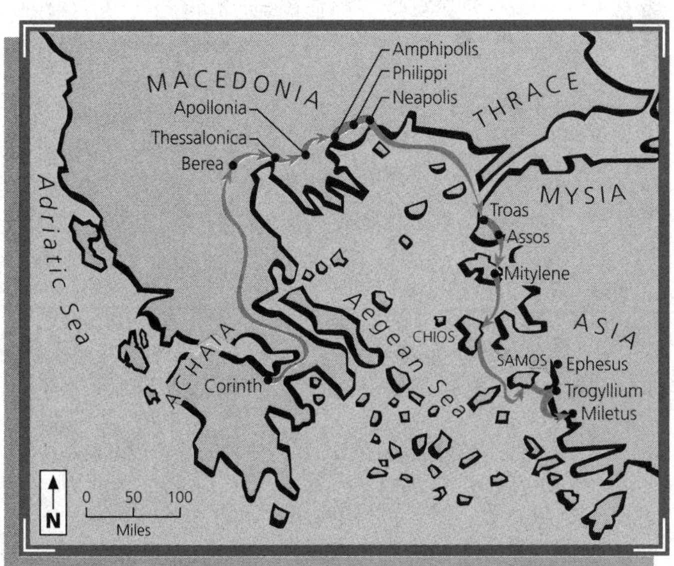

PAUL'S THIRD JOURNEY, PART THREE

MILETUS

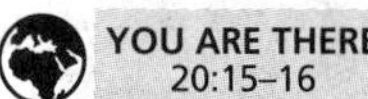
YOU ARE THERE 20:15–16

- **Seaport on the west coast of Asia Minor and southernmost of the great cities of Greek culture.**
- **Located just south of present-day Söke, Turkey.**
- **Hippodamus of Miletus, an urban planner, rebuilt the city after it was destroyed during the Graeco-Persian Wars (c. 546–448 B.C.). Using a grid pattern of right angles with boulevards 30 feet wide, he created the "Hippodamian City," a model recreated throughout the Roman Empire.**
- **Leading merchants founded a marketing empire linking 70 to 90 smaller towns and cities further north, along the coast of the Black Sea.**
- **Exported its culture, Greek philosophy, and a trade language that became the common-speech Greek in which the New Testament was written.**
- **Noted for its civil strife between workers, who wanted a democracy, and the rich, who preferred dictatorship. At Miletus Paul warned the Ephesian elders against similar strife among believers (Acts 20:28–35).**
- **Already in decline commercially and strategically by the time of Paul's visit (c. A.D. 57), due to the silting up of its waterway.**

The Four Daughters of Philip

CONSIDER THIS
21:9

In his Pentecost sermon, Peter declared that the words of the Old Testament prophet Joel were coming to pass: "Your sons and your daughters shall prophesy" (Acts 2:17–18). The four virgin daughters of Philip were proof that it was so (21:9, note w).

In the first century, prophets were recognized (not appointed) through the exercise of their God-given gifts, which they often dis-

(continued on next page)

them, he related one by one the things that God had done
among the Gentiles through his ministry. 20When they
heard it, they praised God. Then they said to him, "You see,
brother, how many thousands of believers there are among
the Jews, and they are all zealous for the law. 21They have
been told about you that you teach all the Jews living
among the Gentiles to forsake Moses, and that you tell
them not to circumcise their children or observe the customs. 22What then is to be done? They will certainly hear
that you have come. 23So do what we tell you. We have
four men who are under a vow. 24Join these men, go
through the rite of purification with them, and pay for the
shaving of their heads. Thus all will know that there is
nothing in what they have been told about you, but that
you yourself observe and guard the law. 25But as for the
Gentiles who have become believers, we have sent a letter
with our judgment that they should abstain from what has
been sacrificed to idols and from blood and from what is
strangled[j] and from fornication." 26Then Paul took the men,

[j]Other ancient authorities lack *and from what is strangled*

CONSIDER THIS
20:33–38

"I Have Not Coveted"

Paul's emotional farewell to the Ephesian elders ended with a significant disclaimer: I have [not] coveted (v. 33). Paul seems to have been at pains to emphasize that he was not a deadbeat while among them, sponging off their generosity. Rather, he worked as a tentmaker, first in order to provide for himself and his companions, and second, to "support [help] the weak" (v. 34–35; see "Paul's 'Real' Job," 18:1–3).

These words merit our attention. First, they reveal a biblical work ethic that forsakes greed in favor of hard, honest labor and a trust in God to provide for basic needs. Then, as God blesses, a worker's abundance should overflow into generosity toward others in need. This pattern recurs throughout the New Testament (for example, Matt. 6:24–34; Luke 16:9–13; Eph. 4:28; 2 Thess. 3:6–15; 1 Tim. 6:6–10, 17–19).

However, Paul's statement also bears upon the reputation of churches and ministries today. A growing number of people regard Christian work and workers with skepticism, as little more than fundraising vehicles for a greedy clergy. Apparently Paul faced similar attitudes, and therefore chose to support himself during his stay in Ephesus. Is

and the next day, having purified himself, he entered the temple with them, making public the completion of the days of purification when the sacrifice would be made for each of them.

A Mob Seeks to Kill Paul

27 When the seven days were almost completed, the
Jews from Asia, who had seen him in the temple, stirred up
the whole crowd. They seized him, 28shouting, "Fellow Israelites, help! This is the man who is teaching everyone
everywhere against our people, our law, and this place;
more than that, he has actually brought Greeks into the
temple and has defiled this holy place." 29For they had previously seen Trophimus the Ephesian with him in the city,
and they supposed that Paul had brought him into the tem-
21:30 ple. 30Then all the city was aroused, and
the people rushed together. They seized
Paul and dragged him out of the temple, and immediately
the doors were shut. 31While they were trying to kill him,

(continued from previous page)

played during worship, bringing a word from the Lord. (The New Testament had not yet been written.) The role was highly esteemed by Paul (Eph. 4:11).

Philip's daughters broke the cultural norm of being wives and mothers, perhaps choosing to remain single in order to carry out their prophetic work.

there any reason why modern Christian leaders shouldn't at least consider that as an option today?

But Paul's words also present a stiff challenge to "laypeople." What about our attitudes toward work, income, and material things? How would we rate on a scale measuring greed versus generosity?

Paul goes beyond saying that generosity is just a nice virtue. "We must support the weak," he urges (v. 35, emphasis added), because it is the very thing that Christ taught. What must that have sounded like to people from the extraordinarily affluent city of Ephesus? It certainly is a powerful exhortation to us today. But it is backed up by two powerful examples—Paul (a tentmaker) and Christ (a carpenter). ◆

Like Paul, Jesus gave a direct, unequivocal command to guard against covetousness—longing for something we don't have. See "Watch Out for Greed!" Luke 12:15.

Paul knew firsthand the wealth and privileges of prominence in the Jewish community and of Roman citizenship. But he also suffered extraordinary hardships in the ministry. He survived both extremes. What was his secret? Find out at Phil. 4:10–13.

The Jerusalem Riots

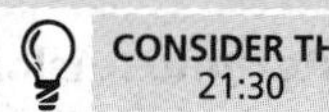

CONSIDER THIS 21:30

By the time Paul was seized (v. 30), many years had passed since the euphoric Pentecost and its aftermath recorded in Acts 2–4. Whatever had happened to the Jerusalem church with its aggressive outreach and bold confidence? Where was it when these events took place? Its silence—or absence—at that point is a reminder that to preach in a city is one thing; to occupy and transform it is quite another. Urbanscapes everywhere, ancient and modern, are marked by steeples over buildings where the city church used to be.

word came to the tribune of the cohort that all Jerusalem
was in an uproar. 32Immediately he took soldiers and centurions and ran down to them. When they saw the tribune
and the soldiers, they stopped beating Paul. 33Then the tribune came, arrested him, and ordered him to be bound
with two chains; he inquired who he was and what he had
done. 34Some in the crowd shouted one thing, some another; and as he could not learn the facts because of the uproar, he ordered him to be brought into the barracks.
35When Paul[k] came to the steps, the violence of the mob
was so great that he had to be carried by the soldiers. 36The
crowd that followed kept shouting, "Away with him!"

Paul Is Allowed to Address the People

37 Just as Paul was about to be brought into the barracks, he said to the tribune, "May I say something to you?"
The tribune[l] replied, "Do you know Greek? 38Then you are
not the Egyptian who recently stirred up a revolt and led
the four thousand assassins out into the wilderness?" 39Paul
replied, "I am a Jew, from Tarsus in Cilicia, a citizen of an
important city; I beg you, let me speak to the people."
40When he had given him permission, Paul stood on the
steps and motioned to the people for silence; and when
there was a great hush, he addressed them in the Hebrew[m]
language, saying:

[k]Gk *he* [l]Gk *He* [m]That is, *Aramaic*

Cos

YOU ARE THERE 21:1

- **A massive, mountainous Greek island just off the west coast of Asia Minor.**
- **Settled by the Greeks, but known to rebel against Greece and side with Rome, which returned the loyalty: Rome's client Herod the Great was the island's benefactor, and Emperor Claudius proclaimed it exempt from paying Roman taxes.**
- **Known for its healthy climate and hot springs; gained prominence as a health resort; traditional site for Greece's first school of medicine and home of the famous physician, Hippocrates; a shrine to Asclepius, god of healing, was built there.**
- **Excavations have located a stadium, a wall, and Roman baths dating to the time of Paul's journey.**
- **Known to modern Greeks as Kos, to Italians as Koo, and to Turks as Istanköy.**

Rhodes

- **Largest and easternmost island in the Aegean Sea, opposite the southwest coast of Asia Minor.**
- **Name may derive from *Rhodē* ("rose"), daughter of the Greek god Poseidon. But some believe it comes from *erod,* the Phoenician word for "snake"; one species of poisonous snakes still survives there.**
- **Important center of commerce, cultural works, and year-round tourism.**
- **Site of the Colossus of Rhodes, which had a symbolic role similar to that of the Statue of Liberty.**
- **Paul only stopped briefly at the island as he hastened to Jerusalem for Pentecost (Acts 21:1).**

(continued on next page)

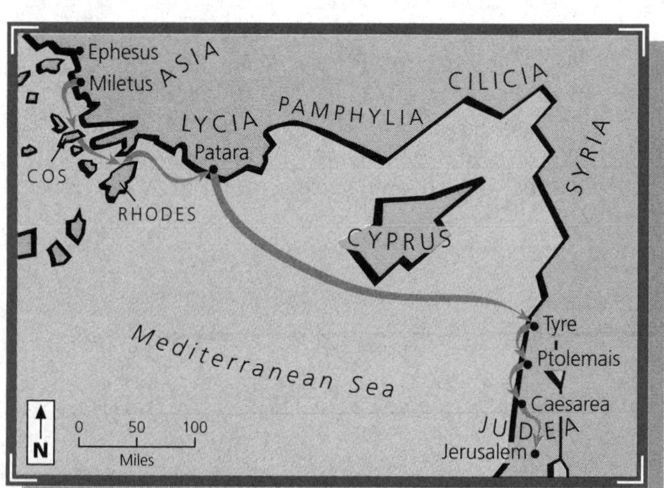

PAUL'S THIRD JOURNEY, PART FOUR

22 "Brothers and fathers, listen to the defense that I
now make before you."
2 When they heard him addressing them in Hebrew,[n]
they became even more quiet. Then he said:
3 "I am a Jew, born in Tarsus in Cilicia, but brought up
in this city at the feet of Gamaliel, educated strictly according to our ancestral law, being zealous for God, just as all of
you are today. 4I persecuted this Way up to the point of
death by binding both men and women and putting them
in prison, 5as the high priest and the whole council of elders can testify about me. From them I also received letters
to the brothers in Damascus, and I went there in order to
bind those who were there and to bring them back to
Jerusalem for punishment.
6 "While I was on my way and approaching Damascus,
about noon a great light from heaven suddenly shone about
me. 7I fell to the ground and heard a voice saying to me,
'Saul, Saul, why are you persecuting me?' 8I answered,
'Who are you, Lord?' Then he said to me, 'I am Jesus of
Nazareth[o] whom you are persecuting.' 9Now those who
were with me saw the light but did not hear the voice of the
one who was speaking to me. 10I asked, 'What am I to do,
Lord?' The Lord said to me, 'Get up and go to Damascus;
there you will be told everything that has been assigned to
you to do.' 11Since I could not see because of the brightness
of that light, those who were with me took my hand and
led me to Damascus.
12 "A certain Ananias, who was a devout man according
to the law and well spoken of by all the Jews living there,
13came to me; and standing beside me, he said, 'Brother
Saul, regain your sight!' In that very hour I regained my
sight and saw him. 14Then he said, 'The God of our ancestors has chosen you to know his will, to see the Righteous
One and to hear his own voice; 15for you will be his witness
to all the world of what you have seen and heard. 16And
now why do you delay? Get up, be baptized, and have your
sins washed away, calling on his name.'
17 "After I had returned to Jerusalem and while I was
praying in the temple, I fell into a trance 18and saw Jesus[p]
saying to me, 'Hurry and get out of Jerusalem quickly, because they will not accept your testimony about me.' 19And
I said, 'Lord, they themselves know that in every synagogue
I imprisoned and beat those who believed in you. 20And
while the blood of your witness Stephen was shed, I myself
was standing by, approving and keeping the coats of those

[n]That is, *Aramaic* [o]Gk *the Nazorean* [p]Gk *him*

(continued from previous page)

PATARA

- **One of the largest and most prosperous cities of Lycia, a rugged coastal area of southwest Asia Minor shut off from the interior by 10,000-foot mountains.**
- **Freed by the Greeks from Persia in 546 B.C., the Lycians adopted Greek ways and language.**
- **With its excellent harbor, Patara enjoyed commercial success as an overhaul and crossover point, with favorable trade winds for ships venturing across the Mediterranean. It became one of the largest cities in the Lycian League, organized for mutual defense.**
- **Boasted a magnificent temple to Apollo, a prominent theater, an archway, and public baths.**

PTOLEMAIS

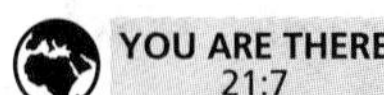

- **Seaport located in northern Palestine, 12 miles south of modern-day Lebanon and just across the bay from the port of Haifa.**
- **Originally Accho, but renamed Ptolemais by Ptolemy I, ruler of Egypt (323-285 B.C.) and descendant of one of Alexander's generals.**
- **The only natural harbor on the eastern Mediterranean coast south of Phoenicia in ancient times.**
- **Likely one of the 20 cities given by King Solomon to Hiram of Tyre in exchange for building materials for the temple (1 Kin. 9:11–14).**
- **A retirement town for veterans under Emperor Claudius' administration, who declared Ptolemais a colony of Rome.**

Faith and Rights

CONSIDER THIS 22:25–29 **"Human rights" is not a new concept. Nearly every social structure has at least some rules to protect its members.**

As a Roman commander arrested Paul and ordered that he be beaten, Paul used his Roman citizenship to protect his rights (vv. 25–29). He had done the same thing at Philippi after being illegally jailed (16:36–40). In Jerusalem, he insisted on due process rather than endure unjust mob retaliation. He set the record straight so that the authorities could intervene appropriately.

Rumor, anger, or distortion regarding the faith need to be met forthrightly, as Paul's example shows. There's no need to allow discrimination to hinder one's practice of Christianity in society, particularly in one's workplace. As believers we need a clear understanding of the laws and rules and their application, and ensure that they are applied fairly on behalf of everyone—including ourselves.

who killed him.' 21Then he said to me, 'Go, for I will send
you far away to the Gentiles.' "
22 Up to this point they listened to him, but then they
shouted, "Away with such a fellow from the earth! For he
should not be allowed to live." 23And while they were
shouting, throwing off their cloaks, and tossing dust into
the air, 24the tribune directed that he was to be brought into
the barracks, and ordered him to be examined by flogging,
22:25–29 to find out the reason for this outcry
against him. 25But when they had tied
him up with thongs,[q] Paul said to the centurion who was
standing by, "Is it legal for you to flog a Roman citizen who
is uncondemned?" 26When the centurion heard that, he
went to the tribune and said to him, "What are you about
to do? This man is a Roman citizen." 27The tribune came
and asked Paul,[r] "Tell me, are you a Roman citizen?" And
he said, "Yes." 28The tribune answered, "It cost me a large
sum of money to get my citizenship." Paul said, "But I was
born a citizen." 29Immediately those who were about to examine him drew back from him; and the tribune also was
afraid, for he realized that Paul was a Roman citizen and
that he had bound him.

Paul Brought before the Jewish Leaders

30 Since he wanted to find out what Paul[s] was being accused of by the Jews, the next day he released him and ordered the chief priests and the entire council to meet. He
brought Paul down and had him stand before them.
23:1 23 While Paul was looking intently
at the council he said, "Brothers,[t]
up to this day I have lived my life with a clear conscience
23:2 before God." 2Then the high priest Ana-
nias ordered those standing near him to
strike him on the mouth. 3At this Paul said to him, "God
will strike you, you whitewashed wall! Are you sitting there
to judge me according to the law, and yet in violation of the
law you order me to be struck?" 4Those standing nearby
23:5 see pg. 512 said, "Do you dare to insult God's high
priest?" 5And Paul said, "I did not realize,
brothers, that he was high priest; for it is written, 'You shall
not speak evil of a leader of your people.' "
6 When Paul noticed that some were Sadducees and
others were Pharisees, he called out in the council,
"Brothers, I am a Pharisee, a son of Pharisees. I am on trial

[q]Or *up for the lashes* [r]Gk *him* [s]Gk *he* [t]Gk *Men, brothers*

concerning the hope of the resurrection[u] of the dead."
7When he said this, a dissension began between the Pharisees and the Sadducees, and the assembly was divided.
8(The Sadducees say that there is no resurrection, or angel,
or spirit; but the Pharisees acknowledge all three.) 9Then a
great clamor arose, and certain scribes of the Pharisees'
group stood up and contended, "We find nothing wrong
with this man. What if a spirit or an angel has spoken to
him?" 10When the dissension became violent, the tribune,
fearing that they would tear Paul to pieces, ordered the soldiers to go down, take him by force, and bring him into the
barracks.
11 That night the Lord stood near him and said, "Keep

[u]Gk *concerning hope and resurrection*

Personality Profile: Ananias the High Priest

FOR YOUR INFO 23:2 **Not to be confused with:** Ananias, the liar (Acts 5:1); Ananias, the disciple who befriended Saul (9:10–19).

Home: Jerusalem.

Occupation: High priest and head of the Jewish council, making him the most powerful Hebrew official in Palestine.

Known to be: Greedy, open to bribes and extortion, and a collaborator with Rome. He was assassinated possibly by Zealots in A.D. 66 or 67 for his pro-Roman activities.

Best known today as: The high priest before whom Paul appeared following his arrest after returning to Jerusalem in about A.D. 58.

As the ranking member of the Jewish council, Ananias enjoyed many powers. See "Stephen's Trial and Murder," Acts 6:12.

Free to Be Bold

CONSIDER THIS 23:1 **The foundation of a believer's witness must be honesty. If we can be open with God about our own sinfulness (Ps. 51) and our continuing struggle with sin (Rom. 7:14—8:1), we won't be prone to mislead others about sin and faith. God knows we aren't sinless and He calls us to be honest (1 John 1:8).**

As Paul stood before the hostile Jewish council, he could honestly declare that he had a clear conscience (Acts 23:1). He said the same thing later when he and his accusers appeared before Governor Felix (24:16). That gave him tremendous freedom and boldness, even though his powerful opponents were hostile and wrong.

Honesty and a clear conscience are not the same as perfection. Paul was by no means perfect, just honest about his failures. He apologized, for example, after lashing out in anger (23:5). But he was real. He didn't cover up in an attempt to look good as a Christian witness.

Jesus does not ask us to project an impossibly perfect image. That would be a lie. Instead, He challenges us to admit our failures. He also delights in forgiving us when we do (Mark 11:25). If we can be honest about ourselves with others, it can give them hope for their own failings and turn them toward our gracious God.

up your courage! For just as you have testified for me in
Jerusalem, so you must bear witness also in Rome."

A Murder Plot Is Uncovered

12 In the morning the Jews joined in a conspiracy and
bound themselves by an oath neither to eat nor drink until
they had killed Paul. 13There were more than forty who
joined in this conspiracy. 14They went to the chief priests
and elders and said, "We have strictly bound ourselves by
an oath to taste no food until we have killed Paul. 15Now
then, you and the council must notify the tribune to bring
him down to you, on the pretext that you want to make a
more thorough examination of his case. And we are ready
to do away with him before he arrives."

16 Now the son of Paul's sister heard about the ambush;
so he went and gained entrance to the barracks and told
Paul. 17Paul called one of the centurions and said, "Take
this young man to the tribune, for he has something to report to him." 18So he took him, brought him to the tribune,
and said, "The prisoner Paul called me and asked me to
bring this young man to you; he has something to tell you."
19The tribune took him by the hand, drew him aside privately, and asked, "What is it that you have to report to
me?" 20He answered, "The Jews have agreed to ask you to
bring Paul down to the council tomorrow, as though they
were going to inquire more thoroughly into his case. 21But
do not be persuaded by them, for more than forty of their
men are lying in ambush for him. They have bound themselves by an oath neither to eat nor drink until they kill
him. They are ready now and are waiting for your consent."
22So the tribune dismissed the young man, ordering him,
"Tell no one that you have informed me of this."

23 Then he summoned two of the centurions and said,
"Get ready to leave by nine o'clock tonight for Caesarea
with two hundred soldiers, seventy horsemen, and two

23:24

hundred spearmen. 24Also provide
mounts for Paul to ride, and take him
safely to Felix the governor." 25He wrote a letter to this effect:

26 "Claudius Lysias to his Excellency the governor Felix,
greetings. 27This man was seized by the Jews and was about

Paul Apologized for Losing His Cool

CONSIDER THIS 23:5 *Attacked in a humiliating and unjust way, Paul lashed out in anger (vv. 1–4). But when told that he had unknowingly insulted the high priest, he apologized (v. 5).*

Paul's example forces us to ask: Would you be willing to apologize for losing your cool, even if your opponent were attacking you and your values?

to be killed by them, but when I had learned that he was a
Roman citizen, I came with the guard and rescued him.
28Since I wanted to know the charge for which they accused him, I had him brought to their council. 29I found
that he was accused concerning questions of their law, but
was charged with nothing deserving death or imprisonment. 30When I was informed that there would be a plot
against the man, I sent him to you at once, ordering his accusers also to state before you what they have against
him.[v]"

[v]Other ancient authorities add *Farewell*

Personality Profile: Felix

FOR YOUR INFO 23:24

Name means: "Happy."

Home: Caesarea, administrative center of Roman rule in Palestine.

Family: Married Drusilla, his third wife, youngest daughter of Herod Agrippa I (see "The Herods," 12:1–2).

Background: A Greek; a favorite of Emperor Claudius, who made him a freedman, and also of Emperor Nero.

Occupation: Procurator (governor) of Judea (A.D. 52–59).

Known for: Ruling with impunity because of his influence over the courts, until he was recalled by Nero; when Paul was brought before him, he tried to collect a bribe; others described him as heavy-handed, a procrastinator, and given to reveling in cruelty and lust, exercising "the powers of a king with the outlook of a slave."

Best known today for: Giving Paul a fair trial and keeping him in protective custody with liberal visitation rights.

Antipatris

YOU ARE THERE 23:31

- **Border town between Judea and Samaria, 25 miles south of Caesarea along a military road from Jerusalem.**
- **Former Canaanite city of Aphek (meaning "fortress"), rebuilt and renamed in the decade before Christ by Herod the Great, king of Judea, as a military outpost in honor of his father Antipater.**
- **Modern Ras el-`Ain, near present-day Petah Tiqwa, Israel. The tell (mound) of the former city is now one of the largest archaeological sites in the country.**

This city was connected to the infamous Herod family. See Acts 12:1–2.

23:31 see pg. 513

31 So the soldiers, according to their
instructions, took Paul and brought him
during the night to Antipatris. 32The next day they let the
horsemen go on with him, while they returned to the barracks. 33When they came to Caesarea and delivered the letter to the governor, they presented Paul also before him.
34On reading the letter, he asked what province he belonged to, and when he learned that he was from Cilicia,
35he said, "I will give you a hearing when your accusers arrive." Then he ordered that he be kept under guard in
Herod's headquarters.[w]

Paul Faces Felix the Governor

24:1–26

24 Five days later the high priest
Ananias came down with some
elders and an attorney, a certain Tertullus, and they reported their case against Paul to the governor. 2When Paul[x]
had been summoned, Tertullus began to accuse him, saying:
"Your Excellency,[y] because of you we have long enjoyed
peace, and reforms have been made for this people because

[w]Gk *praetorium* [x]Gk *he* [y]Gk lacks *Your Excellency*

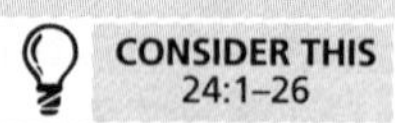

CONSIDER THIS
24:1–26

Truth Can Trigger Opposition

Caring for others, speaking the truth, and living with integrity are not always rewarded in this broken world. God's grace often exposes the sin and guilt of people, sometimes triggering hostility. Believers can become a convenient target of anger.

Paul experienced that from the Jewish leaders in Jerusalem (vv. 1–26). Notice the varied forms of opposition they mobilized against him before Felix:

(1) They enlisted a skilled orator, Tertullus, who flattered the governor as he represented them in their case against Paul (vv. 1–3).

(2) They trumped up a variety of accusations that amounted to little more than name-calling (vv. 5–6). On a previous occasion, Jason of Thessalonica had experienced similar treatment for merely entertaining Paul and his team (17:5–9).

(3) They arrested Paul, and though they accused commander Lysias of violence, it was they who had been on the verge of a riot (23:7–10; 24:6–7).

of your foresight. 3We welcome this in every way and
everywhere with utmost gratitude. 4But, to detain you no
further, I beg you to hear us briefly with your customary
graciousness. 5We have, in fact, found this man a pestilent
fellow, an agitator among all the Jews throughout the
world, and a ringleader of the sect of the Nazarenes.[z] 6He
even tried to profane the temple, and so we seized him.[a]
8By examining him yourself you will be able to learn from
him concerning everything of which we accuse him."
9 The Jews also joined in the charge by asserting that all
this was true.
10 When the governor motioned to him to speak, Paul
replied:
"I cheerfully make my defense, knowing that for many
years you have been a judge over this nation. 11As you can
find out, it is not more than twelve days since I went up to
worship in Jerusalem. 12They did not find me disputing
with anyone in the temple or stirring up a crowd either in
the synagogues or throughout the city. 13Neither can they
prove to you the charge that they now bring against me.
14But this I admit to you, that according to the Way, which

[z]Gk *Nazoreans* [a]Other ancient authorities add *and we would have judged him according to our law. 7But the chief captain Lysias came and with great violence took him out of our hands, 8commanding his accusers to come before you.*

(4) They engineered the testimony of others against him (v. 9).

(5) They apparently played politics with Felix, who was obviously used to settling disputes through bribes and other deals (v. 26; 25:9).

Recognizing this pattern can help us to avoid the mistake of personalizing all attacks on our faith. These are more often rooted in our opponents' sense of guilt or fear of judgment than in any justified assessment of our character or conduct. ◆

QUOTE UNQUOTE

CONSIDER THIS 24:22 *Felix was "rather well informed about the Way" (v. 22). Yet his knowledge did not lead to faith. So it is with many people:*

My non-Christian friends and acquaintances are zealous in what they "know" about Christianity, and which bears little or no relationship to anything I believe.

A friend of mine . . . writes about taking her brain-damaged child to a Jewish doctor. He said, "You people think of us as the people who killed your Christ." Spontaneously she replied, "Oh, no. We think of you as the people who gave him to us."

Madeleine L'Engle, *Walking On Water*, pp. 47–48

they call a sect, I worship the God of our ancestors, believing everything laid down according to the law or written in the prophets. 15I have a hope in God—a hope that they themselves also accept—that there will be a resurrection of both[b] the righteous and the unrighteous. 16Therefore I do my best always to have a clear conscience toward God and all people. 17Now after some years I came to bring alms to my nation and to offer sacrifices. 18While I was doing this, they found me in the temple, completing the rite of purification, without any crowd or disturbance. 19But there were some Jews from Asia—they ought to be here before you to make an accusation, if they have anything against me. 20Or let these men here tell what crime they had found when I stood before the council, 21unless it was this one sentence that I called out while standing before them, 'It is about the resurrection of the dead that I am on trial before you today.' "

24:22 see pg. 515

22 But Felix, who was rather well informed about the Way, adjourned the hearing with the comment, "When Lysias the tribune comes down, I will decide your case." 23Then he ordered the centurion to keep him in custody, but to let him have some liberty and not to prevent any of his friends from taking care of his needs.

24 Some days later when Felix came with his wife Drusilla, who was Jewish, he sent for Paul and heard him speak concerning faith in Christ Jesus. 25And as he discussed justice, self-control, and the coming judgment, Felix became frightened and said, "Go away for the present; when I have an opportunity, I will send for you." 26At the same time he hoped that money would be given him by Paul, and for that reason he used to send for him very often and converse with him.

24:25–26

Paul Faces Festus the Governor

27 After two years had passed, Felix was succeeded by Porcius Festus; and since he wanted to grant the Jews a favor, Felix left Paul in prison.

25:1

25:2

25 Three days after Festus had arrived in the province, he went up from Caesarea to Jerusalem 2where the chief priests and the leaders of the Jews gave him a report against Paul. They appealed to him 3and

Paul and the Structures of Power

CONSIDER THIS 24:25–26 *Chapters 23–25 make it plain that Paul was competent in and comfortable with the Roman judicial system and its procedures. He knew how to address Roman officials, respecting their position. At this point he obviously respected the political system. The state had not yet become the beast that John described in Revelation 13.*

The problems Paul did encounter were not with the system but with its leaders. He faced two politicians, one dealing in bribes (Acts 24:25–26), the other in political favors (25:9). Seeking justice, Paul got caught in the middle.

[b]Other ancient authorities read *of the dead, both of*

requested, as a favor to them against Paul,[c] to have him
transferred to Jerusalem. They were, in fact, planning an
ambush to kill him along the way. 4 Festus replied that Paul
was being kept at Caesarea, and that he himself intended to
go there shortly. 5 "So," he said, "let those of you who have
the authority come down with me, and if there is anything
wrong about the man, let them accuse him."

6 After he had stayed among them not more than eight
or ten days, he went down to Caesarea; the next day he
took his seat on the tribunal and ordered Paul to be
brought. 7 When he arrived, the Jews who had gone down
from Jerusalem surrounded him, bringing many serious
charges against him, which they could not prove. 8 Paul said
in his defense, "I have in no way committed an offense
against the law of the Jews, or against the temple, or against
the emperor." 9 But Festus, wishing to do the Jews a favor,
asked Paul, "Do you wish to go up to Jerusalem and be
tried there before me on these charges?" 10 Paul said, "I am
appealing to the emperor's tribunal; this is where I should
be tried. I have done no wrong to the Jews, as you very well
know. 11 Now if I am in the wrong and have committed
something for which I deserve to die, I am not trying to escape death; but if there is nothing to their charges against
me, no one can turn me over to them. I appeal to the emperor." 12 Then Festus, after he had conferred with his council, replied, "You
have appealed to the emperor; to the emperor you will go."

25:12 see pg. 518

[c] Gk *him*

Personality Profile: Festus

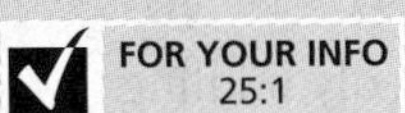

Home: Caesarea.

Occupation: Successor to Felix as governor of Judea (A.D. 59–61; see Acts 24:27).

Best known today for: Insisting that Jewish leaders meet with Paul in Caesarea, where the apostle was protected, thereby foiling a plot to kill him. Later, though, Festus suggested a retrial in Jerusalem as a favor to the Jews.

Caught Between a Novice and the Establishment

CONSIDER THIS 25:2

Paul found himself caught between Festus (v. 1), a brand new local governor appointed by the Romans (24:27), and the well-established Jewish council, the supreme court of the Hebrews (25:2; see "Stephen's Trial and Murder," Acts 6:12). The council could easily have outwitted the new official—at Paul's expense and to their own gain—if the case had been moved to their home turf in Jerusalem (25:9). So Paul appealed to a higher court, Caesar, to regain a balance of power (v. 11).

In doing so, Paul exercised his rights as a Roman citizen (see "Faith and Rights," 22:25–29). At the time of Acts 25, the reigning Caesar was Nero. He had not yet begun to persecute the Christians, as he did later in A.D. 64 (see 25:12).

In light of Paul's example here, it's worth asking: Do you know the proper routes of appeal in your workplace and community?

King Agrippa and Bernice Arrive

 25:13

 25:13–22

13 After several days had passed, King
Agrippa and Bernice arrived at Caesarea
to welcome Festus. [14]Since they were
staying there several days, Festus laid

Agrippa

A CLOSER LOOK 25:13 *King Agrippa came from a long and infamous line of royalty. See "The Herods," Acts 12:1–2.*

A Timely Diplomatic Visit

 FOR YOUR INFO 25:13–22

The visit of King Agrippa and Bernice to Caesarea proved timely (v. 13). As a new, relatively inexperienced Roman governor of Judea, Festus faced a delicate religious conflict between the Jews, led by their council, and the growing Christian movement, represented by Paul. Just as Festus began to rule on the case, Agrippa and Bernice arrived. Festus, the Jews, and Paul all benefited from the couple's expertise in Jewish history and affairs (v. 23; 26:3). The brother and sister had watched their father govern Judea and its population for several years before Agrippa inherited the office himself (see "The Herods," Acts 12:1–2, and "Families of the Early Church," Acts 16:31–34).

Personality Profile: Nero

 FOR YOUR INFO 25:12

Home: Rome.

Family: Son of an insanely controlling mother, Agrippina, who became Emperor Claudius' fourth wife; great-great-grandson of Augustus; raised and tortured by his menacing, mentally deranged uncle, Caligula. The family history bristled with incest, physical abuse, and political conspiracy.

Profession: Emperor of Rome (A.D. 54–68). Though noble in his youth, he made himself out to be a new god. He was the emperor to whom Paul appealed for justice (Acts 25:9–11).

Reputation: Ascetic and maniacal in his devotion to music and the gods, especially during a 15-month arts tour in Greece; capricious as a ruler: he signed countless death warrants, yet once banned capital punishment; he laughed at revolts brewing in the empire; early Christians regarded him as the Antichrist; he died by suicide.

Best known today for: Supposedly fiddling while Rome burned (he was 35 miles away from Rome at his villa at Antium) and for persecuting Christians.

Find out about the other major political leaders of the Roman Empire and Palestine in the first century at "New Testament Political Rulers," Luke 3:1.

Paul's case before the king, saying, "There is a man here
who was left in prison by Felix. 15When I was in Jerusalem,
the chief priests and the elders of the Jews informed me
about him and asked for a sentence against him. 16I told
them that it was not the custom of the Romans to hand
over anyone before the accused had met the accusers face
to face and had been given an opportunity to make a defense against the charge. 17So when they met here, I lost no
time, but on the next day took my seat on the tribunal and
ordered the man to be brought. 18When the accusers stood
up, they did not charge him with any of the crimes[d] that I
was expecting. 19Instead they had certain points of disagreement with him about their own religion and about a
certain Jesus, who had died, but whom Paul asserted to be
alive. 20Since I was at a loss how to investigate these questions, I asked whether he wished to go to Jerusalem and be
tried there on these charges.[e] 21But when Paul had appealed
to be kept in custody for the decision of his Imperial
Majesty, I ordered him to be held until I could send him to
the emperor." 22Agrippa said to Festus, "I would like to
hear the man myself." "Tomorrow," he said, "you will hear
him."

23 So on the next day Agrippa and Bernice came with
great pomp, and they entered the audience hall with the
military tribunes and the prominent men of the city. Then
Festus gave the order and Paul was brought in. 24And Festus said, "King Agrippa and all here present with us, you
see this man about whom the whole Jewish community petitioned me, both in Jerusalem and here, shouting that he
ought not to live any longer. 25But I found that he had done
nothing deserving death; and when he appealed to his Imperial Majesty, I decided to send him. 26But I have nothing
definite to write to our sovereign about him. Therefore I
have brought him before all of you, and especially before
you, King Agrippa, so that, after we have examined him, I
may have something to write— 27for it seems to me unrea-
sonable to send a prisoner without indicating the charges
against him."

26:1–32
see pg. 520

26 Agrippa said to Paul, "You have
permission to speak for your-
self." Then Paul stretched out his hand and began to defend
himself:

2 "I consider myself fortunate that it is before you, King
Agrippa, I am to make my defense today against all the accusations of the Jews, 3because you are especially familiar

(Bible text continued on page 521)

"KING AGRIPPA, I AM TO MAKE MY DEFENSE TODAY. . . ."
—Acts 26:2

[d]Other ancient authorities read *with anything* [e]Gk *on them*

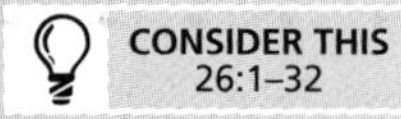

AUDIENCE-SHAPED MESSAGES

As a Christian, do you know how to communicate the message of Christ to the different audiences you encounter? Or do you use the same old formula time after time, no matter who is listening? For that matter, do you remain silent when you have the opportunity to speak up for Christ, because you simply don't know what to say?

Paul had no prepackaged gospel message. He varied his approach with the situation. He was as aware of the differences between his audiences as he was of the content of his faith. Acts records numerous encounters, among them:

(1) Jews in the synagogue at Antioch of Pisidia (Acts 13:14–43).

- Paul reviewed the history of the Jewish faith, summarizing it from the Old Testament (vv. 17–22).
- He told how that history led to Jesus (vv. 23–37).
- He pointed out his audience's need to accept Jesus as their Messiah (vv. 38–41).
- He responded to their resistance by clearly explaining the alternative (vv. 46–48).

Result:

- Many chose to follow the way of Christ (v. 43).
- Others reacted negatively and opposed Paul (v. 45).
- Troublemakers incited city leaders to persecute Paul and his companions (v. 50).

(2) Intellectuals at Athens (17:16–33).

- Paul prepared by observing and reflecting on their culture (v. 16).
- He addressed them on their own turf, the Areopagus (vv. 19, 22).
- He established common ground, beginning with what was familiar and meaningful to them (vv. 22–23a, 28).
- He bridged to a description of God as the Creator and sustainer of life, distinguishing Him from the pagan idols that the Athenians worshiped (vv. 23b-29).
- He challenged them to repentance and appealed to the resurrection of Christ as proof that what he was telling them was true (vv. 30–31).

Result:

- Some mocked (v. 32).
- Some wanted to hear more (v. 32).
- Some believed (v. 34–35).

(3) An angry mob in Jerusalem (21:27—22:21).

- Paul built a bridge by reminding them of his own Jewish heritage (21:30).
- He reminded them that he, too, had once detested Jesus' followers; in fact, he had persecuted them (22:4–5).
- He explained the process by which he had changed his mind and joined a movement that he once opposed (vv. 6–17).

Result:

- Already at fever pitch (21:27–30), the crowd erupted violently, demanding Paul's death (22:22–23).

(4) High officials in a Roman court (26:1–32).

- Paul described his religious heritage (vv. 4–5).
- He related his view of his opponents' charges against him (vv. 6–8).
- He recalled his previous opposition to Jesus' followers (vv. 9–11).
- He recounted his own life-changing encounter with Christ (vv. 12–19).

(continued on next page)

with all the customs and controversies of the Jews; therefore I beg of you to listen to me patiently.
4 "All the Jews know my way of life from my youth, a
life spent from the beginning among my own people and in
Jerusalem. 5They have known for a long time, if they are
willing to testify, that I have belonged to the strictest sect of
our religion and lived as a Pharisee. 6And now I stand here
on trial on account of my hope in the promise made by
God to our ancestors, 7a promise that our twelve tribes
hope to attain, as they earnestly worship day and night. It is
for this hope, your Excellency,[f] that I am accused by Jews!
8Why is it thought incredible by any of you that God raises
the dead?
9 "Indeed, I myself was convinced that I ought to do
many things against the name of Jesus of Nazareth.[g] 10And
that is what I did in Jerusalem; with authority received
from the chief priests, I not only locked up many of the
saints in prison, but I also cast my vote against them when
they were being condemned to death. 11By punishing them
often in all the synagogues I tried to force them to blaspheme; and since I was so furiously enraged at them, I pursued them even to foreign cities.
12 "With this in mind, I was traveling to Damascus with
the authority and commission of the chief priests, 13when at
midday along the road, your Excellency,[f] I saw a light from
heaven, brighter than the sun, shining around me and my
companions. 14When we had all fallen to the ground, I
heard a voice saying to me in the Hebrew[h] language, 'Saul,
Saul, why are you persecuting me? It hurts you to kick
against the goads.' 15I asked, 'Who are you, Lord?' The Lord
answered, 'I am Jesus whom you are persecuting. 16But get
up and stand on your feet; for I have appeared to you for
this purpose, to appoint you to serve and testify to the
things in which you have seen me[i] and to those in which I
will appear to you. 17I will rescue you from your people
and from the Gentiles—to whom I am sending you 18to
open their eyes so that they may turn from darkness to
light and from the power of Satan to God, so that they may
receive forgiveness of sins and a place among those who are
sanctified by faith in me.'
19 "After that, King Agrippa, I was not disobedient to
the heavenly vision, 20but declared first to those in Damascus, then in Jerusalem and throughout the countryside of
Judea, and also to the Gentiles, that they should repent and
turn to God and do deeds consistent with repentance. 21For
this reason the Jews seized me in the temple and tried to
kill me. 22To this day I have had help from God, and so I

[f]Gk *O king* [g]Gk *the Nazorean* [h]That is, *Aramaic* [i]Other ancient authorities read *the things that you have seen*

(continued from previous page)

- He explained the fundamentals of Jesus' message and the implications for his Gentile listeners (vv. 20–23).

Result:

- The rulers listened carefully (vv. 24, 31–32).
- They challenged his application of the gospel to them (vv. 24, 28).
- They passed him on in the Roman judicial process, thereby foiling a Jewish plot against him (vv. 31–32).

The gospel itself is forever the same, but as Christ's followers we are called to shape our message to fit our various audiences. How do your coworkers and friends differ from each other? What effect should that have on your life and message for them? What aspects of the good news would they most likely respond to? Do you know how they view faith? Why not ask them—before you speak? ◆

We can learn a lot about how to communicate the message of Christ by studying carefully how Jesus Himself interacted with people. The four Gospels record more than 40 meetings between Him and various individuals. See "Witnessing—Jesus' Style," Luke 24:48.

stand here, testifying to both small and great, saying nothing but what the prophets and Moses said would take
place: 23that the Messiah[j] must suffer, and that, by being the
first to rise from the dead, he would proclaim light both to
our people and to the Gentiles."
24 While he was making this defense, Festus exclaimed,
"You are out of your mind, Paul! Too much learning is
driving you insane!" 25But Paul said, "I am not out of my
mind, most excellent Festus, but I am speaking the sober
truth. 26Indeed the king knows about these things, and to
him I speak freely; for I am certain that none of these things
has escaped his notice, for this was not done in a corner.
27King Agrippa, do you believe the prophets? I know that
you believe." 28Agrippa said to Paul, "Are you so quickly
persuading me to become a Christian?"[k] 29Paul replied,
"Whether quickly or not, I pray to God that not only you
but also all who are listening to me today might become
such as I am—except for these chains."
30 Then the king got up, and with him the governor and
Bernice and those who had been seated with them; 31and as
they were leaving, they said to one another, "This man is
doing nothing to deserve death or imprisonment."
32Agrippa said to Festus, "This man could have been set
free if he had not appealed to the emperor."

Shipwreck on the Way to Rome

27 When it was decided that we were to sail for Italy,
they transferred Paul and some other prisoners to a

[j] Or *the Christ* [k] Or *Quickly you will persuade me to play the Christian*

Myra

YOU ARE THERE 27:5

- **Port city in the southwest corner of present-day Turkey, on the mouth of Andriacus River, about two miles from the Mediterranean Sea.**
- **Capital of Lycia and a leading city in the Lycean confederation.**
- **Now called Demre by the Turks.**
- **The Alexandrian vessel for which Paul and the party waited (Acts 27:6) was the largest type of ship available in that day, renowned for its seaworthiness.**
- **St. Nicholas—from whom we get the name Santa Claus—was born in nearby Patara and was the city's bishop under Constantine (fourth century A.D.). Legendary miracles have Nicholas appearing to save children and sailors from tragedy; devotion spread rapidly and widely, and he became the patron saint of Greece and Russia, of numerous fraternities and workers' guilds, and of Christmas.**

Fair Havens and Lasea

YOU ARE THERE 27:8

- **Fair Havens was a small bay on the south coast of Crete; Lasea was five miles inland.**
- **One of the more important harbors in the ancient world, according to first-century historian Pliny the Elder. But since the port was separated by five miles from the town, it was unsuitable for wintering.**

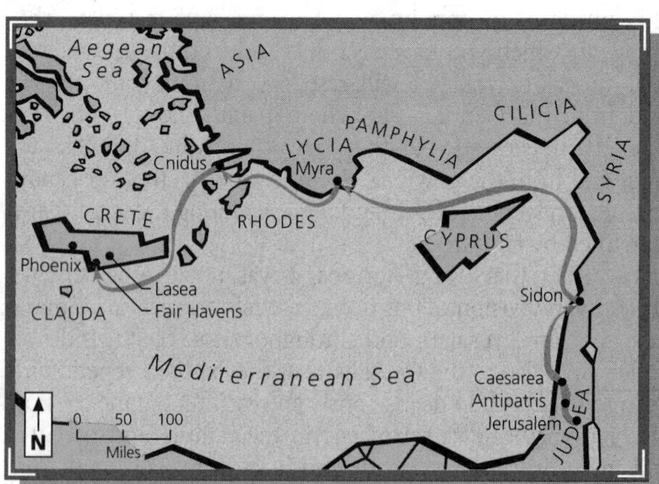

PAUL'S JOURNEY TO ROME, PART ONE

centurion of the Augustan Cohort, named Julius. 2Embark-
ing on a ship of Adramyttium that was about to set sail to
the ports along the coast of Asia, we put to sea, accompanied by Aristarchus, a Macedonian from Thessalonica. 3The
next day we put in at Sidon; and Julius treated Paul kindly,
and allowed him to go to his friends to be cared for.
4Putting out to sea from there, we sailed under the lee of
27:5 Cyprus, because the winds were against
us. 5After we had sailed across the sea
that is off Cilicia and Pamphylia, we came to Myra in Lycia.
6There the centurion found an Alexandrian ship bound for
Italy and put us on board. 7We sailed slowly for a number
of days and arrived with difficulty off Cnidus, and as the
wind was against us, we sailed under the lee of Crete off
27:8 Salmone. 8Sailing past it with difficulty,
we came to a place called Fair Havens,
near the city of Lasea.
27:9–11 9 Since much time had been lost and
sailing was now dangerous, because even
the Fast had already gone by, Paul advised them, 10saying,
"Sirs, I can see that the voyage will be with danger and
much heavy loss, not only of the cargo and the ship, but
also of our lives." 11But the centurion paid more attention
to the pilot and to the owner of the ship than to what Paul
said. 12Since the harbor was not suitable for spending the
winter, the majority was in favor of putting to sea from
there, on the chance that somehow they could reach
Phoenix, where they could spend the winter. It was a harbor of Crete, facing southwest and northwest.
13 When a moderate south wind began to blow, they
thought they could achieve their purpose; so they weighed
anchor and began to sail past Crete, close to the shore.
14But soon a violent wind, called the northeaster, rushed
down from Crete.[l] 15Since the ship was caught and could
not be turned head-on into the wind, we gave way to it and
were driven. 16By running under the lee of a small island
called Cauda[m] we were scarcely able to get the ship's boat
under control. 17After hoisting it up they took measures[n] to
undergird the ship; then, fearing that they would run on
the Syrtis, they lowered the sea anchor and so were driven.
18We were being pounded by the storm so violently that on
the next day they began to throw the cargo overboard,
19and on the third day with their own hands they threw the
ship's tackle overboard. 20When neither sun nor stars appeared for many days, and no small tempest raged, all hope
of our being saved was at last abandoned.

[l]Gk *it* [m]Other ancient authorities read *Claude* [n]Gk *helps*

"It Serves Them Right!"

CONSIDER THIS 27:9–11 **Paul's willingness to speak up (v. 10) is remarkable in that he was on his way to prison and had no need to warn anybody of anything. Nor did he have any control over the situation. Of course, he knew that God could preserve him from any and all dangers. Yet he reached out beyond his own interests and safety and spoke up for the safety of others.**

Is that your perspective, especially when things don't go your way? Or do you keep your mouth shut with the attitude . . .

- **"It serves them right!"**
- **"They won't pay attention anyway."**
- **"Let them stew in their own juices."**
- **"Why should I say anything? My boss doesn't listen anyway. It won't make any difference."**
- **"If they want to play that sort of game, I can, too."**
- **"I'll be out of here in a few weeks anyway."**
- **"She doesn't care about me. Why should I care about what happens to her?"**
- **"He made his bed, now let him lie in it."**

21 Since they had been without food for a long time,
Paul then stood up among them and said, "Men, you
should have listened to me and not have set sail from Crete
and thereby avoided this damage and loss. 22I urge you
now to keep up your courage, for there will be no loss of
life among you, but only of the ship. 23For last night there
stood by me an angel of the God to whom I belong and
whom I worship, 24and he said, 'Do not be afraid, Paul; you
must stand before the emperor; and indeed, God has
granted safety to all those who are sailing with you.' 25So
keep up your courage, men, for I have faith in God that it
will be exactly as I have been told. 26But we will have to
run aground on some island."

27 When the fourteenth night had come, as we were
drifting across the sea of Adria, about midnight the sailors
suspected that they were nearing land. 28So they took
soundings and found twenty fathoms; a little farther on
they took soundings again and found fifteen fathoms.
29Fearing that we might run on the rocks, they let down
four anchors from the stern and prayed for day to come.
30But when the sailors tried to escape from the ship and
had lowered the boat into the sea, on the pretext of putting
out anchors from the bow, 31Paul said to the centurion and
the soldiers, "Unless these men stay in the ship, you cannot
be saved." 32Then the soldiers cut away the ropes of the
boat and set it adrift.

33 Just before daybreak, Paul urged all of them to take
some food, saying, "Today is the fourteenth day that you
have been in suspense and remaining without food, having
eaten nothing. 34Therefore I urge you to take some food, for
it will help you survive; for none of you will lose a hair
from your heads." 35After he had said this, he took bread;
and giving thanks to God in the presence of all, he broke it
and began to eat. 36Then all of them were encouraged and
took food for themselves. 37(We were in all two hundred
seventy-six[o] persons in the ship.) 38After they had satisfied
their hunger, they lightened the ship by throwing the wheat
into the sea.

39 In the morning they did not recognize the land, but
they noticed a bay with a beach, on which they planned to
run the ship ashore, if they could. 40So they cast off the anchors and left them in the sea. At the same time they loos-
ened the ropes that tied the steering-oars; then hoisting the
foresail to the wind, they made for the beach. 41But striking
a reef,[p] they ran the ship aground; the bow stuck and remained immovable, but the stern was being broken up by
the force of the waves. 42The soldiers' plan was to kill the

[o]Other ancient authorities read *seventy-six;* others, *about seventy-six* [p]Gk *place of two seas*

PAUL AND PUBLIUS

CONSIDER THIS 28:7–10 *Paul's encounter with Publius (vv. 7–10) is reminiscent of Peter's meeting with Cornelius (Acts 10). It's interesting that Publius not only responded to the gospel, but also showed the castaways hospitality—something Christians have always valued. This is not uncommon: missionaries often receive from host cultures as much as they give. There is much to be learned from this passage about cross-cultural ministry.*

prisoners, so that none might swim away and escape; 43but
the centurion, wishing to save Paul, kept them from carrying out their plan. He ordered those who could swim to
jump overboard first and make for the land, 44and the rest
to follow, some on planks and others on pieces of the ship.
And so it was that all were brought safely to land.

A Friendly Exchange at Malta

28:1

28 After we had reached safety, we
then learned that the island was
called Malta. 2The natives showed us unusual kindness.
Since it had begun to rain and was cold, they kindled a fire
and welcomed all of us around it. 3Paul had gathered a
bundle of brushwood and was putting it on the fire, when a
viper, driven out by the heat, fastened itself on his hand.
4When the natives saw the creature hanging from his hand,
they said to one another, "This man must be a murderer;
though he has escaped from the sea, justice has not allowed
him to live." 5He, however, shook off the creature into the
fire and suffered no harm. 6They were expecting him to
swell up or drop dead, but after they had waited a long
time and saw that nothing unusual had happened to him,
they changed their minds and began to say that he was a
god.

28:7–10

7 Now in the neighborhood of that
place were lands belonging to the lead-
ing man of the island, named Publius, who received us and
entertained us hospitably for three days. 8It so happened
that the father of Publius lay sick in bed with fever and
dysentery. Paul visited him and cured him by praying and
putting his hands on him. 9After this happened, the rest of
the people on the island who had diseases also came and
were cured. 10They bestowed many honors on us, and
when we were about to sail, they put on board all the provisions we needed.

Paul Arrives at Rome

28:11–13 see pg. 529

11 Three months later we set sail on a
ship that had wintered at the island, an
Alexandrian ship with the Twin Brothers as its figurehead.
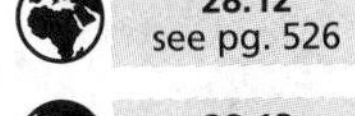
28:12 see pg. 526

12We put in at Syracuse and stayed there
for three days; 13then we weighed anchor
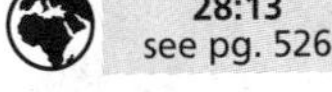
28:13 see pg. 526

and came to Rhegium. After one day
there a south wind sprang up, and on
the second day we came to Puteoli.
28:14–15

14There we found believers[q] and were

(Bible text continued on page 528)

[q]Gk *brothers*

JOY ON THE WAY TO JAIL

CONSIDER THIS 28:14–15

Jail seldom produces joy. The condemnation of society and the grim realities of incarceration bring many reactions, but rarely happy ones. However, when the cause is just (28:25–28), the conscience clear (23:1; 24:16; 26:19), and friends loyal (28:15), imprisonment can take on a new dimension.

As Paul neared the end of his journey to face trial, believers from Rome and its environs welcomed him along the Appian highway from Puteoli to Rome (28:13–15). He had written them three years before, describing his deep longing for them (Rom. 1:9–15; 15:22–29). Even his chains and the prospect of prison could not cloud the joy of connecting with those fellow-believers.

Can Christians today surprise their culture by offering to become true friends to those in jail?

MALTA

YOU ARE THERE 28:1

- **A tiny island grouping in the Mediterranean Sea about 60 miles south of Sicily.**
- **Probably also known as Melita.**
- **Its strategic location has placed Malta between several ancient and modern powers vying for control of the Mediterranean region.**

SYRACUSE

YOU ARE THERE 28:12

- City with a good harbor on the straits of Messina, between Sicily and Italy.
- Initially a Greek colony, the city overthrew its Athenian tyrants during the Peloponnesian War (415–413 B.C.). Syracuse and Carthage (in modern-day Tunisia) shared centuries of prominence as the key cities west of Greece.
- Captured by Rome in 212 B.C.; made into a Roman colony by Caesar Augustus.
- Described by Cicero as the "largest and loveliest of all Greek cities"; boasted impressive public buildings: a temple to Athena, a Greek theater, a large amphitheater, a marketplace flanked by a forum, town hall, senate house, and a temple to Jupiter. Christian catacombs have also been found dating to the third and fourth centuries A.D.
- Noted for shipbuilding and fishing; once boasted the world's best navy.

RHEGIUM

YOU ARE THERE 28:13

- Name means "breach."
- Port city near the Strait of Messina, a treacherous body of water off Sicily. With its shoals, shallows, and narrow width, the strait spelled shipwreck for centuries of sea captains, and was to be passed only under the most favorable of conditions. Ships frequently harbored at Rhegium until the weather or winds changed, contributing to the city's maritime prominence.
- Messina was reputed to be the site of the mythical Scylla, a sea monster dominating shoreline rocks, and Charybdis, a whirlpool large enough to devour entire ships.
- Modern Reggio, Italy.

PUTEOLI

- The best harbor in Italy, located on the Bay of Naples in southern Italy; a stopover for seagoing vehicles and cargo heading to and from Rome.
- The largest ships—including Alexandrian ships such as the one Paul embarked on (Acts 28:11)—could dock there.
- When Paul arrived, a sizable Christian community was already functioning.
- Modern Pozzuoli, Italy.

FORUM OF APPIUS AND THREE TAVERNS

YOU ARE THERE 28:15

- Appii Forum, or the marketplace of Appius, was a town 43 miles southeast of Rome on the Appian Way, an ancient road to the Adriatic Sea built by Appius Claudius.
- Three Taverns was located at a junction of the Appian Way and a road connecting Antium and Norba, 33 miles south of Rome.
- Travelers tended to frequent Three Taverns more than Appii Forum, as the latter was inhospitable, with marshes, gnats, and intolerable drinking water, along with innkeepers and merchants notorious for taking advantage of weary travelers.

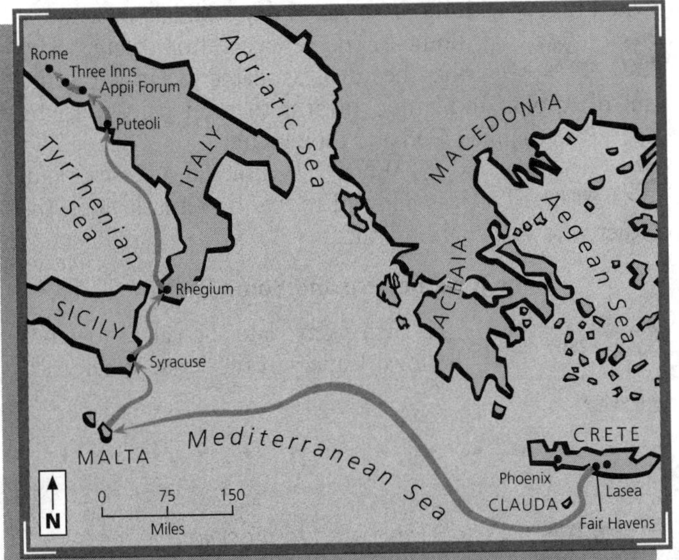

PAUL'S JOURNEY TO ROME, PART TWO

ALL ROADS LEAD TO ROME— AND BEYOND

CONSIDER THIS 28:28–31

Paul felt driven to get to Rome (Acts 19:21; Rom. 1:15), no doubt because it was the capital city. But he also intended to stop there on his way to Spain (Rom. 15:28).

Why was Spain significant? It's impossible to say exactly what Paul had in mind. But the Old Testament prophet Isaiah predicted that in the end times Gentiles would join Jews at Jerusalem to worship God, inaugurating a marvelous new era (Is. 66:19–24). Isaiah's text refers to "Tarshish," thought to mean Spain. Is it possible that Paul believed that getting the gospel to Rome meant being one step closer to the fulfillment of Isaiah's glorious vision (Acts 26:23; 28:28)?

We don't know whether Paul ever made it to Spain. He remained under house arrest in Rome until his trial before the emperor (Acts 28:16, 30–31). He may have been released, but tradition holds that he was eventually condemned and executed under Nero.

ROME

YOU ARE THERE 28:16

- **Political capital of the Roman Empire, which extended by the first century A.D. from the Atlantic Ocean to the Persian Gulf, and north Africa to Britain and northern Europe.**
- **Located on the Tiber river on seven hills, about 15 miles inland from the Tyrrhenian Sea.**
- **One of the two largest cities in the world in the first century (the other being Xian, China), with a population estimated at 1 million people, but declining to 50,000 by the sixth century due to numerous plagues, economic disasters, and a declining birth rate.**
- **A walled city of less than 25 square miles, it boasted the royal palace, ornate fountains, elaborate baths (some of which housed libraries and social clubs), the Circus Maximus, used for chariot racing and other games, and the 50,000-seat Coliseum. The Forum, where citizens engaged in political, religious, and commercial enterprises, was where Paul likely defended himself and the Christian movement.**
- **Some 82 temples were built or remodeled in the first half of the first century.**
- **Eventually became the center of the church in the West.**

When Paul arrived in Rome, he found a community of Christian believers already thriving there. *See the Introduction to Romans.*

invited to stay with them for seven days. And so we came to
28:15 see pg. 526 Rome. 15The believers[r] from there, when
they heard of us, came as far as the Fo-
rum of Appius and Three Taverns to meet us. On seeing
them, Paul thanked God and took courage.
28:16 see pg. 527 16 When we came into Rome, Paul
was allowed to live by himself, with the
soldier who was guarding him.

Some Jews Believe and Some Do Not

28:17–19 17 Three days later he called together
the local leaders of the Jews. When they

[r]*Gk brothers*

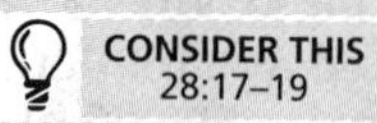

CONSIDER THIS
28:17–19

A Response to Rejection

As believers called to proclaim the message of Christ, our role is not to change people; that's a job for the Holy Spirit (John 16:8). Instead, we need to give a full and careful disclosure of what God has done for us, realizing that it might result in rejection.

Paul knew very well that following Christ would lead to hostility and rejection (Acts 28:19). But in responding to criticism and defending himself legally, he made sure that his judges had the benefit of a full explanation, even though it took a special meeting that lasted all day (v. 23). Yet even that careful effort did not completely set the record straight or convince all of his hearers (vv. 24, 29).

Scripture records a long tradition of God-sent messengers whose words fell on deaf ears. For example:

- *Isaiah, who was told ahead of time that he was being sent to people who would not listen to him (Is. 6:9–12).*
- *the Lord Jesus, who also came to those who would not receive Him (John 1:11; 12:37–43).*
- *Barnabas and Paul, who turned to the Gentiles at Pisidian Antioch after Jews rejected their message (Acts 13:44–46).*
- *Paul, who turned to the Gentiles at Corinth after Jews rejected his message (Acts 18:5–6).*
- *Paul, who grieved over his countrymen's rejection of the gospel (Rom. 11:7–10).*

How should we respond to rejection? The key issue is to make sure that we give our hearers a chance to consider Christ. We must offer them as faithful and convincing a presentation as possible. But it may mean hostility and personal cost. Yet should we expect to suffer any less than Christ did (Phil. 1:29–30)? ◆

had assembled, he said to them, "Brothers, though I had
done nothing against our people or the customs of our ancestors, yet I was arrested in Jerusalem and handed over to
the Romans. 18When they had examined me, the Romans[s]
wanted to release me, because there was no reason for the
death penalty in my case. 19But when the Jews objected, I
was compelled to appeal to the emperor—even though I
had no charge to bring against my nation. 20For this reason
therefore I have asked to see you and speak with you,[t]
since it is for the sake of the hope of Israel that I am bound
with this chain." 21They replied, "We have received no letters from Judea about you, and none of the brothers coming here has reported or spoken anything evil about you.
22But we would like to hear from you what you think, for

[s]Gk *they* [t]Or *I have asked you to see me and speak with me*

Paul's Rented House

CONSIDER THIS 28:30–31

Paul rented a house at his own expense (v. 30), possibly in south Rome. Technically under house arrest, he spent his time in outreach to both Jews and Gentiles, but especially to Gentiles (vv. 28–29).

The restrictions under which Paul lived should have held back his efforts to proclaim the gospel, but they "actually helped to spread the gospel" (Phil. 1:12). Confined to his lodgings and handcuffed to one of the soldiers who guarded him in four-hour shifts, he was free to receive visitors and talk with them about the gospel. The guards and the official in charge of presenting his case were left in no doubt about the reason for his being in Rome. The message of Christ actually became a topic of discussion among them (1:13). This encouraged Christians in Rome to become more bold in their witness to the faith than ever before.

Paul's house in Rome was probably where a runaway slave named Onesimus came to faith. See the Introduction to Philemon.

Hitting the Commercial High Spots

CONSIDER THIS 28:11–13

Springtime on the Mediterranean meant the return of cargo-laden ships from Alexandria, Egypt. They used westerly winds to deliver their goods to the empire's key ports.

Paul was transported from Malta to Rome on one such vessel, a voyage that covered 180 nautical miles in less than two days at sea (v. 11). On the journey he was able to visit three important cities and continue his movement-building work: Syracuse; the dominant city of Sicily; Rhegium, a key harbor town on the Italian side of the Strait of Messina; and Puteoli, gateway to southern Italy, just 33 miles from Rome.

Throughout Christian history, the gospel has invariably traveled the routes of commerce. For example, many have been introduced to the Good News through the witness of:

- **merchants doing business in foreign countries;**
- **employees of multinational corporations stationed overseas;**
- **consultants advising governments and businesses worldwide;**
- **medical personnel serving in developing nations;**
- **faculty and students studying and teaching around the world; and**
- **soldiers in foreign lands during war or occupation.**

Are you taking advantage of strategic opportunities to influence others with the message of Christ through your networks?

"THIS SALVATION OF GOD HAS BEEN SENT TO THE GENTILES. . . ."
—Acts 28:28

with regard to this sect we know that everywhere it is spoken against."
23 After they had set a day to meet with him, they came
to him at his lodgings in great numbers. From morning until evening he explained the matter to them, testifying to
the kingdom of God and trying to convince them about Jesus both from the law of Moses and from the prophets.
24Some were convinced by what he had said, while others
refused to believe. 25So they disagreed with each other; and
as they were leaving, Paul made one further statement:
"The Holy Spirit was right in saying to your ancestors
through the prophet Isaiah,

26 'Go to this people and say,
You will indeed listen, but never understand,
and you will indeed look, but never perceive.
27 For this people's heart has grown dull,
and their ears are hard of hearing,
and they have shut their eyes;
so that they might not look with their eyes,
and listen with their ears,
and understand with their heart and turn—
and I would heal them.'

28:28–31 see pg. 527
28Let it be known to you then that this
salvation of God has been sent to the
Gentiles; they will listen."[u]

Paul Preaches and Teaches

28:30–31 see pg. 529
30 He lived there two whole years at
his own expense[v] and welcomed all who
came to him, 31proclaiming the kingdom of God and teaching about the Lord Jesus Christ with all boldness and without hindrance.

[u]Other ancient authorities add verse 29, *And when he had said these words, the Jews departed, arguing vigorously among themselves* [v]Or *in his own hired dwelling*

The Gospel Explained

What does it mean to be a Christian? Do you know? Many people today who call themselves Christians would be hard pressed to explain the term. Some would talk in generalities about "doing good." Others would say that Christianity means love. Others would say it means "following Jesus," though they have only the vaguest idea of what they are talking about.

Every Christian ought to read the letter to the Romans. It was written to *explain the faith*. The Gospels proclaim the good news (gospel) of Jesus' life, teachings, death, and resurrection. Romans *examines that message*. It shows that the gospel is far more than just nice feelings or high moral sentiments. It is truth. It has intellectual content. It makes a difference in the way people think, and therefore in what they believe.

The Letter of Paul to the

Romans

The gospel is more than high moral sentiments. It is truth.

C O N T E N T S

Have You Ever Wondered . . .

. . . Does it matter what you believe as long as you believe in something?
Read 1:18–23.

. . . Where the Bible refers to homosexuality?
Read 1:24–32.

. . . Why we have to know Jesus to be saved?
Read 3:5–26.

. . . Why doing good isn't good enough for salvation?
Read 3:27—4:25.

. . . Why, if you're saved, you can't just go ahead and sin freely since God forgives and you'll receive eternal life anyway?
Read 6:1–23.

. . . Why you can't help but keep on sinning sometimes, even after you've given your life to God?
Read 7:1–25.

. . . Why there's so much pain and evil, even though God created the world?
Read 8:18–25.

. . . What can separate us from God's love?
Read 8:26–39.

. . . Whether Christians are free from having to obey the government, since we serve a higher authority, God?
Read 13:1–7.

. . . Why Christians even bother with what others think?
Read 14:1—15:13.

A R T I C L E S

A Change of Plans (1:13)
God used Paul, a great visionary, to spread the gospel. Even so, Paul's plans did not always work out.

The Power of the Gospel (1:16)
Are you ever embarrassed to be identified as a follower of Christ?

The Law (2:12)
The Law was given specifically to Israel, but it rests on eternal moral principles that are consistent with God's character. Thus Gentiles will not be judged by the Law, but they will be judged by the same righteous standard that underlies the Law.

Abraham (4:1)
As father of the Hebrews, Abraham features prominently in the New Testament. His faith makes him important to the message of the gospel.

Promises (4:16–25)
Can God be depended on to honor His promises? Do we fulfill our commitments?

Real Freedom (6:15–22)
People throughout the world hunger for freedom. But ultimately, no one is totally "free."

Is Work a Curse? (8:20)
A stubborn myth persists that work is a punishment. Does Scripture support that idea?

Are We One People? (11:13–24)
What are the current challenges to the ethnic, racial, and cultural attitudes of believers?

Do You Suffer from "Comparisonitis"? (12:3)
You won't find this illness listed in medical textbooks, but it's a scourge as widespread and destructive as any physical or emotional malady known today.

Do Not Avenge Yourself (12:19–21)

Romans says vengeance belongs to God. What, then, can you do to those who hurt you?

The High Calling of Government Service (13:6)

If you work in government, you'll want to pay special attention to this article.

Are Sundays Special? (14:5–13)

Should Sunday be treated as a special day in light of God's instructions regarding a Sabbath?

Paul's Female Coworkers (16:12)

Not a few of Paul's most valued associates were women, several of whom are listed in Romans 16.

Who Was Paul's Mother? (16:13)

Meet a woman who played such an important role in Paul's life that he never forgot her.

Why Did Jesus Die?

In Romans we find a carefully constructed argument that answers a crucial question: *Why did Jesus die?* The author, Paul, used his training as a Pharisee in writing this letter. As a rabbi, a teacher of the Law, he knew how to dissect theological issues and philosophical questions. In Romans he works his way through a sophisticated argument, not unlike a modern-day lawyer writing a brief. He asks and answers question after question until he has finished constructing a body of material that hangs together logically and theologically.

Romans shows that the gospel is big enough to deal with the weighty issues of the world—earth's ecology, ethical tensions arising from technology, world wars, humanity's capacity for self-destruction, human dignity, justice. Not everyone needs to look at Christianity on such a scale, but the great thinkers do. Romans does not disappoint: it offers the *big* picture of God's salvation.

This book may not be the easiest reading, but it is profoundly rewarding. Among the peaks of Scripture it looms like the Himalayas; its climax, chapter 8, towers up like Mount Everest. Scaling these vistas will give anyone's mental faculties a real workout—but the view is incomparable! Those who read and study Romans gain a grand perspective on what it means to be a Christian. ◆

THE SUPER-POWERFUL GOSPEL

We know almost nothing about the people to whom Romans was sent. Although Paul mentions the church at Rome (1:7), he wrote a general letter to a general readership, as if addressing it "to whom it may concern." Paul didn't start the church at Rome, nor had he ever visited there before writing this letter (1:13–15). In fact, he even intended to push beyond Rome to Spain (15:22–24).

But even if we know little about Paul's Roman readers, we know much about first-century Rome (see Acts 28:16). Rome was the greatest superpower of its day. Its influence extended from Britain to Africa and from Spain to Persia. This vast empire was governed very effectively by provincial heads, petty kings, and vassals of Rome. A pax Romana *(Roman peace) and a superior road system facilitated transportation and commerce and enabled the rapid spread of Christianity.*

Overall, Rome's government, economy, infrastructure, and defense were formidable enough to last for a thousand years. The Romans were a people in love with power. Perhaps that's why Paul described the gospel to the believers there in terms of power—God's power to save (Rom. 1:16). It's a gospel powerful enough to handle the empire, big enough to address issues on a global scale.

The salvation described in this book extends to . . .

- all aspects of life. *The gospel is not just personal or private, but public and universal as well. It deals with nations, with public policy, with science and technology, with race relations, with good and evil, with the cosmos, with the architecture of the world system.*
- all times and places. *Romans describes the grand sweep of history, from creation to Christ to the culmination of the world. At every point, God is carrying out His strategy for saving His creation from sin.*
- all kinds of people. *Jews and Gentiles, men and women, powerful and powerless, good and bad—all have a place in God's salvation story.*

Rome treated its emperors like gods and gave them dominion over numerous territories and peoples. But the book of Romans affirms Christ as supreme Lord over all creation: over the past (chapters 3–5), over the present (chapters 6–8), over nations (chapters 9–11), and over daily living in a complex society (chapters 12–16). Corrupted as it is and languishing under the crushing domination of Adam's sin, the world yearns for redemption. Fortunately, Adam's power to corrupt is exceeded by Christ's power to restore.

Overall, Romans presents a message for public people to embrace. The gospel is about God's power for anyone who lives and works in public systems and institutions. Is your faith big enough for the issues and tasks you face in your work and your world? If you're a marketplace Christian, Romans is a "must-read." ◆

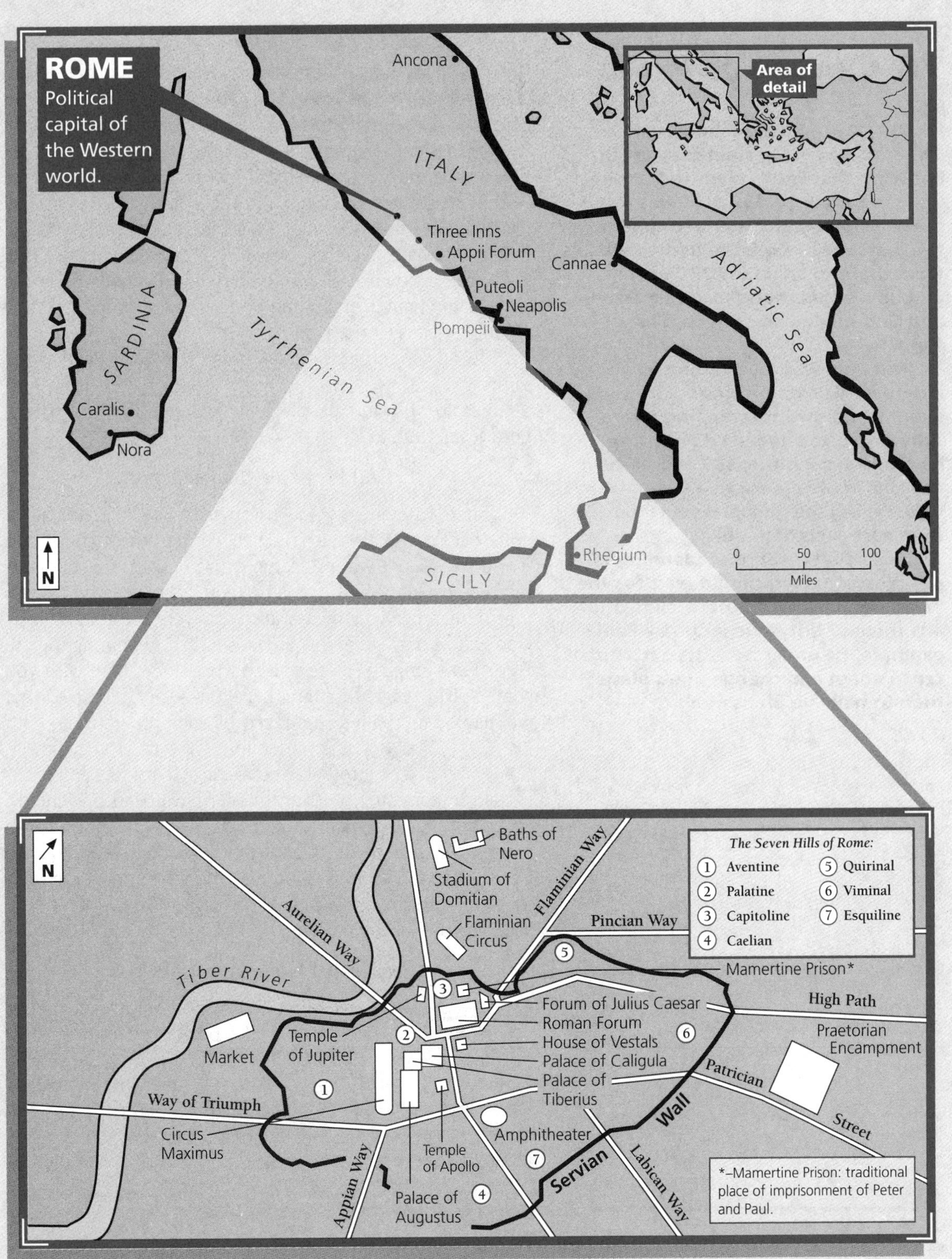
ROME
Political capital of the Western world.
Area of detail
Ancona
ITALY
Three Inns
Appii Forum
Cannae
Adriatic Sea
Puteoli
Neapolis
Pompeii
SARDINIA
Tyrrhenian Sea
Caralis
Nora
Rhegium
SICILY
N
0
50
100
Miles
N
Baths of Nero
Stadium of Domitian
Flaminian Way
Aurelian Way
Flaminian Circus
Pincian Way
Tiber River
Mamertine Prison*
Forum of Julius Caesar
High Path
Roman Forum
Temple of Jupiter
Market
House of Vestals
Palace of Caligula
Praetorian Encampment
Patrician Street
Palace of Tiberius
Way of Triumph
Circus Maximus
Amphitheater
Servian Wall
Temple of Apollo
Appian Way
Labican Way
Palace of Augustus
The Seven Hills of Rome:
1 Aventine
2 Palatine
3 Capitoline
4 Caelian
5 Quirinal
6 Viminal
7 Esquiline
*–Mamertine Prison: traditional place of imprisonment of Peter and Paul.

A Change of Plans

CONSIDER THIS 1:13 **Somehow there's a certain comfort in knowing that Paul's plans did not always work out (v. 13). Paul was a great visionary. He intended to take the message of Christ to Rome, and from there to Spain (15:28). To that end he laid plans and made decisions, and God guided and directed his efforts.**

But Paul was also willing to go wherever God opened doors for him, even if that meant scrapping a carefully organized agenda. For example, he made a complete, 180-degree turn at Troas in obedience to a vision from God, taking the gospel west rather than east (Acts 16:6–10).

Does that mean that planning is pointless, that we should wait for the "leading" of the Lord before making any moves? Not if we judge by Paul's example. He understood that it's better to adapt and change one's plans than to have no plans at all.

Paul felt driven to get to Rome, but Spain was just as significant. See "All Roads Lead to Rome—and Beyond," Acts 28:28–31.

Greetings

1 Paul, a servant[a] of Jesus Christ, called to be an apostle,
set apart for the gospel of God, 2which he promised
beforehand through his prophets in the holy scriptures,
3the gospel concerning his Son, who was descended from
David according to the flesh 4and was declared to be Son of
God with power according to the spirit[b] of holiness by
resurrection from the dead, Jesus Christ our Lord, 5through
whom we have received grace and apostleship to bring
about the obedience of faith among all the Gentiles for the
sake of his name, 6including yourselves who are called to
belong to Jesus Christ,

7 To all God's beloved in Rome, who are called to be
saints:

Grace to you and peace from God our Father and the
Lord Jesus Christ.

Paul Prays for His Readers

8 First, I thank my God through Jesus Christ for all of
you, because your faith is proclaimed throughout the
world. 9For God, whom I serve with my spirit by announcing the gospel[c] of his Son, is my witness that without ceasing I remember you always in my prayers, 10asking that by
God's will I may somehow at last succeed in coming to you.
11For I am longing to see you so that I may share with you
some spiritual gift to strengthen you— 12or rather so that
we may be mutually encouraged by each other's faith, both
1:13 yours and mine. 13I want you to know,
brothers and sisters,[d] that I have often intended to come to you (but thus far have been prevented),
in order that I may reap some harvest among you as I have
among the rest of the Gentiles. 14I am a debtor both to
Greeks and to barbarians, both to the wise and to the foolish 15—hence my eagerness to proclaim the gospel to you
also who are in Rome.

The Gospel Is the Power of God

1:16 16 For I am not ashamed of the
gospel; it is the power of God for salva-
tion to everyone who has faith, to the Jew first and also to
1:17 see pg. 538 the Greek. 17For in it the righteousness
of God is revealed through faith for faith;
as it is written, "The one who is righteous will live by
faith."[e]

[a]Gk *slave* [b]Or *Spirit* [c]Gk *my spirit in the gospel* [d]Gk *brothers* [e]Or *The one who is righteous through faith will live*

God Will Judge Sin

18 For the wrath of God is revealed from heaven against
all ungodliness and wickedness of those who by their
wickedness suppress the truth. 19For what can be known
about God is plain to them, because God has shown it to
them. 20Ever since the creation of the world his eternal
power and divine nature, invisible though they are, have
been understood and seen through the things he has made.
So they are without excuse; 21for though they knew God,
they did not honor him as God or give thanks to him, but
they became futile in their thinking, and their senseless
minds were darkened. 22Claiming to be wise, they became
fools; 23and they exchanged the glory of the immortal God
for images resembling a mortal human being or birds or
four-footed animals or reptiles.

24 Therefore God gave them up in the lusts of their
hearts to impurity, to the degrading of their bodies among
themselves, 25because they exchanged the truth about God
for a lie and worshiped and served the creature rather than
the Creator, who is blessed forever! Amen.

26 For this reason God gave them up to degrading passions. Their women exchanged natural intercourse for unnatural, 27and in the same way also the men, giving up natural intercourse with women, were consumed with passion
for one another. Men committed shameless acts with men
and received in their own persons the due penalty for their
error.

28 And since they did not see fit to acknowledge God,
God gave them up to a debased mind and to things that
should not be done. 29They were filled with every kind of
wickedness, evil, covetousness, malice. Full of envy, murder, strife, deceit, craftiness, they are gossips, 30slanderers,
God-haters,[f] insolent, haughty, boastful, inventors of evil,
rebellious toward parents, 31foolish, faithless, heartless,
ruthless. 32They know God's decree, that those who practice
such things deserve to die—yet they not only do them but
even applaud others who practice them.

All Are Guilty, Whether Jew or Gentile

2 Therefore you have no excuse, whoever you are, when
you judge others; for in passing judgment on another
you condemn yourself, because you, the judge, are doing
the very same things. 2You say,[g] "We know that God's
judgment on those who do such things is in accordance
with truth." 3Do you imagine, whoever you are, that when
you judge those who do such things and yet do them

[f]Or *God-hated* [g]Gk lacks *You say*

The Power of the Gospel

CONSIDER THIS 1:16 **Are you ever embarrassed to be identified as a follower of Christ? Would coworkers or other associates ever assume that you are ashamed of your faith by the way you avoid talking about it or revealing your true thoughts and feelings?**

Paul felt no shame in the message of Christ, for he saw it as *powerful*—powerful enough to transform lives (v. 16).

How powerful is the gospel you believe in? Are you a channel or a barrier for the power of Christ in your workplace?

The first followers of Jesus experienced the power of the gospel in such a profound way that they changed the entire Roman world. *See "Power," Acts 1:8.*

yourself, you will escape the judgment of God? [4]Or do you
despise the riches of his kindness and forbearance and
patience? Do you not realize that God's kindness is meant
to lead you to repentance? [5]But by your hard and
impenitent heart you are storing up wrath for yourself on
the day of wrath, when God's righteous judgment will be
revealed. [6]For he will repay according to each one's deeds:
[7]to those who by patiently doing good seek for glory and
honor and immortality, he will give eternal life; [8]while for
those who are self-seeking and who obey not the truth but
wickedness, there will be wrath and fury. [9]There will be
anguish and distress for everyone who does evil, the Jew
first and also the Greek, [10]but glory and honor and peace
for everyone who does good, the Jew first and also the
Greek. [11]For God shows no partiality.

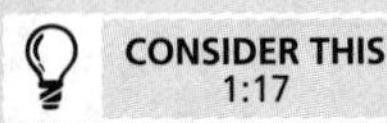
CONSIDER THIS
1:17

Righteousness

One of the greatest challenges confronting believers today is to communicate the message of Christ in terms that everyday people can understand. Words like "righteousness" (v. 17) have become unrecognizable to many in our culture, and even to many in the church.

Yet it's hard to talk about the gospel—and virtually impossible to understand Romans—without coming to terms with the word "righteousness" (Greek, dikaiosune*). In fact, the New Testament uses the term in one form or another no less than 228 times, at least 40 in Romans. What, then, does "righteousness" mean and how does the gospel reveal "the righteousness of God" (v. 17)?*

The word "righteous" goes back to a base, reg, *meaning "move in a straight line." Thus, "righteous"* (rightwise) *means "in the straight (or right) way." Used with reference to morality, "righteous" means living or acting in the* right *way.*

But what is the "right" way? In our society, people commonly say that everyone must determine what is right for oneself. However, Scripture offers a different standard—indeed, the ultimate standard of rightness *or "righteousness," God Himself. God's character reveals what is absolutely* right. *He is the measure of moral right and wrong.*

He is also the source of right living. It's important to understand that righteousness involves more than just determining whether or not one has lived up to the perfect standard that God sets. The fact is, no one has except Je-

2:12
see pg. 540

12 All who have sinned apart from the
law will also perish apart from the law,
and all who have sinned under the law will be judged by
the law. [13]For it is not the hearers of the law who are righteous in God's sight, but the doers of the law who will be
justified. [14]When Gentiles, who do not possess the law, do
instinctively what the law requires, these, though not having the law, are a law to themselves. [15]They show that what
the law requires is written on their hearts, to which their
own conscience also bears witness; and their conflicting
thoughts will accuse or perhaps excuse them [16]on the day
when, according to my gospel, God, through Jesus Christ,
will judge the secret thoughts of all.

sus (Rom. 3:23; 5:18–21). Thus, in a legal sense, all of us stand guilty before God. We are all "unrighteous." We have all "sinned" (literally, "missed the mark").

But the message of Romans is that God has done and is doing everything that needs to be done to restore things to the way He originally intended—to the right *way. For example, He dealt with sin through Jesus' death on the cross (5:6–11), and He transfers the* righteousness *of* Christ *to those who trust in Him (5:1–2). As believers, we can enjoy a restored relationship with God.*

That means that we can begin to live with righteousness, *that is, in a way that pleases God and fulfills His purposes for us. We can do that because He gives us the ability to do it (8:1–17). Rather than trying to "prove" ourselves good enough for Him or live up to impossible moral standards, we can relate to Him in love, expecting Him to help us as we make choices about how to live.*

The gospel, then, is "good news" because it reveals God's right *way. It tells us that He is a good God who, in love and mercy, has done something about the* wrong *way that the world has taken. How have you responded to that good news of God's righteousness?* ◆

Another term that is often misunderstood today is gospel. *To learn more about what it means, see "What Is the Gospel?" Luke 7:22.*

GOD, THROUGH JESUS CHRIST, WILL JUDGE THE SECRET THOUGHTS OF ALL.
—Romans 2:16

Being Jewish Is Not Enough

17 But if you call yourself a Jew and rely on the law and
boast of your relation to God 18and know his will and determine what is best because you are instructed in the law,
19and if you are sure that you are a guide to the blind, a
light to those who are in darkness, 20a corrector of the foolish, a teacher of children, having in the law the embodiment of knowledge and truth, 21you, then, that teach others, will you not teach yourself? While you preach against
stealing, do you steal? 22You that forbid adultery, do you
commit adultery? You that abhor idols, do you rob temples? 23You that boast in the law, do you dishonor God by
breaking the law? 24For, as it is written, "The name of God
is blasphemed among the Gentiles because of you."
25 Circumcision indeed is of value if you obey the law;
but if you break the law, your circumcision has become uncircumcision. 26So, if those who are uncircumcised keep the
requirements of the law, will not their uncircumcision be

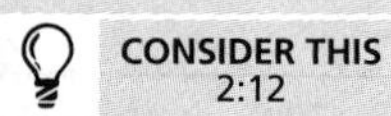

THE LAW

Paul's reference to "law" (v. 12) has to do not with laws in general, but with the specific code of rules and regulations that God gave to Moses on Mount Sinai. The Law was part of the covenant that set Israel apart as God's people. It governed their worship, their relationship to God, and their social relationships with one another. The Ten Commandments form a summary of that Law.

Israel was not the only nation to have a law code. Indeed, such collections were common in the ancient world. Most of them began by explaining that the gods gave the king power to reign, along with a pronouncement about how good and capable he was. Then came the king's laws grouped by subject. Finally, most of the codes closed with a series of curses and blessings.

What set the Mosaic Law apart from these other codes was, first of all, its origin. The Law was given by God Himself. It issued from His very nature; like Him it was holy, righteous, and good. Thus, all crimes in Israel were crimes against God (1 Sam. 12:9–10). He expected all of the people to love and serve Him (Amos 5:21–24). As their final judge, He disciplined those who violated the Law (Ex. 22:21–24; Deut. 10:18; 19:17), though He also held the nation responsible for insuring that justice was carried out (Deut. 13:6–10; 17:7; Num. 15:32–36).

Furthermore, God ruled over Israel, in effect, as the

regarded as circumcision? 27Then those who are physically
uncircumcised but keep the law will condemn you that
have the written code and circumcision but break the law.
28For a person is not a Jew who is one outwardly, nor
is true circumcision something external and physical.
29Rather, a person is a Jew who is one inwardly, and real
circumcision is a matter of the heart—it is spiritual and not
literal. Such a person receives praise not from others but
from God.
3 Then what advantage has the Jew? Or what is the value
of circumcision? 2Much, in every way. For in the first
place the Jews[h] were entrusted with the oracles of God.
3What if some were unfaithful? Will their faithlessness
nullify the faithfulness of God? 4By no means! Although
everyone is a liar, let God be proved true, as it is written,

"So that you may be justified in your words,
and prevail in your judging."[i]

[h]Gk *they* [i]Gk *when you are being judged*

nation's King. Ancient kings often enacted laws to try to outdo their predecessors in image, economic power, and political influence. God, however, gave His law as an expression of love for His people, to advance their best interests (Ex. 19:5–6).

The Law can be divided into three categories—moral laws, ceremonial laws, and civil laws. The latter regulated in great detail matters having to do with leaders, the army, criminal cases, crimes against property, humane treatment, personal and family rights, property rights, and other social behavior.

The ceremonial laws contained specifications regarding public worship and ritual, giving high priority to the concept of holiness. Because God is holy (Lev. 21:8), Israel was to be holy in all its religious practices.

The Law was given specifically to Israel, but it rests on eternal moral principles that are consistent with God's character. Thus it is a summary of fundamental and universal moral standards. It expresses the essence of what God requires of people. That's why when God judges, He can be impartial. Gentiles will not be judged by the Law (Rom. 2:12), since it was not given to them, but they will still be judged by the same righteous standard that underlies the Law. ◆

ALTHOUGH EVERYONE IS A LIAR, LET GOD BE PROVED TRUE. . . .
—Romans 3:4

Nobody's Perfect

CONSIDER THIS 3:9–18 **It's common today for people to excuse their faults with the attitude, "Hey, nobody's perfect!" True enough. People can only be expected to be human—and that means fallible.**

Unfortunately, though, few people take that reality seriously enough. Indeed, when it comes to their standing before God, all too many take a different stance: they may not be perfect, but they're "good enough."

The question is, are they good enough for God? Romans 3 says they are not. That's what Paul means when he writes, all "are under the power of sin" (v. 9) and then cites a number of Old Testament passages to back up his claim (vv. 10–18).

It's not that people are evil through and through, or that they never do any moral good. Quite the contrary. People are capable of impressive acts of courage, compassion, and justice. But in light of God's holy (morally perfect) character, which is the ultimate standard against which people's goodness is measured, people are indeed far from perfect. Their good behavior turns out to be the exception rather than the rule.

The good news that Paul writes about in Romans, however, is that God has reached out to humanity despite its imperfect ways. His attitude has not been one of rejection, as if to say, "They're not good enough for Me," but one of grace and compassion that says, in effect, "I will make them into good people—people as good as I AM—by means of Christ My Son."

Another popular notion today is that humankind is basically good, and that moral problems are simply the result of bad parenting, bad education, and the foibles of "society." Is that true? See "Are People Basically Good?" Rom. 7:21.

5But if our injustice serves to confirm the justice of God,
what should we say? That God is unjust to inflict wrath on
us? (I speak in a human way.) 6By no means! For then how
could God judge the world? 7But if through my falsehood
God's truthfulness abounds to his glory, why am I still being
condemned as a sinner? 8And why not say (as some people
slander us by saying that we say), "Let us do evil so that
good may come"? Their condemnation is deserved!

All Stand Condemned before God

3:9–18 9 What then? Are we any better off?[j]
No, not at all; for we have already
charged that all, both Jews and Greeks, are under the
power of sin, 10as it is written:

"There is no one who is righteous, not even one;
11 there is no one who has understanding,
there is no one who seeks God.
12 All have turned aside, together they have become
worthless;
there is no one who shows kindness,
there is not even one."
13 "Their throats are opened graves;
they use their tongues to deceive."
"The venom of vipers is under their lips."
14 "Their mouths are full of cursing and bitterness."
15 "Their feet are swift to shed blood;
16 ruin and misery are in their paths,
17 and the way of peace they have not known."
18 "There is no fear of God before their eyes."

19 Now we know that whatever the law says, it speaks
to those who are under the law, so that every mouth may be
silenced, and the whole world may be held accountable to
God. 20For "no human being will be justified in his sight"
by deeds prescribed by the law, for through the law comes
the knowledge of sin.

The Way of Righteousness—by Faith

21 But now, apart from law, the righteousness of God
has been disclosed, and is attested by the law and the
prophets, 22the righteousness of God through faith in Jesus
Christ[k] for all who believe. For there is no distinction,
23since all have sinned and fall short of the glory of God;
24they are now justified by his grace as a gift, through the
redemption that is in Christ Jesus, 25whom God put forward as a sacrifice of atonement[l] by his blood, effective
through faith. He did this to show his righteousness, be-

[j]Or at any disadvantage? [k]Or through the faith of Jesus Christ [l]Or a place of atonement

cause in his divine forbearance he had passed over the sins
previously committed; 26it was to prove at the present time
that he himself is righteous and that he justifies the one
who has faith in Jesus.[m]
27 Then what becomes of boasting? It is excluded. By
what law? By that of works? No, but by the law of faith.
28For we hold that a person is justified by faith apart from
works prescribed by the law. 29Or is God the God of Jews
only? Is he not the God of Gentiles also? Yes, of Gentiles
also, 30since God is one; and he will justify the circumcised
on the ground of faith and the uncircumcised through that
same faith. 31Do we then overthrow the law by this faith?
By no means! On the contrary, we uphold the law.

Abraham Was Justified by Faith

4:1
4 What then are we to say was gained
by[n] Abraham, our ancestor accord-
ing to the flesh? 2For if Abraham was justified by works, he
has something to boast about, but not before God. 3For
what does the scripture say? "Abraham believed God, and it
was reckoned to him as righteousness." 4Now to one who
works, wages are not reckoned as a gift but as something
due. 5But to one who without works trusts him who justifies the ungodly, such faith is reckoned as righteousness.
4:6 see pg. 544
6So also David speaks of the blessedness
of those to whom God reckons righteousness apart from works:
7 "Blessed are those whose iniquities are forgiven,
and whose sins are covered;
8 blessed is the one against whom the Lord will not
reckon sin."
9 Is this blessedness, then, pronounced only on the circumcised, or also on the uncircumcised? We say, "Faith was
reckoned to Abraham as righteousness." 10How then was it
reckoned to him? Was it before or after he had been circumcised? It was not after, but before he was circumcised.
11He received the sign of circumcision as a seal of the righteousness that he had by faith while he was still uncircumcised. The purpose was to make him the ancestor of all
who believe without being circumcised and who thus have
righteousness reckoned to them, 12and likewise the ancestor of the circumcised who are not only circumcised but
who also follow the example of the faith that our ancestor
Abraham had before he was circumcised.
13 For the promise that he would inherit the world did
not come to Abraham or to his descendants through the

[m]Or *who has the faith of Jesus* [n]Other ancient authorities read *say about*

ABRAHAM

CONSIDER THIS 4:1 **As father of the Hebrews, Abraham (v. 1) features prominently in the New Testament. Here in Romans 4, he is recalled as an individual. Elsewhere he represents the entire people of Israel, and especially those who have placed faith in God (for example, 9:7; 11:1; Gal. 3:6–9).**

Indeed, Abraham's faith is what makes him so important to the New Testament writers. God made important promises to him and his descendants, Isaac, Jacob, and Jacob's twelve sons—promises that God repeated throughout Israel's history. Abraham is remembered as the man who believed that God would do what He said He would do (Rom. 4:3)—a remarkable thing when we consider that at the time of the promises, Abraham had very little evidence that God would follow through, certainly far less than the New Testament writers or we who live today.

One of the most important promises was that God would send a Messiah, an "anointed one." Jesus claimed to be that Messiah. So the central question of the New Testament becomes, do we believe that? Do we take Jesus at His word? Do we accept His claim and its implications? Abraham believed God; do we?

Another important question raised by the coming of Jesus was, what happens to Israel? Even though many Jews believed Jesus' claims and followed Him, by and large the nation rejected Him. What did that mean for the promises of God? Paul deals with those issues in Romans 9–11 (see "Israel," Rom. 10:1).

DAVID

CONSIDER THIS 4:6 **If Abraham (v. 1) was honored as the patriarch of Israel, David (v. 6) was honored as the king of Israel. He was not the nation's first king, but He was God's choice for king (1 Sam. 16:1–13).**

If anyone might have a claim on being right with God and meriting His favor, then, it was David. After all, he was said to be a man after God's own heart (13:14; Acts 13:22). Furthermore, God established a covenant with him, promising that his heirs would have a right to the throne of Israel forever (2 Sam. 7:12; 22:51). He was even a direct ancestor of Jesus Christ (Matt. 1:6; Luke 3:31).

But David relied on none of these advantages (or "works," Rom. 4:5) when it came to his standing before God. Instead, he threw himself on God's mercy, trusting in His gracious character to forgive his sin and establish his "righteousness" (v. 6), or right standing in relation to God. Psalm 32, from which Romans 4:7–8 quotes, celebrates this delivery from sin that God brings about.

Do you rely on your own good works to establish your relationship with God? Romans 4 says you can never be good enough. That's why God offers an alternative—trusting in Jesus' righteousness to cover your sin and make it possible for you to know God.

It's virtually impossible to understand Romans without coming to terms with the word "righteousness." Learn more about what that word means at Rom. 1:17.

law but through the righteousness of faith. 14If it is the adherents of the law who are to be the heirs, faith is null and
the promise is void. 15For the law brings wrath; but where
there is no law, neither is there violation.

God Rewarded Abraham's Faith

4:16–25

16 For this reason it depends on faith,
in order that the promise may rest on
grace and be guaranteed to all his descendants, not only to
the adherents of the law but also to those who share the
faith of Abraham (for he is the father of all of us, 17as it is
written, "I have made you the father of many nations")—in
the presence of the God in whom he believed, who gives
life to the dead and calls into existence the things that do
not exist. 18Hoping against hope, he believed that he would
become "the father of many nations," according to what
was said, "So numerous shall your descendants be." 19He
did not weaken in faith when he considered his own body,
which was already[o] as good as dead (for he was about a
hundred years old), or when he considered the barrenness
of Sarah's womb. 20No distrust made him waver concerning
the promise of God, but he grew strong in his faith as he
gave glory to God, 21being fully convinced that God was
able to do what he had promised. 22Therefore his faith[p]
"was reckoned to him as righteousness." 23Now the words,
"it was reckoned to him," were written not for his sake
alone, 24but for ours also. It will be reckoned to us who believe in him who raised Jesus our Lord from the dead,
25who was handed over to death for our trespasses and was
raised for our justification.

Through Faith We Have Peace with God

5 Therefore, since we are justified by faith, we[q] have
peace with God through our Lord Jesus Christ,
2through whom we have obtained access[r] to this grace in
which we stand; and we[s] boast in our hope of sharing the
glory of God. 3And not only that, but we[s] also boast in our
sufferings, knowing that suffering produces endurance,
4and endurance produces character, and character produces
hope, 5and hope does not disappoint us, because God's love
has been poured into our hearts through the Holy Spirit
that has been given to us.

6 For while we were still weak, at the right time Christ
died for the ungodly. 7Indeed, rarely will anyone die for a
righteous person—though perhaps for a good person
someone might actually dare to die. 8But God proves his

[o]Other ancient authorities lack *already* [p]Gk *Therefore it* [q]Other ancient authorities read *let us* [r]Other ancient authorities add *by faith* [s]Or *let us*

love for us in that while we still were sinners Christ died for us. [9]Much more surely then, now that we have been justified by his blood, will we be saved through him from the wrath of God.[t] [10]For if while we were enemies, we were reconciled to God through the death of his Son, much more surely, having been reconciled, will we be saved by his life. [11]But more than that, we even boast in God through our Lord Jesus Christ, through whom we have now received reconciliation.

Through Faith Christ Makes Us Alive Again

12 Therefore, just as sin came into the world through one man, and death came through sin, and so death spread to all because all have sinned— [13]sin was indeed in the world before the law, but sin is not reckoned when there is

5:14

no law. [14]Yet death exercised dominion from Adam to Moses, even over those whose sins were not like the transgression of Adam, who is a type of the one who was to come.

15 But the free gift is not like the trespass. For if the many died through the one man's trespass, much more surely have the grace of God and the free gift in the grace of the one man, Jesus Christ, abounded for the many. [16]And the free gift is not like the effect of the one man's sin. For the judgment following one trespass brought condemnation, but the free gift following many trespasses brings justification. [17]If, because of the one man's trespass, death exercised dominion through that one, much more surely will those who receive the abundance of grace and the free gift of righteousness exercise dominion in life through the one man, Jesus Christ.

18 Therefore just as one man's trespass led to condemnation for all, so one man's act of righteousness leads to justification and life for all. [19]For just as by the one man's disobedience the many were made sinners, so by the one man's obedience the many will be made righteous. [20]But law came in, with the result that the trespass multiplied; but where sin increased, grace abounded all the more, [21]so that, just as sin exercised dominion in death, so grace might also exercise dominion through justification[u] leading to eternal life through Jesus Christ our Lord.

Through Faith We Can Obey God

6 What then are we to say? Should we continue in sin in order that grace may abound? [2]By no means! How can we who died to sin go on living in it? [3]Do you not know

(Bible text continued on page 547)

[t]Gk *the wrath* [u]Or *righteousness*

PROMISES

CONSIDER THIS 4:16–25 **Do you believe that God can be depended on to honor His promises? Abraham did (vv. 20–21).**

All of us rely on the promises of others in our daily lives and work. Vendors promise to deliver products in specified quantities and qualities. Project groups promise to deliver results by certain dates. Companies promise to stand behind their products with "satisfaction guaranteed." If we can believe the promises of fallible human beings, how much more can we trust the promises of God, who never fails?

Of course, if we are one of God's people, we need to live and work with the same trustworthiness and reliability. When we give our word, we need to fulfill it. When we make a commitment, we need to honor it. When we enter into a contract, we need to abide by it. Otherwise, we bring discredit to God.

Trustworthiness is one of the traits of a godly "workstyle." See Titus 2:9–10.

ADAM

FOR YOUR INFO 5:14 **Adam (v. 14) is cited as the first man, who, along with his wife, Eve, was placed in the Garden of Eden (Gen. 1:26–28; 2:7–24). Thus they became the ancestors of all humanity.**

But Adam failed to keep God's command, and that disobedience resulted in a dramatic change—indeed, a tragic rupture—in the relationship between God and Adam and Eve and their descendants. His choice to disobey brought sin and death into the world (Rom. 5:12–19; 1 Cor. 15:22).

FOR YOUR INFO
6:16

SLAVES

Paul uses a powerful image when he pictures one's relationship either to sin or to obedience as slavery (v. 16). The Roman Empire was heavily dependent on slaves to take care of its hard labor and menial tasks. In fact, many of Paul's Roman recipients may have been slaves, since perhaps half the population or more were under servitude by one historian's estimate.

Slaves were taken from the many nations that Rome conquered. Those assigned to the empire's widespread construction projects or to its mines had a hard lot. Fed a subsistence diet, they were worked to exhaustion. Injuries and disease were common, and once they were too sick to work, or in rare cases too old, they were abandoned.

Household slaves, however, enjoyed better conditions. Nearly every Roman home owned at least two or three servants, and some had hundreds. They assisted the women in maintaining their homes and raising their children. Slaves with occupational expertise proved particularly valuable in the workplace, and some businesses were entirely dependent on these imported, cheap laborers.

Slavery existed long before the Romans, of course. The Bible records several different forms of slavery in ancient times: domestic slavery, as illustrated by Hagar (Gen. 16:1); state slavery, as illustrated by the Israelites under Egypt (Ex. 5:6–19; 13:3); and temple slavery, as illustrated by the slaves of the Levites for temple service (Num. 31:25–47; Josh. 9:21–27).

Curiously, the Bible does not directly condemn slavery as an institution, though it contains warnings about the practice of slavery (Amos 1:6–9; Rev. 18:13). The Old Testament Law did regulate Israel's treatment of slaves (Ex. 21; Deut. 15). Repeatedly, the people were instructed not to rule over a fellow Israelite harshly (Lev. 25:39; Deut. 15:14). If a master beat a slave or harmed him, the law provided that the slave could go free (Ex. 21:26–27); and the killing of a slave called for a penalty (Ex. 21:20).

In the New Testament, slaves were advised to obey their masters (Eph. 6:5; Col. 3:22; Titus 2:9). Paul appealed to Philemon to receive back Onesimus, a runaway slave who became a Christian and therefore a brother (see the Introduction to Philemon). This was an illustration that in Christ, social distinctions such as slavery no longer apply (Gal. 3:28; Col. 3:11). Elsewhere Paul counseled believing slaves to seek freedom if they could (1 Cor. 7:21).

Under Jewish law, no Hebrew was to be the permanent slave of another Hebrew (Ex. 21:2; Lev. 25:37–43; Deut. 15:12). If a slave desired to continue with his master, he would have a mark made in the ear to signify that he had chosen to remain a slave (Ex. 21:5–6). A slave could also buy his freedom, or another person could buy his freedom for him (Lev. 25:47–49).

Among the Romans, an owner could free a slave outright, or the slave could purchase his freedom by paying his owner. Freedom could also be arranged if ownership was transferred to a god. The slave could then receive his freedom in return for contracting his services. He would continue with his master, but now as a free man.

Perhaps Paul had that sort of arrangement in mind when he described the moral choice of which master one would obey—sin or righteousness (Rom. 6:16). For as believers, we have been freed from sin, and in fact are now owned by God. We are now free to serve God. Yet we still have a choice to serve either sin or God. In light of the realities of slavery, it's worth considering: Which master are you serving? Which one is likely to treat you better? ◆

that all of us who have been baptized into Christ Jesus were
baptized into his death? 4Therefore we have been buried
with him by baptism into death, so that, just as Christ was
raised from the dead by the glory of the Father, so we too
might walk in newness of life.
5 For if we have been united with him in a death like
his, we will certainly be united with him in a resurrection
like his. 6We know that our old self was crucified with him
so that the body of sin might be destroyed, and we might
no longer be enslaved to sin. 7For whoever has died is freed
from sin. 8But if we have died with Christ, we believe that
we will also live with him. 9We know that Christ, being
raised from the dead, will never die again; death no longer
has dominion over him. 10The death he died, he died to
sin, once for all; but the life he lives, he lives to God. 11So
you also must consider yourselves dead to sin and alive to
God in Christ Jesus.
12 Therefore, do not let sin exercise dominion in your
mortal bodies, to make you obey their passions. 13No
longer present your members to sin as instruments[v] of
wickedness, but present yourselves to God as those who
have been brought from death to life, and present your
members to God as instruments[v] of righteousness. 14For sin
will have no dominion over you, since you are not under
law but under grace.

We Are No Longer Enslaved to Sin

6:15–22

6:16

15 What then? Should we sin because
we are not under law but under grace?
By no means! 16Do you not know that if
you present yourselves to anyone as obe-
dient slaves, you are slaves of the one whom you obey, either of sin, which leads to death, or of obedience, which
leads to righteousness? 17But thanks be to God that you,
having once been slaves of sin, have become obedient from
the heart to the form of teaching to which you were entrusted, 18and that you, having been set free from sin, have
become slaves of righteousness. 19I am speaking in human
terms because of your natural limitations.[w] For just as you
once presented your members as slaves to impurity and to
greater and greater iniquity, so now present your members
as slaves to righteousness for sanctification.
20 When you were slaves of sin, you were free in regard
to righteousness. 21So what advantage did you then get
from the things of which you now are ashamed? The end of
those things is death. 22But now that you have been freed
from sin and enslaved to God, the advantage you get is

[v]Or *weapons* [w]Gk *the weakness of your flesh*

Real Freedom

CONSIDER THIS 6:15–22 **One of the greatest motivating factors for people throughout the world today is the quest for freedom, for self-determination. Armies fight for it. Nations vote for it. Individuals work for it.**

But here in Romans 6, Scripture teaches that, ultimately, no one is ever totally "free." In the end, everyone serves either God or sin. In fact, Paul uses the word "slaves" to describe the relationship (vv. 16–20; see related article on "Slaves"). We are either slaves of righteousness or slaves of sin.

What does that imply for our understanding of the nature of freedom? Is complete autonomy possible? Is there such a thing as self-rule or political self-determination? Yes, in a limited sense. But here as elsewhere, Scripture describes real freedom as a change of masters: being set free from slavery to sin in order to become slaves to righteousness instead.

All of us are enslaved to sin from the moment of conception. Our only hope is Christ, who is able to emancipate us from that bondage (7:24–25). Then, having saved us, He enables us through His Holy Spirit to do what we could not do in and of ourselves—live in obedience to God's law (8:3–4). Therein lies true freedom.

sanctification. The end is eternal life. 23For the wages of sin
is death, but the free gift of God is eternal life in Christ Jesus our Lord.

A New View of the Law

7 Do you not know, brothers and sisters[x]—for I am
speaking to those who know the law—that the law is
binding on a person only during that person's lifetime?
2Thus a married woman is bound by the law to her
husband as long as he lives; but if her husband dies, she is
discharged from the law concerning the husband.
3Accordingly, she will be called an adulteress if she lives
with another man while her husband is alive. But if her
husband dies, she is free from that law, and if she marries
another man, she is not an adulteress.
4 In the same way, my friends,[x] you have died to the law
through the body of Christ, so that you may belong to another, to him who has been raised from the dead in order

[x]Gk *brothers*

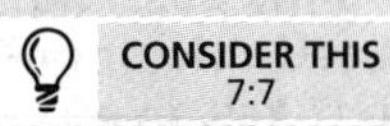

CONSIDER THIS
7:7

SCYLLA AND CHARYBDIS

Ancient Greek mythology told of two dangers at sea known as Scylla and Charybdis. Scylla was a twelve-tentacled monster with six heads that grabbed at least six sailors from the decks of passing ships. Nearby lay Charybdis, an underwater terror able to suck down entire vessels in a giant whirlpool of seawater. These two dangers were arranged so that a ship could sail closer to one or the other, but could avoid neither.

The Christian life has two dangers not unlike Scylla and Charybdis. As believers travel along the journey of faith, they encounter two perils that cannot be avoided—law and lawlessness. Paul addresses both pitfalls in Romans 6–7.

In Romans, the Law (7:7; see 2:12) refers specifically to the Old Testament Law that God gave to Israel, but more generally to the moral expectations that God places on all humanity. Obviously such standards are not evil in themselves. Nevertheless, they become perilous because no one is humanly able to keep them all perfectly.

Paul illustrated that fact by citing the Tenth Commandment, "You shall not covet" (7:7; Ex. 20:17). That was a basic moral principle with which Paul was in total agreement. Yet when he examined his own life, he found "all kinds of covetousness." In other words, the more Paul understood God's Law, the more aware he became of the sin in his life. Nor did knowing God's expectations make him

that we may bear fruit for God. [5]While we were living in
the flesh, our sinful passions, aroused by the law, were at
work in our members to bear fruit for death. [6]But now we
are discharged from the law, dead to that which held us
captive, so that we are slaves not under the old written
code but in the new life of the Spirit.

7:7

7 What then should we say? That the
law is sin? By no means! Yet, if it had not
been for the law, I would not have known sin. I would not
have known what it is to covet if the law had not said, "You
shall not covet." [8]But sin, seizing an opportunity in the
commandment, produced in me all kinds of covetousness.
Apart from the law sin lies dead. [9]I was once alive apart
from the law, but when the commandment came, sin revived [10]and I died, and the very commandment that
promised life proved to be death to me. [11]For sin, seizing
an opportunity in the commandment, deceived me and

capable of doing them. In fact, he found himself incapable of carrying them out (v. 19).

The end result was frustration and wretchedness (v. 24). How many Christians today feel similarly? They are keenly aware of the expectations of the Christian life, yet they are also aware of how poorly they carry out those expectations. As a result, they feel guilt and condemnation. So they become preoccupied with doing acts of morality rather than with the person of Christ. Such an attitude is called legalism.

However, if an overemphasis on law is perilous, its opposite, lawlessness, is just as perilous. Scripture says that all sin is lawlessness (6:19; 1 John 3:4), because to sin is to violate God's law, His moral expectations. But one sinful act has a way of spawning another, and yet another, until things snowball into a lifestyle of lawlessness. Some Christians end up in that condition—especially many who have previously suffered under legalism.

Scylla and Charybdis were myths of the Greeks, but the perils of law and lawlessness are no illusions. They are real dangers that Christians face every day. There is only one way to avoid either pitfall: Christ must produce in us the good that we cannot produce through our own human ability (8:1–4). If we want to fulfill the expectations of God, we must rely on the power of God to enable us to do so. Are you trusting Christ to reproduce His character in you? ◆

WE ARE SLAVES NOT UNDER THE OLD WRITTEN CODE BUT IN THE NEW LIFE OF THE SPIRIT.
—Romans 7:6

ARE PEOPLE BASICALLY GOOD?

CONSIDER THIS 7:21 **Many of us want to believe that we are "basically good" people—or at least better than other people. In fact, it's popular today to subscribe to the view that humankind is basically good, and that moral problems are simply the result of bad parenting, bad education, and the foibles of "society."**

The Bible presents a different view, however. Scripture affirms the inherent dignity and value of every human being (Ps. 139:13–14; see "People At Work," Heb. 2:7). But it insists that each of us is born "in sin"—that is, apart from God, naturally tending toward wrong rather than right. That's what Paul addresses in Romans 7.

Original sin is a sobering concept, one that our pride would dearly love to do away with. But then, pride lies at the root of sin. Therefore, the first step toward rooting it out of our lives is to humbly admit our true condition—not to blame someone else, but rather to confess our sin to God and trust solely in His grace for forgiveness and acceptance (Luke 18:13).

This attitude of humility in light of our sin needs to become a way of life. Sin is so deeply entrenched within us that we can never safely say that we've mastered it (1 Cor. 4:4; 10:12). Instead, we live with limitation, admitting that we don't have all the answers to our own problems, let alone those that plague the world.

This perspective provides insight into the troubles that come our way. Sometimes they come as a result of our own sinful choices. Sometimes

(continued on next page)

through it killed me. 12So the law is holy, and the commandment is holy and just and good.

A Terrible Inner Conflict

13 Did what is good, then, bring death to me? By no
means! It was sin, working death in me through what is
good, in order that sin might be shown to be sin, and
through the commandment might become sinful beyond
measure.
14 For we know that the law is spiritual; but I am of the
flesh, sold into slavery under sin.[y] 15I do not understand
my own actions. For I do not do what I want, but I do the
very thing I hate. 16Now if I do what I do not want, I agree
that the law is good. 17But in fact it is no longer I that do it,
but sin that dwells within me. 18For I know that nothing
good dwells within me, that is, in my flesh. I can will what
is right, but I cannot do it. 19For I do not do the good I
want, but the evil I do not want is what I do. 20Now if I do
what I do not want, it is no longer I that do it, but sin that
dwells within me.

7:21 21 So I find it to be a law that when I
want to do what is good, evil lies close at
hand. 22For I delight in the law of God in my inmost self,
23but I see in my members another law at war with the law
of my mind, making me captive to the law of sin that
dwells in my members. 24Wretched man that I am! Who
will rescue me from this body of death? 25Thanks be to God
through Jesus Christ our Lord!
So then, with my mind I am a slave to the law of God,
but with my flesh I am a slave to the law of sin.

In Christ There Is No More Condemnation

8 There is therefore now no condemnation for those who
are in Christ Jesus. 2For the law of the Spirit[z] of life in
Christ Jesus has set you[a] free from the law of sin and of
death. 3For God has done what the law, weakened by the
flesh, could not do: by sending his own Son in the likeness
of sinful flesh, and to deal with sin,[b] he condemned sin in
the flesh, 4so that the just requirement of the law might be
fulfilled in us, who walk not according to the flesh but
according to the Spirit.[z] 5For those who live according to
the flesh set their minds on the things of the flesh, but
those who live according to the Spirit[z] set their minds on
the things of the Spirit.[z] 6To set the mind on the flesh is
death, but to set the mind on the Spirit[z] is life and peace.
7For this reason the mind that is set on the flesh is hostile

[y] Gk *sold under sin* [z] Or *spirit* [a] Here the Greek word *you* is singular number; other ancient authorities read *me* or *us* [b] Or *and as a sin offering*

to God; it does not submit to God's law—indeed it cannot,
8and those who are in the flesh cannot please God.

Believers Are People of the Spirit

9 But you are not in the flesh; you are in the Spirit,[c] since
the Spirit of God dwells in you. Anyone who does not have
the Spirit of Christ does not belong to him. 10But if Christ is
in you, though the body is dead because of sin, the Spirit[c]
is life because of righteousness. 11If the Spirit of him who
raised Jesus from the dead dwells in you, he who raised
Christ[d] from the dead will give life to your mortal bodies
also through[e] his Spirit that dwells in you.
12 So then, brothers and sisters,[f] we are debtors, not to
the flesh, to live according to the flesh— 13for if you live according to the flesh, you will die; but if by the Spirit you
put to death the deeds of the body, you will live. 14For all
8:15–17 who are led by the Spirit of God are children of God. 15For you did not receive a
spirit of slavery to fall back into fear, but you have received
a spirit of adoption. When we cry, "Abba![g] Father!" 16it is
that very Spirit bearing witness[h] with our spirit that we are
children of God, 17and if children, then heirs, heirs of God
and joint heirs with Christ—if, in fact, we suffer with him
so that we may also be glorified with him.

Believers Receive the Spirit's Help

18 I consider that the sufferings of this present time are
not worth comparing with the glory about to be revealed to
us. 19For the creation waits with eager longing for the re-
8:20 see pg. 552 vealing of the children of God; 20for the
creation was subjected to futility, not of
its own will but by the will of the one who subjected it, in
8:21–22 see pg. 554 hope 21that the creation itself will be set
free from its bondage to decay and will
obtain the freedom of the glory of the children of God.
22We know that the whole creation has been groaning in labor pains until now; 23and not only the creation, but we
ourselves, who have the first fruits of the Spirit, groan inwardly while we wait for adoption, the redemption of our
bodies. 24For in[i] hope we were saved. Now hope that is

(Bible text continued on page 553)

[c]Or *spirit* [d]Other ancient authorities read *the Christ* or *Christ Jesus* or *Jesus Christ* [e]Other ancient authorities read *on account of* [f]Gk *brothers* [g]Aramaic for *Father* [h]Or [15]*a spirit of adoption, by which we cry, "Abba! Father!"* [16]*The Spirit itself bears witness* [i]Or *by*

A CLOSER LOOK 8:15–17

An Inheritance?

As God's adopted children, believers are promised an inheritance (vv. 15–17). What will that involve? See "What's In It for Me?" Eph. 1:11.

(continued from previous page)

God allows them as a way of building our character, especially our faith in Him (Ps. 119:67, 71–72; Heb. 12:7–11; James 1:2–4, 12–18).

Do you want true humility? It comes from seeing yourself in relation to God. See "Humility—The Scandalous Virtue," Phil. 2:3.

TO SET THE MIND ON THE SPIRIT IS LIFE AND PEACE.
—Romans 8:6

CONSIDER THIS
8:20

Is Work a Curse?

What was the curse that God put on creation (v. 20)? One of the most stubborn myths in Western culture is that God imposed work as a curse to punish Adam and Eve's sin (Gen. 3:1–19). As a result, some people view work as something evil. Scripture does not support that idea:

God Himself is a worker. The fact that God works shows that work is not evil, since by definition God cannot do evil. On the contrary, work is an activity that God carries out. See "God: The Original Worker," John 5:17.

God created people in His image to be His coworkers. He gives us ability and authority to manage His creation. See "People At Work," Heb. 2:7.

God established work before the fall. Genesis 1–2 record how God created the world. The account tells how He placed the first humans in a garden "to tend and keep it" (2:15). This work assignment was given before sin entered the world and God pronounced the curse (Gen. 3). Obviously, then, work cannot be a result of the fall since people were working before the fall.

God commends work even after the fall. If work were evil in and of itself, God would never encourage people to engage in it. But He does. For example, He told Noah and his family the same thing He told Adam and Eve—to have dominion over the earth (Gen. 9:1–7). In the New Testament, Christians are commanded to work (Col. 3:23; 1 Thess. 4:11).

Work itself was not cursed in the fall. A careful reading of Genesis 3:17–19 shows that God cursed the *ground* as a result of Adam's sin—but not work:

> "Cursed is the ground because
> of you;
> in toil you shall eat of it all the
> days of your life;
> thorns and thistles it shall
> bring forth for you;
> and you shall eat the plants of
> the field.
> By the sweat of your face
> you shall eat bread
> until you return to the ground,
> for out of it you were taken;
> you are dust,
> and to dust you shall return."

Notice three ways that this curse affected work: (1) Work had been a joy, but now it would be "toil." People would feel burdened down by it, and even come to hate it. (2) "Thorns and thistles" would hamper people's efforts to exercise dominion. In other words, the earth would not be as cooperative as it had been. (3) People would have to "sweat" to accomplish their tasks. Work would require enormous effort and energy.

Most of us know all too well how burdensome work can be. Workplace stresses and pressures, occupational hazards, the daily grind, office politics, crushing boredom, endless routine, disappointments, setbacks, catastrophes, frustration, cutthroat competition, fraud, deception, injustice—there is no end of evils connected with work. But work itself is not evil. Far from naming it a curse, the Bible calls work and its fruit a gift from God (Eccl. 3:13; 5:18–19). ◆

Do you know that your job is actually an extension of Christ's rule over the world? See "People at Work," Heb. 2:7.

seen is not hope. For who hopes[j] for what is seen? 25But if we hope for what we do not see, we wait for it with patience.

26 Likewise the Spirit helps us in our weakness; for we do not know how to pray as we ought, but that very Spirit intercedes[k] with sighs too deep for words. 27And God,[l] who searches the heart, knows what is the mind of the Spirit, because the Spirit[m] intercedes for the saints according to the will of God.[n]

8:28

28 We know that all things work together for good[o] for those who love God, who are called according to his purpose. 29For those whom he foreknew he also predestined to be conformed to the image of his Son, in order that he might be the firstborn within a large family.[p] 30And those whom he predestined he also called; and those whom he called he also justified; and those whom he justified he also glorified.

Believers Are Loved by God

31 What then are we to say about these things? If God is for us, who is against us? 32He who did not withhold his own Son, but gave him up for all of us, will he not with him also give us everything else? 33Who will bring any charge against God's elect? It is God who justifies. 34Who is to condemn? It is Christ Jesus, who died, yes, who was raised, who is at the right hand of God, who indeed intercedes for us.[q] 35Who will separate us from the love of Christ? Will hardship, or distress, or persecution, or famine, or nakedness, or peril, or sword? 36As it is written,

"For your sake we are being killed all day long;
  we are accounted as sheep to be slaughtered."

37No, in all these things we are more than conquerors through him who loved us. 38For I am convinced that neither death, nor life, nor angels, nor rulers, nor things present, nor things to come, nor powers, 39nor height, nor depth, nor anything else in all creation, will be able to separate us from the love of God in Christ Jesus our Lord.

The Implications of Faith for Israel

9:1 see pg. 556

9 I am speaking the truth in Christ—I am not lying; my conscience confirms it by the Holy Spirit— 2I have great sorrow and unceasing anguish in my heart. 3For I could wish that I myself were accursed and cut off from Christ for the sake of my own people,[r] my kindred according to the flesh. 4They are Israelites, and to them belong the adoption, the glory, the covenants, the giving of the law, the worship, and the

[j]Other ancient authorities read *awaits* [k]Other ancient authorities add *for us* [l]Gk *the one* [m]Gk *he or it* [n]Gk *according to God* [o]Other ancient authorities read *God makes all things work together for good,* or *in all things God works for good* [p]Gk *among many brothers* [q]Or *Is it Christ Jesus . . . for us?* [r]Gk *my brothers*

All Things For Good?

CONSIDER THIS 8:28 **Verse 28 is easy to quote to someone else. But what about when it's *your* turn to suffer? Is there comfort in this passage? Notice two important things as you consider Paul's words here:**

(1) All things work together *for* good but not all things *are* good. The loss of a job, a tyrannical boss, physical illness, or family troubles are not good *per se.* In fact, often they are the direct result of evil. That's important to observe. Believers are never promised immunity from the problems and pains of the world. Every day we must put up with much that is not good.

(2) Nevertheless, good can come out of bad! This verse promises that God uses all the circumstances of our lives—both the good and the bad—to shape outcomes that accomplish His purposes for us. And His purposes can only be good, because He is good by definition (James 1:17).

So how can you make this verse work for you as you face tough, troubling times?

- **Affirm your trust in God's presence.**
- **Align your goals with God's purposes.**
- **Accept the reliability of God's promises.**

promises; 5to them belong the patriarchs, and from them,
according to the flesh, comes the Messiah,[s] who is over all,
God blessed forever.[t] Amen.
6 It is not as though the word of God had failed. For not
all Israelites truly belong to Israel, 7and not all of Abraham's
children are his true descendants; but "It is through Isaac
that descendants shall be named for you." 8This means that
it is not the children of the flesh who are the children of
God, but the children of the promise are counted as descendants. 9For this is what the promise said, "About this
time I will return and Sarah shall have a son." 10Nor is that
all; something similar happened to Rebecca when she had
conceived children by one husband, our ancestor Isaac.
11Even before they had been born or had done anything
good or bad (so that God's purpose of election might continue, 12not by works but by his call) she was told, "The elder shall serve the younger." 13As it is written,

"I have loved Jacob,
but I have hated Esau."

[s]Or *the Christ* [t]Or *Messiah, who is God over all, blessed forever*; or *Messiah. May he who is God over all be blessed forever*

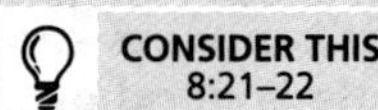

THE LIBERATION OF CREATION

In Romans 8, Paul painted on a cosmic canvas a vast picture of the world, from its origin as God's beautiful creation to the impact of sin, and on to its ultimate restoration at the end of history. If you've ever wondered what's ultimately going to happen to the world, if you've ever worried about environmental disaster, if you've ever wished that evil could somehow be vanquished, this passage is "must reading."

Paul recognized that the world is both delightful and disastrous, orderly and chaotic. He offered a good news/bad news scenario. The bad news is that all of creation, including human beings and their environments, are corrupted by sin. Sin is so prevalent and so destructive that we need more than just a better earth—we need a new earth. Sin is not just personal, it's global. It's infused in the bloodstream of the whole world, where sinful people create systems and cultures that promote and protect evil, as well as good.

So much for the bad news. The good news is that God's salvation is equally universal in its availability and effects. His saving grace starts its work inside people, but eventually works its way out through their influence. God's power and purposes begin to penetrate their values,

God Is Sovereign

14 What then are we to say? Is there injustice on God's
part? By no means! 15For he says to Moses,
"I will have mercy on whom I have mercy,
and I will have compassion on whom I have
compassion."
16So it depends not on human will or exertion, but on God
who shows mercy. 17For the scripture says to Pharaoh, "I
have raised you up for the very purpose of showing my
power in you, so that my name may be proclaimed in all
the earth." 18So then he has mercy on whomever he
chooses, and he hardens the heart of whomever he chooses.
19 You will say to me then, "Why then does he still find
fault? For who can resist his will?" 20But who indeed are
you, a human being, to argue with God? Will what is
molded say to the one who molds it, "Why have you made
me like this?" 21Has the potter no right over the clay, to
make out of the same lump one object for special use and
another for ordinary use? 22What if God, desiring to show
his wrath and to make known his power, has endured with
much patience the objects of wrath that are made for

worldview, relationships, career choices, and community involvements. As God's managers of the earth, they begin to reclaim the devil's territory, as it were, by redirecting social systems and cultural values so that people and places benefit instead of being exploited. What begins as personal conversion results in societal change as God's people slowly impact their families, coworkers, churches, communities, culture, and environment.

But this liberation of creation will be partial and imperfect until Christ returns to redeem it personally. In the meantime, the world groans like a woman in labor (v. 22), waiting for its delivery from sin. Christ calls His followers to participate in the world's systems, to promote His values and love as we have opportunity. As His people, we affirm both the salvation of persons and the transformation of places, participating with Him in the first skirmishes of the liberation of His creation. ◆

WHO INDEED ARE YOU, A HUMAN BEING, TO ARGUE WITH GOD?
—Romans 9:20

destruction; 23 and what if he has done so in order to make
known the riches of his glory for the objects of mercy,
which he has prepared beforehand for glory— 24 including
us whom he has called, not from the Jews only but also
from the Gentiles? 25 As indeed he says in Hosea,

"Those who were not my people I will call 'my people,'
and her who was not beloved I will call 'beloved.' "
26 "And in the very place where it was said to them, 'You
are not my people,'
there they shall be called children of the living God."

27 And Isaiah cries out concerning Israel, "Though the
number of the children of Israel were like the sand of the

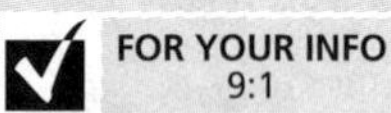

FOR YOUR INFO
9:1

God's Heart for the Whole World

n Romans 9–11, Paul reminds us that God's heart reaches out to the whole world, both Jews and Gentiles:

Good News for the World in Romans 9–11

Passage	Teaching
9:24	•God in His mercy calls not only Jews but Gentiles as well.
9:25	•Gentiles, who were not God's people, have become children of the living God.
9:30	•Gentiles have received righteousness through their faith, just as Jews who have believed in Jesus.
10:3	•But Jews who seek God through the Law's requirements will never find righteousness because they do not seek it through faith. They seek to establish their own righteousness, not God's.
10:4	•Jesus is God's righteousness to everyone who believes.
9:33; 10:9,11	•Faith in Jesus is the key to salvation.
10:12–13	•When it comes to who can be saved, God makes no distinction between Jews and Gentiles.
10:20–21; 11:11	•The Gentiles, who were not looking for God, found Him. But the Jews, whom God continually reached out to, did not want Him.
11:1–2	•God has not given up on the Jews. Many have turned to God; Paul was one of them.
11:14	•The Gentiles found Christ through the witness of the Jews. Paul's great desire was for Jews to come to Christ through the witness of the Gentiles.
11:16–24	•Gentiles were grafted into God's tree of life as Jews rejected God and were broken off. But that leaves no room for pride or arrogance on the part of the Gentiles; rather, humility.
11:19–24	•Jews were "cut off" because they refused to believe. If they repent, God is able to graft them in again.
11:32	•God's desire is to have mercy on all.

By the time Paul wrote Romans, Gentiles had probably become a majority in the church. Paul saw the possibility of a church divided, and the tragedy that would result if that happened. *See "Are We One People?" Rom. 11:13–24.*

sea, only a remnant of them will be saved; 28for the Lord will execute his sentence on the earth quickly and decisively."[u] 29And as Isaiah predicted,

"If the Lord of hosts had not left survivors[v] to
us,
we would have fared like Sodom
and been made like Gomorrah."

30 What then are we to say? Gentiles, who did not strive for righteousness, have attained it, that is, righteousness through faith; 31but Israel, who did strive for the righteousness that is based on the law, did not succeed in fulfilling that law. 32Why not? Because they did not strive for it on the basis of faith, but as if it were based on works. They have stumbled over the stumbling stone, 33as it is written,

"See, I am laying in Zion a stone that will make
people stumble, a rock that will make
them fall,
and whoever believes in him[w] will not be put
to shame."

Paul Longs for Israel's Salvation

10:1 see pg. 558

10 Brothers and sisters,[x] my heart's desire and prayer to God for them is that they may be saved. 2I can testify that they have a zeal for God, but it is not enlightened. 3For, being ignorant of the righteousness that comes from God, and seeking to establish their own, they have not submitted to God's righteousness. 4For Christ is the end of the law so that there may be righteousness for everyone who believes.

5 Moses writes concerning the righteousness that comes from the law, that "the person who does these things will live by them." 6But the righteousness that comes from faith says, "Do not say in your heart, 'Who will ascend into heaven?' " (that is, to bring Christ down) 7"or 'Who will descend into the abyss?' " (that is, to bring Christ up from the dead). 8But what does it say?

"The word is near you,
on your lips and in your heart"

(that is, the word of faith that we proclaim); 9because[y] if you confess with your lips that Jesus is Lord and believe in your heart that God raised him from the dead, you will be saved. 10For one believes with the heart and so is justified, and one confesses with the mouth and so is saved. 11The scripture says, "No one who believes in him will be put to shame." 12For there is no distinction between Jew and Greek; the same Lord is Lord of all and is generous to all who call on him. 13For, "Everyone who calls on the name of the Lord shall be saved."

The Nation Needs to Hear the Gospel

14 But how are they to call on one in whom they have not believed? And how are they to believe in one of whom they have never heard? And how are they to hear without someone to proclaim him? 15And how are they to proclaim him unless they are sent? As it is written, "How beautiful are the feet of those who bring good news!" 16But not all have obeyed the good news;[z] for Isaiah says, "Lord, who has believed our message?" 17So faith comes from what is heard, and what is heard comes through the word of Christ.[a]

18 But I ask, have they not heard? Indeed they have; for

"Their voice has gone out to all the earth,
and their words to the ends of the world."

19Again I ask, did Israel not understand? First Moses says,

"I will make you jealous of those who are not a
nation;
with a foolish nation I will make you angry."

20Then Isaiah is so bold as to say,

"I have been found by those who did not seek
me;
I have shown myself to those who did not ask
for me."

21But of Israel he says, "All day long I have held out my hands to a disobedient and contrary people."

(Bible text continued on page 559)

[u] Other ancient authorities read *for he will finish his work and cut it short in righteousness, because the Lord will make the sentence shortened on the earth* [v] Or *descendants*; Gk *seed* [w] Or *trusts in it* [x] Gk *Brothers*

[y] Or *namely, that* [z] Or *gospel* [a] Or *about Christ*; other ancient authorities read *of God*

FOR YOUR INFO
10:1

ISRAEL

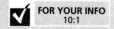

Have you ever wondered what happened to the special relationship between God and the nation of Israel (v. 1)? Are the Jews still God's "chosen people"? Are the promises that God made to Abraham, Moses, David, and other Old Testament Hebrews still in effect? Or did God reject Israel when the nation rejected His Son, Jesus?

These are issues that Paul addresses in Romans 9–11. They are vitally important, because they relate to whether or not God is to be trusted.

Origins

God's relationship with Israel goes back thousands of years to the ancient Near East. The Bible presents Abraham (see Rom. 4:1) as the father of the nation. Abraham came from Ur, a city of ancient Sumer in Mesopotamia (Gen. 11:31), where he prospered before moving to the land of Canaan (Gen. 12:5).

There God entered into a covenant with Abraham, promising to bless his descendants and make them His special people (Gen. 12:1–3). Abraham was to remain faithful to God and to serve as a channel through which God's blessings could flow to the rest of the world.

Abraham's son Isaac had two sons, Esau and Jacob. God chose Jacob for the renewal of His promise to Abraham (Gen. 28:13–15). Jacob's name was changed to Israel after a dramatic struggle with God (Gen. 32:24–30; 35:9–15). The name Israel has been interpreted by different scholars as "prince with God," "he strives with God," "let God rule," or "God strives." The name was later applied to the descendants of Jacob through his twelve sons, the Hebrew people. These twelve tribes were called "Israelites," "children of Israel," and "house of Israel," identifying them clearly as the descendants of Israel.

God's Chosen People

God's covenant with Abraham was far more than a contract. A contract always has an end date, while a covenant, in the biblical sense, is a permanent arrangement. Furthermore, a contract generally involves only one part of a person, such as a skill, while a covenant covers a person's total being. Another striking feature is that God is holy, all-knowing, and all-powerful, yet He consented to enter into a covenant with Abraham and his descendants—weak, sinful, and imperfect as they were.

Thus, through Abraham, Israel became God's "chosen people." This covenant relationship was confirmed at Mount Sinai when the nation promised to perform "all the words that the Lord has spoken" (Ex. 24:3). When the people later broke their side of the agreement, they were called by their leaders to renew the covenant (2 Kin. 23:3).

God, of course, never breaks His promises, and throughout Israel's history, He has always lived up to His side of the covenant. That's why Paul can affirm that God has not "rejected" His people (Rom. 11:1). God's oath to raise up believing children to Abraham (Gen. 22:16–17) remains an "everlasting" covenant (Gen. 17:7).

This is good news for Jew and Gentile alike. For Jews it means that God has not abandoned His people. They still figure prominently in His plans and purposes. For Gentiles, it means that God is totally trustworthy. His word can be taken at face value. Are you basing your hope on the unalterable covenants of God? ◆

Because the Hebrews failed to honor their side of their covenant with God, He promised a new covenant through the prophet Jeremiah that would accomplish what the old covenant had failed to do. See "The New Covenant," 1 Cor. 11:25.

God Has Not Given Up on His People

11 I ask, then, has God rejected his people? By
no means! I myself am an Israelite, a descendant of Abraham, a member of the tribe of
Benjamin. 2God has not rejected his people whom
he foreknew. Do you not know what the scripture
says of Elijah, how he pleads with God against Israel? 3“Lord, they have killed your prophets, they
have demolished your altars; I alone am left, and
they are seeking my life.” 4But what is the divine
reply to him? “I have kept for myself seven thousand who have not bowed the knee to Baal.” 5So
too at the present time there is a remnant, chosen
by grace. 6But if it is by grace, it is no longer on the
basis of works, otherwise grace would no longer be
grace.[b]
7 What then? Israel failed to obtain what it was
seeking. The elect obtained it, but the rest were
hardened, 8as it is written,

“God gave them a sluggish spirit,
eyes that would not see
and ears that would not hear,
down to this very day.”

9And David says,

“Let their table become a snare and a trap,
a stumbling block and a retribution for them;
10 let their eyes be darkened so that they cannot
see,
and keep their backs forever bent.”

The Implications of Faith for Gentiles

11 So I ask, have they stumbled so as to fall? By
no means! But through their stumbling[c] salvation
has come to the Gentiles, so as to make Israel[d] jealous. 12Now if their stumbling[c] means riches for the
world, and if their defeat means riches for Gentiles,
how much more will their full inclusion mean!

11:13–24
see pg. 560

13 Now I am speaking to you
Gentiles. Inasmuch then as I am
an apostle to the Gentiles, I glorify my ministry
14in order to make my own people[e] jealous, and
thus save some of them. 15For if their rejection is
the reconciliation of the world, what will their acceptance be but life from the dead! 16If the part of
the dough offered as first fruits is holy, then the
whole batch is holy; and if the root is holy, then
the branches also are holy.
17 But if some of the branches were broken off,
and you, a wild olive shoot, were grafted in their
place to share the rich root[f] of the olive tree, 18do
not boast over the branches. If you do boast, remember that it is not you that support the root,
but the root that supports you. 19You will say,
“Branches were broken off so that I might be
grafted in.” 20That is true. They were broken off because of their unbelief, but you stand only through
faith. So do not become proud, but stand in awe.
21For if God did not spare the natural branches,
perhaps he will not spare you.[g] 22Note then the
kindness and the severity of God: severity toward
those who have fallen, but God’s kindness toward
you, provided you continue in his kindness; otherwise you also will be cut off. 23And even those of
Israel,[h] if they do not persist in unbelief, will be
grafted in, for God has the power to graft them in
again. 24For if you have been cut from what is by
nature a wild olive tree and grafted, contrary to nature, into a cultivated olive tree, how much more
will these natural branches be grafted back into
their own olive tree.

Israel Will Eventually Be Saved

25 So that you may not claim to be wiser than
you are, brothers and sisters,[i] I want you to understand this mystery: a hardening has come upon
part of Israel, until the full number of the Gentiles
has come in. 26And so all Israel will be saved; as it
is written,

“Out of Zion will come the Deliverer;
he will banish ungodliness from Jacob.”
27 “And this is my covenant with them,
when I take away their sins.”

28As regards the gospel they are enemies of God[j]
for your sake; but as regards election they are
beloved, for the sake of their ancestors; 29for the
gifts and the calling of God are irrevocable. 30Just
as you were once disobedient to God but have now
received mercy because of their disobedience, 31so

[b]Other ancient authorities add *But if it is by works, it is no longer on the basis of grace, otherwise work would no longer be work* [c]Gk *transgression* [d]Gk *them* [e]Gk *my flesh*

[f]Other ancient authorities read *the richness* [g]Other ancient authorities read *neither will he spare you* [h]Gk lacks *of Israel* [i]Gk *brothers* [j]Gk lacks *of God*

they have now been disobedient in order that, by the mercy
shown to you, they too may now[k] receive mercy. 32For God
has imprisoned all in disobedience so that he may be merciful to all.

Paul's Prayer of Praise

33 O the depth of the riches and wisdom and knowledge of God! How unsearchable are his judgments and how
inscrutable his ways!
34 "For who has known the mind of the Lord?
   Or who has been his counselor?"
35 "Or who has given a gift to him,
   to receive a gift in return?"
36For from him and through him and to him are all things.
To him be the glory forever. Amen.

The Believer's Relationship to God

12 I appeal to you therefore, brothers and sisters,[l] by
the mercies of God, to present your bodies as a living sacrifice, holy and acceptable to God, which is your

[k]Other ancient authorities lack *now* [l]Gk *brothers*

CONSIDER THIS
11:13–24

ARE WE ONE PEOPLE?

By the time Paul wrote his letter to the Christians at Rome, Gentiles were probably becoming a majority of believers throughout the church. Jews had less and less influence theologically, culturally, or politically. Gradually—and tragically—the attitudes of pride and prejudice with which Jews had looked down on Gentiles were coming back to haunt them, as Gentile believers began to turn away from their Jewish brothers.

In Romans 9–11, Paul pleaded with his Gentile readers to remember that God has not forgotten Israel. God made promises to the nation that He cannot forsake (11:29). Furthermore, Gentiles have no room for arrogance: they were not originally included among God's people, but were allowed in, like branches grafted onto a tree (vv. 17–18).

Paul saw the possibility of a church divided, with Jewish and Gentile believers going their separate ways. If that happened, Gentiles would ignore the Jewish community altogether rather than show compassion and communicate the gospel so that Jews could be saved. That's why here, as elsewhere, Paul challenged believers to pursue unity in the body of Christ and charity among the peoples of the world.

spiritual[m] worship. 2Do not be conformed to this world,[n]
but be transformed by the renewing of your minds, so that
you may discern what is the will of God—what is good and
acceptable and perfect.[o]

The Believer's Position in the Body of Christ

12:3 see pg. 562

3 For by the grace given to me I say to
everyone among you not to think of
yourself more highly than you ought to think, but to think
with sober judgment, each according to the measure of
faith that God has assigned. 4For as in one body we have
many members, and not all the members have the same
function, 5so we, who are many, are one body in Christ,
and individually we are members one of another. 6We have
gifts that differ according to the grace given to us: prophecy,
in proportion to faith; 7ministry, in ministering; the teacher,
in teaching; 8the exhorter, in exhortation;
the giver, in generosity; the leader, in
diligence; the compassionate, in cheerfulness.
9 Let love be genuine; hate what is evil, hold fast to what

12:8

[m] *Or reasonable* [n] *Gk age* [o] *Or what is the good and acceptable and perfect will of God*

QUOTE UNQUOTE

CONSIDER THIS 12:8

If God has given you the capacity to give, give liberally (v. 8):

We make a living by what we get.
We make a life by what we give.

Anonymous

Are we as believers today carrying out that exhortation? Unfortunately, the legacy that we've inherited is not encouraging. Had the church wholeheartedly embraced Paul's teaching, it would not have kept its tragic silence or participated in some of the great evils of the past 2,000 years. In fact, many of them probably could have been avoided, or at least resisted, had Christians paid careful attention to Romans 9–11.

We need to ask: What are the current challenges to the ethnic, racial, and cultural attitudes of believers? What tragic evils are currently operating that we need to be aware of and actively resisting? God's desire is clear—to have mercy on all (v. 32). Does that describe our heart? ◆

Paul was at pains to show that God's love and mercy extended to the whole world, both Jews and Gentiles. See how Paul accomplished that in Romans 9–11 by looking at the table, "God's Heart for the Whole World," Rom. 9:1.

is good; 10love one another with mutual affection; outdo
one another in showing honor. 11Do not lag in zeal, be ardent in spirit, serve the Lord.[p] 12Rejoice in hope, be patient
in suffering, persevere in prayer. 13Contribute to the needs
of the saints; extend hospitality to strangers.

The Believer's Service to the Community

14 Bless those who persecute you; bless and do not
curse them. 15Rejoice with those who rejoice, weep with
those who weep. 16Live in harmony with one another; do
not be haughty, but associate with the lowly;[q] do not claim
to be wiser than you are. 17Do not repay anyone evil for
evil, but take thought for what is noble in the sight of all.
18If it is possible, so far as it depends on you, live peaceably
with all. 19Beloved, never avenge your-
selves, but leave room for the wrath of
God;[r] for it is written, "Vengeance is mine, I will repay, says
the Lord." 20No, "if your enemies are hungry, feed them; if
they are thirsty, give them something to drink; for by doing

12:19–21

[p]Other ancient authorities read *serve the opportune time* [q]Or *give yourselves to humble tasks* [r]Gk *the wrath*

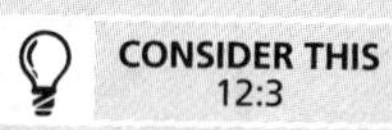

CONSIDER THIS
12:3

Do You Suffer from "Comparison-itis"?

One of the most debilitating diseases of the modern world is "comparisonitis"—the tendency to measure one's worth by comparing oneself to other people. You won't find this illness listed in any of the standard medical textbooks, nor will your company's disability or health insurance or worker's compensation program reimburse you for it. But make no mistake: comparisonitis is a scourge as widespread and destructive as any physical or emotional malady known today.

Do you suffer from it? Do you find ways to look down on others and think highly of yourself because you enjoy greater abilities, intelligence, status, or wealth than they? Or do you look down on yourself and envy others because you feel you are not as capable, smart, powerful, or rich as they?

Comparisonitis is an ancient disease. Certainly Paul was aware of how deadly it could be. That's why he offered an antidote for it—to see ourselves not as we stack up against others, nor as others evaluate us, but as God sees us (v. 3). *Ultimately, His estimation of our worth is what matters. And to Him we matter* a lot!

God does not define us according to culturally defined externals. Even our gender, ethnicity, family heritage, or

this you will heap burning coals on their heads." 21Do not
be overcome by evil, but overcome evil with good.

The Believer's Submission to the State

13:1–7 see pg. 564
13 Let every person be subject to
the governing authorities; for
there is no authority except from God, and those authori-
13:2 see pg. 565
ties that exist have been instituted by
God. 2Therefore whoever resists author-
ity resists what God has appointed, and those who resist
will incur judgment. 3For rulers are not a terror to good
conduct, but to bad. Do you wish to have no fear of the authority? Then do what is good, and you will receive its ap-
13:4 see pg. 564
proval; 4for it is God's servant for your
good. But if you do what is wrong, you
should be afraid, for the authority[s] does not bear the sword
in vain! It is the servant of God to execute wrath on the
wrongdoer. 5Therefore one must be subject, not only be-
13:6 see pg. 566
cause of wrath but also because of conscience. 6For the same reason you also

[s]Gk *it*

body type are not of primary importance to Him. No, He uses an altogether different set of criteria as the basis for how He deals with us, as several people in Scripture indicate:

- Paul *found that God's grace made him who he was (1 Cor. 15:10). He also discovered that despite his past, God had made him into a new person (2 Cor. 5:17).*
- Peter *learned that God's power gave him everything he needed to live his life and pursue godliness (2 Pet. 1:3).*
- Job *realized that all he had—family, friends, possessions, health—was ultimately from God (Job 1:21).*
- One of the psalmists *understood that God Himself had created him, "fearfully and wonderfully." Imagine what that did for his self-image! (Ps. 139:14).*

Do you suffer from comparisonitis? What needs to change in your self-assessment for you to see yourself as God sees you? ◆

Jesus told a parable that illustrates the deadly nature of comparisonitis. See "Comparisonitis Will Kill You," Luke 18:9–14.

Do Not Avenge Yourself

CONSIDER THIS 12:19–21
Scripture is straightforward: no believer should avenge himself on others (v. 19). Why? Because God has reserved vengeance to Himself.

What, then, can you do to those who hurt you? You must do them good, not evil (v. 21). If you do them evil, you will yourself be overcome by evil. You can't be too careful when it comes to vengeance. One of Satan's favorite tactics is to lure someone into doing evil by providing a "good" excuse for it. And retaliation feels so appealing.

But Scripture challenges you to overcome evil, both in yourself (the will to retaliate) and in those who harm you (by doing them good). Doing so will "heap burning coals" on the heads of your enemies (v. 20). In other words, you may magnify their sense of guilt when they see that their evil against you is met by your good toward them. Indeed, their guilty conscience may drive them to repentance.

Does Paul mean that we can never defend ourselves or our property, or that criminals should go unpunished? See "An Eye for an Eye," Matt. 5:38–42; and "The Avengers," Rom. 13:4.

The Avengers

CONSIDER THIS 13:4 **Governmental authorities are called by God to exact vengeance on those who do evil (v. 4). Is that inconsistent with Paul's command to believers not to avenge themselves (12:19–21)?**

No, in Romans 12, Paul was addressing individuals in their private capacities. But in Romans 13, he was writing about representatives of governments in their official, public capacities. Private individuals are not to avenge themselves because God has reserved vengeance to Himself. But in doing so, God reserves the right to decide how He will bring about justice. Verse 4 indicates that one means He uses is government.

Jesus spoke along very similar lines. See "An Eye for an Eye," Matt. 5:38–42.

pay taxes, for the authorities are God's servants, busy with
this very thing. [7]Pay to all what is due them—taxes to
whom taxes are due, revenue to whom revenue is due, respect to whom respect is due, honor to whom honor is
due.

The Believer's Conduct

13:8 see pg. 567

8 Owe no one anything, except to
love one another; for the one who loves
another has fulfilled the law. [9]The commandments, "You
shall not commit adultery; You shall not murder; You shall
not steal; You shall not covet"; and any other commandment, are summed up in this word, "Love your neighbor as
yourself." [10]Love does no wrong to a neighbor; therefore,
love is the fulfilling of the law.

11 Besides this, you know what time it is, how it is now
the moment for you to wake from sleep. For salvation is
nearer to us now than when we became believers; [12]the
night is far gone, the day is near. Let us then lay aside the
works of darkness and put on the armor of light; [13]let us
live honorably as in the day, not in reveling and drunkenness, not in debauchery and licentiousness, not in quarrel-

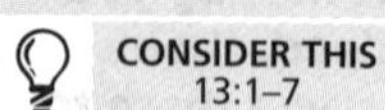

The Limits of Political Authority

When Paul wrote to the Roman believers about governing authorities (v. 1), there was no question as to what authorities he had in mind—the imperial government of Rome, probably led at the time by Nero. According to this passage, even Rome's harsh, corrupt system was established by God and deserved the respect and obedience of Christians.

However, Rome's authority—and all authority—was merely delegated authority. Ultimate authority belongs to God, as Paul pointed out. But that raises a tough question for believers, then as now: If governments are subordinate to God and accountable to Him for what they do, then aren't there limits on the extent to which believers must submit to them? Aren't there times when Christians need to obey God rather than human officials? If so, shouldn't the church pay attention to whether any particular civil government is usurping God's power and undermining His purposes rather than carrying out its intended function?

The early church had to wrestle with these issues.

ing and jealousy. 14Instead, put on the Lord Jesus Christ,
and make no provision for the flesh, to gratify its desires.

Controversial Practices

14:1–23 see pg. 568

14 Welcome those who are weak in
faith,[t] but not for the purpose of
quarreling over opinions. 2Some believe in eating anything,
while the weak eat only vegetables. 3Those who eat must
not despise those who abstain, and those who abstain must
not pass judgment on those who eat; for God has welcomed them. 4Who are you to pass judgment on servants
of another? It is before their own lord that they stand or
fall. And they will be upheld, for the Lord[u] is able to make
them stand.

14:5 see pg. 566

5 Some judge one day to be better
than another, while others judge all days
to be alike. Let all be fully convinced in their own minds.

14:5–13 see pg. 569

6Those who observe the day, observe it
in honor of the Lord. Also those who eat,
eat in honor of the Lord, since they give thanks to God;
while those who abstain, abstain in honor of the Lord and
give thanks to God.

[t]Or *conviction* [u]Other ancient authorities read *for God*

Rome's government was far more tolerant of Christians when Paul likely wrote Romans 13 than in the 90s, when John penned Revelation. Within that span of some 30 years, believers changed their view of Rome from God's "minister for good" (v. 4) to a usurper of power that deserved to fall. In fact, the book of Revelation is seen at one level as the story of Rome's fall.

Throughout church history, believers have struggled with whether to obey or resist evil governments. There are no easy answers. But one principle that Paul clearly affirms here is that government itself is intrinsically good, having been established by God. ◆

Governmental Authority

CONSIDER THIS 13:2 **Scripture challenges us as believers to subject ourselves to whatever governments we live under (vv. 1–7). Submission to authority is never easy. Human nature tends toward resistance and even rebellion, especially if government is imposed, incompetent, and/or corrupt. But as we struggle with how to respond to the systems in which we live, this passage offers some helpful perspectives:**

(1) God is the ultimate authority (v. 1). **Government as an institution has been established by God to serve His purposes. God raises up and does away with leaders.**

(2) Both followers and leaders are ultimately accountable to God (v. 2). **Submission to human authorities reflects our submission to God's authority.**

(3) God uses governments to carry out His good purposes on earth (v. 3). **Without question, some governments sometimes persecute those who do good. Paul had firsthand experience with that. But in the main, it's the lawbreaker, not the law-abiding citizen, who has something to fear from government.**

(4) Obedience is a matter of inner conviction as well as external law (v. 5). **Our motivation to obey must go beyond fear of punishment. As believers, we serve the highest of all authorities, God Himself.**

Tough questions remain when a political leader like Hitler claims for himself the power of God. What do you think?

Our responses to authority tell others much about the sincerity of our commitment to Christ. See 1 Thess. 4:12; 1 Tim. 6:1; and Titus 2:9–10.

QUOTE UNQUOTE

CONSIDER THIS 14:5 *One modern-day believer who has become "fully convinced in his own mind" (v. 5) about Sundays has written:*

It is a gross error to suppose that the Christian cause goes forward solely or chiefly on weekends. What happens on the regular weekdays may be far more important, so far as the Christian faith is concerned, than what happens on Sundays.

Elton Trueblood, *Your Other Vocation*, p. 57

7 We do not live to ourselves, and we do not die to ourselves. 8If we live, we live to the Lord, and if we die, we die
to the Lord; so then, whether we live or whether we die, we
are the Lord's. 9For to this end Christ died and lived again,
so that he might be Lord of both the dead and the living.
10 Why do you pass judgment on your brother or
sister?[v] Or you, why do you despise your brother or sister?[v]
For we will all stand before the judgment seat of God.[w]
11For it is written,

"As I live, says the Lord, every knee shall bow to me,
and every tongue shall give praise to[x] God."

12So then, each of us will be accountable to God.[y]

Pursue Peace with Each Other

13 Let us therefore no longer pass judgment on one another, but resolve instead never to put a stumbling block or
hindrance in the way of another.[z] 14I know and am persuaded in the Lord Jesus that nothing is unclean in itself;
but it is unclean for anyone who thinks it unclean. 15If your

[v]Gk *brother* [w]Other ancient authorities read *of Christ* [x]Or *confess* [y]Other ancient authorities lack *to God* [z]Gk *of a brother*

CONSIDER THIS 13:6

The High Calling of Government Service

The largest category of employment in many nations is government. That outrages some citizens, who see government as a massive, wasteful, scandal-plagued bureaucracy. But God takes a different view. If you work in government—as an elected or appointed official, a letter carrier, a police or military officer, a water-meter reader—you'll want to pay special attention to vv. 1–7.

Paul refers to governmental authorities as God's "servants" (vv. 4, 6). It's the same word translated elsewhere as "deacons." The point is, if you work in government, you are ultimately God's worker. Your authority derives not just from the people, but from God Himself. (This is an amazing statement from Paul. He was not living under a democratically elected government, but under an imperial Roman system, probably headed by Nero!)

Government, then, is established by God. That doesn't mean that He approves of everything governments or their representatives do. But good or bad, He chooses to allow them to exist and have authority. He actually works through them to accomplish His purposes.

As a government employee, you are a "servant for

brother or sister[a] is being injured by what you eat, you are
no longer walking in love. Do not let what you eat cause
the ruin of one for whom Christ died. 16So do not let your
good be spoken of as evil. 17For the kingdom of God is not
food and drink but righteousness and peace and joy in the
Holy Spirit. 18The one who thus serves Christ is acceptable
to God and has human approval. 19Let us then pursue what
makes for peace and for mutual upbuilding. 20Do not, for
the sake of food, destroy the work of God. Everything is indeed clean, but it is wrong for you to make others fall by
what you eat; 21it is good not to eat meat or drink wine or
do anything that makes your brother or sister[a] stumble.[b]
22The faith that you have, have as your own conviction before God. Blessed are those who have no reason to condemn themselves because of what they approve. 23But those
who have doubts are condemned if they eat, because they
do not act from faith;[c] for whatever does not proceed from
faith[c] is sin.[d]

(Bible text continued on page 569)

[a]Gk *brother* [b]Other ancient authorities add *or be upset or be weakened* [c]Or *conviction*
[d]Other authorities, some ancient, add here 16.25-27

good." In what way? This passage describes one important category of governmental authority—policing citizens by motivating them to pursue good and punishing those who do evil. Of course, your work in the system may involve very different tasks. Still, God wants you to be a "servant for good" by helping society function, by meeting the needs of people, by protecting the rights of people, or by defending your country from attack.

With authority comes responsibility and accountability. As a "minister of God" you will answer to Him for your decisions and actions. If God promises to avenge the evil that citizens commit, how much more will He avenge the evil that those in authority commit? ◆

For a larger perspective on everyday work, see "People at Work," Heb. 2:7.

God gives government the right to revenge, but not private citizens. See "The Morality of Christ," Matt. 5:17–48.

DEBT-FREE LIVING

CONSIDER THIS 13:8 **Paul's admonition to owe nothing but love (v. 8) is a powerful reminder of God's distaste for all forms of unpaid debt.**

Usually we think of debt in terms of monetary loans. But in light of the context of this passage (13:1–7, 9–10), Paul seems to have a broader view of debt in mind (v. 7). He speaks to us of:

- ***Taxes,* levies placed on us by governing authorities, such as income and social security taxes.**
- ***Customs,* tolls and tariffs arising from trade and business, such as highway tolls, airport landing fees, and import fees.**
- ***Fear,* the respect we owe to those who enforce the law, such as police officers and military personnel.**
- ***Honor,* the praise we owe to those in high authority, such as judges and elected officials.**

All of us are debtors to God's grace. As He has shown us love, we need to extend love to those around us with whom we live and work—even those who tax and govern us.

CONSIDER THIS
14:1–23

MATTERS OF CONSCIENCE

One noticeable difference between Christianity and most other religions is that Christians are not bound by ritualistic rules. Paul discusses two examples here in Romans 14: special days of religious observance (vv. 5–13) and food (vv. 2–4, 14–23). However, the principles he sets forth apply to all matters of conscience, the "gray" areas of life for which Scripture prescribes no specific behavior one way or another.

Special observances and food were apparently trouble spots for the Roman believers. No doubt those from Jewish backgrounds brought their heritage of strict Sabbath-keeping and were shocked to find Gentile believers to whom Sabbath days were inconsequential. Likewise, some from pagan backgrounds may have encouraged the church to form its own counterparts to the festival days they had practiced in their former religions. Either way, the keeping of "holy days" created tension in the church.

So did the issue of eating meat. The pagan religions of the day offered meat as sacrifices to their idols. The meat was then sold to the general public. As it tended to be among the choicest cuts, it made for good eating. But many believers objected to eating such meat, or meat of any kind, lest they give tacit approval to the practice of idolatry. Others, however, saw no problem (v. 2). Again, Christians lined up on both sides of the issue. Predictably, people began to question each other's spirituality and dispute over whose position was "right" (v. 1).

Do these situations sound familiar? Perhaps meat sacrificed to idols is not an issue for believers today. But plenty of issues have managed to divide believers today. Does Paul offer any perspective on settling such disputes? Yes:

(1) No Christian should judge another regarding disputable things (vv. 3–4, 13). We may have opinions about what is right and wrong. But Christ is the Judge, for us and for others.

(2) Each person needs to come to his or her own convictions regarding matters of conscience (vv. 5, 22–23). God has given us a mind and the responsibility to think things through and decide what is best for ourselves in cases where the Scriptures are not clear. Unexamined morality is as irresponsible as no morality.

(3) We are not totally free to do as we please; we must answer to the Lord for our behavior (vv. 7–8, 12).

(4) We should avoid offending others by flaunting our liberty (v. 13). A "stumbling block" is an ancient metaphor for giving offense. It is easy to offend believers whose consciences are immature—that is, who lack the knowledge and confidence of their liberty in Christ (v. 2; 1 Cor. 8:9–12). This can happen in two ways: through trampling on their sensibilities by deliberately engaging in practices they find offensive; or through tempting them to engage in something they regard as sin. Even actions that are not inherently sinful can produce sin if they cause others to stumble.

(5) We should practice love, pursuing peace in the body and that which builds others up in the faith (vv. 15, 19). Christianity is just as concerned with community and healthy relationships as it is with morality. To be sure, there are matters that are worth fighting for. But where God is either silent or has left room for personal choice, believers need to practice tolerance and consider what is best for all. ◆

In a related text, Paul appeals to conscience for settling controversial issues. See "Gray Areas," 1 Cor. 8:1–13.

Show Compassion to All

15 We who are strong ought to put up with the failings
of the weak, and not to please ourselves. 2Each of
us must please our neighbor for the good purpose of building up the neighbor. 3For Christ did not please himself;
but, as it is written, "The insults of those who insult you
have fallen on me." 4For whatever was written in former
days was written for our instruction, so that by steadfastness and by the encouragement of the scriptures we might
have hope. 5May the God of steadfastness and encouragement grant you to live in harmony with one another, in accordance with Christ Jesus, 6so that together you may with
one voice glorify the God and Father of our Lord Jesus
Christ.

15:7–12 see pg. 570

7 Welcome one another, therefore,
just as Christ has welcomed you, for the
glory of God. 8For I tell you that Christ has become a servant of the circumcised on behalf of the truth of God in order that he might confirm the promises given to the patriarchs, 9and in order that the Gentiles might glorify God for
his mercy. As it is written,

"Therefore I will confess[e] you among the Gentiles,
and sing praises to your name";
10and again he says,
"Rejoice, O Gentiles, with his people";
11and again,
"Praise the Lord, all you Gentiles,
and let all the peoples praise him";
12and again Isaiah says,
"The root of Jesse shall come,
the one who rises to rule the Gentiles;
in him the Gentiles shall hope."
13May the God of hope fill you with all joy and peace in believing, so that you may abound in hope by the power of
the Holy Spirit.

Paul's Confidence in His Readers

14 I myself feel confident about you, my brothers and
sisters,[f] that you yourselves are full of goodness, filled with
all knowledge, and able to instruct one another. 15Never-
theless on some points I have written to you rather boldly
by way of reminder, because of the grace given me by God
16to be a minister of Christ Jesus to the Gentiles in the
priestly service of the gospel of God, so that the offering of

[e]Or *thank* [f]Gk *brothers*

Are Sundays Special?

CONSIDER THIS 14:5–13 **In the Old Testament, God commanded the Hebrews to set aside one day a week as a "sabbath," a holy day of rest (Ex. 20:8–11; Is. 58:13–14; Jer. 17:19–27). Yet here in Romans, Paul seems to take a nondirective posture toward the Sabbath (14:5). Does that mean that there is no such thing as a "Lord's day," that God's people are no longer required to observe a Sabbath, whether it be Saturday or Sunday?**

Not exactly. For Paul, *every day* should be lived for the Lord because we are the Lord's possession (v. 8). If we act as if Sunday is the Lord's day but the other six days belong to us, then we've got a major misunderstanding. All seven days of the week belong to the Lord.

So the real question is, should one of those days be observed in a special way, in light of God's instructions regarding a sabbath? Paul says that neither pressure from other people nor tradition should bind our consciences. Instead, we are to seek guidance from the Spirit of God as to what we should do. Having inspired the Scriptures, God will help us determine what we should do as we study them.

For more on God's intentions regarding the Sabbath, see "The Sabbath," Heb. 4:1–13.

God's Rainbow

CONSIDER THIS 15:7–12 **Societies and their systems tend to encourage people to divide along racial, ethnic, and cultural lines, or else to abandon their distinctives by assimilating into the dominant power group. Paul called for a different approach. He didn't ask Jews to give up their Jewish heritage and become Gentiles, nor did he ask Gentiles to become Jews. Instead, he affirmed the rich ethnic backgrounds of both groups while challenging them to live together in unity (v. 7).**

That kind of unity is costly, and the attempt to practice it is always under attack. Yet that is the church that God calls us to—a diverse body of people who are unified around Christ. Our backgrounds—whether Japanese, Anglo-Saxon, African, Middle Eastern, Puerto Rican, Chinese, Italian, or whatever—are God's gifts to each of us and to the church. He has placed us in our families as He has seen fit. We can rejoice in the background He has given us and be enriched by the background He has given others.

the Gentiles may be acceptable, sanctified by the Holy
Spirit. 17In Christ Jesus, then, I have reason to boast of my
work for God. 18For I will not venture to speak of anything
except what Christ has accomplished[g] through me to win
obedience from the Gentiles, by word and deed, 19by the
power of signs and wonders, by the power of the Spirit of
God,[h] so that from Jerusalem and as far around as Illyricum
I have fully proclaimed the good news[i] of Christ. 20Thus I
make it my ambition to proclaim the good news,[i] not where
Christ has already been named, so that I do not build on
someone else's foundation, 21but as it is written,

"Those who have never been told of him shall see,
and those who have never heard of him shall
understand."

Paul Expects to Preach the Gospel at Rome

22 This is the reason that I have so often been hindered
from coming to you. 23But now, with no further place for
me in these regions, I desire, as I have for many years, to
15:24 come to you 24when I go to Spain. For I
do hope to see you on my journey and to
be sent on by you, once I have enjoyed your company for a
little while. 25At present, however, I am going to Jerusalem
in a ministry to the saints; 26for Macedonia and Achaia have
been pleased to share their resources with the poor among
the saints at Jerusalem. 27They were pleased to do this, and
indeed they owe it to them; for if the Gentiles have come to
share in their spiritual blessings, they ought also to be of
service to them in material things. 28So, when I have completed this, and have delivered to them what has been collected,[j] I will set out by way of you to Spain; 29and I know
that when I come to you, I will come in the fullness of the
blessing[k] of Christ.

30 I appeal to you, brothers and sisters,[l] by our Lord Jesus Christ and by the love of the Spirit, to join me in
earnest prayer to God on my behalf, 31that I may be rescued
from the unbelievers in Judea, and that my ministry[m] to

[g]Gk *speak of those things that Christ has not accomplished* [h]Other ancient authorities read *of the Spirit* or *of the Holy Spirit* [i]Or *gospel* [j]Gk *have sealed to them this fruit* [k]Other ancient authorities add *of the gospel* [l]Gk *brothers* [m]Other ancient authorities read *my bringing of a gift*

Rest Stop in Rome

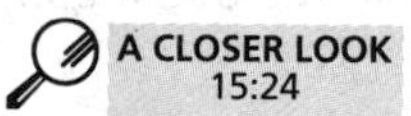

Many Bible readers assume that Paul's main goal in his work was to reach Rome, where he would preach the gospel to the leaders of the empire. But he intended to stop at Rome on his way to another strategic target, Spain (v. 24). He probably never made it that far. But why was Spain so important? See "All Roads Lead to Rome—and Beyond," Acts 28:28–31.

Jerusalem may be acceptable to the saints, 32so that by
God's will I may come to you with joy and be refreshed in
your company. 33The God of peace be with all of you.[n]
Amen.

Personal Greetings

16:1

16 I commend to you our sister
Phoebe, a deacon[o] of the church
at Cenchreae, 2so that you may welcome her in the Lord as
is fitting for the saints, and help her in whatever she may
require from you, for she has been a benefactor of many
and of myself as well.

[n]One ancient authority adds 16.25-27 here [o]Or *minister*

Personality Profile: Priscilla and Aquila

FOR YOUR INFO 16:3–5

Names mean: "Eagle" (Aquila); "ancient" (Priscilla, who was also called Prisca).

Background: Aquila was originally from Pontus in Asia Minor, bordering the Black Sea. They lived in Rome before Claudius forced all Jews to leave Rome. They then relocated to Corinth, and later to Ephesus. Eventually they returned to Rome.

Family: Priscilla might have grown up in a wealthy Roman family; Aquila might have been a Jewish freedman. Marrying across ethnic and socioeconomic lines was unusual in their day.

Occupation: Tentmaking—the manufacture of affordable mobile buildings for living, working, and traveling.

Best known today for: Taking Apollos the speaker aside and explaining to him the way of God more accurately (Acts 18:26); also helping to start at least three churches—at Rome, Corinth, and Ephesus.

Phoebe

CONSIDER THIS 16:1

Paul called Phoebe (v. 1) a *diakonos* (translated here as "deacon," elsewhere as "servant" or "minister") of the church at Cenchreae, the eastern port of Corinth. Does that mean she held a formal position of responsibility? Possibly. Paul frequently referred to himself as a *diakonos* and used the same term in writing about male coworkers such as Apollos, Tychicus, Epaphras, and Timothy (1 Cor. 3:5; Eph. 6:21; Col. 1:7; 4:7; 1 Thess. 3:2).

Our understanding of exactly what it meant to be a *diakonos* in the early church is incomplete. Where the word appears in secular literature of the first century it refers to a helper of any sort who was not a slave. Whatever the role entailed, Paul commended Phoebe to the believers in Rome as a valued sister and one to be esteemed as one of his coworkers.

One important way that Phoebe may have assisted Paul was by taking his letter to Rome. The terms used to describe her suggest that she was a wealthy businesswoman of some influence. Perhaps she agreed to carry the document with her on business to the capital. Since couriers in the ancient world served as representatives of those who sent them, it is possible that Phoebe not only delivered the letter but also read it at different gatherings of Christians and discussed its contents with them.

Junia

CONSIDER THIS 16:7

Paul sends greetings to two fellow countrymen and fellow prisoners, Andronicus and Junia (v. 7). Was Junia a man or a woman? It is impossible to tell from the Greek text. The name could just as well be translated Ju-

(continued on next page)

(continued from previous page)

nias. However, in v. 3 Paul greets a couple, Priscilla and Aquila, then a man, Epaenetus (v. 4) and a woman, Mary (v. 5). Then he comes to Andronicus and Junia, whom he names together. Were they a couple, like Priscilla and Aquila? Again, it is impossible to say with certainty, but it is at least possible.

The interesting thing is that Paul describes these two as "prominent among the apostles." That could mean either that they were actually apostles themselves or simply that the apostles held them in high esteem. If the former, and if Junia was a woman, that would mean that the early church had female apostles as well as male, and that it was not a movement led exclusively by men.

Right from the start the apostles were joined by women who had followed Christ. See "An Inclusive Prayer Meeting," Acts 1:14.

16:3–5 see pg. 571

3 Greet Prisca and Aquila, who work
with me in Christ Jesus, 4and who risked
their necks for my life, to whom not only I give thanks, but
also all the churches of the Gentiles. 5Greet also the church
in their house. Greet my beloved Epaenetus, who was the
first convert[p] in Asia for Christ. 6Greet Mary, who has
16:7 see pg. 571
worked very hard among you. 7Greet
Andronicus and Junia,[q] my relatives[r]
who were in prison with me; they are prominent among the
apostles, and they were in Christ before I was. 8Greet Ampliatus,
my beloved in the Lord. 9Greet Urbanus, our coworker
in Christ, and my beloved Stachys. 10Greet Apelles,
who is approved in Christ. Greet those who belong to the
family of Aristobulus. 11Greet my relative[s] Herodion. Greet
those in the Lord who belong to the family of Narcissus.
16:12
12Greet those workers in the Lord,
Tryphaena and Tryphosa. Greet the

16:13
beloved Persis, who has worked hard in
the Lord. 13Greet Rufus, chosen in the
Lord; and greet his mother—a mother to me also. 14Greet
Asyncritus, Phlegon, Hermes, Patrobas, Hermas, and the

[p]Gk *first fruits* [q]Or *Junias;* other ancient authorities read *Julia* [r]Or *compatriots* [s]Or *compatriot*

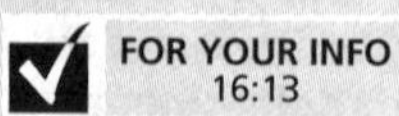
FOR YOUR INFO 16:13

Who Was Paul's Mother?

In greeting Rufus' mother as "a mother to me also" (v. 13), Paul was probably not indicating his own actual mother, but rather a woman who played an important role in Paul's life.

The apostle often used the image of a father or mother to describe his own unique relationship with certain Christians (1 Cor. 4:15; 1 Thess. 2:7), and some believers he called his children (1 Cor. 4:14; 1 Tim. 1:2; 2 Tim. 1:2; 2:1). He never explained exactly what he meant by those terms, but we can assume that those who received his letters knew what he meant. Apparently Paul had been instrumental in their lives in a way that a parent might be with a child.

In a similar way, the woman greeted in Romans 16:13 must have been especially important to Paul. Perhaps she had helped to nurture his faith, somewhat like Priscilla and Aquila with Apollos (see "Marketplace Mentors: Priscilla and Aquila," Acts 18:24–26; and "Apollos," Acts 18:24–28). Or perhaps she had helped to support Paul financially or in prayer. Whatever the case, he felt deeply enough toward her to refer to her as his mother.

Of Paul's actual mother, almost nothing is known. We

brothers and sisters[t] who are with them. 15Greet Philologus,
Julia, Nereus and his sister, and Olympas, and all the saints
who are with them. 16Greet one another with a holy kiss.
All the churches of Christ greet you.

Warnings against False Teachers

17 I urge you, brothers and sisters,[t] to keep an eye on
those who cause dissensions and offenses, in opposition to
the teaching that you have learned; avoid them. 18For such
people do not serve our Lord Christ, but their own appetites,[u] and by smooth talk and flattery they deceive the
hearts of the simple-minded. 19For while your obedience is
known to all, so that I rejoice over you, I want you to be
wise in what is good and guileless in what is evil. 20The
God of peace will shortly crush Satan under your feet. The
grace of our Lord Jesus Christ be with you.[v]

Final Greetings and a Benediction

21 Timothy, my co-worker, greets you; so do Lucius and
Jason and Sosipater, my relatives.[w]

[t]Gk *brothers* [u]Gk *their own belly* [v]Other ancient authorities lack this sentence [w]Or *compatriots*

can deduce that she must have been Jewish, because Paul was a Jew, and a Jewish heritage was determined through the mother. Paul said that he was born a Roman citizen (Acts 22:28), which meant his father must have been a Roman citizen before him. Apparently Paul was not their only child, for Luke mentions a sister (Acts 23:16).

However, we do have a clue as to the identity of the woman mentioned in Romans 16. The context implies that she was Rufus' actual mother. Rufus is probably the same man mentioned as one of the sons of Simon, the man who helped carry Jesus' cross (see Mark 15:21). If so, Rufus and his family were from Cyrene on the northern coast of Africa and were well known to the early church.

Whatever role Rufus' mother had in Paul's life, he certainly didn't forget her. Do you remember your mothers and fathers in the faith? ◆

Learn more about Paul's background through the two profiles, "Saul" and "Paul," Acts 13:2–3.

Paul's Female Coworkers

FOR YOUR INFO 16:12 **As Paul traveled throughout the Mediterranean, many believers labored with him to spread the message of Christ. Not a few of these valuable associates were women, several of whom are listed here in Romans 16.**

Paul literally owed his life to some of these coworkers. In several of his letters he lists their names and expresses his gratitude to them. Here are some of the women mentioned:

Women of the Early Church
Apphia (Philem. 2)
Euodia (Phil. 4:2–3)
Junia (possibly a woman, Rom. 16:7)
Lydia (Acts 16:13–40)
Mary of Rome (Rom. 16:6)
Nympha (Col. 4:15)
Persis (Rom. 16:12)
Phoebe (Rom. 16:1–2)
Priscilla (Acts 18:1–28; Rom. 16:3; 1 Cor. 16:19; 2 Tim. 4:19)
Syntyche (Phil. 4:2–3)
Tryphaena (Rom. 16:12)
Tryphosa (Rom. 16:12)

Women also played a major part in Jesus' life and work, and helped take His message to the far reaches of the Roman world. See "The Women around Jesus," John 19:25; and the table, "Women and the Growth of Christianity," Phil. 4:3.

22 I Tertius, the writer of this letter, greet you in
the Lord.[x]
23 Gaius, who is host to me and to the whole
church, greets you. Erastus, the city treasurer, and
our brother Quartus, greet you.[y]

25 Now to God[z] who is able to strengthen you
according to my gospel and the proclamation of Jesus Christ, according to the revelation of the mystery that was kept secret for long ages 26 but is now
disclosed, and through the prophetic writings is
made known to all the Gentiles, according to the
command of the eternal God, to bring about the
obedience of faith— 27 to the only wise God,
through Jesus Christ, to whom[a] be the glory forever! Amen.[b]

[x]Or *I Tertius, writing this letter in the Lord, greet you* [y]Other ancient authorities add verse 24, *The grace of our Lord Jesus Christ be with all of you. Amen.* [z]Gk *the one*

[a]Other ancient authorities lack *to whom*. The verse then reads, *to the only wise God be the glory through Jesus Christ forever. Amen.* [b]Other ancient authorities lack 16.25-27 or include it after 14.23 or 15.33; others put verse 24 after verse 27

A Collection of Sinners

Have you ever sighed, “I wish my church could be more like the church of the first century”? Perhaps you have in mind a small, closely knit community of believers who are radically committed to each other and, despite their number, are turning the community upside down with the gospel. What an exciting ideal! Unfortunately, the reality of the first churches probably wouldn’t match it.

The church at Corinth is a good case in point. It had several excellent teachers and leaders, yet it struggled with the same problems many churches face today. The Corinthian church was an example of what churches look like, made up as they are of sinners saved by grace.

Depending on your expectations, the two Corinthian letters can make for encouraging reading. They point to the fact that there is no instant spirituality. Discipleship is a process. So if you and other believers around you sometimes seem less than Christlike, take heart! The Corinthians have walked this path before you. Despite their shortcomings, they held a special place in the heart of those who knew them best and helped them get started in the faith.

The First and Second Letters of Paul to the

Corinthians

There is no instant spirituality.

Discipleship is a process.

CONTENTS

FIRST-CENTURY CHRISTIANS, TWENTY-FIRST-CENTURY PROBLEMS

The church at Corinth struggled with . . .

. . . Divisions over personalities and doctrine
(1 Cor. 1:10–17)

. . . Immaturity
(1 Cor. 3:1–9)

. . . Accountability
(1 Cor. 3:10–17; 5:1–2; 2 Cor. 1:12—2:4)

. . . Church discipline
(1 Cor. 5:3–13; 2 Cor. 2:5–11)

. . . Lawsuits
(1 Cor. 6:1–11)

. . . Immorality
(1 Cor. 6:18—7:1)

. . . Marriage and divorce
(1 Cor. 7:2–16)

. . . Insensitivity
(1 Cor. 8:1–13)

. . . Competing religions
(1 Cor. 10:1–14)

. . . Relating to unbelievers
(1 Cor. 10:27–30; 2 Cor. 6:11—7:1)

. . . Styles of worship
(1 Cor. 11:2–34)

. . . Prophecy and tongues
(1 Cor. 14:1–40)

. . . The nature of the gospel
(1 Cor. 15:1–11)

. . . Assistance for the poor
(1 Cor. 16:1–9; 2 Cor. 8:1—9:15)

. . . Money and generosity
(2 Cor. 9:6–15)

ARTICLES

The Power of Foolishness (1 Cor. 1:18)
Nowhere does the gospel appear more foolish than in today's workplace. Yet the irony is that the message of Christ is far more powerful than even the strongest players in the marketplace can imagine.

Workplace Myths (3:9)
A number of distorted views of work have taken on mythical proportions in Western culture, with devastating effect.

The Scandal of Litigating Christians (6:1–11)
Does the Bible categorically rule out litigation between Christians today?

Career Changes (7:17–24)
Paul says to remain in the situations we were in when we came to faith. Yet most people today change careers at least four times in their lives.

Women and Work in the Ancient World (7:32–35)
Learn about the busy lives that first-century women lived, especially in the large cities of the Roman Empire.

Paying Vocational Christian Workers (9:1–23)
How much should pastors, missionaries, and others who work in churches and ministries be paid? Or should they be paid at all?

The Games (9:24–27)
Corinth was home to one of four prestigious athletic festivals of the Greeks at which competitors vied for glory more than for tangible prizes.

Ten Myths about Christianity, Myth #6: People Become Christians through Social Conditioning (15:9–10)
A common notion today is that religious preference is mainly a result of upbringing. Cultural circumstances play a part in people's religious beliefs, but far more is involved than one's background.

Listening In on a Private Conversation

To read 1 & 2 Corinthians is to read someone else's mail. In contrast to Romans, these letters of Paul are very personal, and perhaps for that reason, very enlightening. What we have here are not fancy ideas dressed up in high-sounding words, but straight talk for a church working through everyday problems.

Actually, several letters passed between Paul and the Corinthians, including at least one between 1 & 2 Corinthians (2 Cor. 2:3). As in listening to one side of a telephone conversation, one has to infer what issues and questions made up the correspondence, based on the two letters that survive.

Paul had written a first, unpreserved letter from Ephesus (during his long stay mentioned in Acts 20:31) in which he warned the congregation about mixing with sexually immoral people (1 Cor. 5:9). That was an ever-present danger in Corinth. Most of the believers there had come from pagan backgrounds (12:2), and perhaps some had previously engaged in the idolatrous practices—including ritual prostitution—of the city's dozens of shrines and pagan temples. (The most prominent, the temple of Aphrodite, employed no less than 1,000 temple prostitutes.)

Paul's first letter must have failed to achieve its purpose, because certain problems persisted (1:11; 16:17). Apparently the Corinthians wrote a letter back to Paul, perhaps to justify their behavior, but also to ask him about other matters. He then wrote 1 Corinthians and minced no words in condemning the congregation's divisions and their continued tolerance of immorality. He also addressed their other concerns, as the repeated use of the words, "Now concerning," indicates (7:1, 25; 8:1; 12:1; 16:1).

But for all its stern language, 1 Corinthians also failed to correct the abuses. So Paul paid a visit to the church, but he was rebuffed (2 Cor. 2:1). Upon his return to Ephesus, he penned an extremely strident letter calculated to shock the stubborn Corinthians into obedience to Christ. (Most scholars believe that that letter has been lost. But some posit that it has been preserved in 2 Corinthians as chapters 10–13.)

Paul sent Titus to deliver the bombshell and then waited to hear the outcome. But Titus delayed in returning. As time passed, Paul felt increasingly alarmed that perhaps he had charged the epistle with a bit too much explosive. When he could contain his anxiety no longer, he set out for Corinth by way of Macedonia. But en route he encountered Titus, who, to his relief and joy, reported that the church had at last responded obediently. Heartened by this news, Paul wrote 2 Corinthians to bring healing to the relationship.

Christians today can profit by reading 1 and 2 Corinthians because they get behind the stereotyped images of what the church and the ministry are "supposed" to be. First Corinthians shows that churches are made up of real people living in the real world struggling with real problems. Likewise, 2 Corinthians shows that people in "full-time ministry" struggle with the same problems, doubts, and feelings as anyone else. As we read this correspondence, we need to ask, *If Paul came to my church and my community, what issues and problems would he see? And what would he say?*

Corinth

Beauty mingled with debauchery at Corinth. A "planned" city, it was less than 100 years old at the time of Paul. Stately gates at each city entrance opened onto well-maintained avenues with dozens of buildings and monuments built by the Roman emperors. City walls were lined with picturesque colonnades and countless residential shops. But Corinth was known less for its impressive architecture than its encouragement of gross immorality. See "Corinth" at the Introduction to 2 Corinthians.

The Power of Foolishness

CONSIDER THIS 1:18 **Paul recognized that the gospel appears foolish to most people (v. 18). Nowhere is that more apparent than in the workplace. In a tough, secular business environment, the message of Christ seems wholly out of place. Try to introduce it as relevant and you'll usually find stares of incredulity, if not outright protests.**

The irony is that the gospel is far more powerful than even the strongest players in the marketplace can imagine. But it remains impossible to receive except as the Holy Spirit opens a person's eyes.

This has a tremendous bearing on our witness as believers in the workplace. We need to keep communicating the message as persuasively and persistently as we can, all the while asking the Spirit to work His power, both in our own lives and in the lives of those around us.

One thing is certain about evangelism: both non-Christians and Christians feel uncomfortable with it. Fortunately, both have someone to help them in the process. See "Whose Job Is Evangelism?" John 16:8.

The message of the cross may be foolishness, but it was powerful enough to turn the Roman world upside down. See "Power," Acts 1:8.

A Word of Greeting

1 Paul, called to be an apostle of Christ Jesus by the will of God, and our brother Sosthenes,

2 To the church of God that is in Corinth, to those who are sanctified in Christ Jesus, called to be saints, together with all those who in every place call on the name of our Lord Jesus Christ, both their Lord[a] and ours:

3 Grace to you and peace from God our Father and the Lord Jesus Christ.

4 I give thanks to my[b] God always for you because of the
grace of God that has been given you in Christ Jesus, 5for in
every way you have been enriched in him, in speech and
knowledge of every kind— 6just as the testimony of[c] Christ
has been strengthened among you— 7so that you are not
lacking in any spiritual gift as you wait for the revealing of
our Lord Jesus Christ. 8He will also strengthen you to the
end, so that you may be blameless on the day of our Lord
Jesus Christ. 9God is faithful; by him you were called into
the fellowship of his Son, Jesus Christ our Lord.

The Corinthians Are Divided

10 Now I appeal to you, brothers and sisters,[d] by the
name of our Lord Jesus Christ, that all of you be in agreement and that there be no divisions among you, but that
you be united in the same mind and the same purpose.
11For it has been reported to me by Chloe's people that
there are quarrels among you, my brothers and sisters.[e]
12What I mean is that each of you says, "I
belong to Paul," or "I belong to Apollos,"
or "I belong to Cephas," or "I belong to Christ." 13Has
Christ been divided? Was Paul crucified for you? Or were
you baptized in the name of Paul? 14I thank God[f] that I
baptized none of you except Crispus and Gaius, 15so that
no one can say that you were baptized in my name. 16(I did
baptize also the household of Stephanas; beyond that, I do
not know whether I baptized anyone else.) 17For Christ did
not send me to baptize but to proclaim the gospel, and not
with eloquent wisdom, so that the cross of Christ might not
be emptied of its power.

1:12

[a]Gk *theirs* [b]Other ancient authorities lack *my* [c]Or *to* [d]Gk *brothers* [e]Gk *my brothers* [f]Other ancient authorities read *I am thankful*

Apollos

A CLOSER LOOK 1:12 *The name Apollos means "destroyer," but Apollos probably wouldn't have wanted the destructive factions that afflicted the church at Corinth. See "Apollos" at Acts 18:24–28.*

Wisdom Is Misunderstood

1:18
18 For the message about the cross is
foolishness to those who are perishing,
but to us who are being saved it is the power of God. 19For
it is written,

"I will destroy the wisdom of the wise,
and the discernment of the discerning I will thwart."

20Where is the one who is wise? Where is the scribe? Where
is the debater of this age? Has not God made foolish the
wisdom of the world? 21For since, in the wisdom of God,
the world did not know God through wisdom, God decided, through the foolishness of our proclamation, to save
those who believe. 22For Jews demand signs and Greeks de-
1:23
sire wisdom, 23but we proclaim Christ
crucified, a stumbling block to Jews and
foolishness to Gentiles, 24but to those who are the called,
both Jews and Greeks, Christ the power of God and the
wisdom of God. 25For God's foolishness is wiser than human wisdom, and God's weakness is stronger than human
strength.

1:26 see pg. 580
26 Consider your own call, brothers
and sisters:[g] not many of you were wise
by human standards,[h] not many were powerful, not many
were of noble birth. 27But God chose what is foolish in the
world to shame the wise; God chose what is weak in the
world to shame the strong; 28God chose what is low and
despised in the world, things that are not, to reduce to
nothing things that are, 29so that no one[i] might boast in the
presence of God. 30He is the source of your life in Christ Jesus, who became for us wisdom from God, and righteousness and sanctification and redemption, 31in order that, as
it is written, "Let the one who boasts, boast in[j] the Lord."

Paul's Initial Visit Was in Weakness

2 When I came to you, brothers and sisters,[g] I did not
come proclaiming the mystery[k] of God to you in lofty
words or wisdom. 2For I decided to know nothing among
you except Jesus Christ, and him crucified. 3And I came to
you in weakness and in fear and in much trembling. 4My
speech and my proclamation were not with plausible words
of wisdom,[l] but with a demonstration of the Spirit and of
power, 5so that your faith might rest not on human wisdom
but on the power of God.

(Bible text continued on page 581)

[g]Gk *brothers* [h]Gk *according to the flesh* [i]Gk *no flesh* [j]Or *of* [k]Other ancient authorities read *testimony* [l]Other ancient authorities read *the persuasiveness of wisdom*

QUOTE UNQUOTE

CONSIDER THIS 1:23 *Paul's message was "Christ crucified" (v. 23). The gospel has not changed, and the same bold message is needed today:*

I simply argue that the cross be raised again at the center of the marketplace, as well as on the steeple of the church. I am recovering the claim that Jesus was not crucified between two candles, but on a cross between two thieves; on the town garbage heap; at a crossroad so cosmopolitan that they had to write his title in Latin and Greek . . . at the kind of place where cynics talk smut, and thieves curse, and soldiers gamble. Because that's where He died. And that is what He died about. And that is where churchmen ought to be and what churchmen should be about.

George MacLeod, Founder of the Scottish IONA Community, recipient of the Templeton Award for religious leadership

CONSIDER THIS
1:26

MYTH #5

10 MYTHS ABOUT CHRISTIANITY

MYTH: CHRISTIANITY IS JUST A CRUTCH FOR THE WEAK

Many people today accept a number of myths about Christianity, with the result that they never respond to Jesus as He really is. This is one of ten articles that speak to some of those misconceptions. For a list of all ten, see 1 Tim. 1:3–4.

The believers at Corinth tended to think more highly of themselves than they ought to have. The result was conflict and division in the church. So Paul pointed out that most of them had little of which to boast (v. 26; see also 6:9–11). On the whole they were weak, sinful people saved only by the grace of God.

Today, the grace of God still reaches out to the weak, the downcast, the broken, and the oppressed. Perhaps for that reason, people who pride themselves on their strength and self-sufficiency have little use for the gospel. Indeed, some despise a faith that resists the proud but promises hope to the humble.

Is Christianity just another crutch for people who can't make it on their own? In one sense, yes. "Those who are well have no need of a physician," Jesus said, "but those who are sick. I have come to call not the righteous but sinners to repentance" (Luke 5:31–32). Jesus bypasses those who pretend to be invincible, those who think they have it all together. Instead He reaches out to those who know that something is wrong, that their lives are "sick" with "illnesses" such as greed, lust, cruelty, and selfishness.

Jesus knows that no one is spiritually healthy. No one is righteous enough to stand before a holy God. That's why He came into this world, to restore people to God. The good news is that Christ gives us the power to overcome sin and the ways it pulls us down time after time.

What happens to the "weak" who avail themselves of this "crutch"? Consider Mother Teresa, who emerged from an insignificant nunnery to love the helpless and homeless of Calcutta and became a worldwide symbol of compassion. Or consider Alexander Solzhenitsyn, a forgotten political prisoner rotting away in the gulag system of Stalinist Russia. Surrendering himself to Jesus, he gained renewed strength to challenge a totalitarian regime on behalf of human dignity and freedom.

These are but two examples from the millions who have thrown away the self-styled crutches on which they used to limp along the road of life, opting instead for the seasoned wood of the cross of Christ which has transformed their weakness into strength.

In one sense, Christianity is a crutch for the weak. But those who dismiss it for that reason usually do so to deny their own inadequacies. They use that excuse as a way to evade the claims God has on their lives. They cannot accept that He takes wounded, fractured people and makes them whole. ◆

The Message Was God's Wisdom

6 Yet among the mature we do speak wisdom, though it
is not a wisdom of this age or of the rulers of this age, who
are doomed to perish. 7But we speak God's wisdom, secret
and hidden, which God decreed before the ages for our
glory. 8None of the rulers of this age understood this; for if
they had, they would not have crucified the Lord of glory.
9But, as it is written,

"What no eye has seen, nor ear heard,
nor the human heart conceived,
what God has prepared for those who love him"—

10these things God has revealed to us through the Spirit; for
the Spirit searches everything, even the depths of God.
11For what human being knows what is truly human except
the human spirit that is within? So also no one compre-
hends what is truly God's except the Spirit of God. 12Now
we have received not the spirit of the world, but the Spirit
that is from God, so that we may understand the gifts bestowed on us by God. 13And we speak of these things in
words not taught by human wisdom but taught by the
Spirit, interpreting spiritual things to those who are spiritual.[m]

14 Those who are unspiritual[n] do not receive the gifts of
God's Spirit, for they are foolishness to them, and they are
unable to understand them because they are spiritually dis-
2:15
cerned. 15Those who are spiritual discern
all things, and they are themselves subject to no one else's scrutiny.

16 "For who has known the mind of the Lord
so as to instruct him?"
But we have the mind of Christ.

The Apostles' Role Misunderstood

3 And so, brothers and sisters,[o] I could not speak to you
as spiritual people, but rather as people of the flesh, as
infants in Christ. 2I fed you with milk, not solid food, for
you were not ready for solid food. Even now you are still
not ready, 3for you are still of the flesh. For as long as there
is jealousy and quarreling among you, are you not of the
flesh, and behaving according to human inclinations? 4For
when one says, "I belong to Paul," and another, "I belong to
Apollos," are you not merely human?

3:5–8
see pg. 582

5 What then is Apollos? What is Paul?
Servants through whom you came to be-
lieve, as the Lord assigned to each. 6I planted, Apollos

[m]*Or interpreting spiritual things in spiritual language, or comparing spiritual things with spiritual* [n]*Or natural* [o]*Gk brothers*

ARE WE TO JUDGE ALL THINGS?

CONSIDER THIS 2:15 **Paul's claim about judging all things (v. 15) sounds rather presumptuous. Is he urging believers to become moral policemen, passing judgment on everyone and everything around us?**

Yes and no. Paul was challenging the spiritually immature believers at Corinth to grow up by applying spiritual discernment to the world around them. In this passage he mentions three categories of people:

- ***natural*** **(v. 14), those without Christ, still living in the lost condition in which they were born;**
- ***spiritual*** **(v. 15), believers in Christ who have been born of the Spirit and in whom the Spirit of God lives and is producing growth; and**
- ***carnal*** **(3:1), believers who remain immature in the faith because they don't allow the Spirit to work in their lives.**

Spiritual people "judge" all things that come their way (v. 15) in the sense of scrutinizing, examining, and investigating spiritual value and implications. This is not something that we should do merely as individuals, but also corporately with other believers. For example, in the workplace Christians in various occupations need to band together to explore how the faith applies to particular vocations. By analyzing work situations in light of Scripture, we can discern what the issues are and how we might respond with Christlikeness.

"Judging all things" has nothing to do with damning others, but with recognizing and doing what God would want. Instead of pride, it calls for humility, since God will be the final Judge of everything we do (2 Cor. 5:10).

Who Gets the Credit?

CONSIDER THIS 3:5–8 **Paul pointed out that the work of planting the church at Corinth was a joint venture between himself, Apollos, and the Lord (vv. 5–8). Actually, many others were involved as well. But the point was that cooperation, not competition, is what God desires.**

Paul was speaking about the start-up of a church, but the principles apply in the workplace as well. An attitude of competition worries about who gets the credit for success, which is really a selfish concern. By contrast, cooperative efforts over time generally result in achievements far greater than what any individual could do in isolation. That's because the skill, insight, and energy in an organization's work force have enormous potential. But that potential will never be realized if everyone's chief objective is to take credit for results.

Who gets the credit where you work? Do you promote cooperation toward mutual goals rather than competition between individual agendas?

Apollos was a silver-tongued orator, but he learned much of his theology from a hard-working couple. See his profile, Acts 18:24–28.

The Ultimate Performance Review

CONSIDER THIS 3:13–15 **People often joke about standing before God and having their lives examined. But the picture Paul paints in vv. 9–15 is anything but funny. He is dead serious about a day of accountability for believers. Most of us are familiar with performance reviews on**

(continued on next page)

watered, but God gave the growth. 7So neither the one who
plants nor the one who waters is anything, but only God
who gives the growth. 8The one who plants and the one
who waters have a common purpose, and each will receive
wages according to the labor of each.
9For we are God's servants, working together; you are God's field, God's building.

3:9 see pg. 584

Building on the Foundation

10 According to the grace of God given to me, like a
skilled master builder I laid a foundation, and someone else
is building on it. Each builder must choose with care how
to build on it. 11For no one can lay any foundation other
than the one that has been laid; that foundation is Jesus
Christ. 12Now if anyone builds on the foundation with
gold, silver, precious stones, wood, hay,
straw— 13the work of each builder will
become visible, for the Day will disclose it, because it will
be revealed with fire, and the fire will test what sort of work
each has done. 14If what has been built on the foundation
survives, the builder will receive a reward. 15If the work is
burned up, the builder will suffer loss; the builder will be
saved, but only as through fire.

3:13–15

16 Do you not know that you are God's temple and that
God's Spirit dwells in you?[p] 17If anyone destroys God's temple, God will destroy that person. For God's temple is holy,
and you are that temple.

18 Do not deceive yourselves. If you think that you are
wise in this age, you should become fools so that you may
become wise. 19For the wisdom of this world is foolishness
with God. For it is written,

"He catches the wise in their craftiness,"

20and again,

"The Lord knows the thoughts of the wise,
that they are futile."

21So let no one boast about human leaders. For all things
are yours, 22whether Paul or Apollos or Cephas or the
world or life or death or the present or the future—all belong to you, 23and you belong to Christ, and Christ belongs
to God.

No Room for Boasting

4 Think of us in this way, as servants of Christ and
stewards of God's mysteries. 2Moreover, it is required
of stewards that they be found trustworthy. 3But with me it is a very small

4:3–5 see pg. 586

[p] In verses 16 and 17 the Greek word for *you* is plural

thing that I should be judged by you or by any human
court. I do not even judge myself. 4 I am not aware of
anything against myself, but I am not thereby acquitted. It
is the Lord who judges me. 5 Therefore do not pronounce
judgment before the time, before the Lord comes, who will
bring to light the things now hidden in darkness and will
disclose the purposes of the heart. Then each one will receive commendation from God.
6 I have applied all this to Apollos and myself for your
benefit, brothers and sisters,[q] so that you may learn through
us the meaning of the saying, "Nothing beyond what is
written," so that none of you will be puffed up in favor of
one against another. 7 For who sees anything different in
you?[r] What do you have that you did not receive? And if
you received it, why do you boast as if it were not a gift?

Fools for Christ

8 Already you have all you want! Already you have become rich! Quite apart from us you have become kings! Indeed, I wish that you had become kings, so that we might
be kings with you! 9 For I think that God has exhibited us
apostles as last of all, as though sentenced to death, because
we have become a spectacle to the world, to angels and to
mortals. 10 We are fools for the sake of Christ, but you are
wise in Christ. We are weak, but you are strong. You are
held in honor, but we in disrepute. 11 To the present hour
we are hungry and thirsty, we are poorly clothed and
beaten and homeless, 12 and we grow weary from the work
of our own hands. When reviled, we bless; when persecuted, we endure; 13 when slandered, we speak kindly. We
have become like the rubbish of the world, the dregs of all
things, to this very day.

Paul's Care for the Corinthians

14 I am not writing this to make you ashamed, but to
admonish you as my beloved children. 15 For though you
might have ten thousand guardians in Christ, you do not
have many fathers. Indeed, in Christ Jesus I became your
father through the gospel. 16 I appeal to you, then, be imitators of me. 17 For this reason I sent[s] you Timothy, who is my
beloved and faithful child in the Lord, to remind you of my
ways in Christ Jesus, as I teach them everywhere in every
church. 18 But some of you, thinking that I am not coming
to you, have become arrogant. 19 But I will come to you
soon, if the Lord wills, and I will find out not the talk of
these arrogant people but their power. 20 For the kingdom

(Bible text continued on page 586)

[q]Gk *brothers* [r]Or *Who makes you different from another?* [s]Or *am sending*

(continued from previous page)

the job. Paul describes the ultimate performance review—the moment when we stand before God and He evaluates the worth of our lives on the earth, not for salvation but for reward or loss.

Paul uses the image of metal being purified in a refining fire (vv. 13–15). The fire burns away the worthless impurities, leaving only what is valuable. Based on the values set forth in many passages of Scripture, we can imagine the kinds of things that constitute "gold, silver, [and] precious stones": acts of charity and kindness; ethical decision-making; the pursuit of justice and fair play; keeping our word; courage and perseverance in the face of opposition and persecution; humility; communicating the message of Christ to coworkers; honoring our marriage vows; working diligently at the work God gives us; trusting God to keep His promises. Whatever is left when the fire burns down, Paul says, God will reward us for it (v. 14).

Conversely, we can envision what sorts of "wood, hay, [and] straw" will burn up: the lies we've told; ways we may have cheated customers; abuse heaped on family and relatives; manipulation of situations to our advantage; selfishness of all kinds; the squandering of income on trivial luxuries; turning a deaf ear to the poor; damage allowed to our environment; the systems created to lock ourselves into power and lock others out; the arrogance of self-sufficiency; lack of faith.

When the smoke clears, what will be left of your life?

CONSIDER THIS 3:9

Workplace Myths

Paul called himself one of God's "servants" (v. 9) and spoke of "workers in the Lord" (Rom. 16:12). In a similar way, every one of us is a coworker with God (see "People at Work," Heb. 2:7). Yet certain distorted views of work have taken on mythical proportions in Western culture. They've had devastating effect on both the people and the message of Christ. Here's a sampling of these pernicious myths, along with a few points of rebuttal:

Myth: Church work is the only work that has any real spiritual value.

In other words, everyday work in the "secular" world counts for nothing of lasting value. Only "sacred" work matters to God.

Fact: Christianity makes no distinction between the "sacred" and the "secular."

All of life is to be lived under Christ's lordship. So when it comes to work, all work has essential value to God, and workers will answer to Him for how they have carried out the work He has given to them (1 Cor. 3:13).

Myth: The heroes of the faith are ministers and missionaries. "Lay" workers remain second-class.

This follows from the previous idea. If "sacred" work is the only work with eternal value, then "sacred workers" (clergy) are the most valuable workers. The best that "laypeople" can do is to support the clergy and engage in "ministry" during their spare hours.

Fact: God has delegated His work to everybody, not just clergy.

Among the main characters of Scripture are ranchers, farmers, fishermen, vintners, ironworkers, carpenters, tentmakers, textile manufacturers, public officials, construction supervisors and workers, military personnel, financiers, physicians, judges, tax collectors, musicians, sculptors, dancers, poets, and writers, among others. Nowhere does God view these people or their work as "second class" or "secular." Rather, their work accomplishes God's work in the world. As we do our work each day, we reflect the very image of God, who is a working God (see "God—The Original Worker," John 5:17). He spent six days working on the creation (Gen. 1:31—2:3), so we merely follow God's example when we work five or six days out of the week.

Myth: Work is a part of the curse.

According to this belief, God punished Adam and Eve for their sin by laying the burden of work on them: "By the sweat of your face you shall eat bread until you return to the ground" (Gen. 3:19). That's why work is so often drudgery, and why the workplace is driven by greed and selfishness.

Fact: Work is a gift from God.

The Bible never calls work a curse, but rather a gift from God (Eccl. 3:13; 5:18–19). God gave Adam and Eve work to do long before they ever sinned (Gen. 2:15), and He commends and commands work long after the fall (Gen. 9:1–7; Col. 3:23; 1 Thess. 4:11; see "Is Work a Curse?" Rom. 8:20–22).

Myth: God is no longer involved in His creation.

For many, if not most, modern-day workers, God is irrelevant in the workplace. He may exist, but He has little to do with everyday matters of the work world. These people don't care much about what God does, and they assume He doesn't care much about what they do, either.

Fact: God remains intimately connected with both His world and its workers.

Scripture knows nothing of a detached Creator. He actively holds the creation together (Col. 1:16–17) and works toward its ultimate restoration from sin (John 5:17; Rom. 8:18–25). He uses the work of people to accomplish many of His purposes. Indeed, believers ultimately work for Christ as their Boss (see "Who's the Boss?" Col. 3:22–24). He takes an active interest in how they do their work (Titus 2:9–10).

Myth: You only go around once in life—so you better make the most of it!

This is the "heaven can wait" perspective. Here-and-now is what matters; it's where the excitement is. Heaven is just a make-believe world of gold-paved streets and never-ending choirs. Boring! Why not enjoy your reward right now? Go for it!

Fact: God is saving the greatest rewards for eternity—and work will be among them.

Scripture doesn't offer much detail about life after death, but it does promise a future society remade by God where work goes on—without the sweat, toil, pain, or futility of the curse (Is. 65:17–25; Rev. 22:2–5). And as for the question of rewards, God plans to hand out rewards for how believers have spent their lives—including their work (1 Cor. 3:9–15).

Myth: The most important day of the week is Friday.

"Thank God it's Friday!" the secular work ethic cries. Because work is drudgery, weekends are for escaping—and catching up. There's no idea of a Sabbath, just a couple of days of respite from the grinding routine.

Fact: God wants us to pursue cycles of meaningful work and restorative rest.

A biblical view of work places a high value on rest. God never intended us to work seven days a week. He still invites us to join Him in a day of rest, renewal, and celebration. That restores us to go back to our work with a sense of purpose and mission. "Thank God it's Monday!" we can begin to say. ◆

AVOIDING MORBID INTROSPECTION

CONSIDER THIS 4:3–5 **Paul wisely recognized that even our most conscientious attempts to maintain pure motives fall far short (vv. 3–5). Indwelling sin taints everything we do. But Paul didn't allow that to discourage him from aiming at high motives. Neither did he despair of doing anything good. He was content to do his best in life and let God be his Judge.**

Are you free from the chronic worry that your motives are not always pristine? Are you living under the grace of God?

Paul knew that someday he would face the ultimate performance review, when God would evaluate both his motives and actions. See 1 Cor. 3:9–15.

COVER-UPS DECEIVE EVERYBODY

CONSIDER THIS 5:1–13 **Evil can never be remedied by ignoring or hiding it. In fact, covering it up is the worst that can happen, for like yeast, evil does its terrible work from within (vv. 6–8).**

The same is true of believers who live in consistent disobedience to God's expressed will. Their behavior will badly infect the larger groups of which they are a part. It can even lead to a distorted perception of sin in which the group tolerates or even approves of disobedience among its own members yet condemns outsiders for the very same activity (Rom. 1:32; 1 Cor. 5:9–10).

(continued on next page)

of God depends not on talk but on power. 21What would
you prefer? Am I to come to you with a stick, or with love
in a spirit of gentleness?

Immorality Must Be Dealt With

5:1–13

5 It is actually reported that there is
sexual immorality among you, and
of a kind that is not found even among pagans; for a man is
living with his father's wife. 2And you are arrogant! Should
you not rather have mourned, so that he who has done this
would have been removed from among you?
3 For though absent in body, I am present in spirit; and
as if present I have already pronounced judgment 4in the
name of the Lord Jesus on the man who has done such a
thing.[t] When you are assembled, and my spirit is present
with the power of our Lord Jesus, 5you are to hand this
man over to Satan for the destruction of the flesh, so that
his spirit may be saved in the day of the Lord.[u]
6 Your boasting is not a good thing. Do you not know
that a little yeast leavens the whole batch of dough? 7Clean
out the old yeast so that you may be a new batch, as you really are unleavened. For our paschal lamb, Christ, has been
sacrificed. 8Therefore, let us celebrate the festival, not with
the old yeast, the yeast of malice and evil, but with the unleavened bread of sincerity and truth.
9 I wrote to you in my letter not to associate with sexually immoral persons— 10not at all meaning the immoral of
this world, or the greedy and robbers, or idolaters, since
you would then need to go out of the world. 11But now I
am writing to you not to associate with anyone who bears
the name of brother or sister[v] who is sexually immoral or
greedy, or is an idolater, reviler, drunkard, or robber. Do
not even eat with such a one. 12For what have I to do with
judging those outside? Is it not those who are inside that
you are to judge? 13God will judge those outside. "Drive out
the wicked person from among you."

Lawsuits before Unbelievers

6:1–11

6 When any of you has a grievance
against another, do you dare to take
it to court before the unrighteous, instead of taking it before the saints? 2Do you not know that the saints will judge
the world? And if the world is to be judged by you, are you
incompetent to try trivial cases? 3Do you not know that we

[t]Or *on the man who has done such a thing in the name of the Lord Jesus* [u]Other ancient authorities add *Jesus* [v]Gk *brother*

are to judge angels—to say nothing of ordinary matters? 4If
you have ordinary cases, then, do you appoint as judges
those who have no standing in the church? 5I say this to
your shame. Can it be that there is no one among you wise
enough to decide between one believer[w] and another, 6but a
believer[w] goes to court against a believer[w]—and before unbelievers at that?
7 In fact, to have lawsuits at all with one another is already a defeat for you. Why not rather be wronged? Why
not rather be defrauded? 8But you yourselves wrong and
defraud—and believers[x] at that.
9 Do you not know that wrongdoers will not inherit the
kingdom of God? Do not be deceived! Fornicators, idolaters, adulterers, male prostitutes, sodomites, 10thieves, the
greedy, drunkards, revilers, robbers—none of these will inherit the kingdom of God. 11And this is what some of you
used to be. But you were washed, you were sanctified, you
were justified in the name of the Lord Jesus Christ and in
the Spirit of our God.

Liberty Does Not Mean License

6:12
see pg. 589

12 "All things are lawful for me," but
not all things are beneficial. "All things
are lawful for me," but I will not be dominated by anything.
13"Food is meant for the stomach and the stomach for
food,"[y] and God will destroy both one and the other. The
body is meant not for fornication but for the Lord, and the
Lord for the body. 14And God raised the Lord and will also
raise us by his power. 15Do you not know that your bodies
are members of Christ? Should I therefore take the members of Christ and make them members of a prostitute?
Never! 16Do you not know that whoever is united to a prostitute becomes one body with her? For it is said, "The two
shall be one flesh." 17But anyone united to the Lord becomes one spirit with him. 18Shun fornication! Every sin
that a person commits is outside the body; but the fornicator sins against the body itself. 19Or do you not know that
your body is a temple[z] of the Holy Spirit within you, which
you have from God, and that you are not your own? 20For
you were bought with a price; therefore glorify God in your
body.

Instructions to Married Believers

7:1
see pg. 588

7 Now concerning the matters about
which you wrote: "It is well for a

[w]Gk *brother* [x]Gk *brothers* [y]The quotation may extend to the word *other* [z]Or *sanctuary*

(continued from previous page)

Paul challenged the Corinthians to confront the subtle deterioration they had allowed within their congregation (1 Cor. 5:5). However, once the perpetrator had repented, they were then to seek his restoration. Even though corrective activity among believers may be severe, confrontation should always be to promote healing rather than to expel wrongdoers (compare Matt. 18:15–22; 2 Cor. 10:8). There are no throwaway people in the kingdom of God.

The Scandal of Litigating Christians

CONSIDER THIS 6:1–11 **Scripture is explicit: for a Christian to take another Christian to court is "an utter failure" (v. 7). What, then, should we as believers do when we have disputes that normally call for litigation? Paul recommends that we take the matter before wise believers who can make a judgment (vv. 4–5). But suppose we can't arrange that? Then Paul says it would be better to "accept wrong" than to go before unbelievers for judgment.**

Does that categorically rule out lawsuits between Christians today? Not necessarily. Modern Christians disagree over how to apply this passage. Our society is very different from the first-century Roman Empire. But we know that early churches took Paul's instructions literally. They forbade their members to resort to the pagan courts of the day. Instead, they appointed their own elders to judge civil disputes between members.

Those courts gained such a reputation for justice that they even attracted non-Christians, who found them preferable to the notoriously corrupt imperial courts. Eventually, church courts replaced secular courts

(continued on next page)

(continued from previous page)

and for some six centuries were the most important, if not the only, courts in Europe.

Some Christians today are trying to restore this judicial function of the church. In the United States, Christian attorneys are working with church leaders to arbitrate church members' disputes. The decisions can even be legally binding if the disputants agree to that in advance.

How do you settle legal problems when other believers are involved? Are you willing to try everything short of litigation *first,* before even considering going to court?

man not to touch a woman." 2But because of cases of sexual
immorality, each man should have his own wife and each
7:3–6 see pg. 590
woman her own husband. 3The husband
should give to his wife her conjugal
rights, and likewise the wife to her husband. 4For the wife
does not have authority over her own body, but the husband does; likewise the husband does not have authority
over his own body, but the wife does. 5Do not deprive one
another except perhaps by agreement for a set time, to devote yourselves to prayer, and then come together again, so
that Satan may not tempt you because of your lack of self-
control. 6This I say by way of concession, not of command.
7I wish that all were as I myself am. But each has a particular gift from God, one having one kind and another a different kind.

CONSIDER THIS 7:1

Practical Lessons on Marriage

Have you ever listened in on half of a telephone conversation, trying to figure out what the whole conversation is about? That's what we have in 1 Corinthians 7—half of a very important conversation on marriage between Paul and the Corinthian believers. But we can glean many practical lessons from this passage, for marriage was undergoing profound changes then just as it is today.

Some of the believers in the early church had married before they became Christians. They wondered whether they should divorce their unbelieving spouses in order to remarry Christians and live more wholeheartedly for Christ.

An argument could be made for that. After all, if people's primary loyalty were now to Jesus, shouldn't that invalidate their pre-conversion marriage vows? (Of course, it would also provide them with a convenient excuse to escape bad marriages.)

But Paul didn't recommend that. He viewed the abandonment of one's family as a very serious matter (vv. 10–11), arguing that the believer should stay in the marriage as long as possible (vv. 12–13). However, God desires peace in relationships (v. 15), and that may not be possible in a family where Christian values are not shared. If the unbeliever wants to leave, he or she should be allowed to do so (v. 15).

Many churches in different cultures around the world today are faced with very similar circumstances. For example:

Instructions to Single Believers

8 To the unmarried and the widows I say that it is well
for them to remain unmarried as I am. 9But if they are not
practicing self-control, they should marry. For it is better to
marry than to be aflame with passion.

Instructions to Those Married to Unbelievers

10 To the married I give this command—not I but the
Lord—that the wife should not separate from her husband
11(but if she does separate, let her remain unmarried or else
be reconciled to her husband), and that the husband
should not divorce his wife.
12 To the rest I say—I and not the Lord—that if any believer[a] has a wife who is an unbeliever, and she consents to
live with him, he should not divorce her. 13And if any

[a]Gk *brother*

◆ ◆ ◆ ◆ ◆ ◆ ◆ ◆ ◆ ◆ ◆ ◆ ◆ ◆ ◆ ◆

- *the new believer who wonders what to do, since her husband isn't interested in church or religion.*
- *the inner-city congregation that has members who live in common-law marriages. What should the church tell them?*
- *the recent immigrant who tells his pastor that he has two families, one in each of two countries. "Should I get rid of one or both of those families?" he wonders.*
- *a tribal chief who wants to join the church—along with his five wives. What should he do with the wives? Divorce them all? Keep one? If so, which one?*

Paul offers no simple solutions for any of these situations, but he does share one piece of very good news: it is possible for one believer to "sanctify" a family, that is, to be an agent of God's love and grace, and perhaps to eventually bring other family members into the faith. No matter how unconventional the situation might be, Scripture doesn't counsel sudden changes. God may have work left to do in that family, and He may use the believer to do it—if he or she stays. ◆

What Controls You?

CONSIDER THIS 6:12 **As Christians we live under grace, not law. We enjoy a certain freedom of choice and commitment. But Paul reminds us that our choices and commitments, while freely made, do not always bring freedom (v. 12). Often they overpower us: we no longer possess our possessions—they possess us! We can be consumed by our jobs, our wealth, our houses, our hobbies, even our churches.**

Are there any ways to manage this problem? Here are a few suggestions:

(1) Determine your limits. What can you actually handle? What is realistic?

(2) Let time go by before making decisions and commitments. Sooner or later you need to decide, but very few choices are better made sooner than later.

(3) Pay attention to agreement or disagreement with your spouse and/or a close friend or associate. There is wisdom in mutual decision-making.

(4) To manage the commitment you are taking on, what are you willing to give up? Taking on new responsibilities means trading one set of problems for another. Are you prepared for that?

(5) Commit to giving away as well as taking on. That declares your freedom from the tyranny of things and responsibilities.

A New View of Sexuality

CONSIDER THIS 7:3–6 **In an era when Greek women were often deprived both emotionally and sexually, Paul insisted that the Christian husband should recognize and fulfill the needs of his wife (vv. 3–6). He declared that marriage partners have authority over each other. That means that both husband and wife were forbidden from using sex as a means of control, but were to enjoy mutuality in that aspect of their marriage.**

The gospel required a different understanding of sex and marriage than the surrounding culture's. Two thousand years later, it still does.

woman has a husband who is an unbeliever, and he consents to live with her, she should not divorce him. 14For the
unbelieving husband is made holy through his wife, and
the unbelieving wife is made holy through her husband.
Otherwise, your children would be unclean, but as it is,
they are holy. 15But if the unbelieving partner separates, let
it be so; in such a case the brother or sister is not bound. It
is to peace that God has called you.[b] 16Wife, for all you
know, you might save your husband. Husband, for all you
know, you might save your wife.

Calling and Vocation

7:17

17 However that may be, let each of
you lead the life that the Lord has as-
signed, to which God called you. This is my rule in all the
churches. 18Was anyone at the time of his call already circumcised? Let him not seek to remove the marks of circumcision. Was anyone at the time of his call uncircumcised?
Let him not seek circumcision. 19Circumcision is nothing,
and uncircumcision is nothing; but obeying the commandments of God is everything. 20Let each of you remain in the
condition in which you were called.

21 Were you a slave when called? Do not be concerned
about it. Even if you can gain your freedom, make use of

[b]Other ancient authorities read *us*

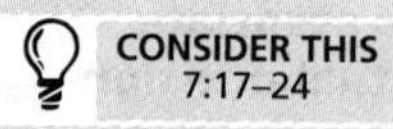

CONSIDER THIS 7:17–24

Career Changes

Modern workers place a high value on mobility and freedom of choice. So how should Christians in our culture deal with Paul's admonition to remain in the situation where God has called us (vv. 17–24)? That sounds terribly antiquated in a society where the average person changes careers at least four times in life. In the ancient world, people normally worked for a lifetime at the same job.

Paul wrote that becoming a believer doesn't necessarily mean a career change. Wherever God has assigned us, that is our calling and we should pursue it to God's glory. On the other hand, there is nothing in the faith that locks a person into a work situation, any more than an unmarried woman must remain single all her life (7:8–9).

Paul's teaching about vocation parallels what he wrote about pre-conversion marriage (7:10–16). A believer is not compelled to leave his or her unbelieving spouse. On the other hand, the marriage may be dissolved if necessary to maintain peace. In the same way, believers should not use conversion as an excuse to leave their jobs.

your present condition now more than ever.[c] 22For whoever
was called in the Lord as a slave is a freed person belonging
to the Lord, just as whoever was free when called is a slave
of Christ. 23You were bought with a price; do not become
slaves of human masters. 24In whatever
condition you were called, brothers and
sisters,[d] there remain with God.

7:17–24

Instructions Regarding Virgins

25 Now concerning virgins, I have no command of the
Lord, but I give my opinion as one who by the Lord's mercy
is trustworthy. 26I think that, in view of the impending[e] crisis, it is well for you to remain as you are. 27Are you bound
to a wife? Do not seek to be free. Are you free from a wife?
Do not seek a wife. 28But if you marry, you do not sin, and
if a virgin marries, she does not sin. Yet those who marry
will experience distress in this life,[f] and I would spare you
that. 29I mean, brothers and sisters,[d] the appointed time has
grown short; from now on, let even those who have wives
be as though they had none, 30and those who mourn as
though they were not mourning, and those who rejoice
as though they were not rejoicing, and those who buy as
though they had no possessions, 31and those who deal with

[c]*Or avail yourself of the opportunity* [d]*Gk brothers* [e]*Or present* [f]*Gk in the flesh*

This is an important point because Christianity introduces new values into our lives that may make us anxious to escape our work environment. The atmosphere of language and jokes, competition and politics, quotas and numbers may begin to feel uncomfortable. Wouldn't it be easier to quit one's job and go to work for a Christian employer—or better yet, pursue a career in a church or ministry? But Paul didn't encourage that choice as the normal path. A job change may be a possibility, as Jesus' disciples found out. But it is not necessarily virtuous to leave our "nets," especially if our only reason is to escape the realities of the work world. ◆

It's actually an advantage for us to work alongside unbelievers so that we can communicate the message of Christ by how we do our jobs. See "Your 'Workstyle,'" Titus 2:9–10.

QUOTE UNQUOTE

CONSIDER THIS 7:17 *Many believers today, like believers in Paul's day, struggle with how to bring their faith into their work. Should they quit their jobs and become vocational Christian workers? Paul did not encourage people to do that (v. 17). Here's a similar perspective from a twentieth-century believer:*

Look: the question is not whether we should bring God into our work or not. We certainly should and must: as MacDonald says, "All that is not God is death." The question is whether we should simply (a) bring Him in by the dedication of our work to Him, by the integrity, diligence, and humility with which we do it, or also (b) make His professed and explicit service our job. The A vocation rests on all men whether they know it or not; the B vocation only on those who are specially called to it. Each vocation has its peculiar dangers and peculiar rewards.

C.S. Lewis, Letter to Sheldon Vanauken, Jan. 8, 1951

Gray Areas

CONSIDER THIS 8:1–13 **In first-century Corinth, meat sacrificed to idols (v. 1) proved to be an issue on which believers vehemently disagreed. It was a "gray" area of life, a matter for which there seemed to be no clear-cut instruction. How should Christians settle such disputes? Through a predetermined set of dos and don'ts? No, Paul offered a different perspective, one that appeals to conscience.**

Paul argued that food and drink

(continued on next page)

the world as though they had no dealings with it. For the
present form of this world is passing away.
7:32–35 32 I want you to be free from anxi-
eties. The unmarried man is anxious
about the affairs of the Lord, how to please the Lord; 33but
the married man is anxious about the affairs of the world,
how to please his wife, 34and his interests are divided. And
the unmarried woman and the virgin are anxious about the
affairs of the Lord, so that they may be holy in body and
spirit; but the married woman is anxious about the affairs
of the world, how to please her husband. 35I say this for
your own benefit, not to put any restraint upon you, but to
promote good order and unhindered devotion to the Lord.
36 If anyone thinks that he is not behaving properly toward his fiancée,[g] if his passions are strong, and so it has to
be, let him marry as he wishes; it is no sin. Let them marry.
37But if someone stands firm in his resolve, being under no

[g] *Gk virgin*

YOU ARE THERE 7:32–35

Women and Work in the Ancient World

Paul's observation that a married woman must care about "the affairs of the world" (v. 34) hints at the busy lives that first century women lived, especially in the large cities of the Roman Empire.

The New Testament shows that women carried out a wide range of tasks: for example, drawing water, grinding grain, manufacturing tents, hosting guests, governing and influencing civic affairs, making clothes, teaching, prophesying and filling other spiritual functions, burying the dead, and doing the work of slaves, to name but a few. Additional evidence from the period reveals that women also served as wool workers, midwives, hairdressers, nurses, vendors, entertainers, political leaders, and even construction workers, among many other occupations.

If a woman was among the upper classes, she enjoyed relative economic security and social privileges. According to the Roman ideal, her role in society was to marry a citizen, produce legitimate heirs for him, and manage the household according to his orders. However, by the first century few families attained that ideal.

Wealthy women used slaves to perform such household tasks as cooking, making clothes, washing laundry, and caring for children (see "Children and Childcare," Matt. 19:14). Slaves also functioned as nurses, midwives, hairdressers, stenographers, and secretaries, and it was common for a high-ranking slave to be designated the household manager.

necessity but having his own desire under control, and has
determined in his own mind to keep her as his fiancée,[h] he
will do well. 38So then, he who marries his fiancée[h] does
well; and he who refrains from marriage will do better.

Instructions Regarding Remarriage

39 A wife is bound as long as her husband lives. But if
the husband dies,[i] she is free to marry anyone she wishes,
only in the Lord. 40But in my judgment she is more blessed
if she remains as she is. And I think that I too have the
Spirit of God.

The Controversy of Food Offered to Idols

8:1–13

8 Now concerning food sacrificed to
idols: we know that "all of us possess knowledge." Knowledge puffs up, but love builds up.
2Anyone who claims to know something does not yet have

[h]Gk *virgin* [i]Gk *falls asleep*

Female slaves were not only considered to be household property, but sexual property as well. The master of the house could legally force a slave to have sex with him, or with anyone he chose. Any children that she bore became his property. In this way a citizen could increase his number of slaves.

Women who were former slaves, or freeborn, lacked the economic security of either the citizen or the slave. Nevertheless, many women sought to buy their way out of slavery. Some of these working-class women earned their living as vendors, selling fish, grain, vegetables, clothing, or perfume. Others became wet nurses, and some chose to become entertainers or prostitutes, occupations that were considered beneath the dignity of respectable women. ◆

In Jewish homes, women were responsible not only for carrying out household tasks, but also for preparing the home for the Sabbath. See "Jewish Homemaking," Mark 1:29–31.

Not all first-century women centered their lives around domestic responsibilities totally. Lydia was a successful businesswoman in the purple trade (see profile at Acts 16:14) and Priscilla manufactured tents with her husband (see profile at Rom. 16:3–5).

(continued from previous page)

do not determine our relationship to God (v. 8). Meat offered to idols is inconsequential because, ultimately, there is no such thing as an idol (vv. 4–6). An idol is not God, so the mere fact that a priest blesses meat and offers it to an idol means nothing. From that point of view, Christians should be able to enjoy whatever food they want.

However, questionable practices may affect one's relationships with fellow believers or unbelievers (v. 9). As members of Christ's family we are obligated not to be a "stumbling block," but a loving neighbor. Our faith is not merely private, but has a corporate ethic and public responsibility as well.

So we live in a tension: God's grace frees us to choose as we please, but God's love requires us to ask questions of conscience about our choices. From what we eat, to whom we live and work with, to where we live, to what we do with our money and time—almost everything we do affects our neighbors (vv. 10–13). So we need to ask, are we treating them with love?

We need not allow others to manipulate us through legalistic criticism. But we do need discretion as to how our choices affect those around us. It's not enough to follow Christ just in our hearts; we also need to follow Him in our consciences.

Several other principles that apply to these issues can be found in "Matters of Conscience," Rom. 14:1–23.

the necessary knowledge; [3]but anyone who loves God is
known by him.

4 Hence, as to the eating of food offered to idols, we
know that "no idol in the world really exists," and that
"there is no God but one." [5]Indeed, even though there may
be so-called gods in heaven or on earth—as in fact there are
many gods and many lords— [6]yet for us there is one God,
the Father, from whom are all things and for whom we exist,
and one Lord, Jesus Christ, through whom are all things
and through whom we exist.

7 It is not everyone, however, who has this knowledge.
Since some have become so accustomed to idols until now,
they still think of the food they eat as food offered to an
idol; and their conscience, being weak, is defiled. [8]"Food
will not bring us close to God."[j] We are no worse off if we
do not eat, and no better off if we do. [9]But take care that
this liberty of yours does not somehow become a stumbling
block to the weak. [10]For if others see you, who possess

[j]The quotation may extend to the end of the verse

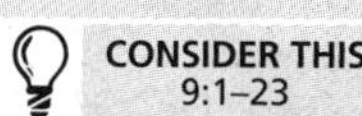
CONSIDER THIS
9:1–23

Paying Vocational Christian Workers

How much should pastors, missionaries, and others who work in churches and ministries be paid? Or should they be paid at all? Paul's example with the Corinthians offers some insight.

In Paul's day, philosophers traveled from city to city, teaching publicly for a fee. The more prestigious the teacher, the larger the fee. However, Paul charged the Corinthians nothing *when he came and delivered the gospel message. As a result, some were criticizing him, asserting that he must not be an authentic leader of the church if he was rendering his services for free.*

In reply, Paul explained himself (chapter 9). First, he insisted that those who labor spiritually should be supported materially by those with whom they work. He pointed to five familiar examples to support his position:

(1) Roman soldiers drew pay for their service (v. 7).
(2) Vintners enjoyed the fruits of their vineyards (v. 7).
(3) Shepherds received food from their flocks (v. 7).
(4) The Old Testament Law affirmed the right of laborers to receive fair compensation (vv. 8–10).
(5) The Law also allowed temple priests and attendants to live off of the sacrifices that the people brought (v. 13).

Paul also explained that the Lord Himself allowed those who preach the gospel to make their living from

knowledge, eating in the temple of an idol, might they not,
since their conscience is weak, be encouraged to the point
of eating food sacrificed to idols? 11So by your knowledge
those weak believers for whom Christ died are destroyed.[k]
12But when you thus sin against members of your family,[l]
and wound their conscience when it is weak, you sin
against Christ. 13Therefore, if food is a cause of their
falling,[m] I will never eat meat, so that I may not cause one
of them[n] to fall.

Paul's Own Example of Christian Liberty

9:1–23

9 Am I not free? Am I not an apostle?
Have I not seen Jesus our Lord? Are
you not my work in the Lord? 2If I am not an apostle to
others, at least I am to you; for you are the seal of my apostleship in the Lord.
3 This is my defense to those who would examine me.

[k]Gk *the weak brother . . . is destroyed* [l]Gk *against the brothers* [m]Gk *my brother's falling* [n]Gk *cause my brother*

QUOTE UNQUOTE

CONSIDER THIS
9:6

Paul had a right to be paid for preaching the gospel (v. 6), but he did not use that right (vv. 12, 15–17). Instead, he made his living as a tentmaker. Perhaps his training as a Pharisee encouraged him in that direction:

Excellent is Torah study together with worldly business, for all Torah without work must ultimately fail and lead to sin.

Pirke Aboth ii:2

that occupation (v. 14). Elsewhere the apostle wrote that church elders who rule well are worthy of "double honor" (1 Tim. 5:17–18). The context shows that Paul had payment in mind. In short, effective vocational Christian workers should be paid fairly for their labor.

Yet Paul refused payment in Corinth. Why? Because He felt that he owed it to God to communicate the gospel for free. When he considered his past and how God had saved him, the foremost sinner (1 Tim. 1:15), it was payment enough to be able to tell people about Jesus (1 Cor. 9:18).

Should workers in churches and ministries be paid? This passage insists that they have a right to a fair wage, and Christians today do well to pay attention to Paul's words here in light of the many workers who are leaving the ministry because of inadequate support. On the other hand, Paul's example opens the door to an alternative—the idea of carrying out ministry for free while supporting oneself through other means. That is also a model worth considering in a day when, for a variety of reasons, an increasing number of churches and ministries are strapped for funds. ◆

RACERS' STARTING BLOCKS

THE GAMES

YOU ARE THERE 9:24–27 **Paul's use of running, boxing, and other athletic feats (vv. 24–27) as metaphors for spiritual discipline was suited perfectly to the Corinthian culture. Corinth hosted numerous athletic events, including the prestigious Isthmian Games, one of four major athletic festivals of the Greeks.**

The Isthmian Games were held every other year and attracted athletes from all over Greece. The competitions were between individuals, not teams, who vied more for glory than for tangible prizes. At the Corinthian games, victors were crowned with pine needle garlands, the "perishable wreath" to which Paul referred (v. 25).

However, when the heroes returned home, their cities might erect statues in their honor, have a parade, and write poems celebrating their feats. Sometimes a champion was even exempted from paying taxes, given free meals, and placed in the seat of honor at public events.

(continued on next page)

4Do we not have the right to our food and drink? 5Do we
not have the right to be accompanied by a believing wife,[o]
as do the other apostles and the brothers of the Lord and
9:6 see pg. 595
Cephas? 6Or is it only Barnabas and I
who have no right to refrain from working for a living? 7Who at any time pays the expenses for doing military service? Who plants a vineyard and does not
eat any of its fruit? Or who tends a flock and does not get
any of its milk?
8 Do I say this on human authority? Does not the law
also say the same? 9For it is written in the law of Moses,
"You shall not muzzle an ox while it is treading out the
grain." Is it for oxen that God is concerned? 10Or does he
not speak entirely for our sake? It was indeed written for
our sake, for whoever plows should plow in hope and whoever threshes should thresh in hope of a share in the crop.
11If we have sown spiritual good among you, is it too much
if we reap your material benefits? 12If others share this
rightful claim on you, do not we still more?

A Servant to All

Nevertheless, we have not made use of this right, but we
endure anything rather than put an obstacle in the way of
the gospel of Christ. 13Do you not know that those who are
employed in the temple service get their food from the temple, and those who serve at the altar share in what is sacrificed on the altar? 14In the same way, the Lord commanded
that those who proclaim the gospel should get their living
by the gospel.
15 But I have made no use of any of these rights, nor am
I writing this so that they may be applied in my case. Indeed, I would rather die than that—no one will deprive me
of my ground for boasting! 16If I proclaim the gospel, this
gives me no ground for boasting, for an obligation is laid
on me, and woe to me if I do not proclaim the gospel! 17For
if I do this of my own will, I have a reward; but if not of my
own will, I am entrusted with a commission. 18What then is
my reward? Just this: that in my proclamation I may make
the gospel free of charge, so as not to make full use of my
rights in the gospel.
19 For though I am free with respect to all, I have made
myself a slave to all, so that I might win more of them. 20To
the Jews I became as a Jew, in order to win Jews. To those
under the law I became as one under the law (though I myself am not under the law) so that I might win those under
the law. 21To those outside the law I became as one outside
the law (though I am not free from God's law but am under
Christ's law) so that I might win those outside the law. 22To

[o] Gk *a sister as wife*

the weak I became weak, so that I might win the weak. I
have become all things to all people, that I might by all
means save some. 23I do it all for the sake of the gospel, so
that I may share in its blessings.

9:24–27

24 Do you not know that in a race the
runners all compete, but only one re-
ceives the prize? Run in such a way that you may win it.
25Athletes exercise self-control in all things; they do it to receive a perishable wreath, but we an imperishable one. 26So
I do not run aimlessly, nor do I box as though beating the
air; 27but I punish my body and enslave it, so that after proclaiming to others I myself should not be disqualified.

The Example of Israel

10 I do not want you to be unaware, brothers and sisters,[p] that our ancestors were all under the cloud,
and all passed through the sea, 2and all were baptized into
Moses in the cloud and in the sea, 3and all ate the same
spiritual food, 4and all drank the same spiritual drink. For
they drank from the spiritual rock that followed them, and
the rock was Christ. 5Nevertheless, God was not pleased
with most of them, and they were struck down in the
wilderness.

6 Now these things occurred as examples for us, so that
we might not desire evil as they did. 7Do not become idolaters as some of them did; as it is written, "The people sat
down to eat and drink, and they rose up to play." 8We must
not indulge in sexual immorality as some of them did, and
twenty-three thousand fell in a single day. 9We must not
put Christ[q] to the test, as some of them did, and were destroyed by serpents. 10And do not complain as some of
them did, and were destroyed by the destroyer. 11These
things happened to them to serve as an example, and they
were written down to instruct us, on whom the ends of the

10:12–13
see pg. 598

ages have come. 12So if you think you are
standing, watch out that you do not fall.
13No testing has overtaken you that is not common to
everyone. God is faithful, and he will not let you be tested
beyond your strength, but with the testing he will also provide the way out so that you may be able to endure it.

Flee from Idolatry

14 Therefore, my dear friends,[r] flee from the worship of
idols. 15I speak as to sensible people; judge for yourselves
what I say. 16The cup of blessing that we bless, is it not a
sharing in the blood of Christ? The bread that we break, is

(Bible text continued on page 599)

[p]Gk *brothers* [q]Other ancient authorities read *the Lord* [r]Gk *my beloved*

(continued from previous page)

One of the important institutions associated with these athletic contests was the *gymnasium,* where young men were educated by the philosophers and trained in various physical routines. The name derived from the fact that the athletes trained and performed naked (*gumnos,* "naked"). That and the fact that gymnastic activities were closely tied to Greek culture made the institution repulsive to most Jewish people. But Paul's Corinthian readers were no doubt well acquainted with this prominent part of Greek life.

PAY ATTENTION TO TEMPTATION!

Paul's warning to "watch out that you do not fall" (v. 12) is as necessary today as it has ever been. For we, like all who have gone before us, are fallen, temptable, and subject to thinking and doing what is wrong. Few teachings of Scripture have more practical implications for day-to-day living.

Opportunities for temptation are almost endless. And since human nature is not getting any better, nor is any of us immune to the corrupted appetites of the flesh, we need to take Paul's warning seriously and watch out for temptation, or we will surely fall. Yet Scripture offers several alternatives for dealing with temptation as we find it:

(1) We should *avoid* temptation whenever possible. Proverbs 4:14–15 urges us, "Do not enter the path of the wicked, and do not walk in the way of evildoers. Avoid it; do not go on it." Often we know beforehand whether a certain set of circumstances is likely to lead to sin. Therefore, the obvious way to avoid sin is to avoid those circumstances. Paul described a "way of escape" from temptation (1 Cor. 10:13). Often the escape is to stay away from the place or the people where temptation lurks.

As believers, we can help others in this regard. We can avoid setting up situations that encourage people to do wrong. Teachers, for example, can help students avoid cheating by making assignments, giving tests, and communicating expectations in ways that reduce the need or incentive to cheat. Likewise, business owners and managers can devise procedures that don't needlessly place employees in a position where they might be tempted to steal cash, inventory, or equipment. It's not that a teacher or employer can't trust students or employees, but that no one can trust human nature to be immune from temptation.

(2) We should *flee* from powerful temptations. Earlier in this letter, Paul warned the Corinthians to flee sexual immorality (6:18). Here he warned them to flee idolatry (v. 14). Elsewhere he warned Timothy to flee the lust for material possessions and wealth (1 Tim. 6:9–11), as well as youthful lusts (2 Tim. 2:22). The message is clear: don't toy with temptation. Flee from it!

(3) Chronic temptation is something we need to *confess* and offer to Christ and ask for His cleansing work. Some temptations are powerful inner struggles, with thoughts and attitudes that graphically remind us of how fallen we really are. What should we do with that kind of temptation? Rather than deny it or try to repress it, we should bring it to Christ. He alone is capable of cleaning up the insides of our minds.

(4) Finally, we must *resist* temptation until it leaves us. When Christ was tempted by the devil, He resisted until the devil went away (Matt. 4:1–11). James encouraged us to do the same (James 4:7). Resistance begins by bathing our minds with the Word of God and standing our ground. We have the promise, after all, that the temptations we experience will never go beyond the common experiences of others, or beyond our ability to deal with them (1 Cor. 10:13). That is great news! ◆

it not a sharing in the body of Christ? [17]Because there is one
bread, we who are many are one body, for we all partake of
the one bread. [18]Consider the people of Israel;[s] are not
those who eat the sacrifices partners in the altar? [19]What do
I imply then? That food sacrificed to idols is anything, or
that an idol is anything? [20]No, I imply that what pagans
sacrifice, they sacrifice to demons and not to God. I do not
want you to be partners with demons. [21]You cannot drink
the cup of the Lord and the cup of demons. You cannot
partake of the table of the Lord and the table of demons.
[22]Or are we provoking the Lord to jealousy? Are we
stronger than he?

Do All to the Glory of God

23 "All things are lawful," but not all things are beneficial. "All things are lawful," but not all things build up.
[24]Do not seek your own advantage, but that of the other.
10:25–26 see pg. 600
[25]Eat whatever is sold in the meat market
without raising any question on the
ground of conscience, [26]for "the earth and its fullness are
the Lord's." [27]If an unbeliever invites you to a meal and you
are disposed to go, eat whatever is set before you without
raising any question on the ground of conscience. [28]But if
someone says to you, "This has been offered in sacrifice,"
then do not eat it, out of consideration for the one who informed you, and for the sake of conscience— [29]I mean the
other's conscience, not your own. For why should my liberty be subject to the judgment of someone else's conscience? [30]If I partake with thankfulness, why should I be
denounced because of that for which I give thanks?
31 So, whether you eat or drink, or whatever you do, do
everything for the glory of God. [32]Give no offense to Jews
or to Greeks or to the church of God, [33]just as I try to
please everyone in everything I do, not seeking my own ad-
11 vantage, but that of many, so that they may be saved.
[1]Be imitators of me, as I am of Christ.

Head Coverings for Women

11:2–16

11:3 see pg. 601

2 I commend you because you remember me in everything and maintain
the traditions just as I handed them on to
you. [3]But I want you to understand that
Christ is the head of every man, and the husband[t] is the
head of his wife,[u] and God is the head of Christ. [4]Any man
who prays or prophesies with something on his head disgraces his head, [5]but any woman who prays or prophesies
with her head unveiled disgraces her head—it is one and

[s]Gk *Israel according to the flesh* [t]The same Greek word means *man* or *husband* [u]Or *head of the woman*

HEAD COVERINGS

CONSIDER THIS 11:2–16 Head coverings (vv. 4–6) were an important part of first-century wardrobes. Outdoors they provided both men and women protection from the intense sun and heat, as well as rain. In addition, a woman's head covering was a sign of modesty and commitment to her husband. Jewish and other women of the Near East wore veils in public, but Roman women never wore veils, and among the Greeks, some did and some did not. In some cultures, a woman without a veil was assumed to have loose morals.

These cultural issues came to bear on the women believers at Corinth. Controversy arose over whether they were required to keep their heads covered during worship or not. Paul wrote that the churches had no universal policy on the matter (v. 16), indicating that the women had some freedom to choose how they would handle the issue.

Observing the custom to wear a

(continued on next page)

(continued from previous page)

covering may have been especially important in Corinth, where a favorite slogan was, "Everything is permissible" (compare 1 Cor. 6:12; 10:23). Paul was eager for Christians to maintain a good reputation and give no cause for offense so that people hearing the gospel would have no barriers to becoming followers of Christ.

the same thing as having her head shaved. 6For if a woman
will not veil herself, then she should cut off her hair; but if
it is disgraceful for a woman to have her hair cut off or to
be shaved, she should wear a veil. 7For a man ought not to
have his head veiled, since he is the image and reflection[v] of
God; but woman is the reflection[v] of man. 8Indeed, man
was not made from woman, but woman from man. 9Nei-
ther was man created for the sake of woman, but woman
for the sake of man. 10For this reason a woman ought to
have a symbol of[w] authority on her head,[x] because of the
angels. 11Nevertheless, in the Lord woman is not independent of man or man independent of woman. 12For just as
woman came from man, so man comes through woman;

[v]Or *glory* [w]Gk lacks *a symbol of* [x]Or *have freedom of choice regarding her head*

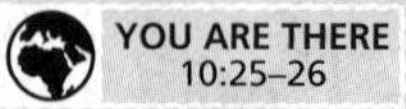

Food in the New Testament World

Meat sold in the Corinthian meat market (v. 25) was meat that had been offered to the Greek gods. Thus Paul had to address the moral question of whether a believer in Christ should buy and eat such food. His conclusion: don't worry about it; the earth and all its products belong to God (vv. 25–26).

Actually, ***beef*** *was something of luxury in ancient Greece and seldom eaten on a regular basis. A far more common source of meat was* ***fish****. Other items in a typical meal might be* ***cheese, leeks, olives, wine, oil, and vinegar****. Greece raised some* ***wheat,*** *but most of its* ***bread*** *was made from imported grain from Egypt or Asia Minor.*

In Palestine, the land of "milk and honey" (Ex. 13:5), Hebrew farmers raised a variety of cereal grains such as ***wheat*** *and related products,* ***spelt, barley, and millet****. They also cultivated* ***cucumbers, squash, beans, lentils,***

but all things come from God. [13]Judge for yourselves: is it
proper for a woman to pray to God with her head unveiled?
[14]Does not nature itself teach you that if a man wears long
hair, it is degrading to him, [15]but if a woman has long hair,
it is her glory? For her hair is given to her for a covering.
[16]But if anyone is disposed to be contentious—we have no
such custom, nor do the churches of God.

Impropriety in Worship

17 Now in the following instructions I do not commend
you, because when you come together it is not for the better but for the worse. [18]For, to begin with, when you come
together as a church, I hear that there are divisions among
you; and to some extent I believe it. [19]Indeed, there have to

◆ ◆ ◆ ◆ ◆ ◆ ◆ ◆ ◆ ◆ ◆ ◆ ◆ ◆ ◆

***leeks, onions, and garlic**. Fruits and nuts included **melons, grapes and raisins, figs, apricots, oranges, almonds, and pistachios**.*

***Honey** was gathered from bees or made from **dates**. Regional spices included **mint, anise, dill, and cummin**. As in the rest of the Mediterranean, **olives** were plentiful. They were eaten green or ripe, or they might be pressed into **oil**, which was used for cooking, seasoning, and as fuel for lamps.*

***Beef and mutton** were a common part of the daily fare in Palestine, along with **milk, butter, and cheese**. A noon meal for a workman might consist of two small loaves of **barley bread**—one filled with cheese, the other with olives.*

*Animals were divided into two classes by the Hebrews, clean and unclean (Lev. 11:1–47; Acts 10:9–15). Only **clean animals**—those that chewed the cud and had divided hooves—could be used for food (Lev. 11:3), except the fat (Lev. 3:16–17). Pigs and camels were ceremonially unclean and therefore unfit for food. **Camel's milk and cheese**, however, were not forbidden.*

*Many kinds of **fish** could be eaten (Lev. 11:9–12), but not oysters or shrimp. Some twenty different species of **birds** were rejected (11:13–19). Insects that had legs and leaped, such as the **grasshopper**, were fit for consumption.*

*The major preservative for these foods was **salt**. An abundant supply was available from the Sea of Salt, or Dead Sea, in the south.* ◆

WHAT IS HEADSHIP?

CONSIDER THIS
11:3

What exactly did Paul mean when he used the word "head" (v. 3)? Some believe that the term by definition implies subordination of one person to another. Others disagree. For example, John Chrysostom, an early church leader, declared that only a heretic would understand "head" as chief or authority over. Rather, he understood the word as meaning absolute oneness, cause, or primal source.

Either way, it's important to note that while "God is the head of Christ" (v. 3), Christ is elsewhere shown to be equal with God (for example, John 1:1–3; 10:30; Col. 1:15). So the term "head" need not exclude the idea of equality. At the same time, even though Christ is the equal of God, He became obedient to the point of death (Phil. 2:5–8), demonstrating that equality need not rule out submission.

be factions among you, for only so will it become clear who
among you are genuine. [20]When you come together, it is
not really to eat the Lord's supper. [21]For when the time
comes to eat, each of you goes ahead with your own supper, and one goes hungry and another becomes drunk.
[22]What! Do you not have homes to eat and drink in? Or do
you show contempt for the church of God and humiliate
those who have nothing? What should I say to you? Should
I commend you? In this matter I do not commend you!

The Proper Observance of the Lord's Supper

23 For I received from the Lord what I also handed on
to you, that the Lord Jesus on the night when he was betrayed took a loaf of bread, [24]and when he had given
thanks, he broke it and said, "This is my body that is for[y]

[y]Other ancient authorities read *is broken for*

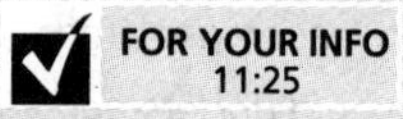

FOR YOUR INFO 11:25

THE NEW COVENANT

Even a casual reader of the Bible soon discovers that it is divided into two major sections, the Old Testament and the New Testament. But how many readers realize that "testament" is just another word for "covenant"? Thus, the New Testament describes the new covenant (v. 25), or agreement, that God has made with humanity, based on the death and resurrection of Jesus Christ.

In the Bible, a covenant involves much more than a contract or simple agreement. A contract has an end date, but a covenant is a permanent arrangement. Furthermore, a contract generally involves only one aspect of a person, such as a skill, while a covenant covers a person's total being.

God entered into numerous covenants with people in the Old Testament. For example: with Adam and Eve (Gen. 3:15); with Noah (Gen. 8:21–22; 2 Pet. 3:7, 15); with Abraham (Gen. 12:1–3); with Israel (Deut. 29:1—30:20); and with David (2 Sam. 7:12–16; 22:51).

The agreement with Israel was especially significant, because it established a special relationship between God and the Hebrews. They were made His "chosen people" through whom He would bring blessing and hope to the rest of the world. However, because the recipients of God's Law could not keep it perfectly, further provision was necessary for them as well as for the rest of humanity.

That's why God promised a new covenant through the prophet Jeremiah (Jer. 31:31). Under the new covenant,

11:25 you. Do this in remembrance of me." [25]In
the same way he took the cup also, after
supper, saying, "This cup is the new covenant in my blood.
Do this, as often as you drink it, in remembrance of me."
[26]For as often as you eat this bread and drink the cup, you
proclaim the Lord's death until he comes.
27 Whoever, therefore, eats the bread or drinks the cup
of the Lord in an unworthy manner will be answerable for
the body and blood of the Lord. [28]Examine yourselves, and
only then eat of the bread and drink of the cup. [29]For all
who eat and drink[z] without discerning the body,[a] eat and
drink judgment against themselves. [30]For this reason many
of you are weak and ill, and some have died.[b] [31]But if we
judged ourselves, we would not be judged. [32]But when we
are judged by the Lord, we are disciplined[c] so that we may
not be condemned along with the world.

[z]Other ancient authorities add *in an unworthy manner,* [a]Other ancient authorities read *the Lord's body* [b]Gk *fallen asleep* [c]Or *When we are judged, we are being disciplined by the Lord*

God would write His Law on human hearts. This suggested a new level of obedience and a new knowledge of the Lord.

The work of Jesus Christ brought the promised new covenant into being. When Jesus ate His final Passover meal with the Twelve, He spoke of the cup as "the new covenant in my blood" (Luke 22:20), the words that Paul quoted to the Corinthians to remind them of the need for purity and propriety in their worship (1 Cor. 11:25–34).

The new covenant in Jesus' blood rests directly on the sacrificial work of Christ on the cross (which was prefigured by Israel's system of sacrifices) and accomplishes the removal of sin and the cleansing of the conscience by faith in Him (Heb. 10:2, 22). So every time Christians celebrate the Lord's Supper, they remind themselves that God has fulfilled His promise: "I will be their God, and they shall be my people . . . I will be merciful toward their iniquities, and I will remember their sins no more" (Heb. 8:10,12; compare Jer. 31:33–34). ◆

One of the striking features of God's covenant with Israel is that God is holy, all-knowing, and all-powerful, yet He consented to enter into a covenant with Abraham and his descendants—weak, sinful, and imperfect as they were. See "Israel," Rom. 10:1.

"THIS IS MY BODY THAT IS FOR YOU."
—1 Corinthians 11:24

33 So then, my brothers and sisters,[d] when you come together to eat, wait for one another. 34If you are hungry, eat at home, so that when you come together, it will not be for your condemnation. About the other things I will give instructions when I come.

The Spirit Gives Gifts to Each Believer

12 Now concerning spiritual gifts,[e] brothers and sisters,[d] I do not want you to be uninformed. 2You
know that when you were pagans, you were enticed and
led astray to idols that could not speak. 3Therefore I want
you to understand that no one speaking by the Spirit of
God ever says "Let Jesus be cursed!" and no one can say
"Jesus is Lord" except by the Holy Spirit.
4 Now there are varieties of gifts, but the same Spirit;
5and there are varieties of services, but the same Lord; 6and
there are varieties of activities, but it is the same God who

[d]Gk *brothers* [e]Or *spiritual persons*

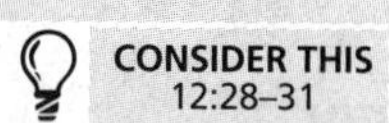
CONSIDER THIS
12:28–31

ARE SOME JOBS MORE IMPORTANT THAN OTHERS?

Does a hierarchy of gifts (vv. 28–31) mean God values some jobs more than others? Judging by popular opinion, one might conclude that He does. In fact, for centuries Christians have subscribed to a subtle yet powerful hierarchy of vocations.

In our culture, that hierarchy tends to position clergy *(missionaries and evangelists, pastors and priests) at the top, members of the* "helping professions" *(doctors and nurses, teachers and educators, social workers) next, and* "secular" workers *(business executives, salespeople, factory laborers and farmers) at the bottom.*

So what determines the spiritual value of a job? How does God assign significance? The hierarchy assumes sacred and secular distinctions, and assigns priority to the sacred. But does God view vocations that way? No . . .

All legitimate work matters to God. *God Himself is a worker. In fact, human occupations find their origin in His work to create the world (Ps. 8:6–8). Work is a gift from Him to meet the needs of people and the creation.*

God creates people to carry out specific kinds of work. *God uniquely designs each of us, fitting us for certain kinds of tasks. He distributes skills, abilities, interests, and personalities among us so that we can carry out His work in the world. That work includes "spiritual" tasks, but also*

activates all of them in everyone. [7]To each is given the manifestation of the Spirit for the common good. [8]To one is
given through the Spirit the utterance of wisdom, and to
another the utterance of knowledge according to the same
Spirit, [9]to another faith by the same Spirit, to another gifts
of healing by the one Spirit, [10]to another the working of
miracles, to another prophecy, to another the discernment
of spirits, to another various kinds of tongues, to another
the interpretation of tongues. [11]All these are activated by
one and the same Spirit, who allots to each one individually
just as the Spirit chooses.

12 For just as the body is one and has many members,
and all the members of the body, though many, are one
body, so it is with Christ. [13]For in the one Spirit we were all
baptized into one body—Jews or Greeks, slaves or free—
and we were all made to drink of one Spirit.

extends to health, education, agriculture, business, law, communication, the arts, and so on.

God cares more about character and conduct than occupational status. *Paul's teaching in this passage is about gifts, not vocations. At the time Paul wrote it, there were few if any "professional" clergy in the church. Paul himself was a tentmaker by occupation, along with his friends, Aquila and Priscilla (1 Cor. 16:19; see Rom. 16:3–5). Other church leaders practiced a wide variety of professions and trades. God* may *assign rank among the spiritual gifts; but there's no indication that He looks at vocations that way.*

Furthermore, Scripture says there is something more important than gifts, a "more excellent way" (1 Cor. 12:31). Chapter 13 reveals it to be the way of Christlike love and character. Implication: If you want status in God's economy, excel at love, no matter what you do for work. Love has the greatest value to God (13:13; Matt. 22:35–40). ◆

Your work is like the work that God does, and it expresses something of who God is and what He wants done in the world. See "People at Work," Heb. 2:7.

Is it possible to hold a "secular" job and still seek the things of Christ? Or would it be better to quit and go into the ministry? See "The Spirituality of Everyday Work," Col. 3:1–2.

IN THE ONE SPIRIT WE WERE ALL BAPTIZED INTO ONE BODY. . . .
—1 Corinthians 12:13

Every Member Is Necessary

14 Indeed, the body does not consist of one
member but of many. 15If the foot would say, "Because I am not a hand, I do not belong to the
body," that would not make it any less a part of the
body. 16And if the ear would say, "Because I am not
an eye, I do not belong to the body," that would
not make it any less a part of the body. 17If the
whole body were an eye, where would the hearing
be? If the whole body were hearing, where would
the sense of smell be? 18But as it is, God arranged
the members in the body, each one of them, as he
chose. 19If all were a single member, where would
the body be? 20As it is, there are many members,
yet one body. 21The eye cannot say to the hand, "I
have no need of you," nor again the head to the
feet, "I have no need of you." 22On the contrary,
the members of the body that seem to be weaker
are indispensable, 23and those members of the
body that we think less honorable we clothe with
greater honor, and our less respectable members
are treated with greater respect; 24whereas our
more respectable members do not need this. But
God has so arranged the body, giving the greater
honor to the inferior member, 25that there may be
no dissension within the body, but the members
may have the same care for one another. 26If one
member suffers, all suffer together with it; if one
member is honored, all rejoice together with it.

27 Now you are the body of Christ and individ-

12:28–31 see pg. 604

ually members of it. 28And God
has appointed in the church first
apostles, second prophets, third teachers; then
deeds of power, then gifts of healing, forms of assistance, forms of leadership, various kinds of
tongues. 29Are all apostles? Are all prophets? Are all
teachers? Do all work miracles? 30Do all possess
gifts of healing? Do all speak in tongues? Do all interpret? 31But strive for the greater gifts. And I will
show you a still more excellent way.

The Way of Love

13:1–13

13 If I speak in the tongues
of mortals and of angels,
but do not have love, I am a noisy gong or a clang-
ing cymbal. 2And if I have prophetic powers, and
understand all mysteries and all knowledge, and if
I have all faith, so as to remove mountains, but do

13:3

not have love, I am nothing. 3If I
give away all my possessions,
and if I hand over my body so that I may boast,[f]
but do not have love, I gain nothing.

4 Love is patient; love is kind; love is not envious or boastful or arrogant 5or rude. It does not insist on its own way; it is not irritable or resentful;
6it does not rejoice in wrongdoing, but rejoices in
the truth. 7It bears all things, believes all things,
hopes all things, endures all things.

8 Love never ends. But as for prophecies, they
will come to an end; as for tongues, they will
cease; as for knowledge, it will come to an end.
9For we know only in part, and we prophesy only
in part; 10but when the complete comes, the partial
will come to an end. 11When I was a child, I spoke
like a child, I thought like a child, I reasoned like a
child; when I became an adult, I put an end to

13:12

childish ways. 12For now we see
in a mirror, dimly,[g] but then we
will see face to face. Now I know only in part; then
I will know fully, even as I have been fully known.
13And now faith, hope, and love abide, these three;
and the greatest of these is love.

The Value of Prophecy

14 Pursue love and strive for the spiritual
gifts, and especially that you may prophesy.
2For those who speak in a tongue do not speak to

[f]Other ancient authorities read *body to be burned* [g]Gk *in a riddle*

A Lifestyle of Love

A CLOSER LOOK 13:1–13 *In chapter 13, Paul described the lifestyle of love that Christ can produce in His followers. Elsewhere he painted a number of other pictures of what Christlikeness looks like. See "New Creatures with New Character," Gal. 5:22–23.*

Giving It All Away

A CLOSER LOOK 13:3 *Just as the Love Chapter suggests (v. 3), Christ told one man to sell all of his possessions and give the proceeds to the poor (Mark 10:17–27). Apparently He felt that doing so would bring eternal profit to the man. But the fellow could not bear to part with his goods. At least he was honest enough to turn away, even if in sadness, rather than fake love and end up with nothing. See "The Man Who Had It All—Almost," Mark 10:17–27.*

How should believers handle their money? See "Christians and Money," 1 Tim. 6:6–19.

other people but to God; for nobody understands them, since they are speaking mysteries in the Spirit. [3]On the other hand, those who prophesy speak to other people for their upbuilding and encouragement and consolation. [4]Those who speak in a tongue build up themselves, but those who prophesy build up the church. [5]Now I would like all of you to speak in tongues, but even more to prophesy. One who prophesies is greater than one who speaks in tongues, unless someone interprets, so that the church may be built up.

6 Now, brothers and sisters,[h] if I come to you speaking in tongues, how will I benefit you unless I speak to you in some revelation or knowledge or prophecy or teaching? [7]It is the same way with lifeless instruments that produce sound, such as the flute or the harp. If they do not give distinct notes, how will anyone know what is being played? [8]And if the bugle gives an indistinct sound, who will get ready for battle? [9]So with yourselves; if in a tongue you utter speech that is not intelligible, how will anyone know what is being said? For you will be speaking into the air. [10]There are doubtless many different kinds of sounds in the world, and nothing is without sound. [11]If then I do not know the meaning of a sound, I will be a foreigner to the speaker and the speaker a foreigner to me. [12]So with yourselves; since you are eager for spiritual gifts, strive to excel in them for building up the church.

The Reason for Tongues

13 Therefore, one who speaks in a tongue should pray for the power to interpret. [14]For if I pray in a tongue, my spirit prays but my mind is unproductive. [15]What should I do then? I will pray with the spirit, but I will pray with the mind also; I will sing praise with the spirit, but I will sing praise with the mind also. [16]Otherwise, if you say a blessing with the spirit, how can anyone in the position of an outsider say the "Amen" to your thanksgiving, since the outsider does not know what you are saying? [17]For you may give thanks well enough, but the other person is not built up. [18]I thank God that I speak in tongues more than all of you; [19]nevertheless, in church I would rather speak five words with my mind, in order to instruct others also, than ten thousand words in a tongue.

20 Brothers and sisters,[h] do not be children in your thinking; rather, be infants in evil, but in thinking be adults. [21]In the law it is written,

"By people of strange tongues
and by the lips of foreigners

[h]Gk *brothers*

QUOTE UNQUOTE

CONSIDER THIS 13:12 *One believer's reflections on seeing in a mirror dimly (v. 12):*

If we see dimly now with God as one image,
How well do we see with another sinner in the communication process here on earth?
No wonder human relations are so distorted.
But someday all hindrances will be removed!

Pete Hammond, *Marketplace Networks*, 1990

Not Permitted to Speak?

CONSIDER THIS 14:34 *When Paul writes that women should keep silent in the churches (v. 34), we are led to ask why in light of previous statements in the letter. He has already mentioned that women prayed and prophesied, presumably during worship services (11:5). Likewise, he has written that the Spirit gave gifts to everyone in the body (12:7, 11), and presumably some of the women received some of the speaking gifts. So why would he exhort the women to keep silent?*

One explanation may be that the women in the congregation at Corinth probably had few opportunities for formal education and little exposure to large gatherings—except for the wild rites of their former religion. So when they came into the church, they may have assumed a similar approach to Christian worship. That would have been inappropriate, so Paul exhorted them to pursue a quieter, more orderly form of worship now that they were following the Lord.

I will speak to this people;
yet even then they will not listen to me,"
says the Lord. 22Tongues, then, are a sign not for believers
but for unbelievers, while prophecy is not for unbelievers
but for believers. 23If, therefore, the whole church comes
together and all speak in tongues, and outsiders or unbelievers enter, will they not say that you are out of your
mind? 24But if all prophesy, an unbeliever or outsider who
enters is reproved by all and called to account by all. 25After
the secrets of the unbeliever's heart are disclosed, that person will bow down before God and worship him, declaring,
"God is really among you."

Order in Worship

26 What should be done then, my friends?[i] When you
come together, each one has a hymn, a lesson, a revelation,
a tongue, or an interpretation. Let all things be done for
building up. 27If anyone speaks in a tongue, let there be
only two or at most three, and each in turn; and let one interpret. 28But if there is no one to interpret, let them be
silent in church and speak to themselves and to God. 29Let
two or three prophets speak, and let the others weigh what
is said. 30If a revelation is made to someone else sitting
nearby, let the first person be silent. 31For you can all
prophesy one by one, so that all may learn and all be encouraged. 32And the spirits of prophets are subject to the
prophets, 33for God is a God not of disorder but of peace.
14:34 (As in all the churches of the saints,
34women should be silent in the
churches. For they are not permitted to speak, but should
be subordinate, as the law also says. 35If there is anything
they desire to know, let them ask their husbands at home.
For it is shameful for a woman to speak in church.[j] 36Or did
the word of God originate with you? Or are you the only
ones it has reached?)
37 Anyone who claims to be a prophet, or to have spiritual powers, must acknowledge that what I am writing to
you is a command of the Lord. 38Anyone who does not recognize this is not to be recognized. 39So, my friends,[k] be eager to prophesy, and do not forbid speaking in tongues;
40but all things should be done decently and in order.

What the Gospel Is

15 Now I would remind you, brothers and sisters,[i] of
the good news[l] that I proclaimed to you, which you
in turn received, in which also you stand, 2through which
also you are being saved, if you hold firmly to the message

[i]Gk *brothers* [j]Other ancient authorities put verses 34-35 after verse 40 [k]Gk *my brothers*
[l]Or *gospel*

that I proclaimed to you—unless you have come to believe
in vain.
3 For I handed on to you as of first importance what I in
turn had received: that Christ died for our sins in accordance with the scriptures, 4and that he was buried, and that
he was raised on the third day in accordance with the scriptures, 5and that he appeared to Cephas, then to the twelve.
6Then he appeared to more than five hundred brothers and
sisters[m] at one time, most of whom are still alive, though
some have died.[n] 7Then he appeared to James, then to all
the apostles. 8Last of all, as to one untimely born, he ap-
15:9–10 see pg. 610
peared also to me. 9For I am the least of
the apostles, unfit to be called an apostle,
because I persecuted the church of God. 10But by the grace
of God I am what I am, and his grace toward me has not
been in vain. On the contrary, I worked harder than any of
them—though it was not I, but the grace of God that is
with me. 11Whether then it was I or they, so we proclaim
and so you have come to believe.

Who Says There Is No Resurrection?

12 Now if Christ is proclaimed as raised from the dead,
how can some of you say there is no resurrection of the
dead? 13If there is no resurrection of the dead, then Christ
has not been raised; 14and if Christ has not been raised,
then our proclamation has been in vain and your faith has
been in vain. 15We are even found to be misrepresenting
God, because we testified of God that he raised Christ—
whom he did not raise if it is true that the dead are not
raised. 16For if the dead are not raised, then Christ has not
been raised. 17If Christ has not been raised, your faith is futile and you are still in your sins. 18Then those also who
have died[n] in Christ have perished. 19If for this life only we
have hoped in Christ, we are of all people most to be
pitied.
20 But in fact Christ has been raised from the dead, the
first fruits of those who have died.[n] 21For since death came
through a human being, the resurrection of the dead has
also come through a human being; 22for as all die in Adam,
so all will be made alive in Christ. 23But each in his own order: Christ the first fruits, then at his coming those who be-
15:24
long to Christ. 24Then comes the end,[o]
when he hands over the kingdom to God
the Father, after he has destroyed every ruler and every
authority and power. 25For he must reign until he has put
all his enemies under his feet. 26The last enemy to be

(Bible text continued on page 611)

[m]Gk *brothers* [n]Gk *fallen asleep* [o]Or *Then come the rest*

The End of Authority

CONSIDER THIS 15:24 **Someday all authority, rule, and power will end—a sobering thought (v. 24). Peter mentioned a similar idea when he asked, in light of the end of the present time, what sort of people should we be (1 Pet. 3:10–13)? How should we live? No matter how hard we've worked to acquire and accrue power and position, it will eventually come to an end. That thought should challenge us to hold on lightly to the trappings of authority and use it wisely and responsibly for God's purposes.**

CONSIDER THIS
15:9–10

MYTH #6

10 MYTHS ABOUT CHRISTIANITY

MYTH: PEOPLE BECOME CHRISTIANS THROUGH SOCIAL CONDITIONING

Many people today accept a number of myths about Christianity, with the result that they never respond to Jesus as He really is. This is one of ten articles that speak to some of those misconceptions. For a list of all ten, see 1 Tim. 1:3–4.

Paul's statement that he persecuted the church prior to his conversion (vv. 9–10) is a strong piece of evidence against the commonly held notion that religious preference is mainly a result of upbringing.

Without question, cultural circumstances play a part in people's religious beliefs. A Hindu background would tend to predispose a person towards Hinduism, a Christian background toward Christianity, and so forth. But can social conditioning alone explain why people believe and behave as they do? After all, a Christian upbringing is no guarantee that a person won't someday abandon the faith. On the other hand, countless people who have had no exposure to Christianity in their youth nevertheless convert as adults.

The fact is, Christian conversion is much misunderstood. It is often regarded as sudden, irrational, selective, and even illusory. But what are its essential elements? Paul's experience is instructive. While certain aspects of his conversion were unique, four elements stand out that are present in every authentic conversion:

(1) *His conversion touched his conscience.* He recognized that he had been fighting God and that his vicious treatment of Christians was wrong (Acts 26:9–11; 1 Tim. 1:13).

(2) *His conversion touched his understanding.* He discovered that the Jesus he was persecuting was no less than the risen Messiah, the Son of God (Acts 9:22).

(3) *His conversion touched his will.* He gave in to Jesus and began following Him (Acts 26:19–20).

(4) *His conversion produced noticeable change in his life.* His ambitions, his character, his relationships, his outlook—everything changed as a result of his encounter with Christ (Phil. 3:7–11).

But suppose, as some have, that it all amounts to nothing but an illusion? Three tests can be applied to determine whether religious experience in general and Christianity in particular is illusory. First, there is the test of history. Christianity makes historical claims. Are those claims valid? Does history bear them out? Yes it does. There is nothing illusory about Jesus or His impact on the world. Nor are His claims illusory (see "Myth #1: Jesus Christ Was Only a Great Moral Teacher," Matt. 13:34–35). Likewise, His death and resurrection are well attested (see "Myth #2: There Is No Evidence That Jesus Rose From the Dead," Matt. 28:1–10). Nor is there any doubt about the reality of the church. In short, Christian faith is rooted in historical fact.

A second test is the test of character. When drunkards become sober and crooks become honest, when animists give up their mysticism and people enslaved by black magic are set free, when self-centered people become generous and unbelievers become giants of faith, it is very difficult to explain it away as illusion. Changed lives are not the only evidence of Christianity's authenticity, but they are certainly an impressive one.

(continued on next page)

destroyed is death. 27 For "God[p] has put all things in subjection under his feet." But when it says, "All things are put in
subjection," it is plain that this does not include the one
who put all things in subjection under him. 28 When all
things are subjected to him, then the Son himself will also
be subjected to the one who put all things in subjection under him, so that God may be all in all.
29 Otherwise, what will those people do who receive
baptism on behalf of the dead? If the dead are not raised at
all, why are people baptized on their behalf?
30 And why are we putting ourselves in danger every
hour? 31 I die every day! That is as certain, brothers and sisters,[q] as my boasting of you—a boast that I make in Christ
Jesus our Lord. 32 If with merely human hopes I fought with
wild animals at Ephesus, what would I have gained by it? If
the dead are not raised,
"Let us eat and drink,
for tomorrow we die."
33 Do not be deceived:
"Bad company ruins good morals."
34 Come to a sober and right mind, and sin no more; for
some people have no knowledge of God. I say this to your
shame.

A New Body

35 But someone will ask, "How are the dead raised?
With what kind of body do they come?" 36 Fool! What you
sow does not come to life unless it dies. 37 And as for what
you sow, you do not sow the body that is to be, but a bare
seed, perhaps of wheat or of some other grain. 38 But God
gives it a body as he has chosen, and to each kind of seed
its own body. 39 Not all flesh is alike, but there is one flesh
for human beings, another for animals, another for birds,
and another for fish. 40 There are both heavenly bodies and
earthly bodies, but the glory of the heavenly is one thing,
and that of the earthly is another. 41 There is one glory of
the sun, and another glory of the moon, and another glory
of the stars; indeed, star differs from star in glory.
15:42 see pg. 612
42 So it is with the resurrection of the
dead. What is sown is perishable, what is
raised is imperishable. 43 It is sown in dishonor, it is raised
in glory. It is sown in weakness, it is raised in power. 44 It is
sown a physical body, it is raised a spiritual body. If there is
a physical body, there is also a spiritual body. 45 Thus it
is written, "The first man, Adam, became a living being";
the last Adam became a life-giving spirit. 46 But it is not the

(Bible text continued on page 613)

[p] *Gk he* [q] *Gk brothers*

(continued from previous page)

Finally there is the test of power. Delusions and neuroses tend to destroy people's character. They produce unbalanced behavior and keep people from achieving their goals. Christianity has precisely the opposite effect. It makes people whole. It even enables people to face death—a time when delusions are usually stripped away—with confidence and courage.

History, character, power: these cannot be attributed to social conditioning. Rather they strongly suggest that something far deeper lies behind Christianity, something good, powerful, and alive. ◆

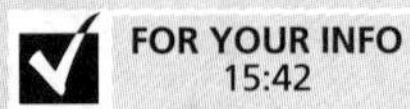

BURIAL

Paul's doctrine of the resurrection (v. 42) flew in the face of prevailing ideas about the afterlife. To the Greek mind, death released a person's spirit from the prison of the body. The last thing a Greek would want was to be reunited with a corruptible body (v. 35).

Burial practices in Corinth and the other cities of the Roman Empire were largely a function of one's status in life. If the deceased was a member of the upper classes, the job of preparing the body was delegated to professional undertakers. They usually dressed the body in a toga adorned with badges and other tokens of the person's accomplishments and offices. Professional mourners and musicians then led a funeral procession to the burial site. Sometimes actors were recruited to follow the cortege, wearing masks that depicted the family's ancestors.

In Greek and Roman cultures, bodies were as likely to be cremated as buried. Either way, the rich tended to bury their dead in elaborate tombs. Some even formed cooperatives in which hundreds of urns were placed.

The poor, by contrast, laid their dead to rest in common, often unmarked graves. Or, if they lived in or near Rome, they might use the catacombs, a maze of underground tunnels outside the city. In the later years of the first century, Christians were not permitted to use regular cemeteries, so they resorted to the catacombs for their funerals. As persecution increased, some eventually fled there for survival.

Among the Hebrews, bodies were laid either in a shallow grave covered with stones or in a cave or tomb hewn out of stone and secured by a circular stone rolled and sealed over the entrance. Graves were often marked with a large, upright stone.

Due to the hot climate of Palestine, dead bodies decayed rapidly, so burial usually took place within a few hours after death. If someone died late in the day, burial took place the next day, but always within twenty-four hours after death.

The Hebrews did not follow the Greek custom of cremation, except in emergencies, nor did they generally use coffins. And even though they had historical ties to Egypt, they did not embalm their dead as the Egyptians did.

Mummification was invented by the Egyptians more than 3,000 years ago. They believed that the preservation of the body insured the continuation of the soul after death.

According to the Greek historian Herodotus, there were three different methods of embalming. The least expensive method involved emptying the intestines by flushing them with a cleaning

(continued on next page)

spiritual that is first, but the physical, and then the spiritual. 47The first man was from the earth, a man of dust; the
second man is[r] from heaven. 48As was the man of dust, so
are those who are of the dust; and as is the man of heaven,
so are those who are of heaven. 49Just as we have borne the
image of the man of dust, we will[s] also bear the image of
the man of heaven.
50 What I am saying, brothers and sisters,[t] is this: flesh
and blood cannot inherit the kingdom of God, nor does the
perishable inherit the imperishable. 51Listen, I will tell you
a mystery! We will not all die,[u] but we will all be changed,
52in a moment, in the twinkling of an eye, at the last trumpet. For the trumpet will sound, and the dead will be raised
imperishable, and we will be changed. 53For this perishable
body must put on imperishability, and this mortal body
must put on immortality. 54When this perishable body puts
on imperishability, and this mortal body puts on immortality, then the saying that is written will be fulfilled:
"Death has been swallowed up in victory."
55 "Where, O death, is your victory?
Where, O death, is your sting?"
56The sting of death is sin, and the power of sin is the law.
57But thanks be to God, who gives us the victory through
our Lord Jesus Christ.
58 Therefore, my beloved,[v] be steadfast, immovable, always excelling in the work of the Lord, because you know
that in the Lord your labor is not in vain.

A Collection for Believers at Jerusalem

16:1–4
see pg. 615

16 Now concerning the collection
for the saints: you should follow
the directions I gave to the churches of Galatia. 2On the
first day of every week, each of you is to put aside and save
whatever extra you earn, so that collections need not be
taken when I come. 3And when I arrive, I will send any
whom you approve with letters to take your gift to
Jerusalem. 4If it seems advisable that I should go also, they
will accompany me.
5 I will visit you after passing through Macedonia—for I
intend to pass through Macedonia— 6and perhaps I will
stay with you or even spend the winter, so that you may
send me on my way, wherever I go. 7I do not want to see
you now just in passing, for I hope to spend some time
with you, if the Lord permits. 8But I will stay in Ephesus
until Pentecost, 9for a wide door for effective work has opened to me, and there
are many adversaries.

16:9–20
see pg. 614

[r]Other ancient authorities add *the Lord* [s]Other ancient authorities read *let us* [t]Gk *brothers* [u]Gk *fall asleep* [v]Gk *beloved brothers*

(continued from previous page)

liquid, after which the body was soaked in natron. A second method called for placing the body in natron after the stomach and intestines had been dissolved by an injection of cedar oil.

The most elaborate method of embalming required the removal of the brain and all internal organs except the heart. The inner cavity of the body was then washed and filled with spices. The corpse was soaked in natron, then washed and wrapped in bandages of linen soaked with gum. Finally, the embalmed body was placed in a wooden coffin. These processes proved remarkably effective in preserving bodies from decay. ◆

Among Jews at the time of Christ, it was chiefly the women's task to prepare bodies for interment. See the article, "Funeral Preparations," John 12:1–8.

Greetings and Conclusion

16:10

10 If Timothy comes, see that he has
nothing to fear among you, for he is do-
ing the work of the Lord just as I am; 11therefore let no one
despise him. Send him on his way in peace, so that he may
come to me; for I am expecting him with the brothers.
12 Now concerning our brother Apollos, I strongly
urged him to visit you with the other brothers, but he was
not at all willing[w] to come now. He will come when he has
the opportunity.
13 Keep alert, stand firm in your faith, be courageous,
be strong. 14Let all that you do be done in love.
15 Now, brothers and sisters,[x] you know that members
of the household of Stephanas were the first converts in
Achaia, and they have devoted themselves to the service of
the saints; 16I urge you to put yourselves at the service of

[w]Or *it was not at all God's will for him* [x]Gk *brothers*

Timothy

A CLOSER LOOK 16:10

Timothy (v. 10) was one of Paul's most trusted and valued companions. To find out more about this promising young man, see his profile at the Introduction to 1 and 2 Timothy.

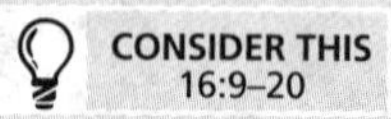

CONSIDER THIS 16:9–20

Enemies Become Family and Friends

Paul had once been a dangerous enemy to the followers of Christ. But his dramatic encounter with the Savior and subsequent change of heart brought him into the family of God (Acts 9:1–30). Courageous Christians such as Ananias (see 9:10) and Barnabas (see 4:36–37) began to nurture and aid the new believer. He had become a brother.

In the same way, Christ makes believers today into a new family. Having experienced the same gift from God—forgiveness and hope—we are now brothers and sisters in Christ.

Paul acknowledged several of his family of faith as he closed 1 Corinthians:

- *Young* Timothy *(1 Cor. 16:10–11), who needed acceptance and affirmation (see Timothy's profile at the Introduction to 1 and 2 Timothy).*
- *Gifted* Apollos *(v. 12), one of the Corinthians' former leaders (1:12) who was unable to go to them at that time (see "Apollos," Acts 18:24–28).*
- Stephanas *(vv. 15–16), baptized by Paul in the early days*

such people, and of everyone who works and toils with
them. [17]I rejoice at the coming of Stephanas and Fortunatus
and Achaicus, because they have made up for your absence; [18]for they refreshed my spirit as well as yours. So
give recognition to such persons.

16:19

19 The churches of Asia send greetings. Aquila and Prisca, together with the
church in their house, greet you warmly in the Lord. [20]All
the brothers and sisters[y] send greetings. Greet one another
with a holy kiss.

21 I, Paul, write this greeting with my own hand. [22]Let
anyone be accursed who has no love for the Lord. Our
Lord, come![z] [23]The grace of the Lord Jesus be with you.
[24]My love be with all of you in Christ Jesus.[a]

[y]Gk *brothers* [z]Gk *Marana tha*. These Aramaic words can also be read *Maran atha*, meaning *Our Lord has come* [a]Other ancient authorities add *Amen*

Aquila and Priscilla

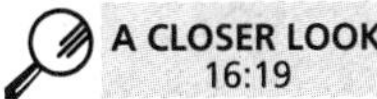

A CLOSER LOOK 16:19

Aquila and Priscilla (v. 19) were old friends of the Corinthians. In fact, they had been instrumental in starting the church at Corinth (Acts 18:1–11). To find out more about these valuable coworkers, business partners, and friends of Paul, see their profile at Rom. 16:3–5.

of the Corinthian church; the Corinthians needed to respect him.

- Fortunatus and Achaicus *(vv. 17–18), encouragers of Paul who may have delivered to him the letter from the Corinthians that he was answering with 1 Corinthians; like Stephanas, they too needed recognition.*
- Priscilla and Aquila *(v. 19), co-founders of the Corinthian work and business partners with Paul (Acts 18:1–4); they now were leading a similar work at Ephesus and sent warm greetings to their brothers and sisters across the "wine dark" Aegean Sea (see "Priscilla and Aquila," Rom. 16:3–5).*

Once an enemy, Paul became a true friend, partner, and advocate of other believers. Just as others had once cared for him and his needs, he wrote to the Corinthians of the needs and concerns of his brothers and sisters in Christ.

Who are some of your friends in the faith? Who among them needs support or advocacy right now? To whom can you appeal on their behalf? ◆

MONEY: COMPASSION AND INTEGRITY

CONSIDER THIS 16:1–4

Money is powerful. It can bring out the best or the worst in a person. In our drive to gain lots of it or use it for personal comfort and convenience, we can become very cold and manipulative (1 Tim. 6:10). But that ought not to be the way for God's followers.

In 1 Corinthians 16, we see that Paul was coordinating a fund-raising drive to help some needy believers. He could have focused on the plight of the recipients. They were Christians in Jerusalem, perhaps suffering from persecution or famine. But instead he concentrated on how the Corinthians should initiate a regular pattern of giving to meet the need (1 Cor. 16:2). Their participation would be an act of loving worship as they met together on the first day of the week.

Paul also pointed out that the transfer of the funds would be carried out by responsible people chosen by the Corinthians themselves (v. 3). That guaranteed accountability and integrity. Apparently Paul was quite realistic about the human tendency toward manipulation and greed.

How are you using your money to alleviate suffering and meet the needs of others?

God is as interested in what Christians do with the money they keep as He is in the money they give away. See "Christians and Money," 1 Tim. 6:6–19.

The Second Letter of Paul to the Corinthians

CONTENTS

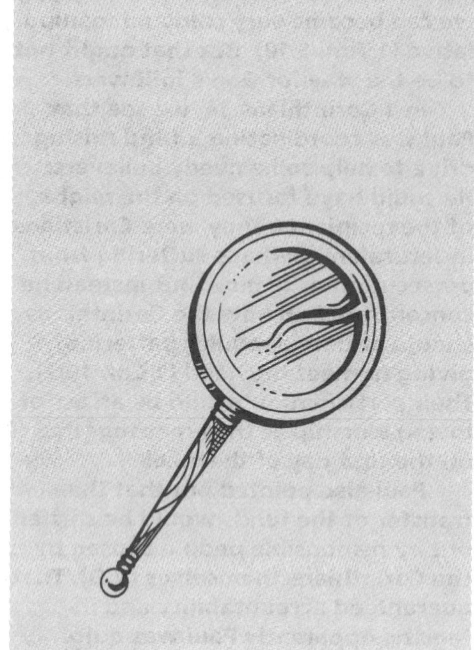

ARTICLES

Integrity in the Face of Competition (10:1)

When you face a competitive situation, are you tempted to do *whatever* it takes to win? Or can you keep the big picture, avoiding short-term gains in order to live with long-term, Christlike values?

When I Am Weak, Then I Am Strong (12:7–10)

It's hard to believe and it flies in the face of our culture's way of thinking, but weakness can make a person strong.

Spiritual Authority (13:10)

Anyone who exercises leadership among other believers will want to carefully study Paul's use of authority.

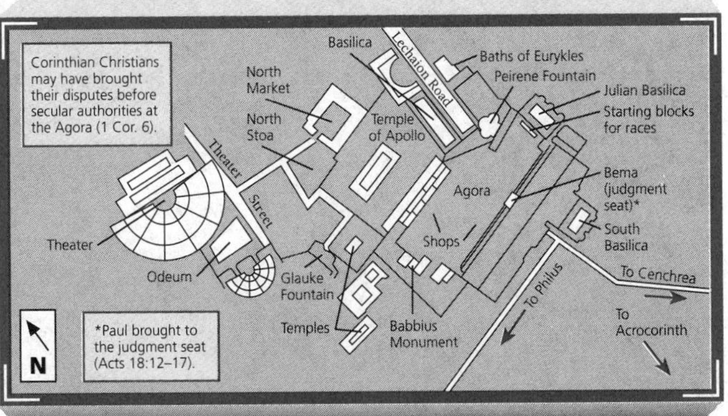

CORINTH

- A major city of Greece situated on the Isthmus of Corinth between the Ionian Sea and the Aegean Sea.
- In New Testament times, perhaps the most celebrated city of the Roman Empire, second only to Rome.
- Less than 100 years old at the time of Paul.
- A "planned" city rebuilt from ashes by the Roman emperors.
- A transportation hub for both land and sea travel. Though not a seaport, its location on an isthmus linked two seaports and two bays. To save time and avoid potential disasters of sailing around Greece, shippers transported passengers and their goods across the isthmus and reloaded them onto ships on the other side.
- Greece's leading commercial center for trade, agriculture, and industry.
- Host city to numerous athletic events, gladiatorial contests, theater productions, and the Isthmian Games, one of four major athletic festivals of the Greeks.
- A major center for pagan religions. More than twelve temples have been excavated at Corinth, including the magnificent temple of Apollo, with its 38 Doric columns 24 feet high. The temple of Aphrodite, goddess of love, employed at least 1,000 temple prostitutes. The city had a widespread reputation for gross immorality.
- A city of diverse peoples and cultures, including Greeks, Roman colonists (mostly retired army veterans and freedmen), and Jews, some of whom migrated there during persecution under the emperor Claudius (Acts 18:1).

The Corinthians were first-century Christians but they struggled with a number of twenty-first-century problems. See the Introduction to 1 and 2 Corinthians.

INSTEAD YOU SHOULD FORGIVE AND CONSOLE HIM. . . . —2 Corinthians 2:7

ASIA MINOR

YOU ARE THERE 1:8

- **A peninsula, also called Anatolia, situated in the extreme western part of the continent of Asia.**
- **Bounded on the north by the Black Sea, the Sea of Marmara, and the Dardanelles; the Aegean Sea on the west; and Syria and the Mediterranean Sea on the south.**
- **Roughly identical with the modern nation of Turkey.**
- **A high plateau crossed by mountains, especially the Taurus Mountains near the southern coast.**
- **In the New Testament, the term "Asia" is ambiguous, sometimes referring to the peninsula of Asia Minor as a whole (Acts 19:26–27), but more often referring to proconsular Asia, situated in the western part of the peninsula (Acts 2:9; 6:9).**

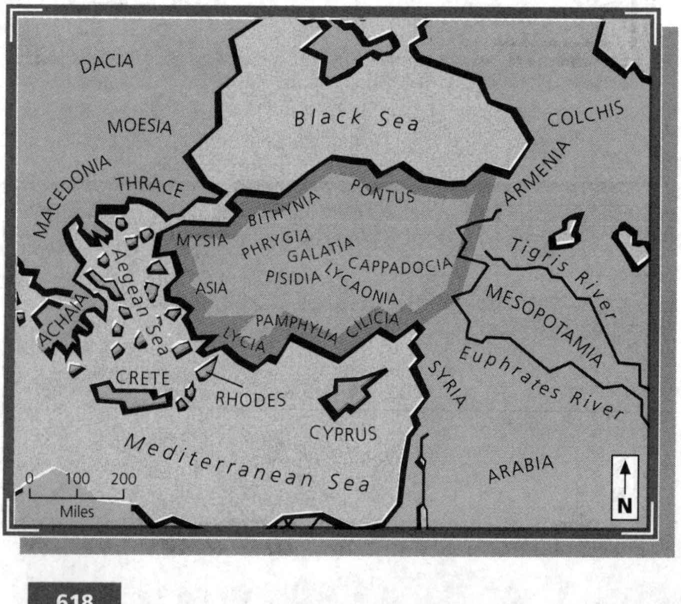

The explosive impact of the gospel at Ephesus reverberated throughout Asia Minor, such that "all who dwelt in Asia heard the word of the Lord Jesus" (Acts 19:10). See "The Ephesus Approach," Acts 19:8–41.

Comfort in the Midst of Trouble

1 Paul, an apostle of Christ Jesus by the will of God, and
Timothy our brother,
To the church of God that is in Corinth, including all the
saints throughout Achaia:
2 Grace to you and peace from God our Father and the
Lord Jesus Christ.

3 Blessed be the God and Father of our Lord Jesus
Christ, the Father of mercies and the God of all consolation, 4who consoles us in all our affliction, so that we may
be able to console those who are in any affliction with the
consolation with which we ourselves are consoled by God.
5For just as the sufferings of Christ are abundant for us, so
also our consolation is abundant through Christ. 6If we are
being afflicted, it is for your consolation and salvation; if we
are being consoled, it is for your consolation, which you
experience when you patiently endure the same sufferings
that we are also suffering. 7Our hope for you is unshaken;
for we know that as you share in our sufferings, so also you
share in our consolation.

1:8

8 We do not want you to be unaware,
brothers and sisters,[a] of the affliction we
experienced in Asia; for we were so utterly, unbearably
crushed that we despaired of life itself. 9Indeed, we felt that
we had received the sentence of death so that we would
rely not on ourselves but on God who raises the dead. 10He
who rescued us from so deadly a peril will continue to res-

[a]Gk *brothers*

cue us; on him we have set our hope that he will rescue us again, 11as you also join in helping us by your prayers, so that many will give thanks on our[b] behalf for the blessing granted us through the prayers of many.

Paul Defends His Integrity

12 Indeed, this is our boast, the testimony of our conscience: we have behaved in the world with frankness[c] and godly sincerity, not by earthly wisdom but by the grace of God—and all the more toward you. 13For we write you nothing other than what you can read and also understand; I hope you will understand until the end— 14as you have already understood us in part—that on the day of the Lord Jesus we are your boast even as you are our boast.

Paul Explains His Plans

15 Since I was sure of this, I wanted to come to you first, so that you might have a double favor;[d] 16I wanted to visit you on my way to Macedonia, and to come back to you from Macedonia and have you send me on to Judea. 17Was I vacillating when I wanted to do this? Do I make my plans according to ordinary human standards,[e] ready to say "Yes, yes" and "No, no" at the same time? 18As surely as God is faithful, our word to you has not been

1:19–20

"Yes and No." 19For the Son of God, Jesus Christ, whom we proclaimed among you, Silvanus and Timothy and I, was not "Yes and No"; but in him it is always "Yes." 20For in him every one of God's promises is a "Yes." For this reason it is through him that we say the "Amen," to the glory of God. 21But it is God who establishes us with you in Christ and has anointed us, 22by putting his seal on us and giving us his Spirit in our hearts as a first installment.

A Letter Instead of a Painful Visit

23 But I call on God as witness against me: it was to spare you that I did not come again to Corinth. 24I do not mean to imply that we lord it over your faith; rather, we are workers with you for your joy, because you stand firm in the faith.

[b]Other ancient authorities read *your* [c]Other ancient authorities read *holiness* [d]Other ancient authorities read *pleasure* [e]Gk *according to the flesh*

2 1So I made up my mind not to make you another painful visit. 2For if I cause you pain, who is there to make me glad but the one whom I have pained? 3And I wrote as I did, so that when I came, I might not suffer pain from those who should have made me rejoice; for I am confident about all of you, that my joy would be the joy of all of you. 4For I wrote you out of much distress and anguish of heart and with many tears, not to cause you pain, but to let you know the abundant love that I have for you.

Forgiving a Repentant Brother

2:5–11 see pg. 620

5 But if anyone has caused pain, he has caused it not to me, but to some extent—not to exaggerate it—to all of you. 6This punishment by the majority is enough for such a person; 7so now instead you should forgive and console him, so that he may not be overwhelmed by excessive sorrow. 8So I urge you to reaffirm your love for him. 9I wrote for this reason: to test you and to know whether you are obedient in everything. 10Anyone whom you forgive, I also forgive. What I have forgiven, if I have forgiven anything, has been for your sake in the presence of Christ. 11And we do this so that we may not be outwitted by Satan; for we are not ignorant of his designs.

Christ Leads in Triumph

12 When I came to Troas to proclaim the good news of Christ, a door was opened for me in the Lord; 13but my mind could not rest because I did not find my brother Titus there. So I said farewell to them and went on to Macedonia.

14 But thanks be to God, who in Christ always leads us in triumphal procession, and through us spreads in every place the fragrance that comes from knowing him. 15For we are the aroma of Christ to God among those who are being saved

(Bible text continued on page 621)

Affirmative Action

A CLOSER LOOK 1:19–20

God doesn't equivocate in what He promises. Christ was His ultimate statement in the affirmative (vv. 19–20). Do you believe that God can be depended on to honor His word? See "Promises," Rom. 4:16–25.

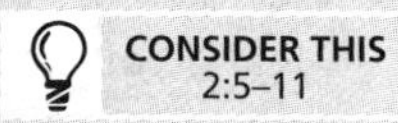

Accountability

The discipline of a Corinthian believer (v. 6) points to one of the important functions of the body of Christ—to hold its members accountable for how they conduct their lives. In the case mentioned here, the censure of the church caused the offender to repent and change his ways, restoring his spiritual life and bringing joy to the church.

Accountability is easy to talk about but difficult to practice. No one likes to be judged by others. In modern society it's especially easy to feel that one's personal life is no one else's business. But a study of Scripture reveals a number of important principles about accountability:

(1) *As believers, we are accountable not only for our actions, but also for our attitudes.* In the performance-oriented work world, evaluations tend to measure results alone—higher sales, greater cost control, more clients served. Everything is quantitative. But God is interested in our innermost heart. He looks at the quality of our character. As God told Samuel, "The Lord does not see as mortals see; they look on the outward appearance, but the Lord looks on the heart" (1 Sam. 16:7).

(2) *Accountability depends on trust.* To hold ourselves accountable to others is to trust their judgment and to believe that they are committed to the same truths and values that we are. It also helps if we can sense that they have our best interests at heart. That's why Paul pleaded with the Corinthians to forsake their divisions and "be united in the same mind and the same purpose" (1 Cor. 1:10). Without that unity, they would never submit to each other.

(3) *Accountability is directly related to the principle of submission.* Every person must struggle with the natural tendency toward rebellion against God. Accountability involves allowing others to enter into that struggle with us. But that means that sometimes we must defer to the judgment or counsel of another, especially when they challenge us with clear-cut Scriptural truth or the wisdom of personal experience. Paul told the Ephesians that part of living in the will of the Lord involves being "subject to one another out of reverence for Christ" (Eph. 5:21).

It's not surprising that participation in the body of Christ would involve accountability, because all of us experience accountability in many other areas of life. For example, the government holds us accountable for obeying the law and paying taxes. Likewise, government officials are accountable to the public for their decisions. Employees are accountable to the boss for their work. Likewise, corporate officers are accountable to stockholders for quarterly financial results. In short, accountability touches us at home, at work, at church, and even at play.

But our attitudes toward accountability in general ultimately reflect our attitude toward accountability to God. If we are rebellious toward the One who created us and loves us most, how able will we be to submit to others? ◆

and among those who are perishing; 16 to the one a fragrance from death to death, to the other a fragrance from
life to life. Who is sufficient for these things? 17 For we are
not peddlers of God's word like so many;[f] but in Christ we
speak as persons of sincerity, as persons sent from God and
standing in his presence.

Paul's Best Defense: The Corinthians Themselves

3 Are we beginning to commend ourselves again? Surely
we do not need, as some do, letters of recommenda-
tion to you or from you, do we? 2 You yourselves are our
letter, written on our[g] hearts, to be known and read by all;
3 and you show that you are a letter of Christ, prepared by
us, written not with ink but with the Spirit of the living
God, not on tablets of stone but on tablets of human hearts.
4 Such is the confidence that we have through Christ toward God. 5 Not that we are competent of ourselves to claim
anything as coming from us; our competence is from God,
3:6 6 who has made us competent to be ministers of a new covenant, not of letter but
of spirit; for the letter kills, but the Spirit gives life.

[f]Other ancient authorities read *like the others* [g]Other ancient authorities read *your*

Image-Conscious

CONSIDER THIS 3:7–18 **When other people look at you, what do they see? What image do you project to coworkers, customers, friends, and neighbors? As Paul traveled through the cities of the Roman Empire, he always gave thought to how he would be perceived, but his biggest concern was whether observers would see Jesus in him.**

To illustrate this principle, Paul recalled a phenomenon that occurred during the period in which Moses received the Law (vv. 7, 13). As Israel wandered through the wilderness, God revealed Himself to the people through what looked like a consuming fire (Ex. 24:17). But to Moses He spoke face to face (33:11). This encounter with the Living God had such an effect on Moses that his face would shine with an afterglow whenever he returned to the people. To dispel their fear, he put a veil over his face to hide the glory that resulted from his proximity to God.

Paul argues that we as believers have an even closer proximity to God than Moses did, for God Himself lives inside us (v. 8). Thus, when we meet others, they ought to see the glory of God shining out of us (vv. 9–11, 18). In other words, they ought to see Jesus.

Is that who people see when they look at us? Do they see Jesus' love, integrity, and power? Or do we "veil" the Light of the World (Matt. 5:14–16) under a mask of selfish ambition and worldly concerns?

The New Covenant

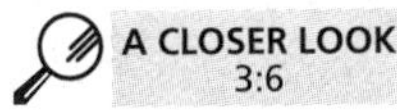

God promised a new covenant through the prophet Jeremiah in which He would write His Law on human hearts. This suggested a new level of obedience and a new knowledge of the Lord. *See "The New Covenant," 1 Cor. 11:25.*

The New Testament Ministry

3:7–18 see pg. 621

7 Now if the ministry of death, chiseled in letters on stone tablets,[h] came in
glory so that the people of Israel could not gaze at Moses'
face because of the glory of his face, a glory now set aside,
8how much more will the ministry of the Spirit come in
glory? 9For if there was glory in the ministry of condemnation, much more does the ministry of justification abound
in glory! 10Indeed, what once had glory has lost its glory
because of the greater glory; 11for if what was set aside
came through glory, much more has the permanent come in
glory!
12 Since, then, we have such a hope, we act with great
boldness, 13not like Moses, who put a veil over his face to
keep the people of Israel from gazing at the end of the glory
that[i] was being set aside. 14But their minds were hardened.
Indeed, to this very day, when they hear the reading of the

[h]*Gk on stones* [i]*Gk of what*

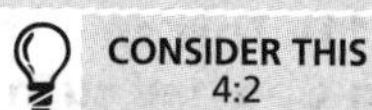
CONSIDER THIS 4:2

A Code of Ethics for Christian Witness

When believers present the message of Christ, we need to be like Paul, absolutely above board in our motives and manners (v. 2). We need to respect our hearers and refuse to do anything that would violate their integrity. Otherwise we become like a cult, peddling spiritual goods (2:17).

Here are some suggestions (from material distributed by Inter Varsity Christian Fellowship) to guide Christians in their witness:

Ethics for Witnessing
(1) We are Christians, called by God to honor Jesus Christ with our lives, abiding by biblically defined ethical standards in every area of life, public and private. This includes our efforts to persuade coworkers and others to believe the good news about Jesus Christ.
(2) Wherever we live and work, we seek to follow the mandate, motives, message, and model of Jesus, who still pursues and reclaims those lost in sin and rebelling against Him.
(3) We believe all people are created in God's image with the capacity to relate to their Creator and Redeemer. We disdain any effort to influence people which depersonalizes them or deprives them of their inherent value as persons.
(4) Since we respect the value of persons, we believe all are worthy of hearing about Jesus Christ. We also affirm the right of every person to survey other religious options. People are free to choose a different belief system than Christianity.

Continued

old covenant, that same veil is still there, since only in
Christ is it set aside. [15]Indeed, to this very day whenever
Moses is read, a veil lies over their minds; [16]but when one
turns to the Lord, the veil is removed. [17]Now the Lord is
the Spirit, and where the Spirit of the Lord is, there is freedom. [18]And all of us, with unveiled faces, seeing the glory
of the Lord as though reflected in a mirror, are being transformed into the same image from one degree of glory to another; for this comes from the Lord, the Spirit.

Christ Is the Message

4 Therefore, since it is by God's mercy that we are
engaged in this ministry, we do not lose heart. [2]We
4:2 have renounced the shameful things that
one hides; we refuse to practice cunning
or to falsify God's word; but by the open statement of the
truth we commend ourselves to the conscience of everyone

Continued

(5) We affirm the role and right of Christians to share the gospel of Christ in the marketplace of ideas. However, this does not justify any means to fulfill that end. We reject coercive techniques or manipulative appeals, especially those that play on emotions and discount or contradict reason or evidence. We will not bypass a person's critical faculties, prey upon psychological weaknesses, undermine a relationship with one's family or religious institution, or mask the true nature of Christian conversion. We will not intentionally mislead.

(6) We respect the individual integrity, intellectual honesty, and academic freedom of others, both believers and skeptics, and so we proclaim Christ without hidden agendas. We reveal our own identity, purpose, theological positions, and sources of information. We will use no false advertising and seek no material gain from presenting the gospel.

(7) We invite people of other religious persuasions to join us in true dialogue. We acknowledge our humanness—that we Christians are just as sinful, needy, and dependent on the grace of God as anyone else. We seek to listen sensitively in order to understand, and thus rid our witness of any stereotypes or fixed formulae which block honest communication.

(8) As our "brothers' keepers," we accept our responsibility to admonish any Christian brother or sister who presents the message of Christ in a way that violates these ethical guidelines.

Just Plain Jars

CONSIDER THIS 4:7

As humans, we are earthen vessels—plain old clay pots (v. 7). We may drape our human frame with fancy clothes, surround it with glittering possessions, transport it in rolling splendor, or rest it on a seat of power. But in the end, we are still just human beings. Certainly we have dignity and value in God's sight, but as believers we hold something of incomparably greater value—the treasure of Christ's grace and light!

A child picks a fragrant bouquet of wildflowers for her mother and places them in an old mayonnaise jar for a vase. What does the mother pay attention to? What delights her heart? The flowers or the mayonnaise jar?

Our value as vessels lies in the incomparable beauty and splendor of what we hold, not in our shape or color.

in the sight of God. 3And even if our gospel is veiled, it is
veiled to those who are perishing. 4In their case the god of
this world has blinded the minds of the unbelievers, to
keep them from seeing the light of the gospel of the glory of
Christ, who is the image of God. 5For we do not proclaim
ourselves; we proclaim Jesus Christ as Lord and ourselves
as your slaves for Jesus' sake. 6For it is the God who said,
"Let light shine out of darkness," who has shone in our
hearts to give the light of the knowledge of the glory of God
in the face of Jesus Christ.

Natural Messengers, Supernatural Power

4:7
see pg. 623

7 But we have this treasure in clay jars,
so that it may be made clear that this extraordinary power belongs to God and does not come from
us. 8We are afflicted in every way, but not crushed; perplexed, but not driven to despair; 9persecuted, but not forsaken; struck down, but not destroyed; 10always carrying in
the body the death of Jesus, so that the life of Jesus may
also be made visible in our bodies. 11For while we live, we
are always being given up to death for Jesus' sake, so that
the life of Jesus may be made visible in our mortal flesh.
12So death is at work in us, but life in you.
13 But just as we have the same spirit of faith that is in
accordance with scripture—"I believed, and so I spoke"—

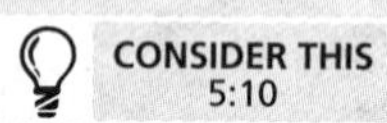

The Judgment Seat

Have you ever felt wronged and had someone say, "Don't worry, you'll have your day in court"? All of us will eventually have our "day in court" before God when we stand before the judgment seat (bēma) *of Christ (v. 10).*

Paul's Corinthian readers must have been quite familiar with the bēma. *As in most cities of Greece, a large, richly decorated rostrum called the* bēma *stood in the middle of the marketplace at Corinth. It was used by the officials for purposes of public proclamations, commendations, and condemnations.*

Paul himself had been brought to the Corinthian bēma *by Jews who opposed his message. The case was heard by Gallio, the Roman proconsul (governor) of the region, who dismissed the complaint (Acts 18:12–17).*

But the bēma *was used for more than just tribunals. It was at the* bēma *that winners of Corinth's prestigious athletic contests were announced (see "The Games," 1 Cor. 9:24–27). Thus, Paul's statement that believers will appear*

we also believe, and so we speak, [14]because we know that
the one who raised the Lord Jesus will raise us also with
Jesus, and will bring us with you into his presence. [15]Yes,
everything is for your sake, so that grace, as it extends to
more and more people, may increase thanksgiving, to the
glory of God.
16 So we do not lose heart. Even though our outer nature is wasting away, our inner nature is being renewed day
by day. [17]For this slight momentary affliction is preparing
us for an eternal weight of glory beyond all measure, [18]be-
cause we look not at what can be seen but at what cannot
be seen; for what can be seen is temporary, but what cannot
be seen is eternal.

We Are Headed for Eternity with God

5 For we know that if the earthly tent we live in is
destroyed, we have a building from God, a house not
made with hands, eternal in the heavens.
5:2–5 [2]For in this tent we groan, longing to be
clothed with our heavenly dwelling— [3]if indeed, when we
have taken it off[j] we will not be found naked. [4]For while we
are still in this tent, we groan under our burden, because
we wish not to be unclothed but to be further clothed, so
that what is mortal may be swallowed up by life. [5]He who

[j]Other ancient authorities read *put it on*

before the bēma of Christ is as much a cause for joy and hope as it is for fear.

One thing is certain: the judgment rendered at the bēma *will be fair, for Christ will be the Judge, and He Himself once stood before Pilate's* bēma *(Matt. 27:19; John 19:10). He knows what it feels like to have one's life weighed in the balance.*

However, the Lord will not be deciding the eternal fate of believers as He sits on His bēma*; that was settled at the moment of salvation (John 5:24). Instead, the* bēma *of Christ will be our chance as believers to look at our lives according to Christ's perfect assessment. It will be the ultimate opportunity to experience honest evaluation and true justice as we stand before Him.*

What will Christ say of you? Are you paying attention to your deeds "done in the body" in light of this moment of accountability? Are you striving to earn the Lord's praise in every area of life? ◆

What Did You Expect?

CONSIDER THIS 5:2–5 **In much of the world, evil abounds and Christians suffer. Yet many Western believers assume that health and wealth ought to be the norm. It's not just that they hope for these—they *expect* them, as if God somehow owes them prosperity in exchange for their faith or integrity or some other Christian virtue.**

What a far cry from Paul's day, when "groaning" was the normal experience of people, believers and unbelievers alike (vv. 2, 4). Certainly Paul exulted in the "new creation" that God brings about (5:17). But having celebrated that marvelous reality, Paul went on to say that life in Christ involves troubles and pain (6:4–10). Only from our glorified bodies will God remove all suffering (5:1).

What does this say to modern Christians in the West? We may enjoy health, wealth, and success, but isn't that the exception rather than the rule, at least judging by the experience of believers throughout history and around the world today? How much do we really know about *normal* Christianity?

Paul directly attacked the idea that God rewards godliness with material blessing. See "The Dangers of Prosperity Theology," 1 Tim. 6:3–6.

has prepared us for this very thing is God, who has given
us the Spirit as a guarantee.
6 So we are always confident; even though we know that
while we are at home in the body we are away from the
Lord— 7for we walk by faith, not by sight. 8Yes, we do have
confidence, and we would rather be away from the body
and at home with the Lord. 9So whether we are at home or
away, we make it our aim to please him.
10For all of us must appear before the
judgment seat of Christ, so that each may receive recom-
pense for what has been done in the body, whether good or
evil.

5:10
see pg. 624

A New Creation in Christ

11 Therefore, knowing the fear of the Lord, we try to
persuade others; but we ourselves are well known to God,
and I hope that we are also well known to your consciences. 12We are not commending ourselves to you again,
but giving you an opportunity to boast about us, so that
you may be able to answer those who boast in outward ap-

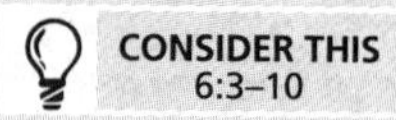

WELCOME TO STRESSFUL LIVING

For many people in the world today, tension, conflict, weariness, and suffering have become commonplace. Nevertheless, some offer the vain hope that life's troubles can be done away with, that we can somehow get to the point where things will always be great. They suggest that faith in Christ will deliver us into a state of serenity and ease and bring prosperity, health, and constant pleasure.

However, that was neither the experience nor the teaching of early Christians such as Paul, James, or Peter, and certainly not of their Lord Jesus. Paul described the life of a servant of God in terms of tribulation, distress, tumult, and sleeplessness (vv. 4–5). But he also linked these stress producers with rich treasures that money cannot buy: purity, kindness, sincere love, honor, good report, joy, and the possession of all things (vv. 6–10).

So as long as we live as God's people on this earth, we can expect a connection between trouble and hope. That connection is never pleasant, but our troubles can bring about lasting benefits:

> Jesus *told us that if we want to follow Him, we must deny ourselves and take up a cross. If we try to save our lives, we will only lose them. But if we lose our lives for His sake, we will find them (Matt. 16:24–25).*

pearance and not in the heart. 13For if we are beside ourselves, it is for God; if we are in our right mind, it is for
you. 14For the love of Christ urges us on, because we are
convinced that one has died for all; therefore all have died.
15And he died for all, so that those who live might live no
longer for themselves, but for him who died and was raised
for them.

16 From now on, therefore, we regard no one from a human point of view;[k] even though we once knew Christ from
a human point of view,[k] we know him no longer in that
way. 17So if anyone is in Christ, there is a
new creation: everything old has passed
away; see, everything has become new! 18All this is from
God, who reconciled us to himself through Christ, and has

5:17

[k]Gk *according to the flesh*

A New Creation

A CLOSER LOOK 5:17 *In what sense do we become "a new creation" in Christ (v. 17)? Paul painted several pictures of what that looks like. See "New Creatures with New Character," Gal. 5:22–23.*

The writer to the Hebrews encouraged us that our troubles are often a sign that we are legitimate children of God, who lovingly disciplines us to train us in righteousness (Heb. 12:8–11).

James encouraged us to rejoice in our various trials, because as they test our faith, they produce patience, which ultimately makes us mature in Christ (James 1:2–4).

Peter knew by personal experience the kind of pressure that can cause one's allegiance to Christ to waiver. He warned us that "fiery trials" are nothing strange, but that they actually allow us to experience something of Christ's sufferings so that we can ultimately experience something of His glory, too (1 Pet. 4:12–13).

We can count on feeling stress if we're going to obey Christ. But we can take hope! That stress is preparing us for riches we will enjoy for eternity. ◆

EVERYTHING OLD HAS PASSED AWAY; SEE, EVERYTHING HAS BECOME NEW!
—2 Corinthians 5:17

given us the ministry of reconciliation; [19]that is, in Christ God was reconciling the world to himself,[l] not counting their trespasses against them, and entrusting the message of reconciliation to us. [20]So we are ambassadors for Christ, since God is making his appeal through us; we entreat you on behalf of Christ, be reconciled to God. [21]For our sake he made him to be sin who knew no sin, so that in him we might become the righteousness of God.

Openness and Authenticity

6 As we work together with him,[m] we urge you also not to accept the grace of God in vain. [2]For he says,

"At an acceptable time I have listened to you,
and on a day of salvation I have helped you."

See, now is the acceptable time; see, now is the day of salvation! [3]We are putting no obstacle in anyone's way, so that no fault may be found with our ministry, [4]but as servants of God we have commended ourselves in every way: through great endurance, in afflictions, hardships, calamities, [5]beatings, imprisonments, riots, labors, sleepless nights, hunger; [6]by purity, knowledge, patience, kindness, holiness of spirit, genuine love, [7]truthful speech, and the power of God; with the weapons of righteousness for the right hand and for the left; [8]in honor and dishonor, in ill repute and good repute. We are treated as impostors, and yet are true; [9]as unknown, and yet are well known; as dying, and see—we are alive; as punished, and yet not killed; [10]as sorrowful, yet always rejoicing; as poor, yet making many rich; as having nothing, and yet possessing everything.

6:3–10
see pg. 626

11 We have spoken frankly to you Corinthians; our heart is wide open to you. [12]There is no restriction in our affections, but only in yours. [13]In return—I speak as to children—open wide your hearts also.

Avoid Immoral Partnerships

14 Do not be mismatched with unbelievers. For what partnership is there between righteousness and lawlessness? Or what fellowship is there between light and darkness? [15]What agreement does Christ have with Beliar? Or what does a believer share with an unbeliever? [16]What agreement has the temple of God with idols? For we[n] are the temple of the living God; as God said,

"I will live in them and walk among them,
and I will be their God,
and they shall be my people.
17 Therefore come out from them,
and be separate from them, says the Lord,
and touch nothing unclean;
then I will welcome you,
18 and I will be your father,
and you shall be my sons and daughters,
says the Lord Almighty."

7 Since we have these promises, beloved, let us cleanse ourselves from every defilement of body and of spirit, making holiness perfect in the fear of God.

Be Open toward Each Other

2 Make room in your hearts[o] for us; we have wronged no one, we have corrupted no one, we have taken advantage of no one. [3]I do not say this to condemn you, for I said before that you are in our hearts, to die together and to live together. [4]I often boast about you; I have great pride in you; I am filled with consolation; I am overjoyed in all our affliction.

5 For even when we came into Macedonia, our bodies had no rest, but we were afflicted in every way—disputes without and fears within. [6]But God, who consoles the downcast, consoled us by the arrival of Titus, [7]and not only by his coming, but also by the consolation with which he was consoled about you, as he told us of your longing, your mourning, your zeal for me, so that I rejoiced still more. [8]For even if I made you sorry with my letter, I do not regret it (though I did regret it, for I see that I grieved you with that letter, though only briefly). [9]Now I rejoice, not because you were grieved, but because your grief led to repentance; for you felt a godly grief, so that you were not harmed in any way by us. [10]For godly grief produces a repentance that leads to salvation and brings no regret, but worldly grief produces death. [11]For see what earnestness this godly grief has produced in you, what eagerness to clear yourselves, what indignation, what alarm, what longing, what zeal, what punishment!

7:6

[l]Or *God was in Christ reconciling the world to himself* [m]Gk *As we work together*

[n]Other ancient authorities read *you* [o]Gk lacks *in your hearts*

At every point you have proved yourselves guiltless in the matter. 12So although I wrote to you, it was not on account of the one who did the wrong, nor on account of the one who was wronged, but in order that your zeal for us might be made known to you before God. 13In this we find comfort.

In addition to our own consolation, we rejoiced still more at the joy of Titus, because his mind has been set at rest by all of you. 14For if I have been somewhat boastful about you to him, I was not disgraced; but just as everything we said to you was true, so our boasting to Titus has proved true as well. 15And his heart goes out all the more to you, as he remembers the obedience of all of you, and how you welcomed him with fear and trembling. 16I rejoice, because I have complete confidence in you.

The Example of the Macedonians

8 We want you to know, brothers and sisters,[p] about the grace of God that has been granted to the churches of Macedonia; 2for during a severe ordeal of affliction, their abundant joy and their extreme poverty have overflowed in a wealth of generosity on their part. 3For, as I can testify, they voluntarily gave according to their means, and even

[p] Gk *brothers*

Personality Profile: Titus

FOR YOUR INFO 7:6

Not to be confused with: The Roman general Titus who destroyed Jerusalem in A.D. 70 (see "Jerusalem Surrounded," Luke 21:20).

Background: Raised as a Greek-speaking Gentile.

Known for: Diplomacy, public relations, project management, and fund-raising. Paul praised him as dependable, reliable, and diligent.

Best known today for: His work with Paul as a traveling companion and coworker in establishing churches throughout the Roman world.

The Man of the Hour

Titus was a man for tough tasks. According to Paul, he was dependable (2 Cor. 8:17), reliable (7:6), and diligent (8:17). He also had a great capacity for human affection (7:13–15). Tradition holds that he was the first bishop of Crete. Possessing both strength and tact, Titus calmed a desperate situation on more than one occasion. He serves as a good model for believers living under trying circumstances.

Titus' ethnic background proved to be important and useful to the early church. As an uncircumcised Gentile, he accompanied Paul and Barnabas to Jerusalem, where many of the Jewish Christians were debating whether non-Jews could be saved. Paul introduced him there as a living example of a great theological truth—that Gentiles need not be circumcised (that is, become Jews) in order to receive the grace of God (Gal. 2:1–3).

Does it really matter what you believe, as long as you do the right thing? Yes it does, thought Paul. That's why he wrote to Titus, his valued associate on Crete, urging him to teach "sound doctrine." He knew that correct living is a product of correct belief. To learn more about the situation, see the Introduction to Titus.

beyond their means, 4begging us earnestly for the privilege[q]
of sharing in this ministry to the saints— 5and this, not
merely as we expected; they gave themselves first to the
Lord and, by the will of God, to us, 6so that we might urge
Titus that, as he had already made a beginning, so he
should also complete this generous undertaking[r] among
you. 7Now as you excel in everything—in faith, in speech,
in knowledge, in utmost eagerness, and in our love for
you[s]—so we want you to excel also in this generous
undertaking.[r]

The Example of Christ

8:8–9

8 I do not say this as a command, but
I am testing the genuineness of your love
against the earnestness of others. 9For you know the generous act[t] of our Lord Jesus Christ, that though he was rich,

[q]Gk *grace* [r]Gk *this grace* [s]Other ancient authorities read *your love for us* [t]Gk *the grace*

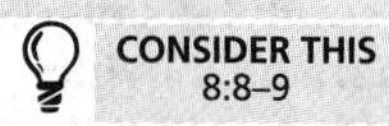

CONSIDER THIS
8:8–9

Christ Became Poor

Almost anyone can "love" people in the abstract. But when it comes time to express that love—by lending a helping hand or writing a check—one can quickly determine the sincerity of a person's love for others. That was Paul's point in vv. 8–9. To illustrate it, he used the ultimate model of tangible love—Jesus Christ.

Christ became poor in order to make us rich. Consider what He gave up when He left heaven and took on a human body:

- *He left His Father, whose immediate presence He would not enjoy again for more than 30 years. How long would you be willing to be away from your closest companion and friend in order to help a group of people—especially if you knew that most of them would reject and despise you, and might even kill you?*
- *We can imagine that He left a joyful crowd that included Abraham, Isaac, Jacob, the angelic hosts, and all the redeemed saints who were worshiping Him, glorifying Him, and having fellowship with Him prior to His incarnation. He left those who loved Him to come and be misunderstood, rejected, scorned, hated, and scourged by most of those He came to help. Would you leave a position of honor and adoration to go help people who would by and large reject you?*
- *He left a heavenly home that far exceeded in splendor, majesty, and comfort the physical environment of His*

yet for your sakes he became poor, so that by his poverty
you might become rich. 10And in this matter I am giving
my advice: it is appropriate for you who began last year not
only to do something but even to desire to do something—
11now finish doing it, so that your eagerness may be
matched by completing it according to your means. 12For if
the eagerness is there, the gift is acceptable according to
what one has—not according to what one does not have.
8:13–15 13I do not mean that there should be relief for others and pressure on you, but it
is a question of a fair balance between 14your present abundance and their need, so that their abundance may be for
your need, in order that there may be a fair balance. 15As it
is written,

> "The one who had much did not have too much,
> and the one who had little did not have too little."

earthly life. Would you give up the best accommodations this earth has to offer in order to help needy people in a bad neighborhood?

- *He left His pre-incarnate existence in the form of God, without limitations, to take on a physical body subject to fatigue, aches, and pains. Would you accept hunger, thirst, fatigue, pain, and limited physical abilities to help people who didn't even care whether you came or not?*

The statement that Christ became poor puts into perspective Jesus' command to the rich young ruler to sell what he had and give the proceeds to the poor (Mark 10:21), and His instruction to the disciples to sell what they had and give alms, providing themselves treasure in heaven (Luke 12:33). What Jesus asked them to do, He had already done—to such a degree, in fact, that their obedience could never equal His selflessness. ◆

Jesus worked as a carpenter and lived responsibly. But the fact remains, He was born poor and lived poor. In fact, He was homeless. See Matt. 8:20.

Christ may have been poor, but many of His followers today are not. How should wealthy believers handle their money? See "Christians and Money," 1 Tim. 6:6–19.

SOLIDARITY

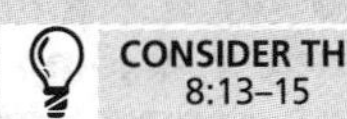

Paul challenged the Corinthian Christians to participate in a fund-raising project to benefit believers at Jerusalem. But he seemed to be concerned with more than money. He wanted Gentile churches like Corinth to start practicing solidarity with their Jewish brothers and sisters (vv. 13–15, 24). It's almost as if the new churches owed something, in a sense, to the original church in Jerusalem.

Reaping the Benefits

CONSIDER THIS 9:6–8 **Paul wanted the Corinthians to give generously toward a fund-raising project to help needy Christians. He linked generosity with spiritual benefits: the more one gives, the more one benefits (vv. 6–11).**

This principle goes beyond financial giving. At work, for example, you may donate toward the local United Way. But when a coworker asks for some of your time to talk about a problem, what is your response? Do you give your attention generously or grudgingly? When your boss gives you a special assignment, do you give the project just enough attention to get it over with, or do you jump in wholeheartedly with energy and creativity?

What about your time and emotional energy after hours? When your spouse or children need you, do you make yourself available generously or grudgingly? Do you give a fair contribution of yourself to assignments that you've volunteered for, or just a token effort?

We are constant recipients of God's generous grace. He promises that if we will give of ourselves, He'll enable us to have an abundance of resources for the work to which He has called us (v. 8).

Giving generously in order to gain spiritual benefits does not mean that God rewards godliness with material blessings. See "The Dangers of Prosperity Theology," 1 Tim. 6:3–6.

A Plan to Provide Material Help

16 But thanks be to God who put in the heart of Titus
the same eagerness for you that I myself have. 17For he not
only accepted our appeal, but since he is more eager than
ever, he is going to you of his own accord. 18With him we
are sending the brother who is famous among all the
churches for his proclaiming the good news;[u] 19and not
only that, but he has also been appointed by the churches
to travel with us while we are administering this generous
undertaking[v] for the glory of the Lord himself[w] and to show
our goodwill. 20We intend that no one should blame us
about this generous gift that we are administering, 21for we
intend to do what is right not only in the Lord's sight but
also in the sight of others. 22And with them we are sending
our brother whom we have often tested and found eager in
many matters, but who is now more eager than ever because of his great confidence in you. 23As for Titus, he is my
partner and co-worker in your service; as for our brothers,
they are messengers[x] of the churches, the glory of Christ.
24Therefore openly before the churches, show them the
proof of your love and of our reason for boasting about
you.

Implementing the Plan

9 Now it is not necessary for me to write you about the
ministry to the saints, 2for I know your eagerness,
which is the subject of my boasting about you to the people
of Macedonia, saying that Achaia has been ready since last
year; and your zeal has stirred up most of them. 3But I am
sending the brothers in order that our boasting about you
may not prove to have been empty in this case, so that you
may be ready, as I said you would be; 4otherwise, if some
Macedonians come with me and find that you are not
ready, we would be humiliated—to say nothing of you—in
this undertaking.[y] 5So I thought it necessary to urge the
brothers to go on ahead to you, and arrange in advance for
this bountiful gift that you have promised, so that it may be
ready as a voluntary gift and not as an extortion.

The Blessings of Generosity

9:6–8

6 The point is this: the one who sows
sparingly will also reap sparingly, and the
one who sows bountifully will also reap bountifully. 7Each
of you must give as you have made up your mind, not re-
luctantly or under compulsion, for God loves a cheerful
giver. 8And God is able to provide you with every blessing

[u]Or *the gospel* [v]Gk *this grace* [w]Other ancient authorities lack *himself* [x]Gk *apostles*
[y]Other ancient authorities add *of boasting*

in abundance, so that by always having enough of everything, you may share abundantly in every good work. 9As it is written,

9:9–10

"He scatters abroad, he gives to the poor;
his righteousness[z] endures forever."

10He who supplies seed to the sower and bread for food will supply and multiply your seed for sowing and increase the harvest of your righteousness.[z] 11You will be enriched in every way for your great generosity, which will produce thanksgiving to God through us; 12for the rendering of this ministry not only supplies the needs of the saints but also overflows with many thanksgivings to God. 13Through the testing of this ministry you glorify God by your obedience to the confession of the gospel of Christ and by the generosity of your sharing with them and with all others, 14while they long for you and pray for you because of the surpassing grace of God that he has given you. 15Thanks be to God for his indescribable gift!

An Appeal for Obedience

10:1 see pg. 634

10 I myself, Paul, appeal to you by the meekness and gentleness of Christ—I who am humble when face to face with you, but bold toward you when I am away!— 2I ask that when I am present I need not show boldness by daring to oppose those who think we are acting according to human standards.[a] 3Indeed, we live as human beings,[b] but we do not wage war according to human standards;[a] 4for the weapons of our warfare are not merely human,[c] but they have divine power to destroy strongholds. We destroy arguments 5and every proud obstacle raised up against the knowledge of God, and we take every thought captive to obey Christ. 6We are ready to punish every disobedience when your obedience is complete.

Paul Defends His Personal Integrity

7 Look at what is before your eyes. If you are confident that you belong to Christ, remind yourself of this, that just as you belong to Christ, so also do we. 8Now, even if I boast a little too much of our authority, which the Lord gave for building you up and not for tearing you down, I will not be ashamed of it. 9I do not want to seem as though I am trying to frighten you with my letters. 10For they say, "His letters are weighty and strong, but his bodily presence is weak, and his speech contemptible." 11Let such people understand that what we say by letter when absent, we will also do when present.

[z]*Or benevolence* [a]*Gk according to the flesh* [b]*Gk in the flesh* [c]*Gk fleshly*

Who Are the Poor?

CONSIDER THIS 9:9–10 **By comparison to the many modern Christians who live in affluence, the Corinthian believers would appear poor. Yet Paul described the Christians of Macedonia as living in "extreme poverty" (8:2), so they were much poorer even than the Corinthians. What does Scripture mean, then, when it says that God "gives to *the poor*" (9:9, italics added)? And what does that mean for believers today who are relatively affluent?**

The word for *poor* (v. 9) described someone who toiled for a living, what we would call a day laborer. Such persons were distinct from the truly destitute. The former may have had a difficult life, but at least they were in no danger of losing it. By contrast, the truly poor were in immediate danger of perishing if they didn't receive charitable aid.

Paul described God as dispersing to the *poor,* the day laborers, not food for survival but seed that they could sow to raise a crop (vv. 9–10). He indicated that God would aid the Corinthians so that they, in turn, could aid the completely destitute believers in Jerusalem.

So what does that mean for us as Christians today if we work at relatively stable, well-paid jobs, own our own homes, and manage to salt away at least some money for retirement? Paul would doubtless identify us as rich. We may work hard, but we have disposable income that most first-century Christians could have only imagined.

12 We do not dare to classify or compare ourselves with
some of those who commend themselves. But when they
measure themselves by one another, and compare themselves with one another, they do not show good sense.
13We, however, will not boast beyond limits, but will keep
within the field that God has assigned to us, to reach out
even as far as you. 14For we were not overstepping our limits when we reached you; we were the first to come all the
way to you with the good news[d] of Christ. 15We do not
boast beyond limits, that is, in the labors of others; but our
hope is that, as your faith increases, our sphere of action
among you may be greatly enlarged, 16so that we may proclaim the good news[d] in lands beyond you, without boasting of work already done in someone else's sphere of action.
17"Let the one who boasts, boast in the Lord." 18For it is not
those who commend themselves that are approved, but
those whom the Lord commends.

[d]*Or the gospel*

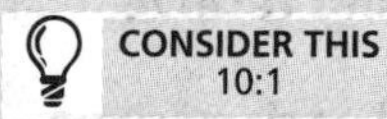

INTEGRITY IN THE FACE OF COMPETITION

When you face a competitive situation, are you tempted to do whatever it takes to win? Paul faced severe competition at Corinth. In chapters 10–12, he described real danger to his work in Corinth:

- *Opposing leaders and teachers were making headway. Paul's people were tempted to cross over to them (10:15; 11:3–4, 12–15).*
- *Paul felt the pain of this loss very deeply (10:2–3; 11:2–3, 29).*
- *He felt threatened (10:8–11, 13–15; 11:5–6, 16–21).*
- *He loved the Corinthians and feared losing them so much that he became angry (11:11–15).*
- *He defended himself as a faithful servant who had suffered for the Corinthians and the gospel (10:13–18; 11:20–30; 12:11).*

As Paul wrestled with mixed feelings and sketchy information, he dealt in known principles of godliness and clear communication:

- *Paul was passionate about the problem. He wrote to the Corinthians extensively (see the Introduction to 1 and 2 Corinthians).*

Paul Defends His Apostleship

11 I wish you would bear with me in a little foolishness. Do bear with me! [2]I feel a divine jealousy for
you, for I promised you in marriage to one husband, to
present you as a chaste virgin to Christ. [3]But I am afraid
that as the serpent deceived Eve by its cunning, your
thoughts will be led astray from a sincere and pure[e] devotion to Christ. [4]For if someone comes and proclaims another Jesus than the one we proclaimed, or if you receive a
different spirit from the one you received, or a different
gospel from the one you accepted, you submit to it readily
enough. [5]I think that I am not in the
least inferior to these super-apostles. [6]I
may be untrained in speech, but not in knowledge; certainly in every way and in all things we have made this evident to you.
7 Did I commit a sin by humbling myself so that you

✓ 11:5

[e]Other ancient authorities lack *and pure*

◆ ◆ ◆ ◆ ◆ ◆ ◆ ◆ ◆ ◆ ◆ ◆ ◆ ◆ ◆ ◆

- *He tried to visit Corinth to discuss matters openly (10:2, 11; 12:14; 13:1).*
- *He encouraged the Corinthians to test his prior works among them if they questioned his loyalty and integrity (10:13, 15; 11:22–27). It's interesting that he felt awkward in this self-defense (11:21, 23; 12:7–10).*
- *He gave a clear statement of the finances involved in his previous work in Corinth (11:7–9; 1 Cor. 16:1–4, 16).*
- *He appealed for negotiations in a way that would honor Christ and not duplicate the world's methods (2 Cor. 10:3–4; 13:8–10).*
- *He urged in-depth analysis of the situation (10:7; 13:1, 5, 8).*

Paul faced a real temptation to resort to any means not to lose his converts in Corinth. As readers we can feel the tension in these letters. But Paul waged spiritual warfare within himself first so that he could rise above vicious, underhanded solutions. He kept the big picture, avoiding short term gains in order to live with long-term, Christlike values. ◆

WHO WERE THE APOSTLES?

✓ FOR YOUR INFO 11:5 **Paul was counted among a group of early church leaders known as "apostles" (v. 5). Each apostle was chosen by Jesus and given authority to carry out certain tasks, especially the task of making disciples of "all nations" (Matt. 28:19).**

The word *apostle* means "messenger." The term was first used of the twelve disciples whom Jesus sent out, two by two, into Galilee to expand His ministry of preaching and healing (Mark 3:14; 6:30). These same disciples, with the exception of Judas Iscariot, were recommissioned as apostles after Jesus' resurrection to be His witnesses throughout the world (Acts 1:8). After Jesus' ascension, the group brought their number to twelve again by choosing Matthias (1:23–26).

However, the term apostle came to apply to others besides the Twelve. It included people like Paul who had seen the risen Christ and were specially commissioned by Him (1 Cor. 15:10). James, the Lord's brother, was counted as an apostle (Gal. 1:19; see profile at the Introduction to James). And when Paul wrote that Jesus was seen not only by James but also by "all the apostles" (1 Cor. 15:7), he seemed to be describing a wider group than the Twelve to whom Jesus appeared earlier (1 Cor. 15:5).

The authority committed to the apostles by Christ was unique and foundational (1 Cor. 12:28; Eph. 4:11). The apostles could install elders or other leaders and teachers in the churches, and they could authorize believers to assume special responsibilities.

might be exalted, because I proclaimed God's good
news[f] to you free of charge? 8I robbed other
churches by accepting support from them in order
to serve you. 9And when I was with you and was
in need, I did not burden anyone, for my needs
were supplied by the friends[g] who came from
Macedonia. So I refrained and will continue to refrain from burdening you in any way. 10As the
truth of Christ is in me, this boast of mine will not
be silenced in the regions of Achaia. 11And why?
Because I do not love you? God knows I do!

12 And what I do I will also continue to do, in
order to deny an opportunity to those who want
an opportunity to be recognized as our equals in
what they boast about. 13For such boasters are false
apostles, deceitful workers, disguising themselves
as apostles of Christ. 14And no wonder! Even Satan
disguises himself as an angel of light. 15So it is not
strange if his ministers also disguise themselves as
ministers of righteousness. Their end will match
their deeds.

Paul's Impeccable Credentials

16 I repeat, let no one think that I am a fool;
but if you do, then accept me as a fool, so that I
too may boast a little. 17What I am saying in regard
to this boastful confidence, I am saying not with
the Lord's authority, but as a fool; 18since many
boast according to human standards,[h] I will also
boast. 19For you gladly put up with fools, being
wise yourselves! 20For you put up with it when
someone makes slaves of you, or preys upon you,
or takes advantage of you, or puts on airs, or gives
you a slap in the face. 21To my shame, I must say,
we were too weak for that!

But whatever anyone dares to boast of—I am
speaking as a fool—I also dare to boast of that.
22Are they Hebrews? So am I. Are they Israelites?
So am I. Are they descendants of Abraham? So am
I. 23Are they ministers of Christ? I am talking like a
madman—I am a better one: with far greater
labors, far more imprisonments, with countless
floggings, and often near death. 24Five times I have
received from the Jews the forty lashes minus one.
25Three times I was beaten with rods. Once I received a stoning. Three times I was shipwrecked;
for a night and a day I was adrift at sea; 26on frequent journeys, in danger from rivers, danger from
bandits, danger from my own people, danger from
Gentiles, danger in the city, danger in the wilderness, danger at sea, danger from false brothers and
sisters;[g] 27in toil and hardship, through many a
sleepless night, hungry and thirsty, often without
food, cold and naked. 28And, besides other things,
I am under daily pressure because of my anxiety
for all the churches. 29Who is weak, and I am not
weak? Who is made to stumble, and I am not indignant?

30 If I must boast, I will boast of the things that
show my weakness. 31The God and Father of the
Lord Jesus (blessed be he forever!) knows that I do
not lie. 32In Damascus, the governor[i] under King
Aretas guarded the city of Damascus in order to[j]
seize me, 33but I was let down in a basket through
a window in the wall,[k] and escaped from his
hands.

A Revelation from the Lord

12 It is necessary to boast; nothing is to be
gained by it, but I will go on to visions and
revelations of the Lord. 2I know a person in Christ
who fourteen years ago was caught up to the third
heaven—whether in the body or out of the body I
do not know; God knows. 3And I know that such a
person—whether in the body or out of the body I
do not know; God knows— 4was caught up into
Paradise and heard things that are not to be told,
that no mortal is permitted to repeat. 5On behalf of
such a one I will boast, but on my own behalf I
will not boast, except of my weaknesses. 6But if I
wish to boast, I will not be a fool, for I will be
speaking the truth. But I refrain from it, so that no
one may think better of me than what is seen in
12:7–10 me or heard from me, 7even considering the exceptional charac-
ter of the revelations. Therefore, to keep[l] me from
being too elated, a thorn was given me in the flesh,
a messenger of Satan to torment me, to keep me
from being too elated.[m] 8Three times I appealed to
the Lord about this, that it would leave me, 9but
he said to me, "My grace is sufficient for you, for
power[n] is made perfect in weakness." So, I will
boast all the more gladly of my weaknesses, so that

[f] Gk *the gospel of God* [g] Gk *brothers* [h] Gk *according to the flesh*

[i] Gk *ethnarch* [j] Other ancient authorities read *and wanted to* [k] Gk *through the wall* [l] Other ancient authorities read *To keep* [m] Other ancient authorities lack *to keep me from being too elated* [n] Other ancient authorities read *my power*

the power of Christ may dwell in me. 10 Therefore I am content with weaknesses, insults, hardships, persecutions, and
calamities for the sake of Christ; for whenever I am weak,
then I am strong.

11 I have been a fool! You forced me to it. Indeed you
should have been the ones commending me, for I am not at
all inferior to these super-apostles, even though I am nothing. 12 The signs of a true apostle were performed among
you with utmost patience, signs and wonders and mighty
works. 13 How have you been worse off than the other
churches, except that I myself did not burden you? Forgive
me this wrong!

Paul Says He Will Visit

14 Here I am, ready to come to you this third time. And
I will not be a burden, because I do not want what is yours
but you; for children ought not to lay up for their parents,
but parents for their children. 15 I will most gladly spend
and be spent for you. If I love you more, am I to be loved
less? 16 Let it be assumed that I did not burden you. Nevertheless (you say) since I was crafty, I took you in by deceit.
17 Did I take advantage of you through any of those whom I
sent to you? 18 I urged Titus to go, and sent the brother with
him. Titus did not take advantage of you, did he? Did we
not conduct ourselves with the same spirit? Did we not
take the same steps?

19 Have you been thinking all along that we have been
defending ourselves before you? We are speaking in Christ
before God. Everything we do, beloved, is for the sake of
building you up. 20 For I fear that when I come, I may find
you not as I wish, and that you may find me not as you
wish; I fear that there may perhaps be quarreling, jealousy,
anger, selfishness, slander, gossip, conceit, and disorder. 21 I
fear that when I come again, my God may humble me before you, and that I may have to mourn over many who
previously sinned and have not repented of the impurity,
sexual immorality, and licentiousness that they have practiced.

Paul Challenges the Corinthians to Prepare

13 This is the third time I am coming to you. "Any
charge must be sustained by the evidence of two or
three witnesses." 2 I warned those who sinned previously
and all the others, and I warn them now while absent, as I
did when present on my second visit, that if I come again, I

When I Am Weak, Then I Am Strong

CONSIDER THIS 12:7–10

Our world prizes strength—the physical strength of athletes, the financial strength of companies, the political strength of office-holders, and the military strength of armies. But Paul put a new twist on the notion of strength: weakness can make a person strong (vv. 7–10).

Most of us would have no problem with God using our natural areas of strength, such as speaking, organizing, managing, or selling. But suppose He chose instead to use us in areas where we are weak? Moses claimed to be a poor speaker (Ex. 4:10), yet God used him as His spokesman on Israel's behalf. Peter tended to be impulsive and even hotheaded, yet God used him as one of the chief architects of the early church.

Weakness has a way of making us rely on God far more than our strengths do. What weakness in your life might God desire to use for His purposes?

SPIRITUAL AUTHORITY

CONSIDER THIS 13:10 **If you exercise leadership among other believers, you'll want to carefully study Paul's comment about his authority (v. 10). Like many of us, Paul liked to be in charge, and he felt frustrated when people failed to follow his lead, as the Corinthians had. As an apostle, he had spiritual authority over them, which at times led him to deal severely with them (1 Cor. 4:21; 5:5; compare Titus 1:13).**

But it's important to notice how Paul exercised his authority, especially as he grew older in the faith. He didn't lord it over others or try to use his authority to personal advantage. Nor did he abuse his power by using it to work out his own anger. Instead, he recognized that spiritual authority is given "for edification and not for destruction" (2 Cor. 10:8; 13:10), for building others up, not for tearing them down.

Is that how you use your position and authority? Do you exercise leadership in order to accomplish the best interests of those who follow you? As they carry out your directives, are they built up in Christ, or torn down?

Paul's method of leadership reflected a unique style of authority that Jesus encouraged. See "Servant-Leaders," Matt. 20:25–28.

will not be lenient— 3since you desire proof that Christ is
speaking in me. He is not weak in dealing with you, but is
powerful in you. 4For he was crucified in weakness, but
lives by the power of God. For we are weak in him,[o] but in
dealing with you we will live with him by the power of
God.

5 Examine yourselves to see whether you are living in
the faith. Test yourselves. Do you not realize that Jesus
Christ is in you?—unless, indeed, you fail to meet the test!
6I hope you will find out that we have not failed. 7But we
pray to God that you may not do anything wrong—not that
we may appear to have met the test, but that you may do
what is right, though we may seem to have failed. 8For we
cannot do anything against the truth, but only for the truth.
9For we rejoice when we are weak and you are strong. This
13:10 is what we pray for, that you may become perfect. 10So I write these things
while I am away from you, so that when I come, I may not
have to be severe in using the authority that the Lord has
given me for building up and not for tearing down.

Final Words

11 Finally, brothers and sisters,[p] farewell.[q] Put things in
order, listen to my appeal,[r] agree with one another, live in
peace; and the God of love and peace will be with you.
12Greet one another with a holy kiss. All the saints greet
you.

13 The grace of the Lord Jesus Christ, the love of God,
and the communion of[s] the Holy Spirit be with all of you.

[o]Other ancient authorities read *with him* [p]Gk *brothers* [q]Or *rejoice* [r]Or *encourage one another* [s]Or *and the sharing in*

The Letter of Paul to the

Galatians

What happens when the gospel spreads from one culture to another? A collision often takes place, a clash of values and perceptions, too often with damage to the cause of Christ and the spiritual well-being of believers. Paul's letter to the Galatians shows that cultural conflicts began right from the start of the Christian movement.

Why should that be? Jesus told His followers to make disciples of "all nations" (Matt. 28:19). The term "nations" (Greek, *ethnē*) literally means "peoples" or "people-groups," what we would call ethnic groups. In other words, Jesus specifically mandated that His followers cross ethnic, national, tribal, linguistic, and cultural lines to spread His message of salvation throughout the world.

In doing so, believers need to consider: What cultural "baggage" do we attach to our faith? Do we make certain assumptions about what Christianity should look like that are based less on biblical grounds than on cultural values and expectations? Is it possible that someone from a different background might serve the same Lord, but do so in a way that feels uncomfortable to us because of cultural differences?

Galatians offers insight into these questions. It is a brief letter, but it offers a powerful message for today, given our increasingly pluralistic society. As we are faced with diversity on every hand, the book reminds us to be clear about the essentials of the gospel, and not to confuse them with externals that really don't matter.

Be clear about the essentials of the gospel.

CONTENTS

ARTICLES

New Creatures with New Character (5:22–23)

If you are in Christ, you are a new creature. What does that look like? Scripture paints several pictures for us.

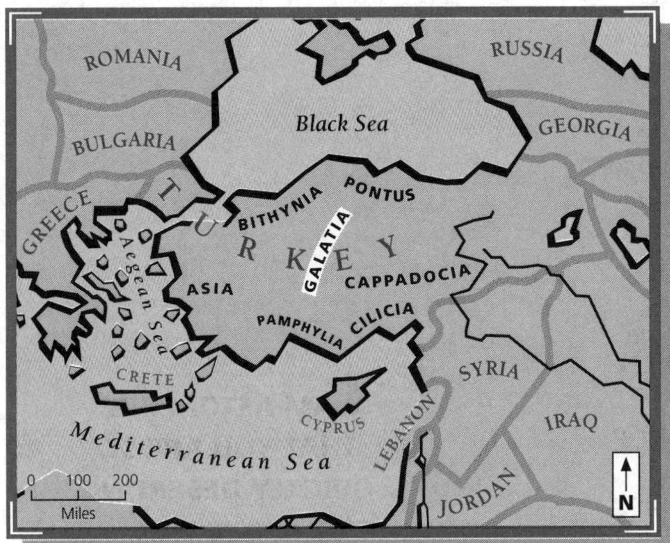

GALATIA AND SURROUNDING REGIONS

GALATIA

- **A loosely defined plateau region of central Asia Minor bounded on the east by Cappadocia, on the west by Asia, on the south by Pamphylia and Cilicia, and on the north by Bithynia and Pontus.**
- **Name derives from Celtic tribes driven out of Gaul (France) that settled the region in the third century B.C.**
- **Interconnected roads in Galatia provided easy access to roving tribes and marching armies. Cities had no walls and citizens cared little for defending themselves as they could always escape to nearby mountains.**
- **Conquered by Rome by 166 B.C. and given freedom on one condition—that the Celts would assist Rome in dividing and conquering the other groups around them. Thus, in Paul's day, Galatia was politically, economically, and militarily significant to Rome.**
- **North Galatia resisted Greek-Roman culture, keeping its own gods and Celtic language.**
- **South Galatia adopted the cult of emperor worship, and Judaism also persisted there for centuries after Christ.**
- **We know that Paul visited and established churches in the south (Acts 13:13—14:25), but we have no reliable record of any visits or churches to the north.**

ONLY CHRIST

Throughout Christian history, people have "added on" various requirements to the gospel message, almost always with an appeal to Scripture. Inevitably the result is a distortion of the faith that does great damage.

In first-century Galatia, the challenge came from Judaizers, followers who insisted that belief in Jesus was not enough for salvation. One must also keep the Law of Moses, they said. In a way, one can understand their point of view. For centuries, Jews had held to the Law as the righteous path to favor with God (see Deut. 6:1–9; 30:15–20; compare Mark 12:28–34; Luke 10:25–28). The Judaizers perceived Jesus as perhaps building on the Law of Moses, but not replacing it.

However, their teaching greatly troubled the young believers in Galatia who had responded to Paul's message (Acts 13:13—14:26). If what the Judaizers said was true, Paul had been wrong and Christ alone did not really save a person.

Not surprisingly, Paul was outraged. He was furious with the deceptive claims of the Judaizers and zealous to defend the integrity of the gospel. So he composed the letter that we call Galatians, which may be his earliest surviving epistle, written perhaps in A.D. 48 or 49.

If Galatians emphasizes anything, it is that Christ alone is sufficient for salvation—nothing more and nothing less. Centuries later, after the church had again embraced add-ons to the faith, a young priest named Martin Luther claimed Galatians for his own, calling it the Magna Charta of Christian liberty. It helped usher in a reclamation of the faith in which salvation is based on Christ's grace, not on people's efforts.

Still, every generation is marked by a tendency to classify believers according to their outward observances. Some are considered first-class, others second-class. In nearly every case, the resegregating of the church results from add-ons to the simple, pure gospel of Christ. But when believers hold to Christ alone, then their faith and the church will grow. That's the message of Galatians. ◆

I AM ASTONISHED THAT YOU ARE SO QUICKLY DESERTING THE ONE WHO CALLED YOU . . . .
—Galatians 1:6

To the Churches of Galatia

1 Paul an apostle—sent neither by human commission
nor from human authorities, but through Jesus Christ
and God the Father, who raised him from the dead— 2and
all the members of God's family[a] who are with me,
To the churches of Galatia:
3 Grace to you and peace from God our Father and the
Lord Jesus Christ, 4who gave himself for our sins to set us
free from the present evil age, according to the will of our
God and Father, 5to whom be the glory forever and ever.
Amen.

Don't Turn Away from the True Gospel

6 I am astonished that you are so quickly deserting the
one who called you in the grace of Christ and are turning
to a different gospel— 7not that there is another gospel, but
there are some who are confusing you and want to pervert
the gospel of Christ. 8But even if we or an angel[b] from
heaven should proclaim to you a gospel contrary to what
we proclaimed to you, let that one be accursed! 9As we
have said before, so now I repeat, if anyone proclaims to
you a gospel contrary to what you received, let that one be
accursed!

The Gospel Was Revealed by God

10 Am I now seeking human approval, or God's approval? Or am I trying to please people? If I were still pleasing people, I would not be a servant[c] of Christ.
1:11–24
11 For I want you to know, brothers
and sisters,[d] that the gospel that was proclaimed by me is not of human origin; 12for I did not receive it from a human source, nor was I taught it, but I
received it through a revelation of Jesus Christ.
1:13–17 see pg. 644
13 You have heard, no doubt, of my
earlier life in Judaism. I was violently
persecuting the church of God and was trying to destroy it.
14I advanced in Judaism beyond many among my people of
the same age, for I was far more zealous for the traditions of
my ancestors. 15But when God, who had set me apart before I was born and called me through his grace, was
pleased 16to reveal his Son to me,[e] so that I might proclaim
him among the Gentiles, I did not confer with any human
being, 17nor did I go up to Jerusalem to those who were already apostles before me, but I went away at once into Arabia, and afterwards I returned to Damascus.
18 Then after three years I did go up to Jerusalem to
visit Cephas and stayed with him fifteen days; 19but I did

[a]Gk *all the brothers* [b]Or *a messenger* [c]Gk *slave* [d]Gk *brothers* [e]Gk *in me*

Hope for You: Watch Paul Grow!

CONSIDER THIS 1:11–24 **The Bible offers many examples of people who struggled as they tried to live for God. Their stories are meant to encourage us. But sometimes comparing ourselves to the "heroes" of the faith only intimidates us. Paul, for instance, was a learned scholar, a fervent evangelist, a compassionate pastor, a competent businessman, and a diplomatic statesman. So when he tells us to follow his example as he follows Christ's example (1 Cor. 11:1), it sounds a bit unrealistic. How could we ever emulate a super-saint like Paul?**

But Paul didn't start out as a super-saint. Nor did he end up that way. In fact, he never saw himself that way. On the contrary, he grew in the faith with some difficulty. Notice how his view of himself changed over time (dates given are estimates):

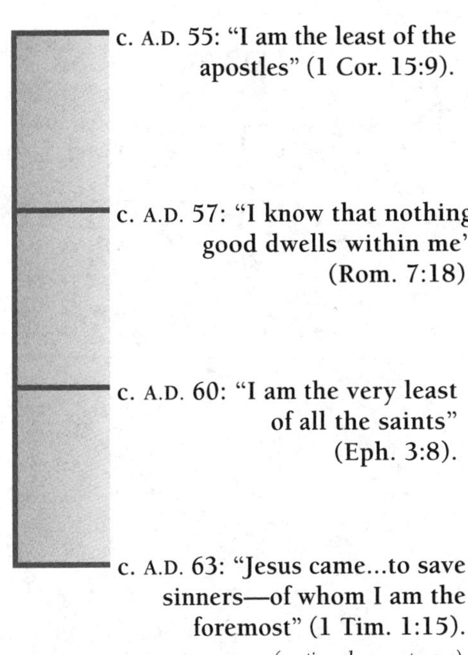
c. A.D. 55: "I am the least of the apostles" (1 Cor. 15:9).
c. A.D. 57: "I know that nothing good dwells within me" (Rom. 7:18).
c. A.D. 60: "I am the very least of all the saints" (Eph. 3:8).
c. A.D. 63: "Jesus came...to save sinners—of whom I am the foremost" (1 Tim. 1:15).

(continued on next page)

(continued from previous page)

Sounds as if Paul was perhaps more "average" than we often think. In fact, look carefully at some of the highlights (and lowlights) in his life (see Paul's profile, Acts 13:2–3). If one changes a few particulars and develops the whole-hearted commitment to God that Paul had, then his story could well be anyone's. That's because Paul was as human as any of us. His life challenges us to ask whether we are growing, struggling, and changing as he did. If so, then there's hope for us!

One of the keys to Paul's growth was the careful tutelage of a man named Barnabas. See "Barnabas—A Model for Mentoring," Acts 9:27.

It's interesting that sometimes when Paul compared himself to other Christians of his day, he was all too aware of his own feet of clay. Apparently he suffered from the deadly disease of "comparisonitis." See Rom. 12:3.

not see any other apostle except James the Lord's brother.
20In what I am writing to you, before God, I do not lie!
21Then I went into the regions of Syria and Cilicia, 22and I
was still unknown by sight to the churches of Judea that are
in Christ; 23they only heard it said, "The one who formerly
was persecuting us is now proclaiming the faith he once
tried to destroy." 24And they glorified God because of me.

The Apostles Approved Paul's Message

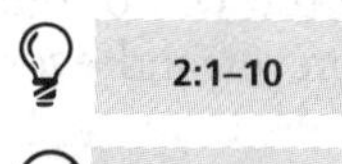

2:2

2 Then after fourteen years I went up
again to Jerusalem with Barnabas,
taking Titus along with me. 2I went up in
response to a revelation. Then I laid be-
fore them (though only in a private meeting with the acknowledged leaders) the gospel that I proclaim among the
Gentiles, in order to make sure that I was not running, or
had not run, in vain. 3But even Titus, who was with me,

A CLOSER LOOK 2:2

Those Who Were Leaders

Who were those described as being "acknowledged leaders" (v. 2)? See "The Twelve," Matt. 10:2, and "Who Were the Apostles?" 2 Cor. 11:5.

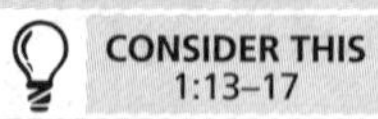

CONSIDER THIS 1:13–17

FROM PERSECUTOR TO APOSTLE

In vv. 13–17, Paul recounts his dramatic confrontation with Christ on the Damascus road and his subsequent conversion (Acts 9:1–30). Imagine the emotional strain that placed on Saul (as he was called at the time): Jesus was alive! What members of the Way (the early Christians) had been saying about Him was all true! And Saul had killed many of them! What a shattering experience for one "advanced in Judaism" and exceedingly "zealous for the traditions" of his fathers (Gal. 1:14).

Perhaps that's why God made Saul blind for three days. He had a lot to sort out after meeting the risen Lord. It's not easy for someone to suddenly revise the entire theological basis on which he's been living, especially as a respected leader. No one wants to admit he's been wrong. No wonder Saul spent much of the time in prayer.

But God not only intended to change Saul's theology; He was determined to transform his narrow view of the world. At the root of Saul's intense hatred of the Christian movement might well have been a belief that it would destroy Judaism by mixing it with foreign, Gentile elements (see "Stephen's Trial and Murder," Acts 6:12).

Imagine Saul's shock, then, when Ananias came to tell

was not compelled to be circumcised, though he was a
Greek. 4But because of false believers[f] secretly brought in,
who slipped in to spy on the freedom we have in Christ
Jesus, so that they might enslave us— 5we did not submit
to them even for a moment, so that the truth of the gospel
might always remain with you. 6And from those who were
supposed to be acknowledged leaders (what they actually
were makes no difference to me; God shows no partiality)—those leaders contributed nothing to me. 7On the
contrary, when they saw that I had been entrusted with the
gospel for the uncircumcised, just as Peter had been entrusted with the gospel for the circumcised 8(for he who
worked through Peter making him an apostle to the circumcised also worked through me in sending me to the
Gentiles), 9and when James and Cephas and John, who
were acknowledged pillars, recognized the grace that had
been given to me, they gave to Barnabas and me the right
hand of fellowship, agreeing that we should go to the Gentiles and they to the circumcised. 10They
asked only one thing, that we remember
the poor, which was actually what I was[g] eager to do.

2:10 see pg. 647

(Bible text continued on page 647)

[f]Gk *false brothers* [g]Or *had been*

him that God had chosen him to bear His name—to the Gentiles (Acts 9:15; 22:14–15; 26:16–18)! Unthinkable! Jews like Saul, who were utterly committed to holy living by all the laws and traditions of Judaism, had nothing to do with Gentiles (Acts 10:28). No wonder it took Saul years to re-evaluate his perspectives and bring them in line with the heart of God for the world (Acts 9:26–30; 22:17–21).

Paul's experience forces us to ask: What attitudes of prejudice keep you from recognizing God's heart for the whole world? What attitudes of bigotry operate where you live or work? Do you in any way challenge that thinking, or do you just keep silent—or worse, go along with it or even promote it? Would God be able to use you to bear His name to people from a different ethnic heritage? ◆

Believers often embrace cultural values whether they are biblical or not. We may reproduce and even defend sinful attitudes and actions that are normal for our surrounding culture. See "Society's Divisions Affect Believers," Acts 6:1.

Wise Believers Seek Counsel

CONSIDER THIS 2:1–10 **If you've ever tried to resolve a deep-seated controversy, you may have found how easy it is to "agree to disagree" over a highly controversial issue, but how difficult it is to actually carry that out. It takes concerted effort. In his exchange with the apostles at Jerusalem (v. 1), Paul demonstrated how believers should honor one another by seeking each other's counsel, especially when strong convictions and difficult issues are at stake.**

In this situation, Jewish followers of Christ were finding that their faith was influenced by deeply rooted ethnic and cultural bias against Gentiles. Paul had once been a champion of Judaism (1:13–14), but then became the apostle to the Gentiles (1:15; see Acts 13:2–3). Paul came to Jerusalem to meet with the leaders of the Jewish believers and discuss his activities.

Note several elements in the encounter between the two different positions:

(1) Paul voluntarily went to the leaders of the other side (vv. 1–2).
(2) He met privately to discuss a potentially volatile situation (v. 2).
(3) He sought the input of recognized leaders (vv. 2–9).

(continued on page 647)

FOR YOUR INFO
2:12

CIRCUMCISION

The fact that a group in the early church was referred to as "the circumcision faction" (v. 12) reflects how deeply controversial the ancient practice of circumcision had become. Originally mandated by God as a sign of His covenant relationship with Israel, circumcision became a mark of exclusivity, not only among the Jews, but among the early Jewish Christians.

Technically speaking, circumcision refers to the surgical removal of the male's foreskin. The procedure was widely practiced in the ancient world, including the Egyptian and Canaanite cultures. But they performed the rite at the beginning of puberty as an initiation into manhood. By contrast, the Hebrews circumcised infants as a sign of their responsibility to serve God as His special, holy people in the midst of a pagan world.

God instructed Abraham to circumcise every male child in his household, including servants (Gen. 17:11) as a visible, physical sign of the covenant between the Lord and His people. Any male not circumcised was to be "cut off from his people" (17:14) and regarded as a covenant breaker (Ex. 22:48). The custom was performed on the eighth day after birth (Gen. 17:12), at which time a name was given to the son (Luke 1:59; 2:21). In the early history of the Jews, the rite was performed by the father, but eventually was carried out by a specialist.

The Hebrew people came to take great pride in circumcision. In fact, it became a badge of their spiritual and national superiority. This attitude fostered a spirit of exclusivism instead of compassion to reach out to other nations as God intended. Gentiles came to be regarded as the "uncircumcision," a term of disrespect implying that non-Jewish peoples were outside the circle of God's love. The terms "circumcised" and "uncircumcised" became charged with emotion, as is plain from the discord the issue brought about in the early church.

A crisis erupted at Antioch when believers from Judea, known as Judaizers, taught the brethren, "Unless you are circumcised according to the custom of Moses, you cannot be saved" (Acts 15:1–2). In effect, the Judaizers insisted that a believer from a non-Jewish background must first become a Jew ceremonially by being circumcised before he could be admitted to the Christian brotherhood.

A council of apostles and elders was convened in Jerusalem to resolve the issue (Acts 15:6–29). Among those attending were Paul, Barnabas, Simon Peter, and James, leader of the Jerusalem church. To insist on circumcision for the Gentiles, Peter argued, would amount to a burdensome yoke (Acts 15:10). This was the decision handed down by the council.

Years later, reinforcing this decision, the apostle Paul wrote the believers at Rome that Abraham, "the ancestor of circumcision" (Rom. 4:12), was saved by faith rather than by circumcision (Rom. 4:9–12). He declared that "real circumcision is a matter of the heart—it is spiritual and not literal" (Rom. 2:29).

Paul also spoke of the "circumcision of Christ" (Col. 2:11), a reference to His atoning death which "condemned sin in the flesh" (Rom. 8:3) and nailed "the record . . . against us" to the cross (Col. 2:14). In essence, Paul declared that the new covenant of Christ's shed blood has made forgiveness available to both Jew and Gentile and has made circumcision unnecessary. All that ultimately matters for both Jew and Gentile, Paul says, is a changed nature—a new creation that makes them one in Jesus Christ (Eph. 2:14–18). ◆

Among the Jews, circumcision was a sign of the covenant that God established with Israel, His chosen people. But in Christ, God established a new covenant, open to all people. *See "The New Covenant," 1 Cor. 11:25.*

A Rebuke for Compromising the Gospel

11 But when Cephas came to Antioch, I opposed him
2:12 to his face, because he stood self-
condemned; 12for until certain people
came from James, he used to eat with the Gentiles. But after
they came, he drew back and kept himself separate for fear
of the circumcision faction. 13And the other Jews joined
him in this hypocrisy, so that even Barnabas was led astray
by their hypocrisy. 14But when I saw that they were not acting consistently with the truth of the gospel, I said to
Cephas before them all, "If you, though a Jew, live like a
Gentile and not like a Jew, how can you compel the Gentiles to live like Jews?"[h]
15 We ourselves are Jews by birth and not Gentile sinners; 16yet we know that a person is justified[i] not by the
works of the law but through faith in Jesus Christ.[j] And we
have come to believe in Christ Jesus, so that we might be
justified by faith in Christ,[k] and not by doing the works of
the law, because no one will be justified by the works of the
law. 17But if, in our effort to be justified in Christ, we ourselves have been found to be sinners, is Christ then a servant of sin? Certainly not! 18But if I build up again the very
things that I once tore down, then I demonstrate that I am
a transgressor. 19For through the law I died to the law, so
that I might live to God. I have been crucified with Christ;
20and it is no longer I who live, but it is Christ who lives in
me. And the life I now live in the flesh I live by faith in the
Son of God,[l] who loved me and gave himself for me. 21I do
not nullify the grace of God; for if justification[m] comes
through the law, then Christ died for nothing.

Abraham Was Justified by Faith

3:1 see pg. 648

3 You foolish Galatians! Who has bewitched you? It was before your eyes
that Jesus Christ was publicly exhibited as crucified! 2The
only thing I want to learn from you is this: Did you receive
the Spirit by doing the works of the law or by believing
what you heard? 3Are you so foolish? Having started with
the Spirit, are you now ending with the flesh? 4Did you experience so much for nothing?—if it really was for nothing.

[h]Some interpreters hold that the quotation extends into the following paragraph [i]Or *reckoned as righteous;* and so elsewhere [j]*Or the faith of Jesus Christ* [k]*Or the faith of Christ* [l]*Or by the faith of the Son of God* [m]*Or righteousness*

Remember the Poor

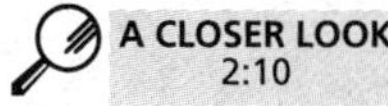

A CLOSER LOOK 2:10

Recounting his meeting with the church leaders (v. 10), Paul reveals his attitude of generosity toward the poor. This was a constant theme throughout his life. In fact, elsewhere he says we must support the weak. See " 'I Have Not Coveted,' " Acts 20:33–38.

(continued from page 645)

(4) He evaluated his position and behavior in light of God's truth, in order to avoid working "in vain" (v. 2).

(5) He brought along an actual test case, uncircumcised Titus, and refused the demand of some that Titus conform to the Jewish rite of circumcision (v. 3–5).

(6) Clarity was achieved, but in this case it did not require uniformity of practice (v. 9).

(7) The leaders reached agreement on another matter, serving the poor among both Jews and Gentiles (v. 10).

Commitment to Christ calls for believers to pay each other honor and respect. Even if they decide to "agree to disagree," they still need each other.

[5]Well then, does God[n] supply you with the Spirit and work
miracles among you by your doing the works of the law, or
by your believing what you heard?

3:6

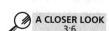

6 Just as Abraham "believed God, and
it was reckoned to him as righteousness,"
[7]so, you see, those who believe are the descendants of
Abraham. [8]And the scripture, foreseeing that God would
justify the Gentiles by faith, declared the gospel beforehand
to Abraham, saying, "All the Gentiles shall be blessed in
you." [9]For this reason, those who believe are blessed with
Abraham who believed.
10 For all who rely on the works of the law are under a
curse; for it is written, "Cursed is everyone who does not
observe and obey all the things written in the book of the
law." [11]Now it is evident that no one is justified before God

[n]Gk *he*

A CLOSER LOOK
3:6

Abraham

As the man who believed God, Abraham (v. 6) features prominently in the New Testament. See "Abraham," Rom. 4:1.

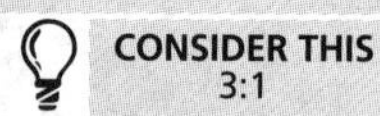

CONSIDER THIS
3:1

A STRONG REBUKE

The book of Ecclesiastes speaks of "a time to love, and a time to hate; a time for war, and a time for peace" (Eccl. 3:8). When it came to a question of altering the gospel about Jesus, Paul realized that it was no time for peace, but for intense conflict. Here in Galatians and elsewhere, he issued a strong rebuke both to those who would pervert the message of Christ in order to preserve their traditions, and to those who followed them (Gal. 3:1).

Notice the strong feelings in some of Paul's statements on this subject (emphasis added):

- "I am astonished *that you are so quickly deserting [Christ] . . . to a different gospel" (Gal. 1:6).*
- *"Even if we or an angel from heaven should proclaim to you a gospel contrary to what we proclaimed to you,* let that one be accursed" *(1:8).*
- *"As we have said before, so now I repeat, if anyone proclaims to you a gospel contrary to what you received,* let that one be accursed" *(1:9).*
- "You foolish Galatians! *Who has* bewitched *you?" (3:1).*
- "I am afraid that my work for you *may have been wasted" (4:11).*

by the law; for "The one who is righteous will live by
faith."[o] 12But the law does not rest on faith; on the contrary,
"Whoever does the works of the law[p] will live by them."
13Christ redeemed us from the curse of the law by becoming a curse for us—for it is written, "Cursed is everyone
who hangs on a tree"— 14in order that in Christ Jesus the
blessing of Abraham might come to the Gentiles, so that we
might receive the promise of the Spirit through faith.

15 Brothers and sisters,[q] I give an example from daily
life: once a person's will[r] has been ratified, no one adds to it
or annuls it. 16Now the promises were made to Abraham
and to his offspring;[s] it does not say, "And to offsprings,"[t] as
of many; but it says, "And to your offspring,"[s] that is, to one
person, who is Christ. 17My point is this: the law, which
came four hundred thirty years later, does not annul a
covenant previously ratified by God, so as to nullify the
promise. 18For if the inheritance comes from the law, it no
longer comes from the promise; but God granted it to Abraham through the promise.

19 Why then the law? It was added because of transgressions, until the offspring[s] would come to whom the

[o]Or *The one who is righteous through faith will live* [p]Gk *does them* [q]Gk *Brothers* [r]Or *covenant* (as in verse 17) [s]Gk *seed* [t]Gk *seeds*

- *"I wish I were present with you now and could change my tone, for* I am perplexed about you" *(4:20).*
- "I wish those who unsettle you would castrate themselves!" *(5:12).*
- "Beware of the dogs, beware of the evil workers, beware of those who mutilate the flesh!" *(Phil. 3:2).*

Believers in Christ are called to be kind, humble, meek, and longsuffering; to bear with one another, to forgive each other, and above all to love one another as they seek the unity of the body (Col. 3:12–15). At the same time, they are called to "stand firm" in the faith (1 Cor. 16:13) and in their freedom in Christ (Gal. 5:1). At times, that may mean anger and conflict when the very truth of the gospel is under attack.

The energy with which Paul defended the fundamentals of the faith should encourage us as believers today to ask: What challenges to the truth do we need to meet? Where are compromises being made to basic biblical principles? Is our commitment to the faith strong enough that we are willing to defend it against those who would pervert it to their own ends? ◆

HAVING STARTED WITH THE SPIRIT, ARE YOU NOW ENDING WITH THE FLESH?
—Galatians 3:3

We Are Family!

CONSIDER THIS 3:28 **In v. 28, Paul emphasizes that three major social distinctions no longer matter in Christ:**

- ***Ethnicity:* "no longer Jew or Greek."**
- ***Socioeconomic status:* "no longer slave or free."**
- ***Gender:* "no longer male and female."**

First-century culture was deeply divided along these lines. So was the church. But Paul stressed, "All of you are *one* in Christ Jesus" (italics added).

Christians have become children of God through faith, which means we are all in the same family. We are no longer divided by ethnicity, social status, or gender, but have become brothers and sisters in God's family.

One powerful symbol of that new unity is baptism (v. 27). As part of the baptismal ceremony, a believer affirms the lordship of Christ and his or her commitment to a new way of life. Paul is possibly quoting from a first-century baptismal creed (v. 28) to remind us of our promise to "put on Christ," not in word but in deed.

In the early Christian communities that meant that both Gentiles and Jews could exercise their spiritual gifts. Both slaves and masters could pray or prophesy. Both women and men could enjoy full membership in the body. "Christ [was] all and in all" (Col. 3:11). The breaking down of traditional barriers wasn't just a future hope. The early church worked to make it a reality.

Which brings us to the question: What walls of ethnicity, status, or gender divide believers today? Are we willing to model reconciliation between different and even antagonistic groups? If not, then is our church truly a sign of God's kingdom, or merely a human institution?

promise had been made; and it was ordained through
angels by a mediator. 20Now a mediator involves more than
one party; but God is one.
21 Is the law then opposed to the promises of God? Certainly not! For if a law had been given that could make alive, then righteousness would indeed come through the
law. 22But the scripture has imprisoned all things under the
power of sin, so that what was promised through faith in
Jesus Christ[u] might be given to those who believe.

Believers Are Children of God by Faith

23 Now before faith came, we were imprisoned and
guarded under the law until faith would be revealed.
24Therefore the law was our disciplinarian until Christ
came, so that we might be justified by faith. 25But now that
faith has come, we are no longer subject to a disciplinarian,
26for in Christ Jesus you are all children of God through
faith. 27As many of you as were baptized into Christ have
3:28 clothed yourselves with Christ. 28There is
no longer Jew or Greek, there is no longer slave or free, there is no longer male and female; for
all of you are one in Christ Jesus. 29And if you belong to
Christ, then you are Abraham's offspring,[v] heirs according to the promise.

No Longer Slaves But Heirs

4:1–18 4 My point is this: heirs, as long as they are minors, are no better than slaves, though they are the owners of all the property; 2but
they remain under guardians and trustees until the date set
by the father. 3So with us; while we were minors, we were
enslaved to the elemental spirits[w] of the world. 4But when
the fullness of time had come, God sent his Son, born of a
woman, born under the law, 5in order to redeem those who
were under the law, so that we might receive adoption as
children. 6And because you are children, God has sent the
Spirit of his Son into our[x] hearts, crying, "Abba![y] Father!"
4:7 7So you are no longer a slave but a child,
and if a child then also an heir, through God.[z]
8 Formerly, when you did not know God, you were en-

[u] Or *through the faith of Jesus Christ* [v] Gk *seed* [w] Or *the rudiments* [x] Other ancient authorities read *your* [y] Aramaic for *Father* [z] Other ancient authorities read *an heir of God through Christ*

The Privileges of God's Children

A CLOSER LOOK 4:7 *Children enjoy privileges that slaves will never know (v. 7). See "What's In It for Me?" at Eph. 1:11, to learn more about the inheritance we will enjoy as God's children.*

slaved to beings that by nature are not gods. 9Now, however, that you have come to know God, or rather to be
known by God, how can you turn back again to the weak
and beggarly elemental spirits?[a] How can you want to be
enslaved to them again? 10You are observing special days,
and months, and seasons, and years. 11I am afraid that my
work for you may have been wasted.

Whose Message Is to Be Believed?

12 Friends,[b] I beg you, become as I am, for I also have
become as you are. You have done me no wrong. 13You
know that it was because of a physical infirmity that I first

[a]Or *beggarly rudiments* [b]Gk *Brothers*

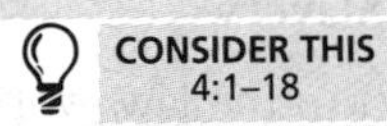

RIGHTS

We live in a time when it seems that everyone is concerned about exercising their "rights." Indeed, society has become somewhat polarized as various groups form around their perceptions of rights that they feel they are being denied. The more intense the struggle to achieve those rights, the more social conflict seems to escalate.

Paul indicated to the Galatians that before God, no one has any rights; whatever rights humanity once had have been forfeited as a result of sin. To bring this situation home to his readers, Paul used the metaphor of a slave (vv. 1–3), an image that the Galatians probably knew well, as the Roman Empire depended heavily on slave labor (see Rom. 6:16).

The Galatians had become children of God, but before that they were in bondage to sin, to the "elemental spirits of the world" (v. 3; compare Col. 2:8, 20). As slaves to sin, they had no rights before God. He owed them nothing. They belonged to sin, which they were forced to serve. Emancipation from that position had to come from a source other than their own power, ingenuity, or morality.

Such is the plight of all sinners before God—helpless and hopeless (Rom. 3:23, John 3:19–20). But just as God gave life, resources, and responsibility to humanity in the beginning (Gen. 1:26—2:4), so now He has given Christ His Son to rescue or "redeem" people from sin and grant them all the privileges of adoption into the family of God (vv. 4–7). No one deserves that, which is why receiving Christ's new life and the rights therein is truly a gift.

If as believers we have received these treasures from God, then we ought to let others know that the same opportunity is available to them. ◆

HAGAR

FOR YOUR INFO 4:24–25

A helpless outcast serves as a metaphor for Paul's warning to the Galatians against turning to the Law for salvation. Hagar (vv. 24–25; Gen. 16:1–16) was an Egyptian slave of Sarah, the wife of the Old Testament patriarch Abraham (see 1 Pet. 3:6).

God promised Abraham and Sarah that He would give them a son. But after ten years of waiting, Sarah presented Hagar to her husband so that he could father a child by her, according to the custom of the day. However, God viewed the substitution as a lack of faith.

When Hagar became pregnant, she mocked her mistress, who dealt with her harshly. Fleeing into the wilderness, Hagar encountered an angel of the Lord. The heavenly messenger revealed that the child she was to bear, Ishmael, would be the father of a great nation even though he was not the son that God had promised to Abraham and Sarah.

Hagar returned to Abraham's camp and bore Ishmael, who was accepted as Abraham's son. But when Ishmael was 14, Sarah gave birth to Isaac, the promised son. Later Ishmael mocked Isaac at the festival of Isaac's weaning. At Sarah's insistence, Hagar and her son were expelled from Abraham's family. However, God took care of them as they wandered in the wilderness.

The Lord also carried out His promise to make a great nation of Ishmael. He had twelve sons who had many descendents who lived as nomads in the deserts of northern Arabia. Tradition holds that all of the Arab peoples are descended from Hagar.

announced the gospel to you; 14though my condition put
you to the test, you did not scorn or despise me, but welcomed me as an angel of God, as Christ Jesus. 15What has
become of the goodwill you felt? For I testify that, had it
been possible, you would have torn out your eyes and
given them to me. 16Have I now become your enemy by
telling you the truth? 17They make much of you, but for no
good purpose; they want to exclude you, so that you may
make much of them. 18It is good to be made much of for a
good purpose at all times, and not only when I am present
with you. 19My little children, for whom I am again in the
pain of childbirth until Christ is formed in you, 20I wish I
were present with you now and could change my tone, for
I am perplexed about you.

Two Alternatives—Freedom or Slavery

21 Tell me, you who desire to be subject to the law, will
you not listen to the law? 22For it is written that Abraham
had two sons, one by a slave woman and the other by a free
woman. 23One, the child of the slave, was born according
to the flesh; the other, the child of the free woman, was
4:24–25 born through the promise. 24Now this
is an allegory: these women are two
covenants. One woman, in fact, is Hagar, from Mount Sinai,
4:25–26 see pg. 655 bearing children for slavery. 25Now Hagar
is Mount Sinai in Arabia[c] and corre-
sponds to the present Jerusalem, for she is in slavery with
her children. 26But the other woman corresponds to the
Jerusalem above; she is free, and she is our mother. 27For it
is written,

"Rejoice, you childless one, you who bear no children,
burst into song and shout, you who endure no birth
pangs;
for the children of the desolate woman are more
numerous
than the children of the one who is married."

28Now you,[d] my friends,[e] are children of the promise, like
Isaac. 29But just as at that time the child who was born
according to the flesh persecuted the child who was born
according to the Spirit, so it is now also. 30But what does
the scripture say? "Drive out the slave and her child; for the
child of the slave will not share the inheritance with the
child of the free woman." 31So then, friends,[e] we are chil-
5:1–12 5 dren, not of the slave but of the free
woman. 1For freedom Christ has set

(Bible text continued on page 654)

[c]Other ancient authorities read *For Sinai is a mountain in Arabia* [d]Other ancient authorities read *we* [e]Gk *brothers*

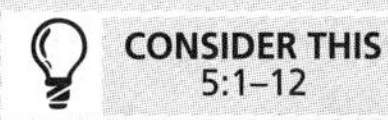

MYTH #7

10 MYTHS ABOUT CHRISTIANITY

MYTH: CHRISTIANITY STIFLES PERSONAL FREEDOM

Many people today accept a number of myths about Christianity, with the result that they never respond to Jesus as He really is. This is one of ten articles that speak to some of those misconceptions. For a list of all ten, see 1 Tim. 1:3–4.

Freedom is the prevailing cry of the world today, the overwhelming preoccupation of individuals and nations. Yet even though Scripture speaks of a liberty that Christ offers (vv. 1–12), some people resist Christianity as itself an obstacle to freedom. Is this view of the faith justified?

On the face of it, it seems strange to identify Christianity as an enemy of freedom. After all, Christians have historically stood up for the poor, the oppressed, the captive, and the underprivileged. Likewise, liberation from ignorance, disease, and political oppression have invariably resulted wherever Christian faith and principles have been adopted. Why, then, would some view the faith as repressive?

Perhaps part of the answer lies in the problem of legalism. Whenever Christianity is made into a list of dos and don'ts, it becomes intolerant and restrictive. Instead of enjoying an intimate relationship with a loving God, the legalist is obsessed with rules and regulations, as if God were a celestial Policeman just waiting to catch us out of line.

To be sure, Christ does make demands on us that sometimes limit our autonomy. But true Christianity sees this as part of a relationship based on love and grace, not unlike a healthy marriage in which both partners sometimes sacrifice their own desires in order to serve the other.

But even if there were no legalists, many people would still resist Christianity because they resist any standards that would place absolute claims on them. To them, freedom means pure autonomy—the right to do whatever they want, with no accountability to anyone else.

But surely that leads to irresponsibility and license rather than freedom. Nor do people really live that way. Sooner or later they choose one course of action over another, based on some set of values. In other words, they surrender their will to standards, whether good or bad, and act accordingly. So it is not just the values of Christianity that "stifle" personal freedom, but values in general.

The real question, of course, is what kind of people are we? What is our character? Christians try to mold their character after the pattern of Jesus. He was the most liberated man who ever lived. His ultimate standard of behavior was, what does My Father want Me to do (John 8:29)? Did that code stifle His freedom? Hardly: He was utterly free of covetousness, hypocrisy, fear of others, and every other vice. At the same time He was free to be Himself, free to tell the truth, free to love people with warmth and purity, and free to surrender His life for others.

True Christian freedom is Christlike freedom. There is no hint of legalism about it. It accepts absolute moral standards that are well known and well proven, and it takes its inspiration from the most liberated human being who ever lived, Jesus of Nazareth. What is stifling about that? ◆

us free. Stand firm, therefore, and do not submit again to a
yoke of slavery.

Live in the Liberty of the Gospel

2 Listen! I, Paul, am telling you that if you let yourselves
be circumcised, Christ will be of no benefit to you. 3Once
again I testify to every man who lets himself be circumcised

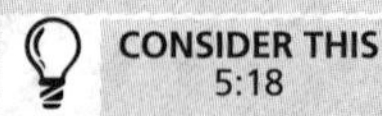
CONSIDER THIS 5:18

TEN COMMANDMENTS—TEN GREAT FREEDOMS

To live under the law is to live under the crushing expectation of fulfilling God's moral standards through one's own human ability. People who try to live that way are likely to end up in misery because sooner or later they are bound to fail (Rom. 7:7–24). Rather than experiencing the joy of a clean conscience, they feel enslaved to legalism and guilt.

The problem is not with God's moral standards but with the sinful nature of humanity. Fortunately, God provides the Holy Spirit to enable believers to carry out His holy standards, as summarized in the Ten Commandments. Thus, living by the Spirit (v. 16) means that one is able to obey the spirit of the Ten Commandments ("the law") and experience powerful new freedoms to be the person God originally intended:

FREEDOMS FOR LIVING

	Original Commandment	New Freedoms
I	"You shall have no other gods before me."	God is our Helper. If we hold onto Him we can find freedom from anxiety about our future, our relationships, our well-being, and our happiness.
II	"You shall not make for yourself an idol."	God is our Teacher. If we hold onto Him we will learn what is true and avoid being talked into that which is false.
III	"You shall not make wrongful use of the name of the Lord your God."	God is our Friend. If we hold onto Him, our prayers will not be futile; we need not try to force Him to help us. Nor should we invoke His name in pursuit of our own self-interest.
IV	"Remember the sabbath day, and keep it holy."	God is our Master. If we hold onto Him, we will find fulfillment. We need not work ourselves to death.
		Continued

that he is obliged to obey the entire law. 4You who want to be justified by the law have cut yourselves off from Christ; you have fallen away from grace. 5For through the Spirit, by faith, we eagerly wait for the hope of righteousness. 6For in Christ Jesus neither circumcision nor uncircumcision counts for anything; the only thing that counts is faith working[f] through love.

[f]Or *made effective*

FREEDOMS FOR LIVING

	Original Commandment	New Freedoms
	Continued	
V	"Honor your father and your mother."	God is our Father in heaven. If we hold onto Him, we will experience His love. We need not be bound by the disappointments of our human relationships.
VI	"You shall not murder."	God is our Protector. If we hold onto Him, we can find freedom from competitiveness with our neighbor and instead act with love.
VII	"You shall not commit adultery."	God is the Author of true happiness. If we hold onto Him, we can find freedom to pursue true love rather than the caricatures of love promoted by our culture.
VIII	"You shall not steal."	God is our Provider. If we hold onto Him, we can learn to give instead of take. We can find freedom from worry about our material well-being and instead work honestly with the abilities He has given us.
IX	"You shall not bear false witness."	God is the Truth. If we hold onto Him, we can learn to speak truth and engender trust.
X	"You shall not covet."	God is the Giver of all good gifts. If we hold onto Him, we can find freedom from greed and instead live with generosity, compassion, and self-respect.

Just as the Ten Commandments provide powerful freedoms for living, they also serve as a guide for workplace behaviors and attitudes. See "Ten Commandments for Practical Living," James 2:8–13.

THE JERUSALEM ABOVE

CONSIDER THIS
4:25–26

Paul distinguished between a "present Jerusalem" (v. 25) and "the Jerusalem above" (v. 26). What was he talking about?

Paul was furious because teachers had come from Jerusalem to lay a Jewish agenda on the new believers in Galatia. It was a legalistic agenda. It claimed that one could not really be a Christian unless one first became a Jew. So when Paul mentioned the "present Jerusalem," he was referring to those teachers. They had enslaved Jerusalem itself with their teaching, and he resented their coming to Galatia to enslave Christians there.

By contrast, "the Jerusalem above" is free (v. 28)—free from legalism and free from sin. It is more than a city; it is a symbol of God's rule and kingdom.

Jerusalem is the place where God has fulfilled His promises in Christ, just as Isaac was delivered on the mountain there (v. 28).

7 You were running well; who prevented you from obeying the truth? 8Such persuasion does not come from the
one who calls you. 9A little yeast leavens the whole batch of
dough. 10I am confident about you in the Lord that you will
not think otherwise. But whoever it is that is confusing you
will pay the penalty. 11But my friends,[g] why am I still being
persecuted if I am still preaching circumcision? In that case
the offense of the cross has been removed. 12I wish those
who unsettle you would castrate themselves!

[g]Gk *brothers*

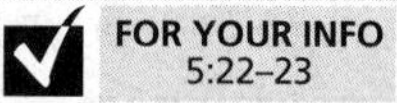
FOR YOUR INFO
5:22–23

New Creatures with New Character

If you are in Christ, you are a new creation. The old habits and character traits that marked your life before Christ are passing away. He is making you entirely new (see 2 Cor. 5:17). What will that look like? Paul paints several pictures of new creatures with new character:

The Traits of New Creatures in Christ

1 Corinthians 13:3–8	Galatians 5:22–23	Philippians 4:8	Colossians 3:12–16
Love... •is patient •is kind •is not envious •is not boastful •is not arrogant •is not rude •does not insist on its own way •is not irritable •is not resentful •does not rejoice in wrongdoing •rejoices in the truth •bears all things •believes all things •hopes all things •endures all things	*The fruit of the Spirit is...* •love •joy •peace •patience •kindness •generosity •faithfulness •gentleness •self-control	*Meditate on whatever things are...* •true •honorable •just •pure •pleasing •commendable •of excellence •worthy of praise	*Put on these things...* •compassion •kindness •humility •meekness •patience •Bear with one another. •Forgive each other. •Above all, clothe yourselves with love. •Let the peace of Christ rule in your hearts. •Be thankful. •Let the word of Christ dwell in you richly. •Teach and admonish one another. •Sing with gratitude in your hearts.
"Now faith, hope, and love abide, these three; and the greatest of these is love" (13:13).	"There is no law against such things... If we live by the Spirit, let us also be guided by the Spirit" (5:23, 25).	"Keep on doing the things that you have learned and received and heard and seen in me, and the God of peace will be with you" (4:9).	"Whatever you do, in word or deed, do everything in the name of the Lord Jesus" (3:17).

Liberty Means Living in Love

13 For you were called to freedom, brothers and sisters;[h] only do not use your freedom as an opportunity for self-indulgence,[i] but through love become slaves to one another. 14 For the whole law is summed up in a single commandment, "You shall love your neighbor as yourself." 15 If, however, you bite and devour one another, take care that you are not consumed by one another.

Liberty Means Living by the Spirit

16 Live by the Spirit, I say, and do not gratify the desires of the flesh. 17 For what the flesh desires is opposed to the Spirit, and what the Spirit desires is opposed to the flesh; for these are opposed to each other, to prevent you from doing what you want. 18 But if you are led by the Spirit, you are not subject to the law. 19 Now the works of the flesh are obvious: fornication, impurity, licentiousness, 20 idolatry, sorcery, enmities, strife, jealousy, anger, quarrels, dissensions, factions, 21 envy,[j] drunkenness, carousing, and things like these. I am warning you, as I warned you before: those who do such things will not inherit the kingdom of God.

5:18 see pg. 654

5:22–23

22 By contrast, the fruit of the Spirit is love, joy, peace, patience, kindness, generosity, faithfulness, 23 gentleness, and self-control. There is no law against such things. 24 And those who belong to Christ Jesus have crucified the flesh with its passions and desires. 25 If we live by the Spirit, let us also be guided by the Spirit. 26 Let us not become conceited, competing against one another, envying one another.

Liberty Means a Concern for Purity

6:1

6 My friends,[k] if anyone is detected in a transgression, you who have received the Spirit should restore such a one in a spirit of gentleness. Take care that you yourselves are not tempted. 2 Bear one another's burdens, and in this way you will fulfill[l] the law of Christ. 3 For if those who are nothing think they are something, they deceive themselves. 4 All must test their own work; then that work, rather than their neighbor's work, will become a cause for pride. 5 For all must carry their own loads.

[h]Gk *brothers* [i]Gk *the flesh* [j]Other ancient authorities add *murder* [k]Gk *Brothers* [l]Other ancient authorities read *in this way fulfill*

Liberty Means Caring about Other Believers

6 Those who are taught the word must share in all good things with their teacher.

7 Do not be deceived; God is not mocked, for you reap whatever you sow. 8 If you sow to your own flesh, you will reap corruption from the flesh; but if you sow to the Spirit, you will reap eternal life from the Spirit. 9 So let us not grow weary in doing what is right, for we will reap at harvest time, if we do not give up. 10 So then, whenever we have an opportunity, let us work for the good of all, and especially for those of the family of faith.

A Handwritten Conclusion

11 See what large letters I make when I am writing in my own hand! 12 It is those who want to make a good showing in the flesh that try to compel you to be circumcised—only that they may not be persecuted for the cross of Christ. 13 Even the circumcised do not themselves obey the law, but they want you to be circumcised so that they may boast about your flesh. 14 May I never boast of anything except the cross of our Lord Jesus Christ, by which[m] the world has been crucified to me, and I to the world. 15 For[n] neither circumcision nor uncircumcision is anything; but a new creation is everything! 16 As for those who will follow this rule—peace be upon them, and mercy, and upon the Israel of God.

17 From now on, let no one make trouble for me; for I carry the marks of Jesus branded on my body.

18 May the grace of our Lord Jesus Christ be with your spirit, brothers and sisters.[h] Amen.

[m]Or *through whom* [n]Other ancient authorities add *in Christ Jesus*

Look to Yourselves!

Paul warns us as believers that while we correct those who have fallen into sin, we should pay attention to our own vulnerability to temptation (v. 1). For more on this important topic, see "Pay Attention to Temptation!" 1 Cor. 10:12–13.

The Letter of Paul to the

Ephesians

In some areas of the world today, Christianity is spreading so rapidly that experts predict that some countries and even some continents will be "Christianized" within a matter of years. However, encouraging as that may be, the roots of that new faith are often shallow and unstable, producing a Christianity that some have described as a mile wide and an inch deep.

Meanwhile, many Christians in the West tend to embrace what might be called a *subjective* gospel: what matters is not so much whether the message of Christ is true, but what it can do for *me*. Can it solve *my* problems, meet *my* needs, help *me* feel okay, improve *my* relationships? It's as if Jesus came primarily for *me*; what difference He makes for others in other times and places is of little consequence.

Paul's letter to the Ephesians was written for believers in both these kinds of circumstances. By unveiling some of what lies behind life in Christ, Ephesians brings depth to our day-to-day experience of the faith. For example, it explains how all three members of the Godhead brought about salvation through a carefully coordinated plan that began in eternity and continues in history. It also reveals the broad, diverse nature of the church. And it makes us aware of the vast forces of evil arrayed against God and His people, and what we must do to withstand the "spiritual forces of evil in the heavenly places" (6:12).

In short, by paying careful attention to this letter, we as believers can develop depth and stability in our faith. We can discover a foundation that goes far beyond cultures and ideologies, and a purpose that transcends personal interests and preoccupations. As Paul says, we can "grow up in every way into him who is the head, into Christ" (4:15).

CONTENTS

ARTICLES

The Ultimate "New Testament Church"

Have you ever longed for your church to be more like the church of the New Testament? If so, carefully study the church at Ephesus. More material in the New Testament pertains historically to Ephesus than to any other community of believers, giving us the best picture we have of what a first-century congregation really looked like:

- *No less than 20 chapters, covering a period of more than 40 years, describe God's work and His people at Ephesus.*
- *More authors write about Ephesus than any other New Testament congregation:*

  Luke *described its founding in three chapters of Acts (18–20);*

  Paul *wrote Ephesians to the congregation there and sent two letters, 1 and 2 Timothy, to its young pastor;*

  John, *repeating a message from Christ, encouraged and warned the Ephesian believers in a letter preserved in the book of Revelation (2:1–7).*

The world of Ephesus feels remarkably like our own—tense with political intrigue and prejudices, divided between affluent, ambitious masters and a needy, dehumanized underclass, and strangely hopeful about its future. A reading of the entire New Testament record on the Ephesian church illustrates what it takes to live out the gospel in a challenging, world-class marketplace.

The start-up congregation in Ephesus proved remarkably fruitful. According to Luke, the message of Christ spread far inland from that major urban center until "all the residents of Asia, both Jews and Greeks, heard the word of the Lord" (Acts 19:10). Judging from Revelation and the letters to Timothy, the Ephesian believers planted several daughter churches. In addition, some church historians believe that a fugitive slave, Onesimus, from Philemon's house church in Laodicea, may have been the same Bishop Onesimus who served at Ephesus around A.D. *110 (see the Introduction to Philemon).*

However, establishing such a thriving center of Christianity was not without cost. Paul probably devoted more time and energy to Ephesus than to any other city. He made at least three visits and spent three years there laying a foundation for the start-up effort. He was aided enormously by Priscilla and Aquila, his business partners (see Rom. 16:3–5). Later, young Timothy, Paul's protégé, carried on the work through tough times and apparently established faithful leadership to follow after him (see the Introduction to 2 Timothy and 2 Tim. 2:2).

Overall, the church at Ephesus serves as a case study in how to establish a community of faith in an increasingly urban world. The study begins with Luke's account of the church's beginnings (Acts 18–20). The letter that follows and 1 and 2 Timothy provide a window on what a growing church and its leaders need to keep in mind. Finally, the church receives an "audit," a warning to beware lest its spiritual life dissipate and its bright promise slip into decline (Rev. 2:1–7). ◆

EPHESUS

- **A major city of Asia between the Croessus mountain range and the Aegean Sea, seated at the mouth of the Cayster River in Paul's day. (Today the site of the ancient city is six miles inland, due to river silting.)**
- **First-century population estimated at 300,000, making Ephesus one of the larger cities of the Roman Empire.**
- **Extraordinarily prosperous as a commercial center, provincial capital, and port city in the eastern Roman Empire.**
- **Boasted numerous monuments, theaters, and temples, notably the temple of Artemis (Acts 19:24–27). Ephesus was an international tourist center, so profitable that its leaders opened the first world bank.**
- **Renowned for religious pluralism, including emperor-worship, mystery cults, occult practices, Hellenized Judaism, and early Christianity.**
- **A frequent stop for Paul, who stayed almost three years and helped establish a church. He may have been jailed there, and probably wrote some of his letters there.**
- **Home to several Christian leaders, including Timothy, Erastus, and Onesiphorus.**
- **Timothy and the apostle John pastored there. The church experienced institutional development but was later denounced as having lost its first love (Rev. 2:4).**
- **Ephesian Christians held firm over four centuries. In A.D. 431 a church council was held there, condemning a false teaching called Nestorianism.**

Paul and the other believers at Ephesus penetrated the city and its systems so effectively that "all . . . of Asia . . . heard the word of the Lord" (Acts 19:10). Find out more about their powerful strategy in "The Ephesus Approach," Acts 19:8–41.

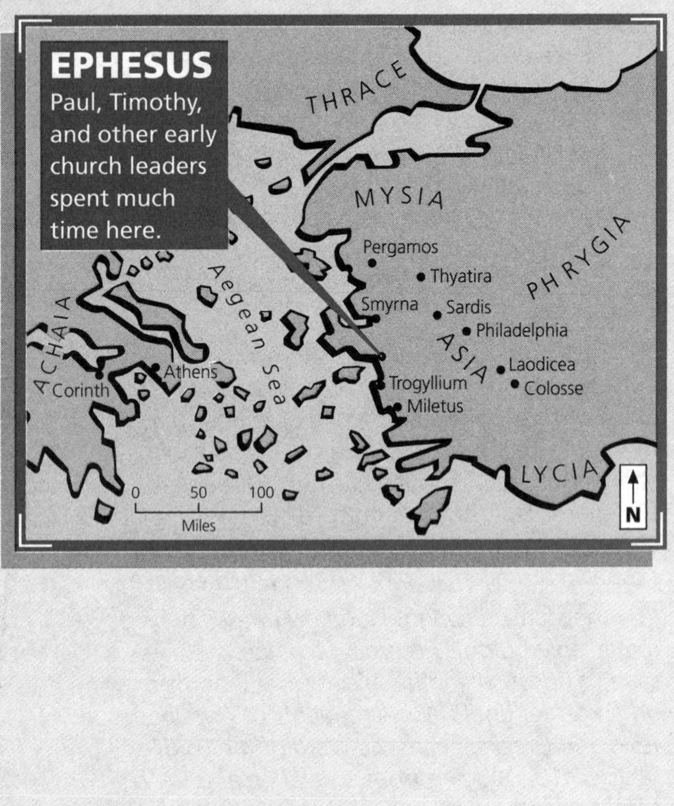

Greeting

1 Paul, an apostle of Christ Jesus by the will of God,
To the saints who are in Ephesus and are faithful[a] in
Christ Jesus:
2 Grace to you and peace from God our Father and the
Lord Jesus Christ.

Blessed Beyond Measure

1:3–14

3 Blessed be the God and Father of
our Lord Jesus Christ, who has blessed
us in Christ with every spiritual blessing in the heavenly
places, 4 just as he chose us in Christ[b] before the foundation
of the world to be holy and blameless before him in love.
5 He destined us for adoption as his children through Jesus
Christ, according to the good pleasure of his will, 6 to the
praise of his glorious grace that he freely bestowed on us in
the Beloved. 7 In him we have redemption through his
blood, the forgiveness of our trespasses, according to the
riches of his grace 8 that he lavished on us. With all wisdom
and insight 9 he has made known to us the mystery of his
will, according to his good pleasure that he set forth in
Christ, 10 as a plan for the fullness of time, to gather up all
things in him, things in heaven and
things on earth. 11 In Christ we have also
obtained an inheritance,[c] having been destined according to
the purpose of him who accomplishes all things according
to his counsel and will, 12 so that we, who were the first to
set our hope on Christ, might live for the praise of his glory.
13 In him you also, when you had heard the word of truth,
the gospel of your salvation, and had believed in him, were
marked with the seal of the promised Holy Spirit; 14 this[d] is
the pledge of our inheritance toward redemption as God's
own people, to the praise of his glory.

1:11 see pg. 664

A Prayer for Eye Opening

15 I have heard of your faith in the Lord Jesus and your
love[e] toward all the saints, and for this reason 16 I do not
cease to give thanks for you as I remember you in my
prayers. 17 I pray that the God of our Lord Jesus Christ, the
Father of glory, may give you a spirit of wisdom and revelation as you come to know him, 18 so that,
with the eyes of your heart enlightened,
you may know what is the hope to which he has called
you, what are the riches of his glorious inheritance among
the saints, 19 and what is the immeasurable greatness of his
power for us who believe, according to the working of his

1:18 see pg. 664

[a]Other ancient authorities lack *in Ephesus,* reading *saints who are also faithful* [b]Gk *in him* [c]Or *been made a heritage* [d]Other ancient authorities read *who* [e]Other ancient authorities lack *and your love*

The Foundation

CONSIDER THIS 1:3–14 **Many islands in the Pacific Ocean appear to be tiny points of land that rise only a few thousand feet above sea level. Yet the foundations of those peaks extend for miles underwater. In fact, if measured from their base, some would tower above the Himalayas.**

In a similar way, the salvation that we enjoy today involves far more than our brief experience of it. It extends back through time and even beyond time into eternity, "before the foundation of the world" (v. 4). Indeed, salvation brings so many things into play that Paul wrote a 202-word run-on sentence (in the Greek) stretching across twelve verses (vv. 3–14) as he began to describe it. The exhaustive, inspiring picture offers a breathtaking vista for the believer.

One thing it shows is that the salvation of every Christian involves all three persons of the Trinity. God the Father has selected us for His grace (vv. 4–5, 11). God the Son offered Himself as the sacrifice for sin, paying our penalty and extending forgiveness (v. 7). And God the Holy Spirit has sealed us in Christ, guaranteeing our relationship with God (vv. 13–14). This work of God began before the world was formed and has continued throughout history.

Thus the foundation of our faith is anchored in God Himself. In His wisdom He has superintended a massive chain of events of which our own lives are but the most recent links.

What's In It for Me?

CONSIDER THIS 1:11

Do you ever wonder what you're going to get out of following Christ? Peter and the other disciples wondered. "We have left everything and followed you," Peter told Jesus. "What then will we have?" (Matt. 19:27). In other words, "What's the payoff? What's in this for me?"

Paul describes some of the "payoff" for believers here in Ephesians 1:3–14. Because so much of it lies in the future, in another mode of existence, the language is strange and hard to understand. But in v. 11 he mentions an inheritance that is coming to us. What is it that we are going to receive "in Christ"?

Simply this: all that God has prepared for Christ in "the fullness of the times" is going to be ours as well (Rom. 8:15–17). This includes salvation from sin (Heb. 1:14), everlasting life (Matt. 19:29), and the kingdom of God (Matt. 25:34). In fact, we will inherit God Himself.

Is this just wishful thinking? No, God is already giving us glimpses of that inconceivable future. The Holy Spirit lives inside us as a guarantee of things to come (v. 14). He seals us, assuring that we remain in God's family and do not lose our inheritance. And while we move toward that day, He works within our lives to make us like Christ. Paul describes what that looks like in chapters 4–6.

Scripture also speaks of the inheritance of material goods that people receive from their parents. See "Will You Get What's Coming to You?" Luke 12:13–15.

great power. 20God[f] put this power to work in Christ when
he raised him from the dead and seated him at his right
hand in the heavenly places, 21far above all rule and authority and power and dominion, and above every name that is
named, not only in this age but also in the age to come.
22And he has put all things under his feet and has made
him the head over all things for the church, 23which is his
body, the fullness of him who fills all in all.

Christ Has Overcome Sin

2:1 see pg. 666

2 You were dead through the trespasses and sins 2in which you once
lived, following the course of this world, following the ruler

[f] Gk *He*

All God's Children

CONSIDER THIS 1:18

In the ancient world, conquering rulers often made a gift of conquered territories and other property to their children or to valued servants (Luke 19:12, 14, 17, 27). Such treasures formed an "inheritance" (Matt. 21:38). A similar idea appears in Ephesians 1:18, where Paul speaks of God's "inheritance among the saints."

God is preparing an inheritance, a kingdom, for His Son, Jesus Christ. It will include people from throughout history, people the Bible calls "saints," or true believers. These are people that God has called and chosen to be His children. Paul wants the Ephesians—and us—to know that believers in Christ will be part of that joyful crowd.

God didn't have to do things that way. When sin entered the world He could have started all over again and created new and perfect creatures to present to His Son. But He chose to gather from the fallen, broken hordes of humanity a people for Himself. By telling us that we are going to be part of His inheritance, He's making a promise: the renovation that has started in our lives will continue until we are perfected and ready to be presented to Christ.

of the power of the air, the spirit that is now at work among
those who are disobedient. 3All of us once lived among
them in the passions of our flesh, following the desires of
flesh and senses, and we were by nature children of wrath,
like everyone else. 4But God, who is rich in mercy, out of
the great love with which he loved us 5even when we were
dead through our trespasses, made us alive together with
Christ[g]—by grace you have been saved— 6and raised us up
with him and seated us with him in the heavenly places in
Christ Jesus, 7so that in the ages to come he might show the
immeasurable riches of his grace in kindness toward us in
Christ Jesus. 8For by grace you have been saved through
faith, and this is not your own doing; it is the gift of God—
9not the result of works, so that no one may boast. 10For we
are what he has made us, created in Christ Jesus for good
works, which God prepared beforehand to be our way of
life.

Christ Has Abolished the Law's Enmity

11 So then, remember that at one time you Gentiles by
birth,[h] called "the uncircumcision" by those who are called
"the circumcision"—a physical circumcision made in the
flesh by human hands— 12remember that you were at that
time without Christ, being aliens from the commonwealth
of Israel, and strangers to the covenants of promise, having
no hope and without God in the world. 13But now in Christ
Jesus you who once were far off have been brought near by

2:14–18

the blood of Christ. 14For he is our peace;
in his flesh he has made both groups into
one and has broken down the dividing wall, that is, the
hostility between us. 15He has abolished the law with its
commandments and ordinances, that he might create in
himself one new humanity in place of the two, thus making
peace, 16and might reconcile both groups to God in one
body[i] through the cross, thus putting to death that hostility
through it.[j] 17So he came and proclaimed peace to you who
were far off and peace to those who were near; 18for
through him both of us have access in one Spirit to the

[g]Other ancient authorities read *in Christ* [h]Gk *in the flesh* [i]Or *reconcile both of us in one body for God* [j]Or *in him*, or *in himself*

This Building Gets Landmark Status

CONSIDER THIS 2:19–22

Many church buildings in the United States and Europe receive special protection from agencies such as the National Register of Historic Places. Historians do research on these landmark buildings, and visitors tour them to learn more about their architectural and cultural significance.

Paul regards the community of believers at Ephesus in a similar way (vv. 19–22). Apostles and prophets are the foundation of the building, and Christ is its cornerstone. Jews and Gentiles are chiseled into living bricks and mortar, until the whole group becomes the "dwelling place for God." Such mixed construction is so unique, so full of grace, that Paul gives the structure special recognition, "landmark status" as it were.

Suppose Paul were to visit your church—not the physical building, but the *people.* Would he find your group deserving of "landmark status"? What are you and your fellow believers doing to construct a holy dwelling place for God on the historic foundation blueprinted in Ephesians 2?

Breaking Down Walls

Paul wrote about breaking down the walls that divide us (vv. 14–22). Antioch, the city from which Paul was sent out to take the gospel to Asia Minor, walled off the four dominant ethnic groups of its population—Greek, Syrian, African, and Jewish. For more, see "Antioch: A Model for the Modern Church?" Acts 13:1.

2:19–22
see pg. 665

Father. 19So then you are no longer
strangers and aliens, but you are citizens
with the saints and also members of the household of God,
20built upon the foundation of the apostles and prophets,
with Christ Jesus himself as the cornerstone.[k] 21In him the
whole structure is joined together and grows into a holy
temple in the Lord; 22in whom you also are built together
spiritually[l] into a dwelling place for God.

The Mystery of the Church

3 This is the reason that I Paul am a prisoner for[m] Christ
Jesus for the sake of you Gentiles— 2for surely you
have already heard of the commission of God's grace that
was given me for you, 3and how the mystery was made
known to me by revelation, as I wrote above in a few
words, 4a reading of which will enable you to perceive my
understanding of the mystery of Christ. 5In former generations this mystery[n] was not made known to humankind, as
it has now been revealed to his holy apostles and prophets

[k]Or *keystone* [l]Gk *in the Spirit* [m]Or *of* [n]Gk *it*

CONSIDER THIS
2:1

Alive Together

In the earliest days of Christianity, the few Gentiles in the church were often looked down on by Jewish believers who found it hard to accept that salvation had been offered to non-Jews. In Ephesus, however, Gentiles made up the majority of the church (see "The Ephesus Approach," Acts 19:8–41). Did they still regard themselves as second-class Christians? Or did they

New Life for Believers of All Kinds

Gentiles were...	God has...
•dead in trespasses and sins (2:1) •children of wrath (2:3) •dead in trespasses (2:5)	•made them alive (2:1) •loved them (2:4) •made them alive together with Christ (2:5) •raised them up (2:6) •seated them with Christ (2:6)
•without Christ (2:12) •aliens from the commonwealth of Israel (2:12) •strangers from the covenants of promise (2:12) •without hope and without God in the world (2:12)	•brought them near by the blood of Christ (2:13)
•far from God (2:17)	•provided access to Himself (2:18)
•strangers and foreigners (2:19)	•made them fellow citizens with the saints and members of the household of God (2:19) •built them into a holy temple or dwelling place of God (2:21–22)

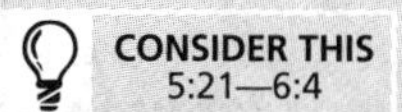

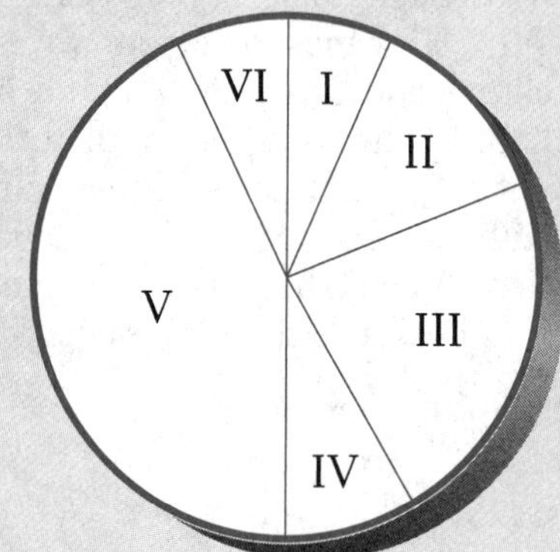

by the Spirit: 6that is, the Gentiles have become fellow
heirs, members of the same body, and sharers in the
promise in Christ Jesus through the gospel.
7 Of this gospel I have become a servant according to
the gift of God's grace that was given me by the working of
his power. 8Although I am the very least of all the saints,
this grace was given to me to bring to the Gentiles the news
of the boundless riches of Christ, 9and to make everyone
see[o] what is the plan of the mystery hidden for ages in[p] God
who created all things; 10so that through the church the
wisdom of God in its rich variety might now be made
known to the rulers and authorities in the heavenly places.
11This was in accordance with the eternal purpose that he
has carried out in Christ Jesus our Lord, 12in whom we
have access to God in boldness and confidence through
faith in him.[q] 13I pray therefore that you[r] may not lose heart
over my sufferings for you; they are your glory.

[o]Other ancient authorities read *to bring to light* [p]Or *by* [q]Or *the faith of him* [r]Or *I*

perhaps reverse the discrimination and treat Jewish believers with prejudice?

Ephesians doesn't tell us, but it does describe in detail the new life that Christ has provided for Gentiles. Apparently they so dominated the Ephesian church that Paul could address them generally with the pronoun "you" as if to mean, "you Gentile believers" (Eph. 2:1, 11). Notice on the accompanying table what God has done for His Gentile children.

The interesting thing is that these privileges have not been provided for Gentiles separately from Jews, but together with them (2:5–6, 21–22; 4:16). In fact, God has torn down the "dividing wall" between the two groups in order to make from them one unified body (2:14–16).

These principles from the early church speak to divisions between Jew and Gentile, but they apply wherever believers face cultural diversity. The challenge of Ephesians is to see past differences to the common grace in which we stand, and "[bear] with one another in love, making every effort to maintain the unity of the Spirit in the bond of peace" (4:2–3). ◆

. . . WE HAVE ACCESS TO GOD IN BOLDNESS AND CONFIDENCE THROUGH FAITH IN HIM.
—Ephesians 3:12

A Prayer to Experience Christ's Love

3:14–21

14 For this reason I bow my knees before the Father,[s] 15from whom every
family[t] in heaven and on earth takes its name. 16I pray that,
according to the riches of his glory, he may grant that you
may be strengthened in your inner being with power
through his Spirit, 17and that Christ may dwell in your
hearts through faith, as you are being rooted and grounded
in love. 18I pray that you may have the power to comprehend, with all the saints, what is the breadth and length
and height and depth, 19and to know the love of Christ that
surpasses knowledge, so that you may be filled with all the
fullness of God.

20 Now to him who by the power at work within us is
able to accomplish abundantly far more than all we can ask
or imagine, 21to him be glory in the church and in Christ
Jesus to all generations, forever and ever. Amen.

Walk Worthy of Your Calling

4 I therefore, the prisoner in the Lord, beg you to lead a
life worthy of the calling to which you have been
called, 2with all humility and gentleness, with patience,
bearing with one another in love, 3making every effort to
maintain the unity of the Spirit in the bond of peace.
4There is one body and one Spirit, just as you were called
to the one hope of your calling, 5one Lord, one faith, one
baptism, 6one God and Father of all, who is above all and
through all and in all.

7 But each of us was given grace according to the measure of Christ's gift. 8Therefore it is said,

"When he ascended on high he made captivity itself a
captive;
he gave gifts to his people."

9(When it says, "He ascended," what does it mean but that
he had also descended[u] into the lower parts of the earth?
10He who descended is the same one who ascended far
above all the heavens, so that he might fill all things.) 11The
gifts he gave were that some would be apostles, some

4:12

prophets, some evangelists, some pastors
and teachers, 12to equip the saints for the
work of ministry, for building up the body of Christ, 13until
all of us come to the unity of the faith and of the knowledge of the Son of God, to maturity, to the measure of the
full stature of Christ. 14We must no longer be children,
tossed to and fro and blown about by every wind of doctrine, by people's trickery, by their craftiness in deceitful

[s]Other ancient authorities add *of our Lord Jesus Christ* [t]Gk *fatherhood* [u]Other ancient authorities add *first*

A Prayer Can Restore Confidence

CONSIDER THIS 3:14–21 Our troubles can easily cause us to lose the larger picture about life. Daily routines and pressures can create doubts about our significance. And because we are bound in a world of time, it's easy to assume that difficulties such as sickness, conflict, loneliness, insecurity, or fear will become a permanent state of affairs.

The Ephesian believers lived with a lot of pressure. Their faith was born in a crucible of riots, courtroom conflict, and economic change (Acts 19:23–40). Later, when Paul wrote this letter to the Ephesians, he encouraged them to develop and maintain God's perspective on their lives and faith:

- ***Looking back* he rehearsed what God had done for them before they were even born (1:3–8).**
- ***Looking forward* he listed the future benefits that their faith would bring (1:9–14).**
- ***In the meantime* he prayed that they would be aware of and comprehend these realities, and experience God's power (1:15–23). He also prayed that their identity would be rooted in eternal truths and in God's present power in them (3:14–21).**

What doubts and stresses have caused you to lose perspective? Ephesians suggests that you relax—and join Paul in prayer. Take a look at the big picture of God's work on your behalf. It began long before you

(continued on next page)

scheming. [15]But speaking the truth in love, we must grow up in every way into him who is the head, into Christ, [16]from whom the whole body, joined and knit together by every ligament with which it is equipped, as each part is working properly, promotes the body's growth in building itself up in love.

Walk Differently than Unbelievers

17 Now this I affirm and insist on in the Lord: you must no longer live as the Gentiles live, in the futility of their minds. [18]They are darkened in their understanding, alienated from the life of God because of their ignorance and hardness of heart. [19]They have lost all sensitivity and have abandoned themselves to licentiousness, greedy to practice every kind of impurity. [20]That is not the way you learned Christ! [21]For surely you have heard about him and were

4:22–24

taught in him, as truth is in Jesus. [22]You were taught to put away your former way of life, your old self, corrupt and deluded by its lusts, [23]and to be renewed in the spirit of your minds, [24]and to clothe yourselves with the new self, created according to the likeness of God in true righteousness and holiness.

Walk in Love

25 So then, putting away falsehood, let all of us speak the truth to our neighbors, for we are members of one another. [26]Be angry but do not sin; do not let the sun go down on your anger, [27]and do not make room for the devil.

4:28 see pg. 670

[28]Thieves must give up stealing; rather let them labor and work honestly with their own hands, so as to have something to share with the needy. [29]Let no evil talk come out of your mouths, but only what is useful for building up,[v] as there is need, so that your words may give grace to those who hear. [30]And do not grieve the Holy Spirit of God, with which you were marked with a seal for the day of redemption. [31]Put away from you all bitterness and wrath and anger and wrangling and slander, together with all malice, [32]and be kind to one another, tenderhearted, forgiving one another, as God in Christ has

[v]Other ancient authorities read *building up faith*

Are You Fashion-conscious?

A CLOSER LOOK 4:22–24 *People who want to succeed in the business world know that they must pay careful attention to how they look. In vv. 22–24, Paul tells how to "dress for success," spiritually speaking: take off the old and put on the new. What do the fashions of faith look like? See "New Creatures with New Character," Gal. 5:22–23.*

(continued from previous page)

arrived and long before your first steps in Christ. It will continue long after you pass from this life. Seeing things in this way can lend perspective to the harsh realities that may dominate your life right now.

QUOTE UNQUOTE

CONSIDER THIS 4:12 *Equipping the saints for the work of ministry (v. 12) is needed today more than ever:*

The First Reformation which came to its climax more than three centuries ago produced a great new power, by something analogous to a change of gears . . . . [T]he crucial step was that of making available the open Bible . . . .

Now, after more than three centuries, we can, if we will, change gears again. Our opportunity for a big step lies in opening the ministry to the ordinary Christian in much the same manner that our ancestors opened Bible reading to the ordinary Christian. To do this means, in one sense, the inauguration of a new Reformation while in another it means the logical completion of the earlier Reformation in which the implications of the position taken were neither fully understood nor loyally followed.

Elton Trueblood, *Your Other Vocation*, pp. 31–32

FROM DEADBEAT TO DONOR

CONSIDER THIS 4:28 **Does Christ affect people's work life? Yes, and Paul gives a concrete illustration of what "clothe yourselves with the new self" means (vv. 24, 28). After Christ comes into his life, a person who has been a no-account thief stops stealing and takes an honest job. He becomes a contributing, productive member of society, doing good work. As a result, he is able to provide for his own needs and those of his family.**

But the transformation doesn't stop there. As God prospers him through his labor, he is able to give money away to help meet the needs of others. Christ changes a deadbeat into a donor!

How is Christ transforming your perspective on work and giving?

One reason that Christ has such a profound effect on people's work is that He gives it meaning and value. See "People at Work," Heb. 2:7.

The Bible has more to say about Christian character in the workplace. See "Who's the Boss?" Col. 3:22–24, and "Your 'Workstyle,'" Titus 2:9–10.

TIME FOR A CHECKUP

CONSIDER THIS 5:1–18 **How can we evaluate the quality of our faith? Are there any ways to assess spiritual progress and growth? Yes, Paul gives us a number of them here in Ephesians 5.**

Ephesians can be viewed as two halves of one big picture about giving

(continued on next page)

5:1–18

5 forgiven you.[w] 1Therefore be imitators of God, as beloved children,
2and live in love, as Christ loved us[x] and gave himself up
for us, a fragrant offering and sacrifice to God.
3 But fornication and impurity of any kind, or greed,
must not even be mentioned among you, as is proper
among saints. 4Entirely out of place is obscene, silly, and
vulgar talk; but instead, let there be thanksgiving. 5Be sure
of this, that no fornicator or impure person, or one who is
greedy (that is, an idolater), has any inheritance in the
kingdom of Christ and of God.

Walk as Children of Light

6 Let no one deceive you with empty words, for because
of these things the wrath of God comes on those who are
disobedient. 7Therefore do not be associated with them.
8For once you were darkness, but now in the Lord you are
light. Live as children of light— 9for the fruit of the light is
found in all that is good and right and true. 10Try to find
out what is pleasing to the Lord. 11Take no part in the unfruitful works of darkness, but instead expose them. 12For
it is shameful even to mention what such people do secretly; 13but everything exposed by the light becomes visible, 14for everything that becomes visible is light. Therefore
it says,

"Sleeper, awake!
Rise from the dead,
and Christ will shine on you."

15 Be careful then how you live, not as unwise people
but as wise, 16making the most of the time, because the
days are evil. 17So do not be foolish, but understand what
the will of the Lord is. 18Do not get drunk with wine, for
that is debauchery; but be filled with the Spirit, 19as you
sing psalms and hymns and spiritual songs among yourselves, singing and making melody to the Lord in your
hearts, 20giving thanks to God the Father at all times and
for everything in the name of our Lord Jesus Christ.

[w]Other ancient authorities read *us* [x]Other ancient authorities read *you*

A Lifestyle of Submission

A CLOSER LOOK 5:21 *Christ calls His people to a lifestyle of submission instead of selfish ambition (v. 21). The New Testament teaches that believers are to submit themselves to God, to their leaders, and to other believers. But what exactly does that mean? See "Submission," James 4:7.*

Instructions to Husbands and Wives

5:21

21 Be subject to one another out of
reverence for Christ.
22 Wives, be subject to your husbands as you are to the
Lord. 23For the husband is the head of the wife just as
Christ is the head of the church, the body of which he is
the Savior. 24Just as the church is subject to Christ, so also
wives ought to be, in everything, to their husbands.
25 Husbands, love your wives, just as Christ loved the
church and gave himself up for her, 26in order to make her
holy by cleansing her with the washing of water by the
word, 27so as to present the church to himself in splendor,
without a spot or wrinkle or anything of the kind—yes, so
that she may be holy and without blemish. 28In the same
way, husbands should love their wives as they do their own

(Bible text continued on page 676)

A New Perspective on Marriage

CONSIDER THIS
5:21–29

In a great many pagan marriages of the first century, the husband was much older than his wife. He frequented other partners for sex, taking on a wife only to father legitimate children. Thus a girl of 13 or 14 entered an arranged marriage, frequently against her will and often with a man she had never previously met. There was little communication, cooperation, or affection—or expectation of these.

But new life in Christ called for new patterns in marriage (vv. 21–29). Paul instructed the husband to love his wife and seek her personal development—a radically new idea in that culture. The wife was to respond with commitment and loyalty. Her submission was not subordination but a wholehearted response to her husband's love.

New life in Christ also called for "A New View of Sexuality," 1 Cor. 7:3–6.

(continued from previous page)

and receiving faith. Chapters 1–3 describe what God has done for us in Christ. Chapters 4–6 describe what we are to do in response to what God has done for us.

We are called to live for God and to be imitators of God (5:1), just as children follow after the patterns seen in their parents. Here are some of the patterns that a godly lifestyle would include:

(1) Living in love, which means giving of ourselves sacrificially for the benefit of others, just as Christ has done for us (v. 2).
(2) Forsaking selfish pursuits such as self-seeking immorality and ruthless greed (vv. 3, 5).
(3) Replacing filthy talk, flippant chatter, and unkind jesting with communication rooted in thanksgiving to God and affirmation of others (vv. 4, 20).
(4) Exercising discernment about what we are told so as not to be susceptible to trickery from others (vv. 6–7, 15).
(5) Bowing out from situations where evil is the agenda (vv. 11–12).
(6) Managing our time well (v. 16).

Perhaps you'll want to develop your own list of Christlike patterns from this passage and others. Consider asking a close believing friend to assess your progress over several days or weeks. Allow these patterns of godliness to affect your own life before using them to evaluate others (Matt. 7:1–6).

The New Testament offers several portraits of what a godly lifestyle would look like. See "New Creatures with New Character," Gal. 5:22–23.

CONSIDER THIS
5:21—6:4

The Family: A Call to Long-Term Work

"Family planning" is a controversial topic today that evokes strong feelings and images. But there is a place for "biblical family planning" in light of the reality of family life as a decades-long process to which God calls His people. Indeed, the family, along with work, is a focal point of life as God has designed it. That's why Paul devoted so much space in Ephesians to the issues of married couples (5:22–33), children (6:1–3), and fathers (6:4).

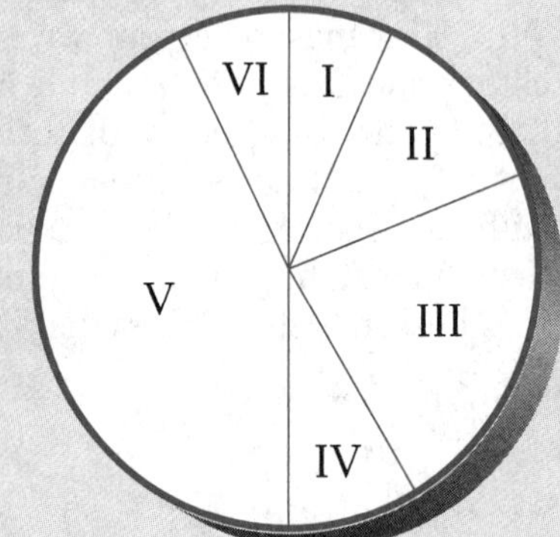

If a couple marry in their mid-20s and live into their mid-70s still married, they will spend 50 or more years of life together. That's a substantial commitment! One would never enter a business contract for that length of time without clarifying the work and costs involved. Yet do young people have any idea of the lifetime of work they are taking on when they repeat their marriage vows? Often not.

Perhaps it would help to know that there are roughly six phases of marriage. Each one requires husband and wife to work together as a team, combining their unique temperaments and strengths. As with any team activity, they must pull in the same direction if they expect to complete all six phases with their marriage intact.

Of course, not every couple or family follows the pattern outlined below. But what matters is not that a family adhere to a certain timetable, but that it recognize that there are seasons of family life, and that building relationships is a lifelong process. The following six periods are by no means distinct categories, but overlap quite a bit.

I. The Honeymoon Years

During this first period of marriage, two people from different family experiences and value systems begin to discover one another. Differences and similarities surface in areas such as finances, sexuality, faith, use of time, and personal habits. Each difference affords an opportunity for conflict and, hopefully, growth. Patterns that the couple establishes during this phase will tend to affect what happens during the next five phases.

The honeymoon typically ends with the birth or adoption of the first child. For some, it ends with the realization that there will be no children. In all too many cases, it ends with the dissolution of the marriage itself.

II. The Childbearing Years

The birth or adoption of the first child brings a rapid transition. New babies, though welcome, can feel like an "invasion," an abrupt intrusion into what up until then had been a relatively cozy twosome. Often the father particularly feels displaced as mother and infant bond through birth, nursing, and nurturing.

The childbearing years can be extraordinarily draining. Young parents often give out more than they take in from their children. They may be able to offset the deficit somewhat by revisiting some of the practices that they so valued during the "courtship" and "honeymoon" phases of their relationship. They'll need to "deposit" lots of emotional support into each other's "reserve bank accounts" if they hope to maintain a positive balance during the demanding child-focused years.

This period typically ends when the last child begins school.

III. The Child-rearing Years

As a couple's children pass through elementary and high school, new authority figures emerge, such as teachers, television personalities, scout masters, coaches, music teachers, youth pastors, and perhaps most influential of all, peers, both friends and bullies. Before, parents had the final word. Now others suggest or impose new values, decisions, and schedules.

That makes child rearing a great time for parents to help children think about themselves and the world. Discussion, prayer, and support can create an atmosphere of unity that is essential if young people are to face the many factors that compete with the family. If the parents are secure in their "bond of perfection," they can help their children tackle the tough issues—issues they themselves have been dealing with all along.

During the child-rearing years, which may stretch out over two decades or more, parents need to keep making deposits in their mate's bank of emotional support. One way to do that is to keep dating and to guard time alone with each other. Again, too many marriages never make it through the stresses and strains of the childbearing and child-rearing phases, and the families break apart.

IV. The Child-launching Years

With the onset of puberty, children begin to notice the opposite sex and discover "love" outside the home. This is the beginning of the "leaving" process, as children become adults in their own right and take steps toward independence, usually through work, college, and/or marriage.

In this phase, young adults tend to experience numerous "trial runs" of freedom, not all of which succeed. It helps for parents to remain available when their children have lost their way. Failure, whether in academic studies, financial matters, experiments in "freedom," or sexuality, offer important moments for learning, and sometimes for forgiveness. If young people never experience the freedom to fail, they may never learn to leave the nest and fly on their own.

V. The Empty-Nest Years

They're gone! Now it's just two again. Now the couple will find out whether they've grown together or apart over the years. Unfortunately, by this point many couples have developed a child- or career-centered marriage rather than a strong relationship between themselves. Though understandable, that can be tragic since the empty-nest phase typically outlasts the first four phases combined. No wonder so many marriages come apart as soon as the children have grown up and left. The couples have built their lives around their kids, and now they have nothing left in common.

By contrast, though, empty-nest couples who have built into each other can experience a joyous recovery of full attention to their marriage. They have more time to spend with each other, and often more money to spend. They may also have the bright privilege of welcoming grandchildren into the world.

VI. The Alone Years

The death of either spouse brings the survivor into the final phase of family life. For so many years, the person has lived in relation to his or her mate and children. Now, the sudden experience of being alone again exposes the level of individual growth experienced during marriage. Some couples never establish patterns that make for strong individuality. They become so intertwined and dependent on each other that the loss of the partner causes the surviving mate to crash or wither. But if the person has cultivated other relationships among friends and family and developed personal interests and hobbies, life can still be somewhat joyful, despite the painful loss of one's lifetime partner.

Where is your family among these six phases of family life? God calls couples to a lifetime of work. Are you practicing "biblical family planning" with a view toward the long haul? ◆

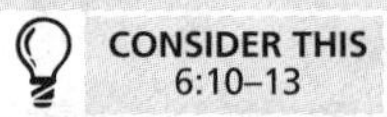

Who Is the Enemy?

No matter who we are or what we do for a living, all of us are bound to face struggles in life. Financial pressures, job loss, personality conflicts, time demands, injury, illness, emotional pain, death—as Job's friend Eliphaz wryly noted, "Human beings are born to trouble just as sparks fly upward" (Job 5:7).

When faced with setbacks like these, people often tend to blame God for their circumstances, or other people, or even themselves. However, Scripture urges us to consider another, more sinister source for troubles, what Paul called the "principalities" and "powers" in the heavenly places. Our struggle is not against God or other people but against "spiritual forces of evil" (Eph. 6:11–12).

Certainly there's a place for human responsibility. But Paul is telling us that ultimately, people are not our enemy, sin and Satan are. If we intend to stand up to the onslaught of these powerful adversaries, we must fight them on their own turf—the spiritual—with weapons appropriate to the conflict (vv. 14–18).

Of course, it can be very difficult to persuade people of that in this day and age. Secular thinking dismisses all talk of the supernatural realm as so much superstition left over from the ancient world. At the same time, advocates of the occult have stimulated people's curiosity and have developed in many a fascination with evil rather than a determination to overcome it.

Nevertheless, the Bible is straightforward. It declares that evil forces exist in the spiritual realm that have a substantial influence on the world and human events. Paul refers to them as "rulers." The Greek word is often used in the New Testament, sometimes, as here, referring to an order of spirits that had power over human life. Elsewhere the word refers to human rulers (Titus 3:1), or sometimes to any type of ruler other than God Himself (Eph. 1:21; Col. 2:10).

Sometimes the presence of evil powers is evident, as in demon possession (see Luke 11:14). However, Satan and his hosts have numerous other ways to influence human activity and carry out their ultimate purpose, the capture of people away from God. For example, two means through which they can work are:

Belief systems. Philosophies and worldviews have a powerful effect on the way people live. By introducing lies into the very principles upon which entire societies are based, the evil one can wreak incredible havoc on the world.

Consider, for instance, the beliefs that fueled Nazism. Eventually they led to the most destructive war in history, which claimed tens of millions of lives. They brought about extermination camps in which millions of Jews and others were slaughtered. They disrupted entire nations and economies. Indeed, the aftermath of that dark era is still with us.

Again, none of this is to suggest that humans are excused from responsibility. But behind the visible, knowable element of human choice, one can detect or at least suspect the activity of forces with supernatural ability and evil intent, prompting people to accept and act on falsehoods.

That's why we cannot be too careful about the ideas we embrace, whether they come from religious teachers, educators, government leaders, or the media. Ideas have consequences, both in individual lives and entire nations. Our best protection against deception is a grounding in biblical truth (Eph. 6:14).

Human institutions and leaders. Human systems and people in authority make ideal targets of Satanic activity because of their influence on others. In the first century, one has only to consider the character and especially the spiritual choices of such groups as the Pharisees (Matt. 23:13–15, 31–36), the Jewish council (Acts 7:51–60), the Herods (see Acts 12:1–2), Caiaphas (see Matt. 26:3), Pilate (John 18:37–38; 19:10–11; 1 Cor. 2:8), and the emperors, especially Nero (see Acts 25:12), to appreciate the counterattack that Satan must have launched after the coming of Christ and the founding of the church.

Scripture asserts that human authorities are established by God to carry out good purposes (Rom. 13:1–7). But because they are operated by humans, they are vulnerable to the influence of evil spiritual forces.

Paul knew that all too well. As he wrote the Ephesians, he sat chained to a Roman soldier for no other crime than the preaching of the gospel (Eph. 6:19–20). On another occasion, he instructed Timothy, the pastor at Ephesus, to have the people pray "for kings and all who are in high positions, so that we may lead a quiet and peaceable life in all godliness and dignity" because God "desires everyone to be saved and to come to the knowledge of the truth" (1 Tim. 2:1–4).

There are many other ways in which the powers of darkness attempt to subvert the purposes of God. But it is pointless for us to try to determine at any moment whether something is being "caused" by a wicked spiritual power. A preoccupation with that leads only to foolish speculation.

Paul gives us a far more positive, constructive strategy for standing firm against our spiritual enemies: "put on the whole armor of God" (Eph. 6:11). That armor is made up entirely of spiritual weapons: truth, righteousness, the gospel of peace, faith, salvation, the word of God, and prayer (vv. 14–18). By learning to wear and to wield these powerful armaments, we can resist the carefully laid plans of the devil and, when the fight is over, still be standing. ◆

WORK—A PLATFORM FOR EVANGELISM?

CONSIDER THIS 6:5–9 **Our jobs put us in touch with people like no other activity. For 40 or more hours a week we toil, laugh, struggle, and interact with others to accomplish tasks. For that reason, many Christians view their workplace as a primary platform for spreading the gospel. Is that legitimate?**

It is certainly legitimate to treat our workplace as an opportunity for unbelievers to see Christianity by looking at us. Indeed, Paul challenges us to display a godly workstyle for that reason (Titus 2:9–10). However, we must never emphasize verbal witness to the detriment of our work, as if God sends us into the work world *only* to use it as a platform for evangelism.

Employers rightly look down on workers who are intruders, deceivers, or sluggards. In Ephesians 6:5–9, Paul challenges us to work with "singleness of heart" and to pay close attention to the work itself, which he calls "doing the will of God." How many ways can you witness to your faith while performing your job responsibly and effectively?

5:21–29 see pg. 671
bodies. He who loves his wife loves himself. 29For no one ever hates his own
body, but he nourishes and tenderly cares for it, just as
Christ does for the church, 30because we are members of
his body.[y] 31"For this reason a man will leave his father and
mother and be joined to his wife, and the two will become
one flesh." 32This is a great mystery, and I am applying it to
Christ and the church. 33Each of you, however, should love
his wife as himself, and a wife should respect her husband.

Instructions to Children and Fathers

6 Children, obey your parents in the Lord,[z] for this is
right. 2"Honor your father and mother"—this is the
first commandment with a promise: 3"so that it may be well
with you and you may live long on the earth."

5:21—6:4 see pg. 672
4 And, fathers, do not provoke your
children to anger, but bring them up in
the discipline and instruction of the Lord.

Instructions to Slaves and Masters

6:5
5 Slaves, obey your earthly masters
with fear and trembling, in singleness of
heart, as you obey Christ; 6not only while being watched,
and in order to please them, but as slaves of Christ, doing
the will of God from the heart. 7Render service with enthu-
6:5–9
siasm, as to the Lord and not to men and
women, 8knowing that whatever good
we do, we will receive the same again from the Lord,
whether we are slaves or free.

6:5–9
9 And, masters, do the same to them.
Stop threatening them, for you know that
both of you have the same Master in heaven, and with him
there is no partiality.

Spiritual Warfare

6:10–13 see pg. 674
10 Finally, be strong in the Lord and
in the strength of his power. 11Put on the
whole armor of God, so that you may be able to stand
against the wiles of the devil. 12For our[a] struggle is not
against enemies of blood and flesh, but against the rulers,
against the authorities, against the cosmic powers of this

[y]Other ancient authorities add *of his flesh and of his bones* [z]Other ancient authorities lack *in the Lord* [a]Other ancient authorities read *your*

What is God's intention for everyday work? See "People at Work," Heb. 2:7.

Some employers have become so disappointed with the work of believers that they no longer hire Christians. See 1 Tim. 6:1–2.

A Promotion

A CLOSER LOOK 6:5–9 *What Paul wrote to "slaves" (v. 5) redefined their occupational status. They were no longer just Roman slaves—they were employees of Jesus Christ! See "Who's the Boss?" Col. 3:22–24.*

present darkness, against the spiritual forces of evil in the
heavenly places. 13Therefore take up the whole armor of
God, so that you may be able to withstand on that evil day,
and having done everything, to stand firm. 14Stand therefore, and fasten the belt of truth around your waist, and put
on the breastplate of righteousness. 15As shoes for your feet
put on whatever will make you ready to proclaim the
gospel of peace. 16With all of these,[b] take the shield of faith,
with which you will be able to quench all the flaming arrows of the evil one. 17Take the helmet of salvation, and the
sword of the Spirit, which is the word of God.

18 Pray in the Spirit at all times in every prayer and supplication. To that end keep alert and always persevere in
supplication for all the saints. 19Pray also for me, so that
when I speak, a message may be given to me to make
known with boldness the mystery of the gospel,[c] 20for
which I am an ambassador in chains. Pray that I may declare it boldly, as I must speak.

Concluding Matters

21 So that you also may know how I am and what I am
doing, Tychicus will tell you everything. He is a dear
brother and a faithful minister in the Lord. 22I am sending
him to you for this very purpose, to let you know how we
are, and to encourage your hearts.

23 Peace be to the whole community,[d] and love with
faith, from God the Father and the Lord Jesus Christ.
24Grace be with all who have an undying love for our Lord
Jesus Christ.[e]

[b]Or *In all circumstances* [c]Other ancient authorities lack *of the gospel* [d]Gk *to the brothers* [e]Other ancient authorities add *Amen*

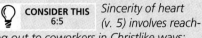

QUOTE UNQUOTE

CONSIDER THIS 6:5 *Sincerity of heart (v. 5) involves reaching out to coworkers in Christlike ways:*

The world is not a fun house hall of mirrors, everywhere reflecting distorted images of myself. The world is a wax museum of individuals needing to warm each other into full humanity through the touch of love.

Mark Quinn, Chicago public school teacher, "Five Guidelines to a Spirituality of Work"

The Letter of Paul to the

Philippians

Some of the most powerful writings in history have been penned by leaders imprisoned for political reasons. Something about the confinement, uncertainty, and (often) mistreatment these prisoners have suffered seems to have helped them focus their minds on their fundamental convictions.

But whereas many imprisoned authors take a martyr's posture and rail against whatever system is oppressing them, Paul sounded a radically different note in his "prison epistle" to the Philippians: he focused on the Christ-centered life, the hallmark of which is joy—a remarkable theme considering that he may have been facing execution (Phil. 1:23), most likely in Rome (1:13; 4:22).

Can Paul's message have any relevance to believers today who live in a free society without threat of imprisonment or death for practicing their religion? Yes, by showing what ultimately matters. In the midst of freedom, affluence, and opportunity, it's easy to lose perspective, to pay more attention to peripheral things that, while attractive, really have little value, rather than substantial things that have great value.

The ultimate value is Christ. Whether elevated to heights of glory or, like Paul, reduced to prisoner status, we need to center our lives on Christ. Whatever happens, we need to hold onto Him. He alone must be our ultimate source of contentment, joy, and life.

The ultimate value is Christ.

C O N T E N T S

A R T I C L E S

The Mind of Christ

The first church founded in the West was the church at Philippi (Acts 16:6–15). Living at a highly favored Roman military colony and a major crossroads on the Egnatian Way (one of the empire's "interstates"), the Philippians were proud and affluent. It's interesting that Paul's first convert was a businesswoman who sold purple, the most expensive of dyes, as valuable as gold and used for tribute and international trade (16:14).

Yet in writing to the believers in this prosperous community, Paul neither condemned the wealthy nor attacked profitable commerce. Rather, he emphasized Christ. Paul was well acquainted with position and power (Phil. 3:4–6). But he had surrendered everything to Christ and could say that "to me, living is Christ" (1:21), that he was a prisoner "for Christ" (1:13), and that "I regard everything as loss because of the surpassing value of knowing Christ" (3:8). Christ had laid hold of Paul (3:12) and Paul's sole passion was to bring glory to Him (3:8–9).

Paul longed for his friends in Philippi to have the same experience of Christ. He prayed that they would abound in Christ's love (1:9), that they would adopt Christ's mind (2:5–11), and that, like himself, they would follow in Christ's footsteps, experiencing His sufferings, death, and resurrection (3:10–11).

How could the Philippians translate their relationship with Christ into daily life? Paul told them that they would have to become "like-minded" with Christ and "set their minds on Christ." What would that look like? Paul painted a picture for them in 2:5–11. (Some scholars believe that this passage was an early hymn of the church. Could it have been among the songs Paul sang with Silas while in jail during his first visit to Philippi, Acts 16:25?)

For Christians in a prestigious city, Christ comes clothed in humility. Later, in Colossians, we see His power, glory, and lordship over creation emphasized. But here, Christ is shown to be human, vulnerable, and accessible. He lays down His rights and takes on a humble, virtually powerless posture of a servant.

Do you want honor and status, power and prestige? Our world offers them through selfish ambition and empty conceit (2:3). An alternative is the "lowliness of mind" that characterized Christ. In the short term, that may involve sacrifice and even suffering. But in the long run it means praise from God and joy in His pleasure. The path to glory is humility. The way to gain is loss. The way up is down. ◆

Philippi

Though "all roads led to Rome," much of the traffic to Rome from the east funneled through Philippi, which served as a gateway to Greece and Italy. To find out more about this strategic crossroads, *see "Philippi," Acts 16:12.*

Grace and Peace

1 Paul and Timothy, servants[a] of Christ Jesus,
To all the saints in Christ Jesus who are in Philippi,
with the bishops[b] and deacons:[c]
2 Grace to you and peace from God our Father and the
Lord Jesus Christ.

Thanks for the Philippians' Gift

3 I thank my God every time I remember you, 4con-
stantly praying with joy in every one of my prayers for all
of you, 5because of your sharing in the gospel from the first
day until now. 6I am confident of this, that the one who began a good work among you will bring it to completion by
the day of Jesus Christ. 7It is right for me to think this way
about all of you, because you hold me in your heart,[d] for all
of you share in God's grace[e] with me, both in my imprisonment and in the defense and confirmation of the gospel.
8For God is my witness, how I long for all of you with the
compassion of Christ Jesus. 9And this is my prayer, that
your love may overflow more and more with knowledge
and full insight 10to help you to determine what is best, so
that in the day of Christ you may be pure and blameless,
11having produced the harvest of righteousness that comes
through Jesus Christ for the glory and praise of God.

In Prison for the Gospel

1:12–18

12 I want you to know, beloved,[f] that
what has happened to me has actually
helped to spread the gospel, 13so that it has become known
throughout the whole imperial guard[g] and to everyone else
that my imprisonment is for Christ; 14and most of the
brothers and sisters,[f] having been made confident in the
Lord by my imprisonment, dare to speak the word[h] with
greater boldness and without fear.
15 Some proclaim Christ from envy and rivalry, but others from goodwill. 16These proclaim Christ out of love,
knowing that I have been put here for the defense of the
gospel; 17the others proclaim Christ out of selfish ambition,
not sincerely but intending to increase my suffering in my
imprisonment. 18What does it matter? Just this, that Christ
is proclaimed in every way, whether out of false motives or
true; and in that I rejoice.
Yes, and I will continue to rejoice, 19for I know that
through your prayers and the help of the Spirit of Jesus
Christ this will turn out for my deliverance. 20It is my eager
expectation and hope that I will not be put to shame in any

[a] Gk *slaves* [b] Or *overseers* [c] Or *overseers and helpers* [d] Or *because I hold you in my heart* [e] Gk *in grace* [f] Gk *brothers* [g] Gk *whole praetorium* [h] Other ancient authorities read *word of God*

PAUL'S BROAD PERSPECTIVE

CONSIDER THIS 1:12–18 *Paul was deeply committed to the truth and integrity of the gospel. But in vv. 12–18 he generously credits others who were doing ministry, even though they had impure motives.*

This sets an important example for Christians today who feel strong loyalty to their particular tradition or institution. Like Paul, we need to accept and celebrate the fact that other believers with different perspectives and approaches may be helping people and accomplishing tasks that we never could.

way, but that by my speaking with all boldness, Christ will
be exalted now as always in my body, whether by life or by
1:21 death. 21For to me, living is Christ and
dying is gain. 22If I am to live in the flesh,
that means fruitful labor for me; and I do not know which I
prefer. 23I am hard pressed between the two: my desire is to
depart and be with Christ, for that is far better; 24but to remain in the flesh is more necessary for you. 25Since I am
convinced of this, I know that I will remain and continue
with all of you for your progress and joy in faith, 26so that I
may share abundantly in your boasting in Christ Jesus
when I come to you again.

A Call to Stand Firm

27 Only, live your life in a manner worthy of the gospel
of Christ, so that, whether I come and see you or am absent
and hear about you, I will know that you are standing firm
in one spirit, striving side by side with one mind for the
faith of the gospel, 28and are in no way intimidated by your
opponents. For them this is evidence of their destruction,
but of your salvation. And this is God's doing. 29For he has
graciously granted you the privilege not only of believing in
Christ, but of suffering for him as well— 30since you are
having the same struggle that you saw I had and now hear
that I still have.

The Humble Example of Christ

2 If then there is any encouragement in Christ, any
consolation from love, any sharing in the Spirit, any
compassion and sympathy, 2make my joy complete: be of
the same mind, having the same love, being in full accord
2:3 see pg. 684 and of one mind. 3Do nothing from
selfish ambition or conceit, but in hu-
mility regard others as better than yourselves. 4Let each of
you look not to your own interests, but to the interests of
2:5–8 others. 5Let the same mind be in you that
was[i] in Christ Jesus,

6 who, though he was in the form of God,
did not regard equality with God
as something to be exploited,
7 but emptied himself,
taking the form of a slave,
being born in human likeness.
And being found in human form,
8 he humbled himself
and became obedient to the point of death—
even death on a cross.

(*Bible text continued on page 685*)

[i]Or *that you have*

To Live Is . . . ?

CONSIDER THIS 1:21 **Facing the prospect of his execution, Paul had to wrestle with what mattered most to him. It didn't take him long to come to a conclusion: Christ (v. 21). He felt that Christ not only made his life worth living, but death worth dying.**

What makes life worth living for you? Your family? Your work? The memory you hope to leave behind?

What makes death worth dying? Anything? Complete these thoughts:

- **"If I live for anything, it's . . . ."**
- **"Above all, I want to gain . . . ."**

Downward Mobility

CONSIDER THIS 2:5–8 *In contrast to the many people today who seek upward mobility, Jesus was, in a sense, downwardly mobile (vv. 5–8), moving from a position of ultimate power to utter powerlessness. In making this transition He set the best possible example of servant-leadership (see Matt. 20:25–28; John 13:2–17).*

However, in Colossians, Paul paints a different portrait of the Lord. See "Christ, the Lord of the World," Col. 1:15–18.

CONSIDER THIS
2:3

HUMILITY—THE SCANDALOUS VIRTUE

By recommending "humility" (v. 3), Paul fired a broadside at the Philippian culture—and our own. Like us, the Greeks and Romans exalted the lifestyles of the rich and famous!

Humility? Who would want that? A lowly or humble person meant a slave—a servile, groveling, wretched individual. Everyone assumed that lowly people had no intelligence, and everyone honored higher thinking and self-conceit.

The idea of humility seemed especially out of place in Philippi. The town hosted a Roman military colony by the pretentious-sounding name of *Colonia Augusta Julia Pilippensis.* Unlike other conquered towns, it enjoyed the *jus Italicum* (law of Italy), which made it a sort of small, self-governing version of the empire. Pride and self-importance were part and parcel of Philippian life in Paul's day (see "Philippi," Acts 16:12).

Yet Paul insisted that Christians there cultivate humility—but not a grovelling, abject demeanor. No, biblical humility means not thinking of oneself more highly than is true (Rom. 12:3), but rather acknowledging what one is—with all of one's strengths and weaknesses, pluses and minuses, successes and failures.

Far from self-loathing, real humility makes people so truthful that they don't hesitate, when necessary, to tell about even their good qualities.

Do you want true humility? It comes from seeing yourself in relation to God. No wonder, then, that this virtue ran counter to the Roman worldview. Their concept of a god was grossly similar to their concept of humanity, and the mythological Roman gods were hardly noble.

By contrast, Jesus praised the humble, "the poor in spirit," (literally, "the destitute," Matt. 5:3). What would that attitude look like? David expresses it in Psalm 39:4–6:

LORD, let me know my end,
and what is the measure of my days;
let me know how fleeting my life is.
You have made my days a few handbreadths,
and my lifetime is as nothing in your sight.
Surely everyone stands as a mere breath.
Surely everyone goes about like a shadow.
Surely for nothing they are in turmoil;
they heap up, and do not know who will gather.

Likewise, the prophet Micah warns that humility is one of three main virtues that ought to govern our lives (Mic. 6:8):

He has told you, O mortal, what is good;
and what does the Lord require of you
but to do justice, and to love kindness,
and to walk humbly with your God?

Humility is not an option for us as believers—it's an essential if we want to walk with God. Over and again, Scripture insists that we either walk humbly with Him, or not at all (Ps. 138:6; Is. 57:15; 1 Pet. 5:5–7). In short, a biblical lifestyle knows nothing of looking out chiefly for Number One. Just the opposite. With John the Baptist we need to say, "He must increase, but I must decrease" (John 3:30). ◆

Humility affects four crucial areas of everyday life:

(1) our view of ourselves. See "The Proper Measure of All Things," Heb. 2:6–8.
(2) our attitude toward controlling our circumstances. See "Who's in Charge Here?" James 4:13–16.
(3) how good or bad we think we are. See "Are People Basically Good?" Rom. 7:21.
(4) our perspective on status and power. See "Leadership Equals Humility?" Luke 22:24–27.

9 Therefore God also highly exalted him
and gave him the name
that is above every name,
10 so that at the name of Jesus
every knee should bend,
in heaven and on earth and under the earth,
11 and every tongue should confess
that Jesus Christ is Lord,
to the glory of God the Father.

Shine as Lights in the World

12 Therefore, my beloved, just as you have always
obeyed me, not only in my presence, but much more now
in my absence, work out your own salvation with fear and
trembling; 13for it is God who is at work in you, enabling
you both to will and to work for his good pleasure.

2:15

14 Do all things without murmuring
and arguing, 15so that you may be blame-
less and innocent, children of God without blemish in the
midst of a crooked and perverse generation, in which you
shine like stars in the world. 16It is by your holding fast to
the word of life that I can boast on the day of Christ that I
did not run in vain or labor in vain. 17But even if I am being poured out as a libation over the sacrifice and the offering of your faith, I am glad and rejoice with all of you—
18and in the same way you also must be glad and rejoice
with me.

Paul Hopes to Send Timothy and to Come Himself

19 I hope in the Lord Jesus to send Timothy to you
soon, so that I may be cheered by news of you. 20I have no
one like him who will be genuinely concerned for your
welfare. 21All of them are seeking their own interests, not
those of Jesus Christ. 22But Timothy's[j] worth you know,
how like a son with a father he has served with me in the
work of the gospel. 23I hope therefore to send him as soon
as I see how things go with me; 24and I trust in the Lord
that I will also come soon.

Epaphroditus Is on His Way

2:25
see pg. 686

25 Still, I think it necessary to send to
you Epaphroditus—my brother and co-
worker and fellow soldier, your messenger[k] and minister to
my need; 26for he has been longing for[l] all of you, and has
been distressed because you heard that he was ill. 27He was
indeed so ill that he nearly died. But God had mercy on
him, and not only on him but on me also, so that I would

[j]Gk *his* [k]Gk *apostle* [l]Other ancient authorities read *longing to see*

Honesty and Ethical Standards

CONSIDER THIS 2:15 **Paul called his generation "crooked and perverse" (v. 15). But was his generation much different than ours? According to the Gallup Poll:**

By a large margin the U.S. public believes that ethics and standards of honesty are getting worse. This is a view held by all age groups and in each socio-economic level.

The public also does not give very high marks to people in most of the 24 occupations tested in a Gallup Poll in terms of honesty and ethical standards. Here is the full list, with the percentages who say the honesty and ethical standards are very high or high:

"Are Their Standards High?"

Occupation	%
Clergymen	64
Druggists, pharmacists	61
Medical doctors	53
Dentists	51
College teachers	47
Engineers	46
Policemen	42
Bankers	38
TV reporters, commentators	33
Funeral directors	29
Newspaper reporters	26
Lawyers	24
Stockbrokers	19
Business executives	18
Senators	17
Building contractors	17
Local political officeholders	16
Congressmen	14
Realtors	13
State political officeholders	13
Insurance salesmen	13
Labor union leaders	12
Advertising practitioners	8
Car salesmen	6

(continued on next page)

(continued from previous page)

Given such a low opinion of the integrity of so many occupations, believers today have an outstanding opportunity to "shine as lights in the world" (v. 15).

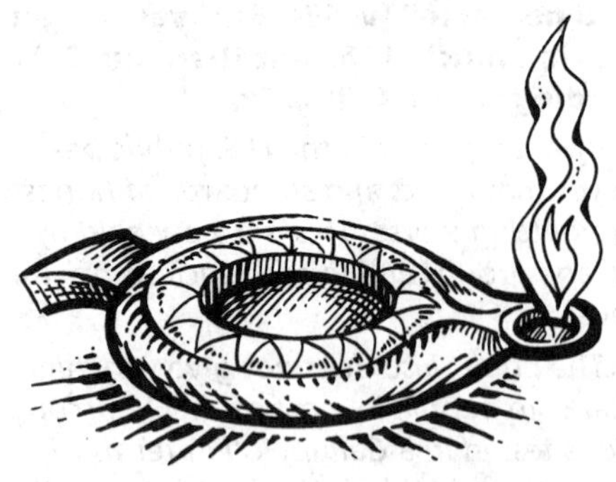

Paul wrote about the need for workplace Christians whose work and ethical integrity would be irresistibly attractive to coworkers. See "Your 'Workstyle,'" Titus 2:9–10.

not have one sorrow after another. 28I am the more eager to
send him, therefore, in order that you may rejoice at seeing
him again, and that I may be less anxious. 29Welcome him
then in the Lord with all joy, and honor such people, 30be-
cause he came close to death for the work of Christ,[m] risking his life to make up for those services that you could not
give me.

A Warning about Judaizers

3 Finally, my brothers and sisters,[n] rejoice[o] in the Lord.

To write the same things to you is not troublesome to me,
and for you it is a safeguard.
2 Beware of the dogs, beware of the evil workers, beware
of those who mutilate the flesh![p] 3For it is we who are the
circumcision, who worship in the Spirit of God[q] and boast
 3:4–6 in Christ Jesus and have no confidence in
the flesh— 4even though I, too, have rea-
son for confidence in the flesh.
If anyone else has reason to be confident in the flesh, I
have more: 5circumcised on the eighth day, a member of
the people of Israel, of the tribe of Benjamin, a Hebrew
born of Hebrews; as to the law, a Pharisee; 6as to zeal, a persecutor of the church; as to righteousness under the law,
blameless.

[m]Other ancient authorities read *of the Lord* [n]Gk *my brothers* [o]Or *farewell* [p]Gk *the mutilation* [q]Other ancient authorities read *worship God in spirit*

Personality Profile: Epaphroditus

FOR YOUR INFO 2:25

Name means: "Charming."

Not to be confused with: Epaphras, an associate of Paul's from Colossae (Col. 1:7; 4:12), whose name also means "charming."

Occupation: Unknown, but he may have been a coworker with Paul in the gospel ministry, for the apostle described him as a brother, fellow worker, and fellow soldier.

Best known today as: The messenger sent by the church at Philippi to take a gift to Paul, who was under house arrest in Rome, and also the bearer of Paul's letter back to the Philippian believers.

What Really Matters

3:7–14 7 Yet whatever gains I had, these I
have come to regard as loss because of
Christ. 8More than that, I regard everything as loss because
of the surpassing value of knowing Christ Jesus my Lord.
For his sake I have suffered the loss of all things, and I regard them as rubbish, in order that I may gain Christ 9and
be found in him, not having a righteousness of my own
that comes from the law, but one that comes through faith in
Christ,[r] the righteousness from God based on faith. 10I want
to know Christ[s] and the power of his resurrection and the
sharing of his sufferings by becoming like him in his death,
11if somehow I may attain the resurrection from the dead.
12 Not that I have already obtained this or have already
reached the goal;[t] but I press on to make it my own, because Christ Jesus has made me his own. 13Beloved,[u] I do
not consider that I have made it my own;[v] but this one
thing I do: forgetting what lies behind and straining forward to what lies ahead, 14I press on toward the goal for the

[r]Or *through the faith of Christ* [s]Gk *him* [t]Or *have already been made perfect* [u]Gk *Brothers* [v]Other ancient authorities read *my own yet*

Paul's Drivenness

CONSIDER THIS 3:4–6 *As we read Paul's description of his younger days (vv. 4–6), we discover a profound drivenness, as if he were out to prove something. Several clues suggest that he probably was. He was born outside of Palestine, in Tarsus, rather than in Judea. He devoted his life to intensive study of the Law. He attacked Christians with unusual vengeance. Perhaps it all added up to an intense desire to be accepted by the Jewish society in Jerusalem.*

There are two major ways that minorities and other outsiders cope with rejection or discrimination by the larger society. One is to turn inward and refuse to participate in the dominant culture. The other is to remove or diminish differences and blend in with the majority. Perhaps one might be accepted, even if never treated as an equal. Paul seems possibly to have chosen the latter course.

Taking Stock

CONSIDER THIS 3:7–14 **In Philippians 3, Paul takes stock of his life to determine what he has done that counts and what doesn't. His list of qualities and the conclusions he draws offer some important guideposts to help us assess our motives for and definitions of success:**

(1) What does success look like to you? How have you arrived at that definition? What or who has influenced your vision of a successful life? What role, if any, have God's perspectives and purposes been given in your definition?

(2) What have you given up or sacrificed in order to pursue success?

(3) What have you determined to be worth your investment of time, energy, and/or money?

(4) How have your priorities and loyalties changed over time? Why?

(5) In what ways do you think God and His purposes are served by the life you are pursuing?

Leading by Example

CONSIDER THIS 3:17 **As Paul recognized (v. 17), leaders always lead by personal example, whether they are aware of it or not. And their example extends far beyond the nature of the task at hand. People pattern their motives and values after executives, supervisors, and other leaders.**

Paul encouraged others to follow his example. What sort of example do you set for others? Are you aware of how you influence them? Are you close enough to the people around you, and in touch enough with your own tendencies, to have confidence in how others might follow you?

Euodia and Syntyche

CONSIDER THIS 4:2 *Paul described Euodia and Syntyche (v. 2) as having "struggled" with him in the gospel (v. 3). His choice of words is significant. Elsewhere he affirmed other women who helped with the spread of the gospel (see "Paul's Female Coworkers," Rom. 16:12).*

Paul doesn't tell us about the exact nature of these two women's work, but he hints at the effectiveness of their ministry: he was eager to have them settle their dispute, probably because it crippled their work with others.

prize of the heavenly[w] call of God in Christ Jesus. 15Let
those of us then who are mature be of the same mind; and if
you think differently about anything, this too God will reveal
to you. 16Only let us hold fast to what we have attained.

Paul Says to Follow His Example

3:17 see pg. 687 17 Brothers and sisters,[x] join in imitating me, and observe those who live ac-
cording to the example you have in us. 18For many live as
enemies of the cross of Christ; I have often told you of
them, and now I tell you even with tears. 19Their end is destruction; their god is the belly; and their glory is in their
shame; their minds are set on earthly things. 20But our citizenship[y] is in heaven, and it is from there that we are expecting a Savior, the Lord Jesus Christ. 21He will transform
the body of our humiliation[z] that it may be conformed to
the body of his glory,[a] by the power that also enables him to
make all things subject to himself. 4 1Therefore, my
brothers and sisters,[b] whom I love and long for, my joy
and crown, stand firm in the Lord in this way, my beloved.

A Word to Euodia and Syntyche

4:2 2 I urge Euodia and I urge Syntyche
to be of the same mind in the Lord. 3Yes,

[w]Gk *upward* [x]Gk *Brothers* [y]Or *commonwealth* [z]Or *our humble bodies* [a]Or *his glorious body* [b]Gk *my brothers*

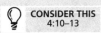

CONSIDER THIS 4:10–13

A Lifestyle of Contentment

Paul sounds so positive in vv. 10–13, so confident! It would be easy to assume that life was rosy when he wrote these words. But where was he? According to 1:12–14, in prison—quite possibly in Rome, facing a death sentence!

Given that sobering context, this passage speaks powerfully to the issue of contentment, not only with material possessions, but with circumstances as well.

Paul makes no idle boast here. He knew firsthand the wealth and privileges of prominence in the Jewish community and of Roman citizenship (3:4–6; Acts 22:3–5, 25–29; 26:4–5). On the other hand, he had suffered extraordinary hardships in his work—jailings, beatings, stonings, forcible ejection from several towns, shipwrecks—to say nothing of emotional and spiritual disappointments and setbacks (2 Cor. 11:23–33).

Either extreme would test a person's character. What was Paul's secret? Christ "who strengthens me." Rather than looking to the possessions he had or didn't have, or

4:3 and I ask you also, my loyal companion,[c]
help these women, for they have strug-
gled beside me in the work of the gospel, together with
Clement and the rest of my co-workers, whose names are
in the book of life.

How to Have the Peace of God

4 Rejoice[d] in the Lord always; again I will say, Rejoice.[d]
5Let your gentleness be known to everyone. The Lord is
near. 6Do not worry about anything, but in everything by
prayer and supplication with thanksgiving let your requests
be made known to God. 7And the peace of God, which surpasses all understanding, will guard your hearts and your
minds in Christ Jesus.

4:8 8 Finally, beloved,[e] whatever is true,
whatever is honorable, whatever is just,
whatever is pure, whatever is pleasing, whatever is com-
mendable, if there is any excellence and if there is anything

[c]Or *loyal Syzygus* [d]Or *Farewell* [e]Gk *brothers*

A New Way of Thinking

A CLOSER LOOK 4:8

The new way of thinking that Paul summarizes in v. 8 is only one of several pictures that Scripture paints of "New Creatures with New Character." See Gal. 5:22–23.

to his circumstances, good or bad, he looked to Christ to satisfy his needs. The result, he says, was contentment.

This passage poses a strong challenge to Christians living and working in today's society. Some of us live at the upper levels of material prosperity—"abounding," as Paul puts it. The temptation is to forget God (Luke 12:16–21). Likewise, much in our culture urges us to feel discontent with our lot—to long for more, for bigger, for better. Jesus warns against that attitude ("Watch Out for Greed!" Luke 12:15). On the other hand, failures and disappointments can also draw us away from trusting in the God who cares (see Luke 12:22–34). ◆

Where does contentment end and responsibility begin? What about setting goals and taking initiative? See "A Command to Work," 2 Thess. 3:6–12.

Women and the Growth of Christianity

FOR YOUR INFO 4:3

Euodia and Syntyche (v. 2) were only two of the many women who played a role in the spread of the gospel and the development of the early church.

What Women Did

Activity	Reference
Prayed	Acts 1:14
Received the Spirit	2:17
Were converted	2:41
Hosted the church in their homes	2:46–47; Col. 4:15
Received help	Acts 6:1–2
Were thrown in prison	8:3
Helped those in need	9:39
Were raised from the dead	9:40
Aided Paul and his companions	16:15
Were freed from evil spirits	16:18
Were often the first converts in a city	17:34
Traveled with Paul	18:18
Taught others	18:26
Served as couriers for Paul's letters	Rom. 16:1
Excelled in ministry and were described as "among the apostles"	Rom. 16:7, according to one possible translation
Worked alongside men in proclaiming the gospel	Phil. 4:3

Women also played a major part in Jesus' life and work. See "The Women around Jesus," John 19:25. For names of some of the women who worked alongside Paul, see the table, "Paul's Female Coworkers," Rom. 16:12.

worthy of praise, think about[f] these things. 9 Keep
on doing the things that you have learned and received and heard and seen in me, and the God of
peace will be with you.

Praise for the Philippians' Gift

4:10–13
see pg. 688

10 I rejoice[g] in the Lord
greatly that now at last you have
revived your concern for me; indeed, you were
concerned for me, but had no opportunity to show
it.[h] 11 Not that I am referring to being in need; for I
have learned to be content with whatever I have.
12 I know what it is to have little, and I know what
it is to have plenty. In any and all circumstances I
have learned the secret of being well-fed and of going hungry, of having plenty and of being in need.
13 I can do all things through him who strengthens
me. 14 In any case, it was kind of you to share my
distress.

15 You Philippians indeed know that in the
early days of the gospel, when I left Macedonia, no
church shared with me in the matter of giving and
receiving, except you alone. 16 For even when I was
in Thessalonica, you sent me help for my needs
more than once. 17 Not that I seek the gift, but I
seek the profit that accumulates to your account.
18 I have been paid in full and have more than
enough; I am fully satisfied, now that I have received from Epaphroditus the gifts you sent, a fragrant offering, a sacrifice acceptable and pleasing
to God. 19 And my God will fully satisfy every need
of yours according to his riches in glory in Christ
Jesus. 20 To our God and Father be glory forever
and ever. Amen.

Greetings for Everyone

21 Greet every saint in Christ Jesus. The friends[i]
who are with me greet you. 22 All the saints greet
you, especially those of the emperor's household.

23 The grace of the Lord Jesus Christ be with
your spirit.[j]

[f]Gk *take account of* [g]Gk *I rejoiced* [h]Gk lacks *to show it*

[i]Gk *brothers* [j]Other ancient authorities add *Amen*

The Letter of Paul to the

Colossians

Can Christianity compete in an age of "Star Wars," New Age thinking, and occult metaphysics? Absolutely! In fact, not only can the faith hold its own, it can be expected to prevail over competing worldviews and systems of thought. It happened before at Colossae.

Christians at Colossae, like many Christians today, were fond of mixing and matching the truths of Christ with ideas and practices from the surrounding non-Christian culture. The results were sometimes wild and always destructive. Some fell into extreme forms of legalism. Others took liberties with their "freedom" in Christ and succumbed to gross immorality. The doctrines of the faith were mingled with incompatible mysteries and the integrity of the gospel was compromised. As a result, Colossian Christianity was hard to distinguish from other religions of the day.

Sound familiar? If so, pay attention to Colossians. It speaks directly to the same kind of situation that exists today. Rather than conceding the idea of Christ as one god among many, Colossians establishes Him as God alone (capital "G")—*the* preeminent Lord of the universe, Creator of all things, the only One deserving of honor, worship, and obedience. If Philippians presents Christ in His humility (Phil. 2:5–11), Colossians presents Him in His exaltation.

In a day of moral and philosophical relativism, when many people hold to the idea that "what's true for you may not be true for me" and "all religions are basically the same," Colossians sounds a clarion call to a crucial absolute: Jesus is Lord! That made all the difference in the first century. It still does today.

CONTENTS

ARTICLES

The Dangers of Syncretism

First-century Colossae was an ideological swamp into which three main cultural streams drained. The first was Hellenism, the vestiges of Greek civilization that had dominated the world before the Romans. Hellenism brought a "dualistic" view of the world, the idea that things are either material or spiritual. A second stream was a form of Judaism that tended to be rigid and puritanical, leading to outright withdrawal from and condemnation of the world. A third influence was the local pagan culture. This included superstitious occultism and primitive, mystical rites.

These three streams blended together into a pseudo-philosophical swamp that mired the Colossian church in debates, divisions, and depravity. The problem was one of syncretism. *Syncretism involves the confusion of various ideas, beliefs, and practices.*

The syncretist has a mind like a blender. The person throws in notions from any number of systems of thought—even notions that contradict each other. Then they are ground into a single philosophical stew to generate a system that satisfies one's intellectual demands and preferences. Result: a custom-made worldview that invariably leads away from biblical truth.

Syncretism flourishes in times of rapid change and cultural upheaval. First-century Colossae experienced a lot of that. The region was dominated by a foreign superpower. The city was quickly being eclipsed by its neighbor, Laodicea. Frequent earthquakes made life precarious. In fact, one tremor in A.D. 61 devastated the town, forcing a relocation three miles to the south.

How the gospel reached Colossae is unknown, though Christians from Ephesus may have played a part (see "The Ephesus Approach," Acts 19:8–41). But once a church was established, it had to contend with the syncretism of its surrounding culture. Paul (who to our knowledge never visited Colossae) attempted to help by sending this letter, which he intended the believers to share with their brothers and sisters in Laodicea (Col. 4:16).

Paul's theme is straightforward: Christ is preeminent. He is Lord. He rules over the world as its Creator and Sustainer. Other religions may offer attractive claims and appealing rituals, but the gospel supersedes them all.

Such a claim has profound implications. It makes Christianity exclusive—not true along with all the other religions, but the true religion. That may not be a popular position in today's world. Anyone who holds it can expect conflict and criticism. But were Paul here to speak to the issue, we can imagine that he would quickly turn to Colossians and affirm his words from the first century: "[Christ] is the image of the invisible God . . . all things have been created through him and for him. He himself is before all things, and in him all things hold together . . . . I am saying this so that no one may deceive you with plausible arguments" (1:15–17; 2:4).

The remarkable thing is that belief in Christ affects one's lifestyle in a positive way that syncretistic religion cannot. As Colossians clearly shows, Christ makes a profound difference in one's relationships, family life, work, and community involvements. Though He rules the world and governs the universe, He enters into the day-to-day lives of His followers. He comes to us where we are in order to bring us to where He is (3:3–4). ◆

COLOSSAE

- **A Roman city of Asia Minor located at the base of 8,000-foot-high Mount Cadmus in the Lycus River Valley east of Ephesus.**
- **Watered by a cascade descending through a gorge from Mount Cadmus.**
- **A prosperous industrial center especially famous for its textiles, but clearly in decline at the time of Christ, squeezed by its increasingly competitive neighbor, Laodicea.**
- **Survived a devastating earthquake in A.D. 61, but later its population moved three miles south to Chonai (modern Honaz).**
- **Judaism, Platonism, and mystery cults from the surrounding mountain peoples blended into strange, often contradictory religious practices. Cultic worship of angels persisted, with Michael as the favorite. He was credited with sparing the town in a time of disaster.**
- **Home of Archippus and Epaphras, associates of Paul who helped spread the gospel throughout Asia, up and down the Lycus Valley. The region was also home to Onesimus, a runaway slave who became a believer (see the Introduction to Philemon).**

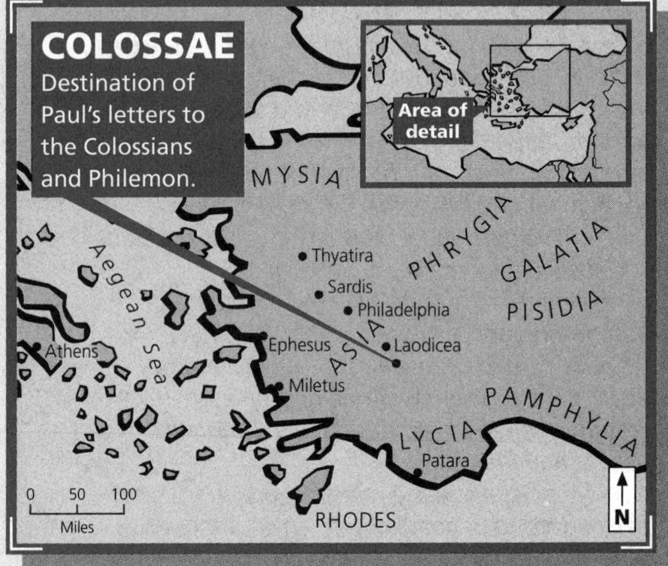

Greeting

1 Paul, an apostle of Christ Jesus by the will of God, and
Timothy our brother,
2 To the saints and faithful brothers and sisters[a] in Christ
in Colossae:
Grace to you and peace from God our Father.

Praise for Faith, Hope, and Love

3 In our prayers for you we always thank God, the
Father of our Lord Jesus Christ, 4for we have heard of your
faith in Christ Jesus and of the love that you have for all the
saints, 5because of the hope laid up for you in heaven. You
have heard of this hope before in the word of the truth, the
gospel 6that has come to you. Just as it is bearing fruit and
growing in the whole world, so it has been bearing fruit
among yourselves from the day you heard it and truly com-
prehended the grace of God. 7This you learned from Epaphras, our beloved fellow servant.[b] He is a faithful minister
of Christ on your[c] behalf, 8and he has made known to us
your love in the Spirit.
9 For this reason, since the day we heard it, we have not
ceased praying for you and asking that you may be filled
with the knowledge of God's[d] will in all spiritual wisdom
and understanding, 10so that you may lead lives worthy of
the Lord, fully pleasing to him, as you bear fruit in every
good work and as you grow in the knowledge of God.
11May you be made strong with all the strength that comes
from his glorious power, and may you be prepared to endure everything with patience, while joyfully 12giving
thanks to the Father, who has enabled[e] you[f] to share in the
inheritance of the saints in the light. 13He has rescued us
from the power of darkness and transferred us into the
kingdom of his beloved Son, 14in whom we have redemption, the forgiveness of sins.[g]

The Preeminence of Christ

1:15–18

15 He is the image of the invisible
God, the firstborn of all creation; 16for in[h]
him all things in heaven and on earth were created, things
visible and invisible, whether thrones or dominions or
rulers or powers—all things have been created through him
and for him. 17He himself is before all
things, and in[h] him all things hold to-
gether. 18He is the head of the body, the church; he is the

1:17 see pg. 696

[a]Gk *brothers* [b]Gk *slave* [c]Other ancient authorities read *our* [d]Gk *his* [e]Other ancient authorities read *called* [f]Other ancient authorities read *us* [g]Other ancient authorities add *through his blood* [h]Or *by*

Christ, the Lord of the World

CONSIDER THIS 1:15–18 *In vv. 15–18, Paul presents Jesus as the cosmic Christ, Creator of the universe, Sustainer of earth and all of its ecological systems, and Ruler over the competing power networks of the world.*

This is quite a contrast from Jesus the Servant, as presented in Philippians 2:5–8. There He is Lord of the personal and the private, the One who speaks to someone's heart. Here in Colossians, Paul offers the Lord of the public who transcends individual needs to deal with global concerns.

These are not two different Christs, but the same Christ, Lord of all. And His rule over both domains—the public and the private—suggests the kinds of activities in which His followers need to engage. On the one hand, Christ lives in us to transform us personally. He wants to affect our individual jobs, our families, our local communities, and our personal relationships. On the other hand, Christ is at work globally, using people to transform societies and their systems, confront principalities and powers, and work for public justice and human rights.

Paul claimed that all things were created through and for Christ. How much of "all" is all? See "Life—The Big Picture," Mark 12:28–34.

EVERY BREATH YOU TAKE

CONSIDER THIS 1:17 **People frequently use the term Mother Nature to describe the natural laws that bring order and predictability to the world. But Paul reminds us that Christ is ultimately the One who holds things together (v. 17), not some impersonal force or random chance. We depend on Him for every breath we draw. Since the first day of creation, He has been sustaining the world and providing for His creatures (Neh. 9:6; Ps. 36:6; Heb. 1:3).**

That lends tremendous dignity to human labor, especially since God has placed humanity over the creation as His managers. He values work that seeks to understand and oversee this world—for example, the work of the climatologist who studies the impact of humans on global ecology; the physicist who looks into the makeup of the atom and the application of that knowledge to human needs; and the publisher who helps distribute information and ideas to people. Jobs like these reflect God's work as Creator, and those who do them are actually partners with Christ in maintaining His creation.

God values everyday work because work is something that He Himself has done and continues to do. See "God—The Original Worker," John 5:17.

For more on how your job can help to accomplish God's purposes in the world, see "People at Work," Heb. 2:7.

beginning, the firstborn from the dead, so that he might
come to have first place in everything. 19For in him all the
fullness of God was pleased to dwell, 20and through him
God was pleased to reconcile to himself all things, whether
on earth or in heaven, by making peace through the blood
of his cross.
21 And you who were once estranged and hostile in
mind, doing evil deeds, 22he has now reconciled[i] in his
fleshly body[j] through death, so as to present you holy and
blameless and irreproachable before him— 23provided that
you continue securely established and steadfast in the faith,
without shifting from the hope promised by the gospel that
you heard, which has been proclaimed to every creature
under heaven. I, Paul, became a servant of this gospel.

Paul's Role in Preaching Christ

24 I am now rejoicing in my sufferings for your sake,
and in my flesh I am completing what is lacking in Christ's
afflictions for the sake of his body, that is, the church. 25I
became its servant according to God's commission that was
given to me for you, to make the word of God fully known,
26the mystery that has been hidden throughout the ages
and generations but has now been revealed to his saints.
27To them God chose to make known how great among the
Gentiles are the riches of the glory of this mystery, which is
Christ in you, the hope of glory. 28It is he whom we proclaim, warning everyone and teaching everyone in all wisdom, so that we may present everyone mature in Christ.
1:29 29For this I toil and struggle with all the
energy that he powerfully inspires within
me.

Paul's Burden for the Colossians

2 For I want you to know how much I am struggling for
you, and for those in Laodicea, and for all who have
not seen me face to face. 2I want their hearts to be
encouraged and united in love, so that they may have all
the riches of assured understanding and have the
knowledge of God's mystery, that is, Christ himself,[k] 3in
whom are hidden all the treasures of wisdom and
knowledge. 4I am saying this so that no one may deceive
you with plausible arguments. 5For though I am absent in
body, yet I am with you in spirit, and I rejoice to see your
morale and the firmness of your faith in Christ.

[i]Other ancient authorities read *you have now been reconciled* [j]Gk *in the body of his flesh* [k]Other ancient authorities read *of the mystery of God, both of the Father and of Christ*

Continue in Christ

2:6 see pg. 698
6 As you therefore have received
Christ Jesus the Lord, continue to live
your lives[l] in him, 7rooted and built up in him and established in the faith, just as you were taught, abounding in
thanksgiving.

Beware of False Teaching

8 See to it that no one takes you captive through philosophy and empty deceit, according to human tradition, according to the elemental spirits of the universe,[m] and not
according to Christ. 9For in him the whole fullness of deity
dwells bodily, 10and you have come to fullness in him, who
is the head of every ruler and authority. 11In him also you
were circumcised with a spiritual circumcision,[n] by putting
off the body of the flesh in the circumcision of Christ;
12when you were buried with him in baptism, you were
also raised with him through faith in the power of God,
who raised him from the dead. 13And when you were dead
in trespasses and the uncircumcision of your flesh, God[o]
made you[p] alive together with him, when he forgave us all
our trespasses, 14erasing the record that stood against us
with its legal demands. He set this aside, nailing it to the
cross. 15He disarmed[q] the rulers and authorities and made a
public example of them, triumphing over them in it.

2:16–17
16 Therefore do not let anyone condemn you in matters of food and drink
or of observing festivals, new moons, or sabbaths. 17These
are only a shadow of what is to come, but the substance belongs to Christ. 18Do not let anyone disqualify you, insisting on self-abasement and worship of angels, dwelling[r] on
visions,[s] puffed up without cause by a human way of thinking,[t] 19and not holding fast to the head, from whom the

(Bible text continued on page 699)

[l]Gk *to walk* [m]Or *the rudiments of the world* [n]Gk *a circumcision made without hands* [o]Gk *he* [p]Other ancient authorities read *made us*; others, *made* [q]Or *divested himself of* [r]Other ancient authorities read *not dwelling* [s]Meaning of Gk uncertain [t]Gk *by the mind of his flesh*

QUOTE UNQUOTE

CONSIDER THIS 1:29 *Just as Paul strived to accomplish God's work, so many Christians today work hard to do the same:*

Using both the* [Wall Street] Journal *and the Bible, at the same time, sure makes our business lives complicated and difficult. But whoever said Christian faithfulness would be simple and easy?

John H. Rudy

Stand Up for Your Convictions!

A CLOSER LOOK 2:16–17 *The community of believers at Colossae was plagued by opinionated people who tried to impose their preferences on others. Paul challenged his readers to stand up for their own convictions, and not to allow others to coerce them through intimidation or condemnation (vv. 16–17). His advice is similar to what he told the Christians at Rome about "Matters of Conscience" (Rom. 14:1–23).*

Jesus constantly faced judgment from religious leaders of His day over His treatment of the Sabbath. See "Jesus Confronts the Legalists," Luke 6:1–11.

Two Portraits of Jesus, Two Sides of Life

Paul urged the Colossians to follow the pattern of Christ (v. 6). But what does that pattern look like? In Philippians and Colossians, Paul paints two contrasting but complementary portraits of the Lord. Hanging side by side in the New Testament, they challenge believers to pay attention to two sides of life—the private and the public. Neither one is more important; both are crucial when it comes to living out the faith.

Notice how Jesus modeled two styles of living, and what that means for those of us who follow Christ today:

Two Ways Jesus Is Portrayed by Paul

Christ the Lord: Power over All	Christ the Servant: Lowest of the Lowly
As portrayed in Colossians, especially 1:15–20.	As portrayed in Philippians, especially 2:5–11.
Original audience: believers at Colossae, a dying town of Asia Minor.	*Original audience:* believers at Philippi, a proud, prosperous Roman colony in Macedonia.
Main features: Christ is... •the ruler of the universe. •the firstborn of creation. •the bodily expression of God. •the One who possesses all authority in heaven and on earth. •the "cosmic Christ" who confronts and exposes every opposing principality and power.	*Main features:* Christ is... •the model of humility, of "downward mobility." •the model of servant leadership. •the obedient Son who surrenders His power in order to accomplish His task among and on behalf of the powerless. •the One who dies in order to save.
Tends to produce a public faith that... is concerned with human rights, feeding the hungry, assisting the poor, and working on community development. Because Christ is Lord of the powers, He is Lord of governments, cities, systems, and economic structures. Christ's people pay attention to the social implications of the gospel.	*Tends to produce a private faith that...* is concerned with personal holiness, spiritual disciplines, individual growth, and one-on-one evangelism. Because Christ modeled servanthood, His people are called to put the interests of others ahead of their own. They especially pay attention to relationships and the personal, inner needs of people.
Examples today: •Running for public office. •Challenging businesses when they appear to have an adverse effect on people. •Serving meals to the homeless. •Advising public officials on matters of public policy. •Learning to initiate and manage institutional change. •Voting.	*Examples today:* •Bible study. •Friendship evangelism. •Missions. •Ministries that strengthen marriages and home life. •Support groups. •Counseling. •Prayer.

◆

whole body, nourished and held together by its ligaments
and sinews, grows with a growth that is from God.
20 If with Christ you died to the elemental spirits of the
universe,[u] why do you live as if you still belonged to the
world? Why do you submit to regulations, 21“Do not handle, Do not taste, Do not touch”? 22All these regulations refer to things that perish with use; they are simply human
commands and teachings. 23These have indeed an appearance of wisdom in promoting self-imposed piety, humility,
and severe treatment of the body, but they are of no value
in checking self-indulgence.[v]

Christ the Focus of Life

3:1–2 see pg. 702

3 So if you have been raised with
Christ, seek the things that are
above, where Christ is, seated at the right hand of God. 2Set
your minds on things that are above, not on things that are
on earth, 3for you have died, and your life is hidden with
Christ in God. 4When Christ who is
your[w] life is revealed, then you also will
be revealed with him in glory.

3:1–4

A Christlike Lifestyle

3:5 see pg. 700

5 Put to death, therefore, whatever in
you is earthly: fornication, impurity, pas-
sion, evil desire, and greed (which is idolatry). 6On account
of these the wrath of God is coming on those who are disobedient.[x] 7These are the ways you also once followed,
when you were living that life.[y] 8But now you must get rid
of all such things—anger, wrath, malice, slander, and abusive[z] language from your mouth. 9Do not lie to one another,
seeing that you have stripped off the old self with its practices 10and have clothed yourselves with the new self,
which is being renewed in knowledge according to the image of its creator. 11In that renewal[a] there
is no longer Greek and Jew, circumcised
and uncircumcised, barbarian, Scythian, slave and free; but
Christ is all and in all!

3:11 see pg. 701

12 As God's chosen ones, holy and
beloved, clothe yourselves with compas-

3:12–17

[u]*Or the rudiments of the world* [v]*Or are of no value, serving only to indulge the flesh* [w]Other authorities read *our* [x]Other ancient authorities lack *on those who are disobedient* (Gk *the children of disobedience*) [y]*Or living among such people* [z]*Or filthy* [a]Gk *its creator,* [11]*where*

A New Wardrobe

A CLOSER LOOK 3:12–17

In vv. 12–17, Paul challenges us as believers to "put on" a new wardrobe, one appropriate to our new life in Christ. For an expanded list of what that wardrobe includes, see "New Creatures with New Character," Gal. 5:22–23.

Where's Your Head At?

CONSIDER THIS 3:1–4

Paul urges us to focus on the "things that are above" rather than the "things that are on earth" (vv. 1–4). The distinction between these two spheres has caused no end of misunderstanding. It has been said that heavenly things matter and earthly things don't. But that's not what Paul says. When he tells us to "set your minds on things that are above," he's challenging us to make Christ the center of our lives, because Christ is what matters, certainly more than anything this world has to offer.

And yet it is precisely because heavenly things matter that earthly things also matter a great deal—and why Paul immediately launches into a long exhortation about everyday issues such as character and conduct, relationships, and work (3:5—4:6). How we handle earthly affairs such as time, money, personal energy, emotions, our thought life, and our relationships reflects the focus of our mind. These "mundane" things show what matters to us.

sion, kindness, humility, meekness, and patience. [13]Bear
with one another and, if anyone has a complaint against another, forgive each other; just as the Lord[b] has forgiven you,
so you also must forgive. [14]Above all, clothe yourselves
with love, which binds everything together in perfect harmony. [15]And let the peace of Christ rule in your hearts, to
which indeed you were called in the one body. And be
thankful. [16]Let the word of Christ[c] dwell in you richly;
teach and admonish one another in all wisdom; and with
gratitude in your hearts sing psalms, hymns, and spiritual
songs to God.[d] [17]And whatever you do, in word or deed, do
everything in the name of the Lord Jesus, giving thanks to
God the Father through him.

Instructions for Christian Households

18 Wives, be subject to your husbands, as is fitting in
the Lord. [19]Husbands, love your wives and never treat them
harshly.

20 Children, obey your parents in everything, for this is
your acceptable duty in the Lord. [21]Fathers, do not provoke
your children, or they may lose heart.
[22]Slaves, obey your earthly masters[e] in

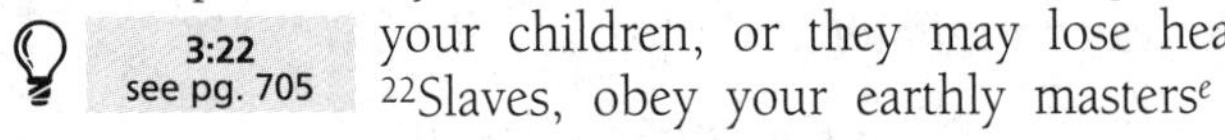
3:22
see pg. 705

[b]Other ancient authorities read *just as Christ* [c]Other ancient authorities read *of God*, or *of the Lord* [d]Other ancient authorities read *to the Lord* [e]In Greek the same word is used for *master* and *Lord*

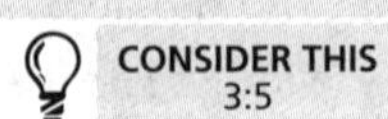
CONSIDER THIS
3:5

Do-It-Yourself Idolatry

Most of us think of idolatry as a pagan bowing down to an image carved from stone or wood, reciting mysterious incantations, and carrying out peculiar rituals. But Paul says that idolatry is much more familiar to us than we realize. All it takes is simple greed (v. 5).

Does that mean it's wrong to want a bigger house, a newer car, a more prestigious job, a more dynamic personality, a more noticeable spirituality? No, none of these things is evil, in and of itself. The question is, what is the heart attitude that makes us want any of these things?

The difference between desire and greed is the difference between a small, blue circle of flame that cooks food on a gas range, and a raging inferno that threatens to burn down the house. Simple desire can be constructive; it motivates us to work and be productive. Proverbs 16:26 says that "the appetite of workers works for them." But greed is dangerous and destructive. It is desire out of control.

Control is the real issue. Will the thing we want serve

everything, not only while being watched and in order to
3:22–24 see pg. 704 please them, but wholeheartedly, fearing
the Lord.[f] 23Whatever your task, put
yourselves into it, as done for the Lord and not for your
3:24 masters,[g] 24since you know that from the
Lord you will receive the inheritance as
your reward; you serve[h] the Lord Christ. 25For the wrongdoer will be paid back for whatever wrong has been
3:22—4:1 see pg. 706 4 done, and there is no partiality.
1Masters, treat your slaves justly and
fairly, for you know that you also have a Master in heaven.

(Bible text continued on page 704)

[f]In Greek the same word is used for *master* and *Lord* [g]Gk *not for men* [h]Or *you are slaves of*, or *be slaves of*

Your Reward

A CLOSER LOOK 3:24 *Do you ever wonder what you're going to get out of serving Christ? Paul promises "the reward of the inheritance" (v. 24). Find out more about it in the article, "What's In It for Me?" Eph. 1:11.*

our needs, or will our needs serve that thing? That's why Paul says that covetousness—or greed—is idolatry *(Eph. 5:5). To covet is to surrender our will to a thing—in effect, to make it our master, our god, the thing that we serve. But God insists: "You shall have no other gods before Me" (Ex. 20:3).*

Greed means that we want something other than God. He is not enough for us; we need something more to satisfy. It also means that we don't trust Him to follow through on His promises to supply what we need (Matt. 6:33; Rom. 8:32). Everyday greed, then, is nothing less than an attack on the very character of God. No wonder Paul warns so sternly against it! ◆

Jesus gives a direct, unequivocal command to guard against longing for something we don't have. See "Watch Out for Greed!" Luke 12:15.

The opposite of covetousness is contentment. What would that look like? See Phil. 4:10–13.

BLOODLINES

CONSIDER THIS 3:11 **The city of Colossae included people from a wide variety of ethnic and cultural backgrounds (v. 11):**

- ***Greeks,* whose cultural heritage dominated the Roman world.**
- ***Jews,* who prided themselves as "God's chosen people."**
- ***Barbarians,* who spoke no Greek and therefore lacked social standing.**
- ***Scythians,* a crude, cruel warlike people from the north.**
- ***Slaves,* menial workers at the bottom of the society.**

Members from all these groups came to faith and joined the community of believers at Colossae. But their ethnic prejudices created problems, which Paul listed (vv. 8–9). He pulled no punches, calling them by their ugly names: anger, wrath, malice, blasphemy, filthy language, and lying. Paul challenged his culturally mixed group of readers to shed such behaviors like an old set of clothes and put on Christ instead, who "is all and in all." He was possibly reminding them of a first-century baptismal creed that reminded new converts that they were joining a new family in Christ (see "We Are Family!" Gal. 3:28).

God's family has no place for prejudice. Radically new ways of relating to others are called for (Col. 3:12–17). If believers today lived out these ideals, we would see God change our churches and begin to transform our culture.

CONSIDER THIS
3:1–2

THE SPIRITUALITY OF EVERYDAY WORK

What do vv. 1–2 imply about everyday work? Is it possible to hold a "secular" job and still "seek the things that are above" rather than "things that are on earth"? Or would it be better to quit one's job and go into the ministry?

The issue here is *spirituality,* the capacity to know, experience, and respond to God. How is it possible to bring spirituality into "secular" work? Consider:

If Christ is Lord over all of life, then He must be Lord over work, too. Colossians 3 does not distinguish between the sacred and the secular, but between the life that Christ offers, (the "things that are above") and its alternative—spiritual death apart from Him (the "things that are on earth"). This is clear from the preceding context (2:20) and the rest of chapter 3: "earthly" things include fornication, uncleanness, passion, etc. (vv. 5, 8); the things above include tender mercies, kindness, humility, etc. (vv. 12– 15). Spirituality has to do with conduct and character, not just vocation.

It also has to do with the lordship of Christ. Christ is Lord over all of creation (1:15–18). Therefore, He is Lord over work. Whatever we do for work, we should do it "in the name of the Lord Jesus" (v. 17), that is, with a concern for His approval and in a manner that honors Him. In fact, Paul specifically addresses two categories of workers—slaves (v. 22–25) and masters (4:1)—in this manner.

The Spirit empowers us to live and work with Christlikeness. Spirituality has to do with character and conduct, regardless of where we work. Christ gives the Holy Spirit to help us live in a way that pleases Him. (Gal. 5:16–25.) That has enormous implications for how we do our jobs, our "workstyle" (Titus 2:9–10).

Furthermore, Scripture calls us "temples" of the Holy Spirit (1 Cor. 6:19). An intriguing image: In Exodus 31 and 35, the Spirit enabled Hebrew workers to use their skills in stonecutting, carpentry, lapidary arts, and so on to construct a beautiful, functional house of worship. In an even greater way, we can expect the Spirit to enable us to use our God-given skills and abilities to bring glory to God.

God values our work even when the product has no eternal value. A common measure of the significance of a job is its perceived value from the eternal perspective. Will the work "last"? Will it "really count" for eternity? The assumption is that God values work for eternity, but not work for the here and now.

By this measure, the work of ministers and missionaries has eternal value because it deals with the spiritual, eternal needs of people. By contrast, the work of the shoe salesman, bank teller, or typist has only limited value, because it meets only earthly needs. Implication: that kind of work doesn't really "count" to God.

But this way of thinking overlooks several important truths:

(1) God Himself has created a world which is time-bound and temporary (2 Pet. 3:10–11). Yet He values His work, declaring it to be "very good," good by its very nature (Gen. 1:31; Ps. 119:68; Acts 14:17).

(2) God promises rewards to people in everyday jobs, based on their attitude and conduct (Eph. 6:7–9; Col. 3:23—4:1).

(3) God cares about the everyday needs of people as well as their spiritual needs. He cares whether people have food, clothing, shelter, and so forth.

(4) God cares about people, who will enter eternity. To the extent that a job serves the needs of people, He values it because He values people. ◆

Because God cares about the everyday needs of people as well as their spiritual needs, He has given people the skills required to meet those everyday needs. See "People at Work," Heb. 2:7.

Are some jobs more important than others? See 1 Cor. 12:28–31.

The Gift of an Ethnic Heritage

CONSIDER THIS 4:10–11 Culture provides people with a common set of experiences and values that bind them together over time. As Paul concludes his letter to the Colossians, he mentions three men who shared his Jewish heritage: Aristarchus, Mark the cousin of Barnabas, and Jesus who was called Justus (vv. 10–11). He says that they were the only Jews still working with him.

Even though Paul was "the apostle to the Gentiles," he still cherished his Jewish roots. No Gentile could fully appreciate what it meant to grow up and live with the traditions of Judaism. But Aristarchus, Mark, and Justus could. No wonder Paul calls them "a comfort" to him.

God never asks us to reject our roots. We can affirm our ethnic heritage as a rich gift from Him, no matter how our surrounding culture regards it. To be sure, ethnicity ought not to create barriers with other people (Gal. 3:28; Col. 3:11). But we need not hide the cultural background from which God has called us. We need never deny who God has created us to be.

Workers for the Kingdom

CONSIDER THIS 4:11 Do you ever wonder what your life contributes to the work of God in the world? If you are in a "secular" occupation, you may conclude that the only way to further the kingdom is to pray for and contribute financially to those who are in "full-time" Christian work. But are those your only options?

Paul described Aristarchus, Mark, and Justus as "co-workers for the kingdom" (v. 11), indicating that they may have been vocational Christian workers. However, there is no way to say whether they were employed in that work as a full-time occupation. In fact, if they followed Paul's example, they probably had other jobs through which they made their living (see "Paul's 'Real' Job," Acts 18:1–3).

The point is that drawing a paycheck for doing "ministry" is not the criterion by which to judge whether someone is a worker for God's kingdom. Kingdom work involves promoting the values, beliefs, and lifestyle of the kingdom. That may involve professional employment such as pastoring a church or serving on a mission field. But kingdom workers are also found among doctors, accountants, engineers, painters, salespeople, auto mechanics, and homemakers. Wherever believers are furthering the goals and objectives of Christ, they are working for His kingdom.

How does your life promote the purposes of God? Do you use your skills and abilities toward that end, whether or not pay is involved? Or have you given up and concluded that because you are not a vocational Christian worker, you aren't really serving the Lord with your life and career? If so, you'll want to reconsider what it means to be a worker for Christ's kingdom!

Is it really possible to hold a "secular" job and still please God with your life? Or would it be better to quit one's job and go into the ministry? See "The Spirituality of Everyday Work," Col. 3:1–2.

Instructions and Requests

4:2 see pg. 707

2 Devote yourselves to prayer, keeping alert in it with thanksgiving. 3At the
same time pray for us as well that God will open to us a
door for the word, that we may declare the mystery of

CONSIDER THIS 3:22–24

Who's the Boss?

He had a menial, dead-end job. They assigned him tasks that no one else wanted—the "dumb-work," the dirty work, the dangerous work. They called him out at all hours of the day and night to satisfy the whims of his supervisors. He had little hope for advancement. In fact, he'd be lucky just to keep his job; plenty of others stood in line, ready to replace him. Whether he even lived or died mattered little. He was a first-century Roman slave.

Yet he mattered to God, and his work mattered, too. In writing to this lowly worker (vv. 22–24), Paul redefined his occupational status: he was not a Roman slave, he was an employee of Christ the Lord! That makes all the difference.

So it is for any Christian in the workplace. You may work for a giant multinational corporation or a mom-'n-pop pizza parlor. You may have 15 levels of bureaucracy over you, or be self-employed. It doesn't matter. Ultimately, Christ is your Boss. Consider what that means:

Christ, for which I am in prison, 4so that I may reveal it
clearly, as I should.
5 Conduct yourselves wisely toward outsiders, making
the most of the time.[i] 6Let your speech always be gracious,
seasoned with salt, so that you may know how you ought
to answer everyone.

(Bible text continued on page 707)

[i]Or opportunity

Christ gives you work to do. *Work is a gift from God. He has created you in His image to be a worker, giving you skills and abilities to accomplish His purposes. He has also sovereignly placed you in your occupation to do His work there. Even if your job is as lowly as a Roman slave's, it still has value and dignity to Christ.*

Christ is your Boss, but He uses human supervisors. *According to Colossians 3, people in authority over you are actually human representatives of Christ. They may not act very Christlike. But in working for them, you are ultimately working for Christ. Do you follow their instructions? Do you shirk your job when they're not around? Are you more interested in impressing them to gain approval and advancement than in getting the job done? How would your work ethic change if you saw Christ as your supervisor?*

Christ asks you to put your heart into your work. *If you serve Christ in your job, you have more reason than anyone else to work with integrity and enthusiasm. The job itself may be unchallenging or unpleasant. But Christ asks you to do it with dignity, to the best of your ability, as though working for Christ Himself.*

Christ will reward you for good, faithful work. *This passage says that Christ will review your work someday. You can expect praise and reward for working in a Christlike manner.* ◆

Many of the first Christians may have been slaves, since perhaps half the population or more of the Roman Empire were under servitude by one historian's estimate. Find out more about this important group in the article, "Slaves," Rom. 6:16.

One of the reasons that your work has dignity and value, even if you are a slave, is that you are a coworker with God. See "People at Work," Heb. 2:7.

Christ cares not only about what job you have, but how you go about doing it. See "Your 'Workstyle,'" Titus 2:9–10.

QUOTE UNQUOTE

CONSIDER THIS 3:22 *Paul's instructions to bondservants (v. 22) are as applicable to employees today as they were to slaves in the first century:*

When I hear someone say, "I couldn't work with a corporation with a profit motive or which demands more than forty hours a week," I say something like this: "Do you know that the Christian slaves to whom Paul wrote were working sixteen hours a day for masters that were fornicating with female slaves, making dirty business deals with traders from other parts of the Roman empire and going to baths and the gymnasium at night for orgies? To these slaves Paul says, 'Treat your masters as though they were Jesus. You are not working for them but for Jesus. And it is worship.'"

Paul Stevens, *Liberating the Laity,* p. 158

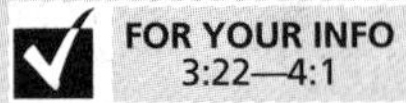
FOR YOUR INFO
3:22—4:1

WORK-WORLD CODES

Paul's letters have much to say to believers as we live out our faith in the work world. As he does here in 3:22—4:1, Paul usually speaks to both leaders and workers about the tough character and choices required to honor Christ in a difficult workplace environment. For example:

Guidelines for Managers and Others in Authority

Finance
- Workers deserve payment for their work (1 Cor. 9:7–14).
- You are accountable for fair employee compensation (Col. 4:1).
- Handle wealth very delicately (1Tim. 6:9–10, 17–18).

Work Relationships
- Bring your walk with Christ into each business relationship (2 Cor. 7:1).
- Value people highly (Gal. 5:14–15; Eph. 4:31–32).
- Treat and motivate employees with respect rather than threats (Eph. 6:5–9).
- Have a reasonable view of yourself (Rom. 12:3).

Communication
- Accusations must be verified (Matt. 18:15–35; 2 Cor. 13:1; 1 Tim. 5:19).
- Communication should always be gracious and truthful (Col. 4:6).

Responsibility
- Fulfill your commitments (Rom. 13:6–8).
- Remember your accountability (1 Cor. 3:9–15).
- Care for the poor and the weak (Rom. 12:13; Gal. 2:10).
- Learn how to handle times of bounty and leanness (Phil. 4:12).
- Remember, God's Son gets the ultimate credit (Col. 1:17–18).
- Be sure to care for your own family (1 Tim. 5:8).
- Discern needs and meet them (Titus 3:14).

Management
- View time not only in terms of time management, but also in light of the long-term implications of your decisions (2 Cor. 4:16–18; 2 Pet. 3:8–13).
- Help each employee discern the best thing to do (1 Thess. 5:14–15).
- Be willing to change your opinions (2 Cor. 5:16–17; Philem. 10–14).

Guidelines for Workers and Those under Authority

Tasks
- Don't try to get out of your current situation too quickly (1 Cor. 7:17–24).
- View stress and trouble in perspective (2 Cor. 4:7–18).

Supervisors
- Develop a respect for authority (Rom. 13:1–8).
- Do your work wholeheartedly and respectfully (Eph. 6:5–8; 1 Thess. 5:12–15).
- Give your employers obedient, hard work (Col. 3:22–25; 1 Thess. 4:11–12).
- Honor bosses, whether they are believers or not (1 Tim. 6:1–2).

Coworkers
- Develop a reasonable self-estimate (Rom. 12:3).
- Acknowledge differences and accept the contributions of others (1 Cor. 12:1–8).
- Help others, but do your job (Gal. 6:1–5).
- Learn to speak appropriately and sensitively (Col. 4:6).
- Understand others and treat them respectfully (1 Tim. 5:1–3).
- Develop a reputation for good relationships (Titus 3:1–2).

Responsibility
- Give your whole self to God (Rom. 12:1).
- Develop the art of discernment in order to live responsibly (Eph. 5:15–18).
- Do your work as if working for God—you are (1 Cor. 3:13; Col. 3:17).
- Don't let your responsibilities weigh you down with worry (Phil. 4:6).
- Take responsibility for yourself (1 Thess. 4:11–12; 2 Thess. 3:8–9).
- Develop a godly "workstyle" (Titus 2:9–10).

Finances
- Live frugally and do not steal—including pilfering (Eph. 4:28).
- Care for your family (1Tim. 5:8).

News, Greetings, and Final Words

7 Tychicus will tell you all the news about me; he is a
beloved brother, a faithful minister, and a fellow servant[j] in
the Lord. 8I have sent him to you for this very purpose, so
that you may know how we are[k] and that he may encourage
your hearts; 9he is coming with Onesimus, the faithful and
beloved brother, who is one of you. They will tell you about
everything here.

4:10–11 see pg. 703

10 Aristarchus my fellow prisoner
greets you, as does Mark the cousin of
Barnabas, concerning whom you have received instructions—if he comes to you, welcome him.

4:11 see pg. 703

11And Jesus who is called Justus greets
you. These are the only ones of the circumcision among my
co-workers for the kingdom of God, and they have been a
comfort to me. 12Epaphras, who is one of you, a servant[j] of
Christ Jesus, greets you. He is always wrestling in his
prayers on your behalf, so that you may stand mature and
fully assured in everything that God wills. 13For I testify for
him that he has worked hard for you and for those in
Laodicea and in Hierapolis. 14Luke, the beloved physician,
and Demas greet you. 15Give my greetings to the brothers
and sisters[l] in Laodicea, and to Nympha and the church in
her house. 16And when this letter has been read among
you, have it read also in the church of the Laodiceans; and
see that you read also the letter from Laodicea. 17And say to
Archippus, "See that you complete the task that you have
received in the Lord."

18 I, Paul, write this greeting with my own hand. Remember my chains. Grace be with you.[m]

[j]Gk *slave* [k]Other authorities read *that I may know how you are* [l]Gk *brothers* [m]Other ancient authorities add *Amen*

QUOTE UNQUOTE

CONSIDER THIS 4:2

Vigilance in prayer is a vital part of working with Christlikeness:

Orare est laborare, laborare est orare.
(To pray is to work, to work is to pray.)

Motto of the Benedictine monks, C. A.D. 500

The First and Second Letters of Paul to the

Thessalonians

What does a church look like when it functions the way it is supposed to? It may well resemble the church at Thessalonica. Of all the congregations mentioned in the New Testament, the Thessalonians were perhaps the model in carrying out the instructions of the apostles. Indeed, the story of their faith spread far and wide in the first century, impressing all who heard it (1:7–9).

Their example still proves instructive today. Many people in our culture are choosing to live increasingly isolated lives, putting distance between themselves and the needs of the world. By contrast, Christians are challenged to engage the world and penetrate it with the light of God's love. The Thessalonians did that in the first century; believers today can do the same. In a world that lacks hope, they can point toward the hope that is found in Christ.

The story of their faith spread far and wide.

C O N T E N T S

A R T I C L E S

When Hope Fades

Judging from his comments in the New Testament, the apostle Paul may have felt greater affection for the church at Thessalonica than for any other congregation (1 Thess. 2:7–8, 11). The believers there didn't just talk about the gospel, they *practiced* it.

In doing so they were emulating Paul, Silas, and Timothy, who had brought them the gospel. The threesome had taken great pains to live an exemplary life among them (2:9–10; 2 Thess. 3:7–9). The demonstration of a Christlike lifestyle lent credibility to the apostles' message, with the result that many Thessalonians were persuaded (Acts 17:1–4). Even those who were not recognized a power in the messengers, claiming they had been "turning the world upside down" (17:6).

For a time the gospel turned Thessalonica upside down. But after the apostles left and things quieted down, the new believers were left with an important reality of the faith—that lasting change occurs over time. That's why Paul's two letters call for responsible, long-term progress and the refusal to let hope fade. He reminds his readers of his example, how he worked among the Thessalonians (1 Thess. 2:9). They should work as well, he says, and keep on working rather than burning out in the midst of doing good (4:11; 5:12–14; 2 Thess. 3:6–13).

The work that Paul calls for is the everyday work of making a living and maintaining a home. And yet there is an inner work that takes place in and through that day-to-day toil. As the Thessalonians carried out their everyday responsibilities, God was building their character, so that Paul could speak of their "work of faith and labor of love and steadfastness of hope" (1 Thess. 1:3).

When hope fades, people lose heart and doubts begin to grow. Perhaps that was happening in Thessalonica. A major question that the two letters address is, what will happen in the end times (see 4:13—5:11; 2 Thess. 2:1–12)? And how should believers live as they await the return of the Lord? Again, Paul exhorts his readers to lifestyles of faithful service and steadfast hope. "The Lord is faithful," he declares (3:3). Therefore, His people should be faithful as well.

Two thousand years after the Thessalonians, believers still await the coming of the Lord. Has your hope faded? Have doubts crowded in so that you wonder whether God will keep His word? Has your lifestyle grown spiritually lax and undisciplined? The message of 1 and 2 Thessalonians remains: keep working, stay faithful, don't lose hope. God will honor His commitments. He challenges you to live in a way that points to that hope. ◆

. . . LET
US NOT
FALL ASLEEP
AS
OTHERS
DO,
BUT LET
US KEEP AWAKE
AND BE
SOBER. . . .
—1 Thessalonians 5:6

Thessalonica

Thessalonica was a thriving commercial and military center with a renowned history. Learn more about it at Acts 17:1.

Work, Labor, and Steadfastness

CONSIDER THIS 1:3 *It's easy to see Paul's emphasis on faith, hope, and love, the trinity of Christian virtues (v. 3). But notice the words that precede these qualities:* work *of faith,* labor *of love, and* steadfastness *of hope. These are marketplace terms. Christians in the workplace understand that useful results come only from hard work, diligent labor, and patience. The same is true in spiritual growth.*

Greeting

1 Paul, Silvanus, and Timothy,
To the church of the Thessalonians in God the Father
and the Lord Jesus Christ:
Grace to you and peace.

The Thessalonians Act as Believers Should

2 We always give thanks to God for all of you and men-
1:3 tion you in our prayers, constantly 3re-
membering before our God and Father
your work of faith and labor of love and steadfastness of
hope in our Lord Jesus Christ. 4For we know, brothers and
sisters[a] beloved by God, that he has chosen you, 5because
our message of the gospel came to you not in word only,
but also in power and in the Holy Spirit and with full conviction; just as you know what kind of persons we proved
to be among you for your sake. 6And you became imitators
of us and of the Lord, for in spite of persecution you re-
1:7 ceived the word with joy inspired by the
Holy Spirit, 7so that you became an ex-
ample to all the believers in Macedonia and in Achaia. 8For
the word of the Lord has sounded forth from you not only
in Macedonia and Achaia, but in every place your faith in
God has become known, so that we have no need to speak
about it. 9For the people of those regions[b] report about us
what kind of welcome we had among you, and how you
turned to God from idols, to serve a living and true God,
10and to wait for his Son from heaven, whom he raised
from the dead—Jesus, who rescues us from the wrath that
is coming.

Fond Memories of Paul's First Visit

2 You yourselves know, brothers and sisters,[a] that our
coming to you was not in vain, 2but though we had
already suffered and been shamefully mistreated at Philippi,
as you know, we had courage in our God to declare to you
the gospel of God in spite of great opposition. 3For our
appeal does not spring from deceit or impure motives or
trickery, 4but just as we have been approved by God to be
entrusted with the message of the gospel, even so we speak,
not to please mortals, but to please God who tests our
2:5 hearts. 5As you know and as God is our
witness, we never came with words of

[a]Gk *brothers* [b]Gk *For they*

QUOTE UNQUOTE

CONSIDER THIS 1:7 *The Thessalonians became examples of what the gospel can do (v. 7). Models of Christlikeness are still needed today:*

People are not particularly interested in our ideas; they are interested in our experiences. They are not searching for theories but for convictions. They want to penetrate our rhetoric in order to discover the reality of our lives.

Richard Halverson, Chaplain, United States Senate, and former pastor of Fourth Presbyterian Church, McLean, Virginia; from a church newsletter

flattery or with a pretext for greed; 6nor did we seek praise
2:7 see pg. 716
from mortals, whether from you or from
others, 7though we might have made
demands as apostles of Christ. But we were gentle[c] among
you, like a nurse tenderly caring for her own children. 8So
deeply do we care for you that we are determined to share
with you not only the gospel of God but also our own
selves, because you have become very dear to us.

2:9

9 You remember our labor and toil,
brothers and sisters;[d] we worked night
and day, so that we might not burden any of you while we
proclaimed to you the gospel of God. 10You are witnesses,
and God also, how pure, upright, and blameless our conduct was toward you believers. 11As you know, we dealt
with each one of you like a father with his children, 12urg-
ing and encouraging you and pleading that you lead a life
worthy of God, who calls you into his own kingdom and
glory.

A Model Church

2:13–14 see pg. 714

13 We also constantly give thanks to
God for this, that when you received the
word of God that you heard from us, you accepted it not as
a human word but as what it really is, God's word, which is
also at work in you believers. 14For you, brothers and sisters,[d] became imitators of the churches of God in Christ
Jesus that are in Judea, for you suffered the same things
from your own compatriots as they did from the Jews,
15who killed both the Lord Jesus and the prophets,[e] and
drove us out; they displease God and oppose everyone 16by
hindering us from speaking to the Gentiles so that they may
be saved. Thus they have constantly been filling up the
measure of their sins; but God's wrath has overtaken them
at last.[f]

(Bible text continued on page 716)

[c]Other ancient authorities read *infants* [d]Gk *brothers* [e]Other ancient authorities read *their own prophets* [f]Or *completely* or *forever*

The Value of Self-Support

A CLOSER LOOK 2:9

As an apostle, Paul had a right to be supported by others. However, he chose to forfeit that right so as not to be a burden on anyone and possibly cause them to reject the gospel (v. 9; compare 1 Cor. 9:7–12).

Paul's example is instructive to clergy and laity alike. For those who make their living in vocational Christian work, it opens the door to the idea of carrying out ministry while supporting oneself through other means. See "Paying Vocational Christian Workers," 1 Cor. 9:1–23. For all believers, it honors the principle of self-support to which every Christian is called. See "A Command to Work," 2 Thess. 3:6–12.

A Straightforward Approach

CONSIDER THIS 2:5

Many people in today's culture have grown cynical about religion. So as we believers think about presenting the gospel to others, we need to be careful to make our message credible and straightforward.

Paul mentions two dangers that he avoided so as not to compromise his credibility (v. 5): the use of flattering words, which amounts to telling people what they want to hear, and "a pretext for greed," which involves hidden motives. To use either of these approaches is to deceive people. That's unacceptable for someone who presents himself as a representative of Christ.

The key to Paul's integrity was his realization that God Himself had entrusted him with the message (v. 4). The task of taking the gospel to the Gentiles was not something that Paul had thought up, but a calling from God (Gal. 1:11–17). Thus his aim was not to please people, but God.

Nor did he need to worry about his material well-being, even less to covet what others had. As a messenger of God, he could rely on God to provide for his needs and remain content in whatever circumstances came his way (Phil. 4:11–12). (This is not to suggest that Paul was irresponsible; he earned his living through his occupation as a tentmaker. See "Paul's 'Real' Job," Acts 18:1–3.)

As we consider ways in which to communicate Christ to people around us, what obstacles to our credibility might there be? Are there things about our methods or motives that conflict with the message with which we've been entrusted?

Some helpful suggestions for communicating the faith with integrity are contained in "A Code of Ethics for Christian Witness," 2 Cor. 4:2.

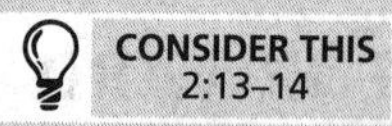

Is Your Church Upside-down or Right Side Up?

The believers at Thessalonica became something of a model church in Paul's estimation by embracing the gospel with unreserved commitment and sincerity (v. 13; 1:8–9). What does a model church look like? We can gain some idea by looking at the New Testament's many glimpses of the early church worshiping the Lord, relating to one another, and effectively reaching out to its surrounding culture with the gospel.

It's interesting that the first believers apparently did not rely on hired staff to carry out most of the church's work, nor did they occupy many formal church buildings until the fourth century A.D. Nevertheless, they were enormously successful at carrying out the Lord's command to be His witnesses "to the ends of the earth" (Acts 1:8). At Ephesus, for example, Christian outreach was so effective that "all the residents of Asia [Minor]. . . heard the word of the Lord" (19:10).

If we compare the pattern that seems to emerge from the New Testament with the way most churches in the West are structured today, we can see two models for describing church life.

The first model shows a chain-of-command, pyramid-like structure. At the top are the professional, "full-time" clergy who make up perhaps 1 percent of any local congregation.

A second level near the top are the "paraclergy," volunteers who are particularly active in congregational life. Their dedicated service within the programs and structures of the church is greatly appreciated by the clergy and is often used as a measure of their Christian commitment.

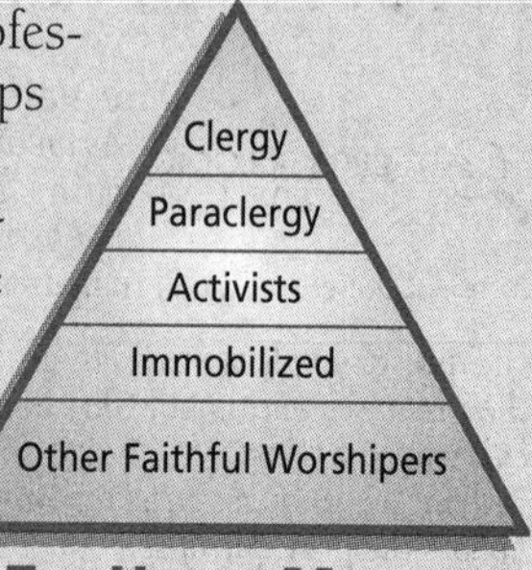

THE USUAL MODEL

Next are the "activists," some of whom may be among the paraclergy. These believers take a special interest in matters requiring action and the taking of a position. For example, they may advocate for a certain public policy, lead programs of social outreach, or lobby within the church to influence a particular decision. Sometimes activists stir up controversy and make others uncomfortable, but their zeal to apply the gospel is never in doubt.

Another important category to consider, especially in our own day, might be called "the immobilized." These are people in the midst of a crisis that dominates their experience, such as death, illness, divorce, or unemployment. Their situation makes it difficult for them to participate in ministry to others. Instead, they need the body to minister to them. Depending on the church, the immobilized and the other groups may comprise 20 to 30 percent or more of the congregation.

That leaves a majority of the church's faithful worshippers—perhaps 70 to 80 percent—available for ministries outside the church, out in the world among unbelievers. However, these potential "Monday ministers" are often overlooked by church leaders because their service is not directed toward the congregation itself. Yet because of their strategic location in the culture, they should be affirmed, equipped, and supported to impact the world for Christ (see "Faith Impacts the World," Mark 16:15–16).

When we examine the New Testament's description of the early church, we find all of the groups mentioned above. However, the way that these believers are organized and deployed for service is "upside-down" from the first model—or "right side up," depending on your point of view. The second model shows the difference.

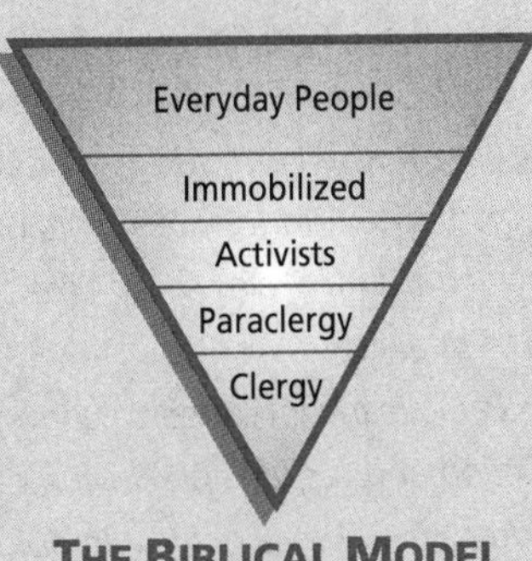

THE BIBLICAL MODEL

This is an outward-looking congregation in which the people of God view themselves as agents of Christ in the world. The pastors, teachers, and paraclergy function to "equip the saints for the work of ministry" (Eph. 4:12). They are, in effect, "internists" whose goal is to make Scripture "rise up and walk" in the minds and wills of everyday people.

As they do that, the larger congregation, the 70 to 80 percent majority above, become the "church scattered" as they live and work in the world, representing Christ.

Actually, both of the two diagrams shown are valid ways of understanding how a group of believers functions. As the first model suggests, the church needs to gather for worship, instruction, and the care of its members. In fact, the New Testament term for congregations of believers is *ekklēsia,* the "assembly." God's people are called out of the world and into the "church gathered," which functions as a home for safety, a hospital for restoration, a school for development, and an orchestra for worship.

This "gathered life," however, has its counterpart in the "scattered life" of God's people. As the second diagram suggests, the church looks outside itself to fulfill Christ's Great Commission (Matt. 28:18–20) in the world. Thus the "church scattered" becomes an army overcoming spiritual opposition, a social agency to meet the needs of wounded, hurting people, an agent of justice promoting righteousness in the community, and a communications company proclaiming the good news of salvation.

The church—gathered for equipping, scattered for service. Both dimensions are crucial. Where does your church place its emphasis? What ways can you think of to strengthen its internal growth and external outreach? ◆

The book of Acts shows a dynamic rhythm in the early church between gathering for the refinement of believers and the scattering of the church for encounter with the world. See "Reconnecting Sunday and Monday," Acts 2:46–47.

Paul Hindered from Visiting

17 As for us, brothers and sisters,[g] when, for a short
time, we were made orphans by being separated from
you—in person, not in heart—we longed with great eagerness to see you face to face. 18For we wanted to come to
you—certainly I, Paul, wanted to again and again—but Satan blocked our way. 19For what is our hope or joy or
crown of boasting before our Lord Jesus at his coming? Is it
not you? 20Yes, you are our glory and joy!

Timothy Sent to Thessalonica

3:1–10 3 Therefore when we could bear it no
longer, we decided to be left alone in
Athens; 2and we sent Timothy, our brother and co-worker
for God in proclaiming[h] the gospel of Christ, to strengthen

[g]Gk *brothers* [h]Gk lacks *proclaiming*

THIS IS THE WILL OF GOD, YOUR SANCTIFICATION.
—1 Thessalonians 4:3

GENTLE AS A NURSING MOTHER

CONSIDER THIS 2:7 *Paul felt great love for the Thessalonian believers, and he drew upon a touching image to communicate his affection, that of a woman nursing an infant (v. 7).*

Most mothers in the first-century world nursed their own infants. However, some wealthy women employed wet nurses. In that case, the child lived in the home of the wet nurse, who agreed to certain conditions such as not nursing other children and avoiding alcohol. The wet nurse took responsibility not only for feeding the child but also for raising it until it was weaned, often up to three years of age. Many contracts specified that the wet nurse's fee had to be returned if the child died.

Paul clearly intended to convey a sense of tender affection and responsible, loving care for his spiritual children, the Thessalonians. In doing so, he showed a side of spiritual leadership and nurture that Christian leaders do well to emulate today.

and encourage you for the sake of your faith, 3so that no one would be shaken by these persecutions. Indeed, you yourselves know that this is what we are destined for. 4In fact, when we were with you, we told you beforehand that we were to suffer persecution; so it turned out, as you know. 5For this reason, when I could bear it no longer, I sent to find out about your faith; I was afraid that somehow the tempter had tempted you and that our labor had been in vain.

Timothy's Encouraging Report

6 But Timothy has just now come to us from you, and has brought us the good news of your faith and love. He has told us also that you always remember us kindly and long to see us—just as we long to see you. 7For this reason, brothers and sisters,[i] during all our distress and persecution we have been encouraged about you through your faith. 8For we now live, if you continue to stand firm in the Lord. 9How can we thank God enough for you in return for all the joy that we feel before our God because of you? 10Night and day we pray most earnestly that we may see you face to face and restore whatever is lacking in your faith.

Paul's Prayer for the Thessalonians

11 Now may our God and Father himself and our Lord Jesus direct our way to you. 12And may the Lord make you increase and abound in love for one another and for all, just as we abound in love for you. 13And may he so strengthen your hearts in holiness that you may be blameless before our God and Father at the coming of our Lord Jesus with all his saints.

Maintain Sexual Purity

4 Finally, brothers and sisters,[i] we ask and urge you in the Lord Jesus that, as you learned from us how you ought to live and to please God (as, in fact, you are doing), you should do so more and more. 2For you know what instructions we gave you through the Lord Jesus. 3For this is the will of God, your sanctification: that you abstain from fornication; 4that each one of you know how to control your own body[j] in holiness and honor, 5not with lustful passion, like the Gentiles who do not know God; 6that no one wrong or exploit a brother or sister[k] in this matter, because the Lord is an avenger in all these things, just as we have already told you beforehand and solemnly warned

[i] *Gk brothers* [j] *Or how to take a wife for himself* [k] *Gk brother*

Encouraging the Mentor

CONSIDER THIS 3:1–10 **Separation from close friends can bring feelings of loneliness and loss, especially when one is facing disappointment or failure. Paul felt that way in Athens. Despite his strident efforts to present and defend the gospel, he met with only lackluster response from the Athenians (Acts 17:16–34). Not surprisingly, his thoughts turned toward the Thessalonians with whom he felt an unusually deep bond (1 Thess. 2:8; 2:17—3:1).**

Anxious for news, Paul sent his valuable associate Timothy north for a visit (3:2). The young man's report buoyed Paul up. Even as one city was resisting Christ, another was responding to Him in powerful and encouraging ways (3:6–10).

Paul's emotional honesty here is refreshing and instructive. Rather than deny or spiritualize his pain, he acknowledged it and took action. He needed the warm affection of the Thessalonians and especially the capable companionship of Timothy. Rather than live as a "Lone Ranger Christian," Paul stayed connected to other believers and relied on them for insight, encouragement, and support. In this way he honored a basic principle of Christian community (Heb. 10:24–25).

Does your mentor in faith need encouragement, affirmation, or help in keeping the big picture? Often when people are under great stress or feeling a sense of failure, the only thing they hear is what's wrong. Can you encourage yours with a word about what is *right?*

QUOTE UNQUOTE

CONSIDER THIS 4:11–12 *Leading a disciplined life of honest work (vv. 11–12) can pay as many spiritual dividends as working in vocational ministry:*

I've always been glad myself that theology is not the thing that I earn my living by. On the whole, I'd advise you to get on with your tent-making. The performance of a duty will probably teach you quite as much about God as academic theology would do. Mind, I'm not certain: but that is the view I incline to.

C.S. Lewis, Letter to Sheldon Vanauken, Jan. 5, 1951

you. 7For God did not call us to impurity but in holiness.
8Therefore whoever rejects this rejects not human authority
but God, who also gives his Holy Spirit to you.

Contribute to Society

9 Now concerning love of the brothers and sisters,[l] you
do not need to have anyone write to you, for you yourselves have been taught by God to love one another; 10and
indeed you do love all the brothers and sisters[l] throughout
Macedonia. But we urge you, beloved,[l] to do so more and
more, 11to aspire to live quietly, to mind
your own affairs, and to work with your
hands, as we directed you, 12so that you
may behave properly toward outsiders
and be dependent on no one.

4:11

4:11–12

Concerning Believers Who Have Died

13 But we do not want you to be uninformed, brothers
and sisters,[l] about those who have died,[m] so that you may
not grieve as others do who have no hope. 14For since we
believe that Jesus died and rose again, even so, through

(Bible text continued on page 720)

[l]Gk *brothers* [m]Gk *fallen asleep*

CONSIDER THIS 4:11

Quiet Living in a Hectic World

If any one word characterizes life in the modern world, it may be the word hectic. *The rat race. The grind. The fast lane. The laser lane. Things seem to move faster and faster, and anyone who can't keep up is in danger of being left behind.*

For that reason, Paul's exhortation to "live quietly" (v. 11) seems out of step with contemporary culture. How can one lead a quiet life when technology accelerates change and increases complexity? When television and other media bring the world into our homes and broadcast private lives to the world? When a global economy makes everybody's business our business?

The challenge to lead a quiet life in a hectic world is considerable, but as believers we can take decisive steps that will benefit us personally and spiritually. Actually, Paul gives us an important first step in the exhortation to "work with your hands." The focus is not on "hands" but on "your": it was not manual labor that Paul insisted on, but self-support (see "A Command to Work," 2 Thess. 3:6–12).

As far as quiet living, Paul was probably not objecting to noise and sound as such, but to needless distraction.

THE BLESSED HOPE

CONSIDER THIS 4:13–18 *Paul encouraged the believers at Thessalonica with the promise that the Lord will intervene (vv. 13–18). The resurrection is real! Fellowship with one another and with God is for real, whether it's here, there, or "in the air." This is the "blessed hope" that Paul offers by way of comfort (v. 18).*

The question this raises, however, is what is the interim hope for the church? Is it to flee the inner city and migrate to the suburbs, leaving behind city problems in search of healthier, wealthier prospects? Is that what Paul would recommend?

◆ ◆ ◆ ◆ ◆ ◆ ◆ ◆ ◆ ◆ ◆ ◆ ◆ ◆ ◆ ◆

One way that most people could bring a little more peace and quiet into their homes would be to cut their television viewing in half. Imagine the time left for family members and neighbors, personal reflection, and prayer!

However, the real thrust of this passage is not so much for believers to lower the noise level around them as to live peaceably with others, without disturbance or conflict (compare Rom. 12:18; Heb. 12:14). Minding our own business and working for ourselves are both means to that end, the end of "[behaving] properly toward outsiders [to the faith]" (1 Thess. 4:12).

How can we live peaceably? By avoiding quarrels and complaints (Col. 3:13); by refusing to take offense when others hurt us (Matt. 5:7–12); by not getting entangled in the affairs of others (Prov. 6:1); and by humbly accepting the circumstances that God sends us for our good, rather than grumbling (Rom. 8:28; Phil. 4:11–12). ◆

QUOTE UNQUOTE

CONSIDER THIS 5:6 *Today there may be a reason why some believers sleep "as others do" (v. 6):*

Many so-called believers have accepted a "decaffeinated" Christianity—it promises not to keep you awake at night.

Anglican Bishop Michael Marshall, as quoted in editor's column, *America Magazine*

Support the Weak

CONSIDER THIS 5:14 **Paul begins the concluding words of his letter with four sharp exhortations (v. 14). The "idlers"—the lazy, the undisciplined, those looking for a free ride—need a bit of a jolt. (Paul later gave them one in 2 Thess. 3:6–12.) Those who are losing heart need encouragement. And everyone needs patience.**

But Paul's third directive, "help the weak," has to do with one's responsibilities toward the poor. Wherever Scripture raises this issue, it challenges us to share at least some of our material wealth with people in desperate need. It is the only Christlike response there is.

Indeed, Christ serves as the ultimate model of compassion (see "Christ Became Poor," 2 Cor. 8:8–9). He even staked His credibility on His work among the downtrodden and destitute when John the Baptist inquired as to whether He was the Christ (see "Some Surprising Evidence," Matt. 11:2–6).

Paul hardly needed to challenge the Thessalonian believers to be generous. He knew by experience that even though they lived in deep poverty, they were willing to give "beyond their means" (2 Cor. 8:3) to help others in need.

If the Thessalonians, poor as they were, could give "beyond their means," what should affluent believers today be giving?

Scripture has a great deal to say about our responsibilities to the poor and needy. See " 'I Have Not Coveted,' " Acts 20:33–38.

Jesus, God will bring with him those who have died.[n] 15For
this we declare to you by the word of the Lord, that we
who are alive, who are left until the coming of the Lord,
will by no means precede those who have died.[n] 16For the
Lord himself, with a cry of command, with the archangel's
call and with the sound of God's trumpet, will descend
from heaven, and the dead in Christ will rise first. 17Then
we who are alive, who are left, will be caught up in the
clouds together with them to meet the Lord in the air; and
so we will be with the Lord forever.
18Therefore encourage one another with
these words.

4:13–18 see pg. 719

Concerning the Times

5 Now concerning the times and the seasons, brothers
and sisters,[o] you do not need to have anything written
to you. 2For you yourselves know very well that the day of
the Lord will come like a thief in the night. 3When they say,
"There is peace and security," then sudden destruction will
come upon them, as labor pains come upon a pregnant
woman, and there will be no escape! 4But you, beloved,[o]
are not in darkness, for that day to surprise you like a thief;
5for you are all children of light and children of the day; we
are not of the night or of darkness. 6So
then let us not fall asleep as others do,
but let us keep awake and be sober; 7for those who sleep
sleep at night, and those who are drunk get drunk at night.
8But since we belong to the day, let us be sober, and put on
the breastplate of faith and love, and for a helmet the hope
of salvation. 9For God has destined us not for wrath but for
obtaining salvation through our Lord Jesus Christ, 10who
died for us, so that whether we are awake or asleep we may
live with him. 11Therefore encourage one another and build
up each other, as indeed you are doing.

5:6 see pg. 719

The Community Life of Believers

12 But we appeal to you, brothers and sisters,[o] to respect
those who labor among you, and have charge of you in the
Lord and admonish you; 13esteem them very highly in love
because of their work. Be at peace among
yourselves. 14And we urge you, beloved,[o]
to admonish the idlers, encourage the faint hearted, help
the weak, be patient with all of them. 15See that none of
you repays evil for evil, but always seek to do good to one
another and to all. 16Rejoice always, 17pray without ceasing,
18give thanks in all circumstances; for this is the will of God

5:14

[n]Gk *fallen asleep* [o]Gk *brothers*

in Christ Jesus for you. 19Do not quench the Spirit. 20Do
not despise the words of prophets,[p] 21but test everything;
hold fast to what is good; 22abstain from every form of evil.

Blessings and Greetings

23 May the God of peace himself sanctify you entirely;
and may your spirit and soul and body be kept sound[q] and
blameless at the coming of our Lord Jesus Christ. 24The one
who calls you is faithful, and he will do this.
25 Beloved,[r] pray for us.
26 Greet all the brothers and sisters[s] with a holy kiss. 27I
solemnly command you by the Lord that this letter be read
to all of them.[t]
28 The grace of our Lord Jesus Christ be with you.[u]

[p]Gk *despise prophecies* [q]Or *complete* [r]Gk *Brothers* [s]Gk *brothers* [t]Gk *to all the brothers* [u]Other ancient authorities add *Amen*

THE ONE WHO CALLS YOU IS FAITHFUL.
—1 Thessalonians 5:24

The Second Letter of Paul to the Thessalonians

CONTENTS

ARTICLES

Greetings

1 Paul, Silvanus, and Timothy,
To the church of the Thessalonians in God our Father
and the Lord Jesus Christ:
2 Grace to you and peace from God our[a] Father and the
Lord Jesus Christ.

Praise for Withstanding Persecution

1:3–12

3 We must always give thanks to God
for you, brothers and sisters,[b] as is right,
because your faith is growing abundantly, and the love of
everyone of you for one another is increasing. 4Therefore
we ourselves boast of you among the churches of God for
your steadfastness and faith during all your persecutions
and the afflictions that you are enduring.
5 This is evidence of the righteous judgment of God,
and is intended to make you worthy of the kingdom of
God, for which you are also suffering. 6For it is indeed just
of God to repay with affliction those who afflict you, 7and
to give relief to the afflicted as well as to us, when the Lord
Jesus is revealed from heaven with his mighty angels 8in
flaming fire, inflicting vengeance on those who do not
know God and on those who do not obey the gospel of our
Lord Jesus. 9These will suffer the punishment of eternal destruction, separated from the presence of the Lord and from
the glory of his might, 10when he comes to be glorified by
his saints and to be marveled at on that day among all who
have believed, because our testimony to you was believed.
11To this end we always pray for you, asking that our God
will make you worthy of his call and will fulfill by his
power every good resolve and work of faith, 12so that the
name of our Lord Jesus may be glorified in you, and you in
him, according to the grace of our God and the Lord Jesus
Christ.

Discerning the Times

2:1–12 see pg. 724

2 As to the coming of our Lord Jesus
Christ and our being gathered to-
gether to him, we beg you, brothers and sisters,[b] 2not to be
quickly shaken in mind or alarmed, either by spirit or by
word or by letter, as though from us, to the effect that the
day of the Lord is already here. 3Let no one deceive you in
any way; for that day will not come unless the rebellion
comes first and the lawless one[c] is revealed, the one

(Bible text continued on page 725)

[a]Other ancient authorities read *the* [b]Gk *brothers* [c]Gk *the man of lawlessness*; other ancient authorities read *the man of sin*

Finishing Well

CONSIDER THIS 1:3–12 **What would be an appropriate epitaph on your tombstone? What statement would describe your life overall rather than whatever current circumstances you are temporarily facing right now?**

When Paul wrote to the believers in Thessalonica, they were in the midst of intense suffering (1:4–5). But Paul encouraged them to look beyond their immediate troubles to the return of Christ and the affirmation they would receive from Him at that time (vv. 6–7). Their enemies, who were really enemies of the Lord, would be judged and dealt with (vv. 8–9). By contrast, they would join with their Savior in joy and praise (v. 10). Paul went on in the next chapter to expand on this theme and its impact on the Thessalonians' current difficulties (2:1–12).

God calls us as His people to finish our lives well by holding on to the truths that last (2:15). He challenges us to maintain lifelong faithfulness and not to be entirely caught up in the here and now, whether good or bad.

As you consider the long-term direction of your life, what memories are you creating in others about your values and reputation? What will people choose to remember about you?

The Dangers of Preoccupations

CONSIDER THIS 2:1–12 Are you anxious about the future of the world? Do dire predictions about coming disasters trouble you? Or do dramatic solutions to the world's many problems hold your curiosity?

Like many people today, the believers in Thessalonica were vulnerable to urgent warnings and announcements related to the future (vv. 1–2). In fact, certain false teachers of the day pandered to people's interest in such things, playing to their greatest hopes and worst fears about the return of Christ (v. 3; 1 Thess. 5:2–5). In response, Paul appealed for reason and critical thinking based on the clear instructions he had given (2 Thess. 2:3–12, 15).

As we read 2 Thessalonians today, we, like the letter's original readers, need to "stand firm and hold fast to the traditions that [we] were taught," the truths of God's Word. We should avoid fanciful, fearful guesswork about events related to the Lord's return and instead be busy about our responsibilities at hand (3:6–13).

Father, Son, and Spirit for You!

CONSIDER THIS 2:13–17 One of the most important teachings of Christianity is the concept of the Trinity, the belief that God is one God, but exists in three Persons—Father, Son, and Holy Spirit. However, the Bible does not offer an explanation of this concept so much as a presentation of it. It assumes a Triune God but does not try to "prove" the Trinity.

In 2 Thessalonians, Paul seeks to enrich his readers' understanding of their new life in Christ by telling them about works done on their behalf by all three Persons of the Godhead. These same benefits are ours as believers today:

The Father *has selected us for salvation, loves us, and gives us consolation and hope (vv. 13, 16).*

The Son *shares His glory with us and provides comfort and stability in the faith (vv. 14, 16).*

The Spirit *purifies (sanctifies) us and develops our faith (v. 13).*

As believers, we have a powerful, caring, active God working on our behalf. For the first-century Christians at Thessalonica, that was a distinct contrast to the many gods of the surrounding Greek and Roman cultures that were often passive, sometimes capricious, and terribly self-absorbed. Likewise in our own day, our God is infinitely more powerful and personal than the vague "higher power" to which many people allude.

The doctrine of the Trinity may be difficult to comprehend, but as always we see in a dim mirror when it comes to ultimate truth (1 Cor. 13:12). Nevertheless, we can obediently respond to what we know clearly and not dwell on things that are cloudy. One thing we know for sure: our God is for us in every way!

A Command to Work

CONSIDER THIS 3:6–12 God wants Christians to take responsibility to provide for their material needs and those of their families. In fact, v. 10 states this as a *command.*

God has created a world of resources for this purpose. He gives us authority, along with strength and skills, to use those resources to earn our living. Work is His gift to us, a means of supplying what we need.

Obviously, there are times when grown children must care for their parents or grand-

(continued on next page)

destined for destruction.[d] 4He opposes and exalts himself
above every so-called god or object of worship, so that he
takes his seat in the temple of God, declaring himself to be
God. 5Do you not remember that I told you these things
when I was still with you? 6And you know what is now restraining him, so that he may be revealed when his time
comes. 7For the mystery of lawlessness is already at work,
but only until the one who now restrains it is removed.
8And then the lawless one will be revealed, whom the Lord
Jesus[e] will destroy[f] with the breath of his mouth, annihilat-
ing him by the manifestation of his coming. 9The coming of
the lawless one is apparent in the working of Satan, who
uses all power, signs, lying wonders, 10and every kind of
wicked deception for those who are perishing, because they
refused to love the truth and so be saved. 11For this reason
God sends them a powerful delusion, leading them to believe what is false, 12so that all who have not believed the
truth but took pleasure in unrighteousness will be condemned.

Thanksgiving, Exhortation, and a Prayer

2:13–17

13 But we must always give thanks
to God for you, brothers and sisters[g]
beloved by the Lord, because God chose you as the first
fruits[h] for salvation through sanctification by the Spirit and
through belief in the truth. 14For this purpose he called you
through our proclamation of the good news,[i] so that you
may obtain the glory of our Lord Jesus Christ. 15So then,
brothers and sisters,[g] stand firm and hold fast to the traditions that you were taught by us, either by word of mouth
or by our letter.
16 Now may our Lord Jesus Christ himself and God our
Father, who loved us and through grace gave us eternal
comfort and good hope, 17comfort your hearts and
strengthen them in every good work and word.

Paul Requests Prayer

3 Finally, brothers and sisters,[g] pray for us, so that the
word of the Lord may spread rapidly and be glorified
everywhere, just as it is among you, 2and that we may be
rescued from wicked and evil people; for not all have faith.
3But the Lord is faithful; he will strengthen you and guard
you from the evil one.[j] 4And we have confidence in the
Lord concerning you, that you are doing and will go on
doing the things that we command. 5May the Lord direct

[d]Gk *the son of destruction* [e]Other ancient authorities lack *Jesus* [f]Other ancient authorities read *consume* [g]Gk *brothers* [h]Other ancient authorities read *from the beginning* [i]Or *through our gospel* [j]Or *from evil*

(continued from previous page)

parents (Mark 7:9–13; 1 Tim. 5:4). Likewise, the church community sometimes must assume responsibility for those in need. But responsibility always starts with the individual, as this passage makes plain.

Earlier, in 1 Thessalonians 4:12, Paul explains why: (1) Because of the testimony that Christians have among unbelievers. Believers who beg, borrow unnecessarily, or steal discredit Christ and the church. (2) Because God doesn't want His children to "lack" what they need. He doesn't call us to poverty, but to adequacy.

Our everyday work is something that God takes seriously. See "People at Work," Heb. 2:7.

God not only wants us to work, He wants us to work with a Christlike "workstyle." See Titus 2:9–10.

The idea that God rewards godliness with material blessing can lead people to be irresponsible about work. See "The Dangers of Prosperity Theology," 1 Tim. 6:3–6.

ARE YOU TIRED?

CONSIDER THIS 3:13

Do you grow weary of holding to high standards of integrity or performance? Do you resent a lack of recognition? Are you fed up as you see others around you maneuvering to get out of work, and do you seethe when they get away with it?

Paul's admonition in v. 13 is meant for believers who are "burned out" on doing good. Keep in mind that God never forgets you. You are the object of His attention and love. He sees the good that you do when no one else is around—and He'll never forget it!

No Work? No Eat!

CONSIDER THIS 3:10 *Paul urged that those who would not work should not eat (v. 10). He may have been dealing with the laziness and idleness of those who thought there would be no tomorrow because they expected the immediate return of the Lord. Two thousand years later, we still anticipate the Second Coming. But it's interesting that nowadays people generally work as if there will be a tomorrow without a return.*

It's worth noting that these Macedonian believers, if they were the same ones that Paul referred to in 2 Corinthians 8:2, lived in abject poverty. It is common in poor communities—where jobs are few and many of those that do exist pay too little to support even the basics—for some to grow discouraged and give up all attempts at finding employment. How does your faith help you encourage those who need hope and nudge those who need to work?

your hearts to the love of God and to the steadfastness of
Christ.

Every Believer Has Work to Do

3:6–12 see pg. 724

6 Now we command you, beloved,[k]
in the name of our Lord Jesus Christ, to
keep away from believers who are[l] living in idleness and
not according to the tradition that they[m] received from us.

3:7–9

7 For you yourselves know how you
ought to imitate us; we were not idle
when we were with you, 8 and we did not eat anyone's bread
without paying for it; but with toil and labor we worked
night and day, so that we might not burden any of you.
9 This was not because we do not have that right, but in or-

3:10

der to give you an example to imitate.
10 For even when we were with you, we
gave you this command: Anyone unwilling to work should
not eat. 11 For we hear that some of you are living in idleness, mere busybodies, not doing any work. 12 Now such
persons we command and exhort in the Lord Jesus Christ
to do their work quietly and to earn their own living.

3:13 see pg. 725

13 Brothers and sisters,[n] do not be weary
in doing what is right.
14 Take note of those who do not obey what we say in
this letter; have nothing to do with them, so that they may
be ashamed. 15 Do not regard them as enemies, but warn
them as believers.[o]

Peace and Grace from the Lord

16 Now may the Lord of peace himself give you peace at
all times in all ways. The Lord be with all of you.
17 I, Paul, write this greeting with my own hand. This is
the mark in every letter of mine; it is the way I write. 18 The
grace of our Lord Jesus Christ be with all of you.[p]

[k] Gk *brothers* [l] Gk *from every brother who is* [m] Other ancient authorities read *you* [n] Gk *Brothers* [o] Gk *a brother* [p] Other ancient authorities add *Amen*

Paul's Example

A CLOSER LOOK 3:7–9 *Paul wrote that he had a right as an apostle to let others take care of him (v. 9). But he chose instead to earn his own living, setting an example of how believers should take responsibility to meet their own needs. Think of it: in effect, Paul was saying that if paid work was good enough for him, it's good enough for any of us.*

Paul's example also bears upon the reputation of churches and ministries today. Is there any reason why modern Christian leaders shouldn't at least consider doing as Paul did—earning a living outside the ministry to support their basic needs? See "I Have Not Coveted," Acts 20:33–38.

The First and Second Letters of Paul to

Timothy

One of the most difficult transitions for any organization to make is the transfer of power from the founders to a second generation of leadership. Countless entrepreneurs have brought disaster on their companies by refusing to relinquish control to others who are younger and, in their view, less competent. And even where visionaries gladly hand the reigns of authority over to qualified successors, there is no guarantee of continuity or success.

That's one reason why 1 and 2 Timothy make for such interesting reading. They are letters about the transfer of leadership to a new generation. Tradition says that Paul was passing the torch to his son in the faith, Timothy, pastor of the church at Ephesus. Paul knew that his own time was drawing to a close, that his work would soon come to an end. Would the Ephesians continue in the faith? Would they hold to the truth of the gospel and practice Christlike love toward one another? Would young Timothy be adequate to the pastoral task? Would he teach his people sound doctrine, navigate through disputes and disappointments, and model a lifestyle of faith?

Whatever the condition of the local church where you worship—whatever its size, form of leadership, or spiritual condition—1 and 2 Timothy will prove instructive. They take us back to one of the very first cases of a church moving into its second generation. As a result, they reveal the essentials of church life and leadership, the key things to which everyone in the body needs to be paying attention.

C O N T E N T S

A R T I C L E S

A Manual for Church Life

As we read Paul's instructions in 1 and 2 Timothy, we can feel his heart reaching out to the believers at Ephesus, where he had spent so much effort (Acts 19:1—20:1), and to his young protégé from Lystra. Paul wanted the congregation not merely to survive, but to thrive. So he wrote these two letters, which are among the earliest manuals we have for church organization. 1 Timothy emphasizes the life of the congregation, and 2 Timothy dwells on the life of the pastor.

Why were such instructions needed? Perhaps it was because of the gospel's unparalleled success at Ephesus. No longer was the Christian community there just a small body of new converts enjoying intimate fellowship on a first-name basis. The group had grown substantially over the years and was having an influence in cities throughout Asia Minor (see "The Ultimate 'New Testament Church' " at the Introduction to Ephesians). It was a diverse, multiethnic church struggling internally with issues of unity and doctrinal purity and externally with a pagan, sometimes hostile environment.

Ephesus was in many ways the church as it is supposed to be. But it had grown to the point where it needed organizational structure. For example:

- The church was attracting teachers who contradicted the gospel of Paul and Timothy, so it needed to think clearly about the content of the faith (1 Tim. 1:3–4, 18–20; 4:1–16).
- The gospel had impacted the commercial life of Ephesus, so church members needed to consider the public side of their faith (2:1–7).
- The worship service needed order (2:8–15).
- Standards were needed by which to appoint leaders (3:1–16) and hold them accountable (5:17–25).
- As its members advanced in years, the group had more and more widows to look after, so criteria were needed for determining who should receive help (5:3–16).
- Both masters and slaves, the rich and the poor, were joining the church, so it needed to develop a statement of policy regarding income and lifestyle (6:1–19).

From Paul's point of view, the key human actor in the work at Ephesus was Timothy. This man enjoyed an unusually close relationship with the apostle. Paul called him "my beloved and faithful child in the Lord" (1 Cor. 4:17) and his "loyal child in the faith" (1 Tim. 1:2). To the Philippians he boasted that no one else would have the same care for them as Timothy. Others were looking after their own affairs, Paul wrote, not the affairs of Christ. But not Timothy: "Timothy's worth you know, how like a son with a father he has served with me in the work of the gospel" (Phil. 2:19–22).

So as he penned 2 Timothy, Paul was doing far more than writing a directive to a subordinate. He was opening his heart as a mentor to a man who would succeed him. He urged Timothy over and over to follow after him, to repeat the truths "that you have heard *from me*" (2 Tim. 1:13; 2:2, italics added), to "continue in what you have learned and firmly believed, *knowing from whom you learned it*" (3:14, italics added). These are more than encouragements to uphold standards or to pass along rituals. This is an older man reaching into the mind and heart and life of a younger man with the most powerful and enduring educational tool of all—his own personality. ◆

Timothy

Paul's young protégé Timothy traveled widely and worked among groups of believers in Greece, Macedonia, and Asia Minor. He also participated in the sending of six New Testament letters. See the profile on Timothy at the Introduction to 2 Timothy.

Sorting Out the Truth

CONSIDER THIS 1:3–11 **It seems as if everybody has one thing or another to sell. Even teachers try to persuade us to accept their ideas and claims about what is true. But when it comes to matters of faith, it's wise to remain slightly skeptical, especially if someone claims to be God's special envoy to you.**

Paul warned young project leader Timothy about exactly that sort of activity—false doctrines, myths, and endless genealogies (vv. 3–4). Here and in other passages, Paul gave guidelines for sorting out and testing what people say about faith issues and practices:

- **Do they call for the practice of love (v. 5)?**
- **Are they ambitious, striving for esteem and acclaim through their teaching (vv. 6–7)?**
- **Does their message promote internal moral standards that produce good behavior (vv. 8–10)?**
- **Is there evidence of a radical change for the better because of their walk with Christ (vv. 12–14)?**
- **Do they offer praise and thanksgiving to God for what they have received (vv. 15–17)?**
- **Does their position build on the wisdom of predecessors (vv. 18–20)? (Paul contrasts those who called Timothy with two others whom he condemns.)**

When people make claims about spiritual things, weigh their words carefully against standards like these. Others around you may criticize any form of doubting, questioning, or evaluation. If so, they need to consider Paul's teaching in this passage. Scripture invites careful examination of statements about spiritual things so that we will distinguish what is from God and will last.

A True Son in the Faith

1 Paul, an apostle of Christ Jesus by the command of God
our Savior and of Christ Jesus our hope,
2 To Timothy, my loyal child in the faith:
Grace, mercy, and peace from God the Father and Christ
Jesus our Lord.

Counter False Teaching

1:3–4 see pg. 732

3 I urge you, as I did when I was on
my way to Macedonia, to remain in Eph-
esus so that you may instruct certain people not to teach
any different doctrine, 4and not to occupy themselves with
myths and endless genealogies that promote speculations
rather than the divine training[a] that is known by faith. 5But
the aim of such instruction is love that comes from a pure
heart, a good conscience, and sincere faith. 6Some people
have deviated from these and turned to meaningless talk,
7desiring to be teachers of the law, without understanding
either what they are saying or the things about which they
make assertions.
8 Now we know that the law is good, if one uses it legitimately. 9This means understanding that the law is laid
down not for the innocent but for the lawless and disobedient, for the godless and sinful, for the unholy and profane,
for those who kill their father or mother, for murderers,
10fornicators, sodomites, slave traders, liars, perjurers, and
whatever else is contrary to the sound

1:3–11

teaching 11that conforms to the glorious
gospel of the blessed God, which he entrusted to me.

Paul's Testimony

12 I am grateful to Christ Jesus our Lord, who has
strengthened me, because he judged me faithful and appointed me to his service, 13even though I was formerly a
blasphemer, a persecutor, and a man of violence. But I received mercy because I had acted ignorantly in unbelief,
14and the grace of our Lord overflowed for me with the
faith and love that are in Christ Jesus. 15The saying is sure
and worthy of full acceptance, that Christ Jesus came into
the world to save sinners—of whom I am the foremost.
16But for that very reason I received mercy, so that in me, as
the foremost, Jesus Christ might display the utmost patience, making me an example to those who would come to
believe in him for eternal life. 17To the King of the ages, immortal, invisible, the only God, be honor and glory forever
and ever.[b] Amen.

[a]Or *plan* [b]Gk *to the ages of the ages*

A Charge to Timothy

18 I am giving you these instructions, Timothy, my child, in accordance with the prophecies made earlier about you, so that by following them you may fight the good fight, 19having faith and a good conscience. By rejecting conscience, certain persons have suffered shipwreck in the faith; 20among them are Hymenaeus and Alexander, whom I have turned over to Satan, so that they may learn not to blaspheme.

Instructions for Men and Women

2:1–7

2 First of all, then, I urge that supplications, prayers, intercessions, and thanksgivings be made for everyone, 2for kings and all who are in high positions, so that we may lead a quiet and peaceable life in all godliness and dignity. 3This is right and is acceptable in the sight of God our Savior, 4who desires everyone to be saved and to come to the knowledge of the truth. 5For

there is one God;
 there is also one mediator between God and
 humankind,
Christ Jesus, himself human,
6 who gave himself a ransom for all

—this was attested at the right time. 7For this I was appointed a herald and an apostle (I am telling the truth,[c] I am not lying), a teacher of the Gentiles in faith and truth.

2:8–15 see pg. 734

8 I desire, then, that in every place the men should pray, lifting up holy hands without anger or argument; 9also that the women should dress themselves modestly and decently in suitable clothing, not with their hair braided, or with gold, pearls, or expensive clothes, 10but with good works, as is proper for women who profess reverence for God. 11Let a woman[d] learn in silence with full submission. 12I permit no woman[d] to teach or to have authority over a man;[e] she is to keep silent. 13For Adam was formed first, then Eve; 14and Adam was not deceived, but the woman was deceived and became a transgressor. 15Yet she will be saved through childbearing, provided they continue in faith and love and holiness, with modesty.

Standards for Leaders

3:1 see pg. 733

3 The saying is sure:[f] whoever aspires to the office of bishop[g] desires a

(Bible text continued on page 733)

[c]Other ancient authorities add *in Christ* [d]Or *wife* [e]Or *her husband* [f]Some interpreters place these words at the end of the previous paragraph. Other ancient authorities read *The saying is commonly accepted* [g]Or *overseer*

The Prayer Breakfast Movement

CONSIDER THIS 2:1–7 **Paul urges prayer for "kings and all who are in high positions" (vv. 1–2). In that spirit, Christians today pray for presidents, cabinet members, legislators, governors, mayors, and judges. In fact, a modern prayer breakfast movement has developed, with events held annually in many major cities.**

City-wide prayer for leaders recalls Abraham, who prayed for the doomed city of Sodom (Gen. 18:16–33). Abraham assumed that his prayers as a righteous man could preserve a city. In the same way, Paul affirms that believers ought to petition God for a "quiet and peaceable" community life (1 Tim. 2:2).

One interesting result of that peace—and a good reason for believers to serve in public office and/or to support in prayer those who do—is more effective witness (vv. 3–7).

CONSIDER THIS
1:3–4

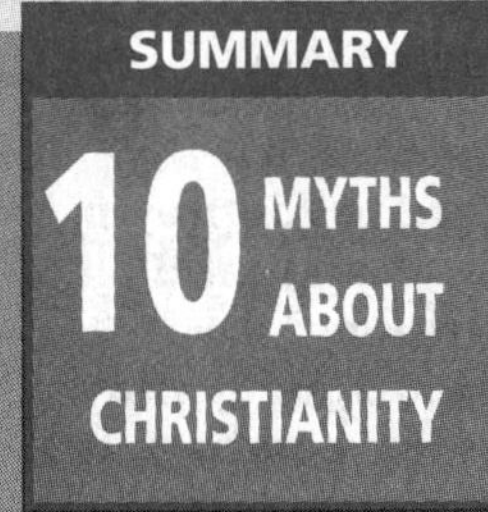

SUMMARY: THE TEN FAVORITE MYTHS PEOPLE BELIEVE ABOUT CHRISTIANITY

Truth and error have battled since the first days of the Christian faith. Paul urged Timothy to counter those who taught strange doctrines at Ephesus (vv. 3–4). Today, Christianity has become a major world religion with a well established set of beliefs. Nevertheless, believers still must contend with doctrinal error and misconceptions about the faith.

Unfortunately, many people have accepted a number of myths about Christianity, with the result that they never respond to Jesus as He really is. They reject the gospel on the basis of half-truths and lies rather than a clear understanding of Christ's message or its consequences. Below is a list of ten myths about Christianity that are common in our culture. Turn to the passages indicated for a discussion of these errors.

THE TEN FAVORITE MYTHS

#	Myth	See
1	Jesus Christ was only a great moral teacher.	Matt. 13:34–35
2	There is no evidence that Jesus rose from the dead.	Matt. 28:1–10
3	Science is in conflict with Christian faith.	John 4:48
4	It doesn't matter what you believe, all religions are basically the same.	Acts 4:12
5	Christianity is just a crutch for the weak.	1 Cor. 1:26
6	People become Christians through social conditioning.	1 Cor. 15:9–10
7	Christianity stifles personal freedom.	Gal. 5:1–12
8	Christianity is other-worldly and irrelevant to modern life.	Heb. 12:1–2
9	The Bible is unreliable and not to be trusted.	2 Pet. 1:16
10	All the evil and suffering in the world prove there is no God.	Rev. 20:1–10

Abandon the Myths—Go for the Truth!

Go for the truth about God. There are many things in the world that point to the truth about God—the kind of God that the Bible talks about, the God who made us, loves us, and communicates Himself to us.

Go for the truth about Jesus. Jesus claimed to be *the* truth (John 14:6). Everything in his life, teaching, death, and resurrection validates that astounding claim. So feel free to take a good, long look at Jesus. He won't disappoint you!

Go for the truth about yourself. Each of us is something of an enigma. At times we can be kind and thoughtful, generous and unselfish. Yet we can also be self-centered and vindictive, lustful and treacherous. What a contradiction! As the Roman poet Ovid put it, "I see the better way and I approve it—but I follow the worse." Or as Paul wrote, "I do not do the good I want, but the evil I do not want is what I do" (Rom. 7:19).

No wonder some people see only the good in human nature and dream of utopia, while others see little but moral squalor

(continued on next page)

noble task. 2 Now a bishop[h] must be above reproach, married only once,[i] temperate, sensible, respectable, hospitable,
3:3 an apt teacher, 3 not a drunkard, not vio-
lent but gentle, not quarrelsome, and not
a lover of money. 4 He must manage his own household
well, keeping his children submissive and respectful in
every way— 5 for if someone does not know how to manage
his own household, how can he take care of God's church?
6 He must not be a recent convert, or he may be puffed up
with conceit and fall into the condemnation of the devil.
7 Moreover, he must be well thought of by outsiders, so that
he may not fall into disgrace and the snare of the devil.
8 Deacons likewise must be serious, not double-
tongued, not indulging in much wine, not greedy for
money; 9 they must hold fast to the mystery of the faith with

[h] *Or an overseer* [i] *Gk the husband of one wife*

No Greedy Leaders!

A CLOSER LOOK 3:3

Many church members today work in the marketplace where the mark of success is making and accumulating wealth. The same was true in Timothy's congregation at Ephesus. So Paul warns about those who are "greedy for money" (v. 3). He has much more to say about wealth in chapter 6. See "Christians and Money," 1 Tim. 6:6–19.

One Standard for All

CONSIDER THIS 3:1

In chapter 3, Paul outlines the criteria that qualify people for leadership in the church community. All of the items mentioned have to do with character. God seems far more concerned with the personal integrity of leaders than with their education, eloquence, or charisma.

Without question, the standards are high, but that doesn't imply a higher standard for church leaders than "ordinary" Christians. All believers are called to these same high standards of Christlikeness. Paul is not creating a class of the spiritually elite here. He is simply indicating that the church should select its leadership from among people who are generally living up to the ideals of the gospel.

(continued from previous page)

and political chaos and fear cosmic destruction ahead. Christianity sees a bit of both: we are like semi-ruined temples that still bear the marks of their original splendor. Only the Architect who designed us can fully repair and restore us to our original purpose and beauty.

Go for the truth about growth. If we're going to be restored to God, change will be required. The first step is to turn our lives over to Him. Then He begins a process of growth that affects every aspect of life. The process takes time—a lifetime, in fact. Indeed, the process won't end until we meet Him after death.

For now, God helps us cultivate a close relationship with Himself. He develops our character so that we gradually become more like Christ. And He especially affects our relationships with other people so that we treat them as Jesus would. ◆

a clear conscience. 10 And let them first be tested; then, if
they prove themselves blameless, let them serve as deacons.
11 Women[j] likewise must be serious, not slanderers, but
temperate, faithful in all things. 12 Let deacons be married
only once,[k] and let them manage their children and their
households well; 13 for those who serve well as deacons gain
a good standing for themselves and great boldness in the
faith that is in Christ Jesus.

Paul's Reason for Writing

14 I hope to come to you soon, but I am writing these
instructions to you so that, 15 if I am delayed, you may
know how one ought to behave in the household of God,
which is the church of the living God, the pillar and bul-
wark of the truth. 16 Without any doubt, the mystery of our
religion is great:

He[l] was revealed in flesh,
  vindicated[m] in spirit,[n]
    seen by angels,
proclaimed among Gentiles,
  believed in throughout the world,
    taken up in glory.

[j]Or *Their wives*, or *Women deacons* [k]Gk *be husbands of one wife* [l]Gk *Who*; other ancient authorities read *God*; others, *Which* [m]Or *justified* [n]Or *by the Spirit*

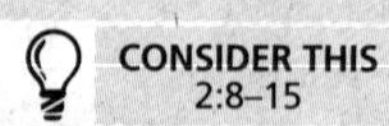

CONSIDER THIS
2:8–15

A New Way to Worship

What is the proper way to worship God? For those who had grown up in the religious climate of Ephesus before the gospel, Christian worship called for altogether different behavior than they were used to practicing. So Paul offered guidelines for worship to the men and women in the Ephesian church (vv. 8–15).

Ephesus (see profile at the Introduction to Ephesians) was world-renowned for its magnificent temple of Artemis. Pagan cults flourished there, along with occult practices. In fact, books with magic recipes came to be known as "Ephesian books."

Nevertheless, the gospel bore great fruit there and the community of believers grew rapidly (see "The Ephesus Approach," Acts 19:8–41). Yet some of the new converts brought their old way of life into the church and began teaching other doctrines (1 Tim. 1:3–7). When it came to worship, many were used to wild rites and festivals. Ephesian women were particularly unacquainted with pub-

Deception in Latter Times

4:1–16

4 Now the Spirit expressly says that in
later[o] times some will renounce the
faith by paying attention to deceitful spirits and teachings
of demons, 2through the hypocrisy of liars whose consciences are seared with a hot iron. 3They forbid marriage
and demand abstinence from foods, which God created to
be received with thanksgiving by those who believe and
know the truth. 4For everything created by God is good,
and nothing is to be rejected, provided it is received with
thanksgiving; 5for it is sanctified by God's word and by
prayer.

Live and Teach the Truth

6 If you put these instructions before the brothers and
sisters,[p] you will be a good servant[q] of Christ Jesus, nourished on the words of the faith and of the sound teaching
that you have followed. 7Have nothing to do with profane
myths and old wives' tales. Train yourself in godliness, 8for,
while physical training is of some value, godliness is valuable in every way, holding promise for both the present life
and the life to come. 9The saying is sure and worthy of full

[o]Or *the last* [p]Gk *brothers* [q]Or *deacon*

lic behavior, having been excluded for the most part from public gatherings, except pagan rituals.

So Paul described the correct way of worship. Men, who were apparently given to anger and doubts, needed to stop wrangling and start praying (v. 8). Likewise, women needed to focus on godliness and good works rather than clothing, jewelry, and hairstyles (vv. 9–10). And because some were apparently disruptive, they needed to practice restraint (v. 11)—not necessarily complete silence, but "quiet" (as the word is translated in 2 Thess. 3:12), since they likely participated in the prayers and other expressive parts of the worship gatherings (compare 1 Cor. 11:5; Eph. 5:19).

Today the message of Christ continues to attract people from a variety of backgrounds. Some, like the Ephesians, need to learn for the first time about worshiping God. Others bring cultural norms and expectations that are worth using in the worship experience, so long as they preserve biblical guidelines such as those that Paul gave to the Ephesians. ◆

Feel Like a Novice?

CONSIDER THIS 4:1–16 **Are you new at work or in your neighborhood? Has marriage recently brought you into a whole new family of relationships? Do you feel that proving yourself and gaining acceptance is an uphill battle? Are you tempted to declare, "I'll show 'em"?**

Timothy was young in age and relatively untested as a trainee under Paul, his mentor. His pastorate in Ephesus was his first solo assignment. So Paul offered him some seasoned wisdom and perspective:

- **Tough times are to be expected in a broken world (vv. 1–3).**
- **We need to accept God's gifts with thanksgiving (vv. 4–5).**
- **Affirm the truth with others who share your faith (v. 6).**
- **Avoid getting caught up in the folklore that occurs in every environment (v. 7). It's not that stories are bad, but always search out the truth and make it your trademark (vv. 8–11).**
- **Overcome the skepticism of others with the basics like love, edifying conversation, and purity (v. 12).**
- **Work on your own skills and abilities with diligence (vv. 13–14).**

Over the long haul, perspectives like these will hold one in good stead, while the shortcuts of dirty politics, competition, and intrigue will fail.

WIDOWS

FOR YOUR INFO 5:3 **Widows (v. 3) were common in the ancient world due to a number of factors. First, women tended to marry earlier in life than men, usually in their early teens, because of societal expectations that they marry as virgins. The same did not apply to men, and most delayed marriage into their twenties and even thirties, as marriage incurred responsibility. That age disparity between husbands and wives, along with disease, wars, and other factors of mortality, created many widows.**

Among the Jews, widows were the responsibility of the community (Deut. 24:19–21). One feature of the system was for a brother of the deceased husband to take the widow as his wife and father an heir if no male heirs had been born (Deut. 25:5). Unremarried widows would be supported by family members or left to manage on their own as best they could. But in many cases widows were reduced to begging, prostitution, or slavery to survive.

Paul and the other leaders of the early church had no intention of tolerating that possibility in the Christian community. Here he gives clear instructions on the care of widows. Earlier, problems in the care of widows, along with ethnic tensions, had created conflict for the church at Jerusalem (Acts 6:1–7).

Today, the care of widows who lack either savings or adequate support from their families is often left to the state or nonprofit agencies. However, there is no reason why Paul's instructions regarding widows do not still apply to believers.

Widows who came in contact with Jesus found Him responsive to their needs. He offered them hope (Luke 7:11–15). He also used them frequently as object lessons of dependence on God and the need for justice (Mark 12:41–44; Luke 18:1–8; 21:1–4).

acceptance. 10For to this end we toil and struggle,[r] because we have our hope set on the living God, who is the Savior of all people, especially of those who believe.

11 These are the things you must insist on and teach. 12Let no one despise your youth, but set the believers an example in speech and conduct, in love, in faith, in purity. 13Until I arrive, give attention to the public reading of scripture,[s] to exhorting, to teaching. 14Do not neglect the gift that is in you, which was given to you through prophecy with the laying on of hands by the council of elders.[t] 15Put these things into practice, devote yourself to them, so that all may see your progress. 16Pay close attention to yourself and to your teaching; continue in these things, for in doing this you will save both yourself and your hearers.

Treatment of Believers

5 Do not speak harshly to an older man,[u] but speak to him as to a father, to younger men as brothers, 2to older women as mothers, to younger women as sisters—with absolute purity.

Care for Widows

5:3

3 Honor widows who are really widows. 4If a widow has children or grandchildren, they should first learn their religious duty to their own family and make some repayment to their parents; for this is pleasing in God's sight. 5The real widow, left alone, has set her hope on God and continues in supplications and prayers night and day; 6but the widow[v] who lives for pleasure is dead even while she lives. 7Give these commands as well, so that they may be above reproach. 8And whoever does not provide for relatives, and especially for family members, has denied the faith and is worse than an unbeliever.

9 Let a widow be put on the list if she is not less than sixty years old and has been married only once;[w] 10she must be well attested for her good works, as one who has brought up children, shown hospitality, washed the saints' feet, helped the afflicted, and devoted herself to doing good in every way. 11But refuse to put younger widows on the list; for when their sensual desires alienate them from Christ, they want to marry, 12and so they incur condemnation for having violated their first pledge. 13Besides that, they learn to be idle, gadding about from house to house; and they are not merely idle, but also gossips and

(Bible text continued on page 738)

[r]Other ancient authorities read *suffer reproach* [s]Gk *to the reading* [t]Gk *by the presbytery* [u]Or *an elder, or a presbyter* [v]Gk *she* [w]Gk *the wife of one husband*

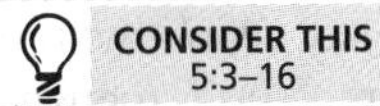

Effective Care for the Needy

Followers of Christ have the potential to be among the world's most effective agents for social service. They have the example of Christ to follow. They have the motivation of doing compassionate work in His name. They have the structure, community life, and pooled resources of their congregations. And they have the model of the early church, which provided standards for the systematic, ongoing care of widows (vv. 3–22).

We can learn a great deal about delivering services to the needy by carefully observing the principles that Paul set forth for Timothy and the believers at Ephesus. For example:

(1) The care described here was regular and ongoing for people who were "put on the list" (v. 9) of continuing recipients of the church's support. Presumably, the church was to give short-term support to people who needed help until they could get back on their feet; but not to able-bodied people who refused to work to support themselves (compare 2 Thess. 3:10).

(2) The care was for "widows who are really widows" (v. 3). The Old Testament described a widow as a woman who had no one to support her and therefore depended on the protection of the community (Ex. 22:22–24; Deut. 14:28–29; 24:17–22; 26:12–13). If a widow had able-bodied children or grandchildren, she needed to depend on them for provision, not the church (1 Tim. 5:4).

(3) A widow who was "put on the list" incurred certain responsibilities in order to maintain her eligibility for the church's charity. For example, she needed to be frugal lest someone reproach her for living an extravagant lifestyle and the fellowship for supporting it (vv. 6–7). Likewise, she needed to meet certain criteria related to her earlier life and character (vv. 9–10). The point was not to keep a widow out of the program, but to ensure that she served her fellow believers in every way she could if she was going to receive support.

(4) Younger widows were expected to remarry and, as was common for that day, bear children (who presumably would care for their parents in old age). Again, the church needed to avoid offering long-term support to someone who had other options. To do so might contribute to wantonness, idleness, and gossip (vv. 11–14).

These instructions to Timothy mirror principles about systematic aid found elsewhere in Scripture. For example, Paul told the Corinthians that financial support should go only to the truly poor (see "Who Are the Poor?" 2 Cor. 9:9–10). Likewise, the aim of providing care is to give people enough food, clothing, and other aid for survival and health. It is not intended to give anyone a free ride, even less to underwrite an inflated standard of living (2 Cor. 8:13–15; 1 Tim. 6:6–10).

First Timothy 5 specifically addresses the care of widows, but its principles apply to a much broader range of human need. By using this and other biblical texts to develop social programs, believers can effectively render care in a way that honors the name of Christ and provides real help to needy people. ◆

QUOTE UNQUOTE

CONSIDER THIS
6:7

One of the world's wealthiest men concurred with Scripture's observation that we can carry nothing out of this world (v. 7) when he said:

It is disgraceful to die a rich man.

Andrew Carnegie

busybodies, saying what they should not say. 14So I would
have younger widows marry, bear children, and manage
their households, so as to give the adversary no occasion to
revile us. 15For some have already turned away to follow
Satan. 16If any believing woman[x] has relatives who are really widows, let her assist
them; let the church not be burdened, so that it can assist
those who are real widows.

5:3–16
see pg. 737

Dealing with Elders

17 Let the elders who rule well be considered worthy of
double honor,[y] especially those who labor in preaching and

[x]Other ancient authorities read *believing man or woman*; others, *believing man* [y]Or *compensation*

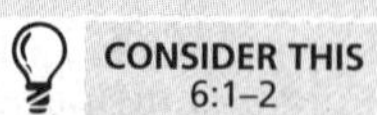

CONSIDER THIS
6:1–2

"I Won't Hire Christians!"

He stood beside a window overlooking the shop floor below. A din of table saws, routers, and other equipment filtered up to the tiny cubicle. His desk was lost under mountains of papers, folders, catalogues, manuals, bills, and an ancient rotary phone.

Turning from the window he sighed and said, "I don't usually hire people who tell me they're Christians. I know that sounds mean. And I don't advertise it. I'm a Christian myself and I try to run this company the way I think God wants it run. But I won't hire Christians!"

"Why not?" he was asked.

"I've been burned once too often," he replied. "I've hired people just because they said they were Christians, and they turned out to be some of the worst employees I ever had.

"I remember one guy was always standing around preaching to the other guys instead of getting his work done. I couldn't afford him! Another guy kept coming in late, day after day. His supervisor warned him. Finally he fired him. Then the fellow came to me to try and get his job back. I told him the supervisor had made the right decision. Know what he said? 'I thought you were a Christian!' Imagine that! He thought he could take advantage of me just because he knew I was a Christian!

"After that I decided: no more Christians!" ◆

Every believer should understand why God has given us work. See "People at Work," Heb. 2:7.

When Christians enter the workplace, they need to exhibit a Christlike "workstyle." See Titus 2:9–10. They also need to remember "Who's the Boss?" Col. 3:22–24.

teaching; 18for the scripture says, "You shall not muzzle an
ox while it is treading out the grain," and, "The laborer deserves to be paid." 19Never accept any accusation against an
elder except on the evidence of two or three witnesses. 20As
for those who persist in sin, rebuke them in the presence of
all, so that the rest also may stand in fear. 21In the presence
of God and of Christ Jesus and of the elect angels, I warn
you to keep these instructions without prejudice, doing
nothing on the basis of partiality. 22Do not ordain[z] anyone
hastily, and do not participate in the sins of others; keep
yourself pure.
23 No longer drink only water, but take a little wine for
the sake of your stomach and your frequent ailments.
24 The sins of some people are conspicuous and precede
them to judgment, while the sins of others follow them
there. 25So also good works are conspicuous; and even
when they are not, they cannot remain hidden.

Slaves Should Respect Masters

6:1–2

6 Let all who are under the yoke of
slavery regard their masters as wor-
thy of all honor, so that the name of God and the teaching
may not be blasphemed. 2Those who have believing masters must not be disrespectful to them on the ground that
they are members of the church;[a] rather they must serve
them all the more, since those who benefit by their service
are believers and beloved.[b]

Godliness and Gain

6:3–6 see pg. 742

Teach and urge these duties. 3Whoever
teaches otherwise and does not agree
with the sound words of our Lord Jesus Christ and the
teaching that is in accordance with godliness, 4is conceited,
understanding nothing, and has a morbid craving for controversy and for disputes about words. From these come
envy, dissension, slander, base suspicions, 5and wrangling
among those who are depraved in mind and bereft of
the truth, imagining that godliness is a
means of gain.[c] 6Of course, there is great
gain in godliness combined with contentment; 7for we brought nothing into the
world, so that[d] we can take nothing out of it; 8but if we
have food and clothing, we will be content with these. 9But
those who want to be rich fall into temptation and are
trapped by many senseless and harmful desires that plunge

6:6–19 see pg. 740

6:7

(Bible text continued on page 743)

[z]Gk *Do not lay hands on* [a]Gk *are brothers* [b]Or *since they are believers and beloved, who devote themselves to good deeds* [c]Other ancient authorities add *Withdraw yourself from such people* [d]Other ancient authorities read *world—it is certain that*

QUOTE UNQUOTE

CONSIDER THIS
6:17–19

Eighteenth-century hymn writer Charles Wesley's instructions regarding money repeat the themes that Paul gave to Timothy and the believers at Ephesus (vv. 17–19):

Gain all you can by honest industry. Use all possible diligence in your calling. Lose no time. Gain all you can, by common sense, by using in your business all the understanding which God has given you. It is amazing to observe how few do this . . . . Having gained all you can by honest wisdom and unwearied diligence, the second rule of Christian prudence is, "Save all you can." Do not throw it away in idle expenses—to gratify pride, etc. If you desire to be a good and faithful steward . . . first provide things needful for yourself, food, raiment, etc. Second, provide these for your wife, your children, your servants, and others who pertain to your household. If then you have an overplus, do good to them that are of the household of faith. If there be still an overplus, do good to all men.

Charles Wesley, *The Use of Money.* (Wesley amassed some $250,000 from his writings, which made him a wealthy man according to the standards of his age.)

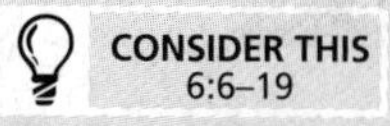
CONSIDER THIS
6:6–19

CHRISTIANS AND MONEY

Paul ridicules the idea that God is in the business of dispensing material gain in exchange for spiritual cooperation (v. 5). That launches him into a discussion of money that modern believers do well to study carefully, given the emphasis on money in our culture. He speaks to three categories of people: those who want to get rich (vv. 6–10), those who want to honor God (vv. 11–16), and those who are rich and want to honor God (vv. 17–19).

Contentment versus Covetousness (vv. 6–10)

Paul warns us strongly against "the love of money" (v. 10). But let's be sure we interpret his words correctly. He does not say that money itself is evil (nor does any other Scripture). Neither does he say that money is *the* fundamental root of evil, or that money lies at the root of *every* evil. Rather, the *love* of money (something inside people, not money itself) can be *a* root (but not the only root) of all *kinds* of evil (but not of all evil).

But don't let those qualifications soften the blow: people who love money are vulnerable to all kinds of evil, the worst of which, Paul points out, is straying from the faith (see "Do-It-Yourself Idolatry," Col. 3:5).

Given that danger, believers should by all means avoid greed. Jesus gave a direct, unequivocal command to that effect. He didn't tell us to guard against it in others, but in ourselves (see "Watch Out for Greed!" Luke 12:15).

Paul offers the alternative to greed, or covetousness, as contentment (vv. 6–8). However, his description of contentment—food and clothing—sounds incredibly spartan in our own culture that extols self-made millionaires and entertains itself by paying video visits to those who live in opulent, even decadent lifestyles. Are believers required to take vows of poverty like Franciscan monks (see "A Prayer of the Laity," Matt. 10:7–10)?

No, but Paul does remind us in this passage what poverty really is: lack of food, clothing, and shelter adequate for survival where one lives. If we have these, we ought to be content. If not, then we are truly destitute and dependent on the charity of others for survival. The biblical concept of poverty is not merely having less than the average income, or some percentage of it, in one's society, as contemporary sociologists and economists tend to define it (see "Who Are the Poor?" 2 Cor. 9:9–10).

Can Paul be serious? Is it really possible to be content, at least in our society, with merely the basics—food, clothing, and shelter? Paul should know. He experienced firsthand the wealth and privileges of prominence in the Jewish community and of Roman citizenship. Yet he also suffered extraordinary hardships in his work. Through it all he learned a secret that helped him maintain contentment. What was it? See "A Lifestyle of Contentment," Phil. 4:10–13.

A Charge to Timothy (vv. 11–16)

Paul's example was especially important to Timothy, his protégé in the faith (see the Introduction to 2 Timothy). He challenges the young pastor to pursue a lifestyle that values character over cash (1 Tim. 6:11). The words are addressed to Timothy, but they apply to anyone who wants to honor God in life. Timothy needed to watch out for greed just like any other believer (see "One Standard for All," 3:1; and "No Greedy Leaders!" 3:3).

Paul was especially on the lookout for greed. Interestingly, one of his main strategies for avoiding it was to earn his own living as a tentmaker, rather than live off the generosity of others (see "I Have Not Coveted!" Acts 20:33–38).

Commands for Rich Christians (vv. 17–19)

Apparently there were wealthy believers in Timothy's church at Ephesus. The city was extraordinarily prosperous. In fact, its tourist trade brought in so much revenue that the town leaders opened the first world bank. Paul had penetrated this vibrant economic life with the gospel, winning many converts (see "The Ephesus Approach," Acts 19:8–41). No doubt some of the rich Christians he addresses here brought their money with them into the faith—just like many in the modern church.

The question, then, especially in light of the teaching in 1 Tim. 6:6–10, is, what should people with money do if they want to honor God? Paul says they should start by examining their attitudes. Money has incredible power to create feelings of pride, superiority, and self-sufficiency (v. 17). So people of means have to learn to look beyond their money to God, the ultimate source of wealth.

But attitude is only half the battle. Sooner or later rich Christians need to take conscious, decisive action with their wealth. They need to put it into play serving God and others (v. 18).

What About You?

What is your deepest desire? Is it to be rich rather than righteous? If so, beware! Longing for wealth leads to many dangers—even to death. God wants you to grasp something far more permanent and satisfying—eternal life (vv. 12, 18). ◆

The ultimate model for how Christians, rich or poor, should handle wealth is Jesus. See Phil. 2:5–8.

IN THEIR EAGERNESS TO BE RICH SOME HAVE WANDERED AWAY FROM THE FAITH. . . .
—1 Timothy 6:10

CONSIDER THIS
6:3–6

THE DANGERS OF PROSPERITY THEOLOGY

Susan is a sales representative. She can make a big sale, but only if she mildly deceives the customer. She decides to tell the truth and she loses the sale. Should she expect God to honor her integrity by helping her make an even bigger sale in the future?

A contractor is deciding whether to award a job to Allen's firm or to another company. Allen really needs the business. So he prays at length that he will get the contract, and asks others to pray, too. Should he anticipate that God will somehow make the contractor award him the job? If not, should he expect God to arrange for other work to come along soon?

John and Joan are reviewing their finances. John has recently received a small bonus from his company, and they're wondering what to do with it. They finally decide to give ten percent of it to their church, and another ten percent to a mission. Can they expect God to bring them more money as a result?

Does God reward godliness with material blessing? Not according to v. 5. In fact, Paul describes those who teach that as being "destitute of the truth." They are guilty of fostering a "prosperity theology." That's a dangerous view:

It encourages perverted motives. God wants us to seek Him for His own sake, not for a "payoff" of physical well-being or financial gain. The reward of loving obedience is a closer relationship to God (John 14:15–18, 21–23). He also wants us to be content with what He provides us, not greedy for more (v. 6).

It misinterprets God's deepest concerns for us. If God wants us to have abundant material benefits, if He sees that they would be in our best interest, then we can trust Him to supply them. Otherwise, such "blessings" would be harmful. God loves us too much to destroy us with what we don't need or can't handle.

It misrepresents God's promises in Scripture. The Old Testament offers plenty of promises about material prosperity and blessing. But for the most part, those benefits were offered to the nation of Israel, not to individual believers.

Furthermore, God's promises are always offered to those who truly love Him, seek His will, and obey Him from a pure heart. The Lord Himself is always the end to be sought; material benefits are never an end in themselves.

A final note: God has established certain "moral laws" that benefit anyone who adheres to them. (The Proverbs are filled with prudent advice that rewards those who keep them.) For example, paying taxes avoids the trouble, fines, prison terms, and public censure associated with nonpayment. In this sense it "pays" to obey the law. But we shouldn't expect special blessing for doing what God wants us to do anyway (Luke 17:7–10). ◆

people into ruin and destruction. [10]For the love of money is a root of all kinds of evil, and in their eagerness to be rich some have wandered away from the faith and pierced themselves with many pains.

Life's Focus Is Christ

11 But as for you, man of God, shun all this; pursue righteousness, godliness, faith, love, endurance, gentleness. [12]Fight the good fight of the faith; take hold of the eternal life, to which you were called and for which you made[e] the good confession in the presence of many witnesses. [13]In the presence of God, who gives life to all things, and of Christ Jesus, who in his testimony before Pontius Pilate made the good confession, I charge you [14]to keep the commandment without spot or blame until the manifestation of our Lord Jesus Christ, [15]which he will bring about at the right time—he who is the blessed and only Sovereign, the King of kings and Lord of lords. [16]It is he alone who has immortality and dwells in unapproachable light, whom no one has ever seen or can see; to him be honor and eternal dominion. Amen.

A Word to the Wealthy

6:17–19 see pg. 739

17 As for those who in the present age are rich, command them not to be haughty, or to set their hopes on the uncertainty of riches, but rather on God who richly provides us with everything for our enjoyment. [18]They are to do good, to be rich in good works, generous, and ready to share, [19]thus storing up for themselves the treasure of a good foundation for the future, so that they may take hold of the life that really is life.

6:18

A Sacred Trust

20 Timothy, guard what has been entrusted to you. Avoid the profane chatter and contradictions of what is falsely called knowledge; [21]by professing it some have missed the mark as regards the faith.

Grace be with you.[f]

[e]Gk *confessed* [f]The Greek word for *you* here is plural; in other ancient authorities it is singular. Other ancient authorities add *Amen*

QUOTE UNQUOTE

CONSIDER THIS 6:18 *Are you rich in good works (v. 18)? A former communist party boss who became a vibrant believer pointed out the strategic importance of doing good with one's work life:*

The most important part of the Communist's day is, or should be, that which he spends at work. He sees his work as giving him wonderful opportunity to do a job for the cause. By way of contrast, the average [Christian] feels that his time for going into action on behalf of his beliefs begins after he has returned from his day's work, had a meal, changed and has just an hour or two left—when he is already tired—to give to his cause.

Douglas Hyde, *Dedication and Leadership*, p. 98

The Second Letter of Paul to

Timothy

CONTENTS

Personality Profile: Timothy

Name means: "Honored of God."

Home: Originally Lystra in Asia Minor. Later, as an associate of Paul, he traveled widely and worked among groups of believers in Macedonia, especially Thessalonica, and in Corinth and Ephesus.

Family: His father was Greek; his mother Eunice and his grandmother Lois were Jewish Christians. His "spiritual father" was Paul.

Occupation: Traveling teacher and short-term pastor; tradition holds that he became bishop of Ephesus. He also helped in the sending of 2 Corinthians, Philippians, Colossians, 1 and 2 Thessalonians, and Philemon.

Best known today for: Joining Paul in his travels and being the recipient of two New Testament letters.

ARTICLES

A Beloved Son

1 Paul, an apostle of Christ Jesus by the will of God, for
the sake of the promise of life that is in Christ Jesus,
2 To Timothy, my beloved child:
Grace, mercy, and peace from God the Father and Christ
Jesus our Lord.

A Valuable Heritage

1:3

3 I am grateful to God—whom I worship with a clear conscience, as my ancestors did—when I remember you constantly in my
prayers night and day. [4]Recalling your tears, I long to see
you so that I may be filled with joy. [5]I am
reminded of your sincere faith, a faith
that lived first in your grandmother Lois and your mother
Eunice and now, I am sure, lives in you.
[6]For this reason I remind you to rekindle
the gift of God that is within you through the laying on of
my hands; [7]for God did not give us a spirit of cowardice, but rather a spirit of power and of love and of self-
discipline.
8 Do not be ashamed, then, of the testimony about our
Lord or of me his prisoner, but join with me in suffering for
the gospel, relying on the power of God, [9]who saved us and
called us with a holy calling, not according to our works
but according to his own purpose and grace. This grace was
given to us in Christ Jesus before the ages began, [10]but it
has now been revealed through the appearing of our Savior
Christ Jesus, who abolished death and brought life and immortality to light through the gospel. [11]For this gospel I
was appointed a herald and an apostle and a teacher,[a] [12]and
for this reason I suffer as I do. But I am not ashamed, for I
know the one in whom I have put my trust, and I am sure
that he is able to guard until that day what I have entrusted
to him.[b] [13]Hold to the standard of sound teaching that you
have heard from me, in the faith and love that are in Christ
Jesus. [14]Guard the good treasure entrusted to you, with the
help of the Holy Spirit living in us.

1:5 see pg. 746

1:6–7 see pg. 747

The Faithful and the Faithless

15 You are aware that all who are in Asia have turned
away from me, including Phygelus and Hermogenes. [16]May
the Lord grant mercy to the household of Onesiphorus, because he often refreshed me and was not ashamed of my

[a]Other ancient authorities add *of the Gentiles* [b]*Or what has been entrusted to me*

PAUL THE JEW—TEACHER OF THE GENTILES

CONSIDER THIS 1:3 **What is your ethnic heritage? Are you proud to be who you are? Paul was. In v. 3 he openly identifies with his background as a Jew, affirming his connection to the "forefathers," people of faith such as Abraham, Isaac, Jacob, Joseph, Moses, and David.**

But wait! Didn't he earlier call that same background a "loss" and "rubbish" as he considered his new life in Christ (Phil. 3:4–8)? Yes, at times he was highly critical of his culture, but only to the extent that it fostered self-righteous pride, exclusive attitudes, or a belief in salvation by the Law rather than by faith in Christ. In other words, Paul had perspective on his roots. He was able to value his heritage for the good things it gave him, yet reject its negative legacies.

Perhaps that was why Paul was so effective as a teacher of the Gentiles (v. 11)—a remarkable calling, given his training as a Pharisee and strict adherence to Hebrew traditions (see "From Persecutor to Apostle," Gal. 1:13–17). God not only helped him reevaluate his ethnicity but in the process transformed his attitude toward non-Jews. He became a man who knew who he was, so he was no longer threatened by people from other cultures.

Consequently, Paul had much to offer Timothy, who came from a mixed background (Acts 16:1–3). Paul also serves as a model for believers today who need perspective on their roots in an increasingly diverse culture where ethnic and racial tensions run high.

God never asks us to reject our roots. We can affirm our ethnic heritage as a rich gift from Him, no matter how our surrounding culture regards it. See "The Gift of an Ethnic Heritage," Col. 4:10–11.

Eunice—A Mother's Legacy

FOR YOUR INFO 1:5 **Eunice (v. 5) was a Jewish Christian, but apparently her father was not very orthodox: he violated one of the clear commands of the Law in arranging a match for his daughter with a Gentile (Acts 16:1). Later, when Timothy was born, he wasn't circumcised (16:3).**

Paul praised Eunice for her "sincere faith," which she shared in common with Lois, her mother (2 Tim. 1:5). Eunice imparted that faith to her son, Timothy, and more than anyone else equipped him for a lifetime of usefulness for God.

Eunice is an encouragement for every woman faced with the daunting task of nurturing the spiritual life of her children, especially if she can't count on the help of a strong male. Eunice may have had no formal religious education and little encouragement from her family, except for Lois. But she had two crucial things going for her that offer hope for mothers today—the inherent power of being a mother and the dynamic power of a loving God.

How did the "genuine faith" that Timothy received from his mother work out in practical terms? See 1 Tim. 3:1–13 for a description.

chain; 17when he arrived in Rome, he eagerly[c] searched for
me and found me 18—may the Lord grant that he will find
mercy from the Lord on that day! And you know very well
how much service he rendered in Ephesus.

Pass On the Teaching

2 You then, my child, be strong in the grace that is in
Christ Jesus; 2and what you have heard from me
2:2 see pg. 748 through many witnesses entrust to
faithful people who will be able to teach
others as well. 3Share in suffering like a good soldier of
Christ Jesus. 4No one serving in the army gets entangled in
everyday affairs; the soldier's aim is to please the enlisting
officer. 5And in the case of an athlete, no one is crowned
without competing according to the rules. 6It is the farmer
who does the work who ought to have the first share of the
crops. 7Think over what I say, for the Lord will give you
understanding in all things.

A Sure Foundation

8 Remember Jesus Christ, raised from the dead, a descendant of David—that is my gospel, 9for which I suffer
hardship, even to the point of being chained like a criminal. But the word of God is not chained. 10Therefore I endure everything for the sake of the elect, so that they may
also obtain the salvation that is in Christ Jesus, with eternal
glory. 11The saying is sure:

If we have died with him, we will also live with him;
12 if we endure, we will also reign with him;
if we deny him, he will also deny us;
2:13
13 if we are faithless, he remains faithful—
for he cannot deny himself.

14 Remind them of this, and warn them before God[d]
that they are to avoid wrangling over words, which does no
good but only ruins those who are listening. 15Do your best
to present yourself to God as one approved by him, a
worker who has no need to be ashamed, rightly explaining
the word of truth. 16Avoid profane chatter, for it will lead
people into more and more impiety, 17and their talk will
spread like gangrene. Among them are Hymenaeus and
Philetus, 18who have swerved from the truth by claiming
that the resurrection has already taken place. They are up-

[c]Or *promptly* [d]Other ancient authorities read *the Lord*

setting the faith of some. 19But God's firm foundation
stands, bearing this inscription: "The Lord knows those
who are his," and, "Let everyone who calls on the name of
the Lord turn away from wickedness."

Character and Conduct

20 In a large house there are utensils not only of gold
and silver but also of wood and clay, some for special use,
some for ordinary. 21All who cleanse themselves of the
things I have mentioned[e] will become special utensils, dedicated and useful to the owner of the house, ready for every
good work. 22Shun youthful passions and pursue righteousness, faith, love, and peace, along with those who call
on the Lord from a pure heart. 23Have nothing to do with
stupid and senseless controversies; you know that they
breed quarrels. 24And the Lord's servant[f] must not be quarrelsome but kindly to everyone, an apt teacher, patient,
25correcting opponents with gentleness. God may perhaps
grant that they will repent and come to know the truth,
26and that they may escape from the snare of the devil, having been held captive by him to do his will.[g]

Perilous Times Will Come

3 You must understand this, that in the last days
distressing times will come. 2For people will be lovers
of themselves, lovers of money, boasters, arrogant, abusive,
disobedient to their parents, ungrateful, unholy, 3inhuman,
implacable, slanderers, profligates, brutes, haters of good,
4treacherous, reckless, swollen with conceit, lovers of
pleasure rather than lovers of God, 5holding to the outward
form of godliness but denying its power. Avoid them! 6For
among them are those who make their way into households
and captivate silly women, overwhelmed by their sins and
swayed by all kinds of desires, 7who are always being
instructed and can never arrive at a knowledge of the truth.
3:8–9 see pg. 751
8As Jannes and Jambres opposed Moses,
so these people, of corrupt mind and
counterfeit faith, also oppose the truth. 9But they will not
make much progress, because, as in the case of those two
men,[h] their folly will become plain to everyone.

Consistency Needed in Hard Times

3:10–11 see pg. 749
10 Now you have observed my teaching, my conduct, my aim in life, my

(Bible text continued on page 749)

[e]Gk *of these things* [f]Gk *slave* [g]Or *by him, to do his* (that is, God's) *will* [h]Gk lacks *two men*

The Spirit of Power

CONSIDER THIS 1:6–7 *Verses 6–7 offer both encouragement and exhortation. Paul links power—the ability to make things happen—with love and a sound mind. Conversely, power exercised without love and wisdom is inevitably destructive.*

A unique power accounted for the rapid spread of the message of Christ in the first century. See "Power," Acts 1:8.

He Remains Faithful

CONSIDER THIS 2:13 **Have you ever reneged on a business agreement? Or skipped out on an appointment? Or gone back on your word to a coworker? Or missed a crucial deadline on which everyone was counting? Have you ever broken promises to your spouse or children?**

Fortunately we can count on God to keep His commitments. Even though we as humans are frequently faithless, He remains faithful to His word (v. 13).

If we want to develop godly character, then one of our main objectives should be to honor our commitments. Psalm 15 describes persons who are moving closer to God as those who "stand by their oath even to their hurt." His word is his bond.

Faithfulness, trustworthiness, and reliability are key aspects of a godly "workstyle." See Titus 2:9–10.

CONSIDER THIS
2:2

Mentoring, Kingdom-Style

Paul describes the powerful process of mentoring in v. 2. Just as he had helped Timothy during a formative stage in his development, he challenged Timothy to mentor others, who in turn could become mentors and keep the reproductive cycle going. Christians today need to recover this pattern of older believers working with younger ones, which dates to the earliest days of the faith. Here are a few examples:

Jethro with Moses

A cattleman and father-in-law to Moses, Jethro took his overworked son-in-law through a performance review and taught him to delegate authority to associates (Ex. 18:1–27).

Boaz with Naomi and Ruth

A wealthy landowner and relative of Naomi, Boaz risked rejection from Jewish peers when he rescued the impoverished widow Naomi and her widowed immigrant daughter-in-law, Ruth. Ruth faced rejection among the Israelites but had respect and honor from Boaz (Ruth 1—4).

Deborah with Barak

A national leader and judge over Israel, Deborah guided Barak into battle and then accepted his call for her help, leading the campaign to victory over a Canaanite king. Together they celebrated in song, and the land enjoyed peace for 40 years (Judg. 4:4—5:31).

Barnabas with Saul/Paul

A wealthy landowner from Cyprus, Barnabas stood up for Saul, the persecutor-turned-convert, introducing him to church leaders and vouching for his conversion. Coached by Barnabas (Acts 4:36–37; 9:26–30; 11:22–30), Paul became an outstanding leader in the burgeoning movement. (Barnabas' example serves as a textbook case in kingdom-style mentoring. See "Barnabas—A Model for Mentoring," Acts 9:27.)

Barnabas with John Mark

In a dramatic split with Paul, Barnabas took young John Mark home with him to Cyprus and rebuilt his confidence (Acts 15:36–39). Years later, Paul changed his opinion, describing John Mark as "useful in my ministry" (2 Tim. 4:11).

Priscilla and Aquila with Apollos

Manufacturers of mobile living units (tents), Priscilla and Aquila drew alongside gifted but confused Apollos, tutoring him in the faith and then sponsoring his ministry (Acts 18:1–3, 24–28. Be sure to see the Priscilla and Aquila profile at Rom. 16:3–5).

Paul with Timothy

Pioneering leader Paul recruited young Timothy and built on the foundation laid by the young man's mother and grandmother (2 Tim. 1:5). Enlisting him as a fellow-traveler and tutoring him in the faith, Paul guided him in his first major assignment, the multiethnic start-up at Ephesus (Acts 16:1–3; Phil. 2:19–23; 2 Tim. 1–4).

Paul with Philemon

Paul helped Philemon, a wealthy leader in Colossae, deal with a runaway slave who had broken the law. He recommended full acceptance—even as a brother in the family—rather than insisting on the usual retribution (see the Introduction to Philemon). ◆

faith, my patience, my love, my steadfastness, 11my persecutions and suffering the things that happened to me in
Antioch, Iconium, and Lystra. What persecutions I endured! Yet the Lord rescued me from all of them. 12Indeed,
all who want to live a godly life in Christ Jesus will be persecuted. 13But wicked people and impostors will go from
bad to worse, deceiving others and being deceived. 14But as
for you, continue in what you have learned and firmly believed, knowing from whom you learned it, 15and how
from childhood you have known the sacred writings that
are able to instruct you for salvation through faith in Christ
3:16–17 see pg. 750
Jesus. 16All scripture is inspired by God
and is[i] useful for teaching, for reproof,
for correction, and for training in righteousness, 17so that
everyone who belongs to God may be proficient, equipped
for every good work.

A Charge to Timothy

4 In the presence of God and of Christ Jesus, who is to
judge the living and the dead, and in view of his
appearing and his kingdom, I solemnly urge you: 2proclaim
the message; be persistent whether the time is favorable or
unfavorable; convince, rebuke, and encourage, with the
utmost patience in teaching. 3For the time is coming when
people will not put up with sound doctrine, but having
itching ears, they will accumulate for themselves teachers to
suit their own desires, 4and will turn away from listening to
the truth and wander away to myths. 5As for you, always be
sober, endure suffering, do the work of an evangelist, carry
out your ministry fully.

PROCLAIM THE MESSAGE; BE PERSISTENT WHETHER THE TIME IS FAVORABLE OR UNFAVORABLE. . . . —2 Timothy 4:2

Paul's Example and Reward

6 As for me, I am already being poured out as a libation,
and the time of my departure has come. 7I have fought
the good fight, I have finished the race, I have kept the
faith. 8From now on there is reserved for me the crown of

(Bible text continued on page 752)

[i]Or *Every scripture inspired by God is also*

Follow the Leader

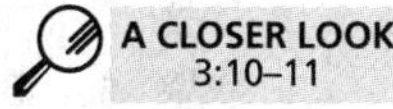

Paul felt confident in encouraging Timothy and others to follow his example (vv. 10–11). In light of his mentoring relationship to Timothy (2:2), it's clear that he realized that the values of Christ are as much caught as taught. See "Leading by Example," Phil. 3:17.

CONSIDER THIS
3:16–17

THE BIBLE: GETTING THE BIG PICTURE

As Paul indicates to Timothy (vv. 16–17) and many other passages affirm, the Bible is the ultimate authority for Christian faith and practice. It is crucial to interpret Scripture in light of its overall context.

The Bible as it has come down to us is laid out in two parts: the Old Testament, covering the period before Christ, and the New Testament, the period after Christ. The biblical record is a three-part story:

Part I: God's Original Creation (Gen. 1–2)

The eternal God created a perfect, beautiful world and put it under the management of Adam and Eve and their successors (Gen. 1–2). No one knows how long this part of the story lasted, but Scripture devotes only the first two of its 1,189 chapters to telling it.

Part II: The Human Dilemma and God's Response (Gen. 3—Rev. 20)

The second part of the story takes up all but the last two chapters of the Bible. Two story lines weave throughout the record. One reveals how the balance and beauty of creation is terribly damaged by sin and rebellion. The other unfolds God's response to rescue His creatures and the creation from this dilemma. His redemptive work is promised through Israel (as recorded in the Old Testament), provided through Christ (as recorded in the gospels), and then applied in and through the church (as told in Acts and the letters). The book of Revelation's first 20 chapters display events related to Christ's return to earth.

Part III: The Achievement of God's Original Design (Rev. 21–22)

The last two chapters of the Bible tell the final third of the story. They offer great hope to the reader by promising a new heaven and earth. God's original intentions for the creation will

(continued on next page)

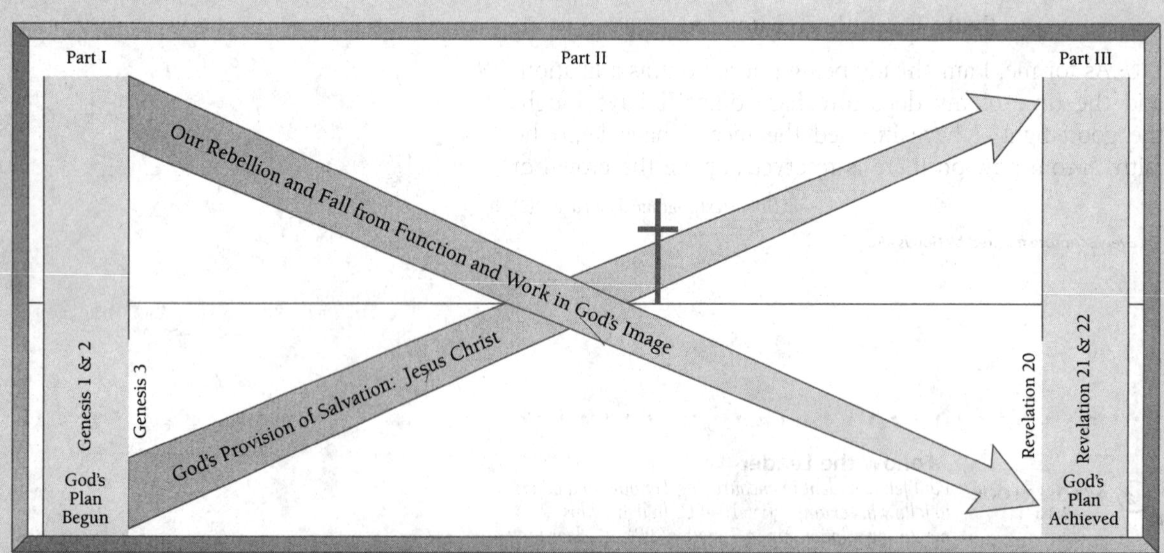

CREATION, REBELLION, AND RESTORATION

COUNTERFEIT CHRISTIANITY

CONSIDER THIS 3:8–9 **Wherever people accept the truth of God and begin practicing it, counterfeits soon surface. That's what Paul found at Ephesus, and what he warns Timothy about (vv. 8–9).**

He mentions two characters, Jannes and Jambres, whose names mean "he who seduces" and "he who is rebellious." Neither name is in the Old Testament, but Jewish legend held that these were the names of two Egyptian magicians who opposed Moses' demand of Pharaoh to free the Israelites. They tried to duplicate the miracles of Moses in an attempt to discredit him. But God showed that Moses' authority was more powerful (Ex. 7:11–12, 22).

Paul faced a similar experience at Ephesus. For two years he taught the message of Christ there, in a culture heavily steeped in pagan idolatry and occultism. God confirmed his teaching through powerful miracles and the release of many from evil spirits. But local exorcists attempted to duplicate the miracles. Their scheme backfired, however, to the benefit of the gospel (Acts 19:8–20).

Counterfeits to the truth of Christ abound today, as Paul predicted they would. If we effectively communicate the gospel to friends and coworkers, we can virtually count on the fact that competing systems and worldviews will soon appear. That's why we must "continue in what you have learned and firmly believed," basing our lives and our witness on the firm foundation of Scripture (2 Tim. 3:14–17).

(continued from previous page)

finally and fully be achieved. This parallels and fulfills Genesis 1–2 and also reflects the values of Christ, who is the focus of the whole Bible.

Reading the Bible

Because the middle third of the account comprises 99 percent of the text, it grabs most of the attention of Bible readers. But to properly understand it, one must keep the first and third parts firmly in mind. Like two bookends, they frame and anchor the big picture of God's work throughout history. They provide the crucial context for the double story line of rebellion and restoration etched through the middle of the account.

That middle part often makes for rather painful reading. With forceful realism it shows the cruelty that sin unleashes on all of creation. Some readers would prefer to skip over or dismiss that aspect of the story. But God refuses to distort reality or put a positive "spin" on it. He includes the horrors of sin in His record as "examples to avoid" (1 Cor. 10:6). He lets nothing escape either exposure or resolution in Jesus Christ. ◆

How did the Bible come to be written? See 2 Pet. 1:21.

Alexander—A Confirmed Enemy

FOR YOUR INFO 4:14–15 **Wherever the gospel enjoys unusual success, believers will soon find someone determined to oppose it. In fact, it seems that the greater the impact that the message of Christ has, the more strident and determined will be the opposition.**

The man Alexander (v. 14) became a confirmed enemy of Paul and the church at Ephesus. Some identify him as a Jew who lived in the city during the riots instigated by Demetrius and the silversmiths to oppose Paul's preaching (Acts 19:21–41). The Jews tried to use Alexander to convince the Gentile Ephesians that they (the Jews) had nothing to do with Paul and the burgeoning Christian movement (v. 33).

Others, however, believe that Alexander was one of two heretical teachers at Ephesus mentioned by Paul (1 Tim. 1:19–20). With his associate Hymenaeus, Alexander was said to have "suffered shipwreck" concerning the faith, indicating that at one point he may have been counted among the believers. But Paul, apparently using his apostolic authority, "delivered [him] to Satan," which may have been some form of excommunication from the church.

Whoever Alexander was, Paul counted him as a confirmed enemy and warned Timothy to watch out for him (2 Tim. 4:15). However, rather than attack him, Paul left his fate in the Lord's hands, to "pay him back for his deeds."

Who are the confirmed enemies of the gospel where you live and work? Are you on guard against their attempts to discredit the cause of Christ?

No matter how mean-spirited people may become toward us or our witness to Christ, people are not really our enemies. We have far more powerful forces opposing us. See "Who Is the Enemy?" Eph. 6:10–13.

righteousness, which the Lord, the righteous judge, will give me on that day, and not only to me but also to all who have longed for his appearing.

Personal News and Requests

9 Do your best to come to me soon, [10]for Demas, in love with this present world, has deserted me and gone to Thessalonica; Crescens has gone to Galatia,[j] Titus to Dalmatia. [11]Only Luke is with me. Get Mark and bring him with you, for he is useful in my ministry. [12]I have sent Tychicus to Ephesus. [13]When you come, bring the cloak that I left with Carpus at Troas, also the books, and above all the parchments. (4:14–15) [14]Alexander the coppersmith did me great harm; the Lord will pay him back for his deeds. [15]You also must beware of him, for he strongly opposed our message.

(4:16–17) 16 At my first defense no one came to my support, but all deserted me. May it not be counted against them! [17]But the Lord stood by me and gave me strength, so that through me the message might be fully proclaimed and all the Gentiles might hear it. So I was rescued from the lion's mouth. [18]The Lord will rescue me from every evil attack and save me for his heavenly kingdom. To him be the glory forever and ever. Amen.

19 Greet Prisca and Aquila, and the household of Onesiphorus. [20]Erastus remained in Corinth; Trophimus I left ill in Miletus. [21]Do your best to come before winter. Eubulus sends greetings to you, as do Pudens and Linus and Claudia and all the brothers and sisters.[k]

22 The Lord be with your spirit. Grace be with you.[l]

[j]Other ancient authorities read *Gaul* [k]Gk *all the brothers* [l]The Greek word for *you* here is plural. Other ancient authorities add *Amen*

"That All the Gentiles Might Hear"

A CLOSER LOOK 4:16–17 *As Paul wrote the last of this letter to Timothy, he knew that the end of his life was near. But right to the end, one goal was paramount—to preach the gospel to the Gentiles (v. 17). See "Paul the Jew—Teacher of the Gentiles," 1:3; and "From Persecutor to Apostle," Gal. 1:13–17.*

The Letter of Paul to

Titus

Some people say that it doesn't really matter what you believe, as long as you do the right thing. However, Paul's letter to Titus contradicts that sort of thinking. He knew that people become what they think, and that everything they do is shaped by what they believe.

That's why he urged Titus, his valued associate who was pastoring a church on the island of Crete, to "teach what is consistent with sound doctrine" (Titus 2:1). He knew that correct living is a product of correct belief. Error can never lead to godliness. Only truth produces genuine Christlikeness.

In our world today, many streams of thought lay claim to being "true." Yet they produce nothing that even approaches the character, integrity, and humility of Christ. That's why believers need to pay careful attention to the teaching they receive. Does it square with Scripture? Does it honor Christ? Does it acknowledge what Paul calls "the truth that is in accordance with godliness" (1:1)?

Only truth produces genuine Christlikeness.

C O N T E N T S

A R T I C L E S

God Cannot Lie (1:2)

Christians are not called to present just a "new and improved" set of deceptions about God. No, we should be "new and improved" people, adjusting distorted perceptions of the faith and of God in our spheres of influence.

Your "Workstyle" (2:9–10)

The attitudes, behaviors, and expectations you have about your work could be termed your "workstyle." Paul highlights five key areas of a Christlike workstyle. See how yours compares.

Evidence Before Information (3:1–8)

Has your own walk with Christ produced any visible fruit in front of your coworkers, such as patience, staying power, compassion, loyalty, better management, hard work, or faithful service? That's the kind of evidence that shows whether faith in Christ has any power and impact.

CRETE

- **An island in the Mediterranean Sea south of the Aegean Sea.**
- **Probably the same as the ancient Caphtor (Deut. 2:23; Amos 9:7) from which the Philistines (Caphtorim) originated.**
- **Associated with many legends, including those of King Minos and the Minotaur, a mythical half-bull, half-man monster.**
- **Captured by the Romans in 68–66 B.C. and made a Roman province.**
- **Inhabited by people known for their excesses. Paul quoted from the Greek poet Epimenides of Knossos (c. 600 B.C.) who wrote, "Cretans are always liars, vicious brutes, lazy gluttons" (Titus 1:12).**

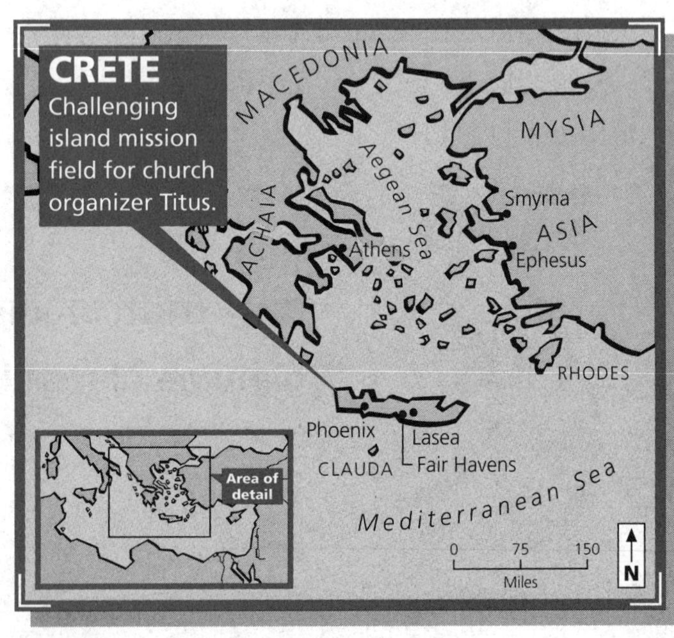

The Genuine Item

Just as 1 and 2 Timothy were meant to provide continuity for the church at Ephesus, Titus was meant to provide continuity for the church at Crete. What did believers there need? In a word, *authenticity.*

Crete had an ancient culture that was notorious for its corruption. In the face of this moral wasteland, believers needed to live counter-culturally. They needed to speak the truth and live the truth.

In the ancient world, people felt no need to emulate their gods (who were, after all, little better than humans, and in some cases much worse). But Christianity was just the opposite: believers needed to look like their God—and their God was not a liar. He was morally perfect or "holy," and His people needed to pursue holiness as well (2:14), no matter what the surrounding culture might sanction.

So Titus was to urge his people to "be an ornament to the doctrine of God" (2:10), that is, to make the teaching about God attractive. Paul's words picture a fine gem that reflects light with beauty and radiance as it is placed in its appropriate setting. (Interestingly, Crete was a center for the jewelry trade.) So believers there were to stand out against the culture, reflecting the light of Christ.

As we read Titus we need to ask, what are the poets of our day saying about our culture? What is the moral reputation of our society? What is the spiritual climate? Like the Cretan believers, we need to speak the truth and live the truth. When people look at us, they need to see authentic Christianity, not a lukewarm, accommodating lifestyle that stands for nothing. We need to make the gospel attractive in such a way that unbelievers will be drawn to the matchless Light of the World. ◆

BE AN ORNAMENT TO THE DOCTRINE OF GOD OUR SAVIOR.
—Titus 2:10

Titus

The man to whom Paul wrote this letter was someone the apostle could rely on in tense situations. Earlier he had represented Paul at Corinth. Now he was left on the island of Crete to bring order to the church there and establish leadership (1:5). Apparently Titus fulfilled his assignment rather well, for tradition holds that he was the first bishop of Crete. Learn more about Paul's "man of the hour" at "Titus," 2 Cor. 7:6.

God Cannot Lie

1 Paul, a servant[a] of God and an apostle of Jesus Christ,
for the sake of the faith of God's elect and the
knowledge of the truth that is in accordance with godliness,
1:2 2in the hope of eternal life that God, who
never lies, promised before the ages
began— 3in due time he revealed his word through the
proclamation with which I have been entrusted by the
command of God our Savior,
4 To Titus, my loyal child in the faith we share:
Grace[b] and peace from God the Father and Christ Jesus
our Savior.

Titus to Establish New Leaders

5 I left you behind in Crete for this reason, so that you
should put in order what remained to be done, and should
appoint elders in every town, as I directed you: 6someone
who is blameless, married only once,[c] whose children are
believers, not accused of debauchery and not rebellious.

[a] Gk *slave* [b] Other ancient authorities read *Grace, mercy,* [c] Gk *husband of one wife*

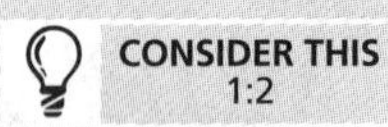

GOD CANNOT LIE

What understanding of God do your coworkers, friends, and family have? Is there a variety of opinion about spiritual issues among your peers? Do you face a mixture of hostility, detachment, distortion, or accusation that reflect badly on the faith?

Such was the case in Crete. New believers on that Mediterranean island heard no end of opinions about their new loyalty to Christ. The Greeks believed in many gods. Each one was to be served, honored, or placated. Jesus seemed to be just one more deity to add to the pantheon. To stabilize the situation, Paul sent his trainee Titus, instructing him to "put in order what remained to be done, and . . . appoint elders in every town" (v. 5).

As he wrote out Titus' job description, Paul emphasized that God does not lie (v. 2). Quite a contrast to the Cretans, who were known for their dishonesty. In fact, one of their own literary heroes, Epimenides, had remarked that "Cretans are always liars, vicious brutes, and lazy gluttons." Paul added his affirmation to the assessment by writing, "That testimony is true" (vv. 12–13). He knew that he was dealing with a culture that thrived on trickery.

If the new believers were going to be faithful to a God who speaks truth, they would have to break that pattern.

7For a bishop,[d] as God's steward, must be blameless; he
must not be arrogant or quick-tempered or addicted to
wine or violent or greedy for gain; 8but he must be hospitable, a lover of goodness, prudent, upright, devout, and
self-controlled. 9He must have a firm grasp of the word that
is trustworthy in accordance with the teaching, so that he
may be able both to preach with sound doctrine and to refute those who contradict it.

Counter False Teachers

10 There are also many rebellious people, idle talkers
and deceivers, especially those of the circumcision; 11they
must be silenced, since they are upsetting whole families by
teaching for sordid gain what it is not right to teach. 12It
was one of them, their very own prophet, who said,

"Cretans are always liars, vicious brutes, lazy gluttons."

13That testimony is true. For this reason rebuke them
sharply, so that they may become sound in the faith, 14not
paying attention to Jewish myths or to commandments of

[d]*Or an overseer*

◆ ◆ ◆ ◆ ◆ ◆ ◆ ◆ ◆ ◆ ◆ ◆ ◆ ◆ ◆ ◆

Therefore, Paul directed Titus to:

- *develop leaders who could be trusted (vv. 6–9).*
- *train all believers—young and old, male and female, slaves or free—to pursue changed lifestyles reflecting integrity, control, and purity (2:1–15).*
- *call all believers to lives characterized by action, not just words (1:16; 2:7, 14; 3:8–9, 14. See also James 1:19–27 and Matt. 7:21–23).*

Through these strategies, Titus and the Cretan believers would silence the critics of the faith (2:5, 8, 15).

God is not a liar. And followers of Christ are not just "wordsmiths" called to outdo the art of their culture in presenting a "new and improved" set of deceptions. No, Christians should be "new and improved" people known for their good deeds in contrast to a previous lifestyle of dishonesty, passion, and malice (3:1–3).

Are there distorted perceptions of the faith and of God in your sphere of influence? How can you live in a way that will speak to those and offer a clearer demonstration of true Christianity? How about gathering with other believers who live or work in similar environments, and together identifying the most strategic witness that could be offered? ◆

QUOTE UNQUOTE

CONSIDER THIS 1:15 *Another way of saying that "to the pure all things are pure" (v. 15) is:*

There is nothing so secular that it cannot be sacred, and that is one of the deepest messages of the Incarnation.

Madeleine L'Engle, *Walking On Water,* p. 50

1:15
see pg. 757
those who reject the truth. [15]To the pure
all things are pure, but to the corrupt
and unbelieving nothing is pure. Their very minds and
consciences are corrupted. [16]They profess to know God,
but they deny him by their actions. They are detestable,
disobedient, unfit for any good work.

Develop Human Resources

2 But as for you, teach what is consistent with sound
doctrine. [2]Tell the older men to be temperate, serious,
prudent, and sound in faith, in love, and in endurance.
3 Likewise, tell the older women to be reverent in behavior, not to be slanderers or slaves to drink; they are to
teach what is good, [4]so that they may encourage the young

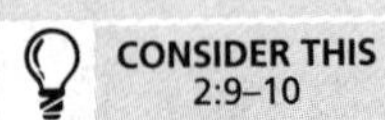
CONSIDER THIS
2:9–10

YOUR "WORKSTYLE"

The term "lifestyle" describes the attitudes, behaviors, and expectations you have toward the life you lead. Similarly, the attitudes, behaviors, and expectations you have about your work could be termed your "workstyle." Paul highlights five key areas of a Christlike workstyle in vv. 9–10. How does yours compare? (See table opposite.)

According to verse 10, there's a purpose behind this godly workstyle: that workers "may be an ornament to the doctrine of God our Savior." Your attitudes and actions on the job can make the gospel of Christ attractive to coworkers and customers. What impression are you making? ◆

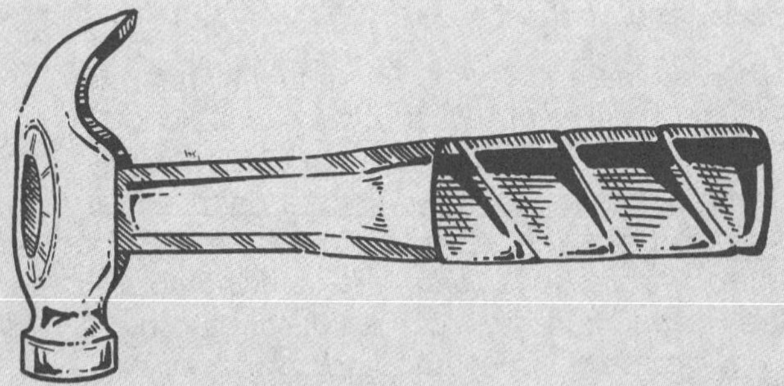

Did you know that in going to work every day, you bear the very image of God? See "People at Work," Heb. 2:7.

Christ never intended His followers to withdraw from the world to set up their own exclusive communities. Engagement, not isolation, is His desire. See "Called into the World," John 17:18.

No matter what position you hold at your job, no matter where you fit in the organization, you have a boss to answer to. See "Who's the Boss?" Col. 3:22–24.

women to love their husbands, to love their children, 5to be
self-controlled, chaste, good managers of the household,
kind, being submissive to their husbands, so that the word
of God may not be discredited.
6 Likewise, urge the younger men to be self-controlled.
2:7 7Show yourself in all respects a model of
good works, and in your teaching show

Moral Leadership

A CLOSER LOOK 2:7 *Do you exhibit moral leadership at work, at home, and in your community? Paul challenges Titus to show "a pattern of good works" (v. 7). He understood that the most effective leaders lead by example. See Phil. 3:17.*

FIVE "WORKSTYLE" CATEGORIES

Description	Issue	Application
"submissive to their masters"	Authority	Do you... •follow instructions? •comply with industry standards? •pay your fair share of taxes?
"give satisfaction in every respect"	Excellence	Do you... •take pride in your work? •use the right tools for the job, in the right way? •work just as hard even when the boss isn't around?
"not to talk back"	Conflict	Do you... •seek to resolve conflicts in a healthy way? •respond with honesty and courtesy? •promote constructive cooperation instead of destructive competition?
"not to pilfer"	Honesty & Integrity	Do you... •keep an honest accounting of your hours? •pay for personal expenses rather than charge them to company expense accounts? •avoid making personal long-distance calls on the company's phone?
"show complete and perfect fidelity"	Loyalty & Dependability	Do you... •keep your word? •do what it takes to meet deadlines? •honor what your company stands for?

TEACH WHAT IS CONSISTENT WITH SOUND DOCTRINE.
—Titus 2:1

integrity, gravity, [8]and sound speech that cannot be censured; then any opponent will be put to shame, having nothing evil to say of us.

2:9–10 see pg. 758

2:9–10

9 Tell slaves to be submissive to their masters and to give satisfaction in every respect; they are not to talk back, [10]not to pilfer, but to show complete and perfect fidelity, so that in everything they may be an ornament to the doctrine of God our Savior.

Build on What God Has Done

11 For the grace of God has appeared, bringing salvation to all,[e] [12]training us to renounce impiety and worldly passions, and in the present age to live lives that are self-controlled, upright, and godly, [13]while we wait for the blessed hope and the manifestation of the glory of our great God and Savior,[f] Jesus Christ. [14]He it is who gave himself

[e]Or *has appeared to all, bringing salvation* [f]Or *of the great God and our Savior*

A CLOSER LOOK 2:9–10

Workplace Evangelism

Paul implies that a believer's approach to work will influence the way coworkers see the gospel (v. 10). Today, many Christians view their job as a soapbox for spreading the gospel. Is that legitimate? See "Work—A Platform for Evangelism?" Eph. 6:5–9.

CONSIDER THIS 3:1–8

EVIDENCE BEFORE INFORMATION

What evidence can new believers offer to validate their new faith? How can their commitment to Christ be seen as more than just one more spiritual path among many? They need to put their best foot forward among nonbelievers, spiritually speaking, but how?

Believers on the island of Crete faced such a challenge, and it was enormous. The Cretan culture had many gods. Its people filled their time with much idle chatter, empty promises, and lies (Titus 1:10–13). So how could the Christians' loyalty to yet one more God be taken seriously, let alone make any difference in the society?

Paul acknowledged the dilemma that these early believers faced by opening his letter to Titus with the affirmation that God never lies (1:2). In the same way, God's people must be people of truth and unimpeachable integrity. How can that happen? Through fewer words and more deeds. That was the way to build consistent evidence of a new and credible lifestyle with lasting impact.

for us that he might redeem us from all iniquity and purify
for himself a people of his own who are zealous for good
deeds.
15 Declare these things; exhort and reprove with all authority.[g] Let no one look down on you.

Believers' Conduct in the Community

3:1

3 Remind them to be subject to rulers
and authorities, to be obedient, to be
ready for every good work, 2 to speak evil of no one, to
avoid quarreling, to be gentle, and to show every courtesy
to everyone. 3 For we ourselves were once foolish, disobedient, led astray, slaves to various passions and pleasures,
passing our days in malice and envy, despicable, hating one
another. 4 But when the goodness and loving kindness of
God our Savior appeared, 5 he saved us, not because of any
works of righteousness that we had done, but according to
his mercy, through the water[h] of rebirth and renewal by the

[g] Gk *commandment* [h] Gk *washing*

Subject to Rulers

A CLOSER LOOK 3:1

Submission to human authorities (v. 1) reflects our submission to God's authority. See "Governmental Authority," Rom. 13:2.

The apostle called for that strategy among several sub-groups of the new believers: older men (2:2), older women (2:3), younger women (2:4–5), younger men (2:6), Titus himself (2:7–8), and slaves (2:9–10). Each of these groups was to carry out the deeds of faith listed in 3:1–8. In fact, Paul insisted that they all "be careful to devote themselves to good works" (v. 8). They were to avoid extended arguments as unprofitable and useless in their witness.

Do your coworkers see the Christlike deeds of believers where you work? Or has their main exposure to the faith been little more than Christians filling the air with statements and ideas? Has your own walk with Christ produced any visible fruit in front of your associates, such as patience, staying power, compassion, loyalty, better management, hard work, or faithful service? That's the kind of evidence that shows whether faith in Christ has any power and impact. ◆

United for the Work

CONSIDER THIS 3:12–15

Working without phones, faxes, cars, or planes, a dedicated, diverse team of first-century believers spread the good news about Jesus throughout the Roman world. Paul mentioned several of these coworkers to Titus—Artemas, Tychicus, Zenas the lawyer, and Apollos (vv. 12–13)—but there were many others; for example, Barnabas (see Acts 4:36–37), Priscilla and Aquila (see Rom. 16:3–5), Silas (see Acts 15:32), and Junia (see Rom. 16:7).

The task of proclaiming the gospel in the face of sometimes fierce opposition knit these early believers together. They planned their travel not only around the tasks of ministry, but also around their relationships with each other. For example, Paul encouraged Titus to come to him at Nicopolis during a seasonal break (Titus 3:12). They also took care to provide necessities for each other (v. 13).

The principle emerges from this pattern that the cause of Christ goes forward even in the face of opposition when the workers are united for the work.

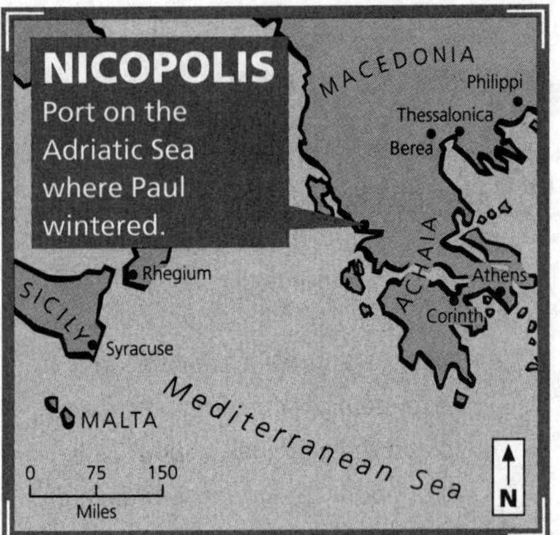

Holy Spirit. 6This Spirit he poured out on us richly through Jesus Christ our Savior, 7so that, having been justified by his grace, we might become heirs according to the hope of eternal life. 8The saying is sure.

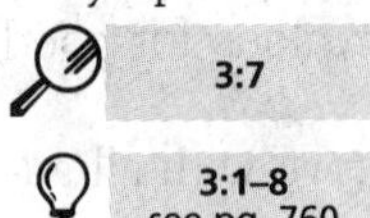

3:1–8 see pg. 760

Unprofitable Disputes

I desire that you insist on these things, so that those who have come to believe in God may be careful to devote themselves to good works; these things are excellent and profitable to everyone. 9But avoid stupid controversies, genealogies, dissensions, and quarrels about the law, for they are unprofitable and worthless. 10After a first and second admonition, have nothing more to do with anyone who causes divisions, 11since you know that such a person is perverted and sinful, being self-condemned.

Plans and Greetings

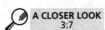

12 When I send Artemas to you, or Tychicus, do your best to come to me at Nicopolis, for I have decided to spend the winter there. 13Make every effort to send Zenas the lawyer and Apollos on their way, and see that they lack nothing. 14And let people learn to devote themselves to good works in order to meet urgent needs, so that they may not be unproductive.

3:12–15 see pg. 761

15 All who are with me send greetings to you. Greet those who love us in the faith.

Grace be with all of you.[i]

[i] Other ancient authorities add *Amen*

Nicopolis

YOU ARE THERE 3:12

- **The name of many cities in the first century, including the one at which Paul decided to spend a winter (Titus 3:12), probably in northwestern Greece on the Adriatic Sea.**
- **Name means "city of victory."**

We Are Heirs

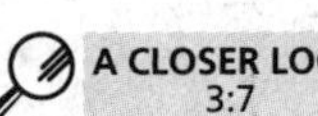

Is the idea of believers being "heirs" (v. 7) just wishful thinking? See "What's In It for Me?" Eph. 1:11.

The Letter of Paul to

Philemon

Does Christ really make a difference in relationships? Does He really bring healing and the resolution of old grievances? Does He really surmount differences in social and economic status? The letter to Philemon offers powerful evidence that He does!

THE BACKGROUND OF THE LETTER

Philemon provides a window on the story of Onesimus, a runaway slave, and Philemon, his master. The story begins with Paul's arrival in Ephesus. According to Acts 19:8–10, his work there for more than two years produced spectacular results: "all the residents of Asia [Minor], both Jews and Greeks, heard the word of the Lord."

Among those who responded to the gospel was Philemon, a wealthy man of Colossae, perhaps one of the many merchants doing business in the thriving economy of Ephesus. Philemon took his newfound faith back to Colossae and started or at least hosted a church in his home—perhaps the same group of believers to whom the letter to the Colossians was written (Col. 4:7–9).

Like most wealthy citizens of the Roman world, Philemon owned slaves. Scholars estimate that perhaps half the population of the empire may have been slaves. One of Philemon's slaves was Onesimus, possibly from Phrygia, the mountainous region in which Colossae sat. Whether Onesimus stole from his master, tired of his bondage, or thought he could take advantage of his master's new religion of love and grace, we don't know, but for some reason he ran away. ◆

THE PRODIGAL RETURNS

Years later, Onesimus surfaced in Rome—where he ran into Paul! The apostle was living in rented quarters (Acts 28:30), perhaps in the Greek-speaking section in south Rome, where Onesimus would likely have gone. Like his former master, the fugitive turned to Christ and began growing in the faith. Paul came to regard him as "my child . . . whose father I have become during my imprisonment" (Philem. 10), indicating a close relationship of mutual affection.

But Paul faced a dilemma. Should he hold onto him? The fellow proved useful and loyal. That's what Paul wanted to do (Philem. 13). But by law he was required to return the runaway slave to his master, or at least turn him over to the authorities. Yet what would happen to this new believer, his spiritual son and friend? Would he be punished or sold? Could Paul live with himself, knowing that in a sense, he had betrayed the man?

Paul's solution was to send Onesimus back to Philemon—but not without protection. He assigned an associate named Tychicus to escort the fugitive back, and to carry three letters—two general ones to the believers in Colossae and Laodicea (Col. 4:16), and a personal one to Philemon. As the latter makes clear, Paul was leaning heavily on his history with Philemon. He was also counting on the master to demonstrate spiritual maturity by forgiving the slave and accepting him as a brother in Christ. No doubt Philemon's standing among the community of believers would add further leverage, as people would be closely watching his response. ◆

THE REST OF THE STORY

The letter to Philemon gives us only half of the conversation between Paul and Philemon. We don't know Philemon's response or what happened to Onesimus upon his return.

However, the name Onesimus appears among letters written by a bishop named Ignatius in about A.D. 110. Ignatius of Antioch was arrested and taken to Rome for trial. During the journey, he wrote a letter from Smyrna to the church at Ephesus in which he addressed the new bishop there, whose name was Onesimus. Many believe that this man was the same Onesimus who, as a slave, had run away from Philemon but later came to faith and returned.

Whatever the case, the Onesimus-Philemon story holds a number of significant lessons:

- **It shows that in Christ, there is always room for reconciliation and a second chance for people.**
- **It illustrates how God works behind the scenes to bring people to faith and restore relationships.**
- **It shows the power of the gospel to work at a distance and effect change from city to city, coast to coast, and continent to continent.**
- **It shows the value of mentoring relationships, the way that older, seasoned believers can help younger followers of Christ work out problems and conflicts.**
- **It shows a measure of irony behind God's patience and providence: He had to send Onesimus thousands of miles away from his Christian master in order to bring him to faith!**
- **It shows that in Christ, people can change. Consider the many stages that Onesimus went through: from slave, to thief and runaway, to refugee, to convert, to penitent, to brother, and possibly to bishop. ◆**

PERSONALITY PROFILE: ONESIMUS

Name means: "Useful" or "profitable."

Home: Originally from Phrygia, he worked in Colossae, lived for a while in Rome, but eventually returned to Colossae.

Occupation: Slave.

Best known today for: Running away from his master, Philemon, but returning to him after coming to faith.

PERSONALITY PROFILE: PHILEMON

Home: Colossae.

Family: His wife may have been Apphia (Philem. 2).

Occupation: Probably a businessman.

Special interests: He hosted a group of believers in his home.

Best known today for: Receiving a letter from Paul regarding the return of his runaway slave, Onesimus.

A General Greeting

1 Paul, a prisoner of Christ Jesus, and Timothy our
brother,[a]

CONSIDER THIS 2 To Philemon our dear friend and coworker, 2to Apphia our sister,[b] to Archippus our fellow soldier, and to the church in your house:
3 Grace to you and peace from God our Father and the
Lord Jesus Christ.

God Praised for Philemon

4 When I remember you[c] in my prayers, I always thank
my God 5because I hear of your love for all the saints and
your faith toward the Lord Jesus. 6I pray that the sharing of
your faith may become effective when you perceive all the
good that we[d] may do for Christ. 7I have indeed received
much joy and encouragement from your love, because the
hearts of the saints have been refreshed through you, my
brother.

[a]Gk *the brother* [b]Gk *the sister* [c]From verse 4 through verse 21, *you* is singular [d]Other ancient authorities read *you* (plural)

Apphia

CONSIDER THIS 2

Apphia (v. 2) may have been the wife of Philemon and possibly the mother or sister of Archippus. In addition, some manuscripts give the phrase "to Apphia the [or our] sister" as "to the beloved Apphia." This as well as the placement of Apphia's name between two men, along with the terms used for each, suggest the possibility that Philemon, Apphia, and Archippus were leaders of the Christian community at Colossae.

Paul was addressing this letter not only to Philemon as the owner of Onesimus, but to all three of those named as well as to their church. Paul apparently did not intend that Philemon should act in isolation as he made his decision about what to do with Onesimus. By including Apphia and Archippus in his greeting, the apostle may have expected them to help Philemon make a wise, Christlike choice.

"Perhaps . . ."

CONSIDER THIS 15–16

"I wonder why God allowed that to happen."

Countless people have uttered statements like that, either to themselves or out loud. In a world of many mysteries and uncertainties, they wonder *why*?

Is it worthwhile to ponder the reasons behind events or to question the ways of God? Some people think not. "God has His own reasons," they say. "Ours is not to know why. We ought not to question the purposes of God. Besides, there are some things we'll never know until we get to heaven, so why bother our heads with them now?"

But judging by Paul's words in vv. 15–16, thinking about what God may be up to in the events that come our way, what we might call "theological reflection," is both useful and encouraged. Paul had no scriptural text to turn to that would fully explain why Onesimus, of all people, had come to faith and was prepared to return to Philemon. So he offered Philemon his own reading of events.

Like Paul, we can and should reflect on the circumstances of our lives. We should think carefully about what God may be trying to show us or teach us. We should pay attention to the unusual or the unexpected, and even to the undesirable events that come our way. Such habits help us bring God and His Word into our understanding of life. We will never discover all the answers, but we may discover a bit more of God in our lives by wondering, "Perhaps . . ."

Paul's Appeal for Onesimus

8 For this reason, though I am bold enough in Christ to
command you to do your duty, 9yet I would rather appeal
to you on the basis of love—and I, Paul, do this as an old
man, and now also as a prisoner of Christ Jesus.[e] 10I am appealing to you for my child, Onesimus, whose father I have
become during my imprisonment. 11Formerly he was useless to you, but now he is indeed useful[f] both to you and to
me. 12I am sending him, that is, my own heart, back to you.
13I wanted to keep him with me, so that he might be of service to me in your place during my imprisonment for the
gospel; 14but I preferred to do nothing without your consent, in order that your good deed might be voluntary and
not something forced. 15Perhaps this is
the reason he was separated from you for
a while, so that you might have him back
forever, 16no longer as a slave but more
than a slave, a beloved brother—especially to me but how
much more to you, both in the flesh and in the Lord.
17 So if you consider me your partner,
welcome him as you would welcome me.
18If he has wronged you in any way, or owes you anything,

15–16 see pg. 765

16

17–19

[e]*Or as an ambassador of Christ Jesus, and now also his prisoner* [f]The name Onesimus means *useful* or (compare verse 20) *beneficial*

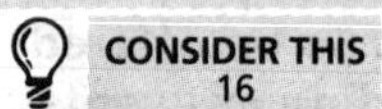

A CHALLENGE TO SLAVERY

Some people have criticized Paul and the early church, claiming that they did not call for an end to slavery. But Paul wrote the believers in Colossae, "There is no longer . . . slave and free; but Christ is all and in all" (Col. 3:11). Similarly, Galatians 3:28 reads, "There is no longer slave or free . . . all of you are one in Christ Jesus."

In Christ, societal divisions and distinctions become immaterial, and practices that degrade and devalue people are condemned. It is true that first-century believers didn't actively campaign for an end to slavery, as far as we know. They never petitioned the government or urged slaves to rebel.

Yet here in Philemon we have a clear case of a believing slave owner being asked to put into practice the Christian ideals cited above. Philemon and Onesimus had an opportunity to demonstrate the gospel's power over slavery.

This was one of a number of cultural divisions that early believers broke down, such as:

17–19 charge that to my account. [19]I, Paul, am writing this with my own hand: I will repay it. I say nothing about your owing me even your own self. [20]Yes, brother, let me have this benefit from you in the Lord! Refresh my heart in Christ. [21]Confident of your obedience, I am writing to you, knowing that you will do even more than I say.

22 One thing more—prepare a guest room for me, for I am hoping through your prayers to be restored to you.

Greetings and Farewell

23 Epaphras, my fellow prisoner in Christ Jesus, sends greetings to you,[g] [24]and so do Mark, Aristarchus, Demas, and Luke, my fellow workers.

25 The grace of the Lord Jesus Christ be with your spirit.[h]

[g]Here *you* is singular [h]Other ancient authorities add *Amen*

Paul Mentors Philemon

A CLOSER LOOK 17–19 *In this letter, Paul carries out a mentoring role for his friend, Philemon. He advises him on the difficult issue of dealing with a runaway slave who is also a brother in Christ. For more on mentoring relationships, see "Discipleship—Or Mentoring?" Acts 9:26–30.*

- *Hellenists and Hebrews (Acts 6:1–7).*
- *Samaritans and Jews (Acts 8:5–8).*
- *Gentiles and Jews (Acts 8:26–40; 10:1–48).*
- *Women and men (Acts 16:14–15; 18:1–4, 24–28).*

Our society has formally done away with slavery. But there are systems still in place that abuse or oppress people. From the standpoint of the gospel, the issue is not whether they are legal, but whether they treat people as God would want them treated. If Paul were writing today, what would he challenge us as believers to do? What does "one in Christ" mean for the systems we participate in from day to day? ◆

Christians are all in the same family, no longer divided by ethnicity, social status, or gender. That has powerful implications for how we live. See "We Are Family!" Gal. 3:28.

Let Me Pick Up the Tab

CONSIDER THIS 17–19 Paul tells Philemon that "if" Onesimus has stolen anything, he should send Paul a bill for it (vv. 18–19). But at this point he is writing somewhat tongue-in-cheek.

Paul knew that Onesimus really had "wronged" Philemon. Not only had he run away, apparently he had stolen property and owed Philemon restitution. Paul never questioned Philemon's right to have his slave returned or receive reimbursement for the theft. Conversion to Christ does not relieve anyone of obligations to others.

Nonetheless, Paul wanted Philemon to forgive Onesimus and receive him back as a brother (v. 16). But just in case the theft created a sticking point in the reconciliation, Paul volunteered to pay for the loss if Philemon was unwilling simply to forgive it. (Notice how Paul was imitating Christ in this regard.)

Of course, Paul anticipated that Philemon would be more than happy to bear the loss. After all, he owed Paul a large, intangible debt of gratitude for all that Paul had done for him (v. 19). So in effect, he would be returning Paul a favor by accepting Onesimus back unconditionally.

Is there a lesson here about favors and paybacks? Consider: often when we impose on others, asking them to do favors for us or for our friends, our main concern is for our own interests. But Paul's main concern was for Philemon—not for his financial loss, which was trifling, but for his spiritual gain, which was considerable.

The Roots of the Gospel

In 1976, Doubleday published Alex Haley's *Roots,* the story of Haley's descent from Africans brought to America as slaves. A subsequent television miniseries catapulted the work into best-seller status, fueling the burgeoning black pride movement and sparking a nationwide passion for tracing one's ancestry.

In many ways, the book of Hebrews is the *Roots* of the New Testament. It celebrates Christ as the fulfillment of Old Testament Judaism. Jewish Christians, who were quickly becoming a minority among first-century believers, were struggling with how their ancient heritage fit with the gospel. While warning them not to slip back into their old ways, the book showed that they need not disparage their background; there was still dignity and value to it, especially since so many of the seeds of Christianity had sprouted from it. Therefore, just as Gentiles did not need to become Jews to be accepted by God (the message of Galatians), so Jews did not need to become Gentiles.

If you've ever struggled to integrate your background, particularly your ethnic or cultural roots, with your faith in Christ, you'll do well to study Hebrews. God has used history—including the history of your own family—to accomplish His will and bring you to Himself.

The Letter to the Hebrews

Christ is the fulfillment of Judaism.

CONTENTS

ARTICLES

Creation: "Very Good," But Not Sacred! (11:3)

Is the universe itself divine? Is "Mother Nature" sacred?

Aiming to Please (11:6)

Sometimes we face conflicts because it's not always possible to please everybody. So when we have to make tough decisions about whom to please—and therefore whom to displease—how can we choose?

CHRIST ALONE!

One of the most divisive issues in the early church was whether non-Jews could become Christians, and if so, to what extent they had to adopt Jewish practices. The church began, of course, among Jews. Since the earliest Christians shared much of the same religious, ethnic, and cultural background, there was little conflict over inclusiveness. But as the gospel spread to other groups, such as the Hellenists (Jews born outside of Palestine who spoke Greek), or the Jews' despised cousins the Samaritans, or Gentiles, tensions rose and conflicts broke out (for example, Acts 6:1; 11:1–2; 15:1–2).

In the case of Gentiles, some Jewish believers stridently opposed their inclusion. The only way that Gentiles could be acceptable to God, they argued, was by satisfying a precondition: they would have to be circumcised according to the Law of Moses. In effect, Gentiles would have to become Jews before they could become Christians.

This issue was first raised by Stephen, who in essence charged the Jewish council with using Judaism as an excuse for not believing in Jesus (Acts 7:2–53). Later, circumcision was hotly debated among church leaders in Jerusalem (11:1–18; 15:1–29; Gal. 2:1–10) and Antioch (Gal. 2:11–16). Eventually the Jerusalem church officially declared that Christ alone was necessary for salvation.

But that didn't stop false teachers from traveling many of the same paths as the apostles. Some arrived in Galatia and disturbed Gentiles there with a "different gospel" (Gal. 1:6–7). With holy indignation, Paul sent a strongly worded letter to the Galatians in which he insisted that salvation depends on Christ alone. Similar messages went to believers in Ephesus (Eph. 2:11–22), Philippi (Phil. 3:2–16), and Rome (Rom. 2:1—3:30; 11:11–32; 15:7–13).

The gospel of "Christ alone" prevailed. Before long, Gentiles outnumbered Jews in the church and the pendulum swung to the other extreme. "There is no longer Jew or Greek," the apostles said (Gal. 3:28; see also Eph. 2:14–18; Col. 3:11). So what value was left in Judaism if Christ alone was necessary for salvation? Why bother with an outdated system?

THE OTHER SIDE OF THE COIN

Such issues troubled Jewish Christians. Although Jews throughout the empire were coming to faith, they were now a minority among believers. Would Christianity prove to be just one more episode in the loss of their Jewish heritage and assimilation into a Gentile world?

The letter to the Hebrews (along with Romans 9–11) spoke to those fears by showing the other side of the coin. Rather than dismiss the Jewish heritage, Hebrews affirmed it (Heb. 6:13–20).

- It celebrated the richness of God's special relationship with Israel (1:1; 6:13–15).
- It showed God's work in Jewish history and the fulfillment of His plans for the nation in Christ (8:7–13; 10:15–17).
- It revealed significant parallels between details of the Old Testament heritage—such as smells, sounds, traditions, and names—and the new way of Christ (6:20—7:28; 9:1—10:14; 13:10–13).

(continued on next page)

- **It recalled many of the heroes of Israel's history, such as Abraham (6:13—7:6; 11:8–19), Moses (2:2–6; 11:23–28), Aaron (4:14—5:10), Joshua (7:8–10), David (7:6–7), and others (11:4–40).**

What a treasure Jewish Christians could have in light of God's partnership with them! They need not be swallowed up by the Gentile cultures around them. Embracing Christ, they could still hold onto their roots and be themselves (6:13–19).

Hebrews was written to Jewish believers (1:1; 2:14–18; 3:1–6), but it encourages each of us to go back and re-examine, accept, and affirm our roots. That doesn't mean that everything in our past is honoring to God and worth preserving. Indeed, we may have to repudiate certain beliefs, traditions, or behaviors because they run counter to biblical truth.

Nevertheless, part of identifying ourselves with Christ involves a recognition of what God has made us to be from our backgrounds. By tracing the paths of history that He has used to prepare us for the gospel, we can discover delightful new insights into His wisdom, sovereignty, and grace. ◆

Who Wrote Hebrews?

Hebrews lacks a greeting or identification of its author, giving rise to numerous suggestions as to who wrote it. *See " 'I Have Written to You,' " Heb. 13:22.*

God Has Spoken through Jesus

1:1
see pg. 774

1:2–3

1 Long ago God spoke to our ancestors
in many and various ways by the
prophets, 2 but in these last days he has
spoken to us by a Son,[a] whom he ap-
pointed heir of all things, through whom he also created
the worlds. 3 He is the reflection of God's glory and the exact imprint of God's very being, and he sustains[b] all things
by his powerful word. When he had made purification for
sins, he sat down at the right hand of the Majesty on high,
4 having become as much superior to angels as the name he
has inherited is more excellent than theirs.

Jesus Is Superior to the Angels

1:5–14
see pg. 776

5 For to which of the angels did God
ever say,

"You are my Son;
today I have begotten you"?

Or again,

"I will be his Father,
and he will be my Son"?

6 And again, when he brings the firstborn into the world, he
says,

"Let all God's angels worship him."

7 Of the angels he says,

"He makes his angels winds,
and his servants flames of fire."

8 But of the Son he says,

"Your throne, O God, is[c] forever and ever,
and the righteous scepter is the scepter of your[d]
kingdom.
9 You have loved righteousness and hated wickedness;
therefore God, your God, has anointed you
with the oil of gladness beyond your companions."

10 And,

"In the beginning, Lord, you founded the earth,
and the heavens are the work of your hands;

[a] *Or the Son* [b] *Or bears along* [c] *Or God is your throne* [d] Other ancient authorities read *his*

. . . A
SON,
WHOM
HE
APPOINTED
HEIR
OF ALL
THINGS . . .
—Hebrews 1:2

He's Got the Whole World in His Hands

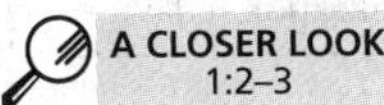
A CLOSER LOOK
1:2–3

We owe our day-to-day existence to God (vv. 2–3), not Mother Nature. See "Every Breath You Take," Col. 1:17.

11 they will perish, but you remain;
they will all wear out like clothing;
12 like a cloak you will roll them up,
and like clothing[e] they will be changed.
But you are the same,
and your years will never end."
13But to which of the angels has he ever said,

[e]Other ancient authorities lack *like clothing*

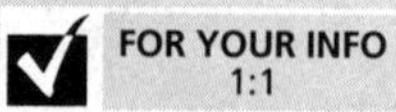
FOR YOUR INFO 1:1

FATHERS AND PROPHETS

Who were the "ancestors" and "prophets" privileged to hear God's voice "long ago" (v. 1)? The writer was referring to some of the Hebrews' most well-known ancestors and others to whom God made astonishing promises and through whom He communicated His Word, now known as the Old Testament. See if you can identify some of these important figures in Israelite history from the descriptions that follow (answers are given at the article, "Who Are These People?" Heb. 11:2):

OLD TESTAMENT FIGURES	
1	The father of three sons in especially evil times, this man is warned of coming disaster and prepares for it despite his neighbors' ridicule. But when calamity strikes and destroys his opponents, he is vindicated by surviving. However, drunkenness leads him into sin with long-term consequences. Nevertheless, God makes an everlasting promise to him and his descendants.
2	A prisoner of war becomes a government trainee who resists cultural assimilation. Later, his coworkers hatch an evil plot which results in orders for his execution. However, by God's power he emerges unscathed and becomes the king's most trusted advisor. Through him God reveals great and awesome visions concerning history.
3	Born in poverty to a minority couple, this man is raised among the wealthy and powerful. But after committing murder, he flees to a remote land and adopts the life of a shepherd. Years later he stages a dramatic comeback, leading his people on the world's largest known expedition back to their homeland. Through him God reveals a moral code that still impacts civilization today.
	Continued

"Sit at my right hand
until I make your enemies a footstool for your feet"?

1:14

14Are not all angels[f] spirits in the divine
service, sent to serve for the sake of those
who are to inherit salvation?

[f]Gk *all of them*

Inheriting Salvation

A CLOSER LOOK 1:14

Who are "those who are to inherit salvation" (v. 14)? And what is it that they will inherit? See "What's In It for Me?" Eph. 1:11.

	Continued
4	One of the youngest sons of a family of shepherds develops musical ability and becomes a military prodigy. However, his prowess causes the existing leadership to view him as such a threat that he is marked for death. Nevertheless, he eventually becomes his nation's leader. Through him God causes to be composed a large portion of the Hebrews' songs of worship.
5	Himself the son of a king, he becomes the most powerful militarist, builder, and judge of his day, trading with foreign nations in military arms, construction materials, treasure cities, and wives. However, frustrations beset him and he writes of the hopelessness of life apart from God. Through him God reveals many practical nuggets of wisdom and the beauty of love.
6	Describing himself as nothing but "a herdsman, and a dresser of sycamore trees," this man rises from obscurity and announces to a rebellious kingdom that God is sending invaders to punish it for its idol worship, corruption, and oppression of the poor. Through his message and its fulfillment, God shows that He can be counted on to keep His Word.
7	The answer to a barren woman's prayer, this man hears as a child the call of God to be His spokesman. Later he serves as a judge of his people and warns them against the perils of establishing a kingdom. Nevertheless, he presides over the anointing of two kings and records the early history of his nation's kingdom era.
8	A poet of deep emotional strength, this man is so outraged by his nation's sin that he cries out to God for judgment. Then when God reveals His plans, he challenges the justice of the proposal. A man of deep faith, he leaves behind a beautiful poem of praise in response to the mysterious ways of God.

For more Old Testament "guess-who's," see "Who Are These People?" Heb. 11:2.

"YOU ARE THE SAME, AND YOUR YEARS WILL NEVER END."
—Hebrews 1:12

A Warning

2 Therefore we must pay greater attention to what we
have heard, so that we do not drift away from it. 2For if
the message declared through angels was valid, and every
transgression or disobedience received a just penalty, 3how
can we escape if we neglect so great a salvation? It was
declared at first through the Lord, and it was attested to us
by those who heard him, 4while God added his testimony
by signs and wonders and various miracles, and by gifts of
the Holy Spirit, distributed according to his will.

Jesus—Lord over All the Earth

5 Now God[g] did not subject the coming world, about
2:6–8 which we are speaking, to angels. 6But
someone has testified somewhere,

"What are human beings that you are mindful of them,[h]
or mortals, that you care for them?[i]
2:7 see pg. 778
7 You have made them for a little while
lower[j] than the angels;
you have crowned them with glory and honor,[k]

[g]Gk *he* [h]Gk *What is man that you are mindful of him?* [i]Gk *or the son of man that you care for him?* In the Hebrew of Psalm 8.4-6 both *man* and *son of man* refer to all humankind [j]Or *them only a little lower* [k]Other ancient authorities add *and set them over the works of your hands*

Many Are Great, But Christ Is the Greatest

The world has seen many great people in its history, but none equal to Jesus, the Son of God (v. 5). The writer shows that Christ is superior to:

- *The angels, Israel's divinely appointed guardians (1:4—2:18).*
- *Moses, Israel's great leader (3:1—4:7).*
- *Joshua, Israel's great general (4:8–13).*
- *Aaron, Israel's great high priest (4:14—7:28).*

Later, Hebrews lists a parade of people who showed great faith in their lives as they looked ahead to the coming of their spiritual brother, Christ (2:11–13; 11:1–40). They believed the promises of God to them, but they realized that the ultimate fulfillment of God's Word was yet to come through His Son.

Christ is the full disclosure of God and serves as the one fixed point amid all the chaotic periods of history—the time past of Old Testament history (1:1), the difficult times that the readers of Hebrews were enduring (12:4–13), and our own times in which we struggle

8 subjecting all things under their feet."
Now in subjecting all things to them, God[l] left nothing outside their control. As it is, we do not yet see everything in
subjection to them, 9but we do see Jesus, who for a little
while was made lower[m] than the angels, now crowned with
glory and honor because of the suffering of death, so that
by the grace of God[n] he might taste death for everyone.
10 It was fitting that God,[l] for whom and through whom
all things exist, in bringing many children to glory, should
make the pioneer of their salvation perfect through sufferings. 11For the one who sanctifies and those who are sanctified all have one Father.[o] For this reason Jesus[l] is not
ashamed to call them brothers and sisters,[p] 12saying,
"I will proclaim your name to my brothers and sisters,[p]
in the midst of the congregation I will praise you."
13And again,
"I will put my trust in him."
And again,
"Here am I and the children whom God has given me."

[l]Gk *he* [m]Or *who was made a little lower* [n]Other ancient authorities read *apart from God* [o]Gk *are all of one* [p]Gk *brothers*

against spiritually hostile forces (see "Who Is the Enemy?" Eph. 6:10–13).

As we face the temptation to doubt God or forsake His ways, this letter assures us that our key resource is the incomparable Christ. He is:

- *God's communication to us (1:2).*
- *The heir of all things (1:2).*
- *The Creator of the worlds (1:3).*
- *A full reflection of God's glory (1:3).*
- *The Sustainer of all things (1:3).*
- *The One who has purged our sins (1:3).*
- *Our representative with God (1:3).*
- *Superior to the angels (1:4).*
- *The possessor of a more excellent name (1:4).*

The book of Hebrews invites us to get to know this incomparable Savior, our Lord and friend, Jesus! ◆

One reason we need to get to know Jesus is that He has faced the temptations we face—and conquered them! See "You Don't Understand!" Matt. 4:3, and "Cocooning," Heb. 4:14–16.

The Proper Measure of All Things

CONSIDER THIS 2:6–8 **"What are human beings?" David asked in Psalm 8:4–6. He found his answer not by looking at humans themselves but *humans in relation to God.* Five hundred years later, the Greek philosopher Protagoras took a completely different approach by offering, "Man is the measure of all things." Today, our culture tends to side with Protagoras.**

But the Bible shows that God is the true measure of all things. Adopting that perspective is the beginning of humility, the doorway to all the other virtues (see "The Way Up Is Down," Matt. 5:3).

Scripture constantly emphasizes the relative insignificance and transitoriness of humanity and the rest of creation in comparison to the greatness of eternal God. David asked, *What are humans* in comparison to their Creator (Ps. 8:3–4)? *What are humans* that they should merit God's attention and affection (Ps. 144:3–4)?

This lends perspective to so many of the idealistic, even utopian, plans to solve the problems of our world. There's nothing wrong with humans working cooperatively to solve problems. But it's a grave mistake to dismiss faith in God and rely instead on the omnipotence of a corporation, a state, or an international collective. To do so smacks of the same blind pride that brought judgment at the Tower of Babel (Gen. 11:1–9). It is cause for God to laugh (Ps. 2:1–4). If we as individuals are as fleeting as grass (Is. 40:6–7), then groups of us, no matter how large, are just as fleeting. We still need the wisdom and strength that only God can supply.

One of the benefits of seeing oneself in relation to God is that it cultivates "Humility—The Scandalous Virtue," Phil. 2:3.

14 Since, therefore, the children share flesh and blood,
he himself likewise shared the same things, so that through
death he might destroy the one who has the power of
death, that is, the devil, 15and free those who all their lives
were held in slavery by the fear of death. 16For it is clear
that he did not come to help angels, but the descendants of
Abraham. 17Therefore he had to become like his brothers
and sisters[q] in every respect, so that he might be a merciful
and faithful high priest in the service of God, to make a sacrifice of atonement for the sins of the people. 18Because he
himself was tested by what he suffered, he is able to help
those who are being tested.

Jesus Superior to Moses

3:1
see pg. 780

3 Therefore, brothers and sisters,[q] holy
partners in a heavenly calling, con-
sider that Jesus, the apostle and high priest of our confes-

[q]Gk *brothers*

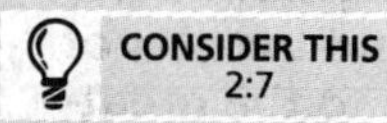

CONSIDER THIS
2:7

People at Work

Do you know that your job is an extension of Christ's rule over the world? Verse 7 cites Psalm 8:4–6 to support its point that Christ is Lord of the earth. But Psalm 8 also shows that God has given people authority over the world. It looks back to the Creation account (Gen. 1:26–30), where God created humanity in His image to be His coworkers in overseeing the creation. Consider what that means:

(1) You bear the very image of God. *Like Him, you are a person, which means you have dignity and value. You matter. Who you are and what you do are significant. God has created you for a reason, which gives your life ultimate meaning and purpose.*

(2) You are created to be a worker. *God is a worker, and since you are made in His image, your work expresses something of who He is and what He wants done in the world. Work (activity that advances your own well-being or that of someone else, or that manages the creation in a godly way) reflects the work that God does. That means your work has dignity and value. It matters to God.*

(3) You are God's coworker. *Genesis 1:26–30 makes it clear that God wants people to manage the world. He gives us authority to "subdue" the earth—to cultivate and develop it, bring it under our control, use it to meet our*

sion, 2was faithful to the one who appointed him, just as
Moses also "was faithful in all[r] God's[s] house." 3Yet Jesus[t] is
worthy of more glory than Moses, just as the builder of a
house has more honor than the house itself. 4(For every
house is built by someone, but the builder of all things is
God.) 5Now Moses was faithful in all God's[s] house as a servant, to testify to the things that would be spoken later.
6Christ, however, was faithful over God's[s] house as a son,
and we are his house if we hold firm[u] the confidence and
the pride that belong to hope.

Listen to Jesus

7 Therefore, as the Holy Spirit says,
"Today, if you hear his voice,
8 do not harden your hearts as in the rebellion,
as on the day of testing in the wilderness,

(Bible text continued on page 782)

[r]Other ancient authorities lack *all* [s]Gk *his* [t]Gk *this one* [u]Other ancient authorities add *to the end*

needs, explore its wonders, and learn to cooperate with its natural laws. He also gives us "dominion" over every plant and animal for similar purposes.

Your job can help accomplish that mandate, as you use your God-given skills and opportunities. He views your work as having not only dignity, but purpose and direction as well. He wants you to accomplish meaningful tasks as you labor with a Christlike work ethic. Ultimately, He wants you to bring Him glory as a faithful manager of the resources and responsibilities He has placed under your control. By approaching work from this perspective, you can find fulfillment and motivation as a partner with God Himself. ◆

Our work isn't exactly the same as God's work, is it? See "Creation: 'Very Good,' But Not Sacred!" Heb. 11:3.

Isn't work a part of the curse put on Adam and Eve? See Rom. 8:20–22.

Work has value in and of itself; it is something that God Himself does. See "God—The Original Worker," John 5:17.

As God's coworker, you have a responsibility to demonstrate Christlike character and conduct on the job. See "Your 'Workstyle,' " Titus 2:9–10.

HE HAD TO BECOME LIKE HIS BROTHERS AND SISTERS IN EVERY RESPECT . . .
—Hebrews 2:17

CONSIDER THIS
3:1

WHO IS "CALLED," ANYWAY?

Nowadays people often speak of a "calling" to signify a career that one has made a lifelong passion, a vocation to which one feels deeply committed. In a similar way, many people use the term "calling" in connection with vocational Christian work. For instance, members of the clergy often describe their "call" to the ministry, a conviction that God has led them into that particular career to accomplish certain work for Him.

Hebrews tells us that all of us as believers partake of the "heavenly calling" (v. 1). What exactly does that mean? The Greek word translated "calling" comes from *kaleō*, meaning to call, invite, or summon. The word and its derivatives are used often in the New Testament. There is no single, definitive discussion of calling, but we can gain a fuller understanding by looking at some of the ways in which this subject is treated. For example, calling is used in connection with:

- An invitation to classes of people for salvation (Mark 2:17; 1 Cor. 1:9, 24; 2 Thess. 2:13–14).
- An invitation to individuals for salvation (Gal. 1:15–16; 2 Tim. 1:9).
- A summons to a Christlike lifestyle (Eph. 4:1; 1 Thess. 2:12).
- A designation of believers' position with God (1 Pet. 2:9; 1 John 3:1) or their identity with Christ, especially when it means suffering (1 Pet. 2:21; James 2:7).

A Summons to Faith and Obedience

It is the sense of identification with Christ and with other believers that Hebrews emphasizes when it calls us "holy partners in a heavenly calling" (Heb. 3:1). Christ became human like us (2:14, 17) in order that we might become like Him—alive, free from sin, and holy.

One overriding theme for all of these treatments of calling is that the call of God is a summons to people to come to Him through faith in Christ and live as servants of His kingdom. Thus, salvation from sin and obedience to God are at the heart of what "calling" means in the New Testament.

A Higher Calling?

Why, then, did the idea of calling come to be connected with vocation? One reason is that Scripture records God calling individuals to particular tasks. Paul, for instance, said that he was "called" to be an apostle (Rom. 1:1; 1 Cor. 1:1). This has led some to propose the idea of a "general call" to all believers but a "special call" or "higher call" to certain believers for specific assignments, notably the "full-time" gospel ministry.

However, there is little evidence that Paul saw his calling chiefly as a "higher calling." Rather, he viewed himself in the main like any other believer, called by God to salvation and obedience. However, that calling had important implications for his vocation, because the Lord made clear from the start of Paul's walk with Christ what He wanted Paul to do: "He is an instrument whom I have chosen to bring my name before Gentiles and kings and before the people of Israel" (Acts 9:15). Henceforth, Paul regarded himself as "called to be an apostle." But the emphasis should be on the word *called* more than the word *apostle*.

Every Christian shares that same basic calling with Paul, as his opening words to the Romans demonstrate. He began the letter, as was his custom, with the greeting, "Paul, a servant of Jesus Christ, called to be an apostle, set apart for the gospel of God" (Rom. 1:1). But the opening sentence (which is unbroken in the original Greek) goes on to say, "*including* yourselves who are called to belong to Jesus Christ" (1:6, emphasis added). The word "including" indicates that the Roman believers' call was basically the same as Paul's. They were not all apostles, but they were all "called to belong to Jesus Christ."

So it is for believers today. Like Paul and the rest of the New Testament Christians, we are all called with the same calling and thus stand as equals before God.

Calling and Careers

As with Paul, our calling has important implications for our jobs and careers. For one thing, it means a change of bosses: as God's children, we ultimately serve Christ (see "Who's the Boss?" Col. 3:22–24). It also means a change of conduct and character: as Christ's followers, we need to work with a Christlike "workstyle" (see Titus 2:9–10). And it means a new motivation when it comes to our paycheck: we work not only to meet our own needs, but to have money to meet the needs of others (see "From Deadbeat to Donor," Eph. 4:28, and "Christians and Money," 1 Tim. 6:6–19).

Does our calling affect our choice of career? It may, but not necessarily. It's interesting that Paul directed the Corinthians to remain in the calling in which they found themselves when they came to faith in Christ (1 Cor. 7:17–24). They did not need to change jobs just because they had become believers. Instead, they needed to be Christ's followers *wherever* they were. On the other hand, their relationship with Christ did not prevent them from changing occupational status if they could and if they wanted to.

The point is that no matter what we do for work—whether "full-time" vocational Christian work or "secular," everyday work—we are all called to serve Christ. In the end, what makes the issue of calling important is not us, but the One who calls us. ◆

Find out more about how God regards careers in the "secular" workplace. See "People at Work," Heb. 2:7.

[9] where your ancestors put me to the test,
though they had seen my works [10]for forty years.
Therefore I was angry with that generation,
and I said, 'They always go astray in their hearts,
and they have not known my ways.'
[11] As in my anger I swore,
'They will not enter my rest.' "
[12]Take care, brothers and sisters,[v] that none of you may
have an evil, unbelieving heart that turns away from the living God. [13]But exhort one another every day, as long as it is
called "today," so that none of you may be hardened by the
deceitfulness of sin. [14]For we have become partners of
Christ, if only we hold our first confidence firm to the end.
[15]As it is said,
"Today, if you hear his voice,
do not harden your hearts as in the rebellion."
[16]Now who were they who heard and yet were rebellious?
Was it not all those who left Egypt under the leadership of
Moses? [17]But with whom was he angry forty years? Was it
not those who sinned, whose bodies fell in the wilderness?

[v]Gk *brothers*

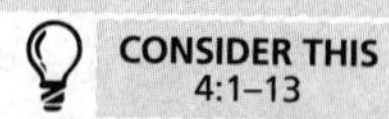

CONSIDER THIS
4:1–13

THE SABBATH

How would you explain the gospel to Jews living in the first century? How would you describe what it means to trust in Christ's work on the cross rather than living by strict observance of the Law? The writer of Hebrews found a useful comparison in the Sabbath (vv. 1–13).

When God completed His work of creation, He rested. He stopped. It wasn't that He was tired and needed a break; He no longer needed to work because His work was finished. Creation was complete (v. 4; Gen. 2:1–2). In the same way, people don't need to work for salvation because in Christ salvation is finished. The way to God is open. We can rest from slavish adherence to the Law in an attempt to make ourselves acceptable to God. We need only trust in Christ's finished work on our behalf (Heb. 4:3; Rom. 10:4).

The writer knew that nothing would dramatize what Christ accomplished like the Sabbath. Every seven days the Jews ceased from their work. They didn't just take a day off to catch up on chores or go to the lake, as many modern people do on Saturdays. They put an emphatic pause

[18]And to whom did he swear that they would not enter his
rest, if not to those who were disobedient? [19]So we see that
they were unable to enter because of unbelief.

A Promise of Rest

4:1–13

4 Therefore, while the promise of entering his rest is still open, let us
take care that none of you should seem to have failed to
reach it. [2]For indeed the good news came to us just as to
them; but the message they heard did not benefit them, because they were not united by faith with those who listened.[w] [3]For we who have believed enter that rest, just as
God[x] has said,

"As in my anger I swore,
'They shall not enter my rest,' "

though his works were finished at the foundation of the
world. [4]For in one place it speaks about the seventh day as
follows, "And God rested on the seventh day from all his
works." [5]And again in this place it says, "They shall not

[w]Other ancient authorities read *it did not meet with faith in those who listened* [x]Gk *he*

in life for an entire day. Society came to a screeching halt to remind everyone of what God had done (Ex. 20:8–11).

So when Hebrews equates rest in Christ with Sabbath rest, it draws on the heart of Jewish culture. Jesus is God's Sabbath rest when it comes to the work of salvation.

Every culture has powerful metaphors and symbols to describe its life. As you consider how to communicate Christ to people in your culture, what are some useful metaphors that you could use? How could you communicate the "old, old story" in "new, new" ways? ◆

Over the centuries Sabbath observance became so rigid that by the time of Christ it was "unlawful" even to do good on that day. See "Jesus Confronts the Legalists," Luke 6:1–11.

Do some of the activities that people engage in on Sundays bother you? Or maybe you wonder why Sundays seem like such a big deal to some Christians. See "Matters of Conscience," Rom. 14:1–23.

THE PROMISE OF ENTERING HIS REST IS STILL OPEN. . . .
—Hebrews 4:1

QUOTE UNQUOTE

CONSIDER THIS 4:7 *Christ wants to start giving us life* today *(v. 7), right now, not at some distant point in the future:*

Many people spend their entire life indefinitely preparing to live.

Paul Tournier

enter my rest." [6]Since therefore it remains open for some to
enter it, and those who formerly received the good news
4:7 failed to enter because of disobedience,
[7]again he sets a certain day—"today"—
saying through David much later, in the words already
quoted,

"Today, if you hear his voice,
do not harden your hearts."

[8]For if Joshua had given them rest, God[y] would not speak
later about another day. [9]So then, a sabbath rest still remains for the people of God; [10]for those who enter God's
rest also cease from their labors as God did from his. [11]Let
us therefore make every effort to enter that rest, so that no
one may fall through such disobedience as theirs.

4:12 12 Indeed, the word of God is living
and active, sharper than any two-edged
sword, piercing until it divides soul from spirit, joints from
marrow; it is able to judge the thoughts and intentions of
the heart. [13]And before him no creature is hidden, but all

[y]Gk *he*

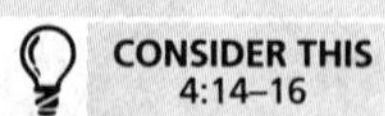

CONSIDER THIS 4:14–16

Cocooning

One of the major developments in modern Western society is the phenomenon of "cocooning"—people pulling in, living private lifestyles in which they shut out the world and its concerns. Cocooners have interest only in what touches them, and they set up their environment so that they control what touches them.

Unfortunately, cocooning has subtly invaded the church, contributing to the "pulling in" of Christian faith. It shows up, for instance, in over-emphasis on the relationship of the individual to Christ and what He can do for each person, to the neglect of what Christ wants to do among communities of His people, including their corporate responsibilities to each other and the larger society.

The book of Hebrews speaks to the danger of cocooning as it describes Christ's work on our behalf (vv. 14–16):

(1) Christ chose to get involved. *He did not remain in His privileged position with the Father, but "passed through the heavens" (v. 14) to come to earth, becoming poor in order to make us spiritually rich. We can't imagine what that move cost Him (see "Christ Became Poor," 2 Cor. 8:8–9).*

are naked and laid bare to the eyes of the one to whom we must render an account.

Trials Are Shared by Christ

4:14–16

14 Since, then, we have a great high priest who has passed through the heavens, Jesus, the Son of God, let us hold fast to our confession.
15For we do not have a high priest who is unable to sympathize with our weaknesses, but we have one who in every respect has been tested[z] as we are, yet without sin.
16Let us therefore approach the throne of grace with boldness, so that we may receive mercy and find grace to help in time of need.

Jesus a Superior Priest

5:1–14 see pg. 786

5 Every high priest chosen from among mortals is put in charge of things pertaining to God on their behalf, to offer gifts and sacrifices for sins.
2He is able to deal gently with the

[z]*Or tempted*

(2) Christ faced reality. *He is no stranger to real life. He never walled Himself off from what people go through every day (v. 15; see "You Don't Understand!" Matt. 4:3).*

(3) Christ empowers people. *He gives His people sufficient power to deal with life. One rationale for cocooning is the attitude, "When I'm done with work, I'm worn out. I can't be bothered with people's problems. I can hardly manage my own! If anything, I need to be a receiver of grace, not a dispenser of it." Result: the many take comfort, help, and peace from the few who give.*

But v. 16 challenges believers—individually and corporately—to "approach the throne of grace with boldness." Why? In order to obtain mercy—a personal need of every individual—and "grace to help in time of need." Notice: grace to help. *God's help relieves some of our cares and allows us the freedom and strength to "pass it on" by helping others.* ◆

The Power of God's Word

CONSIDER THIS 4:12

This publication that you are reading is based on the belief that Scripture really is the living and powerful Word of God (v. 12). As this verse shows, the Word speaks to heart matters—intentions and motives. Ultimately, people make choices and act on the basis of their underlying values and notions about what is true and right. God's Word is the authoritative standard by which all thoughts and actions are to be measured.

ignorant and wayward, since he himself is subject to weakness; [3]and because of this he must offer sacrifice for his
own sins as well as for those of the people. [4]And one does
not presume to take this honor, but takes it only when
called by God, just as Aaron was.
5 So also Christ did not glorify himself in becoming a
high priest, but was appointed by the one who said to him,
"You are my Son,
today I have begotten you";
[6]as he says also in another place,
"You are a priest forever,
according to the order of Melchizedek."
7 In the days of his flesh, Jesus[a] offered up prayers and
supplications, with loud cries and tears, to the one who
was able to save him from death, and he was heard because
of his reverent submission. [8]Although he was a Son, he
learned obedience through what he suffered; [9]and having
been made perfect, he became the source of eternal salvation for all who obey him, [10]having been designated by God
a high priest according to the order of Melchizedek.

Press On to Maturity

11 About this[b] we have much to say that is hard to explain, since you have become dull in understanding. [12]For

[a]Gk *he* [b]Or *him*

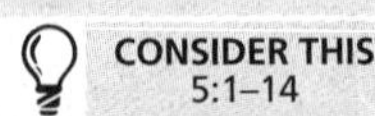

CONSIDER THIS
5:1–14

ELEMENTARY LEADERSHIP LESSONS

Leadership is often understood in terms of power, manipulation, assertiveness, and ambition. The literature of the work world is cluttered with "how to" books that profile the famous and successful who have fought and won by these cruel values. In the first century, the Roman Empire was dominated by very powerful and manipulative family dynasties riddled with competition, violence, greed, and dirty tricks.

But Jesus modeled a different way of leadership. Throughout the New Testament we are shown glimpses of His life and character. In them we discover a stark contrast to our world's soap opera of abuse and distortion.

Hebrews 5 is one such picture. It describes a true leader as a priest who is . . .

- *focused on people and how they connect with God (v. 1).*
- *compassionate with the weak and ignorant (v. 2).*
- *required to face sin head-on (v. 3).*

though by this time you ought to be teachers, you need
someone to teach you again the basic elements of the oracles of God. You need milk, not solid food; 13for everyone
who lives on milk, being still an infant, is unskilled in the
word of righteousness. 14But solid food is for the mature,
for those whose faculties have been trained by practice to
distinguish good from evil.

Grow Beyond the Basics

6:1–20 see pg. 788

6 Therefore let us go on toward perfection,[c] leaving behind the basic
teaching about Christ, and not laying again the foundation:
repentance from dead works and faith toward God, 2in-
struction about baptisms, laying on of hands, resurrection
of the dead, and eternal judgment. 3And we will do[d] this, if
God permits. 4For it is impossible to restore again to repentance those who have once been enlightened, and have
tasted the heavenly gift, and have shared in the Holy Spirit,
5and have tasted the goodness of the word of God and the
powers of the age to come, 6and then have fallen away,
since on their own they are crucifying again the Son of God

(Bible text continued on page 789)

[c]Or *toward maturity* [d]Other ancient authorities read *let us do*

YOU NEED SOMEONE TO TEACH YOU AGAIN THE BASIC ELEMENTS. . . .
—Hebrews 5:12

- *not self-appointed, but rather called by God into his role (v. 4).*

Jesus was the perfect priest (vv. 5–10). The writer admits that this portrait is hard to grasp (vv. 11–14). However, those who seek to grow into Christlike maturity need to consider it carefully. Jesus provides for those who seek His help. All we need to do is ask (4:14–16).

Who are your heroes when it comes to leadership? Why? Do you aspire to a leadership style that lacks the character of Christ? Why not ask peers or friends what patterns they see in you? Use the evaluations of others to rewrite your agenda for growth. ◆

The families of first-century rulers were notorious for their villainy and intrigue. See "The Herods," Acts 12:1–2, and "Nero," Acts 25:12.

CONSIDER THIS
6:1–20

KNOWING *ABOUT* GOD IS NOT THE SAME AS *KNOWING* GOD

Many people have knowledge about religion, Christianity, and the Bible. But as the writer to the Hebrews warns, intellectual knowledge is not the same as vital faith. Knowing about God is not the same as having a personal relationship with Him.

This is clear from everyday relationships. Reading books on marriage is not the same as spending time with one's spouse. Knowing someone's phone number is a far cry from enjoying friendship with that person. Knowing who one's customers are is not the same as dealing with a specific customer.

In the same way, *knowing* God involves far more than knowing *about* Him. Information alone does not produce tangible faith. To be sure, right thinking is involved in faith, but faith is more than mere knowledge. For example, the recipients of Hebrews knew quite a bit about the faith, such as the basic teachings about Christ, the need for repentance and for faith in God (6:1), and the meaning of baptism, ordination, the resurrection, and judgment (v. 2).

Nevertheless, without the constant work of cultivation (watering, weeding, fertilizing, pruning), spiritual weeds soon sprout and in time take over, producing thorns rather than good fruit or grain (vv. 7–8). In that case, the crop (faith) is worthless and destined for burning. To avoid that outcome, diligent tending and development are required (vv. 11–12). Perseverance is crucial: we must never "coast" on past experience or former tidbits of knowledge.

Hebrews 6 is a stern warning and a loving appeal for renewed commitment to Christ. Are you in need of spiritual renewal? What disciplines might help you get started on making your faith vital once again? Perhaps you might:

- Establish a small group with other believers in your workplace, industry, neighborhood, or family to meet regularly for prayer and discussion on how Christ enters into everyday situations.
- Volunteer for a program to serve the needy through your church or a community service agency.
- Speak out on workplace policies, decisions, or practices that you know to be unethical or harmful to others or the environment.
- Begin a regular habit of Bible reading and study in order to apply God's Word to your life.
- Get to know people in international missions work.
- Begin patterns of prayer such as: prayer for people with whom you live and work—even those you may not like; prayers of thanksgiving for the things God has done for you and for the responsibilities He has given to you; prayers of confession and repentance for sin or areas of neglect in your life; prayers that meditate on God and His Word; prayers that express your innermost feelings and thoughts to God.
- Keep a journal of developments and changes in your life.
- Take on a task that uses ability with which God has gifted you, especially if that ability is unused or underused elsewhere in your life.
- Consider whether you have ignored, offended, or hurt someone and need to repent of your error and apologize to that person.

The point is, faith works best when it is the central unifying factor in one's life. Christ must never be just one more thing to occasionally acknowledge;

(continued on next page)

and are holding him up to contempt. 7Ground that drinks
up the rain falling on it repeatedly, and that produces a
crop useful to those for whom it is cultivated, receives a
blessing from God. 8But if it produces thorns and thistles, it
is worthless and on the verge of being cursed; its end is to
be burned over.

Great Expectations

6:9–12 9 Even though we speak in this way,
beloved, we are confident of better things
in your case, things that belong to salvation. 10For God is
not unjust; he will not overlook your work and the love
that you showed for his sake[e] in serving the saints, as you
still do. 11And we want each one of you to show the same
diligence so as to realize the full assurance of hope to the
6:12–15 very end, 12so that you may not become
sluggish, but imitators of those who
through faith and patience inherit the promises.
6:13 13 When God made a promise to
Abraham, because he had no one greater
by whom to swear, he swore by himself, 14saying, "I will
surely bless you and multiply you." 15And thus Abraham,[f]
having patiently endured, obtained the promise. 16Human
beings, of course, swear by someone greater than themselves, and an oath given as confirmation puts an end to all
dispute. 17In the same way, when God desired to show even
more clearly to the heirs of the promise the unchangeable
character of his purpose, he guaranteed it by an oath, 18so
that through two unchangeable things, in which it is impossible that God would prove false, we who have taken
refuge might be strongly encouraged to seize the hope set
before us. 19We have this hope, a sure and steadfast anchor

[e]Gk *for his name* [f]Gk *he*

(continued from previous page)

rather, He must be the Lord of life and be brought into every area of life (see "Is Jesus Really Lord of All?" Luke 6:1–5). Hebrews 6 urges us to take our faith beyond only knowing to being and doing. ◆

Jesus made a connection between belief and practice by immediately following His Sermon on the Mount with "deeds in the valley." After warning His listeners against empty religious talk (Matt. 7:21–28), He demonstrated true spirituality by meeting needs. See "What It Means To Be Like Jesus: To Be Like Jesus Means to Serve Others," Matt. 8:1—9:38.

"GOD PROMISED TO . . ."

CONSIDER THIS 6:12–15 **God has no problem committing Himself to people (v. 13). He has utter confidence that He can fulfill what He has promised. But His promises usually are not carried out for us immediately. God is not a vending machine dispensing treats at the press of a button. Nor should we expect to be able to call Him up and tell Him to send us what we need by overnight express. Like Abraham, we must receive His promises in faith, with great patience (vv. 12–13).**

Actually, trusting in others and waiting for them to deliver is hardly foreign to us. Most of us face that every day in the workplace. We accept contracts for products and services weeks, months, or even years in advance of actual delivery.

Are you asking God to deliver on your time schedule? God wants to *grow* you rather than just *give* to you. He cultivates faith and perseverance by doing His work in our lives in His way and in His time.

Work, Labor, and Patience

A CLOSER LOOK 6:9–12 *Work, labor, and patience (vv. 10, 12)—these are marketplace terms that have important spiritual application. See "Work, Labor, and Steadfastness," 1 Thess. 1:3.*

Promises to Abraham

A CLOSER LOOK 6:13 *God made important promises to Abraham (v. 13), who is remembered as the man who believed God—a remarkable thing in that Abraham had very little evidence that God would follow through. See "Abraham," Rom. 4:1.*

of the soul, a hope that enters the inner shrine behind the
curtain, 20where Jesus, a forerunner on our behalf, has entered, having become a high priest forever according to the
order of Melchizedek.

Melchizedek—An Illustration of Christ

7:1

7 This "King Melchizedek of Salem,
priest of the Most High God, met
Abraham as he was returning from defeating the kings and
blessed him"; 2and to him Abraham apportioned "one-tenth
of everything." His name, in the first place, means "king of
righteousness"; next he is also king of Salem, that is, "king
of peace." 3Without father, without mother, without genealogy, having neither beginning of days nor end of life, but
resembling the Son of God, he remains a priest forever.
4 See how great he is! Even[g] Abraham the patriarch gave
him a tenth of the spoils. 5And those descendants of Levi
who receive the priestly office have a commandment in the
law to collect tithes[h] from the people, that is, from their
kindred,[i] though these also are descended from Abraham.
6But this man, who does not belong to their ancestry, collected tithes[h] from Abraham and blessed him who had received the promises. 7It is beyond dispute that the inferior
is blessed by the superior. 8In the one case, tithes are re-

[g]Other ancient authorities lack *Even* [h]Or *a tenth* [i]Gk *brothers*

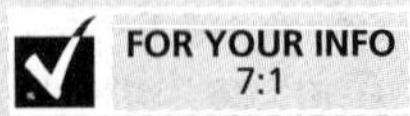

FOR YOUR INFO
7:1

MELCHIZEDEK

One of the most mysterious figures in the Old Testament serves as an illustration for Christ. Melchizedek (v. 1) suddenly appears in the book of Genesis to bless Abraham after his defeat of Chedorlaomer, king of Elam, and his three allies (Gen. 14:18–20). Then, just as suddenly, Melchizedek disappears from the biblical record, until hundreds of years later David refers to him in Psalm 110.

Melchizedek ("king of righteousness") was a real man. Genesis reports that he was the king of Salem (Jerusalem) and a priest of God Most High. It was apparently in this priestly role that he first met Abraham returning from the rescue of his nephew Lot from Chedorlaomer. Melchizedek presented bread and wine, which was probably a demonstration of friendship and religious kinship. Melchizedek also bestowed a blessing on Abraham, praising God for giving him victory in the battle.

In exchange, Abraham presented Melchizedek with a tithe (one-tenth) of the booty he had taken from the field of battle. By this act, Abraham indicated that he

ceived by those who are mortal; in the other, by one of
whom it is testified that he lives. [9]One might even say that
Levi himself, who receives tithes, paid tithes through Abraham, [10]for he was still in the loins of his ancestor when
Melchizedek met him.

Jesus Is Our High Priest

11 Now if perfection had been attainable through the
levitical priesthood—for the people received the law under
this priesthood—what further need would there have been
to speak of another priest arising according to the order of
Melchizedek, rather than one according to the order of
Aaron? [12]For when there is a change in the priesthood,
there is necessarily a change in the law as well. [13]Now the
one of whom these things are spoken belonged to another
tribe, from which no one has ever served at the altar. [14]For
it is evident that our Lord was descended from Judah, and
in connection with that tribe Moses said nothing about
priests.

15 It is even more obvious when another priest arises,
resembling Melchizedek, [16]one who has become a priest,
not through a legal requirement concerning physical descent, but through the power of an indestructible life. [17]For
it is attested of him,

ANOTHER PRIEST ARISES, RESEMBLING MELCHIZEDEK. . . .
—Hebrews 7:15

recognized Melchizedek as a fellow-worshiper of the one true God as well as a priest who ranked higher spiritually than himself. Melchizedek's existence shows that there were people other than Abraham and his family who served the true God in ancient times.

In Psalm 110, a messianic psalm written by David, Melchizedek is seen as a type of Christ (v. 4). It's interesting that Jesus confounded His enemies by quoting from this Psalm (Matt. 22:43). They either failed to understand that Jesus was the Christ of whom David was speaking, or else they knew all too well but chose not to recognize Him as the Messiah.

The writer to the Hebrews recalls the incident between Abraham and Melchizedek and shows the parallels between Melchizedek and Christ. Both are kings of righteousness and peace. Both have a priesthood that is superior to the old Levitical order and the priesthood of Aaron (Heb. 7:1–10). ◆

"You are a priest forever,
according to the order of Melchizedek."
[18]There is, on the one hand, the abrogation of an earlier
commandment because it was weak and
7:19–22
ineffectual [19](for the law made nothing
perfect); there is, on the other hand, the introduction of a
better hope, through which we approach God.
20 This was confirmed with an oath; for others who became priests took their office without an oath, [21]but this
one became a priest with an oath, because of the one who
said to him,
"The Lord has sworn
and will not change his mind,
'You are a priest forever' "—
[22]accordingly Jesus has also become the guarantee of a better covenant.
23 Furthermore, the former priests were many in number, because they were prevented by death from continuing

FOR YOUR INFO
7:19–22

Something Better than Law and Priests

Those who follow Christ enjoy the benefits of a "better hope" (v. 19) and a "better covenant" (v. 22) than the Mosaic Law and the sacrificial system described in the Old Testament (vv. 11–12).

The Mosaic Law:

- *Came from God.*
- *Prepared the way and pointed toward Christ (Matt. 5:17; Rom. 5:20; Gal. 3:19–25).*
- *Set the standard for holiness in every area of life, not just religious dimensions (1 John 3:4). (For example, Leviticus 17–26 and Exodus 21–23 are concentrated collections of what the entire Law teaches. They include laws regarding leaders, the army, criminal cases, property rights and crimes against property, humane treatment, personal and family rights, and social behavior.)*
- *Helped people know of their need for God because it exposed their bondage to sin (Rom. 7:7, 12, 14–25).*

The Levitical Priests:

- *Came from the tribe of Levi (Deut. 18:1).*
- *Functioned to: administer the Law to Israel (Mal. 2:6–7); represent the people before God by offering sacrifices (Lev. 4:20, 26, 31); judge matters in the land as a supreme court (Deut. 17:8–13).*
- *Preserved the Torah, copies of the Law (Deut. 31:24–26).*

in office; [24]but he holds his priesthood permanently, because he continues forever. [25]Consequently he is able for all time to save[j] those who approach God through him, since he always lives to make intercession for them.

26 For it was fitting that we should have such a high priest, holy, blameless, undefiled, separated from sinners, and exalted above the heavens. [27]Unlike the other[k] high priests, he has no need to offer sacrifices day after day, first for his own sins, and then for those of the people; this he did once for all when he offered himself. [28]For the law appoints as high priests those who are subject to weakness, but the word of the oath, which came later than the law, appoints a Son who has been made perfect forever.

A New Covenant

8 Now the main point in what we are saying is this: we have such a high priest, one who is seated at the right

[j]Or *able to save completely* [k]Gk lacks *other*

- *Cared for the temple after it was built.*
- *Foreshadowed the priesthood of Christ's followers (1 Pet. 2:9).*

The writer of Hebrews shows that Christ is superior to the Law and the Old Testament priests. He is God's provision to unite people directly with God.

Christ:

- *Offers a better hope than the Law (Heb. 7:18–20, 22).*
- *Is a permanent priest, no longer vulnerable to death (vv. 23–25).*
- *Always makes intercession for us (v. 25).*
- *Is holy, harmless, undefiled, separate from sinners, and has become higher than the heavens (v. 26).*
- *Has offered the one, final sacrifice for sins on our behalf—Himself (v. 27).*

No wonder we are called to submit to Christ and follow Him (10:19–22). He is our priest and our sacrifice, restoring us to God as beloved children. Have you declared your dependence on Christ and loyalty to Him? ◆

In what way does Jesus establish a "better covenant" than the old covenant? See "The New Covenant," 1 Cor. 11:25.

. . . HOLY, BLAMELESS, UNDEFILED, SEPARATED FROM SINNERS . . . EXALTED ABOVE THE HEAVENS.
—Hebrews 7:26

A New Contract That You'll Like

CONSIDER THIS 8:6–7 **Are you losing hope in your current situation? Do you long for a better arrangement? Perhaps you need a fresh start at work, in your family, your friendships, or your personal life. For too long you've felt trapped in old patterns.**

Hebrews addresses those kinds of circumstances. Thousands of years of Jewish history were built on God's covenant with Israel (see "Israel," Rom. 10:1). But Christ came to rewrite the script of history. He offers a superior covenant rooted in better promises and without fault (Heb. 8:6–7). As the prophet Jeremiah had foreseen, under the new arrangement wickedness will be forgiven, sins will be forgotten, and the old covenant will fade into the shadows before vanishing altogether (vv. 12–13; Jer. 31:31–34).

What an amazing message! We can have a fresh start. Bondage to old, seemingly unbreakable patterns can be broken and replaced. But first we must confess our condition and accept God's provision, which includes His agenda for change (1 John 1:8–10). Therein lies fresh start for our lives.

The same pattern of newness holds true for relationships. Owning our responsibility and admitting our faults opens the door to new ways (see Acts 19:18–20; James 5:16).

Have you learned the joy of confession, apology, and repentance? Do you need some breakthroughs among your peers, friends, or associates? Take the risk to speak the truth to them about your failings and seek a renewal in the relationship.

Many other passages of Scripture talk about the fresh start we can have in Christ, such as 2 Cor. 5:16–17; Col. 3:5–17; Titus 3:3–7; 1 Pet. 2:9–12.

hand of the throne of the Majesty in the heavens, 2a
minister in the sanctuary and the true tent[l] that the Lord,
and not any mortal, has set up. 3For every high priest is
appointed to offer gifts and sacrifices; hence it is necessary
for this priest also to have something to offer. 4Now if he
were on earth, he would not be a priest at all, since there
are priests who offer gifts according to the law. 5They offer
worship in a sanctuary that is a sketch and shadow of the
heavenly one; for Moses, when he was about to erect the
tent,[l] was warned, "See that you make everything according
8:6–7 to the pattern that was shown you on the
mountain." 6But Jesus[m] has now obtained
a more excellent ministry, and to that degree he is the
mediator of a better covenant, which has been enacted
through better promises. 7For if that first covenant had
been faultless, there would have been no need to look for a
second one.

"They Shall Be My People"

8 God[n] finds fault with them when he says:
"The days are surely coming, says the Lord,
when I will establish a new covenant with the house
of Israel
and with the house of Judah;
9 not like the covenant that I made with their ancestors,
on the day when I took them by the hand to lead
them out of the land of Egypt;
for they did not continue in my covenant,
and so I had no concern for them, says the Lord.
10 This is the covenant that I will make with the house of
Israel
after those days, says the Lord:
I will put my laws in their minds,
and write them on their hearts,
and I will be their God,
and they shall be my people.
11 And they shall not teach one another
or say to each other, 'Know the Lord,'
for they shall all know me,
from the least of them to the greatest.
12 For I will be merciful toward their iniquities,
and I will remember their sins no more."
13In speaking of "a new covenant," he has made the first
one obsolete. And what is obsolete and growing old will
soon disappear.

[l] *Or tabernacle* [m] Gk *he* [n] Gk *He*

The Old Covenant

9:1–10

9 Now even the first covenant had
regulations for worship and an
earthly sanctuary. 2For a tent[o] was constructed, the first
one, in which were the lampstand, the table, and the bread
of the Presence;[p] this is called the Holy Place. 3Behind the
second curtain was a tent[o] called the Holy of Holies. 4In it
stood the golden altar of incense and the ark of the
covenant overlaid on all sides with gold, in which there
were a golden urn holding the manna, and Aaron's rod that
budded, and the tablets of the covenant; 5above it were the
cherubim of glory overshadowing the mercy seat.[q] Of these
things we cannot speak now in detail.
6 Such preparations having been made, the priests go
continually into the first tent[o] to carry out their ritual
duties; 7but only the high priest goes into the second, and
he but once a year, and not without taking the blood that
he offers for himself and for the sins committed uninten-
tionally by the people. 8By this the Holy Spirit indicates
that the way into the sanctuary has not yet been disclosed
as long as the first tent[o] is still standing. 9This is a symbol[r]
of the present time, during which gifts and sacrifices are offered that cannot perfect the conscience of the worshiper,
10but deal only with food and drink and various baptisms,
regulations for the body imposed until the time comes to
set things right.

Eternal Redemption—Once for All

11 But when Christ came as a high priest of the good
things that have come,[s] then through the greater and perfect[t] tent[o] (not made with hands, that is, not of this creation), 12he entered once for all into the Holy Place, not
with the blood of goats and calves, but with his own blood,
thus obtaining eternal redemption. 13For if the blood of
goats and bulls, with the sprinkling of the ashes of a heifer,
sanctifies those who have been defiled so that their flesh is
purified, 14how much more will the blood of Christ, who
through the eternal Spirit[u] offered himself without blemish
to God, purify our[v] conscience from dead works to worship
the living God!

[o]Or *tabernacle* [p]Gk *the presentation of the loaves* [q]Or *the place of atonement* [r]Gk *parable* [s]Other ancient authorities read *good things to come* [t]Gk *more perfect* [u]Other ancient authorities read *Holy Spirit* [v]Other ancient authorities read *your*

An Eternal Inheritance?

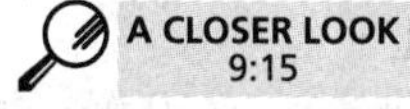

A CLOSER LOOK 9:15 *Because so much of what God has in store for believers is on the other side of death, it is hard to explain. For instance, v. 15 talks about an "eternal inheritance." What is that? See "What's In It for Me?" Eph. 1:11.*

The Freedom of the New Covenant

FOR YOUR INFO 9:1–10 **Have you ever noticed how terms like "binding," "enforceable," and "limits" tend to make their way into negotiations of contracts and agreements? Words like that suggest that contracts rarely free people, but rather hedge them in with terms and commitments.**

The Bible presents two contracts, called *covenants,* between God and people: the old covenant (v. 1) described in the Old Testament ("testament" means covenant), which was based on God's law, and the new covenant described in the New Testament, which is based on God's grace.

Two Covenants Compared

THE OLD COVENANT: (Heb. 9:1–10)	THE NEW COVENANT: (Heb. 9:11–28)
Obsolete now that Christ has come (Heb. 8:13).	A better covenant brought about by Christ (Heb. 7:19; 8:6–7).
Originated at Mount Sinai (Gal. 4:24–25).	Originated from the Jerusalem above (Gal. 4:26–27).
Brought death and condemnation (2 Cor. 3:7–9).	Brings life (Eph. 2:1–13).
Impossible to obey perfectly because of human weakness and sin (Rom. 8:3).	Fulfilled perfectly by Christ (Luke 22:20; 1 Cor. 11:25).
Required annual atonement for sins (Heb. 9:7–8; 10:1–4).	Removes sin once for all and cleanses the conscience (Heb. 9:12; 10:2, 22).
Restricted access to God (Heb. 9:7–8).	Opened access to God for all (Heb. 9:15–16).

Actually, God's new covenant differs from a contract in that it is one-sided in initiative, not unlike a conqueror declaring the terms of victory.

(continued on next page)

(continued from previous page)

However, God's covenant is vastly different from a victor's terms in that God's driving motivation is love, grace, and the desire to restore people into His family.

Based on His new covenant, God offers the forgiveness of sins and eternal life to all who respond and place faith in Jesus. Have you responded? Is there someone you need to tell about God's offer?

God entered into numerous covenants with people in the Old Testament. See "The New Covenant," 1 Cor. 11:25.

9:15
see pg. 795

15 For this reason he is the mediator
of a new covenant, so that those who are
called may receive the promised eternal inheritance, because a death has occurred that redeems them from the
transgressions under the first covenant.[w] 16Where a will[w] is
involved, the death of the one who made it must be established. 17For a will[w] takes effect only at death, since it is not
in force as long as the one who made it is alive. 18Hence not
even the first covenant was inaugurated without blood.
19For when every commandment had been told to all the
people by Moses in accordance with the law, he took the
blood of calves and goats,[x] with water and scarlet wool and
hyssop, and sprinkled both the scroll itself and all the people, 20saying, "This is the blood of the covenant that God
has ordained for you." 21And in the same way he sprinkled
with the blood both the tent[y] and all the vessels used in
worship. 22Indeed, under the law almost everything is purified with blood, and without the shedding of blood there is
no forgiveness of sins.
23 Thus it was necessary for the sketches of the heavenly
things to be purified with these rites, but the heavenly
things themselves need better sacrifices than these. 24For
Christ did not enter a sanctuary made by human hands, a
mere copy of the true one, but he entered into heaven itself,
now to appear in the presence of God on our behalf. 25Nor
was it to offer himself again and again, as the high priest
enters the Holy Place year after year with blood that is not
his own; 26for then he would have had to suffer again and
again since the foundation of the world. But as it is, he has
appeared once for all at the end of the age to remove sin by
the sacrifice of himself. 27And just as it is appointed for
mortals to die once, and after that the judgment, 28so
Christ, having been offered once to bear the sins of many,
will appear a second time, not to deal with sin, but to save
those who are eagerly waiting for him.

The New Covenant Works

10 Since the law has only a shadow of the good things
to come and not the true form of these realities, it[z]
can never, by the same sacrifices that are continually offered
year after year, make perfect those who approach. 2Other-
wise, would they not have ceased being offered, since the
worshipers, cleansed once for all, would no longer have
any consciousness of sin? 3But in these sacrifices there is a
reminder of sin year after year. 4For it is impossible for the
blood of bulls and goats to take away sins. 5Consequently,
when Christ[a] came into the world, he said,

[w]The Greek word used here means both *covenant* and *will* [x]Other ancient authorities lack *and goats* [y]Or *tabernacle* [z]Other ancient authorities read *they* [a]Gk *he*

"Sacrifices and offerings you have not desired,
but a body you have prepared for me;
6 in burnt offerings and sin offerings
you have taken no pleasure.
7 Then I said, 'See, God, I have come to do your will, O God'
(in the scroll of the book[b] it is written of me)."

8When he said above, "You have neither desired nor taken
pleasure in sacrifices and offerings and burnt offerings and
sin offerings" (these are offered according to the law), 9then
he added, "See, I have come to do your will." He abolishes
the first in order to establish the second. 10And it is by
God's will[c] that we have been sanctified through the offering of the body of Jesus Christ once for all.

11 And every priest stands day after day at his service,
offering again and again the same sacrifices that can never
take away sins. 12But when Christ[d] had offered for all time a
single sacrifice for sins, "he sat down at the right hand of
God," 13and since then has been waiting "until his enemies
would be made a footstool for his feet." 14For by a single offering he has perfected for all time those who are sanctified.
15And the Holy Spirit also testifies to us, for after saying,

16 "This is the covenant that I will make with them
after those days, says the Lord:
I will put my laws in their hearts,
and I will write them on their minds,"

17he also adds,

"I will remember[e] their sins and their lawless deeds no more."

18Where there is forgiveness of these, there is no longer any
offering for sin.

Hold Onto Christ

10:19–25 see pg. 798

19 Therefore, my friends,[f] since we
have confidence to enter the sanctuary
by the blood of Jesus, 20by the new and living way that he
opened for us through the curtain (that is, through his
flesh), 21and since we have a great priest
over the house of God, 22let us approach
with a true heart in full assurance of faith, with our hearts
sprinkled clean from an evil conscience and our bodies

10:19–39 see pg. 800

(Bible text continued on page 799)

[b]Meaning of Gk uncertain [c]Gk *by that will* [d]Gk *this one* [e]Gk *on their minds and I will remember* [f]Gk *Therefore, brothers*

"I WILL PUT MY LAWS IN THEIR HEARTS, AND I WILL WRITE THEM ON THEIR MINDS. . . ."
—Hebrews 10:16

He Is Faithful

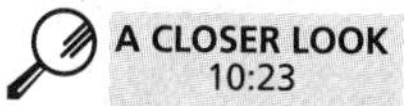

A CLOSER LOOK 10:23

Do you believe that God is faithful *(v. 23), that He can be depended on to honor His promises? See "Promises," Rom. 4:16–25.*

CONSIDER THIS
10:19–25

Coventry

The writer to the Hebrews draws a strong connection between prayer and the ability of believers to encourage each other toward "love and good deeds" (vv. 19–25). One church that has a long history of linking prayer for its people with the work they carry out is Coventry Cathedral in England.

Since 1043, when a Benedictine monastery was established there, parishioners at Coventry have applied the Lord's Prayer to their own work for God in the marketplace. In the fourteenth century, the merchant guild of St. Mary built a cathedral in the town to support the laity in their work, and the prayers continued.

Twice during World War II, German air raids demolished the town center, including Coventry Cathedral. The building lay in ruins until the mid-fifties, when work on a new cathedral was started. Finished in 1962, the new structure incorporates prayer panels that were preserved through the war. The panels, representing various industries in the town, bring together worship and work in a powerful way. They read:

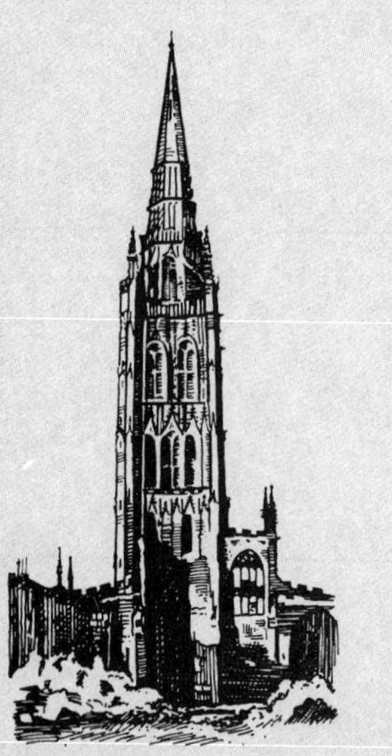

Hallowed be Thy Name in Industry:
God be in my hands and in my making.
[REFRAIN:]
Holy, Holy, Holy; Lord God of Hosts;
Heaven and earth are full of thy glory.

Hallowed be Thy Name in the Arts:
God be in my senses and in my creating.
[REFRAIN]

Hallowed be Thy Name in the Home:
God be in my heart and in my loving.
[REFRAIN]

Hallowed be Thy Name in Commerce:
God be at my desk and in my trading.
[REFRAIN]

Hallowed be Thy Name in Suffering:
God be in my pain and in my enduring.
[REFRAIN]

Hallowed be Thy Name in Government:
God be in my plans and in my deciding.
[REFRAIN]

Hallowed be Thy Name in Education:
God be in my mind and in my growing.
[REFRAIN]

Hallowed be Thy Name in Recreation:
God be in my limbs and in my leisure.
[REFRAIN]

Coventry's fame as a center of commerce and industry dates to the eleventh-century monastery. By 1400, the town had become the center of the Midlands' cloth industry, renowned for its excellent dyeing processes. It also boasted a theater. In 1545, the government chartered the first public school there. In the seventeenth century, industry shifted to watch- and clock-making for the next 200 years. By the late nineteenth century, the manufacture of bicycles and automobiles rose to prominence,

(continued on next page)

10:23 see pg. 797

washed with pure water. 23Let us hold
fast to the confession of our hope with-
out wavering, for he who has promised is faithful. 24And let
us consider how to provoke one another to love and good
deeds, 25not neglecting to meet together, as is the habit of
some, but encouraging one another, and all the more as
you see the Day approaching.

Endurance Is Needed

26 For if we willfully persist in sin after having received
the knowledge of the truth, there no longer remains a sacrifice for sins, 27but a fearful prospect of judgment, and a
fury of fire that will consume the adversaries. 28Anyone
who has violated the law of Moses dies without mercy "on
the testimony of two or three witnesses." 29How much
worse punishment do you think will be deserved by those
who have spurned the Son of God, profaned the blood of
the covenant by which they were sanctified, and outraged
the Spirit of grace? 30For we know the one who said,
"Vengeance is mine, I will repay." And again, "The Lord will
judge his people." 31It is a fearful thing to fall into the
hands of the living God.

32 But recall those earlier days when, after you had been
enlightened, you endured a hard struggle with sufferings,
33sometimes being publicly exposed to abuse and persecution, and sometimes being partners with those so treated.
34For you had compassion for those who were in prison,
and you cheerfully accepted the plundering of your possessions, knowing that you yourselves possessed something
better and more lasting. 35Do not, therefore, abandon that
confidence of yours; it brings a great re-
ward. 36For you need endurance, so that
when you have done the will of God, you may receive what
was promised.

10:36

37 For yet "in a very little while,
the one who is coming will come and will not delay;
38 but my righteous one will live by faith.
My soul takes no pleasure in anyone who shrinks back."
39But we are not among those who shrink back and so are
lost, but among those who have faith and so are saved.

The Hall of Faithfulness

11:1–40

11 Now faith is the assurance of
things hoped for, the conviction

Hang In There!

A CLOSER LOOK 10:36

God can be counted on to keep His promises, but can He count on us to wait until He delivers? See "God Promised To . . . ," Heb. 6:12–15.

(continued from previous page)

followed later by the rayon industry, telephone manufacturing, and electrical equipment. In 1958, England's first civic-funded theater was built there.

This vibrant economic life is certainly reflected in the prayer services at Coventry Cathedral and its support for the various guilds. Believers there have found an important way to stir up "love and good deeds." ◆

The Hall of Faithfulness

CONSIDER THIS 11:1–40

Hebrews 11 takes us through a museum of Hebrew heroes—what we might call the Hall of Faithfulness, since faith is the operative value here (vv. 1–2). This is a remarkable collection of social winners and losers, all of whom are now with God because of their faith.

We look back on the lives of these "greats," but they in turn fill a stadium to watch us run the race of life (11:39—12:1). However, that race is not a solo event or one lonely individual against the world. It's more like a relay race, in which we have received a handoff from those who have preceded us. Now it's our turn to run, in full public view.

Creation: "Very Good," But Not Sacred!

CONSIDER THIS 11:3 **When God made the world, He declared it to be "very good" (Gen. 1:31). But is the universe itself divine? Is Mother Nature sacred? No, because God made the world and its natural systems out of nothing (Heb. 11:3). Nor is the creation self-sustaining; it depends on God for its continued existence (Col. 1:17; Heb. 1:3).**

This means that:

(1) People can work only within the framework of pre-existing physical realities. Humans are not God, and cannot call things into existence from what was nonexistent.

(2) The universe is not God. Some philosophies and religions teach

(continued on next page)

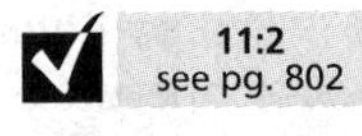
11:2 see pg. 802
of things not seen. 2Indeed, by faith[g] our
ancestors received approval. 3By faith we
11:3
understand that the worlds were prepared by the word of God, so that what
is seen was made from things that are not visible.[h]
4 By faith Abel offered to God a more acceptable[i] sacrifice than Cain's. Through this he received approval as righteous, God himself giving approval to his gifts; he died, but
through his faith[j] he still speaks. 5By faith Enoch was taken
so that he did not experience death; and "he was not found,
because God had taken him." For it was attested before he
11:6
was taken away that "he had pleased
God." 6And without faith it is impossible
to please God, for whoever would approach him must believe that he exists and that he rewards those who seek
him. 7By faith Noah, warned by God about events as yet
unseen, respected the warning and built an ark to save his
household; by this he condemned the world and became
an heir to the righteousness that is in accordance with faith.
8 By faith Abraham obeyed when he was called to set
out for a place that he was to receive as an inheritance; and

[g]*Gk by this* [h]*Or was not made out of visible things* [i]*Gk greater* [j]*Gk through it*

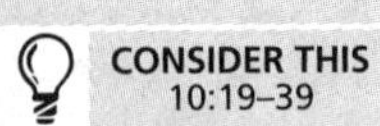
CONSIDER THIS 10:19–39

Toughening Timid Faith

For some followers of Christ, faith is not merely a private matter but a timid one as well. It's as if faith is such a delicate thing that unless one carefully protects it, the world will surely destroy it.

However, Hebrews challenges believers to a different way of living. Faith that is alive and growing need not be treated like a pet bunny rabbit that is periodically brought out of its cage to be adored and fed on special occasions, but then quickly returned to its haven of safety. To be sure, we live in a world of roaring lions (1 Pet. 5:8) and therefore must be on guard. Yet the safest way to live in a world of spiritual dangers is to build up our strength, not to hide our faith in secrecy. Hebrews offers some suggestions:

- *We can take* confidence *by freely entering into God's presence through Christ (vv. 19, 22).*
- *Our faith can* rest in full assurance *that because of Christ's work on our behalf, our sins have been forgiven (vv. 21–22).*
- *We can* keep a firm grip *on the basics of our faith, which rest on the integrity of Christ (v. 23).*

he set out, not knowing where he was going. 9By faith he
stayed for a time in the land he had been promised, as in a
foreign land, living in tents, as did Isaac and Jacob, who
were heirs with him of the same promise. 10For he looked
forward to the city that has foundations, whose architect
11:11 see pg. 804
and builder is God. 11By faith he received
power of procreation, even though he
was too old—and Sarah herself was barren—because he
considered him faithful who had promised.[k] 12Therefore
from one person, and this one as good as dead, descendants were born, "as many as the stars of heaven and as the
innumerable grains of sand by the seashore."

13 All of these died in faith without having received the
promises, but from a distance they saw and greeted them.
They confessed that they were strangers and foreigners on
the earth, 14for people who speak in this way make it clear
that they are seeking a homeland. 15If they had been thinking of the land that they had left behind, they would have
had opportunity to return. 16But as it is, they desire a better
country, that is, a heavenly one. Therefore God is not

(Bible text continued on page 803)

[k]Or *By faith Sarah herself, though barren, received power to conceive, even when she was too old, because she considered him faithful who had promised.*

- *As believers we can* stir each other up *to loving, active faith (v. 24).*
- *We can* meet with other believers *regularly for encouragement, accountability, worship, and prayer (v. 25).*
- *We can* leave judgment and repayment up to God, *who is the ultimate Judge of people (vv. 29–31).*
- *We can* keep a loose grip *on privilege, comfort, and possessions and instead show compassion toward those in need, such as prisoners (vv. 32–33).*
- *We can* condition ourselves for the long haul *so as to finish well (vv. 35–39).*

Spiritual strength and health means integrating our faith with every area of life. Faith is not just one more thing on a list of a hundred things, but rather the foundation of who we are. If our walk with Christ is real, it should become evident to others (James 2:14, 26; 3:13). Faith that is alive and growing is faith unleashed! ◆

(continued from previous page)

that the material universe and all it contains are a form of God, and/or that every human, animal, plant, and object contain a piece of God. But God is distinct from His creation.

(3) The earth is not sacred. Some conservationists ascribe a false value to creation by treating the earth and its flora and fauna as sacred. God wants humanity to manage the earth carefully, but not because the earth is sacred.

(4) The earth is a resource that God has given humans to manage. God has called His creation "very good" and has placed it under our rule for His glory and our benefit (Gen. 1:26–30). We are to tend it, cultivate it, conserve it, reshape it, mine it, and consume it with the certainty that each of us will give a full accounting to God for what we do with and to His world (Rom. 14:11–12; 1 Cor. 4:5).

The fact that God's work was "very good" has enormous implications for work itself. See "God—The Original Worker," John 5:17.

AIMING TO PLEASE

CONSIDER THIS 11:6

Success is pleasing, and we often obtain success by pleasing others—our bosses, customers, shareholders, and so forth. But who do you most seek to please? Yourself? Other people? Or God? There is no inevitable conflict. Sometimes you can, with integrity, please all of these. But sometimes there is a dilemma because it's not always possible to please everybody. Preferences and standards may contradict each other. So when you have to make the tough decision about whom to please and therefore whom to displease, perhaps a better question is how much does pleasing God really matter to you?

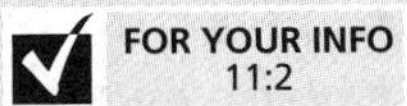

WHO ARE THESE PEOPLE?

Hebrews 11 is the Bible's "Hall of Faith," its review of Old Testament believers, called "our ancestors," who "received approval" by exhibiting trust in God's promises (vv. 2, 39). Their faith is worth our praise and their example is worth following.

See if you can identify some of the "spiritual giants" mentioned in this chapter from the descriptions that follow (answers are given at the end of Hebrews):

EXAMPLES OF FAITH

(1) After deceiving his elderly father in order to trick his brother out of an inheritance, this man gets caught in the vicious intrigue of his wife's family. Struggling to break free and eager to build his own wealth, he resorts to lying. Later he loses most of what he has during a severe famine and dies as a refugee in a foreign land.

(2) The beautiful wife of a wealthy rancher, this woman joins her husband in a deception out of fear that his trading partner will kill him in order to marry her. Later, she resorts to using a surrogate to provide her husband with an heir. The union causes great trouble in the family and among its descendants. However, long after the time when she would be expected to conceive, she bears a son who becomes a sign of God's commitment to honoring His promises.

(3) While doing farm chores one day, this man is called by God to lead an uprising against his people's enemies. Unsure about the veracity of the message, he requests a sign from heaven, not once but twice. Later, after paring his "army" down to a small band of men, he uses stealth, surprise, and good timing to thoroughly rout the opposition.

(4) This wealthy man leaves a prosperous city for a land that he has never visited. Once there, however, his wealth multiplies beyond all expectation, and he and his nephew negotiate a major subdivision of the real estate. God gives him a new name.

(5) Raised in the family herding business, this man has jealous brothers who sell him to foreign slave traders. Eventually he winds up as a top-level manager, only to be imprisoned on false charges of sexual harassment. But a fortunate opportunity distinguishes him before the king and he ends up in a highly responsible position from which he manages large-scale grain storage and distribution.

(6) A handsome body builder with a penchant for charming women, this man is called by God to lead his people but proves unreliable because of weak character. Nevertheless, he wreaks havoc among the nation's enemies. After his foreign-born wife betrays him, he is made into an object of curiosity and scorn before a final prayer leads to a burst of God's power and vengeance on his enemies.

(7) The younger son of displaced parents, this man continues their legacy of working the land. He also takes a special interest in matters of faith and holiness. However, a disagreement with his jealous brother leads to his murder and the anguished grief of his mother.

(8) A manufacturer of dyed linen, this woman escapes the destruction of an invading army by housing two of its soldiers in stalks of flax. Later, she bears a son and through him becomes an ancestor of some of history's most important leaders.

◆

Answers to quiz at "Fathers and Prophets" (Heb. 1:1)

(1) Noah (Gen. 6–9)

(2) Daniel (Dan. 1–12)

(3) Moses (Exodus, Leviticus, Numbers, Deuteronomy)

(4) David (1 Sam. 16–31, Psalms)

(5) Solomon (2 Sam. 12, 1 Kin. 1–12, Proverbs, Ecclesiastes, Song of Solomon)

(6) Amos (Amos)

(7) Samuel (1 and 2 Samuel)

(8) Habakkuk (Habakkuk)

ashamed to be called their God; indeed, he has prepared a
city for them.

The Patriarchs

17 By faith Abraham, when put to the test, offered up
Isaac. He who had received the promises was ready to offer
up his only son, 18of whom he had been told, "It is through
Isaac that descendants shall be named for you." 19He considered the fact that God is able even to raise someone from
the dead—and figuratively speaking, he did receive him
back. 20By faith Isaac invoked blessings for the future on Jacob and Esau. 21By faith Jacob, when dying, blessed each of
the sons of Joseph, "bowing in worship over the top of his
staff." 22By faith Joseph, at the end of his life, made mention
of the exodus of the Israelites and gave instructions about
his burial.[l]

Moses and Israel

23 By faith Moses was hidden by his parents for three
months after his birth, because they saw that the child was
beautiful; and they were not afraid of the king's edict.[m] 24By
faith Moses, when he was grown up, refused to be called a
son of Pharaoh's daughter, 25choosing rather to share ill-
treatment with the people of God than to enjoy the fleeting
pleasures of sin. 26He considered abuse suffered for the
Christ[n] to be greater wealth than the treasures of Egypt, for
he was looking ahead to the reward. 27By faith he left
Egypt, unafraid of the king's anger; for he persevered as
though[o] he saw him who is invisible. 28By faith he kept the
Passover and the sprinkling of blood, so that the destroyer
of the firstborn would not touch the firstborn of Israel.[p]

29 By faith the people passed through the Red Sea as if it
were dry land, but when the Egyptians attempted to do so
they were drowned. 30By faith the walls of Jericho fell after
11:31 they had been encircled for seven days.
31By faith Rahab the prostitute did not
perish with those who were disobedient,[q] because she had
received the spies in peace.

More People of Faith

32 And what more should I say? For time would fail me
to tell of Gideon, Barak, Samson, Jephthah, of David and
Samuel and the prophets— 33who through faith conquered
kingdoms, administered justice, obtained promises, shut
the mouths of lions, 34quenched raging fire, escaped the
edge of the sword, won strength out of weakness, became

[l]Gk *his bones* [m]Other ancient authorities add *By faith Moses, when he was grown up, killed the Egyptian, because he observed the humiliation of his people* (Gk *brothers*) [n]Or *the Messiah* [o]Or *because* [p]Gk *would not touch them* [q]Or *unbelieving*

Rahab

CONSIDER THIS 11:31 *Rahab the prostitute was an example to the early church of a Gentile whose faith was accepted by God (v. 31). As a Canaanite woman of Jericho, she probably worshiped many gods according to elaborate pagan rituals. Yet somehow she recognized the uniqueness of the God of Israel (Josh. 2:11).*

How could she demonstrate her response to that God? One way was by her treatment of Israel's spies (2:1–24). By offering them a haven of safety, she was choosing to be at peace with their God. Through that simple but brave act, she modeled the concept of drawing near to God in faith, believing that He rewards those who seek Him (Heb. 11:6).

Her act of faith was a risky thing. Had she been caught hiding the spies, she would almost certainly have been executed. Thus her faith wasn't just a special feeling, but a conscious choice and a commitment to be for God, even if it meant standing against the entire city of Jericho.

11:35

mighty in war, put foreign armies to
flight. 35 Women received their dead by
resurrection. Others were tortured, refusing to accept release, in order to obtain a better resurrection. 36 Others suffered mocking and flogging, and even chains and imprisonment. 37 They were stoned to death, they were sawn in two,[r]
they were killed by the sword; they went about in skins of
sheep and goats, destitute, persecuted, tormented— 38 of
whom the world was not worthy. They wandered in deserts
and mountains, and in caves and holes in the ground.
39 Yet all these, though they were commended for their
faith, did not receive what was promised, 40 since God had
provided something better so that they would not, apart
from us, be made perfect.

[r] Other ancient authorities add *they were tempted*

Women Received Their Dead Resurrected

A CLOSER LOOK 11:35

To be reminded of women who "received their dead by resurrection" (v. 35) was to be reminded of God's deliverance where it was least expected. Two strikingly similar Old Testament incidents were the prophet Elijah raising the son of a widow of Zarephath (1 Kin. 17:8–24) and his successor Elisha raising the son of a Shunammite woman (2 Kin. 4:8–37).

A New Testament example of the same miraculous response to faith was Jesus' raising of Lazarus, the brother of Mary and Martha. See John 11:1–45.

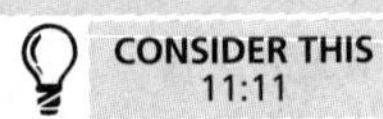

CONSIDER THIS 11:11

WHY BELIEVE ANYONE?

Often many of us confront feelings of disappointment or frustration because people don't do what they promise. If we experience enough pain from enough broken commitments, we tend to become skeptical and unwilling to trust others. That mistrust can even spill over into our relationship with God.

Sarah (v. 11) must have often felt disappointment and confusion during the 75 years that she lived without bearing a child. God had promised her husband Abraham that his descendants would be more numerous than the dust of the earth or the stars in the sky (Gen. 13:16; 15:5). Yet month after month, Sarah remained barren. Was God telling the truth? Could He be trusted?

When Abraham was 99 and Sarah 90, the Lord again told them that they would have a child (17:1–22; 18:1–15). Both of them laughed at the idea of an aged couple conceiving a child. Abraham actually fell on the ground in laughter (17:17), while Sarah laughed to herself (18:12). Could God be serious? Could He be trusted?

Let Us Run the Race

12:1–2 see pg. 806

12 Therefore, since we are surrounded by so great a cloud of
witnesses, let us also lay aside every weight and the sin that
clings so closely,[s] and let us run with perseverance the race
that is set before us, 2looking to Jesus the pioneer and per-
fecter of our faith, who for the sake of[t] the joy that was set
before him endured the cross, disregarding its shame, and
has taken his seat at the right hand of the throne of God.

God's Loving Discipline

12:3–13 see pg. 808

3 Consider him who endured such
hostility against himself from sinners,[u] so
that you may not grow weary or lose heart. 4In your struggle against sin you have not yet resisted to the point of
shedding your blood. 5And you have forgotten the exhortation that addresses you as children—

"My child, do not regard lightly the discipline of the
Lord,
or lose heart when you are punished by him;

(Bible text continued on page 807)

[s]Other ancient authorities read *sin that easily distracts* [t]Or *who instead of* [u]Other ancient authorities read *such hostility from sinners against themselves*

However, Sarah's inclusion in Hebrews' "Hall of Faithfulness" suggests that in the end, hers was not the laugh of a skeptic but of a woman who realized that physically, what had been promised was impossible—but that the One who made the promise could and would keep it. She knew that God meant what He said, and that He was willing and able to do as He promised. Sarah's faith was not based on her lack of ability to conceive, but on her knowledge of God's power and truthfulness.

Faith is not a matter of stirring up feelings or convincing ourselves of what we know to be false. Faith involves getting to know God and learning to trust His character. Then as we consider His promises, we can take confidence, with Sarah, that He will make them come true. ◆

In Hebrews, Sarah serves as a model of faith. In 1 Peter, she serves as a model for Christian women to develop Christlike inner character. See "Sarah," 1 Pet. 3:6.

LET US RUN WITH PERSEVERANCE THE RACE THAT IS SET BEFORE US. . . .
—Hebrews 12:1

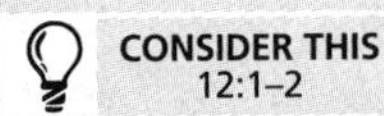

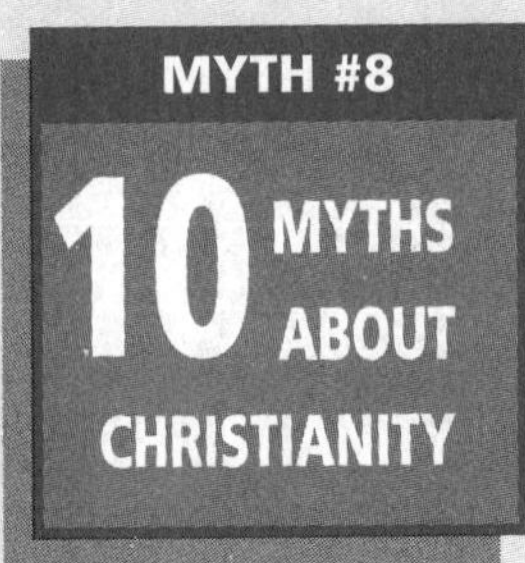

MYTH: CHRISTIANITY IS OTHERWORLDLY AND IRRELEVANT TO MODERN LIFE

Many people today accept a number of myths about Christianity, with the result that they never respond to Jesus as He really is. This is one of ten articles that speak to some of those misconceptions. For a list of all ten, see 1 Tim. 1:3–4.

The writer of Hebrews encourages us to live with an eye toward the "cloud of witnesses" who watch us from heaven (v. 1) and to look to Jesus who sits at God's right hand (v. 2). Perhaps it is images such as these that cause some people to see Christianity as detached from the world. They prefer a worldview that seems more relevant to everyday life.

But the Christian worldview is very relevant. To be sure, Christians look to realities that lie beyond our natural universe. But we do so in order to gain perspective on life, to find a star by which to steer. Belief in the living God changes our outlook dramatically. We can see His hand in history. We can gain insight into His purposes for the world. As a result, we can find tremendous meaning and motivation for our lives and our day-to-day work.

Perhaps the greatest benefit of being absorbed with the person of Christ is that we no longer insulate ourselves from people for whom He cares. Human beings really matter. We take people seriously. As a result, we get involved with them for their welfare.

That means that we have a definite mandate for Christian social involvement. Wherever the tide of faith sweeps in, it brings a corresponding rise in social concern and service to the community. In England in the eighteenth and nineteenth centuries, a dedicated Christian named William Wilberforce led a lifelong struggle to abolish slavery, a fight he eventually won. Nearly all of the later social reforms of that era were brought about, not by the agnostic followers of John Stuart Mill, but by people who responded to the great Christian revivals of the day. The Great Reform Bill was passed largely through the influence of Christian parliamentarians. The Mines Act, forbidding the forced labor of women and children in the mines, and the Factories Act, limiting hours of work, were masterminded by the Earl of Shaftesbury. A believer named Dr. Barnardo founded homes for orphans. A Christian woman named Elizabeth Fry brought about prison reform. Another believer, Josephine Butler, lobbied Parliament to protect women and outlaw child prostitution.

There may be some Christians who are, as they say, "so heavenly minded that they are no earthly good." But believers who cultivate a Christlike mind and heart cannot help but get involved with the world around them. Just as Christ came into the world to do the will of His Father, so His servants go into the world to accomplish the Father's work. ◆

6 for the Lord disciplines those whom he loves,
and chastises every child whom he accepts."
[7]Endure trials for the sake of discipline. God is treating you
as children; for what child is there whom a parent does not
discipline? [8]If you do not have that discipline in which all
children share, then you are illegitimate and not his children. [9]Moreover, we had human parents to discipline us,
and we respected them. Should we not be even more willing to be subject to the Father of spirits and live? [10]For they
disciplined us for a short time as seemed best to them, but
he disciplines us for our good, in order that we may share
his holiness. [11]Now, discipline always seems painful rather
than pleasant at the time, but later it yields the peaceful
fruit of righteousness to those who have been trained by it.
12 Therefore lift your drooping hands and strengthen
your weak knees, [13]and make straight paths for your feet,
so that what is lame may not be put out of joint, but rather
be healed.

New Life Means New Relationships

12:14–29
see pg. 810

14 Pursue peace with everyone, and
the holiness without which no one will
see the Lord. [15]See to it that no one fails to obtain the grace
of God; that no root of bitterness springs up and causes
trouble, and through it many become defiled. [16]See to it
that no one becomes like Esau, an immoral and godless
person, who sold his birthright for a single meal. [17]You
know that later, when he wanted to inherit the blessing, he
was rejected, for he found no chance to repent,[v] even
though he sought the blessing[w] with tears.
18 You have not come to something[x] that can be
touched, a blazing fire, and darkness, and gloom, and a
tempest, [19]and the sound of a trumpet, and a voice whose
words made the hearers beg that not another word be spoken to them. [20](For they could not endure the order that
was given, "If even an animal touches the mountain, it shall
be stoned to death." [21]Indeed, so terrifying was the sight
that Moses said, "I tremble with fear.") [22]But you have come
to Mount Zion and to the city of the living God, the heavenly Jerusalem, and to innumerable angels in festal gathering, [23]and to the assembly[y] of the firstborn who are enrolled
in heaven, and to God the judge of all, and to the spirits of
the righteous made perfect, [24]and to Jesus, the mediator of
a new covenant, and to the sprinkled blood that speaks a
better word than the blood of Abel.

[v]Or *no chance to change his father's mind* [w]Gk *it* [x]Other ancient authorities read *a mountain* [y]Or *angels, and to the festal gathering [23]and assembly*

YOU HAVE COME TO MOUNT ZION AND TO THE CITY OF THE LIVING GOD. . . .
—Hebrews 12:22

25 See that you do not refuse the one who is speaking;
for if they did not escape when they refused the one who
warned them on earth, how much less will we escape if we
reject the one who warns from heaven! 26At that time his
voice shook the earth; but now he has promised, "Yet once
more I will shake not only the earth but also the heaven."
27This phrase, "Yet once more," indicates the removal of
what is shaken—that is, created things—so that what cannot be shaken may remain. 28Therefore, since we are receiv-

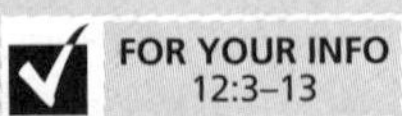

Family Helps in the New Testament Letters

Many of the first generation of believers were in difficult marriages and relationships when they entered the faith. Patterns from their backgrounds needed to be examined in light of their new commitment to Christ. The New Testament letters address these various family issues and talk about relationships based on Biblical values.

Biblical Guidance for Families

Texts	Issue	Summary
Rom. 9:6—11:36	Ethnic attitudes	Paul reviews some of the Jewish attitudes that had existed since the time of the patriarchs and appeals for humility and acceptance.
Rom. 14:1—15:6	Differences in spiritual maturity and convictions	Believers must practice grace and tolerance toward one another.
1 Cor. 5:1–13; 2 Cor. 2:1–11	Sexual immorality within families	Paul deals with a case of continuing incest within a believer's family.
1 Cor. 6:15–20; 1 Thess. 4:1–12	Temptation to sexual immorality	The body is God's temple; believers are to flee from sexual sins.
1 Cor. 7:1–7	Sexuality within marriage	Intimacy is crucial to the marriage relationship.
1 Cor. 7:8–20, 25–38	Singles and marriage	Paul expresses his own preference for singleness over marriage.
1 Cor. 7:39–40	Remarriage of widows	Remarriage to a believer is completely permissible.
Eph. 5:21–33; Col. 3:18–19; 1 Pet. 3:1–7	Spousal relationships	Paul and Peter challenge husbands and wives to mutual love and support.
Eph. 6:1–4; Col. 3:20–21	Child–parent relationships	The home should be characterized by obedient children and nurturing parents.
1 Tim. 3:1–13; Titus 1:5–16	Character	One of the major areas in which spiritual leaders should be evaluated is the home.
1 Tim. 5:3–16; James 1:27	Widows	Paul offers guidelines for the care of widows; James exhorts believers to meet the needs of widows and orphans.

ing a kingdom that cannot be shaken, let us give thanks, by which we offer to God an acceptable worship with reverence and awe; [29]for indeed our God is a consuming fire.

A Lifestyle of Love

13:1–6 see pg. 810

13 Let mutual love continue. [2]Do not neglect to show hospitality to strangers, for by doing that some have entertained angels

(Bible text continued on page 813)

For example, the writer to the Hebrews describes the fatherly discipline through which God develops His children (vv. 3–13). Readers can learn a great deal about parenting by examining the principles presented and following God's example.

The table opposite shows other passages that have at least some bearing on a variety of family-related issues. Believers today face the issues shown along with many others. Obviously, other biblical passages and principles could be mentioned. But by reading and discussing the texts and their implications with members of your family or with others, you can gain tremendous help from the New Testament's teaching on family matters. ◆

One of the most important things to understand about family life is that it goes through seasons in which the nature of the relationships change. In fact, building healthy family relationships is a lifelong process. See "The Family: A Call to Long-Term Work," Eph. 5:21—6:4.

. . . WE ARE RECEIVING A KINGDOM THAT CANNOT BE SHAKEN. . . .
—Hebrews 12:28

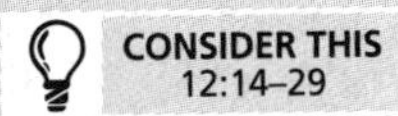

TIME FOR A CHECKUP

A timeworn adage that makes a lot of sense in the world of business and industry is, "If it ain't broke, don't fix it!" However, that definitely does not *apply when it comes to people's health. In fact, health experts report that preventive care can not only lead to better health and reduced risk from disease, but vastly reduce medical costs. People are unwise to neglect their physical condition.*

This truth has its parallel in the spiritual realm, as the writer to the Hebrews shows. Twice the book warns its readers to pay attention to their spiritual condition (Heb. 6:1–20; 12:14–29). Notice the strong language used in chapter 12 to describe what can happen to us if we neglect our walk with Christ:

- *We can fall short of the grace of God (v. 15).*
- *Bitterness can take root and sprout up, causing trouble (v. 15).*
- *Many people can become defiled (v. 15).*
- *We may make a foolish or even catastrophic mistake like Esau did (vv. 16–17; Gen. 25:27–34; 27:1–45).*
- *We may refuse to listen when God speaks to us (v. 25).*
- *God's judgment may consume us (v. 29).*

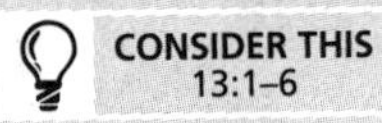

LOVE NEVER FAILS

Are you ever in doubt about what you should do in a given situation? One rule of thumb that always applies is, Do to others as you would have them do to you *(Matt. 7:12).*

This "golden rule" is universally recognized. It summarizes the principle of love as an ethical cornerstone for life. In fact, Jesus taught that the greatest commandment was to love *God with all of one's heart, soul, and mind, and the second greatest was to love one's neighbor as oneself (22:37–39). Likewise, James called love the "royal law" (James 2:8), and Paul wrote that of faith, hope, and love, love was the greatest; it never fails (1 Cor. 13:8, 13).*

We also see this in Hebrews. Having summarized the vast changes brought about by the coming of Christ, the book's final chapter begins with a clear statement about one thing that has not *changed, love. Love among believers must* continue *(Heb. 13:1). The writer goes on to list several ways in which that can happen:*

Those are dire consequences! Fortunately, the writer offers some ways to check our spirituality and make corrections where we detect trouble:

- *Are we pursuing peace with others (v. 14)? For example: how do we respond to conflicts at home, work or school?*
- *Are we pursuing holiness (v. 14)? For example: is our thought life focused on that which purifies (see Phil. 2:1–13; 4:8–9; 1 Thess. 4:1–8)?*
- *Are we listening carefully to God (v. 25)? For example: do we regularly wrestle with Scripture, allowing it to challenge us and keep us accountable?*
- *Do we live in grace, serving God in an acceptable way with reverence and respect (v. 28)? For example: are we growing in our appreciation for God and His salvation, and for other believers? Do we express that clearly and regularly? Would others describe us as "thankful" (see 1 Tim. 4:4; Col. 3:17)?*

How is your spiritual condition? Are there any symptoms to be concerned about? Any functions that seem weak or absent? What changes do you need to make to build yourself up into spiritual health and strength? ◆

◆ ◆ ◆ ◆ ◆ ◆ ◆ ◆ ◆ ◆ ◆ ◆ ◆ ◆ ◆ ◆

- *Hospitality toward strangers; in our day these might include immigrants, the homeless, and people of a different race than we are (v. 2).*
- *Remembrance of prisoners; it would be just as easy to forget them, but the principle of love says we ought to treat them as if imprisoned with them (v. 3).*
- *Faithfulness to our marriage; this goes beyond sexual fidelity to active enrichment and development of our partner (v. 4).*
- *Contentment regarding money and possessions; this is a severe challenge in modern culture (vv. 5–6; see "Watch Out for Greed!" Luke 12:15, and "A Lifestyle of Contentment," Phil. 4:10–13).*

Christlike love is very practical. It seeks expression toward a wide variety of people. Is that love "continuing" in your life? ◆

TEMPORARY CITIES

CONSIDER THIS 13:14

Our world is increasingly urban, far more so than the first century, which boasted many impressive cities. Verse 14 provides a measure of realism and hope for Christians in the city. It says that our urban environments—and therefore our citizenship in earthly urban structures—are temporary. They are not "continuing"; they will eventually pass from the scene. Furthermore, if believers truly live for Christ in the city, we may well be driven out of the city, just as Christ was when He was dragged outside of Jerusalem and crucified (vv. 12–13). However, we also have the hope of a new Jerusalem which is to come—the everlasting city of God that will be our permanent, continuing home.

Researching Your Own Religious Roots

The book of Hebrews shows that God uses history to bring people to Himself. In the case of the Jews, God used generations of people and centuries of political events and religious symbolism to prepare the way for Christ. If you are Jewish, you have much to celebrate as you ponder God's sovereignty and grace in using your ancestors the Hebrews to bless "all the families of the earth" (Gen. 12:3; 22:18; Acts 3:25–26; Gal. 3:8).

However, God's participation in history extends far beyond the Jews. In fact, every believer is indebted to God's grace for superintending the circumstances that brought the gospel to him or her.

Have you ever traced the path between Jesus' proclamation of the gospel in the first century and your reception of it today? Do you know the religious roots of your own family and ancestors? Why not examine that heritage, either on your own or with a small group of believers? Doing so will help to personalize the gospel to your own life and experience. Here are some suggestions for getting started:

Gathering the Data

Begin by collecting as much information as you can about your genealogy. Widespread interest in genealogical studies in recent years has made this process easier. Many books, articles, libraries, data bases, organizations, seminars, and other resources exist to help you. In addition, you'll want to talk with your parents, grandparents, or other relatives who might have information about your family and its heritage. As you carry out your search, consider such questions as:

- When and where did your ancestors live?
- What was their culture like?
- What historical or political events or technological developments occurred during their times? How might those have affected people?
- What was the religious climate in which your ancestors lived? For example, what was the view of God, the nature of evil, the origins of the world, and the afterlife? Was one religion dominant, or were there many alternatives? How did religion affect people's day-to-day lives?
- When was the gospel first introduced to the society in which your ancestors lived? What was the reception? What has been the legacy since?
- Are there any notable religious figures in your ancestry or connected with people in your history?
- Overall, what has been your family's posture toward the message of Christ?
- What has been the role of religion in your family of origin? Where did its religious sentiments come from? Are there any surviving symbols of religion that might hold clues for investigation (family Bibles or other books, letters, documents, pictures, clothing, etc.)?
- When did you personally first hear the gospel?

Evaluating Your Religious Roots

As your knowledge about your ancestry grows, you can begin to piece together some idea of your religious heritage. Be careful not to jump to conclusions or make too much of sketchy details. You probably won't be able to come up with any definitive answers, but you can at least gain an appreciation for how God has worked in your past and what it took for Him to bring you to faith.

Of course, you may discover

(continued on next page)

without knowing it. 3Remember those who are in prison, as
though you were in prison with them; those who are being
tortured, as though you yourselves were being tortured.[z]
4Let marriage be held in honor by all, and let the marriage
bed be kept undefiled; for God will judge fornicators and
adulterers. 5Keep your lives free from the love of money,
and be content with what you have; for he has said, "I will
never leave you or forsake you." 6So we can say with confidence,

"The Lord is my helper;
I will not be afraid.
What can anyone do to me?"

Obey Leaders

7 Remember your leaders, those who spoke the word of
God to you; consider the outcome of their way of life, and
imitate their faith. 8Jesus Christ is the same yesterday and
today and forever. 9Do not be carried away by all kinds of
strange teachings; for it is well for the heart to be strengthened by grace, not by regulations about food,[a] which have
not benefited those who observe them. 10We have an altar
from which those who officiate in the tent[b] have no right to
eat. 11For the bodies of those animals whose blood is
brought into the sanctuary by the high priest as a sacrifice
for sin are burned outside the camp. 12Therefore Jesus also
suffered outside the city gate in order to sanctify the people
by his own blood. 13Let us then go to him outside the camp
and bear the abuse he endured. 14For
here we have no lasting city, but we are
looking for the city that is to come.
15Through him, then, let us continually
offer a sacrifice of praise to God, that is, the fruit of lips that
confess his name. 16Do not neglect to do good and to share
what you have, for such sacrifices are pleasing to God.

13:14 see pg. 811

13:15 see pg. 814

17 Obey your leaders and submit to them, for they are
keeping watch over your souls and will give an account. Let
them do this with joy and not with sighing—for that would
be harmful to you.

Greetings and Blessings

18 Pray for us; we are sure that we have a clear conscience, desiring to act honorably in all things. 19I urge you
all the more to do this, so that I may be restored to you
very soon.

(Bible text continued on page 815)

[z]*Gk were in the body* [a]*Gk not by foods* [b]*Or tabernacle*

(continued from previous page)

elements of your family's religious history that run counter to the gospel. But that, too, is important to know. You need not agree with what others believed or did in the past, but it's worth understanding the bolt of cloth from which you've been cut.

As you evaluate your data, consider such questions as:

- Is the gospel recent in your family's history, or has there been a long legacy of participation in the faith?
- If Christianity has been a part of your cultural or religious roots, what distinguishes your family's expression of Christianity from other traditions within the faith? Why? Where did that tradition come from and how and why did your family identify with it?
- What beliefs and practices among your religious roots would you disagree with or even denounce? Why?
- What has been the reception of your family to your personal faith in Christ? Why? How might the past contribute to their response?
- How might your understanding of the past affect the way in which you present the gospel to any unbelievers among your relatives?
- What is the story of how the gospel traveled from the apostles in the first century to your life today? What response can you make to God for superintending this process? ◆

QUOTE UNQUOTE

CONSIDER THIS 13:15 *Hebrews challenges us to speak up about our faith and give evidence of our relationship with God through the fruit of our lips (v. 15):*

A spiritual enemy in our time is privatization of personal faith. For too many so-called "committed Christians" their relationship with Jesus is like an extramarital affair. It's a secret relationship. The love affair is real but hidden from the public eye. Some Christians become so skilled at concealing their personal faith in Christ that it takes the talent of an undercover agent to reveal their clandestine activity. The tragedy for those individuals is that undisclosed personal faith eventually produces an inner sense of psychological illegitimacy. The tragedy for the Kingdom is that God is silenced in the open forum so that people who ought to know Him do not even see Him as an option.

Donald C. Posterski, *Reinventing Evangelism*

"I Have Written to You"

FOR YOUR INFO 13:22 **The author of Hebrews writes as if the original readers of the letter already knew who it was (v. 22). If only modern readers did! It would perhaps help us to better understand the epistle.**

Hebrews is one of only two letters in the New Testament that lacks a greeting or identification of its author (the other is 1 John). The King James Version calls the letter "The Epistle of Paul the Apostle to the Hebrews." But there is no such indication in the earliest manuscripts. And many people doubt whether Paul wrote the book. Among their reasons:

- **The language, vocabulary, and style differ from Paul's letters.**
- **Certain expressions that Paul often uses—"Christ Jesus," "in Christ," "the resurrection"—are all but absent.**
- **Hebrews approaches certain subjects, such as the law and faith, very differently from Paul's known writings.**
- **Early church sources mention other possible authors.**

Others challenge these points, however. Yet no one has conclusively demonstrated that Paul was the author. But if not, then who was? There has been no shortage of suggestions: Luke, Priscilla, Aquila, Clement of Rome, Silvanus, Philip the evangelist, Apollos, and Barnabas.

In the end, we do not know who wrote this letter. However, the anonymity of the author in no way diminishes the work's integrity, nor has it caused anyone to question its important place among the Scriptures.

20 Now may the God of peace, who brought back from
the dead our Lord Jesus, the great shepherd of the sheep,
by the blood of the eternal covenant, 21make you complete
in everything good so that you may do his will, working
among us[c] that which is pleasing in his sight, through Jesus
Christ, to whom be the glory forever and ever. Amen.

13:22

22 I appeal to you, brothers and sisters,[d] bear with my word of exhortation,
for I have written to you briefly. 23I want you to know that
our brother Timothy has been set free; and if he comes in
time, he will be with me when I see you.
24Greet all your leaders and all the saints.
Those from Italy send you greetings.
25Grace be with all of you.[e]

13:24 see pg. 812

13:25

[c]Other ancient authorities read *you* [d]Gk *brothers* [e]Other ancient authorities add *Amen*

FOR YOUR INFO
13:25

Answers to quiz at "Who Are These People?" (Heb. 11:2)

(1) Jacob (Heb. 11:21; Gen. 25–35, 43–50)

(2) Sarah (Heb. 11:11; Gen. 13–17, 20–22)

(3) Gideon (Heb. 11:32; Judg. 6–8)

(4) Abraham (Heb. 11:8; Gen. 11–26)

(5) Joseph (Heb. 11:22; Gen. 37–48)

(6) Samson (Heb. 11:32; Judg. 13–17)

(7) Abel (Heb. 11:4; Gen. 4)

(8) Rahab (Heb. 11:31; Josh. 2, 6)

Faith and Life

You're a success. Your faith in Christ is helping you live responsibly, and now you're enjoying the fruits of that lifestyle. Your income is up. Your family life is stable. Your church is doing well. You have lots of friends. So what more do you need? What more can the gospel contribute to your life in the here and now than it already has?

To find out, read the letter of James. It was written to people who were prospering as a result of their faith, not unlike many Christians today. The gospel had brought a "social lift" to their lives, bettering their material circumstances. But what about those left behind, people still struggling to "make it"? What about trials and tribulations? Does success change the way one looks at trouble? What about sermons—is it really necessary to take them so seriously when things are going so well?

Perhaps you're finding it easy to be comfortable in the faith. But are you fruitful? James was written to help you consider whether Christ is affecting more than your income and lifestyle.

The Letter of

James

What more can the gospel contribute to your life?

C O N T E N T S

A R T I C L E S

Personality Profile: James

Not to be confused with: James the son of Zebedee and James the son of Alphaeus, two of the Twelve (see Matt. 10:2); James the Less, the son of Mary and brother of Joses (Mark 15:40); James the father of Judas (that is, of Thaddaeus; Matt. 10:3; Mark 3:18; Luke 6:16; Acts 1:13).

Home: Probably Nazareth.

Family: His father was probably Joseph; his mother was Mary; his older brother was Jesus; younger brothers were Joses, Judas, and Simon; he had sisters whom Scripture does not name.

Occupation: Unknown, but since his father and Jesus were carpenters, he may have been a carpenter, too.

Best known today for: Leading the church at Jerusalem and writing the book of James.

James—From Skeptic to True Believer

The James whose name appears as the author of James (1:1) was probably the oldest of Jesus' four younger brothers (Mark 6:3). Apparently he was at first skeptical about his brother's claims and ministry (Matt. 12:46–50; Mark 3:31–35; Luke 8:19–21; John 7:5). But after meeting the resurrected Lord (1 Cor. 15:7), he became a strong believer and was numbered among the apostles. He oversaw the church at Jerusalem, and helped resolve the dispute over Gentiles having to keep the Law (Acts 15:13–21).

Sermons to Successful Believers

James is a compact, hard-hitting letter about *practicing* the faith. It reads like a collection of sermons. In fact, except for a brief introduction, it bears none of the traits of an ancient letter. Each of its five chapters is packed with pointed illustrations and reminders designed to motivate the wills and hearts of relatively prosperous believers. James wanted them to grasp a truth taught by Jesus: "A tree is known by its fruit" (Matt. 12:33; compare James 1:9–11, 18; 3:12–18; 5:7–8, 17–18).

For James, religion is not about church membership, financial contributions, or even teaching in the Sunday school. The acid test of true religion is *doing the truth,* not just hearing it or speaking it. Action is the hallmark of authentic faith. In this respect, James mirrors Jesus' Sermon on the Mount. He forcefully condemns counterfeit religion that substitutes theory for practice. ◆

HUMAN RESOURCE DEVELOPMENT

CONSIDER THIS 1:2–5 **God has a three-stage "human resource development" program for believers (vv. 2–5). Stage one involves *trials*—as many as we need, as hard as they need to be. That leads to stage two, *patience*—waiting for God with trust and perseverance. The final result is stage three, *wisdom,* which is God's goal of growth for personnel in His kingdom.**

Do you want wisdom? Be careful when you ask for it! You could get a healthy dose of trials that demand patience. Eventually the process leads to wisdom—*if* you let it work.

A Greeting to Scattered Believers

1 James, a servant[a] of God and of the Lord Jesus Christ,
To the twelve tribes in the Dispersion:
Greetings.

Trials and Temptations

1:2–5

2 My brothers and sisters,[b] whenever
you face trials of any kind, consider it
nothing but joy, 3because you know that the testing of your
faith produces endurance; 4and let endurance have its full
effect, so that you may be mature and complete, lacking in
nothing.
5 If any of you is lacking in wisdom, ask God, who gives
to all generously and ungrudgingly, and it will be given
you. 6But ask in faith, never doubting, for the one who
doubts is like a wave of the sea, driven and tossed by the
wind; 7, 8for the doubter, being double-minded and unstable in every way, must not expect to receive anything from
the Lord.

1:9–11

9 Let the believer[c] who is lowly boast
in being raised up, 10and the rich in be-
ing brought low, because the rich will disappear like a
flower in the field. 11For the sun rises with its scorching
heat and withers the field; its flower falls, and its beauty
perishes. It is the same way with the rich; in the midst of a
busy life, they will wither away.
12 Blessed is anyone who endures temptation. Such a
one has stood the test and will receive the crown of life that

1:13–18 see pg. 822

the Lord[d] has promised to those who love
him. 13No one, when tempted, should
say, "I am being tempted by God"; for God cannot be
tempted by evil and he himself tempts no one. 14But one is
tempted by one's own desire, being lured and enticed by it;
15then, when that desire has conceived, it gives birth to sin,
and that sin, when it is fully grown, gives birth to death.
16Do not be deceived, my beloved.[e]
17 Every generous act of giving, with every perfect gift,
is from above, coming down from the Father of lights, with
whom there is no variation or shadow due to change.[f] 18In
fulfillment of his own purpose he gave us birth by the word
of truth, so that we would become a kind of first fruits of
his creatures.

[a]Gk *slave* [b]Gk *brothers* [c]Gk *brother* [d]Gk *he;* other ancient authorities read *God* [e]Gk *my beloved brothers* [f]Other ancient authorities read *variation due to a shadow of turning*

True Faith Involves Practical Obedience

19 You must understand this, my beloved:[g] let everyone
be quick to listen, slow tc speak, slow to anger; [20]for your
anger does not produce God's righteousness. [21]Therefore
rid yourselves of all sordidness and rank growth of wickedness, and welcome with meekness the implanted word that
has the power to save your souls.
22 But be doers of the word, and not merely hearers
who deceive themselves. [23]For if any are hearers of the
word and not doers, they are like those who look at themselves[h] in a mirror; [24]for they look at themselves and, on
going away, immediately forget what they were like. [25]But
those who look into the perfect law, the law of liberty, and
persevere, being not hearers who forget but doers who
act—they will be blessed in their doing.
26 If any think they are religious, and do not bridle their
tongues but deceive their hearts, their religion is worthless.
[27]Religion that is pure and undefiled before God, the
Father, is this: to care for orphans and widows in their
distress, and to keep oneself unstained by the world.

True Faith Does Not Play Favorites

2:1–13 see pg. 823

2 My brothers and sisters,[i] do you with
your acts of favoritism really believe
in our glorious Lord Jesus Christ?[j] [2]For if a person with
gold rings and in fine clothes comes into your assembly,
and if a poor person in dirty clothes also comes in, [3]and if
you take notice of the one wearing the fine clothes and say,
"Have a seat here, please," while to the one who is poor you
say, "Stand there," or, "Sit at my feet,"[k] [4]have you not made
distinctions among yourselves, and become judges with evil
thoughts? [5]Listen, my beloved brothers
and sisters.[l] Has not God chosen the
poor in the world to be rich in faith and to be heirs of the
kingdom that he has promised to those who love him? [6]But
you have dishonored the poor. Is it not the rich who oppress you? Is it not they who drag you into court? [7]Is it not
they who blaspheme the excellent name that was invoked
over you?

2:5–6 see pg. 823

The Royal Law

2:1–9 see pg. 822

8 You do well if you really fulfill the
royal law according to the scripture, "You
shall love your neighbor as yourself." [9]But if you show

[g]*Gk my beloved brothers* [h]*Gk at the face of his birth* [i]*Gk My brothers* [j]*Or hold the faith of our glorious Lord Jesus Christ without acts of favoritism* [k]*Gk Sit under my footstool* [l]*Gk brothers*

Why the Rush?

CONSIDER THIS 1:9–11 **We live in a day of the "fast track," the "sound bite," and the "hurried child." But what is so attractive about the rush to achieve quick results? Is that the way life was intended to be?**

A study of James 1 shows that God wants people to *be someone* more than to *get somewhere.* Rather than measuring our worth through achievements and acquisitions, He evaluates our character, looking for such virtues as peace, truth, serenity, and strength of character. He values us for who we are and who we are becoming. He wants us to be:

- **People who can endure testing and trial (v. 4).**
- **People who trust God to provide for their needs and feel free to ask for His help (vv. 5–9).**
- **People who can discern between good and bad choices and make wise decisions (vv. 12–16).**
- **People who give generously to others, just as God has given generously to us (vv. 17–18).**
- **People who listen well and respond thoughtfully (vv. 19–21).**
- **People who act instead of just talking and whose actions benefit others (vv. 22–25).**
- **People who value and show compassion toward others who are in need, especially those forgotten by society (vv. 26–27).**

It takes time to develop character like that. But God is interested in long-term growth, not just a quick fix. We may need to slow down and take a long, hard look at the direction of our lives. If we're driven to gain as much as we can as fast as we can, we're headed down a road toward destruction.

Paul suggests some practical steps that we can take to slow down and become Christlike people. See "Quiet Living in a Hectic World," 1 Thess. 4:11.

THE ROOTS OF SIN

CONSIDER THIS 1:13–18 **Excuses for sin are many: "The devil made me do it"; "I couldn't help myself"; "It's not really my fault"; "I'm only human."**

James mentions another excuse that people give for sin: they blame God (v. 13). "If only He understood how hard it is to overcome temptation," they say. "He put me in a situation that was more than I could handle."

But the problem with that way of thinking is that sin is never rooted outside of us; it always comes from our own heart, often from our desire for what God has not given us (vv. 14–15; compare 1 Cor. 10:6).

In this sense, the roots of sin lie in covetousness or discontentment. We feel that we are worthy of more than what we have. But that means that sin is tied closely to pride—and God resists the proud (James 4:6).

But He gives grace to the humble. Therefore, the surest path to overcoming the temptation is to develop humility, which leads to contentment with the good gifts of God (1:17–18; see "Humility—The Scandalous Virtue," Phil. 2:3).

PLAYING FAVORITES

CONSIDER THIS 2:1–9 **Countless laws and legal battles have been and continue to be fought over civil rights and the effort to end discrimination. James calls on the ultimate law, the "royal law" (v. 8), to speak out against discrimination in the one place it ought least to exist—the church. He specifically condemns favoritism toward the rich and discrimination against the poor. When believers discriminate on the basis of**

(continued on next page)

partiality, you commit sin and are convicted by the law as
transgressors. 10For whoever keeps the whole law but fails
in one point has become accountable for all of it. 11For the
one who said, "You shall not commit adultery," also said,
"You shall not murder." Now if you do not commit adultery
but if you murder, you have become a transgressor of the
law. 12So speak and so act as those who are to be judged by
2:8–13 see pg. 824 the law of liberty. 13For judgment will be
without mercy to anyone who has shown
no mercy; mercy triumphs over judgment.

Faith without Works Is Dead

14 What good is it, my brothers and sisters,[m] if you say
you have faith but do not have works? Can faith save you?
15If a brother or sister is naked and lacks daily food, 16and
one of you says to them, "Go in peace; keep warm and eat
your fill," and yet you do not supply their bodily needs,
what is the good of that? 17So faith by itself, if it has no
works, is dead.
18 But someone will say, "You have faith and I have
works." Show me your faith apart from your works, and I
by my works will show you my faith. 19You believe that
God is one; you do well. Even the demons believe—and
shudder. 20Do you want to be shown, you senseless person,
that faith apart from works is barren? 21Was not our ancestor Abraham justified by works when he offered his son
Isaac on the altar? 22You see that faith was active along with
his works, and faith was brought to completion by the
works. 23Thus the scripture was fulfilled that says, "Abraham believed God, and it was reckoned to him as righteousness," and he was called the friend of God. 24You see
that a person is justified by works and not by faith alone.
2:25 25Likewise, was not Rahab the prostitute
also justified by works when she welcomed the messengers and sent them out by another road?
26For just as the body without the spirit is dead, so faith
without works is also dead.

[m]Gk *brothers*

Rahab

A CLOSER LOOK 2:25 *By offering the Israelite spies a safe haven in Jericho, Rahab the prostitute (v. 25) demonstrated a commitment to the God of Israel. Through her simple but brave act, she was drawing near to Him, giving tangible evidence of her belief that He rewards those who seek Him. Find out more about this remarkable woman at Heb. 11:31.*

The Test of Self-Control

3 Not many of you should become teachers, my brothers
and sisters,[n] for you know that we who teach will be
judged with greater strictness. 2For all of us make many
mistakes. Anyone who makes no mistakes in speaking is
perfect, able to keep the whole body in check with a bridle.
3If we put bits into the mouths of horses to make them
obey us, we guide their whole bodies. 4Or look at ships:
though they are so large that it takes strong winds to drive
them, yet they are guided by a very small rudder wherever
the will of the pilot directs. 5So also the tongue is a small
member, yet it boasts of great exploits.

How great a forest is set ablaze by a small fire! 6And the
tongue is a fire. The tongue is placed among our members
as a world of iniquity; it stains the whole body, sets on fire
the cycle of nature,[o] and is itself set on fire by hell.[p] 7For
every species of beast and bird, of reptile and sea creature,
can be tamed and has been tamed by the human species,
8but no one can tame the tongue—a restless evil, full of
deadly poison. 9With it we bless the Lord and Father, and
with it we curse those who are made in the likeness of God.
10From the same mouth come blessing and cursing. My
brothers and sisters,[q] this ought not to be so. 11Does a
spring pour forth from the same opening both fresh and
brackish water? 12Can a fig tree, my brothers and sisters,[r]
yield olives, or a grapevine figs? No more can salt water
yield fresh.

(Bible text continued on page 825)

[n] *Gk brothers* [o] *Or wheel of birth* [p] *Gk Gehenna* [q] *Gk My brothers* [r] *Gk my brothers*

Ushers on Trial

CONSIDER THIS 2:1–13

To discriminate is to sin. Here in James 2, a congregation is on trial for discrimination, particularly the ushers. Their behavior is an example of how "faith without works" operates: without cause it excludes people on the basis of social standing rather than welcoming them into the household of God.

Paul saw a similar case when he affirmed that, in Christ, "we are all one" (Gal. 3:28).

(continued from previous page)

socioeconomic status, they violate the core of God's law.

Yet it happens all the time, doesn't it? How about where you work, or in your church or community? Are only the wealthy considered likely candidates for church leadership? How do you respond to customers at work, visitors at church, or shoppers at a grocery store who look "down-and-out"?

On the other hand, does James' stern warning against favoring the rich and dishonoring the poor imply that we should favor the poor and dishonor the rich? Do you ever practice "reverse discrimination"? Does your church condemn wealthy people for their wealth? Do you assume that someone who has riches gained them by dishonesty or oppression, rather than by honest work and service?

James says that favoritism is as much a transgression of the law as adultery or murder (vv. 10–11). Apparently God takes economic discrimination seriously!

Rich in . . . Faith?

CONSIDER THIS 2:5–6

James notes the tension between wealth and faith (vv. 5–6). None of us is exempt from the distracting and distorting effect of growing affluence. God does not condemn wealth, but He clearly warns us that we can't pursue wealth or trust in it and also pursue God and trust in His faithfulness (Matt. 6:24–34).

Those of us who have wealth might consider several tough questions:

(1) What plans do we have for giving money away? Are we giving away more in the name of God now than we did last year or the year before?

(continued on next page)

(continued from previous page)

(2) What is our intention—to move to an even higher level of luxury, or to hold steady where we are, or even simplify our lifestyle and give away the excess?

(3) Can we name any ways in which our increased wealth has brought us closer to God?

Paul offers a discussion of wealth that modern believers do well to study carefully, given the emphasis on money in our culture. See "Christians and Money," 1 Tim. 6:6–19.

QUOTE UNQUOTE

CONSIDER THIS 3:13–18

Do you want to be considered a wise person and a leader in the Christian community? James describes the nature of true wisdom and leadership (vv. 13–18). A modern-day writer expands on this theme:

The purpose of Christian leadership training is not just to help ambitious men to the top, or to make little men who have done leadership courses feel bigger than they really are. Still less is it to produce fuehrers, either large or small.

It has much more to do with the making of integrated people. Ones who understand what they believe, are deeply dedicated to it, and who try unceasingly to relate their beliefs to every facet of their own lives and to the society in which they live.

Douglas Hyde, *Dedication and Leadership*, p. 157

TEN COMMANDMENTS FOR PRACTICAL LIVING

CONSIDER THIS 2:8–13

Are the Ten Commandments that James refers to (vv. 8–11; Ex. 20:1–17) still realistic in today's culture? Absolutely. Jesus insisted that His followers honor them (see "The Morality of Christ," Matt. 5:17–48). But what might it look like to fulfill those ancient commandments in today's workplace? Here are some suggestions:

GOD'S LAW IN PRACTICE

	Original Commandment	Modern Application
I	"You shall have no other gods before me."	Show proper respect for authority.
II	"You shall not make for yourself an idol."	Have a singleness of purpose.
III	"You shall not make wrongful use of the name of the Lord your God."	Use effective communication in word and deed.
IV	"Remember the sabbath day, and keep it holy."	Provide proper rest, recreation, and reflection.
V	"Honor your father and your mother."	Show respect for elders.
VI	"You shall not murder."	Show respect for human life, dignity, and rights.
VII	"You shall not commit adultery."	Maintain a stability of the sexes and family.
VIII	"You shall not steal."	Demonstrate the proper allocation of resources.
IX	"You shall not bear false witness."	Demonstate honesty and integrity.
X	"You shall not covet."	Maintain the right of ownership of property.

Adapted from *Ten Commandments for Practical Living*, ©1973 McNair Associates, used by permission.

True Wisdom

3:13–18

13 Who is wise and understanding
among you? Show by your good life that
your works are done with gentleness born of wisdom. 14But
if you have bitter envy and selfish ambition in your hearts,
do not be boastful and false to the truth. 15Such wisdom
does not come down from above, but is earthly, unspiritual,
devilish. 16For where there is envy and selfish ambition,
there will also be disorder and wickedness of every kind.
17But the wisdom from above is first pure, then peaceable,
gentle, willing to yield, full of mercy and good fruits, without a trace of partiality or hypocrisy. 18And a harvest of
righteousness is sown in peace for[s] those who make peace.

Conflict, or Humility before God?

4 Those conflicts and disputes among you, where do
they come from? Do they not come from your cravings
that are at war within you? 2You want something and do
not have it; so you commit murder. And you covet[t]
something and cannot obtain it; so you engage in disputes
and conflicts. You do not have, because you do not ask.
3You ask and do not receive, because you ask wrongly, in
order to spend what you get on your pleasures. 4Adulterers!
Do you not know that friendship with the world is enmity
with God? Therefore whoever wishes to be a friend of the
world becomes an enemy of God. 5Or do you suppose that
it is for nothing that the scripture says, "God[u] yearns
jealously for the spirit that he has made to dwell in us"?
6But he gives all the more grace; therefore it says,

"God opposes the proud,
but gives grace to the humble."

4:7 see pg. 826

7Submit yourselves therefore to God. Resist the devil, and he will flee from you.
8Draw near to God, and he will draw near to you. Cleanse
your hands, you sinners, and purify your hearts, you
double-minded. 9Lament and mourn and weep. Let your
laughter be turned into mourning and your joy into dejec-
tion. 10Humble yourselves before the Lord, and he will exalt you.

Watch Out for Judgmental Attitudes

11 Do not speak evil against one another, brothers and
sisters.[v] Whoever speaks evil against another or judges another, speaks evil against the law and judges the law; but if
you judge the law, you are not a doer of the law but a

(Bible text continued on page 829)

[s]Or *by* [t]Or *you murder and you covet* [u]Gk *He* [v]Gk *brothers*

Who's in Charge Here?

CONSIDER THIS 4:13–16

All of us have hopes, dreams, and plans, and the Bible never discourages us from looking to the future with bright expectation. However, passages like vv. 13–16 enforce a crucial qualification. As we make our plans, whether in business, in relationships, in our personal lives, we must do so with a perspective on who is ultimately in charge—God! In other words, we need to plan with an attitude of humility.

Our tendency as humans is to seek control over our circumstances. Certainly the Bible encourages us to take responsibility for our lives (1 Thess. 4:11; 1 Pet. 2:12). But even so, we must ultimately submit to the sovereignty of God. The Old Testament prophet Isaiah likens us to clay in the hands of a potter; the divine Craftsman can do with us as He wishes (Is. 64:8; 1 Cor. 12:15–18).

As a result, we need to submit every intention to God—even our business proposals and plans. He may allow us to proceed according to our desires; or He may decide to alter our plans according to His own purposes. In either case, we need to accept what He decides to bring into our lives, without arguing and complaining (Rom. 9:20–21; Phil. 2:13–14).

The result: tremendous peace! We can feel confident that an infinitely wise, powerful, and good God ultimately controls our lives and our world. Of course, that doesn't mean that life will always go the way we want. Sometimes, from our human perspective, it will seem unfair, maybe even absurd. Nevertheless, God rules the world. Humility demands that we acknowledge and accept what He allows to happen in it.

Submitting to God involves "Humility—The Scandalous Virtue," Phil. 2:3.

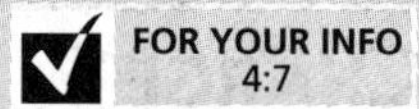

Submission

A popular slogan in recent years has been "peace through strength." But James might change that to "peace through humility." After all, the source of wars and fights are internal "desires for pleasure" (v. 1). Our cravings lead to friendship with the world and enmity toward God (vv. 2–4). Thus, peace in the world depends on peace with God, and that requires humility (v. 6).

The way to show humility before God is to submit to Him (v. 7). In fact, the New Testament calls believers to a lifestyle of submission, as the following table shows:

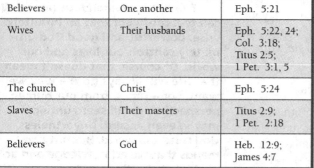

Submission by Believers		
Who Submits?	**To Whom?**	**Text**
Everyone (believers)	Governing authorities	Rom. 13:1, 5; Titus 3:1; 1 Pet. 2:13
Women	The church	1 Cor. 14:34
Corinthian believers	Paul's coworkers	1 Cor. 16:16
Believers	One another	Eph. 5:21
Wives	Their husbands	Eph. 5:22, 24; Col. 3:18; Titus 2:5; 1 Pet. 3:1, 5
The church	Christ	Eph. 5:24
Slaves	Their masters	Titus 2:9; 1 Pet. 2:18
Believers	God	Heb. 12:9; James 4:7
Young people	Those who are older	1 Pet. 5:5

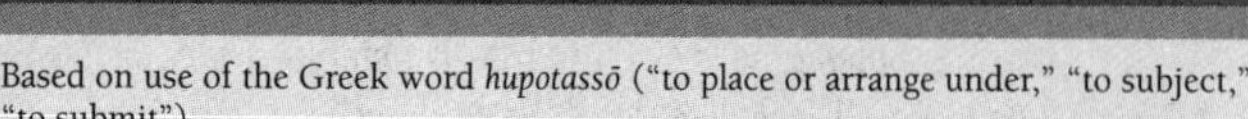
Based on use of the Greek word *hupotassō* ("to place or arrange under," "to subject," "to submit")

In addition to these, the New Testament shows other relationships of submission as well:

FURTHER EXAMPLES OF SUBMISSION		
Who/What Submits?	**To Whom?**	**Text**
Jesus	His parents	Luke 2:51
Demons	The 70 disciples	Luke 10:17, 20
Creation	God	Rom. 8:20
Everything	Christ	1 Cor. 15:27–28; Phil. 3:21
Christ	God the Father	1 Cor. 15:28
The world to come	Christ and His church	Heb. 2:5–8
Angels, authorities, powers	Christ	1 Pet. 3:22

Notice two instances of a lack of submission:

FAILURE TO SUBMIT		
Who Did/Does Not Submit?	**To Whom?**	**Text**
The sinful mind	God and His law	Rom. 8:7
Israel	God's righteousness	Rom. 10:3

The fact that Christ submits to His Father shows that submission need not carry a sense of inferiority. In fact, it shows that submission in the ways that Scripture indicates is a Christlike behavior, and worthy of honor (Phil. 2:1–11).

It's worth mentioning that submission is only half the equation in the relationships shown above. For example, the church is called to submit to Christ, but Christ also has responsibilities toward the church: to love her, to give Himself up for her, to make her pure, to nourish and cherish her, to love her as He loves Himself (Eph. 5:25–33). ◆

Biblical humility does not involve a grovelling, abject demeanor, but rather acknowledging the reality about oneself—all of one's strengths and weaknesses, pluses and minuses, successes and failures. See "Humility—The Scandalous Virtue," Phil. 2:3.

CONSIDER THIS
5:13

Let's Celebrate!

Does Christianity have to be morbid or cheerless? Should nonbelievers have all the fun? Does God disapprove of merrymaking? Is the only way to celebrate with wild wingdings and horrid hangovers?

No! Christians have ample reason to enjoy life, as James hints at when he urges us to sing songs of praise with those who are happy (v. 13). Likewise, Paul says (twice) to "rejoice in the Lord" (Phil. 3:1; 4:4). Even Jesus challenges a too-somber attitude. To be sure, He was "a Man of sorrows and acquainted with grief" (Is. 53:3). Yet His enemies called Him a "winebibber" (Matt. 11:19). He enlivened a wedding with a gift of fine wine (John 2:1–12) and attended a "great feast" with a converted tax collector and his friends (Luke 5:27–39).

We might also note that the Bible opens in celebration. God creates the world and then sets aside an entire day to commemorate what He has done (Gen. 2:1–3). In fact, He tells His people to follow that pattern weekly and annually (Ex. 20:8–11; Lev. 23:1–44). At the other end of Scripture, we find a wedding-like celebration in heaven as God removes all pain and suffering (Rev. 19:1–10). Hallelujah!

How, then, can we cultivate celebration and joy on earth, here and now? Scripture encourages us to be the joyous people of God who have hope:

Weddings

Weddings are a cause for celebration because the "one flesh" union of a man and a woman reflects God's image on earth. The Song of Solomon is an entire love poem that celebrates this theme.

Concerts and Artfests

Major events or accomplishments call for celebration in song, dance, poetry, and other arts. Scripture memorializes the victory or work of God among His people in numerous songs, such as those of Deborah (Judg. 5), Moses and Miriam (Ex. 15:1–21), Hannah (1 Sam. 2:1–10), David (Ps. 18), and Mary (Luke l:46–55). We do not have the words to the songs of Jephthah's daughter (Judg. 11:34), David's followers (1 Sam. 18:6–7), or Paul and Silas (Acts 16:25–26), but their songs of deliverance set a joyous pattern for us to follow.

Harvest Celebrations

Israel's agricultural economy revolved around harvest time, which it celebrated by honoring God in songs of joy and parading samples of produce (Ps. 126:5–6; Is. 9:3). Other festivals included the week-long feasts of unleavened bread, weeks, and tabernacles (Ex. 23:16; Lev. 23; Num. 28–29; Deut. 16:9–17). The Sabbath year festival, held every seven years (Lev. 25:1–7), and the year of jubilee celebrations, held every fiftieth year (Lev. 25:8–55), linked the nation's worship and celebration with social legislation.

Sabbath

Having finished His work, God established one day each week to remind His people that all of creation belongs to Him, that work is not endless, and that His people must depend on Him (Gen. 2:1–3; Ex. 20:8–11). Early Christians moved their weekly observance to the first day of the week to commemorate "Resurrection Day" or the "Lord's Day" (see Rev. 1:10), the day on which Jesus proved that He was "Lord of the Sabbath" (Matt. 12:1–14) by rising from the dead.

As was the Sabbath, the Lord's Day is a time for worship, celebration, rest, and renewal. Unfortunately, both in Jesus' day and our own, the joy of the day has too often been lost under layers of legalistic rules and restrictions, making it more of a burden than a delight. But Jesus declared that "the sabbath was made for humankind, and not humankind for the sabbath" (Mark 2:27).

(continued on next page)

judge. 12There is one lawgiver and judge who is able to save
and to destroy. So who, then, are you to judge your neighbor?

Trust God for the Future

4:13–16 see pg. 825

13 Come now, you who say, "Today or
tomorrow we will go to such and such a
town and spend a year there, doing business and making
money." 14Yet you do not even know what tomorrow will
bring. What is your life? For you are a mist that appears for
a little while and then vanishes. 15Instead you ought to say,
"If the Lord wishes, we will live and do this or that." 16As it
is, you boast in your arrogance; all such boasting is evil.
17Anyone, then, who knows the right thing to do and fails
to do it, commits sin.

True Faith Reacts to Injustice

5:1–6

5 Come now, you rich people, weep
and wail for the miseries that are
coming to you. 2Your riches have rotted, and your clothes
are moth-eaten. 3Your gold and silver have rusted, and their
rust will be evidence against you, and it will eat your flesh
like fire. You have laid up treasure[w] for the last days. 4Lis-
ten! The wages of the laborers who mowed your fields,
which you kept back by fraud, cry out, and the cries of the
harvesters have reached the ears of the Lord of hosts. 5You
have lived on the earth in luxury and in pleasure; you have
fattened your hearts in a day of slaughter. 6You have condemned and murdered the righteous one, who does not resist you.

Patience and Perseverance

7 Be patient, therefore, beloved,[x] until the coming of the
Lord. The farmer waits for the precious crop from the earth,
being patient with it until it receives the early and the late
rains. 8You also must be patient. Strengthen your hearts, for
the coming of the Lord is near.[y] 9Beloved,[z] do not grumble
against one another, so that you may not be judged. See,
the Judge is standing at the doors! 10As an example of suffering and patience, beloved,[x] take the prophets who spoke
in the name of the Lord. 11Indeed we call blessed those who
showed endurance. You have heard of the endurance of
Job, and you have seen the purpose of the Lord, how the
Lord is compassionate and merciful.
12 Above all, my beloved,[x] do not swear, either by
heaven or by earth or by any other oath, but let your "Yes"

[w]Or will eat your flesh, since you have stored up fire [x]Gk brothers [y]Or is at hand [z]Gk Brothers

(continued from previous page)

Special Occasions

Scripture records a variety of occasions that called for special, spontaneous celebrations, such as escape from captivity (Ps. 126:1–3), conversion from sin (Acts 2:40–47; 16:25–34), and miraculous deliverance (Ex. 14:30—15:21). On occasions like these we need to pause to enjoy God's good gift, and to give thanks for what He has done in our lives. ◆

The Sabbath celebrated God's "rest" from His work of creation. Every seven days the Jews ceased from their work. They didn't just take a day off to catch up on chores or go to the lake, as many modern people do on Saturdays. They put an emphatic pause in life for an entire day. See "The Sabbath," Heb. 4:1–13.

GETTING YOURS

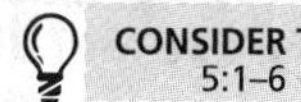

When James blasts the rich (vv. 1–6), is he condemning the possession of wealth? Is wealth inherently evil? No, but he is clearly warning those who get their wealth unjustly (v. 4) and live lavishly while ignoring their neighbors (vv. 5–6). Wealthy people of that kind are storing up judgment for themselves (v. 1).

God will call us to account for how we earn and spend our money. What will He say of you?

James' warning fits with other Scripture that discusses the use and abuse of wealth. See "Christians and Money," 1 Tim. 6:6–19.

be yes and your "No" be no, so that you may not fall under
condemnation.

The Power of Prayer

5:13
see pg. 828

13 Are any among you suffering? They
should pray. Are any cheerful? They
should sing songs of praise. 14Are any among you sick?
They should call for the elders of the church and have them
pray over them, anointing them with oil in the name of the
Lord. 15The prayer of faith will save the sick, and the Lord
will raise them up; and anyone who has committed sins
will be forgiven. 16Therefore confess your sins to one another, and pray for one another, so that you may be healed.

5:17–18

The prayer of the righteous is powerful
and effective. 17Elijah was a human being
like us, and he prayed fervently that it might not rain, and
for three years and six months it did not rain on the earth.
18Then he prayed again, and the heaven gave rain and the
earth yielded its harvest.

19 My brothers and sisters,[a] if anyone among you wanders from the truth and is brought back by another, 20you
should know that whoever brings back a sinner from wandering will save the sinner's[b] soul from death and will cover
a multitude of sins.

[a]Gk *My brothers* [b]Gk *his*

ELIJAH

CONSIDER THIS 5:17–18 **What sort of person does it take to pray effectively? James offers Elijah as a model (vv. 17–18).**

In a way, Elijah seems an unlikely choice to be a model for ordinary people. After all, he was one of Israel's greatest prophets. He took on the evil Ahab and Jezebel, brought a punishment of drought on the land, called down fire from heaven, and was translated to heaven in a whirlwind accompanied by fiery chariots (1 Kin. 17–22, 2 Kin. 1–2). How much do we have in common with such a man? How could our prayers possibly emulate his?

Yet James insists that "Elijah was a human being like us." So apparently he did not pray because he was a great man; perhaps he became a great man because he prayed.

James shows some reasons why Elijah's prayer life was so effective:

- **He prayed; one cannot be effective in prayer unless one prays in the first place.**
- **He prayed fervently; he was aware of what he was praying, and kept praying with diligence and discipline.**
- **He prayed an "effective" prayer (v. 16); that is, he expected results.**
- **He was a righteous man (v. 16); he did not allow sin to cloud his conversation with God.**
- **He prayed specifically, first for a drought, then for rain, in accordance with God's word (for example, Deut. 28:12, 24); he prayed according to Scripture.**

Elijah was a great prophet granted extraordinary results by God. Nevertheless, there is no reason why any believer today cannot pray using the same principles he did. Imagine what God might do in our world if Christians began praying like Elijah!

The First and Second Letters of

Peter

For Christians in the crucible.

Are you feeling beat up by life these days? Perhaps you've lost a job, or your family is in turmoil, or your health is poor. Perhaps a friend has turned against you, or an investment has gone bad, or the system has let you down. Whatever the circumstances, if life has become such a struggle that your faith itself feels under siege, then pay attention to 1 and 2 Peter! They were written for Christians in the crucible.

First Peter offers unique hope to people who "have had to suffer various trials" (1:6), a hope rooted in the power of Jesus' triumph over death (1:3, 21) and the certainty of His return (1:13). What practical difference does that hope make? It dramatically affects one's behavior. Instead of caving in under the stress and pressure of adversity, the person of hope responds with Christlike dignity and moral integrity.

Second Peter shifts the emphasis from a hope by which we can live to a hope on which we can count. We can rely on God to provide us with "everything needed for life and godliness" (1:3). We can trust the Scriptures to guide us in the way of truth (1:16–21) and help us avoid error (2:1—3:7). We can also count on Jesus to return just as He said He would (3:8–18).

One of the great comforts of these letters is that we are not alone when we encounter disappointment, pain, or persecution. Jesus suffered the same kind of "fiery trial" and stands with us in our troubles. Best of all, He gave us an example of how to face the fires of adversity. Now 1 and 2 Peter invite us to "follow in his steps" (1 Pet. 2:21).

C O N T E N T S

A R T I C L E S

Christians Against the System

In our culture, Christians enjoy privileges and freedoms that first-century believers could have only imagined. To be sure, Christians today may disapprove of many things that our increasingly secular society permits or encourages, and here and there we find believers discriminated against for their faith. Nevertheless, the system remains open to us. In fact, believers occupy positions of influence at all levels of society.

Things were far different for followers of Christ in the first century. As the gospel spread throughout the Roman Empire, it ran into hostility at the local level and eventually from Rome itself. Christians were harassed, threatened, arrested, jailed, beaten, and even killed for their unwavering commitment to Christ. During Domitian's reign as emperor (A.D. 81–96), official persecution intensified, turning many believers into migrants and driving some in Rome to live underground in the catacombs.

First Peter speaks to believers enduring "fiery ordeals" (4:12), people who had been rejected by the system. Likewise 2 Peter speaks to Christians whose faith may have been wavering as they endured long years of struggle, waiting for the return of the Lord and a deliverance from their oppressors.

The letters highlight a number of themes for Christians living under these conditions:

(1) The need for clarity as to position. The early Christians were enemies of Rome because the system defined them as enemies, not the other way around. The writer urged believers to submit to authorities, to persevere in the face of injustice, and to love their enemies rather than retaliate (1 Pet. 2:13–20; 3:13–17; 4:12–16).

(2) The need to affirm identity and worth. Some in the first century regarded Christians as evildoers (1 Pet. 2:12; 3:16; 4:4). By contrast, Peter gave the believers names and titles that affirmed their value to God—a chosen generation, a royal priesthood, a holy nation, God's own special people (2:9).

(3) The value of community. People under trial need each other. That's why Peter urged suffering saints to hold onto each other, to take care of each other, and to identify with other believers who are facing tough times (3:8–9).

(4) The crucial importance of character. When squeezed by opposition to their beliefs and morality, many people find it easy to compromise their ethical standards. Peter challenged his readers not to use persecution as an excuse to fail to grow in grace, but to stand firm in their faith and let suffering establish Christlike virtues within them (1:13–16; 2:1–2, 11–12; 2 Pet. 1:5–9; 3:17–18).

(5) The centrality of sound doctrine. Second Peter in particular warns against false teaching (2:1–22; 3:17–18). The author recognized that people under pressure tend to be vulnerable to powerful opportunists who capitalize on suffering to advance their own false ideas. When that happens, the enemy is no longer outside the community of faith, but within it. The result is inevitably a compromise of the truth and accommodation to evil. God deals very harshly with such false teachers (2:4–10).

(6) The importance of perseverance. Sometimes the only thing one can do under persecution is to endure. Peter's letters show believers how to do that, how to cope when they have no control over their circumstances or the outcome of their trials. Coping may be their only alternative to caving in—coping to the glory of God by never losing hope, never trading away their dignity, never letting their spirit give in. Keep on keeping on! That's the message of these books. ◆

QUOTE UNQUOTE

CONSIDER THIS 1:1 *The "exiles" who were dispersed abroad (v. 1) were probably ordinary believers from Jerusalem who had a powerful impact on the cultures where they located:*

The pagan Celsus admitted in the second century that it was the "wool workers, cobblers, laundry workers, and the most illiterate and bucolic yokels" who carried the gospel forth, even more than the bishops, the apologists, and the theologians.

Paul Stevens, *Liberating the Laity,* p. 22

Greetings to Pilgrim Believers

1:1

1 Peter, an apostle of Jesus Christ,
To the exiles of the Dispersion in
Pontus, Galatia, Cappadocia, Asia, and Bithynia, 2who have
been chosen and destined by God the Father and sanctified
by the Spirit to be obedient to Jesus Christ and to be sprinkled with his blood:
May grace and peace be yours in abundance.

Put Your Hope in Christ

3 Blessed be the God and Father of our Lord Jesus
Christ! By his great mercy he has given us a new birth into
a living hope through the resurrection of Jesus Christ from
the dead, 4and into an inheritance that is imperishable, undefiled, and unfading, kept in heaven for you, 5who are being protected by the power of God through faith for a salvation ready to be revealed in the last time. 6In this you
rejoice,[a] even if now for a little while you have had to suffer
various trials, 7so that the genuineness of your faith—being
more precious than gold that, though perishable, is tested
by fire—may be found to result in praise and glory and
honor when Jesus Christ is revealed. 8Although you have
not seen[b] him, you love him; and even though you do not
see him now, you believe in him and rejoice with an indescribable and glorious joy, 9for you are receiving the outcome of your faith, the salvation of your souls.
10 Concerning this salvation, the prophets who prophesied of the grace that was to be yours made careful search
and inquiry, 11inquiring about the person or time that the
Spirit of Christ within them indicated when it testified in
advance to the sufferings destined for Christ and the subsequent glory. 12It was revealed to them that they were serving not themselves but you, in regard to the things that
have now been announced to you through those who
brought you good news by the Holy Spirit sent from
heaven—things into which angels long to look!

An Encouragement to Holiness and Love

13 Therefore prepare your minds for action;[c] discipline
yourselves; set all your hope on the grace that Jesus Christ
will bring you when he is revealed. 14Like obedient children, do not be conformed to the desires that you formerly
had in ignorance. 15Instead, as he who called you is holy, be

[a]Or *Rejoice in this* [b]Other ancient authorities read *known* [c]Gk *gird up the loins of your mind*

holy yourselves in all your conduct; 16for it is written, "You
shall be holy, for I am holy."
17 If you invoke as Father the one who judges all people
impartially according to their deeds, live in reverent fear
during the time of your exile. 18You know that you were
ransomed from the futile ways inherited from your ancestors, not with perishable things like silver or gold, 19but
with the precious blood of Christ, like that of a lamb without defect or blemish. 20He was destined before the foundation of the world, but was revealed at the end of the ages
for your sake. 21Through him you have come to trust in
God, who raised him from the dead and gave him glory, so
that your faith and hope are set on God.
22 Now that you have purified your souls by your obedience to the truth[d] so that you have genuine mutual love,
love one another deeply[e] from the heart.[f] 23You have been
born anew, not of perishable but of imperishable seed,
through the living and enduring word of God.[g] 24For

"All flesh is like grass
  and all its glory like the flower of grass.
The grass withers,
  and the flower falls,
25 but the word of the Lord endures forever."

That word is the good news that was announced to you.

The Way to Spiritual Growth

2 Rid yourselves, therefore, of all malice, and all guile,
insincerity, envy, and all slander. 2Like newborn
infants, long for the pure, spiritual milk, so that by it you
may grow into salvation— 3if indeed you have tasted that
the Lord is good.

God's New People

4 Come to him, a living stone, though rejected by mortals yet chosen and precious in God's sight, and 5like living
stones, let yourselves be built[h] into a spiritual house, to be a
holy priesthood, to offer spiritual sacrifices acceptable to
God through Jesus Christ. 6For it stands in scripture:

"See, I am laying in Zion a stone,
  a cornerstone chosen and precious;
and whoever believes in him[i] will not be put to shame."

7To you then who believe, he is precious; but for those who
do not believe,

[d]Other ancient authorities add *through the Spirit* [e]Or *constantly* [f]Other ancient authorities read *a pure heart* [g]Or *through the word of the living and enduring God* [h]Or *you yourselves are being built* [i]Or *it*

QUOTE UNQUOTE

CONSIDER THIS 2:9 *Peter's reference to "a royal priesthood" (v. 9) supports a Christian teaching known as the priesthood of believers:*

Most Protestants pay lip service to the Reformation doctrine of the priesthood of every believer, but they do not thereby mean to say that every Christian is a minister. Many hasten to add that all they mean by the familiar doctrine is that nobody needs to confess to a priest, since each can confess directly to God. The notion that this doctrine erases the distinction between laymen and minister is seldom presented seriously, and would, to some, be shocking, but it does not take much study of the New Testament to realize that the early Christians actually operated on this revolutionary basis.

Elton Trueblood, *Your Other Vocation,* p. 30

GOD'S FAMILY ALBUM

CONSIDER THIS 2:9–10 **The names that Peter calls believers (vv. 9–10) are important because they reveal our identity. We know *who* we are because we know *whose* we are: we belong to God. We have received His call, mercy, and claim on our lives. As a result, we can commit ourselves to others and work with them to achieve common goals.**

Peter draws on the Exodus account for his language here: "I . . . brought you [out of Egypt] to myself . . . you shall be for me a priestly kingdom" (Ex. 19:4–6). God first identified with and redeemed the people of Israel, then He made covenant agreements with them (see "Israel," Rom. 10:1, and "The New Covenant," 1 Cor. 11:25). Likewise for us, first God's grace secures our identity, then our commitment to His service.

Our modern culture tears at that sense of identity and security. If we want to effect change and serve others, we need to know *whose* we are and why. Do you? Can you find yourself in God's family portrait framed in this passage?

"The stone that the builders rejected
has become the very head of the corner,"
8 and
"A stone that makes them stumble,
and a rock that makes them fall."
They stumble because they disobey the word, as they were
destined to do.

2:9 see pg. 835

9 But you are a chosen race, a royal
priesthood, a holy nation, God's own
people,[j] in order that you may proclaim the mighty acts of
him who called you out of darkness into his marvelous
light.

2:9–10

10 Once you were not a people,
but now you are God's people;
once you had not received mercy,
but now you have received mercy.

Living in the Community

11 Beloved, I urge you as aliens and exiles to abstain
from the desires of the flesh that wage war against the soul.
12 Conduct yourselves honorably among the Gentiles, so
that, though they malign you as evildoers, they may see
your honorable deeds and glorify God when he comes to
judge.[k]
13 For the Lord's sake accept the authority of every human institution,[l] whether of the emperor as supreme, 14 or
of governors, as sent by him to punish those who do wrong
and to praise those who do right. 15 For it is God's will that
by doing right you should silence the ignorance of the foolish. 16 As servants[m] of God, live as free people, yet do not
use your freedom as a pretext for evil. 17 Honor everyone.
Love the family of believers.[n] Fear God. Honor the emperor.

The Challenge of Work Relationships

2:18–21

18 Slaves, accept the authority of your
masters with all deference, not only those
who are kind and gentle but also those who are harsh.
19 For it is a credit to you if, being aware of God, you endure pain while suffering unjustly. 20 If you endure when
you are beaten for doing wrong, what credit is that? But if
you endure when you do right and suffer for it, you have
God's approval. 21 For to this you have been called, because

[j] *Gk a people for his possession* [k] *Gk God on the day of visitation* [l] *Or every institution ordained for human beings* [m] *Gk slaves* [n] *Gk Love the brotherhood*

Christ also suffered for you, leaving you an example, so that
you should follow in his steps.
22 "He committed no sin,
and no deceit was found in his mouth."
23When he was abused, he did not return abuse; when he
suffered, he did not threaten; but he entrusted himself to
the one who judges justly. 24He himself bore our sins in his
body on the cross,[o] so that, free from sins, we might live for
righteousness; by his wounds[p] you have been healed. 25For
you were going astray like sheep, but now you have returned to the shepherd and guardian of your souls.

Christlike Families

3 Wives, in the same way, accept the authority of your
husbands, so that, even if some of them do not obey
the word, they may be won over without a word by their
wives' conduct, 2when they see the purity and reverence of
your lives. 3Do not adorn yourselves outwardly by braiding
your hair, and by wearing gold ornaments or fine clothing;
4rather, let your adornment be the inner self with the
lasting beauty of a gentle and quiet spirit, which is very
precious in God's sight. 5It was in this way long ago that the
holy women who hoped in God used to adorn themselves
by accepting the authority of their husbands. 6Thus Sarah obeyed Abraham and
called him lord. You have become her daughters as long as
you do what is good and never let fears alarm you.

3:6 see pg. 838

7 Husbands, in the same way, show consideration for
your wives in your life together, paying honor to the
woman as the weaker sex,[q] since they too are also heirs of
the gracious gift of life—so that nothing may hinder your
prayers.

Relating to Other Believers

8 Finally, all of you, have unity of spirit, sympathy, love
for one another, a tender heart, and a humble mind. 9Do
not repay evil for evil or abuse for abuse; but, on the contrary, repay with a blessing. It is for this that you were
called—that you might inherit a blessing. 10For
"Those who desire life
and desire to see good days,

[o]Or *carried up our sins in his body to the tree* [p]Gk *bruise* [q]Gk *vessel*

It's Not Fair!

CONSIDER THIS 2:18–21 **Are you suffering at the hands of an unjust superior? Are you paid unfairly, or have you been cheated out of a raise? Have you been loaded down with more than your fair share of work? How should Christians react to injustices in the workplace?**

Healthy confrontation may be called for. There's a time to claim one's own rights or stand up for the rights of others. Scripture provides many examples and guidelines. For instance, Jesus gave instructions on how to deal with a believer in sin (Matt. 18:15–17), and Paul appealed to the emperor when he realized that justice was being withheld from him (Acts 25:8–12).

On the other hand, there is also a time to quietly suffer injustice as a matter of testimony, as Peter indicates (1 Pet. 2:18–21). Jesus told His followers the same thing (Matt. 5:38–42), and Paul discouraged lawsuits among believers for the sake of their testimony (1 Cor. 6:7).

Either way, Christians should never just ignore injustice. We may decide to quit if our employer is grossly unjust. But we should do so not out of cowardice or an unwillingness to endure hardship, but to honor Christ or else to find a constructive, godly alternative elsewhere.

Working for a difficult boss is one of the most important situations where a believer needs to work with a Christlike "workstyle." See Titus 2:9–10.

Faced with injustice, it might seem easier for believers to withdraw from the world. But engagement, not isolation, is Christ's desire for us. See "Called into the World," John 17:18.

let them keep their tongues from evil
  and their lips from speaking deceit;
11 let them turn away from evil and do good;
  let them seek peace and pursue it.
12 For the eyes of the Lord are on the righteous,
  and his ears are open to their prayer.
But the face of the Lord is against those who do evil."

If You Should Suffer

13 Now who will harm you if you are eager to do what
is good? 14But even if you do suffer for doing what is right,
you are blessed. Do not fear what they fear,[r] and do not be
intimidated, 15but in your hearts sanctify
3:15–17
Christ as Lord. Always be ready to make
your defense to anyone who demands from you an accounting for the hope that is in you; 16yet do it with gentleness and reverence.[s] Keep your conscience clear, so that,
when you are maligned, those who abuse you for your
good conduct in Christ may be put to shame. 17For it is
better to suffer for doing good, if suffering should be God's
will, than to suffer for doing evil. 18For Christ also suffered[t]
for sins once for all, the righteous for the unrighteous, in
order to bring you[u] to God. He was put to death in the

[r]Gk *their fear* [s]Or *respect* [t]Other ancient authorities read *died* [u]Other ancient authorities read *us*

Sarah . . . and Her Daughters

Sarah was no doubt well known to the Jewish believers to whom Peter was writing. Just as Jewish men valued their connection with Abraham (compare Matt. 3:9; John 8:39; Acts 13:26), so women regarded themselves as daughters of Sarah. Peter affirmed that desire by describing what it would mean for Christian women facing severe persecution: doing good and not giving in to fear (1 Pet. 3:5–6).

The book of Genesis does not record Sarah calling her husband lord, but the term was commonly used by members of a clan to show esteem to the head of the clan. By using such a title of respect, Sarah would be honoring Abraham and demonstrating her submission to God by following her husband's leadership (vv. 1, 5).

Sarah exerted some leadership of her own by arranging for her servant Hagar to bear Abraham a son (Gen. 16:2–4; see "Hagar," Gal. 4:24–25), and later by urging him to send Hagar and her son Ishmael away (21:10–14). It's interesting that God instructed Abraham to listen to (obey) Sarah, even though Abraham was displeased with her plan.

In holding up Sarah as a model, Peter emphasized her good works and courageous faith (compare Heb. 11:11). She followed Abraham into some risky situations where courage and righteous living were required (Gen. 12:15; 20:2). In a similar way, Peter's readers were undergoing "fiery ordeal" as a result of their faith in Christ (1 Pet. 4:12). The key to their survival was not to capitulate to cultural standards of worth, but to develop a Christlike inner character, which is both beautiful and enduring (3:3–4).

Personality Profile: Sarah

FOR YOUR INFO 3:6

Name means: "Princess."

Also known as: Sarai, until the Lord changed her name (Gen. 17:15).

Home: Originally Haran in Mesopotamia (in modern Iraq); later, Canaan.

Family: Half-sister to her husband, Abraham; they had the same father but different mothers; mother to Isaac.

Best known today for: Bearing a promised son, Isaac, after she was past childbearing years.

flesh, but made alive in the spirit, 19in which also he went
and made a proclamation to the spirits in prison, 20who in
former times did not obey, when God waited patiently in
the days of Noah, during the building of the ark, in which a
few, that is, eight persons, were saved through water. 21And
baptism, which this prefigured, now saves you—not as a
removal of dirt from the body, but as an appeal to God for[v]
a good conscience, through the resurrection of Jesus Christ,
22who has gone into heaven and is at the right hand of God,
with angels, authorities, and powers made subject to him.

A Radically Different Lifestyle

4 Since therefore Christ suffered in the flesh,[w] arm
yourselves also with the same intention (for whoever
has suffered in the flesh has finished with sin), 2so as to live
for the rest of your earthly life[x] no longer by human desires
but by the will of God. 3You have already spent enough
time in doing what the Gentiles like to do, living in
licentiousness, passions, drunkenness, revels, carousing,
and lawless idolatry. 4They are surprised that you no longer
join them in the same excesses of dissipation, and so they
blaspheme.[y] 5But they will have to give an accounting to
him who stands ready to judge the living and the dead.
6For this is the reason the gospel was proclaimed even to
the dead, so that, though they had been judged in the flesh
as everyone is judged, they might live in the spirit as God
does.

Commitment to Other Believers

7 The end of all things is near;[z] therefore be serious and
discipline yourselves for the sake of your prayers. 8Above
all, maintain constant love for one another, for love covers a
multitude of sins. 9Be hospitable to one another without
complaining. 10Like good stewards of the manifold grace of
God, serve one another with whatever gift each of you has
received. 11Whoever speaks must do so as one speaking the
very words of God; whoever serves must do so with the
strength that God supplies, so that God may be glorified in
all things through Jesus Christ. To him belong the glory
and the power forever and ever. Amen.

(Bible text continued on page 841)

[v]*Or a pledge to God from* [w]Other ancient authorities add *for us*; others, *for you* [x]Gk *rest of the time in the flesh* [y]*Or they malign you* [z]*Or is at hand*

QUOTE UNQUOTE

CONSIDER THIS 3:15–17 *Christians must "always be ready to give a defense for the hope that is in [them]" (v. 15). This is especially true at work. But witness involves the work itself as well as words:*

If you are going to be really effective in your place of work, you must set out to be the best man at your job . . . .

I knew a man who . . . arrived on the job and, contrary to expectations, he did not talk, he did not agitate. He just got on with the work. And, for a period of some months, that is all he did . . . . His workmates began to see him in a new light . . . .

Only when he had already, to the surprise of everyone, established himself as a craftsman amongst craftsmen did he go into action. By this time he had the respect of every worker in the factory and in the trade union branch . . . . Within two years . . . he had obtained one of the most influential positions in his union, where he could profoundly influence policies which concerned the working lives and conditions of hundreds of thousands of Britain's key war-workers.

Douglas Hyde, *Dedication and Leadership*, pp. 99–100

Suffering Outweighs Comfort

CONSIDER THIS 4:12–19 **Comfort and ease were never intended for sinners. We can't handle them. As someone has well said, sin gives us the terrible ability to misuse any good thing. We are deluded if we think we can rise above this less-than-perfect condition without outside help.**

Christ's intervention highlights the seriousness of our situation. It took suffering and death for Him to break the bondage that holds all of God's creation in its vicious grip. That made it possible for us to enter into new life. Now His work continues in us and with us throughout our lives, and He gives us an opportunity to co-operate in our re-creation.

As believers, we inevitably find ourselves at war with our old ways, so we should not be surprised at pain and suffering in the walk of faith (1 Pet. 4:1). It is all part of the gift of believing (Phil. 1:29). It is the path to strength and steadiness (1 Pet. 5:10). It is the process of being completed (James 1:2–3).

Do you desire to arrive at a place of peace, joy, and serenity? Someday you will. That is not a false hope. But it is a *hope*: we won't enjoy those until we reach full maturity in Christ in the world to come (Rev. 7:9–17; 21:1–5; 22:1–6).

Don't Fleece the Flock!

CONSIDER THIS 5:2 **Several flagrant abuses by prominent ministers, involving hundreds of millions of dollars, were exposed during the 1980s. As a result, many people adopted a general distrust of Christian ministers and ministries, and giving declined. The situation makes Peter's words to overseers (v. 2) required reading for all vocational Christian workers and their supporters. Clergy need to maintain the utmost integrity when it comes to finances.**

Peter speaks here of *sordid gain*, literally "filthy" or "shameful" money. What brings shame is not the money but the greed, which is nothing less than idolatry (Col. 3:5). No wonder Paul strenuously warned church leaders to beware of using ministry as a pretext for gain (1 Tim. 3:3, 8; 6:3–5; Titus 1:7).

Of course, it is not inevitable that ministers should fall to greed. Peter refused Simon's offer of a bribe in exchange for the power of the Holy Spirit (Acts 8:18–20). Likewise, Paul frequently refused the financial support to which he had a right as an apostle (1 Cor. 9:7–15).

Do you make your living in the ministry? If so, are you doing so willingly and eagerly, as Peter indicates? If not, why are you in the ministry?

Paul bent over backward to avoid any hint of financial impropriety. See "I Have Not Coveted," Acts 20:33–38.

Rejoice in Suffering

4:12–19

12 Beloved, do not be surprised at the fiery ordeal that is taking place among you to test you, as though something strange were happening to you. 13But rejoice insofar as you are sharing Christ's sufferings, so that you may also be glad and shout for joy when his glory is revealed. 14If you are reviled for the name of Christ, you are blessed, because the spirit of glory,[a] which is the Spirit of God, is resting on you.[b] 15But let none of you suffer as a murderer, a thief, a criminal, or even as a mischief maker. 16Yet if any of you suffers as a Christian, do not consider it a disgrace, but glorify God because you bear this name. 17For the time has come for judgment to begin with the household of God; if it begins with us, what will be the end for those who do not obey the gospel of God? 18And

"If it is hard for the righteous to be saved,
what will become of the ungodly and the sinners?"

19Therefore, let those suffering in accordance with God's will entrust themselves to a faithful Creator, while continuing to do good.

Leaders and Followers

5 Now as an elder myself and a witness of the sufferings of Christ, as well as one who shares in the glory to be

5:2

revealed, I exhort the elders among you 2to tend the flock of God that is in your charge, exercising the oversight,[c] not under compulsion but willingly, as God would have you do it[d]—not for sordid gain but eagerly. 3Do not lord it over those in your charge,

5:2–4

but be examples to the flock. 4And when the chief shepherd appears, you will win the crown of glory that never fades away. 5In the same way, you who are younger must accept the authority of the elders.[e] And all of you must clothe yourselves with humility in your dealings with one another, for

"God opposes the proud,
but gives grace to the humble."

Watch Out for the Enemy

6 Humble yourselves therefore under the mighty hand of God, so that he may exalt you in due time. 7Cast all your

[a]Other ancient authorities add *and of power* [b]Other ancient authorities add *On their part he is blasphemed, but on your part he is glorified* [c]Other ancient authorities lack *exercising the oversight* [d]Other ancient authorities lack *as God would have you do it* [e]Or *of those who are older*

The Business of the Church

CONSIDER THIS 5:2–4

There are many reasons why people seek positions of authority in a church. Some do it because they have authority at their normal job and therefore feel they should have authority at church. Some do it for just the opposite reason: authority is denied them at work, so they seek it in the church.

Peter reminds overseers (vv. 2–4) that the presence or absence of authority or success on the job is more or less irrelevant to positions of authority at church. That may shock church members and leaders who have uncritically adopted models of church management from the business world. It's not that churches can't benefit from many of the practices found in business. Certainly in administration and finances, churches have much to learn from the efficient and effective policies of the marketplace. But the church is not a business, and philosophies and practices from that sphere need to be carefully evaluated and sifted in light of Scripture before they are put into effect.

5:8

anxiety on him, because he cares for you.
8Discipline yourselves, keep alert.[f] Like a
roaring lion your adversary the devil prowls around, looking for someone to devour. 9Resist him, steadfast in your
faith, for you know that your brothers and sisters[g] in all the
world are undergoing the same kinds of suffering. 10And after you have suffered for a little while, the God of all grace,
who has called you to his eternal glory in Christ, will himself restore, support, strengthen, and establish you. 11To
him be the power forever and ever. Amen.

Final Greetings

12 Through Silvanus, whom I consider a faithful
brother, I have written this short letter to encourage you and
to testify that this is the true grace of God. Stand fast in it.

5:13

13Your sister church[h] in Babylon, chosen
together with you, sends you greetings;
and so does my son Mark. 14Greet one another with a kiss
of love.

Peace to all of you who are in Christ.[i]

[f]Or *be vigilant* [g]Gk *your brotherhood* [h]Gk *She who is* [i]Other ancient authorities add *Amen*

LIKE A ROARING LION YOUR ADVERSARY THE DEVIL PROWLS AROUND. . . . —1 Peter 5:8

A Hungry Lion

A CLOSER LOOK 5:8

Satan, who stalks the world like a lion (v. 8), knows that spiritual overconfidence is one sure-fire way to catch Christians off-guard. See "Pay Attention to Temptation!" at 1 Cor. 10:12–13.

The Church in "Babylon"

A CLOSER LOOK 5:13

"She who is in Babylon" sent greetings to Peter's readers (v. 13). Describing her as "elect together with you," Peter may have been indicating a group of believers rather than one person. But what did he mean by referring to Babylon? See "A Symbol of Evil," Rev. 14:8.

The Second Letter of Peter

Called, Equipped, and Growing

1 Simeon[a] Peter, a servant[b] and apostle of Jesus Christ,
To those who have received a faith as precious as ours
through the righteousness of our God and Savior Jesus
Christ:[c]
2 May grace and peace be yours in abundance in the
knowledge of God and of Jesus our Lord.
1:3–4
3 His divine power has given us
everything needed for life and godliness,
through the knowledge of him who called us by[d] his own
glory and goodness. 4Thus he has given us, through these
things, his precious and very great promises, so that
through them you may escape from the corruption that is
in the world because of lust, and may become participants
of the divine nature. 5For this very reason, you must make
every effort to support your faith with goodness, and goodness with knowledge, 6and knowledge with self-control,
and self-control with endurance, and endurance with godliness, 7and godliness with mutual[e] affection, and mutual[e]
affection with love. 8For if these things are yours and are increasing among you, they keep you from being ineffective
and unfruitful in the knowledge of our Lord Jesus Christ.
9For anyone who lacks these things is nearsighted and
blind, and is forgetful of the cleansing of past sins. 10There-
fore, brothers and sisters,[f] be all the more eager to confirm
your call and election, for if you do this, you will never
stumble. 11For in this way, entry into the eternal kingdom
of our Lord and Savior Jesus Christ will be richly provided
for you.

Peter's Intent in Writing

12 Therefore I intend to keep on reminding you of these
things, though you know them already and are established
in the truth that has come to you. 13I think it right, as long
as I am in this body,[g] to refresh your memory, 14since I
know that my death[h] will come soon, as indeed our Lord
Jesus Christ has made clear to me. 15And I will make every
effort so that after my departure you may be able at any
time to recall these things.

1:16 see pg. 844

16 For we did not follow cleverly devised myths when we made known to

(Bible text continued on page 845)

[a]Other ancient authorities read *Simon* [b]Gk *slave* [c]Or *of our God and the Savior Jesus Christ* [d]Other ancient authorities read *through* [e]Gk *brotherly* [f]Gk *brothers* [g]Gk *tent* [h]Gk *the putting off of my tent*

Do You Have What It Takes?

CONSIDER THIS 1:3–4 **Do you think you have what it takes to "make it" in life? According to v. 3 you do. Peter says that God's power gives us what we need to experience real life in a way that pleases Him. God wants to affect every area of our lives—work, marriage and family, relationships, church, and community.**

How can you make God's power operational in your experience? Peter says that it comes "through the knowledge of him who called us." In other words, we must grow closer to Christ. Real power comes from having an understanding of our place in God's purposes and relying on His provisions.

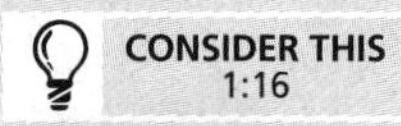

MYTH #9

10 MYTHS ABOUT CHRISTIANITY

MYTH: THE BIBLE IS UNRELIABLE AND NOT TO BE TRUSTED

Many people today accept a number of myths about Christianity, with the result that they never respond to Jesus as He really is. This is one of ten articles that speak to some of those misconceptions. For a list of all ten, see 1 Tim. 1:3–4.

Is the Bible a trustworthy document? Are the Scriptures true as written? Or are they full of myths that may have symbolic value but little if any basis in fact? People have been questioning the biblical record almost from its beginnings. Peter, for instance, encountered skepticism as he presented the gospel in the first century. His claims about Jesus were nothing but cleverly devised fables, some said—a charge he vehemently denied (v. 16).

Today the Bible's credibility and authority are still attacked. Yet how many of its critics have carefully studied its teaching? How many have even looked at the story of how it came to be written?

A careful reader will recognize that the Bible is not so much a single book as a library of sixty-six books. It contains a variety of literary genres: history, poetry, narrative, exposition, parable, and "apocalyptic" (see Rev. 10:1–10). Its many authors wrote during a period of some two thousand years using three languages—Hebrew, Greek, and Aramaic. Probably all but one were Jews.

Remarkably, the writers tell one unified story:

- They offer the same understanding of God throughout. He is one God, Creator, Savior, and Judge. He is all-powerful, all-knowing, and eternal. His character is holy, good, loving, and just.
- They offer the same understanding of human nature. People are made in God's image and are capable of great good. Yet they are also sinful and capable of great wickedness. The great need of humanity is to be reconciled to God and to each another.
- The New Testament offers a common understanding of Jesus Christ. He is both God and man. He became a real human being in order to show the world the God it could not otherwise perceive. Something deeply significant happened as a result of His death on the cross, making it possible for God and humanity to be reconciled.
- They offer the same hope. God will accomplish His purposes for His Creation.

Aside from the internal evidence that Scripture is what it claims to be—the very words of God—is a growing body of external evidence that supports its reliability as a document. For example, scholars have found many contemporary sources that parallel the Scriptural record. For instance, Jesus is mentioned by two Roman writers of the first century, Tacitus (*Annals* 15.44) and Pliny the Younger (*Letters* 19.96), as well as by some Jewish writings of that period, including Josephus (*Antiquities* 18.3.3) and the Mishnah, a collection of traditions under compilation in Jesus' day.

Another body of research that proves invaluable for biblical studies is archaeology. Countless discoveries have helped to verify the text of Scripture, most notably the Dead Sea Scrolls. Likewise, digs throughout the Mediterranean have supported biblical references to various places and people and the

(continued on next page)

you the power and coming of our Lord Jesus Christ, but we
had been eyewitnesses of his majesty. 17For he received
honor and glory from God the Father when that voice was
conveyed to him by the Majestic Glory, saying, "This is my
Son, my Beloved,[i] with whom I am well pleased." 18We ourselves heard this voice come from heaven, while we were
with him on the holy mountain.
19 So we have the prophetic message more fully confirmed. You will do well to be attentive to this as to a lamp
shining in a dark place, until the day dawns and the morning star rises in your hearts. 20First of all you must understand this, that no prophecy of scripture is a matter of
one's own interpretation, 21because no
prophecy ever came by human will, but
men and women moved by the Holy Spirit spoke from God.[j]

1:21

Beware of False Teachers

2 But false prophets also arose among the people, just as
there will be false teachers among you, who will
secretly bring in destructive opinions. They will even deny
the Master who bought them—bringing swift destruction
on themselves. 2Even so, many will follow their licentious
ways, and because of these teachers[k] the way of truth will
be maligned. 3And in their greed they will exploit you with
deceptive words. Their condemnation, pronounced against
them long ago, has not been idle, and their destruction is
not asleep.

God Will Protect

4 For if God did not spare the angels when they sinned,
but cast them into hell[l] and committed them to chains[m] of
deepest darkness to be kept until the judgment; 5and if he
did not spare the ancient world, even though he saved
Noah, a herald of righteousness, with seven others, when
he brought a flood on a world of the un-
godly; 6and if by turning the cities of
Sodom and Gomorrah to ashes he condemned them to extinction[n] and made them an example of what is coming to
the ungodly;[o] 7and if he rescued Lot, a righteous man
greatly distressed by the licentiousness of the lawless 8(for
that righteous man, living among them day after day, was

2:6–9 see pg. 846

[i]Other ancient authorities read *my beloved Son* [j]Other ancient authorities read *but moved by the Holy Spirit saints of God spoke* [k]Gk *because of them* [l]Gk *Tartaros* [m]Other ancient authorities read *pits* [n]Other ancient authorities lack *to extinction* [o]Other ancient authorities read *an example to those who were to be ungodly*

Deliver Us from Temptation

A CLOSER LOOK 2:9 *God has committed Himself to help His children avoid, flee, confess, and resist temptation (v. 9). See "Pay Attention to Temptation!" at 1 Cor. 10:12–13.*

(continued from previous page)

events of which they were a part thousands of years ago.

The more one examines the evidence, the more one becomes convinced that the Bible is more than a cleverly devised tale. It has the ring of authenticity. But in that case, readers ought to pay attention to its message. That is the ultimate issue. As Mark Twain aptly put it, it is not the things in the Bible that people can't understand that prove troublesome, but the things they can understand. Even if people are convinced that the Bible is true from cover to cover, will they heed its message? ♦

How Did the Bible Come to Us?

FOR YOUR INFO 1:21 **Peter wants us to feel confident that the Scriptures are as valid and trustworthy today as they were when they were first written (v. 21). He also gives some information on the process God used to get His Word written down in a permanent form.**

The "older testament," which exists today in 39 books, was written mostly in Hebrew over a thousand-year period, hundreds of years before Christ. The 27 books of the "newer testament" were written in Greek during the first century after Christ's birth. As the various writings came into existence over the centuries, the people of God corporately studied and recognized them as being the Word of God.

(continued on next page)

(continued from previous page)

The two testaments together tell a completed story. *Testament* means "covenant" or "agreement" between God and humanity (see "The New Covenant," 1 Cor. 11:25). The Old Testament is "old" in the sense that it reveals a covenant made at Mount Sinai (Ex. 19:3–6; 24:3–8; see "Israel," Rom. 10:1). The *New* Testament or covenant was accomplished by Christ through His death on the cross (Luke 22:20; 1 Cor. 11:25).

As we read Scripture, we need to make sure that we keep in mind its full context. See "The Bible: Getting the Big Picture," 2 Tim. 3:16–17.

SECOND CHANCES

CONSIDER THIS 2:6–9 **Peter asks us to consider Sodom and Gomorrah, which God did not spare (v. 6; Gen. 19:24). This and fifty other biblical references to those twin cities make two things clear: they could have been saved in spite of their evil, and God wants future generations like ours to avoid their mistakes.**

tormented in his righteous soul by their lawless deeds that
2:9 see pg. 845
he saw and heard), [9]then the Lord knows
how to rescue the godly from trial, and to
keep the unrighteous under punishment until the day of
judgment [10]—especially those who indulge their flesh in
depraved lust, and who despise authority.

Deceptions of False Teachers

Bold and willful, they are not afraid to slander the glorious ones,[p] [11]whereas angels, though greater in might and
power, do not bring against them a slanderous judgment
from the Lord.[q] [12]These people, however, are like irrational
animals, mere creatures of instinct, born to be caught and
killed. They slander what they do not understand, and
when those creatures are destroyed,[r] they also will be de-
2:13
stroyed, [13]suffering[s] the penalty for doing
wrong. They count it a pleasure to revel
in the daytime. They are blots and blemishes, reveling in
their dissipation[t] while they feast with you. [14]They have
eyes full of adultery, insatiable for sin. They entice unsteady
souls. They have hearts trained in greed. Accursed children!
[15]They have left the straight road and have gone astray, following the road of Balaam son of Bosor,[u] who loved the
wages of doing wrong, [16]but was rebuked for his own
transgression; a speechless donkey spoke with a human
voice and restrained the prophet's madness.

17 These are waterless springs and mists driven by a
storm; for them the deepest darkness has been reserved.
[18]For they speak bombastic nonsense, and with licentious
desires of the flesh they entice people who have just[v] escaped from those who live in error. [19]They promise them
freedom, but they themselves are slaves of corruption; for
people are slaves to whatever masters them. [20]For if, after
they have escaped the defilements of the world through the
knowledge of our Lord and Savior Jesus Christ, they are
again entangled in them and overpowered, the last state has
become worse for them than the first. [21]For it would have
been better for them never to have known the way of righteousness than, after knowing it, to turn back from the holy
commandment that was passed on to them. [22]It has happened to them according to the true proverb,

"The dog turns back to its own vomit,"

and,

"The sow is washed only to wallow in the mud."

[p]Or *angels*; Gk *glories* [q]Other ancient authorities read *before the Lord*; others lack the phrase [r]Gk *in their destruction* [s]Other ancient authorities read *receiving* [t]Other ancient authorities read *love feasts* [u]Other ancient authorities read *Beor* [v]Other ancient authorities read *actually*

Scoffers Will Come

3 This is now, beloved, the second letter I am writing to
you; in them I am trying to arouse your sincere
intention by reminding you 2that you should remember the
words spoken in the past by the holy prophets, and the
commandment of the Lord and Savior spoken through your
apostles. 3First of all you must understand this, that in the
last days scoffers will come, scoffing and indulging their
own lusts 4and saying, "Where is the promise of his
coming? For ever since our ancestors died,[w] all things
continue as they were from the beginning of creation!"
5They deliberately ignore this fact, that by the word of God
heavens existed long ago and an earth was formed out of
water and by means of water, 6through which the world of
that time was deluged with water and perished. 7But by the
same word the present heavens and earth have been
reserved for fire, being kept until the day of judgment and
destruction of the godless.

A New View of Time

3:8 see pg. 848

8 But do not ignore this one fact,
beloved, that with the Lord one day is
like a thousand years, and a thousand years are like one
day. 9The Lord is not slow about his promise, as some think
of slowness, but is patient with you,[x] not wanting any to
perish, but all to come to repentance. 10But the day of the
Lord will come like a thief, and then the heavens will pass
away with a loud noise, and the elements will be dissolved
with fire, and the earth and everything that is done on it
will be disclosed.[y]

Pursue Holiness and Maturity

11 Since all these things are to be dissolved in this way,
what sort of persons ought you to be in leading lives of holiness and godliness, 12waiting for and hastening[z] the coming of the day of God, because of which the heavens will be
set ablaze and dissolved, and the elements will melt with
fire? 13But, in accordance with his promise, we wait for new
heavens and a new earth, where righteousness is at home.

14 Therefore, beloved, while you are waiting for these
things, strive to be found by him at peace, without spot or
blemish; 15and regard the patience of our Lord as salvation.
So also our beloved brother Paul wrote to you according
to the wisdom given him, 16speaking of this as he does
in all his letters. There are some things in them hard to

[w]Gk *our fathers fell asleep* [x]Other ancient authorities read *on your account* [y]Other ancient authorities read *will be burned up* [z]Or *earnestly desiring*

QUOTE UNQUOTE

CONSIDER THIS 2:13 *Many people who "revel in the daytime" (v. 13) do so because they are bored:*

Boredom is really a spiritual problem . . . . One way we try to avoid boredom is by owning and using material goods. We also try to escape boredom by pleasure without conscience.

Fr. Jerry Foley, "We Work at Our Leisure," *Connecting Faith and Life,* p. 25

understand, which the ignorant and unstable twist to their
own destruction, as they do the other scriptures. 17You
therefore, beloved, since you are forewarned, beware that
you are not carried away with the error of the lawless and
lose your own stability. 18But grow in the grace and knowledge of our Lord and Savior Jesus Christ. To him be the
glory both now and to the day of eternity. Amen.[a]

[a]Other ancient authorities lack *Amen*

Keeping the Big Picture

CONSIDER THIS 3:8 **Where were you ten years ago? Does it seem like a distant memory, or as if it were only yesterday? Does the here and now totally consume you, dominating your perspective? Where do you expect to be ten years from now?**

As Peter neared the end of his life, he wrote a letter in which he offers some insight into the nature of time and eternity. He beckons us to view time in both thousand-year units and as mere days (3:8), recalling the beginnings of creation (vv. 4–6). He also projects into the future, when judgment will be rendered and new heavens and earth will be home to those who fear God (vv. 10–13). Peter reminds us that God values a day as much as a thousand years, affirming the importance of the here and now (v. 8). But he also affirms God's activity long before we came on the scene (v. 9).

Peter's perspective challenges us to live with a view toward eternity and values that last—purity, holiness, and righteousness (vv. 11, 14). We need to avoid getting caught up in the here and now and losing sight of our eternal destiny. Neither the joys of today nor the problems of this week can quite compare with what God has prepared for us in eternity. Peter urges us to stick with the basics of the faith and resist the fleeting enticements offered in this present moment (vv. 17–18).

The First, Second, and Third Letters of

John

Oxford scholar C.S. Lewis once asked, "If you examined a hundred people who had lost their faith in Christianity, I wonder how many of them would turn out to have been reasoned out of it by honest argument? Do not most people simply drift away?" (*Mere Christianity*, p. 124).

Toward the end of the first century, some Christians began "drifting away" from the truth about Christ. They were losing touch with those who had known Jesus in the flesh as the founders of the church began to die off. They were also being seduced by competing doctrines, especially early forms of *gnosticism* (see 1 John 5:20). As a result, second- and third-generation believers began to grow cold in their love for each other and lukewarm in their commitment to the truth.

One response to this trend was the writing of 1, 2, and 3 John. These letters call Christians back to the basics—the truth about Christ and the love of Christ. For that reason, they are crucial for Christians today.

Back to the basics

C O N T E N T S

A R T I C L E S

Tough Love

John is often described as the "apostle of love" and 1, 2, and 3 John as the "love letters" of the New Testament. But these writings are far from mere sentimentalism. They're about "tough love," love that shoots straight, even if it hurts, because it cares for others and wishes them the best.

The tone of these letters has the feeling of an older believer pleading with a younger. Nine times in 1 John the writer addresses his readers as his "little children" and nine times among the three letters as "beloved." Likewise, he refers to himself as "the elder" (2 John 1, 3 John 1). His writing style is reflective and loosely structured, and he uses some of the simplest Greek in the New Testament.

One of the most notable features of 1 John in particular is the way in which the writer presents his material in formulaic expressions (for example 2:12–14; 5:6–8). These may be the beginnings of creedal statements and catechisms that package truth in a memorable way so as to lock it into the reader's thinking.

Such a strategy would be important in order to counter false teachers who denied Jesus' physical reality. Claiming to have special knowledge, they taught that God could not have become flesh. No wonder John opens his first letter with the powerful declaration that "what we have heard, what we have seen with our eyes, what we have looked at and touched with our hands, concerning the word of life . . . we declare to you what we have seen and heard" (1:1, 3). Here was a man—perhaps the last man in the early church—who had actually walked and talked with Jesus.

How does one discern genuine Christianity? John claims that there is a core truth to believe—that Jesus has come in the flesh—and that the practice of love and righteousness is the test of whether one truly believes in (and follows) that Jesus. His message is similar to Paul's word to the Ephesians that true spirituality involves "speaking the truth in love" (Eph. 4:15).

Two Short Letters with a Powerful Message

Perhaps because they are so brief, 2 and 3 John are often overlooked by Bible readers. Yet their message is crucial. Second John encourages believers to test ideas and spiritual claims against the litmus test of Christology: what do they say about Jesus? Deceivers are coming, the author warns, and God's people need to be on guard against deception. As believers today confront an onslaught of religious systems in a pluralistic society, John's warning remains extremely relevant.

Third John confronts disloyalty in the church. The hospitable and faithful Gaius contrasts with domineering Diotrephes, "who likes to put himself first" (v. 9). Diotrephes apparently felt no need of the apostles or their doctrine. Instead, he had become self-sufficient and, in fact, opposed to the church's leaders. John responds to this problem in an interesting way. He sets descriptions of Gaius and Diotrephes side by side and then simply encourages the rest of his readers to "imitate what is good" (v. 11). Apparently he felt confident that the group would know which man was worthy of imitation. ◆

Those who love God must love their brothers and sisters also.
—1 John 4:21

◆ ◆ ◆ ◆ ◆ ◆ ◆ ◆ ◆ ◆ ◆ ◆ ◆

BINARY FAITH

Modern-day computers are built on the principles of binary mathematics. A binary system breaks down choices into two and only two alternatives—on or off, plus or minus, yes or no. This simple convention has enabled technicians to develop powerful machines and programs to accomplish a variety of complex tasks.

John's writing is somewhat binary in that it treats matters of faith in either-or categories. In contrast to the moral relativism that characterizes much of modern life, John requires that we look at spiritual things in black and white categories. Notice some of the strong contrasts that he draws in 1 John:

THE CHOICES IN JOHN'S FIRST LETTER

Either...	Or...	Texts
Light	Darkness	1:5–7; 2:9–11
Truth	Deception	1:8–10
Keeping God's commandments	Not keeping God's commandments	2:3–6
A new commandment	The old commandment	2:7–8
We love God	We love the world	2:15–16
Christ	The antichrist	2:18, 22
Truth	Error	2:20–21; 4:1–3
Child of God	Child of the devil	3:1–10
Righteousness	Lawlessness	3:4–9
Life	Death	3:13–15; 5:11–12
Love	Hate	3:15–17; 4:20–21
Spirits confessing Christ	Spirits not confessing Christ	4:1–3
We are of God	We are not of God	4:4–11
Love	Fear	4:18–19

With Our Own Eyes

1:1–10

1 We declare to you what was from the
beginning, what we have heard,
what we have seen with our eyes, what we have looked at
and touched with our hands, concerning the word of life—
[2]this life was revealed, and we have seen it and testify to it,
and declare to you the eternal life that was with the Father
and was revealed to us— [3]we declare to you what we have
seen and heard so that you also may have fellowship with
us; and truly our fellowship is with the Father and with his
Son Jesus Christ. [4]We are writing these things so that our[a]
joy may be complete.

God's Offer and Our Response

5 This is the message we have heard from him and proclaim to you, that God is light and in him there is no darkness at all. [6]If we say that we have fellowship with him
while we are walking in darkness, we lie and do not do
what is true; [7]but if we walk in the light as he himself is in
the light, we have fellowship with one another, and the
blood of Jesus his Son cleanses us from all sin. [8]If we say
that we have no sin, we deceive ourselves, and the truth is
not in us. [9]If we confess our sins, he who is faithful and just
will forgive us our sins and cleanse us from all unrighteousness. [10]If we say that we have not sinned, we make him a
liar, and his word is not in us.

Dealing with Sin

2:1–2

2 My little children, I am writing these
things to you so that you may not
sin. But if anyone does sin, we have an advocate with the
Father, Jesus Christ the righteous; [2]and he is the atoning
sacrifice for our sins, and not for ours only but also for the
sins of the whole world.

Loving God and One Another

2:3–6 see pg. 854

3 Now by this we may be sure that we
know him, if we obey his command-
ments. [4]Whoever says, "I have come to know him," but

[a]Other ancient authorities read *your*

The Advocate

A CLOSER LOOK 2:1–2

As Christians we have an Advocate in Christ (v. 1). Not only is He our go-between with the Father when we do sin, but He also helps us avoid sin in the first place. Does that mean we should expect never to sin? See "Sinless Perfection?" 1 John 3:6.

Some Basics of Witness

CONSIDER THIS 1:1–10

A key verb in 1:2 is "testify." Some other versions of the Bible use the word "witness," a term that for many is a stereotyped "turnoff." But think of "testify" and "witness" in the context of a courtroom where a credible witness can mean the difference between life and death. *Everyday,* your testimony can make that difference for *all* who find you to be a credible witness.

What is expected of an effective witness for Christ? In this first chapter, John notes several basic elements of what it means to communicate Christ to others:

- **Our message grows out of our knowledge and experience of Christ (vv. 1–4).**
- **We make clear to others what we have heard from Christ (v. 5).**
- **We live out our faith on a continuous basis, thereby avoiding lives that contradict our message (vv. 6–7). "Walk" is a metaphor for living used often in the New Testament (for example, John 8:12; Rom. 4:12; Col. 3:7).**
- **When we fall short (as we all will, v. 10), we own up to it, avoiding deception about our walk or Christ's work (vv. 8–10).**

Truthfulness, clarity, consistency, and honesty should be basic qualities of an effective witness—and of all of Christ's followers. We should offer nothing less.

RULES THAT LEAD TO JOY

CONSIDER THIS 2:3–6 **Most parents expect obedience from their children as a sign of loyalty and trust. In a similar way, God expects His children to follow His commandments (vv. 4–5). In fact, when we obey God and act like Him, we show ourselves to be His (v. 6).**

We can be thankful that God has established rules and standards. Without such boundaries, we would not experience freedom but chaos. After all, we no longer inhabit Eden, but a broken world of sinners. We need moral safeguards that protect people's rights, delay gratification, enforce commitments, define relationships, ensure privacy, and demonstrate a respect for life.

Furthermore, we can be thankful that God is the One who has defined moral absolutes. Sinners could not be trusted to define goodness or justice.

God's original desire was for humans to have authority over all creation (Gen. 1:26–31). But sin and rebellion made us incapable of carrying out that responsibility (Gen. 3:22–24; Rom. 1:18–32). However, Christ has opened the way for us to re-establish our relationship with God and assume once again the responsibilities for which He created us:

- **He has provided for the forgiveness for our sins (John 3:16–19).**
- **He has provided renewal for all of our life (2 Cor. 5:16–21).**
- **He empowers us to carry out His work (Acts 1:6–8).**
- **He has established guidelines for proper conduct (1 John 2:7–17).**

When we follow God's commandments we experience true liberty. As His obedient children we can be fulfilled, fruitful, and joyful as we look forward to the promise of eternal life (v. 17).

does not obey his commandments, is a liar, and in such a
person the truth does not exist; 5but whoever obeys his
word, truly in this person the love of God has reached perfection. By this we may be sure that we are in him: 6who-
ever says, "I abide in him," ought to walk just as he walked.
7 Beloved, I am writing you no new commandment, but
an old commandment that you have had from the beginning; the old commandment is the word that you have
heard. 8Yet I am writing you a new commandment that is
true in him and in you, because[b] the darkness is passing
away and the true light is already shining. 9Whoever says,
"I am in the light," while hating a brother or sister,[c] is still
in the darkness. 10Whoever loves a brother or sister[d] lives in
the light, and in such a person[e] there is no cause for stumbling. 11But whoever hates another believer[f] is in the darkness, walks in the darkness, and does not know the way to
go, because the darkness has brought on blindness.

Three Stages of Faith

12 I am writing to you, little children,
because your sins are forgiven on account of his name.
13 I am writing to you, fathers,
because you know him who is from the beginning.
I am writing to you, young people,
because you have conquered the evil one.
14 I write to you, children,
because you know the Father.
I write to you, fathers,
because you know him who is from the beginning.
I write to you, young people,
because you are strong
and the word of God abides in you,
and you have overcome the evil one.

Do Not Love the World

15 Do not love the world or the things in the world. The
love of the Father is not in those who love the world; 16for
all that is in the world—the desire of the flesh, the desire of
the eyes, the pride in riches—comes not from the Father
but from the world. 17And the world and its desire[g] are
passing away, but those who do the will of God live forever.
18 Children, it is the last hour! As you have heard that
antichrist is coming, so now many antichrists have come.

[b] *Or that* [c] *Gk hating a brother* [d] *Gk loves a brother* [e] *Or in it* [f] *Gk hates a brother*
[g] *Or the desire for it*

From this we know that it is the last hour. 19They went out
from us, but they did not belong to us; for if they had belonged to us, they would have remained with us. But by going out they made it plain that none of them belongs to us.
20But you have been anointed by the Holy One, and all of
you have knowledge.[h] 21I write to you, not because you do
not know the truth, but because you know it, and you
know that no lie comes from the truth. 22Who is the liar
but the one who denies that Jesus is the Christ?[i] This is the
antichrist, the one who denies the Father and the Son. 23No
one who denies the Son has the Father; everyone who confesses the Son has the Father also. 24Let what you heard
from the beginning abide in you. If what you heard from
the beginning abides in you, then you will abide in the Son
2:25 and in the Father. 25And this is what he
has promised us,[j] eternal life.
26 I write these things to you concerning those who
would deceive you. 27As for you, the anointing that you received from him abides in you, and so you do not need
anyone to teach you. But as his anointing teaches you about
all things, and is true and is not a lie, and just as it has
taught you, abide in him.[k]
28 And now, little children, abide in him, so that when
he is revealed we may have confidence and not be put to
shame before him at his coming.

The Children of God

29 If you know that he is righteous, you may be sure
3 that everyone who does right has been born of him.
1See what love the Father has given us, that we should
be called children of God; and that is what we are. The reason the world does not know us is that it did not know
him. 2Beloved, we are God's children now; what we will be
has not yet been revealed. What we do know is this: when
he[k] is revealed, we will be like him, for we will see him as
he is. 3And all who have this hope in him purify themselves, just as he is pure.
4 Everyone who commits sin is guilty of lawlessness; sin
is lawlessness. 5You know that he was revealed to take away
3:6 see pg. 856 sins, and in him there is no sin. 6No one
who abides in him sins; no one who sins
has either seen him or known him. 7Little children, let no

[h]Other ancient authorities read *you know all things* [i]Or *the Messiah* [j]Other ancient authorities read *you* [k]Or *it*

Eternal Life

CONSIDER THIS 2:25 **From beauty creams to vitamins to aerobics, many people today are pursuing a "fountain of youth." They want to avoid growing old, perhaps because it leads to the final, ultimate reality, death. That reality is so painful to most people that they won't even consider it. They make little or no preparation for their death and its aftermath.**

John offers the one way that a person can actually do something about his or her death. He speaks of a revolutionary promise that God has made—we can have true life forever (vv. 24–25)! God makes that promise of eternal life for those who put their faith in Jesus Christ.

What would it mean for you to live in response to God's promise? Are you trusting in Christ for your eternal life? If not, why not do so now? If you already have, then tell someone else about God's promise today.

one deceive you. Everyone who does what is right is righteous, just as he is righteous. 8Everyone who commits sin is
a child of the devil; for the devil has been sinning from the
beginning. The Son of God was revealed for this purpose,
to destroy the works of the devil. 9Those who have been
born of God do not sin, because God's seed abides in
them;[l] they cannot sin, because they have been born of
God. 10The children of God and the children of the devil
are revealed in this way: all who do not do what is right are
not from God, nor are those who do not love their brothers
and sisters.[m]

Love Cares for Others' Needs

3:11–13

11 For this is the message you have
heard from the beginning, that we should
love one another. 12We must not be like Cain who was from
the evil one and murdered his brother. And why did he
murder him? Because his own deeds were evil and his
brother's righteous. 13Do not be astonished, brothers and
sisters,[n] that the world hates you. 14We know that we have
passed from death to life because we love one another.
Whoever does not love abides in death. 15All who hate a
brother or sister[m] are murderers, and you know that mur-

[l]Or *because the children of God abide in him* [m]Gk *his brother* [n]Gk *brothers*

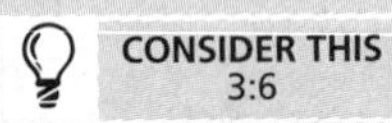

CONSIDER THIS
3:6

SINLESS PERFECTION?

Most followers of Christ would agree that they should pursue the highest moral integrity that they can. But John's statements in v. 6 appear to raise that standard to the point of sinless perfection. In fact, if no one who sins "has either seen [Christ] or known Him," then what hope is there for believers who fail?

Here is a case where the English language fails us. In English the word "sins" appears absolute and final: one sin and you're cut off from God. However, the form of the Greek verb here (hamartanei) *conveys a sense of continuous action: "No one who abides in Christ makes a habit of continually sinning." The point is that true believers diminish their old patterns of sin as they grow in Christ, replacing them with new patterns of faith and love.*

The situation is similar to losing weight by changing one's eating habits. No one obtains instant health, but over time and by sticking to a disciplined diet, one can make great strides in that direction.

3:16–21

derers do not have eternal life abiding in
them. 16We know love by this, that he
laid down his life for us—and we ought to lay down our
lives for one another. 17How does God's love abide in anyone who has the world's goods and sees a brother or sister[o]
in need and yet refuses help?
18 Little children, let us love, not in word or speech, but
in truth and action. 19And by this we will know that we are
from the truth and will reassure our hearts before him
20whenever our hearts condemn us; for God is greater than
our hearts, and he knows everything. 21Beloved, if our
hearts do not condemn us, we have boldness before God;
22and we receive from him whatever we ask, because we
obey his commandments and do what pleases him.
23 And this is his commandment, that we should believe in the name of his Son Jesus Christ and love one

[o]Gk *brother*

Take a Cardiogram

A CLOSER LOOK 3:16–21

John gives us a way to check the condition of our heart (v. 17). He indicates that one vital way to assess our spiritual health is by our reaction to the poor. Of course, anyone can "love" in the abstract. That's why John goes on to challenge us to express our love in practical terms. That's what Jesus did. See "Christ Became Poor," 2 Cor. 8:8–9.

Of course, the fact that we won't obtain sinless perfection in this life does not mean that we should deal lightly with sin. To do so would be an offense to God, as well as destructive to ourselves. Yes, God forgives individual sins, but if we persist in sinful patterns, we keep the power of Christ from operating in our lives. We also risk grave spiritual consequences, such as losing the ability to repent (Heb. 6:1–12).

Do you keep falling into a particular area of sin? John says that the way out of that frustrating predicament is to learn to continually "abide" in Christ. Confess your sins to Him and then concentrate not so much on avoiding sin as on maintaining your relationship with Him. After all, He has come to keep you from sin (1 John 2:1–2). But if you turn away from Him and capitulate to sin's mastery, then, as John has written, you can neither see Him working in your life nor know the joy of His presence. ◆

Murder on the Job

CONSIDER THIS 3:11–13

Why do mediocre workers often resent excellent workers? Why do people who lie to and steal from their employers and customers resent honest coworkers? Why does the person who cuts corners on the job feel ill-at-ease with someone who gives an honest day's work? Because the unrighteous hate the righteous, as John shows (vv. 11–13). They can't stand someone who has integrity. That person's honest lifestyle exposes their evil and wrongdoing, like a light that penetrates moral darkness.

The reference to Cain (v. 12) is sobering. Cain killed his brother, Abel, out of resentment (Gen. 4:3–8; Heb. 11:4). In the same way, a worker with a poor attitude and substandard work usually resents a coworker whose work ethic and performance are consistently higher. Like Cain, he may "murder" his nemesis in his mind and heart, simply by begrudging his conscientious efforts.

The warning is clear: Pay attention to feelings of resentment against coworkers who outperform you. Consider what happened to Cain!

another, just as he has commanded us. 24All who obey his
commandments abide in him, and he abides in them. And
by this we know that he abides in us, by the Spirit that he
has given us.

Discernment

4:1

4 Beloved, do not believe every spirit,
but test the spirits to see whether
they are from God; for many false prophets have gone out
into the world. 2By this you know the Spirit of God: every
spirit that confesses that Jesus Christ has come in the flesh
is from God, 3and every spirit that does not confess Jesus[p] is
not from God. And this is the spirit of the antichrist, of
which you have heard that it is coming; and now it is already in the world. 4Little children, you are from God, and
have conquered them; for the one who is in you is greater
than the one who is in the world. 5They are from the world;
therefore what they say is from the world, and the world
listens to them. 6We are from God. Whoever knows God
listens to us, and whoever is not from God does not listen

[p]Other ancient authorities read *does away with Jesus* (Gk *dissolves Jesus*)

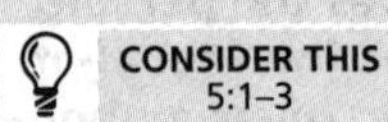

Love Is More than Enthusiasm

John has been called the apostle of love, and 1 John certainly offers plenty of evidence to show why. For example, he writes that one way to know that we are born of God is that we love Him and keep His commandments (v. 2).

But what does John mean by love? People say they "love" all kinds of things today. One minute they "love" peanut butter and in the next they "love" their spouse. Likewise, they "love" pets, food, sports, vacations, cars, children—whatever!

Thankfully, Scripture defines love for us by describing God's love, using both nouns and verbs. As we examine various passages, we find that God's love is:

- *Lasting (Ps. 136; Rom. 8:28–39; 1 Cor. 13:8).*
- *Sacrificial (John 15:12–13; Rom. 5:8; 2 Cor. 5:14–15; Gal. 2:20; 1 John 3:16–17).*
- *Reconciling and healing (Matt. 5:38–48; Luke 6:27–31; 2 Cor. 5:17–19).*
- *Mutual between Father, Son, and Holy Spirit (Matt. 11:27–30; John 14:31).*
- *Effective; it involves not just emotions or words, but deeds that benefit people (1 John 3:18–19; 4:21; 5:1–3).*

to us. From this we know the spirit of truth and the spirit of error.

Love Serves Others

7 Beloved, let us love one another, because love is from
God; everyone who loves is born of God and knows God.
8Whoever does not love does not know God, for God is
love. 9God's love was revealed among us in this way: God
sent his only Son into the world so that we might live
through him. 10In this is love, not that we loved God but
that he loved us and sent his Son to be the atoning sacrifice
for our sins. 11Beloved, since God loved us so much, we
also ought to love one another. 12No one has ever seen
God; if we love one another, God lives in us, and his love is
perfected in us.
13 By this we know that we abide in him and he in us,
because he has given us of his Spirit. 14And we have seen
and do testify that the Father has sent his Son as the Savior
of the world. 15God abides in those who confess that Jesus
is the Son of God, and they abide in God. 16So we have
known and believe the love that God has for us.

- *Fearless (Rom. 1:16; 1 John 4:18).*
- *Discerning (1 Tim. 1:3–7; 1 John 2:15–17; 4:1–7).*
- *Accepting, not condemning (Luke 15:11–32; 18:10–17; John 3:16–17; Rom. 8:1).*
- *Generous (Luke 10:25–37; Rom. 5:8, 15–17; 6:23; 1 Cor. 2:9; 1 Pet. 3:8–9).*

Perhaps the best summary of true, godly love is 1 Corinthians 13, "the love chapter," in which Paul describes the love of God as it needs to be among the believers at Corinth. Likewise, the ultimate expression of God's love is Christ, who offered Himself up for the sins of the world (John 3:16).

In what ways does your love need to develop? Have you grasped the dimensions of God's love for you? How can you cultivate Christlike love and make it more tangible in your life, work, and relationships? ◆

As noted, people use the word "love" to describe very different relationships today. But in the New Testament there are four distinct words for love, each with its own shade of meaning. Find out about them at "What Kind of Love Is This?" Matt. 22:34–40.

Tough-Minded Believers

CONSIDER THIS 4:1 **Christianity has rightly been characterized as a religion of love, but it's important not to take that emphasis to an unhealthy extreme. If, in the name of love, we uncritically accept every idea or value of others, we open ourselves up to error. God never asks us to put our brains in neutral when it comes to matters of faith.**

John repeatedly appeals for love (1 John 2:10; 3:3, 10–24; 4:7–12, 16–21), but he also places a premium on truth—not the wishy-washy opinions that pass for "truth" in our society, but the absolute, eternal truths of God's Word. For example, John challenges us to "test the spirits" (4:1) and learn to discern between truth and error (v. 6). He calls for us to avoid sin, which requires that we discern what is sinful (2:1; 3:4–10). He tells us to distinguish between the things of the world and the will of God (2:15–17), and he appeals for us to identify deceivers and avoid them (2:18–29; 3:7).

Paul echoes this appeal to be tough-minded when it comes to our faith. To be spiritual, he writes, means to be able to "discern" (or test) all things (1 Cor. 2:15). Likewise, we are to have the mind of Christ: tough in discernment, loving toward all, and fearless in the face of judgment (Phil. 2:5–11, 17–18).

Are you discerning on issues of faith and spirituality? If not, consider starting your own study of the Scriptures to understand what they say and mean, or perhaps enroll in a Bible class where you can learn more about God's truth in a systematic way.

God is love, and those who abide in love abide in God,
and God abides in them. 17Love has been perfected among
us in this: that we may have boldness on the day of judgment, because as he is, so are we in this world. 18There is
no fear in love, but perfect love casts out fear; for fear has
to do with punishment, and whoever fears has not reached
perfection in love. 19We love[q] because he first loved us.
20Those who say, "I love God," and hate their brothers or
sisters,[r] are liars; for those who do not love a brother or sister[s] whom they have seen, cannot love God whom they
have not seen. 21The commandment we have from him is

[q]Other ancient authorities add *him*; others add *God* [r]Gk *brothers* [s]Gk *brother*

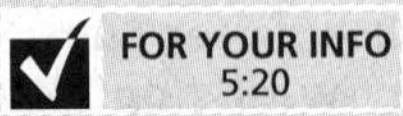

THE DANGER OF GNOSTICISM

One reason John was so concerned that his readers exercise discernment (1 John 4:1; 2 John 1–2, 4; 3 John 3–4) was that a system of false teachings known as gnosticism *was then becoming popular.*

The name gnosticism comes from the Greek word for knowledge, gnōsis. *The gnostics believed that a special knowledge about the nature of the world was the way to salvation. For that reason, several writers of the New Testament condemned early manifestations of the philosophy as false. Paul, for example, emphasized a wisdom and knowledge that comes from God as opposed to idle speculations and fables (Col. 2:8–23; 1 Tim. 1:4; 2 Tim. 2:16–19; Titus 1:10–16). Likewise John, both in his Gospel and the epistles, countered heretical teaching which, in a broad sense, could be considered gnostic.*

Roots in Greek Dualism

The gnostic teachers accepted the Greek idea of a radical dualism between God (spirit) and the world (matter). According to their worldview, the created order was evil, inferior, and opposed to the good. They believed that the earth is surrounded by a number of cosmic spheres which separate humans from God. These spheres are ruled by archōns *(spiritual powers) who guard their spheres by barring the souls of those who are seeking to ascend from the realm of darkness and captivity which is below to the realm of light which is above.*

The gnostics also taught that humans are composed of body, soul, and spirit. Since the body and soul are part of people's earthly existence, they were held to be evil. Enclosed in the soul, they said, is the spirit, the divine sub-

this: those who love God must love their brothers and sisters[t] also.

If You Love God, Obey Him

5:1–3
see pg. 858

5 Everyone who believes that Jesus is
the Christ[u] has been born of God,
and everyone who loves the parent loves the child. 2By this
we know that we love the children of God, when we love
God and obey his commandments. 3For the love of God is
this, that we obey his commandments. And his command-

5:4–5

ments are not burdensome, 4for whatever
is born of God conquers the world. And

[t]*Gk brothers* [u]*Or the Messiah*

stance of man. According to gnostic teaching, this spirit is asleep and ignorant, and needs to be awakened and liberated by knowledge. Thus the aim of salvation in gnosticism is to release the inner man from his earthly dungeon so that he can return to the realm of light where the soul is reunited with God.

These beliefs led to two extremes of ethical behavior. Some gnostics became ascetics, trying to separate themselves from matter in order to avoid contamination by evil. Paul may have been opposing such a view in 1 Timothy 4:1–5. Other gnostics felt that since they had received divine knowledge and were truly informed as to their divine nature, it didn't matter how they lived; they thought their "knowledge" gave them freedom to participate in all sorts of indulgences.

Impact on the Church

Gnostic teachings, when blended with Christian beliefs, created serious heresies. They also had a disruptive effect on fellowship within the church. Those who were "enlightened" thought of themselves as being superior to those who did not have such knowledge, and divisions arose. Again, the New Testament writers severely condemned this attitude of superiority. Christians are "one body," the apostles argued (1 Cor. 12) and should love one another (1 Cor. 13; 1 John 4). Whatever spiritual gifts God has given are for the entire Christian community, not just individual use. Moreover, they should promote humility rather than pride (1 Cor. 12–14; Eph. 4:11–16). ◆

QUOTE UNQUOTE

CONSIDER THIS 5:4–5 *Christians are not those who must leave the world in order to experience life, but those who "conquer the world" (vv. 4–5) through their relationship with Christ:*

When the gnostic escapes the world, it becomes very possible for him to be a christian [sic] ***on the side, even in his spare time. But the christian whose life has been transformed from aimless wandering to determined pilgrimage will find no respite. The christian and the cosmos are inextricably bound together until death do them part.***

Philip J. Lee, Jr., *Against the Protestant Gnostics*, pp. 25–26

this is the victory that conquers the world, our
faith. 5Who is it that conquers the world but the
one who believes that Jesus is the Son of God?

Certainty about Eternal Life

6 This is the one who came by water and blood,
Jesus Christ, not with the water only but with the
water and the blood. And the Spirit is the one that
testifies, for the Spirit is the truth. 7There are three
that testify:[v] 8the Spirit and the water and the
blood, and these three agree. 9If we receive human
testimony, the testimony of God is greater; for this
is the testimony of God that he has testified to his
Son. 10Those who believe in the Son of God have
the testimony in their hearts. Those who do not
believe in God[w] have made him a liar by not believing in the testimony that God has given concerning his Son. 11And this is the testimony: God
gave us eternal life, and this life is in his Son.
12Whoever has the Son has life; whoever does not
have the Son of God does not have life.

[v]A few other authorities read (with variations) *7There are three that testify in heaven, the Father, the Word, and the Holy Spirit, and these three are one. 8And there are three that testify on earth:* [w]Other ancient authorities read *in the Son*

Avoiding Sin

13 I write these things to you who believe in the
name of the Son of God, so that you may know
that you have eternal life.
14 And this is the boldness we have in him, that
if we ask anything according to his will, he hears
us. 15And if we know that he hears us in whatever
we ask, we know that we have obtained the requests made of him. 16If you see your brother or
sister[x] committing what is not a mortal sin, you
will ask, and God[y] will give life to such a one—to
those whose sin is not mortal. There is sin that is
mortal; I do not say that you should pray about
that. 17All wrongdoing is sin, but there is sin that is
not mortal.
18 We know that those who are born of God do
not sin, but the one who was born of God protects
them, and the evil one does not touch them. 19We
know that we are God's children, and that the
whole world lies under the power of the evil one.

5:20 see pg. 860

20And we know that the Son of
God has come and has given us
understanding so that we may know him who is
true;[z] and we are in him who is true, in his Son
Jesus Christ. He is the true God and eternal life.
21 Little children, keep yourselves from idols.[a]

[x]Gk *your brother* [y]Gk *he* [z]Other ancient authorities read *know the true God* [a]Other ancient authorities add *Amen*

The Second Letter of John

To the Elect Lady

1

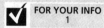

1 The elder to the elect lady and her
children, whom I love in the truth, and
not only I but also all who know the truth, 2because of the
truth that abides in us and will be with us forever:
3 Grace, mercy, and peace will be with us from God the
Father and from[a] Jesus Christ, the Father's Son, in truth and
love.

[a]Other ancient authorities add *the Lord*

THE ELECT LADY

FOR YOUR INFO 1 *The identity of the "elect lady" (v. 1) is unknown. Some believe that she was an individual woman, and that John chose to use this title instead of her personal name in order to protect her from persecution. Most scholars believe that the term is symbolic, referring to a specific church, perhaps the one at Ephesus.*

If, however, John was writing to a specific woman, she must have been a wise and loving mother as John's praise for her children attests (vv. 4–6). He warned her not to welcome those who spread false teaching (vv. 9–10). His closing remarks also hint that the "elect lady" and John shared a close friendship (vv. 12–13). If, on the other hand, John was referring to a church, the symbolism reflects his highest regard for women and for the nurturing care given by mothers.

Although most first-century cultures isolated and even discriminated against women, Christ invited women to follow Him. See "The Women around Jesus," John 19:25. Women also played an important role in the development of early church. See the table, "Women and the Growth of Christianity," Phil. 4:3.

HOSPITALITY AND DISCERNMENT

CONSIDER THIS 7–11 **We live in a day in which any and everything is tolerated. No matter how outlandish or how strenuously we disagree with what others cherish or embrace, we accept their right to their opinion. There seems to be no basis for saying "no" anymore. Ours is an age of "I'm okay, you're okay."**

But that is just not true. It would be more honest to affirm, "I'm *not* okay and you're *not* okay. We both need help that we can count on."

The early church faced a similar predicament. After Jesus' death and resurrection, many claimed to know Him and His message, even though their versions of the story differed remarkably. For instance, Paul faced a conflicting gospel in Galatia and at Philippi and vehemently challenged his opponents' claims (Gal. 1:6–9; Phil. 3:1–4). Likewise, John warned against those who distort the truth (1 John 2:18–29; 4:1–6; 3 John 9–11).

The recipient of 2 John, possibly a woman (v. 1), was given to hospitality (v. 10)—a wonderfully Christlike virtue. But John was concerned to help her become more discerning and not lend the reputation of her household to those who would distort the truth about Christ (vv. 7, 11). He knew that not all who claim Christ are true followers. So believers must develop discernment if they are to remain loyal to truth.

Do you know the basics of what the Bible teaches? Can you detect error in the statements of others? When you do, do you know how to lovingly disagree on major issues of faith and truth?

Joy Over Truth and Love

4 I was overjoyed to find some of your children
walking in the truth, just as we have been commanded by the Father. 5But now, dear lady, I ask
you, not as though I were writing you a new commandment, but one we have had from the beginning, let us love one another. 6And this is love, that
we walk according to his commandments; this is
the commandment just as you have heard it from
the beginning—you must walk in it.

Watch Out for False Teachers

7–11 see pg. 863

7 Many deceivers have gone
out into the world, those who
do not confess that Jesus Christ has come in the
flesh; any such person is the deceiver and the
antichrist! 8Be on your guard, so that you do not
lose what we[b] have worked for, but may receive a
full reward. 9Everyone who does not abide in the
teaching of Christ, but goes beyond it, does not
have God; whoever abides in the teaching has both
the Father and the Son. 10Do not receive into the
house or welcome anyone who comes to you and
does not bring this teaching; 11for to welcome is to
participate in the evil deeds of such a person.

John Plans to Visit in Person

12 Although I have much to write to you, I
would rather not use paper and ink; instead I hope
to come to you and talk with you face to face, so
that our joy may be complete.
13 The children of your elect sister send you
their greetings.[c]

[b]Other ancient authorities read *you* [c]Other ancient authorities add *Amen*

The Third Letter of John

A Greeting

1 The elder to the beloved Gaius, whom I love in truth.

Encouragement for Gaius

2

2 Beloved, I pray that all may go well
with you and that you may be in good
health, just as it is well with your soul. 3I was overjoyed
when some of the friends[a] arrived and testified to your
faithfulness to the truth, namely how you walk in the truth.
4I have no greater joy than this, to hear that my children are
walking in the truth.
5 Beloved, you do faithfully whatever you do for the
friends,[a] even though they are strangers to you; 6they have
testified to your love before the church. You will do well to
send them on in a manner worthy of God; 7for they began
their journey for the sake of Christ,[b] accepting no support
from non-believers.[c] 8Therefore we ought to support such
people, so that we may become co-workers with the truth.

Disappointing Diotrephes

9–11
see pg. 866

9 I have written something to the
church; but Diotrephes, who likes to put
himself first, does not acknowledge our authority. 10So if I
come, I will call attention to what he is doing in spreading
false charges against us. And not content with those
charges, he refuses to welcome the friends,[a] and even prevents
those who want to do so and expels them from the church.

The Testimony of Demetrius

11 Beloved, do not imitate what is evil but imitate what
is good. Whoever does good is from God; whoever does
evil has not seen God. 12Everyone has testified favorably
about Demetrius, and so has the truth itself. We also testify
for him,[d] and you know that our testimony is true.

John Will Come in Person

13 I have much to write to you, but I would rather not
write with pen and ink; 14instead I hope to see you soon,
and we will talk together face to face.
15 Peace to you. The friends send you their greetings.
Greet the friends there, each by name.

[a]*Gk brothers* [b]*Gk for the sake of the name* [c]*Gk the Gentiles* [d]*Gk lacks for him*

Prosperity

CONSIDER THIS 2 **John's greeting (v. 2) raises an important issue. It is clear that he expects God to give physical and material well-being to Gaius. Is that what believers today should be asking God for? Should we expect God to prosper us physically and financially? Is this verse an indication that He will? Notice three important things:**

(1) John is praying for Gaius' prosperity, not Gaius praying for his own prosperity.

(2) This is part of a formal greeting or blessing. We say very similar things today like, "Good luck," or "Have a good day," or "Stay healthy, kid."

(3) The Greek word here for *prosper* means "to travel well on a journey." That fits with its use in a blessing. Furthermore, it is not something one should actively pursue, but rather a gift that one should look for, a sense of "wholeness" like the Old Testament concept of *shalom* that people enjoy when they follow God's precepts and live in His power.

(4) We don't know what Gaius' circumstances may have been, only that his soul was prospering. John may be saying, "You are doing so well in the faith; I wish you were doing as well in your health and the rest of your life."

(5) John's main concern is that Gaius would walk in the truth (vv. 3–4), not that he would have a big bank account or be in tip-top shape.

Overall, it would be foolish to construct a general principle of material blessing from this verse, especially when so many other passages warn against that very thing.

Paul describes those who teach that God rewards godliness with material blessing as being "destitute of the truth." See "The Dangers of Prosperity Theology," 1 Tim. 6:3–6.

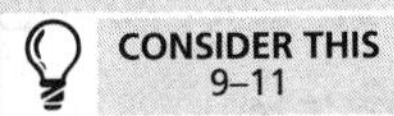

A Study in Contrasts of Faith

What traits does Christ desire in a faithful follower? How does godliness reveal itself? What are the differences between a good representative of the faith and a bad one?

In 3 John, John contrasts two men, Gaius and Diotrephes. Notice the patterns of each one:

A Good Example and a Bad One
Gaius (vv. 1–8)
•Attended to things that made for a godly inner spiritual life (v. 2).
•Was well regarded by other believers for his life and activities (v. 3).
•Made truth central to his communication (vv. 3–4).
•Showed hospitality to believers and others (vv. 5–6).
•Showed generosity to traveling gospel workers, freeing them from dependence on outside sources (v. 7).
•Did not aspire to fame or an exalted position in the fellowship, in contrast to others (v. 9).
Diotrephes (vv. 9–10)
•Loved prominence (v. 9).
•Did not welcome John's communication (v. 9).
•Demeaned John's reputation with malicious information (v. 10).
•Was not hospitable to other believers (v. 10).
•Hindered others in the congregation in their desire to be hospitable (v. 10).
•Expelled believers who resisted his activities (v. 10).

As always, the true test of the integrity of one's faith is whether one's actions are befitting to a follower of Christ. It's easy to talk about religious things, but words are of little value unless they translate into works that benefit others and bring glory to God (compare Matt. 7:21–29; Titus 1:16; 2:7–8; 3:8–11; James 1:19–27; 2:14–26).

Whom are you more like—Gaius or Diotrephes? What could people point to in your life that gives evidence of a faith that benefits others and honors Christ? ◆

Suppose you were on trial as Jesus was. What would be some of the best evidence against you, that you were "guilty" of following Christ? Would there be anything conclusive? Consider the checklist at "Is There Enough Evidence to Convict You?" Mark 14:53–64.

John's juxtaposition of Gaius and Diotrephes is another example of his use of strong contrasts to describe matters of faith. See the table, "Binary Faith," at the Introduction to 1 John.

The Letter of

Jude

An exposé of false teachers.

One of the most popular forms of journalism today is the exposé, the report that unmasks pretenders and brings to light the carefully concealed misdeeds of individuals and institutions. The exposé appeals to people's desire for the truth to be told and for wrongdoers to be subjected to public scrutiny. Such stories carry an implicit warning to others: "You may decide to do wrong, but sooner or later you're going to be found out."

The book of Jude is the New Testament's exposé of false teachers in the body of Christ. Using graphic word pictures and recalling a rogue's gallery of deceivers from the Old Testament, Jude documents a history of subversive forces that threatened to destroy Israel and threatened to destroy the early church. Watch out, the letter warns, because "certain intruders have stolen in among you . . . who pervert the grace of our God into licentiousness and deny our only Master and Lord, Jesus Christ" (Jude 4). By blowing the whistle on such impostors, Jude makes sure that they will no longer be unnoticed.

The author doesn't give us advice on how to do away with false teachers. He merely urges us to guard ourselves by building ourselves up in the faith (vv. 20–21). The best protection against deception is a mature grasp of God's revealed truth.

Contend Earnestly for the Faith

No one knows exactly when Jude was written, but it was apparently late enough in the first century, or even early enough in the second, for Jude to tell his readers, "remember the predictions of the apostles of our Lord Jesus Christ" (v. 17). By the time he wrote, faith had become *the* faith "once for all entrusted to the saints" (v. 3), suggesting a formal and even codified body of belief and practice. That spiritual treasure was under attack, so Jude urged believers to "contend for the faith" (v. 3).

However, the battle was not with outsiders, such as the Jewish council, the Roman government, or the many esoteric philosophies and mystery religions of the day. Instead, the danger came from within. Curiously, Jude never named names, except from the Old Testament: sinful Israel (v. 5; Num. 14:22–23), rebellious angels (v. 6), Sodom and Gomorrah (v. 7; Gen. 19:24–25), Cain (v. 11; Gen. 4:3–8), Balaam (v. 11; Num. 22–24), and Korah (v. 11; Num. 16:19–35).

For Jude's readers, who were probably Jewish Christians, these references were virtual code names for subversion and rebellion against God. They were as well known a warning then as a skull and crossbones marking poison are today. Jude was warning his readers that like those who had caused so much evil for the ancient Hebrews, mockers and false teachers were now infiltrating the church, poisoning it with error. However, the author avoided naming names, perhaps because his readers might have faced reprisals if he did so.

At any rate, the oblique way in which Jude makes these references is an ironic return to Judas Iscariot. The danger is inside the camp, Jude warned, but you don't always know who it is. And just like the disciples at the last supper, the readers of Jude would be asking, "Which of us is it?" (Matt. 26:20–22; John 13:25).

Little has changed in the two thousand years since Jude was written. Believers still need to be on their guard against doctrinal error and persuasive teachers who lead people away from the truth about Jesus. In reading this letter, we are reminded that Christianity is no game. The Old Testament rebels mentioned in Jude came to very bad ends. So will today's false teachers and those who follow them. Jude is a very sobering book. It warns us in stark terms not to play with sin. ◆

The Faithful Judas

Jude is an English form of the name Judas—an infamous name among believers both then and now because of Judas Iscariot, whom the New Testament never mentions without reminding the reader that it was Judas Iscariot who betrayed Jesus to the Jewish leaders (for example, Matt. 10:4; Mark 3:19; John 12:4).

In contrast to Judas Iscariot, the author of Jude was a devoted defender of the Lord and the faith. We know little about the man, except that he called himself "a servant of Jesus Christ and brother of James" (Jude 1).

Whoever this man was, he was very familiar with the Old Testament and with apocryphal books that dated from the intertestamental period. These books, written during a time of political turmoil in the history of the Jewish people, from about 200 B.C. to about A.D. 100, did not meet the requirements of being written in Hebrew during the time of the prophets, and so were excluded from the Hebrew Scriptures.

However, they were quite popular at the time of Christ, and Jesus and Jude probably read them in their youth. In fact, Jude may have used some of these writings in putting together his letter. For example, Jude 14 may be a reference to the apocryphal Book of Enoch 1:9. ◆

Jude

A Bondservant of Jesus

1 Jude,[a] a servant[b] of Jesus Christ and brother of James,
To those who are called, who are beloved[c] in[d] God the
Father and kept safe for[d] Jesus Christ:
2 May mercy, peace, and love be yours in abundance.

Contend for the Faith

3 Beloved, while eagerly preparing to write to you about
the salvation we share, I find it necessary to write and appeal to you to contend for the faith that was once for all entrusted to the saints. 4For certain intruders have stolen in
among you, people who long ago were designated for this
condemnation as ungodly, who pervert the grace of our
God into licentiousness and deny our only Master and
Lord, Jesus Christ.[e]

Examples from History

5 Now I desire to remind you, though you are fully informed, that the Lord, who once for all saved[f] a people out
of the land of Egypt, afterward destroyed those who did not
6–13 believe. 6And the angels who did not
keep their own position, but left their
proper dwelling, he has kept in eternal chains in deepest
darkness for the judgment of the great Day. 7Likewise,
Sodom and Gomorrah and the surrounding cities, which,
in the same manner as they, indulged in sexual immorality
and pursued unnatural lust,[g] serve as an example by undergoing a punishment of eternal fire.

False Teachers Described and Condemned

8–16 see pg. 870 8 Yet in the same way these dreamers
also defile the flesh, reject authority, and
slander the glorious ones.[h] 9But when the archangel
Michael contended with the devil and disputed about the
body of Moses, he did not dare to bring a condemnation of
slander[i] against him, but said, "The Lord rebuke you!" 10But
these people slander whatever they do not understand, and
they are destroyed by those things that, like irrational animals, they know by instinct. 11Woe to them! For they go
the way of Cain, and abandon themselves to Balaam's error
for the sake of gain, and perish in Korah's rebellion. 12These
are blemishes[j] on your love-feasts, while they feast with you
without fear, feeding themselves.[k] They are waterless clouds
carried along by the winds; autumn trees without fruit,
twice dead, uprooted; 13wild waves of the sea, casting up

THE POWER BEHIND PORN

CONSIDER THIS 6–13 *Pornography exposes more than skin. Jude connects the illicit sex in Sodom and Gomorrah (v. 7) with demonic powers (v. 6; see "Who Is the Enemy?" Eph. 6:10–13). The real evil behind porn is not that it is so shameful or unfulfilling, though it is, like "clouds without water" (vv. 12–13). Nor is the evil that the peddling of raw sex and lustful pleasure makes someone else rich, though it does (v. 11). Jude hints at the real sources of power and profit behind the porn market: demonic evil that traffics in human sex.*

[a]Gk *Judas* [b]Gk *slave* [c]Other ancient authorities read *sanctified* [d]Or *by* [e]Or *the only Master and our Lord Jesus Christ* [f]Other ancient authorities read *though you were once for all fully informed, that Jesus* (or *Joshua*) *who saved* [g]Gk *went after other flesh* [h]Or *angels;* Gk *glories* [i]Or *condemnation for blasphemy* [j]Or *reefs* [k]Or *without fear. They are shepherds who care only for themselves*

the foam of their own shame; wandering stars, for whom
the deepest darkness has been reserved forever.
14 It was also about these that Enoch, in the seventh
generation from Adam, prophesied, saying, "See, the Lord
is coming[l] with ten thousands of his holy ones, 15to execute
judgment on all, and to convict everyone of all the deeds of
ungodliness that they have committed in such an ungodly
way, and of all the harsh things that ungodly sinners have
spoken against him." 16These are grumblers and malcon-
tents; they indulge their own lusts; they are bombastic in
speech, flattering people to their own advantage.

Stay in the Love of God

17 But you, beloved, must remember the predictions of
the apostles of our Lord Jesus Christ; 18for they said to you,
"In the last time there will be scoffers, indulging their own
ungodly lusts." 19It is these worldly people, devoid of the
Spirit, who are causing divisions. 20But you, beloved, build

[l] Gk *came*

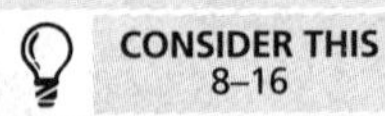

CONSIDER THIS
8–16

Sad Fallouts Are Inevitable

In today's age of acceptance and tolerance, it is not easy or popular to disagree with others. It seems that the one truth everyone must bow to is that everybody has the right to their own beliefs, and what's true for one may not be true for another. To suggest that someone else could be wrong, or worse, to claim that there is such a thing as ultimate, absolute truth, is highly offensive in our culture.

But how can everything be true? That seems to be a contradiction in logic, if we agree with Webster that truth can be defined as fact, the state of something being the case, or as actuality, the body of real things, events, or facts. Jesus claimed to be the *truth, not just* a *truth (John 14:6). He regularly spoke of telling the truth to his listeners (for example, Matt. 5:18, 26; Mark 10:15, 29; Luke 21:3, 32; John 3:3–11; 16:7–23). So what God communicated through Christ is extraordinarily important and must not be compromised.*

But as Jude demonstrates, not all who begin to follow God's truth finish well:

- *When Israel fled from Egypt, some disbelieved—and died (v. 5; Num. 14:26–45).*

yourselves up on your most holy faith; pray in the Holy
Spirit; [21]keep yourselves in the love of God; look forward to
the mercy of our Lord Jesus Christ that leads to[m] eternal
life. [22]And have mercy on some who are wavering; [23]save
others by snatching them out of the fire; and have mercy on
still others with fear, hating even the tunic defiled by their
bodies.[n]

A Doxology

24 Now to him who is able to keep you from falling, and
to make you stand without blemish in the presence of his
glory with rejoicing, [25]to the only God our Savior, through
Jesus Christ our Lord, be glory, majesty, power, and authority, before all time and now and forever. Amen.

[m]Gk *Christ to* [n]Gk *by the flesh*. The Greek text of verses 22-23 is uncertain at several points

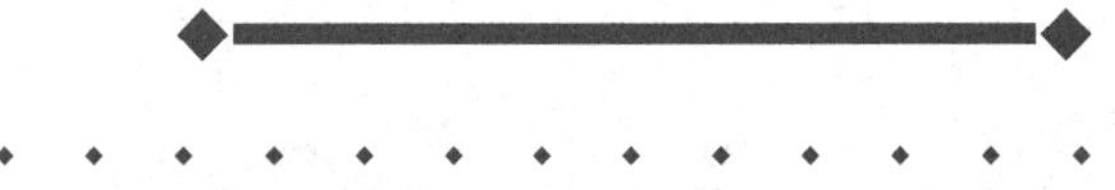

- *Some angels turned away from God and were banished from their positions (v. 6; Matt. 25:41; 2 Pet. 2:4).*
- *Sodom and Gomorrah stand as evidence that sin can bring about destruction (v. 7; Gen. 13:10—19:28).*
- *Cain chose selfishness, greed, hatred and murder (v. 11; Gen. 4:3–8).*
- *Balaam gave in to error and lost his clarity regarding the truth of God (v. 11; Num. 22–24; 2 Pet. 2:15–16).*
- *Korah mistakenly opposed God's leaders and paid for it dearly (v. 11; Num. 16).*

God's people are not called to be bigots who flaunt their connection with the truth. But we are called to be loyal to the truth of Christ, and we should challenge people to avoid anything less than what God offers (Jude 17–23). We're not to be a "truth squad," inflated with our own importance. But neither are we to be spiritual wimps who will agree to anything for the sake of peace. No, we must proclaim God's truth with mercy (v. 22) to those who will perish without it (v. 23). ◆

"IN THE LAST TIME THERE WILL BE SCOFFERS. . . ." —Jude 18

Christ the Lord of History

At the end of the twentieth century, the nations of the world seem to be emerging from under the ominous threat of nuclear holocaust. Yet even as an era of safety seems to be at hand, many warn of new possibilities for global catastrophe through widespread destruction of the world's ecology. In both cases, disaster on a scale described as "apocalyptic" has been forecast—the end of the world as we know it.

How will history end? That is the theme of this last book in the New Testament. Originally known as the *Apocalypse,* which means the "unveiling" or "disclosure" of things known only to God, the book pulls the curtain back to reveal the end of the world. What we find is a dramatic tale told in highly symbolic language. Nevertheless, its ultimate point is easily grasped: Christ will emerge as the Lord of history. The world will change—indeed, it will be made new—but Jesus remains "the Alpha and the Omega . . . who is and who was and who is to come, the Almighty" (Rev. 1:8).

The Revelation to John

Jesus remains "the Alpha and the Omega . . . the Almighty."

C O N T E N T S

A R T I C L E S

Will Evil Ever Get Its Reward? (20:1–5)

Sometimes it seems like fairness never happens in matters of business, government, the law, and world affairs. But God will not turn His back on injustice. Scripture promises that He will deal with evil in absolute, final ways.

There's a Welcome Here (22:17)

Revelation closes with a powerful invitation from Jesus to join Him in an exciting journey that leads to eternal life!

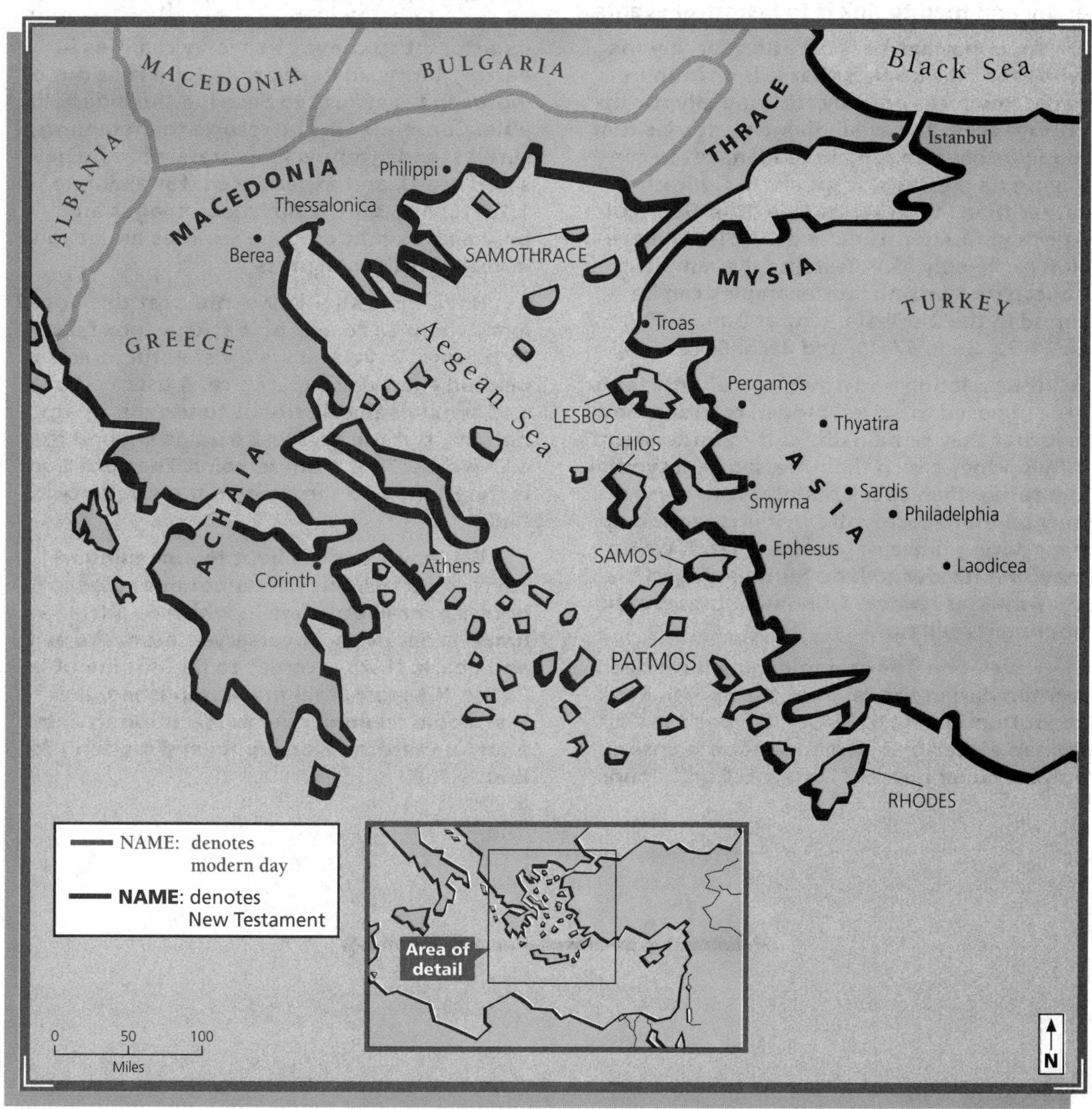

THE AEGEAN SEA AND SURROUNDING REGIONS

John's Vision—Mystery, Not Magic

Revelation has been perhaps the most debated book in the Bible. Throughout history people have offered various interpretations to try to explain its meaning. Some have seen it as allegorical. Others have taken it more literally and tried to link it to historical events.

An important consideration for anyone who reads the book is that it is written in a genre known as *apocalyptic*. Apocalyptic literature seeks to reveal divine mysteries that would otherwise remain hidden. Yet in conveying its message, it speaks in figurative rather than literal terms (see "The Genre of Apocalyptic Literature," Rev. 10:1–10). Revelation is the only New Testament example of apocalyptic writing, but examples can be found in the Old Testament at Dan. 7–12, Is. 24–27, Ezek. 37–41, and Zech. 9–12.

If Revelation and other apocalyptic texts are supposed to unveil hidden realities, how is it that they remain difficult to understand? Why do they couch their messages in symbolism rather than speak plainly? One reason may be that apocalyptic writings tend to appear during times of great danger. A writer may find it safer to hide his meaning in images that his readers will understand but his opponents will not.

Revelation, for example, may have been written during the reign of the Roman Emperor Domitian (A.D. 81–96). He was the first Roman emperor to demand that the entire empire honor him as "Lord and God." John, who had been exiled to the island of Patmos under Domitian (see Rev. 1:9), may have been warning first-century believers not to give in to the emperor's wishes (compare 22:8–9). The apostle's images of "Babylon the great, mother of whores" and of a seven-headed beast that lives on seven mountains (17:1–11) are commonly taken to be a veiled reference to Rome.

However, in addition to the danger of the times, another reason for the mystical nature of apocalyptic literature may have to do with its attempt to convey heavenly realities in earthly terms. In Revelation, John runs out of words in his efforts to describe the indescribable. Consequently, he resorts to metaphors, similes, and symbols to express what he has seen, heard, and experienced (for example, 1:13–16; 4:1, 3, 6–7). But these images are only approximations; the realities are beyond human words to express.

How, then, should we interpret this book? First, we need to accept it as true, not false. To be sure, Revelation is a vision that takes us beyond everyday experience. It uses codes and symbols that invite us to use our imaginations, but the greatest truth is beyond literal words. That truth remains: The Lord God is the Alpha and the Omega, the Almighty (1:8).

We may wonder about the meaning of specific details, but we cannot miss the book's overall outcome in which God triumphs over every adversary—Satan, sin, evil, and death. History comes to its fulfillment in Christ. His eternal reign is established, and His people triumph over persecution to enter a joyful eternity, worshiping and working for Him. ◆

Greetings to All

1 The revelation of Jesus Christ, which God gave him to
show his servants[a] what must soon take place; he
made[b] it known by sending his angel to his servant[c] John,
2who testified to the word of God and to the testimony of
Jesus Christ, even to all that he saw.
3 Blessed is the one who reads aloud the words of the
prophecy, and blessed are those who hear and who keep
what is written in it; for the time is near.

4 John to the seven churches that are in Asia:
Grace to you and peace from him who is and who was
and who is to come, and from the seven spirits who are before his throne, 5and from Jesus Christ, the faithful witness,
the firstborn of the dead, and the ruler of the kings of the
earth.
To him who loves us and freed[d] us from our sins by his
blood, 6and made[b] us to be a kingdom, priests serving[e] his
God and Father, to him be glory and dominion forever and
ever. Amen.

7 Look! He is coming with the clouds;
every eye will see him,
even those who pierced him;
and on his account all the tribes of the earth will wail.
So it is to be. Amen.

8 "I am the Alpha and the Omega," says the Lord God,
who is and who was and who is to come, the Almighty.

John Sees a Vision of Jesus

1:9 see pg. 880

9 I, John, your brother who share
with you in Jesus the persecution and
the kingdom and the patient endurance, was on the island
called Patmos because of the word of God and the testi-

1:10 see pg. 878

mony of Jesus.[f] 10I was in the spirit[g] on
the Lord's day, and I heard behind me a
loud voice like a trumpet 11saying, "Write in a book what
you see and send it to the seven churches, to Ephesus, to
Smyrna, to Pergamum, to Thyatira, to Sardis, to Philadelphia, and to Laodicea."
12 Then I turned to see whose voice it was that spoke to
me, and on turning I saw seven golden lampstands, 13and
in the midst of the lampstands I saw one like the Son of
Man, clothed with a long robe and with a golden sash

[a]Gk *slaves* [b]Gk *and he made* [c]Gk *slave* [d]Other ancient authorities read *washed* [e]Gk *priests to* [f]Or *testimony to Jesus* [g]Or *in the Spirit*

HE IS COMING WITH THE CLOUDS; EVERY EYE WILL SEE HIM. . . .
—Revelation 1:7

across his chest. [14]His head and his hair were white as
white wool, white as snow; his eyes were like a flame of
fire, [15]his feet were like burnished bronze, refined as in a
furnace, and his voice was like the sound of many waters.
[16]In his right hand he held seven stars, and from his mouth
came a sharp, two-edged sword, and his face was like the
sun shining with full force.

17 When I saw him, I fell at his feet as though dead. But
he placed his right hand on me, saying, "Do not be afraid; I
am the first and the last, [18]and the living one. I was dead,
and see, I am alive forever and ever; and I have the keys of
Death and of Hades. [19]Now write what you have seen, what
is, and what is to take place after this.
[20]As for the mystery of the seven stars
that you saw in my right hand, and the seven golden lampstands: the seven stars are the angels of the seven churches,
and the seven lampstands are the seven churches.

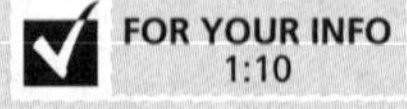
1:20
see pg. 880

Ephesus Has Left Her First Love

2 "To the angel of the church in Ephesus write: These are
the words of him who holds the seven stars in his right
hand, who walks among the seven golden lampstands:

FOR YOUR INFO
1:10

THE LORD'S DAY

John's reference to the Lord's Day (v. 10), generally regarded as referring to Sunday, suggests that to first-century Christians the first day of the week was particularly significant. That raises the question of whether Sundays are special today.

We know that the early church gave special honor to Sunday, the first day of the week, as the day on which Jesus was raised from the dead. Every week on that day they celebrated His resurrection and met for worship and instruction (1 Cor. 16:2). This observance of a special day was both a parallel and a contrast to the Jewish Sabbath, or day of rest, at the end of the week. The Sabbath celebrated God's rest from creation (see "The Sabbath," Heb. 4:1–13).

Some Jewish Christians continued to observe the Sabbath, as well as the Jewish festival days. But many Gentiles in the church did not. Apparently this created tension, especially when the observance of Jewish practices began to be linked by some to salvation. A council of church leaders at Jerusalem did not include a demand for Sabbath obser-

2 "I know your works, your toil and your patient endurance. I know that you cannot tolerate evildoers; you
have tested those who claim to be apostles but are not, and
have found them to be false. 3I also know that you are enduring patiently and bearing up for the sake of my name,
and that you have not grown weary. 4But I have this against
you, that you have abandoned the love you had at first.
5Remember then from what you have fallen; repent, and do
the works you did at first. If not, I will come to you and remove your lampstand from its place, unless you repent.
6Yet this is to your credit: you hate the works of the Nicolaitans, which I also hate. 7Let anyone who has an ear listen
to what the Spirit is saying to the churches. To everyone
who conquers, I will give permission to eat from the tree of
life that is in the paradise of God.

Smyrna Is Suffering

8 "And to the angel of the church in Smyrna write:
These are the words of the first and the last, who was dead
and came to life:

9 "I know your affliction and your poverty, even though
you are rich. I know the slander on the part of those who
say that they are Jews and are not, but are a synagogue of

(Bible text continued on page 881)

LISTEN TO WHAT THE SPIRIT IS SAYING TO THE CHURCHES.
—Revelation 2:7

vance in its decision regarding Gentile converts (Acts 15:20, 28–29).

Likewise, in writing to the Romans, Paul urged everyone to decide for themselves whether one day should be esteemed above another; but by all means, no one should judge another for his convictions (see "Matters of Conscience," Rom. 14:1–23; compare Gal. 4:10; Col. 2:16–17).

It's interesting that the phrase "the Lord's day" occurs only this one time in Rev. 1:10. In Asia Minor, where the churches to which John was writing were located, people celebrated the first day of each month as the Emperor's Day. Some believe that a day of the week was also called by this name. Thus, by calling the first day of the week the Lord's Day, John may have been making a direct challenge to emperor worship, as he does elsewhere in the book. ◆

PATMOS

YOU ARE THERE 1:9

- A small rocky island in the Aegean Sea off the southwest coast of Asia Minor.
- Site of John's exile under Emperor Domitian (A.D. 81–96) and the place where he wrote the book of Revelation. Because of its desolate and barren nature, Patmos was used by the Romans to banish criminals. Prisoners were forced to work at hard labor in the mines and quarries of the island.

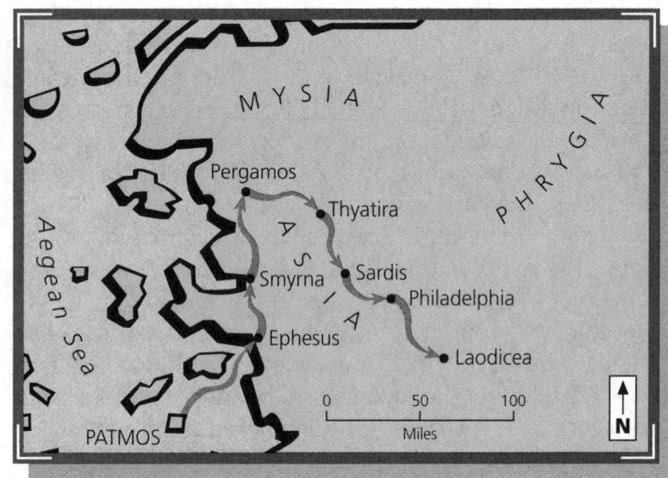

FROM PATMOS TO THE SEVEN CHURCHES

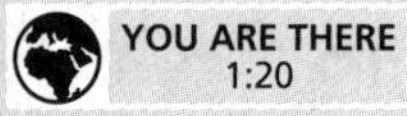

YOU ARE THERE 1:20

THE CHURCH AT THE END OF THE FIRST CENTURY

First-century believers faced stiff opposition from political authorities determined to stop the spread of their message. Nevertheless, despite increasingly harsh treatment, they were able to go a long way toward fulfilling the Lord's mandate to take the gospel "to the ends of the earth" (Acts 1:8). In fact, within about three decades they had won converts throughout the Roman Empire, including the capital, Rome itself.

One reason for these spectacular results was a concentration on reaching cities (see "Paul's Urban Strategy," Acts 16:4). In Ephesus, for example, Christian leaders influenced strategic groups of workers who not only turned the city upside down with their new faith, but took the gospel inland so that "all the residents of Asia . . . heard the word of the Lord" (Acts 19:10; see "The Ephesus Approach," Acts 19:8–41).

In Revelation, John writes letters from the Lord to some of the churches that were probably established through the Ephesus initiative (see the table, "Seven Churches to Study," Rev. 3:1). The seven mentioned were provincial capitals in what is now Turkey. A courier would have taken a circular route to deliver the epistles to the seven cities, which in turn would have served as distribution points to other churches in the region.

By the time John wrote to these churches, Christians were probably facing intense persecution under Emperor Domitian (A.D. 81–96). He extended the practice of emperor worship to demand that all citizens in the empire re-

Satan. 10Do not fear what you are about to suffer. Beware,
the devil is about to throw some of you into prison so that
you may be tested, and for ten days you will have affliction.
Be faithful until death, and I will give you the crown of life.
11Let anyone who has an ear listen to what the Spirit is saying to the churches. Whoever conquers will not be harmed
by the second death.

Pergamum Is Confused

12 "And to the angel of the church in Pergamum write:
These are the words of him who has the sharp two-edged
sword:
13 "I know where you are living, where Satan's throne is.
Yet you are holding fast to my name, and you did not deny
your faith in me[h] even in the days of Antipas my witness,

[h]Or *deny my faith*

fer to him as "Lord and God." He also used political, economic, and social measures to suppress what he perceived to be resistance, including the burgeoning Christian movement. Some emperors had been more tolerant toward Christians and Jews, recognizing how strongly those followers believed in one God. Those emperors settled for an expression of loyalty. Not so for Domitian.

Internally, many of the churches struggled with poverty, heresy, and dissension. In Revelation, heretical teachers are variously referred to as teachers of Balaam (2:14), Jezebel (2:20), the Nicolaitans (2:6, 15), and the Synagogue of Satan (2:9; 3:9). We don't know exactly what the nature of these heresies was, though one possibility is gnosticism (see article at the end of 1 John). But we do know that problems of syncretism and worldliness were common (see the Introduction to Colossians).

John sends the Lord's letters to seven groups of believers living at the end of the first century. But Revelation is an open letter to all Christians, including those of us who follow Christ today. In John's day believers were faced with false teachers and the persecution that resulted from a resurgent cult of emperor worship. Revelation challenged them to loyalty to the truth and perseverance under suffering.

What challenges to their faith do Christians face today? What would Christ say to them? What words of warning might apply to today's life and faith? ◆

THYATIRA

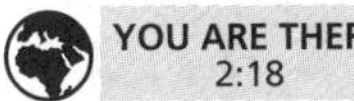

- **A city of the province of Lydia in western Asia Minor located on the road from Pergamum to Sardis.**
- **Situated on the southern bank of the Lycus River, a branch of the Hermus River.**
- **Although never a large city, a thriving manufacturing and commercial center during New Testament times. Archaeologists have uncovered evidence of many trade guilds and unions here. Membership in these guilds, necessary for financial and social success, often involved pagan customs and practices such as superstitious worship, feasts using food sacrificed to idols, and loose sexual morality.**
- **Original home of Lydia of Philippi (see Acts 16:14), the first person known to have responded to the gospel in Europe.**
- **Modern name of Thyatira, Akhisar, means "white castle."**

my faithful one, who was killed among you, where Satan
lives. 14But I have a few things against you: you have some
there who hold to the teaching of Balaam, who taught Balak
to put a stumbling block before the people of Israel, so that
they would eat food sacrificed to idols and practice fornication. 15So you also have some who hold to the teaching of
the Nicolaitans. 16Repent then. If not, I will come to you

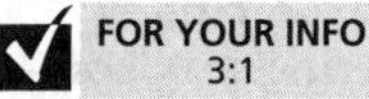

FOR YOUR INFO
3:1

SEVEN CHURCHES TO STUDY

What is your church like? What would be the message to your church if it were addressed alongside the churches of Asia Minor (2:1—3:22)? Here is a comparison of the seven churches mentioned in Revelation. See if there are any parallels between these churches and the congregation with whom you worship today:

Church	Description	Praised for	Warned about
Ephesus (2:1–7)	The Loveless Church	•labor •patience •not bearing those who are evil •testing false apostles •perseverance •hating the deeds of the Nicolaitans	•leaving their first love
Smyrna (2:8–11)	The Persecuted Church	•tribulation •poverty	•faithfulness under persecution
Pergamum (2:12–17)	The Compromising Church	•holding fast to Christ's name •not denying the faith, even faced with martyrdom	•allowing false teaching having to do with immorality and idolatry •holding to the doctrine of the Nicolaitans
Thyatira (2:18–29)	The Corrupt Church	•love •service •faith •patience	•allowing Jezebel to teach and seduce to immorality and idolatry •holding fast and overcoming
Sardis (3:1–6)	The Dead Church	•a few faithful people	•deadness, even though they had a reputation for being alive
Philadelphia (3:7–13)	The Faithful Church	•a little strength •keeping Christ's word •not denying Christ's name •perseverance	•holding fast what they had and overcoming during coming tribulations
Laodicea (3:14–20)	The Lukewarm Church		•being lukewarm •pretending to be well off spiritually when they were impoverished •need for repentance and overcoming

As you study the seven churches to whom Christ dictated letters, with which group do you most identify? What words of warning might apply to your church? What changes might your church need to make?

soon and make war against them with the sword of my
mouth. 17Let anyone who has an ear listen to what the
Spirit is saying to the churches. To everyone who conquers
I will give some of the hidden manna, and I will give a
white stone, and on the white stone is written a new name
that no one knows except the one who receives it.

Thyatira Is Too Tolerant

2:18 see pg. 881

18 "And to the angel of the church in
Thyatira write: These are the words of
the Son of God, who has eyes like a flame of fire, and
whose feet are like burnished bronze:
19 "I know your works—your love, faith, service, and
patient endurance. I know that your last works are greater

2:20–23

than the first. 20But I have this against
you: you tolerate that woman Jezebel,
who calls herself a prophet and is teaching and beguiling
my servants[i] to practice fornication and to eat food sacrificed to idols. 21I gave her time to repent, but she refuses to
repent of her fornication. 22Beware, I am throwing her on a
bed, and those who commit adultery with her I am throwing into great distress, unless they repent of her doings;
23and I will strike her children dead. And all the churches
will know that I am the one who searches minds and
hearts, and I will give to each of you as your works deserve.
24But to the rest of you in Thyatira, who do not hold this
teaching, who have not learned what some call 'the deep
things of Satan,' to you I say, I do not lay on you any other
burden; 25only hold fast to what you have until I come. 26To
everyone who conquers and continues to do my works to
the end,

I will give authority over the nations;
27 to rule[j] them with an iron rod,
as when clay pots are shattered—
28even as I also received authority from my Father. To the
one who conquers I will also give the morning star. 29Let
anyone who has an ear listen to what the Spirit is saying to
the churches.

Sardis Is Sleeping

3:1

3 "And to the angel of the church in
Sardis write: These are the words of
him who has the seven spirits of God and the seven stars:
"I know your works; you have a name of being alive, but

(Bible text continued on page 885)

[i]Gk *slaves* [j]Or *to shepherd*

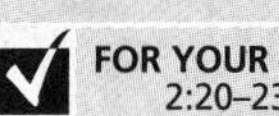

JEZEBEL

FOR YOUR INFO 2:20–23 *The name Jezebel (v. 20) instantly signified evil for John's readers. King Ahab's wife, Jezebel, left a bad taste in Israel (1 Kin. 16:31; 21:25; 2 Kin. 9:7–10, 22). After her passing, Jews avoided naming their daughters Jezebel.*

Here in Revelation 2, a Jezebel is teaching people to worship false gods and encouraging immorality. The pagan religions of the day, including the emperor-worship of the Romans, usually involved idol worship and sometimes included sexual activity.

This Jezebel was no follower of Christ, but a false prophet leading people astray. Yet the believers at Thyatira stood by, watching and tolerating her teaching and promotion of sexual promiscuity in the name of religion.

FOR YOUR INFO
3:17–18

A History of Money

The words attributed to the Laodiceans, "I am rich, I have prospered, and I need nothing" (v. 17) are easy to understand since Laodicea became an extremely wealthy city under the Romans. When the city was destroyed by an earthquake in A.D. 61, the Laodiceans took a posture of self-sufficiency by refusing aid from Rome for rebuilding. In doing so, they continued a long tradition associated with money.

From Barter to Metals

In ancient times, people used a system of barter, or trading of property, to exchange value. Land became an important commodity, but produce, and especially livestock, was more convenient. Grain, oil, wine, and spices were also popular tools of trade.

Gradually metals began to replace goods and services as items of exchange. Copper or bronze was in demand for weapons, farming tools, and religious offerings. The early Egyptians and others shaped gold and silver into rings, bars, or rounded nodules for easier trading. Scripture records that Jacob's children used "bundles of money" (Gen. 42:35), which may have been metal rings tied together with strings.

Silver became especially important in real estate transactions. Omri, for example, purchased the village and hill of Samaria for two talents of silver (1 Kin. 16:24; compare Gen. 23:15–16; 2 Sam. 24:24). Eventually silver became so commonly used as money that the Hebrew word for "silver" came to mean "money" (Gen. 17:13).

Gold, the most valuable of metals, was also used for major transactions. King Hiram of Tyre paid 120 talents of gold to Solomon for several cities near his land (1 Kin. 9:13–14). Later, Hezekiah paid Sennacherib 300 talents of silver and 30 talents of gold to obtain peace (2 Kin. 18:14). Silver, gold, and copper (probably a copper-bronze alloy) were used to mint Israel's first coins.

Standardized Value

In their early use as money, metals were probably in their raw form or in varying stages of refinement. However, in that form it was difficult to transport them and to determine their true value. Thus metals began to be refined into wedges or bars of known weight and value (Josh. 7:21) or into various forms of jewelry. Gold and silver were also kept as ingots, vessels, dust, or small fragments that could be melted and used immediately. These small pieces of metal were often carried in leather pouches that could be easily hidden (Gen. 42:35).

The Bible frequently refers to "pieces" of silver or gold. The confusing term *shekel* did not denote any one value or weight at first, although it later became the name of a Jewish coin. Fractions of the shekel are mentioned in the Old Testament as well (for example, Ex. 38:26; Lev. 27:25; Neh. 10:32). These pieces were probably fragments of gold or silver bars rather than shaped coins.

The largest unit of silver was the talent, shaped in pellets or rings, with approximately the value of one ox.

Eventually pieces of metal were standardized, then stamped to designate their weight and value. Coins still had to be weighed, however, since their edges might have been trimmed or filed. Ancient coins often show other marks, indicating they may have been probed to assure their silver content.

The basic unit of Roman coinage was the silver denarius, probably equal to a laborer's daily wage, as in the parable of the vineyard workers (Matt. 20:9–10, 13). It was also used for paying tribute, or taxes, to the Roman emperor, whose image it carried. Jesus was shown a

(continued on next page)

you are dead. 2Wake up, and strengthen what remains and
is on the point of death, for I have not found your works
perfect in the sight of my God. 3Remember then what you
received and heard; obey it, and repent. If you do not wake
up, I will come like a thief, and you will not know at what
hour I will come to you. 4Yet you have still a few persons in
Sardis who have not soiled their clothes; they will walk
with me, dressed in white, for they are worthy. 5If you conquer, you will be clothed like them in white robes, and I
will not blot your name out of the book of life; I will confess your name before my Father and before his angels. 6Let
anyone who has an ear listen to what the Spirit is saying to
the churches.

Philadelphia Is Working

7 "And to the angel of the church in Philadelphia write:
These are the words of the holy one, the true one,
who has the key of David,
who opens and no one will shut,
who shuts and no one opens:

8 "I know your works. Look, I have set before you an
open door, which no one is able to shut. I know that you
have but little power, and yet you have kept my word and
have not denied my name. 9I will make those of the synagogue of Satan who say that they are Jews and are not, but
are lying—I will make them come and bow down before
your feet, and they will learn that I have loved you. 10Be-
cause you have kept my word of patient endurance, I will
keep you from the hour of trial that is coming on the whole
world to test the inhabitants of the earth. 11I am coming
soon; hold fast to what you have, so that no one may seize
your crown. 12If you conquer, I will make you a pillar in
the temple of my God; you will never go out of it. I will
write on you the name of my God, and the name of the city
of my God, the new Jerusalem that comes down from my
God out of heaven, and my own new name. 13Let anyone
who has an ear listen to what the Spirit is saying to the
churches.

Laodicea Is Lukewarm

14 "And to the angel of the church in Laodicea write:
The words of the Amen, the faithful and true witness, the
origin[k] of God's creation:

15 "I know your works; you are neither cold nor hot. I
wish that you were either cold or hot. 16So, because you are

[k]Or *beginning*

(continued from previous page)

denarius by the Pharisees who wanted to trick him into opposing Roman taxation (Matt. 22:15–22).

Scripture warns believers against "the love of money," but it does not teach that money itself is evil (see "Christians and Money," 1 Tim. 6:6–19). Instead, it encourages Christ's followers to work at a steady job to earn a living in order to provide for one's own needs as well as to help others who have material needs (see "From Deadbeat to Donor," Eph. 4:28, and "A Command to Work," 2 Thess. 3:6–12). ◆

For more on the value of biblical units of coinage, see the table, "Money in the New Testament," Rev. 16:21.

lukewarm, and neither cold nor hot, I am about to spit you
3:17–18 see pg. 884 out of my mouth. 17For you say, 'I am
rich, I have prospered, and I need noth-
ing.' You do not realize that you are wretched, pitiable,
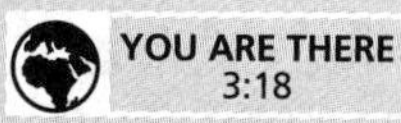
poor, blind, and naked. 18Therefore I
counsel you to buy from me gold refined
by fire so that you may be rich; and white robes to clothe
you and to keep the shame of your nakedness from being
seen; and salve to anoint your eyes so that you may see.
19I reprove and discipline those whom I love. Be earnest,
therefore, and repent. 20Listen! I am standing at the door,

YOU ARE THERE 3:18

CLOTHING

John records the promise of white garments (v. 18), probably a symbol for purity and health. But clothing of the more practical kind was as important to the first-century Laodiceans as it is to modern Westerners.

In the ancient world, wool and flax provided most of the raw material for creating fabric. The more rural the household, the more likely that spinning and weaving were done in the home. Urban households probably depended on merchants for material and even finished garments. Cleaning and dyeing eventually developed into distinct occupations.

Among the Greeks, spinning, weaving, and decorating cloth were so much the responsibility of females that those skills became metaphors for "women's wiles." Women in Roman cities were likewise encouraged to occupy their time working with wool. The task was synonymous with being a virtuous wife and mother. In fact, Emperor Augustus (27 B.C.—A.D. 14) was so eager to re-establish traditional Roman values that he wore woolen clothes made by his wife to encourage women to return to their looms.

Among the Jews, some men but mostly women made fabric. Jews who intended to strictly observe the Law were careful not to mix wool and flax in the same garment, following the prohibitions of Deut. 22:11 and Lev. 19:19. They also sewed fringes with a blue thread on the corners onto their outer garments as a sign of remembrance of the commandments of God (Deut. 22:12, Num. 15:38–40).

knocking; if you hear my voice and open the door, I will
come in to you and eat with you, and you with me. 21To the
one who conquers I will give a place with me on my
throne, just as I myself conquered and sat down with my
Father on his throne. 22Let anyone who has an ear listen to
what the Spirit is saying to the churches."

Worship in Heaven

4 After this I looked, and there in heaven a door stood open! And the first voice, which I had heard speaking to me like a trumpet, said, "Come up here, and I will show

Mediterranean clothing typically consisted of a tunic made of two pieces of wool joined together at the top, with an opening to pass over the head. The garment was often red, yellow, black, or a combination of these colors, and might be decorated with two vertical stripes of a contrasting color. Another garment, the mantle, was a single piece of cloth, often yellow or brown with a pattern woven into it. ◆

"I WILL SHOW YOU WHAT MUST TAKE PLACE AFTER THIS."
—Revelation 4:1

you what must take place after this." 2At once I was in the
spirit,[l] and there in heaven stood a throne, with one seated
on the throne! 3And the one seated there looks like jasper
and carnelian, and around the throne is a rainbow that
looks like an emerald. 4Around the throne are twenty-four
thrones, and seated on the thrones are twenty-four elders,
dressed in white robes, with golden crowns on their heads.
5Coming from the throne are flashes of lightning, and
rumblings and peals of thunder, and in front of the throne
burn seven flaming torches, which are the seven spirits of
God; 6and in front of the throne there is something like a
sea of glass, like crystal.

Around the throne, and on each side of the throne, are
four living creatures, full of eyes in front and behind: 7the
first living creature like a lion, the second living creature
like an ox, the third living creature with a face like a human
face, and the fourth living creature like a flying eagle. 8And

[l]Or *in the Spirit*

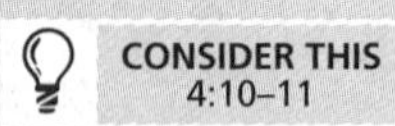

TWO GREAT WORKS OF GOD

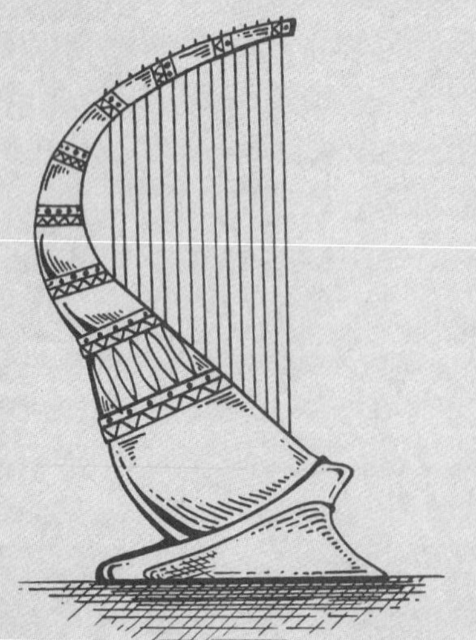

In calling believers to faithfulness, Revelation records several heavenly songs that focus on two great works of God—creation and redemption:

- A creation hymn (4:11). *God created the universe and sustains it for our benefit (Gen. 1:1–31). Four creatures sing, "You are worthy, our Lord and God."*
- A redemption hymn (5:9–12). *In Christ, God has offered up the necessary sacrifice to rescue us from sin. Four creatures, twenty-four elders, and myriads of the heavenly host sing, "You are worthy."*

Finally, these two great gifts of God, creation and redemption, cause every creature in heaven and earth to give praise by singing, "Blessing and honor and glory and might" be to Him (5:13).

Believers today need to give thanks to God for both of these mighty acts. We also need to respond to these acts through our lives and work. For example, through an emphasis on the creative activity of God, believers might participate in efforts on behalf of the environment or on projects to aid the needy who control few of the resources of creation. Likewise, through an emphasis on the re-

the four living creatures, each of them with six wings, are full of eyes all around and inside. Day and night without ceasing they sing,

"Holy, holy, holy,
the Lord God the Almighty,
who was and is and is to come."

9And whenever the living creatures give glory and honor and thanks to the one who is seated on the throne, who

4:10–11

lives forever and ever, 10the twenty-four
elders fall before the one who is seated
on the throne and worship the one who lives forever and ever; they cast their crowns before the throne, singing,

11 "You are worthy, our Lord and God,
to receive glory and honor and power,
for you created all things,
and by your will they existed and were created."

demptive activity of God, believers will work hard to communicate the message of Christ's saving grace to all the people of the earth.

Ideally, followers of Christ will strike a balance between these two, rather than choose one emphasis over another. After all, we have been called by God to obey two mandates: (1) to be good stewards of God's creation by exercising dominion over the earth and its resources (Gen. 1:26–31); and (2) to carry out Christ's mandate to make disciples of all peoples (Matt. 28:18–20).

John reinforces these challenges through two additional passages:

- *"Do not damage the earth or the sea or the trees" (7:3).*
- *"I looked, and there was a great multitude that no one could count, from every nation, from all tribes and peoples and languages, standing before the throne" (7:9).*

Do you tend to emphasize one aspect of God's work—creation or redemption—to the neglect of the other? How can you and your church recover this dual calling from God? ◆

"YOU ARE WORTHY, OUR LORD AND GOD TO RECEIVE GLORY AND HONOR AND POWER."
—Revelation 4:11

FINALLY, FULL EQUALITY

CONSIDER THIS 5:9–10 **Will there ever be an end to discrimination, racism, elitism, and injustice? Will people ever regard each other as equals? John's vision of "every tribe and language and people and nation" standing before God and singing His praise (v. 9) gives us assurance that in the end, we will all experience full equality.**

Scripture begins with a creation that was "very good" (Gen. 1:31). Adam and Eve were given authority over creation and responsibility to tend the garden as full partners. However, the horrible entrance of sin ruins this original design. Is there any reason to hope that God's original intention will be recovered?

Yes, Revelation 5 offers images of the original reality one day coming true again:

- **One who is worthy to provide a renewed future arrives (vv. 1–5).**
- **The Spirits of God pervade the creation (v. 6).**
- **Believers from every tribe and nation are among the leadership (v. 9).**
- **All of them are empowered to be "priests serving our God" who will reign on the earth (v. 10).**
- **Unhindered praise and worship breaks forth, uniting representatives of all peoples before God (vv. 11–14).**

God's original design will ultimately become a reality. Meanwhile, believers today are called to be signposts of Christ's coming kingdom so that others may choose to welcome Him into their lives.

Is there evidence in your life, family, and work that this kingdom is beginning in you?

A Sealed Scroll

5 Then I saw in the right hand of the one seated on the
throne a scroll written on the inside and on the back,
sealed[m] with seven seals; 2and I saw a mighty angel
proclaiming with a loud voice, "Who is worthy to open the
scroll and break its seals?" 3And no one in heaven or on
earth or under the earth was able to open the scroll or to
look into it. 4And I began to weep bitterly because no one
was found worthy to open the scroll or to look into it.
5Then one of the elders said to me, "Do not weep. See, the
Lion of the tribe of Judah, the Root of David, has
conquered, so that he can open the scroll and its seven
seals."

6 Then I saw between the throne and the four living
creatures and among the elders a Lamb standing as if it had
been slaughtered, having seven horns and seven eyes,
which are the seven spirits of God sent out into all the
earth. 7He went and took the scroll from the right hand of
the one who was seated on the throne. 8When he had taken
the scroll, the four living creatures and the twenty-four elders fell before the Lamb, each holding a harp and golden
bowls full of incense, which are the prayers of the saints.

5:9–10 9They sing a new song:

"You are worthy to take the scroll
and to open its seals,
for you were slaughtered and by your blood you
ransomed for God
saints from[n] every tribe and language and people and
nation;
10 you have made them to be a kingdom and priests
serving[o] our God,
and they will reign on earth."

11 Then I looked, and I heard the voice of many angels
surrounding the throne and the living creatures and the elders; they numbered myriads of myriads and thousands of
thousands, 12singing with full voice,

"Worthy is the Lamb that was slaughtered
to receive power and wealth and wisdom and might
and honor and glory and blessing!"

13Then I heard every creature in heaven and on earth and
under the earth and in the sea, and all that is in them,
singing,

"To the one seated on the throne and to the Lamb
be blessing and honor and glory and might
forever and ever!"

[m]*Or written on the inside, and sealed on the back* [n]*Gk ransomed for God from* [o]*Gk priests to*

[14]And the four living creatures said, "Amen!" And the elders fell down and worshiped.

Seals of Wrath and Chaos

6:1–17 see pg. 892

6 Then I saw the Lamb open one of
the seven seals, and I heard one of
the four living creatures call out, as with a voice of thunder,
"Come!"[p] [2]I looked, and there was a white horse! Its rider
had a bow; a crown was given to him, and he came out
conquering and to conquer.
3 When he opened the second seal, I heard the second
living creature call out, "Come!"[p] [4]And out came[q] another
horse, bright red; its rider was permitted to take peace from
the earth, so that people would slaughter one another; and
he was given a great sword.
5 When he opened the third seal, I heard the third living
creature call out, "Come!"[p] I looked, and there was a black
horse! Its rider held a pair of scales in his hand, [6]and I
heard what seemed to be a voice in the midst of the four
living creatures saying, "A quart of wheat for a day's pay,[r]
and three quarts of barley for a day's pay,[r] but do not damage the olive oil and the wine!"
7 When he opened the fourth seal, I heard the voice of
the fourth living creature call out, "Come!"[p] [8]I looked and
there was a pale green horse! Its rider's name was Death,
and Hades followed with him; they were given authority
over a fourth of the earth, to kill with sword, famine, and
pestilence, and by the wild animals of the earth.
9 When he opened the fifth seal, I saw under the altar
the souls of those who had been slaughtered for the word
of God and for the testimony they had given; [10]they cried
out with a loud voice, "Sovereign Lord, holy and true, how
long will it be before you judge and avenge our blood on
the inhabitants of the earth?" [11]They were each given a
white robe and told to rest a little longer, until the number
would be complete both of their fellow servants[s] and of
their brothers and sisters,[t] who were soon to be killed as
they themselves had been killed.
12 When he opened the sixth seal, I looked, and there
came a great earthquake; the sun became black as sackcloth, the full moon became like blood, [13]and the stars of
the sky fell to the earth as the fig tree drops its winter fruit

[p]Or *"Go!"* [q]Or *went* [r]Gk *a denarius* [s]Gk *slaves* [t]Gk *brothers*

Angels—Servants of God

FOR YOUR INFO 7:1 **The four angels that John saw standing at the four corners of the earth (v. 1) are among the countless ministering spirits that serve God and His people (Heb. 1:7, 14). Angels figure prominently in the book of Revelation (for example, 1:20; 5:2, 11; 7:2, 11; 8:2, 6; 12:7; 14:6; 15:1; 18:21; 20:1; 22:8). But they also played a part in many other**

(continued on next page)

when shaken by a gale. 14The sky vanished like a scroll
rolling itself up, and every mountain and island was removed from its place. 15Then the kings of the earth and the
magnates and the generals and the rich and the powerful,
and everyone, slave and free, hid in the caves and among
the rocks of the mountains, 16calling to the mountains and
rocks, "Fall on us and hide us from the face of the one
seated on the throne and from the wrath of the Lamb; 17for
the great day of their wrath has come, and who is able to
stand?"

Representatives from Israel

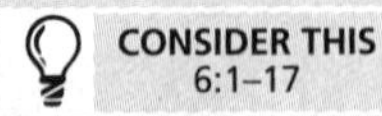

7:1

7 After this I saw four angels standing
at the four corners of the earth,
holding back the four winds of the earth so that no wind
could blow on earth or sea or against any tree. 2I saw an-

CONSIDER THIS 6:1–17

Worship or Wrath?

For some people, Christ makes very little difference in how one looks at life. Faith doesn't really matter. But in Revelation 4–10, John provides us with a peek into the future and the prospect of life or death forever. Clearly, the time we spend on earth is but a brief preamble to something much larger.

Christ Makes All the Difference

With Christ: Worship	Without Christ: Wrath
Splendor and beauty (4:2–8)	Peace gone from earth (6:4)
Praise and adoration (4:8–11)	Killing unleashed (6:5)
Access provided (5:1–8)	Death reigns (6:8)
Outbursts of worship (5:9)	Earth collapses (6:12–17)
Entitlement given (5:10)	Fires and earthquakes (8:5)
Affirmation (5:11–14)	Destruction surges (8:7–10)
Martyrs restored (6:9–11)	Many die (8:11)
Protection given (7:2–8)	Darkness pervades earth (8:12)
Suffering ceases (7:9–17)	Woes are announced (8:13)
God's mystery completed (10:7)	Plagues torment the lost (9:2–11)
Bitter becomes sweet (10:9)	Many die (9:18)
	Repentance is rejected (9:20–21)

other angel ascending from the rising of the sun, having the
seal of the living God, and he called with a loud voice to
the four angels who had been given power to damage earth
and sea, 3saying, "Do not damage the earth or the sea or the
trees, until we have marked the servants[u] of our God with a
seal on their foreheads."
4 And I heard the number of those who were sealed, one
hundred forty-four thousand, sealed out of every tribe of
the people of Israel:

5 From the tribe of Judah twelve thousand sealed,
from the tribe of Reuben twelve thousand,
from the tribe of Gad twelve thousand,
6 from the tribe of Asher twelve thousand,
from the tribe of Naphtali twelve thousand,
from the tribe of Manasseh twelve thousand,
7 from the tribe of Simeon twelve thousand,
from the tribe of Levi twelve thousand,
from the tribe of Issachar twelve thousand,

[u]Gk *slaves*

This section offers us a bird's-eye view of the coming apocalypse on earth and the promised joy of heaven (4:1). The contrasts are severe. Those who embrace Christ and His provision for sin can anticipate a celebration that exceeds their greatest expectations. Those without Christ have cause to tremble for their refusal to accept His offer of deliverance from the wrath to come.

The message is plain: only in Christ is there hope of escaping wrath. That way of escape is offered right now. Waiting to accept Christ's offer only increases the risk of experiencing adverse judgment. It also deprives one of new life today.

If you have not yet responded to Christ's offer of eternal life, why not do so right now? The choice you make has meaning for life here and now as well as eternal consequences. ◆

(continued from previous page)

events of the New Testament, as the following table shows:

The Ministry of Angels
•Calmed Joseph's doubts about Mary's faithfulness (Matt. 1:20–25).
•Warned Joseph to flee from Herod's plan to kill Jesus (Matt. 2:13).
•Encouraged Joseph to return to Israel with his family (Matt. 2:19–20).
•Ministered to Jesus after His temptation in the wilderness (Matt. 4:11).
•Told the women at the empty tomb that Jesus was alive (Matt. 28:2–6).
•Foretold to Zechariah the birth of John the Baptist (Luke 1:11–20).
•Told Mary that she would bear the Christ (Luke 1:26–38).
•Announced Jesus' birth to shepherds near Bethlehem (Luke 2:8–15).
•Appeared to Jesus in the Garden of Gethsemane to give Him strength (Luke 22:43).
•Promised the crowd observing Jesus' ascension that He would return in like manner (Acts 1:10–11).
•Brought Peter and John out of prison (Acts 5:17–20).
•Told Philip to go into the desert where he met the Ethiopian treasurer (Acts 8:26).
•Told the centurion Cornelius to send for Peter (Acts 10:3–8).
•Released Peter from prison (Acts 12:7).
•Struck down Herod for not giving glory to God (Acts 12:23).
•Stood by Paul during a storm at sea to assure him that he would stand before the emperor (Acts 27:23–24).

Learn more about angels and the role they played in Jesus' birth, resurrection, and ascension at the article, "Spiritual Realities Beyond You," Matt. 8:29.

8 from the tribe of Zebulun twelve thousand,
from the tribe of Joseph twelve thousand,
from the tribe of Benjamin twelve thousand sealed.

A Great Multitude from Every Nation

7:9

9 After this I looked, and there was a
great multitude that no one could count,
from every nation, from all tribes and peoples and languages, standing before the throne and before the Lamb,
robed in white, with palm branches in their hands. 10They
cried out in a loud voice, saying,

"Salvation belongs to our God who is seated on the
throne, and to the Lamb!"

11And all the angels stood around the throne and around
the elders and the four living creatures, and they fell on
their faces before the throne and worshiped God, 12singing,

"Amen! Blessing and glory and wisdom
and thanksgiving and honor
and power and might
be to our God forever and ever! Amen."

13 Then one of the elders addressed me, saying, "Who
are these, robed in white, and where have they come from?"
14I said to him, "Sir, you are the one that knows." Then he
said to me, "These are they who have come out of the great
ordeal; they have washed their robes and made them white
in the blood of the Lamb.

15 For this reason they are before the throne of God,
and worship him day and night within his temple,
and the one who is seated on the throne will shelter
them.
16 They will hunger no more, and thirst no more;
the sun will not strike them,
nor any scorching heat;
17 for the Lamb at the center of the throne will be their
shepherd,
and he will guide them to springs of the water of life,
and God will wipe away every tear from their eyes."

One Last Seal

8:1
see pg. 896

8 When the Lamb opened the seventh
seal, there was silence in heaven for
about half an hour. 2And I saw the seven angels who stand
before God, and seven trumpets were given to them.

A Great Multitude of All Nations

CONSIDER THIS 7:9 **Jesus sent His followers to make disciples of all the nations (*ethnē*, "peoples"; see "To All the Nations," Matt. 28:19). As John takes us into the throne room of heaven, we see the fulfillment of Jesus' mandate. There, standing before the Lamb (Christ) is a crowd so large that it cannot be counted, made up from "every nation, from all tribes and peoples and languages" (Rev. 7:9).**

Actually, two groups are present—representatives from God's people, the Jews (vv. 3–8), and countless Gentile believers (vv. 9–10). Just as Jesus said it would, the gospel has spread out from Jerusalem to reach people from "the ends of the earth" (Acts 1:8). Now Jews and Gentiles have come together to receive the salvation that God has promised. Now God dwells among His people. Jesus is their Shepherd, supplying all their needs (Rev. 7:14–17).

In response to this spectacular, worldwide, multiethnic salvation, the creatures of heaven and earth fall down before God in worship and song (vv. 11–12). What a breathtaking picture this is!

But of course this vision lies in the future. For now, we live in a world wracked by ethnic divisions and racial prejudice. Yet knowing that God intends to populate heaven with people from every ethnic background has important implications for those of us who claim to follow Christ. If God's heart reaches out to the whole world, then our hearts need to as well.

3 Another angel with a golden censer came and stood at
the altar; he was given a great quantity of incense to offer
with the prayers of all the saints on the golden altar that is
before the throne. 4And the smoke of the incense, with the
prayers of the saints, rose before God from the hand of the
angel. 5Then the angel took the censer and filled it with fire
from the altar and threw it on the earth; and there were
peals of thunder, rumblings, flashes of lightning, and an
earthquake.

A Sound of Trumpets

6 Now the seven angels who had the seven trumpets
made ready to blow them.
7 The first angel blew his trumpet, and there came hail
and fire, mixed with blood, and they were hurled to the
earth; and a third of the earth was burned up, and a third
of the trees were burned up, and all green grass was burned
up.
8 The second angel blew his trumpet, and something
like a great mountain, burning with fire, was thrown into
the sea. 9A third of the sea became blood, a third of the living creatures in the sea died, and a third of the ships were
destroyed.
10 The third angel blew his trumpet, and a great star fell
from heaven, blazing like a torch, and it fell on a third of
the rivers and on the springs of water. 11The name of the
star is Wormwood. A third of the waters became wormwood, and many died from the water, because it was made
bitter.
12 The fourth angel blew his trumpet, and a third of the
sun was struck, and a third of the moon, and a third of the
stars, so that a third of their light was darkened; a third of
the day was kept from shining, and likewise the night.
13 Then I looked, and I heard an eagle crying with a
loud voice as it flew in midheaven, "Woe, woe, woe to the
inhabitants of the earth, at the blasts of the other trumpets
that the three angels are about to blow!"

Two More Trumpets and Woe

9 And the fifth angel blew his trumpet, and I saw a star
that had fallen from heaven to earth, and he was given
the key to the shaft of the bottomless pit; 2he opened the

"AND THE ONE WHO IS SEATED ON THE THRONE WILL SHELTER THEM."
—Revelation 7:15

shaft of the bottomless pit, and from the shaft rose smoke
like the smoke of a great furnace, and the sun and the air
were darkened with the smoke from the shaft. [3]Then from
the smoke came locusts on the earth, and they were given

9:4
see pg. 898

authority like the authority of scorpions
of the earth. [4]They were told not to dam-

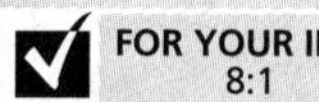

FOR YOUR INFO
8:1

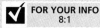

The Structure of Revelation

A cascade of dramatic events pours from the book of Revelation as the book unfolds. John narrates his vision in a torrent of images such as the seventh seal (v. 1), many of which may seem confusing to some readers. However, close observation reveals that the action is not random. John's vision is told in a tightly woven structure that offers important clues to understanding the book.

One way to summarize the material in Revelation is based on the three time frames that Christ told John to write about: "Write what you have seen, what is, and what is to take place after this" (1:19). This yields the following outline for the book:

I. "What you have seen" (1:1–20)
A. Greetings and praise (1:1–8)
B. A vision of the risen Christ (1:9–20)
II. "What is" (2:1—3:22)
A. Letter to the church at Ephesus (2:1–7)
B. Letter to the church at Smyrna (2:8–11)
C. Letter to the church at Pergamum (2:12–17)
D. Letter to the church at Thyatira (2:18–29)
E. Letter to the church at Sardis (3:1–6)
F. Letter to the church at Philadelphia (3:7–13)
G. Letter to the church at Laodicea (3:14–22)
III. "What is to take place after this" (4:1—22:21)
A. Worship in heaven (4:1—5:14)
B. Seven seals (6:1—8:5)
C. Seven trumpets (8:6—11:19)
D. Seven signs or portents (12:1—14:20)
E. Seven bowls (15:1—16:21)
F. The final judgment and the triumph of God (17:1—20:15)
G. A new heaven and new earth (21:1—22:5)
H. Conclusion (22:6–21)

age the grass of the earth or any green growth or any tree, but only those people who do not have the seal of God on their foreheads. 5They were allowed to torture them for five months, but not to kill them, and their torture was like the torture of a scorpion when it stings someone. 6And in those days people will seek death but will not find it; they will long to die, but death will flee from them.

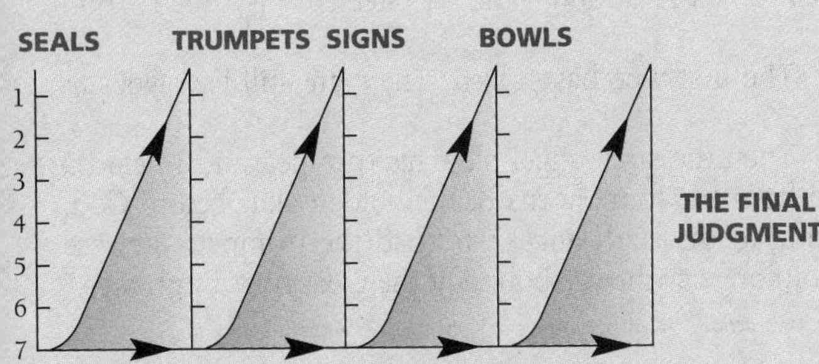

THE STRUCTURE OF REVELATION

In the portion of the book devoted to the seven seals, seven trumpets, seven signs, and seven bowls (6:1—16:21), a common pattern repeats. In each case, six of the seven items play out their action and then there is a break during which God's people are challenged to perseverance and faithfulness. Then the seventh item unfolds.

Some have suggested that the seventh item in each group holds or gives rise to the action that follows: the seventh seal contains the seven trumpets, the seventh trumpet contains the seven signs, the seventh sign contains the seven bowls, and the seventh bowl contains the final judgment. This suggests that the apocalyptic events increase in their intensity with each passing event, spiraling toward the final defeat of evil and the triumph of Christ.

Throughout these events, a message to believers remains clear: God is in control; ultimately His will will be done; therefore His people need to stand firm, trust in His power, and wait for deliverance from whatever trials befall them. ◆

In addition to the structure of Revelation, it's important to read the book as a kind of literature known as apocalyptic in order to appreciate its meaning. See "The Genre of Apocalyptic Literature," Rev. 10:1–10.

IN THOSE DAYS PEOPLE WILL SEEK DEATH BUT WILL NOT FIND IT.
—Revelation 9:6

7 In appearance the locusts were like horses equipped
for battle. On their heads were what looked like crowns of
gold; their faces were like human faces, 8their hair like
women's hair, and their teeth like lions' teeth; 9they had
scales like iron breastplates, and the noise of their wings
was like the noise of many chariots with horses rushing
into battle. 10They have tails like scorpions, with stingers,
and in their tails is their power to harm people for five
months. 11They have as king over them
the angel of the bottomless pit; his name
in Hebrew is Abaddon,[v] and in Greek he is called Apollyon.[w]

9:11

12 The first woe has passed. There are still two woes to
come.

13 Then the sixth angel blew his trumpet, and I heard a
voice from the four[x] horns of the golden altar before God,
14saying to the sixth angel who had the trumpet, "Release
the four angels who are bound at the great river Euphrates."

[v]That is, *Destruction* [w]That is, *Destroyer* [x]Other ancient authorities lack *four*

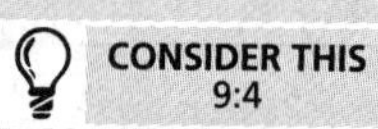

FAITH AND THE ENVIRONMENT

Global warming. Overpopulation. Acid rain. The destruction of rain forests. Is the Bible concerned with the earth's ecology? Or does it teach that the earth's resources exist purely for people's pleasure, to be used as they will, with little thought for long-term consequences?

"The earth is the Lord's, and all that is in it," declared the psalmist (Ps. 24:1). Again, "The earth is full of [God's] creatures" (Ps. 104:24). These and many other passages indicate that creation is not ours to plunder, but rather a resource which God has entrusted to our management, to be used in service to each other (Ps. 104:13, 23, 31). We will ultimately answer to God for its use.

In John's description of the end times, there is much destruction and violence. But not all is to be consumed. Nor does the earth exist only for people's pleasure and consumption. The command given to agents (locusts) of destruction not to harm "the grass of the earth or any green growth or any tree" (v. 4) is a curious echo of Gen. 1:29–30. Thus, even in messages of destruction there is affirmation of God's good creation.

The same concern for earth's resources occurs when God sends one of His angels to cry with a loud voice to the four angels "who had been given power to damage earth and sea . . . 'Do not damage the earth or the sea or the

15 So the four angels were released, who had been held
ready for the hour, the day, the month, and the year, to kill
a third of humankind. 16 The number of the troops of cavalry was two hundred million; I heard their number. 17 And
this was how I saw the horses in my vision: the riders wore
breastplates the color of fire and of sapphire[y] and of sulfur;
the heads of the horses were like lions' heads, and fire and
smoke and sulfur came out of their mouths. 18 By these
three plagues a third of humankind was killed, by the fire
and smoke and sulfur coming out of their mouths. 19 For
the power of the horses is in their mouths and in their tails;
their tails are like serpents, having heads; and with them
they inflict harm.
20 The rest of humankind, who were not killed by these
plagues, did not repent of the works of their hands or give

(Bible text continued on page 902)

[y]Gk *hyacinth*

trees' " (7:2–3). Likewise, the new heaven and earth include a "river of the water of life, bright as crystal . . . the tree of life with its twelve kinds of fruit, producing its fruit each month; and the leaves of the tree are for the healing of the nations" (22:1–2).

When God created the world's resources, He declared them to be "very good" (Gen. 1:31). He assigned people to care for them, develop them, and use them for good (1:26–31). This management role is part of our calling to live according to the image and likeness of God. He has made us to be more than mere consumers who gratify their own desires. He wants us to serve Him as we manage His creation. Our work is a gift from God to develop and deliver the benefits of that resource to other people (see "People at Work," Heb. 2:7).

Do you treat the world with respect as a resource for which God has given you responsibility? Does your work please God and serve other people? Can you think of ways to do a better job of managing the environment in a way that God would approve? ◆

Names for Satan in the New Testament

FOR YOUR INFO 9:11 **Two names are given to the "angel of the bottomless pit" (v. 11), Abaddon ("destruction") and Apollyon ("destroyer"). It is unclear whether this angel was related to Satan or was God's agent for destruction. Elsewhere in the New Testament, however, are names or descriptions for the personification of evil:**

Satan's Many Aliases

- Beelzebul, the ruler of the demons (Matt. 12:24)
- The evil one (Matt. 13:19, 38)
- The enemy (Matt. 13:39)
- Murderer (John 8:44)
- Liar (John 8:44)
- The ruler of this world (John 12:31; 14:30)
- The god of this age (2 Cor. 4:4)
- Beliar (2 Cor. 6:15, according to some interpretations)
- The ruler of the power of the air (Eph. 2:2)
- The tempter (1 Thess. 3:5)
- A roaring lion (1 Pet. 5:8)
- The adversary (1 Pet. 5:8)
- The dragon (Rev. 12:7)
- The accuser of our comrades (Rev. 12:10)
- The ancient serpent (Rev. 20:2)
- The devil who deceived (Rev. 20:10)

Satan leads a vast army of fallen angels who are in open rebellion against God. See "Demons," Luke 11:14.

FOR YOUR INFO
10:1–10

The Genre of Apocalyptic Literature

An angel from heaven, straddling land and sea (vv. 1, 3). A voice from heaven (v. 4). The number seven (vv. 4, 7). Prophecies about "peoples and nations and languages and kings" (v. 11). These are features of the style of literature known as apocalyptic, of which Revelation is the preeminent example. It's important to understand this genre if one wants to understand the book's meaning. Although Revelation is more than just a typical apocalyptic work, in that it is part of Scripture, it pays to study such literature as a category.

The Greek word *apocalypse* means a "revelation," "unveiling," or "disclosure." Thus apocalyptic literature seeks to reveal certain mysteries about heaven and earth, humankind and God, angels and demons, the life of the world today, and the world to come. This type of writing arose among the Jews and Christians during the period from 200 B.C. to A.D. 200.

Characteristics

Apocalyptic literature employs a number of literary devices, styles, and motifs that set it apart from other literature, including:

- *visions* as a way of revealing secrets from heaven about the present and future. Often these visions are caused by some trauma or major event that creates a crisis in the writer's experience (for example, Rev. 1:10). Often one vision leads to others.
- *ethical conclusions* drawn on the basis of the writer's visionary experiences. For instance, John's seven letters to seven churches in Rev. 2–3 are written after the apostle sees a vision and is commissioned by God to write (1:19). The letters call the churches to specific ethical and moral decisions.
- *anonymous or attributed authorship*. Revelation is an exception among apocalyptic works in that it gives the name of its author (1:1, 9). Many non-canonical apocalyptic books attribute their origins to famous prophets of the past, such as Ezra, Enoch, Jeremiah, and Moses. This may be a way to add credibility to the work.

- *the use of powerful symbolism.* Apocalyptic books stretch the reader's imagination through highly dramatic images in which actions and outcomes occur in extremes. Numerology is especially important. Those for whom the books were originally intended presumably knew the meaning of the symbols used by the authors, connecting them to events of the time.
- *a stark contrast between good and evil.* Apocalyptic writing is dualistic in that it separates things into definite categories of good and evil, right and wrong. In Revelation, for example, one is either on the side of God, who is holy, righteous, and just, or on the side of Satan, who is surrounded by abominations, idolatries, and wickedness.
- *a concern with end times.* The future plays prominently in these writings. The authors look ahead to coming events, on the one hand offering hope to those who long for justice and delivery from evil, and on the other issuing warnings to those who are in rebellion against God's ways.

Messages

Through apocalyptic writing, authors communicate important messages to their readers. The following themes occur in all the apocalyptic writings:

- *The end is coming soon.* Apocalyptic writers frequently connect the arrival of the end times with the near future. This sense of immediacy lends urgency to the message.
- *The whole cosmos is involved.* The end of the world is not a solitary event for the earth alone; it extends to the whole universe. Apocalyptic writings emphasize worldwide events and cataclysmic judgments.
- *History is divided into fixed segments.* Along with a pessimistic view of history, apocalyptic literature takes the view that history has been determined by God before creation. World history has been divided into fixed time periods, and people simply live out a predetermined drama. Many of the writings divide history into two major periods—the present world, ruled by Satan and his legions, and the world to come, in which wickedness will be abolished and God will rule supreme.
- *Angels and demons.* Spirits are common figures in the apocalyptic genre who are actively involved in the drama of events. Pointing to Satan and his demons (fallen angels) explains the problem of evil. Likewise, angels who have not fallen are used by God to protect and serve His faithful people.
- *A new heaven and a new earth.* The end times as portrayed in apocalyptic writings bring a return to the beginning of creation. Out of heaven will come a new heaven and a new earth. The old will be destroyed, replaced by a new creation where God will rule.
- *A Messiah.* A Messiah or mediator between God and man appears in most of the apocalyptic writings as one who accomplishes the final salvation of the world. In Revelation, the Messiah is shown to be Christ, the "King of kings and Lord of lords" (19:16).

Dr. Bruce Metzger, a renowned New Testament scholar, encourages us to use "disciplined imagination" in reading Revelation. "Disciplined imagination" involves imagining the symbolisms and poetic imagery in Revelation, but viewing them as part of the big picture—not interpreting them literally as isolated details.

Because the book of Revelation forms a part of God's revealed Word, it is in a class by itself among the apocalyptic works of its period. Like the rest of the inspired Scriptures, it is reliable and authoritative, and possesses an integrity and a trustworthiness not found in uninspired writings that resemble it as to its genre. But studying apocalyptic literature helps us to identify Revelation's themes, and thereby to better understand God's message to us in it. ◆

up worshiping demons and idols of gold and silver and
bronze and stone and wood, which cannot see or hear or
walk. 21And they did not repent of their murders or their
sorceries or their fornication or their thefts.

The Little Scroll

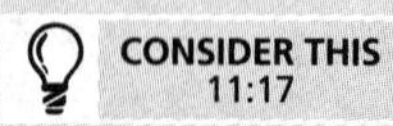

10:1–10 see pg. 900

10 And I saw another mighty angel
coming down from heaven,
wrapped in a cloud, with a rainbow over his head; his face
was like the sun, and his legs like pillars of fire. 2He held a
little scroll open in his hand. Setting his right foot on the
sea and his left foot on the land, 3he gave a great shout, like
a lion roaring. And when he shouted, the seven thunders

CONSIDER THIS
11:17

POWER

Business, government, nonprofit organizations, and churches all feel the impact of people pursuing and defending power. Here in John's vision of God triumphing over evil, God holds the ultimate power (v. 17).

What does the New Testament teach about power?

- *There is tremendous power in humility. It gives us strength that is a gift from God to be used for His purposes. See "The Power of Humility," Matt. 3:11.*
- *Forgiveness is powerful and liberating and is a power that Jesus has delegated to His followers. See "The Power of Forgiveness," Matt. 9:4–8.*
- *When others observe us and the way we use power and authority, they ought to see Jesus. See " 'You Remind Me of . . . ,' " Mark 6:14–16.*
- *Like fire, power can be used to accomplish good. But always lurking in its shadow is the temptation of abuse. See "Three Dangers of Power," Luke 3:14.*
- *Jesus described the power that He supplies as the right and ability to lay down one's life for others. See "The Power of Self-Sacrifice," John 10:17–18.*
- *All power ultimately comes from God, and we are ultimately accountable to Him for how we use power. See "Seeing Behind Power," John 19:10–11.*
- *Jesus gives His followers a unique kind of power to accomplish His tasks. See "Power," Acts 1:8.*
- *God's power has little or nothing to do with outward ap-*

sounded. [4]And when the seven thunders had sounded, I was about to write, but I heard a voice from heaven saying, "Seal up what the seven thunders have said, and do not write it down." [5]Then the angel whom I saw standing on the sea and the land

raised his right hand to heaven
6 and swore by him who lives forever and ever,
who created heaven and what is in it, the earth and what is in it, and the sea and what is in it: "There will be no more delay, [7]but in the days when the seventh angel is to blow his trumpet, the mystery of God will be fulfilled, as he announced to his servants[z] the prophets."

[z]Gk *slaves*

pearances or worldly acclaim. See " 'Give Me Power!' " Acts 8:18–19.

- *Paul was competent in and comfortable with the powerful Roman judicial system and its procedures, even when he faced officials who dealt in bribes and political favors. See "Paul and the Structures of Power," Acts 24:25–26.*
- *The message of Christ is powerful enough to transform lives. See "The Power of the Gospel," Rom. 1:16.*
- *The gospel appears foolish to many people. Yet the irony is that it is far more powerful than even the strongest players in our culture can imagine. See "The Power of Foolishness," 1 Cor. 1:18.*
- *Sometimes we give away the control of our lives to things like status and possessions. When we do, they overpower us: we no longer possess our possessions—they possess us! See "What Controls You?" 1 Cor. 6:12.*
- *Our world prizes strength and power, but Scripture puts a new twist on the notion of strength: weakness can make a person strong. See "When I Am Weak, Then I Am Strong," 2 Cor. 12:7–10.*
- *Do you have what it takes to "make it" in life? Scripture teaches that God's power gives us what we need to experience real life in a way that pleases Him. See "Do You Have What It Takes?" 2 Pet. 1:3–4.* ◆

WHEN HE SHOUTED, THE SEVEN THUNDERS SOUNDED.
—Revelation 10:3

8 Then the voice that I had heard from heaven spoke to me again, saying, "Go, take the scroll that is open in the hand of the angel who is standing on the sea and on the land." 9So I went to the angel and told him to give me the little scroll; and he said to me, "Take it, and eat; it will be bitter to your stomach, but sweet as honey in your mouth." 10So I took the little scroll from the hand of the angel and ate it; it was sweet as honey in my mouth, but when I had eaten it, my stomach was made bitter.

11 Then they said to me, "You must prophesy again about many peoples and nations and languages and kings."

Two Witnesses and a Second Woe

11 Then I was given a measuring rod like a staff, and I was told, "Come and measure the temple of God and the altar and those who worship there, 2but do not measure the court outside the temple; leave that out, for it is given over to the nations, and they will trample over the holy city for forty-two months. 3And I will grant my two witnesses authority to prophesy for one thousand two hundred sixty days, wearing sackcloth."

4 These are the two olive trees and the two lampstands that stand before the Lord of the earth. 5And if anyone wants to harm them, fire pours from their mouth and consumes their foes; anyone who wants to harm them must be killed in this manner. 6They have authority to shut the sky, so that no rain may fall during the days of their prophesying, and they have authority over the waters to turn them into blood, and to strike the earth with every kind of plague, as often as they desire.

7 When they have finished their testimony, the beast that comes up from the bottomless pit will make war on them and conquer them and kill them, 8and their dead bodies will lie in the street of the great city that is prophetically[a] called Sodom and Egypt, where also their Lord was crucified. 9For three and a half days members of the peoples and tribes and languages and nations will gaze at their dead bodies and refuse to let them be placed in a tomb; 10and the inhabitants of the earth will gloat over them and celebrate and exchange presents, because these two prophets had been a torment to the inhabitants of the earth.

11 But after the three and a half days, the breath[b] of life from God entered them, and they stood on their feet, and those who saw them were terrified. 12Then they[c] heard a loud voice from heaven saying to them, "Come up here!" And they went up to heaven in a cloud while their enemies watched them. 13At that moment there was a great earthquake, and a tenth of the city fell; seven thousand people were killed in the earthquake, and the rest were terrified and gave glory to the God of heaven.

14 The second woe has passed. The third woe is coming very soon.

The Seventh Trumpet

15 Then the seventh angel blew his trumpet, and there were loud voices in heaven, saying,

"The kingdom of the world has become the
kingdom of our Lord
and of his Messiah,[d]
and he will reign forever and ever."

16 Then the twenty-four elders who sit on their thrones before God fell on their faces and worshiped God, 17singing,

11:17
see pg. 902

"We give you thanks, Lord
God Almighty,
who are and who were,
for you have taken your great power
and begun to reign.
18 The nations raged,
but your wrath has come,
and the time for judging the dead,
for rewarding your servants,[e] the prophets
and saints and all who fear your name,
both small and great,
and for destroying those who destroy the earth."

19 Then God's temple in heaven was opened, and the ark of his covenant was seen within his

[a]Or *allegorically*; Gk *spiritually*

[b]Or *the spirit* [c]Other ancient authorities read *I* [d]Gk *Christ* [e]Gk *slaves*

temple; and there were flashes of lightning, rumblings, peals of thunder, an earthquake, and heavy hail.

A Woman Gives Birth

12:1–2
see pg. 906

12 A great portent appeared in heaven: a woman clothed with the sun, with the moon under her feet, and on her head a crown of twelve stars. [2]She was pregnant and was crying out in birth pangs, in the agony of giving birth. [3]Then another portent appeared in heaven: a great red dragon, with seven heads and ten horns, and seven diadems on his heads. [4]His tail swept down a third of the stars of heaven and threw them to the earth. Then the dragon stood before the woman who was about to bear a child, so that he might devour her child as soon as it was born. [5]And she gave birth to a son, a male child, who is to rule[f] all the nations with a rod of iron. But her child was snatched away and taken to God and to his throne; [6]and the woman fled into the wilderness, where she has a place prepared by God, so that there she can be nourished for one thousand two hundred sixty days.

War in Heaven

7 And war broke out in heaven; Michael and his angels fought against the dragon. The dragon and his angels fought back, [8]but they were defeated, and there was no longer any place for them in heaven. [9]The great dragon was thrown down, that ancient serpent, who is called the Devil and Satan, the deceiver of the whole world—he was thrown down to the earth, and his angels were thrown down with him.

10 Then I heard a loud voice in heaven, proclaiming,
"Now have come the salvation and the power
and the kingdom of our God
and the authority of his Messiah,[g]
for the accuser of our comrades[h] has been thrown
down,
who accuses them day and night before our God.
11 But they have conquered him by the blood of the Lamb
and by the word of their testimony,
for they did not cling to life even in the face of death.
12 Rejoice then, you heavens
and those who dwell in them!
But woe to the earth and the sea,
for the devil has come down to you
with great wrath,
because he knows that his time is short!"

[f]*Or to shepherd* [g]*Gk Christ* [h]*Gk brothers*

WOMAN AGAINST EVIL

CONSIDER THIS 12:1–17 **Women have often been identified in folk wisdom as a peculiar source of evil. For example, confusion over the temptation in the Garden of Eden (Gen. 3:1–16) has sometimes resulted in holding women particularly responsible for sin.**

But in Revelation 12, John describes a woman who is the source of all life and the parent of the One who will rule the nations, Christ (vv. 2, 5). When she is pursued by a dragon that opposes God's work and seeks its destruction (vv. 3–4), God cares for her and prepares a place of refuge for her (v. 6).

This leads to a cosmic war between the angel Michael and the dragon (vv. 7–13). The evil dragon loses and the woman emerges safe and sound (vv. 13–16). Nevertheless, the dragon, which is mortally wounded, declares war on the woman's children (v. 17). Far from blaming our bondage to sin on a woman, John portrays this woman as a symbol of victorious opposition to evil. Who or what do you think the woman represents? The ideal community? The church? Mary? Something else?

War on Earth

13 So when the dragon saw that he had been thrown
down to the earth, he pursued[i] the woman who had given
birth to the male child. 14But the woman was given the two
wings of the great eagle, so that she could fly from the serpent into the wilderness, to her place where she is nourished for a time, and times, and half a time. 15Then from
his mouth the serpent poured water like a river after the
woman, to sweep her away with the flood. 16But the earth
came to the help of the woman; it opened its mouth and
swallowed the river that the dragon had poured from his
mouth. 17Then the dragon was angry
with the woman, and went off to make

12:1–17 see pg. 905

[i]Or *persecuted*

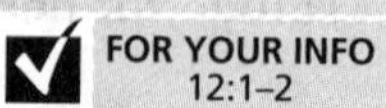

WOMEN IN REVELATION

John's first-century readers no doubt understood more of Revelation than we do today. Nevertheless, even they may have struggled with some of the complex imagery and bizarre descriptions. One interesting group of characters in the narrative is women, such as the woman in labor (vv. 1–2).

The women in Revelation are described in extremes of moral character, either very good or very bad. These heavy contrasts are typical of apocalyptic literature, which tends to be dualistic (see 10:1–10). This, along with the unusual actions that these women take, suggest that we understand them as symbols rather than literal women.

Jezebel (2:20–23)

Christ rebukes the church at Thyatira for allowing "that woman Jezebel" to teach people to worship false gods and to encourage immorality. In the Old Testament, Jezebel was the wife of King Ahab. Together, they were perhaps the most wicked of the Jewish rulers (see "Jezebel," 2:20–23). Note that Christ says that He will judge not only Jezebel, but her children as well—people who follow her ways.

The Woman Giving Birth (12:1–6, 13–17)

This woman stands in marked contrast to Jezebel. Attacked by an evil dragon, she finds protection and refuge provided by God. Her identity has been variously interpreted. Because she bears the child, some have seen her as Mary, the mother of Jesus, others as Israel, the collective "mother" that brought forth the Messiah. The attempts of

war on the rest of her children, those who keep the commandments of God and hold the testimony of Jesus.

The Great Beast from the Sea

18 Then the dragon[j] took his stand on the sand of the
13:1 13 seashore. 1And I saw a beast ris-
ing out of the sea, having ten

[j]Gk *Then he*; other ancient authorities read *Then I stood*

Beastly Rome

A CLOSER LOOK 13:1 *The beast from the sea (v. 1) has long been understood to be a symbol for the Roman Empire. This image of a power that deserved to fall was a far cry from the one that Paul urged Christians to obey. See "The Limits of Political Authority," Rom. 13:1–7.*

the dragon to destroy her, along with "the rest of her children" (v. 17), may be references to Satan's attempts to destroy Israel and disrupt the Messianic line.

Babylon, the Great Whore (14:8; 17:1–6, 15–18; 18:1–24)

Old Testament prophets (for example, Hosea; Ezek. 16:8–58) often referred to adulterers and prostitutes to represent people who practiced idolatry. Just as an adulteress is unfaithful to her husband, so God's people are unfaithful to Him when they allow their hearts to be divided and they worship other gods (see "Understanding Prostitution," Matt. 21:31–32).

The harlot in Revelation 17 is identified as Babylon, which first-century readers would probably have identified as Rome (see "A Symbol of Evil," 14:8). In contrast to the new Jerusalem that descends from heaven with glory and blessing (Rev. 21), Babylon is shattered and destroyed in judgment for persecuting God's people and corrupting the peoples of the earth with wickedness (Rev. 18).

The Wife (Bride) of the Lamb (19:7–8)

As the marriage feast of the Lamb approaches, a bride has made herself ready. The description of this woman clothing herself in righteous acts (19:8) suggests that she may represent the church. ◆

THEN THE DRAGON WAS ANGRY WITH THE WOMAN. . . .
—Revelation 12:17

horns and seven heads; and on its horns were ten diadems,
and on its heads were blasphemous names. 2And the beast
that I saw was like a leopard, its feet were like a bear's, and
its mouth was like a lion's mouth. And the dragon gave it
his power and his throne and great authority. 3One of its
heads seemed to have received a death-blow, but its mortal
wound[k] had been healed. In amazement the whole earth
followed the beast. 4They worshiped the dragon, for he had
given his authority to the beast, and they worshiped the
beast, saying, "Who is like the beast, and who can fight
against it?"

5 The beast was given a mouth uttering haughty and
blasphemous words, and it was allowed to exercise authority for forty-two months. 6It opened its mouth to utter blasphemies against God, blaspheming his name and his
dwelling, that is, those who dwell in heaven. 7Also it was
allowed to make war on the saints and to conquer them.[l] It

[k]Gk *the plague of its death* [l]Other ancient authorities lack this sentence

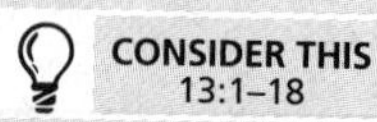

God Restrains Evil

The presence of pain, suffering, and evil in the world causes some people to wonder whether a good God exists, and if He does, why He doesn't put an end to it if He can. There are no easy answers to such questions about evil, but the Bible offers insights to help us explore the questions. John's vision of a beast rising up out of the sea (v. 1) and causing great havoc in the world does not explain why there is evil, but it does sound an important note of encouragement: the evils of the world happen only by "permission" and those that do occur have precise limits imposed on them by God. Notice that the beast was given "authority for forty-two months" *(v. 5, emphasis added).*

Clearly, God has placed restraints on evil. We have not and will not experience the full onslaught of pain and suffering that could be delivered. This restraining work of God can be seen in several incidents in the Old Testament:

- Adam and Eve (Gen. 3:22–24). *After Adam and Eve sinned, God sent them out of the garden and sealed it off. According to Genesis, this was not a matter of retaliation by God but a protection from the possibility of eating from the tree of life and being separated from Him forever.*
- The Tower of Babel (Gen. 11:1–9). *Again, widespread evil threatened to consume the creation. God intervened*

was given authority over every tribe and people and language and nation, 8and all the inhabitants of the earth will
worship it, everyone whose name has not been written
from the foundation of the world in the book of life of the
Lamb that was slaughtered.[m]
9 Let anyone who has an ear listen:
10 If you are to be taken captive,
into captivity you go;
if you kill with the sword,
with the sword you must be killed.
Here is a call for the endurance and faith of the saints.
11 Then I saw another beast that rose out of the earth; it
had two horns like a lamb and it spoke like a dragon. 12It
exercises all the authority of the first beast on its behalf,
and it makes the earth and its inhabitants worship the first
beast, whose mortal wound[n] had been healed. 13It performs

(Bible text continued on page 911)

[m]Or *written in the book of life of the Lamb that was slaughtered from the foundation of the world* [n]Gk *whose plague of its death*

by confusing the languages of the peoples to limit their collusion in wickedness. This was a case of God preserving sinful humanity from itself.

- Job (Job 1:6—2:10). *Satan wanted to prove to God that Job's faithfulness was merely the result of God blessing him. So God granted Satan limited permission to inflict suffering.*

John was writing to believers to help them maintain a realistic view of good and evil in the midst of intense persecution. Today, as we watch televised reports of death and disaster around the world and as we experience pain and suffering in our own families and among our neighbors and associates, we too need to maintain a godly perspective. God has placed limits on evil. The very fact that we have a distaste for it reflects that we do indeed bear God's image as His creatures. ◆

There can be no question that evil and pain are a massive problem to both belief and behavior. But the Bible does give us ground to stand on as we try to live in a world where suffering is real. See "Ten Myths about Christianity, Myth #10: All the Evil and Suffering in the World Proves There Is No God," Rev. 20:1–10.

HERE IS A CALL FOR THE ENDURANCE AND FAITH OF THE SAINTS.
—Revelation 13:10

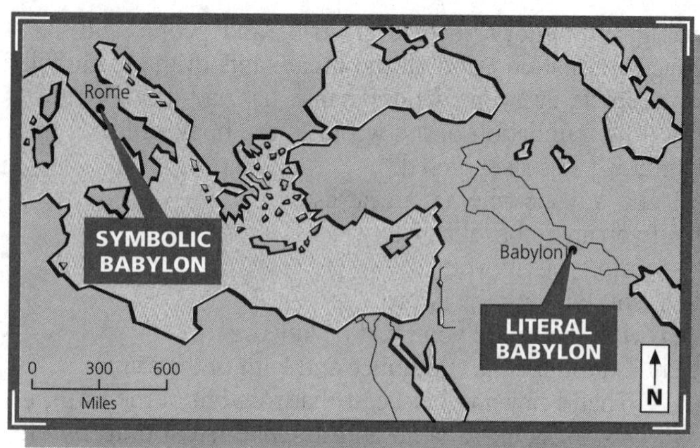

THE TWO BABYLONS

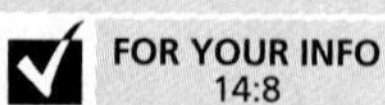
FOR YOUR INFO 14:8

A SYMBOL OF EVIL

In Revelation, Babylon (v. 8) probably represents, more than a city, an entire world system in rebellion against God. The Old Testament prophets often prophesied the fall of Babylon, the capital of an empire that destroyed Jerusalem and carried away God's people into captivity. So here Babylon becomes a fitting image for a society that persecutes believers but which God will ultimately destroy.

In the first century, Babylon may have been a code word for Rome, built as it was on seven hills (17:9). Under the Roman Emperor Domitian (A.D. 81–96), Christians were severely persecuted, especially for refusing to participate in the cult of emperor worship. Each mention of Babylon in Revelation shows that it is linked with evil and resistance to God:

BABYLON IN REVELATION
•Babylon is brought down for making "all nations drink of the wine of the wrath of her fornication" (14:8).
•Babylon is shattered by God, who remembers the city's ways and gives it "the wine-cup of the fury of his wrath" (16:19).
•Babylon is given the title, "Babylon the great, mother of whores and of earth's abominations" (17:5).
•Babylon falls and becomes "a dwelling place of demons, a haunt of every foul spirit, … bird, … and hateful beast" (18:2).
•Babylon is mourned as it wallows in terrifying torment; those who watch cry out, "Alas, alas, the great city, Babylon, the mighty city! For in one hour your judgment has come" (18:10).
•Babylon "will be thrown down, and will be found no more" (18:21).

great signs, even making fire come down from heaven to earth in the sight of all; [14]and by the signs that it is allowed to perform on behalf of the beast, it deceives the inhabitants of earth, telling them to make an image for the beast that had been wounded by the sword[o] and yet lived; [15]and it was allowed to give breath[p] to the image of the beast so that the image of the beast could even speak and cause those who would not worship the image of the beast to be killed. [16]Also it causes all, both small and great, both rich and poor, both free and slave, to be marked on the right hand or the forehead, [17]so that no one can buy or sell who does not have the mark, that is, the name of the beast or

[o]Or *that had received the plague of the sword* [p]Or *spirit*

Historically, Babylon oppressed and captured Judah. In the same way, John's figurative Babylon oppresses the people of God and holds them captive under its mighty grip. History is a war between two cities: "Babylon," the capital of idolatry and oppression, and "Jerusalem," the center of Christ's peace and justice.

John's buildup to the clash of these two titans is epic in scope and drama. The climax comes here in chapter 14, where judgment finally falls on Babylon, and the bowls, plagues, and intoxicating wine of God's wrath are poured out on her. A tremendous tidal wave of evil sloshes back and forth in the passage, like the last great battles of World War II. But the outcome is assured; Christ will prevail. ◆

IT CAUSES ALL . . . TO BE MARKED ON THE RIGHT HAND OR THE FOREHEAD. . . .
—Revelation 13:16

13:1–18
see pg. 908

the number of its name. [18]This calls for wisdom: let anyone with understanding calculate the number of the beast, for it is the number of a person. Its number is six hundred sixty-six.[q]

The Lamb Calls His Own

14 Then I looked, and there was the Lamb, standing
on Mount Zion! And with him were one hundred forty-four thousand who had his name and his Father's
name written on their foreheads. 2And I heard a voice from
heaven like the sound of many waters and like the sound of loud thunder; the voice I heard was like the sound of
harpists playing on their harps, 3and they sing a new song
before the throne and before the four living creatures and before the elders. No one could learn that song except the one hundred forty-four thousand who have been redeemed
from the earth. 4It is these who have not defiled themselves
with women, for they are virgins; these follow the Lamb wherever he goes. They have been redeemed from humankind as first fruits for God and the Lamb, 5and in their
mouth no lie was found; they are blameless.

"**BLESSED ARE THE DEAD WHO FROM NOW ON DIE IN THE LORD.**"
—Revelation 14:13

Angels with Announcements

6 Then I saw another angel flying in midheaven, with an eternal gospel to proclaim to those who live[r] on the earth—to every nation and tribe and language and people. 7He said
in a loud voice, "Fear God and give him glory, for the hour of his judgment has come; and worship him who made heaven and earth, the sea and the springs of water."

14:8
see pg. 910

8 Then another angel, a second, fol-
lowed, saying, "Fallen, fallen is Babylon the great! She has made all nations drink of the wine of the wrath of her fornication."

9 Then another angel, a third, followed them, crying with a loud voice, "Those who worship the beast and its image, and receive a mark on their foreheads or on their
hands, 10they will also drink the wine of God's wrath, poured unmixed into the cup of his anger, and they will be tormented with fire and sulfur in the presence of the holy
angels and in the presence of the Lamb. 11And the smoke of
their torment goes up forever and ever. There is no rest day or night for those who worship the beast and its image and for anyone who receives the mark of its name."

12 Here is a call for the endurance of the saints, those who keep the commandments of God and hold fast to the faith of[s] Jesus.

[q]Other ancient authorities read *six hundred sixteen* [r]Gk *sit* [s]Or *to their faith in*

13 And I heard a voice from heaven saying, "Write this:
Blessed are the dead who from now on die in the Lord."
"Yes," says the Spirit, "they will rest from their labors, for
their deeds follow them."

Reaping the Earth's Harvest

14 Then I looked, and there was a white cloud, and
seated on the cloud was one like the Son of Man, with a
golden crown on his head, and a sharp sickle in his hand!
15Another angel came out of the temple, calling with a loud
voice to the one who sat on the cloud, "Use your sickle and
reap, for the hour to reap has come, because the harvest of
the earth is fully ripe." 16So the one who sat on the cloud
swung his sickle over the earth, and the earth was reaped.
17 Then another angel came out of the temple in
heaven, and he too had a sharp sickle. 18Then another angel came out from the altar, the angel who has authority
over fire, and he called with a loud voice to him who had
the sharp sickle, "Use your sharp sickle and gather the clusters of the vine of the earth, for its grapes are ripe." 19So the
angel swung his sickle over the earth and gathered the vin-
tage of the earth, and he threw it into the great wine press
of the wrath of God. 20And the wine press was trodden outside the city, and blood flowed from the wine press, as high
as a horse's bridle, for a distance of about two hundred
miles.[t]

A Vision of Seven Plagues

15:1–8

15 Then I saw another portent in
heaven, great and amazing: seven
angels with seven plagues, which are the last, for with them
the wrath of God is ended.
2 And I saw what appeared to be a sea of glass mixed
with fire, and those who had conquered the beast and its
image and the number of its name, standing beside the sea
of glass with harps of God in their hands. 3And they sing
the song of Moses, the servant[u] of God, and the song of the
Lamb:

"Great and amazing are your deeds,
  Lord God the Almighty!
Just and true are your ways,
  King of the nations![v]
4 Lord, who will not fear
  and glorify your name?

[t]Gk *one thousand six hundred stadia* [u]Gk *slave* [v]Other ancient authorities read *the ages*

QUOTE UNQUOTE

CONSIDER THIS 15:1–8 *Although Revelation is not fiction, it nevertheless narrates a story that goes beyond ordinary experience. Compare John's description of the evil beasts (13:1–17) with his portrayal of the heavenly temple (15:1–8):*

In all but a few writers the "good" characters are the least successful, and every one who has ever tried to make even the humblest story ought to know why . . . . Heaven understands Hell and Hell does not understand Heaven, and all of us, in our measure, share the Satanic . . . blindness. To project ourselves into a wicked character, we have only to stop doing something, and something that we are already tired of doing; to project ourselves into a good one, we have to do what we cannot and become what we are not.

C. S. Lewis, *A Preface to Paradise Lost*, pp. 100–101

For you alone are holy.
All nations will come
and worship before you,
for your judgments have been revealed."

5 After this I looked, and the temple of the tent[w] of witness in heaven was opened, 6and out of the temple came the
seven angels with the seven plagues, robed in pure bright
linen,[x] with golden sashes across their chests. 7Then one of
the four living creatures gave the seven angels seven golden
bowls full of the wrath of God, who lives forever and ever;
8and the temple was filled with smoke from the glory of
God and from his power, and no one could enter the temple until the seven plagues of the seven angels were ended.

[w]Or *tabernacle* [x]Other ancient authorities read *stone*

Money in the New Testament

The hail that falls from heaven is described as weighing "about a hundred pounds," or, in Greek, "about a talent" (v. 21). A talent was also a measure used as a monetary unit (for example, Matt. 25:15). The table below shows various monetary systems used among New Testament peoples.

New Testament Monetary Units

Unit	Equivalents	Translations
Jewish Weights		
Talent	3,000 shekels; 6,000 bekas	talent
Shekel	4 days' wages; 2 bekas; 20 gerahs	shekel
Beka	1/2 shekel; 10 gerahs	bekah
Gerah	1/20 shekel	gerah
Persian Coins		
Daric	2 days' wages; 1/2 Jewish silver shekel	drachma
Greek Coins		
Tetradrachma (Stater)	4 drachmas	piece of money
Didrachma	2 drachmas	tribute
Drachma	1 day's wage	piece of silver
Lepton	1/2 of a Roman kodrantes	mite
Roman Coins		
Aureus	25 denarii	
Denarius	1 day's wage	denarius
Assarius	1/16 of a denarius	copper coin
Kodrantes	1/4 of an assarius	penny, quadrans

Learn more about the origins and use of money among ancient peoples in the article, "A History of Money," Rev. 3:17–18.

Seven Bowls Pour Out

16 Then I heard a loud voice from the temple telling the seven angels, "Go and pour out on the earth the seven bowls of the wrath of God."
2 So the first angel went and poured his bowl on the earth, and a foul and painful sore came on those who had the mark of the beast and who worshiped its image.
3 The second angel poured his bowl into the sea, and it became like the blood of a corpse, and every living thing in the sea died.
4 The third angel poured his bowl into the rivers and the springs of water, and they became blood.
5And I heard the angel of the waters say,
"You are just, O Holy One, who are and were,
for you have judged these things;
6 because they shed the blood of saints and prophets,
you have given them blood to drink.
It is what they deserve!"
7And I heard the altar respond,
"Yes, O Lord God, the Almighty,
your judgments are true and just!"
8 The fourth angel poured his bowl on the sun, and it was allowed to scorch them with fire;
9they were scorched by the fierce heat, but they cursed the name of God, who had authority over these plagues, and they did not repent and give him glory.
10 The fifth angel poured his bowl on the throne of the beast, and its kingdom was plunged into darkness; people gnawed their tongues in agony,
11and cursed the God of heaven because of their pains and sores, and they did not repent of their deeds.
12 The sixth angel poured his bowl on the great river Euphrates, and its water was dried up in order to prepare the way for the kings from the east.
13And I saw three foul spirits like frogs coming from the mouth of the dragon, from the mouth of the beast, and from the mouth of the false prophet.
14These are demonic spirits, performing signs, who go abroad to the kings of the whole world, to assemble them for battle on the great day of God the Almighty.
15("See, I am coming like a thief! Blessed is the one who stays awake and is clothed,[y] not going about naked and exposed to shame.")
16And they assembled them at the place that in Hebrew is called Harmagedon.
17 The seventh angel poured his bowl into the air, and a loud voice came out of the temple, from the throne, saying,

(Bible text continued on page 918)

[y]*Gk and keeps his robes*

"YOU ARE JUST, O HOLY ONE . . . FOR YOU HAVE JUDGED THESE THINGS."
—Revelation 16:5

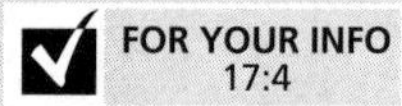
FOR YOUR INFO
17:4

COLORS IN THE BIBLE

The woman that John sees in the wilderness sits on a scarlet beast and wears purple and scarlet (vv. 3–4). In apocalyptic literature, color plays an important role in conveying symbolic meanings (see "The Genre of Apocalyptic Literature," Rev. 10:1–10). Here, the purple and scarlet suggest that the woman has become affluent, probably through evil means.

Individual colors mentioned in the Bible fall into two major types—natural colors and artificial colors.

ARTIFICIAL COLORS IN THE BIBLE	
PURPLE	The most precious of ancient dyes (see "The Trade in Purple," Acts 16:14) made from a shellfish found in the Mediterranean Sea. A total of 250,000 mollusks was required to make one ounce of the dye, which partly accounts for its great price. It was highly valued within the nation of Israel. Used in several features of the tabernacle (Ex. 26:1; 27:16) and the temple (2 Chr. 2:14); the color of royal robes (Judg. 8:26); the garments of the wealthy (Prov. 31:22; Luke 16:19); the vesture of a harlot (Rev. 17:4); and the robe placed on Jesus (Mark 15:17, 20). The color of royalty.
BLUE	Also derived from a species of shellfish; fabric dyed this color used in the tabernacle (Ex. 26:1) and the temple (2 Chr. 2:7); also used for royal trappings (Esth. 1:6; 8:15) and clothing for the rich (Jer. 10:9; Ezek. 23:6).
RED	Existed in several shades; dye extracted from the bodies of insects. Crimson linen used in the temple (2 Chr. 2:7, 14; 3:14); the color must have been indelible or permanent (Jer. 4:30), as crimson is used figuratively of sin (Is. 1:18). Scarlet cord tied around the wrist of Zerah (Gen. 38:28–30); used a great deal in the tabernacle (Ex. 25:4); the color of the cord hung form Rahab's window (Josh. 2:18); a mark of prosperity (2 Sam. 1:24; Prov. 31:21); the color of the robe placed on Jesus (Matt. 27:28), though scarlet and purple were not always distinguished (Mark 15:17); color of the beast ridden by the harlot Babylon (Rev. 17:3) along with some of her garments (Rev. 17:4) and those of her followers (Rev. 18:16). Vermilion used in decorating homes of the wealthy (Jer. 22:14) and in the painting of idols (Ezek. 23:14).

Artificial colors, such as paints and dyes, were used widely in the ancient world. The Israelites had an advanced textile industry. They were skilled not only in weaving but also in dyeing. Since dyes were made from vegetable sources or from shellfish, quality control was difficult. The completed colors were often impure and inexact. These problems were compounded by the fact that many dyes were closely guarded family recipes which were sometimes lost or changed.

Natural Colors in the Bible	
BLUE	Used to describe the color of a wound, but may refer to the wound itself (Prov. 20:30). Sometimes describes the sky.
BROWN	A dark, blackish color referred only to sheep (Gen. 30:32–33, 35, 40).
BLACK	One of the more commonly used colors in Scripture; describes the color of the middle of the night (Prov. 7:9); diseased skin (Job 30:30); healthy hair (Song 5:11; Matt. 5:36); corpses' faces (Lam. 4:8); the sky (Jer. 4:28); the darkening of the sun and the moon (Joel 2:10); horses (Zech. 6:2, 6; Rev. 6:5); and marble (Esth. 1:6). The color of famine and death.
GRAY	Used only to describe the hair of the elderly (Gen. 42:38).
GREEN	Normally describes vegetation; used of pastures (Ps. 23:2); herbage (2 Kin. 19:26); trees in general (Deut. 12:2; Luke 23:31; Rev. 8:7); the marriage bed (in a figurative sense, Song 1:16); a hypocrite compared to a papyrus plant (Job 8:16); and grass (Mark 6:39). A word meaning "greenish" describes plague spots (Lev. 13:49; 14:37) as well as the color of gold.
RED	Describes natural objects such as Jacob's stew (Gen. 25:30); the sacrificial heifer (Num. 19:2); wine (Prov. 23:31); newborn Esau (Gen. 25:25); Judah's eyes (Gen. 49:12, KJV); the eyes of the drunkard (Prov. 23:29); and the dragon (Rev. 12:3). The color of blood, it often symbolizes life; it also suggests the carnage of war.
WHITE	The color of animals (Gen. 30:35); manna (Ex. 16:31); both hair and pustules located in plague sores (Lev. 13:3–39); garments (Eccl. 9:8; Dan. 7:9); the robes of the righteous (Rev. 19:8); horses (Zech. 1:8; Rev. 6:2; 19:11); forgiven sins (Ps. 51:7; Is. 1:18); a refined remnant (Dan. 11:35; 12:10); the beloved one (Song 5:10); the white of an egg (Job 6:6); the shining garments of angels (Rev. 15:6) and of the transfigured Christ (Matt. 17:2); hair (Matt. 5:36); gravestones (Matt. 23:27); and the great throne of judgment (Rev. 20:11). Portrays purity, righteousness, and joy, and a white horse symbolizes victory.
YELLOW	Indicates the greenish cast of gold (Ps. 68:13) and the light-colored hair in a leprous spot (Lev. 13:30, 32).

◆

The Delusions of Luxury

CONSIDER THIS 18:1–24 **Just as overeating can make a person sick and too much insulation in a home can trap toxic air inside, too much wealth can be dangerous to the moral and spiritual health of an individual, a city, or a nation. In fact, Jesus warned about the "lure of wealth" (Matt. 13:22). Luxury can easily delude us into spiritual carelessness, greed, and ultimate ruin.**

Such is the case of Babylon in John's vision of her fall (Rev. 18:2–3, 7–8). Historically, Babylon achieved wealth, power, and dominance through constant warfare, oppression, and deception. It was known throughout the ancient world for plundering others for its own gain. Here in Revelation, Babylon is probably a symbol not only of Rome, but of a world system that operates in open rebellion against God (see "A Symbol of Evil," Rev. 14:8).

But there is a heavy price to pay for the self-indulgent lifestyle that Babylon's people live, and for the injustices they resort to in maintaining it. Cruelty and deception do not go unanswered:

- **The city becomes a dwelling place for demons (v. 2).**
- **Her patterns of luxury become addictive, similar to alcoholism, sexual excess, and a lifestyle of greed (v. 3).**
- **Insulated from pain, she lives in denial of her true condition (vv. 4–8).**
- **Her economic systems are taken away and her trading partnerships are dissolved (vv. 11–18; 22–23).**

(continued on next page)

"It is done!" [18]And there came flashes of lightning, rumblings, peals of thunder, and a violent earthquake, such as
had not occurred since people were upon the earth, so violent was that earthquake. [19]The great city was split into
three parts, and the cities of the nations fell. God remembered great Babylon and gave her the wine-cup of the fury
of his wrath. [20]And every island fled away, and no mountains were to be found; [21]and huge hail-
stones, each weighing about a hundred
pounds,[z] dropped from heaven on people, until they cursed
God for the plague of the hail, so fearful was that plague.

16:21 see pg. 914

The Whore Babylon

17 Then one of the seven angels who had the seven
bowls came and said to me, "Come, I will show you
the judgment of the great whore who is seated on many
waters, [2]with whom the kings of the earth have committed
fornication, and with the wine of whose fornication the
inhabitants of the earth have become drunk." [3]So he carried
me away in the spirit[a] into a wilderness, and I saw a woman
sitting on a scarlet beast that was full of blasphemous
names, and it had seven heads and ten
horns. [4]The woman was clothed in pur-
ple and scarlet, and adorned with gold and jewels and
pearls, holding in her hand a golden cup full of abominations and the impurities of her fornication; [5]and on her
forehead was written a name, a mystery: "Babylon the great,
mother of whores and of earth's abominations." [6]And I saw
that the woman was drunk with the blood of the saints and
the blood of the witnesses to Jesus.

17:4 see pg. 916

When I saw her, I was greatly amazed. [7]But the angel said
to me, "Why are you so amazed? I will tell you the mystery
of the woman, and of the beast with seven heads and ten
horns that carries her. [8]The beast that you saw was, and is
not, and is about to ascend from the bottomless pit and go
to destruction. And the inhabitants of the earth, whose
names have not been written in the book of life from the
foundation of the world, will be amazed when they see the
beast, because it was and is not and is to come.

9 "This calls for a mind that has wisdom: the seven
heads are seven mountains on which the woman is seated;
also, they are seven kings, [10]of whom five have fallen, one
is living, and the other has not yet come; and when he
comes, he must remain only a little while. [11]As for the beast
that was and is not, it is an eighth but it belongs to the
seven, and it goes to destruction. [12]And the ten horns that
you saw are ten kings who have not yet received a king-

[z]Gk *weighing about a talent* [a]Or *in the Spirit*

dom, but they are to receive authority as kings for one
hour, together with the beast. [13]These are united in yielding
their power and authority to the beast; [14]they will make
war on the Lamb, and the Lamb will conquer them, for he
is Lord of lords and King of kings, and those with him are
called and chosen and faithful."
15 And he said to me, "The waters that you saw, where
the whore is seated, are peoples and multitudes and nations
and languages. [16]And the ten horns that you saw, they and
the beast will hate the whore; they will make her desolate
and naked; they will devour her flesh and burn her up with
fire. [17]For God has put it into their hearts to carry out his
purpose by agreeing to give their kingdom to the beast, until the words of God will be fulfilled. [18]The woman you saw
is the great city that rules over the kings of the earth."

Babylon's Corruption

18:1–24

18 After this I saw another angel
coming down from heaven, hav-
ing great authority; and the earth was made bright with his
splendor. [2]He called out with a mighty voice,

"Fallen, fallen is Babylon the great!
It has become a dwelling place of demons,
a haunt of every foul spirit,
a haunt of every foul bird,
a haunt of every foul and hateful beast.[b]
3 For all the nations have drunk[c]
of the wine of the wrath of her fornication,
and the kings of the earth have committed fornication
with her,
and the merchants of the earth have grown rich from
the power[d] of her luxury."

4 Then I heard another voice from heaven saying,
"Come out of her, my people,
so that you do not take part in her sins,
and so that you do not share
in her plagues;
5 for her sins are heaped high as heaven,
and God has remembered her iniquities.
6 Render to her as she herself has rendered,
and repay her double for her deeds;
mix a double draught for her in the cup she mixed.
7 As she glorified herself and lived luxuriously,
so give her a like measure of torment and grief.
Since in her heart she says,
'I rule as a queen;

[b]Other ancient authorities lack the words *a haunt of every foul beast* and attach the words *and hateful* to the previous line so as to read *a haunt of every foul and hateful bird* [c]Other ancient authorities read *she has made all nations drink* [d]Or *resources*

(continued from previous page)

- **All of her possessions disappear and ultimately she is left desolate (v. 19).**

What happens to Babylon is instructive for those of us who follow Christ, especially as we live in a culture of affluence. Is there a note of warning in this text for us?

I am no widow,
and I will never see grief,'
8 therefore her plagues will come in a single day—
pestilence and mourning and famine—
and she will be burned with fire;
for mighty is the Lord God who judges her."
9 And the kings of the earth, who committed fornication
and lived in luxury with her, will weep and wail over her
when they see the smoke of her burning; 10they will stand
far off, in fear of her torment, and say,
"Alas, alas, the great city,
Babylon, the mighty city!
For in one hour your judgment has come."

Collapse of the Global Economy

11 And the merchants of the earth weep and mourn for
her, since no one buys their cargo anymore, 12cargo of gold,
silver, jewels and pearls, fine linen, purple, silk and scarlet,
all kinds of scented wood, all articles of ivory, all articles of
costly wood, bronze, iron, and marble, 13cinnamon, spice,

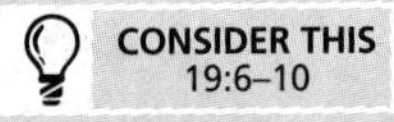
CONSIDER THIS
19:6–10

THERE IS HOPE FOR THE FAMILY

The fact that John's vision ends in a marriage between Christ (the Lamb) and His bride the church (vv. 6–10) offers great hope to families. In this world, almost every family experiences some pain and suffering in its relationships. After all, families are made up of people who struggle under the burden of sin.

Of course, things were not intended to be that way. In the beginning, God instituted the family when He created Adam and Eve and joined them together as "one flesh" (Gen. 2:24). However, their sin and rebellion against God brought havoc into their relationship and into all subsequent families. In their own family they soon experienced violence as Cain murdered his brother Abel, causing an ongoing cycle of trouble (4:1–16).

Even in a fallen world, however, God desires His best for the family structure. Scripture holds out great hope for the restoration of marriage. For example:

- *It encourages parents to raise children in an environment of truth and integrity (Deut. 6:2–9).*
- *It offers a touching illustration of aid to a family devastated by death and the prospect of poverty (Ruth 1–4).*
- *It shows a family destroyed by senseless evil but restored twofold by a faithful God (Job 1:13–21; 2:9; 42:10–17).*

incense, myrrh, frankincense, wine, olive oil, choice flour and wheat, cattle and sheep, horses and chariots, slaves—and human lives.[e]

14 "The fruit for which your soul longed
has gone from you,
and all your dainties and your splendor
are lost to you,
never to be found again!"

15The merchants of these wares, who gained wealth from her, will stand far off, in fear of her torment, weeping and mourning aloud,

16 "Alas, alas, the great city,
clothed in fine linen,
in purple and scarlet,
adorned with gold,
with jewels, and with pearls!
17 For in one hour all this wealth has been laid waste!"

And all shipmasters and seafarers, sailors and all whose trade is on the sea, stood far off
18and cried out as they saw the smoke of her burning,

[e]Or *chariots, and human bodies and souls*

- *It affirms the beauty of sexual love within marriage in terms of passion, fidelity, and integrity (Song of Solomon).*
- *It encourages the restoration of broken relationships, just as God will do with His people (Hos. 1:2—2:23).*
- *It offers guidelines for marriage in terms of mutual submission, loyalty, love, and discipline for children that does not alienate them—a way of relating that is similar to Christ's relationship to His bride the church (Eph. 5:21—6:4).*

God's original design for the family will not be destroyed. Right now you may be experiencing the struggle of human relationships or even the pain of a broken family. But you can take hope from the knowledge that God's healing and love will ultimately win out, and He will "wipe every tear . . . Death . . . mourning and crying and pain will be no more" (21:4). ◆

Scripture offers a great deal of help on a variety of family-related issues. See the table, "Family Helps in the New Testament Letters," Heb. 12:3–13.

"AND THE MERCHANTS OF THE EARTH WEEP AND MOURN FOR HER. . . ."
—Revelation 18:11

MAGIC AND SORCERY

FOR YOUR INFO 18:23 **There is today a growing interest in occult beliefs and practices, such as fortune-telling, witchcraft, and astrology. But John reveals the true nature of the occult when he writes that the sorcery of Babylon has deceived all the nations (v. 23).**

Occult practices were common among the pagan nations of the ancient world. But attempts to contact or control evil spirits were expressly forbidden to the Hebrews, and the prohibition extends to believers today. Among the practices that Deuteronomy 18:10–12 calls "abhorrent to the Lord" are:

- **child sacrifice (making one's son or daughter "pass through the fire").**
- **witchcraft.**
- **soothsaying, a form of divination which may have been similar to tea leaf reading or astrology.**
- **interpreting omens.**
- **sorcery.**
- **conjuring spells.**
- **consulting mediums.**
- **spiritism.**
- **calling up the dead.**

In the New Testament, the gospel exposed two sorcerers, Simon (Acts 8:9–25) and Elymas (Acts 13:6–8). They may have been something like the "itinerant Jewish exorcists," also mentioned in the book of Acts (Acts 19:13), who attempted to drive evil spirits out of people in the name of Jesus.

The New Testament word translated "sorcery" comes from the same Greek word as our English word, "pharmacy." Obviously this has to do with drugs; a more relevant and contemporary application could hardly be found. The denunciations of Revela-

(continued on next page)

"What city was like the great city?"
19And they threw dust on their heads, as they wept and
mourned, crying out,
"Alas, alas, the great city,
where all who had ships at sea
grew rich by her wealth!
For in one hour she has been laid waste."
20 Rejoice over her, O heaven, you saints and apostles
and prophets! For God has given judgment for you against
her.
21 Then a mighty angel took up a stone like a great millstone and threw it into the sea, saying,
"With such violence Babylon the great city
will be thrown down,
and will be found no more;
22 and the sound of harpists and minstrels and of flutists
and trumpeters
will be heard in you no more;
and an artisan of any trade
will be found in you no more;
and the sound of the millstone
will be heard in you no more;
23 and the light of a lamp
will shine in you no more;
and the voice of bridegroom and bride
will be heard in you no more;
for your merchants were the magnates of the earth,
and all nations were deceived by your sorcery.
24 And in you[f] was found the blood of prophets and of
saints,
and of all who have been slaughtered on earth."

18:23

Rejoicing in Heaven

19 After this I heard what seemed to be the loud voice
of a great multitude in heaven, saying,
"Hallelujah!
Salvation and glory and power to our God,
2 for his judgments are true and just;
he has judged the great whore
who corrupted the earth with her fornication,
and he has avenged on her the blood of his servants."[g]
3Once more they said,
"Hallelujah!
The smoke goes up from her forever and ever."
4And the twenty-four elders and the four living creatures
fell down and worshiped God who is seated on the throne,
saying,

[f] Gk *her* [g] Gk *slaves*

"Amen. Hallelujah!"
5 And from the throne came a voice saying,
"Praise our God,
all you his servants,[h]
and all who fear him,
small and great."

19:6–10
see pg. 920

6Then I heard what seemed to be the
voice of a great multitude, like the sound
of many waters and like the sound of mighty thunderpeals,
crying out,
"Hallelujah!
For the Lord our God
the Almighty reigns.
7 Let us rejoice and exult
and give him the glory,
for the marriage of the Lamb has come,
and his bride has made herself ready;
8 to her it has been granted to be clothed
with fine linen, bright and pure"—
for the fine linen is the righteous deeds of the saints.
9 And the angel said[i] to me, "Write this: Blessed are
those who are invited to the marriage supper of the Lamb."
And he said to me, "These are true words of God." 10Then I
fell down at his feet to worship him, but he said to me,
"You must not do that! I am a fellow servant[j] with you and
your comrades[k] who hold the testimony of Jesus.[l] Worship
God! For the testimony of Jesus[l] is the spirit of prophecy."

The Rule of Christ Restored

11 Then I saw heaven opened, and there was a white
horse! Its rider is called Faithful and True, and in righteousness he judges and makes war. 12His eyes are like a flame of
fire, and on his head are many diadems; and he has a name
inscribed that no one knows but himself. 13He is clothed in
a robe dipped in[m] blood, and his name is called The Word
of God. 14And the armies of heaven, wearing fine linen,
white and pure, were following him on white horses.
15From his mouth comes a sharp sword with which to
strike down the nations, and he will rule[n] them with a rod
of iron; he will tread the wine press of the fury of the wrath
of God the Almighty. 16On his robe and on his thigh he has
a name inscribed, "King of kings and Lord of lords."
17 Then I saw an angel standing in the sun, and with a
loud voice he called to all the birds that fly in midheaven,
"Come, gather for the great supper of God, 18to eat the flesh
of kings, the flesh of captains, the flesh of the mighty, the

[h]Gk *slaves* [i]Gk *he said* [j]Gk *slave* [k]Gk *brothers* [l]Or *to Jesus* [m]Other ancient authorities read *sprinkled with* [n]Or *will shepherd*

(continued from previous page)

tion 9:21; 18:23; 21:8; and 22:15 apply to those who use drugs to bring on trances during which they claim to have supernatural knowledge or power.

Will Evil Ever Get Its Reward?

CONSIDER THIS 20:1–5 **Anyone who pays attention to today's headlines is likely to wonder, whatever happened to ethics and justice? Sometimes it seems like fairness never happens in matters of business, government, the law, and world affairs. But for those who long to see justice reign, the Bible offers powerful hope.**

God will not turn His back on injustice. His character demands that He give people what is coming to them. Moreover, Scripture promises that He will deal with evil in absolute, final ways. John's vision foresees that triumphant accomplishment:

- **God will bind evil and cast it into a bottomless pit (vv. 2–3).**
- **He will place a seal on the source of evil (v. 3).**
- **He will administer judgment and restore believers who have been killed unjustly (v. 4).**
- **He will deal finally with Satan after allowing him one last attempt to deceive (vv. 7–9); the devil's punishment will include eternal torment (vv. 10, 14).**
- **the dead will stand before God and be judged (vv. 11–15).**

This picture offers tremendous hope to anyone concerned about the injustices of our world today. As we seek to deliver God's righteousness into our communities, workplaces, and families, it's a relief to know that no human being—no matter how impartial and objective or biased and corrupt—is the final judge. Ultimate justice will someday be administered by One who can be thoroughly trusted—God, through Christ.

flesh of horses and their riders—flesh of all, both free and
slave, both small and great." [19]Then I saw the beast and the
kings of the earth with their armies gathered to make war
against the rider on the horse and against his army. [20]And
the beast was captured, and with it the false prophet who
had performed in its presence the signs by which he deceived those who had received the mark of the beast and
those who worshiped its image. These two were thrown
alive into the lake of fire that burns with sulfur. [21]And the
rest were killed by the sword of the rider on the horse, the
sword that came from his mouth; and all the birds were
gorged with their flesh.

Judgments on Satan

20:1–5

20 Then I saw an angel coming
down from heaven, holding in
his hand the key to the bottomless pit and a great chain.
[2]He seized the dragon, that ancient serpent, who is the
Devil and Satan, and bound him for a thousand years, [3]and
threw him into the pit, and locked and sealed it over him,
so that he would deceive the nations no more, until the
thousand years were ended. After that he must be let out
for a little while.

4 Then I saw thrones, and those seated on them were
given authority to judge. I also saw the souls of those who
had been beheaded for their testimony to Jesus[o] and for the
word of God. They had not worshiped the beast or its image and had not received its mark on their foreheads or
their hands. They came to life and reigned with Christ a
thousand years. [5](The rest of the dead did not come to life
until the thousand years were ended.) This is the first resurrection. [6]Blessed and holy are those who share in the first
resurrection. Over these the second death has no power,
but they will be priests of God and of Christ, and they will
reign with him a thousand years.

7 When the thousand years are ended, Satan will be released from his prison [8]and will come out to deceive the
nations at the four corners of the earth, Gog and Magog, in
order to gather them for battle; they are as numerous as the
sands of the sea. [9]They marched up over the breadth of
the earth and surrounded the camp of the saints and the
beloved city. And fire came down from heaven[p] and consumed them. [10]And the devil who had
deceived them was thrown into the lake of
fire and sulfur, where the beast and the false prophet were,
and they will be tormented day and night forever and ever.

20:1–10 see pg. 926

[o]Or *for the testimony of Jesus* [p]Other ancient authorities read *from God, out of heaven,* or *out of heaven from God*

The Great White Throne Judgment

11 Then I saw a great white throne and the one who sat on it; the earth and the heaven fled from his presence, and no place was found for them. [12]And I saw the dead, great and small, standing before the throne, and books were opened. Also another book was opened, the book of life. And the dead were judged according to their works, as recorded in the books. [13]And the sea gave up the dead that were in it, Death and Hades gave up the dead that were in them, and all were judged according to what they had done. [14]Then Death and Hades were thrown into the lake of fire. This is the second death, the lake of fire; [15]and anyone whose name was not found written in the book of life was thrown into the lake of fire.

A New Heaven and A New Earth

21:1 see pg. 928

21:1–2

21 Then I saw a new heaven and a new earth; for the first heaven and the first earth had passed away, and the sea was no more. [2]And I saw the holy city, the new Jerusalem, coming down out of heaven from God, prepared as a bride adorned for her husband. [3]And I heard a loud voice from the throne saying,

"See, the home[q] of God is among mortals.
He will dwell[r] with them;
they will be his peoples,[s]
and God himself will be with them;[t]
4 he will wipe every tear from their eyes.
Death will be no more;
mourning and crying and pain will be no more,
for the first things have passed away."

5 And the one who was seated on the throne said, "See, I am making all things new." Also he said, "Write this, for these words are trustworthy and true." [6]Then he said to me, "It is done! I am the Alpha and the Omega, the beginning and the end. To the thirsty I will give water as a gift from the spring of the water of life. [7]Those who conquer will inherit these things, and I will be their God and they will be my children. [8]But as for the cowardly, the faithless,[u] the polluted, the murderers, the fornicators, the sorcerers, the idolaters, and all liars, their place will be in the lake that burns with fire and sulfur, which is the second death."

The New Jerusalem

9 Then one of the seven angels who had the seven bowls full of the seven last plagues came and said to me, "Come, I

(Bible text continued on page 927)

[q]Gk *the tabernacle* [r]Gk *will tabernacle* [s]Other ancient authorities read *people* [t]Other ancient authorities add *and be their God* [u]Or *the unbelieving*

The New Jerusalem

CONSIDER THIS 21:1–2 *As John draws Revelation to a close, he offers a glimpse of a new Jerusalem descending from heaven (v. 2). It is Jerusalem as it was intended to be—fulfilling its prophetic calling as a light to the nations, a place of justice and peace, and the capital city and dwelling place of God.*

CONSIDER THIS
20:1–10

MYTH #10

10 MYTHS ABOUT CHRISTIANITY

MYTH: ALL THE EVIL AND SUFFERING IN THE WORLD PROVES THERE IS NO GOD

Many people today accept a number of myths about Christianity, with the result that they never respond to Jesus as He really is. This is one of ten articles that speak to some of those misconceptions. For a list of all ten, see 1 Tim. 1:3–4.

Few stories offer a more dramatic or thrilling climax than the closing chapters of Revelation. The scene of God finally and ultimately destroying Satan and his hosts (vv. 1–10) brings a bright, joyful conclusion not only to the Revelation of John, but to the entire Bible. Once and for all, evil will be banished, never again to trouble God's creation.

Yet while Christians look forward to that day with hope, many other people reject God and the gospel precisely because of evil in the world. Their reasoning goes something like this:

(1) A God who is good and loving would not allow evil and suffering in His world.
(2) Yet evil exists in the world.
(3) If God is all-powerful, He could remove evil if He wanted to.
(4) Yet evil remains. In fact, at times it seems to grow worse.
(5) Therefore, a good and powerful God must not exist.

This is a powerful argument, and there can be no question that evil and pain are a massive problem to both belief and behavior. Christianity offers no knock-down solution, but the Bible does give us ground to stand on as we try to live in a world where suffering is real.

(1) The Bible teaches that God did not create evil. The world He made was utterly good (Gen. 1:31). Where, then, did evil come from? The record finds people themselves turning against God, using His gift of free will to rebel against Him. With that moral rebellion, the perfection of God's world came tumbling down and people began to suffer.

One biblical answer is that behind human wickedness lies a great outside influence, Satan. This fallen angel hates God and everything to do with Him. He is out to destroy both humanity and the environment and does everything He can to attack God and His purposes. To that end he promotes much of the evil and suffering that we see. (See "Spiritual Realities Beyond You," Matt. 8:28–34.)

(2) The Bible teaches that even though God did not create evil, nor does He will it, He nevertheless uses it to accomplish His purposes. For instance, God sometimes uses pain in a profound way to draw people to Himself, especially when they otherwise would not respond to Him. Likewise, the struggle against evil has led many to strive for good. Like an irritating grain of sand in an oyster, it has produced pearls of character in countless people—courage, endurance, self-sacrifice, compassion.

(3) Why then, if God is all-powerful, does He not remove evil from the world? The question assumes, of course, that He has done nothing. But in fact, He has, is, and will. First, God Himself came into this world, with all its sorrow, pain, and wickedness, and lived as a man. Jesus was well acquainted with suffering. He knew poverty, thirst, hunger, injustice, physical abuse, heartbreak, and betrayal. He ended his life in excruciating

(continued on next page)

will show you the bride, the wife of the Lamb." 10And in
the spirit[v] he carried me away to a great, high mountain
and showed me the holy city Jerusalem coming down out
of heaven from God. 11It has the glory of God and a radiance like a very rare jewel, like jasper, clear as crystal. 12It
has a great, high wall with twelve gates, and at the gates
twelve angels, and on the gates are inscribed the names of
the twelve tribes of the Israelites; 13on the east three gates,
on the north three gates, on the south three gates, and on
the west three gates. 14And the wall of the city has twelve
foundations, and on them are the twelve names of the
twelve apostles of the Lamb.
15 The angel[w] who talked to me had a measuring rod of
gold to measure the city and its gates and walls. 16The city
lies foursquare, its length the same as its width; and he
measured the city with his rod, fifteen hundred miles;[x] its
length and width and height are equal. 17He also measured
its wall, one hundred forty-four cubits[y] by human measure-
ment, which the angel was using. 18The wall is built of
jasper, while the city is pure gold, clear as glass. 19The
foundations of the wall of the city are adorned with every
jewel; the first was jasper, the second sapphire, the third
agate, the fourth emerald, 20the fifth onyx, the sixth carnelian, the seventh chrysolite, the eighth beryl, the ninth
topaz, the tenth chrysoprase, the eleventh jacinth, the
twelfth amethyst. 21And the twelve gates are twelve pearls,
each of the gates is a single pearl, and the street of the city
is pure gold, transparent as glass.
22 I saw no temple in the city, for its temple is the Lord
God the Almighty and the Lamb. 23And the city has no
need of sun or moon to shine on it, for the glory of God is
its light, and its lamp is the Lamb. 24The nations will walk
by its light, and the kings of the earth will bring their glory
into it. 25Its gates will never be shut by day—and there will
be no night there. 26People will bring into it the glory and
the honor of the nations. 27But nothing unclean will enter
it, nor anyone who practices abomination or falsehood, but
only those who are written in the Lamb's book of life.

Eden Is Restored

22:1–11 see pg. 929

22:2 see pg. 930

22 Then the angel[z] showed me the
river of the water of life, bright as
crystal, flowing from the throne of God
and of the Lamb 2through the middle of
the street of the city. On either side of the river is the tree of
life[a] with its twelve kinds of fruit, producing its fruit each

[v]Or *in the Spirit* [w]Gk *He* [x]Gk *twelve thousand stadia* [y]That is, almost seventy-five yards [z]Gk *he* [a]Or *the Lamb.* [2]*In the middle of the street of the city, and on either side of the river, is the tree of life*

(continued from previous page)

pain. So God certainly understands our condition. He has personally experienced it.

In the process, God dealt with the problem of evil at its root. On the cross, Jesus took on Himself the wickedness of every man and woman who has ever lived in order to do away with it. We may never fully understand what happened in that incredible act of self-sacrifice. But we know that Christ broke the grip of evil that holds the world captive. Already we can see among God's people a glimpse of the new life that He has brought about (Rom. 8:4, 11).

(4) That brings us to God's final solution to evil, which John describes in Revelation 20. In the end, God will triumph by doing away with evil itself and those who promote it. He will restore His creation and His creatures to their original purpose, to the original relationship they enjoyed with Him. Suffering will be but a memory. Goodness, justice, and peace will characterize the moral climate of God's new heaven and earth. ◆

month; and the leaves of the tree are for the healing of the
nations. 3Nothing accursed will be found there any more.
But the throne of God and of the Lamb will be in it, and his
servants[b] will worship him; 4they will see his face, and his
name will be on their foreheads. 5And there will be no
more night; they need no light of lamp or sun, for the Lord
God will be their light, and they will reign forever and ever.

"I Am Coming Soon!"

6 And he said to me, "These words are trustworthy and
true, for the Lord, the God of the spirits of the prophets,
has sent his angel to show his servants[b] what must soon
take place."

(Bible text continued on page 930)

[b]Gk *slaves*

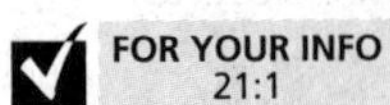

GENESIS AND REVELATION— THE FIRST AND LAST VOLUMES

The word "Bible" comes from the Greek word *biblos*, which means "book." The Bible is a complete book, unified in its theme and message. But it is also a collection of sixty-six books, a virtual library of God's Word to humanity. Genesis, the first book in the Bible, and Revelation, the last, help to define the collection, showing us the beginning and the end of history.

Here in Revelation 21, John reveals a new heaven and earth. In reading it, we can't help but look back to the beginnings of the world:

Genesis	Revelation
God creates the world.	God creates a new heaven and earth.
The devil introduces sin into the world.	The devil is defeated and destroyed; sin is done away with.
Humanity falls into sin.	God restores people to their original sinlessness.
The world is subjected to a curse.	The curse is removed.
People are separate from God.	People live with God forever.
People shed tears and know sorrow.	God wipes away every tear and removes sorrow.
People are barred from the tree of life.	People may eat freely from the tree of life.
Death enters the world.	Death is done away with and people live forever.
The languages of humanity are confused and the peoples scattered.	The peoples of the world are brought together before Christ and they sing His praises together.

One way to view the Bible is to see it as a magnificent three-part story. See "The Bible: Getting the Big Picture," 2 Tim. 3:16–17.

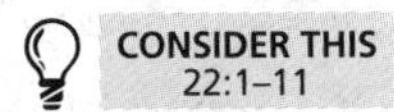

A Glance at Work in the Bible

As John's Revelation draws to a close, we see creation restored to its original intention (vv. 1–11). Since work plays such an important role in the world—whether Eden, today, or the end time—this is a good place to review Scripture's teaching on work, considered according to three different eras: work as it was originally intended, work in a fallen world, and work as it will be when Christ returns.

Main Point	Key Texts	Related Articles
Creation of Work: Work according to God's original design.		
God reveals Himself as the primary Worker and Creator.	Gen. 1:1–25; Ps. 19:1–6	"Our Daily Bread," Matt. 6:11; "The Divine Partnership," John 1:3; "He's Got the Whole World in His Hands," Heb. 1:2–3; "Creation: 'Very Good,' But Not Sacred!" Heb. 11:3
God creates us in His likeness and image as coworkers.	Gen. 1:26–31; 2:15–25; Ps. 8:1–9	"Every Breath You Take," Col. 1:17; "People at Work," Heb. 2:7
Distortion of Work: Work under the curse and influenced by the principalities and powers that oppose God.		
Sin introduces toil, sweat, and pain into work and family.	Gen. 3:16–24; 4:11–12; Rom. 8:20–22	"Is Work a Curse?" Rom. 8:20
Complications intensify in the workplace.	Gen. 39:1–23	"Workplace Myths," 1 Cor. 3:9; "Honesty and Ethical Standards," Phil. 2:15; "It's Not Fair!" 1 Pet. 2:18–21
The danger of exploitation in the workplace appears.	Ex. 1:8–22	"Work-World Codes," Col. 3:22—4:1
Work is not only for our own benefit but for others, including the poor and oppressed.	Ex. 23:10–11; Deut. 15:7–11; Eph. 4:28	"From Deadbeat to Donor," Eph. 4:28
God still equips people for work with His Word and the Spirit.	Ex. 31:2–11	"People at Work," Heb. 2:7
People lack fulfillment by idolizing work or making it an end in itself.	Eccl. 2:4–26; Luke 12:13–34	"Do-It-Yourself Idolatry," Col. 3:5
But God still rules and work can be a gift that fits God's design.	Eccl. 2:24—3:17	"A Command to Work," 2 Thess. 3:6–12
Work is a gift of God and will be blessed.	Ps. 104:1–35; 127:1–5; Eccl. 3:12–13; 5:18–20	"People at Work," Heb. 2:7
Jesus re-established and illustrated God's original design for work.	John 4:34–38; 5:1–18	"Jesus the Carpenter," Mark 6:3; "Paul's 'Real' Job," Acts 18:1–3
Our agony in this life continues as we seek release from sin and the renewal of creation.	Eccl. 1:2–3; Rom. 8:18–30	"Is Work a Curse?" Rom. 8:20
God's people are to illustrate their new citizenship in heaven through good work here and now.	Eph. 6:5–9; Col. 3:17–23; Titus 2:1—3:15; James 2:1–26	"A Promotion," Eph. 6:5–9; "Who's the Boss?" Col. 3:22–24; "'I Won't Hire Christians!'" 1 Tim. 6:1–2; "Your 'Workstyle,'" Titus 2:9–10
Restoration of Work: Work as it will be when Christ returns.		
God will someday restore His original design; His people will work without the burden of sin.	Is. 65:17–25; Rev. 15:1–4; 22:1–11	

Why not use this overview of the Bible's teaching on work as an outline of study for yourself, others at your church, or coworkers who want to know what God has to say on the subject?

To understand more about Scripture's teaching on the three different time periods shown—God's original design, life in a fallen world, and the period after Christ returns—see "The Bible: Getting the Big Picture," 2 Tim. 3:16–17.

7 "See, I am coming soon! Blessed is the one who keeps
the words of the prophecy of this book."
8 I, John, am the one who heard and saw these things.
And when I heard and saw them, I fell down to worship at
the feet of the angel who showed them to me; [9]but he said
to me, "You must not do that! I am a fellow servant[c] with
you and your comrades[d] the prophets, and with those who
keep the words of this book. Worship God!"
10 And he said to me, "Do not seal up the words of the
prophecy of this book, for the time is near. [11]Let the evildoer still do evil, and the filthy still be filthy, and the righteous still do right, and the holy still be holy."

12 "See, I am coming soon; my reward is with me, to repay according to everyone's work. [13]I am the Alpha and the
Omega, the first and the last, the beginning and the end."
14 Blessed are those who wash their robes,[e] so that they
will have the right to the tree of life and may enter the city
by the gates. [15]Outside are the dogs and sorcerers and fornicators and murderers and idolaters, and everyone who
loves and practices falsehood.
16 "It is I, Jesus, who sent my angel to you with this tes-

[c]Gk *slave* [d]Gk *brothers* [e]Other ancient authorities read *do his commandments*

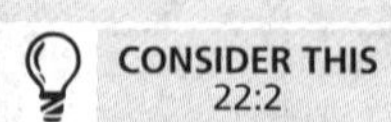

CONSIDER THIS
22:2

FRESH FRUIT SALAD!

When you think of the new heavens and new earth that God will someday create, what images come to mind? John's vision includes a unique species of tree, the tree of life that bears twelve kinds of fruits—a different fruit every month (v. 2)!

Trees that productive will afford little rest for the workers who cultivate and harvest them. Yet surely those fruit pickers will be happy because the text also says, "Nothing accursed will be found there any more*" (v. 3, emphasis added). Work will be free of the painful toil and drudgery that now characterizes it (see also Rev. 21:4).*

This view of the new creation, with delightful work and enjoyable results, is very similar to the description of God's future society in Isaiah 65:17–23. There the picture includes such attractive images as:

- *joy and rejoicing (v. 18).*
- *an end to weeping and crying (v. 19).*
- *building and living in one's own house (v. 21).*
- *owning, planting, and enjoying the fruit of one's vineyard (vv. 21–22).*

timony for the churches. I am the root and the descendant of David, the bright morning star."

22:17 [17] The Spirit and the bride say, "Come."
And let everyone who hears say,
"Come."
And let everyone who is thirsty come.
Let anyone who wishes take the water of life as a gift.

A Final Warning

18 I warn everyone who hears the words of the
prophecy of this book: if anyone adds to them, God will
add to that person the plagues described in this book; [19]if
anyone takes away from the words of the book of this
prophecy, God will take away that person's share in the tree
of life and in the holy city, which are described in this book.
20 The one who testifies to these things says, "Surely I
am coming soon."
Amen. Come, Lord Jesus!
21 The grace of the Lord Jesus be with all the saints.
Amen.[f]

[f]Other ancient authorities lack *all*; others lack *the saints*; others lack *Amen*

- *enjoying the work of one's hands (v. 22).*
- *an end to laboring in vain or bringing children into a world of trouble (v. 23).*

These statements from Revelation and Isaiah recall the original design that God had for His creation, a creation that was "very good" (Gen. 1:31). God created people to be His coworkers in managing the resources of His world for the benefit of all (see "People at Work," Heb. 2:7). God will restore that ideal. As Paul promised, the world will be freed from its sufferings, futility, and bondage to corruption and be made again to fulfill its original design (Rom. 8:18–25).

What a hope to look forward to—the reign of God over a joyful new world where trouble-free families work painlessly together and enjoy fresh fruit salad month after month! ◆

Most of us know all too well how burdensome work can be. Yet the Bible calls it a gift from God. See "Is Work a Curse?" Rom. 8:20–22.

There's a Welcome Here

CONSIDER THIS 22:17 **Perhaps you or someone you know feels hesitant about spiritual things. Matters of faith may feel forbidding, even scary. Religion may seem like nothing but judgment and condemnation.**

Yet Jesus came not to condemn, but to save. His primary purpose was to offer life to dying people, inviting them to experience forgiveness, healing, and hope. "Come!" He says to those who are thirsty, "Let anyone who wishes take the water of life as a gift" (v. 17; see also John 7:37–38).

Centuries prior to Jesus' coming, a prophet foretold this invitation (Is. 55:1, 3):

Ho, everyone who thirsts,
come to the waters;
and you that have no money,
come, buy and eat!
Come, buy wine and milk
without money and without price. . . .
Incline your ear, and come to me;
listen, so that you may live.

This is a powerful invitation because the same Jesus who makes it wields the power to withdraw it from those who refuse His call and continue to live in rebellion and sin (Rev. 22:14–15, 18–19). Just as He has authority to welcome us into eternal life, so He has the authority not to welcome us. Yet in His grace He chooses to offer life to sinful people.

You may be confused about many issues of religion, but hear God's gracious offer: Jesus wants to forgive your sins and welcome you into new life. If you haven't already accepted His invitation, why not do so now and begin the exciting journey that leads to eternal life!

Acknowledgments

Weights and Measures

Themes to Study in the New Testament

Index to Key New Testament Passages

The Four Gospels Side by Side

Jobs and Occupations Index

Acknowledgments

Matthew 13:34–35: "Ten Myths About Christianity, Myth #1: Jesus Christ Was Only a Great Moral Teacher." Adapted by permission from *Ten Myths About Christianity* by Michael Green and Gordon Carkner, Lion Publishing, 1988. Quotation from C.S. Lewis, *Mere Christianity,* Macmillan, 1978, used by permission of HarperCollins Publishers.

Matthew 20:28: quotation from *Honest To God,* by John A.T. Robinson, SCM Press Ltd. 1963. Used by permission. © J.A.T. Robinson, 1963.

Matthew 23:1–30: excerpt from *A Severe Mercy* by Sheldon Vanauken. Copyright ©1977, 1980 by Sheldon Vanauken. Reprinted by permission of HarperCollins Publishers Inc.

Matthew 28:1–10: "Ten Myths About Christianity, Myth #2: There Is No Evidence That Jesus Rose from the Dead." Adapted by permission from *Ten Myths About Christianity* by Michael Green and Gordon Carkner, Lion Publishing, 1988.

Mark 2:17: quotation reprinted from *Walking on Water* by Madeleine L'Engle, ©1980 by Crosswicks. Used by permission of Harold Shaw Publishers, Wheaton, IL.

Mark 16:15: quotation from *National Catholic Reporter,* October 27, 1989.

John 4:48: "Ten Myths About Christianity, Myth #3: Science Is In Conflict with Christian Faith." Adapted by permission from *Ten Myths About Christianity* by Michael Green and Gordon Carkner, Lion Publishing, 1988.

John 5:17: "God—The Original Worker." Adapted by permission from Doug Sherman and William Hendricks, *Your Work Matters to God,* NavPress, 1987.

John 15:18–20: quotation from A. W. Tozer, *A Treasury of A.W. Tozer,* Baker Book House, 1980.

John 18:37–38: quotation reprinted from *Walking on Water* by Madeleine L'Engle, ©1980 by Crosswicks. Used by permission of Harold Shaw Publishers, Wheaton, IL.

Acts 4:12: "Ten Myths About Christianity, Myth #4: It Doesn't Matter What You Believe, All Religions Are Basically the Same." Adapted by permission from *Ten Myths About Christianity* by Michael Green and Gordon Carkner, Lion Publishing, 1988.

Acts 4:13: quotation from Elton Trueblood, *Your Other Vocation,* Harper & Brothers, 1952, used by permission of HarperCollins Publishers.

Acts 24:22: quotation reprinted from *Walking on Water* by Madeleine L'Engle, ©1980 by Crosswicks. Used by permission of Harold Shaw Publishers, Wheaton, IL.

Romans 8:20: "Is Work a Curse?" Adapted by permission from Doug Sherman and William Hendricks, *Your Work Matters to God,* NavPress, 1987.

Romans 14:5: quotation from Elton Trueblood, *Your Other Vocation,* Harper & Brothers, 1952, used by permission of HarperCollins Publishers.

1 Corinthians 1:26: "Ten Myths About Christianity, Myth #5: Christianity Is Just a Crutch for the Weak." Adapted by permission from *Ten Myths About Christianity* by Michael Green and Gordon Carkner, Lion Publishing, 1988.

1 Corinthians 7:17: excerpt from *A Severe Mercy* by Sheldon Vanauken. Copyright ©1977, 1980 by Sheldon Vanauken. Reprinted by permission of HarperCollins Publishers Inc.

1 Corinthians 13:12: quotation from Pete Hammond, *Marketplace Networks,* InterVarsity Christian Fellowship of the USA, 1990.

1 Corinthians 15:9–10: "Ten Myths About Christianity, Myth #6: People Become Christians Through Social Conditioning." Adapted by permission from *Ten Myths About Christianity* by Michael Green and Gordon Carkner, Lion Publishing, 1988.

2 Corinthians 4:2: "A Code of Ethics for Christian Witness." Used by permission of InterVarsity Christian Fellowship of the USA.

Galatians 5:1–12: "Ten Myths About Christianity, Myth #7: Christianity Stifles Personal Freedom." Adapted by permission from *Ten Myths About Christianity* by Michael Green and Gordon Carkner, Lion Publishing, 1988.

Galatians 5:18: "Ten Commandments—Ten Great Freedoms." Used by permission of InterVarsity Christian Fellowship of the USA.

Ephesians 4:12: quotation from Elton Trueblood, *Your Other Vocation,* Harper & Brothers, 1952, used by permission of HarperCollins Publishers.

Ephesians 6:5: quotation from Mark Quinn, "Five Guidelines to a Spirituality of Work," *Initiatives,* newsletter of the National Center for the Laity, 1989.

Philippians 2:15: "Honesty & Ethical Standards." From a speech given by George Gallup, Jr., December 2, 1987, as reported in *Emerging Trends,* Princeton Religion Research Center, 1988.

Colossians 3:22: reprinted from *Liberating the Laity* by R. Paul Stevens. ©1985 by InterVarsity Christian Fellowship of the USA. Used by permission of InterVarsity Press, P.O. Box 1400, Downers Grove, IL 60515.

1 Thessalonians 1:7: quotation from speech by Richard Halverson as reported in the newsletter of Fourth Presbyterian Church, McLean, VA.

1 Thessalonians 4:11–12: excerpt from *A Severe Mercy* by Sheldon Vanauken. Copyright ©1977, 1980 by Sheldon Vanauken. Reprinted by permission of HarperCollins Publishers Inc.

1 Thessalonians 5:6: remarks by Anglican Bishop Michael Marshall, as quoted in editor's column, *America Magazine,* 1990.

1 Timothy 1:3–4: "Ten Myths About Christianity." Adapted by permission from *Ten Myths About Christianity* by Michael Green and Gordon Carkner, Lion Publishing, 1988.

1 Timothy 6:18: quotation from *Dedication and Leadership* by Douglas Hyde. ©1966 by the University of Notre Dame Press. Reprinted by permission.

Titus 1:15: quotation reprinted from *Walking on Water* by Madeleine L'Engle, ©1980 by Crosswicks. Used by permission of Harold Shaw Publishers, Wheaton, IL.

Hebrews 2:7: "People at Work." Adapted by permission from Doug Sherman and William Hendricks, *Your Work Matters to God,* NavPress, 1987.

Hebrews 12:1–2: "Ten Myths About Christianity, Myth #8: Christianity Is Otherwordly and Irrelevant to Modern Life." Adapted by permission from *Ten Myths About Christianity* by Michael Green and Gordon Carkner, Lion Publishing, 1988.

Hebrews 13:15: reprinted from *Reinventing Evangelism* by Donald C. Posterski. ©1989 by Donald C. Posterski. Used by permission of InterVarsity Press, P.O. Box 1400, Downers Grove, IL 60515.

James 2:8–13: "Ten Commandments for Practical Living." Adapted from *Ten Commandments for Practical Living,* ©1973, McNair Associates, used by permission.

James 3:13–18: quotation from *Dedication and Leadership* by Douglas Hyde. ©1966 by the University of Notre Dame Press. Reprinted by permission.

1 Peter 1:1: reprinted from *Liberating the Laity* by R. Paul Stevens. ©1985 by InterVarsity Christian Fellowship of the USA. Used by permission of InterVarsity Press, P.O. Box 1400, Downers Grove, IL 60515.

1 Peter 2:9: quotation from Elton Trueblood, *Your Other Vocation,* Harper & Brothers, 1952, used by permission of HarperCollins Publishers.

1 Peter 3:15–17: quotation from *Dedication and Leadership* by Douglas Hyde. ©1966 by the University of Notre Dame Press. Reprinted by permission.

2 Peter 1:16: "Ten Myths About Christianity, Myth #9: The Bible Is Unreliable and Not to Be Trusted." Adapted by permission from *Ten Myths About Christianity* by Michael Green and Gordon Carkner, Lion Publishing, 1988.

2 Peter 2:13: quotation from Fr. Jerry Foley, "We Work At Our Leisure," from *Connecting Faith and Life,* Sheed and Ward, 1986.

1 John 5:4–5: quotation from Philip J. Lee, Jr., *Against the Protestant Gnostics,* Oxford University Press, 1989.

Revelation 15:1–8: quotation from C.S. Lewis, *A Preface to Paradise Lost,* Oxford University Press, 1942.

Revelation 20:1–10: "Ten Myths About Christianity, Myth #10: Evil and Suffering in the World Proves There Is No God." Adapted by permission from *Ten Myths About Christianity* by Michael Green and Gordon Carkner, Lion Publishing, 1988.

A diligent effort has been made to secure permission to reprint previously published material. Any oversight should be brought to the attention of the publisher for rectification in a subsequent printing.

Use of material does not necessarily imply endorsement of all of the author's other views.

WEIGHTS AND MEASURES

WEIGHTS

Unit	Weight	Equivalents	Translations
Jewish Weights			
Talent	c. 75 pounds for common talent, c. 150 pounds for royal talent	60 minas; 3,000 shekels	talent
Mina (Maneh)	1.25 pounds	50 shekels	mina
Shekel	c. .4 ounce (11.4 grams) for common shekel c. .8 ounce for royal shekel	2 bekas; 20 gerahs	shekel
Beka	c. .2 ounce (5.7 grams)	1/2 shekel; 10 gerahs	half a shekel
Gerah	c. .02 ounce (.57 grams)	1/20 shekel	gerah
Roman Weight			
Litra	12 ounces		pound

MEASURES OF LENGTH

Unit	Length	Equivalents	Translations
Day's journey	c. 20 miles		day's journey
Roman mile	4,854 feet	8 stadia	mile
Sabbath day's journey	3,637 feet	6 stadia	Sabbath day's journey
Stadion	606 feet	1/8 Roman mile	furlong
Rod	9 feet (10.5 feet in Ezekiel)	3 paces; 6 cubits	measuring reed, reed
Fathom	6 feet	4 cubits	fathom
Pace	3 feet	1/3 rod; 2 cubits	pace
Cubit	18 inches	1/2 pace; 2 spans	cubit
Span	9 inches	1/2 cubit; 3 handbreadths	span
Handbreadth	3 inches	1/3 span; 4 fingers	handbreadth
Finger	.75 inchs	1/4 handbreadth	finger

LIQUID MEASURES

Unit	Measure	Equivalents	Translations
Kor	60 gallons	10 baths	kor
Metretes	10.2 gallons		gallons
Bath	6 gallons	6 hins	measure, bath
Hin	1 gallon	2 kabs	hin
Kab	2 quarts	4 logs	kab
Log	1 pint	1/4 kab	log

DRY MEASURES

Unit	Measure	Equivalents	Translations
Homer	6.52 bushels	10 ephahs	homer
Kor	6.52 bushels	1 homer; 10 ephahs	kor, measure
Lethech	3.26 bushels	1/2 kor	half homer
Ephah	.65 bushel, 20.8 quarts	1/10 homer	ephah
Modius	7.68 quarts		basket
Seah	7 quarts	1/3 ephah	measure
Omer	2.08 quarts	1/10 ephah; 1 4/5 kab	omer
Kab	1.16 quarts	4 logs	kab
Choenix	1 quart		measure
Xestes	1 1/6 pints		pot
Log	.58 pint	1/4 kab	log

For a table of monetary units see Rev. 16:21.

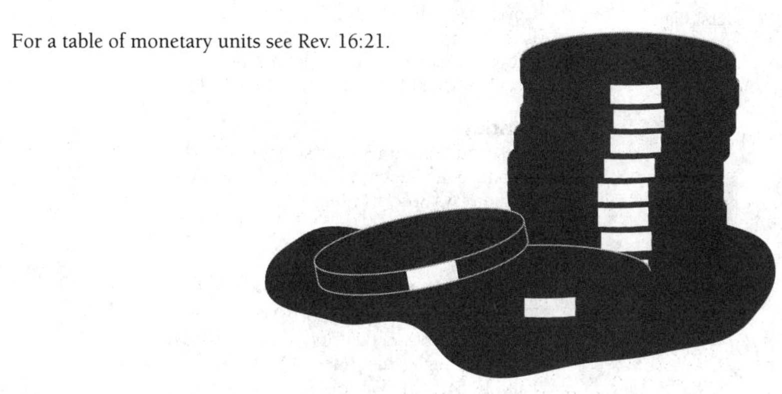

Themes to Study in the New Testament

The New Testament speaks to numerous practical themes, as shown below. Studying the texts associated with a given issue will help you apply God's Word to your experience. To study a theme, refer to the articles listed for that theme. Within the articles you'll find references to additional helps, Bible texts, and related themes.

The Church

What is the church? A building? An institution? A community of believers? Is there such a thing as an "ideal" or "model" church? What can we learn about the church as we study its infancy recorded in the New Testament? What implications are there for the church today? The articles below and their related texts will help you get started as you think about the church and your place in it:

The Nature of the Church

The King Declares His Kingdom (Matt. 4:17)
Significance for Little People (Mark 2:3–17)
Is Jesus Really Lord of All? (Luke 6:1–5)
Sorting Out Membership (Luke 13:22–23)
With Us (John 14:16–18)
The Network (John 15:1–10)
A New Reality Gets a New Name (Acts 11:26)
Ten Myths about Christianity, Myth #5: Christianity Is Just a Crutch for the Weak (1 Cor. 1:26)
This Building Gets Landmark Status (Eph. 2:19–22)
Is Your Church Upside-down or Right Side Up? (1 Thess. 2:13–14)
God's Family Album (1 Pet. 2:9–10)
Worship or Wrath? (Rev. 6:1–17)

The Character of the Church

To Be Like Jesus Means to Commit to Other Believers (Matt. 3:1–17)
To Be Like Jesus Means to Serve Others (Matt. 8:1—9:38)
To Be Like Jesus Means to Affirm Other Leaders (Matt. 10:1–42)
Are You Confused about Greatness, Too? (Mark 9:33–37)
The Hallmark of Love (John 13:31–35)
Society's Divisions Affect Believers (Acts 6:1)
The Scandal of Litigating Christians (1 Cor. 6:1–11)
Support the Weak (1 Thess. 5:14)
One Standard for All (1 Tim. 3:1)
Ushers on Trial (James 2:1–13)
Playing Favorites (James 2:1–9)
Rules That Lead to Joy (1 John 2:3–6)
Sad Fallouts Are Inevitable (Jude 8–16)

The Early Church

The Women Who Followed Jesus (Luke 8:1–3)
Jesus—A Rabbi for Women, Too (Luke 23:49)
Families of the Early Church (Acts 16:31–34)
"Not Many Mighty"...But a Few (Acts 18:7–8)
The Church at the End of the First Century (Rev. 1:20)
Seven Churches to Study (Rev. 3:1)

"Making Disciples of All the Nations"

Pluralism at Pentecost (Acts 2:5)
Come One, Come All! (Acts 10:34)
Ethnic Walls Break Down (Acts 10:44–45)
Antioch: A Model for the Modern Church? (Acts 13:1)
A Church That Defies Market Research (Acts 15:22–35)
Are We One People? (Rom. 11:13–24)
Enemies Become Family and Friends (1 Cor. 16:9–20)
A Strong Rebuke (Gal. 3:1)
We Are Family! (Gal. 3:28)
Breaking Down Walls (Eph. 2:14–18)

The Church Gathered for Refinement

To Be Like Jesus Means to Serve Others (Matt. 8:1—9:38)
The Synagogue (Mark 1:21)
The Network (John 15:1–10)
Reconnecting Sunday and Monday (Acts 2:46–47)
Sharing Things in Common (Acts 4:32–35)
Society's Divisions Affect Believers (Acts 6:1)
Barnabas—A Model for Mentoring (Acts 9:27)
A Church That Defies Market Research (Acts 15:22–35)
Not Permitted to Speak? (1 Cor. 14:34)
Work, Labor, and Steadfastness (1 Thess. 1:3)
Is Your Church Upside-down or Right Side Up? (1 Thess. 2:13–14)
A New Way to Worship (1 Tim. 2:8–15)
Widows (1 Tim. 5:3)
Effective Care for the Needy (1 Tim. 5:3–16)
Mentoring, Kingdom-Style (2 Tim. 2:2)
Coventry (Heb. 10:19–25)
Let's Celebrate! (James 5:13)
Tough-minded Believers (1 John 4:1)
Hospitality and Discernment (2 John 7–11)

Sundays

Does God Work on Sundays? (John 5:16–17)
Reconnecting Sunday and Monday (Acts 2:46–47)
Are Sundays Special? (Rom. 14:5–13)
The Sabbath (Heb. 4:1–13)
The Lord's Day (Rev. 1:10)

The Church Scattered for Impact

To All the Nations (Matt. 28:19)
People Priorities in the City (Mark 5:21–43)
Life—The Big Picture (Mark 12:28–34)
Faith Impacts the World (Mark 16:15–16)
Jesus' First Sermon Included Surprises (Luke 4:16–27)
The Spirit of the Lord Is upon...You! (Luke 4:18)
The Underclass (Luke 7:20–23)
Can Laity Get the Job Done? (Luke 9:1–62)
Sorting Out Membership (Luke 13:22–23)
You Alone Can't Bring Them to Jesus (John 6:44)
Whose Job Is Evangelism? (John 16:8)
Called into the World (John 17:18)
Reconnecting Sunday and Monday (Acts 2:46–47)

Where Has God Placed You? (Acts 8:26–39)
The Ephesus Approach (Acts 19:8–41)
The Power of the Gospel (Rom. 1:16)
A Straightforward Approach (1 Thess. 2:5)
Is Your Church Upside-down or Right Side Up? (1 Thess. 2:13–14)

Leaders

To Be Like Jesus Means to Serve Others (Matt. 8:1—9:38)
To Be Like Jesus Means to Affirm Other Leaders (Matt. 10:1–42)
The Twelve (Matt. 10:2)
Would You Choose These for Leaders? (Matt. 26:35–74)
Can Laity Get the Job Done? (Luke 9:1–62)
Leadership Equals Humility? (Luke 22:24–27)
The Order of the Towel (John 13:1–20)
An International Work Group (Acts 20:4)
"I Have Not Coveted" (Acts 20:33–38)
Paying Vocational Christian Workers (1 Cor. 9:1–23)
Who Were the Apostles? (2 Cor. 11:5)
A Straightforward Approach (1 Thess. 2:5)
Is Your Church Upside-down or Right Side Up? (1 Thess. 2:13–14)
One Standard for All (1 Tim. 3:1)
No Greedy Leaders! (1 Tim. 3:3)
Mentoring, Kingdom-Style (2 Tim. 2:2)
United for the Work (Titus 3:12–15)
Don't Fleece the Flock (1 Pet. 5:2)
The Business of the Church (1 Pet. 5:2–4)

The Church in the World

"The Gates of Hell" (Matt. 16:18)
Faith Impacts the World (Mark 16:15–16)
Is Jesus Really Lord of All? (Luke 6:1–5)
Whose Job Is Evangelism? (John 16:8)
Called into the World (John 17:18)
Reconnecting Sunday and Monday (Acts 2:46–47)
A Confusing Reputation (Acts 5:12–16)
Where Has God Placed You? (Acts 8:26–39)
Confusing Responses (Acts 14:11–19)
Paul's Urban Strategy (Acts 16:4)
The Ephesus Approach (Acts 19:8–41)
Truth Can Trigger Opposition (Acts 24:1–26)
Audience-shaped Messages (Acts 26:1–32)
The Power of the Gospel (Rom. 1:16)
God's Heart for the Whole World (Rom. 9:1)
A Straightforward Approach (1 Thess. 2:5)
Quiet Living in a Hectic World (1 Thess. 4:11)

Ethics and Character

God calls His people to integrity and compassion. But because all of us are sinners who have rebelled against God and come into bondage to our own self-interests, following God's calling does not come naturally. Instead we find in ourselves agendas and patterns of behavior that fall far short of Christ's example of goodness and humane treatment of others.

How can we change? How can born sinners develop into ethical people? To find out, start by studying the categories, articles, and passages below:

Accountability

Do You Suffer From "Comparisonitis"? (Rom. 12:3)
The Ultimate Performance Review (1 Cor. 3:13–15)
Taking Stock (Phil. 3:7–14)

Behavior on the Job

See "Work"

Christlike Character

Being Like Jesus (series; Matt. 10:25)
The Spirit of the Lord Is Upon...You! (Luke 4:18)
The Cost of Following Jesus (Luke 14:25–32)
Sinless Perfection? (1 John 3:6)

Decision Making

Judge Not! (Matt. 7:1–5)
Trick Questions Foiled (Matt. 22:23–33)
A Reckless Choice (Mark 6:23)
Convenience Makes for Odd Choices (Luke 23:1–25)
A Double Standard? (John 8:2–3)
The Blessing of a Clean Conscience (John 18:1–11)
Matters of Conscience (Rom. 14:1–23)
Are We to Judge All Things? (1 Cor. 2:15)
Gray Areas (1 Cor. 8:1–13)
Welcome to Stressful Living (2 Cor. 6:3–10)

Humility

The Power of Humility (Matt. 3:11)
The Way Up Is Down (Matt. 5:3)
Are You a Friend of Someone in Need? (Luke 5:17–26)
Competition versus Compassion (Luke 9:46–48)
The Right Kind of Fear (Luke 12:4–7)
Compassion and Anger in One Person? (Luke 19:41–46)
Leadership Equals Humility? (Luke 22:24–27)
The Quest for Greatness (Luke 22:24–30)
The Power of Self-Sacrifice (John 10:17–18)
The Order of the Towel (John 13:1–20)
Paul Apologized for Losing His Cool (Acts 23:5)
Humility—The Scandalous Virtue (Phil. 2:3)

Integrity

Is Evasion Ethical? (Matt. 21:24–27)
Trick Questions Foiled (Matt. 22:23–33)
Can You Be Trusted? (Luke 1:18–19)
Convenience Makes for Odd Choices (Luke 23:1–25)
The Blessing of a Clean Conscience (John 18:1–11)
Real Estate Deal Deadly (Acts 5:2–10)
Promises (Rom. 4:16–25)
Matters of Conscience (Rom. 14:1–23)
Cover-ups Deceive Everybody (1 Cor. 5:1–13)
Integrity in the Face of Competition (2 Cor. 10:1)
New Creatures with New Character (Gal. 5:22–23)
Honesty and Ethical Standards (Phil. 2:15)
Work-World Codes (Col. 3:22—4:1)
Finishing Well (2 Thess. 1:3–12)
One Standard for All (1 Tim. 3:1)
"I Won't Hire Christians!" (1 Tim. 6:1–2)

Justice

An Eye for an Eye (Matt. 5:38–42)
Judge Not! (Matt. 7:1–5)
No Forgiveness! (Matt. 12:31–32)
Seventy Times Seven—Still Not Enough! (Matt. 18:21–35)
Jesus and Unjust Pay (Matt. 20:1–16)
The Final Exam (Matt. 25:31–46)
Jesus' First Sermon Included Surprises (Luke 4:16–27)
Running to Extremes (Luke 6:29)
The Underclass (Luke 7:20–23)
Are You the Elder Brother? (Luke 15:25–30)
Doing Your Duty (Luke 17:5–10)
A Double Standard? (John 8:2–3)
Discrimination on the Basis of Wealth (John 19:1–6)

Forgiveness Abounds (John 21:15–23)
Faith and Rights (Acts 22:25–29)
Do Not Avenge Yourself (Rom. 12:19–21)
The Avengers (Rom. 13:4)
Rights (Gal. 4:1–18)
God Restrains Evil (Rev. 13:1–18)
Will Evil Ever Get Its Reward? (Rev. 20:1–15)

Love
What Kind of Love Is This? (Matt. 22:34–40)
Love My Enemies? (Luke 6:27–31)
Love Your Neighbor (Luke 10:27–28)
The Good Neighbor (Luke 10:30–37)
The Hallmark of Love (John 13:31–35)
New Creatures with New Character (Gal. 5:22–23)
Love Is More than Enthusiasm (1 John 5:1–3)

Money and Wealth
Living Within Your Limits (Matt. 16:22–23)
Jesus and Unjust Pay (Matt. 20:1–16)
Tainted Money (Matt. 27:3–10)
It's All Relative (Mark 12:43–44)
Running to Extremes (Luke 6:29)
The Underclass (Luke 7:20–23)
The Real Bottom Line (Luke 9:25)
Watch Out for Greed! (Luke 12:15)
Confused Value? (Luke 15:1–31)
Holding Wealth or Serving Others? (Luke 18:18–30)
A Remedy for Tax Fraud (Luke 19:1–10)
Discrimination on the Basis of Wealth (John 19:1–6)
Wealth: Hold It Lightly (Acts 4:37—5:11)
Gospel and Property Conflicts (Acts 19:23–27)
Debt-Free Living (Rom. 13:8)
What Controls You? (1 Cor. 6:12)
Money: Compassion and Integrity (1 Cor. 16:1–4)
Who Are the Poor? (2 Cor. 9:9–10)
A Lifestyle of Contentment (Phil. 4:10–13)
Support the Weak (1 Thess. 5:14)
No Greedy Leaders! (1 Tim. 3:3)
The Dangers of Prosperity Theology (1 Tim. 6:3–6)
Christians and Money (1 Tim. 6:6–19)
Don't Fleece the Flock (1 Pet. 5:2)
The Delusions of Luxury (Rev. 18:1–24)

Morality
The Morality of Christ (Matt. 5:17–48)
What About Old Testament Law? (Matt. 5:19)
An Eye for an Eye (Matt. 5:38–42)
Always the Poor (Mark 14:7)
Jesus Confronts the Legalists (Luke 6:1–11)
The Letter and the Spirit (Luke 14:1–6)
A Double Standard? (John 8:2–3)
The Blessing of a Clean Conscience (John 18:1–11)
The Law (Rom. 2:12)
Are People Basically Good? (Rom. 7:21)
Matters of Conscience (Rom. 14:1–23)
Gray Areas (1 Cor. 8:1–13)
New Creatures with New Character (Gal. 5:22–23)
One Standard for All (1 Tim. 3:1)
Ten Commandments for Practical Living (James 2:8–13)
Rules That Lead to Joy (1 John 2:3–6)

Power and Authority
To Be Like Jesus Means to Serve Others (Matt. 8:1—9:38)
Under Authority (Matt. 8:5–13)
The Power of Forgiveness (Matt. 9:4–8)
Servant-Leaders (Matt. 20:25–28)
A New Style of Fame (Matt. 21:8–11)
Would You Choose These for Leaders? (Matt. 26:35–74)
Significance for Little People (Mark 2:3–17)
Are You Confused about Greatness, Too? (Mark 9:33–37)
Three Dangers of Power (Luke 3:14)
Authority and Responsibility (Luke 12:35–48)
A Shrewd Manager (Luke 16:1–13)
Leadership Equals Humility? (Luke 22:24–27)
The Quest for Greatness (Luke 22:24–30)
Wait for Power (Luke 24:49)
The Power of Self-Sacrifice (John 10:17–18)
Under Authority (John 12:49)
The Order of the Towel (John 13:1–20)
A Model of Servant Leadership (John 13:2–17)
Leaders Start as Servants (Acts 6:5–6)
"It Serves Them Right" (Acts 27:9–11)
Who Gets the Credit? (1 Cor. 3:5–8)
One Standard for All (1 Tim. 3:1)
No Greedy Leaders! (1 Tim. 3:3)
Mentoring, Kingdom-Style (2 Tim. 2:2)
Elementary Leadership Lessons (Heb. 5:1–14)
Don't Fleece the Flock (1 Pet. 5:2)

Public Ethics
Sulfa Drugs and Street Lights (Matt. 5:13–16)
The Public Side of Faith (Matt. 14:13–14)
Jesus and Taxation (Matt. 17:24–27)
Taxes (Mark 12:14)
Faith Impacts the World (Mark 16:15–16)
Jesus' First Sermon Included Surprises (Luke 4:16–27)
What Does Leprosy Have to Do with AIDS? (Luke 5:12–15)
The Underclass (Luke 7:20–23)
God and the Environment (Luke 12:6–7)
A Remedy for Tax Fraud (Luke 19:1–10)
Be Willing to Pay the Price (Acts 16:16–24)
Free to Be Bold (Acts 23:1)
The Limits of Political Authority (Rom. 13:1–7)
The Avengers (Rom. 13:4)
The Scandal of Litigating Christians (1 Cor. 6:1–11)
A Code of Ethics for Christian Witness (2 Cor. 4:2)
Rights (Gal. 4:1–18)
Honesty and Ethical Standards (Phil. 2:15)
Support the Weak (1 Thess. 5:14)
A Command to Work (2 Thess. 3:6–12)
A Challenge to Slavery (Philem. 16)

Right and Wrong
The Morality of Christ (Matt. 5:17–48)
Jesus Confronts the Legalists (Luke 6:1–11)
The Letter and the Spirit (Luke 14:1–6)
The Blessing of a Clean Conscience (John 18:1–11)
Righteousness (Rom. 1:17)
Are People Basically Good? (Rom. 7:21)

Success
True Success Means Faithfulness (Matt. 25:14–30)
A Kingdom Perspective on Significance (Mark 13:33)
The Real Bottom Line (Luke 9:25)
Competition versus Compassion (Luke 9:46–48)
Success (John 3:30)
Who Gets the Credit? (1 Cor. 3:5–8)

Temptation
Wealth's Temptation (Matt. 4:8–10)
"It Will All Be Yours" (Luke 4:5–8)

Watch Out for Greed (Luke 12:15)
Real Estate Deal Deadly (Acts 5:2–10)
Are People Basically Good? (Rom. 7:21)
Pay Attention to Temptation! (1 Cor. 10:12–13)
The Delusions of Luxury (Rev. 18:1–24)

Miscellaneous

City Kids Die over Adult Matters (Matt. 2:16–18)
Does Change Threaten You? (Luke 5:36–39)
Who Is Blessed? (Luke 11:27–28)
The Value of a Disabled Woman (Luke 13:10–17)
Holy Interruptions (Luke 18:35–43)
The Road Less Traveled (John 4:4–42)
Resistance—Unpopular Obedience (Acts 7:57–60)
Conflict Resolution (Acts 11:2–18)
Confusing Responses (Acts 14:11–19)
When I Am Weak, Then I Am Strong (2 Cor. 12:7–10)
Hope For You: Watch Paul Grow! (Gal. 1:11–24)
Feel Like a Novice? (1 Tim. 4:1–16)
Let Me Pick Up the Tab (Philem. 17–19)
Knowing *About* God Is Not the Same as *Knowing* God (Heb. 6:1–20)

The Family

There is great confusion in society today about the family. On the one hand, expectations are often high and unmet. On the other hand, many people's expectations are so low as to render the concept of the family meaningless. Tension, conflict, pain, and loss often dominate family relationships so that positive qualities such as love, commitment, pleasure, and security are all but impossible.

Scripture has much to say about the nature of the family. The articles listed below will help you study this theme in order to apply biblical truth to your own family relationships:

Jesus' Family

Jesus' Roots (Matt. 1:1–16)
The Women in Jesus' Genealogy (Matt. 1:3–6)
Asian-born Jesus Becomes a Refugee in Africa (Matt. 2:13–15)
Jesus—A Homeless Man? (Matt. 8:20)
Is Jesus For or Against Family? (Mark 3:31–35)
Jesus the Carpenter (Mark 6:3)
Mary, the Mother of Jesus (Luke 1:26–56)
A Poor Family's Sacrifice (Luke 2:22–24)
Jesus, the Son of...(Luke 3:23–28)
Jesus' Family Experienced Pain, Too (Luke 3:36–38)
James (Introduction to James)
Jude (Introduction to Jude)

Families of the New Testament

A Poor Family Comes into Wealth (Matt. 2:11)
A Surprise in Peter's Household (Matt. 8:14–15)
Hateful Herodias (Matt. 14:3)
A Pushy Mother (Matt. 20:20–23)
Families of the Gospels (Luke 20:34)
Ananias and Sapphira (Acts 5:1)
The Herods (Acts 12:1–2)
Families of the Early Church (Acts 16:31–34)
The Four Daughters of Philip (Acts 21:9)

See also the personality profiles of individual family members listed elsewhere.

Family Backgrounds

Jesus' Roots (Matt. 1:1–16)
To Be Like Jesus Means to Accept Our Roots (Matt. 1:1–17)
The Women in Jesus' Genealogy (Matt. 1:3–6)
Jesus, the Son of...(Luke 3:23–28)
Jesus' Family Experienced Pain, Too (Luke 3:36–38)
Researching Your Own Religious Roots (Heb. 13:24)

Family Life Issues

Family Loyalty (Matt. 12:46–50)
Children and Childcare (Matt. 19:14)
Jewish Homemaking (Mark 1:29–31)
Honor Your Parents (Mark 7:9–13)
Divorce (Mark 10:2–12)
A Poor Family's Sacrifice (Luke 2:22–24)
How Poor Was the Widow? (Luke 21:1–4)
Practical Lessons on Marriage (1 Cor. 7:1)
A New View of Sexuality (1 Cor. 7:3–6)
What Is Headship? (1 Cor. 11:3)
The Family: A Call to Long-Term Work (Eph. 5:21—6:4)
A New Form of Marriage (Eph. 5:21–29)
The Value of Self-Support (1 Thess. 2:9)
Widows (1 Tim. 5:3)
Effective Care for the Needy (1 Tim. 5:3–16)
Family Helps in the New Testament Letters (Heb. 12:14–29)
Love Is More than Enthusiasm (1 John 5:1–3)

Other

A Poor Family Comes into Wealth (Matt. 2:11)
City Kids Die over Adult Matters (Matt. 2:16–18)
Jesus Weeps for the Children (Matt. 23:37–39)
Jewish Homemaking (Mark 1:29–31)
The Friend of Children (Mark 10:13–16)
Betrothal (Luke 1:27)
Please Bless Our Children (Luke 18:15–17)
A Woman in Labor (John 16:21–22)
Enemies Become Family and Friends (1 Cor. 16:9–20)
We Are Family! (Gal. 3:28)
All God's Children (Eph. 1:18)
God's Family Album (1 Pet. 2:9–10)
There Is Hope for the Family (Rev. 19:6–10)

Getting to Know Jesus

Jesus Christ is the center around which Christianity and all of Scripture revolve. He invites everyone to know Him, and the New Testament helps us do that by recording His life, work, teaching, death, and resurrection. To know Jesus is to know God. It is also the way to know what God intended us to be like, before sin began its terrible work on us. The articles listed below will help you get started in learning about the Son of God:

Being Like Jesus

A good place to begin your study would be to read the series of articles in Matthew under the heading, "What It Means to Be Like Jesus." The lead article can be found at Matt. 10:25.

The Life and Work of Jesus

Jesus' Roots (Matt. 1:1–16)
Asian-born Jesus Becomes a Refugee in Africa (Matt. 2:13)
Jesus' Galilean Ministry (map, Matt. 4:25)
Jesus—A City Preacher (Matt. 9:35)
Jesus the Carpenter (Mark 6:3)
The Miracles of Jesus (Mark 8:11–12)
Jesus the Student (Luke 2:46–47)
Jesus, the Son of... (Luke 3:23–28)
Jesus' Family Experienced Pain, Too (Luke 3:36–38)
Jesus' First Sermon Included Surprises (Luke 4:16–27)

Herod Finally Meets Jesus (Luke 23:8)
Jesus—A Rabbi for Women, Too (Luke 23:49)

Jesus' Nature and Character

Ten Myths about Christianity, Myth #1: Jesus Christ Was Only a Great Moral Teacher (Matt. 13:34–35)
The Names of Jesus (Matt. 17:5)
For or Against Family? (Mark 3:31–35)
You Are the Messiah (Mark 8:27–33)
Is Jesus Really Lord of All? (Luke 6:1–5)
Compassion and Anger in One Person? (Luke 19:41–46)
Many Men Would Be Gods, But Only One God Would Be Man (John 8:52–59)
A Model of Servant Leadership (John 13:2–17)
Christ, the Lord of the World (Col. 1:15–18)
Many Are Great, But Christ Is the Greatest (Heb. 1:5–14)

Jesus and People

Jesus' Roots (Matt. 1:1–16)
Jesus' Global Connections (Matt. 8:10)
Jews, Gentiles and Jesus (Matt. 15:24)
The Great Physician (Mark 1:32–34)
Jesus and Ethnicity (Mark 7:24–30)
The Miracles of Jesus (Mark 8:11–12)
Compassion and Anger in One Person? (Luke 19:41–46)
Herod Finally Meets Jesus (Luke 23:8)
Jesus—The Name You Can Trust (Acts 3:1)
Alive Together (Eph. 2:1)

Jesus Our Example

Jesus—A Homeless Man? (Matt. 8:20)
Jesus—A City Preacher (Matt. 9:35)
Jesus and Taxation (Matt. 17:24–27)
Jesus and Unjust Pay (Matt. 20:1–16)
Trick Questions Foiled (Matt. 22:23–33)
Jesus Weeps for the Children (Matt. 23:37–39)
Jesus the Carpenter (Mark 6:3)
Jesus Died Poor (Mark 15:24)
Jesus Is for Gentiles, Too (Luke 1:1–4)
An International Savior (Luke 2:29–32)
Jesus the Student (Luke 2:46–47)
Jesus' Family Experienced Pain, Too (Luke 3:36–38)
Jesus' First Sermon Included Surprises (Luke 4:16–27)
Good Men Care (Luke 13:34)
Compassion and Anger in One Person? (Luke 19:41–46)
His Last Words (Luke 24:45–49)
Witnessing—Jesus' Style (Luke 24:48)
A Model of Servant Leadership (John 13:2–17)
Christ Became Poor (2 Cor. 8:8–9)
Humility—The Scandalous Virtue (Phil. 2:3)
Downward Mobility (Phil. 2:5–8)
Two Portraits of Jesus, Two Sides of Life for Christians (Col. 2:6)

Jesus' Parables

Another way to learn about Christ is to study His teaching through His stories, called parables. For a listing see "The Parables of Jesus," Luke 8:4.

Four Gospels

The New Testament offers four accounts of Jesus' life, known as the four Gospels—Matthew, Mark, Luke, and John. Each one offers a different perspective. If you are unfamiliar with the life and teaching of Jesus, consider reading an entire Gospel at one sitting. The shortest of the four is Mark.

Government

What should be the Christian's relationship to governmental authorities? How did Jesus deal with the political authorities of His day? How did the early church not only survive but thrive in an increasingly hostile political climate? To find out the answers to these and related questions, study the articles below and the passages to which they relate:

The Nature and Value of Government

Under Authority (John 12:49)
The Limits of Political Authority (Rom. 13:1–7)
Governmental Authority (Rom. 13:2)
The Avengers (Rom. 13:4)
The High Calling of Government Service (Rom. 13:6)
The Church at the End of the First Century (Rev. 1:20)
A Symbol of Evil (Rev. 14:8)

The Church and Government

Faith Impacts the World (Mark 16:15–16)
"We Must Obey God Rather than Any Human Authority" (Acts 5:22–32)
Stephen's Trial and Murder (Acts 6:12)
Where Has God Placed You? (Acts 8:26–39)
"Not Many Mighty"...But a Few (Acts 18:7–8)
The Ephesus Approach (Acts 19:8–41)
Faith and Rights (Acts 22:25–29)
Paul and the Structures of Power (Acts 24:25–26)
Caught Between a Novice and the Establishment (Acts 25:2)

New Testament Government Officials

Party Politics of Jesus' Day (Matt. 16:1)
Caiaphas (Matt. 26:3)
Augustus (Luke 2:1)
New Testament Political Rulers (Luke 3:1)
Roman Politics in the First Century A.D. (Luke 22:25)
The Treasurer of Ethiopia (Acts 8:27–39)
Cornelius (Acts 10:1)
Claudius (Acts 11:28)
The Herods (Acts 12:1–2)
Sosthenes the Attorney (Acts 18:17)
Felix (Acts 23:24)
Festus (Acts 25:1)
Nero (Acts 25:12)

Laity in the New Testament

When we examine the New Testament's description of the early church, we find that pastors, teachers, and other leaders functioned for the equipping of "the saints for the work of ministry" (Eph. 4:12). In other words, ministry belonged to the saints or "laity" (from *laos*, "people"), Christians who live and work in the everyday world. Study the articles below to find out what the New Testament has to say about the value, calling, and work of laypeople:

Laypeople and the Church

A Prayer of the Laity (Matt. 10:7–10)
Reconnecting Sunday and Monday (Acts 2:46–47)
Discipleship—Or Mentoring? (Acts 9:26–30)
Who Were the Apostles? (2 Cor. 11:5)
Spiritual Authority (2 Cor. 13:10)
Is Your Church Upside-down or Right Side Up? (1 Thess. 2:13–14)
Who Is "Called," Anyway? (Heb. 3:1)
Coventry (Heb. 10:19–25)

Laypeople and the Community
Faith Impacts the World (Mark 16:15–16)
Called into the World (John 17:18)
The Ephesus Approach (Acts 19:8–41)
Quiet Living in a Hectic World (1 Thess. 4:11)
The Prayer Breakfast Movement (1 Tim. 2:1–7)

Laypeople and Work
Work-World Stories Describe the Kingdom (Matt. 13:1)
Is Work a Curse? (Rom. 8:20–22)
Workplace Myths (1 Cor. 3:9)
Career Changes (1 Cor. 7:17–24)
Are Some Jobs More Important than Others? (1 Cor. 12:28–31)
Work—A Platform for Evangelism? (Eph. 6:5–9)
The Spirituality of Everyday Work (Col. 3:1–2)
Workers for the Kingdom (Col. 4:11)
A Command to Work (2 Thess. 3:6–12)
People at Work (Heb. 2:7)
Ten Commandments for Practical Living (James 2:8–13)

Other
The Twelve (Matt. 10:2)
Being Like Jesus (series; Matt. 10:25)
Would You Choose These for Leaders? (Matt. 26:35–74)
Wealthy People in the New Testament (Matt. 27:57)
Significance for Little People (Mark 2:3–17)
A Kingdom Perspective on Significance (Mark 13:33)
Can Laity Get the Job Done? (Luke 9:1–62)
Delegation and Affirmation (Luke 10:1)
Barnabas—A Model for Mentoring (Acts 9:27)
Just Plain Jars (2 Cor. 4:7)
Hope for You—Watch Paul Grow! (Gal. 1:11–24)
Mentoring, Kingdom-Style (2 Tim. 2:2)
The Hall of Faithfulness (Heb. 11:1–40)
God's Family Album (1 Pet. 2:9–10)

Also study the lives of individual laypeople through the list of personality profiles presented elsewhere in this section.

MEN
What does it mean to be a man? How can men live with Christlike character? By studying the men of the New Testament and the passages that speak to masculine concerns, you can begin to learn what God intends for a man, and how men can grow and serve Christ in every area of life:

The Man Jesus
Jesus' Roots (Matt. 1:1–16)
Jesus: A Homeless Man? (Matt. 8:20)
Jesus the Carpenter (Mark 6:3)
Jesus and Ethnicity (Mark 7:24–30)
The Friend of Children (Mark 10:13–16)
Is Jesus Really Lord of All? (Luke 6:5)
Compassion and Anger in One Person? (Luke 19:41–46)
Jesus—A Rabbi for Women, Too (Luke 23:49)
Witnessing, Jesus' Style (Luke 24:48)
Jesus Speaks to a Woman (John 4:27)
Many Men Would Be Gods, But Only One God Would Be Man (John 8:52–59)
A Model of Servant-Leadership (John 13:2–17)
The Proper Measure of All Things (Heb. 2:6–8)

Men in the New Testament
Matthew, the Social Outcast (Introduction to Matthew).
A Rich Man Enters the Kingdom (Matt. 9:9–13)
The Twelve (Matt. 10:2)
Caiaphas, the Religious Power Broker (Matt. 26:3)
Judas Iscariot, the Betrayer (Matt. 26:14)
John the Baptist, a Voice Crying in the Wilderness (Mark 1:6)
Peter, the First Disciple (Mark 1:16)
Significance for Little People (Mark 2:3–17)
A Respected Leader Takes a Risk (Mark 5:22–23)
Jesus the Carpenter (Mark 6:3)
The Man Who Had It All—Almost (Mark 10:17–27)
Barabbas (Mark 15:7)
Luke, the Gentile Author (Introduction to Luke)
Zechariah (Luke 1:5–25)
Augustus (Luke 2:1)
Simeon (Luke 2:25–35)
Isaiah (Luke 4:17)
Who Was the Neighbor? (Luke 10:37)
Are You the Elder Brother? (Luke 15:25–30)
Families of the Gospels (Luke 20:34)
John—The Apostle of Love (Introduction to John)
Andrew the Networker (John 1:40)
Lazarus (John 11:1–45)
Skeptics Welcome (John 20:24–31)
Barnabas—"Joe Encouragement" (Acts 4:36–37; 9:27)
Ananias and Sapphira (Acts 5:1)
Stephen's Trial and Murder (Acts 6:12)
Philip the Evangelist (Acts 8:5–13)
Simon the Magician (Acts 8:9)
The Treasurer of Ethiopia (Acts 8:27–29)
Ananias the Disciple (Acts 9:10)
Cornelius (Acts 10:1)
Claudius (Acts 11:28)
Saul/Paul (Acts 13:2–3)
Why Did John Mark Go Home? (Acts 13:13)
Silas (Acts 15:34)
John Mark (Acts 15:37)
Families of the Early Church (Acts 16:31–34)
Apollos (Acts 18:24–28)
Demetrius the Silversmith (Acts 19:24)
An International Work Group (Acts 20:4)
Ananias the High Priest (Acts 23:2)
Felix (Acts 23:24)
Festus (Acts 25:1)
Nero (Acts 25:12)
Abraham (Rom. 4:1)
David (Rom. 4:6)
Priscilla and Aquila (Rom. 16:3–5)
Enemies Become Family and Friends (1 Cor. 16:9–20)
Titus, The Man of the Hour (2 Cor. 7:6)
Hope for You—Watch Paul Grow! (Gal. 1:11–24)
From Persecutor to Apostle (Gal. 1:13–17)
Epaphroditus (Phil. 2:25)
The Gift of an Ethnic Heritage (Col. 4:10–11)
Timothy (Introduction to 2 Timothy)
Philemon (Introduction to Philemon)
Onesimus (Introduction to Philemon)
Fathers and Prophets (Heb. 1:1)
The Hall of Faithfulness (Heb. 11:1–40)
Who Are These People? (Heb. 11:2)
James (Introduction to James)
Elijah (James 5:17–18)
A Study in Contrasts of Faith (3 John 9–11)

A Man's Character
See "Ethics and Character"

Other
A New Respect for Women (Matt. 5:32)

Those Women Again! (Luke 24:11)
Gentle as a Nursing Mother (1 Thess. 2:7)

People to Know in the New Testament

Scripture provides many things to many people, such as doctrine, comfort, guidance, and principles for day-to-day life. Another treasure in God's Word is a host of people who lived and worked in public and private places. Their stories are told so we can learn from their examples (whether good or bad) as we see how they struggled with issues of faith and life:

Matthew, the Social Outcast (Introduction to Matthew)
The Women in Jesus' Genealogy (Matt. 1:3–6)
A Rich Man Enters the Kingdom (Matt. 9:9–13)
The Hemorrhaging Woman (Matt. 9:20–22)
The Twelve (Matt. 10:2)
A Pushy Mother (Matt. 20:20–23)
Judas Iscariot, the Betrayer (Matt. 26:14)
Would You Choose These for Leaders? (Matt. 26:35–74)
Wealthy People in the New Testament (Matt. 27:57)
John the Baptist, a Voice Crying in the Wilderness (Mark 1:6)
Peter, the First Disciple (Mark 1:16)
Significance for Little People (Mark 2:3–17)
A Respected Leader Takes a Risk (Mark 5:22–23)
The Man Who Had It All—Almost (Mark 10:17–27)
Barabbas (Mark 15:7)
Why So Many Marys? (Mark 15:40)
Luke, the Gentile Author (Introduction to Luke)
Zechariah (Luke 1:5–25)
Elizabeth (Luke 1:24)
Mary, the Mother of Jesus (Luke 1:26–56)
Simeon (Luke 2:25–35)
Anna (Luke 2:36–38)
Isaiah (Luke 4:17)
The Women Who Followed Jesus (Luke 8:1–3)
Mary of Magdala (Luke 8:2)
Who Was the Neighbor? (Luke 10:37)
Martha of Bethany (Luke 10:38–42)
Who Was the Queen of Sheba? (Luke 11:31)
The Value of a Disabled Woman (Luke 13:10–17)
Are You the Elder Brother? (Luke 15:25–30)
Families of the Gospels (Luke 20:34)
The Servant Girl (Luke 22:56–57)
Jesus—A Rabbi for Women, Too (Luke 23:49)
Those Women Again! (Luke 24:11)
John—The Apostle of Love (Introduction to John)
Andrew the Networker (John 1:40)
Lazarus (John 11:1–45)
Mary of Bethany (John 11:1–2)
The Women Around Jesus (John 19:25)
Skeptics Welcome (John 20:24–31)
Barnabas—"Joe Encouragement" (Acts 4:36–37; 9:27)
Ananias and Sapphira (Acts 5:1)
Stephen's Trial and Murder (Acts 6:12)
The Conversion of Samaritans to the Gospel—and of Peter and John to Samaritans (Acts 8:4–25)
Philip the Evangelist (Acts 8:5–13)
Simon the Magician (Acts 8:9)
The Treasurer of Ethiopia (Acts 8:27–29)
Ananias the Disciple (Acts 9:10)
Tabitha (Acts 9:36)
Cornelius (Acts 10:1)
Saul/Paul (Acts 13:2–3)
Why Did John Mark Go Home? (Acts 13:13)
Silas (Acts 15:34)
John Mark (Acts 15:37)
Lydia (Acts 16:14)
Families of the Early Church (Acts 16:31–34)
Apollos (Acts 18:24–28)
An International Work Group (Acts 20:4)
The Four Daughters of Philip (Acts 21:9)
Abraham (Rom. 4:1)
David (Rom. 4:6)
Phoebe (Rom. 16:1–2)
Priscilla and Aquila (Rom. 16:3–5)
Junia (Rom. 16:7)
Paul's Female Coworkers (Rom. 16:12)
Who Was Paul's Mother? (Rom. 16:13)
Enemies Become Family and Friends (1 Cor. 16:9–20)
Titus, the Man of the Hour (2 Cor. 7:6)
Hope for You—Watch Paul Grow! (Gal. 1:11–24)
From Persecutor to Apostle (Gal. 1:13–17)
Epaphroditus (Phil. 2:25)
The Gift of an Ethnic Heritage (Col. 4:10–11)
Timothy (Introduction to 2 Timothy)
Eunice—A Mother's Legacy (2 Tim. 1:5)
Mentoring, Kingdom-Style (2 Tim. 2:2)
Philemon (Introduction to Philemon)
Onesimus (Introduction to Philemon)
Apphia (Philem. 2)
Fathers and Prophets (Heb. 1:1)
The Hall of Faithfulness (Heb. 11:1–40)
Who Are These People? (Heb. 11:2)
Rahab (Heb. 11:31)
Women Received Their Dead Raised (Heb. 11:35)
James (Introduction to James)
Elijah (James 5:17–18)
Sarah (1 Pet. 3:6)
The Elect Lady (2 John 1)
A Study in Contrasts of Faith (3 John 9–11)

Power

Our society places a great deal of emphasis on power. What does the New Testament teach on this issue? See the following articles and their related texts:

Exercising of Power

The Power of Humility (Matt. 3:11)
The Power of Forgiveness (Matt. 9:4–8)
Three Dangers of Power (Luke 3:14)
The Power of Self-Sacrifice (John 10:17–18)
Seeing Behind Power (John 19:10–11)
The Power of Foolishness (1 Cor. 1:18)
Are We to Judge All Things? (1 Cor. 2:15)
Who Gets the Credit? (1 Cor. 3:5–8)
Power (Rev. 11:17)

Leadership

To Be Like Jesus Means to Serve Others (Matt. 8:1—9:38)
Under Authority (Matt. 8:5–13)
Servant-Leaders (Matt. 20:25–28)
A New Style of Fame (Matt. 21:8–11)
Significance for Little People (Mark 2:3–17)
Are You Confused about Greatness, Too? (Mark 9:33–37)
Authority and Responsibility (Luke 12:35–48)
A Shrewd Manager (Luke 16:1–13)
Leadership Equals Humility? (Luke 22:24–27)
The Quest for Greatness (Luke 22:24–30)
Under Authority (John 12:49)

The Order of the Towel (John 13:1–20)
A Model of Servant-Leadership (John 13:2–17)
Empowering Leadership (John 14:13)
One Standard for All (1 Tim. 3:1)
No Greedy Leaders! (1 Tim. 3:3)
Don't Fleece the Flock! (1 Pet. 5:2)
Do You Have What It Takes? (2 Pet. 1:3–4)

Spiritual Power

Spiritual Realities Beyond You (Matt. 8:29)
Power (Acts 1:8)
"Give Me Power!" (Acts 8:18–19)
The Power of the Gospel (Rom. 1:16)
Who Is the Enemy? (Eph. 6:10–13)
The Spirit of Power (2 Tim. 1:6–7)
The Power of God's Word (Heb. 4:12)

Other

"You Remind Me of..." (Mark 6:14–16)
Paul and the Structures of Power (Acts 24:25–26)
"It Serves Them Right" (Acts 27:9–11)
What Controls You (1 Cor. 6:12)
Just Plain Jars (2 Cor. 4:7)
When I Am Weak, Then I Am Strong (2 Cor. 12:7–10)
The Power Behind Porn (Jude 6–13)

Race and Ethnicity

We all have roots. No matter who we are, the history of our family has had a profound impact on us. Yet these powerful influences are often unrecognized, and they frequently cause people to misunderstand others from different backgrounds. Nevertheless, God values all the people of the world and seeks to bring them into His eternal family. To that end, Scripture calls Christ's followers to overcome barriers of race, ethnicity, language, and culture. While our ultimate allegiance must be to Christ, we need not deny our own roots or those of others. We can celebrate the riches of diversity. Find out more of what the New Testament has to say about this crucial issue through the following articles and their related texts:

Jesus and Ethnicity

Jesus' Roots (Matt. 1:1–16)
Asian-born Jesus Becomes a Refugee in Africa (Matt. 2:13–15)
Jesus' Global Connections (Matt. 8:10)
Jews, Gentiles, and Jesus (Matt. 15:24)
Jesus the Galilean (Mark 1:14)
Jesus and Ethnicity (Mark 7:24–30)
Jesus Is for Gentiles, Too (Luke 1:1–4)
An International Savior (Luke 2:29–32)
Jesus, the Son of... (Luke 3:23–28)
Ethnic Games with Religious Roots (John 4:19–23)
Jesus Is Called a Samaritan Demoniac (John 8:48)
Jesus Excludes Only the Faithless (John 12:20–36)

The Early Church Confronts Ethnic Barriers

Opportunities Look like Barriers (Acts 1:4)
Jerusalem—Merely the Beginning (Acts 1:12–26)
Off to a Good Start (Acts 2:1)
Pluralism at Pentecost (Acts 2:5)
A Surprising First Fulfillment of Acts 1:8 (Acts 2:8–11)
Society's Divisions Affect Believers (Acts 6:1)
A Growing Movement Confronts Ethnic Prejudice (Acts 6:2–6)
Stephen's New View of History (Acts 7:1–53)
The Message Leaves Jerusalem (Acts 8:1)
The Conversion of the Samaritans to the Gospel—And of Peter and John to Samaritans (Acts 8:4–25)
Come One, Come All! (Acts 10:34)
Ethnic Walls Break Down (Acts 10:44–45)
The Movement Expands Beyond Palestine (Acts 11:19–26)
A New Reality Gets a New Name (Acts 11:26)
"Sure You're Saved...Sort Of" (Acts 15:1–21)
A Church That Defies Market Research (Acts 15:22–25)
The Ephesus Approach (Acts 19:8–41)
Rome or Bust (Acts 19:21)
An International Work Group (Acts 20:4)
All Roads Lead to Rome—And Beyond (Acts 28:28–31)

The Inclusiveness of the Gospel

To Be Like Jesus Means to Accept Our Roots (Matt. 1:1–17)
The Twelve (Matt. 10:2)
To All the Nations (Matt. 28:19)
Luke, the Gentile Author (Introduction to Luke)
A Soldier's Surprising Faith (Luke 7:1–10)
The Gospel in a Pluralistic Society (John 3:21)
Samaria (John 4:4)
Called Into the World (John 17:18)
The Treasurer of Ethiopia (Acts 8:27–39)
Saul/Paul (Acts 13:2–3)
Lydia (Acts 16:14)
God's Heart for the Whole World (Rom. 9:1)
God's Rainbow (Rom. 15:7–12)
Circumcision (Gal. 2:12)
We Are Family! (Gal. 3:28)
Breaking Down Walls (Eph. 2:14–18)
Bloodlines (Col. 3:11)
God's Family Album (1 Pet. 2:9–10)
Finally, Full Equality (Rev. 5:9–10)
A Great Multitude of All Nations (Rev. 7:9)

Rebukes against Prejudice

No Better than Gentiles (Mark 10:32–45)
Condemnation or Compassion? (Luke 9:51–56)
Who Was the Neighbor? (Luke 10:37)
Where Are the Others? (Luke 17:11–19)
Are We One People? (Rom. 11:13–24)
From Persecutor to Apostle (Gal. 1:13–17)
A Strong Rebuke (Gal. 3:1)
Paul's Drivenness (Phil. 3:4–6)
A Challenge to Slavery (Philem. 15–16)
Ushers on Trial (James 2:1–13)

The Value of Diversity

The Gift of an Ethnic Heritage (Col. 4:10–11)
Paul the Jew—Teacher of the Gentiles (2 Tim. 1:3, 11)
Fathers and Prophets (Heb. 1:1)
Who Are These People? (Heb. 11:2)
Researching Your Own Religious Roots (Heb. 13:24)

The Roman World Transformed

The Roman Empire was one of the greatest superpowers the world has ever seen. Nevertheless, much of its greatness was fueled by the normal human drives of power and pleasure. One has only to look at the legacy of the emperors, such as Nero (Acts 25:12), or the rulers that Rome installed or tolerated, such as the Herods (12:1–2) and Pontius Pilate, to realize that much of the empire's foundation ultimately rested on the self-interest of its leaders.

But an upstart movement with a radically different approach to leadership and change challenged and eventually overcame that pattern. Quietly at first, but with determination and mounting effectiveness, Jesus and His followers transformed their world, as the New Testament and other writings of that period show. Here is an overview of some of the revolutionary changes brought on by the burgeoning movement that came to be known as Christianity:

The Significance of People Changed

Little people took center stage in importance and focus. See...

- The Twelve (Matt. 10:2)
- Significance for Little People (Mark 2:3–17)
- Personality Profile: Mary of Magdala (Luke 8:2)
- Personality Profile: Mary of Bethany (John 11:1–2)
- The Hall of Faithfulness (Heb. 11:1–40)

Rich and poor connected in new ways. See...

- A Rich Man Enters the Kingdom (Matt. 9:9–13)
- A Burial Fit for a King (Mark 15:42—16:1)
- The Women Who Followed Jesus (Luke 8:1–3)
- Barnabas—"Joe Encouragement" (Acts 4:36–37; 9:27)
- "Not Many Mighty"...But a Few (Acts 18:7–8)

Women were affirmed in a culture that devalued them. See...

- Jesus—A Rabbi for Women, Too (Luke 23:49)
- An Inclusive Prayer Meeting (Acts 1:14)
- Personality Profile: Tabitha (Acts 9:36)
- Personality Profile: Lydia (Acts 16:14)
- Personality Profile: Priscilla and Aquila (Rom. 16:3–5)
- Paul's Female Coworkers (Rom. 16:12)
- Widows (1 Tim. 5:3)

Children were valued in a world that devalued them. See...

- Children and Childcare (Matt. 19:14)
- Jesus Weeps for the Children (Matt. 23:37–39)
- The Friend of Children (Mark 10:13–16)
- The Family: A Call to Long-term Work (Eph. 5:21—6:4)
- There Is Hope for the Family (Rev. 19:6–10)

Entire Systems Changed

Submissiveness and humility were urged in place of oppression and injustice. See...

- The Way Up Is Down (Matt. 5:3)
- Leaders Start as Servants (Acts 6:5–6)
- Do Not Avenge Yourself (Rom. 12:19–21)
- Humility—The Scandalous Virtue (Phil. 2:3)
- Work World Codes (Col. 3:22—4:1)
- Submission (James 4:7)

Opponents, criminals, and ne'er-do-wells were rehabilitated and became leaders. See...

- Matthew, the Social Outcast (Introduction to Matthew)
- Simon the Magician (Acts 8:9)
- Profiles of Saul/Paul (Acts 13:2–3)
- From Deadbeat to Donor (Eph. 4:28)
- Personality Profile: Onesimus (Introduction to Philemon)

People from different races and ethnic backgrounds were reconnected. See...

- A Growing Movement Confronts Ethnic Prejudice (Acts 6:2–6)
- Personality Profile: the Treasurer of Ethiopia (Acts 8:27–39)
- Ethnic Walls Break Down (Acts 10:44–45)
- A Church That Defies Market Research (Acts 15:22–35)
- From Persecutor to Apostle (Gal. 1:13–17)

Slavery was quietly but effectively challenged at its roots. See...

- Slaves (Rom. 6:16)
- Work World Codes (Col. 3:22—4:1)
- Personality Profile: Philemon (Introduction to Philemon)
- Personality Profile: Onesimus (Introduction to Philemon)
- A Challenge to Slavery (Philem. 16)

Competing religions and worldviews were challenged and displaced. See..

- Paul, Apostle to the Intellectuals (Acts 17:15–34)
- The Ephesus Approach (Acts 19:8–41)
- God Cannot Lie (Titus 1:2)
- The Dangers of Syncretism (Introduction to Colossians)
- Gnosticism (1 John 5:20)

Government was called to be more honorable. See...

- Paul and the Structures of Power (Acts 24:25–26)
- Governmental Authority (Rom. 13:2)
- The High Calling of Government Service (Rom. 13:6)

Rights were restructured. See...

- The Power of Self-Sacrifice (John 10:17–18)
- Do Not Avenge Yourself (Rom. 12:19–21)
- Rights (Gal. 4:1–18)
- A Challenge to Slavery (Philem. 16)

Values Changed

Wealth was re-evaluated. See...

- The Man Who Had It All—Almost (Mark 10:17–27)
- Wealth: Hold It Lightly (Acts 4:37—5:11)
- Downward Mobility (Phil. 2:5–8)
- Christians and Money (1 Tim. 6:6–19)
- Prosperity (3 John 2)

Possessions were seen as a call to stewardship. See...

- Gospel and Property Conflicts (Acts 19:23–27)
- Giving It All Away (1 Cor. 13:3)
- Money: Compassion and Integrity (1 Cor. 16:1–4)
- A Lifestyle of Contentment (Phil. 4:10–13)

People were given new worth. See...

- The Underclass (Luke 7:20–23)
- People, Property, and Profitability (Acts 16:19)
- Mentoring, Kingdom-Style (2 Tim. 2:2)
- Let Me Pick Up the Tab (Philem. 17–19)

Morality was redefined. See...

- New Creatures with New Character (Gal. 5:22–23)
- Honesty and Ethical Standards (Phil. 2:15)
- Your "Workstyle" (Titus 2:9–10)
- Ten Commandments for Practical Living (James 2:8–13)

Are you a part of a group of believers in which the faith is producing some of these changes? Do you know of congregations or home fellowships that accomplish these kinds of "faith works"? Can you take initiative to begin something along these lines among your own Christian associates?

Urban Life

For the first time in history, more of the world's people soon will live in cities than in rural areas. Modern technology will further "urbanize" the world by delivering the values and attitudes of city dwellers to even the most remote villages.

How does faith function in this "modern" era? To find out, consider some of what the New Testament has to say about the impact of society on people of faith, and vice versa:

The City

City Kids Die over Adult Matters (Matt. 2:16–18)
Can a Noisy, Dirty, Smelly City Also Be Holy? (Matt. 4:5)
The Holy City (Matt. 23:37)
The Underclass (Luke 7:20–23)
The Septuagint: Alexandria's Gift to Christianity (Acts 18:24)
The Jerusalem Above (Gal. 4:25–26)
Temporary Cities (Heb. 13:14)
Beastly Rome (Rev. 13:1)
A Symbol of Evil (Rev. 14:8)
The New Jerusalem (Rev. 21:1–2)

Jesus and the City

To Be Like Jesus Means to Engage the World's Pain (Matt. 1:18—2:23)
The King Declares His Kingdom (Matt. 4:17)
Jesus' Global Connections (Matt. 8:10)
Jesus—A Homeless Man? (Matt. 8:20)
A Public Statement (Luke 1:46–55)
An International Savior (Luke 2:29–32)
Jesus' First Sermon Included Surprises (Luke 4:16–27)
He Healed Them All (Luke 4:40)
Jesus Confronts the Legalists (Luke 6:1–11)
The Value of a Disabled Woman (Luke 13:10–17)
Good Men Care (Luke 13:34)
Confused Value? (Luke 15:1–31)
Called into the World (John 17:18)

The Church and the City

Sulfa Drugs and Street Lights (Matt. 5:13–16)
People Priorities in the City (Mark 5:21–43)
What Does Leprosy Have to Do with AIDS? (Luke 5:12–15)
The Gospel in a Pluralistic Society (John 3:21)
Churches—Keys to the Cities (Acts 11:22)
Antioch: A Model for the Modern Church? (Acts 13:1)
A Church That Defies Market Research (Acts 15:22–35)
Paul's Urban Strategy (Acts 16:4)
Afraid in the City? (Acts 18:9–10)
The Ephesus Approach (Acts 19:8–41)
Boom Box (Acts 19:10)
Rome or Bust (Acts 19:21)
The Jerusalem Riots (Acts 21:30)
Solidarity (2 Cor. 8:13–15)
This Building Gets Landmark Status (Eph. 2:19–22)
Quiet Living in a Hectic World (1 Thess. 4:11)
The Prayer Breakfast Movement (1 Tim. 2:1–7)
The Church at the End of the First Century (Rev. 1:20)
Seven Churches to Study (Rev. 3:1)

The Environment

God and the Environment (Luke 12:6–7)
The Liberation of Creation (Rom. 8:21)
Faith and the Environment (Rev. 9:4)

Faith in the Public Arena

The Public Side of Our Faith (Matt. 14:13–14)
The Final Exam (Matt. 25:31–46)
Faith Impacts the World (Mark 16:15–16)
Sacred Space (John 1:51)
Be Willing to Pay the Price (Acts 16:16–24)
Free to Be Bold (Acts 23:1)
Matters of Conscience (Rom. 14:1–23)
Gray Areas (1 Cor. 8:1–13)
A Code of Ethics for Christian Witness (2 Cor. 4:2)
Honesty and Ethical Standards (Phil. 2:15)

Pluralism and Diversity

The Twelve: Similar or Diverse? (Luke 6:12–16)
Pluralism at Pentecost (Acts 2:5)
A Growing Movement Confronts Ethnic Prejudice (Acts 6:2–6)
Ethnic Walls Break Down (Acts 10:44–45)
Issues of Faith and Culture (Acts 15:6)
Rights (Gal. 4:1–18)
Who Is the Enemy? (Eph 6:10–13)
Christ, the Lord of the World (Col. 1:15–18)
Support the Weak (1 Thess. 5:14)
(Introduction to Philemon)
A Great Multitude of All Nations (Rev. 7:9)

The Poor

Always the Poor (Mark 14:7)
The Underclass (Luke 7:20–23)
The Good Neighbor (Luke 10:30–37)
Holding Wealth or Serving Others? (Luke 18:18–30)
Sharing Things in Common (Acts 4:32–35)

Urban Systems and Structures

Party Politics of Jesus' Day (Matt. 16:1)
Jesus and Taxation (Matt. 17:24–27)
Centurions (Mark 15:39)
The Census (Luke 2:1–3)
New Testament Political Rulers (Luke 3:1)
A Remedy for Tax Fraud (Luke 19:1–10)
Banking (Luke 19:23)
Owners or Tenants? (Luke 20:9–19)
Roman Politics in the First Century A.D. (Luke 22:25)
Paul and the Structures of Power (Acts 24:25–26)
The Limits of Political Authority (Rom. 13:1–7)
The Scandal of Litigating Christians (1 Cor. 6:1–11)
Who Is the Enemy? (Eph. 6:10–13)
The Power Behind Porn (Jude 6–13)

See also the separate listing of city profiles in the New Testament.

Wealth and Poverty

If you can afford to own this Bible it probably means that you are "rich" in that you have choices in life. By contrast, poverty means not having options such as what to eat, where to live, or to whom to relate. Wealth and poverty are major topics in Scripture. For example, the Gospels preserve more of what Jesus spoke about money than about heaven. So serving and following Christ involves acting responsibly in regard to money, whether we consider ourselves rich or poor. Consider discussing the following articles and their related passages with other believers, especially among your coworkers:

Wealthy People in the New Testament

A Rich Man Enters the Kingdom (Matt. 9:9–13)
Who Were Those Tax Collectors? (Matt. 9:10)
Wealthy People in the New Testament (Matt. 27:57)

The Man Who Had It All—Almost (Mark 10:17–27)
A Burial Fit for a King (Mark 15:42—16:1)
Set for Life—But What about Eternity? (Luke 16:19–31)
"Not Many Mighty"...But a Few (Acts 18:7–8)
Demetrius the Silversmith (Acts 19:24)

Words to the Wealthy

Growing Fat at the Poor's Expense (Matt. 23:14)
True Success Means Faithfulness (Matt. 25:14–30)
The Real Bottom Line (Luke 9:25)
Watch Out for Greed (Luke 12:15)
Confused Value? (Luke 15:1–31)
A Shrewd Manager (Luke 16:1–13)
Holding Wealth or Serving Others? (Luke 18:18–30)
Success (John 3:30)
Discrimination on the Basis of Wealth (John 19:1–6)
Wealth—Hold It Lightly (Acts 4:37—5:11)
Downward Mobility (Phil. 2:5–8)
The Dangers of Prosperity Theology (1 Tim. 6:3–6)
Christians and Money (1 Tim. 6:6–19)
Cocooning (Heb. 4:14–16)
Rich in...Faith? (James 2:5–6)
Prosperity (3 John 2)
The Delusions of Luxury (Rev. 18:1–24)

Poor People in the New Testament

A Poor Family Comes into Wealth (Matt. 2:11)
Jesus—A Homeless Man? (Matt. 8:20)
A Poor Family's Sacrifice (Luke 2:22–24)
The Underclass (Luke 7:20–23)
How Poor Was the Widow? (Luke 21:1–4)
Slaves (Rom. 6:16)
Christ Became Poor (2 Cor. 8:8–9)
Who Are the Poor? (2 Cor. 9:9–10)

Words Concerning the Poor

Growing Fat at the Poor's Expense (Matt. 23:14)
Always the Poor (Mark 14:7)
Discrimination on the Basis of Wealth (John 19:1–6)
Little Is Much with God (Acts 7:3–44)
The Value of Self-Support (1 Thess. 2:9)
Support the Weak (1 Thess. 5:14)
No Work? No Eat! (2 Thess. 3:10)
Effective Care for the Needy (1 Tim. 5:3–16)

The Challenge of Wealth

Wealth's Temptation (Matt. 4:8–10)
Living Within Your Limits (Matt. 16:22–23)
Tainted Money (Matt. 27:3–10)
It's All Relative (Mark 12:43–44)
Running to Extremes (Luke 6:29)
The Real Bottom Line (Luke 9:25)
Watch Out for Greed (Luke 12:15)
Confused Value? (Luke 15:1–31)
Holding Wealth or Serving Others? (Luke 18:18–30)
Owners or Tenants? (Luke 20:9–19)
New Life Means New Lifestyles (Acts 2:42–47)
Sharing Things in Common (Acts 4:32–35)
People, Property, and Profitability (Acts 16:19)
"I Have Not Coveted" (Acts 20:33–38)
Giving It All Away (1 Cor. 13:3)
Money: Compassion and Integrity (1 Cor. 16:1–4)
To Live Is...? (Phil. 1:21)
A Lifestyle of Contentment (Phil. 4:10–13)
The Dangers of Prosperity Theology (1 Tim. 6:3–6)
Christians and Money (1 Tim. 6:6–19)
Cocooning (Heb. 4:14–16)
Rich in...Faith? (James 2:5–6)
Prosperity (3 John 2)
The Delusions of Luxury (Rev. 18:1–24)

Charitable Contributions

Anonymous Donors (Matt. 6:1–4)
Tithing (Matt. 23:23–24)
A Parting Gift (Mark 14:3–9)
From Deadbeat to Donor (Eph. 4:28)
The Value of Self-Support (1 Thess. 2:9)
No Work? No Eat! (2 Thess. 3:10)
Effective Care for the Needy (1 Tim. 5:3–16)
Let Me Pick Up the Tab (Philem. 17–19)

Inheritance

Will You Get What's Coming to You? (Luke 12:13–15)
What's In It for Me? (Eph. 1:11)
Getting Yours (James 5:1–6)

Money

Banking (Luke 19:23)
Trade in Ancient Israel (End of John)
A History of Money (Rev. 3:17–19)
Money in the New Testament (Rev. 16:21)

Taxes

Jesus and Taxation (Matt. 17:24–27)
Taxes (Mark 12:14)
A Remedy for Tax Fraud (Luke 19:1–10)

Other

Some Surprising Evidence (Matt. 11:2–6)
Jesus and Unjust Pay (Matt. 20:1–16)
Jesus' First Sermon Included Surprises (Luke 4:16–27)
A Job to Do (Luke 19:11–27)
Debt-Free Living (Rom. 13:8)
The Scandal of Litigating Christians (1 Cor. 6:1–11)
Paying Vocational Christian Workers (1 Cor. 9:1–23)
All God's Children (Eph. 1:18)
Taking Stock (Phil. 3:7–14)
No Greedy Leaders! (1 Tim. 3:3)
Aiming to Please (Heb. 11:6)
Ushers on Trial (James 2:1–13)
Don't Fleece the Flock! (1 Pet. 5:2)
Clothing (Rev. 3:18)
A Symbol of Evil (Rev. 14:8)

Witness and Evangelism

What does it mean to "be a witness" for Christ? What is evangelism all about? How can believers influence others to consider and accept the message about Jesus?

The topics of witness, evangelism, the gospel, and missions are vitally important to the story of the New Testament and to the church today. Study the following articles and their related passages to learn more about the Scriptures' teaching in these areas:

The Gospel Message

Evidence for the Resurrection—Jesus' Appearances (Mark 16:1–8)
What is the Gospel? (Luke 7:22)
Many Men Would Be Gods, But Only One God Would Be Man (John 8:52–59)
The Power of the Gospel (Rom. 1:16)

Righteousness (Rom. 1:17)
Nobody's Perfect (Rom. 3:9–18)
Are People Basically Good? (Rom. 7:21)
Ten Myths about Christianity (series; 1 Tim. 1:3–4)
Knowing *About* God Is Not the Same as *Knowing* God (Heb. 6:13)
Worship or Wrath? (Rev. 6:1–17)
There's a Welcome Here (Rev. 22:17)

The Example of Jesus

Being Like Jesus (series, Matt. 10:25)
Jews, Gentiles, and Jesus (Matt. 15:24)
The Miracles of Jesus (Mark 8:11–12)
Jesus Is for Gentiles, Too (Luke 1:1–4)
Jesus' First Sermon Included Surprises (Luke 4:16–27)
The Spirit of the Lord Is upon...You! (Luke 4:18)
Jesus Excludes Only the Faithless (John 12:20–36)

The Church's Mandate

The Public Side of Our Faith (Matt. 14:13–14)
To All the Nations (Matt. 28:19)
Faith Impacts the World (Mark 16:15–16)
Can Laity Get the Job Done? (Luke 9:1–62)
The Gospel in a Pluralistic Society (John 3:21)
Whose Job Is Evangelism? (John 16:8)
Power (Acts 1:8)
The Ephesus Approach (Acts 19:8–41)
The Spirit of Power (2 Tim. 1:6–7)

Communicating the Message by What We Say

Is Your Witness Falling on Deaf Ears? (Mark 4:3–20)
Witnessing—Jesus' Style (Luke 24:48)
Carrots, Not Sticks (Acts 2:37–38)
Adapt Your Witness! (Acts 17:17)
Free to Be Bold (Acts 23:1)
Truth Can Trigger Opposition (Acts 24:1–26)
Audience-shaped Messages (Acts 26:1–32)
Some Basics of Witness (1 John 1:1–10)

Communicating the Message by What We Do

Being Like Jesus (series, Matt. 10:25)
Is There Enough Evidence to Convict You? (Mark 14:53–64)
Are You a Friend of Someone in Need? (Luke 5:17–26)
Does Anyone Believe You? (John 7:5)
A Confusing Reputation (Acts 5:12–16)
New Creatures with New Character (Gal. 5:22–23)
"I Won't Hire Christians!" (1 Tim. 6:1–2)
Your "Workstyle" (Titus 2:9–10)
Evidence before Information (Titus 3:1–8)

Strategic Evangelism

Opportunities Look like Barriers (Acts 1:4)
Where Has God Placed You? (Acts 8:26–39)
A Church That Defies Market Research (Acts 15:22–35)
A Code of Ethics for Christian Witness (2 Cor. 4:2)
Work—A Platform for Evangelism? (Eph. 6:5–9)

Other

Faith Unfolds Slowly (Mark 4:33–34)
Set for Life—But What about Eternity? (Luke 16:19–31)
You Alone Can't Bring Them to Jesus (John 6:44)
A Radically Changed Perspective (Acts 9:15)
Come One, Come All (Acts 10:34)
A New Reality Gets a New Name (Acts 11:26)
Be Willing to Pay the Price (Acts 16:16–24)
God's Heart for the Whole World (Rom. 9:1)
Paul the Jew—Teacher of the Gentiles (2 Tim. 1:3)
God Cannot Lie (Titus 1:2)
A Great Multitude of All Nations (Rev. 7:9–17)

Women

The New Testament was written in an age when women faced very different roles and expectations than they experience today. Nevertheless, Jesus took women seriously. He enjoyed important friendships with a number of women and affirmed their value and significance. Here are some articles to study as you consider what Scripture has to say about women and subjects that pertain to them:

Jesus and Women

The Women in Jesus' Genealogy (Matt. 1:3–6)
A New Respect for Women (Matt. 5:32)
Family Loyalty (Matt. 12:46–50)
Persistence Pays Off (Matt. 15:21–28)
Significance for Little People (Mark 2:3–17)
People Priorities in the City (Mark 5:21–43)
The Women Who Followed Jesus (Luke 8:1–3)
The Value of a Disabled Woman (Luke 13:10–17)
Jesus—A Rabbi for Women, Too (Luke 23:49)
Those Women Again! (Luke 24:11)
The Road Less Traveled (John 4:4–42)
A Double Standard? (John 8:2–3)
The Women around Jesus (John 19:25)
The Proper Measure of All Things (Heb. 2:6–8)

Women in the New Testament

The Women in Jesus' Genealogy (Matt. 1:3–6)
The Hemorrhaging Woman (Matt. 9:20–22)
Hateful Herodias (Matt. 14:3)
Persistence Pays Off (Matt. 15:21–28)
Children and Childcare (Matt. 19:14)
A Pushy Mother (Matt. 20:20–23)
"Prostitutes Are Going into the Kingdom" (Matt. 21:31–32)
Jewish Homemaking (Mark 1:29–31)
Significance for Little People (Mark 2:3–17)
Why So Many Marys? (Mark 15:40)
Elizabeth (Luke 1:24)
Mary, the Mother of Jesus (Luke 1:26–56)
Anna (Luke 2:36–38)
The Women Who Followed Jesus (Luke 8:1–3)
Mary of Magdala (Luke 8:2)
Martha of Bethany (Luke 10:38–42)
Who Was the Queen of Sheba? (Luke 11:31)
The Value of a Disabled Woman (Luke 13:10–17)
Families of the Gospels (Luke 20:34)
The Servant Girl (Luke 22:56–57)
Jesus—A Rabbi for Women, Too (Luke 23:49)
Those Women Again! (Luke 24:11)
Mary of Bethany (John 11:1–2)
Funeral Preparations (John 12:1–8)
A Woman in Labor (John 16:21–22)
The Women around Jesus (John 19:25)
An Inclusive Prayer Meeting (Acts 1:14)
Ananias and Sapphira (Acts 5:1)
Tabitha (Acts 9:36)
Lydia (Acts 16:14)
Families of the Early Church (Acts 16:31–34)
The Four Daughters of Philip (Acts 21:9)
Phoebe (Rom. 16:1)
Priscilla and Aquila (Rom. 16:3–5)
Junia (Rom. 16:7)
Paul's Female Coworkers (Rom. 16:12)

Who Was Paul's Mother? (Rom. 16:13)
Women and Work in the Ancient World (1 Cor. 7:32–35)
Euodia and Syntyche (Phil. 4:2)
Widows (1 Tim. 5:3)
Eunice—A Mother's Legacy (2 Tim. 1:5)
Apphia (Philem. 2)
The Hall of Faithfulness (Heb. 11:1–40)
Who Are These People? (Heb. 11:2)
Rahab (Heb. 11:31)
Women Received Their Dead Raised (Heb. 11:35)
Sarah (1 Pet. 3:6)
The Elect Lady (2 John 1)
Jezebel (Rev. 2:20–23)
Woman Against Evil (Rev. 12:1–17)

A Woman's Character

See "Ethics and Character"

Other

The Way Up Is Down (Matt. 5:3)
A New Respect for Women (Matt. 5:32)
Children and Childcare (Matt. 19:14)
A New View of Sexuality (1 Cor. 7:3–6)
Head Coverings (1 Cor. 11:2–16)
What Is Headship? (1 Cor. 11:3)
Not Permitted to Speak? (1 Cor. 14:34)
We Are Family! (Gal. 3:28)
Gentle as a Nursing Mother (1 Thess. 2:7)
A New Way to Worship (1 Tim. 2:8–15)
Submission (James 4:7)
Finally, Full Equality (Rev. 5:9–10)

Work

In today's world some people see their work as a long, dark tunnel between leisurely weekends, others as a passion bordering on addiction; some as a curse from God, others as a divine calling. What does the New Testament say about this crucial area that so dominates day-to-day life? Find out by studying the articles listed below and their related passages:

The Nature and Value of Work

Our Daily Bread (Matt. 6:11)
Life—The Big Picture (Mark 12:28–34)
Is Jesus Really Lord of All? (Luke 6:1–5)
A Job to Do (Luke 19:11–27)
God—The Original Worker (John 5:17)
Reconnecting Sunday and Monday (Acts 2:46–47)
Is Work a Curse? (Rom. 8:20)
Workplace Myths (1 Cor. 3:9)
Are Some Jobs More Important than Others? (1 Cor. 12:28–31)
Every Breath You Take (Col. 1:17)
The Spirituality of Everyday Work (Col. 3:1–2)
A Command to Work (2 Thess. 3:6–12)
No Work? No Eat! (2 Thess. 3:10)
People at Work (Heb. 2:7)
Who Is "Called," Anyway? (Heb. 3:1)
A Glance at Work in the Bible (Rev. 22:1–11)
Fresh Fruit Salad (Rev. 22:2)

The Believer's "Workstyle"

Conflict Resolution (Acts 11:2–18)
The Ultimate Performance Review (1 Cor. 3:13–15)
New Creatures with New Character (Gal. 5:22–23)
Honesty and Ethical Standards (Phil. 2:15)
Work World Codes (Col. 3:22—4:1)
Work, Labor, and Patience (1 Thess. 1:3)
One Standard for All (1 Tim. 3:1)
"I Won't Hire Christians!" (1 Tim. 6:1–2)
Your "Workstyle" (Titus 2:9–10)
Ten Commandments for Practical Living (James 2:8–13)

Career Changes and Planning

Levi's Feast—A Career Transition Party (Luke 5:28–29)
Career Changes (1 Cor. 7:17–24)
From Deadbeat to Donor (Eph. 4:28)

Communicating the Gospel in the Workplace

Sulfa Drugs and Street Lights (Matt. 5:13–16)
The Public Side of Our Faith (Matt. 14:13–14)
Faith Impacts the World (Mark 16:15–16)
Called into the World (John 17:18)
Where Has God Placed You? (Acts 8:26–39)
A Code of Ethics for Christian Witness (2 Cor. 4:2)
Work: A Platform for Evangelism? (Eph. 6:5–9)
"I Won't Hire Christians!" (1 Tim. 6:1–2)
Your "Workstyle" (Titus 2:9–10)

Competition and Conflict

Competition versus Compassion (Luke 9:46–48)
Compassion and Anger in One Person? (Luke 19:41–46)
Paul Apologized for Losing His Cool (Acts 23:5)
"It Serves Them Right" (Acts 27:9–11)
Integrity in the Face of Competition (2 Cor. 10:1)
Murder on the Job (1 John 3:11–13)

Honesty and Integrity

Doing Your Duty (Luke 17:5–10)
The Blessing of a Clean Conscience (John 18:1–11)
Real Estate Deal Deadly (Acts 5:2–10)
Welcome to Stressful Living (2 Cor. 6:3–10)

Money and Profits

Jesus and Unjust Pay (Matt. 20:1–16)
Growing Fat at the Poor's Expense (Matt. 23:14)
People, Property, and Profitability (Acts 16:19)
Debt-Free Living (Rom. 13:8)
From Deadbeat to Donor (Eph. 4:28)
Downward Mobility (Phil. 2:5–8)
Prosperity (3 John 2)

Success and Significance

True Success Means Faithfulness (Matt. 25:14–30)
A Kingdom Perspective on Significance (Mark 13:33)
The Real Bottom Line (Luke 9:25)
Success (John 3:30)
To Live Is...? (Phil 1:21)
Taking Stock (Phil. 3:7–14)
Aiming to Please (Heb. 11:6)

Supervisors and Subordinates

The Dangers of Power (Luke 3:14)
Delegation and Affirmation (Luke 10:1)
A Shrewd Manager (Luke 16:1–13)
The Quest for Greatness (Luke 22:24–30)
Under Authority (John 12:49)
A Model of Servant-Leadership (John 13:2–17)
Barnabas—A Model for Mentoring (Acts 9:27)
People, Property, and Profitability (Acts 16:19)
Who Gets the Credit? (1 Cor. 3:5–8)
The Ultimate Performance Review (1 Cor. 3:13–15)
Who's the Boss? (Col. 3:22–24)
Encouraging the Mentor (1 Thess. 3:1–10)
Submission (James 4:7)
Who's in Charge Here? (James 4:13–16)
Power (Rev. 11:17)

See also the Jobs and Occupations Index, and the list of articles under "Ethics" in this section.

INDEX TO LARGE ARTICLES

See also the introduction to each book in the New Testament.

INDEX TO MAPS

A number of maps help you put the events of the New Testament into geographical perspective:

The Lands of the Gospels (Introduction to Matthew)
To Egypt and Back (Matt. 2:13–15)
Jerusalem (Matt. 4:5)
Jesus' Galilean Ministry (Matt. 4:25)
Cities of Palestine in Christ's Time (Matt. 9:35)
Jesus' Entry (Matt. 21:1)
"To All the Nations" (Matt. 28:19)
Resurrection Appearances (Mark 16:1–8)
Roman Power in Bible Lands (Luke 3:1)
The Sea of Galilee (Luke 5:1–11)
Bypassing Samaria (Luke 9:51–56)
Sheba (Luke 11:31)
The Jordan River Valley (John 10:40–42)
The World of the Early Church (Introduction to Acts)
The Spread of the Gospel (Acts 1:4)
Nations of Pentecost (Acts 2:8–11)
Philip's Journey to Samaria (Acts 8:5–13)
Ethiopia (Acts 8:27)
Philip and the Ethiopian Treasurer (Acts 8:27–39)
Peter's Journey to the Sea (Acts 9:32)
Early Church Expansion (Acts 11:19–26)
Major Land Routes (Acts 13:3–4)
Paul's First Journey, Part One (Acts 13:5)
Paul's First Journey, Part Two (Acts 14:8)
Paul's First Journey, Part Three (Acts 14:20)
Paul's Second Journey, Part One (Acts 16:4)
Paul's Second Journey, Part Two (Acts 16:8)
Paul's Second Journey, Part Three (Acts 17:10)
Paul's Second Journey, Part Four (Acts 17:15)
Paul's Third Journey, Part One (Acts 19:8–41)
Jerusalem to Rome (Acts 19:21)
Paul's Third Journey, Part Two (Acts 20:15)
Paul's Third Journey, Part Three (Acts 20:15–16)
Paul's Third Journey, Part Four (Acts 21:1)
Paul's Journey to Rome, Part One (Acts 27:8)
Paul's Journey to Rome, Part Two (Acts 28:16)
First-Century Rome (Introduction to Romans)
Downtown Corinth (Introduction to 2 Corinthians)
Asia Minor (2 Cor. 1:8)
Galatia Region (Introduction to Galatians)
Aegean Sea Region (Introduction to Revelation)
From Patmos to the Seven Churches (Rev. 1:20)

LOCATOR MAPS

A locator map shows where a certain place is with reference to the surrounding area:

Chorazin (Matt. 11:21)
Magdala (Matt. 15:39)
Jerusalem (Matt. 23:37)
Judea (Mark 1:5)
Galilee (Mark 1:14)
Gadara (Mark 5:1)
Decapolis (Mark 5:20)
Bethsaida (Mark 6:45)
Gennesaret (Mark 6:53)
Caesarea Philippi (Mark 8:27)
Bethphage (Mark 11:1)
Cyrene (Mark 15:21)
Bethlehem (Luke 2:11)
Capernaum (Luke 4:31)
Sidon and Tyre (Luke 6:17)
Nain (Luke 7:11)
Bethabara (John 1:28)
Nazareth (John 1:45)
Cana (John 2:1)
Samaria (John 4:4)
Sychar (John 4:5)
Bethany (John 11:18)
Ephraim (John 11:54)
Damascus (Acts 9:2)
Caesarea (Acts 10:24)
Tarsus (Acts 11:25)
Antioch (Acts 13:1)
Cyprus (Acts 13:4–12)
Athens (Acts 17:15)
Alexandria (Acts 18:24)
Ephesus (Acts 19:8–41)
Rome (Introduction to Romans)
Corinth (Introduction to 2 Corinthians)
Ephesus (Introduction to Ephesians)
Colosse (Introduction to Colossians)
Crete (Introduction to Titus)
Nicopolis (Titus 3:12)
The Two Babylons (Rev. 14:8)

Index to City and Regional Profiles

The world of the Bible was far more urban than many modern readers realize. Jesus, Paul, and others in the first century grew up and carried out most of their work among the cities of the Roman Empire, which were connected by an extensive network of relatively safe, well-maintained roads. Many of the profiles below tell about these important urban centers.

City and Regional Profiles By Reference

Index to City and Regional Profiles

Index to Personality Profiles

In writing to the Corinthian believers, Paul pointed out that the things that happened to Old Testament people happened to them as examples, and were written for their instruction (1 Cor. 10:11). In a similar way, the New Testament provides believers today with many illustrations of people responding to God in one way or another. By studying the personality profiles below and reading the related biblical texts, you can learn much about these individuals, whose lives the Holy Spirit chose to record in Scripture for our benefit.

Index to Tables, Lists, and Diagrams

Index to Tables, Lists, and Diagrams

INDEX TO KEY NEW TESTAMENT PASSAGES

The following index provides access to selected passages of the New Testament that speak most directly to practical concerns in today's world. Use this index along with the other helps and annotations to see quickly what the New Testament says about each subject.

(Passages are listed alphabetically by brief content summaries. The words 'a' and 'the' are ignored in the alphabetizing.)

Passages referred to in a Gospel might also be found in one or more other Gospels, in slightly different form. See "The Four Gospels Side by Side" for a listing of such parallel passages.)

Worship

Youth

THE FOUR GOSPELS SIDE BY SIDE

(The publishers gratefully acknowledge the use of *Gospel Parallels,* edited by Burton H. Throckmorton, Jr., in preparing this chart.)

	MATTHEW	MARK	LUKE	JOHN
I. Before Jesus' Public Ministry				
1. Introductions	—	—	1:1–4	1:1–18
2. The promise of John the Baptist's birth	—	—	1:5–25	—
3. An angel greets Mary; Mary visits Elizabeth	—	—	1:26–56	—
4. John the Baptist born	—	—	1:57–80	—
5. Jesus born; the shepherds see Him	1:18–25	—	2:1–20	—
6. The wise men visit	2:1–12	—	—	—
7. Jesus circumcised and presented in the temple	—	—	2:21–40	—
8. Escape to Egypt; Herod kills children; return from Egypt	2:13–23	—	—	—
9. Jesus at age twelve	—	—	2:41–52	—
II. Preparation for Jesus' Public Ministry				
10. The preaching of John the Baptist	3:1–12	1:1–8	3:1–18	1:19–34
11. John put in prison	—	—	3:19–20	—
12. The baptism of Jesus	3:13–17	1:9–11	3:21–22	—
13. The ancestors of Jesus	1:1–17	—	3:23–38	—
14. The devil tests Jesus	4:1–11	1:12–13	4:1–13	—
III. Jesus' Public Ministry in Galilee				
15. Jesus makes wine from water; visits Capernaum	—	—	—	2:1–12
16. Jesus clears out the temple during Passover	—	—	—	2:13–15
17. Nicodemus visits Jesus at night	—	—	—	3:1–21
18. Jesus baptizes (through His followers) in Judea; John the Baptist again tells of Jesus	—	—	—	3:22—4:3
19. Jesus speaks with a woman of Samaria	—	—	—	4:4–42
20. Jesus arrives in Galilee; His first preaching there	4:12–17	1:14–15	4:14–15	4:43–45
21. Jesus first rejected in Nazareth	—	—	4:16–30	—
22. Many fish caught; the first disciples called	4:18–22	1:16–20	5:1–11	1:35–41
23. Jesus in Capernaum; a man with an evil spirit healed	7:28–29	1:21–28	4:31–37	7:46
24. Peter's mother-in-law and others healed	8:14–17	1:29–34	4:38–41	—
25. Jesus leaves Capernaum	—	1:35–38	4:42–43	—
26. Jesus travels and preaches in Galilee	4:23–25	1:39	4:44	—
A. The Sermon on the Mount (or the Plain)				
27. Introduction	5:1–2	—	6:20	—
28. Blessings promised	5:3–12	—	6:20–23	—
29. Warnings of troubles	—	—	6:24–26	—
30. Stories about salt and about light	5:13–16	9:50	11:33–36; 14:34–35	—
31. About the law	5:17–20	—	16:16–17	—

	MATTHEW	MARK	LUKE	JOHN
A. The Sermon on the Mount (or the Plain) *(continued)*				
32. About murder	5:21–26	—	12:57–59	—
33. About being faithful in marriage	5:27–30	—	—	—
34. About divorce	5:31–32	—	16:18	—
35. About promises and revenge	5:33–42	—	6:29–30	—
36. About love for enemies	5:43–48	—	6:27–28, 32–36	—
37. About giving and prayer	6:1–8	—	—	—
38. The Lord's Prayer	6:9–15	—	11:1–4	—
39. About going without eating; about treasures	6:16–21	—	12:33–34	—
40. About eyes and light	6:22–23	—	11:34–36	—
41. Serving two masters	6:24	—	16:13	—
42. About worry	6:25–34	—	12:22–31	—
43. About judging others	7:1–5	—	6:37–42	—
44. What belongs to God	7:6	—	—	—
45. God's answer to prayer	7:7–11	—	11:9–13	—
46. The Golden Rule	7:12	—	6:31	—
47. The narrow gate	7:13–14	—	13:23–24	—
48. A tree and its fruit	7:15–20	—	6:43–45	—
49. A warning to obey God	7:21–23	—	6:46; 13:26–27	—
50. Two builders	7:24–27	—	6:47–49	—
51. The end of the Sermon	7:28–29	—	—	7:26
B. Continuing Jesus' Public Ministry in Galilee				
52. A man healed of leprosy	8:1–4	1:40–45	5:12–16	—
53. An army officer's servant healed	8:5–13	—	7:1–10	4:46–54
54. A widow's son healed at Nain	—	—	7:11–17	—
55. What it means to follow Jesus	8:18–22	—	9:57–62	—
56. A crippled man healed at Capernaum	9:1–8	2:1–12	5:17–26	5:8–9
57. Jesus chooses Matthew	9:9–13	2:13–17	5:27–32	—
58. People ask about going without eating	9:14–17	2:18–22	5:33–39	—
59. A man healed at a pool; witnesses about Jesus	—	—	—	5:1–47
60. Two blind men healed	9:27–31	—	—	—
61. Jesus heals a man who could not talk	9:32–34	3:22–27	11:14–23	—
62. The twelve apostles sent out	9:35—10:16	—	10:1–16	1:42; 4:35
63. The disciples warned about trouble	10:17–25	13:9–13	21:12–17	13:16; 14:26; 15:20
64. Don't be afraid of people	10:26–33	—	12:2–12	14:26
65. Division in families	10:34–36	—	12:49–56	—
66. The cost of following Jesus	10:37–39	—	14:25–33	12:25
67. End of Jesus' talk with His disciples	10:40—11:1	—	10:16	5:23; 12:44–45
68. John the Baptist's question to Jesus	11:2–6	—	7:18–23	—
69. Jesus talks about John the Baptist	11:7–19	—	7:24–35	—
70. Jesus predicts trouble for unbelieving towns	11:20–24	—	10:13–15	—
71. Jesus gives thanks to the Father	11:25–27	—	10:21–22	3:35; 7:29; 10:14–15; 17:2

	MATTHEW	MARK	LUKE	JOHN
B. Continuing Jesus' Public Ministry in Galilee *(continued)*				
72. Comfort for the tired	11:28–30	—	—	—
73. Picking grains of wheat on the Sabbath	12:1–8	2:23–28	6:1–5	5:10
74. Jesus heals a man with a crippled hand	12:9–14	3:1–6	6:6–11	—
75. Jesus heals many people	12:15–21	3:7–12	6:17–19	—
76. Twelve apostles chosen	10:1–4	3:13–19	6:12–16	1:42
77. A woman pours perfume on Jesus	26:6–13	14:3–9	7:36–50	12:1–8
78. Women who helped Jesus	—	—	8:1–3	—
79. Jesus accused; lesson about when people fight	12:22–37	3:20–30	11:14–23	7:20; 8:48, 52
80. Looking for signs from heaven	12:38–42	8:11–12	11:29–32	—
81. The return of an evil spirit	12:43–45	—	11:24–26	—
82. Jesus' mother and brothers	12:46–50	3:31–35	8:19–21	15:14
83. Jesus teaches with stories: a farmer, weeds, seed growing, a mustard seed, leaven, hidden treasure, a pearl, a fish net, new and old treasures	13:1–52	4:1–34	8:4–18; 10:23–24; 13:18–21	12:40
84. Jesus calms a storm	8:23–27	4:35–41	8:22–25	—
85. The man near Gadara with evil spirits	8:28–34	5:1–20	8:26–39	—
86. A dying girl and a sick woman's faith	9:18–26	5:21–43	8:40–56	—
87. The people of Nazareth reject Jesus again	13:53–58	6:1–6	—	4:44; 6:42; 7:5, 15
88. The twelve apostles sent out	9:35; 10:1–14	6:6–13	9:1–6	—
89. Herod thinks Jesus is John the Baptist back from death	14:1–2	6:14–16	9:7–9	—
90. The death of John the Baptist	14:3–12	6:17–29	—	—
91. The twelve apostles return; five thousand people fed	14:13–21	6:30–44	9:10–17	6:1–14
92. Jesus walks on water	14:22–33	6:45–52	—	6:15–21
93. Jesus speaks of the bread of life	—	—	—	6:22–71
94. Healings at Gennesaret	14:34–36	6:53–56	—	—
95. What really makes people unclean	15:1–20	7:1–23	—	—
96. A Canaanite woman's daughter healed	15:21–28	7:24–30	—	—
97. Many healed, including a man who was deaf and mute	15:29–31	7:31–37	—	—
98. Four thousand people fed	15:32–39	8:1–10	—	—
99. Pharisees want a sign from heaven	16:1–4	8:11–13	11:29–32; 12:54–56	6:30
100. A teaching about yeast	16:5–12	8:14–21	12:1	—
101. A blind man at Bethsaida healed	—	8:22–26	—	9:1–7
102. Who Jesus is; He predicts His suffering and death	16:13–23	8:27–33	9:18–22	6:68–69; 20:21–23
103. What it means to follow Jesus	16:24–28	8:34—9:1	9:23–27	12:25
104. The glory of Jesus	17:1–8	9:2–8	9:28–36	1:14
105. The coming of Elijah	17:9–13	9:9–13	—	—
106. A boy with epilepsy healed	17:14–21	9:14–29	9:37–43a	14:9
107. Jesus predicts His suffering and death a second time	17:22–23	9:30–32	9:43b–45	7:1
108. Paying the temple tax	17:24–27	—	—	—
109. A discussion about greatness	18:1–5	9:33–37	9:46–48	3:3, 5; 12:44–45; 13:20

	MATTHEW	MARK	LUKE	JOHN
B. Continuing Jesus' Public Ministry in Galilee *(continued)*				
110. For or against Jesus	—	9:38–41	9:49–50	—
111. Temptations to sin	18:6–9	9:42–48	17:1–2	—
112. About salt	5:13	9:49–50	14:34–35	—
113. About a lost sheep	18:10–14	—	15:1–10	—
114. When someone sins	18:15–20	—	17:3	20:23
115. Forgiving many times	18:21–22	—	17:3–4	—
116. An official who refused to forgive	18:23–35	—	—	—
117. Jesus teaches in Jerusalem at the festival of Booths	—	—	—	7:1–53
118. A woman caught in sin	—	—	—	8:1–11
119. Jesus is the light of the world; some people try to stone Him	—	—	—	8:12–59
120. Jesus heals a man born blind	—	—	—	9:1–41
121. The good shepherd	—	—	—	10:1–20
C. Luke's Special Section				
122. Samaritan villagers refuse to welcome Jesus	—	—	9:51–56	—
123. What it means to be a follower of Jesus	8:18:22	—	9:57–62	—
124. Seventy followers sent out	9:35—10:16	—	10:1–16	4:35; 5:23
125. The seventy followers return	—	—	10:17–20	12:31
126. Jesus thanks His Father	11:25–27	—	10:21–22	10:15; 17:2
127. The disciples are blessed	13:16–17	—	10:23–24	—
128. An expert in the Law questions Jesus	22:34–40	12:28–31	10:25–28	—
129. The good Samaritan	—	—	10:29–37	—
130. Martha and Mary	—	—	10:38–42	11:1–3
131. The friend at midnight	—	—	11:5–8	—
132. Answer to prayer	7:7–11	—	11:9–13	—
133. Jesus and the ruler of demons	9:32–34; 12:22–30	—	11:14–23	—
134. Being really blessed	—	—	11:27–28	—
135. A sign from God for the people	12:38–42; 16:1–4	8:11–12	11:29–32	—
136. About light	5:14–16; 6:22–23	—	11:33–36	—
137. Jesus condemns the Pharisees	23:1–36	12:37–40	11:37—12:1	—
138. Telling others about Jesus without fear	10:19–20, 26–33; 12:32	4:22; 8:38	12:2–12	14:26
139. About a rich fool	—	—	12:13–21	—
140. Worries about earthly things	6:16–21; 25–34	—	12:22–34	—
141. Watchfulness and faithfulness	24:43–51	13:32–33	12:35–46	13:4–5
142. What a master expects	—	—	12:47–48	—
143. Knowing what to do	10:34–36; 16:1–4	—	12:49–56	12:27
144. Settling with an accuser	5:25–26	—	12:57–59	—
145. Turn back to God; a tree without figs	—	—	13:1–9	—
146. Jesus heals a woman on the Sabbath	—	—	13:10–17	—
147. About a mustard seed; about yeast	13:31–33	4:30–32	13:18–21	—

	MATTHEW	MARK	LUKE	JOHN
C. Luke's Special Section *(continued)*				
148. Being kept out of God's kingdom	7:13–14; 25:10–12; 7:22–23	—	13:22–30	—
149. Leaving Galilee	—	—	13:31–33	—
150. Jesus loves Jerusalem	23:37–39	—	13:34–35	—
151. A man with dropsy (swollen legs) healed	—	—	14:1–6	—
152. Being a humble guest	—	—	14:7–14	—
153. The great banquet	22:1–14	—	14:15–24	—
154. The cost of being a disciple	10:26–33, 37–39	—	14:25–35	—
155. A lost sheep; a lost coin	18:12–14	—	15:1–10	—
156. A lost son comes home	—	—	15:11–32	—
157. A dishonest manager	6:24	—	16:1–13	—
158. God sees the heart	—	—	16:14–15	—
159. About the law and about divorce	5:17–20, 31–32; 11:12–13	—	16:16–18	—
160. A rich man and Lazarus	—	—	16:19–31	—
161. About causing sin	18:6–9	9:42–48	17:1–2	—
162. About forgiving	18:15, 21–22	—	17:3–4	—
163. About faith	17:20	—	17:5–6	—
164. A servant's duty	—	—	17:7–10	—
165. Jesus heals ten men with leprosy	—	—	17:11–19	—
166. About God's kingdom	24:23–25	13:21–23	17:20–21	—
167. The day of the Son of Man	24:26–28, 37–41	—	17:22–37	—
168. About a widow and a crooked judge	—	—	18:1–8	—
169. About a Pharisee and a tax collector	—	—	18:9–14	—
IV. The Judean Ministry				
A. The Journey to Jerusalem				
170. About divorce	19:1–12	10:1–12	—	—
171. Jesus blesses children	19:13–15	10:13–16	18:15–17	3:3, 5
172. A rich young man	19:16–30	10:17–31	18:18–30	—
173. Workers in a vineyard	20:1–16	—	—	—
174. Jesus again tells about His death	20:17–19	10:32–34	18:31–34	—
175. James and John want to be first	20:20–28	10:35–45	22:24–27	—
176. Jesus heals the blind	20:29–34	10:46–52	18:35–43	—
177. Zacchaeus meets Jesus	—	—	19:1–10	—
178. A man who left his servants with money	25:14–30	—	19:11–27	—
B. The Days in Jerusalem				
179. Entry into Jerusalem; Jesus in the temple	21:1–17	11:1–11	19:28–46	12:12–50; 2:13–15
180. Jesus at the festival of Dedication in Jerusalem	—	—	—	10:22–39
181. Jesus brings Lazarus to life at Bethany	—	—	—	10:40—11:44
182. The plot to kill Jesus	—	—	—	11:45–53
183. Jesus at Ephraim; the coming of the Passover	—	—	—	11:54–57

	MATTHEW	MARK	LUKE	JOHN
B. The Days in Jerusalem *(continued)*				
184. Jesus puts a curse on a fig tree	21:18–19	11:12–14	—	—
185. Jesus clears out the temple	21:12–13	11:15–19	19:45–48	2:13–17
186. The meaning of the dried-up fig tree	21:20–22	11:20–26	—	14:13–14
187. A question about Jesus' authority	21:23–27	11:27–33	20:1–8	2:18
188. About two sons	21:28–32	—	—	—
189. About the renters of a vineyard	21:33–46	12:1–12	20:9–19	—
190. The great banquet	22:1–14	—	14:16–24	—
191. Paying taxes to Caesar	22:15–22	12:13–17	20:20–26	3:2
192. Life in the future world	22:23–33	12:18–27	20:27–40	—
193. The most important commandment	22:34–40	12:28–34	10:25–28	—
194. About David's son	22:41–46	12:35–37	20:41–44	—
195. Pharisees and teachers of the Law condemned	23:1–36	12:38–40	20:45–47; 11:37–52	—
196. Jesus loves Jerusalem	23:37–39	—	13:34–35	—
197. A widow's offering	—	12:41–44	21:1–4	—
198. The temple to be destroyed	24:1–3	13:1–4	21:5–7	—
199. Signs of Christ's coming	24:4–8	13:5–8	21:8–11	—
200. Warning about trouble	24:9–14	13:9–13	21:12–19	14:26; 15:21; 16:2
201. The abomination of desolation	24:15–22	13:14–20	21:20–24	—
202. False messiahs to come	24:23–25	13:21–23	17:20–23	—
203. The coming of the Son of Man	24:26–28	—	17:23–24, 37	—
204. When the Son of Man appears	24:29–31	13:24–27	21:25–28	—
205. A lesson from a fig tree	24:32–33	13:28–29	21:29–31	—
206. The time of Christ's appearing unknown	24:34–36	13:30–32	21:32–33	—
207. Be on guard	—	13:33–37	—	—
208. A warning to watch out	—	—	21:34–36	—
209. The Son of Man's appearing to be sudden	24:37–41	—	7:26–27, 34–35	—
210. Watchfulness and faithfulness	24:42–51	—	12:39–46	—
211. About ten virgins	25:1–13	—	—	—
212. About three servants	25:14–30	—	19:12–27	—
213. The final judgment	25:31–46	—	—	5:28–29
214. Jesus teaches in the temple each day	—	—	21:37–38	—
C. Jesus Is Arrested and Crucified				
215. The plot to kill Jesus	26:1–5	14:1–2	22:1–2	11:47–53
216. Perfume poured on Jesus at Bethany	26:6–13	14:3–9	7:36–50	12:1–11
217. Judas betrays Jesus	26:14–16	14:10–11	22:3–6	18:2–5
218. Preparing for the Passover meal	26:17–19	14:12–16	22:7–13	—
219. Jesus washes the feet of His disciples	—	—	—	13:1–20
220. The one who will betray Jesus	26:20–25	14:17–21	22:14, 21–23	13:21–30
221. The Lord's Supper	26:26–29	14:22–25	22:15–20	—
222. Betrayal predicted; greatness in the kingdom; two swords	19:28; 20:25–28	10:42–45	22:21–38	13:4–5, 12–14, 36–38
223. Jesus the true vine; He teaches and prays for His followers	—	—	—	13:31—17:26
224. They go to the Mount of Olives; Peter promises to be loyal	26:30–35	14:26–31	22:39; 22:31–34	13:36–38; 16:32; 18:1

	MATTHEW	MARK	LUKE	JOHN
C. Jesus Is Arrested and Crucified *(continued)*				
225. Jesus prays in Gethsemane	26:36–46	14:32–42	22:40–46	18:1; 12:27; 14:31; 18:11
226. Jesus is arrested	26:47–56	14:43–52	22:47–53	18:2–12, 20
227. The council questions Jesus; Peter says he doesn't know Him	26:57–75	14:53–72	22:54–71	18:13–27
228. Jesus taken to Pilate	27:1–2	15:1	23:1	18:28–32
229. The death of Judas	27:3–10	—	—	—
230. Pilate questions Jesus	27:11–14	15:2–5	23:2–5	18:33–37; 19:6, 9–10
231. Jesus brought to Herod	—	—	23:6–16	—
232. Jesus sentenced to death	27:15–26	15:6–15	23:17–25	18:38–40; 19:4–16
233. Soldiers mock Jesus	27:27–31	15:16–20	—	19:1–3
234. Jesus nailed to a cross at Golgotha	27:32–44	15:21–32	23:26–43	19:17–24
235. Jesus dies and is buried	27:45–61	15:33–47	23:44–56	19:25–42
236. The guards at the tomb	27:62–66	—	—	—
V. The Resurrection				
237. The empty tomb	28:1–10	16:1–11	24:1–12	20:1–18
238. The Roman soldiers bribed	28:11–15	—	—	—
239. Jesus appears to two disciples on the road to Emmaus	—	16:12–13	24:13–35	—
240. Jesus appears in Jerusalem	—	—	24:36–39	—
241. Jesus appears to the disciples twice	—	—	—	20:19–29
242. Jesus appears at Lake Tiberias	—	—	—	21:1–24
243. Jesus appears on a mountain in Galilee	28:16–20	16:14–16	—	—
244. Believers to do wondrous things	—	16:17–18	—	—
245. Jesus ascends to heaven	—	16:19	24:50–53	—
246. The disciples go and preach everywhere	—	16:20	—	—
247. The end of John's gospel	—	—	—	20:30–31; 21:25

JOBS AND OCCUPATIONS INDEX

The ancient Near East has often been called the "cradle of civilization." Highly developed cultures flourished in the region long before Abraham (about 2100 B.C.). Many skills that eventually developed into occupations and trades originated there. The following are mentioned or inferred in the Bible. Where Old Testament references are given, we suggest that you consult a copy of the complete Bible.

This listing mentions translations of words from the New King James Version (NKJV), the King James Version (KJV), the New Revised Standard Version (NRSV), the New International Version (NIV), and the New American Standard Bible (NASB).

(Related terms that are treated separately in this index are indicated by bold type. Other terms are expressed in italics.)

◆ACCOUNTANT

Even though the word *accountant* does not appear in the Bible, the principles and methods of accounting do. Wherever a census or an inventory of financial assets or offerings is recorded (Ex. 30:11–15; 2 Sam. 24; 2 Chron. 13–28; Ezra 2; Neh. 7:6–72; Luke 2:2; see "The Census," Luke 2:1–3), accountants were probably involved. In the New Testament, the language of accounting (adding, reasoning, computing) is used with regard to rational conclusions and moral inventory rather than fiscal reckoning. Paul, for example, "added up" his works of the flesh and counted them as a net "loss" compared to the unsurpassable worth of knowing Christ (Phil. 3:4–8).

◆ACTOR, ACTRESS

The Bible does not refer specifically to professional actors and actresses, perhaps because the acting profession was forbidden to the Jews because of its pagan associations. However, when Jesus called the Pharisees "hypocrites" (Matt. 23:13–30), he was using a word that had come to mean "play-actors." The deceptive religious leaders feigned biblical virtues in order to win people's praise. For example, they "disfigured" their faces with a sad countenance while fasting, essentially putting on a mask, in order to look contrite (Matt. 6:16).

In the first century, actors traveled a circuit of Greek and Roman cities to perform before large audiences in the culture's many theaters, some with a seating capacity of 20,000 or more. The riot at Ephesus began at such a forum (see Acts 19:29).

◆ADVOCATE

One who "pleads another's case" or is "called alongside to give advice" or counsel was known as an advocate, not unlike a modern-day **lawyer**. The word is used primarily in the New Testament, mostly of Jesus or the Holy Spirit. Jesus acts as a righteous Advocate, pleading our case as lost sinners before a righteous God (1 John 2:1). When the term is applied to the Holy Spirit (John 14:16; 15:26; 16:7), it is variously translated as *Advocate* (NRSV), *Helper* (NKJV, NASB), *Comforter* (KJV), or **Counselor** (NIV). (See **Counselor**; **Lawyer**.)

◆AMBASSADOR

In ancient times, kings and rulers spoke to other nations through official representatives, or *envoys*. These ambassadors offered congratulations (1 Kin. 5:1; Is. 39:2), sought favors (Num. 20:14), made treaties (Josh. 9:4–6), and registered protests (Judg. 11:12). The treatment that an ambassador received represented the host nation's response to the ambassador's ruler. Insults could lead to war (2 Sam. 10:4–6). In the New Testament, Paul describes himself as "Christ's ambassador" (Eph. 6:20), as are all Christians (2 Cor. 5:20, according to one interpretation).

◆ANNOUNCER

Modern-day television hosts and radio disc jockeys may have had forerunners in biblical **heralds** who were responsible for bearing a message, often in preparation for the appearance of a king or other royal figure (Dan. 3:4). The Aramaic word for herald is sometimes translated "to proclaim" (Matt. 3:1; 4:17); consequently, New Testament preachers are heralds of the King, Jesus (1 Tim. 2:7; 2 Tim. 1:11). (See **Messenger**.)

◆APOTHECARY

Some translations use this word or *confectioner* for the *pharmacist* who prepared or sold drugs, medicines, and perfumes. (See **Perfumer**; **Physician**.)

◆ARCHER

Archers were trained from childhood to serve in ancient armies. These warriors were the first to engage the enemy from a distance. To draw an ancient war bow required an estimated 100-pound pull. Arrows could pierce almost any armor. A number of Old Testament nations had men who were famous archers (1 Sam. 31:3; 1 Chr. 8:40; Is. 22:6). Abraham's son Ishmael (Gen. 21:20) and Isaac's son Esau (Gen. 27:3) grew up to be archers, though probably not in an army. (See **Hunter**; **Soldier**.)

◆ARCHITECT

Biblical references to the tabernacle, temple, palaces, fortifications, and the like, attest to the need for architects. Walled cities in biblical times required architects (see, for example, the book of Nehemiah). The New Testament speaks of God as the preeminent Architect, calling Him the "builder" and "architect" of the heavenly city, the New Jerusalem (Heb. 11:10). (See **Builder**.)

◆ARMORBEARER

An armorbearer carried weapons for a military commander or champion. They were also responsible for finishing the job of killing enemies brought down by their masters, using clubs or swords. The Old Testament leaders Abimelech (Judg. 9:54), Jonathan (1 Sam. 14:6–17), and Joab (2 Sam. 18:15) had armorbearers. David acted as Saul's armorbearer for a time (1 Sam. 16:21). However, after David became king, commanders fought from chariots, and armorbearers are no longer mentioned in the Bible.

◆ARMORER

This person was a smith skilled in making armor or a leather worker who made shields. In the days of Saul, armorers were primarily Philistines. Armorers are not mentioned directly in the Bible, but their presence is inferred from the Hebrew soldiers' use of shields, helmets, breastplates of scale-like plates, and leg armor. Paul

◆ARMORER *(continued)*

speaks of God in a figurative sense as the great armorer of spiritual soldiers (Eph. 6:14–17).

◆ARTIFICER

(See **Metalworker**.)

◆ARTISAN

(See **Metalworker**.)

◆ARTIST

The Bible makes no direct mention of artists, but the fact that they existed in Hebrew culture is evident from the many paintings and etchings found on clay tablets, bas-reliefs, and engraved images in ivory and stone. Jews construed the Second Commandment (Ex. 20:4) as prohibiting the artistic portrayal of humans.

◆ASTROLOGER

(See **Astronomer**.)

◆ASTRONOMER

Although the model of the universe adopted by ancient peoples was inaccurate, their attempts to explain how the universe works can be traced back thousands of years. In ancient times, the positions of the planets in relation to each other was thought to have an impact on the course of history. This accounts for astronomy's origins in *astrology,* the study of the heavenly bodies and their movements in an attempt to predict the future.

Isaiah taunted the Babylonians to go to "those who study the heavens" for their salvation (Is. 47:13). The Aramaic word for astrologer or enchanter appears eight times in Daniel, in association with **magicians**, *sorcerers, Chaldeans, wise men,* and **diviners** (Dan. 1:20; 2:2, 10, 27; 4:7; 5:7, 11, 15). Some Bible scholars believe the wise men or Magi who saw the star of the infant Jesus (Matt. 2:1–12) were astrologers from Mesopotamia.

In the Bible, astronomical references are often poetic (Amos 5:8). Their main purpose is to show God's glory rather than provide scientific details about the universe. The important truth for the Hebrews as they observed the stars was that "the heavens are telling the glory of God; and the firmament proclaims his handiwork" (Ps. 19:1).

◆ATHLETE

Of all the biblical writers, Paul used the most metaphors from the world of sports to describe spiritual realities. The Greeks of Paul's day celebrated four major athletic festivals, including the original Olympic games (see "The Games," 1 Cor. 9:24–27). The apostle likened the Christian life to that of a track and field **runner** (Acts 20:24; Rom. 9:16; Gal. 2:2; 5:7; Phil. 2:16; 2 Tim. 4:7; compare Heb. 12:1–2), a *wrestler* who struggles (Eph. 6:12), and a *boxer* (1 Cor. 9:26; 2 Tim. 4:7). He noted that athletes were obliged to compete according to rules (2 Tim. 2:5), and that they competed for a prize (1 Cor. 9:24–27; Phil. 3:12–14; 1 Thess. 2:19; 2 Tim. 4:8).

Among the Romans, sporting events evolved beyond vigorous competition into life-and-death struggles. In Nero's day, for example, Christians were sometimes sent into an amphitheater to fight for their lives (1 Cor. 4:9; 15:32; Heb. 10:32–33).

◆ATHLETE *(continued)*

Jewish culture apparently did not develop the same appreciation for athletic contests or train athletes professionally, partly because of the nudity that was often involved. Yet Jews did esteem the ancient sport of running. (See **Runner**.)

◆ATTENDANT

Some translations use this word for one who rendered household services. (See **Servant**.)

◆AUTHOR

The books collected in the Bible were written by about forty writers from various walks of life. Yet even though the Bible is itself a written work, the usual sense of the word author is not mentioned as a profession. In a broader sense, Jesus is called the Author of life, salvation, and faith (Acts 3:15; see Heb. 5:9; 12:2). (See **Writer**.)

B

◆BAKER

Bread was a major food in the ancient world (Gen. 3:19; Judg. 7:13; John 6:13). Most baking was done by women in the home (Gen. 18:6; Lev. 26:26; 1 Sam. 8:13; see "Jewish Homemaking," Mark 1:29–31, and "Grinding the Grain," Luke 17:35). However, the Pharaoh of Egypt employed a chief baker (Gen. 40:2, 16), and a street in old Jerusalem was renowned for its bakers and their shops (Jer. 37:21). Bakers prepared dough from cereal grains, mostly wheat and barley, but sometimes beans, lentils, millet, and spelt (Ezek. 4:9). They baked it on an open fire of wood or coals (Is. 44:19) or in a clay, bell-shaped oven (Lev. 7:9; Hos. 7:4; Matt. 6:30), using iron grids or pans (1 Chr. 9:31; 23:29; Ezek. 4:3).

◆BANKER

Bankers and banking were not part of the Jewish culture until the Babylonian captivity. Money as such did not exist at that time. Lending to other Jews for profit was forbidden (Deut. 23:19–20), though loans to foreigners were permitted. Even so, the Law recognized that there would inevitably be some people in debt to others, and it made provision to keep debtors from falling hopelessly behind (Deut. 15:1–6). National wealth was safeguarded in the temple or at the king's palace, while common people hid their treasures and valuables. When Nebuchadnezzar's troops ransacked the temple (2 Kin. 25:13–17), they were in effect robbing a bank.

In the New Testament, Jesus urged His followers to go beyond the letter of the Law, which said to lend without interest, to the spirit of the Law, by giving without expecting a return of even the principal (Luke 6:35). By Roman times, bankers were becoming common among the Jews (Matt. 25:27; see "Banking," Luke 19:23). Under Roman law, bankers could put a debtor in prison. But echoing the Law, Jesus challenged His followers to cancel others' debts, just as God has cancelled our debts (Matt. 6:25–26; 18:25, 30). (See "A History of Money," Rev. 3:17–18, and "Money in the New Testament," Rev. 16:21.)

◆BARBER

Both men and women in Old Testament times normally wore their hair long, eliminating the need for barbering as a profession. In fact, Israelite men were forbidden to cut the forelocks of their hair (Lev. 19:27), and a shaved or bald head was a sign of disgrace (2 Kin. 2:23–24; Is. 3:24; 15:2; Jer. 48:37). Both men and women prized beautifully styled hair (Song 4:1; 5:11). Long hair contributed to Samson's strength, but also to his capture (Judg. 16:13–19). Likewise, Absalom's locks gave

◆BARBER *(continued)*

him a handsome appeal (2 Sam. 14:25–26), but also brought about his death (2 Sam. 18:9–15).

There were some circumstances that called for barbering. Men who took a Nazirite vow shaved their heads (Num. 6:18). And God ordered Ezekiel's barber to shave the prophet's head as a sign of judgment (Ezek. 5:1).

By New Testament times, men apparently wore their hair shorter than women's, especially in the Roman cities such as Corinth (1 Cor. 11:14–15), so barbers were more in demand. Even so, barbers tended to work for the rich and for royalty. Christian women were urged to style their hair simply, not expensively (1 Tim. 2:9; 1 Pet. 3:3).

◆BASKETMAKER

Ancient Near Eastern societies required lightweight containers to transport goods by hand or donkey. Thus women wove baskets from natural fibers such as palm fronds, straw, reeds, rushes, sedges, and grasses. Baskets came in all sizes and shapes, but a shape resembling earthenware pots was common. Scripture mentions baskets large enough to hold a person (Acts 9:25) or a human head (2 Kin. 10:7), and small enough to house birds (Jer. 5:27) and carry bread (Ex. 29:3).

◆BEEKEEPER

From the many biblical references to honey (for example, Ex. 3:8, 17; 16:31; Prov. 24:13; Matt. 3:4), it is possible to infer that beekeepers were common in Palestine. But honey could also have been obtained wild (Judg. 14:8–9), and the word might have been used of a syrup made from grapes and dates.

◆BEGGAR

Scripture describes people reduced to begging because of divine judgment or wickedness (1 Sam. 2:7–8; Ps. 109:10; Luke 16:3), physical handicaps (Mark 10:46; Luke 18:35; John 9:8), or laziness (Prov. 20:4). Nearly every society and every city in biblical times had a large "underclass," people scraping by on the margins of society. Few cultures provided for these desperate, destitute wanderers, though God did command Israel to care for the poor (Deut. 15:1–11; see "The Underclass," Luke 7:20–23).

◆BLACKSMITH

Some translations use this word for the craftsman who worked with metals, especially in making swords and spears (1 Sam. 13:19). (See **Armorer**; **Metalworker**.)

◆BLEACHER

(See **Fuller**.)

◆BODYGUARD

Many bodyguards mentioned in Scripture may also have been **soldiers**, **armor-bearers**, *prison guards*, **runners**, **slaves**, or *servants*. Examples include bodyguards for the Pharaoh of Egypt (Gen. 37:36; 39:1), Joseph (Gen. 40:3), David (2 Sam. 23:22), certain Israelite kings (2 Kin. 11:19), and Paul (Acts 28:16).

◆BOTANIST

The presence of botanists in Bible times is easily inferred from the thriving agricultural economies of the ancient Near East (see "Trade in Ancient Israel" at the end of John). Apparently Solomon was rather knowledgeable in this area, as vari-

◆BOTANIST *(continued)*

ous gardens and orchards are listed among his great accomplishments (1 Kin. 4:33; Eccl. 2:5–6). In the New Testament, Paul alluded to the techniques of botany when he spoke of the Gentiles as a wild olive tree being "grafted" into God's tree of salvation (Rom. 11:17–21). (See **Gardener**.)

◆BREWER

"Strong" or intoxicating drink is mentioned some twenty times in the Bible, and wine more than 240 times. Ancient brewers are known to have produced beers from various cereals beginning more than 8,000 years ago, and beer was known in Egypt and Mesopotamia. The process involved burying barley in pots to force germination, then mixing it with water to ferment naturally. Sometime between the tenth and seventh centuries B.C., hops were added to the process (see "Winemaking," John 2:3). (See **Winemaker**.)

◆BRICKLAYER

The biblical record of brickmaking goes back to the construction of a tower at Babel (Gen. 11:3). Excavations and wall paintings in Egypt show Hebrews making clay bricks (compare Ex. 1:14) and that the Egyptians used bricks that were sun-dried and large by today's standards (10 by 20 by 4 inches). Clay bricks were made with straw which decomposed to release chemicals that made the bricks stronger (compare Ex. 5:6–19). It's interesting that after the Hebrews had been slaves in Egypt, they later made brickworkers of their prisoners of war (2 Sam. 12:31).

◆BUILDER

The first building project mentioned in Scripture is the walled dwelling that Cain constructed to protect himself (Gen. 4:17). Later, descendants of Noah built a tower at Babel to go up to heaven, to make a name for themselves (Gen. 11:4). Hebrew slaves built storage cities for the Pharaoh of Egypt (Ex. 1:11). Later in Palestine, their descendants built walled cities and unwalled towns, houses, palaces, the temple, and many other structures. After the Babylonian exile, Nehemiah served as a *general contractor* to rebuild the walls of Jerusalem.

In the New Testament era, the Herods were especially active in sponsoring construction projects (see profile at Acts 12:1–2). One of the major ones was the city of Sepphoris in Galilee, which Herod Antipas rebuilt as a provincial capital during the time of Jesus' youth. It is easy to imagine that Jesus and His father, Joseph, who were both **carpenters**, worked on projects in the city, given its proximity to Nazareth. In a similar way, the Roman emperors built Corinth as a "planned" city, favoring it with numerous imperial building projects (see Introduction to 2 Corinthians). (See **Architect**; **Carpenter**.)

◆BUTCHER

The work of the many wild game hunters and livestock ranchers in the ancient world gave rise to the occupation of butcher. In the Old Testament, the Law prescribed that some animals be considered "clean" and others "unclean" (Lev. 11), perhaps partially for reasons of health and survival. In the New Testament, an issue related to meat surfaced in Corinth and other Gentile cities, where meat offered to idols was for sale. Paul affirmed that it was all right, in good conscience, for believers to eat whatever the butchers prepared and sold at the Gentile meat markets (1 Cor. 10:25). (See **Cook**.)

◆BUTLER

The only mention of a butler in Scripture is the chief butler whom Joseph met in prison (Gen. 40). However, the occupation was closely related to that of *cupbearer.* Ancient rulers had to be very cautious about what they ate or drank, as the prospect of poisoning was ever present, either from attempts on their lives or from spoiled food. The butler or cupbearer tasted the ruler's food first in order to test its safety.

Solomon employed cupbearers and waiters (1 Kin. 10:5; 2 Chr. 9:4), and Pharaoh's butler mentioned above probably oversaw a staff of such officials. Nehemiah was a cupbearer to King Artaxerxes (Neh. 1:11), which made him a very powerful official with an expense account and direct access to the king. This enabled him to arrange for the rebuilding of the wall at Jerusalem.

◆BUYER

While the word *buyer* occurs just four times in Scripture (Deut. 28:68; Prov. 20:14; Is. 24:2; Ezek. 7:12), the concept of buying and selling occurs often. A wide range of commodities were sold in and exported from Palestine, including oil, wine, wheat, barley, nuts, honey, fruits, fish, salt, and spices. A list of some of the many commodities being imported into Palestine in Solomon's time is recorded in Ezekiel 27 (see "Trade in Ancient Israel" at the end of John). (See **Merchant**.)

◆CAMEL DRIVER

The camel driver was one who herded and rode camels. Camels were used to cross the desert between Mesopotamia and Palestine about 1800 B.C. The Old Testament mentions the Midianites, who were desert nomads and camel drivers whose thousands of camels were used to wage war (Judg. 6:1–6) and peace (Is. 60:6). David named a camel driver, Obil the Ishmaelite, to his state government to head up the camel division (1 Chr. 27:30). The Queen of Sheba probably brought many camel drivers with her on her visit to Jerusalem to see Solomon's riches (1 Kin. 10:2).

◆CANDYMAKER

The Hebrews enjoyed making and giving royal "dainties," sweet "delicacies," and rich and splendid foodstuffs (Gen. 49:20; Ps. 141:4; Prov. 23:3; Rev. 18:14). This implies that candymaking has a long history. Women were the principal candymakers, using dates, honey, nuts, and gum extract.

◆CAPTAIN

In the Bible, the term captain can mean **prince**, *officer, chief, ruler, leader,* **author**, *initiator,* or **commander**—in a military, civilian, or spiritual sense. In the New Testament period, military captains commanded as many as 1,000 Roman soldiers constituting a military cohort, tribune, or garrison (Mark 6:21; Acts 21:31–37; Rev. 6:15; 19:18). Civilian captains in government were called **magistrates** (Acts 16:20–38). The chief officer on duty in the temple precinct was a *temple captain* (Luke 22:4, 52; Acts 4:1; 5:24, 26). In a spiritual sense, the Pioneer or Initiator of our salvation is Jesus Christ (Heb. 2:10; 12:2; see Josh. 5:14–15; 2 Chr. 13:12). (See **Government Official**.)

◆CAPTAIN (SHIP)

(See **Sailor**.)

◆CARPENTER

Carpenters worked with wood, metal, and stone to produce furniture and farm implements, and to construct houses and public buildings. During the reigns of David and Solomon, Israel relied almost exclusively on foreign carpenters, especially those from Tyre (2 Sam. 5:11; 1 Kin. 5:18; 1 Chr. 14:1). Later, however, Jewish carpenters were used to repair the temple (2 Kin. 22:5–6; 2 Chr. 24:12).

Scripture makes reference to handtools such as the axe and hatchet (Deut. 19:5; Ps. 74:6; Jer. 10:3), the hammer (Judg. 4:21), the saw (Is. 10:15), the plumb line, the ruler, the plane, and the compass (Is. 44:13–14; Amos 7:7; Zech. 2:1).

Two of the best known carpenters in the Bible are Noah (Gen. 6) and Jesus (see "Jesus the Carpenter," Mark 6:3). (See **Builder**.)

◆CARVER

Artisans known as carvers were skilled at whittling, cutting, or chipping wood, stone, ivory, clay, bronze, gold, silver, or glass. Bezalel and Oholiab received special mention in Moses' day for their work on the tabernacle (Ex. 31:1–6). Skilled carvers were sought after (2 Chr. 2:7), and carved panels, windows, and woodwork were signs of great wealth. Some carvers specialized in making idols (Jer. 10:4; Rev. 18:12), thus bringing judgment from God. (See **Metalworker**.)

◆CATTLEMAN

Scripture presents Jabal as "the ancestor of those who live in tents and have livestock" (Gen. 4:20). A similar description applied to Abraham (Gen. 13:2). To own many cattle was a sign of God's blessing (Ps. 107:38). God provides for cattle (2 Kin. 3:17; Ps. 104:14); indeed, He owns "the cattle on a thousand hills" (Ps. 50:10). Some translations classify livestock of all kinds—cows, sheep, goats, donkeys—as "cattle," and the word can also be translated "beasts" or "animals." (See **Shepherd**.)

◆CAULKER

Some carpenters were skilled at applying tar to the hulls of boats to make them watertight (Ezek. 27:9, 27). In the Old Testament, the best caulkers were the "wise men" of Phoenicia, a nation renowned in the ancient world for its shipbuilding. (See **Shipbuilder**.)

◆CENSUS TAKER

The job of the census taker was associated with military conscription and tax collection. Consequently, it was unpopular in Bible times. Several censuses are mentioned in the Bible: Moses' censuses during the Exodus (Ex. 30:11–16; Num. 1), David's numbering of the people (2 Sam. 24), a census under Solomon (2 Chr. 2:17), and the Roman census that brought Joseph and Mary to Bethlehem where Jesus was born (Luke 2:1–5). (See **Accountant**, **Tax Collector**.)

◆CENTURION

The centurion was the backbone of the relatively small but well-organized citizen army of Rome (see "Centurions," Mark 15:39). A centurion was a non-commissioned officer commanding at least 100 men. Six centuries of men made up a cohort or regiment. Ten cohorts, about 6,000 men, made up a legion.

It's interesting that all of the individual centurions mentioned in the New Testament are reported to have been of good repute, and even exceptional faith. Jesus commended a centurion who cared for his dying servant (Luke 7:1–10). The Gospel writers report that the centurion who oversaw Jesus' crucifixion confessed

◆CENTURION *(continued)*

faith in Christ (Matt. 27:54; Mark 15:39; Luke 23:47). In Acts, the centurion Cornelius embraced the gospel, opening the door to Gentiles in the early church (Acts 10). A centurion named Julius saved Paul's life (Acts 27:1–11). (See **Soldier**.)

◆CHAMBERLAIN

(See **Eunuch**.)

◆CHANCELLOR

Some translations use this word for a bureaucratic chief or **magistrate**. (See **Government Official**.)

◆CHARIOTEER

A charioteer was a soldier who fought from a chariot. Chariots were introduced in Mesopotamia about 2800 B.C. These machines served as mobile firing platforms. They came in many different forms. They could be two-wheeled or four-wheeled, drawn by two to four horses. As the technology developed, chariots were made to hold a driver, a bowman, and a shield-bearer to protect both the warrior and the driver.

In Bible times, Solomon employed the most charioteers outside of Egypt. At one point, he deployed 1,400 chariots throughout the land in fortified "chariot cities" (1 Kin. 10:26), and later built 4,000 stalls for his horses and chariots (2 Chr. 9:25). (See **Soldier**.)

◆CHEESEMAKER

Cheesemaking has a long history, dating at least to Job's day (Job 10:10). David and his brothers enjoyed cheese or "curds" (1 Sam. 17:18; 2 Sam. 17:29). A cheese made from sweet milk was probably like our cottage cheese (Deut. 32:14) or goat cheese (Prov. 27:27). A valley outside Jerusalem was named The Valley of the Cheesemakers due to the cottage industry carried on there. (See **Dairyman**.)

◆CHOIRMASTER

More than one-third of the Psalms are by or dedicated to a choirmaster or chief musician. Several choirmasters were named by David to the task of leading corporate worship—Asaph, Heman, Ethan, Jeduthun, Chenaniah, and their descendants (1 Chr. 15:16–24; 25:1–7). These choir directors no doubt helped to organize and instruct the 288 men said to be skilled as temple musicians (1 Chr. 25:7). (See **Musician**; **Singer**.)

◆CITY CLERK

City clerks were important officials in the Greek city-states. They were responsible for record-keeping, recording minutes of official assemblies, caring for the city archives, handling official communications such as public readings, and annually distributing money to the poor. They also served on a number of boards and handled countless administrative details. The city clerk of Ephesus (Acts 19:35) was also president of the assembly. His importance and prominence are shown by the fact that his name frequently appeared on coins of the period.

◆COMMANDER

This word can imply either civilian governance or military service, similar to the word **captain**. (See **Captain**; **Government Official**.)

◆COMPTROLLER

(See **Government Official**.)

◆CONFECTIONER

(See **Apothecary**; **Perfumer**.)

◆CONTROLLER

(See **Government Official**.)

◆COOK

The Hebrew word usually translated cook literally means "slaughterer," one who kills and dresses animals. Thus the king's cooks apparently killed animals to be prepared for the royal table. Cooks may have been either women servants (1 Sam. 8:13) or male professionals (Luke 17:8). In most Hebrew households, cooking was the woman's job (Gen. 18:6; 27:9; see "Jewish Homemaking," Mark 1:29–31), while men did the butchering (Gen. 18:7). Gideon is named as a cook and a baker (Judg. 6:19). (See **Butcher**.)

◆COPPERSMITH

Scripture makes many references to copper and coppersmiths (Ex. 38:8; Deut. 8:9; Ezra 8:27; Job 28:2; Ezek. 22:18). Archaeological excavations of copper tools, vases, polished mirrors, and the like show that coppersmithing was a common occupation in ancient times. Copper mines in Tyre and Cyprus supplied the artisans of Palestine. In time they learned to make bronze, an alloy of copper and tin which could take a finer polish and was harder than pure copper. The first coppersmith mentioned in the Bible is Tubal-cain, a descendant of Cain who instructed others in working with "bronze and iron" (Gen. 4:22). In the New Testament, Paul mentions Alexander the coppersmith as having done him and the gospel much harm (2 Tim. 4:14). (See **Metalworker**.)

◆COPYIST

(See **Scribe**.)

◆COSMETOLOGIST

Cosmetology as a profession is not mentioned in Scripture, but archaeologists have found ancient toilet kits, ointment pots, small make-up instruments, and even a cosmetics factory from 2,500 years ago. The practice of beautifying the skin and eyes with cosmetics, salves, alabaster ointments, and the like is very old (Ex. 30:25; Neh. 3:8; Ezek. 23:40). However, early Christian women were admonished to distinguish themselves by focusing more on the beauty of their souls than that of their bodies (1 Tim. 2:9; 1 Pet. 3:3–4). (See **Perfumer**.)

◆COUNSELOR

Ancient kings had trusted officials who served as counselors (1 Chr. 27:32; Ezra 4:5), though not all counselors were professionals (2 Chr. 22:3). In the New Testament, Joseph of Arimathea is called a counselor, reflecting his membership in the Jewish council, or Sanhedrin (Mark 15:43; Luke 23:50, KJV). Israel anticipated that the coming Messiah would be a Counselor (Is. 9:6). (See **Advocate**.)

◆COURT REPORTER

(See **Government Official**.)

◆CRAFTSMAN

(See **Designer, Metalworker**.)

◆CREDITOR

(See **Banker**.)

◆CRIMINAL

The first criminal mentioned in Scripture, in the sense of one human sinning against another, was Cain, who murdered his brother (Gen. 4:8). Apparently a criminal mentality and rebellion against God's law characterized Cain's descendants (Gen. 4:23–24). In Hebrew society, the Law punished various criminals by mutilation, scourging, paying monetary damages and fines, enslavement, and death (Gen. 9:6; Ex. 21–22). One means of capital punishment was stoning (see John 10:31). Among the Romans and other Gentile empires, crucifixion was practiced (see Luke 23:33).

Paul described the transformation that can occur when a criminal turns to Christ and follows Him (see "From Deadbeat to Donor," Eph. 4:28).

◆CUPBEARER

(See **Butler**.)

◆CUSTODIAN

(See **Keeper**; **Watchman**.)

◆CUSTOMS OFFICER

This occupation was similar to that of the **tax collector**, as taxes and customs were often collected by the same person. In the first century, both taxes and customs were owed to Rome (Rom. 13:7). The KJV has Matthew, the tax collector, sitting at "the receipt of custom" when called by Jesus to follow Him (Matt. 9:9). (See **Census Taker**; **Tax Collector**.)

◆DAIRYMAN

Along with bread, dairy products were staples of the Hebrew diet (Prov. 30:33; 1 Sam. 17:18). Milkers of cows, goats, sheep, and camels had to make use of the milk right away, as there was no way to keep fresh milk from spoiling. However, one way to give it a longer "shelf life" was to culture it into butter (Ps. 55:21), curds (Is. 7:22), or cheese (Job 10:10). Dairymen sold these products in the marketplaces of towns and cities, probably transporting them there on donkeys. (See **Cheesemaker**.)

◆DANCER

Apparently the Hebrews did not have professional dancers as did Egypt, Babylon, and other pagan nations. However, Scripture indicates that children danced in play (Job 21:11; Luke 7:32) and adults danced in joy, notably Miriam (Ex. 15:20) and David (2 Sam. 6:14; Ps. 30:11). God's people were encouraged to dance before Him as a joyous act of congregational worship (Ps. 149:3; 150:4). And other occasions called for dance—festivals (Judg. 21:23), the celebration of war heroes (1 Sam. 18:6–7), and family reunions (Luke 15:25). The Hebrew words associated with dancing reveal that it involved skipping, whirling about, and leaping.

◆DEALER

(See **Merchant**.)

◆DEPUTY

(See **Government Official**.)

◆DESIGNER

The skills of designers were used in commissioned public works of art for the tabernacle, the temple, and other building projects. Designers often worked in concert with *engravers,* **weavers**, **metalworkers**, **carpenters**, and other craftsmen (Ex. 35:35; 38:23). Bezalel and Oholiab were two designers called by God to oversee the construction of the tabernacle. They were filled with the Spirit and knowledgeable in several crafts (Ex. 31:1–11). (See **Metalworker**.)

◆DIVINER

The Old Testament Law condemned the practitioner of magic, sorcery, and divination as a "false prophet." Diviners used a variety of occult practices to contact or control evil spirits or foretell the future: trances, dreams, mediums, enchantments, clairvoyance, the stars, even examining the livers of animals. (see "Magic and Sorcery," Rev. 18:23).

Divination was widespread in the ancient Near East from earliest times: in Egypt (Ex. 7:11), Canaan (Lev. 18:3, 21; 19:26, 31), Arabia (Is. 2:6), Babylon (Ezek. 21:21; Dan. 5:11), Samaria (Acts 8:9), Macedonia (Acts 16:16), and Asia (Acts 19:13, 19). Even the Israelites lapsed at times into the use of divination (2 Kin. 17:17; 21:6).

Because of their idolatry and deception, diviners and similar practitioners are strongly condemned in Scripture, for example by the Law (Deut. 18:9–14), the prophets (Is. 2:6; 8:19; 47:9, 12; Jer. 14:14; 29:8) and Paul (Acts 13:6–12).

◆DOCTOR

The KJV calls the "learned" men in Scripture "doctors of the law" (Luke 2:46; 5:17; Acts 5:34), meaning teachers and experts of the Mosaic Law. In some other translations the term doctor is used to refer to members of the medical profession. (See **Lawyer**, **Physician**.)

◆DOORKEEPER

(See **Eunuch**; **Porter**.)

◆DRESSMAKER

(See **Tailor**.)

◆DRIVER

(See **Camel Driver**, **Charioteer**, **Overseer**.)

◆DYER

Dyeing was an ancient art among families working in linen (1 Chr. 4:21). Dyers often developed specialized formulas for their craft which they passed on to successive generations. One of the most important dyes of the Mediterranean world was purple, made from the shell of the murex, a species of clam. Purple cloth and dye were extremely valuable. The first known Christian in Europe, Lydia, was a "dealer in purple cloth" (see profile and "The Trade in Purple," Acts 16:14).

In the Old Testament, the patriarch Jacob made a "long robe" for his favored son Joseph (Gen. 37:3), which probably involved the use of various dyes. Later, the Israelite tabernacle made use of purple dye that was probably imported from Phoenicia.

◆DYER *(continued)*

The dyer of wool was usually the **fuller** of wool, as well, so that he or she cleansed and dressed the wool before coloring it. (See **Fuller**.)

◆EMBALMER

Egyptian embalmers prepared the dead for burial by treating the body to prevent decay. Modern-day discoveries by archaeologists show that they developed this skill to near perfection. Joseph, who became a ruler in Egypt and the adopted son of a Pharaoh, had his father Jacob embalmed (Gen. 50:2–3) and was himself embalmed (Gen. 50:26). However, this was probably done to preserve the bodies for an anticipated trip back to Palestine (Gen. 50:13–14; Josh. 24:32). Otherwise the Hebrews did not embalm the dead, nor did they cremate bodies as the Greeks and Romans often did. Rather they washed and scented the body before dressing it in the person's own clothes or else wrapping it in specially prepared sheets (see "Funeral Preparations," John 12:1–8, and "Burial," 1 Cor. 15:42). These funeral preparations were frequently carried out by women. (See **Undertaker**.)

◆EMBROIDERER

Decorative needlework, or "painting with a needle," was the work of an embroiderer. Ancient embroiderers decorated clothes with colorful, highly stylized geometric designs, particularly for the rich (Judg. 5:30; Ps. 45:14; Luke 20:46). In Israel, embroiderers decorated priestly garments and the appointments of the tabernacle (Ex. 26:1, 36; 27:16; 28:4, 15). Embroidering, **weaving**, and **tapestry making** were separate occupations, but some translations use the terms interchangeably. (See **Tailor**, **Tapestry Maker**, **Weaver**.)

◆ENCHANTER

(See **Diviner**.)

◆ENGRAVER

(See **Metalworker**.)

◆ENVOY

(See **Ambassador**.)

◆EUNUCH

The eunuch or chamberlain was responsible for guarding the king's bedroom and harem (Esth. 1:10–15). These men were castrated so as to remove all possibility of unfaithfulness (Is. 56:3). They were highly trusted and influential officials. The Ethiopian eunuch under Queen Candace apparently also was in charge of her royal treasury (Acts 8:27). (See **Porter**.)

◆EXECUTIONER

The Old Testament distinguishes between murder (illegally taking another's life, Ex. 20:13) and execution. Under the Law, many crimes were punishable by death (Gen. 9:6; Deut. 13:10; 21:22). It was the executioner's task to carry out that punishment, though some crimes called for stoning by the men of the community (see "Stoning," John 10:31). Personal vengeance was prohibited (Deut. 24:16). The New Testament records several executions that were legal under Roman law (Matt. 14:10; Acts 12:1–2). The most infamous was the crucifixion of Jesus (see "Crucifixion," Luke 23:33).

◆EXORCIST

Peoples of the ancient world generally believed in spirit powers and that a person could be taken over by an evil power. Many methods were used to cast out these demons, including potions, spells, and chanting. Acts even records an attempt by one group of exorcists to use Jesus' name as a magic spell.

New Testament teaching affirms the existence of evil spirits, but it also emphasizes Christ's total victory over them (see "Demons," Luke 11:14, and "Who Is the Enemy?" Eph. 6:10–13). Jesus expelled demons quickly and easily (see "Whatever Became of 'Demon Possession'?" Luke 9:38–42). He did not practice the mysterious and often complicated rituals of the exorcist (Matt. 12:24–28).

◆FANNER

Some translations use this word for the one who sifts wheat from the chaff using a forked fanning instrument. (See **Winnower**.)

◆FARMER

Terms in the Bible that refer to farmer include *plowman* (Is. 28:24), **husbandman** (2 Chr. 26:10, KJV), **vinedresser** (Is. 61:5; John 15:1–8), **gardener** (John 20:15), and *tiller* (Gen. 4:2). This was one of the major occupations of the ancient Hebrews, along with **shepherding**. Cain was the first farmer (Gen. 4:2). Olive and fig trees were the principal crops among fruit farmers in ancient Palestine. Other crops included almonds, apples, dates, grapes, mulberries, pomegranates (Joel 1:11–12). Farmers of ancient times were responsible for all aspects of farming. The plowing, planting, tending, and harvesting were done by farmers and their own families. Very prosperous farmers could hire helpers (see **Laborer**). In the New Testament, a farmer is one who owns the land or rents it and raises crops (Matt. 21:33).

◆FISHERMAN

Fishing was one of the most important and common occupations held in Bible times. Fishermen used various kinds of spears, nets, hooks, and lines (Job 41:7; Is. 19:8; Matt. 13:47–48; Mark 1:16; Luke 5:2; see "The World of the Fishermen," Luke 5:1–11). Several of Jesus' disciples were professional fishermen (Matt. 4:18–22).

◆FOOTMAN

Heralds who ran before a king's chariot to announce his coming were sometimes called footmen (Jer. 12:5). Most biblical references are to "foot soldiers" or infantrymen (for example, 1 Sam. 4:10; 15:4; 22:17, KJV). (See **Announcer**; **Messenger**; **Soldier**.)

◆FOREMAN

(See **Overseer**.)

◆FORESTER

The Bible makes frequent reference to forests. Yet the forests of Palestine were depleted during a brief 13–year period to enable the construction of Solomon's aptly named House of the Forest of Lebanon (1 Kin. 7:2). Nevertheless, loggers were said to be conservationists who practiced reforestation (Is. 44:14). A man named Asaph was "the keeper of the king's forest" in Nehemiah's time (Neh. 2:8). He was a regional governor responsible for land use and for developing and restricting the

◆FORESTER *(continued)*

lumber industry. Nehemiah secured a logging permit from Asaph to fell timber for use in reconstructing the walls of Jerusalem. (See **Builder**; **Carpenter**; **Woodworker**.)

◆FOUNDRY WORKER, FOUNDER, FORGER

The foundry worker melted, refined, and cast ore into precious or other useful metals (Jer. 6:29). Once cast, the metal could be pounded flat or engraved (Jer. 10:9). It was hot, dirty work involving stoking and cleaning furnaces, making castings, and pouring molten metal into clay molds. Hiram of Tyre was brought to Jerusalem by Solomon to cast two bronze pillars, topped with capitals and laced with a pomegranate design, for the temple (1 Kin. 7:13–22). (See **Refiner**; **Metalworker**.)

◆FOWLER

The Egyptians had a particular taste for fowl and so became innovative as "fowlers." Ancient fowlers used a variety of devices to seek, catch, and kill wild fowl, such as decoys, traps (Amos 3:5), nets (Prov. 1:17), bait, bows and arrows, slings, lures, dogs, and bird lime smeared on branches. The Mosaic Law forbade taking a mother bird and her young together; only the young were to be taken (Deut. 22:6–7). Used figuratively, the fowler depicts the wicked, scheming enemies of the righteous (Ps. 91:3; 124:7; Hos. 9:8). (See **Hunter**.)

◆FULLER (BLEACHER)

The fuller's job was to clean, shrink, thicken, and sometimes dye newly cut wool or cloth. The Hebrew term means "to trample" or "to tread," suggesting at least one means by which the fuller carried out the craft.

Fullers removed oily and gummy substances from the material so that it would be fit for use. They used "fuller's soap," probably containing alkaline as found in white clay, putrid urine, or niter; the kind of soap known today did not exist then. The alkaline was washed out by treading on the material repeatedly in clean, running water. The material was then dried and bleached in the sun.

The fulling process created an unpleasant odor, and therefore fullers usually worked outside the city gates. A location outside of Jerusalem was known as the Fuller's Field (2 Kin. 18:17; Is. 7:3).

The day of God's judgment is compared to "fullers' soap" (Mal. 3:2, KJV; "launderers'," NKJV). Likewise, Jesus' garments at the transfiguration are described as having been whiter than any human fuller could make them (Mark 9:3, KJV; launderer, NKJV). (See **Dyer**.)

G

◆GARDENER

Scripture references to gardens, plants and orchards are as abundant as the varieties (for example, 1 Kin. 4:33; Eccl. 2:5; Amos 9:14). With more than 300 botanical terms and incidental reference to gardens, we can conclude that gardening was an important skill in Bible times. Adam was the first gardener (Gen. 2:15). Yet the one gardener directly mentioned in Scripture, the person that Mary Magdalene supposed the resurrected Jesus to be (John 20:15), was probably not one who did actual gardening, but functioned as a watchman. (See **Botanist**; **Farmer**; **Watchman**.)

◆GATEKEEPER

(See **Porter**.)

◆GLASSWORKER

Glass was known as early as 2600 B.C. Around 1400 B.C., the Egyptians were able to make glass similar to pottery by winding hot glass rods around a sand core and then joining the layers by reheating them. While glassworkers are not mentioned specifically in the Bible, several New Testament references to transparent glass suggest the existence of the occupation by that time.

◆GLEANER

Fruit and grain farmers were instructed to leave certain gleanings in the field, unharvested, for poor laborers or gleaners (Lev. 19:9–10; Ruth 2). (See **Laborer**.)

◆GOATHERDER

(See **Shepherd**.)

◆GOLDSMITH

Goldsmiths refined, purified, and worked with gold (Is. 41:7). Israelite goldsmiths fashioned gold-plated vessels and interior furnishings for the tabernacle (Ex. 25:11, 24; 26:29, 32; 30:3), along with solid gold pieces (Ex. 25:18, 29, 31). They also made fine gold wire, thread, and bells for embroidering the priests' garments (Ex. 28). However, some molded and hammered out idols (Ex. 32; Ps. 115:4; Is. 2:7). The New Testament describes God as like a goldsmith, molding Christian character like "gold refined by fire" (1 Cor. 3:12–13; 1 Pet. 1:7; Rev. 3:18). (See **Metalworker**; **Refiner**.)

◆GOVERNOR

The English word governor, meaning "to lead" or "to rule," is used to translate eleven different Hebrew words and four different Greek words. As applied to Joseph, the term indicates that he was second in command in Egypt as a *chief deputy*, **prince**, or *viceroy* in Pharaoh's court (Gen. 41:40; 42:6; 45:26; Acts 7:10). In the New Testament, the term is used of several Roman officials including Pilate (Matt. 27:2), Quirinius (Luke 2:2), Felix (Acts 23:26), and Festus (Acts 26:30), where governor also implied a sort of *chief financial officer* (see "New Testament Political Rulers," Luke 3:1, and "Roman Politics in the First Century A.D.," Luke 22:25). These political appointees were responsible to Rome for the military, judicial, and financial administration of their districts. In one place the KJV uses the word "governor" to mean a *custodian* or *manager* of property or people (Gal. 4:2). (See **Steward**.)

◆GOVERNMENT OFFICIAL

Many different officials are mentioned in Scripture. Depending on the translation, one finds **chancellors**, *commissioners, comptrollers, controllers, courtiers, deputies,* **magistrates**, *officers, presidents, procurers, quartermasters,* **recorders**, **secretaries**, **treasurers**, *trustees,* and *viceroys,* to name several. These officials may have been *government administrators* (Gen. 41:34), religious or military **overseers** (1 Kin. 4:5), **secretaries** (Ex. 5:6–8), **commanders** (Num. 11:16), or *assistants* to the king (Esth. 1:8). However, little is known about most of these positions. For an extended account of one government official, read the life of Joseph (Gen. 39–50).

◆GUARD

(See **Keeper**; **Jailer**; **Soldier**; **Watchman**.)

H

◆HARLOT

(See **Prostitute**.)

◆HARVESTER

(See **Laborer**.)

◆HEALER

(See **Nurse**; **Physician**.)

◆HELMSMAN

(See **Sailor**.)

◆HERALD

(See **Announcer**.)

◆HERDSMAN

(See **Cattleman**; **Shepherd**.)

◆HEWER

(See **Woodworker**.)

◆HEWER OF STONE

(See **Mason**.)

◆HISTORIAN

The fact that the Scriptures exist points to the important role of the historian, *chronicler,* or **recorder**. The Bible names several historians, such as Jehoshaphat (2 Sam. 8:16; 20:24) and Joah (2 Kin. 18:18; Is. 36:22). These chroniclers recorded significant events and stories from their nation's history. Often the events were compiled in chronological order and presented in a way intended to explain the cause of events. Biblical histories also served a spiritual purpose, as we see in Luke's writings especially. (See **Recorder**; **Scribe**.)

◆HORSEMAN

Horses are mentioned often in the Bible but were of little importance to the average Hebrew, who found it more practical to keep a donkey to ride or an ox to pull a plow. Sometimes horsemen were used as mail carriers (Esth. 8:10), but for the most part, horses were thought of in terms of war.

God warned the Israelites not to place their faith in the strength and speed of horses (Ps. 20:7) or to acquire many horses (Deut. 17:16). Nevertheless, David and Solomon built up large mounted forces, even importing horses from other countries. Solomon had a sizeable cavalry as well as horses to draw war chariots. (See **Charioteer**; **Soldier**.)

◆HOUSEHOLDER

Householders were what we would call heads of households, persons with authority over what went on in a given home. Jesus also called them *landowners* or *masters of the house.* He frequently included such figures in His teaching (see "Treasures New and Old," Matt. 13:52; 20:1; 21:33).

◆HUNTER

Hunting was a common means of food and fur provision in ancient times, but there are few references to hunters as such in the Bible. Only two are mentioned by name: Nimrod, the "mighty hunter before the LORD" (Gen. 10:9; 1 Chr. 1:10), and Esau, the skillful hunter and brother of Jacob (Gen. 25:27; 27:3, 30).

A variety of wild game are mentioned in Scripture: roe deer, gazelles, harts, antelope, mountain sheep, and wild goats, among others (Deut. 12:15, 22; 14:5; Lev. 17:13). Methods of hunting included bows and arrows (Gen. 21:20), digging pits, and nets, snares and traps (Is. 24:17; Ezek. 19:4–8; Amos 3:5). Hunting for sport was popular among ancient kings. Landowners also became hunters at times to protect their crops. (See **Archer**; **Fowler**.)

◆HUSBANDMAN

Some translations use this older word for one who plows and cultivates land. (See **Farmer**.)

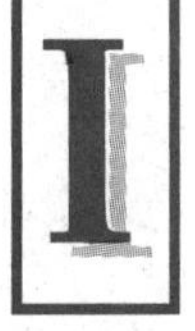

◆INNKEEPER

In Old Testament times, most travelers stayed in private dwellings or slept in the open. But by New Testament times, some people managed inns (Luke 10:34–35). However, these facilities were often neither comfortable nor safe and provided no food and few amenities. According to tradition, innkeepers were infamous for their dishonesty, which may be one reason why Christians were encouraged to open their homes in hospitality to strangers. The inn at which Mary and Joseph stopped but found full could have been a large private dwelling, as it was customary for such homeowners to rent out dwelling quarters during festival times (Luke 2:7). (See "Travel in the Ancient World," Acts 13:3–4.)

◆INSTRUCTOR

Instructors of all kinds—priestly catechists, pastor-evangelists, guardians, and godly parents—were charged with teaching, mentoring, and discipling successive generations. Luke was an instructor in the faith for Theophilus (Luke 1:1–4). Paul chided the Corinthians that though they might have "ten thousand guardians in Christ," he was their spiritual father (1 Cor. 4:15). Many of the Proverbs praise parents who take on the role of instructor (Prov. 1:8; 4:1). God frequently used angels to instruct people when a difficult message needed fuller explanation (Luke 1–2; Acts 10:22).

◆INTERPRETER

The job of an interpreter sometimes resembles that of an instructor in that the term implies one who can "explain fully or give the understanding of something in different words." In the Bible, interpreters were used to translate languages (Gen. 42:23), explain dreams (Gen. 40:8; 41:8), or reveal the meaning of tongues or prophecies (1 Cor. 12:10, 30; 14:26–28). Ambassadors often served kings as interpreters (2 Chr. 32:31; Ezra 4:7), along with magicians, astrologers, and sorcerers (Dan. 2:2–4; 4:6). Daniel and his friends were recruited for this purpose (Dan. 1:3–5; 2:14–49; 4:19–27; 5:13–29). Angels also served as interpreters of God's message (Luke 1–2; Acts 10:22). (See **Ambassador**; **Astrologer**; **Instructor**; **Magician**.)

◆IRONWORKER

(See **Metalworker**.)

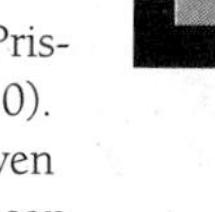

◆JAILER

Jailers and *keepers of prisons* were usually soldiers in Bible times. Prisons were damp, dark, and rigorous places of detention (Ps. 107:10). Numerous biblical persons spent time in jail: Joseph, who was given responsibility over other prisoners (Gen. 39:20–23; 40:3–4); Samson (Judg. 16:21, 25); the prophet Jeremiah, who was imprisoned in four different places of detention (Jer. 37–38); John the Baptist (Mark 6:17, 27); and Peter and John (Acts 4:3; 5:18; 12:3–5). Before his conversion, Paul arrested Christians and had them put into prison (Acts 8:3). Later, he was himself frequently imprisoned on behalf of the gospel (Acts 16:23; 28:30). However, he used the opportunity to bring his jailers to faith (Acts 16:23–37; Phil. 1:12–14). (See **Keeper**.)

◆JEWELER

Ancient peoples were fond of jewelry. The Old Testament mentions jewelry as a sign of wealth and blessing (Ezek. 23:26; Is. 61:10). It was given to brides as a present (Gen. 24:22, 30, 53), or as part of a dowry. The priestly garments, especially the breastplate, were adorned with beautiful gem stones, rings, and chains crafted by a skilled jeweler (Ex. 28:15–28). In the New Testament, Jesus told a story about a woman who lost a coin that may have been part of a set of ten silver coins worn as jewelry, as was common in that day (see "The Woman Who Searched as God Searches," Luke 15:8–10). (See **Metalworker**.)

◆JUDGE

Judges in the Bible dispensed justice, governed, and provided legal protection. It's interesting that the first and last judge mentioned in Scripture is God Himself (Gen. 18:25; Rev. 19:11; 20:1–13). To some extent following this divine model, the Old Testament patriarchs acted as judges in matters of their households (Gen. 21; 22; 27). Moses was judge over all Israel and he appointed elders to be subsidiary judges under him (Ex. 18:13–27; Deut. 1:12–17). After Israel entered the Promised Land, the nation was ruled by a cycle of judges or deliverers such as Othniel, Ehud, Deborah, Gideon, Jephthah, and Samson. Under the monarchy, justice ultimately resided with the king (1 Kin. 3:16–28). All along, however, God was viewed as Israel's final Judge, Deliverer, and King (Judg. 8:23; 11:27; Is. 33:22).

By the time of the New Testament, the high court of Israel had become the Sanhedrin, although there were also judges in every town (Luke 18:2; see "Stephen's Trial and Murder," Acts 6:12). In the early church, members were forbidden to use the pagan courts. Instead, believers appointed their own elders to judge civil disputes between Christians (see "The Scandal of Litigating Christians," 1 Cor. 6:1–11). Christ is the ultimate Judge over His people (see "The Judgment Seat," 2 Cor. 5:10).

◆KEEPER

This generic job description applied to many occupations in the Bible: *trustees* or **treasurers** of the city treasury (Rom. 16:23); keepers of prisons, also known as *guards* or **jailers** (Gen. 39:20–23; 40:3–4); night **watchmen** (2 Kin. 11:5); **foresters** (Neh. 2:8); keepers of the vineyard, or **vinedressers** (Is. 5:1–30; Matt. 21:33–44); and keepers of the wardrobe (2 Kin. 22:14), the doors (2 Kin. 23:4), and the gates, also known as *gatekeepers, doorkeepers,* or **porters** (1 Chr. 9:19). Keepers of a harem (Esth. 2:3, 14) were called **eunuchs** or *chamberlains.* Keepers of animals included **shepherds** (Gen. 4:2; 1 Sam. 17:20) and *herdsmen* or **cattlemen** (Gen. 4:20).

◆KING, QUEEN

The majority of the large ancient civilizations were controlled by kings and queens who usually inherited their position and power and ruled for life. Much has been written about the dynasties of the Pharaohs in Egypt, as well as the bright but brief monarchy in Israel. Unlike the rulers of the Gentiles, the Hebrew kings were not viewed as gods, though their right to rule was given by God.

In the New Testament, several kings are mentioned, including Herod (Matt. 2:1) and his grandson Agrippa (Acts 25:24). However, they were not really kings but **governors** over Roman territories (see "The Herods," Acts 12:1–2). Interestingly, even though Herod was called the "king of the Jews," it was Jesus who was born into that position and later crucified by Pilate under that title (Matt. 27:37). Elsewhere, Scripture affirms that Jesus is the King of kings and Lord of lords (1 Tim. 6:15; Rev. 17:14; 19:16).

◆LABORER (WORKER)

The term *laborer* indicates either a field hand (Matt. 9:37–38; 20:1, 2, 8; James 5:4; see **Farmer**; **Harvester**; **Gleaner**; **Reaper**) or a worker in a general sense (Matt. 10:10, some translations; 1 Tim. 5:18). A laborer's job might entail more manual work, less pay, and less skill (but no less value) than a skilled occupation, but not necessarily: for example, Luke calls the fellow craftsmen of the silversmiths at Ephesus "*workers* of the same trade" (Acts 19:25, emphasis added). While laborers are often poor and oppressed, their heritage in life is good, joyful and worthwhile, even a "gift of God" (Eccl. 5:18–20). Jesus called for more "laborers" to harvest fields of souls (Matt. 9:37–38).

◆LAUNDERER

(See **Fuller**.)

◆LAWYER

The term *lawyer* is found only in the New Testament and means something entirely different from the profession of lawyers today. By the first century, the Law (the first five books of the Old Testament) had been expounded upon by generations of Jewish teachers. Their intent was to interpret and apply the Law to every situation of life. This ongoing work created a vast body of commentary which its custodians claimed was just as binding as the actual commandments of Moses. These experts in the Law, known as lawyers, **scribes**, or **teachers** of the law (Luke 2:46; 5:17; Acts 5:34), were employed in studying, interpreting, and expounding the Law. They also acted as court **judges**. In the New Testament they are found opposing John the Baptist (Luke 7:30) and Jesus (Matt. 22:34–40; Luke 14:3). (See **Advocate**; **Doctor**; **Judges**; **Scribe**.)

◆LEATHERWORKER

(See **Tanner**.)

◆LENDER

The practice of moneylending was under strict regulation in the Old Testament (Deut. 15:1–11; 23:19–20; 24:10–11; 28:12, 44). The Law prohibited interest-bearing loans to the poor, especially to fellow Hebrews. The people were urged instead to give generously and without taking anything in pledge. Nonetheless, Israel repeatedly broke these regulations and had to take corrective measures. Even Nehemiah was guilty of lending at interest and had to make amends (Neh. 5). Jesus brought the concept of canceling debts into sharper focus by applying it to forgiveness (Matt. 18:23–35).

◆LIBRARIAN

Scrolls and parchments were readily available to visiting speakers in a synagogue (Luke 4:17). The Book of the Law (possibly Deuteronomy) was found "in the house of the Lord" by Hilkiah (2 Kin. 22:8; see Ezra 6:1). This finding implies temple archives or perhaps a temple library, and thus a librarian.

◆LINEN WORKER

(See **Dyer**.)

◆LOBBYIST

Moses and Aaron were perhaps the prototype of lobbyists who attempt to persuade those in power to adopt a particular course of action. With God's help, the two leaders ultimately were able to convince Pharaoh to allow the Israelites to leave Egypt (Ex. 7–12). Another effective lobbyist was Nehemiah, who persuaded King Artaxerxes to rebuild Jerusalem, and in fact to underwrite the project. It's interesting to observe some of the methods that Nehemiah used to lobby his cause: prayer, pouting, bold speech, carefully written letters, first-hand inspections, and progress reports. In a similar way, the Old Testament prophets often went to great lengths to convince others to accept God's ways. Ezekiel staged a hunger strike and shaved off all of his hair (Ezek. 4–5). Jeremiah used props to illustrate his message—a ruined, useless belt (Jer. 13:1–11), a broken clay pot (Jer. 19:1–12), and yoked straps and crossbars (Jer. 27). In the New Testament, Paul lobbied the authorities in Rome and Jerusalem to accept the gospel, or at least permit its advance (see "Faith and Rights," Acts 22:25–29, and "Paul and the Structures of Power," Acts 24:25–26). (See **Orator**; **Prophet**.)

◆LOGGER

(See **Forester**.)

◆MAGICIAN

Occult practices, such as fortune-telling and witchcraft, were common among the pagan nations of the ancient world. But attempts to contact or control evil spirits were expressly forbidden to the Hebrews, and the prohibition extends to believers today (see "Magic and Sorcery," Rev. 18:23).

◆MAGISTRATE

This term has many meanings, depending on its context. Sometimes a magistrate was like a **judge** (Ezra 7:25; Luke 12:58; Acts 16:20), with ruling, even priestly, authority (Judg. 18:7; Acts 23:5). Among the Jews in Jesus' day, some magistrates were "rulers of synagogues" (Matt. 9:18, 23; Luke 8:41; 12:11), subject to a larger ruling body known as the Sanhedrin (see "The Synagogue," Mark 1:21, and "Stephen's Trial and Murder," Acts 6:12).

◆MAID, MAIDSERVANT

Two Hebrew words are variously translated *bond-*, *hand-*, or *maidservant*, *maiden*, *bondwoman*, or *female servant*, or **slave**. In general, these girls or women served the wives and daughters of rich or important men (Gen. 16:1–3). They were treated more like property than their male counterparts; some were even sold into slavery by their fathers (Ex. 21:7). They performed menial tasks, such as grinding flour (Ex. 11:5; see "Slaves," Rom. 6:16, and "Women and Work in the Ancient World," 1 Cor. 7:32–35). Some functioned as surrogate mothers (1 Sam. 1:11) and as con-

♦MAID, MAIDSERVANT *(continued)*

cubines (Judg. 19:9). Sarah's maidservant Hagar was given to Abraham so that he could father a child by her, according to the custom of the day (see Gal. 4:24–25). (See **Servant**; **Slave**.)

♦MANAGER

(See **Overseer**.)

♦MARINER

(See **Sailor**.)

♦MASON

Masons were employed in cutting stone to make hedges, walls, buildings, memorials, and other functional or ornamental objects. Stoneworkers also hewed out wine vats, cisterns, tombs, and water tunnels. Judging from the many examples of stone works in Scripture (2 Sam. 5:11; 2 Kin. 22:6; 1 Chr. 22:2; 2 Chr. 24:12), this was an important occupation. The Jews may have learned the craft from their sojourn in Egypt (Ex. 1:11, 14) or from the master builders at Phoenicia (2 Sam. 5:11; 1 Chr. 14:1).

In quarrying out rock, masons drove wooden wedges into stone and soaked them until they expanded, causing the rock to crack. After separating a block of rough stone, they trimmed it with a saw, axe, or pick. Some masons were known for their ability to "square" or "quarry" stone so it joined neatly with other stones to create a smooth face (1 Kin. 5:17–18; 6:7).

The Old Testament likened the Word of God to the quarry worker's hammer (Jer. 23:29).

Other names for stonemasons include *stonecutters* and *hewers of stone*. (See **Builder**.)

♦MEDIATOR

(See **Messenger**; **Priest**.)

♦MERCHANT

Merchants are referred to by various Bible translations as *traders, dealers,* and *merchandisers.* Merchants sold their merchandise in open bazaars or marketplaces in the cities of the Mediterranean (Neh. 3:32; 13:16; Ezek. 27:24; Matt. 11:16; Mark 7:4). Scripture warned them against being unscrupulous by using false weights and measures (Deut. 25:13–16; Hos. 12:7; Amos 8:5), and the book of Revelation depicts how they could take their trade to scandalous excess (Rev. 18:3–23). By contrast, the virtuous woman of Proverbs 31 is praised for her honest merchandising skills.

♦MESSENGER

The job of messenger in Scripture is related to several other occupations: **ambassador** (Prov. 13:17), *mediator* (Job 33:23), and *military courier* (1 Sam. 4:17; 23:27; 2 Sam. 2:19; 11:22–25). The messenger is also associated with the **footman** or **runner** (2 Kin. 6:32–33; Jer. 51:31) and with the **horseman** and **watchman** (2 Kin. 9:18). The word is also used of the **prophets** (Hag. 1:13), the Lord's servant (Is. 42:19), and John the Baptist (Mal. 3:1; Mark 1:2). (See **Announcer**.)

◆METALWORKER

This category includes those who dug ore out of the ground, refined the ore into metal, and worked the metal into useful objects. Refining metal is an ancient skill that was well developed by the time of Abraham, when smiths were using bellows to increase the heat of their furnaces in order to melt iron ore for extraction. Even before then, copper was mixed with tin to form bronze, or mixed with zinc to form brass. Metalworkers produced high quality items such as vessels, jewelry, and coins.

Smiths were commonly named for the metals they worked. The first metalworker mentioned in the Bible is Tubal-cain, a descendant of Cain who instructed others in working with "bronze and iron" (Gen. 4:22). Two metalworkers named in the New Testament are Demetrius, a silversmith at Ephesus (Acts 19:24–28), and Alexander the coppersmith (2 Tim. 4:14).

Various translations use different terms to describe metalworkers: *artificer, artisan,* **blacksmith**, *bronze worker, craftsman, engraver,* **forger, founder**, *metalsmith,* **refiner**, and *smelter.* (See **Foundry Worker**.)

◆MIDWIFE

Midwives helped other women give birth to their babies (Gen. 35:17; see "A Woman in Labor," John 16:21–22). The task involved coaching the mother through the delivery, cutting the umbilical cord, bathing the baby, and rubbing it with salt in the belief that it promoted good health (Ezek. 16:4). Newborns were "swaddled" or wrapped snugly in cloth in a way that bound the baby's arms to its body. If twins were born, the midwife marked the firstborn (Gen. 38:28). Midwives were sometimes relatives or friends of the mother, but often professionals such as the Hebrew midwives who refused to obey the Egyptian Pharaoh's orders to kill all the boy babies at birth (Ex. 1:15–22). (See **Nurse**.)

◆MILITARY RECRUITER

(See **Census Taker**.)

◆MILLER

Grinding the grain was the work of a miller, often a maidservant (Ex. 11:5). In the division of labor, men were usually in the fields gathering grain, while women did the grinding of grain (Matt. 24:40–41) using a household hand-mill (see "Grinding the Grain," Luke 17:35). Thus the millstone became an invaluable asset, never to be used as a pledge and thus put at risk of being lost (Deut. 24:6). The saying, "to have a large millstone hung around one's neck" (Matt. 18:6; Mark 9:42; Luke 17:2; compare Judg. 9:53) indicated humiliating and unbearable punishment, similar to Samson's being forced to push a heavy grinder that would normally have been turned by donkeys or oxen (Judg. 16:21).

◆MINER

(See **Foundry Worker**.)

◆MONEY CHANGER

Money changers set up open-air stalls outside the temple to change ceremonially unclean foreign currency into local money for offerings. These cashiers often cheated their customers, a practice especially irksome since their service was indispensable. Jesus turned over the tables of corrupt money changers, charging that they had made His father's house a den of thieves and a house of merchandise (Mark 11:15–17; John 2:13–20). (See **Banker**.)

◆MOURNER

Many ancient Near Eastern cultures employed professional mourners, usually women, for public expressions of grief at funerals (Eccl. 12:5; Jer. 9:17–18; Amos 5:16; see "The Mourners," Matt. 9:23). Even the poor hired pipers, flute players, and at least one wailer to make the proper lamentations. Men sometimes joined women as singers and wailers at funerals (2 Chr. 35:24–25). An entourage of women mourned Jesus' death (Luke 23:27–28).

◆MUSICIAN

Scripture provides ample evidence that music was a major part of Israel's worship, suggesting that musicians were vital to the culture. While temple music was mostly a voluntary service, paid musicians were called upon for special occasions (Matt. 9:23; Mark 5:38). The study and practice of musical instruments goes back to Cain's family and Jubal, who apparently invented the harp and the flute (Gen. 4:21). David's early fame as a harp player came to the attention of Saul, who employed David as a "music therapist" for his sin-sick soul (1 Sam. 16:14–23). Other stringed instruments noted in Scripture include the lyre, the psaltery, and the sackbut. Wind instruments include the flute, the ram's horn, and the trumpet. The silver or brass cymbal was a main feature of the temple orchestra. (English translations vary in their rendering of instruments' names.) (See **Singer**; **Mourner**.)

◆NOBLEMAN

(See **Prince**.)

◆NURSE

One term for nurse in Hebrew applied in some of its usages to males as well as females and meant "to foster." The more common term meant "to give milk." One well-known biblical nurse was the Hebrew woman fetched by the Pharaoh's daughter to raise Moses (Ex. 2:7–9)—a case in which the biological mother became a paid professional nurse to her own child. Moses later came to see himself as a "nursing [foster] father" (KJV) in relation to the Hebrews (Num. 11:12). Likewise, Paul was like a nurse to his spiritual children (1 Thess. 2:7). The word meaning "to foster" is applied to Mordecai, the man who raised Esther (Esth. 2:7). Both words are used, respectively, with reference to the kings and queens in Isaiah's prophecy who will serve and wait upon God's chosen people (Is. 49:23).

The tasks of a female nurse included suckling the children of Hebrew women and carrying infants on their shoulders or hips (Is. 49:22; see "Children and Childcare," Matt. 19:14). Some family nurses were honored and shared between the generations (Gen. 24:59; 35:8; Ruth 4:16). Some heroic nurses took endangered children into protective custody to raise on their own (2 Kin. 11:2; 2 Chr. 22:11; 2 Sam. 4:4). (See **Midwife**; **Physician**.)

◆OARSMAN

(See **Sailor**.)

◆OFFICER

(See **Government Official**.)

◆ORATOR

Perhaps because communication in ancient societies tended to be oral rather than visual, rhetoricians and their teachers, coaches, and speech writers were in great demand. For example, the Jews who opposed Paul in Jerusalem employed Tertullus, a professional orator, to make their case before the Gentile governor Felix (Acts 24:1–9). Roman courts operated according to rules of etiquette and oratory. One could lose one's case simply by crudeness of speech. Paul was a highly trained speaker who was able to defend himself in such settings (Acts 24:10–21; 25:9–12; 26:1–28). A study of Paul's speech at the Areopagus (Acts 17:22–31) demonstrates the range of his abilities, even though the power of his preaching did not depend on such skill (1 Cor. 2:4; see "Paul, Apostle to the Intellectuals," Acts 17:15, and "Adapt Your Witness!" Acts 17:17).

◆ORNITHOLOGIST

Bird lovers, watchers, and cultivators were many in Scripture, which refers to birds more than 300 times and mentions about 50 species. (Modern-day ornithologists have catalogued almost 400 kinds of birds in the Palestine area.) Adam and Noah included birds in their work as "zoologist" and "zookeeper" (Gen. 2:19–21; 6:19—7:3). The food list in Leviticus 11:2–23 includes a great number of birds, but 44 other books of the Bible name at least one. Among those mentioned: the bittern, chicken, cormorant, crane, cuckoo, dove, eagle, falcon, hawk, heron, osprey, ostrich, owl, partridge, peacock, pelican, pigeon, quail, raven, sparrow, stork, swallow, turtledove, and vulture (translations vary). Migratory patterns, food, songs, nesting, and the habitats of birds are also noted.

◆OVERSEER

An overseer controlled or managed groups of people or projects. In the Old Testament, a captain in Pharaoh's guard bought Joseph from slave traders and made him the "overseer" of his house (Gen. 39:4–5). This was a position of great authority (38:8–9). Elsewhere, overseers were responsible for getting tasks done (2 Chr. 2:8) and sometimes helped to rule others (Neh. 11:9). Overseers responsible for slaves were sometimes called *taskmasters* (see "Slaves," Rom. 6:16, and "Philemon" at the Introduction to Philemon). Those who oversaw the Israelite slaves in Egypt were remembered as particularly cruel (Ex. 1:11–14). Overseers also were known as *drivers, foremen,* and *slavemasters.* In the New Testament, certain leaders in the churches are referred to as overseers, sometimes translated as "bishops" (Acts 20:28; Phil. 1:1; 1 Tim. 3:2; Titus 1:7).

◆PERFUMER

Perfume making is an ancient art, as perfumes were used to mask unpleasant body odors in a world where bathing tended to be infrequent. Perfumers and cooks are frequently associated in ancient literature, since their skills were related. Egyptian tomb paintings of the fifteenth century B.C. depict the process of making perfume from flowers. In the Old Testament, tabernacle and temple worship required professional perfumers to make scents for the priest and incense for burning (Ex. 30:25, 35; 1 Chr. 9:30). These perfumers formed professional guilds (Neh. 3:8). In the KJV, perfumers are sometimes called *apothecaries* or *confectioners.* (See **Cosmetologist**.)

◆PHARMACIST

(See **Apothecary**.)

◆PHILOSOPHER

A philosopher is literally a "lover of wisdom." The only philosophers directly mentioned in Scripture are the Epicureans and Stoics whom Paul encountered at Athens (Acts 17:18). However, their presence in the account reflects the fact that philosophers heavily influenced the thinking of the Greek and Roman cultures.

Elsewhere Scripture offers what could be called philosophical reflection and discussion. The book of Job, for example, records the thinking of Job and his three friends as they struggled to make sense of the evils that befell Job. Ecclesiastes presents the conclusions of a person looking back on life to determine what is of value and significance. Many of Paul's letters, while not philosophical treatises, offer a starting point for philosophical inquiry.

It has sometimes been said that philosophy by its very nature is opposed to faith. However, while philosophers have often started from assumptions and come to conclusions that go against Scripture, there is no indication that God discourages intellectual inquiry (see "The Value of Learning," Acts 7:22, and "Paul, Apostle to the Intellectuals," Acts 17:15–34). At the same time, Scripture reminds us that ultimately Christ is the "wisdom of God," a concept that may appear to be foolishness to some (1 Cor. 1:24).

◆PHYSICIAN

The Bible alludes frequently to sickness and health issues. The practice of medicine began in ancient times and gradually developed in knowledge and technique. Simple but relatively effective medicines were made from mineral, animal, and plant substances. Eventually specialists began to experiment with surgery and other invasive medical procedures. For example, archaeologists have found skulls from the sixth century B.C. which show evidence of *trepanning*, an attempt to surgically relieve pressure on the brain.

The only type of surgery mentioned directly in the Bible is circumcision, the ceremonial removal of the Hebrew male's foreskin eight days after birth (Gen. 17:10–14; see "Circumcision," Gal. 2:12).

The only physician mentioned by name in Scripture is Luke (Col. 4:14; see profile at the Introduction to Luke). However, Jesus and His followers performed miraculous healings of numerous people as a sign that He is indeed the Messiah.

◆PILOT

(See **Sailor**.)

◆PLASTERER

Plastering the walls of a home to form a smooth surface (Lev. 14:42–43) is an ancient and widespread craft, known to have been done sometimes by homeowners themselves. Higher quality plaster was made with heated broken limestone and gypsum; lower quality, used only in very dry climates, was made with clay and straw. Plaster, sometimes called "whitewash" (Deut. 27:2–4), was applied to the altar in the tabernacle and engraved while still wet. Years later in Babylon, a hand suddenly appeared and inscribed a message from God on a plastered wall in King Belshazzar's palace (Dan. 5:5). (See **Bricklayer**.)

◆PLOWMAN

(See **Farmer**.)

◆POET

Poetry was important throughout the ancient world, and nearly every culture had skilled lyricists to capture the essential experiences and emotions of the society.

◆POET *(continued)*

The Hebrew poets were especially prolific; in fact, an entire section of the Old Testament is made up of poetry composed under the inspiration of the Holy Spirit (Job, Psalms, Proverbs, Ecclesiastes, and Song of Solomon), and verse can also be found in other books. Poetry is seen as well in the structure of several New Testament passages (such as Luke 1:46–55, 68–79).

◆POLICEMAN

(See **Keeper**; **Sergeant**.)

◆PORTER

Porters and gatekeepers were essentially security guards who stood at the entrance to public buildings, the temple (1 Chr. 9:23; 26:12; 2 Chr. 23:19), and the homes of public officials (John 18:17) and the wealthy (Mark 13:34). Jesus also referred to a doorkeeper at the entrance to a sheepfold (John 10:3). The job required watchful attention and the ability to handle sudden developments. Nevertheless, it must have been a relatively lowly position as implied by the Psalmist's statement that he would "rather be a doorkeeper in the house of my God than live in the tents of wickedness" (Ps. 84:10). (See "The Gates of Hell," Matt. 16:18.)

◆POTTER

The pottery wheel is known to have been in use for thousands of years. Israel employed professional potters who sat at the edge of a small pit, turning the pottery wheel with their feet. Before working with the clay, however, the potter would tread it by foot, kneading it into the right consistency. Otherwise, weak spots could develop when he threw the piece on his wheel, leading to cracks when the piece was baked or put to use. Jeremiah enacted the role of a potter to make a powerful point that people are like unformed, pliable clay in the hands of God (Jer. 18–19).

◆PREACHER

The words associated with preachers and preaching are found primarily in the New Testament. Preaching was not seen as it is today in terms of an occupation, but more generally as a task or function involving the duties of a herald. For example, Peter described Noah as a "herald of righteousness" (2 Pet. 2:5). Paul referred to himself as a "herald of the gospel" (1 Tim. 2:7; 2 Tim. 1:11). To the Romans he pointed out the importance of a "proclaimer" in the spread of the gospel, meaning one who has been sent to communicate the message of Christ to unbelievers (Rom. 10:14–15). (See **Announcer**.)

◆PRIEST

In Israel, priests were official ministers and worship leaders who represented the people before God and conducted various rituals to atone for their sins. Originally this function was carried out by the father of a family (Job 1:5). But with the appointment of Aaron by God as the first *high priest* over Israel, the priesthood was formally established (Num. 8:9–18).

By the time of the New Testament, the position of priests had changed considerably. The temple functions were taken over by the *chief priests*. Rank-and-file priests were overshadowed by the **scribes** and Pharisees, two groups that arose to interpret the Law for the people.

The office of priest was ultimately fulfilled in Jesus Christ. The Son of God became a man in order to offer Himself as a sacrifice "once to bear the sins of many" (Heb. 2:9–14; 9:28). As a result, there is no longer a need for human priests to

◆PRIEST *(continued)*

offer a sacrifice to atone for people's sins. Christ made Himself a permanent sacrifice through His death on the cross (see "Something Better than Law and Priests," Heb. 7:19–22).

◆PRINCE, PRINCESS

This term applied not only to royalty, but to persons in positions of authority and responsibility (Gen. 12:15; 17:20; Ex. 2:14). (See **King**; **Queen**.)

◆PROCURER

(See **Buyer**.)

◆PROGNOSTICATOR

(See **Astronomer**.)

◆PROPHET

Prophets were people who spoke for God and communicated His message, often at great risk to themselves. The Old Testament prophets received a call directly from God, sometimes even before birth (Jer. 1:5; compare Luke 1:13–16). Otherwise, they had no special qualifications and came from all walks of life. Some were called for a lifetime, others were given only a brief ministry. But one trait characterized them all: a faithful proclamation of God's word and not their own (Jer. 23:16; Ezek. 13:2).

Sometimes prophets made their points by dramatic means. For example, Isaiah went barefoot and unclothed for three years (Is. 20:2–3). Ezekiel lay on his left side for 390 days and on his right side for 40 more (Ezek. 4:1–8). Zechariah broke two staffs (Zech. 11:7–14). A prophet's activities aroused curiosity and caused people to think, but sometimes they also invited scorn (Jer. 11:21).

In the early church, some believers were given the gift of prophecy, such as Agabus and the four daughters of Philip (Acts 21:8–11). These people, who spoke by the Holy Spirit, gave direction to the church in the period before the New Testament had been fully written.

◆PROSTITUTE

Prostitution is known to have been a part of pagan religious rites since at least 3000 B.C. Intercourse with a temple prostitute was believed to induce fertility. In Israel, ritual prostitution was forbidden (Deut. 23:17). However, commercial prostitutes practiced their trade and made themselves easily recognizable (Prov. 5:3–20; 6:24–29; 7:6–27), accepting payment in money, grain, wine, or livestock (see "Prostitutes Are Going into the Kingdom," Matt. 21:31–32).

In contrast to the religious elite of His day, Jesus became known as a friend of sinners who welcomed those in need of forgiveness, including prostitutes (Matt. 11:19; Luke 7:36–50).

The prostitute Rahab was praised in the New Testament as an example of a Gentile whose faith was accepted by God (see Heb. 11:31; compare Josh. 2:1–24; 6:22–25; James 2:25).

◆PUBLICAN

The derivation of the word "publican" from the Latin, *publicanus,* suggests a "provincial general." The publican is not to be confused with the **customs officer** or **tax collector**. Publicans were wealthy men, usually Gentiles, who contracted with the Roman government to be responsible for the taxes of a particular district.

◆PUBLICAN *(continued)*

Each province was assessed a certain amount of taxes by Rome, and the publican employed tax collectors to bring in that amount. Anything he could gather over and above the assessed amount was his to keep as a commission or "collection fee."

The shrewd publican, often backed by military force, collected import-export surcharges, road and bridge user fees, and as many other levies as he could (see "Taxes," Mark 12:14). This led to unscrupulous practices, and to hatred by the Jews toward these Gentile "sinners" who were in league with Rome (Matt. 9:9–11). (See **Tax Collector**.)

◆PUBLISHER

One can find no evidence of publishing as an industry in Scripture, as technologies such as the printing press and papermaking were undeveloped in Bible times. Furthermore, ancient cultures tended to concentrate information in the hands of a few powerful leaders rather than disperse it throughout the societies. Nevertheless, a form of publishing can be seen in Esther, when laws from the king were distributed to the people, apparently in some written form (Esth. 3:14; 8:13). In a similar manner, the king of Nineveh "published" a decree mandating acts of repentance after Jonah's warning of impending judgment (Jon. 3:6–9). (See **Author**; **Scribe**; **Writer**.)

◆QUARRY WORKER

(See **Mason**.)

◆RABBI

This title, meaning "my teacher," showed honor and respect to a teacher of the Jewish Law. In Jesus' day, the term did not signify an ordained person, as it does today, but was simply a term of dignity given by the Jews to a distinguished teacher. (See **Instructor**; **Scribe**.)

◆REAPER

(See **Laborer**.)

◆RECORDS CLERK (RECORDER)

This government worker was a functionary with some official standing, ranked with scribes and priests (2 Sam. 20:24; 1 Kin. 4:3). The job was mostly concerned with calling to remembrance the history of a particular sovereign's reign. In that sense, the records clerk was like a *registrar* or *court reporter*. Apparently, he mostly registered deeds of property and genealogies of people. Genealogical records were important, for example, to certify eligibility for the priesthood (Neh. 7:63). When foreign dignitaries visited, the recorder played a prominent ceremonial role (2 Kin. 18:18; Is. 36:3, 22). (See **Government Official**; **Scribe**; **Historian**.)

◆REFINER

Allusions to this profession are made in the Bible wherever God examines or purifies His people as if refining ore in a furnace (Ps. 66:10; Is. 48:10; Ezek. 22:17–22; Zech. 13:9; Mal. 3:2–3). In the New Testament, the refiner's fire is symbolic of the fire of God's testing (Matt. 3:10–12; 1 Cor. 3:13–15; 1 Pet. 1:6–7). (See **Foundry Worker**.)

◆REGISTRAR

(See **Government Official**; **Records Clerk**; **Scribe**; **Historian**.)

◆ROADMAKER

While the Bible does not mention roadmakers as such, it refers to "paths" (Prov. 8:2) and to "roads and lanes" (Luke 14:23). Palestine was crossed by the Way of the Sea (Is. 9:1), also called "the way of the land of the Philistines" (Ex. 13:17) and, under the Romans, the Via Maris, the most important international highway throughout the biblical period. A second major highway in the region was the King's Highway (Num. 20:17; 21:22; Judg. 21:19), which provided a secondary road to Egypt and access to the spice routes of Arabia. In addition, an internal system of secondary roads provided links between the many cities of the area (see "Travel in the Ancient World," Acts 13:3–4).

The call to prepare for the Messiah by "mak[ing] straight in the desert a highway for our God" (Is. 40:1–5; Matt. 3:3–5) evokes the imagery of roadmaking. In a way, that call was literally carried out: The relative peace established by Rome in the years before Christ enabled an extensive system of ancient roads in the Mediterranean world to be refurbished—just in time to aid the spread of the gospel.

◆ROBBER

(See **Criminal**.)

◆ROPEMAKER

Scripture refers frequently to rope and, by inference, ropemakers. Thus these artisans had a hand in helping the Philistines capture Samson (Judg. 15:13; 16:7) and in helping the spies escape from Jericho (Josh. 2:15). Ropemakers also contributed the cords that held the tabernacle together (Ex. 35:18), as well as the rope by which Judas hung himself (Matt. 27:5). In the shipbuilding trade, ropemakers produced the tackle and sheets that helped trim sails and steer rudders on ships (Is. 33:23; Acts 27:40). They also made heavy-duty bowstrings, animal traps, pulley systems, and plumb lines.

◆RUNNER

Runners were employed as royal messengers for kings. They sometimes competed with chariots and horsemen (1 Sam. 8:11; 2 Sam. 15:1; 1 Kin. 1:5), where "the race is not to the swift" (Eccl. 9:11). In this sense, they were **athletes**, but were more akin to mail carriers. (See **Announcer**; **Messenger**.)

◆SAGE

(See **Astrologer**.)

◆SAILOR

Despite their proximity to the Mediterranean, the Hebrews had little affinity for the sea and apparently had no navy. Nevertheless, the Bible makes frequent reference to sailing and shipping (Ps. 104:26; 107:23; Acts 27). Solomon built a merchant fleet, but many of the crews were Phoenician (1 Kin. 9:27). When Jonah ran away from God's call to Nineveh, he traveled on a Phoenician ship (Jon. 1:3). Later, dur-

◆SAILOR *(continued)*

ing the New Testament era, the headquarters of shipping shifted to Alexandria, which was renowned for its cargo ships (see Acts 18:24, and "Travel in the Ancient World," Acts 13:3–4; compare Acts 27:6; 28:11).

The ship's **captain** (Jon. 1:6) is sometimes called the *pilot* (Ezek. 27:27–29), the *helmsman* (Acts 27:11), or the *shipmaster* (Rev. 18:17). He was responsible for the safety of the vessel, its crew, and its cargo. (See **Shipbuilder**.)

◆SCRIBE

The title of "scribe" can be confusing. Sometimes the term is used interchangeably with **lawyer**, meaning a *teacher* of the law. During some periods of Jewish history, particularly the reigns of David and Solomon, the scribe was a significant administrator similar to a secretary of state or **chancellor** (2 Sam. 8:17; 20:25; 1 Kin. 4:3). In other times, scribes were more like **recorders**, *chroniclers*, or **historians**, recording history as it happened and keeping the official archives. The two books of Chronicles, for example, are believed to have been compiled from historical archives by an authoritative scribe, perhaps Ezra. He was particularly noted for his commitment to studying and promoting the Law (Ezra 7:6; Neh. 8:1–9).

In Jesus' day, scribes had become a learned class in Israel who studied the Scriptures and served as *copyists, editors*, and *teachers* (see "Scribes," Luke 20:39). To become a scribe required a lifetime of study, often beginning at age 14 and continuing to the age of 40. Once qualified, scribes could act as **judges**, be called **rabbis**, and occupy positions in law, government, and education. They joined the *chief* **priests** and aristocratic families who made up the Jewish council. They were held in great esteem by the people.

One category of scribes were the *copyists* who copied by hand the various Hebrew and Greek Scriptures onto rolls of parchment or sheets of papyrus. This time-consuming work was done by a team of scribes gathered at a *scriptorium*, in some ways the precursor to the modern publishing house. At first the documents were reproduced on scrolls. But eventually the bound book was invented, enabling the copyist to write on both sides of a page. These *codices*, as the documents were subsequently called, were a major advance in publishing technology. (See **Author**; **Lawyer**; **Writer**.)

◆SCULPTOR

(See **Stoneworker**.)

◆SEAMSTER, SEAMSTRESS

(See **Tailor**.)

◆SECRETARY

In Hebrew society, the job of writing and corresponding for others was done by a **scribe** or **recorder** (Jer. 36:26, 32). However, scribes typically had many more administrative and teaching duties to fulfill (see "Scribes," Luke 20:39). Like many secretaries today, secretaries in the ancient world took dictation, usually in shorthand, and also composed letters for a communicator. Paul may have dictated some of his letters to such a person, called by some an *amanuensis* or *stenographer* (Rom. 16:22; Gal. 6:11; 2 Thess. 3:17). (See **Scribe**.)

◆SECURITY GUARD

(See **Watchman**.)

◆SENTRY

(See **Watchman**.)

◆SERVANT

(See **Slave**.)

◆SHEEPBREEDER

(See **Shepherd**.)

◆SHEEPSHEARER

(See **Shepherd**.)

◆SHEPHERD (SHEEPHERDER)

The first shepherd mentioned in Scripture is Abel (Gen. 4:2). Later, Abraham, Isaac, and Jacob owned vast herds of livestock, including sheep (Gen. 13:7; 26:20; 30:36). However, when Jacob relocated his family to Egypt, his son Joseph counseled him to tell Pharaoh that his family's occupation was raising livestock, resulting in their isolation in Goshen, "because all shepherds are abhorrent to the Egyptians" (Gen. 46:31–34). Among the other prominent biblical people who spent at least part of their lives as shepherds were Rachel, Moses, David, and Amos.

Sheep and goat herding were major occupations of Palestine throughout its history. Sheep and goats were sometimes herded together, sometimes separately. Other occupations grew up around sheep herding, including breeders and shearers who cut the sheep's wool.

Shepherds were expected to be faithful and diligent, so much so that their occupation was often used as a metaphor for spiritual direction and leadership, either positively or negatively (Jer. 23:1–4; John 10:1–5). Sheep came to know their shepherd's voice so well that they would follow only him. Shepherds provided water and food for their flocks (Ps. 23:2; Jer. 31:10), and when an animal was lost, they were expected to go out and find it (Ezek. 34:12; Luke 15:4–5). Small lambs, unable to keep up with the flock, were often carried by the shepherd (Is. 40:11). Shepherds also protected their flocks, risking their lives if necessary (1 Sam. 17:34–37; Amos 3:12; John 10:11).

In the Old Testament, God is often called a Shepherd (Ps. 23; Is. 40:11). He protects and seeks out His flock, Israel (Jer. 31:10; Ezek. 34:12). Likewise, in the New Testament Jesus refers to Himself as the Good Shepherd who cares for, protects, and redeems His people (John 10:2–16). He even suffers for the sheep (Matt. 26:31) and separates them from the goats at the day of judgment (Matt. 25:32). As the Great Shepherd of the sheep (Heb. 13:20), Jesus calls spiritual leaders to be under-shepherds (Acts 20:28–30; 1 Pet. 5:2).

◆SHIPBUILDER

Shipbuilding stems from the days of Noah (Gen. 6:13–22). However, the Hebrews were not much of a seafaring people, and they mainly relied on others to build and sail their ships, especially the Phoenicians. Hebrew poetry extols the Phoenician shipbuilders for their perfect ships, tall masts, inlaid decks, strong oars, and embroidered sails (Ezek. 27:3–7). In the New Testament, the cargo ships of Alexandria (see Acts 18:24) were prized by sailors and merchants of the Mediterranean (See "Travel in the Ancient World" Acts 13:3–4). Paul sailed on such a vessel on the last leg of his trip to Rome (Acts 28:11). (See **Caulker**; **Ropemaker**; **Sailor**.)

◆SHIPMASTER

(See **Sailor**.)

◆SILVERSMITH

The silversmith refined and molded silver into bowls, cups, trumpets, basins, jewelry, candlesticks, coins (Gen. 23:16; Matt. 22:19–20), and the like. Scripture contains more than 200 references to silver and those who worked it. During Solomon's era, however, the silversmith was virtually out of work as gold was apparently so plenteous that silver "was not considered as anything" (1 Kin. 10:21). In the New Testament, Demetrius, a silversmith of Ephesus, led a guild of related craftsmen in a protest against the gospel, which was destroying their extremely profitable trade in shrines to the goddess Artemis (Acts 19:24–28). (See **Metalworker**.)

◆SINGER

More than fifty singers are named and their songs recorded in Scripture, in addition to the 150 compositions collected in Psalms. Singers were professional vocalists, usually trained. David's royal court enjoyed the singing of both male and female vocalists (2 Sam. 19:35), and he also organized 4,000 Levites and skilled men as temple musicians (1 Chr. 25). Many of these were choir members "trained in singing to the Lord" (25:7). Temple singers were originally all men, aged 30 to 50, and may have belonged to a performing artists' guild. They were employed in the work "day and night" (1 Chr. 9:33). They lodged together, took separate purification vows, and were supported by others to do their work (Neh. 12:29, 45–47). After the Babylonian exile, women also participated in the choirs (Ezra 2:65). Women also sang as professional **mourners** (see "The Mourners," Matt. 9:23, and "Burial," 1 Cor. 15:42). (See **Mourner**; **Musician**.)

◆SLAVE

Virtually every major ancient civilization depended heavily on the service of slaves, conquered peoples set to a variety of tasks by their masters. Scripture states that the Hebrews became slaves of the Egyptians, under whom they carried out forced labor in mortar, in brick, and in every kind of field labor (Ex. 1:8–14). In the Roman Empire of Paul's day, half the population or more may have been slaves, according to one historian's estimate.

Slave labor varied widely, depending on the interests of the ruling masters and the abilities of individual slaves. Joseph was sold as a slave to the Egyptian Potiphar, who made him an **overseer** of his household with a high level of responsibility (Gen. 39:1–9). Likewise Daniel and other young Hebrew males were brought in captivity to Babylon, where they were trained for high levels of government service (Dan. 1:1–7, 18–21). Later the Romans preferred Greek slaves as **tutors** or **instructors** to their young.

However, the majority of slaves in the ancient world were little more than property to be bought and sold as needed. Male slaves were often assigned to construction projects or the mines, where they were worked to exhaustion (see "Slaves," Rom. 6:16). Female slaves or **maidservants** were sold to men for service to their wives and daughters, and in many cultures for the sexual pleasure of the men as well (see "Women and Work in the Ancient World," 1 Cor. 7:32–35).

Not all slavery was between nations, however. According to the Old Testament, the Israelites had both Jewish and Gentile slaves. Jews who were too poor to pay their debts or who were convicted of theft sometimes sold themselves into slavery. In contrast to other cultures of the day, Jewish Law protected slaves and even granted them certain rights (Ex. 21:2–11; Lev. 25:39–55; Deut. 21:10–14).

Often Scripture refers to **servants**, or those who were "under the authority of

◆SLAVE *(continued)*

another." Some were like *day laborers* or *hired hands* who were paid for their work and free to leave when the job was finished (Ex. 21:1–11; compare Matt. 20:1–15). Jacob was such a servant for a time to Laban (Gen. 29). Jesus spoke of a household servant plowing, tending sheep, and preparing a meal (Luke 17:7–10).

Curiously, the Bible does not directly condemn slavery as an institution, though it contains oblique warnings about the practice of slavery (Amos 1:6–9; Rev. 18:13). The New Testament teaches that in Christ, the hierarchy of master over slave is done away (Gal. 3:28; Col. 3:11). Paul appealed to Philemon to put that ideal into practice by receiving back Onesimus, a runaway slave who became a Christian, as a brother (see the Introduction to Philemon and "A Challenge to Slavery," Philem. 16). Even so, Scripture exhorts slaves to obey their masters (Eph. 6:5; Col. 3:22; Titus 2:9). (See **Maid**; **Maidservant**; **Steward**.)

◆SLAVEMASTER

(See **Overseer**.)

◆SMELTER

(See **Foundry Worker**.)

◆SMITH

Some translations use this generic word for one who worked with metals. (See **Metalworker**.)

◆SOLDIER

Even though Israel conquered the Promised Land by waging war, it did not have a standing army until Solomon's time (1 Kin. 10:26). However, all 20-year-old males were liable for emergency military duty (Num. 1:3), with a few exceptions (Deut. 20:5–8). Saul maintained a body of chosen capable fighters (1 Sam. 13:15), and David recruited a force of "mighty men" (1 Sam. 22:2; 1 Chr. 11:10–47). Under David, each tribe had a well-delineated chain of command and trained its adult males to use military weapons (1 Chr. 12).

The Bible mentions several specific kinds of soldiers, including the *guard*, **bodyguard**, or *escort* assigned to protect a particular person or place, such as *prison guards* (Gen. 40:3–4) and *palace guards* (2 Kin. 11:4–11); and the **charioteer** who was often a skilled **horseman** and commanded by a captain of the chariots (1 Kin. 22:33–34). (See **Archer**; **Armorbearer**; **Armorer**; **Captain**; **Centurion**; **Horseman**.)

◆SOOTHSAYER

Soothsaying is rarely mentioned in the Bible, but it appears to describe some form of divination (Deut. 18:10). Because the Hebrew word for "soothsaying" sounds like the word for cloud, some scholars believe it refers to cloud reading. It may have been similar to tea leaf reading or astrology, which is a reading of the stars. In any case, God forbids this occult practice (Deut. 18:10, 14; Lev. 19:26). Wicked King Manasseh was guilty of soothsaying (2 Kin. 21:6; 2 Chr. 33:6), and the Old Testament prophets strongly condemned it (Is. 2:6; 57:3; Jer. 27:9; Mic. 5:12). (See **Astrologer**; **Diviner**; **Magician**.)

◆SORCERER, SORCERESS

(See **Diviner**; **Magician**; **Witch**; **Wizard**.)

◆SPY

Moses sent twelve spies to scout out the Promised Land. Ten returned with discouraging reports, while two, Joshua and Caleb, encouraged the people to go forward (Num. 13). Later, Joshua sent spies into Jericho, who escaped capture only through the help of Rahab (Josh. 2). Another group of five spies for the tribe of Dan compromised in their mission by adopting the idolatry of Micah of Ephraim (Judg. 18).

In the New Testament, the chief priests and scribes had Jesus followed and sent spies to catch Him saying something treasonous (Luke 20:20). Later, Paul accused the Judaizers of sending spies among the leaders of the church (Gal. 2:4). However, on one occasion Paul benefitted from the intelligence brought by a "spy," his sister's son, who reported on a plot to kill the apostle (Acts 23:16–21). (See **Watchman**.)

◆STARGAZER

(See **Astrologer**.)

◆STENOGRAPHER

(See **Secretary**.)

◆STEWARD

Stewards, like **overseers**, were entrusted with responsibility for their superiors' goods (Gen. 43:19). In the New Testament, a steward is sometimes referred to as a *guardian* or *curator* (Matt. 20:8; Gal. 4:2), or as a manager or household superintendent (Luke 8:2–3; 1 Cor. 4:1–2). Paul called himself a "steward" of Christ's household, responsible to Christ for carrying out his task of preaching the gospel to the Gentiles (1 Cor. 4:1). All Christians have been given resources and responsibilities by God and are accountable to Him for their stewardship over those gifts (1 Pet. 4:10). (See **Overseer**.)

◆STONECUTTER

(See **Mason**.)

T

◆TAILOR

The work of tailoring is implied rather than specifically mentioned in Scripture. In Israel, most of a family's clothing was made by the women (see "Jewish Homemaking," Mark 1:29–31). For instance, Hannah made a "little robe" for her son Samuel (1 Sam. 2:19). Likewise, the "virtuous woman of Proverbs" is praised for her skill in making clothing for her family (Prov. 31:13–24).

This work began by spinning thread or yarn and weaving cloth. Everyday clothing tended to be loose fitting and thus did not require much shaping. However, the rich and royalty demanded more ornate design in their garments. Intricate weaving and embroidery were required for the beautiful, stone-studded priestly garments prescribed by Moses (Ex. 28). In the New Testament, Lydia became a successful businesswoman by trading in *purple,* the name for both an expensive dye and the clothing dyed that color (see profile at Acts 16:14). (See **Weaver**.)

◆TANNER

Tanners converted animal skins into leather and fashioned useful or ornamental items from it. Tanning was widespread in the ancient world. Originally, Israelite

◆TANNER *(continued)*

families did their own tanning, but with the growth of cities, leather craftsmen arose. Peter stayed with one such tanner named Simon (Acts 10:6).

Tanning skins was an involved process, requiring much skill. The hides were soaked until the fat, blood, and hair were removed. After the leather was tanned, it was used for many purposes, including tents (Ex. 26:14), sandals (Ezek. 16:10), hats, skirts, and aprons.

◆TAPESTRY MAKER

Sometimes called *carpetmakers* or *rugmakers,* the more inclusive term is tapestry maker. Rugs in Bible times were braided with strips of cotton, wool, or other fibers. Because these braided strands varied in color and length, they were coiled and sewn together to obtain the desired pattern and size. The virtuous woman of Proverbs is praised for making her own tapestries (Prov. 31:22). By contrast, the seductive prostitute of Proverbs 7 has her bedroom chamber adorned with rugs and blankets or wall-hangings from a tapestry maker (7:16). (See **Weaver**.)

◆TASKMASTER

(See **Overseer**.)

◆TAX COLLECTOR

Tax collectors were contract workers who collected taxes for the government during Bible times. Some translations call them "publicans," but publicans were actually the ones who employed tax collectors to do the actual collecting of monies. Between Rome, the temple system, and other taxing authorities, Jews in Jesus' time were probably paying between 30 and 40 percent of their income in taxes and religious dues. Not surprisingly, tax collectors were despised by their fellow citizens who viewed them as mercenaries working for the Romans (see "Who Were Those Tax Collectors?" Matt. 9:10, and "Taxes," Mark 12:14). (See **Publicans**.)

◆TEACHER

(See **Instructor**; **Lawyer**.)

◆TENTMAKER

This ancient craft had to do with the manufacture of affordable, mobile shelters for living, working, and traveling. Construction involved cutting and sewing together cloth, often made of goat's hair, and attaching ropes and loops. Paul's native province of Cilicia exported cilicium cloth made from goat's hair, and his hometown of Tarsus was known for its tentmaking industry (see Acts 11:25). Thus Paul may have picked up the trade as a boy (see "Paul's 'Real' Job," Acts 18:1–3). Later he partnered with Priscilla and Aquila (see profile at Rom. 16:3–5) and earned his living in that manner while preaching the gospel.

◆TETRARCH

The term tetrarch is a title meaning "ruler of a fourth part." Sometimes it is translated "king." Four members of the Herod family named in the New Testament were Roman tetrarchs (see "The Herods," Acts 12:1–2): Herod the Great (Matt. 2), who was tetrarch before he was king (according to the historian Josephus); his son Herod Antipas, called "Herod the Tetrarch" (Matt. 14:1; Acts 13:1); Herod Philip, the brother of Antipas (Mark 6:17); and Lysanias, tetrarch of Abilene (Luke 3:1). A tetrarch's privileges and power were royal, but inferior to those of a real king or emperor. (See **Government Official**.)

◆THIEF

(See **Criminal**.)

◆TILLER

(See **Farmer**.)

◆TOWN CLERK

(See **City Clerk**.)

◆TRADER

(See **Merchant**.)

◆TRAPPER

(See **Hunter**.)

◆TREASURER

The Bible mentions several treasurers, powerful government officials who could sometimes even be heir to a throne (2 Chr. 26:21). They advised and reported to ancient monarchs on financial matters. Ezra was given authority by King Artaxerxes over the treasurers in the districts near Jerusalem (Ezra 7:21).

Nehemiah appointed several treasurers to work in concert with one another in distributing resources (Neh. 13:13). The New Testament highlights an Ethiopian treasurer who became a believer (Acts 8:26–40). (See **Government Official**.)

◆TRUSTEE

(See **Government Official**.)

◆TUTOR

Tutors are hardly mentioned in Scripture, but they were quite common in the ancient world, especially among the Greeks and Romans. Usually the trusted slave of a wealthy family, a tutor supervised the activities of the family's children, especially its sons, acting as a guide and guardian. When boys reached the age of 16, they were considered adults and no longer in need of a tutor. Paul wrote that the Law was a tutor to bring us to Christ (Gal. 3:24–25). In the Old Testament, a man named Jehiel functioned as a tutor to the sons of King David (1 Chr. 27:32). (See **Instructor**.)

◆UNDERTAKER

Most undertakers in Israel were not professionals but family of the deceased (Luke 9:59), or in Jesus' case, friends (Mark 16:1; John 19:38–40; see "A Burial Fit for a King," Mark 15:42). The early church possibly appointed a certain group of people to undertake this responsibility and attend to the dead person's property (Acts 5:6; 8:2).

Haste characterized the burial customs of the ancient Near East due to the hot climate of Palestine, where dead bodies decayed rapidly (see "Funeral Preparations," John 12:1–8, and "Burial," 1 Cor. 15:42). Among the Hebrews, preparation for burial involved washing the body, scenting it with oils and spices, and wrapping it in sheets (John 19:38–40) or the person's own clothes. Bodies were buried in a shallow grave covered with stones or placed in a cave or tomb hewn out of stone. The Jews did not embalm bodies as the Egyptians did, or cremate them as the Greeks and Romans did. (See **Embalmer**.)

◆VICEROY

(See **Government Official**.)

◆VINEDRESSER

Scripture highlights the vocation of the vinedresser in many ways. Isaiah warns Israel of judgment in the woeful song of the vineyard (Is. 5:1–30). Jesus warns the Pharisees of similar judgment in His parable of the wicked vinedressers (Matt. 21:33–44). Jesus also called Himself the true vine and His Father the vinedresser (John 15:1–8). Grape vines required constant digging, weeding, and pruning to bring growth to the fruit and not to the shoots, lest the vines be overcome by thorns and weeds (Prov. 24:30–31; Luke 13:7). During the captivity of Judah in Babylon, God raised up the poor, even the foreigners, to dress the vines (2 Kin. 25:12; Is. 61:5; Jer. 52:16), not unlike today's migrant farm workers. (See **Farmer**; **Laborer**.)

◆WAITER, WAITRESS

(See **Butler**.)

◆WARRIOR

(See **Soldier**.)

◆WATCHMAN

The duty of a watchman was to stand guard over or "watch" over something valuable, perhaps a treasure, a person, or a city. From the height and protection of a watch tower, a guard watched over cities and fields, looking for thieves or ravaging animals (Ps. 80:13; Song 2:15). Nehemiah appointed watchmen to guard the walls of Jerusalem during their rebuilding (Neh. 4:9; 7:3). Some watchmen also worked as *guardians* or *policemen,* patrolling a city (Ps. 127:1; Song 5:7).

The Jews divided the night into three military watches, which the watchman was required to call out (2 Sam. 18:24–27; Is. 21:11–12; see "Telling Time," Matt. 14:25). Under the Romans they adopted the Roman method of dividing the night into four watches (Mark 13:35). A 24–hour, round-the-clock watch was posted at Jesus' tomb (Matt. 27:64–66; 28:11).

In a metaphorical or spiritual sense, prophets and teachers were God's appointed watchmen to keep His people morally alert (Ezek. 33:2–7; 2 Tim. 4:5).

◆WATER CARRIER

Going to the well or spring to bring back a household's daily water supply was lowly work. Wells and springs were generally situated outside city gates (John 4:5–8). Sometimes the task was assigned to young men (Ruth 2:9), but usually to women (Gen. 24:3; 1 Sam. 9:11) or servants (John 2:5–9). Water was carried home in water pots and goatskin bags, sometimes borne by a donkey. Some translations refer to this occupation as *drawer of water.*

◆WEAVER

Weaving was known in the ancient world from about 2000 B.C. Almost every household had a loom, and in Israel women spent much time at this task (Prov. 31:13–24). Women also made their own yarn or thread from animal hair or plant

◆WEAVER *(continued)*

fibers. Among other peoples, however, such as the Egyptians and Assyrians, weaving was a man's job. Professional weavers in urban areas created professional weaver guilds. (See **Embroiderer**.)

◆WELL DIGGER

Well diggers were relatively skilled workers in ancient Palestine, where little rain fell during most of the year. Wells and cisterns were crucial to the region's economy. Wars were sometimes fought over wells and water rights (Gen. 21:25–30; 26:20–22). In David's time, Jerusalem was provided with an elaborate underground system of shafts and tunnels that led to a water source (2 Sam. 5:8). Some wells bore specific names and survive to this day; for example, Jacob's Well (John 4:6).

◆WINE MAKER

Wine was a valuable trade commodity for ancient peoples, including the Israelites (2 Chr. 2:10, 15–16; Ezra 6:9; 7:22). Wine was an important part of the everyday diet and a popular beverage for special occasions (Ps. 104:15). Apparently shouts of joy typified the occasion of treading grapes in the wine presses (Is. 16:10; Jer. 48:33; see "Winemaking," John 2:3). Even ordinary people owned wine presses and gave the firstfruits of them in worship (Num. 18:27, 30; Deut. 14:15). Times of reformation and renewal called for bringing "new wine" into the storehouses (2 Chr. 31:5; Neh. 13:5). Jesus made use of this image by saying that the "wine" of the good news called for new wineskins to hold it (Luke 5:36–38).

It's interesting that of the more than 240 references to wine in the Bible, only about a tenth have to do with "strong" drink or drunkenness. Most use wine to refer to abundance, sustenance, and the blessing of God (for example, Gen. 27:28; Neh. 5:18; Esth. 1:7; Hos. 2:8). Jesus blessed a wedding party at Cana with gallons of new wine (see "Water into Wine," John 2:1–12), and initiated His new covenant with wine (Luke 22:17–20).

Winepressing is also used as a symbol of God's wrath in judgment (Lam. 1:15; Joel 3:13; Rev. 14:18–20; 19:15). (See **Brewer**; **Vinedresser**.)

◆WINNOWER

Those who winnowed or separated grain from the chaff are sometimes called **fanners** (Jer. 51:2, KJV). The grain was beaten to loosen the kernels. The kernels were then trampled underfoot to loosen the chaff covering the grain. After each stage, the fanner would pitch the grain into the air with a winnowing fork, or fan, an implement still used by Syrian farmers. The wind blew the useless chaff away to be burned (Ruth 3:2; Job 21:18; Ps. 1:4; Matt. 3:12) while the valuable grain fell to the ground. The winnower used a five- or six-pronged pitchfork in the first stage and a shovel for the second stage (Is. 30:24). Most references in the Bible to winnowing or fanning are metaphorical. Just as a winnower separates wheat and chaff, so God separates true believers from unbelievers and hypocrites at the Last Day (Jer. 23:28–29; Luke 3:17).

◆WITCH, WIZARD

Witchcraft involved divination or sorcery that attempted to avoid or alter God's revealed will. In the Old Testament, God condemned pagan nations for practicing witchcraft (Deut. 18:9–14; Jer. 27:8–11; 29:8–9; Nah. 3:1–4). Saul was punished for visiting the witch of Endor (1 Sam. 28; 1 Chr. 10:13). (See **Diviner**; **Magician**.)

◆WOODWORKER

This general term covers a variety of trades involved in making wood into usable items. Archaeology has confirmed Scripture's testimony that ancient Palestine had forests. Even so, wood was scarce and rather expensive. Thus, good woodworkers also practiced conservation and reforestation (Is. 44:14). Their projects involved many people working in concert. *Lumberjacks* and *woodcutters* felled trees (1 Kin. 5:6). *Hewers* trimmed and readied the lumber for transportation. **Laborers** transported it (1 Kin. 5:13–14). **Carpenters** fashioned it into houses, furniture, tools, and other useful items (2 Kin. 22:6). Those who specialized as **carvers** carved wood into bas-relief and statues (Is. 40:20; Jer. 10:3–4). (See **Builder**; **Carpenter**; **Forester**.)

◆WRESTLER

(See **Athlete**.)

◆WRITER

More than 400 terms for writing can be found in the Bible. The origins of this craft can be traced to crude inscriptions on clay tablets made in prehistoric times. Writing and writing instruments were well developed by the time of Moses, enabling him to write down the Law (Ex. 17:14; 24:4). Note, however, that the two stone tablets of the Law were said to be written with "the finger of God" (Ex. 31:18). Another form of writing mentioned in Scripture is the "inward [or spiritual] writing" in which a message is written on the "tablet of your heart" (Prov. 3:3; 7:3; Jer. 17:1; 2 Cor. 3:3).

Materials on which ancient peoples wrote included clay, wax, stone, bricks, metal, and the inner side of papyrus bark. The latter was called *biblos,* from which we derive the word *bible.* Papyrus manuscripts were perishable, and some penmen were kept busy full-time transcribing records onto new papyrus. Needless to say, were it not for faithful copywriters, we would have no Bible today. (See **Author**; **Scribe**.)

◆ZOOLOGIST

God brought "every animal of the field and every bird of the air" to Adam for him to name and classify according to its kind (Gen. 2:19–20), making Adam the first "zoologist." Likewise, Noah also classified animals and birds according to their kind (Gen. 6:19—7:3). Scripture reports that he took aboard the ark complete sets (seven) of all the "clean" animals and birds, plus two of the "unclean" variety, plus a 40–day supply of food for all, making Noah a "zookeeper" as well as a "zoologist." (See **Ornithologist**.)

Jobs and Occupations Index— By Category

To read about job classifications in a certain category, see the alphabetical listings in the main Jobs and Occupations Index, as indicated under each category name.

Notes

Notes

Notes

Notes

Notes